Microsoft Press

Programming
Applications
for Microsoft
Windows
Fourth Edition

Jeffrey
Richter

PUBLISHED BY
Microsoft Press
A Division of Microsoft Corporation
One Microsoft Way
Redmond, Washington 98052-6399

Library of Congress Cataloging-in-Publication Data
Richter, Jeffrey.
    Programming Applications for Microsoft Windows / Jeffrey Richter.
        p.   cm.
    ISBN 1-57231-996-8
    1. Application software--Development.   2. Microsoft Windows
(Computer file)   I. Title.
QA76.76.A65R54   1999
005.26'8--dc21   99-40456
                                                                        CIP

Printed and bound in the United States of America.

4 5 6 7 8 9   QWT   7 6 5 4 3 2

Distributed in Canada by Penguin Books Canada Limited.

A CIP catalogue record for this book is available from the British Library.

Microsoft Press books are available through booksellers and distributors worldwide. For further information about international editions, contact your local Microsoft Corporation office or contact Microsoft Press International directly at fax (425) 936-7329. Visit our Web site at www.microsoft.com/mspress. Send comments to *mspinput@microsoft.com*.

Intel is a registered trademark of Intel Corporation. Developer Studio, Microsoft, Microsoft Press, MS-DOS, Visual Basic, Visual C++, Visual Studio, Windows, and Windows NT are either registered trademarks or trademarks of Microsoft Corporation in the United States and/or other countries. Other product and company names mentioned herein may be the trademarks of their respective owners.

The example companies, organizations, products, people, and events depicted herein are fictitious. No association with any real company, organization, product, person, or event is intended or should be inferred.

Acquisitions Editor: Ben Ryan
Project Editor: Rebecca McKay
Technical Editors: Jack Beaudry, Donnie Cameron
Manuscript Editors: Ina Chang, Rebecca McKay

To Kristin,
With the few words I have left, I want to tell you how much you mean to me.
Your energy and exuberance always lift me higher.
Your smile brightens my every day.
Your zest makes my heart sing.
I love you (and Max too). Hap'm.

To my mother, Arlene,
I admire you for your bravery and courage
through the most difficult and trying of times.
Your love and support have shaped me into the person I am.
You're with me wherever I go.

CONTENTS AT A GLANCE

PART I: REQUIRED READING

CHAPTER ONE
ERROR HANDLING **3**

CHAPTER TWO
UNICODE **17**

CHAPTER THREE
KERNEL OBJECTS **41**

PART II: GETTING WORK DONE

CHAPTER FOUR
PROCESSES **69**

CHAPTER FIVE
JOBS **137**

CHAPTER SIX
THREAD BASICS **181**

CHAPTER SEVEN
THREAD SCHEDULING,
PRIORITIES, AND AFFINITIES **213**

CHAPTER EIGHT
THREAD SYNCHRONIZATION
IN USER MODE **257**

CHAPTER NINE

THREAD SYNCHRONIZATION
WITH KERNEL OBJECTS **285**

CHAPTER TEN

THREAD SYNCHRONIZATION
TOOLKIT **337**

CHAPTER ELEVEN

THREAD POOLING **399**

CHAPTER TWELVE

FIBERS **417**

PART III: MEMORY MANAGEMENT

CHAPTER THIRTEEN

WINDOWS MEMORY ARCHITECTURE **435**

CHAPTER FOURTEEN

EXPLORING VIRTUAL MEMORY **471**

CHAPTER FIFTEEN

USING VIRTUAL MEMORY
IN YOUR OWN APPLICATIONS **513**

CHAPTER SIXTEEN

A THREAD'S STACK **559**

CHAPTER SEVENTEEN

MEMORY-MAPPED FILES **577**

CHAPTER EIGHTEEN

HEAPS **655**

PART IV: DYNAMIC-LINK LIBRARIES

CHAPTER NINETEEN

DLL BASICS **675**

CHAPTER TWENTY

DLL ADVANCED TECHNIQUES **695**

CHAPTER TWENTY-ONE

THREAD-LOCAL STORAGE **743**

CHAPTER TWENTY-TWO

DLL INJECTION AND API HOOKING **751**

PART V: STRUCTURED EXCEPTION HANDLING

CHAPTER TWENTY-THREE

TERMINATION HANDLERS **823**

CHAPTER TWENTY-FOUR

EXCEPTION HANDLERS
AND SOFTWARE EXCEPTIONS **843**

CHAPTER TWENTY-FIVE

UNHANDLED EXCEPTIONS
AND C++ EXCEPTIONS **875**

PART VI: WINDOWING

CHAPTER TWENTY-SIX

WINDOW MESSAGING **911**

CHAPTER TWENTY-SEVEN

THE HARDWARE INPUT
MODEL AND LOCAL INPUT STATE **945**

TABLE OF CONTENTS

Introduction .... *xxiii*

PART I: REQUIRED READING

CHAPTER ONE

ERROR HANDLING 3
You Can Do This Too 8
The ErrorShow Sample Application 9

CHAPTER TWO

UNICODE 17
Character Sets 17
    Single-Byte and Double-Byte Character Sets 18
    Unicode: The Wide-Byte Character Set 18
Why You Should Use Unicode 20
Windows 2000 and Unicode 20
Windows 98 and Unicode 21
Windows CE and Unicode 22
Keeping Score 22
A Quick Word About COM 22
How to Write Unicode Source Code 23
    Unicode Support in the C Run-Time Library 23
    Unicode Data Types Defined by Windows 26
    Unicode and ANSI Functions in Windows 26
    Windows String Functions 28
Making Your Application ANSI- and Unicode-Ready 29
    Windows String Functions 30
    Resources 33
    Determining If Text Is ANSI or Unicode 34
    Translating Strings Between Unicode and ANSI 35

CHAPTER THREE

KERNEL OBJECTS **41**

What Is a Kernel Object? 41

Usage Counting 42

Security 43

A Process's Kernel Object Handle Table 46

Creating a Kernel Object 46

Closing a Kernel Object 48

Sharing Kernel Objects

Across Process Boundaries 49

Object Handle Inheritance 50

Named Objects 55

Duplicating Object Handles 60

PART II: GETTING WORK DONE

CHAPTER FOUR

PROCESSES **69**

Writing Your First Windows Application 71

A Process's Instance Handle 76

A Process's Previous Instance Handle 77

A Process's Command Line 78

A Process's Environment Variables 79

A Process's Affinity 83

A Process's Error Mode 83

A Process's Current Drive and Directory 84

The System Version 86

The *CreateProcess* Function 90

pszApplicationName and *pszCommandLine* 91

psaProcess, *psaThread*, and *bInheritHandles* 94

fdwCreate 96

pvEnvironment 99

pszCurDir 100

psiStartInfo 100

ppiProcInfo 105

Terminating a Process 107
    The Primary Thread's Entry-Point Function Returns 107
    The *ExitProcess* Function 108
    The *TerminateProcess* Function 110
    When All the Threads in the Process Die 110
    When a Process Terminates 111
Child Processes 112
    Running Detached Child Processes 114
Enumerating the Processes Running in the System 114
    The Process Information Sample Application 115

CHAPTER FIVE

JOBS 137

Placing Restrictions on a Job's Processes 140
Placing a Process in a Job 149
Terminating All Processes in a Job 150
Querying Job Statistics 151
Job Notifications 155
The JobLab Sample Application 158

CHAPTER SIX

THREAD BASICS 181

When to Create a Thread 182
When Not to Create a Thread 184
Writing Your First Thread Function 185
The *CreateThread* Function 186
    psa 187
    cbStack 187
    pfnStartAddr and *pvParam* 188
    fdwCreate 190
    pdwThreadID 190
Terminating a Thread 191
    The Thread Function Returns 191
    The *ExitThread* Function 191
    The *TerminateThread* Function 192
    When a Process Terminates 193
    When a Thread Terminates 193

Some Thread Internals 194

C/C++ Run-Time Library Considerations 198

Oops—I Called *CreateThread* Instead of
_beginthreadex by Mistake 208

C/C++ Run-Time Library Functions
That You Should Never Call 208

Gaining a Sense of One's Own Identity 209

Converting a Pseudo-Handle to a Real Handle 210

CHAPTER SEVEN

THREAD SCHEDULING,
PRIORITIES, AND AFFINITIES **213**

Suspending and Resuming a Thread 215

Suspending and Resuming a Process 216

Sleeping 218

Switching to Another Thread 219

A Thread's Execution Times 219

Putting the Context in Context 223

Thread Priorities 228

An Abstract View of Priorities 230

Programming Priorities 235

Dynamically Boosting Thread Priority Levels 238

Tweaking the Scheduler for the Foreground Process 240

The Scheduling Lab Sample Application 241

Affinities 250

CHAPTER EIGHT

THREAD SYNCHRONIZATION
IN USER MODE **257**

Atomic Access:
The Interlocked Family of Functions 258

Cache Lines 265

Advanced Thread Synchronization 267

A Technique to Avoid 268

Critical Sections 269

Critical Sections: The Fine Print 273

Critical Sections and Spinlocks 277

Critical Sections and Error Handling 278

Useful Tips and Techniques 279

CHAPTER NINE

THREAD SYNCHRONIZATION WITH KERNEL OBJECTS **285**

Wait Functions 287

Successful Wait Side Effects 291

Event Kernel Objects 293

The Handshake Sample Application 297

Waitable Timer Kernel Objects 305

Having Waitable Timers Queue APC Entries 309

Timer Loose Ends 312

Semaphore Kernel Objects 313

Mutex Kernel Objects 315

Abandonment Issues 317

Mutexes vs. Critical Sections 318

The Queue Sample Application 319

A Handy Thread Synchronization Object Chart 331

Other Thread Synchronization Functions 332

Asynchronous Device I/O 332

WaitForInputIdle 332

MsgWaitForMultipleObjects(Ex) 333

WaitForDebugEvent 334

SignalObjectAndWait 334

CHAPTER TEN

THREAD SYNCHRONIZATION TOOLKIT **337**

Implementing a Critical Section: The Optex 337

The Optex Sample Application 340

**Creating Thread-Safe Datatypes
and Inverse Semaphores** 353

The InterlockedType Sample Application 358

The Single Writer/Multiple Reader Guard (SWMRG) 368

The SWMRG Sample Application 371

**Implementing a
WaitForMultipleExpressions Function** 380

The WaitForMultipleExpressions Sample Application 382

CHAPTER ELEVEN

THREAD POOLING 399
Scenario 1: Call Functions Asynchronously 401
Scenario 2: Call Functions at Timed Intervals 403
　The TimedMsgBox Sample Application 407
Scenario 3: Call Functions When
**　Single Kernel Objects Become Signaled** 412
Scenario 4: Call Functions When
**　Asynchronous I/O Requests Complete** 415

CHAPTER TWELVE

FIBERS 417
Working with Fibers 417
　The Counter Sample Application 421

PART III: MEMORY MANAGEMENT

CHAPTER THIRTEEN

WINDOWS MEMORY ARCHITECTURE 435
A Process's Virtual Address Space 435
How a Virtual Address Space Is Partitioned 436
　Null-Pointer Assignment Partition
　　(Windows 2000 and Windows 98) 438
　MS-DOS/16-Bit Windows Application Compatibility
　　Partition (Windows 98 Only) 438
　User-Mode Partition (Windows 2000 and Windows 98) 439
　64-KB Off-Limits Partition (Windows 2000 Only) 441
　Shared MMF Partition (Windows 98 Only) 442
　Kernel-Mode Partition (Windows 2000 and Windows 98) 442
Regions in an Address Space 443
Committing Physical Storage Within a Region 444
Physical Storage and the Paging File 444
　Physical Storage Not Maintained in the Paging File 447
Protection Attributes 449
　Copy-On-Write Access 450
　Special Access Protection Attribute Flags 452

Bringing It All Home 452

Inside the Regions 456

Address Space Differences for Windows 98 461

The Importance of Data Alignment 465

CHAPTER FOURTEEN

EXPLORING VIRTUAL MEMORY 471

System Information 471

The System Information Sample Application 473

Virtual Memory Status 481

The Virtual Memory Status Sample Application 483

Determining the State of an Address Space 489

The *VMQuery* Function 490

The Virtual Memory Map Sample Application 499

CHAPTER FIFTEEN

USING VIRTUAL MEMORY IN YOUR OWN APPLICATIONS 513

Reserving a Region in an Address Space 513

Committing Storage in a Reserved Region 516

Reserving a Region and Committing Storage Simultaneously 517

When to Commit Physical Storage 518

Decommitting Physical Storage and Releasing a Region 520

When to Decommit Physical Storage 521

The Virtual Memory Allocation Sample Application 523

Changing Protection Attributes 534

Resetting the Contents of Physical Storage 536

The MemReset Sample Application 537

Address Windowing Extensions (Windows 2000 only) 540

The AWE Sample Application 546

CHAPTER SIXTEEN

A THREAD'S STACK 559

A Thread's Stack Under Windows 98 563

The C/C++ Run-Time Library's Stack-Checking Function 565

The Summation Sample Application 567

CHAPTER SEVENTEEN

MEMORY-MAPPED FILES **577**

Memory-Mapped Executables and DLLs 578
Static Data Is Not Shared
by Multiple Instances of an Executable or a DLL 579
Sharing Static Data
Across Multiple Instances of an Executable or a DLL 582
The AppInst Sample Application 588
Memory-Mapped Data Files 594
Method 1: One File, One Buffer 595
Method 2: Two Files, One Buffer 595
Method 3: One File, Two Buffers 596
Method 4: One File, Zero Buffers 596
Using Memory-Mapped Files 597
Step 1: Creating or Opening a File Kernel Object 597
Step 2: Creating a File-Mapping Kernel Object 599
Step 3: Mapping the File's Data into
the Process's Address Space 603
Step 4: Unmapping the File's Data
from the Process's Address Space 606
Steps 5 and 6: Closing the File-Mapping Object
and the File Object 608
The File Reverse Sample Application 609
Processing a Big File Using Memory-Mapped Files 620
Memory-Mapped Files and Coherence 621
Specifying the Base Address of a Memory-Mapped File 622
Implementation Details of Memory-Mapped Files 624
Using Memory-Mapped Files to Share Data Among Processes 627
Memory-Mapped Files Backed by the Paging File 628
The Memory-Mapped File Sharing Sample Application 630
Sparsely Committed Memory-Mapped Files 636
The Sparse Memory-Mapped File Sample Application 638

CHAPTER EIGHTEEN

HEAPS **655**
A Process's Default Heap 656
Reasons to Create Additional Heaps 657
    Component Protection 657
    More Efficient Memory Management 658
    Local Access 659
    Avoiding Thread Synchronization Overhead 660
    Quick Free 660
How to Create an Additional Heap 660
    Allocating a Block of Memory from a Heap 662
    Changing the Size of a Block 664
    Obtaining the Size of a Block 665
    Freeing a Block 665
    Destroying a Heap 665
    Using Heaps with C++ 666
Miscellaneous Heap Functions 670

PART IV: DYNAMIC-LINK LIBRARIES

CHAPTER NINETEEN

DLL BASICS **675**
DLLs and a Process's Address Space 677
The Overall Picture 679
Building the DLL Module 683
    What Exporting Really Means 685
    Creating DLLs for Use with Non–Visual C++ Tools 688
Building the Executable Module 689
    What Importing Really Means 690
Running the Executable Module 692

CHAPTER TWENTY

DLL ADVANCED TECHNIQUES **695**

Explicit DLL Module Loading and Symbol Linking 695

    Explicitly Loading the DLL Module 697

    Explicitly Unloading the DLL Module 698

    Explicitly Linking to an Exported Symbol 701

The DLL's Entry-Point Function 702

    The DLL_PROCESS_ATTACH Notification 703

    The DLL_PROCESS_DETACH Notification 705

    The DLL_THREAD_ATTACH Notification 707

    The DLL_THREAD_DETACH Notification 708

    Serialized Calls to *DllMain* 709

    DllMain and the C/C++ Run-Time Library 712

Delay-Loading a DLL 714

    The DelayLoadApp Sample Application 719

Function Forwarders 727

Known DLLs 728

DLL Redirection 729

Rebasing Modules 730

Binding Modules 738

CHAPTER TWENTY-ONE

THREAD-LOCAL STORAGE **743**

Dynamic TLS 744

    Using Dynamic TLS 747

Static TLS 749

CHAPTER TWENTY-TWO

DLL INJECTION AND API HOOKING **751**

DLL Injection: An Example 752

Injecting a DLL Using the Registry 754

Injecting a DLL Using Windows Hooks 757

    The Desktop Item Position Saver (DIPS) Utility 759

Injecting a DLL Using Remote Threads 774

    The Inject Library Sample Application 779

    The Image Walk DLL 789

Injecting a DLL with a Trojan DLL 792

Injecting a DLL as a Debugger 793

Injecting Code with a Memory-Mapped File on Windows 98 793
Injecting Code with *CreateProcess* 794
API Hooking: An Example 795
    API Hooking by Overwriting Code 796
    API Hooking by Manipulating a Module's Import Section 797
    The LastMsgBoxInfo Sample Application 801

PART V: STRUCTURED EXCEPTION HANDLING

CHAPTER TWENTY-THREE

TERMINATION HANDLERS 823

Understanding Termination Handlers by Example 825
    Funcenstein1 825
    Funcenstein2 826
    Funcenstein3 828
    Funcfurter1 829
    Pop Quiz Time: *FuncaDoodleDoo* 830
    Funcenstein4 831
    Funcarama1 832
    Funcarama2 833
    Funcarama3 834
    Funcarama4: The Final Frontier 835
    Notes About the *finally* Block 837
    Funcfurter2 838
    The SEH Termination Sample Application 839

CHAPTER TWENTY-FOUR

EXCEPTION HANDLERS AND SOFTWARE EXCEPTIONS 843

Understanding Exception Filters and
Exception Handlers by Example 844
    Funcmeister1 844
    Funcmeister2 845
EXCEPTION_EXECUTE_HANDLER 847
    Some Useful Examples 848
    Global Unwinds 851
    Halting Global Unwinds 855

EXCEPTION_CONTINUE_EXECUTION 856
    Use EXCEPTION_CONTINUE_EXECUTION with Caution 857
EXCEPTION_CONTINUE_SEARCH 858
GetExceptionCode 861
    Memory-Related Exceptions 861
    Exception-Related Exceptions 862
    Debugging-Related Exceptions 862
    Integer-Related Exceptions 862
    Floating Point–Related Exceptions 863
GetExceptionInformation 866
Software Exceptions 870

CHAPTER TWENTY-FIVE

UNHANDLED EXCEPTIONS
AND C++ EXCEPTIONS **875**
Just-In-Time Debugging 878
Turning Off the Exception Message Box 880
    Forcing the Process to Die 880
    Wrapping a Thread Function 880
    Wrapping All Thread Functions 881
    Automatically Invoking the Debugger 882
Calling *UnhandledExceptionFilter* Yourself 882
Inside the *UnhandledExceptionFilter* Function 883
Exceptions and the Debugger 885
    The Spreadsheet Sample Application 889
C++ Exceptions Versus Structured Exceptions 904
    Catching Structured Exceptions with C++ 906

PART VI: WINDOWING

CHAPTER TWENTY-SIX

WINDOW MESSAGING **911**
A Thread's Message Queue 912
Posting Messages to a Thread's Message Queue 914
Sending Messages to a Window 915

Waking a Thread 922

    The Queue Status Flags 923

    The Algorithm for Extracting Messages
        from a Thread's Queue 925

    Waking a Thread with Kernel Objects
        or with Queue Status Flags 928

Sending Data with Messages 932

    The CopyData Sample Application 935

How Windows Handle
ANSI/Unicode Characters and Strings 941

CHAPTER TWENTY-SEVEN

THE HARDWARE INPUT
MODEL AND LOCAL INPUT STATE **945**

The Raw Input Thread 945

Local Input State 947

    Keyboard Input and Focus 948

    Mouse Cursor Management 953

Attaching Virtualized Input Queues and
Local Input State Together 955

    The Local Input State Laboratory (LISLab)
        Sample Application 957

    The Local Input State Watch (LISWatch) Sample Application 978

APPENDIX A

THE BUILD ENVIRONMENT **989**

The CmnHdr.h Header File 989

    Windows Version Build Option 990

    Unicode Build Option 990

    Windows Definitions and Warning Level 4 991

    The Pragma Message Helper Macro 991

    The chINRANGE and chDIMOF Macros 992

    The chBEGINTHREADEX Macro 992

    DebugBreak Improvement for *x86* Platforms 994

    Creating Software Exception Codes 994

The chMB Macro 995

The chASSERT and chVERIFY Macros 995

The chHANDLE_DLGMSG Macro 995

The chSETDLGICONS Macro 995

The OS Version Check Inline Functions 995

Making Sure the Host System Supports Unicode 996

Forcing the Linker to Look
      for a (w)WinMain Entry-Point Function 996

APPENDIX B

MESSAGE CRACKERS, CHILD CONTROL MACROS, AND API MACROS   **1005**

Message Crackers 1006

Child Control Macros 1009

API Macros 1010

Index 1011

INTRODUCTION

Microsoft Windows is a complex operating system. It offers so many features and does so much that it's impossible for any one person to fully understand the entire system. This complexity also makes it difficult for someone to decide where to start concentrating the learning effort. Well, I always like to start at the lowest level by gaining a solid understanding of the system's basic building blocks. Once you understand the basics, it's easy to incrementally add any higher-level aspects of the system to your knowledge.

For example, I don't explicitly discuss the Component Object Model (COM) in this book. But COM is an architecture built using processes, threads, memory management, DLLs, thread local storage, Unicode, and so on. If you know these basic building blocks, understanding COM is just a matter of understanding how the building blocks are used. I have great sympathy for people who attempt to jump-start into learning COM's architecture. They have a long road ahead and are bound to have gaping holes in their knowledge, which is bound to negatively affect their code and their schedules.

So that's what this book is all about: the basic Windows building blocks that every Windows developer (at least in my opinion) should be intimately aware of. As each block is discussed, I also describe how the system uses these blocks and how your own applications can best take advantage of these blocks. In many chapters, I show you how to create building blocks of your own. These building blocks, typically implemented as generic functions or C++ classes, group a set of Windows building blocks together to create a whole that is much greater than the sum of its parts.

Today's Windows Platforms

Currently Microsoft ships three different operating system kernels. Each kernel is optimized for a particular computing scenario. Microsoft is trying to lure software developers to Windows by stating that each platform offers the same *application programming interface* (API). This simply means that when you learn how to write a Windows application for one kernel, you know how to write a Windows application for any of the kernels.

Since this book explains how to write applications using the Windows API, whatever you learn from this book applies—theoretically—to all the kernels. In reality, the kernels are different and so the operating system's functions are implemented in different ways. This means that the underlying concepts are the same for the different kernels, but the details might vary.

Let me start by introducing the three different Windows kernels.

The Windows 2000 Kernel

Windows 2000 is Microsoft's high-end operating system. It has a long shopping list of features. Here are some of them (in no particular order):

- It is designed to run as a workstation, server, or data center.

- The system is robust, which prevents a poorly written application from crashing the system.

- The system is secure, which prevents unauthorized access to resources (such as files and printers) managed by the system.

- The tools and utilities used to manage the system are very rich for the administrators within an organization.

- The kernel is mostly written in C and C++, which makes the system easily portable to other CPU architectures.

- The system natively supports Unicode, which makes localization and working with international languages easy.

- The memory-management features offer extremely rich capabilities and high efficiency.

- Structured exception handling (SEH) features allow for easy error recovery.

- Dynamic-Link Libraries (DLLs) allow for easy extensibility.

- Multithreading and support for multiple processors offer easy scalability to improve performance.

- File system features offer great ways of tracking how users manipulate data on their machines.

The Windows 98 Kernel

Windows 98 is Microsoft's consumer-oriented operating system kernel. It has many of the features of Windows 2000 but it is missing some of the key features. For example, Windows 98 is not robust (an application can crash the system), it is not secure, it is a uniprocessor kernel (which restricts its ability to scale), and it does not offer the same degree of Unicode support.

Microsoft's goal is to kill off the Windows 98 kernel. This is because the Windows 98 kernel does not offer the features of the Windows 2000 kernel, and changing the Windows 98 kernel to support these features is too difficult. Plus, if they did modify the kernel to support these features, the kernel would match the Windows 2000 kernel anyway. So the Windows 2000 kernel should be with us for a long time, and the Windows 98 kernel has just a few years (if that) left in it.

Why does the Windows 98 kernel exist at all? The answer is that Windows 98 is more end user–friendly than Windows 2000. Consumers don't like to log on to their computers, they don't like to administer their computers, and so on. Plus, consumers (arguably) tend to play games more than corporate employees do. Many older games tend to access hardware directly, which can crash the machine. Windows 2000—a robust operating system kernel—doesn't allow this. Any application that attempts direct hardware access on Windows 2000 is immediately terminated with no ill effect on the machine or other applications.

For these reasons, Windows 98 is still with us, and the consumer market for it is quite large. Microsoft is actively working on making Windows 2000 more end user–friendly, and a version of the Windows 2000 kernel will soon be available for the consumer market. Because the Windows 2000 and Windows 98 kernels have similar feature sets, and because both kernels have a huge installed base, I have decided to concentrate on these two kernels in this book.

Throughout the book, I discuss various Windows features. Where appropriate, I have placed notes with kernel-specific icons in the text—as shown here—to draw attention to implementation details particular to one kernel or the other.

WINDOWS 98

> This is an implementation detail specific to the Windows 98 platform.

WINDOWS 2000

> This is an implementation detail specific to the Windows 2000 platform.

Even though I don't explicitly mention Windows 95 in this book, the information that I present for Windows 98 applies equally well to Windows 95 since both operating systems use the exact same kernel. I simply refer to Windows 98 in the book—rather than always mentioning both Windows 95 and Windows 98—to allow for a more readable text.

The Windows CE Kernel

Windows CE is Microsoft's most recent Windows kernel. This new operating system was created to fit the needs of small hardware devices such as handheld computers, auto PCs, smart terminals, toasters, microwave ovens, and vending machines. These devices typically must use a minimal amount of power, have small amounts of memory, and have little (if any) persistent storage (such as a disk drive). Because of these hardware restrictions, Microsoft was forced to create a new operating system kernel that had a smaller footprint than that of either Windows 2000 or Windows 98.

Amazingly enough, Windows CE is quite powerful and offers many features. Since Windows CE machines are geared toward the individual, the kernel does not need a lot of support for administration, scalability, and so on. Although I don't specifically cover Windows CE in this book, many of the concepts discussed throughout apply to this platform. Differences that do exist are usually due to the limitations Windows CE has on the various functions. The material presented in this book should be thought of as a companion to any additional information regarding Windows CE.

Tomorrow's Windows Platforms (64-Bit Windows 2000)

The future is upon us. As I write this, Microsoft is hard at work porting the Windows 2000 kernel so that it is a true 64-bit operating system. The expected title is *64-bit Windows 2000,* and the expected ship date is the year 2000. Initially, this 64-bit kernel will run on Compaq's Alpha CPU architecture (AXP64) and Intel's new 64-bit CPU architecture (IA-64).

Compaq's Alpha CPUs have always been 64-bit architectures. So if you already own an Alpha machine, you will just need to install 64-bit Windows 2000 when it ships in order to run a full 64-bit operating system. Intel's Pentium series (and earlier) CPUs use a 32-bit architecture (IA-32). Machines with these CPUs cannot run 64-bit Windows 2000. Intel is currently designing a new 64-bit CPU architecture. The first chip to use this architecture is code-named Merced. Machines based on the Merced CPU should ship in the year 2000.

64-bit Windows 2000 interests me a great deal, and I have been preparing my code for this day. Today Microsoft's Web site has a number of articles about 64-bit Windows 2000 and how it will look to software developers. I'm happy to report the following:

- The 64-bit Windows 2000 kernel is a port of the existing 32-bit Windows 2000 kernel. This means that all the details and intricacies that you've learned about 32-bit Windows 2000 will still apply in the 64-bit world. In fact, Microsoft has modified the 32-bit Windows source code so that it can be compiled to produce a 32-bit or a 64-bit system. They have just one source-code base, so new features and bug fixes are simultaneously applied to both systems.

- Since the kernels use the same code and underlying concepts, the Windows API is identical on both platforms. This means that you do not have to redesign or reimplement your application to work on 64-bit Windows. You can simply make slight modifications to your source code and then rebuild.

- Since it is so easy to port 32-bit applications, we should soon see tools (such as Microsoft's Developer Studio) supporting 64-bit development.

- For backward compatibility, 64-bit Windows can execute 32-bit applications. However, it is promised that your application's performance will improve greatly if built as a true 64-bit application.

- There is little new for you to learn. You'll be happy to know that most data types remain 32 bits wide. These include *int*s, DWORDs, LONGs, BOOLs, and so on. In fact, you mostly just need to worry about pointers and some handles, since they are now 64-bit values.

Since Microsoft's Web site offers much information on how to modify your existing source code to be 64-bit ready, I will not go into those details in this book. However, I thought about 64-bit Windows as I wrote each chapter. Where appropriate, I have included information specific to 64-bit Windows. In addition, I have compiled all the sample applications in this book using a 64-bit compiler, and I was able to test the applications on a very early version of 64-bit Windows for the Alpha CPU. So, if you follow the sample applications in this book, and do as I've done, you should have no trouble creating a single source-code base that you can easily compile for 32-bit or 64-bit Windows.

What's New in the Fourth Edition

Readers of *Advanced Windows* will notice one big change right away: the book's title. Microsoft Press and I both felt that *Advanced Windows* didn't convey enough information about the book's content. For starters, the previous title didn't indicate that the book is for developers. Consequently, bookstores filed the book in the wrong category. Second, I received much e-mail from potential readers who thought my book was "advanced" and wanted me to recommend a more beginner- or intermediate-level Windows programming book.

As for content, the fourth edition is practically a whole new book. I focused on shorter chapters, better isolation of material, and reorganization. I hope that these changes will make the material easier to follow and understand. For example, the Unicode chapter is now at the front of the book, since Unicode influences most of the other topics in one way or another.

In addition, I give each topic much more depth than in previous editions. Specifically, I explain more of the system's inner workings so that you'll know exactly what the system is doing under the covers. I also give much more coverage of how the C/C++ run-time library interacts with the operating system—particularly on process and thread creation and destruction, as well as dynamic-link libraries.

In addition to the new organization and greater depth, I added a ton of new content. Here is a partial list of enhancements made for this edition:

- **New Windows 2000 features.** Of course, the book would not be a true revision unless it covered new features offered in Windows 2000. This edition has new information on the job kernel object, thread pooling functions, thread scheduling issues, address windowing extensions, toolhelp functions, sparse files, and more.

- **64-bit Windows support.** The text addresses 64-bit Windows-specific issues; all sample applications have been built and tested on 64-bit Windows.

- **Practical sample applications.** I have replaced many of the old sample applications with more relevant sample applications that show how to solve real-world programming problems.

- **Use of C++.** The sample applications now use C++ since many readers have requested it. As a result, the sample applications require fewer lines of code, and their logic is easier to follow and understand.

- **Reusable code.** Whenever possible, I created the source code to be generic and reusable. This should allow you to take individual functions or entire C++ classes and drop them into your own applications with little or no modification. The use of C++ made reusability much easier.

- **The VMMap utility.** This particular sample application from the earlier editions has been greatly enhanced. The new VMMap sample can now walk any process's address space, show the pathnames of any data files that have been memory-mapped into the address space, refresh its display, copy the memory information to the clipboard, and (optionally) show only the regions or blocks within the regions.

- **The ProcessInfo utility.** This sample application is new. It shows which processes are running on the system and which DLLs are being used by that module. Once you select a process, this utility can spawn the VMMap utility to walk that process's entire address space. ProcessInfo can also show which modules are loaded in the system and which executables are using that module. It also shows which modules have been relocated because of improper basing.

- **The LISWatch utility.** This sample application is also new. It monitors the system-wide and thread-specific local input state changes for windows. This utility can greatly help you track down user-interface focus change problems.

- **Performance issues.** I give much more information and numerous tips on how to make smaller, faster-running code. Specifically, I've added coverage on data alignment, processor affinity, CPU cache line boundary issues, thread synchronization concerns, module rebasing, module binding, and delay-loading DLLs.

- **Greatly improved threading synchronization material.** I completely rewrote and reorganized all of the thread synchronization material. The new presentation introduces the high-performance thread synchronization methods first and the lower-performance methods last. I've added a new "thread synchronization toolkit" chapter that offers reusable code for solving common thread synchronization scenarios.

- **Executable file format details.**   I go into much more detail about executable and DLL module file formats. I discuss the various sections of these modules and show special linker switches that allow you to do some pretty cool things to a module.

- **More detailed DLL information.**   I've rewritten and reorganized the DLL chapters. The first DLL chapter answers the two basic DLL questions: "What is a DLL?" and "How do I create a DLL?" The remaining DLL chapters dig into advanced DLL features (many of which are new) such as explicit linking, delay loading, function forwarders, DLL redirection (new for Windows 2000), module rebasing, and binding.

- **API hooking.**   Yes, it's true. I've received so much e-mail over the years about API hooking that I have finally added it to the book. I present C++ classes that make it trivial to hook APIs in one or all modules of a process. My code even traps run-time calls to *Load-Library* and *GetProcAddress* so that your API hooks are enforced.

- **Structured exception handling improvements.**   I have rewritten and reorganized much of the structured exception handling material. I have more information on unhandled exceptions, and I offer a C++ class that wraps the proper way of handling virtual memory with structured exception handling. I've added coverage on debugging exceptions and how C++ exception handling relates to structured exception handling.

- **Error handling.**   This new chapter shows how to properly detect errors when calling Windows functions. The chapter also describes some debugging techniques and how to have your functions report errors.

- **Windows Installer.**   Oh yeah, before I forget: The sample applications on the CD-ROM take advantage of the new Windows Installer built into Windows 2000. This allows you fine control over the parts that you want to install and also allows you to easily uninstall the book's sample applications and executable files using the Add/Remove Programs Control Panel applet. If you are using Windows 95, Windows 98, or Windows NT 4.0, the Setup program on the CD-ROM will automatically install the Windows Installer first. Of course, you can always just access the source files and executable files directly off the CD-ROM if you prefer.

This Book Has No Mistakes

This section's caption clearly states what I want to say. But, of course, we both know that it is a flat-out lie. My editors and I have worked hard to bring you the most accurate, up-to-date, in-depth, easy-to-read, painless-to-understand, bug-free information. Even with the fantastic team assembled, we all know that things have slipped through the cracks. If you find any mistakes in this book (especially bugs), I would greatly appreciate it if you would send the mistakes to me via my web site: *http://www.JeffreyRichter.com.*

About the CD-ROM/System Requirements

The companion CD-ROM contains the source code and executable files for all the sample applications presented in the book. All samples were written and compiled with Microsoft Visual C++ 6.0. Most of the applications run on Windows 95, Windows 98, Windows NT 4.0, and Windows 2000, but some of the applications require features that exist only in Windows NT 4.0 or Windows 2000. You'll need Microsoft Visual C++ 6.0 or later to compile all of the applications.

In the root directory of the CD-ROM, you will find the Visual Studio workspace file and the common header file. Under the root directory, there is a separate directory for each sample application. The *x*86 and Alpha32 directories contain the debug versions of all the sample applications so that you can run them directly from the CD-ROM.

When you insert the CD-ROM into the drive, the Welcome screen will present itself automatically. If the screen does not appear, go into the drive's Welcome directory and execute the PressCD.exe application.

Support

Microsoft Press provides corrections for this book at *http://mspress.microsoft.com/mspress/support.*

If you have comments, questions, or ideas regarding this book, please send them to Microsoft Press using postal mail or e-mail:

Microsoft Press
Attn: *Programming Applications for Microsoft Windows,* 4th ed., editor
One Microsoft Way
Redmond, WA 98052-6399
mspinput@microsoft.com

Thanks for Your Help

I could not have written this book without the help and technical assistance of several people. In particular, I'd like to thank:

Members of Microsoft Press editorial team: Jack Beaudry, Donnie Cameron, Ina Chang, Carl Diltz, Stephen Guty, Robert Lyon, Rebecca McKay, Rob Nance, Jocelyn Paul, Shawn Peck, John Pierce, Barb Runyan, Ben Ryan, Eric Stroo, and William Teel.

Members of the Windows 2000 team: Asmus Freytag, Dave Hart, Lee Hart, Jeff Havens, Lokesh Srinivas Koppolu, On Lee, Scott Ludwig, Lou Perazzoli, Mark Lucovsky, Landy Wang, and Steve Wood.

Members of the Windows 95 and Windows 98 team: Brian Smith, Jon Thomason, and Michael Toutonghi.

Members of the Visual C++ team: Jonathan Mark, Chuck Mitchell, Steve Salisbury, and Dan Spalding.

Members of Intel's IA-64 team: Geoff Murray, Juan Rodriguez, Jason Waxman, Koichi Yamada, Keith Yedlin, and Wilfred Yu.

Members of Compaq's AXP64 team: Tom Van Baak, Bill Baxter, Jim Lane, Rich Peterson, Annie Poh, and Joseph Sirimarco.

Members of InstallShield's Installer team: Bob Baker, Kevin Foote, and Tyler Robinson.

Members of the Entertainment and Festivities Party: Jeff Cooperstein and Stephanie, Keith Pleas and Susan, Susan Ramee and Sanjeev Surati, Scott Ludwig and Val Horvath and their son Nicholas, Darren and Shaula Massena, David Solomon, Jeff Prosise, Jim Harkins, Tony Spica.

Members of the Brotherhood: Ron, Maria, Joey (Hoops of Fire), and Brandy Richter

Members of the Raising Jeff Squad: Arlene and Sylvan Richter

Member of the Fleece Faction: Max

Member of the Devotion Division: Kristin Trace.

PART I

REQUIRED READING

ERROR HANDLING

Before we jump in and start examining the many features that Microsoft Windows has to offer, you should understand how the various Windows functions perform their error handling.

When you call a Windows function, it validates the parameters that you pass to it and then attempts to perform its duty. If you pass an invalid parameter or if for some other reason the action cannot be performed, the function's return value indicates that the function failed in some way. Table 1-1 shows the return value data types that most Windows functions use.

Data Type	Value to Indicate Failure
VOID	This function cannot possibly fail. Very few Windows functions have a return type of VOID.
BOOL	If the function fails, the return value is 0; otherwise, the return value is nonzero. It is always best to test this return value to see if it is 0 or nonzero. Avoid testing the return value to see if it is TRUE.
HANDLE	If the function fails, the return value is usually NULL; otherwise, the HANDLE identifies an object that you can manipulate. Be careful with this one because some functions return a handle value of INVALID_HANDLE_VALUE, which is defined as −1. The Platform SDK documentation for the function will clearly state whether the function returns NULL or INVALID_HANDLE_VALUE to indicate failure.
PVOID	If the function fails, the return value is NULL; otherwise, the PVOID identifies the memory address of a data block.

Table 1-1.   *(continued)*
Common return types for Windows functions

Table 1-1. *continued*

Data Type	Value to Indicate Failure
LONG/DWORD	This is a tough one. Functions that return counts usually return a LONG or DWORD. If for some reason the function can't count the thing you want counted, the function usually returns 0 or −1 (depending on the function). If you are calling a function that returns a LONG/DWORD, please read the Platform SDK documentation carefully to ensure that you are properly checking for potential errors.

When a Windows function returns with an error code, it's frequently useful to understand why the function failed. Microsoft has compiled a list of all possible error codes and has assigned each error code a 32-bit number.

Internally, when a Windows function detects an error, it uses a mechanism called thread-local storage to associate the appropriate error-code number with the calling thread. (Thread-local storage is discussed in Chapter 21.) This allows threads to run independently of each other without affecting each other's error codes. When the function returns to you, its return value will indicate that an error has occurred. To see exactly which error this is, call the *GetLastError* function:

```
DWORD GetLastError();
```

This function simply returns the thread's 32-bit error code.

Now that you have the 32-bit error code number, you need to translate that number into something more useful. The WinError.h header file contains the list of Microsoft-defined error codes. I'll reproduce some of it here so you can see what it looks like:

```
// MessageId: ERROR_SUCCESS
//
// MessageText:
//
//  The operation completed successfully.
//
#define ERROR_SUCCESS                   0L

#define NO_ERROR 0L                                 // dderror
#define SEC_E_OK                        ((HRESULT)0x00000000L)

//
// MessageId: ERROR_INVALID_FUNCTION
```

(continued)

4

```
//
// MessageText:
//
//   Incorrect function.
//
#define ERROR_INVALID_FUNCTION           1L      // dderror


//
// MessageId: ERROR_FILE_NOT_FOUND
//
// MessageText:
//
//   The system cannot find the file specified.
//
#define ERROR_FILE_NOT_FOUND             2L


//
// MessageId: ERROR_PATH_NOT_FOUND
//
// MessageText:
//
//   The system cannot find the path specified.
//
#define ERROR_PATH_NOT_FOUND             3L


//
// MessageId: ERROR_TOO_MANY_OPEN_FILES
//
// MessageText:
//
//   The system cannot open the file.
//
#define ERROR_TOO_MANY_OPEN_FILES        4L


//
// MessageId: ERROR_ACCESS_DENIED
//
// MessageText:
//
//   Access is denied.
//
#define ERROR_ACCESS_DENIED              5L
```

As you can see, each error has three representations: a message ID (a macro that you can use in your source code to compare against the return value of *GetLastError*), message text (an English text description of the error), and a number (which you should avoid using and instead use the message ID). Keep in mind that I selected only a very tiny portion of the WinError.h header file to show you; the complete file is more than 21,000 lines long!

When a Windows function fails, you should call *GetLastError* right away or the value is very likely to be overwritten if you call another Windows function.

> **NOTE**
>
> *GetLastError* returns the last error generated by the thread. If the thread calls a Windows function that succeeds, the last error code is not over-written and will not indicate success. A few Windows functions violate this rule and do change the last error code; however, the Platform SDK documentation usually indicates that the function changes the last error code when the function succeeds.

> **WINDOWS 98**
>
> Many Windows 98 functions are actually implemented in 16-bit code that originated from Microsoft's 16-bit Windows 3.1 product. This older code did not report errors via a function like *GetLastError*, and Microsoft did not "fix" the 16-bit code in Windows 98 to support this error handling. What this means to us is that many Win32 functions in Windows 98 do not set the last error code when they fail. The function will return a value that indicates failure so that you can detect that the function did, in fact, fail. But you will not be able to determine the cause of the failure.

Some Windows functions can succeed for several reasons. For example, attempting to create a named event kernel object can succeed either because you actually create the object or because an event kernel object with the same name already exists. Your application might need to know the reason for success. To return this information to you, Microsoft chose to use the last error-code mecha-nism. So when certain functions succeed, you can determine additional infor-mation by calling *GetLastError*. For functions with this behavior, the Platform SDK documentation clearly states that *GetLastError* can be used this way. See the documentation for the *CreateEvent* function for an example.

While debugging, I find it extremely useful to monitor the thread's last error code. In Microsoft Visual Studio 6.0, Microsoft's debugger supports a useful feature—you can configure the Watch window to always show you the thread's last error code number and the English text description of the error. This is done by selecting a row in the Watch window and typing "@err,hr". Examine Figure 1-1. You'll see that I've called the *CreateFile* function. This function returned a HANDLE of INVALID_HANDLE_VALUE (–1), indicating that it failed to open the specified file. But the Watch window shows us that the last error code (the error code that would be returned by the *GetLastError* function if I called it) is 0x00000002. The Watch window further indicates that error code 2 is "The system cannot find the file specified." You'll notice that this is the same string mentioned in the WinError.h header file for error code number 2.

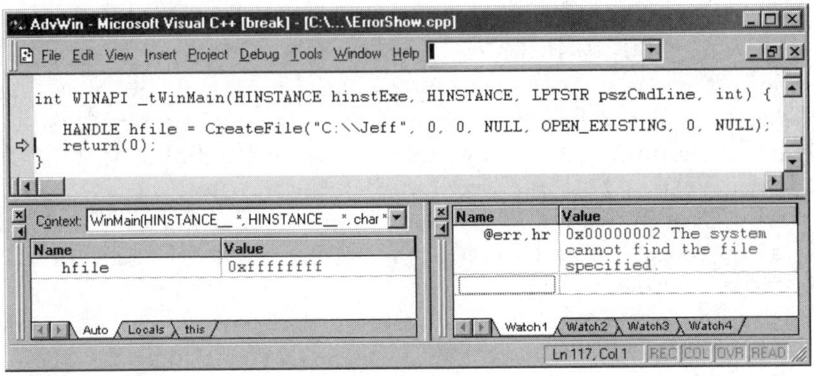

Figure 1-1.
Using "@err,hr" in Visual Studio 6.0's Watch window to view the current thread's last error code

Visual Studio also ships with a small utility called Error Lookup. You can use Error Lookup to convert an error code number into its textual description.

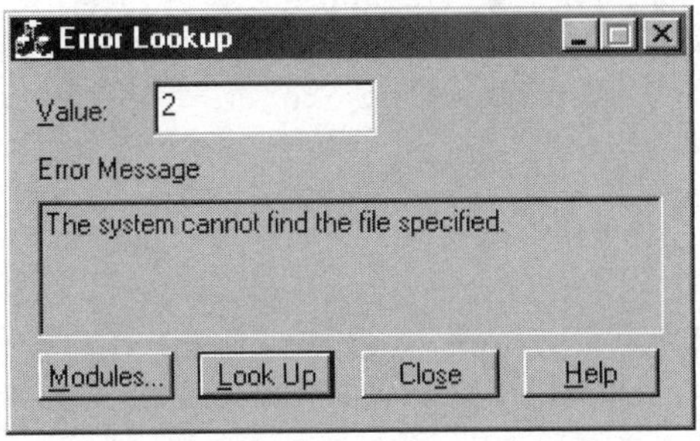

If I detect an error in an application I've written, I might want to show the text description to the user. Windows offers a function that will convert an error code into its text description. This function is called *FormatMessage* and is shown on the next page.

```
DWORD FormatMessage(
   DWORD dwFlags,
   LPCVOID pSource,
   DWORD dwMessageId,
   DWORD dwLanguageId,
   PTSTR pszBuffer,
   DWORD nSize,
   va_list *Arguments);
```

FormatMessage is actually quite rich in functionality and is the preferred way of constructing strings that are to be shown to the user. One reason for this function's usefulness is that it works easily with multiple languages. This function detects the user's preferred language (as set in the Regional Settings Control Panel applet) and returns the appropriate text. Of course, first you must translate the strings yourself and embed the translated message table resource inside your .exe or DLL module, but then the function will select the correct one. The ErrorShow sample application (shown later in this chapter) demonstrates how to call this function to convert a Microsoft-defined error code number into its text description.

Every now and then, someone asks me if Microsoft produces a master list indicating all the possible error codes that can be returned from every Windows function. The answer, unfortunately, is no. What's more, Microsoft will never produce this list—it's just too difficult to construct and maintain as new versions of the system are created.

The problem with assembling such a list is that you can call one Windows function, but internally that function might call another function, and so on. Any of these functions could fail, for lots of different reasons. Sometimes when a function fails the higher-level function can recover and still perform what you want it to. To create this master list, Microsoft would have to trace the path of every function and build the list of all possible error codes. This is difficult. And as new versions of the system were created, these function-execution paths would change.

You Can Do This Too

OK, I've shown you how Windows functions indicate errors to their callers. Microsoft also makes this mechanism available to you for use in your own functions. Let's say you're writing a function that you expect others to call. Your function might fail for one reason or another and you need to indicate that failure back to your caller.

To indicate failure, simply set the thread's last error code and then have your function return FALSE, INVALID_HANDLE_VALUE, NULL, or whatever is appropriate. To set the thread's last error code, you simply call

```
VOID SetLastError(DWORD dwErrCode);
```

passing into the function whatever 32-bit number you think is appropriate. I try to use codes that already exist in WinError.h—as long as the code maps well to the error I'm trying to report. If you don't think that any of the codes in WinError.h accurately reflect the error, you can create your own code. The error code is a 32-bit number that is divided up into the fields shown in the following table.

Bits:	31–30	29	28	27–16	15–0
Contents	Severity	Microsoft/customer	Reserved	Facility code	Exception code
Meaning	0 = Success 1 = Informational 2 = Warning 3 = Error	0 = Microsoft-defined code 1 = customer-defined code	Must be 0	Microsoft-defined	Microsoft/customer-defined

These fields are discussed in detail in Chapter 24. For now, the only important field you need to be aware of is in bit 29. Microsoft promises that all error codes they produce will have a 0 in this bit. If you create your own error codes, you must put a 1 in this bit. This way, you're guaranteed that your error code will never conflict with a Microsoft-defined error code that currently exists or is created in the future.

The ErrorShow Sample Application

The ErrorShow application, "01 ErrorShow.exe" (listed in Figure 1-2 on page 11), demonstrates how to get the text description for an error code. The source code and resource files for the application are in the 01-ErrorShow directory on this book's companion CD-ROM. Basically, this application shows how the debugger's Watch window and Error Lookup programs do their things. When you start the program, the following window appears.

You can type any error number into the edit control. When you click the Look Up button, the error's text description is displayed in the scrollable window at the bottom. The only interesting feature of this application is how to call *FormatMessage*. Here's how I use this function:

```
// Get the error code
DWORD dwError = GetDlgItemInt(hwnd, IDC_ERRORCODE, NULL, FALSE);

HLOCAL hlocal = NULL;    // Buffer that gets the error message string

// Get the error code's textual description
BOOL fOk = FormatMessage(
   FORMAT_MESSAGE_FROM_SYSTEM | FORMAT_MESSAGE_ALLOCATE_BUFFER,
   NULL, dwError, MAKELANGID(LANG_ENGLISH, SUBLANG_ENGLISH_US),
   (LPTSTR) &hlocal, 0, NULL);
   :
   :

if (hlocal != NULL) {
   SetDlgItemText(hwnd, IDC_ERRORTEXT, (PCTSTR) LocalLock(hlocal));
   LocalFree(hlocal);
} else {
   SetDlgItemText(hwnd, IDC_ERRORTEXT, TEXT("Error number not found."));
}
```

The first line retrieves the error code number out of the edit control. Then, a handle to a memory block is instantiated and initialized to NULL. The *FormatMessage* function internally allocates the block of memory and returns its handle back to us.

When calling *FormatMessage*, I pass the FORMAT_MESSAGE_FROM_ SYSTEM flag. This flag tells *FormatMessage* that we want the string for a system-defined error code. I also pass the FORMAT_MESSAGE_ALLOCATE_ BUFFER flag to tell the function to allocate a block of memory large enough for the error's text description. The handle to this block will be returned in the *hlocal* variable. The third parameter indicates the error number we want looked up, and the fourth parameter indicates what language we want the text description in.

If *FormatMessage* returns success, the text description is in the memory block and I copy it to the scrollable window at the bottom of the dialog box. If *FormatMessage* fails, I try to look up the message code in the NetMsg.dll module to see if the error is network-related. Using the handle of the NetMsg.dll module, I again call *FormatMessage*. You see, each DLL (or .exe) can have its own set of error codes that you can add to the module using the Message Compiler (MC.exe) and adding a resource to the module. This is what Visual Studio's Error Lookup tool allows you to do using the Modules dialog box.

ErrorShow.cpp

```cpp
/**********************************************************************
Module:  ErrorShow.cpp
Notices: Copyright (c) 2000 Jeffrey Richter
**********************************************************************/


#include "..\CmnHdr.h"      /* See Appendix A. */
#include <Windowsx.h>
#include <tchar.h>
#include "Resource.h"


///////////////////////////////////////////////////////////////////////


#define ESM_POKECODEANDLOOKUP     (WM_USER + 100)
const TCHAR g_szAppName[] = TEXT("Error Show");


///////////////////////////////////////////////////////////////////////


BOOL Dlg_OnInitDialog(HWND hwnd, HWND hwndFocus, LPARAM lParam) {

   chSETDLGICONS(hwnd, IDI_ERRORSHOW);

   // Don't accept error codes more than 5 digits long
   Edit_LimitText(GetDlgItem(hwnd, IDC_ERRORCODE), 5);

   // Look up the command-line passed error number
   SendMessage(hwnd, ESM_POKECODEANDLOOKUP, lParam, 0);
   return(TRUE);
}


///////////////////////////////////////////////////////////////////////


void Dlg_OnCommand(HWND hwnd, int id, HWND hwndCtl, UINT codeNotify) {
```

Figure 1-2. *(continued)*
The ErrorShow sample application

Figure 1-2. *continued*

```
switch (id) {

case IDCANCEL:
   EndDialog(hwnd, id);
   break;

case IDC_ALWAYSONTOP:
   SetWindowPos(hwnd, IsDlgButtonChecked(hwnd, IDC_ALWAYSONTOP)
      ? HWND_TOPMOST : HWND_NOTOPMOST, 0, 0, 0, 0, SWP_NOMOVE | SWP_NOSIZE);
   break;

case IDC_ERRORCODE:
   EnableWindow(GetDlgItem(hwnd, IDOK), Edit_GetTextLength(hwndCtl) > 0);
   break;

case IDOK:
   // Get the error code
   DWORD dwError = GetDlgItemInt(hwnd, IDC_ERRORCODE, NULL, FALSE);

   HLOCAL hlocal = NULL;   // Buffer that gets the error message string

   // Get the error code's textual description
   BOOL fOk = FormatMessage(
      FORMAT_MESSAGE_FROM_SYSTEM | FORMAT_MESSAGE_ALLOCATE_BUFFER,
      NULL, dwError, MAKELANGID(LANG_ENGLISH, SUBLANG_ENGLISH_US),
      (PTSTR) &hlocal, 0, NULL);

   if (!fOk) {
      // Is it a network-related error?
      HMODULE hDll = LoadLibraryEx(TEXT("netmsg.dll"), NULL,
         DONT_RESOLVE_DLL_REFERENCES);

      if (hDll != NULL) {
         FormatMessage(
            FORMAT_MESSAGE_FROM_HMODULE | FORMAT_MESSAGE_FROM_SYSTEM,
            hDll, dwError, MAKELANGID(LANG_ENGLISH, SUBLANG_ENGLISH_US),
            (PTSTR) &hlocal, 0, NULL);
         FreeLibrary(hDll);
      }
   }

   if (hlocal != NULL) {
      SetDlgItemText(hwnd, IDC_ERRORTEXT, (PCTSTR) LocalLock(hlocal));
      LocalFree(hlocal);
```

(continued)

Figure 1-2. *continued*

```
    } else {
       SetDlgItemText(hwnd, IDC_ERRORTEXT, TEXT("Error number not found."));
    }
    break;
  }
}


//////////////////////////////////////////////////////////////////////////////


INT_PTR WINAPI Dlg_Proc(HWND hwnd, UINT uMsg, WPARAM wParam, LPARAM lParam) {

   switch (uMsg) {
      chHANDLE_DLGMSG(hwnd, WM_INITDIALOG, Dlg_OnInitDialog);
      chHANDLE_DLGMSG(hwnd, WM_COMMAND,      Dlg_OnCommand);

   case ESM_POKECODEANDLOOKUP:
      SetDlgItemInt(hwnd, IDC_ERRORCODE, (UINT) wParam, FALSE);
      FORWARD_WM_COMMAND(hwnd, IDOK, GetDlgItem(hwnd, IDOK), BN_CLICKED,
         PostMessage);
      SetForegroundWindow(hwnd);
      break;
   }

   return(FALSE);
}


//////////////////////////////////////////////////////////////////////////////


int WINAPI _tWinMain(HINSTANCE hinstExe, HINSTANCE, PTSTR pszCmdLine, int) {

   HWND hwnd = FindWindow(TEXT("#32770"), TEXT("Error Show"));
   if (IsWindow(hwnd)) {
      // An instance is already running, activate it and send it the new #
      SendMessage(hwnd, ESM_POKECODEANDLOOKUP, _ttoi(pszCmdLine), 0);
   } else {
      DialogBoxParam(hinstExe, MAKEINTRESOURCE(IDD_ERRORSHOW),
         NULL, Dlg_Proc, _ttoi(pszCmdLine));
   }
   return(0);
}

////////////////////////////// End of File //////////////////////////////////
```

(continued)

Figure 1-2. *continued*

ErrorShow.rc

```
//Microsoft Developer Studio generated resource script.
//
#include "resource.h"

#define APSTUDIO_READONLY_SYMBOLS
/////////////////////////////////////////////////////////////////////////////
//
// Generated from the TEXTINCLUDE 2 resource.
//
#include "afxres.h"


/////////////////////////////////////////////////////////////////////////////
#undef APSTUDIO_READONLY_SYMBOLS


/////////////////////////////////////////////////////////////////////////////
// English (U.S.) resources

#if !defined(AFX_RESOURCE_DLL) || defined(AFX_TARG_ENU)
#ifdef _WIN32
LANGUAGE LANG_ENGLISH, SUBLANG_ENGLISH_US
#pragma code_page(1252)
#endif //_WIN32


/////////////////////////////////////////////////////////////////////////////
//
// Dialog
//

IDD_ERRORSHOW DIALOGEX 0, 0, 182, 42
STYLE DS_SETFOREGROUND | DS_3DLOOK | DS_CENTER | WS_MINIMIZEBOX | WS_VISIBLE |
    WS_CAPTION | WS_SYSMENU
CAPTION "Error Show"
FONT 8, "MS Sans Serif"
BEGIN
    LTEXT           "Error:",IDC_STATIC,4,4,19,8
    EDITTEXT        IDC_ERRORCODE,24,2,24,14,ES_AUTOHSCROLL | ES_NUMBER
    DEFPUSHBUTTON   "Look up",IDOK,56,2,36,14
    CONTROL         "&On top",IDC_ALWAYSONTOP,"Button",BS_AUTOCHECKBOX |
                    WS_TABSTOP,104,4,38,10
```

(continued)

14

Figure 1-2. *continued*

```
        EDITTEXT            IDC_ERRORTEXT,4,20,176,20,ES_MULTILINE | ES_AUTOVSCROLL |
                            ES_READONLY | NOT WS_BORDER | WS_VSCROLL,
                            WS_EX_CLIENTEDGE
END


/////////////////////////////////////////////////////////////////////////////
//
// DESIGNINFO
//

#ifdef APSTUDIO_INVOKED
GUIDELINES DESIGNINFO DISCARDABLE
BEGIN
    IDD_ERRORSHOW, DIALOG
    BEGIN
        LEFTMARGIN, 7
        RIGHTMARGIN, 175
        TOPMARGIN, 7
        BOTTOMMARGIN, 35
    END
END
#endif    // APSTUDIO_INVOKED


#ifdef APSTUDIO_INVOKED
/////////////////////////////////////////////////////////////////////////////
//
// TEXTINCLUDE
//

1 TEXTINCLUDE DISCARDABLE
BEGIN
    "resource.h\0"
END

2 TEXTINCLUDE DISCARDABLE
BEGIN
    "#include ""afxres.h""\r\n"
    "\0"
END

3 TEXTINCLUDE DISCARDABLE
```

(continued)

15

Figure 1-2. *continued*

```
BEGIN
    "\r\n"
    "\0"
END

#endif    // APSTUDIO_INVOKED


/////////////////////////////////////////////////////////////////////////
//
// Icon
//

// Icon with lowest ID value placed first to ensure application icon
// remains consistent on all systems.
IDI_ERRORSHOW           ICON    DISCARDABLE     "ErrorShow.ico"
#endif    // English (U.S.) resources
/////////////////////////////////////////////////////////////////////////


#ifndef APSTUDIO_INVOKED
/////////////////////////////////////////////////////////////////////////
//
// Generated from the TEXTINCLUDE 3 resource.
//


/////////////////////////////////////////////////////////////////////////
#endif    // not APSTUDIO_INVOKED
```

UNICODE

With Microsoft Windows becoming more and more popular around the world, it is increasingly important that we, as developers, target the various international markets. It was once common for U.S. versions of software to ship as much as six months prior to the shipping of international versions. But increasing international support in the operating system is making it easier to produce applications for international markets and therefore is reducing the time lag between distribution of the U.S. and international versions of our software.

Windows has always offered support to help developers localize their applications. An application can get country-specific information from various functions and can examine Control Panel settings to determine the user's preferences. Windows even supports different fonts for our applications.

I decided to present this chapter early in the book because considering Unicode is a fundamental step in the development of any application. Issues regarding Unicode are discussed in just about every chapter and all the sample applications presented in this book are "Unicode-ready." If you are developing for Microsoft Windows 2000 or Microsoft Windows CE, you should be developing with Unicode, period. If you are developing for Microsoft Windows 98, you have some decisions to make. Windows 98 concerns are also discussed in this chapter.

Character Sets

The real problem with localization has always been manipulating different character sets. For years, most of us have been coding text strings as a series of single-byte characters with a zero at the end. This is second nature to us. When we call *strlen*, it returns the number of characters in a zero-terminated array of single-byte characters.

The problem is that some languages and writing systems (Japanese kanji being the classic example) have so many symbols in their character sets that a single byte, which offers no more than 256 different symbols at best, is just not enough. So double-byte character sets (DBCSs) were created to support these languages and writing systems.

Single-Byte and Double-Byte Character Sets

In a double-byte character set, each character in a string consists of either 1 or 2 bytes. With kanji, for example, if the first character is between 0x81 and 0x9F or between 0xE0 and 0xFC, you must look at the next byte to determine the full character in the string. Working with double-byte character sets is a programmer's nightmare because some characters are 1 byte wide and some are 2 bytes wide.

Simply placing a call to *strlen* doesn't really tell you how many characters are in the string—it tells you the number of bytes before you hit a terminating zero. The ANSI C run-time library has no functions that allow you to manipulate double-byte character sets. However, the Microsoft Visual C++ run-time library does include a number of functions, such as *_mbslen*, that allow you to manipulate multibyte (that is, both single-byte and double-byte) character strings.

To help manipulate DBCS strings, Windows offers the following set of helper functions.

Function	Description
PTSTR *CharNext* (PCTSTR *pszCurrentChar);*	Returns the address of the next character in a string
PTSTR *CharPrev* (PCTSTR *pszStart,* PCTSTR *pszCurrentChar);*	Returns the address of the previous character in a string
BOOL *IsDBCSLeadByte* (BYTE *bTestChar);*	Returns TRUE if the byte is the first byte of a DBCS character

The first two functions, *CharNext* and *CharPrev*, allow you to traverse forward or backward through a DBCS string one character at a time. The third function, *IsDBCSLeadByte*, returns TRUE if the byte passed to it is the first byte of a 2-byte character.

Although these functions make manipulating DBCS strings a little easier, a better approach is definitely needed. Enter Unicode.

Unicode: The Wide-Byte Character Set

Unicode is a standard founded by Apple and Xerox in 1988. In 1991, a consortium was created to develop and promote Unicode. The consortium consists of companies such as Apple, Compaq, Hewlett-Packard, IBM, Microsoft, Oracle, Silicon Graphics, Inc., Sybase, Unisys, and Xerox. (A complete and updated list of consortium members is available at *www.Unicode.org.*) This group of companies is responsible for maintaining the Unicode standard. The full description of Unicode can be found in *The Unicode Standard,* published by Addison-Wesley. (This book is available through *www.Unicode.org.*)

Unicode offers a simple and consistent way of representing strings. All characters in a Unicode string are 16-bit values (2 bytes). There are no special bytes that indicate whether the next byte is part of the same character or is a new character. This means that you can traverse the characters in a string by simply incrementing or decrementing a pointer. Calls to functions such as *Char-Next*, *CharPrev*, and *IsDBCSLeadByte* are no longer necessary.

Because Unicode represents each character with a 16-bit value, more than 65,000 characters are available, making it possible to encode all the characters that make up written languages throughout the world. This is a far cry from the 256 characters available with a single-byte character set.

Currently, Unicode code points[1] are defined for the Arabic, Chinese bopomofo, Cyrillic (Russian), Greek, Hebrew, Japanese kana, Korean hangul, and Latin (English) alphabets—and more. A large number of punctuation marks, mathematical symbols, technical symbols, arrows, dingbats, diacritics, and other characters are also included in the character sets. When you add together all these alphabets and symbols, they total about 35,000 different code points, which leaves about half of the 65,000 total code points available for future expansion.

These 65,536 characters are divided into regions. The following table shows some of the regions and the characters that are assigned to them.

16-Bit Code	Characters	16-Bit Code	Characters
0000–007F	ASCII	0300–036F	Generic diacritical marks
0080–00FF	Latin1 characters	0400–04FF	Cyrillic
0100–017F	European Latin	0530–058F	Armenian
0180–01FF	Extended Latin	0590–05FF	Hebrew
0250–02AF	Standard phonetic	0600–06FF	Arabic
02B0–02FF	Modified letters	0900–097F	Devanagari

---

1. A code point is the position of a symbol in a character set.

Approximately 29,000 code points are currently unassigned, but they are reserved for future use. And approximately 6000 code points are reserved for your own personal use.

Why You Should Use Unicode

When developing an application, you should definitely consider taking advantage of Unicode. Even if you're not planning to localize your application today, developing with Unicode in mind will certainly simplify conversion in the future. In addition, Unicode does the following:

- Enables easy data exchange between languages

- Allows you to distribute a single binary .exe or DLL file that supports all languages

- Improves the efficiency of your application (discussed in more detail later in the chapter)

Windows 2000 and Unicode

Windows 2000 is built from the ground up using Unicode. All of the core functions for creating windows, displaying text, performing string manipulations, and so forth require Unicode strings. If you call any Windows function and pass it an ANSI string, the system first converts the string to Unicode and then passes the Unicode string to the operating system. If you are expecting ANSI strings back from a function, the system converts the Unicode string to an ANSI string before returning to your application. All these conversions occur invisibly to you. Of course, there is time and memory overhead involved for the system to carry out all these string conversions.

For example, if you call *CreateWindowEx* and pass non-Unicode strings for the class name and window caption text, *CreateWindowEx* must allocate blocks of memory (in your process's default heap), convert the non-Unicode strings to Unicode strings and store the result in the allocated memory blocks, and make a function call to the Unicode version of *CreateWindowEx*.

For functions that fill buffers with strings, the system must convert from Unicode to non-Unicode equivalents before your application can process the string. Because the system must perform all these conversions, your application requires more memory and runs slower. You can make your application perform more efficiently by developing your application using Unicode from the start.

Windows 98 and Unicode

Windows 98 is not a completely new operating system. It has a 16-bit Windows heritage that was not designed to handle Unicode. Adding Unicode support would have been too large a task and was dropped from the product's feature list. For this reason, Windows 98—like its predecessors—does almost everything internally using ANSI strings.

You can still write a Windows application that processes Unicode characters and strings, but it is much harder to use the Windows functions. For example, if you want to call *CreateWindowEx* and pass it ANSI strings, the call is very fast; no buffers need to be allocated from your process's default heap, and no string conversions need to be done. However, if you want to call *CreateWindowEx* and pass it Unicode strings, you must explicitly allocate buffers and call functions to perform the conversion from Unicode to ANSI. You can then call *CreateWindowEx*, passing the ANSI strings. When *CreateWindowEx* returns, you can free the temporary buffers. This is far less convenient than using Unicode on Windows 2000. I will describe how you can perform these conversions under Windows 98 later in this chapter.

Although it is true that most implementations of Unicode functions do nothing in Windows 98, a few Unicode functions do have useful implementations. These functions are

- EnumResourceLanguagesW
- EnumResourceNamesW
- EnumResourceTypesW
- ExtTextOutW
- FindResourceW
- FindResourceExW
- GetCharWidthW
- GetCommandLineW

- GetTextExtentPoint32W
- GetTextExtentPointW
- lstrlenW
- MessageBoxExW
- MessageBoxW
- TextOutW
- WideCharToMultiByte
- MultiByteToWideChar

Unfortunately, many of these functions exhibit all kinds of bugs in Windows 98. Some of them don't work with certain fonts, some of them corrupt the heap, some of them crash printer drivers, and so on. You're going to have to do a lot of testing if you use these. Even then you might not be able to fix the problems—you'll just have to tell your users about them.

Windows CE and Unicode

The Windows CE operating system was created for small footprint machines: machines with little memory and no disk storage. You would think that since a primary goal was to create as small a system as possible, Microsoft would have used ANSI as the native character set. However, Microsoft was not shortsighted. They knew that Windows CE machines were going to be sold all over the world, and they wanted to reduce software development costs so that applications could more easily be created. Therefore, Windows CE is natively Unicode.

However, to keep Windows CE small, Microsoft decided not to support ANSI Windows functions at all. So if you are developing for Windows CE, you must understand and use Unicode throughout your application.

Keeping Score

For those of you keeping score at home, let's review the "Microsoft Unicode Story":

- Windows 2000 supports Unicode and ANSI—you can develop for either one
- Windows 98 supports ANSI only—you must develop for ANSI
- Windows CE supports Unicode only—you must develop for Unicode

While Microsoft has tried to make it easy for developers to implement software that runs on these three platforms, the Unicode/ANSI difference can make things difficult and is typically one of the biggest problems I run into. Don't get me wrong, Microsoft is firmly behind Unicode and I strongly encourage you to use it. Just be aware that you will run into issues that take time to resolve. My suggestion to you is to try to work with Unicode as much as possible and, if you're running on Windows 98, convert to ANSI only if and when you have to.

Unfortunately, there is yet another small issue that you should be aware of: COM.

A Quick Word About COM

When Microsoft was porting COM from 16-bit Windows to Win32, an executive decision was made that all COM interface methods requiring a string would only accept Unicode strings. This was a great decision because COM is typically used to allow different components to talk to each other and Unicode is the richest way to pass strings around.

If you are developing for Windows 2000 or Windows CE and are also using COM, you have it made. Using Unicode throughout your source code will make talking to the operating system and talking to COM objects a breeze.

If you're developing for Windows 98 and also using COM, you have problems. COM requires that you use Unicode strings. Most of the operating system functions require that you use ANSI strings. What a nightmare! I have worked on several projects in which I have written a lot of code solely to convert strings back and forth.

How to Write Unicode Source Code

Microsoft designed the Windows API for Unicode so that it would have as little impact on your code as possible. In fact, it is possible to write a single source code file so that it can be compiled with or without using Unicode—you need only define two macros (UNICODE and _UNICODE) to make the change and then recompile.

Unicode Support in the C Run-Time Library

To take advantage of Unicode character strings, some data types have been defined. The standard C header file, String.h, has been modified to define a data type named *wchar_t*, which is the data type of a Unicode character:

```
typedef unsigned short wchar_t;
```

For example, if you want to create a buffer to hold a Unicode string of up to 99 characters and a terminating zero character, you can use the following statement:

```
wchar_t szBuffer[100];
```

This statement creates an array of one hundred 16-bit values. Of course, the standard C run-time string functions, such as *strcpy*, *strchr*, and *strcat*, operate on ANSI strings only; they don't correctly process Unicode strings. So, ANSI C also has a complementary set of functions. Figure 2-1 shows some of the standard ANSI C string functions followed by their equivalent Unicode functions.

```
char * strcat(char *, const char *);
wchar_t * wcscat(wchar_t *, const wchar_t *);
```

Figure 2-1. *(continued)*
Standard ANSI C string functions and their Unicode equivalents

23

Figure 2-1. *continued*

```
char * strchr(const char *, int);
wchar_t * wcschr(const wchar_t *, wchar_t);

int strcmp(const char *, const char *);
int wcscmp(const wchar_t *, const wchar_t *);

char * strcpy(char *, const char *);
wchar_t * wcscpy(wchar_t *, const wchar_t *);

size_t strlen(const char *);
size_t wcslen(const wchar_t *);
```

Notice that all the Unicode functions begin with *wcs*, which stands for *wide character string*. To call the Unicode function, simply replace the *str* prefix of any ANSI string function with the *wcs* prefix.

> One very important point that most developers don't remember is that the C run-time library provided by Microsoft conforms to the ANSI standard C run-time library. ANSI C dictates that the C run-time library supports Unicode characters and strings. This means that you can always call C run-time functions to manipulate Unicode characters and strings—even if you're running on Windows 98. In other words, *wcscat*, *wcslen*, *wcstok*, and so on all work just fine on Windows 98; it's the operating system functions you need to worry about.

Code that includes explicit calls to either the *str* functions or the *wcs* functions cannot be compiled easily for both ANSI and Unicode. Earlier in this chapter, I said that it's possible to make a single source code file that can be compiled for both. To set up the dual capability, you include the TChar.h file instead of including String.h.

TChar.h exists for the sole purpose of helping you create ANSI/Unicode generic source code files. It consists of a set of macros that you should use in your source code instead of making direct calls to either the *str* or the *wcs* functions. If you define _UNICODE when you compile your source code, the macros reference the *wcs* set of functions. If you do not define _UNICODE, the macros reference the *str* set of functions.

For example, there is a macro called *_tcscpy* in TChar.h. If _UNICODE is not defined when you include this header file, *_tcscpy* expands to the ANSI *strcpy* function. However, if _UNICODE is defined, *_tcscpy* expands to the

Unicode *wcscpy* function. All C run-time functions that take string arguments have a generic macro defined in TChar.h. If you use the generic macros instead of the ANSI/Unicode specific function names, you'll be well on your way to creating source code that can be compiled natively for ANSI or Unicode.

Unfortunately, you need to do a little more work than just use these macros. TChar.h includes some additional macros.

To define an array of string characters that is ANSI/Unicode generic, use the following TCHAR data type. If _UNICODE is defined, TCHAR is declared as follows:

```
typedef wchar_t TCHAR;
```

If _UNICODE is not defined, TCHAR is declared as

```
typedef char TCHAR;
```

Using this data type, you can allocate a string of characters as follows:

```
TCHAR szString[100];
```

You can also create pointers to strings:

```
TCHAR *szError = "Error";
```

However, there is a problem with the previous line. By default, Microsoft's C++ compiler compiles all strings as though they were ANSI strings, not Unicode strings. As a result, the compiler will compile this line correctly if _UNICODE is not defined, but will generate an error if _UNICODE is defined. To generate a Unicode string instead of an ANSI string, you would have to rewrite the line as follows:

```
TCHAR *szError = L"Error";
```

An uppercase *L* before a literal string informs the compiler that the string should be compiled as a Unicode string. When the compiler places the string in the program's data section, it intersperses zero bytes between every character. The problem with this change is that now the program will compile successfully only if _UNICODE is defined. We need another macro that selectively adds the uppercase *L* before a literal string. This is the job of the _TEXT macro, also defined in TChar.h. If _UNICODE is defined, _TEXT is defined as

```
#define _TEXT(x) L ## x
```

If _UNICODE is not defined, _TEXT is defined as

```
#define _TEXT(x) x
```

Using this macro, we can rewrite the line above so that it compiles correctly whether or not the _UNICODE macro is defined, as shown here:

```
TCHAR *szError = _TEXT("Error");
```

The _TEXT macro can also be used for literal characters. For example, to check whether the first character of a string is an uppercase *J*, write the following code:

```
if (szError[0] == _TEXT('J')) {
   // First character is a 'J'
   ⋮
} else {
   // First character is not a 'J'
   ⋮
}
```

Unicode Data Types Defined by Windows

The Windows header files define the data types listed in the following table.

Data Type	Description
WCHAR	Unicode character
PWSTR	Pointer to a Unicode string
PCWSTR	Pointer to a constant Unicode string

These data types always refer to Unicode characters and strings. The Windows header files also define the ANSI/Unicode generic data types PTSTR and PCTSTR. These data types point to either an ANSI string or a Unicode string, depending on whether the UNICODE macro is defined when you compile the module.

Notice that this time the UNICODE macro is not preceded by an underscore. The _UNICODE macro is used for the C run-time header files and the UNICODE macro is used for the Windows header files. You usually need to define both macros when compiling a source code module.

Unicode and ANSI Functions in Windows

I implied earlier that two functions are called *CreateWindowEx*: a *CreateWindowEx* that accepts Unicode strings and a second *CreateWindowEx* that accepts ANSI strings. This is true, but the two functions are actually prototyped as follows:

```
HWND WINAPI CreateWindowExW(
    DWORD dwExStyle,
    PCWSTR pClassName,
    PCWSTR pWindowName,
    DWORD dwStyle,
    int X,
    int Y,
    int nWidth,
    int nHeight,
    HWND hWndParent,
    HMENU hMenu,
    HINSTANCE hInstance,
    PVOID pParam);

HWND WINAPI CreateWindowExA(
    DWORD dwExStyle,
    PCSTR pClassName,
    PCSTR pWindowName,
    DWORD dwStyle,
    int X,
    int Y,
    int nWidth,
    int nHeight,
    HWND hWndParent,
    HMENU hMenu,
    HINSTANCE hInstance,
    PVOID pParam);
```

CreateWindowExW is the version that accepts Unicode strings. The uppercase *W* at the end of the function name stands for *wide*. Unicode characters are 16 bits each, so they are frequently referred to as wide characters. The uppercase *A* at the end of *CreateWindowExA* indicates that the function accepts ANSI character strings.

But usually we just include a call to *CreateWindowEx* in our code and don't directly call either *CreateWindowExW* or *CreateWindowExA*. In WinUser.h, *CreateWindowEx* is actually a macro defined as

```
#ifdef UNICODE
#define CreateWindowEx CreateWindowExW
#else
#define CreateWindowEx CreateWindowExA
#endif // !UNICODE
```

Whether UNICODE is defined when you compile your source code module determines which version of *CreateWindowEx* is called. When you port a 16-bit Windows application, you probably won't define UNICODE when you compile. Any calls you make to *CreateWindowEx* expand the macro to call *CreateWindowExA*—the ANSI version of *CreateWindowEx*. Because 16-bit Windows offers only an ANSI version of *CreateWindowEx*, your porting will go much easier.

Under Windows 2000, Microsoft's source code for *CreateWindowExA* is simply a thunking, or translation, layer that allocates memory to convert ANSI strings to Unicode strings; the code then calls *CreateWindowExW*, passing the converted strings. When *CreateWindowExW* returns, *CreateWindowExA* frees its memory buffers and returns the window handle to you.

If you're creating dynamic-link libraries (DLLs) that other software developers will use, consider using this technique: supply two exported functions in the DLL—an ANSI version and a Unicode version. In the ANSI version, simply allocate memory, perform the necessary string conversions, and call the Unicode version of the function. (I'll demonstrate this process later in this chapter.)

Under Windows 98, Microsoft's source code for *CreateWindowExA* is the function that does the work. Windows 98 offers all the entry points to all the Windows functions that accept a Unicode parameter, but these functions do not translate Unicode strings to ANSI strings—they just return failure. A call to *GetLastError* returns ERROR_CALL_NOT_IMPLEMENTED. Only ANSI versions of these functions work properly. If your compiled code makes calls to any of the wide-character functions, your application will not run under Windows 98.

Certain functions in the Windows API, such as *WinExec* and *OpenFile*, exist solely for backward compatibility with 16-bit Windows programs and should be avoided. You should replace any calls to *WinExec* and *OpenFile* with calls to the *CreateProcess* and *CreateFile* functions. Internally, the old functions call the new functions anyway. The big problem with the old functions is that they don't accept Unicode strings. When you call these functions, you must pass ANSI strings. All the new and nonobsolete functions, on the other hand, do have both ANSI and Unicode versions on Windows 2000.

Windows String Functions

Windows also offers a comprehensive set of string manipulation functions. These functions are similar to the C run-time string functions, such as *strcpy* and *wcscpy*. However, the operating system functions are part of the OS, and many OS components use these functions instead of the C run-time library. I recommend that you favor the OS functions over the C run-time string functions. This will help your application's performance slightly because the OS string functions are used frequently by heavyweight applications such as the operating system's shell process, Explorer.exe. Since the functions are used heavily, they will probably already be loaded into RAM while your application runs.

To use these functions, the system must be running Windows 2000 or Windows 98. The functions are also available on earlier versions of Windows if Internet Explorer 4.0 or later is installed.

In classic OS function style, the OS string function names contain both uppercase and lowercase letters and look like this: *StrCat*, *StrChr*, *StrCmp*, and *StrCpy* (to name just a few). To use these functions, you must include the ShlWApi.h header file. Also, as previously discussed, these string functions come in both ANSI and Unicode versions, such as *StrCatA* and *StrCatW*. Because these are operating system functions, the symbols will expand to their wide versions if you define UNICODE (without the preceding underscore) when you build your application.

Making Your Application ANSI- and Unicode-Ready

It's a good idea to start converting your application to be Unicode-ready even if you don't plan to use Unicode right away. Here are the basic guidelines you should follow:

- Start thinking of text strings as arrays of characters, not as arrays of *char*s or arrays of bytes.

- Use generic data types (such as TCHAR and PTSTR) for text characters and strings.

- Use explicit data types (such as BYTE and PBYTE) for bytes, byte pointers, and data buffers.

- Use the TEXT macro for literal characters and strings.

- Perform global replaces. (For example, replace PSTR with PTSTR.)

- Modify string arithmetic problems. For example, functions usually expect you to pass a buffer's size in characters, not bytes. This means that you should not pass *sizeof(szBuffer)* but should instead pass *(sizeof(szBuffer) / sizeof(TCHAR))*. Also, if you need to allocate a block of memory for a string and you have the number of characters in the string, remember that you allocate memory in bytes. This means that you must call *malloc(nCharacters * sizeof(TCHAR))* and not call *malloc(nCharacters)*. Of all the guidelines I've just listed, this is the most difficult one to remember, and the compiler offers no warnings or errors if you make a mistake.

When I was developing the sample programs for the first edition of this book, I originally wrote them so that they compiled natively as ANSI-only. Then, when I began to write this chapter, I knew that I wanted to encourage the use of Unicode and was going to create sample programs to demonstrate how easy it is to create programs that can be compiled in both Unicode and ANSI. I decided that the best course of action was to convert all the sample programs in the book so that they could be compiled in both Unicode and ANSI.

I converted all the programs in about four hours, which isn't bad, considering that I didn't have any prior conversion experience.

Windows String Functions

Windows also offers a set of functions for manipulating Unicode strings, as described in the following table.

Function	Description
lstrcat	Concatenates one string onto the end of another
lstrcmp	Performs case-sensitive comparison of two strings
lstrcmpi	Performs case-insensitive comparison of two strings
lstrcpy	Copies one string to another location in memory
lstrlen	Returns the length of a string in characters

These functions are implemented as macros that call either the Unicode version of the function or the ANSI version of the function, depending on whether UNICODE is defined when the source module is compiled. For example, if UNICODE is not defined, *lstrcat* will expand to *lstrcatA*. If UNICODE is defined, *lstrcat* will expand to *lstrcatW*.

Two string functions, *lstrcmp* and *lstrcmpi*, behave differently from their equivalent C run-time functions. The C run-time functions *strcmp*, *strcmpi*, *wcscmp*, and *wcscmpi* simply compare the values of the code points in the strings; that is, the functions ignore the meaning of the actual characters and simply check the numeric value of each character in the first string with the numeric value of the character in the second string. The Windows functions *lstrcmp* and *lstrcmpi*, on the other hand, are implemented as calls to the Windows function *CompareString*:

```
int CompareString(
   LCID lcid,
   DWORD fdwStyle,
   PCWSTR pString1,
   int cch1,
   PCTSTR pString2,
   int cch2);
```

This function compares two Unicode strings. The first parameter to *Compare-String* specifies a locale ID (LCID), a 32-bit value that identifies a particular language. *CompareString* uses this LCID to compare the two strings by checking the meaning of the characters as they apply to a particular language. This action is much more meaningful than the simple number comparison performed by the C run-time functions.

When any of the *lstrcmp* family of functions calls *CompareString*, the function passes the result of calling the Windows *GetThreadLocale* function as the first parameter:

```
LCID GetThreadLocale();
```

Every time a thread is created, it is assigned a locale. This function returns the current locale setting for the thread.

The second parameter of *CompareString* identifies flags that modify the method used by the function to compare the two strings. The following table shows the possible flags.

Flag	Meaning
NORM_IGNORECASE	Ignore case differences
NORM_IGNOREKANATYPE	Do not differentiate between hiragana and katakana characters
NORM_IGNORENONSPACE	Ignore nonspacing characters
NORM_IGNORESYMBOLS	Ignore symbols
NORM_IGNOREWIDTH	Do not differentiate between a single-byte character and the same character as a double-byte character
SORT_STRINGSORT	Treat punctuation the same as symbols

When *lstrcmp* calls *CompareString*, it passes 0 for the *fdwStyle* parameter. But when *lstrcmpi* calls *CompareString*, it passes NORM_IGNORECASE. The remaining four parameters of *CompareString* specify the two strings and their respective lengths. If you pass −1 for the *cch1* parameter, the function assumes that the *pString1* string is zero-terminated and calculates the length of the string. This also is true for the *cch2* parameter with respect to the *pString2* string.

Other C run-time functions don't offer good support for manipulating Unicode strings. For example, the *tolower* and *toupper* functions don't properly convert characters with accent marks. To compensate for these deficiencies in the C run-time library, you'll need to call the following Windows functions to convert the case of a Unicode string. These functions also work correctly for ANSI strings.

The first two functions,

```
PTSTR CharLower(PTSTR pszString);
```

and

```
PTSTR CharUpper(PTSTR pszString);
```

convert either a single character or an entire zero-terminated string. To convert an entire string, simply pass the address of the string. To convert a single character, you must pass the individual character as follows:

```
TCHAR cLowerCaseChar = CharLower((PTSTR) szString[0]);
```

Casting the single character to a PTSTR calls the function, passing it a value in which the low 16 bits contain the character and the high 16 bits contain 0. When the function sees that the high bits are 0, the function knows that you want to convert a single character rather than a whole string. The value returned will be a 32-bit value with the converted character in the low 16 bits.

The next two functions are similar to the previous two except that they convert the characters contained inside a buffer (which does not need to be zero-terminated):

```
DWORD CharLowerBuff(
    PTSTR pszString,
    DWORD cchString);
DWORD CharUpperBuff(
    PTSTR pszString,
    DWORD cchString);
```

Other C run-time functions, such as *isalpha*, *islower*, and *isupper*, return a value that indicates whether a given character is alphabetic, lowercase, or uppercase. The Windows API offers functions that return this information as well, but the Windows functions also consider the language indicated by the user in the Control Panel:

```
BOOL IsCharAlpha(TCHAR ch);
BOOL IsCharAlphaNumeric(TCHAR ch);
BOOL IsCharLower(TCHAR ch);
BOOL IsCharUpper(TCHAR ch);
```

The *printf* family of functions is the last group of C run-time functions we'll discuss. If you compile your source module with _UNICODE defined, the *printf* family of functions expects that all the character and string parameters represent Unicode characters and strings. However, if you compile without defining _UNICODE, the *printf* family expects that all the characters and strings passed to it are ANSI.

Microsoft has added some special field types to their C run-time's *printf* family of functions. Some of these field types have not been adopted by ANSI C. The new types allow you to easily mix and match ANSI and Unicode characters and strings. The operating system's *wsprintf* function has also been enhanced. Here are some examples (note the use of capital *S* and lowercase *s*):

```
char   szA[100];     // An ANSI string buffer
WCHAR szW[100];      // A Unicode string buffer

// Normal sprintf: all strings are ANSI
sprintf(szA,   "%s",   "ANSI Str");

// Converts Unicode string to ANSI
sprintf(szA,   "%S",  L"Unicode Str");

// Normal swprintf: all strings are Unicode
swprintf(szW, L"%s",  L"Unicode Str");

// Converts ANSI string to Unicode
swprintf(szW, L"%S",   "ANSI Str");
```

Resources

When the resource compiler compiles all your resources, the output file is a binary representation of the resources. String values in your resources (string tables, dialog box templates, menus, and so on) are always written as Unicode strings. Under both Windows 98 and Windows 2000, the system performs internal conversions if your application doesn't define the UNICODE macro.

For example, if UNICODE is not defined when you compile your source module, a call to *LoadString* will actually call the *LoadStringA* function. *LoadStringA* will then read the string from your resources and convert the string to ANSI. The ANSI representation of the string will be returned from the function to your application.

Determining If Text Is ANSI or Unicode

To date, there have been very few Unicode text files. In fact, most of Microsoft's own products do not ship with any Unicode text files. However, I expect that this trend could change in the future (albeit a long way into the future). Certainly, the Windows 2000 Notepad application allows you to open both Unicode and ANSI files as well as create them. In fact, Figure 2-2 shows Notepad's File Save As dialog box. Notice the different ways that you can save a text file.

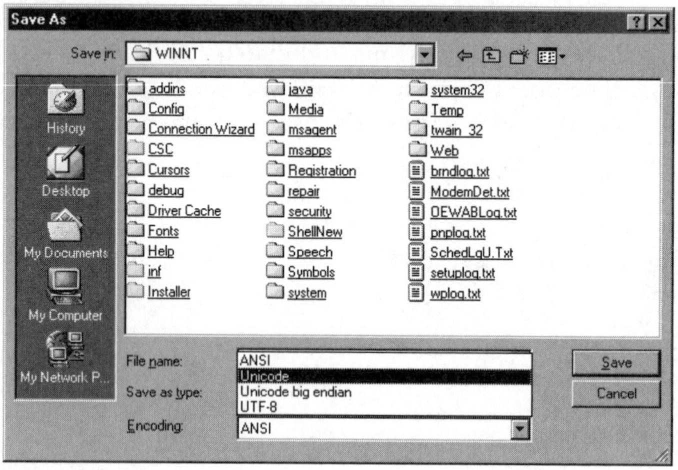

Figure 2-2.
The Windows 2000 Notepad File Save As dialog box

For many applications that open text files and process them, such as compilers, it would be convenient if, after opening a file, the application could determine whether the text file contained ANSI characters or Unicode characters. The *IsTextUnicode* function can help make this distinction:

```
DWORD IsTextUnicode(CONST PVOID pvBuffer, int cb, PINT pResult);
```

The problem with text files is that there are no hard and fast rules as to their content. This makes it extremely difficult to determine whether the file contains ANSI or Unicode characters. *IsTextUnicode* uses a series of statistical and deterministic methods in order to guess at the content of the buffer. Because this is not an exact science, it is possible that *IsTextUnicode* will return an incorrect result.

The first parameter, *pvBuffer*, identifies the address of a buffer that you want to test. The data is a void pointer because you don't know whether you have an array of ANSI characters or an array of Unicode characters.

The second parameter, *cb*, specifies the number of bytes that *pvBuffer* points to. Again, because you don't know what's in the buffer, *cb* is a count of bytes rather than a count of characters. Note that you do not have to specify the entire length of the buffer. Of course, the more bytes *IsTextUnicode* can test, the more accurate a response you're likely to get.

The third parameter, *pResult*, is the address of an integer that you must initialize before calling *IsTextUnicode*. You initialize this integer to indicate which tests you want *IsTextUnicode* to perform. You can also pass NULL for this parameter, in which case *IsTextUnicode* will perform every test it can. (See the Platform SDK documentation for more details.)

If *IsTextUnicode* thinks that the buffer contains Unicode text, TRUE is returned; otherwise, FALSE is returned. That's right, the function actually returns a Boolean even though Microsoft prototyped it as returning a DWORD. If specific tests were requested in the integer pointed to by the *pResult* parameter, the function sets the bits in the integer before returning to reflect the results of each test.

WINDOWS 98

> Under Windows 98, the *IsTextUnicode* function has no useful implementation and simply returns FALSE; calling *GetLastError* returns ERROR_CALL_NOT_IMPLEMENTED.

The FileRev sample application presented in Chapter 17 demonstrates the use of the *IsTextUnicode* function.

Translating Strings Between Unicode and ANSI

The Windows function *MultiByteToWideChar* converts multibyte-character strings to wide-character strings. *MultiByteToWideChar* is shown at the top of page 36.

```
int MultiByteToWideChar(
   UINT uCodePage,
   DWORD dwFlags,
   PCSTR pMultiByteStr,
   int cchMultiByte,
   PWSTR pWideCharStr,
   int cchWideChar);
```

The *uCodePage* parameter identifies a code page number that is associated with the multibyte string. The *dwFlags* parameter allows you to specify additional control that affects characters with diacritical marks such as accents. Usually the flags aren't used, and 0 is passed in the *dwFlags* parameter. The *pMultiByteStr* parameter specifies the string to be converted, and the *cchMultiByte* parameter indicates the length (in bytes) of the string. The function determines the length of the source string if you pass −1 for the *cchMultiByte* parameter.

The Unicode version of the string resulting from the conversion is written to the buffer located in memory at the address specified by the *pWideCharStr* parameter. You must specify the maximum size of this buffer (in characters) in the *cchWideChar* parameter. If you call *MultiByteToWideChar*, passing 0 for the *cchWideChar* parameter, the function doesn't perform the conversion and instead returns the size of the buffer required for the conversion to succeed. Typically, you will convert a multibyte-character string to its Unicode equivalent by performing the following steps:

1. Call *MultiByteToWideChar*, passing NULL for the *pWideCharStr* parameter and 0 for the *cchWideChar* parameter.

2. Allocate a block of memory large enough to hold the converted Unicode string. This size is returned by the previous call to *MultiByteToWideChar*.

3. Call *MultiByteToWideChar* again, this time passing the address of the buffer as the *pWideCharStr* parameter and passing the size returned by the first call to *MultiByteToWideChar* as the *cchWideChar* parameter.

4. Use the converted string.

5. Free the memory block occupying the Unicode string.

The function *WideCharToMultiByte* converts a wide-character string to its multibyte string equivalent, as shown here:

```
int WideCharToMultiByte(
   UINT uCodePage,
   DWORD dwFlags,
   PCWSTR pWideCharStr,
   int cchWideChar,
   PSTR pMultiByteStr,
   int cchMultiByte,
   PCSTR pDefaultChar,
   PBOOL pfUsedDefaultChar);
```

This function is similar to the *MultiByteToWideChar* function. Again, the *uCodePage* parameter identifies the code page to be associated with the newly converted string. The *dwFlags* parameter allows you to specify additional control over the conversion. The flags affect characters with diacritical marks and characters that the system is unable to convert. Usually you won't need this degree of control over the conversion, and you'll pass 0 for the *dwFlags* parameter.

The *pWideCharStr* parameter specifies the address in memory of the string to be converted, and the *cchWideChar* parameter indicates the length (in characters) of this string. The function determines the length of the source string if you pass –1 for the *cchWideChar* parameter.

The multibyte version of the string resulting from the conversion is written to the buffer indicated by the *pMultiByteStr* parameter. You must specify the maximum size of this buffer (in bytes) in the *cchMultiByte* parameter. Passing 0 as the *cchMultiByte* parameter of the *WideCharToMultiByte* function causes the function to return the size required by the destination buffer. You'll typically convert a wide-byte character string to a multibyte-character string using a sequence of events similar to those discussed when converting a multibyte string to a wide-byte string.

You'll notice that the *WideCharToMultiByte* function accepts two parameters more than the *MultiByteToWideChar* function: *pDefaultChar* and *pfUsedDefaultChar*. These parameters are used by the *WideCharToMultiByte* function only if it comes across a wide character that doesn't have a representation in the code page identified by the *uCodePage* parameter. If the wide character cannot be converted, the function uses the character pointed to by the *pDefaultChar* parameter. If this parameter is NULL, which is most common, the function uses a system default character. This default character is usually a question mark. This is dangerous for filenames because the question mark is a wildcard character.

The *pfUsedDefaultChar* parameter points to a Boolean variable that the function sets to TRUE if at least one character in the wide-character string could not be converted to its multibyte equivalent. The function sets the variable to

FALSE if all the characters convert successfully. You can test this variable after the function returns to check whether the wide-character string was converted successfully. Again, you usually pass NULL for this parameter.

For a more complete description of how to use these functions, please refer to the Platform SDK documentation.

You could use these two functions to easily create both Unicode and ANSI versions of functions. For example, you might have a dynamic-link library containing a function that reverses all the characters in a string. You could write the Unicode version of the function as shown here:

```
BOOL StringReverseW(PWSTR pWideCharStr) {

   // Get a pointer to the last character in the string.
   PWSTR pEndOfStr = pWideCharStr + wcslen(pWideCharStr) - 1;
   wchar_t cCharT;
   // Repeat until we reach the center character in the string.
   while (pWideCharStr < pEndOfStr) {
      // Save a character in a temporary variable.
      cCharT = *pWideCharStr;

      // Put the last character in the first character.
      *pWideCharStr = *pEndOfStr;

      // Put the temporary character in the last character.
      *pEndOfStr = cCharT;

      // Move in one character from the left.
      pWideCharStr++;

      // Move in one character from the right.
      pEndOfStr--;
   }

   // The string is reversed; return success.
   return(TRUE);
}
```

And you could write the ANSI version of the function so that it doesn't perform the actual work of reversing the string at all. Instead, you could write the ANSI version so that it converts the ANSI string to Unicode, passes the Unicode string to the *StringReverseW* function, and then converts the reversed string back to ANSI. The function would look like this:

```
BOOL StringReverseA(PSTR pMultiByteStr) {
   PWSTR pWideCharStr;
   int nLenOfWideCharStr;
   BOOL fOk = FALSE;

   // Calculate the number of characters needed to hold
   // the wide-character version of the string.
   nLenOfWideCharStr = MultiByteToWideChar(CP_ACP, 0,
      pMultiByteStr, -1, NULL, 0);

   // Allocate memory from the process's default heap to
   // accommodate the size of the wide-character string.
   // Don't forget that MultiByteToWideChar returns the
   // number of characters, not the number of bytes, so
   // you must multiply by the size of a wide character.
   pWideCharStr = HeapAlloc(GetProcessHeap(), 0,
      nLenOfWideCharStr * sizeof(WCHAR));

   if (pWideCharStr == NULL)
      return(fOk);

   // Convert the multibyte string to a wide-character string.
   MultiByteToWideChar(CP_ACP, 0, pMultiByteStr, -1,
      pWideCharStr, nLenOfWideCharStr);

   // Call the wide-character version of this
   // function to do the actual work.
   fOk = StringReverseW(pWideCharStr);

   if (fOk) {
      // Convert the wide-character string back
      // to a multibyte string.
      WideCharToMultiByte(CP_ACP, 0, pWideCharStr, -1,
         pMultiByteStr, strlen(pMultiByteStr), NULL, NULL);
   }

   // Free the memory containing the wide-character string.
   HeapFree(GetProcessHeap(), 0, pWideCharStr);

   return(fOk);
}
```

Finally, in the header file that you distribute with the dynamic-link library, you would prototype the two functions as follows:

```
BOOL StringReverseW(PWSTR pWideCharStr);
BOOL StringReverseA(PSTR pMultiByteStr);

#ifdef UNICODE
#define StringReverse StringReverseW
#else
#define StringReverse StringReverseA
#endif // !UNICODE
```

CHAPTER THREE

KERNEL OBJECTS

We begin our understanding of the Windows API by examining kernel objects and their handles. This chapter covers relatively abstract concepts—we're not going to discuss the particulars of any specific kernel object. Instead, we're going to discuss features that apply to all kernel objects.

I would have preferred to start off with a more concrete topic, but a solid understanding of kernel objects is critical to becoming a proficient Windows software developer. Kernel objects are used by the system and by the applications we write to manage numerous resources such as processes, threads, and files (to name just a few). The concepts presented in this chapter will appear throughout most of the remaining chapters in this book. However, I do realize that some of the material covered in this chapter won't sink in until you start manipulating kernel objects using actual functions. So, as you read various other chapters in this book, you'll probably want to refer back to this chapter from time to time.

What Is a Kernel Object?

As a Windows software developer, you create, open, and manipulate kernel objects regularly. The system creates and manipulates several types of kernel objects, such as access token objects, event objects, file objects, file-mapping objects, I/O completion port objects, job objects, mailslot objects, mutex objects, pipe objects, process objects, semaphore objects, thread objects, and waitable timer objects. These objects are created by calling various functions. For example, the *CreateFileMapping* function causes the system to create a file-mapping object. Each kernel object is simply a memory block allocated by the kernel and is accessible only by the kernel. This memory block is a data structure whose members maintain information about the object. Some members (security descriptor, usage count, and so on) are the same across all object types, but most are specific to a particular object type. For example, a process object has a process ID, a base priority, and an exit code, whereas a file object has a byte offset, a sharing mode, and an open mode.

Because the kernel object data structures are accessible only by the kernel, it is impossible for an application to locate these data structures in memory and directly alter their contents. Microsoft enforces this restriction deliberately to ensure that the kernel object structures maintain a consistent state. This restriction also allows Microsoft to add, remove, or change the members in these structures without breaking any applications.

If we cannot alter these structures directly, how do our applications manipulate these kernel objects? The answer is that Windows offers a set of functions that manipulate these structures in well-defined ways. These kernel objects are always accessible via these functions. When you call a function that creates a kernel object, the function returns a handle that identifies the object. Think of this handle as an opaque value that can be used by any thread in your process. You pass this handle to the various Windows functions so that the system knows which kernel object you want to manipulate. We'll talk a lot more about these handles later in this chapter.

To make the operating system robust, these handle values are process-relative. So if you were to pass this handle value to a thread in another process (using some form of interprocess communication), the calls that this other process would make using your process's handle value would fail. In the section "Sharing Kernel Objects Across Process Boundaries" (at the end of this chapter), we'll look at three mechanisms that allow multiple processes to successfully share a single kernel object.

Usage Counting

Kernel objects are owned by the kernel, not by a process. In other words, if your process calls a function that creates a kernel object and then your process terminates, the kernel object is not necessarily destroyed. Under most circumstances, the object will be destroyed; but if another process is using the kernel object your process created, the kernel knows not to destroy the object until the other process has stopped using it. The important thing to remember is that a kernel object can outlive the process that created it.

The kernel knows how many processes are using a particular kernel object because each object contains a usage count. The usage count is one of the data members common to all kernel object types. When an object is first created, its usage count is set to 1. Then when another process gains access to an existing kernel object, the usage count is incremented. When a process terminates, the kernel automatically decrements the usage count for all the kernel objects the process still has open. If the object's usage count goes to 0, the kernel destroys the object. This ensures that no kernel object will remain in the system if no processes are referencing the object.

Security

Kernel objects can be protected with a security descriptor. A security descriptor describes who created the object, who can gain access to or use the object, and who is denied access to the object. Security descriptors are usually used when writing server applications; you can ignore this feature of kernel objects if you are writing client-side applications.

WINDOWS 98

> Windows 98 is not designed for use as a server-side operating system. For this reason, Microsoft did not implement security features in Windows 98. However, if you are designing software for Windows 98 today, you should still be aware of security issues and use the proper access information when implementing your application to ensure that it runs correctly on Microsoft Windows 2000.

Almost all functions that create kernel objects have a pointer to a SECURITY_ATTRIBUTES structure as an argument, as shown here with the *CreateFileMapping* function:

```
HANDLE CreateFileMapping(
   HANDLE hFile,
   PSECURITY_ATTRIBUTES psa,
   DWORD flProtect,
   DWORD dwMaximumSizeHigh,
   DWORD dwMaximumSizeLow,
   PCTSTR pszName);
```

Most applications will simply pass NULL for this argument so that the object is created with default security. Default security means that any member of the administrators group and the creator of the object have full access to the object; all others are denied access. However, you can allocate a SECURITY_ATTRIBUTES structure, initialize it, and pass the address of the structure for this parameter. A SECURITY_ATTRIBUTES structure looks like this:

```
typedef struct _SECURITY_ATTRIBUTES {
   DWORD nLength;
   LPVOID lpSecurityDescriptor;
   BOOL bInheritHandle;
} SECURITY_ATTRIBUTES;
```

Even though this structure is called SECURITY_ATTRIBUTES, it really includes only one member that has anything to do with security: *lpSecurity-Descriptor*. If you want to restrict access to a kernel object you create, you must create a security descriptor and then initialize the SECURITY_ATTRIBUTES structure as follows:

```
SECURITY_ATTRIBUTES sa;
sa.nLength = sizeof(sa);            // Used for versioning
sa.lpSecurityDescriptor = pSD;      // Address of an initialized SD
sa.bInheritHandle = FALSE;          // Discussed later
HANDLE hFileMapping = CreateFileMapping(INVALID_HANDLE_VALUE, &sa,
    PAGE_READWRITE, 0, 1024, "MyFileMapping");
    :
    :
```

Since this member has nothing to do with security, I'm going to postpone discussing the *bInheritHandle* member until the section on inheritance later in this chapter.

When you want to gain access to an existing kernel object (rather than create a new one), you must specify the operations you intend to perform on the object. For example, if I wanted to gain access to an existing file-mapping kernel object so that I could read data from it, I would call *OpenFileMapping* as follows:

```
HANDLE hFileMapping = OpenFileMapping(FILE_MAP_READ, FALSE,
    "MyFileMapping");
```

By passing FILE_MAP_READ as the first parameter to *OpenFileMapping*, I am indicating that I intend to read from this file mapping after I gain access to it. The *OpenFileMapping* function performs a security check first, before it returns a valid handle value. If I (the logged-on user) am allowed access to the existing file-mapping kernel object, *OpenFileMapping* returns a valid handle. However, if I am denied this access, *OpenFileMapping* returns NULL, and a call to *GetLastError* will return a value of 5 (ERROR_ACCESS_DENIED). Again, most applications do not use security, so I won't go into this issue any further.

While many applications do not need to be concerned about security, many Windows functions require that you pass desired security access information. Several applications designed for Windows 98 do not work properly on Windows 2000 because security was not given enough consideration when the application was implemented.

For example, imagine an application that, when started, reads some data from a registry subkey. To do this properly, your code should call *RegOpenKeyEx*, passing KEY_QUERY_VALUE for the desired access.

(continued)

However, many applications were originally developed for Windows 98 without any consideration for Windows 2000. Since Windows 98 does not secure the registry, software developers frequently called *RegOpenKeyEx*, passing KEY_ALL_ACCESS as the desired access. Developers did this because it was a simpler solution and meant that the developer didn't have to really think about what access was required. The problem is that the registry subkey might be readable to the user, but not writable. So, when this application now runs on Windows 2000, the call to *RegOpenKeyEx* with KEY_ALL_ACCESS fails, and without proper error checking the application could run with totally unpredictable results.

If the developer had thought about security just a little and had changed KEY_ALL_ACCESS to KEY_QUERY_VALUE (which is all that is necessary in this example), the product would work on both operating system platforms.

Neglecting proper security access flags is one of the biggest mistakes that developers make. Using the correct flags will certainly make it much easier to port an application originally designed for Windows 98 to Windows 2000.

In addition to kernel objects, your application might use other types of objects, such as menus, windows, mouse cursors, brushes, and fonts. These objects are User objects or Graphics Device Interface (GDI) objects, not kernel objects. When you first start programming for Windows, you might be confused when you try to differentiate a User object or a GDI object from a kernel object. For example, is an icon a User object or a kernel object? The easiest way to determine whether an object is a kernel object is to examine the function that creates the object. Almost all functions that create kernel objects have a parameter that allows you to specify security attribute information, as did the *CreateFileMapping* function shown earlier.

None of the functions that create User or GDI objects have a PSECURITY_ATTRIBUTES parameter. For example, take a look at the *CreateIcon* function:

```
HICON CreateIcon(
    HINSTANCE hinst,
    int nWidth,
    int nHeight,
    BYTE cPlanes,
    BYTE cBitsPixel,
    CONST BYTE *pbANDbits,
    CONST BYTE *pbXORbits);
```

A Process's Kernel Object Handle Table

When a process is initialized, the system allocates a handle table for it. This handle table is used only for kernel objects, not for User objects or GDI objects. The details of how the handle table is structured and managed are undocumented. Normally I would refrain from discussing undocumented parts of the operating system. In this case, however, I'm making an exception because I believe that a competent Windows programmer must understand how a process's handle table is managed. Because this information is undocumented, I will not have all of the details completely correct, and the internal implementation is certainly different among Windows 2000, Windows 98, and Windows CE. So read the following discussion to improve your understanding, not to learn how the system really does it.

Table 3-1 shows what a process's handle table looks like. As you can see, it is simply an array of data structures. Each structure contains a pointer to a kernel object, an access mask, and some flags.

Index	Pointer to Kernel Object Memory Block	Access Mask (DWORD of Flag Bits)	Flags (DWORD of Flag Bits)
1	0x???????	0x???????	0x???????
2	0x???????	0x???????	0x???????
...	...	...	...

Table 3-1.
The structure of a process's handle table

Creating a Kernel Object

When a process first initializes, its handle table is empty. Then when a thread in the process calls a function that creates a kernel object, such as *CreateFileMapping*, the kernel allocates a block of memory for the object and initializes it; the kernel then scans the process's handle table for an empty entry. Because the handle table in Table 3-1 is empty, the kernel finds the structure at index 1 and initializes it. The pointer member will be set to the internal memory address of the kernel object's data structure, the access mask will be set to full access, and the flags will be set. (We'll discuss the flags in the inheritance section later in this chapter.)

Here are some of the functions that create kernel objects (this is in no way a complete list):

```
HANDLE CreateThread(
    PSECURITY_ATTRIBUTES psa,
    DWORD dwStackSize,
    LPTHREAD_START_ROUTINE pfnStartAddr,
    PVOID pvParam,
    DWORD dwCreationFlags,
    PDWORD pdwThreadId);

HANDLE CreateFile(
    PCTSTR pszFileName,
    DWORD dwDesiredAccess,
    DWORD dwShareMode,
    PSECURITY_ATTRIBUTES psa,
    DWORD dwCreationDistribution,
    DWORD dwFlagsAndAttributes,
    HANDLE hTemplateFile);

HANDLE CreateFileMapping(
    HANDLE hFile,
    PSECURITY_ATTRIBUTES psa,
    DWORD flProtect,
    DWORD dwMaximumSizeHigh,
    DWORD dwMaximumSizeLow,
    PCTSTR pszName);

HANDLE CreateSemaphore(
    PSECURITY_ATTRIBUTES psa,
    LONG lInitialCount,
    LONG lMaximumCount,
    PCTSTR pszName);
```

All functions that create kernel objects return process-relative handles that can be used successfully by any and all threads that are running in the same process. This handle value is actually the index into the process's handle table that identifies where the kernel object's information is stored. So when you debug an application and examine the actual value of a kernel object handle, you'll see small values such as 1, 2, and so on. Remember that the meaning of the handle is undocumented and is subject to change. In fact, in Windows 2000 the value returned identifies the number of bytes into the process's handle table for the object rather than the index number itself.

Whenever you call a function that accepts a kernel object handle as an argument, you pass the value returned by one of the *Create* * functions. Internally, the function looks in your process's handle table to get the address of the kernel object you want to manipulate and then manipulates the object's data structure in a well-defined fashion.

If you pass an invalid index (handle), the function returns failure and *GetLastError* returns 6 (ERROR_INVALID_HANDLE). Because handle values are actually indexes into the process's handle table, these handles are process-relative and cannot be used successfully from other processes.

If you call a function to create a kernel object and the call fails, the handle value returned is usually 0 (NULL). The system would have to be very low on memory or encountering a security problem for this to happen. Unfortunately, a few functions return a handle value of −1 (INVALID_HANDLE_VALUE) when they fail. For example, if *CreateFile* fails to open the specified file, it returns INVALID_HANDLE_VALUE instead of NULL. You must be very careful when checking the return value of a function that creates a kernel object. Specifically, you can compare the value with INVALID_HANDLE_VALUE only when you call *CreateFile*. The following code is incorrect:

```
HANDLE hMutex = CreateMutex(…);
if (hMutex == INVALID_HANDLE_VALUE) {
   // We will never execute this code because
   // CreateMutex returns NULL if it fails.
}
```

Likewise, the following code is also incorrect:

```
HANDLE hFile = CreateFile(…);
if (hFile == NULL) {
   // We will never execute this code because CreateFile
   // returns INVALID_HANDLE_VALUE(-1) if it fails.
}
```

Closing a Kernel Object

Regardless of how you create a kernel object, you indicate to the system that you are done manipulating the object by calling *CloseHandle*:

```
BOOL CloseHandle(HANDLE hobj);
```

This function first checks the calling process's handle table to ensure that the index (handle) passed to it identifies an object that the process does in fact have access to. If the index is valid, the system gets the address of the kernel object's data structure and decrements the usage count member in the structure; if the count is zero, the kernel destroys the kernel object from memory.

If an invalid handle is passed to *CloseHandle,* one of two things might happen. If your process is running normally, *CloseHandle* returns FALSE and *GetLastError* returns ERROR_INVALID_HANDLE. Or, if your process is being debugged, the system notifies the debugger so that you can debug the error.

Right before *CloseHandle* returns, it clears out the entry in the process's handle table—this handle is now invalid for your process and you should not attempt to use it. The clearing happens whether or not the kernel object has been destroyed! After you call *CloseHandle*, you will no longer have access to the kernel object; however, if the object's count did not decrement to zero, the object has not been destroyed. This is OK; it just means that one or more other processes are still using the object. When the other processes stop using the object (by calling *CloseHandle*), the object will be destroyed.

Let's say that you forget to call *CloseHandle*—will there be a memory leak? Well, yes and no. It is possible for a process to leak resources (such as kernel objects) while the process runs. However, when the process terminates, the operating system ensures that any and all resources used by the process are freed—this is guaranteed. For kernel objects, the system performs the following actions: When your process terminates, the system automatically scans the process's handle table. If the table has any valid entries (objects that you didn't close before terminating), the system closes these object handles for you. If the usage count of any of these objects goes to zero, the kernel destroys the object.

So, your application can leak kernel objects while it runs, but when your process terminates, the system guarantees that everything is cleaned up properly. By the way, this is true for *all* objects, resources, and memory blocks: when a process terminates, the system ensures that your process leaves nothing behind.

Sharing Kernel Objects
Across Process Boundaries

Frequently, threads running in different processes need to share kernel objects. Here are some of the reasons why:

- File-mapping objects allow you to share blocks of data between two processes running on a single machine.

- Mailslots and named pipes allow applications to send blocks of data between processes running on different machines connected to the network.

- Mutexes, semaphores, and events allow threads in different processes to synchronize their continued execution, as in the case of an application that needs to notify another application when it has completed some task.

Because kernel object handles are process-relative, performing these tasks is difficult. However, Microsoft had several good reasons for designing the handles to be process-relative. The most important reason was robustness. If kernel object handles were system-wide values, one process could easily obtain the handle to an object that another process was using and wreak havoc on that process. Another reason for process-relative handles is security. Kernel objects are protected with security, and a process must request permission to manipulate an object before attempting to manipulate it. The creator of the object can prevent an unauthorized user from touching the object simply by denying access to it.

In the following section, we'll look at the three different mechanisms that allow processes to share kernel objects.

Object Handle Inheritance

Object handle inheritance can be used only when processes have a parent-child relationship. In this scenario, one or more kernel object handles are available to the parent process, and the parent decides to spawn a child process, giving the child access to the parent's kernel objects. For this type of inheritance to work, the parent process must perform several steps.

First, when the parent process creates a kernel object, the parent must indicate to the system that it wants the object's handle to be inheritable. Keep in mind that although kernel object *handles* are inheritable, kernel objects themselves are not.

To create an inheritable handle, the parent process must allocate and initialize a SECURITY_ATTRIBUTES structure and pass the structure's address to the specific *Create* function. The following code creates a mutex object and returns an inheritable handle to it:

```
SECURITY_ATTRIBUTES sa;
sa.nLength = sizeof(sa);
sa.lpSecurityDescriptor = NULL;
sa.bInheritHandle = TRUE;   // Make the returned handle inheritable.

HANDLE hMutex = CreateMutex(&sa, FALSE, NULL);
:
:
```

This code initializes a SECURITY_ATTRIBUTES structure indicating that the object should be created using default security (ignored in Windows 98) and that the returned handle should be inheritable.

Even though Windows 98 does not have complete security support, it does support inheritance; therefore, Windows 98 correctly uses the value of the *bInheritHandle* member.

Now we come to the flags that are stored in a process's handle table entry. Each handle table entry has a flag bit indicating whether the handle is inheritable. If you pass NULL as the PSECURITY_ATTRIBUTES parameter when you create a kernel object, the handle returned is not inheritable and this bit is zero. Setting the *bInheritHandle* member to TRUE causes this flag bit to be set to 1.

Imagine a process's handle table that looks like the one shown in Table 3-2.

Index	Pointer to Kernel Object Memory Block	Access Mask (DWORD of Flag Bits)	Flags (DWORD of Flag Bits)
1	0xF0000000	0x???????	0x00000000
2	0x00000000	(N/A)	(N/A)
3	0xF0000010	0x???????	0x00000001

Table 3-2.
A process's handle table containing two valid entries

Table 3-2 indicates that this process has access to two kernel objects (handles 1 and 3). Handle 1 is not inheritable and handle 3 is inheritable.

The next step to perform when using object handle inheritance is for the parent process to spawn the child process. This is done using the *CreateProcess* function:

```
BOOL CreateProcess(
    PCTSTR pszApplicationName,
    PTSTR pszCommandLine,
    PSECURITY_ATTRIBUTES psaProcess,
    PSECURITY_ATTRIBUTES pszThread,
    BOOL bInheritHandles,
    DWORD dwCreationFlags,
    PVOID pvEnvironment,
    PCTSTR pszCurrentDirectory,
    LPSTARTUPINFO pStartupInfo,
    PPROCESS_INFORMATION pProcessInformation);
```

We'll examine this function in detail in the next chapter, but for now I want to draw your attention to the *bInheritHandles* parameter. Usually, when you spawn a process, you will pass FALSE for this parameter. This value tells the system that you do not want the child process to inherit the inheritable handles that are in the parent process's handle table.

If you pass TRUE for this parameter, however, the child will inherit the parent's inheritable handle values. When you pass TRUE, the operating system creates the new child process but does not allow the child process to begin executing its code right away. Of course, the system creates a new, empty process handle table for the child process—just as it would for any new process. But because you passed TRUE to *CreateProcess*'s *bInheritHandles* parameter, the system does one more thing: it walks the parent process's handle table, and for each entry it finds that contains a valid inheritable handle, the system copies the entry exactly into the child process's handle table. The entry is copied to the exact same position in the child process's handle table as in the parent's handle table. This fact is important because it means that the handle value that identifies a kernel object is identical in both the parent and the child processes.

In addition to copying the handle table entry, the system increments the usage count of the kernel object because two processes are now using the object. For the kernel object to be destroyed, both the parent process and the child process must either call *CloseHandle* on the object or terminate. The child does not have to terminate first—but neither does the parent. In fact, the parent process can close its handle to the object immediately after the *CreateProcess* function returns without affecting the child's ability to manipulate the object.

Table 3-3 shows the child process's handle table immediately before the process is allowed to begin execution. You can see that entries 1 and 2 are not initialized and are therefore invalid handles for the child process to use. However, index 3 does identify a kernel object. In fact, it identifies the kernel object at address 0xF0000010, the same object as in the parent process's handle table. The access mask is identical to the mask in the parent, and the flags are also identical. This means that if the child process were to spawn its own child process (a grandchild process of the parent), this grandchild process would also inherit this kernel object handle with the same handle value, same access, and same flags, and the usage count on the object would again be incremented.

Index	Pointer to Kernel Object Memory Block	Access Mask (DWORD of Flag Bits)	Flags (DWORD of Flag Bits)
1	0x00000000	(N/A)	(N/A)
2	0x00000000	(N/A)	(N/A)
3	0xF0000010	0x???????	0x00000001

Table 3-3.
A child process's handle table after inheriting the parent process's inheritable handle

Be aware that object handle inheritance applies only at the time the child process is spawned. If the parent process were to create any new kernel objects with inheritable handles, an already-running child process would not inherit these new handles.

Object handle inheritance has one very strange characteristic: when you use it, the child has no idea that it has inherited any handles. Kernel object handle inheritance is useful only when the child process documents the fact that it expects to be given access to a kernel object when spawned from another process. Usually, the parent and child applications are written by the same company; however, a different company can write the child application if that company documents what the child application expects.

By far the most common way for a child process to determine the handle value of the kernel object that it's expecting is to have the handle value passed as a command-line argument to the child process. The child process's initialization code parses the command line (usually by calling *sscanf*) and extracts the handle value. Once the child has the handle value, it has unlimited access to the object. Note that the only reason handle inheritance works is because the handle value of the shared kernel object is identical in both the parent process and the child process; this is why the parent process is able to pass the handle value as a command-line argument.

Of course, you can use other forms of interprocess communication to transfer an inherited kernel object handle value from the parent process into the child process. One technique is for the parent to wait for the child to complete initialization (using the *WaitForInputIdle* function discussed in Chapter 9); then the parent can send or post a message to a window created by a thread in the child process.

Another technique is for the parent process to add an environment variable to its environment block. The variable's name would be something that the child process knows to look for, and the variable's value would be the handle value of the kernel object to be inherited. Then when the parent spawns the child process, the child process inherits the parent's environment variables and can easily call *GetEnvironmentVariable* to obtain the inherited object's handle value. This approach is excellent if the child process is going to spawn another child process, because the environment variables can be inherited again.

Changing a Handle's Flags

Occasionally, you might encounter a situation in which a parent process creates a kernel object retrieving an inheritable handle and then spawns two child processes. The parent process wants only one child to inherit the kernel object handle. In other words, you might at times want to control which child processes inherit kernel object handles. To alter the inheritance flag of a kernel object handle, you can call the *SetHandleInformation* function:

```
BOOL SetHandleInformation(
   HANDLE hObject,
   DWORD dwMask,
   DWORD dwFlags);
```

As you can see, this function takes three parameters. The first, *hObject*, identifies a valid handle. The second parameter, *dwMask*, tells the function which flag or flags you want to change. Currently, two flags are associated with each handle:

```
#define HANDLE_FLAG_INHERIT      0x00000001
#define HANDLE_FLAG_PROTECT_FROM_CLOSE 0x00000002
```

You can bitwise OR both of these flags together if you want to change both of the object's flags simultaneously. *SetHandleInformation*'s third parameter, *dwFlags*, indicates what you want to set the flags to. For example, to turn on the inheritance flag for a kernel object handle, do the following:

```
SetHandleInformation(hobj, HANDLE_FLAG_INHERIT, HANDLE_FLAG_INHERIT);
```

To turn off this flag, do this:

```
SetHandleInformation(hobj, HANDLE_FLAG_INHERIT, 0);
```

The HANDLE_FLAG_PROTECT_FROM_CLOSE flag tells the system that this handle should not be allowed to close:

```
SetHandleInformation(hobj, HANDLE_FLAG_PROTECT_FROM_CLOSE,
   HANDLE_FLAG_PROTECT_FROM_CLOSE);
CloseHandle(hobj);   // Exception is raised
```

If a thread attempts to close a protected handle, *CloseHandle* raises an exception. You rarely want to protect a handle from being closed. However, this flag might be useful if you had a process that spawned a child that in turn spawned a grandchild process. The parent process might be expecting the grandchild to inherit the object handle given to the immediate child. It is possible, however, that the immediate child might close the handle before spawning the grandchild. If this were to happen, the parent might not be able to communicate with the grandchild because the grandchild did not inherit the kernel object. By marking the handle as "protected from close," the grandchild will inherit the object.

This approach has one flaw, however: the immediate child process might call the following code to turn off the HANDLE_FLAG_PROTECT_FROM_CLOSE flag and then close the handle.

```
SetHandleInformation(hobj, HANDLE_FLAG_PROTECT_FROM_CLOSE, 0);
CloseHandle(hobj);
```

The parent process is gambling that the child process will not execute this code. Of course, the parent is also gambling that the child process will spawn the grandchild, so this bet is not that risky.

For the sake of completeness, I'll also mention the *GetHandleInformation* function:

```
BOOL GetHandleInformation(
    HANDLE hObj,
    PDWORD pdwFlags);
```

This function returns the current flag settings for the specified handle in the DWORD pointed to by *pdwFlags*. To see if a handle is inheritable, do the following:

```
DWORD dwFlags;
GetHandleInformation(hObj, &dwFlags);
BOOL fHandleIsInheritable = (0 != (dwFlags & HANDLE_FLAG_INHERIT));
```

Named Objects

The second method available for sharing kernel objects across process boundaries is to name the objects. Many—though not all—kernel objects can be named. For example, all of the following functions create named kernel objects:

```
HANDLE CreateMutex(
    PSECURITY_ATTRIBUTES psa,
    BOOL bInitialOwner,
    PCTSTR pszName);

HANDLE CreateEvent(
    PSECURITY_ATTRIBUTES psa,
    BOOL bManualReset,
    BOOL bInitialState,
    PCTSTR pszName);

HANDLE CreateSemaphore(
    PSECURITY_ATTRIBUTES psa,
    LONG lInitialCount,
    LONG lMaximumCount,
    PCTSTR pszName);

HANDLE CreateWaitableTimer(
    PSECURITY_ATTRIBUTES psa,
    BOOL bManualReset,
    PCTSTR pszName);
```

(continued)

```
HANDLE CreateFileMapping(
    HANDLE hFile,
    PSECURITY_ATTRIBUTES psa,
    DWORD flProtect,
    DWORD dwMaximumSizeHigh,
    DWORD dwMaximumSizeLow,
    PCTSTR pszName);

HANDLE CreateJobObject(
    PSECURITY_ATTRIBUTES psa,
    PCTSTR pszName);
```

All of these functions have a common last parameter, *pszName*. When you pass NULL for this parameter, you are indicating to the system that you want to create an unnamed (anonymous) kernel object. When you create an unnamed object, you can share the object across processes by using either inheritance (as discussed in the previous section) or *DuplicateHandle* (discussed in the next section). To share an object by name, you must give the object a name.

If you don't pass NULL for the *pszName* parameter, you should pass the address of a zero-terminated string name. This name can be up to MAX_PATH (defined as 260) characters long. Unfortunately, Microsoft offers no guidance for assigning names to kernel objects. For example, if you attempt to create an object called "JeffObj," there's no guarantee that an object called "JeffObj" doesn't already exist. To make matters worse, all of these objects share a single name space. Because of this, the following call to *CreateSemaphore* will always return NULL:

```
HANDLE hMutex = CreateMutex(NULL, FALSE, "JeffObj");
HANDLE hSem = CreateSemaphore(NULL, 1, 1, "JeffObj");
DWORD dwErrorCode = GetLastError();
```

If you examine the value of *dwErrorCode* after executing the code above, you'll see a return code of 6 (ERROR_INVALID_HANDLE). This error code is not very descriptive, but what can you do?

Now that you know how to name an object, let's see how to share objects this way. Let's say that Process A starts up and calls the following function:

```
HANDLE hMutexProcessA = CreateMutex(NULL, FALSE, "JeffMutex");
```

This function call creates a brand new mutex kernel object and assigns it the name "JeffMutex". Notice that in Process A's handle, *hMutexProcessA* is not an inheritable handle—and it doesn't have to be when you're only naming objects.

Some time later, some process spawns Process B. Process B does not have to be a child of Process A; it might be spawned from the Explorer or any other application. The fact that Process B need not be a child of Process A is an advantage of using named objects instead of inheritance. When Process B starts executing, it executes the following code:

```
HANDLE hMutexProcessB = CreateMutex(NULL, FALSE, "JeffMutex");
```

When Process B's call to *CreateMutex* is made, the system first checks to find out whether a kernel object with the name "JeffMutex" already exists. Because an object with this name does exist, the kernel then checks the object type. Since we are attempting to create a mutex and the object with the name "JeffMutex" is also a mutex, the system then makes a security check to see if the caller has full access to the object and if so, the system locates an empty entry in Process B's handle table and initializes the entry to point to the existing kernel object. If the object types don't match or if the caller is denied access, *CreateMutex* fails (returns NULL).

When Process B's call to *CreateMutex* is successful, a mutex is not actually created. Instead, Process B is simply assigned a process-relative handle value that identifies the existing mutex object in the kernel. Of course, because a new entry in Process B's handle table references this object, the mutex object's usage count is incremented; the object will not be destroyed until both Process A and Process B have closed their handles to the object. Notice that the handle values in the two processes are most likely going to be different values. This is OK: Process A will use its handle value, and Process B will use its own handle value to manipulate the one mutex kernel object.

> **NOTE**
>
> When you have kernel objects sharing names, be aware of one extremely important detail. When Process B calls *CreateMutex*, it passes security attribute information and a second parameter to the function. These parameters are ignored if an object with the specified name already exists! An application can determine if it did, in fact, create a new kernel object versus simply opening an existing object by calling *GetLastError* immediately after the call to the *Create** function:
>
> ```
> HANDLE hMutex = CreateMutex(&sa, FALSE, "JeffObj");
> if (GetLastError() == ERROR_ALREADY_EXISTS) {
>    // Opened a handle to an existing object.
>    // sa.lpSecurityDescriptor and the second parameter
>    // (FALSE) are ignored.
> } else {
>    // Created a brand new object.
>    // sa.lpSecurityDescriptor and the second parameter
>    // (FALSE) are used to construct the object.
> }
> ```

An alternative method exists for sharing objects by name. Instead of calling a *Create** function, a process can call one of the *Open** functions shown here:

```
HANDLE OpenMutex(
   DWORD dwDesiredAccess,
   BOOL bInheritHandle,
   PCTSTR pszName);

HANDLE OpenEvent(
   DWORD dwDesiredAccess,
   BOOL bInheritHandle,
   PCTSTR pszName);

HANDLE OpenSemaphore(
   DWORD dwDesiredAccess,
   BOOL bInheritHandle,
   PCTSTR pszName);

HANDLE OpenWaitableTimer(
   DWORD dwDesiredAccess,
   BOOL bInheritHandle,
   PCTSTR pszName);

HANDLE OpenFileMapping(
   DWORD dwDesiredAccess,
   BOOL bInheritHandle,
   PCTSTR pszName);

HANDLE OpenJobObject(
   DWORD dwDesiredAccess,
   BOOL bInheritHandle,
   PCTSTR pszName);
```

Notice that all of these functions have the same prototype. The last parameter, *pszName*, indicates the name of a kernel object. You cannot pass NULL for this parameter; you must pass the address of a zero-terminated string. These functions search the single name space of kernel objects attempting to find a match. If no kernel object with the specified name exists, the functions return NULL and *GetLastError* returns 2 (ERROR_FILE_NOT_FOUND). However, if a kernel object with the specified name does exist, and if it is the same type of object, the system then checks to see if the requested access (via the *dwDesiredAccess* parameter) is allowed; if it is, the calling process's handle table is updated and the object's usage count is incremented. The returned handle will be inheritable if you pass TRUE for the *bInheritHandle* parameter.

The main difference between calling a *Create** function versus calling an *Open** function is that if the object doesn't already exist, the *Create** function will create it, whereas the *Open** function will simply fail.

As I mentioned earlier, Microsoft offers no real guidelines on how to create unique object names. In other words, it would be a problem if a user attempted to run two programs from different companies and each program attempted to create an object called "MyObject". For uniqueness, I recommend that you create a GUID and use the string representation of the GUID for your object names.

Named objects are commonly used to prevent multiple instances of an application from running. To do this, simply call a *Create** function in your *main* or *WinMain* function to create a named object (it doesn't matter what type of object you create). When the *Create** function returns, call *GetLastError*. If *GetLastError* returns ERROR_ALREADY_EXISTS, another instance of your application is running and the new instance can exit. Here's some code that illustrates this:

```
int WINAPI WinMain(HINSTANCE hinstExe, HINSTANCE, PSTR pszCmdLine,
   int nCmdShow) {
   HANDLE h = CreateMutex(NULL, FALSE,
      "{FA531CC1-0497-11d3-A180-00105A276C3E}");
   if (GetLastError() == ERROR_ALREADY_EXISTS) {
      // There is already an instance of this application running.
      return(0);
   }

   // This is the first instance of this application running.
   :
   :

   // Before exiting, close the object.
   CloseHandle(h);
   return(0);
}
```

Terminal Server Name Spaces

Note that Terminal Server changes the above scenario a little bit. A Terminal Server machine will have multiple name spaces for kernel objects. There is one global name space, which is used by kernel objects that are meant to be accessible by any and all client sessions. This name space is mostly used by services. In addition, each client session has its own name space. This keeps two or more sessions that are running the same application from trampling over each other—one session cannot access another session's objects even though the objects share the same name. On a machine without Terminal Server, services and applications share the same kernel object name space as described above; this is not true on a Terminal Server machine.

A service's named kernel objects always go in the global name space. By default, in Terminal Server, an application's named kernel object goes in the session's name space. However, it is possible to force the named object to go into the global name space by prefixing the name with "Global\", as in the example below:

```
HANDLE h = CreateEvent(NULL, FALSE, FALSE, "Global\\MyName");
```

You can also explicitly state that you want a kernel object to go in the session's name space by prefixing the name with "Local\", as in

```
HANDLE h = CreateEvent(NULL, FALSE, FALSE, "Local\\MyName");
```

Microsoft considers Global and Local to be reserved keywords that you should not use in object names except to force a particular name space. Microsoft also considers Session to be a reserved keyword, although it currently has no meaning. Note that all of these reserved keywords are case-sensitive. Finally, these keywords are ignored if the host machine is not running Terminal Server.

Duplicating Object Handles

The last technique for sharing kernel objects across process boundaries requires the use of the *DuplicateHandle* function:

```
BOOL DuplicateHandle(
    HANDLE hSourceProcessHandle,
    HANDLE hSourceHandle,
    HANDLE hTargetProcessHandle,
    PHANDLE phTargetHandle,
    DWORD dwDesiredAccess,
    BOOL bInheritHandle,
    DWORD dwOptions);
```

Simply stated, this function takes an entry in one process's handle table and makes a copy of the entry into another process's handle table. *Duplicate-Handle* takes several parameters but is actually quite straightforward. The most general usage of the *DuplicateHandle* function involves three different processes that are running in the system.

When you call *DuplicateHandle*, the first and third parameters—*hSourceProcessHandle* and *hTargetProcessHandle*—are kernel object handles. The handles themselves must be relative to the process that is calling the *Duplicate-Handle* function. In addition, these two parameters must identify process kernel objects; the function fails if you pass handles to any other type of kernel object. We'll discuss process kernel objects in more detail in Chapter 4; for now, all you need to know is that a process kernel object is created whenever a new process is invoked in the system.

The second parameter, *hSourceHandle*, is a handle to any type of kernel object. However, the handle value is not relative to the process that calls *DuplicateHandle*. Instead, this handle must be relative to the process identified by the *hSourceProcessHandle* handle. The fourth parameter, *phTargetHandle*, is the address of a HANDLE variable that will receive the index of the entry that gets the copy of the source's handle information. The handle value that comes back is relative to the process identified by *hTargetProcessHandle*.

DuplicateHandle's last three parameters allow you to indicate the value of the access mask and the inheritance flag that should be used in the target's entry for this kernel object handle. The *dwOptions* parameter can be 0 (zero) or any combination of the following two flags: DUPLICATE_SAME_ACCESS and DUPLICATE_CLOSE_SOURCE.

Specifying DUPLICATE_SAME_ACCESS tells *DuplicateHandle* that you want the target's handle to have the same access mask as the source process's handle. Using this flag causes *DuplicateHandle* to ignore its *dwDesiredAccess* parameter.

Specifying DUPLICATE_CLOSE_SOURCE has the effect of closing the handle in the source process. This flag makes it easy for one process to hand a kernel object over to another process. When this flag is used, the usage count of the kernel object is not affected.

I'll use an example to show you how *DuplicateHandle* works. For this demonstration, Process S is the source process that currently has access to some kernel object and Process T is the target process that will gain access to this kernel object. Process C is the catalyst process that will execute the call to *DuplicateHandle*.

Process C's handle table (Table 3-4) contains two handle values, 1 and 2. Handle value 1 identifies Process S's process kernel object, and handle value 2 identifies Process T's process kernel object.

Index	Pointer to Kernel Object Memory Block	Access Mask (DWORD of Flag Bits)	Flags (DWORD of Flag Bits)
1	0xF0000000 (Process S's kernel object)	0x????????	0x00000000
2	0xF0000010 (Process T's kernel object)	0x????????	0x00000000

Table 3-4.
Process C's handle table

Table 3-5 is Process S's handle table, which contains a single entry with a handle value of 2. This handle can identify any type of kernel object—it doesn't have to be a process kernel object.

Index	Pointer to Kernel Object Memory Block	Access Mask (DWORD of Flag Bits)	Flags (DWORD of Flag Bits)
1	0x00000000	(N/A)	(N/A)
2	0xF0000020 (any kernel object)	0x???????	0x00000000

Table 3-5.
Process S's handle table

Table 3-6 shows what Process T's handle table contains before Process C calls the *DuplicateHandle* function. As you can see, Process T's handle table contains only a single entry with a handle value of 2; handle entry 1 is currently unused.

Index	Pointer to Kernel Object Memory Block	Access Mask (DWORD of Flag Bits)	Flags (DWORD of Flag Bits)
1	0x00000000	(N/A)	(N/A)
2	0xF0000030 (any kernel object)	0x???????	0x00000000

Table 3-6.
Process T's handle table before calling DuplicateHandle

If Process C now calls *DuplicateHandle* using the following code, only Process T's handle table has changed, as shown in Table 3-7.

```
DuplicateHandle(1, 2, 2, &hObj, 0, TRUE, DUPLICATE_SAME_ACCESS);
```

Index	Pointer to Kernel Object Memory Block	Access Mask (DWORD of Flag Bits)	Flags (DWORD of Flag Bits)
1	0xF0000020	0x???????	0x00000001
2	0xF0000030 (any kernel object)	0x???????	0x00000000

Table 3-7.
Process T's handle table after calling DuplicateHandle

The second entry in Process S's handle table has been copied to the first entry in Process T's handle table. *DuplicateHandle* has also filled in Process C's *hObj* variable with a value of 1, which is the index in process T's handle table where the new entry was placed.

Because the DUPLICATE_SAME_ACCESS flag was passed to *Duplicate-Handle*, the access mask for this handle in Process T's table is identical to the access mask in Process S's table entry. Also, passing the DUPLICATE_SAME-_ACCESS flag causes *DuplicateHandle* to ignore its *dwDesiredAccess* parameter. Finally, notice that the inheritance bit flag has been turned on because TRUE was passed for *DuplicateHandle's bInheritHandle* parameter.

Obviously, you would never call *DuplicateHandle* passing in hard-coded numeric values as I have done in this example. I have used hard-coded numbers only to demonstrate how the function operates. In real applications, you would have the various handle values in variables and you would pass the variables as arguments to the function.

Like inheritance, one of the odd things about the *DuplicateHandle* function is that the target process is not given any notification that a new kernel object is now accessible to it. So, Process C must somehow notify Process T that it now has access to a kernel object and must use some form of interprocess communication to pass the handle value in *hObj* to Process T. Obviously, using a command-line argument or changing Process T's environment variables is out of the question since the process is already up and running. A window message or some other IPC mechanism must be used.

What I have just explained is the most general usage of *DuplicateHandle*. As you can see, it is a very flexible function. However, it is rarely used with the involvement of three different processes (partly because it is unlikely that Process C would know the handle value of an object in use by Process S). Usually, *DuplicateHandle* is called when only two processes are involved. Imagine a situation in which one process has access to an object that another process wants access to, or a case in which one process wants to give access to a kernel object to another process. For example, let's say that Process S has access to a kernel object and wants to give Process T access to this object. To do this, you would call *DuplicateHandle* as follows:

```
// All of the following code is executed by Process S.

// Create a mutex object accessible by Process S.
HANDLE hObjProcessS = CreateMutex(NULL, FALSE, NULL);

// Open a handle to Process T's kernel object.
HANDLE hProcessT = OpenProcess(PROCESS_ALL_ACCESS, FALSE,
   dwProcessIdT);

HANDLE hObjProcessT;   // An uninitialized handle relative to Process T.

// Give Process T access to our mutex object.
DuplicateHandle(GetCurrentProcess(), hObjProcessS, hProcessT,
   &hObjProcessT, 0, FALSE, DUPLICATE_SAME_ACCESS);

// Use some IPC mechanism to get the handle
// value in hObjProcessS into Process T.
.
.
.
// We no longer need to communicate with Process T.
CloseHandle(hProcessT);
.
.
.
// When Process S no longer needs to use the mutex, it should close it.
CloseHandle(hObjProcessS);
```

The call to *GetCurrentProcess* returns a pseudo-handle that always identifies the calling process—Process S in this example. Once *DuplicateHandle* returns, *hObjProcessT* is a handle relative to Process T that identifies the same object that *hObjProcessS*'s handle does when referenced by code in Process S. Process S should never execute the following code:

```
// Process S should never attempt to close the
// duplicated handle.
CloseHandle(hObjProcessT);
```

If Process S were to execute this code, the call might or might not fail. The call would succeed if Process S happened to have access to a kernel object with the same handle value as *hObjProcessT*. This call would have the effect of closing some object so that Process S no longer had access to it, which would certainly cause the application to behave undesirably (to put it nicely).

Here is another way to use *DuplicateHandle*: Suppose that a process has read and write access to a file-mapping object. At some point a function is called that is supposed to access the file-mapping object by reading it. To make our application more robust, we can use *DuplicateHandle* to create a new handle for the existing object and ensure that this new handle has read-only access on it. We would then pass this read-only handle to the function; this way, the code in the function would never be able to accidentally write to the file-mapping object. The following code illustrates this example:

```
int WINAPI WinMain(HINSTANCE hinstExe, HINSTANCE,
   LPSTR szCmdLine, int nCmdShow) {

   // Create a file-mapping object; the handle has read/write access.
   HANDLE hFileMapRW = CreateFileMapping(INVALID_HANDLE_VALUE,
      NULL, PAGE_READWRITE, 0, 10240, NULL);

   // Create another handle to the file-mapping object;
   // the handle has read-only access.
   HANDLE hFileMapRO;
   DuplicateHandle(GetCurrentProcess(), hFileMapRW, GetCurrentProcess(),
      &hFileMapRO, FILE_MAP_READ, FALSE, 0);

   // Call the function that should only read from the file mapping.
   ReadFromTheFileMapping(hFileMapRO);

   // Close the read-only file-mapping object.
   CloseHandle(hFileMapRO);

   // We can still read/write the file-mapping object using hFileMapRW.
   :
   :

   // When the main code doesn't access the file mapping anymore,
   // close it.
   CloseHandle(hFileMapRW);
}
```

PART II

GETTING
WORK DONE

CHAPTER FOUR

PROCESSES

This chapter discusses how the system manages all of the running applications. I'll begin by explaining what a process is and how the system creates a process kernel object to manage each process. I'll then show you how to manipulate a process using its associated kernel object. Following that, I'll discuss the various attributes, or properties, of a process as well as several functions for querying and changing these properties. I'll also examine the functions that allow you to create or spawn additional processes in the system. And, of course, no discussion of processes would be complete without an in-depth look at how they terminate. OK, let's begin.

A process is usually defined as an instance of a running program and consists of two components:

■ A kernel object that the operating system uses to manage the process. The kernel object is also where the system keeps statistical information about the process.

■ An address space that contains all the executable or DLL module's code and data. It also contains dynamic memory allocations such as thread stacks and heap allocations.

Processes are inert. For a process to accomplish anything, it must have a thread that runs in its context; this thread is responsible for executing the code contained in the process's address space. In fact, a single process might contain several threads, all of them executing code "simultaneously" in the process's address space. To do this, each thread has its own set of CPU registers and its own stack. Each process has at least one thread that executes code in the process's address space. If there were no threads executing code in the process's address space, there would be no reason for the process to continue to exist, and the system would automatically destroy the process and its address space.

For all of these threads to run, the operating system schedules some CPU time for each thread. It creates the illusion that all the threads run concurrently by offering time slices (called *quantums*) to the threads in a round-robin fashion. Figure 4-1 shows how this works on a machine with a single CPU. If the machine has multiple CPUs, the operating system's algorithm is much more complex to load balance the threads over the CPUs.

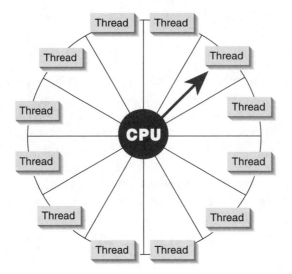

Figure 4-1.
The operating system offers quantums to individual threads in a round-robin fashion on a single-CPU machine.

When a process is created, the system automatically creates its first thread, called the *primary thread*. This thread can then create additional threads, and these can in turn create even more threads.

WINDOWS
2000

Microsoft Windows 2000 can use machines with multiple CPUs. For example, the machine I am using to write this manuscript contains two processors. Windows 2000 can have different threads executing on each CPU so that multiple threads do truly run simultaneously. The Windows 2000 kernel handles all the management and scheduling of threads on this type of system. You do not have to do anything special in your code to gain the advantages offered by a multiprocessor machine.

WINDOWS
98

> Windows 98 can take advantage of only a single processor. Even if the machine contains more than one processor, Windows 98 can schedule only a single thread at a time; any other processors sit dormant.

Writing Your First Windows Application

Windows supports two types of applications: those based on a graphical user interface (GUI) and those based on a console user interface (CUI). A GUI-based application has a graphical front end. It can create windows, have menus, interact with the user via dialog boxes, and use all the standard "Windowsy" stuff. Almost all the accessory applications that ship with Windows (such as Notepad, Calculator, and WordPad) are GUI-based applications. Console-based applications are text-based. They don't usually create windows or process messages, and they don't require a graphical user interface. Although CUI-based applications are contained within a window on the screen, the window contains only text. The command shells—CMD.EXE (for Windows 2000) and COMMAND.COM (for Windows 98)—are typical examples of CUI-based applications.

The line between these two types of applications is very fuzzy. It is possible to create CUI-based applications that display dialog boxes. For example, the command shell could have a special command that causes it to display a graphical dialog box, in which you can select the command you want to execute, instead of having to remember the various commands supported by the shell. You can also create a GUI-based application that outputs text strings to a console window. I frequently create GUI-based applications that create a console window in which I can view debugging information as the application executes. You are certainly encouraged to use a GUI in your applications instead of the old-fashioned character interface, which is much less user-friendly.

When you use Microsoft Visual C++ to create an application project, the integrated environment sets up various linker switches so that the linker embeds the proper type of subsystem in the resulting executable. This linker switch is /SUBSYSTEM:CONSOLE for CUI applications and /SUBSYSTEM-:WINDOWS for GUI applications. When the user runs an application, the operating system's loader looks inside the executable image's header and grabs this subsystem value. If the value indicates a CUI-based application, the loader automatically ensures that a text console window is created for the application.

If the value indicates a GUI-based application, the loader doesn't create the console window and just loads the application. Once the application starts running, the operating system doesn't care what type of UI your application has.

Your Windows application must have an entry-point function that is called when the application starts running. There are four possible entry-point functions:

```
int WINAPI WinMain(
   HINSTANCE hinstExe,
   HINSTANCE,
   PSTR pszCmdLine,
   int nCmdShow);

int WINAPI wWinMain(
   HINSTANCE hinstExe,
   HINSTANCE,
   PWSTR pszCmdLine,
   int nCmdShow);

int __cdecl main(
   int argc,
   char *argv[],
   char *envp[]);

int __cdecl wmain
   int argc,
   wchar_t *argv[],
   wchar_t *envp[]);
```

The operating system doesn't actually call the entry-point function you write. Instead, it calls a C/C++ run-time startup function. This function initializes the C/C++ run-time library so that you can call functions such as *malloc* and *free*. It also ensures that any global and static C++ objects that you have declared are constructed properly before your code executes. The following table tells you which entry point to implement in your source code and when.

Application Type	Entry Point	Startup Function Embedded in Your Executable
GUI application that wants ANSI characters and strings	*WinMain*	*WinMainCRTStartup*
GUI application that wants Unicode characters and strings	*wWinMain*	*wWinMainCRTStartup*

(continued)

Application Type	Entry Point	Startup Function Embedded in Your Executable
CUI application that wants ANSI characters and strings	*main*	*mainCRTStartup*
CUI application that wants Unicode characters and strings	*wmain*	*wmainCRTStartup*

The linker is responsible for choosing the proper C/C++ run-time startup function when it links your executable. If the /SUBSYSTEM:WINDOWS linker switch is specified, the linker expects to find either a *WinMain* or *wWinMain* function. If neither of these functions is present, the linker returns an "unresolved external symbol" error; otherwise, it chooses either the *WinMainCRTStartup* or *wWinMainCRTStartup* function, respectively.

Likewise, if the /SUBSYSTEM:CONSOLE linker switch is specified, the linker expects to find either a *main* or *wmain* function and chooses either the *mainCRTStartup* or *wmainCRTStartup* function, respectively. Again, if neither *main* nor *wmain* exists, the linker returns an "unresolved external symbol" error.

However, it is a little-known fact that you can remove the /SUBSYSTEM linker switch from your project altogether. When you do this, the linker automatically determines which subsystem your application should be set to. When linking, the linker checks to see which of the four functions (*WinMain*, *wWinMain*, *main*, or *wmain*) is present in your code and then infers which subsystem your executable should be and which C/C++ startup function should be embedded in your executable.

One mistake that new Windows/Visual C++ developers commonly make is to accidentally select the wrong project type when they create a new project. For example, a developer might create a new Win32 Application project but create an entry-point function of *main*. When building the application, the developer will get a linker error because a Win32 Application project sets the /SUBSYSTEM:WINDOWS linker switch but no *WinMain* or *wWinMain* function exists. At this point, the developer has four options:

- Change the *main* function to *WinMain*. This is usually not the best choice because the developer probably wants to create a console application.

- Create a new Win32 Console Application in Visual C++ and add the existing source code modules to the new project. This option is tedious because it feels like you're starting over and you have to delete the original project file.

73

- Click on the Link tab of the Project Settings dialog box and change the /SUBSYSTEM:WINDOWS switch to /SUBSYSTEM :CONSOLE. This is an easy way to fix the problem; few people are aware that this is all they have to do.

- Click on the Link tab of the Project Settings dialog box and delete the /SUBSYSTEM:WINDOWS switch entirely. This is my favorite choice because it gives you the most flexibility. Now, the linker will simply do the right thing based on which function you implement in your source code. I have no idea why this isn't the default when you create a new Win32 Application or Win32 Console Application project with Visual C++'s Developer Studio.

All of the C/C++ run-time startup functions do basically the same thing. The difference is in whether they process ANSI or Unicode strings and which entry-point function they call after they initialize the C run-time library. Visual C++ ships with the source code to the C run-time library. You can find the code for the four startup functions in the CRt0.c file; I'll summarize here what the startup functions do:

- Retrieve a pointer to the new process's full command line.

- Retrieve a pointer to the new process's environment variables.

- Initialize the C/C++ run time's global variables. Your code can access these variables if you include StdLib.h. The variables are listed in Table 4-1.

- Initialize the heap used by the C run-time memory allocation functions (*malloc* and *calloc*) and other low-level input/output routines.

- Call constructors for all global and static C++ class objects.

After all of this initialization, the C/C++ startup function calls your application's entry-point function. If you wrote a *wWinMain* function, it is called as follows:

```
GetStartupInfo(&StartupInfo);
int nMainRetVal = wWinMain(GetModuleHandle(NULL), NULL, pszCommandLineUnicode,
   (StartupInfo.dwFlags & STARTF_USESHOWWINDOW)
      ? StartupInfo.wShowWindow : SW_SHOWDEFAULT);
```

If you wrote a *WinMain* function, it is called as follows:

```
GetStartupInfo(&StartupInfo);
int nMainRetVal = WinMainGetModuleHandle(NULL), NULL, pszCommandLineAnsi,
   (StartupInfo.dwFlags & STARTF_USESHOWWINDOW)
      ? StartupInfo.wShowWindow : SW_SHOWDEFAULT);
```

If you wrote a *wmain* function, it is called as follows:

```
int nMainRetVal = wmain(__argc, __wargv, _wenviron);
```

If you wrote a *main* function, it is called as follows:

```
int nMainRetVal = main(__argc, __argv, _environ);
```

When your entry-point function returns, the startup function calls the C run-time *exit* function, passing it your return value (*nMainRetVal*). The *exit* function does the following:

- Calls any functions registered by calls to the *_onexit* function.

- Calls destructors for all global and static C++ class objects.

- Calls the operating system's *ExitProcess* function, passing it *nMainRetVal*. This causes the operating system to kill your process and set its exit code.

Variable Name	Type	Description
_osver	*unsigned int*	The build version of the operating system. For example, Windows 2000 Beta 3 was build 2031. Thus, *_osver* has a value of 2031.
_winmajor	*unsigned int*	A major version of Windows in hexadecimal notation. For Windows 2000, the value is 5.
_winminor	*unsigned int*	A minor version of Windows in hexadecimal notation. For Windows 2000, the value is 0.
_winver	*unsigned int*	(*_winmajor* << 8) + *_winminor*
__argc	*unsigned int*	The number of arguments passed on the command line.
__argv *__wargv*	*char *** *wchar_t ***	An array of size *__argc* with pointers to ANSI/ Unicode strings. Each array entry points to a command-line argument.
_environ *_wenviron*	*char *** *wchar_t ***	An array of pointers to ANSI/Unicode strings. Each array entry points to an environment string.
_pgmptr *_wpgmptr*	*char ** *wchar_t **	The ANSI/Unicode full path and name of the running program.

Table 4-1.
The C/C++ run-time global variables that are available to your programs

A Process's Instance Handle

Every executable or DLL file loaded into a process's address space is assigned a unique instance handle. Your executable file's instance is passed as *(w)WinMain*'s first parameter, *hinstExe*. The handle's value is typically needed for calls that load resources. For example, to load an icon resource from the executable file's image, you need to call this function:

```
HICON LoadIcon(
   HINSTANCE hinst,
   PCTSTR pszIcon);
```

The first parameter to *LoadIcon* indicates which file (executable or DLL) contains the resource you want to load. Many applications save *(w)WinMain*'s *hinstExe* parameter in a global variable so that it is easily accessible to all the executable file's code.

The Platform SDK documentation states that some functions require a parameter of the type HMODULE. An example is the *GetModuleFileName* function, shown here:

```
DWORD GetModuleFileName(
   HMODULE hinstModule,
   PTSTR pszPath,
   DWORD cchPath);
```

NOTE As it turns out, HMODULEs and HINSTANCEs are exactly the same thing. If the documentation for a function indicates that an HMODULE is required, you can pass an HINSTANCE, and vice versa. There are two data types because in 16-bit Windows HMODULEs and HINSTANCEs identified different things.

The actual value of *(w)WinMain*'s *hinstExe* parameter is the base memory address where the system loaded the executable file's image into the process's address space. For example, if the system opens the executable file and loads its contents at address 0x00400000, *(w)WinMain*'s *hinstExe* parameter has a value of 0x00400000.

The base address where an executable file's image loads is determined by the linker. Different linkers can use different default base addresses. The Visual C++ linker uses a default base address of 0x00400000 because this is the lowest address an executable file image can load to when you run Windows 98. You can change the base address that your application loads to by using the /BASE: *address* linker switch for Microsoft's linker.

If you attempt to load an executable that has a base address below 0x00400000 on Windows 98, the Windows 98 loader must relocate the executable to a different address. This increases the loading time of the application, but at least the application can run. If you are developing an application that will run on both Windows 98 and Windows 2000, you should make sure that the application's base address is at 0x00400000 or above.

The *GetModuleHandle* function, shown below, returns the handle/base address where an executable or DLL file is loaded in the process's address space:

```
HMODULE GetModuleHandle(PCTSTR pszModule);
```

When you call this function, you pass a zero-terminated string that specifies the name of an executable or DLL file loaded into the calling process's address space. If the system finds the specified executable or DLL name, *GetModuleHandle* returns the base address where that executable or DLL's file image is loaded. The system returns NULL if it cannot find the file. You can also call *GetModuleHandle*, passing NULL for the *pszModule* parameter; *GetModuleHandle* returns the calling executable file's base address. This is what the C run-time startup code does when it calls your *(w)WinMain* function, as discussed on page 74.

Keep in mind two important characteristics of the *GetModuleHandle* function. First, it examines only the calling process's address space. If the calling process does not use any common dialog functions, calling *GetModuleHandle* and passing it "ComDlg32" causes NULL to be returned even though ComDlg32.dll is probably loaded into other processes' address spaces. Second, calling *GetModuleHandle* and passing a value of NULL returns the base address of the executable file in the process's address space. So even if you call *GetModuleHandle(NULL)* from code that is contained inside a DLL, the value returned is the executable file's base address—not the DLL file's base address.

A Process's Previous Instance Handle

As noted earlier, the C/C++ run-time startup code always passes NULL to *(w)WinMain*'s *hinstExePrev* parameter. This parameter was used in 16-bit Windows and remains a parameter to *(w)WinMain* solely to ease porting of 16-bit Windows applications. You should never reference this parameter inside your code. For this reason, I always write my *(w)WinMain* functions as follows:

```
int WINAPI WinMain(
   HINSTANCE hinstExe,
   HINSTANCE,
   PSTR pszCmdLine,
   int nCmdShow);
```

Because no parameter name is given for the second parameter, the compiler does not issue a "parameter not referenced" warning.

A Process's Command Line

When a new process is created, it is passed a command line. The command line is almost never blank; at the very least, the name of the executable file used to create the new process is the first token on the command line. However, as you'll see later when we discuss the *CreateProcess* function, a process can receive a command line that consists of a single character: the string-terminating zero. When the C run time's startup code begins executing, it retrieves the process's command line, skips over the executable file's name, and passes a pointer to the remainder of the command line to *WinMain*'s *pszCmdLine* parameter.

It's important to note that the *pszCmdLine* parameter always points to an ANSI string. However, if you change *WinMain* to *wWinMain*, you can access a Unicode version of your process's command line.

An application can parse and interpret the command-line string any way it chooses. You can actually write to the memory buffer pointed to by the *pszCmdLine* parameter—but you should not, under any circumstances, write beyond the end of the buffer. Personally, I always consider this a read-only buffer. If I want to make changes to the command line, I first copy the command-line buffer to a local buffer in my application, and then I modify my local buffer.

You can also obtain a pointer to your process's complete command line by calling the *GetCommandLine* function:

```
PTSTR GetCommandLine();
```

This function returns a pointer to a buffer containing the full command line, including the full pathname of the executed file.

Many applications prefer to have the command line parsed into its separate tokens. An application can gain access to the command line's individual components by using the global _ _*argc* and _ _*argv* (or _ _*wargv*) variables. The following function, *CommandLineToArgvW*, separates any Unicode string into its separate tokens:

```
PWSTR CommandLineToArgvW(
   PWSTR pszCmdLine,
   int* pNumArgs);
```

As the *W* at the end of the function name implies, this function exists in a Unicode version only. (The *W* stands for *wide*.) The first parameter, *pszCmdLine*, points to a command-line string. This is usually the return value from an earlier call to *GetCommandLineW*. The *pNumArgs* parameter is the address of an integer; the integer is set to the number of arguments in the command line. *CommandLineToArgvW* returns the address to an array of Unicode string pointers.

CommandLineToArgvW allocates memory internally. Most applications do not free this memory—they count on the operating system to free it when the process terminates. This is totally acceptable. However, if you want to free the memory yourself, the proper way to do so is by calling *HeapFree* as follows:

```
int nNumArgs;
PWSTR *ppArgv = CommandLineToArgvW(GetCommandLineW(), &nNumArgs);

// Use the arguments…
if (*ppArgv[1] == L'x') {
   :
   :

}
// Free the memory block
HeapFree(GetProcessHeap(), 0, ppArgv);
```

A Process's Environment Variables

Every process has an environment block associated with it. An environment block is a block of memory allocated within the process's address space. Each block contains a set of strings with the following appearance:

```
VarName1=VarValue1\0
VarName2=VarValue2\0
VarName3=VarValue3\0
:

VarNameX=VarValueX\0
\0
```

The first part of each string is the name of an environment variable. This is followed by an equal sign, which is followed by the value you want to assign to the variable. All strings in the environment block must be sorted alphabetically by environment variable name.

Because the equal sign is used to separate the name from the value, an equal sign cannot be part of the name. Also, spaces are significant. For example, if you declare the following two variables and then compare the value of *XYZ* with the value of *ABC*, the system will report that the two variables are different because any white space that appears immediately before or after the equal sign is taken into account.

```
XYZ= Windows   (Notice the space after the equal sign.)
ABC=Windows
```

For example, if you were to add the following two strings to the environment block, the environment variable *XYZ* with a space after it would contain *Home* and the environment variable *XYZ* without the space would contain *Work*.

```
XYZ =Home  (Notice the space before the equal sign.)
XYZ=Work
```

Finally, you must place an additional 0 character at the end of all the environment variables to mark the end of the block.

To create an initial set of environment variables for Windows 98, you must modify the system's AutoExec.bat file by placing a series of SET lines in the file. Each line must be in the following form:

```
SET VarName=VarValue
```

When you reboot your system, the contents of the AutoExec.bat file are parsed, and any environment variables you have set will be available to any processes you invoke during your Windows 98 session.

When a user logs on to Windows 2000, the system creates the shell process and associates a set of environment strings with it. The system obtains the initial set of environment strings by examining two keys in the Registry.

The first key contains the list of all environment variables that apply to the system:

```
HKEY_LOCAL_MACHINE\SYSTEM\CurrentControlSet\Control\
    Session Manager\Environment
```

The second key contains the list of all environment variables that apply to the user currently logged on:

```
HKEY_CURRENT_USER\Environment
```

A user can add, delete, or change any of these entries by selecting the Control Panel's System applet, clicking on the Advanced tab, and clicking on the Environment Variables button to bring up the following dialog box:

(continued)

Only a user who has administrator privileges can alter the variables contained in the System Variables list.

Your application can also use the various Registry functions to modify these Registry entries. However, for the changes to take effect for all applications, the user must log off and then log back on. Some applications, such as Explorer, Task Manager, and the Control Panel, can update their environment block with the new Registry entries when their main windows receive a WM_SETTINGCHANGE message. For example, if you update the Registry entries and want to have the interested applications update their environment blocks, you can make the following call:

```
SendMessage(HWND_BROADCAST, WM_SETTINGCHANGE,
   0, (LPARAM) TEXT("Environment"));
```

Normally, a child process inherits a set of environment variables that are the same as those of its parent process. However, the parent process can control what environment variables a child inherits, as you'll see later when we discuss the *CreateProcess* function. By inherit, I mean that the child process gets its own copy of the parent's environment block; the child and parent do not share the same block. This means that a child process can add, delete, or modify a variable in its block and the change will not be reflected in the parent's block.

An application usually uses environment variables to let the user fine-tune its behavior. The user creates an environment variable and initializes it. Then, when the user invokes the application, the application examines the environment block for the variable. If it finds the variable, it parses the value of the variable and adjusts its own behavior.

The problem with environment variables is that they are not easy for users to set or to understand. Users need to spell variable names correctly, and they must also know the exact syntax expected of the variable's value. Most (if not all) graphical applications, on the other hand, allow users to fine-tune an application's behavior using dialog boxes. This approach is far more user-friendly.

If you still want to use environment variables, there are a few functions that your applications can call. The *GetEnvironmentVariable* function allows you to determine the existence and value of an environment variable:

```
DWORD GetEnvironmentVariable(
   PCTSTR pszName,
   PTSTR pszValue,
   DWORD cchValue);
```

When calling *GetEnvironmentVariable*, *pszName* points to the desired variable name, *pszValue* points to the buffer that will hold the variable's value, and *cchValue* indicates the size of the buffer in characters. The function returns either the number of characters copied into the buffer or 0 if the variable name cannot be found in the environment.

Many strings contain replaceable strings within them. For example, I found this string somewhere in the registry:

```
%USERPROFILE%\My Documents
```

The portion in percent signs (%) indicates a replaceable string. In this case, the value of the environment variable, USERPROFILE, should be placed in the string. On my machine, the value of my USERPROFILE environment variable is:

```
C:\Documents and Settings\Administrator
```

So, after performing the string replacement, the resulting string becomes:

```
C:\Documents and Settings\Administrator\My Documents
```

Because this type of string replacement is common, Windows offers the *ExpandEnvironmentStrings* function:

```
DWORD ExpandEnvironmentStrings(
   PCSTR pszSrc,
   PSTR pszDst,
   DWORD nSize);
```

When you call this function, the *pszSrc* parameter is the address of the string that contains replaceable environment variable strings. The *pszDst* parameter is the address of the buffer that will receive the expanded string, and the *nSize* parameter is the maximum size of this buffer, in characters.

Finally, you can use the *SetEnvironmentVariable* function to add a variable, delete a variable, or modify a variable's value:

```
BOOL SetEnvironmentVariable(
   PCTSTR pszName,
   PCTSTR pszValue);
```

This function sets the variable identified by the *pszName* parameter to the value identified by the *pszValue* parameter. If a variable with the specified name already exists, *SetEnvironmentVariable* modifies the value. If the specified variable doesn't exist, the variable is added and, if *pszValue* is NULL, the variable is deleted from the environment block.

You should always use these functions for manipulating your process's environment block. As I said earlier, the strings in an environment block must be sorted alphabetically by variable name so that *GetEnvironmentVariable* can locate them faster. The *SetEnvironmentVariable* function is smart enough to keep the environment variables in sorted order.

A Process's Affinity

Normally, threads within a process can execute on any of the CPUs in the host machine. However, a process's threads can be forced to run on a subset of the available CPUs. This is called *processor affinity* and is discussed in detail in Chapter 7. Child processes inherit the affinity of their parent processes.

A Process's Error Mode

Associated with each process is a set of flags that tells the system how the process should respond to serious errors, which include disk media failures, unhandled exceptions, file-find failures, and data misalignment. A process can tell the system how to handle each of these errors by calling the *SetErrorMode* function:

```
UINT SetErrorMode(UINT fuErrorMode);
```

The *fuErrorMode* parameter is a combination of any of the flags in the following table bitwise ORed together.

Flag	Description
SEM_FAILCRITICALERRORS	The system does not display the critical-error-handler message box and returns the error to the calling process.
SEM_NOGPFAULTERRORBOX	The system does not display the general-protection-fault message box. This flag should be set only by debugging applications that handle general protection (GP) faults themselves with an exception handler.
SEM_NOOPENFILEERRORBOX	The system does not display a message box when it fails to find a file.
SEM_NOALIGNMENTFAULTEXCEPT	The system automatically fixes memory alignment faults and makes them invisible to the application. This flag has no effect on *x*86 processors.

By default, a child process inherits the error mode flags of its parent. In other words, if a process has the SEM_NOGPFAULTERRORBOX flag turned on and then spawns a child process, the child process will also have this flag turned on. However, the child process is not notified of this, and it might not have been written to handle GP fault errors. If a GP fault occurs in one of the child's threads, the child process might terminate without notifying the user. A parent process can prevent a child process from inheriting its error mode by specifying the CREATE_DEFAULT_ERROR_MODE flag when calling *CreateProcess*. (We'll discuss *CreateProcess* later in this chapter.)

A Process's Current Drive and Directory

When full pathnames are not supplied, the various Windows functions look for files and directories in the current directory of the current drive. For example, if a thread in a process calls *CreateFile* to open a file (without specifying a full pathname), the system looks for the file in the current drive and directory.

The system keeps track of a process's current drive and directory internally. Because this information is maintained on a per-process basis, a thread in the process that changes the current drive or directory changes this information for all the threads in the process.

A thread can obtain and set its process's current drive and directory by calling the following two functions:

```
DWORD GetCurrentDirectory(
   DWORD cchCurDir,
   PTSTR pszCurDir);
BOOL SetCurrentDirectory(PCTSTR pszCurDir);
```

A Process's Current Directories

The system keeps track of the process's current drive and directory, but it does not keep track of the current directory for each and every drive. However, there is some operating system support for handling current directories for multiple drives. This support is offered via the process's environment strings. For example, a process can have two environment variables, as shown here:

```
=C:=C:\Utility\Bin
=D:=D:\Program Files
```

These variables indicate that the process's current directory for drive C is \Utility\Bin and that its current directory for drive D is \Program Files.

If you call a function, passing a drive-qualified name indicating a drive that is not the current drive, the system looks in the process's environment block for the variable associated with the specified drive letter. If the variable for the drive exists, the system uses the variable's value as the current directory. If the variable does not exist, the system assumes that the current directory for the specified drive is its root directory.

For example, if your process's current directory is C:\Utility\Bin and you call *CreateFile* to open D:ReadMe.Txt, the system looks up the environment variable =D:. Because the =D: variable exists, the system attempts to open the ReadMe.Txt file from the D:\Program Files directory. If the =D: variable did not exist, the system would attempt to open the ReadMe.Txt file from the root directory of drive D. The Windows file functions never add or change a drive-letter environment variable—they only read the variables.

NOTE

> You can use the C run-time function *_chdir* instead of the Windows *SetCurrentDirectory* function to change the current directory. The *_chdir* function calls *SetCurrentDirectory* internally, but *_chdir* also adds or modifies the environment variables so that the current directory of different drives is preserved.

If a parent process creates an environment block that it wants to pass to a child process, the child's environment block does not automatically inherit the parent process's current directories. Instead, the child process's current directories default to the root directory of every drive. If you want the child process to inherit the parent's current directories, the parent process must create these drive-letter environment variables and add them to the environment block before spawning the child process. The parent process can obtain its current directories by calling *GetFullPathName*:

```
DWORD GetFullPathName(
    PCTSTR pszFile,
    DWORD cchPath,
    PTSTR pszPath,
    PTSTR *ppszFilePart);
```

For example, to get the current directory for drive C, you call *GetFullPathName* as follows:

```
TCHAR szCurDir[MAX_PATH];
DWORD GetFullPathName(TEXT("C:"), MAX_PATH, szCurDir, NULL);
```

Keep in mind that a process's environment variables must always be kept in alphabetical order. As a result, the drive letter environment variables usually must be placed at the beginning of the environment block.

The System Version

Frequently, an application needs to determine which version of Windows the user is running. For example, an application might take advantage of security features by calling the security functions. However, these functions are fully implemented only on Windows 2000.

For as long as I can remember, the Windows API has had a *GetVersion* function:

```
DWORD GetVersion();
```

This function has quite a history behind it. It was first designed for 16-bit Windows. The idea was simple—to return the MS-DOS version number in the high-word and return the Windows version number in the low-word. For each word, the high-byte would represent the major version number and the low-byte would represent the minor version number.

Unfortunately, the programmer who wrote this code made a small mistake, coding the function so that the Windows version numbers were reversed— the major version number was in the low-byte and the minor number was in the high-byte. Since many programmers had already started using this function, Microsoft was forced to leave the function as it was and change the documentation to reflect the mistake.

Because of all the confusion surrounding *GetVersion*, Microsoft added a new function, *GetVersionEx*:

```
BOOL GetVersionEx(POSVERSIONINFO pVersionInformation);
```

This function requires you to allocate an OSVERSIONINFOEX structure in your application and pass the structure's address to *GetVersionEx*. The OSVERSIONINFOEX structure is shown here:

```
typedef struct {
    DWORD dwOSVersionInfoSize;
    DWORD dwMajorVersion;
    DWORD dwMinorVersion;
    DWORD dwBuildNumber;
    DWORD dwPlatformId;
    TCHAR szCSDVersion[128];
    WORD  wServicePackMajor;
    WORD  wServicePackMinor;
    WORD  wSuiteMask;
    BYTE  wProductType;
    BYTE  wReserved;
} OSVERSIONINFOEX, *POSVERSIONINFOEX;
```

The OSVERSIONINFOEX structure is new in Windows 2000. Other versions of Windows use the older OSVERSIONINFO structure, which does not have the service pack, suite mask, product type, and reserved members.

Notice that the structure has different members for each component of the system's version number. This was done so programmers would not have to bother with extracting low-words, high-words, low-bytes, and high-bytes, which should make it much easier for applications to compare their expected version number with the host system's version number. Table 4-2 describes the OSVERSIONINFOEX structure's members.

Member	Description
dwOSVersionInfoSize	Must be set to *sizeof(OSVERSIONINFO)* or *sizeof(OSVERSIONINFOEX)* prior to calling the *GetVersionEx* function.
dwMajorVersion	Major version number of the host system.
dwMinorVersion	Minor version number of the host system.
dwBuildNumber	Build number of the current system.
dwPlatformId	Identifies the platform supported by the current system. This can be VER_PLATFORM_WIN32s (Win32s), VER_PLATFORM_WIN32_WINDOWS (Windows 95/Windows 98), VER_PLATFORM_WIN32_NT (Windows NT/Windows 2000), or VER_PLATFORM_WIN32_CEHH (Windows CE).
szCSDVersion	This field contains additional text that provides further information about the installed operating system.
wServicePackMajor	Major version number of latest installed service pack.
wServicePackMinor	Minor version number of latest installed service pack.
wSuiteMask	Identifies which suite(s) are available on the system (VER_SUITE_SMALLBUSINESS, VER_SUITE_ENTERPRISE, VER_SUITE_BACKOFFICE, VER_SUITE_COMMUNICATIONS, VER_SUITE_TERMINAL, VER_SUITE_SMALLBUSINESS_RESTRICTED, VER_SUITE_EMBEDDEDNT, and VER_SUITE_DATACENTER).
wProductType	Identifies which one of the following operating system products is installed: VER_NT_WORKSTATION, VER_NT_SERVER, or VER_NT_DOMAIN_CONTROLLER.
wReserved	Reserved for future use.

Table 4-2.
The OSVERSIONINFOEX structure's members

To make things even easier, Windows 2000 offers a new function, *VerifyVersionInfo*, which compares the host system's version with the version your application requires:

```
BOOL VerifyVersionInfo(
    POSVERSIONINFOEX pVersionInformation,
    DWORD dwTypeMask,
    DWORDLONG dwlConditionMask);
```

To use this function, you must allocate an OSVERSIONINFOEX structure, initialize its *dwOSVersionInfoSize* member to the size of the structure, and then initialize any other members of the structure that are important to your application. When you call *VerifyVersionInfo*, the *dwTypeMask* parameter indicates which members of the structure you have initialized. The *dwTypeMask* parameter is any of the following flags ORed together: VER_MINORVERSION, VER_MAJORVERSION, VER_BUILDNUMBER, VER_PLATFORMID, VER_SERVICEPACKMINOR, VER_SERVICEPACKMAJOR, VER_SUITE-NAME, and VER_PRODUCT_TYPE. The last parameter, *dwlConditionMask*, is a 64-bit value that controls how the function compares the system's version information to your desired information.

The *dwlConditionMask* describes the comparison using a complex set of bit combinations. To create the desired bit combination, you use the VER_SET_CONDITION macro:

```
VER_SET_CONDITION(
    DWORDLONG dwlConditionMask,
    ULONG dwTypeBitMask,
    ULONG dwConditionMask)
```

The first parameter, *dwlConditionMask*, identifies the variable whose bits you are manipulating. Note that you do not pass the address of this variable because VER_SET_CONDITION is a macro, not a function. The *dwTypeBitMask* parameter indicates a single member in the OSVERSIONINFOEX structure that you want to compare. To compare multiple members, you must call VER_SET_CONDITION multiple times, once for each member. The flags you pass to *VerifyVersionInfo*'s *dwTypeMask* parameter (VER_MINORVERSION, VER_BUILDNUMBER, and so on) are the same flags that you use for VER_SET_CONDITION's *dwTypeBitMask* parameter.

VER_SET_CONDITION's last parameter, *dwConditionMask*, indicates how you want the comparison made. This can be one of the following values: VER_EQUAL, VER_GREATER, VER_GREATER_EQUAL, VER_LESS, or VER_LESS_EQUAL. Note that you can use these values when comparing VER_PRODUCT_TYPE information. For example, VER_NT_WORK-STATION is less than VER_NT_SERVER. However, for the VER_SUITE-NAME information, you cannot use these test values. Instead, you must use VER_AND (all suite products must be installed) or VER_OR (at least one of the suite products must be installed).

After you build up the set of conditions, you call *VerifyVersionInfo* and it returns nonzero if successful (if the host system meets all of your application's requirements). If *VerifyVersionInfo* returns 0, the host system does not meet your requirements or you called the function improperly. You can determine why the function returned 0 by calling *GetLastError*. If *GetLastError* returns ERROR_OLD_WIN_VERSION, you called the function correctly but the system doesn't meet your requirements.

Here is an example of how to test whether the host system is exactly Windows 2000:

```
// Prepare the OSVERSIONINFOEX structure to indicate Windows 2000.
OSVERSIONINFOEX osver = { 0 };
osver.dwOSVersionInfoSize = sizeof(osver);
osver.dwMajorVersion = 5;
osver.dwMinorVersion = 0;
osver.dwPlatformId = VER_PLATFORM_WIN32_NT;

// Prepare the condition mask.
DWORDLONG dwlConditionMask = 0; // You MUST initialize this to 0.
VER_SET_CONDITION(dwlConditionMask, VER_MAJORVERSION, VER_EQUAL);
VER_SET_CONDITION(dwlConditionMask, VER_MINORVERSION, VER_EQUAL);
VER_SET_CONDITION(dwlConditionMask, VER_PLATFORMID, VER_EQUAL);

// Perform the version test.
if (VerifyVersionInfo(&osver, VER_MAJORVERSION | VER_MINORVERSION | VER_PLATFORMID,
   dwlConditionMask)) {
   // The host system is Windows 2000 exactly.
} else {
   // The host system is NOT Windows 2000.
}
```

The *CreateProcess* Function

You create a process with the *CreateProcess* function:

```
BOOL CreateProcess(
   PCTSTR pszApplicationName,
   PTSTR pszCommandLine,
   PSECURITY_ATTRIBUTES psaProcess,
   PSECURITY_ATTRIBUTES psaThread,
   BOOL bInheritHandles,
   DWORD fdwCreate,
   PVOID pvEnvironment,
   PCTSTR pszCurDir,
   PSTARTUPINFO psiStartInfo,
   PPROCESS_INFORMATION ppiProcInfo);
```

When a thread calls *CreateProcess*, the system creates a process kernel object with an initial usage count of 1. This process kernel object is not the process itself but a small data structure that the operating system uses to manage the process—you can think of the process kernel object as a small data structure that consists of statistical information about the process. The system then creates a virtual address space for the new process and loads the code and data for the executable file and any required DLLs into the process's address space.

The system then creates a thread kernel object (with a usage count of 1) for the new process's primary thread. Like the process kernel object, the thread kernel object is a small data structure that the operating system uses to manage the thread. This primary thread begins by executing the C/C++ run-time startup code, which eventually calls your *WinMain*, *wWinMain*, *main*, or *wmain* function. If the system successfully creates the new process and primary thread, *CreateProcess* returns TRUE.

NOTE

CreateProcess returns TRUE before the process has fully initialized. This means that the operating system loader has not attempted to locate all the required DLLs yet. If a DLL can't be located or fails to initialize correctly, the process is terminated. Since *CreateProcess* returned TRUE, the parent process is not aware of any initialization problems.

OK, that's the broad overview. The following sections dissect each of *CreateProcess*'s parameters.

pszApplicationName and pszCommandLine

The *pszApplicationName* and *pszCommandLine* parameters specify the name of the executable file the new process will use and the command-line string that will be passed to the new process, respectively. Let's talk about the *pszCommandLine* parameter first.

NOTE

Notice that the *pszCommandLine* parameter is prototyped as a PTSTR. This means that *CreateProcess* expects that you are passing the address of a non-constant string. Internally, *CreateProcess* actually does modify the command-line string that you pass to it. But before *CreateProcess* returns, it restores the string to its original form.

This is important because an access violation will occur if your command-line string is contained in a read-only portion of your file

(continued)

(continued)

image. For example, the following code causes an access violation because Visual C++ 6.0 places the "NOTEPAD" string in read-only memory:

```
STARTUPINFO si = { sizeof(si) };
PROCESS_INFORMATION pi;
CreateProcess(NULL, TEXT("NOTEPAD"), NULL, NULL,
    FALSE, 0, NULL, NULL, &si, &pi);
```

When *CreateProcess* attempts to modify the string, an access violation occurs. (Earlier versions of Visual C++ placed the string in read/write memory so calls to *CreateProcess* did not cause access violations.)

The best way to solve this problem is to copy the constant string to a temporary buffer before calling *CreateProcess* as follows:

```
STARTUPINFO si = { sizeof(si) };
PROCESS_INFORMATION pi;
TCHAR szCommandLine[] = TEXT("NOTEPAD");
CreateProcess(NULL, szCommandLine, NULL, NULL,
    FALSE, 0, NULL, NULL, &si, &pi);
```

You might also look into using Visual C++'s /Gf and /GF compiler switches, which control the elimination of duplicate strings and determine whether those strings are placed in a read-only section. (Also note that the /ZI switch, which allows the use of Visual Studio's Edit & Continue debugging feature, implies the /GF switch.) The best thing you can do is to use the /GF compiler switch and a temporary buffer. The best thing Microsoft can do is fix *CreateProcess* so that it takes over the responsibility of making a temporary copy of the string so we don't have to do it. Maybe this will happen in a future version of Windows.

By the way, if you are calling the ANSI version of *CreateProcess* on Windows 2000, you will not get an access violation because a temporary copy of the command-line string is made. (For more information about this, see Chapter 2.)

You use the *pszCommandLine* parameter to specify a complete command line that *CreateProcess* uses to create the new process. When *CreateProcess* parses the *pszCommandLine* string, it examines the first token in the string and assumes that this token is the name of the executable file you want to run. If the executable file's name does not have an extension, an .exe extension is assumed. *CreateProcess* also searches for the executable in the following order:

1. The directory containing the .exe file of the calling process

2. The current directory of the calling process

3. The Windows system directory

4. The Windows directory

5. The directories listed in the PATH environment variable

Of course, if the filename includes a full path, the system looks for the executable using the full path and does not search the directories. If the system finds the executable file, it creates a new process and maps the executable's code and data into the new process's address space. The system then calls the C/C++ run-time startup routine. As noted earlier, the C/C++ run-time startup routine examines the process's command line and passes the address to the first argument after the executable file's name as *(w)WinMain*'s *pszCmdLine* parameter.

All of this happens as long as the *pszApplicationName* parameter is NULL (which should be the case more than 99 percent of the time). Instead of passing NULL, you can pass the address to a string containing the name of the executable file you want to run in the *pszApplicationName* parameter. Note that you must specify the file's extension; the system will not automatically assume that the filename has an .exe extension. *CreateProcess* assumes that the file is in the current directory unless a path precedes the filename. If the file can't be found in the current directory, *CreateProcess* doesn't look for the file in any other directory—it simply fails.

Even if you specify a filename in the *pszApplicationName* parameter, however, *CreateProcess* passes the contents of the *pszCommandLine* parameter to the new process as its command line. For example, say that you call *CreateProcess* like this:

```
// Make sure that the path is in a read/write section of memory.
TCHAR szPath[] = TEXT("WORDPAD README.TXT");

// Spawn the new process.
CreateProcess(TEXT("C:\\WINNT\\SYSTEM32\\NOTEPAD.EXE"),szPath,...);
```

The system invokes the Notepad application, but Notepad's command line is WORDPAD README.TXT. This quirk is certainly a little strange, but that's how *CreateProcess* works. This capability provided by the *pszApplicationName* parameter was actually added to *CreateProcess* to support Windows 2000's POSIX subsystem.

psaProcess, *psaThread*, and *bInheritHandles*

To create a new process, the system must create a process kernel object and a thread kernel object (for the process's primary thread). Because these are kernel objects, the parent process gets the opportunity to associate security attributes with these two objects. You use the *psaProcess* and *psaThread* parameters to specify the desired security for the process object and the thread object, respectively. You can pass NULL for these parameters, in which case the system gives these objects default security descriptors. Or you can allocate and initialize two SECURITY_ATTRIBUTES structures to create and assign your own security privileges to the process and thread objects.

Another reason to use SECURITY_ATTRIBUTES structures for the *psaProcess* and *psaThread* parameters is if you want either of these two object handles to be inheritable by any child processes spawned in the future by this parent process. (I discussed the theory behind kernel object handle inheritance in Chapter 3.)

Figure 4-2 is a short program that demonstrates kernel object handle inheritance. Let's say that Process A creates Process B by calling *CreateProcess* and passing the address of a SECURITY_ATTRIBUTES structure for the *psaProcess* parameter in which the *bInheritHandle* member is set to TRUE. In this same call, the *psaThread* parameter points to another SECURITY_ATTRIBUTES structure in which its *bInheritHandle* member is set to FALSE.

When the system creates Process B, it allocates both a process kernel object and a thread kernel object and returns handles back to Process A in the structure pointed to by the *ppiProcInfo* parameter (discussed shortly). Process A can now manipulate the newly created process object and thread object by using these handles.

Now let's say that Process A will call *CreateProcess* a second time to create Process C. Process A can decide whether to grant Process C the ability to manipulate some of the kernel objects that Process A has access to. The *bInheritHandles* parameter is used for this purpose. If *bInheritHandles* is set to TRUE, the system causes Process C to inherit any inheritable handles in Process A. In this case, the handle to Process B's process object is inheritable. The handle to Process B's primary thread object is not inherited no matter what the value of the *bInheritHandles* parameter to *CreateProcess* is. Also, if Process A calls *CreateProcess*, passing FALSE for the *bInheritHandles* parameter, Process C does not inherit any of the handles currently used by Process A.

Inherit.c

```
/**************************************************************
Module name: Inherit.c
Notices: Copyright (c) 2000 Jeffrey Richter
**************************************************************/


#include <Windows.h>


int WINAPI WinMain (HINSTANCE hinstExe, HINSTANCE,
   PSTR pszCmdLine, int nCmdShow) {

   // Prepare a STARTUPINFO structure for spawning processes.
   STARTUPINFO si = { sizeof(si) };
   SECURITY_ATTRIBUTES saProcess, saThread;
   PROCESS_INFORMATION piProcessB, piProcessC;
   TCHAR szPath[MAX_PATH];

   // Prepare to spawn Process B from Process A.
   // The handle identifying the new process
   // object should be inheritable.
   saProcess.nLength = sizeof(saProcess);
   saProcess.lpSecurityDescriptor = NULL;
   saProcess.bInheritHandle = TRUE;

   // The handle identifying the new thread
   // object should NOT be inheritable.
   saThread.nLength = sizeof(saThread);
   saThread.lpSecurityDescriptor = NULL;
   saThread.bInheritHandle = FALSE;

   // Spawn Process B.
   lstrcpy(szPath, TEXT("ProcessB"));
   CreateProcess(NULL, szPath, &saProcess, &saThread,
      FALSE, 0, NULL, NULL, &si, &piProcessB);

   // The pi structure contains two handles
   // relative to Process A:
   // hProcess, which identifies Process B's process
   // object and is inheritable; and hThread, which identifies
   // Process B's primary thread object and is NOT inheritable.
```

Figure 4-2.   *(continued)*
An example of kernel object handle inheritance

Figure 4-2. *continued*

```
// Prepare to spawn Process C from Process A.
// Since NULL is passed for the psaProcess and psaThread
// parameters, the handles to Process C's process and
// primary thread objects default to "noninheritable."

// If Process A were to spawn another process, this new
// process would NOT inherit handles to Process C's process
// and thread objects.

// Because TRUE is passed for the bInheritHandles parameter,
// Process C will inherit the handle that identifies Process
// B's process object but will not inherit a handle to
// Process B's primary thread object.
lstrcpy(szPath, TEXT("ProcessC"));
CreateProcess(NULL, szPath, NULL, NULL,
    TRUE, 0, NULL, NULL, &si, &piProcessC);

return(0);
}
```

fdwCreate

The *fdwCreate* parameter identifies flags that affect how the new process is created. You can specify multiple flags if you combine them with the bitwise OR operator.

■ The DEBUG_PROCESS flag tells the system that the parent process wants to debug the child process and any processes spawned by the child process in the future. This flag tells the system to notify the parent process (now the debugger) when certain events occur in any of the child processes (the debuggees).

■ The DEBUG_ONLY_THIS_PROCESS flag is similar to DEBUG_PROCESS except that the debugger is notified only of special events occurring in the immediate child process. If the child process spawns any additional processes, the debugger is not notified of events in these processes.

■ The CREATE_SUSPENDED flag causes the new process to be created, but its primary thread is suspended. This allows the parent process to modify memory in the child process's address space, alter the child process's primary thread's priority, or add the process to a job before the process has had a chance to execute any code. Once the parent process has modified the child process, the parent process allows the child process to execute code by calling the *ResumeThread* function (discussed in Chapter 7).

■ The DETACHED_PROCESS flag blocks a CUI-based process's access to its parent's console window and tells the system to send its output to a new console window. If a CUI-based process is created by another CUI-based process, the new process will, by default, use the parent's console window. (When you run the C compiler from the command shell, a new console window isn't created; the output is simply appended to the bottom of the existing console window.) By specifying this flag, the new process will send its output to a new console window.

■ The CREATE_NEW_CONSOLE flag tells the system to create a new console window for the new process. Specifying both the CREATE_NEW_CONSOLE and DETACHED_PROCESS flags results in an error.

■ The CREATE_NO_WINDOW flag tells the system not to create any console window for the application. You can use this flag to execute a console application without a user interface.

■ The CREATE_NEW_PROCESS_GROUP flag modifies the list of processes that are notified when the user presses the Ctrl+C or Ctrl+Break keys. If you have several CUI-based processes running when the user presses one of these key combinations, the system notifies all the processes in a process group that the user wants to break out of the current operation. By specifying this flag when creating a new CUI-based process, you create a new process group. If the user presses Ctrl+C or Ctrl+Break while a process in this group is active, the system notifies only processes in this group of the user's request.

■ The CREATE_DEFAULT_ERROR_MODE flag tells the system that the new process should not inherit the error mode used by the parent process. (See the *SetErrorMode* function discussion earlier in this chapter.)

■ The CREATE_SEPARATE_WOW_VDM flag is useful only when you invoke a 16-bit Windows application on Windows 2000. It tells the system to create a separate Virtual DOS Machine (VDM) and run the 16-bit Windows application in this VDM. By default, all 16-bit Windows applications execute in a single shared VDM. The advantage of running an application in a separate VDM is that if the application crashes, it kills only the single VDM; any other programs running in distinct VDMs continue to function normally. Also, 16-bit Windows applications that run in separate VDMs have separate input queues. This means that if one application hangs momentarily, applications in separate VDMs continue to receive input. The disadvantage of running multiple VDMs is that each VDM consumes a significant amount of physical storage. Windows 98 runs all 16-bit Windows applications in a single virtual machine—you cannot override this.

- The CREATE_SHARED_WOW_VDM flag is useful only when you invoke a 16-bit Windows application on Windows 2000. By default, all 16-bit Windows applications run in a single VDM unless the CREATE_SEPARATE_WOW_VDM flag is specified. However, you can override this default behavior by setting the DefaultSeparate VDM value in the registry under HKEY_LOCAL_MACHINE\System-\CurrentControlSet\Control\WOW to yes. The CREATE_SHARED_ WOW_VDM flag then runs the 16-bit Windows application in the system's shared VDM. (You must reboot after changing this registry setting.)

- The CREATE_UNICODE_ENVIRONMENT flag tells the system that the child process's environment block should contain Unicode characters. By default, a process's environment block contains ANSI strings.

- The CREATE_FORCEDOS flag forces the system to run the MS-DOS application that is embedded inside a 16-bit OS/2 application.

- The CREATE_BREAKAWAY_FROM_JOB flag allows a process in a job to spawn a new process that is disassociated from the job. (See Chapter 5 for more information.)

The *fdwCreate* parameter also allows you to specify a priority class. However, you don't have to do this, and for most applications you shouldn't—the system will assign a default priority class to the new process. The following table shows the possible priority classes.

Priority Class	Flag Identifier
Idle	IDLE_PRIORITY_CLASS
Below normal	BELOW_NORMAL_PRIORITY_CLASS
Normal	NORMAL_PRIORITY_CLASS
Above normal	ABOVE_NORMAL_PRIORITY_CLASS
High	HIGH_PRIORITY_CLASS
Realtime	REALTIME_PRIORITY_CLASS

These priority classes affect how the threads contained within the process are scheduled with respect to other processes' threads. See the section titled "An Abstract View of Priorities" in Chapter 7 for more information.

> **NOTE**
>
> The BELOW_NORMAL_PRIORITY_CLASS and ABOVE_NORMAL_PRIORITY_CLASS priority classes are new in Windows 2000; they are not supported on Windows NT 4 (or earlier), Windows 95, or Windows 98.

pvEnvironment

The *pvEnvironment* parameter points to a block of memory that contains environment strings that the new process will use. Most of the time, NULL is passed for this parameter, causing the child process to inherit the set of environment strings that its parent is using. Alternatively, you can use the *GetEnvironmentStrings* function:

```
PVOID GetEnvironmentStrings();
```

This function gets the address of the environment string data block that the calling process is using. You can use the address returned by this function as the *pvEnvironment* parameter of *CreateProcess*. This is exactly what *CreateProcess* does if you pass NULL for the *pvEnvironment* parameter. When you no longer need this block of memory, you should free it by calling *FreeEnvironmentStrings*:

```
BOOL FreeEnvironmentStrings(PTSTR pszEnvironmentBlock);
```

pszCurDir

The *pszCurDir* parameter allows the parent process to set the child process's current drive and directory. If this parameter is NULL, the new process's working directory will be the same as that of the application spawning the new process. If this parameter is not NULL, *pszCurDir* must point to a zero-terminated string containing the desired working drive and directory. Notice that you must specify a drive letter in the path.

psiStartInfo

The *psiStartInfo* parameter points to a STARTUPINFO structure:

```
typedef struct _STARTUPINFO {
    DWORD cb;
    PSTR lpReserved;
    PSTR lpDesktop;
    PSTR lpTitle;
    DWORD dwX;
    DWORD dwY;
    DWORD dwXSize;
    DWORD dwYSize;
    DWORD dwXCountChars;
    DWORD dwYCountChars;
    DWORD dwFillAttribute;
    DWORD dwFlags;
    WORD wShowWindow;
    WORD cbReserved2;
    PBYTE lpReserved2;
    HANDLE hStdInput;
    HANDLE hStdOutput;
    HANDLE hStdError;
} STARTUPINFO, *LPSTARTUPINFO;
```

Windows uses the members of this structure when it creates the new process. Most applications will want the spawned application simply to use default values. At a minimum, you should initialize all the members in this structure to zero and then set the *cb* member to the size of the structure:

```
STARTUPINFO si = { sizeof(si) };
CreateProcess(..., &si, ...);
```

If you fail to zero the contents of the structure, the members will contain whatever garbage is on the calling thread's stack. Passing this garbage to *CreateProcess* means that sometimes the new process will be created and sometimes it won't, depending on the garbage. It is important to set the unused members of this structure to zero so that *CreateProcess* will work consistently. Failing to do so is one of the most common mistakes I see developers make.

Now, if you want to initialize some of the members of the structure, you simply do so before the call to *CreateProcess*. We'll discuss each member in turn. Some members are meaningful only if the child application creates an overlapped window; others are meaningful only if the child performs CUI-based input and output. Table 4-3 describes the usefulness of each member.

Member	Window, Console, or Both	Purpose
cb	Both	Contains the number of bytes in the STARTUPINFO structure. Acts as a version control in case Microsoft expands this structure in the future. Your application must initialize *cb* to *sizeof(STARTUPINFO)*.
lpReserved	Both	Reserved. Must be initialized to NULL.
lpDesktop	Both	Identifies the name of the desktop on which to start the application. If the desktop exists, the new process is associated with the specified desktop. If the desktop does not exist, a desktop with default attributes is created with the specified name for the new process. If *lpDesktop* is NULL (which is most common), the process is associated with the current desktop.
lpTitle	Console	Specifies the window title for a console window. If *lpTitle* is NULL, the name of the executable file is used as the window title.
dwX *dwY*	Both	Specify the *x* and *y* coordinates (in pixels) of the location where the application's window should be placed on the screen. These coordinates are used only if the child process creates its first overlapped window with CW_USEDEFAULT as the *x* parameter of *CreateWindow*. For applications that create console windows, these members indicate the upper left corner of the console window.
dwXSize *dwYSize*	Both	Specify the width and height (in pixels) of an application's window. These values are used only if the child process creates its first overlapped window with CW_USEDEFAULT as the *nWidth* parameter of *CreateWindow*. For applications that create console windows, these members indicate the width and height of the console window.

Table 4-3. *(continued)*
The members of the STARTUPINFO structure

Table 4-3. *continued*

Member	Window, Console, or Both	Purpose
dwXCountChars *dwYCountChars*	Console	Specify the width and height (in characters) of a child's console windows.
dwFillAttribute	Console	Specifies the text and background colors used by a child's console window.
dwFlags	Both	See the following section and the table below.
wShowWindow	Window	Specifies how the child's first overlapped window should appear if the application's first call to *ShowWindow* passes SW_SHOWDEFAULT as the *nCmdShow* parameter. This member can be any of the SW_* identifiers normally used with the *ShowWindow* function.
cbReserved2	Both	Reserved. Must be initialized to 0.
lpReserved2	Both	Reserved. Must be initialized to NULL.
hStdInput *hStdOutput* *hStdError*	Console	Specify handles to buffers for console input and output. By default, the *hStdInput* identifies a keyboard buffer; *hStdOutput* and *hStdError* identify a console window's buffer.

Now, as promised, I'll discuss the *dwFlags* member. This member contains a set of flags that modify how the child process is to be created. Most of the flags simply tell *CreateProcess* whether other members of the STARTUPINFO structure contain useful information or whether some of the members should be ignored. The following table shows the list of possible flags and their meanings.

Flag	Meaning
STARTF_USESIZE	Use the *dwXSize* and *dwYSize* members.
STARTF_USESHOWWINDOW	Use the *wShowWindow* member.
STARTF_USEPOSITION	Use the *dwX* and *dwY* members.
STARTF_USECOUNTCHARS	Use the *dwXCountChars* and *dwYCountChars* members.
STARTF_USEFILLATTRIBUTE	Use the *dwFillAttribute* member.
STARTF_USESTDHANDLES	Use the *hStdInput*, *hStdOutput*, and *hStdError* members.
STARTF_RUN_FULLSCREEN	Forces a console application running on an *x86* computer to start in full-screen mode.

Two additional flags, STARTF_FORCEONFEEDBACK and STARTF_FORCEOFFFEEDBACK, give you control over the mouse cursor when you invoke a new process. Because Windows supports true preemptive multitasking, you can invoke an application and, while the process is initializing, use another program. To give visual feedback to the user, *CreateProcess* temporarily changes the system's arrow cursor to a new cursor called a start glass:

This cursor indicates that you can wait for something to happen or you can continue to use the system. The *CreateProcess* function gives you more control over the cursor when invoking another process. When you specify the STARTF_FORCEOFFFEEDBACK flag, *CreateProcess* does not change the cursor into the start glass.

STARTF_FORCEONFEEDBACK causes *CreateProcess* to monitor the new process's initialization and to alter the cursor based on the result. When *CreateProcess* is called with this flag, the cursor changes into the start glass. If, after two seconds, the new process does not make a GUI call, *CreateProcess* resets the cursor to an arrow.

If the process makes a GUI call within two seconds, *CreateProcess* waits for the application to show a window. This must occur within five seconds after the process makes the GUI call. If a window is not displayed, *CreateProcess* resets the cursor. If a window is displayed, *CreateProcess* keeps the start glass cursor on for another five seconds. If at any time the application calls the *GetMessage* function, indicating that it is finished initializing, *CreateProcess* immediately resets the cursor and stops monitoring the new process.

Before concluding this section, I'd like to mention STARTUPINFO's *wShowWindow* member. You initialize this member to the value that is passed to *(w)WinMain*'s last parameter, *nCmdShow*. This member indicates the value you want passed to the new process's *(w)WinMain* function's last parameter, *nCmdShow*. It is one of the identifiers that can be passed to the *ShowWindow* function. Usually, *nCmdShow*'s value is either SW_SHOWNORMAL or SW_SHOWMINNOACTIVE. However, it can sometimes be SW_SHOWDEFAULT.

When you invoke an application from the Explorer, the application's *(w)WinMain* function is called with SW_SHOWNORMAL passed as the *nCmdShow* parameter. If you create a shortcut for the application, you can use the shortcut's property page to tell the system how the application's window should first appear. Figure 4-3 shows the property page for a shortcut that runs Notepad. Notice that the Run option's combo box allows you to specify how Notepad's window is displayed.

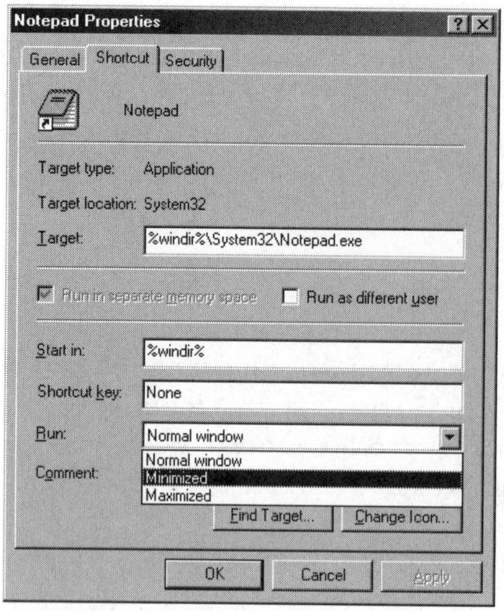

Figure 4-3.
The property page for a shortcut that runs Notepad

When you use Explorer to invoke this shortcut, Explorer prepares the STARTUPINFO structure properly and calls *CreateProcess*. Notepad executes and its *(w)WinMain* function is passed SW_SHOWMINNOACTIVE for the *nCmdShow* parameter.

In this way, the user can easily start an application with its main window showing in the normal state, minimized state, or maximized state.

Finally, an application can call the following function to obtain a copy of the STARTUPINFO structure that was initialized by the parent process. The child process can examine this structure and alter its behavior based on the values of the structure's members.

```
VOID GetStartupInfo(LPSTARTUPINFO pStartupInfo);
```

> **NOTE**
>
> Although the Windows documentation does not explicitly say so, you must initialize the *cb* member of the structure before calling *GetStartupInfo* as follows:
>
> ```
> STARTUPINFO si = { sizeof(si) };
> GetStartupInfo(&si);
>     :
>     :
> ```

ppiProcInfo

The *ppiProcInfo* parameter points to a PROCESS_INFORMATION structure that you must allocate; *CreateProcess* initializes the members of this structure before it returns. The structure appears as follows:

```
typedef struct _PROCESS_INFORMATION {
    HANDLE hProcess;
    HANDLE hThread;
    DWORD  dwProcessId;
    DWORD  dwThreadId;
} PROCESS_INFORMATION;
```

As already mentioned, creating a new process causes the system to create a process kernel object and a thread kernel object. At creation time, the system gives each object an initial usage count of 1. Then, just before *CreateProcess* returns, the function opens the process object and the thread object and places the process-relative handles for each in the *hProcess* and *hThread* members of the PROCESS_INFORMATION structure. When *CreateProcess* opens these objects internally, the usage count for each becomes 2.

This means that before the system can free the process object, the process must terminate (decrementing the usage count by 1) and the parent process must call *CloseHandle* (decrementing the usage count again by 1 making it 0). Similarly, to free the thread object, the thread must terminate and the parent process must close the handle to the thread object. (See the "Child Processes" section at the end of this chapter for more information about freeing thread objects.)

NOTE

You must close the handles to the child process and its primary thread to avoid resource leaks while your application is running. Of course, the system will clean up these leaks automatically when your process terminates, but well-written software explicitly closes these handles (by calling the *CloseHandle* function) when the process no longer needs to access the child process and its primary thread. Failure to close these handles is one of the most common mistakes developers make.

For some reason, many developers believe that closing the handle to a process or thread forces the system to kill that process or thread. This is absolutely not true. Closing the handle simply tells the system that you are not interested in the process or thread's statistical data. The process or thread will continue to execute until it terminates on its own.

When a process kernel object is created, the system assigns the object a unique identifier; no other process kernel object in the system will have the same ID number. The same is true for thread kernel objects. When a thread kernel object is created, the object is assigned a unique, system-wide ID number. Process IDs and thread IDs share the same number pool. This means that it is impossible for a process and a thread to have the same ID. In addition, an object is never assigned an ID of 0. Before *CreateProcess* returns, it fills the *dwProcessId* and *dwThreadId* members of the PROCESS_INFORMATION structure with these IDs. IDs simply make it easy for you to identify the processes and threads in the system. IDs are mostly used by utility applications (such as the Task Manager) and rarely by productivity applications. For this reason, most applications ignore IDs altogether.

If your application uses IDs to track processes and threads, you must be aware that the system reuses process and thread IDs immediately. For example, let's say that when a process is created, the system allocates a process object and assigns it the ID value 122. If a new process object is created, the system doesn't assign the same ID number. However, if the first process object is freed, the system might assign 122 to the next process object created. Keep this in mind so you avoid writing code that references an incorrect process object or thread. It's easy to acquire a process ID and save the ID; but the next thing you know, the process identified by the ID is freed and a new process is created and given the same ID. When you use the saved process ID, you end up manipulating the new process, not the process whose ID you originally acquired.

Occasionally, you'll work on an application that wants to determine its parent process. The first thing you should know is that a parent-child relationship exists between processes only at the time when the child is spawned. Just before the child process begins executing code, Windows does not consider a parent-child relationship to exist anymore. Earlier versions of Windows didn't offer functions that allowed a process to query its parent process. The ToolHelp functions now make this possible via the PROCESSENTRY32 structure. Inside this structure is a *th32ParentProcessID* member that the documentation claims will return the ID of the process's parent.

The system does remember the ID of each process's parent process, but since IDs are immediately reused, by the time you get your parent process's ID, that ID might identify a completely different process running in the system. Your parent process will probably have terminated. If your application needs to communicate with its "creator," you are better off not using IDs; instead, you should define a more persistent mechanism to communicate—kernel objects, window handles, and so forth.

The only way to guarantee that a process or thread ID isn't reused is to make sure that the process or thread kernel object doesn't get destroyed. If you have just created a new process or thread, you can do this simply by not closing the handles to these objects. Then, once your application has finished using the ID, call *CloseHandle* to release the kernel object(s) and remember that it is no longer safe for you to use or rely on the process ID. If you are the child process, you can do nothing to ensure the validity of your parent's process or thread IDs unless the parent process duplicates handles for its own process or thread objects and allows you, the child process, to inherit these handles.

Terminating a Process

A process can be terminated in four ways:

- The primary thread's entry-point function returns. (This is highly recommended.)

- One thread in the process calls the *ExitProcess* function. (Avoid this method.)

- A thread in another process calls the *TerminateProcess* function. (Avoid this method.)

- All the threads in the process just die on their own. (This hardly ever happens.)

This section discusses all four methods and describes what actually happens when a process ends.

The Primary Thread's Entry-Point Function Returns

You should always design an application so that its process terminates only when your primary thread's entry-point function returns. This is the only way to guarantee that all your primary thread's resources are cleaned up properly.

Having your primary thread's entry-point function return ensures the following:

- Any C++ objects created by this thread will be destroyed properly using their destructors.

- The operating system will properly free the memory used by the thread's stack.

- The system will set the process's exit code (maintained in the process kernel object) to your entry-point function's return value.

- The system will decrement the process kernel object's usage count.

The *ExitProcess* Function

A process terminates when one of the threads in the process calls *ExitProcess*:

```
VOID ExitProcess(UINT fuExitCode);
```

This function terminates the process and sets the exit code of the process to *fuExitCode*. *ExitProcess* doesn't return a value because the process has terminated. If you include any code following the call to *ExitProcess*, that code will never execute.

When your primary thread's entry-point function (*WinMain, wWinMain, main,* or *wmain*) returns, it returns to the C/C++ run-time startup code, which properly cleans up all the C run-time resources used by the process. After the C run-time resources have been freed, the C run-time startup code explicitly calls *ExitProcess*, passing it the value returned from your entry-point function. This explains why simply returning from your primary thread's entry-point function terminates the entire process. Note that any other threads running in the process terminate along with the process.

The Windows Platform SDK documentation states that a process does not terminate until all its threads terminate. As far as the operating system goes, this statement is true. However, the C/C++ run time imposes a different policy on an application: the C/C++ run-time startup code ensures that the process terminates when your application's primary thread returns from its entry-point function—whether or not other threads are running in the process—by calling *ExitProcess*. However, if you call *ExitThread* in your entry-point function instead of calling *ExitProcess* or simply returning, the primary thread for your application will stop executing but the process will not terminate if at least one other thread in the process is still running.

Note that calling *ExitProcess* or *ExitThread* causes a process or thread to die while inside a function. As far the operating system is concerned, this is fine and all of the process's or thread's operating system resources will be cleaned up perfectly. However, a C/C++ application should avoid calling these functions because the C/C++ run time might not be able to clean up properly. Examine the following code:

```
#include <windows.h>
#include <stdio.h>
```

(continued)

```
class CSomeObj {
public:
    CSomeObj()  { printf("Constructor\r\n"); }
    ~CSomeObj() { printf("Destructor\r\n"); }
};


CSomeObj g_GlobalObj;


void main () {
    CSomeObj LocalObj;
    ExitProcess(0);      // This shouldn't be here

    // At the end of this function, the compiler automatically added
    // the code necessary to call LocalObj's destructor.
    // ExitProcess prevents it from executing.
}
```

When the code above executes, you'll see:

```
Constructor
Constructor
```

Two objects are being constructed: a global object and a local object. However, you'll never see the word *Destructor* appear. The C++ objects are not properly destructed because *ExitProcess* forces the process to die on the spot: the C/C++ run time is not given a chance to clean up.

As I said, you should never call *ExitProcess* explicitly. If I remove the call to *ExitProcess* in the code above, running the program yields this:

```
Constructor
Constructor
Destructor
Destructor
```

By simply allowing the primary thread's entry point function to return, the C/C++ run time can perform its cleanup and properly destruct any and all C++ objects. By the way, this discussion does not apply only to C++ objects. The C/C++ run time does many things on behalf of your process; it is best to allow the run time to clean it up properly.

> **NOTE**
>
> Making explicit calls to *ExitProcess* and *ExitThread* is a common problem that causes an application to not clean itself up properly. In the case of *ExitThread*, the process continues to run but can leak memory or other resources.

The *TerminateProcess* Function

A call to *TerminateProcess* also ends a process:

```
BOOL TerminateProcess(
   HANDLE hProcess,
   UINT fuExitCode);
```

This function is different from *ExitProcess* in one major way: any thread can call *TerminateProcess* to terminate another process or its own process. The *hProcess* parameter identifies the handle of the process to be terminated. When the process terminates, its exit code becomes the value you passed as the *fuExitCode* parameter.

You should use *TerminateProcess* only if you can't force a process to exit by using another method. The process being terminated is given absolutely no notification that it is dying—the application cannot clean up properly and cannot prevent itself from being killed (except by normal security mechanisms). For example, the process cannot flush any information it might have in memory out to disk.

While it is true that the process will not have a chance to do its own cleanup, the operating system does clean up completely after the process so that no operating system resources remain. This means that all memory used by the process is freed, any open files are closed, all kernel objects have their usage counts decremented, and all User and GDI objects are destroyed.

Once a process terminates (no matter how), the system guarantees that the process will not leave any parts of itself behind. There is absolutely no way of knowing whether that process had ever run. *A process will leak absolutely nothing once it has terminated.* I hope that this is clear.

> **NOTE** The *TerminateProcess* function is asynchronous—that is, it tells the system that you want the process to terminate but the process is not guaranteed to be killed by the time the function returns. So you might want to call *WaitForSingleObject* (described in Chapter 9) or a similar function, passing the handle of the process if you need to know for sure that the process has terminated.

When All the Threads in the Process Die

If all the threads in a process die (either because they've all called *ExitThread* or because they've been terminated with *TerminateThread*), the operating system assumes that there is no reason to keep the process's address space around. This is a fair assumption, since there are no more threads executing any code in the address space. When the system detects that no threads are running any more, it terminates the process. When this happens, the process's exit code is set to the same exit code as the last thread that died.

When a Process Terminates

When a process terminates, the following actions are set in motion:

1. Any remaining threads in the process are terminated.

2. All the User and GDI objects allocated by the process are freed, and all the kernel objects are closed. (These kernel objects are destroyed if no other process has open handles to them. However, the kernel objects are not destroyed if other processes do have open handles to them.)

3. The process's exit code changes from STILL_ACTIVE to the code passed to *ExitProcess* or *TerminateProcess*.

4. The process kernel object's status becomes signaled. (See Chapter 9 for more information about signaling.) Other threads in the system can suspend themselves until the process is terminated.

5. The process kernel object's usage count is decremented by 1.

Note that a process's kernel object always lives at least as long as the process itself. However, the process kernel object might live well beyond its process. When a process terminates, the system automatically decrements the usage count of its kernel object. If the count goes to 0, no other process has an open handle to the object and the object is destroyed when the process is destroyed.

However, the process kernel object's count will not go to 0 if another process in the system has an open handle to the dying process's kernel object. This usually happens when parent processes forget to close their handle to a child process. This is a feature, not a bug. Remember that the process kernel object maintains statistical information about the process. This information can be useful even after the process has terminated. For example, you might want to know how much CPU time the process required. Or, more likely, you might want to obtain the now-defunct process's exit code by calling *GetExitCodeProcess*.

```
BOOL GetExitCodeProcess(
   HANDLE hProcess,
   PDWORD pdwExitCode);
```

This function looks into the process kernel object (identified by the *hProcess* parameter) and extracts the member within the kernel object's data structure that identifies the process's exit code. The exit code value is returned in the DWORD pointed to by the *pdwExitCode* parameter.

You can call this function at any time. If the process hasn't terminated when *GetExitCodeProcess* is called, the function fills the DWORD with the STILL_ACTIVE identifier (defined as 0x103). If the process has terminated, the actual exit code value is returned.

You might think that you can write code to determine whether a process has terminated by calling *GetExitCodeProcess* periodically and checking the exit code. This would work in many situations, but it would be inefficient. I'll explain the proper way to determine when a process has terminated in the next section.

Once again, let me remind you that you should tell the system when you are no longer interested in a process's statistical data by calling *CloseHandle*. If the process has already terminated, *CloseHandle* will decrement the count on the kernel object and free it.

Child Processes

When you design an application, you might encounter situations in which you want another block of code to perform work. You assign work like this all the time by calling functions or subroutines. When you call a function, your code cannot continue processing until the function has returned. And in many situations, this single-tasking synchronization is needed. An alternative way to have another block of code perform work is to create a new thread within your process and have it help with the processing. This lets your code continue processing while the other thread performs the work you requested. This technique is useful, but it creates synchronization problems when your thread needs to see the results of the new thread.

Another approach is to spawn off a new process—a child process—to help with the work. Let's say that the work you need to do is pretty complex. To process the work, you simply create a new thread within the same process. You write some code, test it, and get some incorrect results. You might have an error in your algorithm, or maybe you dereferenced something incorrectly and accidentally overwrote something important in your address space. One way to protect your address space while having the work processed is to have a new process perform the work. You can then wait for the new process to terminate before continuing with your own work, or you can continue working while the new process works.

Unfortunately, the new process probably needs to perform operations on data contained in your address space. In this case, it might be a good idea to have the process run in its own address space and simply give it access to the relevant data contained in the parent process's address space, thus protecting all the data not relevant to the task at hand. Windows offers several methods for transferring data between different processes: Dynamic Data Exchange (DDE), OLE, pipes, mailslots, and so on. One of the most convenient ways to share the data is to use memory-mapped files. (See Chapter 17 for a detailed discussion of memory-mapped files.)

If you want to create a new process, have it do some work, and wait for the result, you can use code similar to the following:

```
PROCESS_INFORMATION pi;
DWORD dwExitCode;

// Spawn the child process.
BOOL fSuccess = CreateProcess(..., &pi);
if (fSuccess) {

    // Close the thread handle as soon as it is no longer needed!
    CloseHandle(pi.hThread);

    // Suspend our execution until the child has terminated.
    WaitForSingleObject(pi.hProcess, INFINITE);

    // The child process terminated; get its exit code.
    GetExitCodeProcess(pi.hProcess, &dwExitCode);

    // Close the process handle as soon as it is no longer needed.
    CloseHandle(pi.hProcess);
}
```

In the code fragment above, you create the new process and, if it is successful, you call the *WaitForSingleObject* function:

```
DWORD WaitForSingleObject(HANDLE hObject, DWORD dwTimeout);
```

We'll discuss the *WaitForSingleObject* function exhaustively in Chapter 9. For now, all you need to know is that it waits until the object identified by the *hObject* parameter becomes *signaled*. Process objects become signaled when they terminate. So the call to *WaitForSingleObject* suspends the parent's thread until the child process terminates. After *WaitForSingleObject* returns, you can get the exit code of the child process by calling *GetExitCodeProcess*.

The calls to *CloseHandle* in the code fragment above cause the system to decrement the usage count for the thread and process objects to 0, allowing the objects' memories to be freed.

You'll notice that in the code fragment, we close the handle to the child process's primary thread kernel object immediately after *CreateProcess* returns.

This does not cause the child's primary thread to terminate—it simply decrements the usage count of the child's primary thread object. Here's why this practice is a good idea: Suppose that the child process's primary thread spawns off another thread and then the primary thread terminates. At this point, the system can free the child's primary thread object from its memory if the parent process doesn't have an outstanding handle to this thread object. But if the parent process does have a handle to the child's thread object, the system can't free the object until the parent process closes the handle.

Running Detached Child Processes

Most of the time, an application starts another process as a *detached process*. This means that after the process is created and executing, the parent process doesn't need to communicate with the new process or doesn't require it to complete its work before the parent process continues. This is how the Explorer works. After the Explorer creates a new process for the user, it doesn't care whether that process continues to live or whether the user terminates it.

To give up all ties to the child process, the Explorer must close its handles to the new process and its primary thread by calling *CloseHandle*. The following code example shows how to create a new process and how to let it run detached.

```
PROCESS_INFORMATION pi;

// Spawn the child process.
BOOL fSuccess = CreateProcess(..., &pi);
if (fSuccess) {

    // Allow the system to destroy the process & thread kernel
    // objects as soon as the child process terminates.
    CloseHandle(pi.hThread);
    CloseHandle(pi.hProcess);
}
```

Enumerating the Processes Running in the System

Many software developers try to write tools or utilities for Windows that require the set of running processes to be enumerated. The Windows API originally had no functions that enumerated the running processes. However, Windows NT has a constantly updating database called the Performance Data database. This database contains a ton of information and is available through registry functions such as *RegQueryValueEx* with the HKEY_PERFORMANCE_DATA root key. Few Windows programmers know about the performance database for these reasons:

- It has no functions that are specific to it; it simply uses existing registry functions.

- It is not available on Windows 95 and Windows 98.

- The layout of information in the database is complex; many developers avoid using it. This prevents knowledge of its existence from spreading by word of mouth.

To make working with this database easier, Microsoft created a Performance Data Helper set of functions (contained in PDH.dll). For more information about this library, search for Performance Data Helper in the Platform SDK documentation.

As I mentioned above, Windows 95 and 98 do not offer this performance database. Instead, they have their own set of functions to enumerate processes and information about them. These are in the ToolHelp API. For more information, search for the *Process32First* and *Process32Next* functions in the Platform SDK documentation.

To make things more fun, Microsoft's Windows NT team, which doesn't like the ToolHelp functions, did not add them to Windows NT. Instead, they produced their own Process Status functions to enumerate processes (contained in PSAPI.dll). For more information, search for the *EnumProcesses* function in the Platform SDK documentation.

Microsoft might appear to be making life difficult for tool and utility developers, but I'm happy to report that it has added the ToolHelp functions to Windows 2000. Finally, developers have a way to write tools and utilities that have common source code for Windows 95, Windows 98, and Windows 2000!

The Process Information Sample Application

The ProcessInfo application, "04 ProcessInfo.exe" (listed in Figure 4-6 on page 118), shows how to use the ToolHelp functions to produce a very useful utility. The source code and resource files for the application are in the 04-ProcessInfo directory on the companion CD-ROM. When you start the program, the window shown in Figure 4-4 appears.

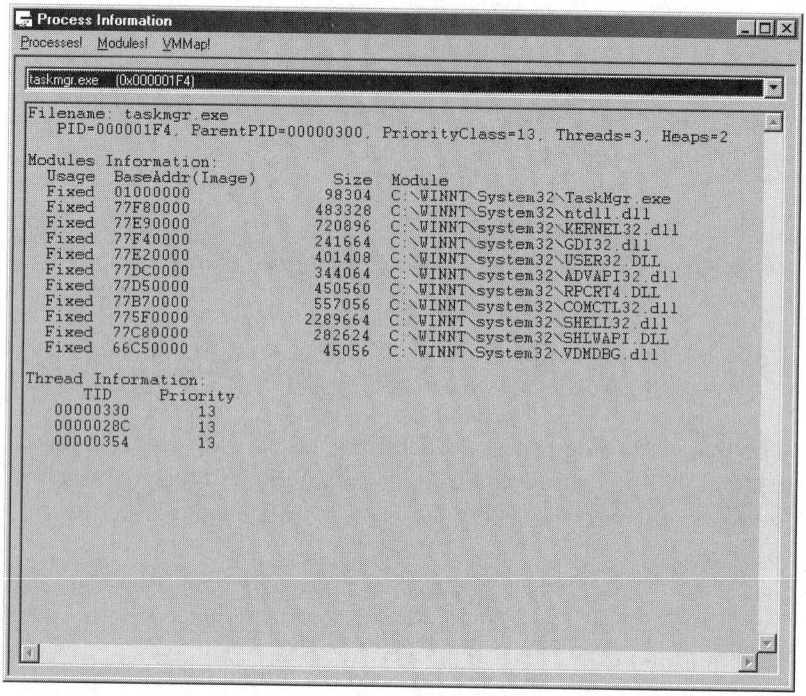

Figure 4-4.
ProcessInfo in action

ProcessInfo first enumerates the set of processes currently running and places each process's name and ID in the top combo box. Then the first process is selected and information about that process is shown in the large read-only edit control. As you can see, the process's ID is shown along with its parent process's ID, the priority class of the process, and the number of threads currently running in the context of the process. Much of the information is beyond the scope of this chapter but will be discussed in later chapters.

When you look at the process list, the VMMap menu item is available. (This item is disabled when you look at the module information.) Selecting the VMMap menu item causes the VMMap sample application (discussed in Chapter 14) to run. This application walks the address space of the selected process.

The module information portion shows the list of modules (executables and DLLs) that are mapped into the process's address space. A fixed module is one that was implicitly loaded when the process initialized. For explicitly loaded DLLs, the DLL's usage count is shown. The second field shows the memory address where the module is mapped. If the module is not mapped at its preferred base address, the preferred base address also appears in parentheses. The third field shows the size of the module in bytes, and finally, the full pathname of the module is displayed. The thread information portion shows the set of threads currently running in the context of this process. Each thread's ID and priority is shown.

In addition to the process information, you can choose the Modules! menu item. This causes ProcessInfo to enumerate the set of modules currently loaded throughout the system and places each module's name in the top combo box. Then ProcessInfo selects the first module and displays information about it, as Figure 4-5 shows.

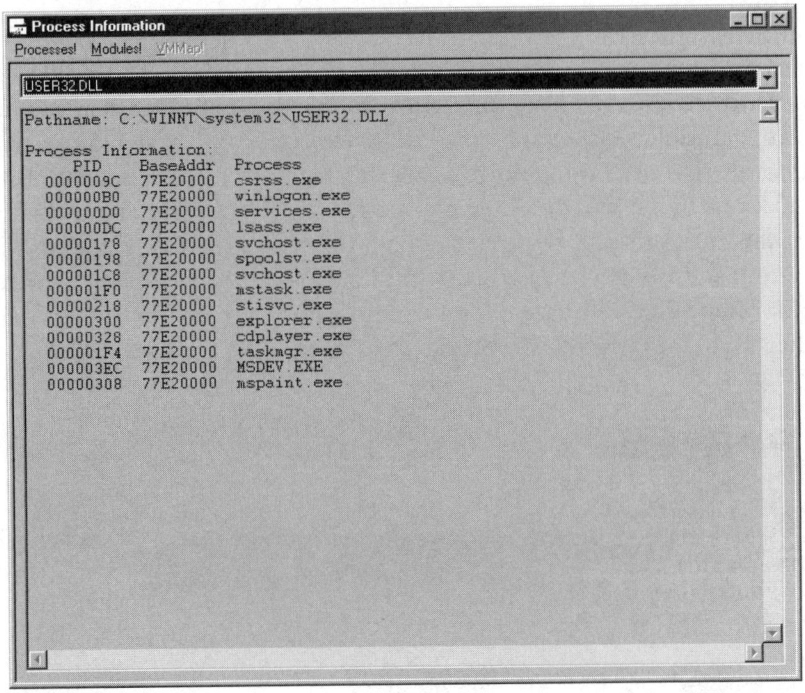

Figure 4-5.
ProcessInfo showing all processes that have User32.dll loaded in their address space

When you use the ProcessInfo utility in this way, you can easily determine which processes are using a particular module. As you can see, the module's full pathname is shown at the top. The Process Information section then shows the list of processes that contain the module. In addition to each process's ID and name, the address where the module is loaded in each process is shown.

Basically, all of the information displayed by the ProcessInfo application is produced by calling the various ToolHelp functions. To make working with the ToolHelp functions a little easier, I created a CToolhelp C++ class (contained in the Toolhelp.h file). This C++ class encapsulates a ToolHelp snapshot and makes calling the other ToolHelp functions a bit easier.

The *GetModulePreferredBaseAddr* function inside ProcessInfo.cpp is particularly interesting:

```
PVOID GetModulePreferredBaseAddr(
    DWORD dwProcessId,
    PVOID pvModuleRemote);
```

This function accepts a process ID and the address of a module in that process. It then looks in that process's address space, locates that module, and reads the module's header information to determine the module's preferred base address. A module should always load at its preferred base address; otherwise applications that use the module require more memory and take a performance hit while initializing. Since this is such a horrible situation, I added this function and I show when a module doesn't load at its preferred base address. You'll see more on preferred base addresses and this time/memory performance hit in the "Rebasing Modules" section of Chapter 20.

 ProcessInfo.cpp

```
/**********************************************************************************
Module:  ProcessInfo.cpp
Notices: Copyright (c) 2000 Jeffrey Richter
**********************************************************************************/

#include "..\CmnHdr.h"        /* See Appendix A. */
#include <windowsx.h>
#include <tlhelp32.h>
#include <tchar.h>
#include <stdarg.h>
#include <stdio.h>
#include "Toolhelp.h"
#include "Resource.h"
```

Figure 4-6.
The ProcessInfo application

(continued)

Figure 4-6. *continued*

```
///////////////////////////////////////////////////////////////////////


// Adds a string to an edit control
void AddText(HWND hwnd, PCTSTR pszFormat, ...) {

   va_list argList;
   va_start(argList, pszFormat);

   TCHAR sz[20 * 1024];
   Edit_GetText(hwnd, sz, chDIMOF(sz));
   _vstprintf(_tcschr(sz, 0), pszFormat, argList);
   Edit_SetText(hwnd, sz);
   va_end(argList);
}


///////////////////////////////////////////////////////////////////////


VOID Dlg_PopulateProcessList(HWND hwnd) {

   HWND hwndList = GetDlgItem(hwnd, IDC_PROCESSMODULELIST);
   SetWindowRedraw(hwndList, FALSE);
   ComboBox_ResetContent(hwndList);

   CToolhelp thProcesses(TH32CS_SNAPPROCESS);
   PROCESSENTRY32 pe = { sizeof(pe) };
   BOOL fOk = thProcesses.ProcessFirst(&pe);
   for (; fOk; fOk = thProcesses.ProcessNext(&pe)) {
     TCHAR sz[1024];

     // Place the process name (without its path) & ID in the list
     PCTSTR pszExeFile = _tcsrchr(pe.szExeFile, TEXT('\\'));
     if (pszExeFile == NULL) pszExeFile = pe.szExeFile;
     else pszExeFile++; // Skip over the slash
     wsprintf(sz, TEXT("%s     (0x%08X)"), pszExeFile, pe.th32ProcessID);
     int n = ComboBox_AddString(hwndList, sz);

     // Associate the process ID with the added item
     ComboBox_SetItemData(hwndList, n, pe.th32ProcessID);
   }
   ComboBox_SetCurSel(hwndList, 0);  // Select the first entry
```

(continued)

119

Figure 4-6. *continued*

```
   // Simulate the user selecting this first item so that the
   // results pane shows something interesting
   FORWARD_WM_COMMAND(hwnd, IDC_PROCESSMODULELIST,
      hwndList, CBN_SELCHANGE, SendMessage);

   SetWindowRedraw(hwndList, TRUE);
   InvalidateRect(hwndList, NULL, FALSE);
}


///////////////////////////////////////////////////////////////////////////////////////

VOID Dlg_PopulateModuleList(HWND hwnd) {

   HWND hwndModuleHelp = GetDlgItem(hwnd, IDC_MODULEHELP);
   ListBox_ResetContent(hwndModuleHelp);

   CToolhelp thProcesses(TH32CS_SNAPPROCESS);
   PROCESSENTRY32 pe = { sizeof(pe) };
   BOOL fOk = thProcesses.ProcessFirst(&pe);
   for (; fOk; fOk = thProcesses.ProcessNext(&pe)) {

      CToolhelp thModules(TH32CS_SNAPMODULE, pe.th32ProcessID);
      MODULEENTRY32 me = { sizeof(me) };
      BOOL fOk = thModules.ModuleFirst(&me);
      for (; fOk; fOk = thModules.ModuleNext(&me)) {
        int n = ListBox_FindStringExact(hwndModuleHelp, -1, me.szExePath);
         if (n == LB_ERR) {
         // This module hasn't been added before
            ListBox_AddString(hwndModuleHelp, me.szExePath);
         }
      }
   }


   HWND hwndList = GetDlgItem(hwnd, IDC_PROCESSMODULELIST);
   SetWindowRedraw(hwndList, FALSE);
   ComboBox_ResetContent(hwndList);
   int nNumModules = ListBox_GetCount(hwndModuleHelp);
   for (int i = 0; i < nNumModules; i++) {
      TCHAR sz[1024];
      ListBox_GetText(hwndModuleHelp, i, sz);
      // Place module name (without its path) in the list
      int nIndex = ComboBox_AddString(hwndList, _tcsrchr(sz, TEXT('\\')) + 1);
```

(continued)

Figure 4-6. *continued*

```
        // Associate the index of the full path with the added item
        ComboBox_SetItemData(hwndList, nIndex, i);
    }

    ComboBox_SetCurSel(hwndList, 0);  // Select the first entry

    // Simulate the user selecting this first item so that the
    // results pane shows something interesting
    FORWARD_WM_COMMAND(hwnd, IDC_PROCESSMODULELIST,
        hwndList, CBN_SELCHANGE, SendMessage);

    SetWindowRedraw(hwndList, TRUE);
    InvalidateRect(hwndList, NULL, FALSE);
}


///////////////////////////////////////////////////////////////////////////////


PVOID GetModulePreferredBaseAddr(DWORD dwProcessId, PVOID pvModuleRemote) {

    PVOID pvModulePreferredBaseAddr = NULL;
    IMAGE_DOS_HEADER idh;
    IMAGE_NT_HEADERS inth;

    // Read the remote module's DOS header
    Toolhelp32ReadProcessMemory(dwProcessId,
        pvModuleRemote, &idh, sizeof(idh), NULL);

    // Verify the DOS image header
    if (idh.e_magic == IMAGE_DOS_SIGNATURE) {
        // Read the remote module's NT header
        Toolhelp32ReadProcessMemory(dwProcessId,
            (PBYTE) pvModuleRemote + idh.e_lfanew, &inth, sizeof(inth), NULL);

        // Verify the NT image header
        if (inth.Signature == IMAGE_NT_SIGNATURE) {
            // This is valid NT header, get the image's preferred base address
            pvModulePreferredBaseAddr = (PVOID) inth.OptionalHeader.ImageBase;
        }
    }
    return(pvModulePreferredBaseAddr);
}
```

(continued)

Figure 4-6. *continued*

//

```
VOID ShowProcessInfo(HWND hwnd, DWORD dwProcessID) {

   SetWindowText(hwnd, TEXT(""));   // Clear the output box

   CToolhelp th(TH32CS_SNAPALL, dwProcessID);

   // Show Process details
   PROCESSENTRY32 pe = { sizeof(pe) };
   BOOL fOk = th.ProcessFirst(&pe);
   for (; fOk; fOk = th.ProcessNext(&pe)) {
      if (pe.th32ProcessID == dwProcessID) {
         AddText(hwnd, TEXT("Filename: %s\r\n"), pe.szExeFile);
         AddText(hwnd, TEXT("   PID=%08X, ParentPID=%08X, ")
            TEXT("PriorityClass=%d, Threads=%d, Heaps=%d\r\n"),
            pe.th32ProcessID, pe.th32ParentProcessID,
            pe.pcPriClassBase, pe.cntThreads,
            th.HowManyHeaps());
         break;   // No need to continue looping
      }
   }


   // Show Modules in the Process
   // Number of characters to display an address
   const int cchAddress = sizeof(PVOID) * 2;
   AddText(hwnd, TEXT("\r\nModules Information:\r\n")
      TEXT(" Usage  %-*s(%-*s)  %8s  Module\r\n"),
      cchAddress, TEXT("BaseAddr"),
      cchAddress, TEXT("ImagAddr"), TEXT("Size"));

   MODULEENTRY32 me = { sizeof(me) };
   fOk = th.ModuleFirst(&me);
   for (; fOk; fOk = th.ModuleNext(&me)) {
      if (me.ProccntUsage == 65535) {
         // Module was implicitly loaded and cannot be unloaded
         AddText(hwnd, TEXT("  Fixed"));
      } else {
         AddText(hwnd, TEXT("  %5d"), me.ProccntUsage);
      }
      PVOID pvPreferredBaseAddr =
         GetModulePreferredBaseAddr(pe.th32ProcessID, me.modBaseAddr);
```

(continued)

Figure 4-6. *continued*

```
        if (me.modBaseAddr == pvPreferredBaseAddr) {
            AddText(hwnd, TEXT("  %p %*s    %8u  %s\r\n"),
                me.modBaseAddr, cchAddress, TEXT(""),
                me.modBaseSize, me.szExePath);
        } else {
            AddText(hwnd, TEXT("  %p(%p)  %8u  %s\r\n"),
                me.modBaseAddr, pvPreferredBaseAddr, me.modBaseSize, me.szExePath);
        }
    }


    // Show threads in the process
    AddText(hwnd, TEXT("\r\nThread Information:\r\n")
        TEXT("      TID    Priority\r\n"));
    THREADENTRY32 te = { sizeof(te) };
    fOk = th.ThreadFirst(&te);
    for (; fOk; fOk = th.ThreadNext(&te)) {
        if (te.th32OwnerProcessID == dwProcessID) {
            int nPriority = te.tpBasePri + te.tpDeltaPri;
            if ((te.tpBasePri < 16) && (nPriority > 15)) nPriority = 15;
            if ((te.tpBasePri > 15) && (nPriority > 31)) nPriority = 31;
            if ((te.tpBasePri < 16) && (nPriority <  1)) nPriority =  1;
            if ((te.tpBasePri > 15) && (nPriority < 16)) nPriority = 16;
            AddText(hwnd, TEXT("   %08X      %2d\r\n"),
                te.th32ThreadID, nPriority);
        }
    }
}


///////////////////////////////////////////////////////////////////////////


VOID ShowModuleInfo(HWND hwnd, LPCTSTR pszModulePath) {

    SetWindowText(hwnd, TEXT(""));   // Clear the output box

    CToolhelp thProcesses(TH32CS_SNAPPROCESS);
    PROCESSENTRY32 pe = { sizeof(pe) };
    BOOL fOk = thProcesses.ProcessFirst(&pe);
    AddText(hwnd, TEXT("Pathname: %s\r\n\r\n"), pszModulePath);
    AddText(hwnd, TEXT("Process Information:\r\n"));
    AddText(hwnd, TEXT("     PID    BaseAddr  Process\r\n"));
    for (; fOk; fOk = thProcesses.ProcessNext(&pe)) {
```

(continued)

123

Figure 4-6. *continued*

```
      CToolhelp thModules(TH32CS_SNAPMODULE, pe.th32ProcessID);
      MODULEENTRY32 me = { sizeof(me) };
      BOOL fOk = thModules.ModuleFirst(&me);
      for (; fOk; fOk = thModules.ModuleNext(&me)) {
         if (_tcscmp(me.szExePath, pszModulePath) == 0) {
            AddText(hwnd, TEXT(" %08X  %p  %s\r\n"),
               pe.th32ProcessID, me.modBaseAddr, pe.szExeFile);
         }
      }
   }
}


///////////////////////////////////////////////////////////////////////////


BOOL Dlg_OnInitDialog(HWND hwnd, HWND hwndFocus, LPARAM lParam) {

   chSETDLGICONS(hwnd, IDI_PROCESSINFO);

   // Hide the module-helper listbox.
   ShowWindow(GetDlgItem(hwnd, IDC_MODULEHELP), SW_HIDE);

   // Have the results window use a fixed-pitch font
   SetWindowFont(GetDlgItem(hwnd, IDC_RESULTS),
      GetStockFont(ANSI_FIXED_FONT), FALSE);

   // By default, show the running processes
   Dlg_PopulateProcessList(hwnd);

   return(TRUE);
}


///////////////////////////////////////////////////////////////////////////


BOOL Dlg_OnSize(HWND hwnd, UINT state, int cx, int cy) {

   RECT rc;
   int n = LOWORD(GetDialogBaseUnits());

   HWND hwndCtl = GetDlgItem(hwnd, IDC_PROCESSMODULELIST);
   GetClientRect(hwndCtl, &rc);
   SetWindowPos(hwndCtl, NULL, n, n, cx - n - n, rc.bottom, SWP_NOZORDER);
```

(continued)

Figure 4-6. *continued*

```
    hwndCtl = GetDlgItem(hwnd, IDC_RESULTS);
    SetWindowPos(hwndCtl, NULL, n, n + rc.bottom + n,
      cx - n - n, cy - (n + rc.bottom + n) - n, SWP_NOZORDER);

    return(0);
}


//////////////////////////////////////////////////////////////////////////////


void Dlg_OnCommand(HWND hwnd, int id, HWND hwndCtl, UINT codeNotify) {

    static BOOL s_fProcesses = TRUE;

    switch (id) {
      case IDCANCEL:
         EndDialog(hwnd, id);
         break;

      case ID_PROCESSES:
         s_fProcesses = TRUE;
         EnableMenuItem(GetMenu(hwnd), ID_VMMAP, MF_BYCOMMAND | MF_ENABLED);
         DrawMenuBar(hwnd);
         Dlg_PopulateProcessList(hwnd);
         break;

      case ID_MODULES:
         EnableMenuItem(GetMenu(hwnd), ID_VMMAP, MF_BYCOMMAND | MF_GRAYED);
         DrawMenuBar(hwnd);
         s_fProcesses = FALSE;
         Dlg_PopulateModuleList(hwnd);
         break;

      case IDC_PROCESSMODULELIST:
         if (codeNotify == CBN_SELCHANGE) {
            DWORD dw = ComboBox_GetCurSel(hwndCtl);
            if (s_fProcesses) {
               dw = (DWORD) ComboBox_GetItemData(hwndCtl, dw); // Process ID
               ShowProcessInfo(GetDlgItem(hwnd, IDC_RESULTS), dw);
            } else {
               // Index in helper listbox of full path
               dw = (DWORD) ComboBox_GetItemData(hwndCtl, dw);
               TCHAR szModulePath[1024];
```

(continued)

Figure 4-6. *continued*

```
            ListBox_GetText(GetDlgItem(hwnd, IDC_MODULEHELP),
            dw, szModulePath);
            ShowModuleInfo(GetDlgItem(hwnd, IDC_RESULTS), szModulePath);
        }
    }
    break;

case ID_VMMAP:
    STARTUPINFO si = { sizeof(si) };
    PROCESS_INFORMATION pi;
    TCHAR szCmdLine[1024];
    HWND hwndCB = GetDlgItem(hwnd, IDC_PROCESSMODULELIST);
    DWORD dwProcessId = (DWORD)
        ComboBox_GetItemData(hwndCB, ComboBox_GetCurSel(hwndCB));
    wsprintf(szCmdLine, TEXT("\"14 VMMap\" %d"), dwProcessId);
    BOOL fOk = CreateProcess(NULL, szCmdLine, NULL, NULL,
        FALSE, 0, NULL, NULL, &si, &pi);
    if (fOk) {
        CloseHandle(pi.hProcess);
        CloseHandle(pi.hThread);
    } else {
        chMB("Failed to execute VMMAP.EXE.");
    }
    break;
    }
}


///////////////////////////////////////////////////////////////////////////////


INT_PTR WINAPI Dlg_Proc(HWND hwnd, UINT uMsg, WPARAM wParam, LPARAM lParam) {

    switch (uMsg) {
        chHANDLE_DLGMSG(hwnd, WM_INITDIALOG, Dlg_OnInitDialog);
        chHANDLE_DLGMSG(hwnd, WM_SIZE,       Dlg_OnSize);
        chHANDLE_DLGMSG(hwnd, WM_COMMAND,    Dlg_OnCommand);
    }
    return(FALSE);
}


///////////////////////////////////////////////////////////////////////////////
```

(continued)

Figure 4-6. *continued*

```
int WINAPI _tWinMain(HINSTANCE hinstExe, HINSTANCE, PTSTR pszCmdLine, int) {

    CToolhelp::EnableDebugPrivilege(TRUE);
    DialogBox(hinstExe, MAKEINTRESOURCE(IDD_PROCESSINFO), NULL, Dlg_Proc);
    CToolhelp::EnableDebugPrivilege(FALSE);
    return(0);
}


///////////////////////////////// End of File /////////////////////////////////
```

ProcessInfo.rc

```
//Microsoft Developer Studio generated resource script.
//
#include "resource.h"

#define APSTUDIO_READONLY_SYMBOLS
/////////////////////////////////////////////////////////////////////////////
//
// Generated from the TEXTINCLUDE 2 resource.
//
#include "afxres.h"


/////////////////////////////////////////////////////////////////////////////
#undef APSTUDIO_READONLY_SYMBOLS


/////////////////////////////////////////////////////////////////////////////
// English (U.S.) resources

#if !defined(AFX_RESOURCE_DLL) || defined(AFX_TARG_ENU)
#ifdef _WIN32
LANGUAGE LANG_ENGLISH, SUBLANG_ENGLISH_US
#pragma code_page(1252)
#endif //_WIN32

/////////////////////////////////////////////////////////////////////////////
//
// Dialog
//

IDD_PROCESSINFO DIALOGEX 0, 0, 400, 317
STYLE DS_3DLOOK | DS_NOFAILCREATE | DS_CENTER | WS_MINIMIZEBOX |
    WS_MAXIMIZEBOX | WS_VISIBLE | WS_CAPTION | WS_SYSMENU | WS_THICKFRAME
```

(continued)

Figure 4-6. *continued*

```
EXSTYLE WS_EX_NOPARENTNOTIFY | WS_EX_CLIENTEDGE
CAPTION "Process Information"
MENU IDR_PROCESSINFO
FONT 8, "MS Sans Serif"
BEGIN
    COMBOBOX        IDC_PROCESSMODULELIST,4,4,392,156,CBS_DROPDOWNLIST |
                    CBS_AUTOHSCROLL | CBS_SORT | WS_VSCROLL | WS_TABSTOP
    LISTBOX         IDC_MODULEHELP,0,0,48,40,NOT LBS_NOTIFY | LBS_SORT |
                    LBS_NOINTEGRALHEIGHT | NOT WS_VISIBLE | NOT WS_BORDER |
                    WS_TABSTOP
    EDITTEXT        IDC_RESULTS,4,24,392,284,ES_MULTILINE | ES_AUTOVSCROLL |
                    ES_AUTOHSCROLL | ES_READONLY | WS_VSCROLL | WS_HSCROLL
END


/////////////////////////////////////////////////////////////////////////////
//
// DESIGNINFO
//

#ifdef APSTUDIO_INVOKED
GUIDELINES DESIGNINFO DISCARDABLE
BEGIN
    IDD_PROCESSINFO, DIALOG
    BEGIN
        LEFTMARGIN, 7
        RIGHTMARGIN, 393
        TOPMARGIN, 7
        BOTTOMMARGIN, 310
    END
END
#endif    // APSTUDIO_INVOKED


#ifdef APSTUDIO_INVOKED
/////////////////////////////////////////////////////////////////////////////
//
// TEXTINCLUDE
//

1 TEXTINCLUDE DISCARDABLE
BEGIN
    "resource.h\0"
END
```

(continued)

128

Figure 4-6. *continued*

```
2 TEXTINCLUDE DISCARDABLE
BEGIN
    "#include ""afxres.h""\r\n"
    "\0"
END

3 TEXTINCLUDE DISCARDABLE
BEGIN
    "\r\n"
    "\0"
END

#endif    // APSTUDIO_INVOKED


/////////////////////////////////////////////////////////////////////////////
//
// Menu
//

IDR_PROCESSINFO MENU DISCARDABLE
BEGIN
    MENUITEM "&Processes!",              ID_PROCESSES
    MENUITEM "&Modules!",                ID_MODULES
    MENUITEM "&VMMap!",                  ID_VMMAP
END


/////////////////////////////////////////////////////////////////////////////
//
// Icon
//

// Icon with lowest ID value placed first to ensure application icon
// remains consistent on all systems.
IDI_PROCESSINFO         ICON    DISCARDABLE     "ProcessInfo.ico"
#endif    // English (U.S.) resources
/////////////////////////////////////////////////////////////////////////////



#ifndef APSTUDIO_INVOKED
/////////////////////////////////////////////////////////////////////////////
//
```

(continued)

Figure 4-6. *continued*

```
// Generated from the TEXTINCLUDE 3 resource.
//



/////////////////////////////////////////////////////////////////////////////
#endif    // not APSTUDIO_INVOKED
```

Toolhelp.h

```
/*****************************************************************************
Module:  Toolhelp.h
Notices: Copyright (c) 2000 Jeffrey Richter
*****************************************************************************/


#include "..\CmnHdr.h"     /* See Appendix A. */
#include <tlhelp32.h>
#include <tchar.h>



/////////////////////////////////////////////////////////////////////////////


class CToolhelp {
private:
   HANDLE m_hSnapshot;

public:
   CToolhelp(DWORD dwFlags = 0, DWORD dwProcessID = 0);
   ~CToolhelp();

   BOOL CreateSnapshot(DWORD dwFlags, DWORD dwProcessID = 0);

   BOOL ProcessFirst(PPROCESSENTRY32 ppe) const;
   BOOL ProcessNext(PPROCESSENTRY32 ppe) const;
   BOOL ProcessFind(DWORD dwProcessId, PPROCESSENTRY32 ppe) const;

   BOOL ModuleFirst(PMODULEENTRY32 pme) const;
   BOOL ModuleNext(PMODULEENTRY32 pme) const;
   BOOL ModuleFind(PVOID pvBaseAddr, PMODULEENTRY32 pme) const;
   BOOL ModuleFind(PTSTR pszModName, PMODULEENTRY32 pme) const;
```

(continued)

130

Figure 4-6. *continued*

```
    BOOL ThreadFirst(PTHREADENTRY32 pte) const;
    BOOL ThreadNext(PTHREADENTRY32 pte) const;

    BOOL HeapListFirst(PHEAPLIST32 phl) const;
    BOOL HeapListNext(PHEAPLIST32 phl) const;
    int  HowManyHeaps() const;

    // Note: The heap block functions do not reference a snapshot and
    // just walk the process's heap from the beginning each time. Infinite
    // loops can occur if the target process changes its heap while the
    // functions below are enumerating the blocks in the heap.
    BOOL HeapFirst(PHEAPENTRY32 phe, DWORD dwProcessID,
        UINT_PTR dwHeapID) const;
    BOOL HeapNext(PHEAPENTRY32 phe) const;
    int  HowManyBlocksInHeap(DWORD dwProcessID, DWORD dwHeapId) const;
    BOOL IsAHeap(HANDLE hProcess, PVOID pvBlock, PDWORD pdwFlags) const;

public:
    static BOOL EnableDebugPrivilege(BOOL fEnable = TRUE);
    static BOOL ReadProcessMemory(DWORD dwProcessID, LPCVOID pvBaseAddress,
        PVOID pvBuffer, DWORD cbRead, PDWORD pdwNumberOfBytesRead = NULL);
};


///////////////////////////////////////////////////////////////////////////////


inline CToolhelp::CToolhelp(DWORD dwFlags, DWORD dwProcessID) {

    m_hSnapshot = INVALID_HANDLE_VALUE;
    CreateSnapshot(dwFlags, dwProcessID);
}


///////////////////////////////////////////////////////////////////////////////


inline CToolhelp::~CToolhelp() {

    if (m_hSnapshot != INVALID_HANDLE_VALUE)
        CloseHandle(m_hSnapshot);
}
```

(continued)

Figure 4-6. *continued*

```
//////////////////////////////////////////////////////////////////////////


inline CToolhelp::CreateSnapshot(DWORD dwFlags, DWORD dwProcessID) {

   if (m_hSnapshot != INVALID_HANDLE_VALUE)
      CloseHandle(m_hSnapshot);

   if (dwFlags == 0) {
      m_hSnapshot = INVALID_HANDLE_VALUE;
   } else {
      m_hSnapshot = CreateToolhelp32Snapshot(dwFlags, dwProcessID);
   }
   return(m_hSnapshot != INVALID_HANDLE_VALUE);
}



//////////////////////////////////////////////////////////////////////////


inline BOOL CToolhelp::EnableDebugPrivilege(BOOL fEnable) {

   // Enabling the debug privilege allows the application to see
   // information about service applications
   BOOL fOk = FALSE;     // Assume function fails
   HANDLE hToken;

   // Try to open this process's access token
   if (OpenProcessToken(GetCurrentProcess(), TOKEN_ADJUST_PRIVILEGES,
      &hToken)) {

      // Attempt to modify the "Debug" privilege
      TOKEN_PRIVILEGES tp;
      tp.PrivilegeCount = 1;
      LookupPrivilegeValue(NULL, SE_DEBUG_NAME, &tp.Privileges[0].Luid);
      tp.Privileges[0].Attributes = fEnable ? SE_PRIVILEGE_ENABLED : 0;
      AdjustTokenPrivileges(hToken, FALSE, &tp, sizeof(tp), NULL, NULL);
      fOk = (GetLastError() == ERROR_SUCCESS);
      CloseHandle(hToken);
   }
   return(fOk);
}
```

(continued)

Figure 4-6. *continued*

```
///////////////////////////////////////////////////////////////////////////


inline BOOL CToolhelp::ReadProcessMemory(DWORD dwProcessID,
   LPCVOID pvBaseAddress, PVOID pvBuffer, DWORD cbRead,
   PDWORD pdwNumberOfBytesRead) {

   return(Toolhelp32ReadProcessMemory(dwProcessID, pvBaseAddress, pvBuffer,
      cbRead, pdwNumberOfBytesRead));
}



///////////////////////////////////////////////////////////////////////////


inline BOOL CToolhelp::ProcessFirst(PPROCESSENTRY32 ppe) const {

   BOOL fOk = Process32First(m_hSnapshot, ppe);
   if (fOk && (ppe->th32ProcessID == 0))
      fOk = ProcessNext(ppe); // Remove the "[System Process]" (PID = 0)
   return(fOk);
}


inline BOOL CToolhelp::ProcessNext(PPROCESSENTRY32 ppe) const {

   BOOL fOk = Process32Next(m_hSnapshot, ppe);
   if (fOk && (ppe->th32ProcessID == 0))
      fOk = ProcessNext(ppe); // Remove the "[System Process]" (PID = 0)
   return(fOk);
}


inline BOOL CToolhelp::ProcessFind(DWORD dwProcessId, PPROCESSENTRY32 ppe)
   const {

   BOOL fFound = FALSE;
   for (BOOL fOk = ProcessFirst(ppe); fOk; fOk = ProcessNext(ppe)) {
      fFound = (ppe->th32ProcessID == dwProcessId);
      if (fFound) break;
   }
   return(fFound);
}
```

(continued)

133

Figure 4-6. *continued*

```
//////////////////////////////////////////////////////////////////////////

inline BOOL CToolhelp::ModuleFirst(PMODULEENTRY32 pme) const {

   return(Module32First(m_hSnapshot, pme));
}

inline BOOL CToolhelp::ModuleNext(PMODULEENTRY32 pme) const {

   return(Module32Next(m_hSnapshot, pme));
}

inline BOOL CToolhelp::ModuleFind(PVOID pvBaseAddr, PMODULEENTRY32 pme) const {

   BOOL fFound = FALSE;
   for (BOOL fOk = ModuleFirst(pme); fOk; fOk = ModuleNext(pme)) {
      fFound = (pme->modBaseAddr == pvBaseAddr);
      if (fFound) break;
   }
   return(fFound);
}

inline BOOL CToolhelp::ModuleFind(PTSTR pszModName, PMODULEENTRY32 pme) const {
   BOOL fFound = FALSE;
   for (BOOL fOk = ModuleFirst(pme); fOk; fOk = ModuleNext(pme)) {
      fFound = (lstrcmpi(pme->szModule,  pszModName) == 0) ||
               (lstrcmpi(pme->szExePath, pszModName) == 0);
      if (fFound) break;
   }
   return(fFound);
}

//////////////////////////////////////////////////////////////////////////

inline BOOL CToolhelp::ThreadFirst(PTHREADENTRY32 pte) const {

   return(Thread32First(m_hSnapshot, pte));
}

inline BOOL CToolhelp::ThreadNext(PTHREADENTRY32 pte) const {

   return(Thread32Next(m_hSnapshot, pte));
}
```

(continued)

Figure 4-6. *continued*

```
//////////////////////////////////////////////////////////////////////////////

inline int CToolhelp::HowManyHeaps() const {

   int nHowManyHeaps = 0;
   HEAPLIST32 hl = { sizeof(hl) };
   for (BOOL fOk = HeapListFirst(&hl); fOk; fOk = HeapListNext(&hl))
      nHowManyHeaps++;
   return(nHowManyHeaps);
}

inline int CToolhelp::HowManyBlocksInHeap(DWORD dwProcessID,
   DWORD dwHeapID) const {

   int nHowManyBlocksInHeap = 0;
   HEAPENTRY32 he = { sizeof(he) };
   BOOL fOk = HeapFirst(&he, dwProcessID, dwHeapID);
   for (; fOk; fOk = HeapNext(&he))
      nHowManyBlocksInHeap++;
   return(nHowManyBlocksInHeap);
}

inline BOOL CToolhelp::HeapListFirst(PHEAPLIST32 phl) const {

   return(Heap32ListFirst(m_hSnapshot, phl));
}

inline BOOL CToolhelp::HeapListNext(PHEAPLIST32 phl) const {

   return(Heap32ListNext(m_hSnapshot, phl));
}

inline BOOL CToolhelp::HeapFirst(PHEAPENTRY32 phe, DWORD dwProcessID,
   UINT_PTR dwHeapID) const {

   return(Heap32First(phe, dwProcessID, dwHeapID));
}

inline BOOL CToolhelp::HeapNext(PHEAPENTRY32 phe) const {

   return(Heap32Next(phe));
}
```

(continued)

Figure 4-6. *continued*

```
inline BOOL CToolhelp::IsAHeap(HANDLE hProcess, PVOID pvBlock,
   PDWORD pdwFlags) const {

   HEAPLIST32 hl = { sizeof(hl) };
   for (BOOL fOkHL = HeapListFirst(&hl); fOkHL; fOkHL = HeapListNext(&hl)) {
      HEAPENTRY32 he = { sizeof(he) };
      BOOL fOkHE = HeapFirst(&he, hl.th32ProcessID, hl.th32HeapID);
      for (; fOkHE; fOkHE = HeapNext(&he)) {
         MEMORY_BASIC_INFORMATION mbi;
         VirtualQueryEx(hProcess, (PVOID) he.dwAddress, &mbi, sizeof(mbi));
         if (chINRANGE(mbi.AllocationBase, pvBlock,
            (PBYTE) mbi.AllocationBase + mbi.RegionSize)) {

            *pdwFlags = hl.dwFlags;
            return(TRUE);
         }
      }
   }
   return(FALSE);
}


//////////////////////////////// End of File ////////////////////////////////
```

JOBS

You often need to treat a group of processes as a single entity. For example, when you tell Microsoft Developer Studio to build a project, it spawns Cl.exe, which might have to spawn additional processes (such as the individual passes of the compiler). But if the user wants to prematurely stop the build, Developer Studio must somehow be able to terminate Cl.exe and all its child processes. Solving this simple (and common) problem in Windows has been notoriously difficult because Windows doesn't maintain a parent/child relationship between processes. In particular, child processes continue to execute even after their parent process has been terminated.

When you design a server, you must also treat a set of processes as a single group. For instance, a client might request that a server execute an application (which might spawn children of its own) and return the results back to the client. Since many clients might connect to this server, it would be nice if the server could somehow restrict what a client can request to prevent any single client from monopolizing all of its resources. These restrictions might include: maximum CPU time that can be allocated to the client's request, minimum and maximum working set sizes, preventing the client's application from shutting down the computer, and security restrictions.

Microsoft Windows 2000 offers a new job kernel object that lets you group processes together and create a "sandbox" that restricts what the processes can do. It is best to think of a job object as a container of processes. However, it is useful to create jobs that contain a single process because you can place restrictions on that process that you normally cannot.

My *StartRestrictedProcess* function (Figure 5-1) places a process in a job that restricts the process's ability to do certain things.

WINDOWS 98

Windows 98 does not support jobs.

```
void StartRestrictedProcess() {
   // Create a job kernel object.
   HANDLE hjob = CreateJobObject(NULL, NULL);

   // Place some restrictions on processes in the job.

   // First, set some basic restrictions.
   JOBOBJECT_BASIC_LIMIT_INFORMATION jobli = { 0 };

   // The process always runs in the idle priority class.
   jobli.PriorityClass = IDLE_PRIORITY_CLASS;

   // The job cannot use more than 1 second of CPU time.
   jobli.PerJobUserTimeLimit.QuadPart = 10000000; // 1 sec in 100-ns intervals

   // These are the only 2 restrictions I want placed on the job (process).
   jobli.LimitFlags = JOB_OBJECT_LIMIT_PRIORITY_CLASS
      | JOB_OBJECT_LIMIT_JOB_TIME;
   SetInformationJobObject(hjob, JobObjectBasicLimitInformation, &jobli,
      sizeof(jobli));

   // Second, set some UI restrictions.
   JOBOBJECT_BASIC_UI_RESTRICTIONS jobuir;
   jobuir.UIRestrictionsClass = JOB_OBJECT_UILIMIT_NONE;      // A fancy zero

   // The process can't log off the system.
   jobuir.UIRestrictionsClass |= JOB_OBJECT_UILIMIT_EXITWINDOWS;

   // The process can't access USER objects (such as other windows)
   // in the system.
   jobuir.UIRestrictionsClass |= JOB_OBJECT_UILIMIT_HANDLES;

   SetInformationJobObject(hjob, JobObjectBasicUIRestrictions, &jobuir,
      sizeof(jobuir));

   // Spawn the process that is to be in the job.
   // Note: You must first spawn the process and then place the process in
   //       the job. This means that the process's thread must be initially
   //       suspended so that it can't execute any code outside of the job's
   //       restrictions.
```

Figure 5-1. *(continued)*
The StartRestrictedProcess *function*

Figure 5-1. *continued*

```
STARTUPINFO si = { sizeof(si) };
PROCESS_INFORMATION pi;
CreateProcess(NULL, "CMD", NULL, NULL, FALSE,
    CREATE_SUSPENDED, NULL, NULL, &si, &pi);
// Place the process in the job.
// Note: If this process spawns any children, the children are
//       automatically part of the same job.
AssignProcessToJobObject(hjob, pi.hProcess);

// Now we can allow the child process's thread to execute code.
ResumeThread(pi.hThread);
CloseHandle(pi.hThread);

// Wait for the process to terminate or
// for all the job's allotted CPU time to be used.
HANDLE h[2];
h[0] = pi.hProcess;
h[1] = hjob;
DWORD dw = WaitForMultipleObjects(2, h, FALSE, INFINITE);
switch (dw - WAIT_OBJECT_0) {
    case 0:
        // The process has terminated...
        break;
    case 1:
        // All of the job's allotted CPU time was used...
        break;
}

// Clean up properly.
CloseHandle(pi.hProcess);
CloseHandle(hjob);
}
```

Now, let me explain how *StartRestrictedProcess* works. I first create a new job kernel object by calling the following:

```
HANDLE CreateJobObject(
    PSECURITY_ATTRIBUTES psa,
    PCTSTR pszName);
```

Like all kernel objects, the first parameter associates security information with the new job object and tells the system whether you want the returned handle to be inheritable. The last parameter names the job object so that it can be accessed by another process via the *OpenJobObject* function shown at the top of page 140.

```
HANDLE OpenJobObject(
   DWORD dwDesiredAccess,
   BOOL bInheritHandle,
   PCTSTR pszName);
```

As always, if you know that you will no longer access the job object in your code, you must close its handle by calling *CloseHandle*. You can see this at the end of my *StartRestrictedProcess* function. Be aware that closing a job object does not force all the processes in the job to be terminated. The job object is actually marked for deletion and is destroyed automatically only after all of the processes within the job have been terminated.

Note that closing the job's handle causes the job to be inaccessible to all processes even though the job still exists, as shown in the following code:

```
// Create a named job object.
HANDLE hjob = CreateJobObject(NULL, TEXT("Jeff"));

// Put our own process in the job.
AssignProcessToJobObject(hjob, GetCurrentProcess());

// Closing the job does not kill our process or the job.
// But the name ("Jeff") is immediately disassociated with the job.
CloseHandle(hjob);

// Try to open the existing job.
hjob = OpenJobObject(JOB_OBJECT_ALL_ACCESS, FALSE, TEXT("Jeff"));
// OpenJobObject fails and returns NULL here because the name ("Jeff")
// was disassociated from the job when CloseHandle was called.
// There is no way to get a handle to this job now.
```

Placing Restrictions on a Job's Processes

After creating a job, you will typically want to set up the sandbox (set restrictions) on what processes within the job can do. You can place several different types of restrictions on a job:

- The basic limit and extended basic limit prevent processes within a job from monopolizing the system's resources.

- Basic UI restrictions prevent processes within a job from altering the user interface.

- Security limits prevent processes within a job from accessing secure resources (files, registry subkeys, and so on).

You place restrictions on a job by calling the following:

```
BOOL SetInformationJobObject(
    HANDLE hJob,
    JOBOBJECTINFOCLASS JobObjectInformationClass,
    PVOID pJobObjectInformation,
    DWORD cbJobObjectInformationLength);
```

The first parameter identifies the job you want to restrict. The second parameter is an enumerated type and indicates the type of restriction you want to apply. The third parameter is the address of a data structure containing the restriction settings, and the fourth parameter indicates the size of this structure (used for versioning). The following table summarizes how to set restrictions.

Limit Type	Value of Second Parameter	Structure of Third Parameter
Basic limit	*JobObjectBasicLimitInformation*	JOBOBJECT_BASIC_ LIMIT_INFORMATION
Extended basic limit	*JobObjectExtendedLimitInformation*	JOBOBJECT_EXTENDED_ LIMIT_INFORMATION
Basic UI restrictions	*JobObjectBasicUIRestrictions*	JOBOBJECT_BASIC_ UI_RESTRICTIONS
Security limit	*JobObjectSecurityLimitInformation*	JOBOBJECT_SECURITY_ LIMIT_INFORMATION

In my *StartRestrictedProcess* function, I set only some basic restrictions on the job. I allocated a JOB_OBJECT_BASIC_LIMIT_INFORMATION structure, initialized it, and then called *SetInformationJobObject*. A JOB_OBJECT_ BASIC_LIMIT_INFORMATION structure looks like this:

```
typedef struct _JOBOBJECT_BASIC_LIMIT_INFORMATION {
    LARGE_INTEGER PerProcessUserTimeLimit;
    LARGE_INTEGER PerJobUserTimeLimit;
    DWORD         LimitFlags;
    DWORD         MinimumWorkingSetSize;
    DWORD         MaximumWorkingSetSize;
    DWORD         ActiveProcessLimit;
    DWORD_PTR     Affinity;
    DWORD         PriorityClass;
    DWORD         SchedulingClass;
} JOBOBJECT_BASIC_LIMIT_INFORMATION, *PJOBOBJECT_BASIC_LIMIT_INFORMATION;
```

Table 5-1 briefly describes the members.

Member	Description	Notes
PerProcessUser-TimeLimit	Specifies the maximum user-mode time allotted to each process (in 100 ns intervals).	The system automatically terminates any process that uses more than its allotted time. To set this limit, specify the JOB_OBJECT_LIMIT_PROCESS_TIME flag in the *LimitFlags* member.
PerJobUser-TimeLimit	Specifies how much more user-mode time the processes in this job can use (in 100 ns intervals).	By default, the system automatically terminates all processes when this time limit is reached. You can change this value periodically as the job runs. To set this limit, specify the JOB_OBJECT_LIMIT_JOB_TIME flag in the *LimitFlags* member.
LimitFlags	Indicates which restrictions to apply to the job.	See the section that follows this table for more information.
Minimum WorkingSetSize/ Maximum WorkingSetSize	Specifies the minimum and maximum working set size for each process (not for all processes within the job).	Normally, a process's working set can grow above its maximum; setting *MaximumWorkingSetSize* forces a hard limit. Once the process's working set reaches this limit, the process pages against itself. Calls to *SetProcessWorkingSetSize* by an individual process are ignored unless the process is just trying to empty its working set. To set this limit, specify the JOB_OBJECT_LIMIT_WORKINGSET flag in the *LimitFlags* member.
ActiveProcessLimit	Specifies the maximum number of processes that can run concurrently in the job.	Any attempt to go over this limit causes the new process to be terminated with a "not enough quota" error. To set this limit, specify the JOB_OBJECT_LIMIT_ACTIVE_PROCESS flag in the *LimitFlags* member.

Table 5-1.
JOBOBJECT_BASIC_LIMIT_INFORMATION members

(continued)

Table 5-1. *continued*

Member	Description	Notes
Affinity	Specifies the subset of the CPU(s) that can run the processes.	Individual processes can limit this even further. To set this limit, specify the JOB_OBJECT_LIMIT_AFFINITY flag in the *LimitFlags* member.
PriorityClass	Specifies the priority class used by all processes.	If a process calls *SetPriorityClass*, the call will return successfully even though it actually fails. If the process calls *GetPriorityClass*, the function returns what the process has set the priority class to even though this might not be process's actual priority class. In addition, *SetThreadPriority* fails to raise threads above normal priority but can be used to lower a thread's priority. To set this limit, specify the JOB_OBJECT_LIMIT_PRIORITY_CLASS flag in the *LimitFlags* member.
SchedulingClass	Specifies a relative time quantum difference assigned to threads in the job.	Value can be from 0 to 9 inclusive; 5 is the default. See the text after this table for more information. To set this limit, specify the JOB_OBJECT_LIMIT_SCHEDULING_CLASS flag in the *LimitFlags* member.

I'd like to explain a few things about this structure that I don't think are clear in the Platform SDK documentation. You set bits in the *LimitFlags* member to indicate the restrictions you want applied to the job. For example, in my *StartRestrictedProcess* function, I set the JOB_OBJECT_LIMIT_PRIORITY_CLASS and JOB_OBJECT_LIMIT_JOB_TIME bits. This means that these are the only two restrictions that I place on the job. I impose no restrictions on CPU affinity, working set size, per-process CPU time, and so on.

As the job runs, it maintains accounting information—such as how much CPU time the processes in the job have used. Each time you set the basic limit using the JOB_OBJECT_LIMIT_JOB_TIME flag, the job subtracts the CPU time accounting information for processes that have terminated. This shows you how much CPU time is used by the currently active processes. But what if you want to change the affinity of the job but not reset the CPU time accounting information? To do this, you have to set a new basic limit using the JOB_OBJECT_LIMIT_AFFINITY flag, and you have to leave off the JOB_OBJECT_LIMIT_JOB_TIME flag. But by doing this, you tell the job that you no longer want to enforce a CPU time restriction. This is not what you want.

What you want is to change the affinity restriction and keep the existing CPU time restriction; you just don't want the CPU time accounting information for the terminated processes to be subtracted. To solve this problem, use a special flag: JOB_OBJECT_LIMIT_PRESERVE_JOB_TIME. This flag and the JOB_OBJECT_LIMIT_JOB_TIME flag are mutually exclusive. The JOB_OBJECT_LIMIT_PRESERVE_JOB_TIME flag indicates that you want to change the restrictions without subtracting the CPU time accounting information for the terminated processes.

We should also talk about the JOBOBJECT_BASIC_LIMIT_INFORMATION structure's *SchedulingClass* member. Imagine that you have two jobs running and you set the priority class of both jobs to NORMAL_PRIORITY_CLASS. But you also want processes in one job to get more CPU time than processes in the other job. You can use the *SchedulingClass* member to change the relative scheduling of jobs that have the same priority class. You can set a value between 0 and 9, inclusive; 5 is the default. On Windows 2000, a higher value tells the system to give a longer time quantum to threads in processes in a particular job; a lower value reduces the threads' time quantum.

For example, let's say that I have two normal priority class jobs. Each job contains one process, and each process has just one (normal priority) thread. Under ordinary circumstances, these two threads would be scheduled in a round-robin fashion and each would get the same time quantum. However, if we set the *SchedulingClass* member of the first job to 3, when threads in this job are scheduled CPU time, their quantum is shorter than for threads that are in the second job.

If you use the *SchedulingClass* member, you should avoid using large numbers and hence larger time quantums because larger time quantums reduce the overall responsiveness of the other jobs, processes, and threads in the system. Also, I have just described what happens on Windows 2000. Microsoft plans to make more significant changes to the thread scheduler in future versions of Windows because it recognizes a need for the operating system to offer a wider range of thread scheduling scenarios to jobs, processes, and threads.

One last limit that deserves special mention is the JOB_OBJECT_LIMIT_ DIE_ON_UNHANDLED_EXCEPTION limit flag. This limit causes the system to turn off the "unhandled exception" dialog box for each process associated with the job. The system does this by calling the *SetErrorMode* function, passing it the SEM_NOGPFAULTERRORBOX flag for each process in the job. A process in a job that raises an unhandled exception is immediately terminated without any user interface being displayed. This is a useful limit flag for services and other batch-oriented jobs. Without it, a process in a job can raise an exception and never terminate, thereby wasting system resources.

In addition to the basic limits, you can set extended limits on a job using the JOBOBJECT_EXTENDED_LIMIT_INFORMATION structure:

```
typedef struct _JOBOBJECT_EXTENDED_LIMIT_INFORMATION {
    JOBOBJECT_BASIC_LIMIT_INFORMATION BasicLimitInformation;
    IO_COUNTERS IoInfo;
    SIZE_T ProcessMemoryLimit;
    SIZE_T JobMemoryLimit;
    SIZE_T PeakProcessMemoryUsed;
    SIZE_T PeakJobMemoryUsed;
} JOBOBJECT_EXTENDED_LIMIT_INFORMATION, *PJOBOBJECT_EXTENDED_LIMIT_INFORMATION;
```

As you can see, this structure contains a JOBOBJECT_BASIC_LIMIT_ INFORMATION structure, which makes it a superset of the basic limits. This structure is a little strange because it includes members that have nothing to do with setting limits on a job. First, the *IoInfo* member is reserved; you should not access it in any way. I'll discuss how you can query I/O counter information later in the chapter. In addition, the *PeakProcessMemoryUsed* and *PeakJobMemoryUsed* members are read-only and tell you the maximum amount of committed storage that has been required for any one process and for all processes within the job, respectively.

The two remaining members, *ProcessMemoryLimit* and *JobMemoryLimit*, restrict the amount of committed storage used by any one process or by all processes in the job, respectively. To set either of these limits, you specify the JOB_OBJECT_LIMIT_JOB_MEMORY and the JOB_OBJECT_LIMIT_ PROCESS_MEMORY flags in the *LimitFlags* member, respectively.

Now let's turn our attention back to other restrictions that you can place on a job. A JOBOBJECT_BASIC_UI_RESTRICTIONS structure looks like this:

```
typedef struct _JOBOBJECT_BASIC_UI_RESTRICTIONS {
    DWORD UIRestrictionsClass;
} JOBOBJECT_BASIC_UI_RESTRICTIONS, *PJOBOBJECT_BASIC_UI_RESTRICTIONS;
```

This structure has only one data member, *UIRestrictionsClass*, which holds a set of bit flags briefly described in Table 5-2.

Flag	Description
JOB_OBJECT_UILIMIT_EXITWINDOWS	Prevents processes from logging off, shutting down, rebooting, or powering off the system via the *ExitWindowsEx* function
JOB_OBJECT_UILIMIT_READCLIPBOARD	Prevents processes from reading the clipboard
JOB_OBJECT_UILIMIT_WRITECLIPBOARD	Prevents processes from erasing the clipboard
JOB_OBJECT_UILIMIT_SYSTEMPARAMETERS	Prevents processes from changing system parameters via the *SystemParametersInfo* function
JOB_OBJECT_UILIMIT_DISPLAYSETTINGS	Prevents processes from changing the display settings via the *ChangeDisplaySettings* function
JOB_OBJECT_UILIMIT_GLOBALATOMS	Gives the job its own global atom table and restricts processes in the job to accessing only the job's table
JOB_OBJECT_UILIMIT_DESKTOP	Prevents processes from creating or switching desktops using the *CreateDesktop* or *SwitchDesktop* function
JOB_OBJECT_UILIMIT_HANDLES	Prevents processes in a job from using USER objects (such as HWNDs) created by processes outside the same job

Table 5-2.
Bit flags for basic user-interface restrictions for a job object

The last flag, JOB_OBJECT_UILIMIT_HANDLES, is particularly interesting. This restriction means that no processes in the job can access USER objects created by processes outside the job. So if you try to run Microsoft Spy++ inside a job, you won't see any windows except the windows that Spy++ itself creates. Figure 5-2 shows Spy++ with two MDI child windows open. Notice that the Threads 1 window contains a list of threads in the system. Only one of those threads, 000006AC SPYXX, seems to have created any windows. This is because I ran Spy++ in its own job and restricted its use of UI handles. In the same window, you can see the MSDEV and EXPLORER threads, but it appears that they have not created any windows. I assure you that these threads have definitely created windows, but Spy++ cannot access them. On the right side, you see the Windows 3 window, in which Spy++ shows the hierarchy of all windows existing on the desktop. Notice that there is only one entry, 00000000. Spy++ must just put this here as a placeholder.

Note that this UI restriction is only one-way. That is, processes outside of a job can see USER objects created by processes within a job. For example, if I run Notepad in a job and Spy++ outside of a job, Spy++ can see Notepad's window even if the job that Notepad is in specifies the JOB_OBJECT_ UILIMIT_HANDLES flag. Also, if Spy++ is in its own job, it can also see Notepad's window unless the job has the JOB_OBJECT_UILIMIT_HANDLES flag specified.

The restricting of UI handles is awesome if you want to create a really secure sandbox for your job's processes to play in. However, it is useful to have a process that is part of a job communicate with a process outside of the job.

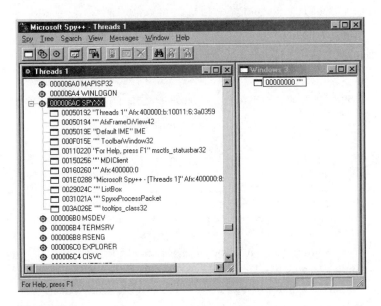

Figure 5-2.
Microsoft Spy++ running in a job that restricts access to UI handles

One easy way to accomplish this is to use window messages, but if the job's processes can't access UI handles, a process in the job can't send or post a window message to a window created by a process outside the job. Fortunately, you can solve this problem using a new function:

```
BOOL UserHandleGrantAccess(
   HANDLE hUserObj,
   HANDLE hjob,
   BOOL fGrant);
```

The *hUserObj* parameter indicates a single USER object whose access you want to grant or deny to processes within the job. This is almost always a window handle, but it can be another USER object, such as a desktop, hook, icon, or menu. The last two parameters, *hjob* and *fGrant*, indicate which job you are granting or denying access to. Note that this function fails if it is called from a process within the job identified by *hjob*—this prevents a process within a job from simply granting itself access to an object.

The last type of restriction that you place on a job is related to security. (Note that once applied, security restrictions cannot be revoked.) A JOB-OBJECT_SECURITY_LIMIT_INFORMATION structure looks like this:

```
typedef struct _JOBOBJECT_SECURITY_LIMIT_INFORMATION {
   DWORD SecurityLimitFlags;
   HANDLE JobToken;
   PTOKEN_GROUPS SidsToDisable;
   PTOKEN_PRIVILEGES PrivilegesToDelete;
   PTOKEN_GROUPS RestrictedSids;
} JOBOBJECT_SECURITY_LIMIT_INFORMATION, *PJOBOBJECT_SECURITY_LIMIT_INFORMATION;
```

The following table briefly describes the members.

Member	Description
SecurityLimitFlags	Indicates whether to disallow administrator access, disallow unrestricted token access, force a specific access token, or disable certain security identifiers (SIDs) and privileges
JobToken	Access token to be used by all processes in the job
SidsToDisable	Indicates which SIDs to disable for access checking
PrivilegesToDelete	Indicates which privileges to delete from the access token
RestrictedSids	Indicates a set of deny-only SIDs that should be added to the access token

Naturally, once you have placed restrictions on a job, you might want to query those restrictions. You can do so easily by calling

```
BOOL QueryInformationJobObject(
    HANDLE hJob,
    JOBOBJECTINFOCLASS JobObjectInformationClass,
    PVOID pvJobObjectInformation,
    DWORD cbJobObjectInformationLength,
    PDWORD pdwReturnLength);
```

You pass this function the handle of the job (like you do with *SetInformationJobObject*)—an enumerated type that indicates what restriction information you want, the address of the data structure to be initialized by the function, and the length of the data block containing that structure. The last parameter, *pdwReturnLength*, points to a DWORD that is filled in by the function, which tells you how many bytes were placed in the buffer. You can (and usually will) pass NULL for this parameter if you don't care.

> **NOTE**
>
> A process in a job can call *QueryInformationJobObject* to obtain information about the job to which it belongs by passing NULL for the job handle parameter. This can be very useful because it allows a process to see what restrictions have been placed on it. However, the *SetInformationJobObject* function fails if you pass NULL for the job handle parameter because this would allow a process to remove restrictions placed on it.

Placing a Process in a Job

OK, that's it for setting and querying restrictions. Now let's get back to my *StartRestrictedProcess* function. After I place some restrictions on the job, I spawn the process that I intend to place in the job by calling *CreateProcess*. However, notice that I use the CREATE_SUSPENDED flag when calling *CreateProcess*. This creates the new process but doesn't allow it to execute any code. Since the *StartRestrictedProcess* function is being executed from a process that is not part of a job, the child process will also not be part of a job. If I were to allow the child process to immediately start executing code, it would run out of my sandbox and could successfully do things that I want to restrict it from doing. So after I create the child process and before I allow it to start running, I must explicitly place the process in my newly created job by calling the following:

```
BOOL AssignProcessToJobObject(
    HANDLE hJob,
    HANDLE hProcess);
```

This function tells the system to treat the process (identified by *hProcess*) as part of an existing job (identified by *hJob*). Note that this function allows only a process that is not assigned to any job to be assigned to a job. Once a process is part of a job, it cannot be moved to another job and it cannot become job-less (so to speak). Also note that when a process that is part of job spawns another process, the new process is automatically made part of the parent's job. However, you can alter this behavior in the following ways:

- Turn on the JOB_OBJECT_BREAKAWAY_OK flag in JOBOBJECT_BASIC_LIMIT_INFORMATION's *LimitFlags* member to tell the system that a newly spawned process can execute outside the job. To make this happen, you must call *CreateProcess* with the new CREATE_BREAKAWAY_FROM_JOB flag. If you call *CreateProcess* with the CREATE_BREAKAWAY_FROM_JOB flag but the job does not have the JOB_OBJECT_BREAKAWAY_OK limit flag turned on, *CreateProcess* fails. This mechanism is useful if the newly spawned process also controls jobs.

- Turn on the JOB_OBJECT_SILENT_BREAKAWAY_OK flag in the JOBOBJECT_BASIC_LIMIT_INFORMATION's *LimitFlags* member. This flag also tells the system that newly spawned processes should not be part of the job. However, there is no need to pass any additional flags to *CreateProcess*. In fact, this flag forces new processes to not be part of the job. This flag is useful for processes that were originally designed knowing nothing about job objects.

As for my *StartRestrictedProcess* function, after I call *AssignProcessToJobObject*, my new process is part of my restricted job. I then call *ResumeThread* so that the process's thread can execute code under the job's restrictions. At this point, I also close the handle to the thread since I no longer need it.

Terminating All Processes in a Job

Well, certainly one of the most popular things that you will want to do with a job is kill all of the processes within it. At the beginning of this chapter, I mentioned that Developer Studio doesn't have an easy way to stop a build that is in progress because it would have to know which processes were spawned from the first process that it spawned. (This is very tricky. I explain how Developer Studio accomplishes this in my Win32 Q & A column in the June 1998 issue of Microsoft Systems Journal.) I suspect that future versions of Developer Studio will use jobs instead because the code is a lot easier to write and you can do much more with it.

To kill all the processes within a job, you simply call

```
BOOL TerminateJobObject(
    HANDLE hJob,
    UINT uExitCode);
```

This is similar to calling *TerminateProcess* for every process contained within the job, setting all their exit codes to *uExitCode*.

Querying Job Statistics

We've already discussed how to use the *QueryInformationJobObject* function to get the current restrictions on a job. You can also use it to get statistical information about a job. For example, to get basic accounting information, you call *QueryInformationJobObject*, passing *JobObjectBasicAccountingInformation* for the second parameter and the address of a JOBOBJECT_BASIC_ ACCOUNTING_INFORMATION structure:

```
typedef struct _JOBOBJECT_BASIC_ACCOUNTING_INFORMATION {
    LARGE_INTEGER TotalUserTime;
    LARGE_INTEGER TotalKernelTime;
    LARGE_INTEGER ThisPeriodTotalUserTime;
    LARGE_INTEGER ThisPeriodTotalKernelTime;
    DWORD TotalPageFaultCount;
    DWORD TotalProcesses;
    DWORD ActiveProcesses;
    DWORD TotalTerminatedProcesses;
} JOBOBJECT_BASIC_ACCOUNTING_INFORMATION,
    *PJOBOBJECT_BASIC_ACCOUNTING_INFORMATION;
```

Table 5-3 briefly describes the members.

Member	Description
TotalUserTime	Specifies how much user-mode CPU time processes in the job have used
TotalKernelTime	Specifies how much kernel-mode CPU time processes in the job have used
ThisPeriodTotal- UserTime	Like *TotalUserTime*, except this value is reset to 0 when *Set-InformationJobObject* is called to change basic limit information and the JOB_OBJECT_LIMIT_PRESERVE_JOB_TIME limit flag is not used

Table 5-3. *(continued)*
JOBOBJECT_BASIC_ACCOUNTING_INFORMATION members

Table 5-3. *continued*

Member	Description
ThisPeriodTotal-KernelTime	Like *ThisPeriodTotalUserTime*, except this value shows kernel-mode time
TotalPageFaultCount	Specifies the total number of page faults that processes in the job have accrued
TotalProcesses	Specifies the total number of processes that have ever been part of the job
ActiveProcesses	Specifies the number of processes that are currently part of the job
TotalTerminated-Processes	Specifies the number of processes that have been killed because they have exceeded their allotted CPU time limit

In addition to querying this basic accounting information, you can make a single call to query both basic accounting and I/O accounting information. To do this, you pass *JobObjectBasicAndIoAccountingInformation* for the second parameter and the address of a JOBOBJECT_BASIC_AND_IO_ACCOUNTING_INFORMATION structure:

```
typedef struct JOBOBJECT_BASIC_AND_IO_ACCOUNTING_INFORMATION {
    JOBOBJECT_BASIC_ACCOUNTING_INFORMATION BasicInfo;
    IO_COUNTERS IoInfo;
} JOBOBJECT_BASIC_AND_IO_ACCOUNTING_INFORMATION;
```

As you can see, this structure simply returns a JOBOBJECT_BASIC_ACCOUNTING_INFORMATION and an IO_COUNTERS structure:

```
typedef struct _IO_COUNTERS {
    ULONGLONG ReadOperationCount;
    ULONGLONG WriteOperationCount;
    ULONGLONG OtherOperationCount;
    ULONGLONG ReadTransferCount;
    ULONGLONG WriteTransferCount;
    ULONGLONG OtherTransferCount;
} IO_COUNTERS;
```

This structure tells you the number of read, write, and non-read/write operations (as well as total bytes transferred during those operations) that have been performed by processes in the job. By the way, you can use the new *GetProcessIoCounters* function to obtain this information for processes that are not in jobs:

```
BOOL GetProcessIoCounters(
   HANDLE hProcess,
   PIO_COUNTERS pIoCounters);
```

You can also call *QueryInformationJobObject* at any time to get the set of process IDs for processes that are currently running in the job. To do this, you must first guess how many processes you expect to see in the job, and then you have to allocate a block of memory large enough to hold an array of these process IDs plus the size of a JOBOBJECT_BASIC_PROCESS_ID_LIST structure:

```
typedef struct _JOBOBJECT_BASIC_PROCESS_ID_LIST {
   DWORD NumberOfAssignedProcesses;
   DWORD NumberOfProcessIdsInList;
   DWORD ProcessIdList[1];
} JOBOBJECT_BASIC_PROCESS_ID_LIST, *PJOBOBJECT_BASIC_PROCESS_ID_LIST;
```

So, to get the set of Process IDs currently in a job, you must execute code similar to the following:

```
void EnumProcessIdsInJob(HANDLE hjob) {

   // I assume that there will never be more
   // than 10 processes in this job.
   #define MAX_PROCESS_IDS    10

   // Calculate the number of bytes needed for structure & process IDs.
   DWORD cb = sizeof(JOBOBJECT_BASIC_PROCESS_ID_LIST) +
      (MAX_PROCESS_IDS - 1) * sizeof(DWORD);

   // Allocate the block of memory.
   PJOBOBJECT_BASIC_PROCESS_ID_LIST pjobpil = _alloca(cb);

   // Tell the function the maximum number of processes
   // that we allocated space for.
   pjobpil->NumberOfAssignedProcesses = MAX_PROCESS_IDS;

   // Request the current set of process IDs.
   QueryInformationJobObject(hjob, JobObjectBasicProcessIdList,
      pjobpil, cb, &cb);

   // Enumerate the process IDs.
   for (int x = 0; x < pjobpil->NumberOfProcessIdsInList; x++) {
      // Use pjobpil->ProcessIdList[x]...
   }

   // Since _alloca was used to allocate the memory,
   // we don't need to free it here.
}
```

This is all the information you get using these functions, but the operating system actually keeps a lot more information about jobs. It does this using performance counters; you can retrieve the information using the functions in the Performance Data Helper function library (PDH.dll). You can also use the Microsoft Management Console (MMC) Performance Monitor Snap-In to view the job information. The dialog box in Figure 5-3 shows some of the counters available for job objects in the system. Figure 5-4 shows some of the available job object details counters. You can also see that Jeff's job has four processes in it: calc, cmd, notepad, and wordpad.

Note that you can obtain performance counter information only for jobs that were assigned names when *CreateJobObject* was called. For this reason, you might want to create job objects with names even though you do not intend to share these objects across process boundaries by name.

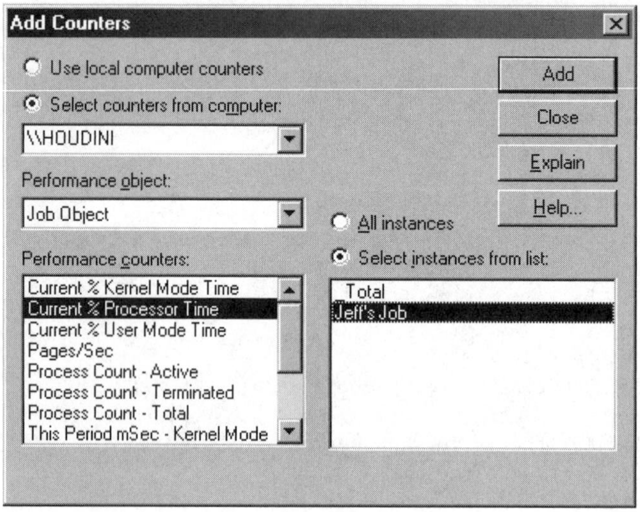

Figure 5-3.
MMC Performance Monitor: job object counters

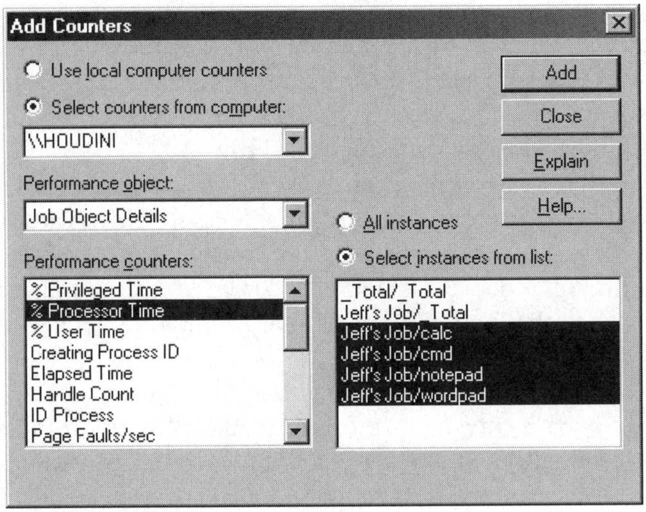

Figure 5-4.
MMC Performance Monitor: job object details counters

Job Notifications

At this point, you certainly know the basics about job objects; the only thing left to cover is notifications. For example, wouldn't you like to know when all of the processes in the job terminate or if all the allotted CPU time has expired? Or maybe you'd like to know when a new process is spawned within a job or when a process in the job terminates. If you don't care about these notifications—and many applications won't care— working with jobs is as easy as what I've already described. If you do care about these events, you have a little more to do.

If all you care about is whether all the allotted CPU time has expired, you can easily get this notification. Job objects are nonsignaled while the processes in the job have not used up the allotted CPU time. Once all the allotted CPU time has been used, Windows forcibly kills all the processes in the job and signals the job object. You can easily trap this event by calling *WaitForSingleObject* (or a similar function). Incidentally, you can reset the job object back to the nonsignaled state later by calling *SetInformationJobObject* and granting the job more CPU time.

When I first started working with jobs, it seemed to me that the job object should be signaled when no processes are running within it. After all, process and thread objects are signaled when they stop running; so it seemed that a job should be signaled when it stops running. In this way, you could easily determine when a job had run to completion. However, Microsoft chose to signal the job when the allotted time expires because that signals an error condition. Since many jobs start off with one parent process that hangs around until all its children are done, you can simply wait on the parent process's handle to know when the entire job is finished. My *StartRestrictedProcess* function shows how to determine when the job's allotted time has expired or when the parent process in the job has terminated.

Well, I've described how to get some simple notifications, but I haven't explained what you need to do to get more "advanced" notifications such as process creation/termination. If you want these additional notifications, you must put a lot more infrastructure into your application. In particular, you must create an I/O completion port kernel object and associate your job object or objects with the completion port. Then you must have one or more threads that wait on the completion port for job notifications to arrive so that they can be processed.

Once you create the I/O completion port, you associate a job with it by calling *SetInformationJobObject*, as follows:

```
JOBOBJECT_ASSOCIATE_COMPLETION_PORT joacp;
joacp.CompletionKey  = 1;    // Any value to uniquely identify this job
joacp.CompletionPort = hIOCP;   // Handle of completion port that
                                // receives notifications
SetInformationJobObject(hJob, JobObjectAssociateCompletionPortInformation,
   &joacp,  sizeof(jaocp));
```

After the code above executes, the system monitors the job, and as events occur it posts them to the I/O completion port. (By the way, you can call *Query-InformationJobObject* to retrieve the completion key and completion port handle, but it is rare that you ever have to do this.) Threads monitor an I/O completion port by calling *GetQueuedCompletionStatus*:

```
BOOL GetQueuedCompletionStatus(
    HANDLE hIOCP,
    PDWORD pNumBytesTransferred,
    PULONG_PTR pCompletionKey,
    POVERLAPPED *pOverlapped,
    DWORD dwMilliseconds);
```

When this function returns a job event notification, *pCompletionKey* contains the completion key value set when *SetInformationJobObject* was called to associate the job with the completion port. This lets you know which job had an event. The value in *pNumBytesTransferred* indicates which event occurred. (See Table 5-4.) Depending on the event, the value in *pOverlapped* will indicate a process ID.

Event	Description
JOB_OBJECT_MSG_ACTIVE_PROCESS_ZERO	Posted when no processes are running in the job.
JOB_OBJECT_MSG_END_OF_PROCESS_TIME	Posted when a process's allotted CPU time is exceeded. The process is terminated and the process's ID is given.
JOB_OBJECT_MSG_ACTIVE_PROCESS_LIMIT	Posted when attempting to exceed the number of active processes in the job.
JOB_OBJECT_MSG_PROCESS_MEMORY_LIMIT	Posted when a process attempts to commit storage over the process's limit. The process's ID is given.
JOB_OBJECT_MSG_JOB_MEMORY_LIMIT	Posted when a process attempts to commit storage over the job's limit. The process's ID is given.
JOB_OBJECT_MSG_NEW_PROCESS	Posted when a process is added to a job. The process's ID is given.
JOB_OBJECT_MSG_EXIT_PROCESS	Posted when a process terminates. The process's ID is given.
JOB_OBJECT_MSG_ABNORMAL_EXIT_PROCESS	Posted when a process terminates due to an unhandled exception. The process's ID is given.
JOB_OBJECT_MSG_END_OF_JOB_TIME	Posted when the job's allotted CPU time is exceeded. The processes are not terminated. You can allow them to continue running, set a new time limit, or call *TerminateJobObject* yourself.

Table 5-4.
Job event notifications that the system can send to a job's associated completion port

Just one last note: by default, a job object is configured so that when the job's allotted CPU time expires, all the job's processes are automatically terminated and the JOB_OBJECT_MSG_END_OF_JOB_TIME notification does not get posted. If you want to prevent the job object from killing the processes and instead just notify you that the time has been exceeded, you must execute code like this:

```
// Create a JOBOBJECT_END_OF_JOB_TIME_INFORMATION structure
// and initialize its only member.
JOBOBJECT_END_OF_JOB_TIME_INFORMATION joeojti;
joeojti.EndOfJobTimeAction = JOB_OBJECT_POST_AT_END_OF_JOB;

// Tell the job object what we want it to do when the job time is
// exceeded.
SetInformationJobObject(hJob, JobObjectEndOfJobTimeInformation,
   &joeojti, sizeof(joeojti));
```

The only other value you can specify for an end-of-job-time action is JOB_OBJECT_TERMINATE_AT_END_OF_JOB, which is the default when jobs are created anyway.

The JobLab Sample Application

The JobLab application, "05 JobLab.exe" (listed in Figure 5-6), allows you to easily experiment with jobs. The source code and resource files for the application are in the 05-JobLab directory on the companion CD-ROM. When you start the program, the window shown in Figure 5-5 appears.

When the process initializes, it creates a job object. I created this job object with the name JobLab so you can use the MMC Performance Monitor Snap-In to see it and monitor its performance. The application also creates an I/O completion port and associates the job object with it. This allows notifications from the job to be monitored and displayed in the list box at the bottom of the window.

Initially, the job has no processes and no limits or restrictions. The fields at the top set basic and extended limits on the job object. All you do is fill them in with valid values and click on the Apply Limits button. If you leave a field empty, that limit will not be applied. Besides the basic and extended limits, you can turn various UI restrictions on and off. Note that the Preserve Job Time When Applying Limits check box does not set a limit; it simply allows you to change the job's limits without resetting the *ThisPeriodTotalUserTime* and *ThisPeriodTotalKernelTime* members when querying the basic accounting information. This check box is disabled when you apply a per-job time limit.

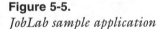

Figure 5-5.
JobLab sample application

The remaining buttons let you manipulate the job in other ways. The Terminate Processes button kills all the processes in the job. The Spawn CMD In Job button spawns a command shell process that is associated with the job. From this command shell, you can spawn additional child processes and see how they behave as part of the job. I found this very useful for experimenting. The last button, Put PID In Job, lets you associate an existing jobless process with the job.

The list box at the bottom of the window shows updated status information about the job. Every 10 seconds, this window shows the basic and I/O accounting information as well as the peak process/job memory usage. The process ID for each process currently in the job is also shown.

In addition to all this statistical information, the list box displays any notifications that come from the job to the application's I/O completion port. Whenever a notification is posted to the list box, the status information at that time is also displayed.

One last note: if you modify the source code and create the job kernel object without a name, you can run multiple copies of this application to create two or more job objects on the same machine and perform more experiments that way.

As far as the source code goes, there isn't anything special to discuss because the source code is well annotated. I did, however, create a Job.h file that defines a CJob C++ class that encapsulates the operating system's job object. This made things a little easier to work with since I didn't have to pass around the job's handle. This class also reduces the amount of casting that I would ordinarily need to do when calling the *QueryInformationJobObject* and *SetInformationJobObject* functions.

JobLab.cpp

```
/*****************************************************************************
Module:  JobLab.cpp
Notices: Copyright (c) 2000 Jeffrey Richter
*****************************************************************************/


#include "..\CmnHdr.h"
#include <windowsx.h>
#include <process.h>     // for _beginthreadex
#include <tchar.h>
#include <stdio.h>
#include "Resource.h"
#include "Job.h"



///////////////////////////////////////////////////////////////////////////


CJob    g_job;              // Job object

HWND    g_hwnd;             // Handle to dialog box (accessible by all threads)

HANDLE g_hIOCP;            // Completion port that receives Job notifications
HANDLE g_hThreadIOCP;      // Completion port thread

// Completion keys for the completion port
#define COMPKEY_TERMINATE    ((UINT_PTR) 0)
#define COMPKEY_STATUS       ((UINT_PTR) 1)
#define COMPKEY_JOBOBJECT    ((UINT_PTR) 2)



///////////////////////////////////////////////////////////////////////////
```

Figure 5-6.
The JobLab sample application

(continued)

Figure 5-6. *continued*

```
DWORD WINAPI JobNotify(PVOID) {
   TCHAR sz[2000];
   BOOL fDone = FALSE;

   while (!fDone) {
      DWORD dwBytesXferred;
      ULONG_PTR CompKey;
      LPOVERLAPPED po;
      GetQueuedCompletionStatus(g_hIOCP,
         &dwBytesXferred, &CompKey, &po, INFINITE);

      // The app is shutting down, exit this thread
      fDone = (CompKey == COMPKEY_TERMINATE);

      HWND hwndLB = FindWindow(NULL, TEXT("Job Lab"));
      hwndLB = GetDlgItem(hwndLB, IDC_STATUS);


      if (CompKey == COMPKEY_JOBOBJECT) {
         lstrcpy(sz, TEXT("--> Notification: "));
         LPTSTR psz = sz + lstrlen(sz);
         switch (dwBytesXferred) {
         case JOB_OBJECT_MSG_END_OF_JOB_TIME:
            wsprintf(psz, TEXT("Job time limit reached"));
            break;

         case JOB_OBJECT_MSG_END_OF_PROCESS_TIME:
            wsprintf(psz, TEXT("Job process (Id=%d) time limit reached"), po);
            break;

         case JOB_OBJECT_MSG_ACTIVE_PROCESS_LIMIT:
            wsprintf(psz, TEXT("Too many active processes in job"));
            break;

         case JOB_OBJECT_MSG_ACTIVE_PROCESS_ZERO:
            wsprintf(psz, TEXT("Job contains no active processes"));
            break;

         case JOB_OBJECT_MSG_NEW_PROCESS:
            wsprintf(psz, TEXT("New process (Id=%d) in Job"), po);
            break;

         case JOB_OBJECT_MSG_EXIT_PROCESS:
            wsprintf(psz, TEXT("Process (Id=%d) terminated"), po);
            break;
```

(continued)

Figure 5-6. *continued*

```
        case JOB_OBJECT_MSG_ABNORMAL_EXIT_PROCESS:
            wsprintf(psz, TEXT("Process (Id=%d) terminated abnormally"), po);
            break;

        case JOB_OBJECT_MSG_PROCESS_MEMORY_LIMIT:
            wsprintf(psz, TEXT("Process (Id=%d) exceeded memory limit"), po);
            break;

        case JOB_OBJECT_MSG_JOB_MEMORY_LIMIT:
            wsprintf(psz,
                TEXT("Process (Id=%d) exceeded job memory limit"), po);
            break;

        default:
            wsprintf(psz, TEXT("Unknown notification: %d"), dwBytesXferred);
            break;
        }
        ListBox_SetCurSel(hwndLB, ListBox_AddString(hwndLB, sz));
        CompKey = 1;    // Force a status update when a notification arrives
}


    if (CompKey == COMPKEY_STATUS) {

        static int s_nStatusCount = 0;
        _stprintf(sz, TEXT("--> Status Update (%u)"), s_nStatusCount++);
        ListBox_SetCurSel(hwndLB, ListBox_AddString(hwndLB, sz));

        // Show the basic accounting information
        JOBOBJECT_BASIC_AND_IO_ACCOUNTING_INFORMATION jobai;
        g_job.QueryBasicAccountingInfo(&jobai);

        _stprintf(sz, TEXT("Total Time: User=%I64u, Kernel=%I64u        ")
            TEXT("Period Time: User=%I64u, Kernel=%I64u"),
            jobai.BasicInfo.TotalUserTime.QuadPart,
            jobai.BasicInfo.TotalKernelTime.QuadPart,
            jobai.BasicInfo.ThisPeriodTotalUserTime.QuadPart,
            jobai.BasicInfo.ThisPeriodTotalKernelTime.QuadPart);
        ListBox_SetCurSel(hwndLB, ListBox_AddString(hwndLB, sz));

        _stprintf(sz, TEXT("Page Faults=%u, Total Processes=%u, ")
            TEXT("Active Processes=%u, Terminated Processes=%u"),
            jobai.BasicInfo.TotalPageFaultCount,
            jobai.BasicInfo.TotalProcesses,
```

(continued)

Figure 5-6. *continued*

```
            jobai.BasicInfo.ActiveProcesses,
            jobai.BasicInfo.TotalTerminatedProcesses);
      ListBox_SetCurSel(hwndLB, ListBox_AddString(hwndLB, sz));

      // Show the I/O accounting information
      _stprintf(sz, TEXT("Reads=%I64u (%I64u bytes), ")
         TEXT("Write=%I64u (%I64u bytes), Other=%I64u (%I64u bytes)"),
         jobai.IoInfo.ReadOperationCount,  jobai.IoInfo.ReadTransferCount,
         jobai.IoInfo.WriteOperationCount, jobai.IoInfo.WriteTransferCount,
         jobai.IoInfo.OtherOperationCount, jobai.IoInfo.OtherTransferCount);
      ListBox_SetCurSel(hwndLB, ListBox_AddString(hwndLB, sz));

      // Show the peak per-process and job memory usage
      JOBOBJECT_EXTENDED_LIMIT_INFORMATION joeli;
      g_job.QueryExtendedLimitInfo(&joeli);
      _stprintf(sz, TEXT("Peak memory used: Process=%I64u, Job=%I64u"),
         (__int64) joeli.PeakProcessMemoryUsed,
         (__int64) joeli.PeakJobMemoryUsed);
      ListBox_SetCurSel(hwndLB, ListBox_AddString(hwndLB, sz));

      // Show the set of Process IDs
      DWORD dwNumProcesses = 50, dwProcessIdList[50];
      g_job.QueryBasicProcessIdList(dwNumProcesses,
         dwProcessIdList, &dwNumProcesses);
      _stprintf(sz, TEXT("PIDs: %s"),
         (dwNumProcesses == 0) ? TEXT("(none)") : TEXT(""));
      for (DWORD x = 0; x < dwNumProcesses; x++) {
         _stprintf(_tcschr(sz, 0), TEXT("%d "), dwProcessIdList[x]);
      }
      ListBox_SetCurSel(hwndLB, ListBox_AddString(hwndLB, sz));
   }
}
return(0);
}


/////////////////////////////////////////////////////////////////////////////


BOOL Dlg_OnInitDialog (HWND hwnd, HWND hwndFocus, LPARAM lParam) {

   chSETDLGICONS(hwnd, IDI_JOBLAB);

   // Save our window handle so that the completion port thread can access it
   g_hwnd = hwnd;
```

(continued)

Figure 5-6. *continued*

```
    HWND hwndPriorityClass = GetDlgItem(hwnd, IDC_PRIORITYCLASS);
    ComboBox_AddString(hwndPriorityClass, TEXT("No limit"));
    ComboBox_AddString(hwndPriorityClass, TEXT("Idle"));
    ComboBox_AddString(hwndPriorityClass, TEXT("Below normal"));
    ComboBox_AddString(hwndPriorityClass, TEXT("Normal"));
    ComboBox_AddString(hwndPriorityClass, TEXT("Above normal"));
    ComboBox_AddString(hwndPriorityClass, TEXT("High"));
    ComboBox_AddString(hwndPriorityClass, TEXT("Realtime"));
    ComboBox_SetCurSel(hwndPriorityClass, 0); // Default to "No Limit"

    HWND hwndSchedulingClass = GetDlgItem(hwnd, IDC_SCHEDULINGCLASS);
    ComboBox_AddString(hwndSchedulingClass, TEXT("No limit"));
    for (int n = 0; n <= 9; n++) {
        TCHAR szSchedulingClass[2] = { (TCHAR) (TEXT('0') + n), 0 };
        ComboBox_AddString(hwndSchedulingClass, szSchedulingClass);
    }
    ComboBox_SetCurSel(hwndSchedulingClass, 0); // Default to "No Limit"
    SetTimer(hwnd, 1, 10000, NULL);                // 10 second accounting update
    return(TRUE);
}


///////////////////////////////////////////////////////////////////////////////


void Dlg_ApplyLimits(HWND hwnd) {
    const int nNanosecondsPerSecond = 100000000;
    const int nMillisecondsPerSecond = 1000;
    const int nNanosecondsPerMillisecond =
        nNanosecondsPerSecond / nMillisecondsPerSecond;
    BOOL f;
    __int64 q;
    SIZE_T s;
    DWORD d;

    // Set Basic and Extended Limits
    JOBOBJECT_EXTENDED_LIMIT_INFORMATION joeli = { 0 };
    joeli.BasicLimitInformation.LimitFlags = 0;

    q = GetDlgItemInt(hwnd, IDC_PERPROCESSUSERTIMELIMIT, &f, FALSE);
    if (f) {
        joeli.BasicLimitInformation.LimitFlags |= JOB_OBJECT_LIMIT_PROCESS_TIME;
        joeli.BasicLimitInformation.PerProcessUserTimeLimit.QuadPart =
            q * nNanosecondsPerMillisecond / 100;
    }
```

(continued)

Figure 5-6. *continued*

```
q = GetDlgItemInt(hwnd, IDC_PERJOBUSERTIMELIMIT, &f, FALSE);
if (f) {
   joeli.BasicLimitInformation.LimitFlags |= JOB_OBJECT_LIMIT_JOB_TIME;
   joeli.BasicLimitInformation.PerJobUserTimeLimit.QuadPart =
      q * nNanosecondsPerMillisecond / 100;
}

s = GetDlgItemInt(hwnd, IDC_MINWORKINGSETSIZE, &f, FALSE);
if (f) {
   joeli.BasicLimitInformation.LimitFlags |= JOB_OBJECT_LIMIT_WORKINGSET;
   joeli.BasicLimitInformation.MinimumWorkingSetSize = s * 1024 * 1024;
   s = GetDlgItemInt(hwnd, IDC_MAXWORKINGSETSIZE, &f, FALSE);
   if (f) {
      joeli.BasicLimitInformation.MaximumWorkingSetSize = s * 1024 * 1024;
   } else {
      joeli.BasicLimitInformation.LimitFlags &=~JOB_OBJECT_LIMIT_WORKINGSET;
      chMB("Both minimum and maximum working set sizes must be set.\n"
         "The working set limits will NOT be in effect.");
   }
}

d = GetDlgItemInt(hwnd, IDC_ACTIVEPROCESSLIMIT, &f, FALSE);
if (f) {
   joeli.BasicLimitInformation.LimitFlags |=
      JOB_OBJECT_LIMIT_ACTIVE_PROCESS;
   joeli.BasicLimitInformation.ActiveProcessLimit = d;
}

s = GetDlgItemInt(hwnd, IDC_AFFINITYMASK, &f, FALSE);
if (f) {
   joeli.BasicLimitInformation.LimitFlags |= JOB_OBJECT_LIMIT_AFFINITY;
   joeli.BasicLimitInformation.Affinity = s;
}

joeli.BasicLimitInformation.LimitFlags |= JOB_OBJECT_LIMIT_PRIORITY_CLASS;
switch (ComboBox_GetCurSel(GetDlgItem(hwnd, IDC_PRIORITYCLASS))) {
   case 0:
      joeli.BasicLimitInformation.LimitFlags &=
         ~JOB_OBJECT_LIMIT_PRIORITY_CLASS;
      break;

   case 1:
      joeli.BasicLimitInformation.PriorityClass =
         IDLE_PRIORITY_CLASS;
      break;
```

(continued)

Figure 5-6. *continued*

```
    case 2:
        joeli.BasicLimitInformation.PriorityClass =
            BELOW_NORMAL_PRIORITY_CLASS;
        break;

    case 3:
        joeli.BasicLimitInformation.PriorityClass =
            NORMAL_PRIORITY_CLASS;
        break;

    case 4:
        joeli.BasicLimitInformation.PriorityClass =
            ABOVE_NORMAL_PRIORITY_CLASS;
        break;

    case 5:
        joeli.BasicLimitInformation.PriorityClass =
            HIGH_PRIORITY_CLASS;
        break;

    case 6:
        joeli.BasicLimitInformation.PriorityClass =
            REALTIME_PRIORITY_CLASS;
        break;
}

int nSchedulingClass =
    ComboBox_GetCurSel(GetDlgItem(hwnd, IDC_SCHEDULINGCLASS));
if (nSchedulingClass > 0) {
    joeli.BasicLimitInformation.LimitFlags |=
        JOB_OBJECT_LIMIT_SCHEDULING_CLASS;
    joeli.BasicLimitInformation.SchedulingClass = nSchedulingClass - 1;
}

s = GetDlgItemInt(hwnd, IDC_MAXCOMMITPERJOB, &f, FALSE);
if (f) {
    joeli.BasicLimitInformation.LimitFlags |= JOB_OBJECT_LIMIT_JOB_MEMORY;
    joeli.JobMemoryLimit = s * 1024 * 1024;
}

s = GetDlgItemInt(hwnd, IDC_MAXCOMMITPERPROCESS, &f, FALSE);
if (f) {
    joeli.BasicLimitInformation.LimitFlags |=
        JOB_OBJECT_LIMIT_PROCESS_MEMORY;
    joeli.ProcessMemoryLimit = s * 1024 * 1024;
}
```

(continued)

Figure 5-6. *continued*

```
    if (IsDlgButtonChecked(hwnd, IDC_CHILDPROCESSESCANBREAKAWAYFROMJOB))
        joeli.BasicLimitInformation.LimitFlags |= JOB_OBJECT_LIMIT_BREAKAWAY_OK;

    if (IsDlgButtonChecked(hwnd, IDC_CHILDPROCESSESDOBREAKAWAYFROMJOB))
        joeli.BasicLimitInformation.LimitFlags |=
        JOB_OBJECT_LIMIT_SILENT_BREAKAWAY_OK;

    if (IsDlgButtonChecked(hwnd, IDC_TERMINATEPROCESSONEXCEPTIONS))
        joeli.BasicLimitInformation.LimitFlags |=
        JOB_OBJECT_LIMIT_DIE_ON_UNHANDLED_EXCEPTION;

    f = g_job.SetExtendedLimitInfo(&joeli,
        ((joeli.BasicLimitInformation.LimitFlags & JOB_OBJECT_LIMIT_JOB_TIME)
            != 0) ? FALSE :
            IsDlgButtonChecked(hwnd, IDC_PRESERVEJOBTIMEWHENAPPLYINGLIMITS));
    chASSERT(f);

    // Set UI Restrictions
    DWORD jobuir = JOB_OBJECT_UILIMIT_NONE;  // A fancy zero (0)
    if (IsDlgButtonChecked(hwnd, IDC_RESTRICTACCESSTOOUTSIDEUSEROBJECTS))
        jobuir |= JOB_OBJECT_UILIMIT_HANDLES;

    if (IsDlgButtonChecked(hwnd, IDC_RESTRICTREADINGCLIPBOARD))
        jobuir |= JOB_OBJECT_UILIMIT_READCLIPBOARD;

    if (IsDlgButtonChecked(hwnd, IDC_RESTRICTWRITINGCLIPBOARD))
        jobuir |= JOB_OBJECT_UILIMIT_WRITECLIPBOARD;

    if (IsDlgButtonChecked(hwnd, IDC_RESTRICTEXITWINDOW))
        jobuir |= JOB_OBJECT_UILIMIT_EXITWINDOWS;

    if (IsDlgButtonChecked(hwnd, IDC_RESTRICTCHANGINGSYSTEMPARAMETERS))
        jobuir |= JOB_OBJECT_UILIMIT_SYSTEMPARAMETERS;

    if (IsDlgButtonChecked(hwnd, IDC_RESTRICTDESKTOPS))
        jobuir |= JOB_OBJECT_UILIMIT_DESKTOP;

    if (IsDlgButtonChecked(hwnd, IDC_RESTRICTDISPLAYSETTINGS))
        jobuir |= JOB_OBJECT_UILIMIT_DISPLAYSETTINGS;

    if (IsDlgButtonChecked(hwnd, IDC_RESTRICTGLOBALATOMS))
        jobuir |= JOB_OBJECT_UILIMIT_GLOBALATOMS;

    chVERIFY(g_job.SetBasicUIRestrictions(jobuir));
}
```

(continued)

Figure 5-6. *continued*

```
/////////////////////////////////////////////////////////////////////////////

void Dlg_OnCommand(HWND hwnd, int id, HWND hwndCtl, UINT codeNotify) {

   switch (id) {
      case IDCANCEL:
         // User is terminating our app, kill the job too.
         KillTimer(hwnd, 1);
         g_job.Terminate(0);
         EndDialog(hwnd, id);
         break;

      case IDC_PERJOBUSERTIMELIMIT:
         {
         // The job time must be reset if setting a job time limit
         BOOL f;
         GetDlgItemInt(hwnd, IDC_PERJOBUSERTIMELIMIT, &f, FALSE);
         EnableWindow(
            GetDlgItem(hwnd, IDC_PRESERVEJOBTIMEWHENAPPLYINGLIMITS), !f);
         }
         break;

      case IDC_APPLYLIMITS:
         Dlg_ApplyLimits(hwnd);
         PostQueuedCompletionStatus(g_hIOCP, 0, COMPKEY_STATUS, NULL);
         break;

      case IDC_TERMINATE:
         g_job.Terminate(0);
         PostQueuedCompletionStatus(g_hIOCP, 0, COMPKEY_STATUS, NULL);
         break;

      case IDC_SPAWNCMDINJOB:
         {
         // Spawn a command shell and place it in the job
         STARTUPINFO si = { sizeof(si) };
         PROCESS_INFORMATION pi;
         TCHAR sz[] = TEXT("CMD");
         CreateProcess(NULL, sz, NULL, NULL,
            FALSE, CREATE_SUSPENDED, NULL, NULL, &si, &pi);
         g_job.AssignProcess(pi.hProcess);
         ResumeThread(pi.hThread);
         CloseHandle(pi.hProcess);
         CloseHandle(pi.hThread);
         }
         PostQueuedCompletionStatus(g_hIOCP, 0, COMPKEY_STATUS, NULL);
         break;
```

(continued)

Figure 5-6. *continued*

```
      case IDC_ASSIGNPROCESSTOJOB:
          {
          DWORD dwProcessId = GetDlgItemInt(hwnd, IDC_PROCESSID, NULL, FALSE);
          HANDLE hProcess = OpenProcess(
              PROCESS_SET_QUOTA | PROCESS_TERMINATE, FALSE, dwProcessId);
          if (hProcess != NULL) {
              chVERIFY(g_job.AssignProcess(hProcess));
              CloseHandle(hProcess);
          } else chMB("Could not assign process to job.");
          }
          PostQueuedCompletionStatus(g_hIOCP, 0, COMPKEY_STATUS, NULL);
          break;
      }
}


///////////////////////////////////////////////////////////////////////////


void WINAPI Dlg_OnTimer(HWND hwnd, UINT id) {

   PostQueuedCompletionStatus(g_hIOCP, 0, COMPKEY_STATUS, NULL);
}


///////////////////////////////////////////////////////////////////////////


INT_PTR WINAPI Dlg_Proc (HWND hwnd, UINT uMsg, WPARAM wParam, LPARAM lParam) {

   switch (uMsg) {
      chHANDLE_DLGMSG(hwnd, WM_INITDIALOG, Dlg_OnInitDialog);
      chHANDLE_DLGMSG(hwnd, WM_TIMER,      Dlg_OnTimer);
      chHANDLE_DLGMSG(hwnd, WM_COMMAND,    Dlg_OnCommand);
   }

   return(FALSE);
}


///////////////////////////////////////////////////////////////////////////


int WINAPI _tWinMain(HINSTANCE hinstExe, HINSTANCE, LPTSTR pszCmdLine, int) {

   // Create the completion port that receives job notifications
   g_hIOCP = CreateIoCompletionPort(INVALID_HANDLE_VALUE, NULL, 0, 0);

   // Create a thread that waits on the completion port
   g_hThreadIOCP = chBEGINTHREADEX(NULL, 0, JobNotify, NULL, 0, NULL);
```

(continued)

Figure 5-6. *continued*

```
    // Create the job object
    g_job.Create(NULL, TEXT("JobLab"));
    g_job.SetEndOfJobInfo(JOB_OBJECT_POST_AT_END_OF_JOB);
    g_job.AssociateCompletionPort(g_hIOCP, COMPKEY_JOBOBJECT);

    DialogBox(hinstExe, MAKEINTRESOURCE(IDD_JOBLAB), NULL, Dlg_Proc);

    // Post a special key that tells the completion port thread to terminate
    PostQueuedCompletionStatus(g_hIOCP, 0, COMPKEY_TERMINATE, NULL);

    // Wait for the completion port thread to terminate
    WaitForSingleObject(g_hThreadIOCP, INFINITE);

    // Clean up everything properly
    CloseHandle(g_hIOCP);
    CloseHandle(g_hThreadIOCP);

    // NOTE: The job is closed when the g_job's destructor is called.
    return(0);
}


///////////////////////////////// End Of File /////////////////////////////////
```

Job.h

```
/******************************************************************************
Module:  Job.h
Notices: Copyright (c) 2000 Jeffrey Richter
******************************************************************************/


#pragma once


//////////////////////////////////////////////////////////////////////////////


#include <malloc.h>  // for _alloca


//////////////////////////////////////////////////////////////////////////////
```

(continued)

Figure 5-6. *continued*

```
class CJob {
public:
   CJob(HANDLE hJob = NULL);
   ~CJob();

   operator HANDLE() const { return(m_hJob); }

   // Functions to create/open a job object
   BOOL Create(LPSECURITY_ATTRIBUTES psa = NULL, LPCTSTR pszName = NULL);
   BOOL Open(LPCTSTR pszName, DWORD dwDesiredAccess,
      BOOL fInheritHandle = FALSE);

   // Functions that manipulate a job object
   BOOL AssignProcess(HANDLE hProcess);
   BOOL Terminate(UINT uExitCode = 0);

   // Functions that set limits/restrictions on the job
   BOOL SetExtendedLimitInfo(PJOBOBJECT_EXTENDED_LIMIT_INFORMATION pjoeli,
      BOOL fPreserveJobTime = FALSE);
   BOOL SetBasicUIRestrictions(DWORD fdwLimits);
   BOOL GrantUserHandleAccess(HANDLE hUserObj, BOOL fGrant = TRUE);
   BOOL SetSecurityLimitInfo(PJOBOBJECT_SECURITY_LIMIT_INFORMATION pjosli);

   // Functions that query job limits/restrictions
   BOOL QueryExtendedLimitInfo(PJOBOBJECT_EXTENDED_LIMIT_INFORMATION pjoeli);
   BOOL QueryBasicUIRestrictions(PDWORD pfdwRestrictions);
   BOOL QuerySecurityLimitInfo(PJOBOBJECT_SECURITY_LIMIT_INFORMATION pjosli);

   // Functions that query job status information
   BOOL QueryBasicAccountingInfo(
      PJOBOBJECT_BASIC_AND_IO_ACCOUNTING_INFORMATION pjobai);
   BOOL QueryBasicProcessIdList(DWORD dwMaxProcesses,
      PDWORD pdwProcessIdList, PDWORD pdwProcessesReturned = NULL);

   // Functions that set/query job event notifications
   BOOL AssociateCompletionPort(HANDLE hIOCP, ULONG_PTR CompKey);
   BOOL QueryAssociatedCompletionPort(
      PJOBOBJECT_ASSOCIATE_COMPLETION_PORT pjoacp);
   BOOL SetEndOfJobInfo(
      DWORD fdwEndOfJobInfo = JOB_OBJECT_TERMINATE_AT_END_OF_JOB);
   BOOL QueryEndOfJobTimeInfo(PDWORD pfdwEndOfJobTimeInfo);

private:
   HANDLE m_hJob;
};
```

(continued)

Figure 5-6. *continued*

```
/////////////////////////////////////////////////////////////////////////////////


inline CJob::CJob(HANDLE hJob) {

   m_hJob = hJob;
}


/////////////////////////////////////////////////////////////////////////////////


inline CJob::~CJob() {

   if (m_hJob != NULL)
      CloseHandle(m_hJob);
}


/////////////////////////////////////////////////////////////////////////////////


inline BOOL CJob::Create(PSECURITY_ATTRIBUTES psa, PCTSTR pszName) {

   m_hJob = CreateJobObject(psa, pszName);
   return(m_hJob != NULL);
}


/////////////////////////////////////////////////////////////////////////////////


inline BOOL CJob::Open(
   PCTSTR pszName, DWORD dwDesiredAccess, BOOL fInheritHandle) {

   m_hJob = OpenJobObject(dwDesiredAccess, fInheritHandle, pszName);
   return(m_hJob != NULL);
}


/////////////////////////////////////////////////////////////////////////////////
```

(continued)

Figure 5-6. *continued*

```
inline BOOL CJob::AssignProcess(HANDLE hProcess) {

   return(AssignProcessToJobObject(m_hJob, hProcess));
}


////////////////////////////////////////////////////////////////////////////////


inline BOOL CJob::AssociateCompletionPort(HANDLE hIOCP, ULONG_PTR CompKey) {

   JOBOBJECT_ASSOCIATE_COMPLETION_PORT joacp = { (PVOID) CompKey, hIOCP };
   return(SetInformationJobObject(m_hJob,
      JobObjectAssociateCompletionPortInformation, &joacp, sizeof(joacp)));
}


////////////////////////////////////////////////////////////////////////////////


inline BOOL CJob::SetExtendedLimitInfo(
   PJOBOBJECT_EXTENDED_LIMIT_INFORMATION pjoeli, BOOL fPreserveJobTime) {

   if (fPreserveJobTime)
      pjoeli->BasicLimitInformation.LimitFlags |=
         JOB_OBJECT_LIMIT_PRESERVE_JOB_TIME;

   // If we are to preserve the job's time information,
   // the JOB_OBJECT_LIMIT_JOB_TIME flag must not be on
   const DWORD fdwFlagTest =
      (JOB_OBJECT_LIMIT_PRESERVE_JOB_TIME | JOB_OBJECT_LIMIT_JOB_TIME);

   if ((pjoeli->BasicLimitInformation.LimitFlags & fdwFlagTest)
      == fdwFlagTest) {
      // These flags are mutually exclusive but both are on, error
      DebugBreak();
   }

   return(SetInformationJobObject(m_hJob,
      JobObjectExtendedLimitInformation, pjoeli, sizeof(*pjoeli)));
}


////////////////////////////////////////////////////////////////////////////////
```

(continued)

Figure 5-6. *continued*

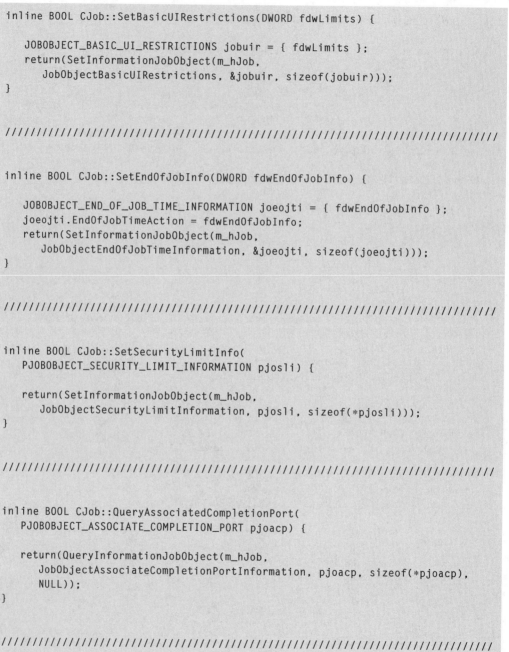

```
inline BOOL CJob::SetBasicUIRestrictions(DWORD fdwLimits) {

   JOBOBJECT_BASIC_UI_RESTRICTIONS jobuir = { fdwLimits };
   return(SetInformationJobObject(m_hJob,
      JobObjectBasicUIRestrictions, &jobuir, sizeof(jobuir)));
}


///////////////////////////////////////////////////////////////////////////////


inline BOOL CJob::SetEndOfJobInfo(DWORD fdwEndOfJobInfo) {

   JOBOBJECT_END_OF_JOB_TIME_INFORMATION joeojti = { fdwEndOfJobInfo };
   joeojti.EndOfJobTimeAction = fdwEndOfJobInfo;
   return(SetInformationJobObject(m_hJob,
      JobObjectEndOfJobTimeInformation, &joeojti, sizeof(joeojti)));
}


///////////////////////////////////////////////////////////////////////////////


inline BOOL CJob::SetSecurityLimitInfo(
   PJOBOBJECT_SECURITY_LIMIT_INFORMATION pjosli) {

   return(SetInformationJobObject(m_hJob,
      JobObjectSecurityLimitInformation, pjosli, sizeof(*pjosli)));
}


///////////////////////////////////////////////////////////////////////////////


inline BOOL CJob::QueryAssociatedCompletionPort(
   PJOBOBJECT_ASSOCIATE_COMPLETION_PORT pjoacp) {

   return(QueryInformationJobObject(m_hJob,
      JobObjectAssociateCompletionPortInformation, pjoacp, sizeof(*pjoacp),
      NULL));
}


///////////////////////////////////////////////////////////////////////////////
```

(continued)

Figure 5-6. *continued*

```
inline BOOL CJob::QueryBasicAccountingInfo(
   PJOBOBJECT_BASIC_AND_IO_ACCOUNTING_INFORMATION pjobai) {

   return(QueryInformationJobObject(m_hJob,
      JobObjectBasicAndIoAccountingInformation, pjobai, sizeof(*pjobai),
      NULL));
}


///////////////////////////////////////////////////////////////////////////


inline BOOL CJob::QueryExtendedLimitInfo(
   PJOBOBJECT_EXTENDED_LIMIT_INFORMATION pjoeli) {

   return(QueryInformationJobObject(m_hJob, JobObjectExtendedLimitInformation,
      pjoeli, sizeof(*pjoeli), NULL));
}


///////////////////////////////////////////////////////////////////////////


inline BOOL CJob::QueryBasicProcessIdList(DWORD dwMaxProcesses,
   PDWORD pdwProcessIdList, PDWORD pdwProcessesReturned) {

   // Calculate the # of bytes necessary
   DWORD cb = sizeof(JOBOBJECT_BASIC_PROCESS_ID_LIST) +
      (sizeof(DWORD) * (dwMaxProcesses - 1));

   // Allocate those bytes from the stack
   PJOBOBJECT_BASIC_PROCESS_ID_LIST pjobpil =
      (PJOBOBJECT_BASIC_PROCESS_ID_LIST) _alloca(cb);

   // Were those bytes allocated OK? If so, keep going
   BOOL fOk = (pjobpil != NULL);

   if (fOk) {
      pjobpil->NumberOfProcessIdsInList = dwMaxProcesses;
      fOk = ::QueryInformationJobObject(m_hJob, JobObjectBasicProcessIdList,
         pjobpil, cb, NULL);

      if (fOk) {
         // We got the information, return it to the caller
         if (pdwProcessesReturned != NULL)
            *pdwProcessesReturned = pjobpil->NumberOfProcessIdsInList;
```

(continued)

175

Figure 5-6. *continued*

```
        CopyMemory(pdwProcessIdList, pjobpil->ProcessIdList,
            sizeof(DWORD) * pjobpil->NumberOfProcessIdsInList);
    }
  }
  return(fOk);
}


///////////////////////////////////////////////////////////////////////////////


inline BOOL CJob::QueryBasicUIRestrictions(PDWORD pfdwRestrictions) {

  JOBOBJECT_BASIC_UI_RESTRICTIONS jobuir;
  BOOL fOk = QueryInformationJobObject(m_hJob, JobObjectBasicUIRestrictions,
    &jobuir, sizeof(jobuir), NULL);
  if (fOk)
    *pfdwRestrictions = jobuir.UIRestrictionsClass;
  return(fOk);
}


///////////////////////////////////////////////////////////////////////////////


inline BOOL CJob::QueryEndOfJobTimeInfo(PDWORD pfdwEndOfJobTimeInfo) {

  JOBOBJECT_END_OF_JOB_TIME_INFORMATION joeojti;
  BOOL fOk = QueryInformationJobObject(m_hJob, JobObjectBasicUIRestrictions,
    &joeojti, sizeof(joeojti), NULL);
  if (fOk)
    *pfdwEndOfJobTimeInfo = joeojti.EndOfJobTimeAction;
  return(fOk);
}


///////////////////////////////////////////////////////////////////////////////


inline BOOL CJob::QuerySecurityLimitInfo(
  PJOBOBJECT_SECURITY_LIMIT_INFORMATION pjosli) {

  return(QueryInformationJobObject(m_hJob, JobObjectSecurityLimitInformation,
    pjosli, sizeof(*pjosli), NULL));
}
```

(continued)

Figure 5-6. *continued*

```
//////////////////////////////////////////////////////////////////////


inline BOOL CJob::Terminate(UINT uExitCode) {

   return(TerminateJobObject(m_hJob, uExitCode));
}


//////////////////////////////////////////////////////////////////////


inline BOOL CJob::GrantUserHandleAccess(HANDLE hUserObj, BOOL fGrant) {

   return(UserHandleGrantAccess(hUserObj, m_hJob, fGrant));
}


/////////////////////////////// End of File //////////////////////////////
```

JobLab.rc

```
//Microsoft Developer Studio generated resource script.
//
#include "resource.h"

#define APSTUDIO_READONLY_SYMBOLS
//////////////////////////////////////////////////////////////////////
//
// Generated from the TEXTINCLUDE 2 resource.
//
#include "afxres.h"

//////////////////////////////////////////////////////////////////////
#undef APSTUDIO_READONLY_SYMBOLS

//////////////////////////////////////////////////////////////////////
// English (U.S.) resources

#if !defined(AFX_RESOURCE_DLL) || defined(AFX_TARG_ENU)
#ifdef _WIN32
LANGUAGE LANG_ENGLISH, SUBLANG_ENGLISH_US
```

(continued)

Figure 5-6. *continued*

```
#pragma code_page(1252)
#endif //_WIN32


/////////////////////////////////////////////////////////////////////////////
//
// Icon
//

// Icon with lowest ID value placed first to ensure application icon
// remains consistent on all systems.
IDI_MEMRESET            ICON    DISCARDABLE     "MemReset.ico"

#ifdef APSTUDIO_INVOKED
/////////////////////////////////////////////////////////////////////////////
//
// TEXTINCLUDE
//
```

```
1 TEXTINCLUDE DISCARDABLE
BEGIN
    "resource.h\0"
END

2 TEXTINCLUDE DISCARDABLE
BEGIN
    "#include ""afxres.h""\r\n"
    "\0"
END

3 TEXTINCLUDE DISCARDABLE
BEGIN
    "\r\n"
    "\0"
END

#endif    // APSTUDIO_INVOKED

#endif    // English (U.S.) resources
/////////////////////////////////////////////////////////////////////////////
```

(continued)

Figure 5-6. *continued*

```
#ifndef APSTUDIO_INVOKED
/////////////////////////////////////////////////////////////////////////////
//
// Generated from the TEXTINCLUDE 3 resource.
//


/////////////////////////////////////////////////////////////////////////////
#endif    // not APSTUDIO_INVOKED
```

CHAPTER SIX

THREAD BASICS

It is critical that you understand threads because every process requires at least one thread. In this chapter, I'll go into much more detail about threads. In particular, I'll explain how processes and threads differ and what responsibility each has. I'll also explain how the system uses thread kernel objects to manage the threads. Like process kernel objects, thread kernel objects have properties, and we'll examine many of the functions that are available for querying and changing these properties. I'll also examine the functions you can use to create or spawn additional threads in a process.

In Chapter 4, we discussed how a process actually consists of two components: a process kernel object and an address space. Similarly, a thread consists of two components:

- A kernel object that the operating system uses to manage the thread. The kernel object is also where the system keeps statistical information about the thread.

- A thread stack that maintains all the function parameters and local variables required as the thread executes code. (In Chapter 16, I'll go into detail about how the system manages a thread's stack.)

I said in Chapter 4 that processes are inert. A process never executes anything; it is simply a container for threads. Threads are always created in the context of some process and live their entire life within that process. What this really means is that the thread executes code within its process's address space and manipulates data within its process's address space. So if you have two or more threads running in the context of a single process, the threads share a single address space. The threads can execute the same code and manipulate the same data. Threads can also share kernel object handles because the handle table exists for each process, not each thread.

As you can see, processes use a lot more system resources than threads do. The reason for this is the address space. Creating a virtual address space for a process requires a lot of system resources. A lot of record keeping takes place in the system, and this requires a lot of memory. Also, since .exe and .dll files get loaded into an address space, file resources are required as well. A thread, on the other hand, uses significantly fewer system resources. In fact, a thread has just a kernel object and a stack; little record keeping is involved, and little memory is required.

Because threads require less overhead than processes, you should always try to solve your programming problems using additional threads and avoid creating new processes. However, don't take this recommendation as law. Many designs are better implemented using multiple processes. You should be aware of the tradeoffs, and experience will guide you.

Before we get into the nitty-gritty details of threads, let's spend a little time discussing how to appropriately use threads in your application's architecture.

When to Create a Thread

A thread describes a path of execution within a process. Every time a process is initialized, the system creates a primary thread. This thread begins executing with the C/C++ run-time library's startup code, which in turn calls your entry-point function (*main*, *wmain*, *WinMain*, or *wWinMain*) and continues executing until the entry-point function returns and the C/C++ run-time library's startup code calls *ExitProcess*. For many applications, this primary thread is the only thread the application requires. However, processes can create additional threads to help them do their work.

Every computer has an extremely powerful resource: the CPU. There is absolutely no reason in the world why the CPU should be idle (if you ignore power conservation issues). To keep the CPU busy, you give it varied tasks to perform. Here are a few examples:

■ You can turn on the content indexing service that ships with Microsoft Windows 2000. It creates a low-priority thread that periodically wakes up and indexes the contents of the files on your disk drives. To locate a file, you invoke the Search Results window (by clicking the Start button, then selecting For Files Or Folders from the Search menu) and enter your search criteria in the Containing Text field. The index is searched and the relevant files are immediately displayed. The content indexing service improves performance greatly because each search doesn't have to open, scan, and close every file on your disk drives.

- You can use the disk defragmenting software that ships with Windows 2000. Normally, this type of utility has many administrative options that the average user can't understand, such as how often the utility should run and when. Using lower-priority threads, you can run the utility in the background and defragment the drive when the system is otherwise idle.

- You can easily imagine a future version of the compiler that automatically compiles your source code file whenever you pause typing. The output window would show you warnings and errors in (almost) real time. You would see immediately when you mistyped a variable or function name. To some extent, Microsoft Visual Studio does this already; you can see it using the Workspace's ClassView pane.

- Spreadsheet applications can perform recalculations in the background.

- Word processors can perform repagination, spelling and grammar checking, and printing in the background.

- Files can be copied to other media in the background.

- Web browsers can communicate with their servers in the background. A user can thus resize the browser's window or go to another Web site before the results from the current Web site have come in.

One important thing that you should notice about many of these examples is that multithreading allows the application's user interface to be simplified. If the compiler builds your application whenever you stop typing, there is no need to offer a Build menu option. The word processor application doesn't need Check Spelling and Check Grammar menu options.

In the Web browser example, notice that using a separate thread for I/O (be it network, file, or other) allows the application's user interface to stay responsive. You can imagine an application that sorts the records of a database, prints a document, or copies files. By using a separate thread for this I/O-bound task, a user can continue to use your application's interface to cancel the operation while in progress.

Designing an application to be multithreaded allows that application to scale. As we'll see in the next chapter, each thread is assigned a CPU. So if you have two CPUs in your computer and two threads in your application, both CPUs will be busy. In effect, you get two tasks done in the time it would take for one.

Every process has at least one thread in it. So if you do nothing special in your application, you already get a lot of benefit just from running on a multithreaded operating system. For example, you can build an application and use the word processor at the same time (something I do a lot). If the computer has two CPUs, the build executes on one processor while the other processor handles a document. In other words, the user notices no degradation in performance. Also, if the compiler has a bug that causes its thread to enter an infinite loop, you can still use other processes. (This is not true of 16-bit Windows and MS-DOS applications.)

When Not to Create a Thread

So far, I've been singing the praises of multithreaded applications. While there are a lot of great things about multithreaded applications, there are also some not-so-nice things. Some developers out there believe that the way to solve *any* problem is to divide it up into threads. They could not be more wrong!

Threads are incredibly useful and have a place, but when you use threads you can create new problems while trying to solve the old ones. For example, let's say you're developing a word processing application and want to allow the printing function to run as its own thread. This sounds like a good idea because the user can immediately go back and start editing the document while it's printing. But wait—this means that the data in the document might be changed while the document is printing. Maybe it would be best not to have the printing take place in its own thread, but this "solution" seems a bit drastic. How about if you let the user edit another document but lock the printing document so that it can't be modified until the printing has been completed? Or here's a third idea: copy the document to a temporary file, print the contents of the temporary file, and let the user modify the original. When the temporary file containing the document has finished printing, delete the temporary file.

As you can see, threads can solve some problems while creating new ones. Another common misuse of threads can arise during the development of an application's user interface. In almost all applications, all the user interface components (windows) should share the same thread. A single thread should definitely create all of a window's child windows. Sometimes creating different windows on different threads is useful, but these occasions are rare indeed.

Usually, an application has one user interface thread that creates all windows and has a *GetMessage* loop. Any other threads in the process are worker threads that are compute-bound or I/O-bound—these threads never create windows. Also, the one user interface thread usually has a higher priority than the worker threads, so the user interface is responsive to the user.

While it is unusual for a single process to have multiple user interface threads, there are some valid uses for this. The Windows Explorer creates a separate thread for each folder's window. This allows you to copy files from one folder to another and still explore other folders on your system. Also, if Explorer has a bug in it, the thread handling one folder might crash, but you can still manipulate other folders—at least until you do the thing that causes the other folder to crash too. (For more information on threads and the user interface, see Chapters 26 and 27.)

The moral of this story is that you should use multiple threads judiciously. Don't use them just because you can. You can still write many useful and powerful applications using nothing more than the primary thread assigned to the process.

Writing Your First Thread Function

Every thread must have an entry-point function where it begins execution. We already discussed this entry-point function for your primary thread: *main*, *wmain*, *WinMain*, or *wWinMain*. If you want to create a secondary thread in your process, it must also have an entry-point function, which should look something like this:

```
DWORD WINAPI ThreadFunc(PVOID pvParam){
    DWORD dwResult = 0;.
        ⋮
        ⋮
    return(dwResult);
}
```

Your thread function can perform any task you want it to. Ultimately, your thread function will come to an end and return. At this point, your thread stops running, the memory for its stack is freed, and the usage count of your thread's kernel object is decremented. If the usage count becomes 0, the thread kernel object is destroyed. Like process kernel objects, thread kernel objects always live at least as long as the thread they are associated with, but the object might live well beyond the lifetime of the thread itself.

Let me point out a few things about thread functions:

■ Unlike a primary thread's entry-point function, which must be named *main*, *wmain*, *WinMain*, or *wWinMain*, a thread function can have any name. In fact, if you have multiple thread functions in your application, you have to give them different names or the compiler/linker will think that you've created multiple implementations for a single function.

- Because your primary thread's entry-point function is passed string parameters, ANSI/Unicode versions of the entry-point functions are available: *main/wmain* and *WinMain/wWinMain*. Thread functions are passed a single parameter whose meaning is defined by you, not the operating system. Therefore, you do not have to worry about ANSI/Unicode issues.

- Your thread function must return a value, which becomes the thread's exit code. This is analogous to the C/C++ run-time library's policy of making your primary thread's exit code your process's exit code.

- Your thread function (and really all your functions) should try to use function parameters and local variables as much as possible. When you use static and global variables, multiple threads can access the variables at the same time, potentially corrupting the variables' contents. However, parameters and local variables are created on the thread's stack and are therefore far less likely to be corrupted by another thread.

Now that you know how to implement a thread function, let's talk about how to actually get the operating system to create a thread that executes your thread function.

The *CreateThread* Function

We've already discussed how a process's primary thread comes into being when *CreateProcess* is called. If you want to create one or more secondary threads, you simply have an already running thread call *CreateThread*:

```
HANDLE CreateThread(
   PSECURITY_ATTRIBUTES psa,
   DWORD cbStack,
   PTHREAD_START_ROUTINE pfnStartAddr,
   PVOID pvParam,
   DWORD fdwCreate,
   PDWORD pdwThreadID);
```

When *CreateThread* is called, the system creates a thread kernel object. This thread kernel object is not the thread itself but a small data structure that the operating system uses to manage the thread. You can think of the thread kernel object as a small data structure that consists of statistical information about the thread. This is identical to the way processes and process kernel objects relate to each other.

The system allocates memory out of the process's address space for use by the thread's stack. The new thread runs in the same process context as the creating thread. The new thread therefore has access to all of the process's kernel object handles, all of the memory in the process, and the stacks of all other threads that are in this same process. This makes it really easy for multiple threads in a single process to communicate with each other.

> **NOTE**
>
> The *CreateThread* function is the Windows function that creates a thread. However, if you are writing C/C++ code, you should never call *CreateThread*. Instead, you should use the Visual C++ run-time library function *_beginthreadex*. If you do not use Microsoft's Visual C++ compiler, your compiler vendor will have its own alternative to *CreateThread*. Whatever this alternative is, you must use it. I'll explain what *_beginthreadex* does and why it is so important later in this chapter.

OK, that's the broad overview. The following sections explain each of *CreateThread*'s parameters.

psa

The *psa* parameter is a pointer to a SECURITY_ATTRIBUTES structure. You can (and usually will) pass NULL if you want the default security attributes for the thread kernel object. If you want any child processes to be able to inherit a handle to this thread object, you must specify a SECURITY_ATTRIBUTES structure, whose *bInheritHandle* member is initialized to TRUE. See Chapter 3 for more information.

cbStack

The *cbStack* parameter specifies how much address space the thread can use for its own stack. Every thread owns its own stack. When *CreateProcess* starts a process, it internally calls *CreateThread* to initialize the process's primary thread. For the *cbStack* parameter, *CreateProcess* uses a value stored inside the executable file. You can control this value using the linker's /STACK switch:

```
/STACK:[reserve] [,commit]
```

The *reserve* argument sets the amount of address space the system should reserve for the thread's stack. The default is 1 MB. The *commit* argument specifies the amount of physical storage that should be initially committed to the stack's reserved region. The default is one page. As the code in your thread executes, you might require more than one page of storage. When your thread overflows its stack, an exception is generated. (See Chapter 16 for more information about a thread's stack and stack overflow exceptions; see Chapter 23 for more information about general exception handling.) The system catches the exception and commits another page (or whatever you specified for the *commit* argument) to the reserved space, which allows a thread's stack to grow dynamically as needed.

When you call *CreateThread*, passing a value other than 0 causes the function to reserve and commit all storage for the thread's stack. Since all the storage is committed up front, the thread is guaranteed to have the specified amount of stack storage available. The amount of reserved space is either the amount specified by the /STACK linker switch or the value of *cbStack*, whichever is larger. The amount of storage committed matches the value you passed for *cbStack*. If you pass 0 to the *cbStack* parameter, *CreateThread* reserves a region and commits the amount of storage indicated by the /STACK linker switch information embedded in the .exe file by the linker.

The reserve amount sets an upper limit for the stack so that you can catch endless recursion bugs in your code. For example, let's say that you're writing a function that calls itself recursively. This function also has a bug that causes endless recursion. Every time the function calls itself, a new stack frame is created on the stack. If the system didn't set a maximum limit on the stack size, the recursive function would never stop calling itself. All of the process's address space would be allocated, and enormous amounts of physical storage would be committed to the stack. By setting a stack limit, you prevent your application from using up enormous amounts of physical storage, and you also know much sooner when a bug exists in your program. (The Summation sample application in Chapter 16 shows how to trap and handle stack overflows in your application.)

pfnStartAddr and *pvParam*

The *pfnStartAddr* parameter indicates the address of the thread function that you want the new thread to execute. A thread function's *pvParam* parameter is the same as the *pvParam* parameter that you originally passed to *CreateThread*. *CreateThread* does nothing with this parameter except pass it on to the thread function when the thread starts executing. This parameter provides a way to pass an initialization value to the thread function. This initialization data can be either a numeric value or a pointer to a data structure that contains additional information.

It is perfectly legal and actually quite useful to create multiple threads that have the same function address as their starting point. For example, you can implement a Web server that creates a new thread to handle each client's request.

Each thread knows which client it is processing because you pass a different *pvParam* value as you create each thread.

Remember that Windows is a preemptive multithreading system, which means that the new thread and the thread that called *CreateThread* can execute simultaneously. Because the threads run simultaneously, problems can occur. Watch out for code like this:

```
DWORD WINAPI FirstThread(PVOID pvParam) {
   // Initialize a stack-based variable
   int x = 0;
   DWORD dwThreadID;

   // Create a new thread.
   HANDLE hThread = CreateThread(NULL, 0, SecondThread, (PVOID) &x,
      0, &dwThreadId);

   // We don't reference the new thread anymore,
   // so close our handle to it.
   CloseHandle(hThread);

   // Our thread is done.
   // BUG: our stack will be destroyed, but
   //      SecondThread might try to access it.
   return(0);
}


DWORD WINAPI SecondThread(PVOID pvParam) {
   // Do some lengthy processing here.

      .
      .
      .

   // Attempt to access the variable on FirstThread's stack.
   // NOTE: This may cause an access violation - it depends on timing!
   * ((int *) pvParam) = 5;

      .
      .
      .

   return(0);
}
```

In the code above, *FirstThread* might finish its work before *SecondThread* assigns 5 to *FirstThread*'s *x*. If this happens, *SecondThread* won't know that *FirstThread* no longer exists and will attempt to change the contents of what is now an invalid address. This causes *SecondThread* to raise an access violation because *FirstThread*'s stack is destroyed when *FirstThread* terminates. One way to solve this problem is to declare x as a static variable so the compiler will create a storage area for x in the application's data section rather than on the stack.

However, this makes the function nonreentrant. In other words, you can't create two threads that execute the same function because the static variable would be shared between the two threads. Another way to solve this problem (and its more complex variations) is to use proper thread synchronization techniques (discussed in Chapters 8, 9, and 10).

fdwCreate

The *fdwCreate* parameter specifies additional flags that control the creation of the thread. It can be one of two values. If the value is 0, the thread is schedulable immediately after it is created. If the value is CREATE_SUSPENDED, the system fully creates and initializes the thread but suspends the thread so that it is not schedulable.

The CREATE_SUSPENDED flag allows an application to alter some properties of a thread before it has a chance to execute any code. Because this is rarely necessary, this flag is not commonly used. The JobLab application presented in Chapter 5 demonstrates a correct use of this flag.

pdwThreadID

The last parameter of *CreateThread*, *pdwThreadID*, must be a valid address of a DWORD in which *CreateThread* stores the ID that the system assigns to the new thread. (Process and thread IDs were discussed in Chapter 4.)

NOTE

Under Windows 2000 (and Windows NT 4), you can (and usually do) pass NULL for this parameter. This tells the function that you're not interested in the thread's ID, but the thread is created. On Windows 95 and Windows 98, passing NULL for this parameter causes the function to fail because the function tries to write the ID to address NULL, which is illegal. The thread is not created.

Of course, this inconsistency between operating systems can cause problems for developers. For example, let's say you develop and test an application on Windows 2000 (which creates the thread even if you pass NULL for the *pdwThreadID* parameter). When you later run your application on Windows 98, *CreateThread* will not create the new thread. You must always thoroughly test your applications on all operating systems (and versions) that you claim to support.

Terminating a Thread

A thread can be terminated in four ways:

■ The thread function returns. (This is highly recommended.)

■ The thread kills itself by calling the *ExitThread* function. (Avoid this method.)

■ A thread in the same or in another process calls the *TerminateThread* function. (Avoid this method.)

■ The process containing the thread terminates. (Avoid this method.)

This section discusses all four methods for terminating a thread and describes what happens when a thread ends.

The Thread Function Returns

You should always design your thread functions so that they return when you want the thread to terminate. This is the only way to guarantee that all your thread's resources are cleaned up properly.

Having your thread function return ensures the following:

■ Any and all C++ objects created in your thread function will be destroyed properly via their destructors.

■ The operating system will properly free the memory used by the thread's stack.

■ The system will set the thread's exit code (maintained in the thread's kernel object) to your thread function's return value.

■ The system will decrement the usage count of the thread's kernel object.

The *ExitThread* Function

You can force your thread to terminate by having it call *ExitThread*:

```
VOID ExitThread(DWORD dwExitCode);
```

This function terminates the thread and causes the operating system to clean up all of the operating system resources that were used by the thread. However, your C/C++ resources (such as C++ class objects) will not be destroyed. For this reason, it is much better to simply return from your thread function instead of calling *ExitThread* yourself. (For more information, see the section titled "The *ExitProcess* Function" in Chapter 4.)

Of course, you use *ExitThread*'s *dwExitCode* parameter to tell the system what to set the thread's exit code to. The *ExitThread* function does not return a value because the thread has terminated and cannot execute any more code.

NOTE The recommended way to have a thread terminate is by having its thread function simply return (as described in the previous section). However, if you use the method described in this section, be aware that the *ExitThread* function is the Windows function that kills a thread. If you are writing C/C++ code, you should never call *ExitThread*. Instead, you should use the Visual C++ run-time library function *_endthreadex*. If you do not use Microsoft's Visual C++ compiler, your compiler vendor will have its own alternative to *ExitThread*. Whatever this alternative is, you must use it. I will explain what *_endthreadex* does and why it is so important later in this chapter.

The *TerminateThread* Function

A call to *TerminateThread* also kills a thread:

```
BOOL TerminateThread(
   HANDLE hThread,
   DWORD dwExitCode);
```

Unlike *ExitThread*, which always kills the calling thread, *TerminateThread* can kill any thread. The *hThread* parameter identifies the handle of the thread to be terminated. When the thread terminates, its exit code becomes the value you passed as the *dwExitCode* parameter. Also, the thread's kernel object has its usage count decremented.

NOTE The *TerminateThread* function is asynchronous. That is, it tells the system that you want the thread to terminate but the thread is not guaranteed to be killed by the time the function returns. If you need to know for sure that the thread has terminated, you might want to call *WaitForSingleObject* (described in Chapter 9) or a similar function, passing the handle of the thread.

A well-designed application never uses this function because the thread being terminated receives no notification that it is dying. The thread cannot clean up properly and it cannot prevent itself from being killed.

> **NOTE**
>
> When a thread dies by returning or calling *ExitThread*, the stack for the thread is destroyed. However, if *TerminateThread* is used, the system does not destroy the thread's stack until the process that owned the thread terminates. Microsoft purposely implemented *TerminateThread* in this way. If other still-executing threads were to reference values on the forcibly killed thread's stack, these other threads would raise access violations. By leaving the killed thread's stack in memory, other threads can continue to execute just fine.
>
> In addition, DLLs usually receive notifications when a thread is terminating. If a thread is forcibly killed with *TerminateThread*, however, the DLLs do not receive this notification, which can prevent proper cleanup. (See Chapter 20 for more information.)

When a Process Terminates

The *ExitProcess* and *TerminateProcess* functions discussed in Chapter 4 also terminate threads. The difference is that these functions terminate all the threads contained in the process being terminated. Also, since the entire process is being shut down, all resources in use by the process are guaranteed to be cleaned up. This certainly includes any and all thread stacks. These two functions cause the remaining threads in the process to be forcibly killed, as if *TerminateThread* were called for each remaining thread. Obviously, this means that proper application cleanup does not occur: C++ object destructors aren't called, data isn't flushed to disk, and so on.

When a Thread Terminates

The following actions occur when a thread terminates:

■ All User object handles owned by the thread are freed. In Windows, most objects are owned by the process containing the thread that creates the objects. However, a thread owns two User objects: windows and hooks. When a thread dies, the system automatically destroys any windows and uninstalls any hooks that were created or installed by the thread. Other objects are destroyed only when the owning process terminates.

■ The thread's exit code changes from STILL_ACTIVE to the code passed to *ExitThread* or *TerminateThread*.

■ The state of the thread kernel object becomes signaled.

■ If the thread is the last active thread in the process, the system considers the process terminated as well.

■ The thread kernel object's usage count is decremented by 1.

When a thread terminates, its associated thread kernel object doesn't automatically become freed until all the outstanding references to the object are closed.

Once a thread is no longer running, there isn't much any other thread in the system can do with the thread's handle. However, these other threads can call *GetExitCodeThread* to check whether the thread identified by *hThread* has terminated and, if it has, determine its exit code:

```
BOOL GetExitCodeThread(
   HANDLE hThread,
   PDWORD pdwExitCode);
```

The exit code value is returned in the DWORD pointed to by *pdwExitCode*. If the thread hasn't terminated when *GetExitCodeThread* is called, the function fills the DWORD with the STILL_ACTIVE identifier (defined as 0x103). If the function is successful, TRUE is returned. (Chapter 9 has more on using the thread's handle to determine when the thread has terminated.)

Some Thread Internals

So far, I've explained how to implement a thread function and how to have the system create a thread to execute that function. In this section, we'll look at how the system pulls this off.

Figure 6-1 shows what the system must do to create and initialize a thread. Let's look closely at this figure to understand exactly what's going on. A call to *CreateThread* causes the system to create a thread kernel object. This object has an initial usage count of 2. (The thread kernel object is not destroyed until the thread stops running *and* the handle returned from *CreateThread* is closed.) Other properties of the thread's kernel object are also initialized: the suspension count is set to 1, the exit code is set to STILL_ACTIVE (0x103), and the object is set to the nonsignaled state.

Once the kernel object has been created, the system allocates memory, which is used for the thread's stack. This memory is allocated from the process's address space since threads don't have an address space of their own. The system then writes two values to the upper end of the new thread's stack. (Thread stacks always build from high memory addresses to low memory addresses.) The first value written to the stack is the value of the *pvParam* parameter that you passed to *CreateThread*. Immediately below it is the *pfnStartAddr* value that you also passed to *CreateThread*.

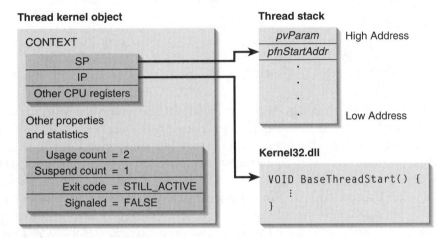

Figure 6-1.
How a thread is created and initialized

Each thread has its own set of CPU registers, called the thread's *context*. The context reflects the state of the thread's CPU registers when the thread last executed. The set of CPU registers for the thread is saved in a CONTEXT structure (defined in the WinNT.h header file). The CONTEXT structure is itself contained in the thread's kernel object.

The instruction pointer and stack pointer registers are the two most important registers in the thread's context. Remember that threads always run in the context of a process. So both these addresses identify memory in the owning process's address space. When the thread's kernel object is initialized, the CONTEXT structure's stack pointer register is set to the address of where *pfnStartAddr* was placed on the thread's stack. The instruction pointer register is set to the address of an undocumented (and unexported) function called *BaseThreadStart*. This function is contained inside the Kernel32.dll module (which is also where the *CreateThread* function is implemented). Figure 6-1 shows all of this.

Here is what *BaseThreadStart* basically does:

```
VOID BaseThreadStart(PTHREAD_START_ROUTINE pfnStartAddr, PVOID pvParam) {
   __try {
      ExitThread((pfnStartAddr)(pvParam));
   }
   __except(UnhandledExceptionFilter(GetExceptionInformation())) {
      ExitProcess(GetExceptionCode());
   }
   // NOTE: We never get here.
}
```

After the thread has completely initialized, the system checks to see whether the CREATE_SUSPENDED flag was passed to *CreateThread*. If this flag was not passed, the system decrements the thread's suspend count to 0 and the thread can be scheduled to a processor. The system then loads the actual CPU registers with the values that were last saved in the thread's context. The thread can now execute code and manipulate data in its process's address space.

Because a new thread's instruction pointer is set to *BaseThreadStart*, this function is really where the thread begins execution. *BaseThreadStart*'s prototype makes you think that the function receives two parameters, but this implies that the function is called from another function, which is not true. The new thread simply comes into existence and starts executing here. *BaseThreadStart* believes that it was called from another function because it has access to two parameters. But access to these parameters works because the operating system explicitly wrote the values to the thread's stack (which is how parameters are normally passed to a function). Note that some CPU architectures pass parameters using CPU registers instead of the stack. For these architectures, the system initializes the proper registers correctly before allowing the thread to execute the *BaseThreadStart* function.

When the new thread executes the *BaseThreadStart* function, the following things happen:

■ A structured exception handling (SEH) frame is set up around your thread function so that any exceptions raised while your thread executes get some default handling by the system. (See Chapters 23, 24, and 25 for more information about structured exception handling.)

■ The system calls your thread function, passing it the *pvParam* parameter that you passed to the *CreateThread* function.

■ When your thread function returns, *BaseThreadStart* calls *ExitThread*, passing it your thread function's return value. The thread kernel object's usage count is decremented and the thread stops executing.

■ If your thread raises an exception that is not handled, the SEH frame set up by the *BaseThreadStart* function handles the exception. Usually, this means that a message box is presented to the user and that when the user dismisses the message box, *BaseThreadStart* calls *ExitProcess* to terminate the entire process, not just the offending thread.

Notice that within *BaseThreadStart*, the thread calls either *ExitThread* or *ExitProcess*. This means that the thread cannot ever exit this function; it always dies inside it. This is why *BaseThreadStart* is prototyped as returning VOID—it never returns.

Also, your thread function can return when it's done processing because of *BaseThreadStart*. When *BaseThreadStart* calls your thread function, it pushes its return address on the stack so your thread function knows where to return. But *BaseThreadStart* is not allowed to return. If it didn't forcibly kill the thread and simply tried to return, an access violation would almost definitely be raised because there is no function return address on the thread's stack and *BaseThreadStart* would try to return to some random memory location.

When a process's primary thread is initialized, its instruction pointer is set to another undocumented function called *BaseProcessStart*. This function is almost identical to *BaseThreadStart* and looks something like this:

```
VOID BaseProcessStart(PPROCESS_START_ROUTINE pfnStartAddr) {
   __try {
      ExitThread((pfnStartAddr)());
   }
   __except(UnhandledExceptionFilter(GetExceptionInformation())) {
      ExitProcess(GetExceptionCode());
   }
   // NOTE: We never get here.
}
```

The only real difference is that there is no reference to the *pvParam* parameter. When *BaseProcessStart* begins executing, it calls the C/C++ run time library's startup code, which initializes and then calls your *main, wmain, WinMain,* or *wWinMain* function. When your entry-point function returns, the C/C++ run-time library startup code calls *ExitProcess*. So for a C/C++ application, the primary thread never returns to the *BaseProcessStart* function.

C/C++ Run-Time Library Considerations

Six C/C++ run-time libraries ship with Visual C++. The following table describes them.

Library Name	Description
LibC.lib	Statically linked library for single-threaded applications. (This is the default library when you create a new project.)
LibCD.lib	Statically linked debug version of the library for single-threaded applications.
LibCMt.lib	Statically linked release version of the library for multithreaded applications.
LibCMtD.lib	Statically linked debug version of the library for multithreaded applications.
MSVCRt.lib	Import library for dynamically linking the release version of the MSVCRt.dll library. This library supports both single-threaded and multithreaded applications.
MSVCRtD.lib	Import library for dynamically linking the debug version of the MSVCRtD.dll library. The library supports both single-threaded and multithreaded applications.

When you implement any type of project, you must know which library you're linking your project with. You select a library using the Project Settings dialog box, shown below. On the C/C++ tab, in the Code Generation category, select one of the six options from the Use Run-Time Library combo box.

The first thing you're probably wondering is, "Why do I need one library for single-threaded applications and another library for multithreaded applications?" The reason is that the standard C run-time library was invented around 1970, long before threads were available on any operating system. The inventors of the library didn't consider the problems of using the C run-time library with multithreaded applications.

Consider the standard C run-time global variable *errno*. Some functions set this variable when an error occurs. Let's say you have the following code fragment:

```
BOOL fFailure = (system("NOTEPAD.EXE README.TXT") == -1);

if (fFailure) {
   switch (errno) {
   case E2BIG:   // Argument list or environment too big
      break;
   case ENOENT:  // Command interpreter cannot be found
      break;
   case ENOEXEC: // Command interpreter has bad format
      break;
   case ENOMEM:  // Insufficient memory to run command
      break;
   }
}
```

Now let's say that the thread executing the code above is interrupted after the call to the *system* function and before the *if* statement. And imagine that the thread is being interrupted to allow a second thread in the same process to execute and that this new thread will execute another C run-time function that sets the global variable *errno*. When the CPU is later assigned back to the first thread, the value of *errno* no longer reflects the proper error code for the call to *system* in the code above. To solve this problem, each thread requires its own *errno* variable. In addition, there must be some mechanism that allows a thread to reference its own *errno* variable but not touch another thread's *errno* variable.

This is only one example of how the standard C/C++ run-time library was not originally designed for multithreaded applications. The C/C++ run-time library variables and functions that have problems in multithreaded environments include *errno*, *_doserrno*, *strtok*, *_wcstok*, *strerror*, *_strerror*, *tmpnam*, *tmpfile*, *asctime*, *_wasctime*, *gmtime*, *_ecvt*, and *_fcvt*—to name just a few.

For multithreaded C and C++ programs to work properly, a data structure must be created and associated with each thread that uses C/C++ run-time library functions. Then, when you make C/C++ run-time library calls, those functions must know to look in the calling thread's data block so that no other thread is adversely affected.

So how does the system know to allocate this data block when a new thread is created? The answer is that it doesn't. The system has no idea that your application is written in C/C++ and that you are calling functions that are not natively thread-safe. The onus is on you to do everything correctly. To create a new thread, you must not call the operating system's *CreateThread* function—you must call the C/C++ run-time library function *_beginthreadex*:

```
unsigned long _beginthreadex(
   void *security,
   unsigned stack_size,
   unsigned (*start_address)(void *),
   void *arglist,
   unsigned initflag,
   unsigned *thrdaddr);
```

The *_beginthreadex* function has the same parameter list as the *CreateThread* function, but the parameter names and types are not exactly the same. This is because Microsoft's C/C++ run-time library group believes that C/C++ run-time library functions should not have any dependencies on Windows data types. The *_beginthreadex* function also returns the handle of the newly created thread, just like *CreateThread* does. So, if you've been calling *CreateThread* in your source code, it is fairly easy to globally replace all these calls with calls to *_beginthreadex*. However, since the data types are not quite the same, you might have to perform some casting to make the compiler happy. To make things easier, I've created a macro, *chBEGINTHREADEX*, to use in my source code:

```
typedef unsigned (__stdcall *PTHREAD_START) (void *);

#define chBEGINTHREADEX(psa, cbStack, pfnStartAddr, \
   pvParam, fdwCreate, pdwThreadID)                 \
      ((HANDLE) _beginthreadex(                      \
         (void *) (psa),                            \
         (unsigned) (cbStack),                      \
         (PTHREAD_START) (pfnStartAddr),            \
         (void *) (pvParam),                        \
         (unsigned) (fdwCreate),                    \
         (unsigned *) (pdwThreadID)))
```

Note that the *_beginthreadex* function exists only in the multithreaded versions of the C/C++ run-time library. If you are linking to a single-thread run-time library, you get an "unresolved external symbol" error reported from the linker. This is by design, of course, because the single-threaded library does not work properly in a multithreaded application. Also note that Visual Studio defaults to selecting the single-threaded library when you create a new project.

This is not the safest default, and for multithreaded applications you must explicitly change to a multithreaded C/C++ run-time library.

Since Microsoft ships the source code to the C/C++ run-time library, it's easy to determine exactly what *_beginthreadex* does that *CreateThread* doesn't do. In fact, I searched the Visual Studio CD-ROM and found the source code for *_beginthreadex* in Threadex.c. Rather than reprint the source code for it here, I'll give you a pseudocode version of it and highlight the interesting points.

```
unsigned long __cdecl _beginthreadex (
   void *psa,
   unsigned cbStack,
   unsigned (__stdcall * pfnStartAddr) (void *),
   void * pvParam,
   unsigned fdwCreate,
   unsigned *pdwThreadID) {

   _ptiddata ptd;          // Pointer to thread's data block
   unsigned long thdl;     // Thread's handle

   // Allocate data block for the new thread.
   if ((ptd = _calloc_crt(1, sizeof(struct tiddata))) == NULL)
      goto error_return;

   // Initialize the data block.
   initptd(ptd);

   // Save the desired thread function and the parameter
   // we want it to get in the data block.
   ptd->_initaddr = (void *) pfnStartAddr;
   ptd->_initarg = pvParam;

   // Create the new thread.
   thdl = (unsigned long) CreateThread(psa, cbStack,
      _threadstartex, (PVOID) ptd, fdwCreate, pdwThreadID);
   if (thdl == NULL) {
      // Thread couldn't be created, cleanup and return failure.
      goto error_return;
   }

   // Create created OK, return the handle.
   return(thdl);

error_return:
   // Error: data block or thread couldn't be created.

   _free_crt(ptd);
   return((unsigned long)0L);
}
```

Here are the important things to note about _beginthreadex:

■ Each thread gets its very own *tiddata* memory block allocated from the C/C++ run-time library's heap. (The *tiddata* structure is in the Visual C++ source code in the Mtdll.h file). Just for fun, I'll reproduce the structure in Figure 6-2.

■ The address of the thread function passed to _beginthreadex is saved in the *tiddata* memory block. The parameter to be passed to this function is also saved in this data block.

■ _beginthreadex does call *CreateThread* internally since this is the only way that the operating system knows how to create a new thread.

■ When *CreateThread* is called, it is told to start executing the new thread with a function called _threadstartex, not *pfnStartAddr*. Also, note that the parameter passed to the thread function is the address of the *tiddata* structure, not *pvParam*.

■ If all goes well, the thread handle is returned just like *CreateThread*. If any operation fails, NULL is returned.

```
struct _tiddata {
    unsigned long   _tid;         /* thread ID */

    unsigned long   _thandle;     /* thread handle */

    int     _terrno;              /* errno value */
    unsigned long   _tdoserrno;   /* _doserrno value */
    unsigned int    _fpds;        /* Floating Point data segment */
    unsigned long   _holdrand;    /* rand() seed value */
    char *      _token;           /* ptr to strtok() token */
#ifdef _WIN32
    wchar_t *   _wtoken;          /* ptr to wcstok() token */
#endif  /* _WIN32 */
    unsigned char * _mtoken;      /* ptr to _mbstok() token */

    /* following pointers get malloc'd at runtime */
    char *      _errmsg;          /* ptr to strerror()/_strerror() buff */
    char *      _namebuf0;        /* ptr to tmpnam() buffer */
#ifdef _WIN32
    wchar_t *   _wnamebuf0;       /* ptr to _wtmpnam() buffer */
#endif  /* _WIN32 */
    char *      _namebuf1;        /* ptr to tmpfile() buffer */
```

Figure 6-2.   *(continued)*
The C/C++ run-time library's thread local tiddata *structure*

Figure 6-2. *continued*

```
#ifdef _WIN32
    wchar_t *    _wnamebuf1;      /* ptr to _wtmpfile() buffer */
#endif  /* _WIN32 */
    char *       _asctimebuf;     /* ptr to asctime() buffer */
#ifdef _WIN32
    wchar_t *    _wasctimebuf;    /* ptr to _wasctime() buffer */
#endif  /* _WIN32 */
    void *       _gmtimebuf;      /* ptr to gmtime() structure */
    char *       _cvtbuf;         /* ptr to ecvt()/fcvt buffer */

    /* following fields are needed by _beginthread code */
    void *       _initaddr;       /* initial user thread address */
    void *       _initarg;        /* initial user thread argument */

    /* following three fields are needed to support signal handling and
     * runtime errors */
    void *       _pxcptacttab;    /* ptr to exception-action table */
    void *       _tpxcptinfoptrs; /* ptr to exception info pointers */
    int          _tfpecode;       /* float point exception code */

    /* following field is needed by NLG routines */
    unsigned long    _NLG_dwCode;

    /*
     * Per-Thread data needed by C++ Exception Handling
     */
    void *       _terminate;      /* terminate() routine */
    void *       _unexpected;     /* unexpected() routine */
    void *       _translator;     /* S.E. translator */
    void *       _curexception;   /* current exception */
    void *       _curcontext;     /* current exception context */
#if defined (_M_MRX000)
    void *       _pFrameInfoChain;
    void *       _pUnwindContext;
    void *       _pExitContext;
    int          _MipsPtdDelta;
    int          _MipsPtdEpsilon;
#elif defined (_M_PPC)
    void *       _pExitContext;
    void *       _pUnwindContext;
    void *       _pFrameInfoChain;
    int          _FrameInfo[6];
#endif  /* defined (_M_PPC) */
};

typedef struct _tiddata * _ptiddata;
```

So now that a *tiddata* structure has been allocated and initialized for the new thread, we need to see how this structure is associated with the thread. Let's take a look at the *_threadstartex* function (which is also in the C/C++ run-time library's Threadex.c file). Here is my pseudocode version of this function:

```
static unsigned long WINAPI threadstartex (void* ptd) {
   // Note: ptd is the address of this thread's tiddata block.

   // Associate the tiddata block with this thread.
   TlsSetValue(__tlsindex, ptd);

   // Save this thread ID in the tiddata block.
   ((_ptiddata) ptd)->_tid = GetCurrentThreadId();

   // Initialize floating-point support (code not shown).

   // Wrap desired thread function in SEH frame to
   // handle run-time errors and signal support.
   __try {
      // Call desired thread function, passing it the desired parameter.
      // Pass thread's exit code value to _endthreadex.
      _endthreadex(
         ( (unsigned (WINAPI *)(void *))(((_ptiddata)ptd)->_initaddr) )
            ( ((_ptiddata)ptd)->_initarg ) ) ;
   }
   __except(_XcptFilter(GetExceptionCode(), GetExceptionInformation())){
      // The C run-time's exception handler deals with run-time errors
      // and signal support; we should never get it here.
      _exit(GetExceptionCode());
   }

   // We never get here; the thread dies in this function.
   return(0L);
}
```

Here are the important things to note about *_threadstartex*:

- The new thread begins executing with *BaseThreadStart* (in Kernel32.dll) and then jumps to *_threadstartex*.

- *_threadstartex* is passed the address to this new thread's *tiddata* block as its only parameter.

- *TlsSetValue* is an operating system function that associates a value with the calling thread. This is called Thread Local Storage (TLS) and is discussed in Chapter 21. The *_threadstartex* function associates the *tiddata* block with the new thread.

■ An SEH frame is placed around the desired thread function. This frame handles many things related to the run-time library—for example, run-time errors (such as throwing C++ exceptions that are not caught) and the C/C++ run-time library's *signal* function. This is critically important. If you were to create a thread using *CreateThread* and then call the C/C++ run-time library's *signal* function, the function would not work correctly.

■ The desired thread function is called and passed the desired parameter. Recall that the address of the function and the parameter were saved in the *tiddata* block by *_beginthreadex*.

■ The return value from the desired thread function is supposed to be the thread's exit code. Note that *_threadstartex* does not simply return back to *BaseThreadStart*. If it were to do that, the thread would die and its exit code would be set correctly but the thread's *tiddata* memory block would not be destroyed. This would cause a leak in your application. To prevent this leak, another C/C++ run-time library function, *_endthreadex*, is called and passed the exit code.

The last function that we need to look at is *_endthreadex* (which is also in the C run-time library's Threadex.c file). Here is my pseudocode version of this function:

```
void __cdecl _endthreadex (unsigned retcode) {
    _ptiddata ptd;          // Pointer to thread's data block

    // Clean up floating-point support (code not shown).

    // Get the address of this thread's tiddata block.
    ptd = _getptd();

    // Free the tiddata block.
    _freeptd(ptd);

    // Terminate the thread.
    ExitThread(retcode);
}
```

Here are the important things to note about *_endthreadex*:

■ The C run-time library's *_getptd* function internally calls the operating system's *TlsGetValue* function, which retrieves the address of the calling thread's *tiddata* memory block.

■ This data block is then freed and the operating system's *ExitThread* function is called to truly destroy the thread. Of course, the exit code is passed and set correctly.

Earlier in this chapter, I said that you should always try to avoid using the *ExitThread* function. This is true and I'm not going to go back on my word. I said that it kills the calling thread and doesn't allow it to return from the currently executing function. Because the function doesn't return, any C++ objects you can construct will not be destructed. Here's another reason not to call *ExitThread*: it prevents the thread's *tiddata* memory block from being freed, so your application will leak memory (until the whole process is terminated).

Microsoft's Visual C++ team realizes that developers like to call *ExitThread* anyway, so they have made this possible without forcing your application to leak memory. If you really want to forcibly kill your thread, you can have it call *_endthreadex* (instead of *ExitThread*) to free the thread's *tiddata* block and then exit. Still, I discourage you from calling *_endthreadex*.

By now you should understand why the C/C++ run-time library's functions need a separate data block for each thread created, and you should also see how calling *_beginthreadex* allocates, initializes, and associates this data block with the newly created thread. You should also understand how the *_endthreadex* function frees the data block when the thread terminates.

Once this data block is initialized and associated with the thread, any C/C++ run-time library functions the thread calls that require per-thread instance data can easily retrieve the address to the calling thread's data block (via *TlsGetValue*) and manipulate the thread's data. This is fine for functions, but you might wonder how this works for a global variable such as *errno*. Well, *errno* is defined in the standard C headers, like this:

```
#if defined(_MT) || defined(_DLL)
extern int * __cdecl _errno(void);
#define errno (*_errno())
#else /* ndef _MT && ndef _DLL */
extern int errno;
#endif /* _MT || _DLL */
```

If you're creating a multithreaded application, you must specify the /MT (multithreaded application) or /MD (multithreaded DLL) switch on the compiler's command line. This causes the compiler to define the _MT identifier. Then, whenever you reference *errno*, you actually make a call to the internal C/C++ run-time library function *_errno*. This function returns the address to the *errno* data member in the calling thread's associated data block. You'll notice that the *errno* macro is defined as taking the contents of this address. This definition is necessary because it's possible to write code like this:

```
int *p = &errno;
if (*p == ENOMEM) {
    .
    .
    .
}
```

If the internal *_errno* function simply returned the value of *errno*, the above code wouldn't compile.

The multithreaded version of the C/C++ run-time library also places synchronization primitives around certain functions. For example, if two threads simultaneously call *malloc*, the heap can become corrupted. The multithreaded version of the C/C++ run-time library prevents two threads from allocating memory from the heap at the same time. It does this by making the second thread wait until the first has returned from *malloc*. Then the second thread is allowed to enter. (Thread synchronization is discussed in more detail in Chapters 8, 9, and 10.)

Obviously, all this additional work affects the performance of the multithreaded version of the C/C++ run-time library. This is why Microsoft supplies the single-threaded version of the statically linked C/C++ run-time library in addition to the multithreaded version.

The dynamically linked version of the C/C++ run-time library was written to be generic so that it can be shared by any and all running applications and DLLs using the C/C++ run-time library functions. For this reason, the library exists only in a multithreaded version. Because the C/C++ run-time library is supplied in a DLL, applications (.exe files) and DLLs don't need to include the code for the C/C++ run-time library function and are smaller as a result. Also, if Microsoft fixes a bug in the C/C++ run-time library DLL, applications automatically gain the fix as well.

As you might expect, the C/C++ run-time library's startup code allocates and initializes a data block for your application's primary thread. This allows the primary thread to safely call any of the C/C++ run-time functions. When your primary thread returns from its entry-point function, the C/C++ run-time library frees the associated data block. In addition, the startup code sets up the proper structured exception handling code so that the primary thread can successfully call the C/C++ run-time library's *signal* function.

Oops—I Called *CreateThread* Instead of *_beginthreadex* by Mistake

You might wonder what happens if you create your new threads by calling *CreateThread* instead of the C/C++ run-time library's *_beginthreadex* function. When a thread calls a C/C++ run-time library function that requires the *tiddata* structure, here is what happens. (Most C/C++ run-time library functions are thread-safe and do not require this structure.) First, the C/C++ run-time function attempts to get the address of the thread's data block (by calling *TlsGetValue*). If NULL is returned as the address of the *tiddata* block, the calling thread doesn't have a *tiddata* block associated with it. At this point, the C/C++ run-time function allocates and initializes a *tiddata* block for the calling thread right on the spot. The block is then associated with the thread (via *TlsSetValue*) and this block stays with the thread for as long as the thread continues to run. The C/C++ run-time function can now use the thread's *tiddata* block, and so can any C/C++ run-time functions that are called in the future.

This, of course, is fantastic because your thread runs without a hitch (almost). Well, actually there are a few problems. First, if the thread uses the C/C++ run-time library's *signal* function, the entire process terminates because the structured exception handling frame has not been prepared. Second, if the thread terminates without calling *_endthreadex*, the data block cannot be destroyed and a memory leak occurs. (And who would call *_endthreadex* for a thread created with *CreateThread*?)

> **NOTE**
>
> If your module links to the multithreaded DLL version of the C/C++ run-time library, the library receives a DLL_THREAD_DETACH notification when the thread terminates and frees the *tiddata* block (if allocated). Even though this prevents the leaking of the *tiddata* block, I strongly recommend that you create your threads using *_beginthreadex* instead of *CreateThread*.

C/C++ Run-Time Library Functions That You Should Never Call

The C/C++ run-time library also contains two other functions:

```
unsigned long _beginthread(
   void (__cdecl *start_address)(void *),
   unsigned stack_size,
   void *arglist);
```

and

```
void _endthread(void);
```

These two functions were originally created to do the work of the new _beginthreadex_ and _endthreadex_ functions, respectively. However, as you can see, the _beginthread_ function has fewer parameters and is therefore more limited than the full-featured _beginthreadex_ function. For example, if you use _beginthread_, you cannot create the new thread with security attributes, you cannot create the thread suspended, and you cannot obtain the thread's ID value. The _endthread_ function has a similar story: it takes no parameters, which means that the thread's exit code is hard-coded to 0.

The _endthread_ function has another significant problem that you can't see. Just before _endthread_ calls _ExitThread_, it calls _CloseHandle_, passing the handle of the new thread. To see why this is a problem, examine the following code:

```
DWORD dwExitCode;
HANDLE hThread = _beginthread(...);
GetExitCodeThread(hThread, &dwExitCode);
CloseHandle(hThread);
```

The newly created thread might execute, return, and terminate before the first thread can call _GetExitCodeThread_. If this happens, the value in _hThread_ will be invalid because _endthread_ has closed the new thread's handle. Needless to say, the call to _CloseHandle_ will also fail for the same reason.

The new _endthreadex_ function does not close the thread's handle, so the code fragment above will work correctly if we replace the call to _beginthread_ with a call to _beginthreadex_. Remember that when your thread function returns, _beginthreadex_ calls _endthreadex_, while _beginthread_ calls _endthread_.

Gaining a Sense of One's Own Identity

As threads execute, they frequently want to call Windows functions that change their execution environment. For example, a thread might want to alter its priority or its process's priority. (Priorities are discussed in Chapter 7.) Since it is common for a thread to alter its (or its process's) environment, Windows offers functions that make it easy for a thread to refer to its process kernel object or to its own thread kernel object:

```
HANDLE GetCurrentProcess();
HANDLE GetCurrentThread();
```

Both of these functions return a pseudo-handle to the calling thread's process or thread kernel object. These functions do not create new handles in the calling process's handle table. Also, calling these functions has no effect on the usage count of the process or thread kernel object. If you call _CloseHandle_, passing a pseudo-handle as the parameter, _CloseHandle_ simply ignores the call and returns FALSE.

When you call a Windows function that requires a handle to a process or thread, you can pass a pseudo-handle, which causes the function to perform its action on the calling process or thread. For example, a thread can query its process's time usage by calling *GetProcessTimes* as follows:

```
FILETIME ftCreationTime, ftExitTime, ftKernelTime, ftUserTime;
GetProcessTimes(GetCurrentProcess(),
    &ftCreationTime, &ftExitTime, &ftKernelTime, &ftUserTime);
```

Likewise, a thread can query its own thread times by calling *GetThreadTimes*:

```
FILETIME ftCreationTime, ftExitTime, ftKernelTime, ftUserTime;
GetThreadTimes(GetCurrentThread(),
    &ftCreationTime, &ftExitTime, &ftKernelTime, &ftUserTime);
```

A few Windows functions allow you to identify a specific process or thread by its unique system-wide ID. The following functions allow a thread to query its process's unique ID or its own unique ID:

```
DWORD GetCurrentProcessId();
DWORD GetCurrentThreadId();
```

These functions are generally not as useful as the functions that return pseudo-handles, but occasionally they come in handy.

Converting a Pseudo-Handle to a Real Handle

Sometimes you might need to acquire a real handle to a thread instead of a pseudo-handle. By "real," I mean a handle that unambiguously identifies a unique thread. Examine the following code:

```
DWORD WINAPI ParentThread(PVOID pvParam) {
   HANDLE hThreadParent = GetCurrentThread();
   CreateThread(NULL, 0, ChildThread, (PVOID) hThreadParent, 0, NULL);
   // Function continues...
}

DWORD WINAPI ChildThread(PVOID pvParam) {
   HANDLE hThreadParent = (HANDLE) pvParam;
   FILETIME ftCreationTime, ftExitTime, ftKernelTime, ftUserTime;
   GetThreadTimes(hThreadParent,
       &ftCreationTime, &ftExitTime, &ftKernelTime, &ftUserTime);
   // Function continues...
}
```

Can you see the problem with this code fragment? The idea is to have the parent thread pass to the child thread a thread handle that identifies the parent thread. However, the parent thread passes a pseudo-handle, not a real handle. When the child thread begins executing, it passes the pseudo-handle to the

GetThreadTimes function, which causes the child thread to get its own CPU times, not the parent thread's CPU times. This happens because a thread pseudo-handle is a handle to the current thread—that is, a handle to whichever thread is making the function call.

To fix this code, we must turn the pseudo-handle into a real handle. The *DuplicateHandle* function (discussed in Chapter 3) can do this transformation:

```
BOOL DuplicateHandle(
    HANDLE hSourceProcess,
    HANDLE hSource,
    HANDLE hTargetProcess,
    PHANDLE phTarget,
    DWORD fdwAccess,
    BOOL bInheritHandle,
    DWORD fdwOptions);
```

Usually you use this function to create a new process-relative handle from a kernel object handle that is relative to another process. However, we can use it in an unusual way to correct the code fragment discussed earlier. The corrected code fragment is as follows:

```
DWORD WINAPI ParentThread(PVOID pvParam) {
    HANDLE hThreadParent;

    DuplicateHandle(
        GetCurrentProcess(),      // Handle of process that thread
                                  // pseudo-handle is relative to
        GetCurrentThread(),       // Parent thread's pseudo-handle
        GetCurrentProcess(),      // Handle of process that the new, real,
                                  // thread handle is relative to
        &hThreadParent,           // Will receive the new, real, handle
                                  // identifying the parent thread
        0,                        // Ignored due to DUPLICATE_SAME_ACCESS
        FALSE,                    // New thread handle is not inheritable
        DUPLICATE_SAME_ACCESS);   // New thread handle has same
                                  // access as pseudo-handle

    CreateThread(NULL, 0, ChildThread, (PVOID) hThreadParent, 0, NULL);
    // Function continues...
}
DWORD WINAPI ChildThread(PVOID pvParam) {
    HANDLE hThreadParent = (HANDLE) pvParam;
    FILETIME ftCreationTime, ftExitTime, ftKernelTime, ftUserTime;
    GetThreadTimes(hThreadParent,
        &ftCreationTime, &ftExitTime, &ftKernelTime, &ftUserTime);
    CloseHandle(hThreadParent);
    // Function continues...
}
```

Now when the parent thread executes, it converts the ambiguous pseudo-handle identifying the parent thread to a new, real handle that unambiguously identifies the parent thread, and it passes this real handle to *CreateThread*. When the child thread starts executing, its *pvParam* parameter contains the real thread handle. Any calls to functions passing this handle will affect the parent thread, not the child thread.

Because *DuplicateHandle* increments the usage count of the specified kernel object, it is important to decrement the object's usage count by passing the target handle to *CloseHandle* when you finish using the duplicated object handle. This is shown in the code fragment above. Immediately after the call to *GetThreadTimes*, the child thread calls *CloseHandle* to decrement the parent thread object's usage count. In this code fragment, I assumed that the child thread would not call any other functions using this handle. If other functions are to be called passing the parent thread's handle, the call to *CloseHandle* should not be made until the child thread no longer requires the handle.

I should also point out that the *DuplicateHandle* function can be used to convert a pseudo-handle for a process to a real process handle as follows:

```
HANDLE hProcess;
DuplicateHandle(
    GetCurrentProcess(),    // Handle of process that the process
                            // pseudo-handle is relative to
    GetCurrentProcess(),    // Process's pseudo-handle
    GetCurrentProcess(),    // Handle of process that the new, real,
                            // process handle is relative to
    &hProcess,              // Will receive the new, real
                            // handle identifying the process
    0,                      // Ignored because of DUPLICATE_SAME_ACCESS
    FALSE,                  // New thread handle is not inheritable
    DUPLICATE_SAME_ACCESS); // New process handle has same
                            // access as pseudo-handle
```

CHAPTER SEVEN

THREAD SCHEDULING, PRIORITIES, AND AFFINITIES

A preemptive operating system must use some algorithm to determine which threads should be scheduled when and for how long. In this chapter, we'll look at the algorithms that Microsoft Windows 98 and Windows 2000 use.

In Chapter 6, we discussed how every thread has a context structure, which is maintained inside the thread's kernel object. This context structure reflects the state of the thread's CPU registers when the thread was last executing. Every 20 milliseconds or so, Windows looks at all of the thread kernel objects currently in existence. Of these objects, only some are considered schedulable. Windows selects one of the schedulable thread kernel objects and loads the CPU's registers with the values that were last saved in the thread's context. This action is called a *context switch*. Windows actually keeps a record of how many times each thread gets a chance to run. You can see this using a tool such as Microsoft Spy++. The figure below shows the properties for a thread. Notice that this thread has been scheduled 37,379 times.

213

At this point, the thread is executing code and manipulating data in its process's address space. After another 20 milliseconds or so, Windows saves the CPU's registers back into the thread's context. The thread is no longer running. The system again examines the remaining schedulable thread kernel objects, selects another thread's kernel object, loads this thread's context into the CPU's registers, and continues. This operation of loading a thread's context, letting the thread run, saving the context, and repeating the operation begins when the system boots and continues until the system is shut down.

That, in short, is how the system schedules multiple threads. We'll discuss more details later, but that is basically it. Simple, isn't it? Windows is called a preemptive multithreaded operating system because a thread can be stopped at any time and another thread can be scheduled. As you'll see, you have some control over this, but not much. Just remember that you cannot guarantee that your thread will always be running, that your thread will get the whole processor, that no other thread will be allowed to run, and so on.

> **NOTE**
>
> Developers frequently ask me how they can guarantee that their thread will start running within some time period of some event—for example, how can you ensure that a particular thread will start running within 1 millisecond of data coming from the serial port? I have an easy answer: You can't. Real-time operating systems can make these promises, but Windows is not a real-time operating system. A real-time operating system requires intimate knowledge of the hardware it is running on so that it knows the latency associated with its hard disk controllers, keyboards, and so on. Microsoft's goal with Windows is to make it work on a wide variety of hardware: different CPUs, different drives, different networks, and so forth. In short, Windows is not designed to be a real-time operating system.

I stress the idea that the system only schedules schedulable threads, but as it turns out, most of the threads in the system are not schedulable. For example, some thread objects might have a suspend count greater than 0. This means that the thread is suspended and should not be scheduled any CPU time. You can create a suspended thread by calling *CreateProcess* or *CreateThread* using the CREATE_SUSPENDED flag. (Later in this chapter, I'll also discuss the *SuspendThread* and *ResumeThread* functions.)

In addition to suspended threads, many other threads are not schedulable because they are waiting for something to happen. For example, if you run Notepad and don't type, Notepad's thread has nothing to do. The system does not assign CPU time to threads that have nothing to do. When you move Notepad's window, or if Notepad's window needs to repaint its contents, or if you type into Notepad, the system automatically makes Notepad's thread schedulable. This does not mean that Notepad's thread gets CPU time immediately. It's just that Notepad's thread has something to do and the system will get around to scheduling it at some time—in the near future, we hope.

Suspending and Resuming a Thread

Inside a thread kernel object is a value that indicates the thread's suspend count. When you call *CreateProcess* or *CreateThread*, the thread kernel object is created and the suspend count is initialized to 1. This prevents the thread from being scheduled to a CPU. This is, of course, desirable because it takes time for the thread to be initialized and you don't want the system to start executing the thread before it is fully ready.

After the thread is fully initialized, *CreateProcess* or *CreateThread* checks to see whether you've passed the CREATE_SUSPENDED flag. If you have, the functions return and the new thread is left in the suspended state. If you have not, the function decrements the thread's suspend count to 0. When a thread's suspend count is 0, the thread is schedulable unless it is waiting for something else to happen (such as keyboard input).

Creating a thread in the suspended state allows you to alter the thread's environment (such as priority, discussed later in the chapter) before the thread has a chance to execute any code. Once you alter the thread's environment, you must make the thread schedulable. You do this by calling *ResumeThread* and passing it the thread handle returned by the call to *CreateThread* (or the thread handle from the structure pointed to by the *ppiProcInfo* parameter passed to *CreateProcess*):

```
DWORD ResumeThread(HANDLE hThread);
```

If *ResumeThread* is successful, it returns the thread's previous suspend count; otherwise, it returns 0xFFFFFFFF.

A single thread can be suspended several times. If a thread is suspended three times, it must be resumed three times before it is eligible for assignment

215

to a CPU. In addition to using the CREATE_SUSPENDED flag when you create a thread, you can suspend a thread by calling *SuspendThread*:

```
DWORD SuspendThread(HANDLE hThread);
```

Any thread can call this function to suspend another thread (as long as you have the thread's handle). It goes without saying (but I'll say it anyway) that a thread can suspend itself but cannot resume itself. Like *ResumeThread*, *SuspendThread* returns the thread's previous suspend count. A thread can be suspended as many as MAXIMUM_SUSPEND_COUNT times (defined as 127 in WinNT.h). Note that *SuspendThread* is asynchronous with respect to kernel mode execution, but user-mode execution does not occur until the thread is resumed.

In real life, an application must be careful when it calls *SuspendThread* because you have no idea what the thread might be doing when you attempt to suspend it. If the thread is attempting to allocate memory from a heap, for example, the thread will have a lock on the heap. As other threads attempt to access the heap, their execution will be halted until the first thread is resumed. *SuspendThread* is safe only if you know exactly what the target thread is (or might be doing) and you take extreme measures to avoid problems or deadlocks caused by suspending the thread. (Deadlocking and other thread synchronization issues are discussed in Chapters 8, 9, and 10.)

Suspending and Resuming a Process

The concept of suspending or resuming a process doesn't exist for Windows since processes are never scheduled CPU time. However, I have been asked numerous times how to suspend all of the threads in a process. Windows does allow one process to suspend all the threads in another process, but the process doing the suspending must be a debugger. Specifically, the process must call functions such as *WaitForDebugEvent* and *ContinueDebugEvent*.

Windows doesn't offer any other way to suspend all threads in a process because of race conditions. For example, while the threads are suspended, a new thread might be created. Somehow the system must suspend any new threads during this window of time. Microsoft has integrated this functionality into the debugging mechanism of the system.

While you cannot create an absolutely perfect *SuspendProcess* function, you can create an implementation of this function that works well in many situations. Here is my implementation of a *SuspendProcess* function:

```
VOID SuspendProcess(DWORD dwProcessID, BOOL fSuspend) {

   // Get the list of threads in the system.
   HANDLE hSnapshot = CreateToolhelp32Snapshot(
      TH32CS_SNAPTHREAD, dwProcessID);

   if (hSnapshot != INVALID_HANDLE_VALUE) {

      // Walk the list of threads.
      THREADENTRY32 te = { sizeof(te) };
      BOOL fOk = Thread32First(hSnapshot, &te);
      for (; fOk; fOk = Thread32Next(hSnapshot, &te)) {

         // Is this thread in the desired process?
         if (te.th32OwnerProcessID == dwProcessID) {

            // Attempt to convert the thread ID into a handle.
            HANDLE hThread = OpenThread(THREAD_SUSPEND_RESUME,
               FALSE, te.th32ThreadID);

            if (hThread != NULL) {

               // Suspend or resume the thread.
               if (fSuspend)
                  SuspendThread(hThread);
               else
                  ResumeThread(hThread);
            }
            CloseHandle(hThread);
         }
      }
      CloseHandle(hSnapshot);
   }
}
```

My *SuspendProcess* function uses the ToolHelp functions (discussed in Chapter 4) to enumerate the list of threads in the system. As I locate threads that are part of the specified process, I call *OpenThread*:

```
HANDLE OpenThread(
   DWORD dwDesiredAccess,
   BOOL bInheritHandle,
   DWORD dwThreadID);
```

This new Windows 2000 function locates the thread kernel object with the matching thread ID, increments the kernel object's usage count, and returns a handle to the object. With this handle, I call *SuspendThread* (or *Resume-Thread*). Because *OpenThread* is new in Windows 2000, my *SuspendProcess* function will not work on Windows 95 or Windows 98, or on Windows NT 4.0 or earlier.

You probably understand why *SuspendProcess* does not work 100 percent of the time: while enumerating the set of threads, new threads can be created and destroyed. So after I call *CreateToolhelp32Snapshot*, a new thread might appear in the target process, which my function will not suspend. Later, when you call *SuspendProcess* to resume the threads, it will resume a thread that it never suspended. Even worse, while enumerating the thread IDs, an existing thread might be destroyed and a new thread might be created, and both of these threads might have the same ID. This would cause the function to suspend some arbitrary thread (probably in a process other than the target process).

Of course, these situations are unlikely, and if you have intimate knowledge of how the target process operates, these issues might not be problems at all. I offer you this function to use at your own risk.

Sleeping

A thread can also tell the system that it does not want to be schedulable for a certain amount of time. This is accomplished by calling *Sleep*:

```
VOID Sleep(DWORD dwMilliseconds);
```

This function causes the thread to suspend itself until *dwMilliseconds* have elapsed. There are a few important things to notice about *Sleep*:

- Calling *Sleep* allows the thread to voluntarily give up the remainder of its time slice.

- The system makes the thread not schedulable for *approximately* the number of milliseconds specified. That's right—if you tell the system you want to sleep for 100 milliseconds, you will sleep approximately that long but possibly several seconds or minutes more. Remember that Windows is not a real-time operating system. Your thread will probably wake up at the right time, but whether it does depends on what else is going on in the system.

- You can call *Sleep* and pass INFINITE for the *dwMilliseconds* parameter. This tells the system to never schedule the thread. This is not a useful thing to do. It is much better to have the thread exit and to recover its stack and kernel object.

■ You can pass 0 to *Sleep*. This tells the system that the calling thread relinquishes the remainder of its time slice and forces the system to schedule another thread. However, the system can reschedule the thread that just called *Sleep*. This will happen if there are no more schedulable threads at the same priority.

Switching to Another Thread

The system offers a function called *SwitchToThread* that allows another schedulable thread to run if one exists:

```
BOOL SwitchToThread();
```

When you call this function, the system checks to see whether there is a thread that is being starved of CPU time. If no thread is starving, *SwitchToThread* returns immediately. If there is a starving thread, *SwitchToThread* schedules that thread (which might have a lower priority than the thread calling *SwitchToThread*). The starving thread is allowed to run for one time quantum and then the system scheduler operates as usual.

This function allows a thread that wants a resource to force a lower-priority thread that might currently own the resource to relinquish the resource. If no other thread can run when *SwitchToThread* is called, the function returns FALSE; otherwise, it returns a nonzero value.

Calling *SwitchToThread* is similar to calling *Sleep* and passing it a timeout of 0 milliseconds. The difference is that *SwitchToThread* allows lower-priority threads to execute. *Sleep* reschedules the calling thread immediately even if lower-priority threads are being starved.

WINDOWS 98

> Windows 98 does not have a useful implementation for this function.

A Thread's Execution Times

Sometimes you want to time how long it takes a thread to perform a particular task. What many people do is write code similar to the following:

```
// Get the current time (start time).
DWORD dwStartTime = GetTickCount();

// Perform complex algorithm here.

// Subtract start time from current time to get duration.
DWORD dwElapsedTime = GetTickCount() - dwStartTime;
```

This code makes a simple assumption: it won't be interrupted. However, in a preemptive operating system, you never know when your thread will be scheduled CPU time. When CPU time is taken away from your thread, it becomes more difficult to time how long it takes your thread to perform various tasks. What we need is a function that returns the amount of CPU time that the thread has received. Fortunately, Windows offers a function called *GetThread-Times* that returns this information:

```
BOOL GetThreadTimes(
   HANDLE hThread,
   PFILETIME pftCreationTime,
   PFILETIME pftExitTime,
   PFILETIME pftKernelTime,
   PFILETIME pftUserTime);
```

GetThreadTimes returns four different time values, as shown in the following table.

Time Value	Meaning
Creation time	An absolute value expressed in 100-nanosecond intervals past midnight on January 1, 1601, at Greenwich, England, indicating when the thread was created.
Exit time	An absolute value expressed in 100-nanosecond intervals past midnight on January 1, 1601, at Greenwich, England, indicating when the thread exited. If the thread is still running, the exit time is undefined.
Kernel time	A relative value indicating how many 100-nanosecond intervals of CPU time the thread has spent executing operating system code.
User time	A relative value indicating how many 100-nanosecond intervals of CPU time the thread has spent executing application code.

Using this function, you can determine the amount of time needed to execute a complex algorithm by using code such as this:

```
__int64 FileTimeToQuadWord (PFILETIME pft) {
   return(Int64ShllMod32(pft->dwHighDateTime, 32) | pft->dwLowDateTime);
}


void PerformLongOperation () {
```

(continued)

```
FILETIME ftKernelTimeStart, ftKernelTimeEnd;
FILETIME ftUserTimeStart,   ftUserTimeEnd;
FILETIME ftDummy;
__int64 qwKernelTimeElapsed, qwUserTimeElapsed,
   qwTotalTimeElapsed;

// Get starting times.
GetThreadTimes(GetCurrentThread(), &ftDummy, &ftDummy,
   &ftKernelTimeStart, &ftUserTimeStart);


// Perform complex algorithm here.


// Get ending times.
GetThreadTimes(GetCurrentThread(), &ftDummy, &ftDummy,
   &ftKernelTimeEnd, &ftUserTimeEnd);

// Get the elapsed kernel and user times by converting the start
// and end times from FILETIMEs to quad words, and then subtract
// the start times from the end times.
qwKernelTimeElapsed = FileTimeToQuadWord(&ftKernelTimeEnd) -
   FileTimeToQuadWord(&ftKernelTimeStart);

qwUserTimeElapsed = FileTimeToQuadWord(&ftUserTimeEnd) -
   FileTimeToQuadWord(&ftUserTimeStart);

// Get total time duration by adding the kernel and user times.
qwTotalTimeElapsed = qwKernelTimeElapsed + qwUserTimeElapsed;

// The total elapsed time is in qwTotalTimeElapsed.
}
```

Note that *GetProcessTimes*, a function similar to *GetThreadTimes*, applies to all of the threads in a process:

```
BOOL GetProcessTimes(
   HANDLE hProcess,
   PFILETIME pftCreationTime,
   PFILETIME pftExitTime,
   PFILETIME pftKernelTime,
   PFILETIME pftUserTime);
```

GetProcessTimes returns times that apply to all the threads in a specified process (even threads that have terminated). For example, the kernel time returned is the sum of all the elapsed times that all of the process's threads have spent in kernel code.

221

> Unfortunately, the *GetThreadTimes* and *GetProcessTimes* functions are not functional in Windows 98. Under Windows 98, there is no reliable mechanism for an application to determine how much CPU time a thread or process has used.

For high-resolution profiling, the *GetThreadTimes* function is not good enough. Windows does offer these high-resolution performance functions:

```
BOOL QueryPerformanceFrequency(LARGE_INTEGER* pliFrequency);

BOOL QueryPerformanceCounter(LARGE_INTEGER* pliCount);
```

These functions assume that the executing thread does not get preempted, but most high-resolution profiling is done for short-lived blocks of code anyway. To make working with these functions a little easier, I have created the following C++ class:

```cpp
class CStopwatch {
public:
   CStopwatch() { QueryPerformanceFrequency(&m_liPerfFreq); Start(); }

   void Start() { QueryPerformanceCounter(&m_liPerfStart); }

   __int64 Now() const {    //
 Returns # of milliseconds since Start was called
      LARGE_INTEGER liPerfNow;
      QueryPerformanceCounter(&liPerfNow);
      return(((liPerfNow.QuadPart - m_liPerfStart.QuadPart) * 1000)
         / m_liPerfFreq.QuadPart);
   }

private:
   LARGE_INTEGER m_liPerfFreq;    // Counts per second
   LARGE_INTEGER m_liPerfStart;   // Starting count
};
```

I use this class as follows:

```cpp
// Create a stopwatch timer (which defaults to the current time).
CStopwatch stopwatch;

// Execute the code I want to profile here.

// Get how much time has elapsed up to now.
__int64 qwElapsedTime = stopwatch.Now();

// qwElapsedTime indicates how long the profiled code
// executed in milliseconds.
```

Putting the Context in Context

By now, you should understand the important role that the context structure plays in thread scheduling. The context structure allows the system to remember a thread's state so that the thread can pick up where it left off the next time it has a CPU to run on.

You might be surprised to learn that such a low-level data structure is completely documented in the Platform SDK. However, if you look up the CONTEXT structure in the documentation, all you'll see is this:

"A CONTEXT structure contains processor-specific register data. The system uses CONTEXT structures to perform various internal operations. Currently, there are CONTEXT structures defined for Intel, MIPS, Alpha, and PowerPC processors. Refer to the header file WinNT.h for definitions of these structures."

The documentation does not show you the structure's members and does not describe the members in any way whatsoever because the members depend on which CPU Windows 2000 is running on. In fact, of all the data structures Windows defines, the CONTEXT structure is the only data structure that is CPU-specific.

So what's in the CONTEXT structure? Well, it contains a data member for each register on the host CPU. On an *x86* machine, the members are *Eax*, *Ebx*, *Ecx*, *Edx*, and so on. For the Alpha processor, the members are *IntV0*, *IntT0*, *IntT1*, *IntS0*, *IntRa*, *IntZero*, and so on. The code fragment below shows the complete CONTEXT structure for an *x86* CPU.

```
typedef struct _CONTEXT {

    //
    // The flags values within this flag control the contents of
    // a CONTEXT record.
    //
    // If the context record is used as an input parameter, then
    // for each portion of the context record controlled by a flag
    // whose value is set, it is assumed that that portion of the
    // context record contains valid context. If the context record
    // is being used to modify a threads context, then only that
    // portion of the threads context will be modified.
    //
    // If the context record is used as an IN OUT parameter to capture
    // the context of a thread, then only those portions of the thread's
    // context corresponding to set flags will be returned.
```

(continued)

```
//
// The context record is never used as an OUT only parameter.
//

DWORD ContextFlags;

//
// This section is specified/returned if CONTEXT_DEBUG_REGISTERS is
// set in ContextFlags.  Note that CONTEXT_DEBUG_REGISTERS is NOT
// included in CONTEXT_FULL.
//

DWORD    Dr0;
DWORD    Dr1;
DWORD    Dr2;
DWORD    Dr3;
DWORD    Dr6;
DWORD    Dr7;

//
// This section is specified/returned if the
// ContextFlags word contians the flag CONTEXT_FLOATING_POINT.
//

FLOATING_SAVE_AREA FloatSave;

//
// This section is specified/returned if the
// ContextFlags word contians the flag CONTEXT_SEGMENTS.
//

DWORD    SegGs;
DWORD    SegFs;
DWORD    SegEs;
DWORD    SegDs;

//
// This section is specified/returned if the
// ContextFlags word contians the flag CONTEXT_INTEGER.
//

DWORD    Edi;
DWORD    Esi;
DWORD    Ebx;
DWORD    Edx;
DWORD    Ecx;
DWORD    Eax;
```

(continued)

```
//
// This section is specified/returned if the
// ContextFlags word contians the flag CONTEXT_CONTROL.
//

DWORD    Ebp;
DWORD    Eip;
DWORD    SegCs;           // MUST BE SANITIZED
DWORD    EFlags;          // MUST BE SANITIZED
DWORD    Esp;
DWORD    SegSs;


//
// This section is specified/returned if the ContextFlags word
// contains the flag CONTEXT_EXTENDED_REGISTERS.
// The format and contexts are processor specific
//

BYTE     ExtendedRegisters[MAXIMUM_SUPPORTED_EXTENSION];

} CONTEXT;
```

A CONTEXT structure has several sections. CONTEXT_CONTROL contains the control registers of the CPU, such as the instruction pointer, stack pointer, flags, and function return address. (Unlike the *x*86 processor, which pushes a function's return address on the stack when it makes a call, the Alpha CPU places a function's return address in a register when it makes a call.) CONTEXT_INTEGER identifies the CPU's integer registers; CONTEXT_ FLOATING_POINT identifies the CPU's floating-point registers; CONTEXT_SEGMENTS identifies the CPU's segment registers (*x*86 only); CONTEXT_DEBUG_REGISTERS identifies the CPU's debug registers (*x*86 only); and CONTEXT_ EXTENDED_REGISTERS identifies the CPU's extended registers (*x*86 only).

Windows actually lets you look inside a thread's kernel object and grab its current set of CPU registers. To do this, you simply call *GetThreadContext*:

```
BOOL GetThreadContext(
   HANDLE hThread,
   PCONTEXT pContext);
```

To call this function, just allocate a CONTEXT structure, initialize some flags (the structure's *ContextFlags* member) indicating which registers you want to get back, and pass the address of the structure to *GetThreadContext*. The function then fills in the members you've requested.

You should call *SuspendThread* before calling *GetThreadContext*, otherwise, the thread might be scheduled and the thread's context might be different from what you get back. A thread actually has two contexts: user mode and kernel mode. *GetThreadContext* can return only the user-mode context of a thread. If you call *SuspendThread* to stop a thread but that thread is currently executing in kernel mode, its user-mode context is stable even though *SuspendThread* hasn't actually suspended the thread yet. But the thread cannot execute any more user-mode code until it is resumed, so you can safely consider the thread suspended and *GetThreadContext* will work.

The CONTEXT structure's *ContextFlags* member does not correspond to any CPU registers. This member exists in all CONTEXT structure definitions regardless of the CPU architecture. The *ContextFlags* member indicates to the *GetThreadContext* function which registers you want to retrieve. For example, if you want to get the control registers for a thread, you can write something like this:

```
// Create a CONTEXT structure.
CONTEXT Context;

// Tell the system that we are interested in only the
// control registers.
Context.ContextFlags = CONTEXT_CONTROL;

// Tell the system to get the registers associated with a thread.
GetThreadContext(hThread, &Context);

// The control register members in the CONTEXT structure
// reflect the thread's control registers. The other members
// are undefined.
```

Notice that you must first initialize the *ContextFlags* member in the CONTEXT structure before calling *GetThreadContext*. If you want to get a thread's control and integer registers, you should initialize *ContextFlags* as follows:

```
// Tell the system that we are interested
// in the control and integer registers.
Context.ContextFlags = CONTEXT_CONTROL | CONTEXT_INTEGER;
```

Here is the identifier you can use to get all of the thread's important registers (that is, the ones Microsoft deems to be most commonly used):

```
// Tell the system we are interested in the important registers.
Context.ContextFlags = CONTEXT_FULL;
```

CONTEXT_FULL is defined in WinNT.h as shown in the following table.

CPU Type	Definition of CONTEXT_FULL
*x*86	CONTEXT_CONTROL | CONTEXT_INTEGER | CONTEXT_SEGMENTS
Alpha	CONTEXT_CONTROL | CONTEXT_FLOATING_POINT | CONTEXT_INTEGER

When *GetThreadContext* returns, you can easily examine any of the thread's register values, but remember that this means writing CPU-dependent code. The following table lists the instruction pointer and stack pointer members of a CONTEXT structure according to the CPU type.

CPU Type	Instruction Pointer	Stack Pointer
*x*86	CONTEXT.Eip	CONTEXT.Esp
Alpha	CONTEXT.Fir	CONTEXT.IntSp

It's amazing how much power Windows offers the developer! But, if you think that's cool, you're gonna love this: Windows lets you change the members in the CONTEXT structure and then place the new register values back into the thread's kernel object by calling *SetThreadContext*:

```
BOOL SetThreadContext(
   HANDLE hThread,
   CONST CONTEXT *pContext);
```

Again, the thread whose context you're changing should be suspended first or the results will be unpredictable.

Before calling *SetThreadContext*, you must initialize the *ContextFlags* member of CONTEXT again, as shown here:

```
CONTEXT Context;

// Stop the thread from running.
SuspendThread(hThread);

// Get the thread's context registers.
Context.ContextFlags = CONTEXT_CONTROL;
GetThreadContext(hThread, &Context);
```

(continued)

227

```
// Make the instruction pointer point to the address of your choice.
// Here I've arbitrarily set the address instruction pointer to
// 0x00010000.
#if defined(_ALPHA_)
Context.Fir = 0x00010000;
#elif defined(_X86_)
Context.Eip = 0x00010000;
#else
#error Module contains CPU-specific code; modify and recompile.
#endif


// Set the thread's registers to reflect the changed values.
// It's not really necessary to reset the ControlFlags member
// because it was set earlier.
Context.ControlFlags = CONTEXT_CONTROL;
SetThreadContext(hThread, &Context);

// Resuming the thread will cause it to begin execution
// at address 0x00010000.
ResumeThread(hThread);
```

This will probably cause an access violation in the remote thread; the unhandled exception message box will be presented to the user, and the remote process will be terminated. That's right—the remote process will be terminated, not your process. You will have successfully crashed another process while yours continues to execute just fine!

The *GetThreadContext* and *SetThreadContext* functions give you a lot of control over threads, but you should use them with caution. In fact, few applications ever call these functions at all. The functions were added to help debuggers and other tools. But any application can call them.

I'll talk about the CONTEXT structure more in Chapter 24.

Thread Priorities

At the beginning of this chapter, I explained how a CPU can run a thread for only about 20 milliseconds before the scheduler assigns another schedulable thread to that CPU. This happens if all the threads have the same priority, but in reality threads are assigned a lot of different priorities and this affects which thread the scheduler picks as the next thread to run.

Every thread is assigned a priority number ranging from 0 (the lowest) to 31 (the highest). When the system decides which thread to assign to a CPU, it examines the priority 31 threads first and schedules them in a round-robin fashion. If a priority 31 thread is schedulable, it is assigned to a CPU. At the end of this thread's time slice, the system checks to see whether there is another priority 31 thread that can run; if so, it allows that thread to be assigned to a CPU.

As long as a priority 31 thread is schedulable, the system never assigns any thread with a priority of 0 through 30 to a CPU. This condition is called *starvation*. Starvation occurs when higher-priority threads use so much CPU time that they prevent lower-priority threads from executing. Starvation is much less likely to occur on a multiprocessor machine because on such a machine a priority 31 thread and a priority 30 thread can run simultaneously. The system always tries to keep the CPUs busy, and CPUs sit idle only if no threads are schedulable.

You might assume that lower-priority threads never get a chance to run in a system designed like this. But as I've pointed out, at any one time most threads in the system are not schedulable. For example, if your process's primary thread calls *GetMessage* and the system sees that no messages are pending, the system suspends your process's thread, relinquishes the remainder of the thread's time slice, and immediately assigns the CPU to another, waiting, thread.

If no messages show up for *GetMessage* to retrieve, the process's primary thread stays suspended and is never assigned to a CPU. However, when a message is placed in the thread's queue, the system knows that the thread should no longer be suspended and assigns the thread to a CPU if no higher-priority threads need to execute.

Let me point out another issue. Higher-priority threads always preempt lower-priority threads, regardless of what the lower-priority threads are executing. For example, if a priority 5 thread is running and the system determines that a higher-priority thread is ready to run, the system immediately suspends the lower-priority thread (even if it's in the middle of its time slice) and assigns the CPU to the higher-priority thread, which gets a full time slice.

By the way, when the system boots, it creates a special thread called the *zero page thread*. This thread is assigned priority 0 and is the only thread in the entire system that runs at priority 0. The zero page thread is responsible for zeroing any free pages of RAM in the system when there are no other threads that need to perform work.

229

An Abstract View of Priorities

When Microsoft developers designed the thread scheduler, they realized that it would not fit everyone's needs all the time. They also realized that the "purpose" of the computer would change over time. When Windows NT first came out, object linking and embedding (OLE) applications were just starting to be written. Now, OLE applications are commonplace. Game software is much more prevalent, and certainly the Internet wasn't discussed much in Windows NT's early days.

The scheduling algorithm has a significant effect on the types of applications that users run. From the beginning, Microsoft developers realized that they would need to modify the scheduling algorithm over time as the purpose of the system changed. But software developers need to write software today and Microsoft guarantees that your software will run on future versions of the system. How can Microsoft change the way the system works and still keep your software running? Here are a few answers:

- Microsoft doesn't fully document the behavior of the scheduler.

- Microsoft doesn't let applications take full advantage of the scheduler's features.

- Microsoft tells you that the scheduler's algorithm is subject to change so that you can code defensively.

The Windows API exposes an abstract layer over the system's scheduler, so you never talk to the scheduler directly. Instead, you call Windows functions that "interpret" your parameters depending on the version of the system you're running on. So, in this chapter, I'll be discussing this abstract layer.

When you design an application, you should think about what other applications your user might run along with your application. Then you should choose a priority class based on how responsive you need the threads in your application to be. I know that this sounds vague; it's supposed to. Microsoft doesn't want to make any promises that will break your code in the future.

Windows supports six priority classes: idle, below normal, normal, above normal, high, and real-time. Of course, normal is the most common priority class and is used by 99 percent of the applications out there. The table below describes the priority classes.

Priority Class	Description
Real-time	The threads in this process must respond immediately to events in order to execute time-critical tasks. Threads in this process also preempt operating system components. Use this priority class with extreme caution.
High	The threads in this process must respond immediately to events in order to execute time-critical tasks. The Task Manager runs at this class so a user can kill runaway processes.
Above normal	The threads in this process run between the normal and high priority classes (new in Windows 2000).
Normal	The threads in this process have no special scheduling needs.
Below normal	The threads in this process run between the normal and idle priority classes (new in Windows 2000).
Idle	The threads in this process run when the system is otherwise idle. This process is typically used by screensavers or background utility and statistic-gathering software.

The idle priority class is perfect for applications that run when the system is all but doing nothing. A computer that is not being used interactively might still be busy (acting as a file server, for example) and should not have to compete for CPU time with a screensaver. Statistic-tracking applications that periodically update some state about the system usually should not interfere with more critical tasks.

You should use the high priority class only when absolutely necessary. You might be surprised to learn that Windows Explorer runs at high priority. Most of the time Explorer's threads are suspended, waiting to be awakened when the user presses a key or clicks a mouse button. While Explorer's threads are suspended, the system doesn't assign its threads to a CPU, which allows lower-priority threads to execute. However, once the user presses a key or key combination, such as Ctrl+Esc, the system wakes up Explorer's thread. (The Start menu also appears when the user presses Ctrl+Esc.) If any lower-priority threads are executing, the system preempts those threads immediately and allows Explorer's thread to run.

Microsoft designed Explorer this way because users expect the shell to be extremely responsive, regardless of what else is going on in the system. In fact, Explorer's windows can be displayed even when lower-priority threads are hung in infinite loops. Because Explorer's threads have higher priority levels, the thread executing the infinite loop is preempted and Explorer lets the user terminate the hung process. Explorer is very well behaved—most of the time its threads have nothing to do and require no CPU time. If this were not the case, the whole system would perform much more slowly and many applications would not respond.

You should avoid the real-time priority class if possible. In fact, the early betas of Windows NT 3.1 did not expose this priority class to applications even though the operating system supported it. Real-time priority is extremely high and can interfere with operating systems tasks because most operating system threads execute at a lower priority. So real-time threads can prevent required disk I/O and network traffic from occurring. In addition, keyboard and mouse input are not processed in a timely manner; the user might think that the system is hung. Basically, you should have a good reason for using real-time priority—such as the need to respond to hardware events with short latency or to perform some short-lived task that just can't be interrupted.

> **NOTE**
>
> A process cannot run in the real-time priority class unless the user has the Increase Scheduling Priority privilege. Any user designated an administrator or a power user has this privilege by default.

Of course, most processes are part of the normal priority class. The two other priority classes, below normal and above normal, are new in Windows 2000. Microsoft added these because several companies complained that the existing priority classes didn't offer enough flexibility.

Once you select a priority class, you should stop thinking about how your application interrelates with other applications and just concentrate on the threads within your application. Windows supports seven relative thread priorities: idle, lowest, below normal, normal, above normal, highest, and time-critical.

These priorities are relative to the process's priority class. Again, most threads use the normal thread priority. The table below describes the relative thread priorities.

Relative Thread Priority	Description
Time-critical	Thread runs at 31 for the real-time priority class and at 15 for all other priority classes.
Highest	Thread runs two levels above normal.
Above normal	Thread runs one level above normal.
Normal	Thread runs normally for the process's priority class.
Below normal	Thread runs one level below normal.
Lowest	Thread runs two levels below normal.
Idle	Thread runs at 16 for the real-time priority class and at 1 for all other priority classes.

So, to summarize, your process is part of a priority class and you assign the threads within the process relative thread priorities. You'll notice that I haven't said anything about priority levels 0 through 31. Application developers never work with priority levels. Instead, the system maps the process's priority class and a thread's relative priority to a priority level. It is precisely this mapping that Microsoft does not want to commit to. In fact, this mapping has changed between versions of the system.

The table on page 234 shows how this mapping works for Windows 2000, but be aware that earlier versions of Windows NT and certainly Windows 95 and Windows 98 have slightly different mappings. Also be aware that the mapping will change in future versions of Windows.

For example, a normal thread in a normal process is assigned a priority level of 8. Since most processes are of the normal priority class and most threads are of normal thread priority, most threads in the system have a priority level of 8.

If you have a normal thread in a high-priority process, the thread will have a priority level of 13. If you change the process's priority class to idle, the thread's priority level becomes 4. Remember that thread priorities are relative to the process's priority class. If you change a process's priority class, the thread's relative priority will not change but its priority level will.

Relative Thread Priority	Process Priority Class					
	Idle	Below Normal	Normal	Above Normal	High	Real-Time
Time-critical	15	15	15	15	15	31
Highest	6	8	10	12	15	26
Above normal	5	7	9	11	14	25
Normal	4	6	8	10	13	24
Below normal	3	5	7	9	12	23
Lowest	2	4	6	8	11	22
Idle	1	1	1	1	1	16

Notice that the table above does not show any way for a thread to have a priority level of 0. This is because the 0 priority is reserved for the zero page thread and the system does not allow any other thread to have a priority of 0. Also, the following priority levels are not obtainable: 17, 18, 19, 20, 21, 27, 28, 29, or 30. If you are writing a device driver that runs in kernel mode, you can obtain these levels; a user-mode application cannot. Also note that a thread in the real-time priority class can't be below priority level 16. Likewise, a thread in a non-real-time priority class cannot be above 15.

NOTE The concept of a process priority class confuses some people. They think that this somehow means that processes are scheduled. Processes are never scheduled; only threads are scheduled. The process priority class is an abstract concept that Microsoft created to help isolate you from the internal workings of the scheduler; it serves no other purpose.

NOTE In general, a thread with a high priority level should not be schedulable most of the time. When the thread has something to do, it quickly gets CPU time. At this point, the thread should execute as few CPU instructions as possible and go back to sleep, waiting to be schedulable again. In contrast, a thread with a low priority level can remain schedulable and execute a lot of CPU instructions to do its work. If you follow these rules, the entire operating system will be responsive to its users.

Programming Priorities

So how is a process assigned a priority class? Well, when you call *CreateProcess*, you can pass the desired priority class in the *fdwCreate* parameter. The table below shows the priority class identifiers.

Priority Class	Symbolic Identifiers
Real-time	REALTIME_PRIORITY_CLASS
High	HIGH_PRIORITY_CLASS
Above normal	ABOVE_NORMAL_PRIORITY_CLASS
Normal	NORMAL_PRIORITY_CLASS
Below normal	BELOW_NORMAL_PRIORITY_CLASS
Idle	IDLE_PRIORITY_CLASS

It might seem odd that the process that creates a child process chooses the priority class at which the child process runs. Let's consider Explorer as an example. When you use Explorer to run an application, the new process runs at normal priority. Explorer has no idea what the process does or how often its threads need to be scheduled. However, once the child process is running, it can change its own priority class by calling *SetPriorityClass*:

```
BOOL SetPriorityClass(
   HANDLE hProcess,
   DWORD fdwPriority);
```

This function changes the priority class identified by *hProcess* to the value specified in the *fdwPriority* parameter. The *fdwPriority* parameter can be one of the identifiers shown in the table above. Because this function takes a process handle, you can alter the priority class of any process running in the system as long as you have a handle to it and sufficient access.

Normally, a process will attempt to alter its own priority class. Here is an example of how to have a process set its own priority class to idle:

```
BOOL SetPriorityClass(
   GetCurrentProcess(),
   IDLE_PRIORITY_CLASS);
```

Here is the complementary function used to retrieve the priority class of a process:

```
DWORD GetPriorityClass(HANDLE hProcess);
```

As you might expect, this function returns one of the identifiers listed in the table above.

When you invoke a program using the command shell, the program's starting priority is normal. However, if you invoke the program using the Start command, you can use a switch to specify the starting priority of the application. For example, the following command entered at the command shell causes the system to invoke the Calculator and initially run it at idle priority:

```
C:\>START /LOW CALC.EXE
```

The Start command also recognizes the /BELOWNORMAL, /NORMAL, /ABOVENORMAL, /HIGH, and /REALTIME switches to start executing an application at their respective priority classes. Of course, once an application starts executing, it can call *SetPriorityClass* to alter its own priority to whatever it chooses.

WINDOWS 98

> The Windows 98 Start command does not support any of these switches. Processes started from the Windows 98 command shell always run using the normal priority class.

The Windows 2000 Task Manager allows the user to change the priority class of a process. The figure below shows the Task Manager's Processes tab, which shows all the processes currently running. The Base Pri column shows each process's priority class. You can alter a process's priority class by selecting a process and then selecting an option from the context menu's Set Priority submenu.

When a thread is first created, its relative thread priority is always set to normal. It has always seemed odd to me that *CreateThread* doesn't offer a way for the caller to set the new thread's relative priority. To set and get a thread's relative priority, you must call these functions:

```
BOOL SetThreadPriority(
   HANDLE hThread,
   int nPriority);
```

Of course, the *hThread* parameter identifies the single thread whose priority you want to change, and the *nPriority* parameter is one of the seven identifiers listed in the following table.

Relative Thread Priority	Symbolic Constant
Time-critical	THREAD_PRIORITY_TIME_CRITICAL
Highest	THREAD_PRIORITY_HIGHEST
Above normal	THREAD_PRIORITY_ABOVE_NORMAL
Normal	THREAD_PRIORITY_NORMAL
Below normal	THREAD_PRIORITY_BELOW_NORMAL
Lowest	THREAD_PRIORITY_LOWEST
Idle	THREAD_PRIORITY_IDLE

Here is the complementary function for retrieving a thread's relative priority:

```
int GetThreadPriority(HANDLE hThread);
```

This function returns one of the identifiers listed in the table above.

To create a thread with an idle relative thread priority, you execute code similar to the following:

```
DWORD dwThreadID;
HANDLE hThread = CreateThread(NULL, 0, ThreadFunc, NULL,
   CREATE_SUSPENDED, &dwThreadID);
SetThreadPriority(hThread, THREAD_PRIORITY_IDLE);
ResumeThread(hThread);
CloseHandle(hThread);
```

Note that *CreateThread* always creates a new thread with a normal relative thread priority. To have the thread execute using idle priority, you pass the CREATE_SUSPENDED flag to *CreateThread*; this prevents the thread from executing any code at all. Then you call *SetThreadPriority* to change the thread to an idle relative thread priority. You then call *ResumeThread* so that the thread can be schedulable. You don't know when the thread will get CPU time, but the scheduler takes into account the fact that this thread has an idle thread priority. Finally, you close the handle to the new thread so that the kernel object can be destroyed as soon as the thread terminates.

> **NOTE**
>
> Windows does not offer a function that returns a thread's priority level. This omission is deliberate. Remember that Microsoft reserves the right to change the scheduling algorithm at any time. You should not design an application that requires specific knowledge of the scheduling algorithm. If you stick with process priority classes and relative thread priorities, your application should run well today and on future versions of the system.

Dynamically Boosting Thread Priority Levels

The system determines the thread's priority level by combining a thread's relative priority with the priority class of the thread's process. This is sometimes referred to as the thread's *base priority level*. Occasionally, the system boosts the priority level of a thread—usually in response to some I/O event such as a window message or a disk read.

For example, a thread with a normal thread priority in a high priority class process has a base priority level of 13. If the user presses a key, the system places a WM_KEYDOWN message in the thread's queue. Because a message has appeared in the thread's queue, the thread is schedulable. In addition, the keyboard device driver can tell the system to temporarily boost the thread's level. So the thread might be boosted by 2 and have a current priority level of 15.

The thread is scheduled for one time slice at priority 15. Once that time slice expires, the system drops the thread's priority by 1 to 14 for the next time slice. The thread's third time slice is executed with a priority level of 13. Any additional time slices required by the thread are executed at priority level 13, the thread's base priority level.

Note that a thread's current priority level never goes below the thread's base priority level. Also note that the device driver that causes the thread to be schedulable determines the amount of the boost. Again, Microsoft does not document how much boost a thread will get by any individual device driver. This allows Microsoft to continuously fine-tune the dynamic boosts to determine the best overall responsiveness.

The system only boosts threads that have a base priority level between 1 and 15. In fact, this is why this range is referred to as the dynamic priority range. In addition, the system never boosts a thread into the real-time range (above

15). Since threads in the real-time range perform most operating system functions, enforcing a cap on the boost prevents an application from interfering with the operating system. Also, the system never dynamically boosts threads in the real-time range (16 through 31).

Some developers complained that the system's dynamic boosts had an adverse affect on their threads' performance, so Microsoft added the following two functions to let you disable the system's dynamic boosting of thread priority levels:

```
BOOL SetProcessPriorityBoost(
    HANDLE hProcess,
    BOOL DisablePriorityBoost);
BOOL SetThreadPriorityBoost(
    HANDLE hThread,
    BOOL DisablePriorityBoost);
```

SetProcessPriorityBoost tells the system to enable or disable priority boosting for all threads within a process; *SetThreadPriorityBoost* lets you enable or disable priority boosting for individual threads. These two functions have counterparts that allow you to determine whether priority boosting is enabled or disabled:

```
BOOL GetProcessPriorityBoost(
    HANDLE hProcess,
    PBOOL pDisablePriorityBoost);
BOOL GetThreadPriorityBoost(
    HANDLE hThread,
    PBOOL pDisablePriorityBoost);
```

To each of these functions, you pass the handle of the process or thread that you want to query along with the address of a BOOL that will be set by the function.

WINDOWS 98

> Windows 98 offers no useful implementation of these four functions. They all return FALSE, and a subsequent call to *GetLastError* returns ERROR_CALL_NOT_IMPLEMENTED.

Another situation causes the system to dynamically boost a thread's priority level. Imagine a priority 4 thread that is ready to run but cannot because a priority 8 thread is constantly schedulable. In this scenario, the priority 4 thread is being starved of CPU time. When the system detects that a thread has been starved of CPU time for about three to four seconds, it dynamically boosts the starving thread's priority to 15 and allows that thread to run for twice its time quantum. When the double time quantum expires, the thread's priority immediately returns to its base priority.

Tweaking the Scheduler for the Foreground Process

When the user works with windows of a process, that process is said to be the *foreground process* and all other processes are *background processes*. Certainly, a user would prefer the process that he or she is using to behave more responsively than the background processes. To improve the responsiveness of the foreground process, Windows tweaks the scheduling algorithm for threads in the foreground process. For Windows 2000, the system gives foreground process threads a larger time quantum than they would usually receive. This tweak is performed only if the foreground process is of the normal priority class. If it is of any other priority class, no tweaking is performed.

Windows 2000 actually allows a user to configure this tweaking. On the Advanced tab of the System Properties dialog box, the user can click the Performance Options button, which causes the following dialog box to appear.

If the user chooses to optimize performance for applications, the system performs the tweaking. If the user chooses to optimize performance for background services, no tweaking is performed. When you install Windows 2000 Professional Edition, Applications is selected by default. For all other editions of Windows 2000, Background Services is the default because it is expected that the machine will be used primarily by noninteractive users.

Windows 98 also tweaks the threads in a normal priority class process when it moves to the foreground. When a normal process is brought to the foreground, the system increases the priority of the lowest, below normal, normal, above normal, and highest threads by 1 when the process is moved to the foreground; the idle and time-critical threads do not have their priorities boosted. So a thread with normal relative thread priority running in a normal priority class process has a priority level of 9 instead of 8. When the process returns to the background, the threads within the process automatically return to their defined base priority level.

WINDOWS
98

> Windows 98 does not offer any user interface that allows a user to con-
> figure this tweaking because Windows 98 is not designed to run as a
> dedicated server machine.

The reason for this change to foreground processes is to make them react faster to the user's input. Without this change, a normal process printing in
the background and a normal process accepting user input in the foreground
would compete equally for the CPU's time. The user, of course, would see that
text is not appearing smoothly in the foreground application. But because the
system alters the foreground process's threads, the foreground process's threads
can process the user's input more responsively.

The Scheduling Lab Sample Application

Using the Scheduling Lab application, "07 SchedLab.exe" (listed in Figure 7-1
on page 243), you can experiment with process priority classes and relative thread
priorities to see their effect on the system's overall performance. The source code
and resource files for the application are in the 07-SchedLab directory on the companion CD-ROM. When you start the program, the window shown here appears.

Initially, the primary thread is always busy so your CPU usage immediately
jumps to 100 percent. The primary thread constantly increments a number and
adds it to the list box on the right. The number doesn't have any meaning—it
simply shows that the thread is busy doing something. To get a feel for how
thread scheduling actually affects the system, I recommend that you run at least
two instances of this sample application simultaneously to see how changing the
priorities of one instance affects the other instances. You can also run Task
Manager and monitor the CPU usage of all instances.

When you perform these tests, the CPU usage will initially go to 100
percent and all instances of the application will get about equal CPU time. (Task
Manager should show about the same percentage of CPU usage for all instances.)

If you change one instance's priority class to above normal or high, you should see it get the bulk of the CPU usage. The scrolling of numbers in the other instances will become erratic. However, the other instances do not stop scrolling completely because of the dynamic boosting that the system automatically performs for starving threads. Anyway, you can play with the priority class and relative thread priorities to see how they affect the other instances. I purposely coded the Scheduling Lab application so it doesn't allow you to change the process to the real-time priority class because this prevents operating system threads from performing properly. If you want to experiment with real-time priority, you must modify the source code yourself.

You can use the Sleep field to stop the primary thread from being schedulable for any number of milliseconds from 0 to 9999. Experiment with this and see how much CPU processing time you recover by passing a sleep value of just 1 millisecond. On my 300 MHz Pentium II Notebook computer, I gain back 99 percent—quite a drop!

Clicking on the Suspend button causes the primary thread to spawn a secondary thread. This secondary thread suspends the primary thread and displays the following message box.

While this message box is displayed, the primary thread is completely suspended and uses no CPU time. The secondary thread also does not use any CPU time because it is simply waiting for the user to do something. While the message box is displayed, you can move it over the application's main window and then move it away so you can see the main window. Because the primary thread is suspended, the main window will not receive any window messages (including WM_PAINT). This is proof positive that the thread is suspended. When you dismiss the message box, the primary thread is resumed and the CPU usage goes back up to 100 percent.

For one more test, display the Performance Options dialog box discussed in the previous section, and change the setting from Application to Background Services or vice versa. Then take multiple instances of the SchedLab program, set them all to the normal priority class, and activate one of them to make it the foreground process. You'll see what effect the performance setting has on the foreground/background processes.

SchedLab.cpp

```
/*****************************************************************************
Module:  SchedLab.cpp
Notices: Copyright (c) 2000 Jeffrey Richter
*****************************************************************************/


#include "..\CmnHdr.H"       /* See Appendix A. */
#include <windowsx.h>
#include <tchar.h>
#include <process.h>         // For _beginthreadex
#include "Resource.H"


///////////////////////////////////////////////////////////////////////////


DWORD WINAPI ThreadFunc(PVOID pvParam) {
   HANDLE hThreadPrimary = (HANDLE) pvParam;
   SuspendThread(hThreadPrimary);
   chMB(
      "The Primary thread is suspended.\n"
      "It no longer responds to input and produces no output.\n"
      "Press OK to resume the primary thread & exit this secondary thread.\n");
   ResumeThread(hThreadPrimary);
   CloseHandle(hThreadPrimary);

   // To avoid deadlock, call EnableWindow after ResumeThread.
   EnableWindow(
      GetDlgItem(FindWindow(NULL, TEXT("Scheduling Lab")), IDC_SUSPEND),
      TRUE);
   return(0);
}


///////////////////////////////////////////////////////////////////////////


BOOL Dlg_OnInitDialog (HWND hwnd, HWND hwndFocus, LPARAM lParam) {

   chSETDLGICONS(hwnd, IDI_SCHEDLAB);
```

Figure 7-1.   *(continued)*
The SchedLab sample application

Figure 7-1. *continued*

```
// Initialize process priority classes
HWND hwndCtl = GetDlgItem(hwnd, IDC_PROCESSPRIORITYCLASS);

int n = ComboBox_AddString(hwndCtl, TEXT("High"));
ComboBox_SetItemData(hwndCtl, n, HIGH_PRIORITY_CLASS);

// Save our current priority class
DWORD dwpc = GetPriorityClass(GetCurrentProcess());

if (SetPriorityClass(GetCurrentProcess(), BELOW_NORMAL_PRIORITY_CLASS)) {

   // This system supports the BELOW_NORMAL_PRIORITY_CLASS class

   // Restore our original priority class
   SetPriorityClass(GetCurrentProcess(), dwpc);

   // Add the Above Normal priority class
   n = ComboBox_AddString(hwndCtl, TEXT("Above normal"));
   ComboBox_SetItemData(hwndCtl, n, ABOVE_NORMAL_PRIORITY_CLASS);

   dwpc = 0;  // Remember that this system supports below normal
}

int nNormal = n = ComboBox_AddString(hwndCtl, TEXT("Normal"));
ComboBox_SetItemData(hwndCtl, n, NORMAL_PRIORITY_CLASS);

if (dwpc == 0) {

   // This system supports the BELOW_NORMAL_PRIORITY_CLASS class

   // Add the Below Normal priority class
   n = ComboBox_AddString(hwndCtl, TEXT("Below normal"));
   ComboBox_SetItemData(hwndCtl, n, BELOW_NORMAL_PRIORITY_CLASS);
}

n = ComboBox_AddString(hwndCtl, TEXT("Idle"));
ComboBox_SetItemData(hwndCtl, n, IDLE_PRIORITY_CLASS);

ComboBox_SetCurSel(hwndCtl, nNormal);

// Initialize thread relative priorities
hwndCtl = GetDlgItem(hwnd, IDC_THREADRELATIVEPRIORITY);

n = ComboBox_AddString(hwndCtl, TEXT("Time critical"));
ComboBox_SetItemData(hwndCtl, n, THREAD_PRIORITY_TIME_CRITICAL);
```

(continued)

Figure 7-1. *continued*

```
  n = ComboBox_AddString(hwndCtl, TEXT("Highest"));
  ComboBox_SetItemData(hwndCtl, n, THREAD_PRIORITY_HIGHEST);

  n = ComboBox_AddString(hwndCtl, TEXT("Above normal"));
  ComboBox_SetItemData(hwndCtl, n, THREAD_PRIORITY_ABOVE_NORMAL);

  nNormal = n = ComboBox_AddString(hwndCtl, TEXT("Normal"));
  ComboBox_SetItemData(hwndCtl, n, THREAD_PRIORITY_NORMAL);

  n = ComboBox_AddString(hwndCtl, TEXT("Below normal"));
  ComboBox_SetItemData(hwndCtl, n, THREAD_PRIORITY_BELOW_NORMAL);

  n = ComboBox_AddString(hwndCtl, TEXT("Lowest"));
  ComboBox_SetItemData(hwndCtl, n, THREAD_PRIORITY_LOWEST);

  n = ComboBox_AddString(hwndCtl, TEXT("Idle"));
  ComboBox_SetItemData(hwndCtl, n, THREAD_PRIORITY_IDLE);

  ComboBox_SetCurSel(hwndCtl, nNormal);

  Edit_LimitText(GetDlgItem(hwnd, IDC_SLEEPTIME), 4);    // Maximum of 9999

  return(TRUE);
}


///////////////////////////////////////////////////////////////////////////


void Dlg_OnCommand (HWND hwnd, int id, HWND hwndCtl, UINT codeNotify) {

  switch (id) {
    case IDCANCEL:
      PostQuitMessage(0);
      break;

    case IDC_PROCESSPRIORITYCLASS:
      if (codeNotify == CBN_SELCHANGE) {
        SetPriorityClass(GetCurrentProcess(), (DWORD)
          ComboBox_GetItemData(hwndCtl, ComboBox_GetCurSel(hwndCtl)));
      }
      break;
```

(continued)

Figure 7-1. *continued*

```
      case IDC_THREADRELATIVEPRIORITY:
         if (codeNotify == CBN_SELCHANGE) {
            SetThreadPriority(GetCurrentThread(), (DWORD)
               ComboBox_GetItemData(hwndCtl, ComboBox_GetCurSel(hwndCtl)));
         }
         break;

      case IDC_SUSPEND:
         // To avoid deadlock, call EnableWindow before creating
         // the thread which calls SuspendThread.
         EnableWindow(hwndCtl, FALSE);

         HANDLE hThreadPrimary;
         DuplicateHandle(GetCurrentProcess(), GetCurrentThread(),
            GetCurrentProcess(), &hThreadPrimary,
            THREAD_SUSPEND_RESUME, FALSE, DUPLICATE_SAME_ACCESS);
         DWORD dwThreadID;
         CloseHandle(chBEGINTHREADEX(NULL, 0, ThreadFunc,
            hThreadPrimary, 0, &dwThreadID));
         break;
   }
}


///////////////////////////////////////////////////////////////////////////


INT_PTR WINAPI Dlg_Proc (HWND hwnd, UINT uMsg, WPARAM wParam, LPARAM lParam) {

   switch (uMsg) {
      chHANDLE_DLGMSG(hwnd, WM_INITDIALOG, Dlg_OnInitDialog);
      chHANDLE_DLGMSG(hwnd, WM_COMMAND,    Dlg_OnCommand);
   }

   return(FALSE);
}


///////////////////////////////////////////////////////////////////////////


int WINAPI _tWinMain (HINSTANCE hinstExe, HINSTANCE, LPTSTR pszCmdLine, int) {
```

(continued)

Figure 7-1. *continued*

```
HWND hwnd =
   CreateDialog(hinstExe, MAKEINTRESOURCE(IDD_SCHEDLAB), NULL, Dlg_Proc);
BOOL fQuit = FALSE;

while (!fQuit) {
   MSG msg;
   if (PeekMessage(&msg, NULL, 0, 0, PM_REMOVE)) {

      // IsDialogMessage allows keyboard navigation to work properly.
      if (!IsDialogMessage(hwnd, &msg)) {

         if (msg.message == WM_QUIT) {
            fQuit = TRUE;  // For WM_QUIT, terminate the loop.
         } else {
            // Not a WM_QUIT message. Translate it and dispatch it.
            TranslateMessage(&msg);
            DispatchMessage(&msg);
         }
      }  // if (!IsDialogMessage())
   } else {

      // Add a number to the listbox
      static int s_n = -1;
      TCHAR sz[20];
      wsprintf(sz, TEXT("%u"), ++s_n);
      HWND hwndWork = GetDlgItem(hwnd, IDC_WORK);
      ListBox_SetCurSel(hwndWork, ListBox_AddString(hwndWork, sz));

      // Remove some strings if there are too many entries
      while (ListBox_GetCount(hwndWork) > 100)
         ListBox_DeleteString(hwndWork, 0);

      // How long should the thread sleep
      int nSleep = GetDlgItemInt(hwnd, IDC_SLEEPTIME, NULL, FALSE);
      if (chINRANGE(1, nSleep, 9999))
         Sleep(nSleep);
   }
}
DestroyWindow(hwnd);
return(0);
}


/////////////////////////////// End of File ///////////////////////////////
```

(continued)

247

Figure 7-1. *continued*

SchedLab.rc

```
//Microsoft Developer Studio generated resource script.
//
#include "resource.h"

#define APSTUDIO_READONLY_SYMBOLS
/////////////////////////////////////////////////////////////////////////////
//
// Generated from the TEXTINCLUDE 2 resource.
//
#include "afxres.h"


/////////////////////////////////////////////////////////////////////////////
#undef APSTUDIO_READONLY_SYMBOLS


/////////////////////////////////////////////////////////////////////////////
// English (U.S.) resources

#if !defined(AFX_RESOURCE_DLL) || defined(AFX_TARG_ENU)
#ifdef _WIN32
LANGUAGE LANG_ENGLISH, SUBLANG_ENGLISH_US
#pragma code_page(1252)
#endif //_WIN32


/////////////////////////////////////////////////////////////////////////////
//
// Dialog
//

IDD_SCHEDLAB DIALOGEX 0, 0, 209, 70
STYLE DS_3DLOOK | DS_CENTER | WS_MINIMIZEBOX | WS_VISIBLE | WS_CAPTION |
    WS_SYSMENU
EXSTYLE WS_EX_NOPARENTNOTIFY | WS_EX_CLIENTEDGE
CAPTION "Scheduling Lab"
FONT 8, "MS Sans Serif"
BEGIN
    LTEXT           "&Process priority class:",IDC_STATIC,4,6,68,8
    COMBOBOX        IDC_PROCESSPRIORITYCLASS,84,4,72,80,CBS_DROPDOWNLIST |
                    WS_TABSTOP
    LTEXT           "&Thread relative priority:",IDC_STATIC,4,20,72,8
    COMBOBOX        IDC_THREADRELATIVEPRIORITY,84,18,72,76,CBS_DROPDOWNLIST |
                    WS_TABSTOP
```

(continued)

Figure 7-1. *continued*

```
        LTEXT           "Sleep (0 to 9999 &ms):",IDC_STATIC,4,36,68,8
        EDITTEXT        IDC_SLEEPTIME,84,34,32,14,ES_NUMBER
        PUSHBUTTON      "&Suspend",IDC_SUSPEND,4,52,49,14
        LISTBOX         IDC_WORK,160,4,48,60,NOT LBS_NOTIFY |
                        LBS_NOINTEGRALHEIGHT | LBS_NOSEL | WS_TABSTOP
END


/////////////////////////////////////////////////////////////////////////////
//
// DESIGNINFO
//

#ifdef APSTUDIO_INVOKED
GUIDELINES DESIGNINFO DISCARDABLE
BEGIN
    IDD_SCHEDLAB, DIALOG
    BEGIN
        LEFTMARGIN, 7
        RIGHTMARGIN, 202
        TOPMARGIN, 7
        BOTTOMMARGIN, 63
    END
END
#endif    // APSTUDIO_INVOKED


#ifdef APSTUDIO_INVOKED
/////////////////////////////////////////////////////////////////////////////
//
// TEXTINCLUDE
//

1 TEXTINCLUDE DISCARDABLE
BEGIN
    "resource.h\0"
END

2 TEXTINCLUDE DISCARDABLE
BEGIN
    "#include ""afxres.h""\r\n"
    "\0"
END
```

(continued)

Figure 7-1. *continued*

```
3 TEXTINCLUDE DISCARDABLE
BEGIN
    "\r\n"
    "\0"
END


#endif    // APSTUDIO_INVOKED



/////////////////////////////////////////////////////////////////////////////
//
// Icon
//

// Icon with lowest ID value placed first to ensure application icon
// remains consistent on all systems.
IDI_SCHEDLAB           ICON    DISCARDABLE     "SchedLab.ico"
#endif    // English (U.S.) resources
/////////////////////////////////////////////////////////////////////////////



#ifndef APSTUDIO_INVOKED
/////////////////////////////////////////////////////////////////////////////
//
// Generated from the TEXTINCLUDE 3 resource.
//



/////////////////////////////////////////////////////////////////////////////
#endif    // not APSTUDIO_INVOKED
```

Affinities

By default, Windows 2000 uses *soft affinity* when assigning threads to processors. This means that if all other factors are equal, it tries to run the thread on the processor it ran on last. Having a thread stay on a single processor helps reuse data that is still in the processor's memory cache.

There is a new computer architecture called NUMA (Non-Uniform Memory Access) in which a machine consists of several boards. Each board has four CPUs and its own bank of memory. The following figure shows a machine with 3 boards in it, making 12 CPUs available so that any single thread can run on any of the 12 CPUs.

NUMA Machine

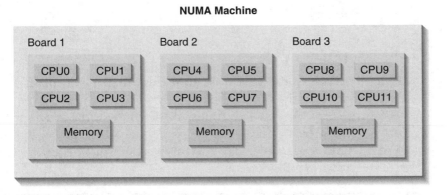

A NUMA system performs best when a CPU accesses the memory that is on its own board. If the CPU needs to touch memory that is on another board, an enormous performance hit is incurred. In such an environment, it is desirable to have threads from one process run on CPUs 0 through 3 and have threads in another process run on CPUs 4 through 7, and so on. To accommodate such machine architectures, Windows 2000 allows you to set process and thread affinities. In other words, you can control which CPUs can run certain threads. This is called *hard affinity*.

The system determines how many CPUs are available in the machine at boot time. An application can query the number of CPUs on the machine by calling *GetSystemInfo* (discussed in Chapter 14). By default, any thread can be scheduled to any of these CPUs. To limit threads in a single process to run on a subset of the available CPUs, you can call *SetProcessAffinityMask*:

```
BOOL SetProcessAffinityMask(
    HANDLE hProcess,
    DWORD_PTR dwProcessAffinityMask);
```

The first parameter, *hProcess*, indicates which process to affect. The second parameter, *dwProcessAffinityMask*, is a bitmask indicating which CPUs the threads can run on. For example, passing 0x00000005 means that threads in this process can run on CPU 0 and CPU 2 but not on CPU 1 and CPUs 3 through 31.

Note that child processes inherit process affinity. So if a process has an affinity mask of 0x00000005, any threads in its child processes have the same mask and share the same CPUs. In addition, you can use the job kernel object (discussed in Chapter 5) to restrict a set of processes to a desired set of CPUs.

Of course, there is also a function that returns a process's affinity mask, *GetProcessAffinityMask*, shown at the top of page 252.

```
BOOL GetProcessAffinityMask(
   HANDLE hProcess,
   PDWORD_PTR pdwProcessAffinityMask,
   PDWORD_PTR pdwSystemAffinityMask);
```

Here, you also pass the handle of the process whose affinity mask you want and the function fills in the variable pointed to by *pdwProcessAffinityMask*. This function also returns the system's affinity mask (in the variable pointed to by *pdwSystemAffinityMask*). The system's affinity mask indicates which of the system's CPUs can process threads. A process's affinity mask is always a proper subset of the system's affinity mask.

> Windows 98 uses only one CPU regardless of how many are actually in the machine. Therefore, *GetProcessAffinityMask* always fills both variables with 1.

So far, we've discussed how to limit the threads of a process to a set of CPUs. Sometimes you might want to limit a thread within a process to a set of CPUs. For example, you might have a process containing four threads running on a machine with four CPUs. If one of these threads is doing important work and you want to increase the likelihood that a CPU will always be available for it, you limit the other three threads so they cannot run on CPU 0 and can only run on CPUs 1, 2, and 3.

You can set affinity masks for individual threads by calling *SetThreadAffinityMask*:

```
DWORD_PTR SetThreadAffinityMask(
   HANDLE hThread,
   DWORD_PTR dwThreadAffinityMask);
```

The *hThread* parameter indicates which thread to limit and the *dwThreadAffinityMask* indicates which CPUs the thread can run on. The *dwThreadAffinityMask* must be a proper subset of the process's affinity mask. The return value is the thread's previous affinity mask. So, to limit three threads to CPUs 1, 2, and 3, you do this:

```
// Thread 0 can only run on CPU 0.
SetThreadAffinityMask(hThread0, 0x00000001);

// Threads 1, 2, 3 run on CPUs 1, 2, 3.
SetThreadAffinityMask(hThread1, 0x0000000E);
SetThreadAffinityMask(hThread2, 0x0000000E);
SetThreadAffinityMask(hThread3, 0x0000000E);
```

WINDOWS 98

> Since Windows 98 uses only one CPU regardless of how many are actually in the machine, the *dwThreadAffinityMask* parameter must always be 1.

When an *x*86 system boots, the system executes code that detects which CPUs on the host machine experience the famous Pentium floating-point bug. The system must test this for each CPU by setting a thread's affinity to the first CPU, performing the potentially faulty divide operation, and comparing the result with the known correct answer. Then this sequence is attempted again for the next CPU, and so on.

NOTE

> In most environments, altering thread affinities interferes with the scheduler's ability to effectively migrate threads across CPUs that make the most efficient use of CPU time. The table below shows an example.
>
> | Thread | Priority | Affinity Mask | Result |
> |--------|----------|---------------|-----------|
> | A | 4 | 0x00000001 | CPU 0 |
> | B | 8 | 0x00000003 | CPU 1 |
> | C | 6 | 0x00000002 | Can't run |
>
> When Thread A wakes, the scheduler sees that the thread can run on CPU 0 and is assigned to CPU 0. Thread B then wakes and the scheduler sees that the thread can be assigned to CPU 0 or 1 but since CPU 0 is in use, the scheduler assigns it to CPU 1. So far, so good.
>
> Now Thread C wakes, and the scheduler sees that it can run only on CPU 1. But CPU 1 is in use by thread B, a priority 8 thread. Since Thread C is a priority 6 thread, it can't preempt Thread B. Thread C can preempt Thread A, a priority 4 thread, but the scheduler will not preempt Thread A because Thread C can't run on CPU 0.
>
> This demonstrates how setting hard affinities for threads can interfere with the scheduler's priority scheme.

Sometimes forcing a thread to a specific CPU is not the best idea. For example, you might have three threads all limited to CPU 0, but CPUs 1, 2, and 3 might be sitting idle. It would be better if you could tell the system that you want a thread to run on a particular CPU but allow the thread to migrate to another CPU if one is available.

To set an ideal CPU for a thread, you call *SetThreadIdealProcessor*:

```
DWORD SetThreadIdealProcessor(
   HANDLE hThread,
   DWORD dwIdealProcessor);
```

The *hThread* parameter indicates which thread to set a preferred CPU for. However, unlike all the other functions we've been discussing, the *dwIdeal-Processor* is not a bitmask; it is an integer from 0 through 31 that indicates the preferred CPU for the thread. You can pass a value of MAXIMUM_ PROCESSORS (defined as 32 in WinNT.h) to indicate that the thread has no ideal CPU. The function returns the previous ideal CPU or MAXIMUM_ PROCESSORS if the thread doesn't have an ideal CPU set for it.

You can also set processor affinity in the header of an executable file. Oddly, there doesn't seem to be a linker switch for this, but you can use code similar to this:

```
// Load the EXE into memory.
PLOADED_IMAGE pLoadedImage = ImageLoad(szExeName, NULL);

// Get the current load configuration information for the EXE.
IMAGE_LOAD_CONFIG_DIRECTORY ilcd;
GetImageConfigInformation(pLoadedImage, &ilcd);

// Change the processor affinity mask.
ilcd.ProcessAffinityMask = 0x00000003; // I desire CPUs 0 and 1

// Save the new load configuration information.
SetImageConfigInformation(pLoadedImage, &ilcd);

// Unload the EXE from memory.
ImageUnload(pLoadedImage);
```

I won't bother to explain all these functions in detail; you can look them up in the Platform SDK documentation if you're interested. Also, you can use a utility called ImageCfg.exe to change some flags in an executable module's header. When you run ImageCfg.exe, it displays the following usage:

```
usage: IMAGECFG [switches] image-names...
             [-?] display this message
             [-a Process Affinity mask value in hex]
             [-b BuildNumber]
             [-c Win32 GetVersionEx Service Pack return value in hex]
             [-d decommit thresholds]
```

(continued)

254

```
[-g bitsToClear bitsToSet]
[-h 1|0 (Enable/Disable Terminal Server Compatible bit)
[-k StackReserve[.StackCommit]
[-l enable large (>2GB) addresses
[-m maximum allocation size]
[-n bind no longer allowed on this image
[-o default critical section timeout
[-p process heap flags]
[-q only print config info if changed
[-r run with restricted working set]
[-s path to symbol files]
[-t VirtualAlloc threshold]
[-u Marks image as uniprocessor only]
[-v MajorVersion.MinorVersion]
[-w Win32 GetVersion return value in hex]
[-x Mark image as Net - Run From Swapfile
[-y Mark image as Removable - Run From Swapfile
```

To change the application's allowed affinity mask, you execute ImageCfg and specify the -a switch. Of course, all this utility does is call the functions shown in the code fragment above. Also notice the -u switch, which tells the system that the executable file can run only on single-CPU systems.

Finally, the Windows 2000 Task Manager allows a user to alter a process's CPU affinity by selecting a process and displaying its context menu. If you run on a multiprocessor machine, you see a Set Affinity menu item. (This menu item is not available on uniprocessor machines.) When you choose this menu item, you see the following dialog box, in which you can select which CPUs the threads in the chosen process can run on.

Processor Affinity

The Processor Affinity setting controls which CPUs the process will be allowed to execute on.

☑ CPU 0	☐ CPU 8	☐ CPU 16	☐ CPU 24
☑ CPU 1	☐ CPU 9	☐ CPU 17	☐ CPU 25
☐ CPU 2	☐ CPU 10	☐ CPU 18	☐ CPU 26
☐ CPU 3	☐ CPU 11	☐ CPU 19	☐ CPU 27
☐ CPU 4	☐ CPU 12	☐ CPU 20	☐ CPU 28
☐ CPU 5	☐ CPU 13	☐ CPU 21	☐ CPU 29
☐ CPU 6	☐ CPU 14	☐ CPU 22	☐ CPU 30
☐ CPU 7	☐ CPU 15	☐ CPU 23	☐ CPU 31

OK   Cancel

WINDOWS 2000

When Windows 2000 boots on an *x*86 machine, you can limit the number of CPUs that the system will use. During the boot cycle, the system examines a file called Boot.ini, which is in the root directory of the boot drive. Here is the Boot.ini file that I have on my dual processor machine:

```
[boot loader]
timeout=2
default=multi(0)disk(0)rdisk(0)partition(1)\WINNT
[operating systems]
multi(0)disk(0)rdisk(0)partition(1)\WINNT="Windows 2000 Server"
    /fastdetect
multi(0)disk(0)rdisk(0)partition(1)\WINNT="Windows 2000 Server"
    /fastdetect /NumProcs=1
```

This Boot.ini file was produced by the Windows 2000 installation, but I added the last line using Notepad. This line tells the system that at boot time it should use just one of the processors on the machine. The /NumProcs=1 switch is the piece of magic that makes this happen. I occasionally find this useful for debugging. (Usually I want to use all of my processors.)

Please note that, because of printing considerations only, the options appear on a separate (indented) line in the listing above. The Boot.ini file requires that the options and the ARC path to the boot partition appear on one line.

CHAPTER EIGHT

THREAD SYNCHRONIZATION IN USER MODE

Microsoft Windows runs best when all of the threads can go about their business without having to communicate with each other. However, a thread can rarely act independently all the time. Usually, threads are spawned to handle some task. When the task is complete, another thread will probably want to know about it.

All threads in the system must have access to system resources such as heaps, serial ports, files, windows, and countless others. If one thread requests exclusive access to a resource, other threads cannot get their work done. On the flip side, you can't just let any thread touch any resource at any time. Imagine a thread writing to a memory block while another thread reads from the same memory block. This would be analogous to reading a book while someone is changing the text on the page. The thoughts on the page are all jumbled and nothing useful comes of it.

Threads need to communicate with each other in two basic situations:

■ When you have multiple threads accessing a shared resource in such a way that the resource does not become corrupt

■ When one thread needs to notify one or more other threads that a specific task has been completed

Thread synchronization has many aspects, which I'll discuss over the next few chapters. The good news is that Windows offers many facilities to make thread synchronization easy. The bad news is that anticipating what a bunch of threads might attempt to do at any time is extremely difficult. Our minds just don't work asynchronously; we like to think things through in an orderly fashion, one step at a time. But that's not how a multithreaded environment works.

I first started working with multiple threads around 1992. At first, I made many programming mistakes and actually published book chapters and magazine articles that had thread synchronization–related bugs in them. Today, I'm much more skilled, but hardly perfect, and I truly believe that everything in this book is bug free (even though I should know better by now). The only way to get good at thread synchronization is by doing it. In these chapters, I'll explain how the system works and show you how to properly synchronize threads, but you should face the music now: you'll make mistakes as you gain experience.

Atomic Access:
The Interlocked Family of Functions

A big part of thread synchronization has to do with *atomic access*—a thread's ability to access a resource with the guarantee that no other thread will access that same resource at the same time. Let's look at a simple example:

```
// Define a global variable.
long g_x = 0;

DWORD WINAPI ThreadFunc1(PVOID pvParam) {
    g_x++;
    return(0);
}

DWORD WINAPI ThreadFunc2(PVOID pvParam) {
    g_x++;
    return(0);
}
```

I've declared a global variable, g_x, and initialized it to 0. Now let's say that I create two threads: one thread executes *ThreadFunc1*, and the other thread executes *ThreadFunc2*. The code in these two functions is identical: they both add 1 to the global variable g_x. So when both threads stop running, you might expect to see the value *2* in g_x. But do you? The answer is…maybe. The way the code is written, you can't tell what g_x will ultimately contain. Here's why. Let's say that the compiler generates the following code for the line that increments g_x by 1:

```
MOV EAX, [g_x]       ; Move the value in g_x into a register.
INC EAX              ; Increment the value in the register.
MOV [g_x], EAX       ; Store the new value back in g_x.
```

Both threads are unlikely to execute this code at exactly the same time. So if one thread executes this code followed by another thread, here is what effectively executes:

```
MOV EAX, [g_x]        ; Thread 1: Move 0 into a register.
INC EAX               ; Thread 1: Increment the register to 1.
MOV [g_x], EAX        ; Thread 1: Store 1 back in g_x.

MOV EAX, [g_x]        ; Thread 2: Move 1 into a register.
INC EAX               ; Thread 2: Increment the register to 2.
MOV [g_x], EAX        ; Thread 2: Store 2 back in g_x.
```

After both threads are done incrementing g_x, the value in g_x is 2. This is great and is exactly what we expect: take zero (0), increment it by 1 twice, and the answer is 2. Beautiful. But wait—Windows is a preemptive, multithreaded environment. So a thread can be switched away from at any time and another thread might continue executing at any time. So the code above might not execute exactly as I've written it. Instead, it might execute as follows:

```
MOV EAX, [g_x]        ; Thread 1: Move 0 into a register.
INC EAX               ; Thread 1: Increment the register to 1.

MOV EAX, [g_x]        ; Thread 2: Move 0 into a register.
INC EAX               ; Thread 2: Increment the register to 1.
MOV [g_x], EAX        ; Thread 2: Store 1 back in g_x.

MOV [g_x], EAX        ; Thread 1: Store 1 back in g_x.
```

If the code executes this way, the final value in g_x is 1—not 2 as you expect! This is pretty scary, especially since you have so little control over the scheduler. In fact, if you have 100 threads executing similar thread functions, after all of them exit, the value in g_x might still be 1! Obviously, software developers can't work in an environment like this. We expect that incrementing 0 twice results in 2 all the time. Also, let's not forget that the results might be different depending on how the compiler generates codes, what CPU is executing the code, and how many CPUs are installed in the host computer. This is how the environment works, and there is nothing we can do about that. But Windows does offer some functions that, when used correctly, guarantee the outcome of our application's code.

To solve the problem above, we need something simple. We need a way to guarantee that the incrementing of the value is done atomically—that is, without interruption. The interlocked family of functions provides the solution we need. The interlocked functions are awesome and underused by most software developers, even though they are incredibly helpful and easy to understand. All of the functions manipulate a value atomically. Take a look at *InterlockedExchangeAdd*:

```
LONG InterlockedExchangeAdd(
    PLONG plAddend,
    LONG lIncrement);
```

What could be simpler? You call this function, passing the address of a long variable and indicating by how much to increment this value. But this function guarantees that the adding of the value is accomplished atomically. So we can rewrite the code presented earlier as follows:

```
// Define a global variable.
long g_x = 0;

DWORD WINAPI ThreadFunc1(PVOID pvParam) {
    InterlockedExchangeAdd(&g_x, 1);
    return(0);
}

DWORD WINAPI ThreadFunc2(PVOID pvParam) {
    InterlockedExchangeAdd(&g_x, 1);
    return(0);
}
```

By making this small change, g_x is incremented atomically and therefore you are guaranteed that the final value in g_x will be 2. Don't you feel better already? Note that all the threads should attempt to modify the shared long variable by calling these functions; no thread should ever attempt to modify the shared variable by using simple C statements:

```
// The long variable shared by many threads
LONG g_x;
    :
    :
// Incorrect way to increment the long
g_x++;
    :
    :
// Correct way to increment the long
InterlockedExchangeAdd(&g_x, 1);
```

How do the interlocked functions work? The answer depends on the CPU platform that you're running on. For the *x*86 family of CPUs, interlocked functions assert a hardware signal on the bus that prevents another CPU from accessing the same memory address. On the Alpha platform, the interlocked functions do something like this:

1. Turn on a special bit flag in the CPU and note the memory address being accessed.

2. Read the value from memory into a register.

3. Modify the register.

4. If the special bit flag in the CPU is off, go to step 2. Otherwise, the special bit flag is still on and the register's value is stored back into memory.

You might wonder how the special CPU bit flag is ever turned off by the time step 4 is executed. Here's the answer: If another CPU in the system attempts to modify the same memory address, it can turn off our CPU's special bit flag, causing the interlocked function to loop back to step 2.

You need not understand exactly how the interlocked functions work. What's important to know is that they guarantee that a value will be modified atomically, no matter how the compiler generates code and no matter how many CPUs are installed in the host machine. You must also ensure that the variable addresses that you pass to these functions are properly aligned or the functions might fail. (I'll discuss data alignment in Chapter 13.)

Another important thing to know about the interlocked functions is that they execute extremely quickly. A call to an interlocked function usually causes just a few CPU cycles (usually less than 50) to execute, and there is no transition from user mode to kernel mode (which usually requires more than 1000 cycles to execute).

Of course, you can use *InterlockedExchangeAdd* to subtract a value—you simply pass a negative value for the second parameter. *InterlockedExchangeAdd* returns the original value that was in **plAddend*.

Here are two more interlocked functions:

```
LONG InterlockedExchange(
   PLONG plTarget,
   LONG lValue);

PVOID InterlockedExchangePointer(
   PVOID* ppvTarget,
   PVOID pvValue);
```

InterlockedExchange and *InterlockedExchangePointer* atomically replace the current value whose address is passed in the first parameter with a value passed in the second parameter. For a 32-bit application, both functions replace a 32-bit value with another 32-bit value. But for a 64-bit application, *InterlockedExchange* replaces a 32-bit value while *InterlockedExchangePointer* replaces a 64-bit value. Both functions return the original value. *InterlockedExchange* is extremely useful when you implement a spinlock:

```
// Global variable indicating whether a shared resource is in use or not
BOOL g_fResourceInUse = FALSE;
:
:

void Func1() {
   // Wait to access the resource.
   while (InterlockedExchange (&g_fResourceInUse, TRUE) == TRUE)
      Sleep(0);

   // Access the resource.
   :
   :


   // We no longer need to access the resource.
   InterlockedExchange(&g_fResourceInUse, FALSE);
}
```

The *while* loop spins repeatedly, changing the value in *g_fResourceInUse* to TRUE and checking its previous value to see if it was TRUE. If the value was previously FALSE, the resource was not in use but the calling thread just set it to in-use and exits the loop. If the previous value was TRUE, the resource was in use by another thread and the *while* loop continues to spin.

If another thread were to execute similar code, it would spin in its *while* loop until the *g_fResourceInUse* was changed back to FALSE. The call to *InterlockedExchange* at the end of the function shows how *g_fResourceInUse* should be set back to FALSE.

You must take extreme care when using this technique because a spinlock wastes CPU time. The CPU must constantly compare two values until one "magically" changes due to another thread. Also, this code assumes that all threads using the spinlock run at the same priority level. You might also want to disable thread priority boosting (call *SetProcessPriorityBoost* or *SetThread-PriorityBoost*) for threads that execute spinlocks.

In addition, you should ensure that the lock variable and the data that the lock protects are maintained in different cache lines (discussed later in this chapter). If the lock variable and data share the same cache line, a CPU using the resource will contend with any CPUs attempting access of the resource. This hurts performance.

You should avoid using spinlocks on single-CPU machines. If a thread is spinning, it's wasting precious CPU time, which prevents the other thread from changing the value. My use of *Sleep* in the *while* loop above improves this situation somewhat. If you use *Sleep*, you might want to sleep a random amount of time, and each time the request to access the resource is denied, you might want to increase the sleep time even more. This prevents threads from simply wasting CPU time. Depending on your situation, it might be better to remove the call to *Sleep* altogether. Or you might want to replace it with a call to *SwitchToThread* (not available on Windows 98). I hate to say it, but trial and error might be your best approach.

Spinlocks assume that the protected resource is always accessed for short periods of time. This makes it more efficient to spin and then transition to kernel mode and wait. Many developers spin some number of times (say 4000), and if access to the resource is still denied, the thread transitions to kernel mode, where it waits (consuming no CPU time) until the resource becomes available. This is how critical sections are implemented.

Spinlocks are useful on multiprocessor machines because one thread can spin while the other thread runs on another CPU. However, even in this scenario, you must be careful. You do not want a thread to spin for a long time, or you'll waste more CPU time. We'll discuss spinlocks further later in this chapter. Also, the section titled "Implementing a Critical Section: The Optex" in Chapter 10 shows how to use spinlocks.

Here are the last two interlocked functions:

```
PVOID InterlockedCompareExchange(
    PLONG plDestination,
    LONG lExchange,
    LONG lComparand);
```

```
PVOID InterlockedCompareExchangePointer(
    PVOID* ppvDestination,
    PVOID pvExchange,
    PVOID pvComparand);
```

These two functions perform an atomic test and set operation: for a 32-bit application, both functions operate on 32-bit values, but in a 64-bit application, *InterlockedCompareExchange* operates on 32-bit values while

InterlockedCompareExchangePointer operates on 64-bit values. In pseudocode, here is what happens:

```
LONG InterlockedCompareExchange(PLONG plDestination,
   LONG lExchange, LONG lComparand) {

   LONG lRet = *plDestination;    // Original value

   if (*plDestination == lComparand)
      *plDestination = lExchange;
   return(lRet);
}
```

The function compares the current value (pointed to by the *plDestination* parameter) with the value passed in the *lComparand* parameter. If the values are the same, **plDestination* is changed to the value of the *lExchange* parameter. If what is in **plDestination* doesn't match the value of *lComparand*, **plDestination* is not changed. The function returns the original value in **plDestination*. Remember that all of these operations are performed as one atomic unit of execution.

There is no interlocked function that simply reads a value (without changing it) because no such function is necessary. If a thread simply attempts to read the contents of a value that is always modified with an interlocked function, the value read is always a good value. You don't know if you'll read the original value or the updated value, but you know that it will be one of them. For most applications, this is sufficient. In addition, the interlocked functions might be used by threads in multiple processes when you're synchronizing access to a value that is in a shared memory section such as a memory-mapped file. (Chapter 9 includes a few sample applications that show how to properly use the interlocked functions.)

Windows offers a few other interlocked functions, but the functions I've described do everything that the other functions do and more. Here are two other functions:

```
LONG InterlockedIncrement(PLONG plAddend);
```

```
LONG InterlockedDecrement(PLONG plAddend);
```

InterlockedExchangeAdd replaces both of these older functions. The new function can add or subtract any value; the old functions are limited to adding or subtracting 1.

Cache Lines

If you want to build a high-performance application that runs on multiprocessor machines, you must be aware of CPU cache lines. When a CPU reads a byte from memory, it does not just fetch the single byte; it fetches enough bytes to fill a cache line. Cache lines consist of 32 or 64 bytes (depending on the CPU) and are always aligned on 32-byte or 64-byte boundaries. Cache lines exist to improve performance. Usually, an application manipulates a set of adjacent bytes. If these bytes are in the cache, the CPU does not have to access the memory bus, which requires much more time.

However, cache lines make memory updates more difficult in a multiprocessor environment, as you can see in this example:

1. CPU1 reads a byte, causing this byte and its adjacent bytes to be read into CPU1's cache line.

2. CPU2 reads the same byte, which causes the same bytes in step 1 to be read into CPU2's cache line.

3. CPU1 changes the byte in memory, causing the byte to be written to CPU1's cache line. But the information is not yet written to RAM.

4. CPU2 reads the same byte again. Since this byte was already in CPU2's cache line, it doesn't have to access memory. But CPU2 will not see the new value of the byte in memory.

This scenario would be disastrous. Of course, chip designers are well aware of this problem and design their CPUs to handle this. Specifically, when a CPU changes bytes in a cache line, the other CPUs in the machine are made aware of this and their cache lines are invalidated. So in the scenario above, CPU2's cache is invalidated when CPU1 changes the value of the byte. In step 4, CPU1 has to flush its cache to RAM and CPU2 has to access memory again to refill its cache line. As you can see, the cache lines can help performance, but they can also be a detriment on multiprocessor machines.

What all of this means is that you should group your application's data together in cache line–size chunks and on cache-line boundaries. The goal is to make sure that different CPUs access different memory addresses separated by at least a cache line boundary. Also, you should separate your read-only data (or infrequently read data) from read-write data. And you should group together pieces of data that are accessed around the same time.

Here is an example of a poorly designed data structure:

```
struct CUSTINFO {
   DWORD    dwCustomerID;     // Mostly read-only
   int      nBalanceDue;      // Read-write
   char     szName[100];      // Mostly read-only
   FILETIME ftLastOrderDate;  // Read-write
};
```

Here is an improved version of this structure:

```
// Determine the cache line size for the host CPU.
#ifdef _X86_
#define CACHE_ALIGN   32
#endif
#ifdef _ALPHA_
#define CACHE_ALIGN   64
#endif
#ifdef _IA64_
#define CACHE_ALIGN   ??
#endif

#define CACHE_PAD(Name, BytesSoFar) \
   BYTE Name[CACHE_ALIGN - ((BytesSoFar) % CACHE_ALIGN)]

struct CUSTINFO {
   DWORD    dwCustomerID;     // Mostly read-only
   char     szName[100];      // Mostly read-only

   // Force the following members to be in a different cache line.
   CACHE_PAD(bPad1, sizeof(DWORD) + 100);

   int      nBalanceDue;      // Read-write
   FILETIME ftLastOrderDate;  // Read-write

   // Force the following structure to be in a different cache line.
   CACHE_PAD(bPad2, sizeof(int) + sizeof(FILETIME));
};
```

The CACHE_ALIGN macro defined above is good but not great. The problem is that you must manually enter each member variable's byte size in the macro. If you add, move, or remove a data member, you must also update the call to the CACHE_PAD macro. In the future, Microsoft's C/C++ compiler will support a new syntax that makes aligning data members easier. It will look something like __declspec(align(32)).

> **NOTE** It is best for data to be always accessed by a single thread (function parameters and local variables are the easiest way to ensure this) or for the data to be always accessed by a single CPU (using thread affinity). If you do either of these, you avoid cache line issues entirely.

Advanced Thread Synchronization

The interlocked family of functions is great when you need to atomically modify a single value. You should definitely try them first. But most real-life programming problems deal with data structures that are far more complex than a single 32-bit or 64-bit value. To get "atomic" access of more sophisticated data structures, you must leave the interlocked functions behind and use some other features offered by Windows.

In the previous section, I stressed that you should not use spinlocks on uniprocessor machines and you should use them cautiously even on multiprocessor machines. Again, the reason is that CPU time is a terrible thing to waste. So we need a mechanism that allows our thread to not waste CPU time while waiting to access a shared resource.

When a thread wants to access a shared resource or be notified of some "special event," the thread must call an operating system function, passing it parameters that indicate what the thread is waiting for. If the operating system detects that the resource is available or that the special event has occurred, the function returns and the thread remains schedulable. (The thread might not execute right away; it is schedulable and will be assigned to a CPU using the rules described in the previous chapter.)

If the resource is unavailable or the special event hasn't yet occurred, the system places the thread in a wait state, making the thread unschedulable. This prevents the thread from wasting any CPU time. While your thread is waiting, the system acts as an agent on your thread's behalf. The system remembers what your thread wants and automatically takes it out of the wait state when the resource becomes available—the thread's execution is synchronized with the special event.

As it turns out, most threads are almost always in a wait state. And the system's power management kicks in when the system detects that all threads are in a wait state for several minutes.

A Technique to Avoid

Without synchronization objects and the operating system's ability to watch for special events, a thread would be forced to synchronize itself with special events by using the technique that I am about to demonstrate. However, because the operating system has built-in support for thread synchronization, you should never use this technique.

In this technique, one thread synchronizes itself with the completion of a task in another thread by continuously polling the state of a variable that is shared by or accessible to multiple threads. The following code fragment illustrates this:

```
volatile BOOL g_fFinishedCalculation = FALSE;

int WINAPI WinMain(...) {
   CreateThread(..., RecalcFunc, ...);
   :
   :

   // Wait for the recalculation to complete.
   while (!g_fFinishedCalculation)
       ;
   :
   :
}


DWORD WINAPI RecalcFunc(PVOID pvParam) {
   // Perform the recalculation.
   :
   :
   g_fFinishedCalculation = TRUE;
   return(0);
}
```

As you can see, the primary thread (executing *WinMain*) doesn't put it-self to sleep when it needs to synchronize itself with the completion of the *RecalcFunc* function. Because the primary thread does not sleep, it is continuously scheduled CPU time by the operating system. This takes precious time cycles away from other threads.

Another problem with the polling method used in the previous code fragment is that the BOOL variable *g_fFinishedCalculation* might never be set to TRUE. This can happen if the primary thread has a higher priority than the thread executing the *RecalcFunc* function. In this case, the system never assigns any time slices to the *RecalcFunc* thread, which never executes the statement that sets *g_fFinishedCalculation* to TRUE. If the thread executing the *WinMain* function is put to sleep instead of polling, it is not scheduled time and the system can schedule time to lower-priority threads, such as the *RecalcFunc* thread, allowing them to execute.

I'll admit that sometimes polling comes in handy. After all, this is what a spinlock does. But there are proper ways to do this and improper ways to do this. As a general rule, you should not use spinlocks and you should not poll. Instead, you should call the functions that place your thread into a wait state until what your thread wants is available. I'll explain a proper way in the next section.

First, let me point out one more thing: At the top of the previous code fragment, you'll notice the use of *volatile*. For this code fragment to even come close to working, the *volatile* type qualifier must be there. This tells the compiler that the variable can be modified by something outside of the application itself, such as the operating system, hardware, or a concurrently executing thread. Specifically, the *volatile* qualifier tells the compiler to exclude the variable from any optimizations and always reload the value from the variable's memory location. Let's say that the compiler has generated the following pseudocode for the *while* statement shown in the previous code fragment:

```
MOV    Reg0, [g_fFinishedCalculation]   ; Copy the value into a register
Label: TEST  Reg0, 0                     ; Is the value 0?
JMP    Reg0 == 0, Label                  ; The register is 0, try again
...                                      ; The register is not 0 (end of loop)
```

Without making the Boolean variable volatile, it's possible that the compiler might optimize your C code as shown here. For this optimization, the compiler loads the value of the BOOL variable into a CPU register just once. Then it repeatedly performs tests against the CPU register. This certainly yields better performance than constantly rereading the value in a memory address and retesting it; therefore, an optimizing compiler might write code like that shown above. However, if the compiler does this, the thread enters an infinite loop and never wakes up. By the way, making a structure *volatile* ensures that all of its members are volatile and are always read from memory when referenced.

You might wonder whether my spinlock variable, *g_fResourceInUse* (used in the spinlock code shown on page 262), should be declared as *volatile*. The answer is no because we are passing the address of this variable to the various interlocked functions and not the variable's value itself. When you pass a variable's address to a function, the function must read the value from memory. The optimizer cannot affect this.

Critical Sections

A *critical section* is a small section of code that requires exclusive access to some shared resource before the code can execute. This is a way to have several lines of code "atomically" manipulate a resource. By atomic, I mean that the code knows that no other thread will access the resource. Of course, the system can still preempt your thread and schedule other threads. However, it will not schedule any other threads that want to access the same resource until your thread leaves the critical section.

Here is some problematic code that demonstrates what happens without the use of a critical section:

```
const int MAX_TIMES = 1000;
int    g_nIndex = 0;
DWORD g_dwTimes[MAX_TIMES];

DWORD WINAPI FirstThread(PVOID pvParam) {

   while (g_nIndex < MAX_TIMES) {
      g_dwTimes[g_nIndex] = GetTickCount();
      g_nIndex++;
   }
   return(0);
}


DWORD WINAPI SecondThread(PVOID pvParam) {

   while (g_nIndex < MAX_TIMES) {
      g_nIndex++;
      g_dwTimes[g_nIndex - 1] = GetTickCount();
   }
   return(0);
}
```

Taken independently, both thread functions are supposed to produce the same result, although each is coded a bit differently. If the *FirstThread* function were to run by itself, it would fill the *g_dwTimes* array with ascending values. The same thing would happen if the *SecondThread* function were to run by itself. Ideally, we want both threads to run concurrently and still have the *g_dwTimes* array produce ascending values. However, the code above has a problem: the *g_dwTimes* array won't be filled properly because the two thread functions access the same global variables simultaneously.

Here is an example of how this could happen. Let's say that we just started executing both threads on a system with one CPU. The operating system starts running *SecondThread* first (which could very well happen), and right after *SecondThread* increments *g_nIndex* to 1, the system preempts the thread and allows *FirstThread* to run. *FirstThread* then sets *g_dwTimes[1]* to the system time, and the system preempts the thread and gives time back to *SecondThread*. *SecondThread* then sets *g_dwTimes[1 -1]* to the new system time. Because this operation occurred later, the new system time is a higher value than that of the time placed into *FirstThread*'s array. Also notice that index 1 of *g_dwTimes* was filled in before index 0. The data in the array is corrupted.

I'll admit that this example is a bit contrived—it's difficult to come up with a real-life example that doesn't require several pages of source code. However, you can see how this problem could extend to real-life examples. Consider the case of managing a linked list of objects. If access to the linked list is not synchronized, one thread can add an item to the list while another thread is trying to search for an item in the list. The situation can become more chaotic if the two threads add items to the list at the same time. By using critical sections, you can ensure that access to the data structures is coordinated among threads.

Now that you see all of the problems, let's correct the code using a critical section:

```
const int MAX_TIMES = 1000;
int   g_nIndex = 0;
DWORD g_dwTimes[MAX_TIMES];
CRITICAL_SECTION g_cs;

DWORD WINAPI FirstThread(PVOID pvParam) {

   while (g_nIndex < MAX_TIMES) {
      EnterCriticalSection(&g_cs);
      g_dwTimes[g_nIndex] = GetTickCount();
      g_nIndex++;
      LeaveCriticalSection(&g_cs);
   }
   return(0);
}


DWORD WINAPI SecondThread(PVOID pvParam) {

   while (g_nIndex < MAX_TIMES) {
      EnterCriticalSection(&g_cs);
      g_nIndex++;
      g_dwTimes[g_nIndex - 1] = GetTickCount();
      LeaveCriticalSection(&g_cs);
   }
   return(0);
}
```

I allocated a CRITICAL_SECTION data structure, *g_cs*, and then I wrapped any code that touches the shared resource (*g_nIndex* and *g_dwTimes* in this example) inside calls to *EnterCriticalSection* and *LeaveCriticalSection*. Notice that I passed the address of *g_cs* in all calls to *EnterCriticalSection* and *LeaveCriticalSection*.

What are the key points to remember? When you have a resource that is accessed by multiple threads, you should create a CRITICAL_SECTION structure. Since I'm writing this on an airplane flight, let me draw the following analogy. A CRITICAL_SECTION structure is like an airplane's lavatory, and the toilet is the data that you want protected. Since the lavatory is small, only one person (thread) at a time can be inside the lavatory (critical section) using the toilet (protected resource).

If you have multiple resources that are always used together, you can place them all in a single lavatory: create just one CRITICAL_SECTION structure to guard them all.

If you have multiple resources that are not always used together—for example, threads 1 and 2 access one resource and threads 1 and 3 access another resource—you should create a separate lavatory, or CRITICAL_SECTION structure, for each resource.

Now, wherever you have code that touches a resource, you must place a call to *EnterCriticalSection*, passing it the address of the CRITICAL_SECTION structure that identifies the resource. This is like saying that when a thread wants to access a resource, it must first check the Occupied sign on the lavatory door. The CRITICAL_SECTION structure identifies which lavatory the thread wants to enter and the *EnterCriticalSection* function is what the thread uses to check the Occupied sign.

If *EnterCriticalSection* sees that no other thread is in the lavatory (the door shows Unoccupied), the calling thread is allowed to use it. If *EnterCriticalSection* sees that another thread is in the lavatory, the calling thread must wait outside the lavatory door until the other thread in the lavatory leaves.

When a thread no longer executes code that touches the resource, it should call *LeaveCriticalSection*. This is how the thread tells the system that it has left the lavatory containing the resource. If you forget to call *LeaveCriticalSection*, the system will think that the resource is still in the lavatory and will not allow any waiting threads in. This is similar to leaving the lavatory without changing the sign on the door back to Unoccupied.

The hardest thing to remember is that any code you write that touches a shared resource must be wrapped inside *EnterCriticalSection* and *LeaveCriticalSection* functions. If you forget to wrap your code in just one place, the shared resource will be subject to corruption. For instance, if I remove *FirstThread*'s calls to *EnterCriticalSection* and *LeaveCriticalSection*, the *g_nIndex* and *g_dwTimes* variables become corrupted. This happens even though *SecondThread* still calls *EnterCriticalSection* and *LeaveCriticalSection* properly.

Forgetting calls to *EnterCriticalSection* and *LeaveCriticalSection* is like not requesting permission to enter the lavatory. The thread just muscles its way in and manipulates the resource. As you can imagine, if just one thread exhibits this rather rude behavior, the resource is corrupted.

When you can't solve your synchronization problem with interlocked functions, you should try using critical sections. The great thing about critical sections is that they are easy to use and they use the interlocked functions internally, so they execute quickly. The major disadvantage of critical sections is that you cannot use them to synchronize threads in multiple processes. However, in Chapter 10, I'll create my own synchronization object, called an Optex. This object shows how critical sections can be implemented by the operating system, and it also works with threads in multiple processes.

Critical Sections: The Fine Print

By now, you have the theory behind critical sections—why they're useful and how they allow "atomic" access to a shared resource. Now let's look more closely at how critical sections tick. We'll start with the CRITICAL_SECTION data structure. If you look up this structure in the Platform SDK documentation, you won't even find an entry for it. What's this all about?

It's not that the CRITICAL_SECTION structure is undocumented; it's just that Microsoft doesn't think you need to understand what this structure is all about—and rightly so. To us, this structure is opaque—the structure is documented, but the member variables within it are not. Of course, since this is just a data structure, you can look it up in the Windows header files and see the data members. (CRITICAL_SECTION is defined in WinNT.h as RTL_CRITICAL_SECTION; the RTL_CRITICAL_SECTION structure is typedefed in WinBase.h.) But you should never write code that references these members.

To manipulate a CRITICAL_SECTION structure, you call a Windows function, passing it the address of the structure. The function knows how to manipulate the members and guarantees that the structure's state is always consistent. So now, let's turn our attention to these functions.

Normally, CRITICAL_SECTION structures are allocated as global variables to allow all threads in the process an easy way to reference the structure: by variable name. However, CRITICAL_SECTION structures can be allocated as local variables or dynamically allocated from a heap. There are just two requirements. The first is that all threads that want to access the resource must know the address of the CRITICAL_SECTION structure that protects the resource. You can get this address to these threads using any mechanism you like. The second requirement is that the members within the CRITICAL_SECTION structure be initialized before any threads attempt to access the protected resource. The structure is initialized via a call to:

```
VOID InitializeCriticalSection(PCRITICAL_SECTION pcs);
```

This function initializes the members of a CRITICAL_SECTION structure (pointed to by *pcs*). Since this function simply sets some member variables, it cannot fail and is therefore prototyped with a return value of VOID. This function must be called before any thread calls *EnterCriticalSection*. The Platform SDK documentation clearly states that the results are undefined if a thread attempts to enter an uninitialized CRITICAL_SECTION.

When you know that your process's threads will no longer attempt to access the shared resource, you should clean up the CRITICAL_SECTION structure by calling this function:

```
VOID DeleteCriticalSection(PCRITICAL_SECTION pcs);
```

DeleteCriticalSection resets the member variables inside the structure. Naturally, you should not delete a critical section if any threads are still using it. Again, the Platform SDK documentation clearly states that the results are undefined if you do.

When you write code that touches a shared resource, you must prefix that code with a call to:

```
VOID EnterCriticalSection(PCRITICAL_SECTION pcs);
```

EnterCriticalSection examines the member variables inside the structure. The variables indicate which thread, if any, is currently accessing the resource. *EnterCriticalSection* performs the following tests:

■ If no thread is accessing the resource, *EnterCriticalSection* updates the member variables to indicate that the calling thread has been granted access and returns immediately, allowing the thread to continue executing (accessing the resource).

■ If the member variables indicate that the calling thread was already granted access to the resource, *EnterCriticalSection* updates the variables to indicate how many times the calling thread was granted access and returns immediately, allowing the thread to continue executing. This situation is rare and occurs only if the thread calls *EnterCriticalSection* twice in a row without an intervening call to *LeaveCriticalSection*.

■ If the member variables indicate that a thread (other than the calling thread) was granted access to the resource, *EnterCriticalSection* places the calling thread in a wait state. This is terrific because the waiting thread does not waste any CPU time! The system remembers that the thread wants access to the resource and automatically updates the CRITICAL_SECTION's member variables and allows the thread to be schedulable as soon as the thread currently accessing the resource calls *LeaveCriticalSection*.

EnterCriticalSection isn't too complicated internally; it performs just a few simple tests. What makes this function so valuable is that it can perform all of these tests atomically. If two threads call *EnterCriticalSection* at exactly the same time on a multiprocessor machine, the function still behaves correctly: one thread is granted access to the resource, and the other thread is placed in a wait state.

If *EnterCriticalSection* places a thread in a wait state, the thread might not be scheduled again for a long time. In fact, in a poorly written application, the thread might never be scheduled CPU time again. If this happens, the thread is said to be *starved*.

In reality, threads waiting for a critical section never starve. Calls to *EnterCriticalSection* eventually time out, causing an exception to be raised. You can then attach a debugger to your application to determine what went wrong. The amount of time that must expire is determined by the *CriticalSectionTimeout* data value contained in the following registry subkey:

```
HKEY_LOCAL_MACHINE\System\CurrentControlSet\Control\Session Manager
```

This value is in seconds and defaults to 2,592,000 seconds, or about 30 days. Do not set this value too low (below 3 seconds, for example) or you will adversely affect threads in the system and other applications that normally wait more than 3 seconds for a critical section.

You can use this function instead of *EnterCriticalSection:*

```
BOOL TryEnterCriticalSection(PCRITICAL_SECTION pcs);
```

TryEnterCriticalSection never allows the calling thread to enter a wait state. Instead, its return value indicates whether the calling thread was able to gain access to the resource. So if *TryEnterCriticalSection* sees that the resource is being accessed by another thread, it returns FALSE. In all other cases, it returns TRUE.

With this function, a thread can quickly check to see if it can access a certain shared resource and, if not, continue doing something else instead of waiting. If *TryEnterCriticalSection* does return TRUE, the CRITICAL_SECTION's member variables have been updated to reflect that the thread is accessing the resource. Therefore, every call to *TryEnterCriticalSection* that returns TRUE must be matched with a call to *LeaveCriticalSection*.

Windows 98 does not have a useful implementation for the *TryEnterCriticalSection* function. Calling this function always returns FALSE.

At the end of your code that touches the shared resource, you must call this function:

```
VOID LeaveCriticalSection(PCRITICAL_SECTION pcs);
```

LeaveCriticalSection examines the member variables inside the structure. The function decrements by 1 a counter that indicates how many times the calling thread was granted access to the shared resource. If the counter is greater than 0, *LeaveCriticalSection* does nothing else and simply returns.

If the counter becomes 0, it checks to see whether any other threads are waiting in a call to *EnterCriticalSection*. If at least one thread is waiting, it updates the member variables and makes one of the waiting threads (selected "fairly") schedulable again. If no threads are waiting, *LeaveCriticalSection* updates the member variables to indicate that no thread is accessing the resource.

Like *EnterCriticalSection*, *LeaveCriticalSection* performs all of these tests and updates atomically. However, *LeaveCriticalState* never places a thread in a wait state; it always returns immediately.

Critical Sections and Spinlocks

When a thread attempts to enter a critical section owned by another thread, the calling thread is placed immediately into a wait state. This means that the thread must transition from user mode to kernel mode (about 1000 CPU cycles). This transition is very expensive. On a multiprocessor machine, the thread that currently owns the resource might execute on a different processor and might relinquish control of the resource shortly. In fact, the thread that owns the resource might release it before the other thread has completed executing its transition into kernel mode. If this happens, a lot of CPU time is wasted.

To improve the performance of critical sections, Microsoft has incorporated spinlocks into them. So when *EnterCriticalSection* is called, it loops using a spinlock to try to acquire the resource some number of times. Only if all the attempts fail does the thread transition to kernel mode to enter a wait state.

To use a spinlock with a critical section, you should initialize the critical section by calling this function:

```
BOOL InitializeCriticalSectionAndSpinCount(
    PCRITICAL_SECTION pcs,
    DWORD dwSpinCount);
```

As in *InitializeCriticalSection*, the first parameter of *InitializeCriticalSectionAndSpinCount* is the address of the critical section structure. But in the second parameter, *dwSpinCount*, you pass the number of times you want the spinlock loop to iterate as it tries to acquire the resource before making the thread wait. This value can be any number from 0 through 0x00FFFFFF. If you call this function while running on a single processor machine, the *dwSpinCount* parameter is ignored and the count is always set to 0. This is good because setting a spin count on a single-processor machine is useless: the thread owning the resource can't relinquish it if another thread is spinning.

You can change a critical section's spin count by calling this function:

```
DWORD SetCriticalSectionSpinCount(
    PCRITICAL_SECTION pcs,
    DWORD dwSpinCount);
```

277

Again, the *dwSpinCount* value is ignored if the host machine has just one processor.

In my opinion, you should always use spinlocks with critical sections since you have nothing to lose. The hard part is determining what value to pass for the *dwSpinCount* parameters. For the best performance, you simply have to play with numbers until you're happy with the performance results. As a guide, the critical section that guards access to your process's heap uses a spin count of 4000.

In Chapter 10, I'll show you how to implement critical sections. This implementation incorporates spinlocks.

Critical Sections and Error Handling

There is a small chance that the *InitializeCriticalSection* function can fail. Microsoft didn't really think about this when it originally designed the function, which is why the function is prototyped as returning VOID. The function might fail because it allocates a block of memory so that the system can have some internal debugging information. If this memory allocation fails, a STATUS_NO_MEMORY exception is raised. You can trap this in your code using structured exception handling (discussed in Chapters 23, 24, and 25).

You can more easily trap this problem using the newer *InitializeCriticalSectionAndSpinCount* function. This function also allocates the memory block for debugging information but returns FALSE if the memory could not be allocated.

Another problem can arise when you use critical sections. Internally, critical sections use an event kernel object if two or more threads contend for the critical section at the same time. (I'll show how this kernel object is used when I explain the COptex C++ class in Chapter 10.) Since contention is rare, the system does not create the event kernel object until the first time it is required. This saves a lot of system resources since most critical sections never have contention.

In a low-memory situation, a critical section might have contention, and the system might be unable to create the required event kernel object. The *EnterCriticalSection* function will then raise an EXCEPTION_INVALID_HANDLE exception. Most developers simply ignore this potential error and have no special handling in their code since this error is extremely rare. However, if you want to be prepared for this situation, you do have two options.

You can use structured exception handling and trap the error. When the error occurs, you can either not access the resource protected with the critical section or wait for some memory to become available and then call *EnterCriticalSection* again.

Your other option is to create the critical section using *InitializeCritical-SectionAndSpinCount*, making sure that you set the high bit of the *dwSpinCount* parameter. When this function sees that the high bit is set, it creates the event kernel object and associates it with the critical section at initialization time. If the event cannot be created, the function returns FALSE and you can handle this more gracefully in your code. If the event is created successfully, you know that *EnterCriticalSection* will always work and never raise an exception. (Always preallocating the event kernel objects can waste system resources. You should do this only if your code cannot tolerate *EnterCriticalSection* failing, if you are sure that contention will occur, or if you expect the process to be run in very low-memory environments.)

Useful Tips and Techniques

When you use critical sections, there are some good habits to get into and some things to avoid. Here are several tips and techniques to help you when you use critical sections. These techniques also apply to kernel object synchronization (discussed in the next chapter).

Use One CRITICAL_SECTION Variable per Shared Resource

If you have several unrelated data structures in your application, you should create a CRITICAL_SECTION variable for each data structure. This is better than having a single CRITICAL_SECTION structure that guards access to all shared resources. Examine this code fragment:

```
int   g_nNums[100];      // A shared resource
TCHAR g_cChars[100];     // Another shared resource
CRITICAL_SECTION g_cs;   // Guards both resources


DWORD WINAPI ThreadFunc(PVOID pvParam) {

   EnterCriticalSection(&g_cs);

   for (int x = 0; x < 100; x++) {
      g_nNums[x]  = 0;
      g_cChars[x] = TEXT('X');
   }

   LeaveCriticalSection(&g_cs);
   return(0);

}
```

This code uses a single critical section to protect both the *g_nNums* array and the *g_cChars* array while they are being initialized. But the two arrays have nothing to do with one another. While this loop executes, no thread can gain access to either array. If the *ThreadFunc* function is implemented as shown below, the two arrays are initialized separately:

```
DWORD WINAPI ThreadFunc(PVOID pvParam) {

   EnterCriticalSection(&g_cs);

   for (int x = 0; x < 100; x++)
      g_nNums[x] = 0;

   for (x = 0; x < 100; x++)
      g_cChars[x] = TEXT('X');

   LeaveCriticalSection(&g_cs);
   return(0);
}
```

Theoretically, after the *g_nNums* array has been initialized, a different thread that needs access only to the *g_nNums* array and not to the *g_cChars* array can begin executing while *ThreadFunc* continues to initialize the *g_cChars* array. But alas, this is not possible because a single critical section is protecting both data structures. To fix this, you can create two critical sections as follows:

```
int g_nNum[100];            // A shared resource
CRITICAL_SECTION g_csNums;  // Guards g_nNums

TCHAR g_cChars[100];        // Another shared resource
CRITICAL_SECTION g_csChars; // Guards g_cChars

DWORD WINAPI ThreadFunc(PVOID pvParam) {

   EnterCriticalSection(&g_csNums);

   for (int x = 0; x < 100; x++)
      g_nNums[x] = 0;

   LeaveCriticalSection(&g_csNums);

   EnterCriticalSection(&g_csChars);

   for (x = 0; x < 100; x++)
      g_cChars[x] = TEXT('X');

   LeaveCriticalSection(&g_ csChars);
   return(0);
}
```

With this implementation, another thread can start using the *g_nNums* array as soon as *ThreadFunc* has finished initializing it. You might also consider having one thread initialize the *g_nNums* array and a separate thread function initialize the *g_cChars* array.

Access Multiple Resources Simultaneously

Sometimes you'll need to access two resources simultaneously. If this were a requirement of *ThreadFunc*, it would be implemented like this:

```
DWORD WINAPI ThreadFunc(PVOID pvParam) {

   EnterCriticalSection(&g_csNums);
   EnterCriticalSection(&g_csChars);

   // This loop requires simultaneous access to both resources.
   for (int x = 0; x < 100; x++)
      g_nNums[x] = g_cChars[x];

   LeaveCriticalSection(&g_csChars);
   LeaveCriticalSection(&g_csNums);
   return(0);
}
```

Suppose another thread in the process, written as follows, also requires access to the two arrays:

```
DWORD WINAPI OtherThreadFunc(PVOID pvParam) {

   EnterCriticalSection(&g_csChars);
   EnterCriticalSection(&g_csNums);

   for (int x = 0; x < 100; x++)
      g_nNums[x] = g_cChars[x];

   LeaveCriticalSection(&g_csNums);
   LeaveCriticalSection(&g_csChars);
   return(0);
}
```

All I did in the function above was switch the order of the calls to *EnterCriticalSection* and *LeaveCriticalSection*. But because the two functions are written the way they are, a deadlock might occur. Suppose that *ThreadFunc* begins executing and gains ownership of the *g_csNums* critical section. Then the thread executing the *OtherThreadFunc* function is given some CPU time and gains ownership of the *g_csChars* critical section. Now you have a deadlock situation. When either *ThreadFunc* or *OtherThreadFunc* tries to continue executing, neither function can gain ownership of the other critical section it requires.

To solve this problem, you must always request access to the resources in exactly the same order. Notice that order does not matter when you call *LeaveCriticalSection* because this function never causes a thread to enter a wait state.

Don't Hold Critical Sections for a Long Time

When a critical section is held for a long time, other threads might enter wait states, which will hurt your application's performance. Here is a technique you can use to minimize the time spent inside a critical section. The following code prevents other threads from changing the value in *g_s* before the WM_SOMEMSG message is sent to a window:

```
SOMESTRUCT g_s;
CRITICAL_SECTION g_cs;

DWORD WINAPI SomeThread(PVOID pvParam) {
   EnterCriticalSection(&g_cs);

   // Send a message to a window.
   SendMessage(hwndSomeWnd, WM_SOMEMSG, &g_s, 0);

   LeaveCriticalSection(&g_cs);
   return(0);
}
```

It's impossible to tell how much time the window procedure requires for processing the WM_SOMEMSG message—it might be a few milliseconds or a few years. During that time, no other threads can gain access to the *g_s* structure. It's better to write the code as follows:

```
SOMESTRUCT g_s;
CRITICAL_SECTION g_cs;

DWORD WINAPI SomeThread(PVOID pvParam) {

   EnterCriticalSection(&g_cs);
   SOMESTRUCT sTemp = g_s;
   LeaveCriticalSection(&g_cs);

   // Send a message to a window.
   SendMessage(hwndSomeWnd, WM_SOMEMSG, &sTemp, 0);
   return(0);
}
```

This code saves the value in *sTemp*, a temporary variable. You can probably guess how long the CPU requires to execute this line—only a few CPU cycles. Immediately after the temporary variable is saved, *LeaveCriticalSection* is called because the global structure no longer needs to be protected. This second implementation is much better than the first because other threads are stopped from using the *g_s* structure for only a few CPU cycles instead of for an unknown amount of time. Of course, this technique assumes that the "snapshot" of the structure is good enough for the window procedure to read. It also assumes that the window procedure doesn't need to change the members in the structure.

CHAPTER NINE

THREAD SYNCHRONIZATION WITH KERNEL OBJECTS

In the last chapter, we discussed how to synchronize threads using mechanisms that allow your threads to remain in user mode. The wonderful thing about user-mode synchronization is that it is very fast. If you are concerned about your thread's performance, you should first determine whether a user-mode thread synchronization mechanism will work for you.

While user-mode thread synchronization mechanisms offer great performance, they do have limitations, and for many applications they simply do not work. For example, the interlocked family of functions operates only on single values and never places a thread into a wait state. You can use critical sections to place a thread in a wait state, but you can use them only to synchronize threads contained within a single process. Also, you can easily get into deadlock situations with critical sections because you cannot specify a timeout value while waiting to enter the critical section.

In this chapter, we'll discuss how to use kernel objects to synchronize threads. As you'll see, kernel objects are far more versatile than the user-mode mechanisms. In fact, the only bad side to kernel objects is their performance. When you call any of the new functions mentioned in this chapter, the calling thread must transition from user mode to kernel mode. This transition is costly: it takes about 1000 CPU cycles on the *x*86 platform for a round-trip—and this, of course, does not include the execution of the kernel-mode code that actually implements the function your thread is calling.

Throughout this book, we've discussed several kernel objects, including processes, threads, and jobs. You can use almost all of these kernel objects for synchronization purposes. For thread synchronization, each of these kernel objects is said to be in a signaled or nonsignaled state. The toggling of this state is determined by rules that Microsoft has created for each object. For example, process kernel objects are always created in the nonsignaled state. When the process terminates, the operating system automatically makes the process kernel object signaled. Once a process kernel object is signaled, it remains that way forever; its state never changes back to nonsignaled.

A process kernel object is nonsignaled while the process is running, and it becomes signaled when the process terminates. Inside a process kernel object is a Boolean value that is initialized to FALSE (nonsignaled) when the object is created. When the process terminates, the operating system automatically changes the corresponding object's Boolean value to TRUE, indicating that the object is signaled.

If you want to write code that checks whether a process is still running, all you do is call a function that asks the operating system to check the process object's Boolean value. That's easy enough. You might also want to tell the system to put your thread in a wait state and wake it up automatically when the Boolean changes from FALSE to TRUE. This way, you can write code in which a thread in a parent process that needs to wait for the child process to terminate can simply put itself to sleep until the kernel object identifying the child process becomes signaled. As you'll see, Microsoft Windows offers functions that accomplish all this easily.

I've just described the rules that Microsoft has defined for a process kernel object. As it turns out, thread kernel objects follow the same rules. That is, thread kernel objects are always created in the nonsignaled state. When the thread terminates, the operating system automatically changes the thread object's state to signaled. Therefore, you can use the same technique in your application to determine whether a thread is no longer executing. Just like process kernel objects, thread kernel objects never return to the nonsignaled state.

The following kernel objects can be in a signaled or nonsignaled state:

- Processes
- Threads
- Jobs
- Files
- Console input
- File change notifications
- Events
- Waitable timers
- Semaphores
- Mutexes

Threads can put themselves into a wait state until an object becomes signaled. Note that the rules that govern the signaled/nonsignaled state of each object depend on the type of object. I've already mentioned the rules for process and thread objects. I discuss the rules for jobs in Chapter 5.

In this chapter, we'll look at the functions that allow a thread to wait for a specific kernel object to become signaled. Then we'll look at the kernel objects that Windows offers specifically to help you synchronize threads: events, waitable timers, semaphores, and mutexes.

When I was first learning this stuff, it helped if I imagined that kernel objects contained a flag (the wave-in-the-air kind, not the bit kind). When the object was signaled, the flag was raised; when the object was nonsignaled, the flag was lowered.

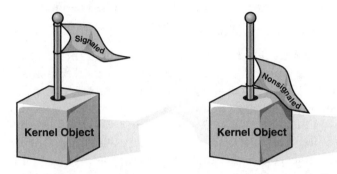

Threads are not schedulable when the objects they are waiting for are nonsignaled (the flag is lowered). However, as soon as the object becomes signaled (the flag goes up), the thread sees the flag, becomes schedulable, and shortly resumes execution.

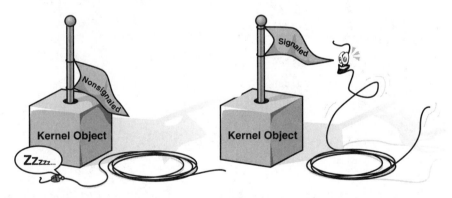

Wait Functions

Wait functions cause a thread to voluntarily place itself into a wait state until a specific kernel object becomes signaled. By far the most common of these functions is *WaitForSingleObject*:

```
DWORD WaitForSingleObject(
   HANDLE hObject,
   DWORD dwMilliseconds);
```

When a thread calls this function, the first parameter, *hObject*, identifies a kernel object that supports being signaled/nonsignaled. (Any object mentioned in the list on page 286 works just great.) The second parameter, *dwMilliseconds*, allows the thread to indicate how long it is willing to wait for the object to become signaled.

The following function call tells the system that the calling thread wants to wait until the process identified by the *hProcess* handle terminates:

```
WaitForSingleObject(hProcess, INFINITE);
```

The second parameter tells the system that the calling thread is willing to wait forever (an infinite amount of time) until this process terminates.

Usually, INFINITE is passed as the second parameter to *WaitForSingleObject*, but you can pass any value (in milliseconds). By the way, INFINITE is defined as 0xFFFFFFFF (or –1). Of course, passing INFINITE can be a little dangerous. If the object never becomes signaled, the calling thread never wakes up—it is forever deadlocked but, fortunately, not wasting precious CPU time.

Here's an example of how to call *WaitForSingleObject* with a timeout value other than INFINITE:

```
DWORD dw = WaitForSingleObject(hProcess, 5000);
switch (dw) {

   case WAIT_OBJECT_0:
     // The process terminated.
     break;

   case WAIT_TIMEOUT:
     // The process did not terminate within 5000 milliseconds.
     break;

   case WAIT_FAILED:
     // Bad call to function (invalid handle?)
     break;
}
```

The code above tells the system that the calling thread should not be schedulable until either the specified process has terminated or 5000 milliseconds have expired, whichever comes first. So this call returns in less than 5000 milliseconds if the process terminates, and it returns in about 5000 milliseconds if the process hasn't terminated. Note that you can pass 0 for the *dwMilliseconds* parameter. If you do this, *WaitForSingleObject* always returns immediately.

WaitForSingleObject's return value indicates why the calling thread became schedulable again. If the object the thread is waiting on became signaled, the return value is WAIT_OBJECT_0; if the timeout expires, the return value is WAIT_TIMEOUT. If you pass a bad parameter (such as an invalid handle) to *WaitForSingleObject*, the return value is WAIT_FAILED (call *GetLastError* for more information).

The function below, *WaitForMultipleObjects*, is similar to *WaitForSingle-Object* except that it allows the calling thread to check the signaled state of several kernel objects simultaneously:

```
DWORD WaitForMultipleObjects(
    DWORD dwCount,
    CONST HANDLE* phObjects,
    BOOL fWaitAll,
    DWORD dwMilliseconds);
```

The *dwCount* parameter indicates the number of kernel objects you want the function to check. This value must be between 1 and MAXIMUM_WAIT_OBJECTS (defined as 64 in the Windows header files). The *phObjects* parameter is a pointer to an array of kernel object handles.

You can use *WaitForMultipleObjects* in two different ways—to allow a thread to enter a wait state until any one of the specified kernel objects becomes signaled, or to allow a thread to wait until all of the specified kernel objects become signaled. The *fWaitAll* parameter tells the function which way you want it to work. If you pass TRUE for this parameter, the function will not allow the calling thread to execute until all of the objects have become signaled.

The *dwMilliseconds* parameter works exactly as it does for *WaitForSingle-Object*. If, while waiting, the specified time expires, the function returns anyway. Again, INFINITE is usually passed for this parameter, but you should write your code carefully to avoid the possibility of deadlock.

The *WaitForMultipleObjects* function's return value tells the caller why it got rescheduled. The possible return values are WAIT_FAILED and WAIT_TIMEOUT, which are self-explanatory. If you pass TRUE for *fWaitAll* and all of the objects become signaled, the return value is WAIT_OBJECT_0. If you pass FALSE for *fWaitAll*, the function returns as soon as any of the objects becomes signaled. In this case, you probably want to know which object became signaled. The return value is a value between WAIT_OBJECT_0 and (WAIT_OBJECT_0 + *dwCount* − 1). In other words, if the return value is not WAIT_TIMEOUT and is not WAIT_FAILED, you should subtract

WAIT_OBJECT_0 from the return value. The resulting number is an index into the array of handles that you passed as the second parameter to *WaitForMultiple-Objects*. The index tells you which object became signaled.

Here's some sample code to make this clear:

```
HANDLE h[3];
h[0] = hProcess1;
h[1] = hProcess2;
h[2] = hProcess3;
DWORD dw = WaitForMultipleObjects(3, h, FALSE, 5000);
switch (dw) {
   case WAIT_FAILED:
      // Bad call to function (invalid handle?)
      break;

   case WAIT_TIMEOUT:
      // None of the objects became signaled within 5000 milliseconds.
      break;

   case WAIT_OBJECT_0 + 0:
      // The process identified by h[0] (hProcess1) terminated.
      break;

   case WAIT_OBJECT_0 + 1:
      // The process identified by h[1] (hProcess2) terminated.
      break;

   case WAIT_OBJECT_0 + 2:
      // The process identified by h[2] (hProcess3) terminated.
      break;
}
```

If you pass FALSE for the *fWaitAll* parameter, *WaitForMultipleObjects* scans the handle array from index 0 on up, and the first object that is signaled terminates the wait. This can have some undesirable ramifications. For example, your thread might be waiting for three child processes to terminate by passing three process handles to this function. If the process at index 0 in the array terminates, *WaitForMultipleObjects* returns. Now the thread can do whatever it needs to and then loop back around, waiting for another process to terminate. If the thread passes the same three handles, the function returns immediately with WAIT_OBJECT_0 again. Unless you remove the handles that you've already received notifications from, your code will not work correctly.

Successful Wait Side Effects

For some kernel objects, a successful call to *WaitForSingleObject* or *WaitFor-MultipleObjects* actually alters the state of the object. A successful call is one in which the function sees that the object was signaled and returns a value relative to WAIT_OBJECT_0. A call is unsuccessful if the function returns WAIT_TIMEOUT or WAIT_FAILED. Objects never have their state altered for unsuccessful calls.

When an object has its state altered, I call this a *successful wait side effect*. For example, let's say that a thread is waiting on an auto-reset event object (discussed later in this chapter). When the event object becomes signaled, the function detects this and can return WAIT_OBJECT_0 to the calling thread. However, just before the function returns, the event is set to the nonsignaled state—the side effect of the successful wait.

This side effect is applied to auto-reset event kernel objects because it is one of the rules that Microsoft has defined for this type of object. Other objects have different side effects, and some objects have no side effects at all. Process and thread kernel objects have no side effects at all—that is, waiting on one of these objects never alters the object's state. As we discuss various kernel objects in this chapter, we'll go into detail about their successful wait side effects.

What makes *WaitForMultipleObjects* so useful is that it performs all of its operations atomically. When a thread calls *WaitForMultipleObjects*, the function can test the signaled state of all the objects and perform the required side effects all as a single operation.

Let's look at an example. Two threads call *WaitForMultipleObjects* in exactly the same way:

```
HANDLE h[2];
h[0] = hAutoResetEvent1;   // Initially nonsignaled
h[1] = hAutoResetEvent2;   // Initially nonsignaled
WaitForMultipleObjects(2, h, TRUE, INFINITE);
```

When *WaitForMultipleObjects* is called, both event objects are nonsignaled; this forces both threads to enter a wait state. Then the *hAutoResetEvent1* object becomes signaled. Both threads see that the event has become signaled, but neither can wake up because the *hAutoResetEvent2* object is still nonsignaled. Because neither thread has successfully waited yet, no side effect happens to the *hAutoResetEvent1* object.

Next, the *hAutoResetEvent2* object becomes signaled. At this point, one of the two threads detects that both objects it is waiting for have become signaled. The wait is successful, both event objects are set to the nonsignaled state, and the thread is schedulable. But what about the other thread? It continues to wait until it sees that both event objects are signaled. Even though it originally detected that *hAutoResetEvent1* was signaled, it now sees this object as nonsignaled.

As I mentioned, it's important to note that *WaitForMultipleObjects* works atomically. When it checks the state of the kernel objects, no other thread can alter any object's state behind its back. This prevents deadlock situations. Imagine what would happen if one thread saw that *hAutoResetEvent1* was signaled and reset the event to nonsignaled and then the other thread saw that *hAutoResetEvent2* was signaled and reset this event to nonsignaled. Both threads would be frozen: one thread would wait for an object that another thread had gotten, and vice versa. *WaitForMultipleObjects* ensures that this never happens.

This brings up an interesting question: If multiple threads wait for a single kernel object, which thread does the system decide to wake up when the object becomes signaled? Microsoft's official response to this question is, "The algorithm is fair." Microsoft doesn't want to commit to the internal algorithm used by the system. All it says is that the algorithm is fair, which means that if multiple threads are waiting, each should get its own chance to wake up each time the object becomes signaled.

This means that thread priority has no effect: the highest-priority thread does not necessarily get the object. It also means that the thread waiting the longest does not necessarily get the object. And it is possible for a thread that got the object to loop around and get it again. However, this wouldn't be fair to the other threads, so the algorithm tries to prevent this. But there is no guarantee.

In reality, the algorithm Microsoft uses is simply the popular "first in, first out" scheme. The thread that has waited the longest for an object gets the object. However, actions can occur in the system that alter this behavior, making it less predictable. This is why Microsoft doesn't explicitly state how the algorithm works. One such action is a thread getting suspended. If a thread waits for an object and then the thread is suspended, the system forgets that the thread is waiting for the object. This is a feature because there is no reason to schedule a suspended thread. When the thread is later resumed, the system thinks that the thread just started waiting on the object.

While you debug a process, all threads within that process are suspended when breakpoints are hit. So debugging a process makes the "first in, first out" algorithm highly unpredictable because threads are frequently suspended and resumed.

Event Kernel Objects

Of all the kernel objects, events are by far the most primitive. They contain a usage count (as all kernel objects do), a Boolean value indicating whether the event is an auto-reset or manual-reset event, and another Boolean value indicating whether the event is signaled or nonsignaled.

Events signal that an operation has completed. There are two different types of event objects: manual-reset events and auto-reset events. When a manual-reset event is signaled, all threads waiting on the event become schedulable. When an auto-reset event is signaled, only one of the threads waiting on the event becomes schedulable.

Events are most commonly used when one thread performs initialization work and then signals another thread to perform the remaining work. The event is initialized as nonsignaled, and then after the thread completes its initial work, it sets the event to signaled. At this point, another thread, which has been waiting on the event, sees that the event is signaled and becomes schedulable. This second thread knows that the first has completed its work.

Here is the *CreateEvent* function, which creates an event kernel object:

```
HANDLE CreateEvent(
    PSECURITY_ATTRIBUTES psa,
    BOOL fManualReset,
    BOOL fInitialState,
    PCTSTR pszName);
```

In Chapter 3, we discussed the mechanics of kernel objects—how to set their security, how usage counting is done, how their handles can be inheritable, and how objects can be shared by name. Since all of this should be familiar to you by now, I won't discuss the first and last parameters of this function.

The *fManualReset* parameter is a Boolean value that tells the system whether to create a manual-reset event (TRUE) or an auto-reset event (FALSE). The *fInitialState* parameter indicates whether the event should be initialized to signaled (TRUE) or nonsignaled (FALSE). After the system creates the event object, *CreateEvent* returns the process-relative handle to the event object. Threads in other processes can gain access to the object by calling *CreateEvent* using the same value passed in the *pszName* parameter; by using inheritance; by using the *DuplicateHandle* function; or by calling *OpenEvent*, specifying a name in the *pszName* parameter that matches the name specified in the call to *CreateEvent*:

```
HANDLE OpenEvent(
    DWORD fdwAccess,
    BOOL fInherit,
    PCTSTR pszName);
```

As always, you should call the *CloseHandle* function when you no longer require the event kernel object.

Once an event is created, you control its state directly. When you call *SetEvent*, you change the event to the signaled state:

```
BOOL SetEvent(HANDLE hEvent);
```

When you call *ResetEvent*, you change the event to the nonsignaled state:

```
BOOL ResetEvent(HANDLE hEvent);
```

It's that easy.

Microsoft has defined a successful wait side effect rule for an auto-reset event: an auto-reset event is automatically reset to the nonsignaled state when a thread successfully waits on the object. This is how auto-reset events got their name. It is usually unnecessary to call *ResetEvent* for an auto-reset event because the system automatically resets the event. In contrast, Microsoft has not defined a successful wait side effect for manual-reset events.

Let's run through a quick example of how you can use event kernel objects to synchronize threads. Here's the setup:

```
// Create a global handle to a manual-reset, nonsignaled event.
HANDLE g_hEvent;

int WINAPI WinMain(...) {

   // Create the manual-reset, nonsignaled event.
   g_hEvent = CreateEve\nt(NULL, TRUE, FALSE, NULL);

   // Spawn 3 new threads.
   HANDLE hThread[3];
   DWORD dwThreadID;
   hThread[0] = _beginthreadex(NULL, 0, WordCount, NULL, 0, &dwThreadID);
   hThread[1] = _beginthreadex(NULL, 0, SpellCheck, NULL, 0, &dwThreadID);
   hThread[2] = _beginthreadex(NULL, 0, GrammarCheck, NULL, 0, &dwThreadID);


   OpenFileAndReadContentsIntoMemory(...);

   // Allow all 3 threads to access the memory.
   SetEvent(g_hEvent);
   ...
}

DWORD WINAPI WordCount(PVOID pvParam) {
```

(continued)

```
    // Wait until the file's data is in memory.
    WaitForSingleObject(g_hEvent, INFINITE);

    // Access the memory block.
    ...
    return(0);
}

DWORD WINAPI SpellCheck (PVOID pvParam) {

    // Wait until the file's data is in memory.
    WaitForSingleObject(g_hEvent, INFINITE);

    // Access the memory block.
    ...
    return(0);
}

DWORD WINAPI GrammarCheck (PVOID pvParam) {

    // Wait until the file's data is in memory.
    WaitForSingleObject(g_hEvent, INFINITE);

    // Access the memory block.
    ...
    return(0);
}
```

When this process starts, it creates a manual-reset, nonsignaled event and saves the handle in a global variable. This makes it easy for other threads in this process to access the same event object. Now three threads are spawned. These threads wait until a file's contents are read into memory, and then each thread accesses the data: one thread does a word count, another runs the spelling checker, and the third runs the grammar checker. The code for these three thread functions starts out identically: each thread calls *WaitForSingleObject*, which suspends the thread until the file's contents have been read into memory by the primary thread.

Once the primary thread has the data ready, it calls *SetEvent*, which signals the event. At this point, the system makes all three secondary threads schedulable—they all get CPU time and access the memory block. Notice that all three threads will access the memory in a read-only fashion. This is the only reason why all three threads can run simultaneously. Also note that if the machine has multiple CPUs on it, all of these threads can truly execute simultaneously, getting a lot of work done in a short amount of time.

If you use an auto-reset event instead of a manual-reset event, the application behaves quite differently. The system allows only one secondary thread to become schedulable after the primary thread calls *SetEvent*. Again, there is no guarantee as to which thread the system will make schedulable. The remaining two secondary threads will continue to wait.

The thread that becomes schedulable has exclusive access to the memory block. Let's rewrite the thread functions so that each function calls *SetEvent* (just like the *WinMain* function does) just before returning. The thread functions now look like this:

```
DWORD WINAPI WordCount(PVOID pvParam) {

   // Wait until the file's data is in memory.
   WaitForSingleObject(g_hEvent, INFINITE);

   // Access the memory block.
   ...
   SetEvent(g_hEvent);
   return(0);
}


DWORD WINAPI SpellCheck (PVOID pvParam) {

   // Wait until the file's data is in memory.
   WaitForSingleObject(g_hEvent, INFINITE);

   // Access the memory block.
   ...
   SetEvent(g_hEvent);
   return(0);
}


DWORD WINAPI GrammarCheck (PVOID pvParam) {

   // Wait until the file's data is in memory.
   WaitForSingleObject(g_hEvent, INFINITE);

   // Access the memory block.
   ...
   SetEvent(g_hEvent);
   return(0);
}
```

When a thread has finished its exclusive pass over the data, it calls *SetEvent,* which allows the system to make one of the two waiting threads schedulable.

Again, we don't know which thread the system will choose, but this thread will have its own exclusive pass over the memory block. When this thread is done, it will call *SetEvent* as well, causing the third and last thread to get its exclusive pass over the memory block. Note that when you use an auto-reset event, there is no problem if each secondary thread accesses the memory block in a read/write fashion; the threads are no longer required to consider the data read-only. This example clearly demonstrates the difference between using a manual-reset event and an auto-reset event.

For the sake of completeness, I'll mention one more function that you can use with events:

```
BOOL PulseEvent(HANDLE hEvent);
```

PulseEvent makes an event signaled and then immediately nonsignaled; it's just like calling *SetEvent* immediately followed by *ResetEvent*. If you call *PulseEvent* on a manual-reset event, any and all threads waiting on the event when it is pulsed are schedulable. If you call *PulseEvent* on an auto-reset event, only one waiting thread becomes schedulable. If no threads are waiting on the event when it is pulsed, there is no effect.

PulseEvent is not very useful. In fact, I've never used it in any practical application because you have no idea what threads, if any, will see the pulse and become schedulable. Since you can't know the state of any threads when you call *PulseEvent*, the function is just not that useful. That said, I'm sure that in some scenarios *PulseEvent* might come in handy—but none spring to mind. See the discussion of the *SignalObjectAndWait* function later in this chapter for a little more information on *PulseEvent*.

The Handshake Sample Application

The Handshake ("09 Handshake.exe") application, listed in Figure 9-1, demonstrates the use of auto-reset events. The source code files and resource files for the application are in the 09-Handshake directory on the companion CD-ROM. When you run Handshake, the following dialog box appears.

Handshake accepts a request string, reverses all the characters in the string, and places the result in the Result field. What makes Handshake exciting is the way it accomplishes this heroic task.

Handshake solves a common programming problem. You have a client and a server that want to talk to each other. Initially, the server has nothing to do, so it enters a wait state. When the client is ready to submit a request to the server, it places the request into a shared memory buffer and then signals an event so that the server thread knows to examine the data buffer and process the client's request. While the server thread is busy processing the request, the client's thread needs to enter a wait state until the server has the request's result ready. So the client enters a wait state until the server signals a different event that indicates that the result is ready to be processed by the client. When the client wakes up again, it knows that the result is in the shared data buffer and can present the result to the user.

When the application starts, it immediately creates two nonsignaled, auto-reset event objects. One event, *g_hevtRequestSubmitted*, indicates when a request is ready for the server. This event is waited on by the server thread and is signaled by the client thread. The second event, *g_hevtResultReturned*, indicates when the result is ready for the client. The client thread waits on this event and the server thread is responsible for signaling it.

After the events are created, the server thread is spawned and executes the *ServerThread* function. This function immediately has the server wait for a client's request. Meanwhile, the primary thread, which is also the client thread, calls *DialogBox*, which displays the application's user interface. You can enter some text in the Request field, and then, when you click the Submit Request To Server button, the request string is placed in a buffer that is shared between the client and the server threads and the *g_hevtRequestSubmitted* event is signaled. The client thread then waits for the server's result by waiting on the *g_hevtResultReturned* event.

The server wakes, reverses the string in the shared memory buffer, and then signals the *g_hevtResultReturned* event. The server's thread loops back around, waiting for another client request. Notice that this application never calls *ResetEvent* because it is unnecessary: auto-reset events are automatically reset to the nonsignaled state after a successful wait. Meanwhile, the client thread detects that the *g_hevtResultReturned* event has becomes signaled. It wakes and copies the string from the shared memory buffer into the Result field of the user interface.

Perhaps this application's only remaining notable feature is how it shuts down. To shut down the application, you simply close the dialog box. This causes the call to *DialogBox* in *_tWinMain* to return. At this point, the primary thread copies a special string into the shared buffer and wakes the server's thread to process this special request. The primary thread waits for the server thread to acknowledge receipt of the request and for the server thread to terminate. When the server thread detects this special client request string, it exits its loop and the thread just terminates.

I chose to have the primary thread wait for the server thread to die by calling *WaitForMultipleObjects* so that you would see how this function is used. In reality, I could have just called *WaitForSingleObject*, passing in the server thread's handle, and everything would have worked exactly the same.

Once the primary thread knows that the server thread has stopped executing, I call *CloseHandle* three times to properly destroy all the kernel objects that the application was using. Of course, the system would do this for me automatically, but it just feels better to me when I do it myself. I like being in control of my code at all times.

 Handshake.cpp

```
/*****************************************************************************
Module:  Handshake.cpp
Notices: Copyright (c) 2000 Jeffrey Richter
*****************************************************************************/


#include "..\CmnHdr.h"      /* See Appendix A. */
#include <windowsx.h>
#include <tchar.h>
#include <process.h>        // For beginthreadex
#include "Resource.h"



///////////////////////////////////////////////////////////////////////////


// This event is signaled when the client has a request for the server
HANDLE g_hevtRequestSubmitted;

// This event is signaled when the server has a result for the client
HANDLE g_hevtResultReturned;

// The buffer shared between the client and server threads
TCHAR  g_szSharedRequestAndResultBuffer[1024];
```

Figure 9-1. *(continued)*
The Handshake sample application

Figure 9-1. *continued*

```
// The special value sent from the client that causes the
// server thread to terminate cleanly.
TCHAR  g_szServerShutdown[] = TEXT("Server Shutdown");


///////////////////////////////////////////////////////////////////////////


// This is the code executed by the server thread
DWORD WINAPI ServerThread(PVOID pvParam) {

   // Assume that the server thread is to run forever
   BOOL fShutdown = FALSE;

   while (!fShutdown) {

      // Wait for the client to submit a request
      WaitForSingleObject(g_hevtRequestSubmitted, INFINITE);

      // Check to see if the client wants the server to terminate
      fShutdown =
         (lstrcmpi(g_szSharedRequestAndResultBuffer, g_szServerShutdown) == 0);

      if (!fShutdown) {
         // Process the client's request (reverse the string)
         _tcsrev(g_szSharedRequestAndResultBuffer);
      }

      // Let the client process the request's result
      SetEvent(g_hevtResultReturned);
   }

   // The client wants us to shutdown, exit
   return(0);
}


///////////////////////////////////////////////////////////////////////////


BOOL Dlg_OnInitDialog(HWND hwnd, HWND hwndFocus, LPARAM lParam) {

   chSETDLGICONS(hwnd, IDI_HANDSHAKE);

   // Initialize the edit control with some test data request
   Edit_SetText(GetDlgItem(hwnd, IDC_REQUEST), TEXT("Some test data"));
```

(continued)

Figure 9-1. *continued*

```
    return(TRUE);
}


/////////////////////////////////////////////////////////////////////////


void Dlg_OnCommand(HWND hwnd, int id, HWND hwndCtl, UINT codeNotify) {

    switch (id) {

        case IDCANCEL:
            EndDialog(hwnd, id);
            break;

        case IDC_SUBMIT:   // Submit a request to the server thread

            // Copy the request string into the shared data buffer
            Edit_GetText(GetDlgItem(hwnd, IDC_REQUEST),
                g_szSharedRequestAndResultBuffer,
                chDIMOF(g_szSharedRequestAndResultBuffer));

            // Let the server thread know that a request is ready in the buffer
            SetEvent(g_hevtRequestSubmitted);

            // Wait for the server to process the request and give us the result
            WaitForSingleObject(g_hevtResultReturned, INFINITE);

            // Let the user know the result
            Edit_SetText(GetDlgItem(hwnd, IDC_RESULT),
                g_szSharedRequestAndResultBuffer);

            break;
    }
}


/////////////////////////////////////////////////////////////////////////


INT_PTR WINAPI Dlg_Proc(HWND hwnd, UINT uMsg, WPARAM wParam, LPARAM lParam) {

    switch (uMsg) {
        chHANDLE_DLGMSG(hwnd, WM_INITDIALOG, Dlg_OnInitDialog);
        chHANDLE_DLGMSG(hwnd, WM_COMMAND,    Dlg_OnCommand);
    }
```

(continued)

Figure 9-1. *continued*

```
    return(FALSE);
}


//////////////////////////////////////////////////////////////////////////////


int WINAPI _tWinMain(HINSTANCE hinstExe, HINSTANCE, PTSTR pszCmdLine, int) {

   // Create & initialize the 2 nonsignaled, auto-reset events
   g_hevtRequestSubmitted = CreateEvent(NULL, FALSE, FALSE, NULL);
   g_hevtResultReturned   = CreateEvent(NULL, FALSE, FALSE, NULL);

   // Spawn the server thread
   DWORD dwThreadID;
   HANDLE hThreadServer = chBEGINTHREADEX(NULL, 0, ServerThread, NULL,
      0, &dwThreadID);

   // Execute the client thread's user-interface
   DialogBox(hinstExe, MAKEINTRESOURCE(IDD_HANDSHAKE), NULL, Dlg_Proc);

   // The client's UI is closing, have the server thread shutdown
   lstrcpy(g_szSharedRequestAndResultBuffer, g_szServerShutdown);
   SetEvent(g_hevtRequestSubmitted);

   // Wait for the server thread to acknowledge the shutdown AND
   // wait for the server thread to fully terminate
   HANDLE h[2];
   h[0] = g_hevtResultReturned;
   h[1] = hThreadServer;
   WaitForMultipleObjects(2, h, TRUE, INFINITE);

   // Properly clean up everything
   CloseHandle(hThreadServer);
   CloseHandle(g_hevtRequestSubmitted);
   CloseHandle(g_hevtResultReturned);

   // The client thread terminates with the whole process
   return(0);
}


//////////////////////////// End of File ////////////////////////////////////
```

(continued)

Figure 9-1. *continued*

Handshake.rc

```
//Microsoft Developer Studio generated resource script.
//
#include "resource.h"

#define APSTUDIO_READONLY_SYMBOLS
/////////////////////////////////////////////////////////////////////////////
//
// Generated from the TEXTINCLUDE 2 resource.
//
#include "afxres.h"


/////////////////////////////////////////////////////////////////////////////
#undef APSTUDIO_READONLY_SYMBOLS


/////////////////////////////////////////////////////////////////////////////
// English (U.S.) resources

#if !defined(AFX_RESOURCE_DLL) || defined(AFX_TARG_ENU)
#ifdef _WIN32
LANGUAGE LANG_ENGLISH, SUBLANG_ENGLISH_US
#pragma code_page(1252)
#endif //_WIN32


/////////////////////////////////////////////////////////////////////////////
//
// Dialog
//

IDD_HANDSHAKE DIALOG DISCARDABLE  0, 0, 256, 81
STYLE DS_CENTER | WS_MINIMIZEBOX | WS_CAPTION | WS_SYSMENU
CAPTION "Handshake"
FONT 8, "MS Sans Serif"
BEGIN
    GROUPBOX        "Client side",IDC_STATIC,4,4,248,72
    LTEXT           "&Request:",IDC_STATIC,12,18,30,8
    EDITTEXT        IDC_REQUEST,48,16,196,14,ES_AUTOHSCROLL
    DEFPUSHBUTTON   "&Submit Request to Server",IDC_SUBMIT,80,36,96,14
    LTEXT           "Result:",IDC_STATIC,12,58,23,8
    EDITTEXT        IDC_RESULT,48,56,196,16,ES_AUTOHSCROLL | ES_READONLY
END
```

(continued)

303

Figure 9-1. *continued*

```
//////////////////////////////////////////////////////////////////////
//
// DESIGNINFO
//

#ifdef APSTUDIO_INVOKED
GUIDELINES DESIGNINFO DISCARDABLE
BEGIN
    IDD_HANDSHAKE, DIALOG
    BEGIN
        LEFTMARGIN, 7
        RIGHTMARGIN, 249
        TOPMARGIN, 7
        BOTTOMMARGIN, 74
    END
END
#endif    // APSTUDIO_INVOKED


#ifdef APSTUDIO_INVOKED
//////////////////////////////////////////////////////////////////////
//
// TEXTINCLUDE
//

1 TEXTINCLUDE DISCARDABLE
BEGIN
    "resource.h\0"
END

2 TEXTINCLUDE DISCARDABLE
BEGIN
    "#include ""afxres.h""\r\n"
    "\0"
END

3 TEXTINCLUDE DISCARDABLE
BEGIN
    "\r\n"
    "\0"
END

#endif    // APSTUDIO_INVOKED
```

(continued)

Figure 9-1. *continued*

```
/////////////////////////////////////////////////////////////////////////
//
// Icon
//

// Icon with lowest ID value placed first to ensure application icon
// remains consistent on all systems.
IDI_HANDSHAKE           ICON    DISCARDABLE     "Handshake.ico"
#endif    // English (U.S.) resources
/////////////////////////////////////////////////////////////////////////


#ifndef APSTUDIO_INVOKED
/////////////////////////////////////////////////////////////////////////
//
// Generated from the TEXTINCLUDE 3 resource.
//


/////////////////////////////////////////////////////////////////////////
#endif    // not APSTUDIO_INVOKED
```

Waitable Timer Kernel Objects

Waitable timers are kernel objects that signal themselves at a certain time or at regular intervals. They are most commonly used to have some operation performed at a certain time.

To create a waitable timer, you simply call *CreateWaitableTimer*:

```
HANDLE CreateWaitableTimer(
   PSECURITY_ATTRIBUTES psa,
   BOOL fManualReset,
   PCTSTR pszName);
```

The *psa* and *pszName* parameters are discussed in Chapter 3. Of course, a process can obtain its own process-relative handle to an existing waitable timer by calling *OpenWaitableTimer*:

```
HANDLE OpenWaitableTimer(
   DWORD dwDesiredAccess,
   BOOL bInheritHandle,
   PCTSTR pszName);
```

As with events, the *fManualReset* parameter indicates a manual-reset or an auto-reset timer. When a manual-reset timer is signaled, all threads waiting on the timer become schedulable. When an auto-reset timer is signaled, only one waiting thread becomes schedulable.

Waitable timer objects are always created in the nonsignaled state. You must call the *SetWaitableTimer* function to tell the timer when you want it to become signaled:

```
BOOL SetWaitableTimer(
    HANDLE hTimer,
    const LARGE_INTEGER *pDueTime,
    LONG lPeriod,
    PTIMERAPCROUTINE pfnCompletionRoutine,
    PVOID pvArgToCompletionRoutine,
    BOOL fResume);
```

This function takes several parameters and can be quite confusing to use. Obviously, the *hTimer* parameter indicates the timer that you want to set. The next two parameters, *pDueTime* and *lPeriod*, are used together. The *pDueTime* parameter indicates when the timer should go off for the first time, and the *lPeriod* parameter indicates how frequently the timer should go off after that. The following code sets a timer to go off for the first time on January 1, 2002, at 1:00 P.M., and then to go off every six hours after that:

```
// Declare our local variables.
HANDLE hTimer;
SYSTEMTIME st;
FILETIME ftLocal, ftUTC;
LARGE_INTEGER liUTC;

// Create an auto-reset timer.
hTimer = CreateWaitableTimer(NULL, FALSE, NULL);

// First signaling is at January 1, 2002, at 1:00 P.M. (local time).
st.wYear         = 2002; // Year
st.wMonth        = 1;    // January
st.wDayOfWeek    = 0;    // Ignored
st.wDay          = 1;    // The first of the month
st.wHour         = 13;   // 1PM
st.wMinute       = 0;    // 0 minutes into the hour
st.wSecond       = 0;    // 0 seconds into the minute
st.wMilliseconds = 0;    // 0 milliseconds into the second

SystemTimeToFileTime(&st, &ftLocal);
```

(continued)

```
// Convert local time to UTC time.
LocalFileTimeToFileTime(&ftLocal, &ftUTC);
// Convert FILETIME to LARGE_INTEGER because of different alignment.
liUTC.LowPart  = ftUTC.dwLowDateTime;
liUTC.HighPart = ftUTC.dwHighDateTime;

// Set the timer.
SetWaitableTimer(hTimer, &liUTC, 6 * 60 * 60 * 1000,
   NULL, NULL, FALSE);
  .
  .
  .
```

The code above first initializes a SYSTEMTIME structure that indicates when the timer should first go off (be signaled). I set this time in local time—the correct time for the machine's time zone. *SetWaitableTimer*'s second parameter is prototyped as a *const* LARGE_INTEGER * and therefore cannot accept a SYSTEMTIME structure directly. However, a FILETIME structure and a LARGE_INTEGER structure have identical binary formats: both structures contain two 32-bit values. So we can convert our SYSTEMTIME structure to a FILETIME structure. The next problem is that *SetWaitableTimer* expects the time always to be passed to it in Coordinated Universal Time (UTC) time. You can call *LocalFileTimeToFileTime* to easily make this conversion.

Since FILETIME and LARGE_INTEGER structures have identical binary formats, you might be tempted to pass the address of the FILETIME structure directly to *SetWaitableTimer*, as follows:

```
// Set the timer.
SetWaitableTimer(hTimer, (PLARGE_INTEGER) &ftUTC,
   6 * 60 * 60 * 1000, NULL, NULL, FALSE);
```

In fact, this is what I originally did. However, this is a big mistake! Though FILETIME and LARGE_INTEGER structures have identical binary format, the alignment requirements of both structures are different. The address of all FILETIME structures must begin on a 32-bit boundary, but the address of all LARGE_INTEGER structures must begin on a 64-bit boundary. Whether calling *SetWaitableTimer* and passing it a FILETIME structure works correctly depends on whether the FILETIME structure happens to be on a 64-bit boundary. However, the compiler ensures that LARGE_INTEGER structures always begin on 64-bit boundaries, so the proper thing to do (the thing that is guaranteed to work all the time) is to copy the FILETIME's members into a LARGE_INTEGER's members and then pass the address of the LARGE_INTEGER to *SetWaitableTimer*.

NOTE

> The *x*86 processors deal with unaligned data references silently. So passing the address of a FILETIME to *SetWaitableTimer* always works when your application is running on an *x*86 CPU. However, other processors, such as the Alpha, do not handle unaligned references as silently. In fact, most other processors raise an EXCEPTION_DATATYPE_MISALIGNMENT exception that causes your process to terminate. Alignment errors are the biggest cause of problems when you port code that works on *x*86 computers to other processors. If you pay attention to alignment issues now, you can save months of porting effort later! For more information about alignment issues, see Chapter 13.

Now, to have the timer go off every six hours after January 1, 2002, at 1:00 P.M., we turn our attention to the *lPeriod* parameter. This parameter indicates, in milliseconds, how often the timer should go off after it initially goes off. For six hours, I pass 21,600,000 (6 hours * 60 minutes per hour * 60 seconds per minute * 1000 milliseconds per second). By the way, *SetWaitableTimer* does not fail if you pass it an absolute time in the past such as January 1, 1975, at 1:00 P.M.

Instead of setting an absolute time that the timer should first go off, you can have the timer go off at a time relative to calling *SetWaitableTimer*. You simply pass a negative value in the *pDueTime* parameter. The value you pass must be in 100-nanosecond intervals. Since we don't normally think in intervals of 100 nanoseconds, you might find this useful: 1 second = 1,000 milliseconds = 1,000,000 microseconds = 10,000,000 100-nanoseconds.

The following code sets a timer to initially go off 5 seconds after the call to *SetWaitableTimer*:

```
// Declare our local variables.
HANDLE hTimer;
LARGE_INTEGER li;

// Create an auto-reset timer.
hTimer = CreateWaitableTimer(NULL, FALSE, NULL);

// Set the timer to go off 5 seconds after calling SetWaitableTimer.
// Timer unit is 100-nanoseconds.
const int nTimerUnitsPerSecond = 10000000;

// Negate the time so that SetWaitableTimer knows we
// want relative time instead of absolute time.
li.QuadPart = -(5 * nTimerUnitsPerSecond);
```

(continued)

```
// Set the timer.
SetWaitableTimer(hTimer, &li, 6 * 60 * 60 * 1000,
    NULL, NULL, FALSE);
```

$$\vdots$$

Usually, you want a one-shot timer that signals itself once and never signals itself again. To accomplish this, you simply pass 0 for the *lPeriod* parameter. You can then call *CloseHandle* to close the timer or you can call *SetWaitableTimer* again to reset the time, giving it new criteria to follow.

SetWaitableTimer's last parameter, *fResume,* is useful for computers that support suspend and resume. Usually, you pass FALSE for this argument, as I've done in the code fragments above. However, if you're writing a meeting planner–type application in which you want to set timers that remind the user of scheduled meetings, you should pass TRUE. When the timer goes off, it takes the machine out of suspend mode (if it's in suspend mode) and wakes up the threads that are waiting on the timer. The application then plays a wave file and presents a message box telling the user of the upcoming meeting. If you pass FALSE for the *fResume* parameter, the timer object becomes signaled but any threads that it wakes up do not get CPU time until the machine is somehow resumed (usually by the user waking it up).

Our discussion of waitable timers would not be complete without talking about *CancelWaitableTimer:*

```
BOOL CancelWaitableTimer(HANDLE hTimer);
```

This simple function takes the handle of a timer and cancels it so that the timer never goes off unless there is a subsequent call to *SetWaitableTimer* to reset the timer. If you ever want to change the criteria for a timer, you don't have to call *CancelWaitableTimer* before calling *SetWaitableTimer*. Each call to *SetWaitableTimer* cancels the criteria for the timer before setting the new criteria.

Having Waitable Timers Queue APC Entries

So far, you've learned how to create a timer and how to set the timer. You also know how to wait on the timer by passing its handle to the *WaitForSingleObject* or *WaitForMultipleObjects* functions. Microsoft also allows timers to queue an asynchronous procedure call (APC) to the thread that calls *SetWaitableTimer* when the timer is signaled.

Normally, when you call *SetWaitableTimer*, you pass NULL for both the *pfnCompletionRoutine* and *pvArgToCompletionRoutine* parameters. When *SetWaitableTimer* sees NULL for these parameters, it knows to signal the timer object when the time comes due. However, if you prefer to have the timer queue an APC when the time comes due, you must pass the address of a timer APC routine, which you must implement. The function should look like this:

```
VOID APIENTRY TimerAPCRoutine(PVOID pvArgToCompletionRoutine,
   DWORD dwTimerLowValue, DWORD dwTimerHighValue) {

   // Do whatever you want here.
}
```

I've named the function *TimerAPCRoutine*, but you can name it anything you like. This function is called using the same thread that called *SetWaitable-Timer* when the timer goes off if and only if the calling thread is in an alertable state. In other words, the thread must be waiting in a call to *SleepEx*, *WaitForSingleObjectEx*, *WaitForMultipleObjectsEx*, *MsgWaitForMultipleObjectsEx*, or *SignalObjectAndWait*. If the thread is not waiting in one of these functions, the system does not queue the timer APC routine. This prevents the thread's APC queue from becoming overloaded with timer APC notifications, which can waste an enormous amount of memory inside the system.

If your thread is in an alertable wait when the timer goes off, the system makes your thread call the callback routine. The first parameter to the callback routine is the same value that you passed to *SetWaitableTimer*'s *pvArgToCompletionRoutine* parameter. You can pass some context information (usually a pointer to a structure that you define) to the *TimerAPCRoutine*. The remaining two parameters, *dwTimerLowValue* and *dwTimerHighValue*, indicate when the timer went off. The following code takes this information and shows it to the user:

```
VOID APIENTRY TimerAPCRoutine(PVOID pvArgToCompletionRoutine,
   DWORD dwTimerLowValue, DWORD dwTimerHighValue) {

   FILETIME ftUTC, ftLocal;
   SYSTEMTIME st;
   TCHAR szBuf[256];

   // Put the time in a FILETIME structure.
   ftUTC.dwLowDateTime = dwTimerLowValue;
   ftUTC.dwHighDateTime = dwTimerHighValue;

   // Convert the UTC time to the user's local time.
   FileTimeToLocalFileTime(&ftUTC, &ftLocal);

   // Convert the FILETIME to the SYSTEMTIME structure
   // required by GetDateFormat and GetTimeFormat.
   FileTimeToSystemTime(&ftLocal, &st);
```

(continued)

310

```
   // Construct a string with the
   // date/time that the timer went off.
   GetDateFormat(LOCALE_USER_DEFAULT, DATE_LONGDATE,
      &st, NULL, szBuf, sizeof(szBuf) / sizeof(TCHAR));
   _tcscat(szBuf, __TEXT(" "));
   GetTimeFormat(LOCALE_USER_DEFAULT, 0,
      &st, NULL, _tcschr(szBuf, 0),
      sizeof(szBuf) / sizeof(TCHAR) - _tcslen(szBuf));

   // Show the time to the user.
   MessageBox(NULL, szBuf, "Timer went off at...", MB_OK);
}
```

Only after all APC entries have been processed does an alertable function return. Therefore, you must make sure that your *TimerAPCRoutine* function finishes executing before the timer becomes signaled again so that APC entries are not queued faster than they can be processed.

This code shows the proper way to use timers and APCs:

```
void SomeFunc() {
   // Create a timer. (It doesn't matter whether it's manual-reset
   // or auto-reset.)
   HANDLE hTimer = CreateWaitableTimer(NULL, TRUE, NULL);

   // Set timer to go off in 5 seconds.
   LARGE_INTEGER li = { 0 };
   SetWaitableTimer(hTimer, &li, 5000, TimerAPCRoutine, NULL, FALSE);

   // Wait in an alertable state for the timer to go off.
   SleepEx(INFINITE, TRUE);

   CloseHandle(hTimer);
}
```

One final word: a thread should not wait on a timer's handle and wait on a timer alertably. Take a look at this code:

```
HANDLE hTimer = CreateWaitableTimer(NULL, FALSE, NULL);
SetWaitableTimer(hTimer, ..., TimerAPCRoutine,...);
WaitForSingleObjectEx(hTimer, INFINITE, TRUE);
```

You should not write code like this because the call to *WaitForSingle-ObjectEx* is actually waiting on the timer twice: alertably and with a kernel object handle. When the timer becomes signaled, the wait is successful and the thread wakes, which takes the thread out of the alertable state, and the APC routine is not called. As I said earlier, you won't often have a reason to use an APC routine with waitable timers because you can always wait for the timer to be signaled and then do what you want.

Timer Loose Ends

Timers are frequently used in communication protocols. For example, if a client makes a request of a server and the server doesn't respond in a certain amount of time, the client assumes that the server is not available. Today, client machines typically communicate with many servers simultaneously. If you were to create a timer kernel object for every single request, system performance would be hampered. You can imagine that it would be possible, for most applications, to create a single timer object and simply change the due time as necessary.

This managing of due times and resetting of the timer can be tedious; few applications go to the effort. However, among the new thread pooling functions (covered in Chapter 11) is a new function called *CreateTimerQueueTimer* that does all of this work for you. If you find yourself creating and managing several timer objects, take a look at this function to reduce your application's overhead.

While it is nice that timers can queue APC entries, most applications written today do not use APCs; they use the I/O completion port mechanism. In the past, I have needed a thread in my own thread pool (managed with an I/O completion port) to wake up at specific timer intervals. Unfortunately, waitable timers do not offer this facility. To accomplish this, I have had to create a single thread whose sole job is to set and wait on a waitable timer. When the timer becomes signaled, the thread calls *PostQueuedCompletionStatus* to force an event to a thread in my thread pool.

One last note: any seasoned Windows developer will immediately compare waitable timers and User timers (set with the *SetTimer* function). The biggest difference is that User timers require a lot of additional user interface infrastructure in your application, which makes them more resource intensive. Also, waitable timers are kernel objects, which means that they can be shared by multiple threads and are securable.

User timers generate WM_TIMER messages that come back to the thread that called *SetTimer* (for callback timers) or the thread that created the window (for window-based timers). So only one thread is notified when a User timer goes off. Multiple threads, on the other hand, can wait on waitable timers, and several threads can be scheduled if the timer is a manual-reset timer.

If you are going to perform user-interface-related events in response to a timer, it is probably easier to structure your code using User timers because using a waitable timer requires that your threads wait for messages as well as kernel objects. (If you want to restructure your code, use the *MsgWaitForMultiple-Objects* function, which exists for exactly this purpose.) Finally, with waitable timers, you're more likely to be notified when the time actually expires. As

Chapter 27 explains, WM_TIMER messages are always the lowest-priority messages and are retrieved when no other messages are in a thread's queue. Waitable timers are not treated any differently than other kernel objects; if the timer goes off and your thread is waiting, your thread will wake up.

Semaphore Kernel Objects

Semaphore kernel objects are used for resource counting. They contain a usage count, as all kernel objects do, but they also contain two additional signed 32-bit values: a maximum resource count and a current resource count. The maximum resource count identifies the maximum number of resources that the semaphore can control; the current resource count indicates the number of these resources that are currently available.

To put this in perspective, let's see how an application might use semaphores. Let's say that I'm developing a server process in which I have allocated a buffer that can hold client requests. I've hard-coded the size of the buffer so that it can hold a maximum of five client requests at a time. If a new client attempts to contact the server while five requests are outstanding, the new client is turned away with an error indicating that the server is busy and the client should try again later. When my server process initializes, it creates a thread pool consisting of five threads, each thread ready to process individual client requests as they come in.

Initially, no clients have made any requests, so my server doesn't allow any of the threads in the pool to be schedulable. However, if three client requests come in simultaneously, three threads in the pool should be schedulable. You can handle this monitoring of resources and scheduling of threads very nicely using a semaphore: the maximum resource count is set to 5 since that is the size of my hard-coded buffer. The current resource count is initially set to 0 since no clients have made any requests. As client requests are accepted, the current resource count is incremented, and as client requests are handed off to server pool threads, the current resource count is decremented.

The rules for a semaphore are as follows:

- If the current resource count is greater than 0, the semaphore is signaled.

- If the current resource count is 0, the semaphore is nonsignaled.

- The system never allows the current resource count to be negative.

- The current resource count can never be greater than the maximum resource count.

When you use a semaphore, do not confuse the semaphore object's usage count with its current resource count.

This function creates a semaphore kernel object:

```
HANDLE CreateSemaphore(
    PSECURITY_ATTRIBUTE psa,
    LONG lInitialCount,
    LONG lMaximumCount,
    PCTSTR pszName);
```

The *psa* and *pszName* parameters are discussed in Chapter 3. Of course, another process can obtain its own process relative handle to an existing semaphore by calling *OpenSemaphore*:

```
HANDLE OpenSemaphore(
    DWORD fdwAccess,
    BOOL bInheritHandle,
    PCTSTR pszName);
```

The *lMaximumCount* parameter tells the system the maximum number of resources that your application can handle. Since this is a signed, 32-bit value, you can have as many as 2,147,483,647 resources. The *lInitialCount* parameter indicates how many of these resources are initially (currently) available. When my server process initializes, there are no client requests, so I call *CreateSemaphore* as follows:

```
HANDLE hsem = CreateSemaphore(NULL, 0, 5, NULL);
```

This creates a semaphore with a maximum resource count of 5, but initially 0 resources are available. (Incidentally, the kernel object's usage count is 1 since I just created this kernel object; don't get the counters confused.) Since the current resource count is initialized to 0, the semaphore is nonsignaled. Any threads that wait on the semaphore are therefore placed in a wait state.

A thread gains access to a resource by calling a wait function, passing the handle of the semaphore guarding the resource. Internally, the wait function checks the semaphore's current resource count and if its value is greater than 0 (the semaphore is signaled), the counter is decremented by 1 and the calling thread remains schedulable. The nifty thing about semaphores is that they perform this test-and-set operation atomically; that is, when you request a resource from a semaphore, the operating system checks whether the resource is available and decrements the count of available resources without letting another thread interfere. Only after the resource count has been decremented does the system allow another thread to request access to a resource.

If the wait function determines that the semaphore's current resource count is 0 (the semaphore is nonsignaled), the system places the calling thread in a wait state. When another thread increments the semaphore's current resource count, the system remembers the waiting thread (or threads) and allows it to become schedulable (decrementing its current resource count appropriately).

A thread increments a semaphore's current resource count by calling *ReleaseSemaphore*:

```
BOOL ReleaseSemaphore(
    HANDLE hsem,
    LONG lReleaseCount,
    PLONG plPreviousCount);
```

This function simply adds the value in *lReleaseCount* to the semaphore's current resource count. Usually, you pass 1 for the *lReleaseCount* parameter, but this is certainly not required; I often pass values of 2 or more. The function also returns the current resource count's original value in **plPreviousCount*. Few applications actually care about this value, so fortunately you can pass NULL to ignore it.

Sometimes it is useful to know the current resource count of a semaphore without actually altering the count, but there is no function that queries a semaphore's current resource count value. At first, I thought that calling *ReleaseSemaphore* and passing 0 for the *lReleaseCount* parameter might work by returning the actual count in **plPreviousCount*. But this doesn't work; *ReleaseSemaphore* fills the long variable with 0. Next, I tried passing a really big number as the second parameter, hoping that it would not affect the current resource count because it would take it over the maximum. Again, *Release-Semaphore* filled **plPreviousCount* with 0. Unfortunately, there is just no way to get the current resource count of a semaphore without altering it.

Mutex Kernel Objects

Mutex kernel objects ensure that a thread has mutual exclusive access to a single resource. In fact, this is how the mutex got its name. A mutex object contains a usage count, a thread ID, and a recursion counter. Mutexes behave identically to critical sections, but mutexes are kernel objects, while critical sections are user-mode objects. This means that mutexes are slower than critical sections. But it also means that threads in different processes can access a single mutex, and it means that a thread can specify a timeout value while waiting to gain access to a resource.

The thread ID identifies which thread in the system currently owns the mutex, and the recursion counter indicates the number of times that this thread owns the mutex. Mutexes have many uses and are among the most frequently used kernel objects. Typically, they are used to guard a block of memory that is accessed by multiple threads. If multiple threads were to access the memory block simultaneously, the data in the block would be corrupted. Mutexes ensure that any thread accessing the memory block has exclusive access to the block so that the integrity of the data is maintained.

The rules for a mutex are as follows:

- If the thread ID is 0 (an invalid thread ID), the mutex is not owned by any thread and is signaled.

- If the thread ID is nonzero, a thread owns the mutex and the mutex is nonsignaled.

- Unlike all the other kernel objects, mutexes have special code in the operating system that allows them to violate the normal rules. (I'll explain this exception shortly.)

To use a mutex, one process must first create the mutex by calling *CreateMutex*:

```
HANDLE CreateMutex(
    PSECURITY_ATTRIBUTES psa,
    BOOL fInitialOwner,
    PCTSTR pszName);
```

The *psa* and *pszName* parameters are discussed in Chapter 3. Of course, another process can obtain its own process relative handle to an existing mutex by calling *OpenMutex*:

```
HANDLE OpenMutex(
    DWORD fdwAccess,
    BOOL bInheritHandle,
    PCTSTR pszName);
```

The *fInitialOwner* parameter controls the initial state of the mutex. If you pass FALSE (the usual case), both the mutex object's thread ID and recursion counter are set to 0. This means that the mutex is unowned and is therefore signaled.

If you pass TRUE for *fInitialOwner*, the object's thread ID is set to the calling thread's ID and the recursion counter is set to 1. Since the thread ID is nonzero, the mutex is initially nonsignaled.

A thread gains access to the shared resource by calling a wait function, passing the handle of the mutex guarding the resource. Internally, the wait function checks the thread ID to see if it is 0 (the mutex is signaled). If the thread ID is 0, the thread ID is set to the calling thread's ID, the recursion counter is set to 1, and the calling thread remains schedulable.

If the wait function detects that the thread ID is not 0 (the mutex is nonsignaled), the calling thread enters a wait state. The system remembers this and when the mutex's thread ID is set back to 0, the system sets the thread ID to the waiting thread's ID, sets the recursion counter to 1, and allows the waiting thread to be schedulable again. As always, these checks and changes to the mutex kernel object are performed atomically.

For mutexes, there is one special exception to the normal kernel object signaled/nonsignaled rules. Let's say that a thread attempts to wait on a nonsignaled mutex object. In this case, the thread is usually placed in a wait state. However, the system checks to see whether the thread attempting to acquire the mutex has the same thread ID as recorded inside the mutex object. If the thread IDs match, the system allows the thread to remain schedulable—even though the mutex was nonsignaled. We don't see this "exceptional" behavior applied to any other kernel object anywhere in the system. Every time a thread successfully waits on a mutex, the object's recursion counter is incremented. The only way the recursion counter can have a value greater than 1 is if the thread waits on the same mutex multiple times, taking advantage of this rule exception.

Once a thread has successfully waited on a mutex, the thread knows that it has exclusive access to the protected resource. Any other threads that attempt to gain access to the resource (by waiting on the same mutex) are placed in a wait state. When the thread that currently has access to the resource no longer needs its access, it must release the mutex by calling the *ReleaseMutex* function:

```
BOOL ReleaseMutex(HANDLE hMutex);
```

This function decrements the object's recursion counter by 1. If a thread successfully waits on a mutex object multiple times, that thread has to call *ReleaseMutex* the same number of times before the object's recursion counter becomes 0. When the recursion counter hits 0, the thread ID is also set to 0 and the object becomes signaled.

When the object becomes signaled, the system checks to see whether any other threads are waiting on the mutex. If so, the system "fairly" selects one of the waiting threads and gives it ownership of the mutex. This means, of course, that the thread ID is set to the selected thread's ID and the recursion counter is set to 1. If no other thread is waiting on the mutex, the mutex stays in the signaled state so that the next thread that waits on the mutex immediately gets it.

Abandonment Issues

Mutex objects are different from all other kernel objects because they have a notion of "thread ownership." None of the other kernel objects that we've discussed in this chapter remembers which thread successfully waited on it; only mutexes keep track of this. This thread ownership concept for mutexes is the reason why mutexes have the special rule exception that allows a thread to acquire the mutex even when it is nonsignaled.

This exception applies not only to a thread that is attempting to acquire a mutex, it also applies to threads attempting to release a mutex. When a thread calls *ReleaseMutex*, the function checks to see whether the calling thread's ID matches the thread ID in the mutex object. If the IDs match, the recursion counter is decremented as described earlier. If the thread IDs don't match, *ReleaseMutex* does nothing and returns FALSE (indicating failure) back to the caller. Making a call to *GetLastError* at this time will return ERROR_NOT_OWNER (attempt to release mutex not owned by caller).

So if a thread owning a mutex terminates (using *ExitThread*, *TerminateThread*, *ExitProcess*, or *TerminateProcess*) before releasing the mutex, what happens to the mutex and the other threads that are waiting on it? The answer is that the system considers the mutex to be *abandoned*—the thread that owns it can never release it because the thread has died.

Because the system keeps track of all mutex and thread kernel objects, it knows exactly when mutexes become abandoned. When a mutex becomes abandoned, the system automatically resets the mutex object's thread ID to 0 and its recursion counter to 0. Then the system checks to see whether any threads are currently waiting for the mutex. If so, the system "fairly" selects a waiting thread, sets the thread ID to the selected thread's ID, and sets the recursion counter to 1; the selected thread becomes schedulable.

This is the same as before except that the wait function does not return the usual WAIT_OBJECT_0 value to the thread. Instead, the wait function returns the special value of WAIT_ABANDONED. This special return value (which applies only to mutex objects) indicates that the mutex the thread was waiting on was owned by another thread that was terminated before it finished using the shared resource. This is not the best situation to be in. The newly scheduled thread has no idea what state the resource is currently in—the resource might be totally corrupt. You have to decide for yourself what your application should do in this case.

In real life, most applications never check explicitly for the WAIT_ABANDONED return value because a thread is rarely just terminated. (This whole discussion provides another great example of why you should never call the *TerminateThread* function.)

Mutexes vs. Critical Sections

Mutexes and critical section have identical semantics with respect to scheduling waiting threads. However, they differ in some of their other attributes. The following table compares them.

Characteristic	Mutex	Critical Section
Performance	Slow	Fast
Can be used across process boundaries	Yes	No
Declaration	HANDLE *hmtx*;	CRITICAL_SECTION *cs*;
Initialization	*hmtx = CreateMutex (NULL, FALSE, NULL);*	*InitializeCriticalSection (&cs);*
Cleanup	*CloseHandle (hmtx);*	*DeleteCriticalSection (&cs);*
Infinite wait	*WaitForSingleObject (hmtx, INFINITE);*	*EnterCriticalSection (&cs);*
0 wait	*WaitForSingleObject (hmtx, 0);*	*TryEnterCriticalSection (&cs);*
Arbitrary wait	*WaitForSingleObject (hmtx, dwMilliseconds);*	Not possible
Release	*ReleaseMutex (hmtx);*	*LeaveCriticalSection (&cs);*
Can be waited on with other kernel objects	Yes (use *WaitForMultipleObjects* or similar function)	No

The Queue Sample Application

The Queue ("09 Queue.exe") application, listed in Figure 9-2, uses a mutex and a semaphore to control a queue of data elements. The source code and resource files for the application are in the 09-Queue directory on the companion CD-ROM. When you run Queue, the following dialog box appears.

When Queue initializes, it creates four client threads and two server threads. Each client thread sleeps for some period of time and then appends a request element to a queue. As each element is queued, the Client Threads list box is updated. Each entry indicates which client thread appended the entry and which entry it was. For example, the first entry in the list box indicates that client thread 0 appended its first request. Then client threads 1 through 3 appended their first request, followed by client thread 0 appending its second request, and so on.

The server threads have nothing to do until at least one element appears in the queue. When an element appears, a single server thread wakes up to process the request. The Server Threads list box shows the status of the server threads. The first entry shows that server thread 0 is processing a request from client thread 0. The request being processed is the client thread's first request. The second entry shows server thread 1 processing client thread 1's first request, and so on.

In this example, the server threads cannot process the client's requests quickly enough and the queue fills to maximum capacity. I initialize the queue data structure so it can hold no more than 10 elements at a single time; this causes the queue to fill quickly. Plus, there are four client threads and only two server threads. We see that the queue is full when client thread 3 attempts to append its fifth request to the queue.

OK, so that's what you see; what's more interesting is how it works. The queue is managed and controlled by a C++ class, CQueue:

```
class CQueue {
public:
   struct ELEMENT {
      int m_nThreadNum, m_nRequestNum;
      // Other element data should go here.
   };
   typedef ELEMENT* PELEMENT;

private:
   PELEMENT m_pElements;        // Array of elements to be processed
   int      m_nMaxElements;     // # of elements in the array
   HANDLE   m_h[2];             // Mutex & semaphore handles
   HANDLE   &m_hmtxQ;           // Reference to m_h[0]
   HANDLE   &m_hsemNumElements; // Reference to m_h[1]

public:
   CQueue(int nMaxElements);
   ~CQueue();

   BOOL Append(PELEMENT pElement, DWORD dwMilliseconds);
   BOOL Remove(PELEMENT pElement, DWORD dwMilliseconds);
};
```

The public ELEMENT structure inside this class defines what a queue data element looks like. The actual content is not particularly important. For this sample application, clients place their client thread number and their request number in this element so that the servers can display this information in their list box when they process the retrieved element. A real-life application would generally not require this information.

For the private members, we have *m_pElements*, which points to a fixed-size array of ELEMENT structures. This is the data that needs protecting from the multiple client/server threads. The *m_nMaxElements* member indicates how large this array is initialized to when the CQueue object is constructed. The next member, *m_h*, is an array of two kernel object handles. To properly protect the queue's data elements, you need two kernel objects: a mutex and a semaphore. In the CQueue constructor, these two objects are created and their handles are placed in this array.

As you'll see shortly, the code sometimes calls *WaitForMultipleObjects*, passing the address to the handle array. You'll also see that sometimes the code needs to refer to just one of these kernel object handles. To make the code more readable and maintainable, I also declare two handle reference members, *m_hmtxQ* and *m_hsemNumElements*. When the CQueue constructor executes, it initializes these handle reference members to *m_h[0]* and *m_h[1]*, respectively.

You should now have no trouble understanding CQueue's constructor and destructor methods, so let's turn our attention to the *Append* method. This method attempts to append an ELEMENT to the queue. But first, the thread must make sure that it has exclusive access to the queue. The *Append* method does this by calling *WaitForSingleObject*, passing the handle of the *m_hmtxQ* mutex. If WAIT_OBJECT_0 is returned, the thread has exclusive access to the queue.

Next, the *Append* method must attempt to increment the number of elements in the queue by calling *ReleaseSemaphore* and passing a release count of 1. If *ReleaseSemaphore* is successful, the queue is not full and the new element can be appended. Fortunately, *ReleaseSemaphore* also returns the previous count of queue elements in the *lPreviousCount* variable. This tells you exactly which array index the new element should be placed in. After copying the element into the queue's array, the function returns. Once the element is completely appended to the queue, *Append* calls *ReleaseMutex* so that other threads can access the queue. The remaining parts of the *Append* function have to do with failure cases and error handling.

Now let's look at how a server thread calls the *Remove* method to extract an element from the queue. First, the thread must make sure that it has exclusive access to the queue, and the queue must have at least one element in it. Certainly, a server thread has no reason to wake if no elements are in the queue.

So the *Remove* method first calls *WaitForMultipleObjects*, passing both the mutex and the semaphore's handles. Only when both of these objects are signaled should a server thread wake up.

If WAIT_OBJECT_0 is returned, the thread has exclusive access to the queue and at least one element must be in the queue. At this point, the code extracts the element at index 0 in the array and then shifts the remaining elements in the array down one. This is not the most efficient way to implement a queue because memory copies like this are expensive, but our purpose here is to demonstrate thread synchronization. Finally, *ReleaseMutex* is called so that other threads can safely access the queue.

Note that the semaphore object keeps track of how many elements are in the queue at any given time. You can see how this number is incremented: the *Append* method calls *ReleaseSemaphore* when a new element is appended to the queue. But you don't immediately see how this count is decremented when an element is removed from the queue. The decrementing is done by the *Remove* method's call to *WaitForMultipleObjects*. Remember that the side effect of successfully waiting on a semaphore is that its count is decremented by one. This is very convenient for us.

Now that you understand how the CQueue class works, the rest of the source code is easy to understand.

 Queue.cpp

```
/*********************************************************************************
Module:  Queue.cpp
Notices: Copyright (c) 2000 Jeffrey Richter
*********************************************************************************/


#include "..\CmnHdr.h"        /* See Appendix A. */
#include <windowsx.h>
#include <tchar.h>
#include <process.h>          // For _beginthreadex
#include "Resource.h"


///////////////////////////////////////////////////////////////////////////////


class CQueue {
public:
   struct ELEMENT {
      int m_nThreadNum, m_nRequestNum;
```

Figure 9-2.
The Queue sample application

(continued)

Figure 9-2. *continued*

```
      // Other element data should go here
   };
   typedef ELEMENT* PELEMENT;

private:
   PELEMENT m_pElements;        // Array of elements to be processed
   int      m_nMaxElements;     // Maximum # of elements in the array
   HANDLE   m_h[2];             // Mutex & semaphore handles
   HANDLE   &m_hmtxQ;           // Reference to m_h[0]
   HANDLE   &m_hsemNumElements; // Reference to m_h[1]

public:
   CQueue(int nMaxElements);
   ~CQueue();

   BOOL Append(PELEMENT pElement, DWORD dwMilliseconds);
   BOOL Remove(PELEMENT pElement, DWORD dwMilliseconds);
};


///////////////////////////////////////////////////////////////////////////


CQueue::CQueue(int nMaxElements)
   : m_hmtxQ(m_h[0]), m_hsemNumElements(m_h[1]) {

   m_pElements = (PELEMENT)
      HeapAlloc(GetProcessHeap(), 0, sizeof(ELEMENT) * nMaxElements);
   m_nMaxElements = nMaxElements;
   m_hmtxQ = CreateMutex(NULL, FALSE, NULL);
   m_hsemNumElements = CreateSemaphore(NULL, 0, nMaxElements, NULL);
}


///////////////////////////////////////////////////////////////////////////


CQueue::~CQueue() {

   CloseHandle(m_hsemNumElements);
   CloseHandle(m_hmtxQ);
   HeapFree(GetProcessHeap(), 0, m_pElements);
}


///////////////////////////////////////////////////////////////////////////
```

(continued)

Figure 9-2. *continued*

```
BOOL CQueue::Append(PELEMENT pElement, DWORD dwTimeout) {

   BOOL fOk = FALSE;
   DWORD dw = WaitForSingleObject(m_hmtxQ, dwTimeout);

   if (dw == WAIT_OBJECT_0) {
      // This thread has exclusive access to the queue

      // Increment the number of elements in the queue
      LONG lPrevCount;
      fOk = ReleaseSemaphore(m_hsemNumElements, 1, &lPrevCount);
      if (fOk) {
         // The queue is not full; append the new element
         m_pElements[lPrevCount] = *pElement;
      } else {

         // The queue is full; set the error code and return failure
         SetLastError(ERROR_DATABASE_FULL);
      }

      // Allow other threads to access the queue
      ReleaseMutex(m_hmtxQ);

   } else {
      // Timeout, set error code and return failure
      SetLastError(ERROR_TIMEOUT);
   }

   return(fOk);   // Call GetLastError for more info
}


///////////////////////////////////////////////////////////////////////////////


BOOL CQueue::Remove(PELEMENT pElement, DWORD dwTimeout) {

   // Wait for exclusive access to queue and for queue to have element.
   BOOL fOk = (WaitForMultipleObjects(chDIMOF(m_h), m_h, TRUE, dwTimeout)
      == WAIT_OBJECT_0);

   if (fOk) {
      // The queue has an element; pull it from the queue
      *pElement = m_pElements[0];

      // Shift the remaining elements down
      MoveMemory(&m_pElements[0], &m_pElements[1],
```

(continued)

Figure 9-2. *continued*

```
        sizeof(ELEMENT) * (m_nMaxElements - 1));

    // Allow other threads to access the queue
    ReleaseMutex(m_hmtxQ);

  } else {
    // Timeout, set error code and return failure
    SetLastError(ERROR_TIMEOUT);
  }

  return(fOk);    // Call GetLastError for more info
}


///////////////////////////////////////////////////////////////////////////


CQueue g_q(10);                     // The shared queue
volatile BOOL g_fShutdown = FALSE;  // Signals client/server threads to die
HWND g_hwnd;                        // How client/server threads give status


// Handles to all client/server threads & number of client/server threads
HANDLE g_hThreads[MAXIMUM_WAIT_OBJECTS];
int    g_nNumThreads = 0;


///////////////////////////////////////////////////////////////////////////


DWORD WINAPI ClientThread(PVOID pvParam) {

  int nThreadNum = PtrToUlong(pvParam);
  HWND hwndLB = GetDlgItem(g_hwnd, IDC_CLIENTS);

  for (int nRequestNum = 1; !g_fShutdown; nRequestNum++) {

    TCHAR sz[1024];
    CQueue::ELEMENT e = { nThreadNum, nRequestNum };

    // Try to put an element on the queue
    if (g_q.Append(&e, 200)) {

      // Indicate which thread sent it and which request
      wsprintf(sz, TEXT("Sending %d:%d"), nThreadNum, nRequestNum);
    } else {
```

(continued)

Figure 9-2. *continued*

```
            // Couldn't put an element on the queue
            wsprintf(sz, TEXT("Sending %d:%d (%s)"), nThreadNum, nRequestNum,
               (GetLastError() == ERROR_TIMEOUT)
                  ? TEXT("timeout") : TEXT("full"));
         }

         // Show result of appending element
         ListBox_SetCurSel(hwndLB, ListBox_AddString(hwndLB, sz));
         Sleep(2500);   // Wait before appending another element
      }

   return(0);
}


//////////////////////////////////////////////////////////////////////////////


DWORD WINAPI ServerThread(PVOID pvParam) {

   int nThreadNum = PtrToUlong(pvParam);
   HWND hwndLB = GetDlgItem(g_hwnd, IDC_SERVERS);

   while (!g_fShutdown) {

      TCHAR sz[1024];
      CQueue::ELEMENT e;

      // Try to get an element from the queue
      if (g_q.Remove(&e, 5000)) {

         // Indicate which thread is processing it, which thread
         // sent it, and which request we're processing
         wsprintf(sz, TEXT("%d: Processing %d:%d"),
            nThreadNum, e.m_nThreadNum, e.m_nRequestNum);

         // The server takes some time to process the request
         Sleep(2000 * e.m_nThreadNum);

      } else {
         // Couldn't get an element from the queue
         wsprintf(sz, TEXT("%d: (timeout)"), nThreadNum);
      }

      // Show result of processing element
      ListBox_SetCurSel(hwndLB, ListBox_AddString(hwndLB, sz));
```

(continued)

Figure 9-2. *continued*

```
   }

   return(0);
}


//////////////////////////////////////////////////////////////////////


BOOL Dlg_OnInitDialog(HWND hwnd, HWND hwndFocus, LPARAM lParam) {

   chSETDLGICONS(hwnd, IDI_QUEUE);

   g_hwnd = hwnd; // Used by client/server threads to show status

   DWORD dwThreadID;

   // Create the client threads
   for (int x = 0; x < 4; x++)
      g_hThreads[g_nNumThreads++] =
         chBEGINTHREADEX(NULL, 0, ClientThread, (PVOID) (INT_PTR) x,
            0, &dwThreadID);

   // Create the server threads
   for (x = 0; x < 2; x++)
      g_hThreads[g_nNumThreads++] =
         chBEGINTHREADEX(NULL, 0, ServerThread, (PVOID) (INT_PTR) x,
            0, &dwThreadID);

   return(TRUE);
}


//////////////////////////////////////////////////////////////////////


void Dlg_OnCommand(HWND hwnd, int id, HWND hwndCtl, UINT codeNotify) {

   switch (id) {
      case IDCANCEL:
         EndDialog(hwnd, id);
         break;
   }
}


//////////////////////////////////////////////////////////////////////
```

(continued)

Figure 9-2. *continued*

```
INT_PTR WINAPI Dlg_Proc(HWND hwnd, UINT uMsg, WPARAM wParam, LPARAM lParam) {

    switch (uMsg) {
        chHANDLE_DLGMSG(hwnd, WM_INITDIALOG, Dlg_OnInitDialog);
        chHANDLE_DLGMSG(hwnd, WM_COMMAND,    Dlg_OnCommand);
    }
    return(FALSE);
}


//////////////////////////////////////////////////////////////////////////////


int WINAPI _tWinMain(HINSTANCE hinstExe, HINSTANCE, PTSTR pszCmdLine, int) {

    DialogBox(hinstExe, MAKEINTRESOURCE(IDD_QUEUE), NULL, Dlg_Proc);
    InterlockedExchangePointer((PVOID*) &g_fShutdown, (PVOID) TRUE);

    // Wait for all the threads to terminate & then cleanup
    WaitForMultipleObjects(g_nNumThreads, g_hThreads, TRUE, INFINITE);
    while (g_nNumThreads--)
        CloseHandle(g_hThreads[g_nNumThreads]);

    return(0);
}


/////////////////////////////// End of File ///////////////////////////////////
```

Queue.rc

```
//Microsoft Developer Studio generated resource script.
//
#include "Resource.h"

#define APSTUDIO_READONLY_SYMBOLS
//////////////////////////////////////////////////////////////////////////////
//
// Generated from the TEXTINCLUDE 2 resource.
//
#include "afxres.h"


//////////////////////////////////////////////////////////////////////////////
#undef APSTUDIO_READONLY_SYMBOLS
```

(continued)

Figure 9-2. *continued*

```
////////////////////////////////////////////////////////////////////////////
// English (U.S.) resources

#if !defined(AFX_RESOURCE_DLL) || defined(AFX_TARG_ENU)
#ifdef _WIN32
LANGUAGE LANG_ENGLISH, SUBLANG_ENGLISH_US
#pragma code_page(1252)
#endif //_WIN32


////////////////////////////////////////////////////////////////////////////
//
// Dialog
//


IDD_QUEUE DIALOG DISCARDABLE  38, 36, 298, 225
STYLE WS_MINIMIZEBOX | WS_VISIBLE | WS_CAPTION | WS_SYSMENU
CAPTION "Queue"
FONT 8, "MS Sans Serif"
BEGIN
    GROUPBOX        "&Client threads",IDC_STATIC,4,4,140,216
    LISTBOX         IDC_CLIENTS,8,16,132,200,NOT LBS_NOTIFY |
                    LBS_NOINTEGRALHEIGHT | WS_VSCROLL | WS_TABSTOP
    GROUPBOX        "&Server threads",IDC_STATIC,156,4,140,216
    LISTBOX         IDC_SERVERS,160,16,132,200,NOT LBS_NOTIFY |
                    LBS_NOINTEGRALHEIGHT | WS_VSCROLL | WS_TABSTOP

END


////////////////////////////////////////////////////////////////////////////
//
// Icon
//


// Icon with lowest ID value placed first to ensure application icon
// remains consistent on all systems.
IDI_QUEUE               ICON    DISCARDABLE     "Queue.Ico"


#ifdef APSTUDIO_INVOKED
////////////////////////////////////////////////////////////////////////////
//
// TEXTINCLUDE
//


1 TEXTINCLUDE DISCARDABLE
BEGIN
    "Resource.h\0"
END
```

(continued)

Figure 9-2. *continued*

```
2 TEXTINCLUDE DISCARDABLE
BEGIN
    "#include ""afxres.h""\r\n"
    "\0"
END

3 TEXTINCLUDE DISCARDABLE
BEGIN
    "\r\n"
    "\0"
END

#endif    // APSTUDIO_INVOKED


/////////////////////////////////////////////////////////////////////////
//
// DESIGNINFO
//

#ifdef APSTUDIO_INVOKED
GUIDELINES DESIGNINFO DISCARDABLE
BEGIN
    IDD_QUEUE, DIALOG
    BEGIN
        RIGHTMARGIN, 244
        BOTTOMMARGIN, 130
    END
END
#endif    // APSTUDIO_INVOKED

#endif    // English (U.S.) resources
/////////////////////////////////////////////////////////////////////////


#ifndef APSTUDIO_INVOKED
/////////////////////////////////////////////////////////////////////////
//
// Generated from the TEXTINCLUDE 3 resource.
//


/////////////////////////////////////////////////////////////////////////
#endif    // not APSTUDIO_INVOKED
```

A Handy Thread Synchronization Object Chart

The following chart summarizes how the various kernel objects behave with respect to thread synchronization.

Object	When Nonsignaled	When Signaled	Successful Wait Side Effect
Process	While process is still active	When process terminates (*ExitProcess*, *TerminateProcess*)	None
Thread	While thread is still active	When thread terminates (*ExitThread*, *Terminate-Thread*)	None
Job	When job's time has not expired	When job time expires	None
File	When I/O request is pending	When I/O request completes	None
Console input	No input exists	When input is available	None
File change notifications	No files have changed	When file system detects changes	Resets notification
Auto-reset event	*ResetEvent, PulseEvent,* or successful wait	When *SetEvent/PulseEvent* is called	Resets event
Manual-reset event	*ResetEvent* or *PulseEvent*	When *SetEvent/PulseEvent* is called	None
Auto-reset waitable timer	*CancelWaitableTimer* or successful wait	When time comes due (*SetWaitableTimer*)	Resets timer
Manual-reset waitable timer	*CancelWaitableTimer*	When time comes due (*SetWaitableTimer*)	None
Semaphore	Successful wait	When count > 0 (*ReleaseSemaphore*)	Decrements count by 1
Mutex	Successful wait	When unowned by a thread (*ReleaseMutex*)	Gives ownership to thread
Critical section (user-mode)	Successful wait (*(Try)EnterCriticalSection*)	When unowned by a thread (*LeaveCriticalSection*)	Gives ownership to thread

Interlocked (user-mode) functions never cause a thread to be unschedulable; they alter a value and return immediately.

Other Thread Synchronization Functions

WaitForSingleObject and *WaitForMultipleObjects* are the most commonly used functions for performing thread synchronization. However, Windows offers a few more functions that have slight variations. If you understand *WaitForSingleObject* and *WaitForMultipleObjects*, you'll have no trouble understanding how these other functions work. In this section, I'll briefly introduce some of them.

Asynchronous Device I/O

Asynchronous device I/O allows a thread to start a read or write operation without having to wait for the read or write operation to complete. For example, if a thread needs to load a large file into memory, the thread can tell the system to load the file into memory. Then, as the system loads the file, the thread can be busy performing other tasks—creating windows, initializing internal data structures, and so on. When the initialization is complete, the thread can suspend itself, waiting for the system to notify it that the file has been read.

Device objects are synchronizable kernel objects, which means that you can call *WaitForSingleObject*, passing the handle of a file, socket, communication port, and so on. While the system performs the asynchronous I/O, the device object is in the nonsignaled state. As soon as the operation is complete, the system changes the state of the object to signaled so that the thread knows that the operation has completed. At this point, the thread continues execution.

WaitForInputIdle

A thread can also suspend itself by calling *WaitForInputIdle*:

```
DWORD WaitForInputIdle(
   HANDLE hProcess,
   DWORD dwMilliseconds);
```

This function waits until the process identified by *hProcess* has no input pending in the thread that created the application's first window. This function is useful for a parent process. The parent process spawns a child process to do some work. When the parent process's thread calls *CreateProcess*, the parent's thread continues to execute while the child process initializes. The parent's thread might need to get the handle of a window created by the child. The only way for the parent's thread to know when the child process has been fully initialized is to wait until the child is no longer processing any input. So after the call to *CreateProcess*, the parent's thread places a call to *WaitForInputIdle*.

You can also use *WaitForInputIdle* when you need to force keystrokes into an application. Let's say that you post the following messages to the main window of an application:

WM_KEYDOWN	with a virtual key of VK_MENU
WM_KEYDOWN	with a virtual key of VK_F
WM_KEYUP	with a virtual key of VK_F
WM_KEYUP	with a virtual key of VK_MENU
WM_KEYDOWN	with a virtual key of VK_O
WM_KEYUP	with a virtual key of VK_O

This sequence sends Alt+F, O to an application, which, for most English-language applications, chooses the Open command from the application's File menu. This command opens a dialog box, but before the dialog box can appear, Windows must load the dialog box template from the file and cycle through all the controls in the template, calling *CreateWindow* for each one. This can take some time. So the application that posted the WM_KEY* messages can call *WaitForInputIdle*, which causes the application to wait until the dialog box has been completely created and is ready for user input. The application can now force additional keys into the dialog box and its controls so that it can continue doing whatever it needs to do.

Developers who wrote for 16-bit Windows often faced this problem. Applications wanted to post messages to a window but didn't know exactly when the window was created and ready. The *WaitForInputIdle* function solves this problem.

MsgWaitForMultipleObjects(Ex)

A thread can call the *MsgWaitForMultipleObjects* or *MsgWaitForMultiple-ObjectsEx* functions to cause the thread to wait for its own messages:

```
DWORD MsgWaitForMultipleObjects(
    DWORD dwCount,
    PHANDLE phObjects,
    BOOL fWaitAll,
    DWORD dwMilliseconds,
    DWORD dwWakeMask);

DWORD MsgWaitForMultipleObjectsEx(
    DWORD dwCount,
    PHANDLE phObjects,
    DWORD dwMilliseconds,
    DWORD dwWakeMask,
    DWORD dwFlags);
```

These functions are similar to the *WaitForMultipleObjects* function. The difference is that they allow a thread to be scheduled when a kernel object becomes signaled or when a window message needs dispatching to a window created by the calling thread.

A thread that creates windows and performs user-interface related tasks should use *MsgWaitForMultipleObjectsEx* instead of *WaitForMultipleObjects* because the latter prohibits the thread's user-interface from responding to the user. This function is discussed in more detail in Chapter 27.

WaitForDebugEvent

Windows has excellent debugging support built right into the operating system. When a debugger starts executing, it attaches itself to a debuggee. The debugger simply sits idle, waiting for the operating system to notify it of debug events related to the debuggee. A debugger waits for these events by calling the *WaitForDebugEvent* function:

```
BOOL WaitForDebugEvent(
   PDEBUG_EVENT pde,
   DWORD dwMilliseconds);
```

When a debugger calls this function, the debugger's thread is suspended. The system notifies the debugger that a debug event has occurred by allowing the call to *WaitForDebugEvent* to return. The structure pointed to by the *pde* parameter is filled by the system before it awakens the thread. This structure contains information about the debug event that has just occurred.

SignalObjectAndWait

The *SignalObjectAndWait* function signals a kernel object and waits on another kernel object in a single atomic operation:

```
DWORD SignalObjectAndWait(
   HANDLE hObjectToSignal,
   HANDLE hObjectToWaitOn,
   DWORD dwMilliseconds,
   BOOL fAlertable);
```

When you call this function, the *hObjectToSignal* parameter must identify a mutex, semaphore, or an event. Any other type of object causes the function to return WAIT_FAILED, and *GetLastError* returns ERROR_INVALID_ HANDLE. Internally, the function examines the type of object and performs the equivalent of *ReleaseMutex*, *ReleaseSemaphore* (with a count of 1), or *ResetEvent*, respectively.

The *hObjectToWaitOn* parameter can identify any of the following kernel objects: mutex, semaphore, event, timer, process, thread, job, console input, and change notification. As usual, the *dwMilliseconds* parameter indicates how long the function should wait for this object to become signaled, and the *fAlertable* flag indicates whether the thread should be able to process any queued asynchronous procedure calls while the thread is waiting.

The function returns one of the following values: WAIT_OBJECT_0, WAIT_TIMEOUT, WAIT_FAILED, WAIT_ABANDONED (discussed earlier in this chapter), or WAIT_IO_COMPLETION.

This function is a welcome addition to Windows for two reasons. First, because you often need to signal one object and wait on another, having a single function that does both operations saves processing time. Each time you call a function that causes your thread to jump from user-mode to kernel-mode code, approximately 1000 CPU cycles need to execute (on *x86* platforms). For example, code such as this causes at least 2000 CPU cycles to execute:

```
ReleaseMutex(hMutex);
WaitForSingleObject(hEvent, INFINITE);
```

In high-performance server applications, *SignalObjectAndWait* saves a lot of processing time.

Second, without the *SignalObjectAndWait* function, one thread cannot know when another thread is in a wait state. This knowledge is useful for functions such as *PulseEvent*. As mentioned earlier in this chapter, *PulseEvent* signals an event and immediately resets it. If no threads are currently waiting on the event, no events catch the pulse. I've seen people write code like this:

```
// Perform some work.
   ⋮
SetEvent(hEventWorkerThreadDone);
WaitForSingleObject(hEventMoreWorkToBeDone, INFINITE);
// Do more work.
   ⋮
```

A worker thread performs some code and then calls *SetEvent* to indicate that the work is done. Another thread executes code like this:

```
WaitForSingleObject(hEventWorkerThreadDone);
PulseEvent(hEventMoreWorkToBeDone);
```

The worker thread's code fragment is poorly designed because it does not work reliably. After the worker thread calls *SetEvent*, the other thread might wake up immediately and call *PulseEvent*. The worker thread is preempted and hasn't had a chance to return from its call to *SetEvent*, let alone call *WaitForSingle-Object*. The result is that the signaling of the *hEventMoreWorkToBeDone* event is missed entirely by the worker thread.

If you rewrite the worker thread's code to call *SignalObjectAndWait* as shown here, the code will work reliably because the signaling and wait is performed atomically.

```
// Perform some work.
  .
  .
  .
SignalObjectAndWait(hEventWorkerThreadDone,
   hEventMoreWorkToBeDone, INFINITE, FALSE);
// Do more work.
  .
  .
  .
```

When the nonworker thread wakes up, it can be 100 percent sure that the worker thread is waiting on the *hEventMoreWorkToBeDone* event and is therefore guaranteed to see the event pulsed.

Windows 98 does not have a useful implementation for this function.

C H A P T E R   T E N

THREAD SYNCHRONIZATION TOOLKIT

Over the years, I've done a lot of work with thread synchronization and have written some C++ classes and components that I'll share with you in this chapter. I hope you'll find this code useful and that it will save you a lot of development time. At the very least, I hope that you learn something from what I offer here.

I'll begin the chapter by showing you how to implement a critical section and add features to it. In particular, you'll learn how to use a critical section in multiple processes. Then you'll learn how to wrap your own datatypes in a C++ class so that the objects are thread-safe. Using these classes, I'll also present an object that behaves opposite of a semaphore.

Next, we'll look at how to solve a common programming problem—when you have multiple threads reading a resource and only one thread writing to a resource. Windows has no built-in primitive that makes this type of synchronization easy, so I wrote a C++ class to do this.

Finally, I'll show you how to implement my *WaitForMultipleExpressions* function, which lets you create complex expressions to indicate when a thread should wake. (It works much like the *WaitForMultipleObjects* function, which lets you wait for any single object to be signaled or for all objects to be signaled.)

Implementing a Critical Section: The Optex

Critical sections have always fascinated me. After all, if they're just user-mode objects, why can't I implement them myself? Why do I need operating system support to make critical sections work? Also, if I write my own critical section, I might want to add features to it and enhance it in some way. At the very least, I would want it to track which thread currently owns the resource. A critical section implementation that did so would help me to resolve deadlock problems in my code; I could use a debugger to discover which thread was not releasing the resource.

So without further ado, let's take a look at how critical sections are implemented. I keep saying that critical sections are user-mode objects. In reality, this isn't 100 percent true. If a thread attempts to enter a critical section that is owned by another thread, the thread is placed in a wait state. The only way for it to enter a wait state is for it to transition from user mode to kernel mode. A user-mode thread can stop doing useful work by spinning, but that is hardly an efficient wait state, hence you should avoid it.

So critical sections must include some kernel object that can cause a thread to enter an efficient wait state. A critical section is fast because this kernel object is used only if there is contention for the critical section. As long as threads can immediately gain access to a resource, use the resource, and release it without contention from other threads, the kernel object is not used and the thread never leaves user mode. In most applications, two (or more) threads rarely contend for a critical section simultaneously.

The Optex.h and Optex.cpp files (shown in Figure 10-1) show my implementation of a critical section. I call my critical section an *optex* (which stands for *optimized mutex*) and have implemented it as a C++ class. Once you understand this code, you'll see why critical sections are faster than mutex kernel objects.

Since I implement my own critical section, I can add useful features to it. For instance, my COptex class allows threads in different processes to synchronize themselves on it. This is a fantastic addition—now I have a high-performance mechanism for communicating between threads in different processes.

To use my optex, you simply declare a COptex object. There are three possible constructors for this object:

```
COptex::(DWORD dwSpinCount = 4000);
COptex::(PCSTR  pszName, DWORD dwSpinCount = 4000);
COptex::(PCWSTR pszName, DWORD dwSpinCount = 4000);
```

The first constructor creates a COptex object that you can use only to synchronize threads of a single process. This type of optex has much less overhead than a cross-process optex. The other two constructors let you create an optex that can be used by threads in multiple processes. For the *pszName* parameter, you must pass an ANSI or Unicode string that uniquely identifies each shared optex. To have two or more processes share a single optex, both processes must instantiate a COptex object, passing the same string name.

A thread enters and leaves a COptex object by calling its *Enter* and *Leave* methods:

```
void COptex::Enter();
void COptex::Leave();
```

I've even included methods that are the equivalent of a critical section's *TryEnterCriticalSection* and *SetCriticalSectionSpinCount* functions:

```
BOOL COptex::TryEnter();
void COptex::SetSpinCount(DWORD dwSpinCount);
```

You can call the last method, shown below, if you need to know whether an optex is a single-process or cross-process optex. (You rarely need to call this function, but the internal method functions call it occasionally.)

```
BOOL COptex::IsSingleProcessOptex() const;
```

Those are all the (public) functions you need to know to use the optex. Now I'll explain how the optex works. Basically, an optex (and a critical section, for that matter) contains a number of member variables. These variables reflect the state of the optex. In my Optex.h file, most of these members are in a SHAREDINFO structure and a few are members of the class itself. The table below describes each member's purpose.

Member	Description
m_lLockCount	Indicates the number of times that threads attempt to enter the optex. This value is 0 if no thread is entering the optex.
m_dwThreadId	Indicates the unique ID of the thread owning the optex. The value is 0 if no thread owns the optex.
m_lRecurseCount	Indicates the number of times the optex is owned by the owning thread. The value is 0 if the optex is unowned.
m_hevt	This is the handle of an event kernel object, which is used only if a thread attempts to enter the optex while another thread owns it. Kernel handles are process-relative, which is why this member is not in the SHAREDINFO structure.
m_dwSpinCount	Indicates the number of times that the thread attempting to enter the optex should try before waiting on the event kernel object. This value is always 0 on a uniprocessor machine.
m_hfm	This is the handle of a file-mapping kernel object, which is used when multiple processes share a single optex. Kernel handles are process-relative, which is why this member is not in the SHAREDINFO structure. This value is always NULL for a single-process optex.
m_psi	This is the pointer to the potentially shared optex data members. Memory addresses are process-relative, which is why this member is not in the SHAREDINFO structure. For a single-process optex, this points to a heap-allocated block. For a multiprocess optex, it points to a memory-mapped file.

The source code is sufficiently commented, so you should have no trouble understanding how the optex works. The important thing to note is that the optex gets its speed because it makes heavy use of the interlocked family of functions. This keeps the code executing in user mode and avoids transitions.

The Optex Sample Application

The Optex ("10 Optex.exe") application, listed in Figure 10-1, tests the COptex class to make sure that it works properly. The source code and resource files for the application are in the 10-Optex directory on this book's companion CD-ROM. I always run the application in the debugger so I can closely watch all the member functions and variables.

When you run the application, it first detects whether it is the first instance of this application running. I do this by creating a named event kernel object. I don't actually use the event object anywhere in the application; I just create it to see if *GetLastError* returns ERROR_ALREADY_EXISTS. If so, I know that this is the second running instance of the application. I'll explain later why I run two instances of this application.

If this is the first instance, I create a single-process COptex object and call my *FirstFunc* function. This function performs a series of manipulations on the optex object. A second thread is created that also manipulates the same optex object. At this point, the two threads manipulating the optex are in the same process. You can examine the source code to see what tests I perform. I tried to cover all possible scenarios so that all the code in the COptex class gets a chance to execute.

After testing a single-process optex, I test the cross-process optex. In *_tWinMain*, when the first call to *FirstFunc* returns, I create another COptex optex object. But this time, I give the optex a string name of *CrossOptexTest*. Simply creating an optex with a name makes it a cross-process optex. Next, I call *FirstFunc* a second time, passing it the address of the cross-process optex. *FirstFunc* executes basically the same code as it did before. But now, instead of spawning a second thread, it spawns a child process.

This child process is just another instance of the same application. But when it starts executing, it creates the event kernel object and detects that the event object already exists. This is how the second instance of the application knows that it's the second instance and executes different code than the first instance. The first thing that the second instance does is call *DebugBreak*:

```
VOID DebugBreak();
```

This handy function forces a debugger to run and connect itself to the process. This makes it easy for me to debug both instances of this application.

The second instance then creates a cross-process optex, passing the same string name. Since the string names are identical, both processes share the optex. By the way, more than two processes can share the same optex.

Now the second instance of the application calls *SecondFunc*, passing it the address of the cross-process optex. At this point, the same set of tests is performed, but the two threads manipulating the optex are in different processes.

Optex.cpp

```
/******************************************************************************
Module:  Optex.cpp
Notices: Copyright (c) 2000 Jeffrey Richter
******************************************************************************/


#include "..\CmnHdr.h"      /* See Appendix A. */
#include "Optex.h"


///////////////////////////////////////////////////////////////////////////////


// 0=multi-CPU, 1=single-CPU, -1=not set yet
BOOL COptex::sm_fUniprocessorHost = -1;


///////////////////////////////////////////////////////////////////////////////


PSTR COptex::ConstructObjectName(PSTR pszResult,
  PCSTR pszPrefix, BOOL fUnicode, PVOID pszName) {

  pszResult[0] = 0;
  if (pszName == NULL)
     return(NULL);

  wsprintfA(pszResult, fUnicode ? "%s%S" : "%s%s", pszPrefix, pszName);
  return(pszResult);
}


///////////////////////////////////////////////////////////////////////////////
```

Figure 10-1. *(continued)*
The Optex sample application

Figure 10-1. *continued*

```
void COptex::CommonConstructor(DWORD dwSpinCount,
   BOOL fUnicode, PVOID pszName) {

   if (sm_fUniprocessorHost == -1) {
      // This is the 1st object constructed, get the number of CPUs
      SYSTEM_INFO sinf;
      GetSystemInfo(&sinf);
      sm_fUniprocessorHost = (sinf.dwNumberOfProcessors == 1);
   }

   m_hevt = m_hfm = NULL;
   m_psi  = NULL;

   if (pszName == NULL) {  // Creating a single-process optex

      m_hevt = CreateEventA(NULL, FALSE, FALSE, NULL);
      chASSERT(m_hevt != NULL);

      m_psi = new SHAREDINFO;
      chASSERT(m_psi != NULL);
      ZeroMemory(m_psi, sizeof(*m_psi));

   } else {                   // Creating a cross-process optex

      // Always use ANSI so that this works on Win9x and Windows 2000
      char szResult[100];
      ConstructObjectName(szResult, "Optex_Event_", fUnicode, pszName);
      m_hevt = CreateEventA(NULL, FALSE, FALSE, szResult);
      chASSERT(m_hevt != NULL);

      ConstructObjectName(szResult, "Optex_MMF_", fUnicode, pszName);
      m_hfm = CreateFileMappingA(INVALID_HANDLE_VALUE, NULL,
         PAGE_READWRITE, 0, sizeof(*m_psi), szResult);
      chASSERT(m_hfm != NULL);

      m_psi = (PSHAREDINFO) MapViewOfFile(m_hfm,
         FILE_MAP_WRITE, 0, 0, 0);
      chASSERT(m_psi != NULL);

      // Note: SHAREDINFO's m_lLockCount, m_dwThreadId, and m_lRecurseCount
      // members need to be initialized to 0. Fortunately, a new pagefile
      // MMF sets all of its data to 0 when created. This saves us from
      // some thread synchronization work.
   }
```

(continued)

Figure 10-1. *continued*

```
   SetSpinCount(dwSpinCount);
}


//////////////////////////////////////////////////////////////////////////////


COptex::~COptex() {

#ifdef _DEBUG
   if (IsSingleProcessOptex() && (m_psi->m_dwThreadId != 0)) {
      // A single-process optex shouldn't be destroyed if any thread owns it
      DebugBreak();
   }

   if (!IsSingleProcessOptex() &&
      (m_psi->m_dwThreadId == GetCurrentThreadId())) {

      // A cross-process optex shouldn't be destroyed if our thread owns it
      DebugBreak();
   }
#endif

   CloseHandle(m_hevt);

   if (IsSingleProcessOptex()) {
      delete m_psi;
   } else {
      UnmapViewOfFile(m_psi);
      CloseHandle(m_hfm);
   }
}


//////////////////////////////////////////////////////////////////////////////


void COptex::SetSpinCount(DWORD dwSpinCount) {

   // No spinning on single CPU machines
   if (!sm_fUniprocessorHost)
      InterlockedExchangePointer((PVOID*) &m_psi->m_dwSpinCount,
         (PVOID) (DWORD_PTR) dwSpinCount);
}
```

(continued)

Figure 10-1. *continued*

```
/////////////////////////////////////////////////////////////////////////////////


void COptex::Enter() {

   // Spin, trying to get the optex
   if (TryEnter())
      return;  // We got it, return

   // We couldn't get the optex, wait for it.
   DWORD dwThreadId = GetCurrentThreadId();

   if (InterlockedIncrement(&m_psi->m_lLockCount) == 1) {

      // Optex is unowned, let this thread own it once
      m_psi->m_dwThreadId = dwThreadId;
      m_psi->m_lRecurseCount = 1;

   } else {

      if (m_psi->m_dwThreadId == dwThreadId) {

         // If optex is owned by this thread, own it again
         m_psi->m_lRecurseCount++;

      } else {

         // Optex is owned by another thread, wait for it
         WaitForSingleObject(m_hevt, INFINITE);

         // Optex is unowned, let this thread own it once
         m_psi->m_dwThreadId = dwThreadId;
         m_psi->m_lRecurseCount = 1;
      }
   }
}


/////////////////////////////////////////////////////////////////////////////////


BOOL COptex::TryEnter() {

   DWORD dwThreadId = GetCurrentThreadId();
```

(continued)

344

Figure 10-1. *continued*

```
    BOOL fThisThreadOwnsTheOptex = FALSE;    // Assume a thread owns the optex
    DWORD dwSpinCount = m_psi->m_dwSpinCount; // How many times to spin

    do {
       // If lock count = 0, optex is unowned, we can own it
       fThisThreadOwnsTheOptex = (0 ==
          InterlockedCompareExchange(&m_psi->m_lLockCount, 1, 0));

       if (fThisThreadOwnsTheOptex) {

          // Optex is unowned, let this thread own it once
          m_psi->m_dwThreadId = dwThreadId;
          m_psi->m_lRecurseCount = 1;

       } else {

          if (m_psi->m_dwThreadId == dwThreadId) {

             // If optex is owned by this thread, own it again
             InterlockedIncrement(&m_psi->m_lLockCount);
             m_psi->m_lRecurseCount++;
             fThisThreadOwnsTheOptex = TRUE;
          }
       }

    } while (!fThisThreadOwnsTheOptex && (dwSpinCount-- > 0));

    // Return whether or not this thread owns the optex
    return(fThisThreadOwnsTheOptex);
}


/////////////////////////////////////////////////////////////////////////////


void COptex::Leave() {

#ifdef _DEBUG
    // Only the owning thread can leave the optex
    if (m_psi->m_dwThreadId != GetCurrentThreadId())
       DebugBreak();
#endif

    // Reduce this thread's ownership of the optex
    if (--m_psi->m_lRecurseCount > 0) {
```

(continued)

345

Figure 10-1. *continued*

```
        // We still own the optex
        InterlockedDecrement(&m_psi->m_lLockCount);

    } else {

        // We don't own the optex anymore
        m_psi->m_dwThreadId = 0;

        if (InterlockedDecrement(&m_psi->m_lLockCount) > 0) {

            // Other threads are waiting, the auto-reset event wakes one of them
            SetEvent(m_hevt);
        }
    }
}

/////////////////////////////// End of File ///////////////////////////////////
```

Optex.h

```
/******************************************************************************
Module name: Optex.h
Written by:   Jeffrey Richter
******************************************************************************/


#pragma once


///////////////////////////////////////////////////////////////////////////////


class COptex {
public:
    COptex(DWORD dwSpinCount = 4000);
    COptex(PCSTR  pszName, DWORD dwSpinCount = 4000);
    COptex(PCWSTR pszName, DWORD dwSpinCount = 4000);
    ~COptex();

    void SetSpinCount(DWORD dwSpinCount);
    void Enter();
```

(continued)

Figure 10-1. *continued*

```
   BOOL TryEnter();
   void Leave();
   BOOL IsSingleProcessOptex() const;

private:
   typedef struct {
      DWORD m_dwSpinCount;
      long  m_lLockCount;
      DWORD m_dwThreadId;
      long  m_lRecurseCount;
   } SHAREDINFO, *PSHAREDINFO;

   HANDLE      m_hevt;
   HANDLE      m_hfm;
   PSHAREDINFO m_psi;

private:
   static BOOL sm_fUniprocessorHost;

private:
   void CommonConstructor(DWORD dwSpinCount, BOOL fUnicode, PVOID pszName);
   PSTR ConstructObjectName(PSTR pszResult,
      PCSTR pszPrefix, BOOL fUnicode, PVOID pszName);
};


///////////////////////////////////////////////////////////////////////////


inline COptex::COptex(DWORD dwSpinCount) {

   CommonConstructor(dwSpinCount, FALSE, NULL);
}


///////////////////////////////////////////////////////////////////////////


inline COptex::COptex(PCSTR pszName, DWORD dwSpinCount) {

   CommonConstructor(dwSpinCount, FALSE, (PVOID) pszName);
}


///////////////////////////////////////////////////////////////////////////
```

(continued)

Figure 10-1. *continued*

```
inline COptex::COptex(PCWSTR pszName, DWORD dwSpinCount) {

   CommonConstructor(dwSpinCount, TRUE, (PVOID) pszName);
}


/////////////////////////////////////////////////////////////////////////////


inline COptex::IsSingleProcessOptex() const {

   return(m_hfm == NULL);
}


//////////////////////////////// End of File /////////////////////////////////
```

Optex.rc

```
//Microsoft Developer Studio generated resource script.
//
#include "resource.h"

#define APSTUDIO_READONLY_SYMBOLS
/////////////////////////////////////////////////////////////////////////////
//
// Generated from the TEXTINCLUDE 2 resource.
//
#include "afxres.h"

/////////////////////////////////////////////////////////////////////////////
#undef APSTUDIO_READONLY_SYMBOLS

/////////////////////////////////////////////////////////////////////////////
// English (U.S.) resources

#if !defined(AFX_RESOURCE_DLL) || defined(AFX_TARG_ENU)
#ifdef _WIN32
LANGUAGE LANG_ENGLISH, SUBLANG_ENGLISH_US
#pragma code_page(1252)
#endif //_WIN32
```

(continued)

Figure 10-1. *continued*

```
//////////////////////////////////////////////////////////////////////////
//
// Icon
//

// Icon with lowest ID value placed first to ensure application icon
// remains consistent on all systems.
IDI_OPTEX                ICON    DISCARDABLE     "Optex.ICO"

#ifdef APSTUDIO_INVOKED
//////////////////////////////////////////////////////////////////////////
//
// TEXTINCLUDE
//

1 TEXTINCLUDE DISCARDABLE
BEGIN
    "resource.h\0"
END

2 TEXTINCLUDE DISCARDABLE
BEGIN
    "#include ""afxres.h""\r\n"
    "\0"
END

3 TEXTINCLUDE DISCARDABLE
BEGIN
    "\r\n"
    "\0"
END

#endif    // APSTUDIO_INVOKED

#endif    // English (U.S.) resources
//////////////////////////////////////////////////////////////////////////



#ifndef APSTUDIO_INVOKED
//////////////////////////////////////////////////////////////////////////
//
// Generated from the TEXTINCLUDE 3 resource.
//
```

(continued)

Figure 10-1. *continued*

```
///////////////////////////////////////////////////////////////////////////
#endif    // not APSTUDIO_INVOKED
```

OptexTest.cpp

```
/***************************************************************************
Module name: OptexTest.cpp
Written by:  Jeffrey Richter
***************************************************************************/


#include "..\CmnHdr.h"      /* See Appendix A. */
#include <tchar.h>
#include <process.h>
#include "Optex.h"


///////////////////////////////////////////////////////////////////////////


DWORD WINAPI SecondFunc(PVOID pvParam) {

   COptex& optex = * (COptex*) pvParam;

   // The primary thread should own the optex here, this should fail
   chVERIFY(optex.TryEnter() == FALSE);

   // Wait for the primary thread to give up the optex
   optex.Enter();

   optex.Enter();   // Test recursive ownership
   chMB("Secondary: Entered the optex\n(Dismiss me 2nd)");

   // Leave the optex but we still own it once
   optex.Leave();
   chMB("Secondary: The primary thread should not display a box yet");
   optex.Leave();   // The primary thread should be able to run now

   return(0);
}


///////////////////////////////////////////////////////////////////////////
```

(continued)

Figure 10-1. *continued*

```
VOID FirstFunc(BOOL fLocal, COptex& optex) {

   optex.Enter();  // Gain ownership of the optex

   // Since this thread owns the optex, we should be able to get it again
   chVERIFY(optex.TryEnter());

   HANDLE hOtherThread = NULL;
   if (fLocal) {
      // Spawn a secondary thread for testing purposes (pass it the optex)

      DWORD dwThreadId;
      hOtherThread = chBEGINTHREADEX(NULL, 0,
         SecondFunc, (PVOID) &optex, 0, &dwThreadId);

   } else {
      // Spawn a secondary process for testing purposes
      STARTUPINFO si = { sizeof(si) };
      PROCESS_INFORMATION pi;
      TCHAR szPath[MAX_PATH];
      GetModuleFileName(NULL, szPath, chDIMOF(szPath));
      CreateProcess(NULL, szPath, NULL, NULL,
         FALSE, 0, NULL, NULL, &si, &pi);
      hOtherThread = pi.hProcess;
      CloseHandle(pi.hThread);
   }

   // Wait for the second thread to own the optex
   chMB("Primary: Hit OK to give optex to secondary");

   // Let the second thread gain ownership of the optex
   optex.Leave();
   optex.Leave();

   // Wait for the second thread to own the optex
   chMB("Primary: Hit OK to wait for the optex\n(Dismiss me 1st)");

   optex.Enter();  // Try to gain ownership back

   WaitForSingleObject(hOtherThread, INFINITE);
   CloseHandle(hOtherThread);
   optex.Leave();
}
```

(continued)

Figure 10-1. *continued*

```
/////////////////////////////////////////////////////////////////////////////////


int WINAPI _tWinMain(HINSTANCE hinstExe, HINSTANCE, PTSTR pszCmdLine, int) {

   // This event is just used to determine which instance this is.
   HANDLE hevt = CreateEvent(NULL, FALSE, FALSE, TEXT("OptexTest"));

   if (GetLastError() != ERROR_ALREADY_EXISTS) {

      // This is the first instance of this test application

      // First, let's test the single-process optex
      COptex optexSingle;   // Create a single-process optex
      FirstFunc(TRUE, optexSingle);

      // Now, let's test the cross-process optex
      COptex optexCross("CrossOptexTest");   // Create a cross-process optex
      FirstFunc(FALSE, optexCross);

   } else {

      // This is the second instance of this test application
      DebugBreak();  // Force debugger connection for tracing

      // Test the cross-process optex
      COptex optexCross("CrossOptexTest");   // Create a cross-process optex
      SecondFunc((PVOID) &optexCross);
   }

   CloseHandle(hevt);
   return(0);
}


//////////////////////////////// End of File //////////////////////////////////
```

Creating Thread-Safe Datatypes and Inverse Semaphores

One day I was writing some code and reached a point where I needed a kernel object whose behavior was opposite that of a semaphore object. I needed the object to be signaled when its current resource count was 0 and nonsignaled when its current resource count was greater than 0.

I could see many uses for this type of object. For example, you might have a thread that needs to wake up after you execute some operation 100 times. To pull this off, you would need a kernel object that you could initialize to 100. When the kernel object's count is greater than 0, the object should not be signaled. Each time you execute some operation, you would want to decrement the count in the kernel object. When the count reaches 0, the object should be signaled so that your other thread can wake up to process something. This is a common problem, and I don't understand why Windows doesn't offer such a built-in primitive.

Actually, Microsoft could easily solve this problem by allowing a semaphore's current resource count to be negative. You could initialize the semaphore's count to −99 and then call *ReleaseSemaphore* after each operation. When the semaphore's count reached 1, the object would be signaled and your other thread could wake up to do its processing. Alas, Microsoft prohibits a semaphore's count from being negative, and I don't expect them to change this code in the foreseeable future.

In this section, I'll present a set of C++ template classes that have the behavior of an inverse semaphore plus a whole lot more. The code for these classes is in the Interlocked.h file. (See Figure 10-2 beginning on page 359.)

When I first set out to tackle this problem, I realized that a thread-safe way to manipulate a variable was at the heart of the solution. I wanted to design an elegant solution that would make code that references the variable trivially easy to write. Obviously, the easiest way to make a resource thread-safe is to protect it with a critical section. Using C++, it is fairly easy to endow a data object with thread safety. All you do is create a C++ class that contains the variable you want to protect and a CRITICAL_SECTION data structure. Then, in the constructor, you call *InitializeCriticalSection*, and in the destructor you call *DeleteCriticalSection*. For all the other member variables you call *EnterCriticalSection*, you manipulate the variable, and then you call *LeaveCriticalSection*. If you implement a C++ class this way, it is easy to write code that accesses a data structure in a thread-safe fashion. This is the founding principle of all the C++ classes I present in this section. (Of course, I could have used the optex presented in the previous section instead of critical sections.)

353

The first class is a resource guard class called CResGuard. It contains a CRITICAL_SECTION data member and a LONG data member. The LONG data member keeps track of how many times the owning thread has entered the critical section. This information can be useful for debugging. The CResGuard object's constructor and destructor call *InitializeCriticalSection* and *Delete-CriticalSection*, respectively. Since only a single thread can create an object, a C++ object's constructor and destructor do not have to be thread-safe. The *IsGuarded* member function simply returns whether *EnterCriticalSection* has been called at least once against this object. As I said before, this is for debugging purposes. Placing a CRITICAL_SECTION inside a C++ object ensures that the critical section is properly initialized and deleted.

The CResGuard class also offers a nested public C++ class: CGuard. A CGuard object contains a reference to a CResGuard object and offers only a constructor and a destructor. The constructor calls the CResGuard's *Guard* member function, which calls *EnterCriticalSection*, and the CGuard's destructor calls the CResGuard's *Unguard* member function, which calls *LeaveCritical-Section*. Setting up these classes this way makes it easy to manipulate a CRITICAL_SECTION. Here is small code fragment that uses these classes:

```
struct SomeDataStruct {
   ...
} g_SomeSharedData;

// Create a CResGuard object that protects g_SomeSharedData.
// Note: The constructor initializes the critical section and
//       the destructor deletes the critical section.
CResGuard g_rgSomeSharedData;


void AFunction() {

   // This function touches the shared data.

   // Protect the resource from being accessed from multiple threads.
   CResGuard::CGuard gDummy(g_rgSomeSharedData); //Enter critical section
   // Touch the g_SomeSharedData resource.
   ...

}  // Note: LeaveCriticalSection is called when gDummy goes out of scope.
```

The next C++ class, CInterlockedType, contains all the parts necessary to create a thread-safe data object. I made the CInterlockedType class a template class so that it can be used to make any data type thread-safe. So, for example, you can use this class to make a thread-safe integer, a thread-safe string, or a thread-safe data structure.

Each instance of a CInterlockedType object contains two data members. The first data member is an instance of the template data type that you want to make thread-safe. This data member is private and can be manipulated only using CInterlockedType's member functions. The second data member is an instance of a CResGuard object, which guards access to the data member. The CResGuard object is a protected data member so a class derived from CInterlockedType can easily protect its data.

You are expected to always derive a new class using the CInterlockedType class as a base class. Earlier, I said that the CInterlockedType class provides all of the parts necessary to create a thread-safe object, but the derived class is responsible for using these parts correctly to access the data value in a thread-safe fashion.

The CInterlockedType class offers only four public functions: a constructor that does not initialize the data value, another constructor that does initialize the data value, a virtual destructor that does nothing, and a cast operator. The cast operator simply ensures thread-safe access to the data value by guarding the resource and returning the object's current value. (The resource is automatically unguarded when the local variable *x* goes out of scope.) The cast operator makes it easy to examine the data object's value contained in the class in a thread-safe fashion.

The CInterlockedType class also offers three nonvirtual protected functions that a derived class will call. Two *GetVal* functions return the current value of the data object. In debug builds of the file, both of these functions first check to see whether the data object is guarded. If the object were not guarded, *GetVal* could return a value for the object and then allow another thread to change the object's value before the original caller examined it.

I assume that a caller is getting the value of the object so that it can change the value in some way. Based on this assumption, the *GetVal* functions require that the caller have guarded access to the data value. If the *GetVal* functions determine that the data is guarded, the current value of the data is returned. The two *GetVal* functions are identical except that one of them operates on a constant version of the object. The two versions allow you to write code that works with constant data types and nonconstant data types without the compiler generating warnings.

The third nonvirtual protected member function is *SetVal*. When a derived class's member function wants to modify the data value, the derived class's function should guard access to the data and then call the *SetVal* function. Like the

GetVal functions, the *SetVal* function first performs a debug check to make sure that the derived class's code didn't forget to guard access to the data value. Then *SetVal* checks to see whether the data value is actually changing. If it is, *SetVal* saves the old value, changes the object to its new value, and then calls a virtual, protected member function, *OnValChanged*, which is passed the old and new data values. The CInterlockedType class implements an *OnValChanged* member function, which does nothing. You can use the *OnValChanged* member function to add some powerful capabilities to the derived class, as you'll see later when we discuss the CWhenZero class.

Thus far, we have talked about a lot of abstract classes and concepts. Now let's see how you can use all of this architecture for the good of all humankind. I present to you the CInterlockedScalar class—a template class derived from CInterlockedType. You can use this class to create a thread-safe scalar data type such as a byte, a character, a 16-bit integer, a 32-bit integer, a 64-bit integer, a floating point value, and so on. Because the CInterlockedScalar class is derived from the CInterlockedType class, it does not have any data members of its own. CInterlockedScalar's constructor simply calls CInterlockedType's constructor, passing an initial value for the scalar. Since the CInterlockedScalar class always works with numeric values, I set the default constructor parameter to 0 so our object is always constructed in a known state. CInterlockedScalar's destructor does nothing at all.

All of CInterlockedScalar's remaining member functions change the scalar value. One member function exists for each operation that can be performed on a scalar value. In order for the CInterlockedScalar class to manipulate its data object in a thread-safe fashion, all of these member functions guard the data value before manipulating it. The member functions are simple, so I won't explain them in any detail; you can examine the code to see what they do. However, I'll show you how to use these classes. The following code declares a thread-safe BYTE and manipulates it:

```
CInterlockedScalar<BYTE> b = 5;    // A thread-safe BYTE
BYTE b2 = 10;                      // A non-thread-safe BYTE
b2 = b++;                          // b2=5, b=6
b *= 4;                            // b=24
b2 = b;                            // b2=24, b=24
b += b;                            // b=48
b %= 2;                            // b=0
```

Manipulating a thread-safe scalar value is as simple as manipulating a non-thread-safe scalar. In fact, the code is identical, thanks to C++'s operator overloading! With the C++ classes I've shown you so far, you can easily turn any

77777777777777

non-thread-safe variable into a thread-safe variable with only small changes to your source code.

I had a specific destination in mind when I started designing all these classes: I wanted to create an object whose behavior was the opposite of a semaphore's. The C++ class that offers this behavior is my CWhenZero class. The CWhenZero class is derived from the CInterlockedScalar class. When the scalar value is 0, the CWhenZero object is signaled; when the data value is not 0, the CWhenZero object is not signaled. This is the opposite behavior of a semaphore.

As you know, C++ objects cannot be signaled; only kernel objects can be signaled and used for thread synchronization. So a CWhenZero object must contain some additional data members, which are handles to event kernel objects. A CWhenZero object contains two data members: *m_hevtZero*, a handle to an event kernel object that is signaled when the data value is 0, and *m_hevtNotZero*, a handle to an event kernel object that is signaled when the data value is not 0.

CWhenZero's constructor accepts an initial value for the data object and also lets you specify whether these two event kernel objects should be manual-reset (the default) or auto-reset. The constructor then calls *CreateEvent* to create the two event kernel objects and set them to the signaled or nonsignaled state, depending on whether the data's initial value is 0. CWhenZero's destructor is merely responsible for closing the two event handles. Because CWhenZero's class publicly inherits the CInterlockedScalar class, all of the overloaded operator member functions are available to users of a CWhenZero object.

Remember the *OnValChanged* protected member function declared inside the CInterlockedType class? The CWhenZero class overrides this virtual function. This function is responsible for keeping the event kernel objects signaled or nonsignaled based on the value of the data object. Whenever the data value changes, *OnValChanged* is called. CWhenZero's implementation of this function checks to see whether the new value is 0, and if so, it sets the *m_hevtZero* event and resets the *m_hevtNotZero* event. If the new value is not 0, *OnValChanged* does the reverse.

Now, when you want a thread to wait until the data value is 0, all you have to do is the following:

```
CWhenZero<BYTE> b = 0;            // A thread-safe BYTE

// Returns immediately because b is 0
WaitForSingleObject(b, INFINITE);

b = 5;

//Returns only if another thread sets b to 0
WaitForSingleObject(b, INFINITE);
```

You can write the call to *WaitForSingleObject* as I did on the preceding page because the CWhenZero class also includes a cast operator member function that casts a CWhenZero object to a kernel object HANDLE. In other words, if you pass a CWhenZero C++ object to any function that expects a HANDLE object, this cast operator function gets called and its return value is passed to the function. CWhenZero's HANDLE cast operator function returns the handle of the *m_hevtZero* event kernel object.

The *m_hevtNotZero* event handle inside the CWhenZero class lets you write code that waits for the data value to not be 0. Unfortunately, I already have a HANDLE cast operator so I can't have another one that returns the *m_hevtNotZero* handle. So to get at this handle, I have added the *GetNotZeroHandle* member function. Using this function, I can write the following code:

```
CWhenZero<BYTE> b = 5;      // A thread-safe BYTE

// Returns immediately because b is not 0
WaitForSingleObject(b.GetNotZeroHandle(), INFINITE);

b = 0;

// Returns only if another thread sets b to not 0
WaitForSingleObject(b.GetNotZeroHandle(), INFINITE);
```

The InterlockedType Sample Application

The InterlockedType ("10 InterlockedType.exe") application, shown in Figure 10-2, tests the C++ classes I just described. The source code and resource files for the application are in the 10-InterlockedType directory on this book's companion CD-ROM. I always run the application in the debugger so I can closely watch all the class member functions and variables change.

The code shows a common programming scenario that goes like this: A thread spawns several worker threads and then initializes a block of memory. Then the main thread wakes the worker threads so that they can start processing the memory block. At this point, the main thread must suspend itself until all the worker threads have finished. Then the main thread reinitializes the memory block with new data and wakes up the worker threads to start the whole process all over again.

By looking at the code, you can see how trivial it is to solve this common programming problem with readable and maintainable C++ code. As you can see, the CWhenZero class gives us a whole lot more than the opposite behavior of a semaphore. We now have a thread-safe number, which is signaled when its value is 0! You can increment and decrement a semaphore's value, but you can add, subtract, multiply, divide, modulo, set explicitly to any value, or even perform bit operations with a CWhenZero object! A CWhenZero object is substantially more powerful than a semaphore kernel object.

It is fun to come up with ideas for these C++ template classes. For example, you can create a CInterlockedString class derived from the CInterlockedType class. You can use the CInterlockedString class to manipulate a character string in a thread-safe fashion. Then you can derive a CWhenCertainString class from your CInterlockedString class, which signals an event kernel object when the character string becomes a certain value or values. The possibilities are endless.

 IntLockTest.cpp

```
/***********************************************************************
Module:  IntLockTest.cpp
Notices: Copyright (c) 2000 Jeffrey Richter
***********************************************************************/


#include "..\CmnHdr.h"      /* See Appendix A. */
#include <tchar.h>
#include "Interlocked.h"



///////////////////////////////////////////////////////////////////////


// Set to TRUE when worker threads should terminate cleanly.
volatile BOOL g_fQuit = FALSE;


///////////////////////////////////////////////////////////////////////


DWORD WINAPI WorkerThread(PVOID pvParam) {

   CWhenZero<BYTE>& bVal = * (CWhenZero<BYTE> *) pvParam;

   // Should worker thread terminate?
   while (!g_fQuit) {

      // Wait for something to do
      WaitForSingleObject(bVal.GetNotZeroHandle(), INFINITE);
```

Figure 10-2.   *(continued)*
The InterlockedType sample application

Figure 10-2. *continued*

```
      // If we should quit, quit
      if (g_fQuit)
        continue;

      // Do something
      chMB("Worker thread: We have something to do");

      bVal--;      // We're done

      // Wait for all worker threads to stop
      WaitForSingleObject(bVal, INFINITE);
   }

   chMB("Worker thread: terminating");
   return(0);
}


/////////////////////////////////////////////////////////////////////////////


int WINAPI _tWinMain(HINSTANCE hinstExe, HINSTANCE, PTSTR pszCmdLine, int) {

   // Initialize to indicate that NO worker threads have anything to do
   CWhenZero<BYTE> bVal = 0;

   // Create the worker threads
   const int nMaxThreads = 2;
   HANDLE hThreads[nMaxThreads];
   for (int nThread = 0; nThread < nMaxThreads; nThread++) {
      DWORD dwThreadId;
      hThreads[nThread] = CreateThread(NULL, 0,
         WorkerThread, (PVOID) &bVal, 0, &dwThreadId);
   }

   int n;
   do {
      // Do more work or stop running?
      n = MessageBox(NULL,
         TEXT("Yes: Give worker threads something to do\nNo: Quit"),
         TEXT("Primary thread"), MB_YESNO);

      // Tell worker threads that we're quitting
      if (n == IDNO)
```

(continued)

Figure 10-2. *continued*

```
        InterlockedExchangePointer((PVOID*) &g_fQuit, (PVOID) TRUE);

   bVal = nMaxThreads;  // Wake the worker threads

   if (n == IDYES) {

      // There is work to do, wait for the worker threads to finish
      WaitForSingleObject(bVal, INFINITE);
   }

} while (n == IDYES);

// There is no more work to do, the process wants to die.
// Wait for the worker threads to terminate
WaitForMultipleObjects(nMaxThreads, hThreads, TRUE, INFINITE);

// Close the worker thread handles.
for (nThread = 0; nThread < nMaxThreads; nThread++)
   CloseHandle(hThreads[nThread]);

// Tell the user that the process is dying
chMB("Primary thread: terminating");

   return(0);
}


///////////////////////////////// End of File /////////////////////////////////
```

Interlocked.h

```
/******************************************************************************
Module:  Interlocked.h
Notices: Copyright (c) 2000 Jeffrey Richter
******************************************************************************/


#pragma once


///////////////////////////////////////////////////////////////////////////////


// Instances of this class will be accessed by multiple threads. So,
// all members of this class (except the constructor and destructor)
// must be thread-safe.
```

(continued)

Figure 10-2. *continued*

```
class CResGuard {
public:
    CResGuard()  { m_lGrdCnt = 0; InitializeCriticalSection(&m_cs); }
    ~CResGuard() { DeleteCriticalSection(&m_cs); }

    // IsGuarded is used for debugging
    BOOL IsGuarded() const { return(m_lGrdCnt > 0); }

public:
    class CGuard {
    public:
        CGuard(CResGuard& rg) : m_rg(rg) { m_rg.Guard(); };
        ~CGuard() { m_rg.Unguard(); }

    private:
        CResGuard& m_rg;
    };

private:
    void Guard()   { EnterCriticalSection(&m_cs); m_lGrdCnt++; }
    void Unguard() { m_lGrdCnt--; LeaveCriticalSection(&m_cs); }

    // Guard/Unguard can only be accessed by the nested CGuard class.
    friend class CResGuard::CGuard;

private:
    CRITICAL_SECTION m_cs;
    long m_lGrdCnt;    // # of EnterCriticalSection calls
};


///////////////////////////////////////////////////////////////////////////


// Instances of this class will be accessed by multiple threads. So,
// all members of this class (except the constructor and destructor)
// must be thread-safe.
template <class TYPE>
class CInterlockedType {

public:         // Public member functions
    // Note: Constructors & destructors are always thread-safe
    CInterlockedType() { }
    CInterlockedType(const TYPE& TVal) { m_TVal = TVal; }
    virtual ~CInterlockedType()  { }
```

(continued)

Figure 10-2. *continued*

```
   // Cast operator to make writing code that uses
   // thread-safe data type easier
   operator TYPE() const {
      CResGuard::CGuard x(m_rg);
      return(GetVal());
   }

protected:  // Protected function to be called by derived class
   TYPE& GetVal() {
      chASSERT(m_rg.IsGuarded());
      return(m_TVal);
   }

   const TYPE& GetVal() const {
      assert(m_rg.IsGuarded());
      return(m_TVal);
   }

   TYPE SetVal(const TYPE& TNewVal) {
      chASSERT(m_rg.IsGuarded());
      TYPE& TVal = GetVal();
      if (TVal != TNewVal) {
         TYPE TPrevVal = TVal;
         TVal = TNewVal;
         OnValChanged(TNewVal, TPrevVal);
      }
      return(TVal);
   }

protected:  // Overridable functions
   virtual void OnValChanged(
      const TYPE& TNewVal, const TYPE& TPrevVal) const {
      // Nothing to do here
   }

protected:
   // Protected guard for use by derived class functions
      mutable CResGuard m_rg;

private:    // Private data members
   TYPE m_TVal;
};


///////////////////////////////////////////////////////////////////////////
```

(continued)

Figure 10-2. *continued*

```
// Instances of this class will be accessed by multiple threads. So,
// all members of this class (except the constructor and destructor)
// must be thread-safe.
template <class TYPE>
class CInterlockedScalar : protected CInterlockedType<TYPE> {

public:
   CInterlockedScalar(TYPE TVal = 0) : CInterlockedType<TYPE>(TVal) {
   }

   ~CInterlockedScalar() { /* Nothing to do */ }

   // C++ does not allow operator cast to be inherited.
   operator TYPE() const {
      return(CInterlockedType<TYPE>::operator TYPE());
   }

   TYPE operator=(TYPE TVal) {
      CResGuard::CGuard x(m_rg);
      return(SetVal(TVal));
   }

   TYPE operator++(int) {      // Postfix increment operator
      CResGuard::CGuard x(m_rg);
      TYPE TPrevVal = GetVal();
      SetVal((TYPE) (TPrevVal + 1));
      return(TPrevVal);        // Return value BEFORE increment
   }

   TYPE operator--(int) {      // Postfix decrement operator.
      CResGuard::CGuard x(m_rg);
      TYPE TPrevVal = GetVal();
      SetVal((TYPE) (TPrevVal - 1));
      return(TPrevVal);        // Return value BEFORE decrement
   }

   TYPE operator += (TYPE op)
      { CResGuard::CGuard x(m_rg); return(SetVal(GetVal() +  op)); }
   TYPE operator++()
      { CResGuard::CGuard x(m_rg); return(SetVal(GetVal() +   1)); }
   TYPE operator -= (TYPE op)
      { CResGuard::CGuard x(m_rg); return(SetVal(GetVal() -  op)); }
```

(continued)

Figure 10-2. *continued*

```
   TYPE operator--()
      { CResGuard::CGuard x(m_rg); return(SetVal(GetVal() -    1)); }
   TYPE operator *= (TYPE op)
      { CResGuard::CGuard x(m_rg); return(SetVal(GetVal() *  op)); }
   TYPE operator /= (TYPE op)
      { CResGuard::CGuard x(m_rg); return(SetVal(GetVal() /  op)); }
   TYPE operator %= (TYPE op)
      { CResGuard::CGuard x(m_rg); return(SetVal(GetVal() %  op)); }
   TYPE operator ^= (TYPE op)
      { CResGuard::CGuard x(m_rg); return(SetVal(GetVal() ^  op)); }
   TYPE operator &= (TYPE op)
      { CResGuard::CGuard x(m_rg); return(SetVal(GetVal() &  op)); }
   TYPE operator |= (TYPE op)
      { CResGuard::CGuard x(m_rg); return(SetVal(GetVal() |  op)); }
   TYPE operator <<=(TYPE op)
      { CResGuard::CGuard x(m_rg); return(SetVal(GetVal() << op)); }
   TYPE operator >>=(TYPE op)
      { CResGuard::CGuard x(m_rg); return(SetVal(GetVal() >> op)); }
};


///////////////////////////////////////////////////////////////////////////////


// Instances of this class will be accessed by multiple threads. So,
// all members of this class (except the constructor and destructor)
// must be thread-safe.
template <class TYPE>
class CWhenZero : public CInterlockedScalar<TYPE> {
public:
   CWhenZero(TYPE TVal = 0, BOOL fManualReset = TRUE)
      : CInterlockedScalar<TYPE>(TVal) {

      // The event should be signaled if TVal is 0
      m_hevtZero = CreateEvent(NULL, fManualReset, (TVal == 0), NULL);

      // The event should be signaled if TVal is NOT 0
      m_hevtNotZero = CreateEvent(NULL, fManualReset, (TVal != 0), NULL);
   }

   ~CWhenZero() {
      CloseHandle(m_hevtZero);
      CloseHandle(m_hevtNotZero);
   }
```

(continued)

Figure 10-2. *continued*

```
    // C++ does not allow operator= to be inherited.
    TYPE operator=(TYPE x) {
        return(CInterlockedScalar<TYPE>::operator=(x));
    }

    // Return handle to event signaled when value is zero
    operator HANDLE() const { return(m_hevtZero); }

    // Return handle to event signaled when value is not zero
    HANDLE GetNotZeroHandle() const { return(m_hevtNotZero); }

    // C++ does not allow operator cast to be inherited.
    operator TYPE() const {
        return(CInterlockedScalar<TYPE>::operator TYPE());
    }

protected:
    void OnValChanged(const TYPE& TNewVal, const TYPE& TPrevVal) const {
        // For best performance, avoid jumping to
        // kernel mode if we don't have to
        if ((TNewVal == 0) && (TPrevVal != 0)) {
            SetEvent(m_hevtZero);
            ResetEvent(m_hevtNotZero);
        }
        if ((TNewVal != 0) && (TPrevVal == 0)) {
            ResetEvent(m_hevtZero);
            SetEvent(m_hevtNotZero);
        }
    }

private:
    HANDLE m_hevtZero;       // Signaled when data value is 0
    HANDLE m_hevtNotZero;    // Signaled when data value is not 0
};


/////////////////////////////////// End of File ///////////////////////////////////
```

InterlockedType.rc

```
//Microsoft Developer Studio generated resource script.
//
#include "resource.h"
```

(continued)

Figure 10-2. *continued*

```
#define APSTUDIO_READONLY_SYMBOLS
/////////////////////////////////////////////////////////////////////////
//
// Generated from the TEXTINCLUDE 2 resource.
//
#include "afxres.h"


/////////////////////////////////////////////////////////////////////////
#undef APSTUDIO_READONLY_SYMBOLS


/////////////////////////////////////////////////////////////////////////
// English (U.S.) resources

#if !defined(AFX_RESOURCE_DLL) || defined(AFX_TARG_ENU)
#ifdef _WIN32
LANGUAGE LANG_ENGLISH, SUBLANG_ENGLISH_US
#pragma code_page(1252)
#endif //_WIN32


/////////////////////////////////////////////////////////////////////////
//
// Icon
//

// Icon with lowest ID value placed first to ensure application icon
// remains consistent on all systems.
IDI_INTERLOCKEDTYPE     ICON     DISCARDABLE     "InterLockedType.ICO"


#ifdef APSTUDIO_INVOKED
/////////////////////////////////////////////////////////////////////////
//
// TEXTINCLUDE
//

1 TEXTINCLUDE DISCARDABLE
BEGIN
    "resource.h\0"
END

2 TEXTINCLUDE DISCARDABLE
BEGIN
    "#include ""afxres.h""\r\n"
    "\0"
END
```

(continued)

Figure 10-2. *continued*

```
3 TEXTINCLUDE DISCARDABLE
BEGIN
    "\r\n"
    "\0"
END

#endif    // APSTUDIO_INVOKED

#endif    // English (U.S.) resources
/////////////////////////////////////////////////////////////////////////////


#ifndef APSTUDIO_INVOKED
/////////////////////////////////////////////////////////////////////////////
//
// Generated from the TEXTINCLUDE 3 resource.
//


/////////////////////////////////////////////////////////////////////////////
#endif    // not APSTUDIO_INVOKED
```

The Single Writer/Multiple Reader Guard (SWMRG)

Many applications have a basic synchronization problem commonly referred to as a single-writer/multiple-readers scenario. The problem involves an arbitrary number of threads that attempt to access a shared resource. Some of these threads (the writers) need to modify the contents of the data, and some of the threads (the readers) need only to read the data. Synchronization is necessary because of the following four rules:

1. When one thread is writing to the data, no other thread can write to the data.

2. When one thread is writing to the data, no other thread can read from the data.

3. When one thread is reading from the data, no other thread can write to the data.

4. When one thread is reading from the data, other threads can also read from the data.

Let's look at this problem in the context of a database application. Let's say we have five end users, all accessing the same database. Two employees are entering records into the database, and three employees are retrieving records from the database.

In this scenario, rule 1 is necessary because we certainly can't have both Employee 1 and Employee 2 updating the same record at the same time. If both employees attempt to modify the same record, Employee 1's changes and Employee 2's changes might be made at the same time, and the information in the record might become corrupted.

Rule 2 prohibits an employee from accessing a record in the database if another employee is updating that record. If this situation is not prevented, Employee 4 might read the contents of a record while Employee 1 is altering the same record. When Employee 4's computer displays the record, the record will contain some of the old information and some of the updated information— this is certainly unacceptable. Rule 3 is needed to solve the same problem. The difference in the wording of rules 2 and 3 prevents the situation regardless of who gains access to the database record first—an employee who is trying to write or an employee who is trying to read.

Rule 4 exists for performance reasons. It makes sense that if no employees are attempting to modify records in the database, the content of the database is not changing and therefore any and all employees who are simply retrieving records from the database should be allowed to do so. It is also assumed that there are more readers than there are writers.

OK, you have the gist of the problem. Now the question is, how do we solve it?

> **NOTE**
>
> The code that I present here is new. Previously, I published solutions to this problem that were criticized for two reasons. First, my previous implementations were too slow because they were designed to be useful in many scenarios. For example, they used more kernel objects so that threads in different processes could synchronize their access to the database. Of course, my implementation still worked even in a single-process scenario, but the heavy use of kernel objects added a great deal of overhead when all threads were running in a single process. I must concede that the single-process case is probably much more common.
>
> The second criticism was that my implementation could potentially lock out writer threads altogether. From the rules stated on the preceding page, if a lot of reader threads accessed the database, writer threads could never get access to the resource.
>
> I have addressed both of these issues with the implementation I present here. It avoids kernel objects as much as possible and uses a critical section for most of the synchronization.

To simplify things, I have encapsulated my solution in a C++ class, called CSWMRG (which I pronounce "swimerge"); it stands for single-writer/multiple-reader guard. The SWMRG.h and SWMRG.cpp files (in Figure 10-3 beginning on page 372) show my implementation.

Using a CSWMRG couldn't be easier. You simply create an object of the CSWMRG C++ class and then call the appropriate member functions as your application dictates. There are only three methods in the C++ class (not including the constructor and destructor):

```
VOID CSWMRG::WaitToRead();   // Call this to gain shared read access.
VOID CSWMRG::WaitToWrite();  // Call this to gain exclusive write access.
VOID CSWMRG::Done();         // Call this when done accessing the resource.
```

You call the first method, *WaitToRead*, just before you execute code that reads from the shared resource. You call the second method, *WaitToWrite*, just before you execute code that reads or writes to the shared resource. You call the last method, *Done*, when your code is no longer accessing the shared resource. Pretty simple, huh?

Basically, a CSWMRG object contains a number of member variables that reflect the state of how threads are accessing the shared resource. The table below describes each member's purpose and summarizes how the whole thing works. See the source code for the details.

Member	Description
m_cs	This guards all the other members so that manipulating them can be accomplished atomically.
m_nActive	This reflects the current state of the shared resource. If the value is 0, no thread is accessing the resource. If the value is greater than 0, the value indicates the number of threads that are currently reading from the resource. If the number is negative, a writer is writing to the resource. The only valid negative number is −1.
m_nWaitingReaders	This value indicates the number of reader threads that want to access the resource. This value is initialized to 0 and is incremented every time a thread calls *WaitToRead* while *m_nActive* is −1.

(continued)

Member	Description
m_nWaitingWriters	This value indicates the number of writer threads that want to access the resource. This value is initialized to 0 and is incremented every time a thread calls *WaitToWrite* while *m_nActive* is greater than 0.
m_hsemWriters	When threads call *WaitToWrite* but are denied access because *m_nActive* is greater than 0, the writer threads all wait on this semaphore. While a writer thread is waiting, new reader threads are denied access to the resource. This prevents reader threads from monopolizing the resource. When the last reader thread that currently has access to the resource calls *Done*, this semaphore is released with a count of 1, waking one waiting writer thread.
m_hsemReaders	When threads call *WaitToRead* but are denied access because *m_nActive* is −1, the reader threads all wait on this semaphore. When the last waiting writer thread calls *Done*, this semaphore is released with a count of *m_nWaitingReaders*, waking all waiting reader threads.

The SWMRG Sample Application

The SWMRG application ("10 SWMRG.exe"), listed in Figure 10-3, tests the CSWMRG C++ class. The source code and resource files for the application are in the 10-SWMRG directory on this book's companion CD-ROM. I always run the application in the debugger so I can closely watch all the class member functions and variable changes.

When you run the application, the primary thread spawns several threads that all execute the same thread function. Then the primary thread waits for all these threads to terminate by calling *WaitForMultipleObjects*. When all the threads have terminated, their handles are closed and the process exits.

Each secondary thread displays a message that looks like this.

If you want this thread to simulate reading the resource, click the Yes button; if you want the thread to simulate writing to the resource, click No. These actions simply cause the thread to call the SWMRG object's *WaitToRead* or *WaitToWrite* function, respectively.

After calling one of these two functions, the thread displays another message box that looks like one of these.

SWMRG Test: Thread 7 ☒	SWMRG Test: Thread 6 ☒
OK stops READING	OK stops WRITING
[OK]	[OK]

The message box suspends the thread and simulates the time that it takes the thread to manipulate the resource that it now has access to.

Of course, if a thread is currently reading from the resource and you instruct a different thread to write to the resource, the writer thread's message box does not appear because the thread is waiting inside its call to *WaitToWrite*. Similarly, if you instruct a thread to read while a writer thread's message box is displayed, the thread that wants to read is suspended inside its call to *WaitToRead*—its message box won't appear until any and all writer threads have finished their simulated access of the resource.

When you click on the OK button to dismiss either of these message boxes, the thread that had access to the resource calls *Done* and the SWMRG object tends to any waiting threads.

SWMRG.cpp

```
/******************************************************************************
Module:  SWMRG.cpp
Notices: Copyright (c) 2000 Jeffrey Richter
******************************************************************************/


#include "..\CmnHdr.h"      /* See Appendix A. */
#include "SWMRG.h"



///////////////////////////////////////////////////////////////////////////////
```

Figure 10-3.
The SWMRG application

(continued)

Figure 10-3. *continued*

```
CSWMRG::CSWMRG() {

   // Initially no readers want access, no writers want access, and
   // no threads are accessing the resource
   m_nWaitingReaders = m_nWaitingWriters = m_nActive = 0;
   m_hsemReaders = CreateSemaphore(NULL, 0, MAXLONG, NULL);
   m_hsemWriters = CreateSemaphore(NULL, 0, MAXLONG, NULL);
   InitializeCriticalSection(&m_cs);
}



/////////////////////////////////////////////////////////////////////////////


CSWMRG::~CSWMRG() {

#ifdef _DEBUG
   // A SWMRG shouldn't be destroyed if any threads are using the resource
   if (m_nActive != 0)
      DebugBreak();
#endif

   m_nWaitingReaders = m_nWaitingWriters = m_nActive = 0;
   DeleteCriticalSection(&m_cs);
   CloseHandle(m_hsemReaders);
   CloseHandle(m_hsemWriters);
}



/////////////////////////////////////////////////////////////////////////////


VOID CSWMRG::WaitToRead() {

   // Ensure exclusive access to the member variables
   EnterCriticalSection(&m_cs);

   // Are there writers waiting or is a writer writing?
   BOOL fResourceWritePending = (m_nWaitingWriters || (m_nActive < 0));

   if (fResourceWritePending) {

      // This reader must wait, increment the count of waiting readers
      m_nWaitingReaders++;
```

(continued)

Figure 10-3. *continued*

```
    } else {

      // This reader can read, increment the count of active readers
      m_nActive++;
    }

    // Allow other threads to attempt reading/writing
    LeaveCriticalSection(&m_cs);

    if (fResourceWritePending) {

      // This thread must wait
      WaitForSingleObject(m_hsemReaders, INFINITE);
    }
}


///////////////////////////////////////////////////////////////////////////////

VOID CSWMRG::WaitToWrite() {

  // Ensure exclusive access to the member variables
  EnterCriticalSection(&m_cs);

  // Are there any threads accessing the resource?
  BOOL fResourceOwned = (m_nActive != 0);

  if (fResourceOwned) {

    // This writer must wait, increment the count of waiting writers
    m_nWaitingWriters++;
  } else {

    // This writer can write, decrement the count of active writers
    m_nActive = -1;
  }

  // Allow other threads to attempt reading/writing
  LeaveCriticalSection(&m_cs);

  if (fResourceOwned) {

    // This thread must wait
    WaitForSingleObject(m_hsemWriters, INFINITE);
  }
}
```

(continued)

Figure 10-3. *continued*

```
/////////////////////////////////////////////////////////////////////////

VOID CSWMRG::Done() {

   // Ensure exclusive access to the member variables
   EnterCriticalSection(&m_cs);

   if (m_nActive > 0) {

      // Readers have control so a reader must be done
      m_nActive--;
   } else {

      // Writers have control so a writer must be done
      m_nActive++;
   }

   HANDLE hsem = NULL;  // Assume no threads are waiting
   LONG lCount = 1;     // Assume only 1 waiter wakes; always true for writers

   if (m_nActive == 0) {

      // No thread has access, who should wake up?
      // NOTE: It is possible that readers could never get access
      //       if there are always writers wanting to write

      if (m_nWaitingWriters > 0) {

         // Writers are waiting and they take priority over readers
         m_nActive = -1;            // A writer will get access
         m_nWaitingWriters--;       // One less writer will be waiting
         hsem = m_hsemWriters;      // Writers wait on this semaphore
         // NOTE: The semaphore will release only 1 writer thread

      } else if (m_nWaitingReaders > 0) {

         // Readers are waiting and no writers are waiting
         m_nActive = m_nWaitingReaders;   // All readers will get access
         m_nWaitingReaders = 0;           // No readers will be waiting
         hsem = m_hsemReaders;            // Readers wait on this semaphore
         lCount = m_nActive;              // Semaphore releases all readers
      } else {

         // There are no threads waiting at all; no semaphore gets released

      }
   }
```

(continued)

Figure 10-3. *continued*

```
   // Allow other threads to attempt reading/writing
   LeaveCriticalSection(&m_cs);

   if (hsem != NULL) {

      // Some threads are to be released
      ReleaseSemaphore(hsem, lCount, NULL);
   }
}


/////////////////////////////// End of File ///////////////////////////////////
```

SWMRG.h

```
/******************************************************************************
Module:  SWMRG.h
Notices: Copyright (c) 2000 Jeffrey Richter
******************************************************************************/


#pragma once


///////////////////////////////////////////////////////////////////////////////

class CSWMRG {
public:
   CSWMRG();                    // Constructor
   ~CSWMRG();                   // Destructor

   VOID WaitToRead();           // Call this to gain shared read access
   VOID WaitToWrite();          // Call this to gain exclusive write access
   VOID Done();                 // Call this when done accessing the resource

private:
   CRITICAL_SECTION m_cs;       // Permits exclusive access to other members
   HANDLE m_hsemReaders;        // Readers wait on this if a writer has access
   HANDLE m_hsemWriters;        // Writers wait on this if a reader has access
   int    m_nWaitingReaders;    // Number of readers waiting for access
   int    m_nWaitingWriters;    // Number of writers waiting for access
   int    m_nActive;            // Number of threads currently with access
                                //   (0=no threads, >0=# of readers, -1=1 writer)
};


/////////////////////////////// End of File ///////////////////////////////////
```

(continued)

Figure 10-3. *continued*

SWMRG.rc

```
//Microsoft Developer Studio generated resource script.
//
#include "resource.h"

#define APSTUDIO_READONLY_SYMBOLS
/////////////////////////////////////////////////////////////////////////////
//
// Generated from the TEXTINCLUDE 2 resource.
//
#include "afxres.h"


/////////////////////////////////////////////////////////////////////////////
#undef APSTUDIO_READONLY_SYMBOLS


/////////////////////////////////////////////////////////////////////////////
// English (U.S.) resources

#if !defined(AFX_RESOURCE_DLL) || defined(AFX_TARG_ENU)
#ifdef _WIN32
LANGUAGE LANG_ENGLISH, SUBLANG_ENGLISH_US
#pragma code_page(1252)
#endif //_WIN32


/////////////////////////////////////////////////////////////////////////////
//
// Icon
//

// Icon with lowest ID value placed first to ensure application icon
// remains consistent on all systems.
IDI_SWMRG                ICON    DISCARDABLE     "SWMRG.ico"

#ifdef APSTUDIO_INVOKED
/////////////////////////////////////////////////////////////////////////////
//
// TEXTINCLUDE
//

1 TEXTINCLUDE DISCARDABLE
BEGIN
    "resource.h\0"
END
```

(continued)

Figure 10-3. *continued*

```
2 TEXTINCLUDE DISCARDABLE
BEGIN
    "#include """"afxres.h""""\r\n"
    "\0"
END

3 TEXTINCLUDE DISCARDABLE
BEGIN
    "\r\n"
    "\0"
END

#endif    // APSTUDIO_INVOKED

#endif    // English (U.S.) resources
/////////////////////////////////////////////////////////////////////////////


#ifndef APSTUDIO_INVOKED
/////////////////////////////////////////////////////////////////////////////
//
// Generated from the TEXTINCLUDE 3 resource.
//


/////////////////////////////////////////////////////////////////////////////
#endif    // not APSTUDIO_INVOKED
```

SWMRGTest.cpp

```
/******************************************************************************
Module:  SWMRGTest.Cpp
Notices: Copyright (c) 2000 Jeffrey Richter
******************************************************************************/


#include "..\CmnHdr.h"       /* See Appendix A. */
#include <tchar.h>
#include <process.h>          // for _beginthreadex
#include "SWMRG.h"
```

(continued)

Figure 10-3. *continued*

```
///////////////////////////////////////////////////////////////////////////


// Global Single-Writer/Multiple-Reader Guard synchronization object
CSWMRG g_swmrg;


///////////////////////////////////////////////////////////////////////////


DWORD WINAPI Thread(PVOID pvParam) {

   TCHAR sz[50];
   wsprintf(sz, TEXT("SWMRG Test: Thread %d"), PtrToShort(pvParam));
   int n = MessageBox(NULL,
      TEXT("YES: Attempt to read\nNO: Attempt to write"), sz, MB_YESNO);

   // Attempt to read or write
   if (n == IDYES)
      g_swmrg.WaitToRead();
   else
      g_swmrg.WaitToWrite();

   MessageBox(NULL,
      (n == IDYES) ? TEXT("OK stops READING") : TEXT("OK stops WRITING"),
      sz, MB_OK);

   // Stop reading/writing
   g_swmrg.Done();
   return(0);
}


///////////////////////////////////////////////////////////////////////////


int WINAPI _tWinMain(HINSTANCE hinstExe, HINSTANCE, PTSTR pszCmdLine, int) {

   // Spawn a bunch of threads that will attempt to read/write
   HANDLE hThreads[MAXIMUM_WAIT_OBJECTS];
   for (int nThreads = 0; nThreads < 8; nThreads++) {
      DWORD dwThreadId;
      hThreads[nThreads] =
         chBEGINTHREADEX(NULL, 0, Thread, (PVOID) (DWORD_PTR) nThreads,
            0, &dwThreadId);
   }
```

(continued)

379

Figure 10-3. *continued*

```
    // Wait for all the threads to exit
    WaitForMultipleObjects(nThreads, hThreads, TRUE, INFINITE);
    while (nThreads--)
        CloseHandle(hThreads[nThreads]);

    return(0);
}



/////////////////////////////// End of File ////////////////////////////////////
```

Implementing a *WaitForMultipleExpressions* Function

A while ago, I was developing an application and I needed to solve a complex thread synchronization problem. The *WaitForMultipleObjects* function, which allows a thread to wait for a single object or for all objects, was insufficient for my needs. What I wanted was a function that allowed me to express a richer waiting criteria. I had three kernel objects: a process, a semaphore, and an event. I needed a way to have my thread wait until the process and semaphore were both signaled or until the process and event were both signaled.

With a little creative use of the existing Windows functions, I created exactly the function I needed: *WaitForMultipleExpressions*. It has the following prototype:

```
DWORD WINAPI WaitForMultipleExpressions(
    DWORD nExpObjects,
    CONST HANDLE* phExpObjects,
    DWORD dwMilliseconds);
```

To call this function, you must first allocate an array of HANDLEs and initialize all the array entries. The *nExpObjects* parameter indicates the number of entries in the array pointed to by the *phExpObjects* parameter. This array contains multiple sets of kernel object handles, each set separated by a NULL handle entry. *WaitForMultipleExpressions* treats objects within a single set as being ANDed together and the individual sets as being ORed together. So a call to *WaitForMultipleExpressions* suspends the calling thread until all the objects within a single set are signaled at the same time.

Here's an example. Suppose that we're working with the four kernel objects in the following table.

Object	Handle Value
Thread	0x1111
Semaphore	0x2222
Event	0x3333
Process	0x4444

Initializing the array of handles as follows instructs *WaitForMultipleObjects* to suspend the calling thread until the thread AND the semaphore are signaled OR the semaphore AND the event AND the process are signaled OR the thread AND the process are signaled, as shown here.

Index	Handle Value	Set
0	0x1111 (thread)	0
1	0x2222 (semaphore)	
2	0x0000 (OR)	
3	0x2222 (semaphore)	1
4	0x3333 (event)	
5	0x4444 (process)	
6	0x0000 (OR)	
7	0x1111 (thread)	2
8	0x4444 (process)	

You might recall that you cannot use *WaitForMultipleObjects* to pass an array of handles that exceeds 64 (MAXIMUM_WAIT_OBJECTS) entries. With *WaitForMultipleExpressions*, the handle array can be much larger than 64 entries. However, you must not have more than 64 expressions and each expression can contain no more than 63 handles. Also, *WaitForMultipleExpressions* does not work correctly if you pass the handle of a mutex into it. (I'll explain why later.)

The table on the following page shows the possible return values for *WaitForMultipleExpressions*. If an expression does become true, *WaitForMultipleExpressions* returns the WAIT_OBJECT_0-based index of that expression. Using the example, if the thread and the process object become signaled, *WaitForMultipleExpressions* returns an index of WAIT_OBJECT_0 + 2.

Return Value	Description
WAIT_OBJECT_0 to (WAIT_OBJECT_0 + # of expressions −1)	Indicates which expression came true.
WAIT_TIMEOUT	No expression came true within the specified time.
WAIT_FAILED	An error occurred. Call *GetLastError* for more information. An error of ERROR_TOO_MANY_SECRETS means that you specified more than 64 expressions. An error of ERROR_SECRET_TOO_LONG means that at least one expression had more than 63 objects specified. Other error codes might be returned. (I just couldn't resist using these two error codes for my own purposes.)

The WaitForMultipleExpressions Sample Application

The WaitForMultipleExpressions application ("10 WaitForMultExp.exe"), listed in Figure 10-4 beginning on page 387, tests the *WaitForMultipleExpressions* function. The source code and resource files for the application are in the 10-WaitForMultExp directory on this book's companion CD-ROM. When you run it, the following dialog box appears.

If you don't change any of the settings and click on the Wait For Multiple Expressions button, the dialog box looks like this.

Internally, the application creates four event kernel objects that are all initially not signaled, and it places one entry in the multicolumn, multiselection list box for each kernel object. Then the application parses the expression field and constructs the array of handles. I have chosen four kernel objects and an expression that coincides with my earlier example.

Since I specified a timeout of 30000 milliseconds, you have 30 seconds to select and deselect the event objects by toggling entries in the list box on and off. Selecting an entry calls *SetEvent* to signal the object and deselecting an entry calls *ResetEvent* to make the event nonsignaled. After you toggle enough entries to satisfy one of the expressions, *WaitForMultipleExpressions* returns and indicates at the bottom of the dialog box which expression was satisfied. If no expressions are satisfied within the 30 seconds, the word "Timeout" appears.

Now I'll discuss how I implemented *WaitForMultipleExpressions*. This was not an easy function to implement, and you definitely have to be concerned with some overhead issues when you use this function. As you know, Windows offers the *WaitForMultipleObjects* function, which allows a thread to wait on a single AND expression:

```
DWORD WaitForMultipleObjects(
    DWORD dwObjects,
    CONST HANDLE* phObjects,
    BOOL fWaitAll,
    DWORD dwMilliseconds);
```

To extend this functionality to include ORing expressions, I must spawn multiple threads: one thread for each ORed expression. Each of these individual threads waits on a single AND expression using *WaitForMultipleObjectsEx*. (I use *WaitForMultipleObjectsEx* instead of the more common *WaitForMultipleObjects*—for reasons that I'll discuss later.) When one of the expressions comes true, one of the spawned threads wakes up and terminates.

The thread that called *WaitForMultipleExpressions* (which is the same thread that spawned all the OR threads) must wait until one of the OR expressions comes true. It does this by calling the *WaitForMultipleObjectsEx* function. The number of threads spawned (OR expressions) is passed for the *dwObjects* parameter, and the *phObjects* parameter points to an array containing the list of spawned thread handles. For the *fWaitAll* parameter, FALSE is passed so that the main thread wakes up as soon as any of the expressions comes true. Finally, the *dwTimeout* value passed to *WaitForMultipleExpressions* is passed to *WaitForMultipleObjectsEx*.

If none of the expressions comes true in the specified time, WAIT_TIMEOUT is returned from *WaitForMultipleObjectsEx* and WAIT_TIMEOUT is returned from *WaitForMultipleExpressions* as well. If an expression does come true, *WaitForMultipleObjectsEx* returns the index indicating which thread terminated. Since each thread is a separate expression, this index also indicates which expression came true and the same index is returned from *WaitForMultipleExpressions*.

That's it for the executive summary of how *WaitForMultipleExpressions* works. However, three small details still need to be addressed. First, we don't want it to be possible for multiple OR threads to wake up from their call to *WaitForMultipleObjectsEx* simultaneously because successfully waiting on some kernel objects causes the object to alter its state. For example, waiting on a semaphore causes its count to decrement by 1. *WaitForMultipleExpressions* waits for just one expression to come true; therefore, I must prevent an object from altering its state more than once.

The solution to this problem is actually quite simple. Before I spawn the OR threads, I create a semaphore object of my own with an initial count of 1. Then each OR thread's call to *WaitForMultipleObjectsEx* includes the handle to this semaphore along with the other handles in the expression. This explains why each set can specify no more than 63 handles. In order for an OR thread to wake up, all the objects that it's waiting on must be signaled—including my special semaphore. Since I gave my semaphore an initial count of 1, no more than one OR thread will ever wake up, and therefore no other objects will accidentally have their states altered.

The second detail that needs to be addressed is how to force a waiting thread to stop waiting in order to clean up properly. Adding the semaphore guarantees that no more than one thread wakes up, but once I know which expression came true, I must force the remaining threads to wake up so they can terminate cleanly, freeing their stack. You should always avoid calling *TerminateThread*, so we need another mechanism. After thinking a while, I remembered that waiting threads are forced to wake up if they are in an alertable state when an entry enters their Asynchronous Procedure Call (APC) queue.

My implementation of *WaitForMultipleExpressions* uses *QueueUserAPC* to force waiting threads to wake up. After my main thread's call to *WaitForMultipleObjects* returns, I queue an APC entry to each of the still-waiting OR threads:

```
// Break all the waiting expression threads out of their
// wait state so that they can terminate cleanly.
for (dwExpNum = 0; dwExpNum < dwNumExps; dwExpNum++) {

   if ((WAIT_TIMEOUT == dwWaitRet) ||
      (dwExpNum != (dwWaitRet - WAIT_OBJECT_0))) {

      QueueUserAPC(WFME_ExpressionAPC, ahThreads[dwExpNum], 0);
   }
}
```

The callback function, *WFME_ExpressionAPC*, looks like this because I really don't have anything to do—I just want the thread to stop waiting.

```
// This is the APC callback routine function.
VOID WINAPI WFME_ExpressionAPC(DWORD dwData) {

   // This function intentionally left blank
}
```

The third and last small detail has to do with handling timeouts correctly. If none of the expressions comes true while waiting, the main thread's call to *WaitForMultipleObjects* returns with a value of WAIT_TIMEOUT. If this happens, I want to prevent any of the expressions from coming true, which could cause objects to alter their state. The following code accomplishes this:

```
// Wait for an expression to come TRUE or for a timeout.
dwWaitRet = WaitForMultipleObjects(dwExpNum, ahThreads,
   FALSE, dwMilliseconds);

if (WAIT_TIMEOUT == dwWaitRet) {
```

(continued)

```
// We timed out; check if any expressions were satisfied by
// checking the state of the hsemOnlyOne semaphore.
dwWaitRet = WaitForSingleObject(hsemOnlyOne, 0);

if (WAIT_TIMEOUT == dwWaitRet) {

   // If the semaphore was not signaled, some thread expression
   // was satisfied; we need to determine which expression.
   dwWaitRet = WaitForMultipleObjects(dwExpNum,
      ahThreads, FALSE, INFINITE);

} else {

   // No expression was satisfied and WaitForSingleObject just gave
   // us the semaphore, so we know that no expression can ever be
   // satisfied now -- waiting for an expression has timed out.
   dwWaitRet = WAIT_TIMEOUT;
}
}
```

I prevent the other expressions from coming true by waiting on the semaphore. This decrements the semaphore's count to 0, and none of the OR threads can wake up. But somewhere after the main thread's call to *WaitForMultipleObjects* and its call to *WaitForSingleObject*, an expression might have come true. This is why I check the return value of calling *WaitForSingleObject*. If it returns WAIT_OBJECT_0, the main thread got the semaphore and none of the expressions can come true. But if WAIT_TIMEOUT is returned, an expression did come true before the main thread got the semaphore. To determine which expression came true, the main thread calls *WaitForMultipleObjects* again with a timeout of INFINITE, which is OK because I know that an OR thread got the semaphore and is about to terminate. At this point, I must force the OR threads to wake up so they exit cleanly. The loop that calls *QueueUserAPC* (shown on the preceding page) does this.

Since *WaitForMultipleExpressions* is implemented internally by using different threads to wait on each set of ANDed objects, it's easy to see why you cannot use mutexes. Unlike the other kernel objects, mutex objects can be owned by a thread. So if one of my AND threads gets ownership of a mutex, it abandons the mutex when the thread terminates. If Microsoft ever adds a function to Windows that allows one thread to transfer ownership of a mutex to another thread, my *WaitForMultipleExpressions* function can easily be fixed to support mutexes properly. Until this function exists, there is no good, clean way for *WaitForMultipleExpressions* to support mutexes.

WaitForMultExp.cpp

```
/****************************************************************************
Module:  WaitForMultExp.cpp
Notices: Copyright (c) 2000 Jeffrey Richter
****************************************************************************/


#include "..\CmnHdr.h"      /* See Appendix A. */
#include <malloc.h>
#include <process.h>
#include "WaitForMultExp.h"


///////////////////////////////////////////////////////////////////////////


// Internal data structure representing a single expression.
// Used to tell OR-threads what objects to wait on.
typedef struct {
   PHANDLE m_phExpObjects;   // Points to set of handles
   DWORD   m_nExpObjects;    // Number of handles
} EXPRESSION, *PEXPRESSION;


///////////////////////////////////////////////////////////////////////////


// The OR-thread function
DWORD WINAPI WFME_ThreadExpression(PVOID pvParam) {

   // This thread function just waits for an expression to come true.
   // The thread waits in an alertable state so that it can be forced
   // to stop waiting by queuing an entry to its APC queue.
   PEXPRESSION pExpression = (PEXPRESSION) pvParam;
   return(WaitForMultipleObjectsEx(
      pExpression->m_nExpObjects, pExpression->m_phExpObjects,
      TRUE, INFINITE, TRUE));
}


///////////////////////////////////////////////////////////////////////////
```

Figure 10-4. *(continued)*
The WaitForMultipleExpressions sample application

Figure 10-4. *continued*

```
// This is the APC callback routine function
VOID WINAPI WFME_ExpressionAPC(ULONG_PTR dwData) {

   // This function intentionally left blank
}



//////////////////////////////////////////////////////////////////////////////


// Function to wait on multiple Boolean expressions
DWORD WINAPI WaitForMultipleExpressions(DWORD nExpObjects,
   CONST HANDLE* phExpObjects, DWORD dwMilliseconds) {

   // Allocate a temporary array because we modify the passed array and
   // we need to add a handle at the end for the hsemOnlyOne semaphore.
   PHANDLE phExpObjectsTemp = (PHANDLE)
      _alloca(sizeof(HANDLE) * (nExpObjects + 1));
   CopyMemory(phExpObjectsTemp, phExpObjects, sizeof(HANDLE) * nExpObjects);
   phExpObjectsTemp[nExpObjects] = NULL;  // Put sentinel at end

   // Semaphore to guarantee that only one expression gets satisfied
   HANDLE hsemOnlyOne = CreateSemaphore(NULL, 1, 1, NULL);

   // Expression information: 1 per possible thread
   EXPRESSION Expression[MAXIMUM_WAIT_OBJECTS];

   DWORD dwExpNum  = 0;    // Current expression number
   DWORD dwNumExps = 0;    // Total number of expressions

   DWORD dwObjBegin = 0;   // First index of a set
   DWORD dwObjCur   = 0;   // Current index of object in a set

   DWORD dwThreadId, dwWaitRet = 0;

   // Array of thread handles for threads: 1 per expression
   HANDLE ahThreads[MAXIMUM_WAIT_OBJECTS];

   // Parse the callers handle list by initializing a structure for
   // each expression and adding hsemOnlyOne to each expression.
   while ((dwWaitRet != WAIT_FAILED) && (dwObjCur <= nExpObjects)) {

      // While no errors, and object handles are in the caller's list...
```

(continued)

Figure 10-4. *continued*

```
    // Find next expression (OR-expressions are separated by NULL handles)
    while (phExpObjectsTemp[dwObjCur] != NULL)
        dwObjCur++;

    // Initialize Expression structure which an OR-thread waits on
    phExpObjectsTemp[dwObjCur] = hsemOnlyOne;
    Expression[dwNumExps].m_phExpObjects =  &phExpObjectsTemp[dwObjBegin];
    Expression[dwNumExps].m_nExpObjects  =  dwObjCur - dwObjBegin + 1;

    if (Expression[dwNumExps].m_nExpObjects > MAXIMUM_WAIT_OBJECTS) {
        // Error: Too many handles in single expression
        dwWaitRet = WAIT_FAILED;
        SetLastError(ERROR_SECRET_TOO_LONG);
    }

    // Advance to the next expression
    dwObjBegin = ++dwObjCur;
    if (++dwNumExps == MAXIMUM_WAIT_OBJECTS) {
        // Error: Too many expressions
        dwWaitRet = WAIT_FAILED;
        SetLastError(ERROR_TOO_MANY_SECRETS);
    }
}

if (dwWaitRet != WAIT_FAILED) {

    // No errors occurred while parsing the handle list

    // Spawn thread to wait on each expression
    for (dwExpNum = 0; dwExpNum < dwNumExps; dwExpNum++) {

        ahThreads[dwExpNum] = chBEGINTHREADEX(NULL,
            1, // We only require a small stack
            WFME_ThreadExpression, &Expression[dwExpNum],
            0, &dwThreadId);
    }

    // Wait for an expression to come TRUE or for a timeout
    dwWaitRet = WaitForMultipleObjects(dwExpNum, ahThreads,
        FALSE, dwMilliseconds);

    if (WAIT_TIMEOUT == dwWaitRet) {

        // We timed-out, check if any expressions were satisfied by
```

(continued)

Figure 10-4. *continued*

```
            // checking the state of the hsemOnlyOne semaphore.
            dwWaitRet = WaitForSingleObject(hsemOnlyOne, 0);

            if (WAIT_TIMEOUT == dwWaitRet) {

                // If the semaphore was not signaled, some thread expressions
                // was satisfied; we need to determine which expression.
                dwWaitRet = WaitForMultipleObjects(dwExpNum,
                    ahThreads, FALSE, INFINITE);

            } else {

                // No expression was satisfied and WaitForSingleObject just gave
                // us the semaphore so we know that no expression can ever be
                // satisfied now -- waiting for an expression has timed-out.
                dwWaitRet = WAIT_TIMEOUT;
            }
        }

        // Break all the waiting expression threads out of their
        // wait state so that they can terminate cleanly.
        for (dwExpNum = 0; dwExpNum < dwNumExps; dwExpNum++) {

            if ((WAIT_TIMEOUT == dwWaitRet) ||
                (dwExpNum != (dwWaitRet - WAIT_OBJECT_0))) {

                QueueUserAPC(WFME_ExpressionAPC, ahThreads[dwExpNum], 0);
            }
        }

#ifdef _DEBUG
        // In debug builds, wait for all of expression threads to terminate
        // to make sure that we are forcing the threads to wake up.
        // In non-debug builds, we'll assume that this works and
        // not keep this thread waiting any longer.
        WaitForMultipleObjects(dwExpNum, ahThreads, TRUE, INFINITE);
#endif

        // Close our handles to all the expression threads
        for (dwExpNum = 0; dwExpNum < dwNumExps; dwExpNum++) {
            CloseHandle(ahThreads[dwExpNum]);
        }
    } // error occurred while parsing
```

(continued)

Figure 10-4. *continued*

```
    CloseHandle(hsemOnlyOne);
    return(dwWaitRet);
}



//////////////////////////////// End of File ////////////////////////////////////
```

WaitForMultExp.h

```
/***********************************************************************************
Module:  WaitForMultExp.h
Notices: Copyright (c) 2000 Jeffrey Richter
***********************************************************************************/


#pragma once


///////////////////////////////////////////////////////////////////////////////


DWORD WINAPI WaitForMultipleExpressions(DWORD nExpObjects,
    CONST HANDLE* phExpObjects, DWORD dwMilliseconds);


//////////////////////////////// End of File /////////////////////////////////////
```

WfMETest.cpp

```
/***********************************************************************************
Module: WfMETest.cpp
Notices: Copyright (c) 2000 Jeffrey Richter
***********************************************************************************/


#include "..\CmnHdr.h"      /* See Appendix A. */
#include <windowsx.h>
#include <tchar.h>
#include <process.h>
#include "resource.h"
#include "WaitForMultExp.h"
```

(continued)

Figure 10-4. *continued*

```
//////////////////////////////////////////////////////////////////////


// g_ahObjs contains the list of event kernel object
// handles referenced in the Boolean expression.
#define MAX_KERNEL_OBJS     1000
HANDLE g_ahObjs[MAX_KERNEL_OBJS];


// ahExpObjs contains all the expressions. A single expression
// consists of a contiguous set of kernel object handles that
// is TRUE when all the objects are signaled at the same time.
// A NULL handle is used to separate OR expressions.

// A handle value may NOT appear multiple times within an AND
// expression but the same handle value may appear in
// different OR expressions.

// An expression can have a maximum of 64 sets with no more
// than 63 handles/set plus a NULL handle to separate each set
#define MAX_EXPRESSION_SIZE   ((64 * 63) + 63)


// m_nExpObjects is the number of entries used in the ahExpObjects array.
typedef struct {
   HWND      m_hwnd;                                // Where to send results
   DWORD     m_dwMilliseconds;                      // How long before timeout
   DWORD     m_nExpObjects;                         // # of entries in object list
   HANDLE    m_ahExpObjs[MAX_EXPRESSION_SIZE];  // List of objs
} AWFME, *PAWFME;
AWFME g_awfme;


// This message is posted to the UI thread when an expression
// comes true or when we timeout while waiting for an
// expression to come TRUE.
#define WM_WAITEND      (WM_USER + 101)


//////////////////////////////////////////////////////////////////////


BOOL Dlg_OnInitDialog(HWND hwnd, HWND hwndFocus, LPARAM lParam) {
```

(continued)

Figure 10-4. *continued*

```
   chSETDLGICONS(hwnd, IDI_WFMETEXT);

   // Initialize the controls in the dialog box
   SetDlgItemInt(hwnd, IDC_NUMOBJS, 4, FALSE);
   SetDlgItemInt(hwnd, IDC_TIMEOUT, 30000, FALSE);
   SetDlgItemText(hwnd, IDC_EXPRESSION,
     _T("1 2 | 2 3 4 | 1 4"));

   // Set the multicolumn listbox's column size
   ListBox_SetColumnWidth(GetDlgItem(hwnd, IDC_OBJLIST),
     LOWORD(GetDialogBaseUnits()) * 4);

   return(TRUE);  // Accept default focus window.
}


///////////////////////////////////////////////////////////////////////////


DWORD WINAPI AsyncWaitForMultipleExpressions(PVOID pvParam) {

   PAWFME pawfme = (PAWFME) pvParam;

   DWORD dw = WaitForMultipleExpressions(pawfme->m_nExpObjects,
     pawfme->m_ahExpObjs, pawfme->m_dwMilliseconds);
   PostMessage(pawfme->m_hwnd, WM_WAITEND, dw, 0);
   return(0);
}


///////////////////////////////////////////////////////////////////////////


LRESULT Dlg_OnWaitEnd(HWND hwnd, WPARAM wParam, LPARAM lParam) {

   // Close all the event kernel object handles
   for (int n = 0; g_ahObjs[n] != NULL; n++)
     CloseHandle(g_ahObjs[n]);

   // Tell the user the result of running the test
   if (wParam == WAIT_TIMEOUT)
     SetDlgItemText(hwnd, IDC_RESULT, __TEXT("Timeout"));
   else
     SetDlgItemInt(hwnd, IDC_RESULT, (DWORD) wParam - WAIT_OBJECT_0, FALSE);
```

(continued)

Figure 10-4. *continued*

```
    // Allow the user to change values and run the test again
    EnableWindow(GetDlgItem(hwnd, IDC_NUMOBJS),     TRUE);
    EnableWindow(GetDlgItem(hwnd, IDC_TIMEOUT),     TRUE);
    EnableWindow(GetDlgItem(hwnd, IDC_EXPRESSION),  TRUE);
    EnableWindow(GetDlgItem(hwnd, IDOK),            TRUE);
    SetFocus(GetDlgItem(hwnd, IDC_EXPRESSION));

    return(0);
}


///////////////////////////////////////////////////////////////////////////////


void Dlg_OnCommand(HWND hwnd, int id, HWND hwndCtl, UINT codeNotify) {

    // Obtain the user's settings from the dialog box controls.
    TCHAR szExpression[100];
    ComboBox_GetText(GetDlgItem(hwnd, IDC_EXPRESSION), szExpression,
        sizeof(szExpression) / sizeof(szExpression[0]));

    int nObjects = GetDlgItemInt(hwnd, IDC_NUMOBJS, NULL, FALSE);

    switch (id) {
    case IDCANCEL:
        EndDialog(hwnd, id);
        break;

    case IDC_OBJLIST:
        switch (codeNotify) {
        case LBN_SELCHANGE:
            // An item changed state, reset all items and set the selected ones.
            for (int n = 0; n < nObjects; n++)
                ResetEvent(g_ahObjs[n]);

            for (n = 0; n < nObjects; n++) {
                if (ListBox_GetSel(GetDlgItem(hwnd, IDC_OBJLIST), n))
                    SetEvent(g_ahObjs[n]);
            }
            break;
        }
        break;
```

(continued)

Figure 10-4. *continued*

```
case IDOK:
    // Prevent the user from changing values while the test is running
    SetFocus(GetDlgItem(hwnd, IDC_OBJLIST));
    EnableWindow(GetDlgItem(hwnd, IDC_NUMOBJS),     FALSE);
    EnableWindow(GetDlgItem(hwnd, IDC_TIMEOUT),     FALSE);
    EnableWindow(GetDlgItem(hwnd, IDC_EXPRESSION),  FALSE);
    EnableWindow(GetDlgItem(hwnd, IDOK),            FALSE);

    // Notify the user that the test is running
    SetDlgItemText(hwnd, IDC_RESULT, TEXT("Waiting..."));

    // Create all of the desired kernel objects
    ZeroMemory(g_ahObjs, sizeof(g_ahObjs));
    g_awfme.m_nExpObjects = 0;
    ZeroMemory(g_awfme.m_ahExpObjs, sizeof(g_awfme.m_ahExpObjs));
    g_awfme.m_hwnd = hwnd;
    g_awfme.m_dwMilliseconds = GetDlgItemInt(hwnd, IDC_TIMEOUT, NULL, FALSE);

    ListBox_ResetContent(GetDlgItem(hwnd, IDC_OBJLIST));
    for (int n = 0; n < nObjects; n++) {
        TCHAR szBuf[20];
        g_ahObjs[n] = CreateEvent(NULL, FALSE, FALSE, NULL);

        wsprintf(szBuf, TEXT("  %d"), n + 1);
        ListBox_AddString(GetDlgItem(hwnd, IDC_OBJLIST),
            &szBuf[lstrlen(szBuf) - 3]);
    }

    PTSTR p = _tcstok(szExpression, TEXT(" "));
    while (p != NULL) {
        g_awfme.m_ahExpObjs[g_awfme.m_nExpObjects++] =
            (*p == TEXT('|')) ? NULL : g_ahObjs[_ttoi(p) - 1];
        p = _tcstok(NULL, TEXT(" "));
    }

    DWORD dwThreadId;
    CloseHandle(chBEGINTHREADEX(NULL, 0,
        AsyncWaitForMultipleExpressions, &g_awfme,
        0, &dwThreadId));
    break;
    }
}

//////////////////////////////////////////////////////////////////////////
```

(continued)

Figure 10-4. *continued*

```
INT_PTR WINAPI Dlg_Proc(HWND hwnd, UINT uMsg, WPARAM wParam, LPARAM lParam) {

   switch (uMsg) {
      chHANDLE_DLGMSG(hwnd, WM_INITDIALOG, Dlg_OnInitDialog);
      chHANDLE_DLGMSG(hwnd, WM_COMMAND,    Dlg_OnCommand);

      case WM_WAITEND:
         return(Dlg_OnWaitEnd(hwnd, wParam, lParam));
   }

   return(FALSE);
}


/////////////////////////////////////////////////////////////////////////////


int WINAPI _tWinMain(HINSTANCE hinstExe, HINSTANCE, PTSTR pszCmdLine, int) {

   DialogBox(hinstExe, MAKEINTRESOURCE(IDD_TESTW4ME), NULL, Dlg_Proc);
   return(0);
}


////////////////////////////////// End of File //////////////////////////////////
```

WfMETest.rc

```
//Microsoft Developer Studio generated resource script.
//
#include "resource.h"

#define APSTUDIO_READONLY_SYMBOLS
/////////////////////////////////////////////////////////////////////////////
//
// Generated from the TEXTINCLUDE 2 resource.
//
#include "afxres.h"


/////////////////////////////////////////////////////////////////////////////
#undef APSTUDIO_READONLY_SYMBOLS
```

(continued)

Figure 10-4. *continued*

```
//////////////////////////////////////////////////////////////////////
// English (U.S.) resources

#if !defined(AFX_RESOURCE_DLL) || defined(AFX_TARG_ENU)
#ifdef _WIN32
LANGUAGE LANG_ENGLISH, SUBLANG_ENGLISH_US
#pragma code_page(1252)
#endif //_WIN32


//////////////////////////////////////////////////////////////////////
//
// Dialog
//

IDD_WFMETEST DIALOGEX 0, 0, 168, 185
STYLE DS_3DLOOK | DS_CENTER | WS_MINIMIZEBOX | WS_VISIBLE | WS_CAPTION |
    WS_SYSMENU
EXSTYLE WS_EX_APPWINDOW
CAPTION "WaitForMultipleExpressions"
FONT 8, "MS Sans Serif", 0, 0, 0x1
BEGIN
    LTEXT           "How many different &kernel objects are referenced in the expression:",
                    IDC_STATIC,3,4,121,17
    EDITTEXT        IDC_NUMOBJS,138,6,27,14,ES_AUTOHSCROLL
    LTEXT           "&Timeout (in milliseconds):",IDC_STATIC,4,28,83,8
    EDITTEXT        IDC_TIMEOUT,138,26,27,14,ES_AUTOHSCROLL
    LTEXT           "&Expression (use space for AND and | for OR):",
                    IDC_STATIC,4,44,143,8
    COMBOBOX        IDC_EXPRESSION,4,56,160,76,CBS_DROPDOWN | WS_VSCROLL |
                    WS_TABSTOP
    DEFPUSHBUTTON   "&Wait for Multiple Expressions",IDOK,34,72,99,14
    LTEXT           "&Signal which kernel objects:",IDC_STATIC,4,92,83,8
    LISTBOX         IDC_OBJLIST,4,102,160,68,LBS_MULTIPLESEL |
                    LBS_NOINTEGRALHEIGHT | LBS_MULTICOLUMN | WS_VSCROLL |
                    WS_HSCROLL | WS_TABSTOP
    LTEXT           "Expression satisfied:",IDC_STATIC,32,172,63,8
    LTEXT           "Timeout",IDC_RESULT,100,172,36,8
END

#ifdef APSTUDIO_INVOKED
//////////////////////////////////////////////////////////////////////
//
// TEXTINCLUDE
//
```

(continued)

Figure 10-4. *continued*

```
1 TEXTINCLUDE DISCARDABLE
BEGIN
    "resource.h\0"
END

2 TEXTINCLUDE DISCARDABLE
BEGIN
    "#include ""afxres.h""\r\n"
    "\0"
END

3 TEXTINCLUDE DISCARDABLE
BEGIN
    "\r\n"
    "\0"
END


#endif    // APSTUDIO_INVOKED



/////////////////////////////////////////////////////////////////////////////
//
// Icon
//

// Icon with lowest ID value placed first to ensure application icon
// remains consistent on all systems.
IDI_WFMETEXT            ICON    DISCARDABLE    "WaitForMultExp.ico"
#endif    // English (U.S.) resources
/////////////////////////////////////////////////////////////////////////////



#ifndef APSTUDIO_INVOKED
/////////////////////////////////////////////////////////////////////////////
//
// Generated from the TEXTINCLUDE 3 resource.
//


/////////////////////////////////////////////////////////////////////////////
#endif    // not APSTUDIO_INVOKED
```

THREAD POOLING

In Chapter 8, we discussed how to synchronize threads using mechanisms that allow your threads to remain in user mode. The wonderful thing about user-mode synchronization is its speed. If you are concerned about your thread's performance, you should always start by seeing if a user-mode thread synchronization mechanism will work for you.

By now, you know that creating multithreaded applications is difficult. You face two big issues: managing the creation and destruction of threads and synchronizing the threads' access to resources. For synchronizing resource access, Windows offers many primitives to help you: events, semaphores, mutexes, critical sections, and so on. These are all fairly easy to use. The only thing that would make things easier is if the system could automatically protect shared resources. Unfortunately, we have a ways to go before Windows can offer this protection in a way that makes everybody happy.

Everybody has opinions on how to manage the creation and destruction of threads. I've created several different implementations of thread pools myself over the past years, each one fine-tuned for a particular scenario. Microsoft Windows 2000 offers some new thread pooling functions to make thread creation, destruction, and general management easier. This new general-purpose thread pool is definitely not right for every situation, but it often fits the bill and can save you countless hours of development time.

The new thread pooling functions let you do the following:

- Call functions asynchronously
- Call functions at timed intervals
- Call functions when single kernel objects become signaled
- Call functions when asynchronous I/O requests complete

To accomplish these tasks, the thread pool consists of four separate components. Table 11-1 shows the components and describes the rules that govern their behavior.

399

	Component			
	Timer	*Wait*	*I/O*	*Non-I/O*
Initial Number of Threads	Always 1	1	0	0
When a Thread Is Created	When first thread pool timer function is called	One thread for every 63 registered objects	The system uses heuristics, but here are some factors that affect the creation of a thread: ■ Some time (in seconds) has passed since the thread was added ■ The WT_EXECUTELONG-FUNCTION flag is used ■ The number of queued work items exceeds a certain threshold	
When a Thread Is Destroyed	When process terminates	When the number of registered wait objects is 0	When the thread has no pending I/O requests and has been idle for a threshold period (about a minute)	When the thread is idle for a threshold period (about a minute)
How a Thread Waits	Alertable	*WaitFor-MultipleObjectsEx*	Alertable	*GetQueued CompletionStatus*
What Wakes Up a Thread	Waitable timer is signaled queuing a user APC	Kernel object becomes signaled	Queued user APC or completed I/O request	Posted completion status or completed I/O request (The completion port allows at most 2 * number of CPUs threads to run concurrently)

Table 11-1.
Thread pool components and their behavior

When a process initializes, it doesn't have any of the overhead associated with these components. However, as soon as one of the new thread pooling functions is called, some of the components are created for the process and some stay around until the process terminates. As you can see, the overhead of using the thread pool is not trivial: quite a few threads and internal data structures become part of your process. So you must carefully consider what the thread pool will and won't do for you: don't just blindly use these functions.

OK, enough with the disclaimers. Let's see what this stuff does.

Scenario 1: Call Functions Asynchronously

Let's say that you have a server process with a main thread that waits for a client's request. When the main thread receives this request, it spawns a separate thread for handling the request. This allows your application's main thread to cycle and wait for another client's request. This scenario is a typical implementation of a client/server application. It's already straightforward enough to implement, but you can also implement it using the new thread pool functions.

When the server process's main thread receives the client's request, it can call this function:

```
BOOL QueueUserWorkItem(
   PTHREAD_START_ROUTINE pfnCallback,
   PVOID pvContext,
   ULONG dwFlags);
```

This function queues a "work item" to a thread in the thread pool and returns immediately. A work item is simply a function (identified by the *pfnCallback* parameter) that is called and passed a single parameter, *pvContext*. Eventually, some thread in the pool will process the work item, causing your function to be called. The callback function you write must have the following prototype:

```
DWORD WINAPI WorkItemFunc(PVOID pvContext);
```

Even though you must prototype this function as returning a DWORD, the return value is actually ignored.

Notice that you never call *CreateThread* yourself. A thread pool is automatically created for your process and a thread within the pool calls your function. Also, this thread is not immediately destroyed after it processes the client's request. It goes back into the thread pool so that it is ready to handle any other queued work items. Your application might become much more efficient because you are not creating and destroying threads for every single client request. Also, because the threads are bound to a completion port, the number of concurrently runnable threads is limited to twice the number of CPUs. This reduces thread context switches.

What happens under the covers is that *QueueUserWorkItem* checks the number of threads in the non-I/O component and, depending on the load (number of queued work items), might add another thread to this component.

QueueUserWorkItem then performs the equivalent of calling *PostQueued-CompletionStatus*, passing your work item information to an I/O completion port. Ultimately, a thread waiting on the completion port extracts your message (by calling *GetQueuedCompletionStatus*) and calls your function. When your function returns, the thread calls *GetQueuedCompletionStatus* again, waiting for another work item.

The thread pool expects to frequently handle asynchronous I/O requests—whenever a thread queues an I/O request to a device driver. While the device driver performs the I/O, the thread that queued the request is not blocked and can continue executing other instructions. Asynchronous I/O is the secret to creating high-performance, scalable applications because it allows a single thread to handle requests from various clients as they come in; the thread doesn't have to handle the requests serially or block while waiting for I/O requests to complete.

However, Windows places a restriction on asynchronous I/O requests: if a thread issues an asynchronous I/O request to a device driver and then terminates, the I/O request is lost and no thread is notified when the I/O request actually completes. In a well-designed thread pool, the number of threads expands and shrinks depending on the needs of its clients. So if a thread issues an asynchronous I/O request and then dies because the pool is shrinking, the I/O request dies too. This is usually not what you want, so you need a solution.

If you want to queue a work item that issues an asynchronous I/O request, you cannot post the work item to the thread pool's non-I/O component. You must queue the work item to the I/O component of the thread pool. The I/O component consists of a set of threads that never die if they have a pending I/O request; therefore, you should use them only for executing code that issues asynchronous I/O requests.

To queue a work item for the I/O component, you still call *QueueUserWorkItem*, but for the *dwFlags* parameter you pass WT_EXECUTEINIOTHREAD. Normally, you just pass WT_EXECUTEDEFAULT (defined as 0), which causes the work item to be posted to the non-I/O component's threads.

Windows offers functions (such as *RegNotifyChangeKeyValue*) that perform non-I/O-related tasks asynchronously. These functions also require that the calling thread not terminate. If you want to call one of these functions using a persistent thread pool thread, you can use the WT_EXECUTEINPERSISTENTTHREAD flag, which causes the timer component's thread to execute the queued work item callback function. Since the timer component's thread never terminates, the asynchronous operation is guaranteed to eventually occur. You should make sure that the callback function does not block and that it executes quickly so that the timer component's thread is not adversely affected.

A well-designed thread pool must also try to keep threads available to handle requests. If a pool contains 4 threads and 100 work items are queued, only 4 work items can be handled at a time. This might not be a problem if a work item takes only a few milliseconds to execute, but if your work items require much more time, you won't be able to handle requests in a timely fashion.

Certainly, the system isn't smart enough to anticipate what your work item functions will do, but if you know that a work item might take a long time to execute, you should call *QueueUserWorkItem*, passing it the WT_EXECUTE-LONGFUNCTION flag. This flag helps the thread pool decide whether to add a new thread to the pool; it forces the thread pool to create a new thread if all of the threads in the pool are busy. So if you queue 10,000 work items (with the WT_EXECUTELONGFUNCTION flag) at the same time, 10,000 threads are added to the thread pool. If you don't want 10,000 threads created, you must space out the calls to *QueueUserWorkItem* so that some work items get a chance to complete.

The thread pool can't place an upper limit on the number of threads in the pool, or starvation or deadlock might occur. Imagine queuing 10,000 work items that all block on an event that is signaled by the 10,001st item. If you've set a maximum of 10,000 threads, the 10,001st work item won't be executed and all 10,000 threads will be blocked forever.

When you use thread pool functions, you should look for potential deadlock situations. Of course, you must be careful if your work item functions block on critical sections, semaphores, mutexes, and so on—this makes deadlocks more likely. Always be aware of which component's (I/O, non-I/O, wait, or timer) thread is executing your code. Also be careful if your work item functions are in DLLs that might be dynamically unloaded. A thread that calls a function in an unloaded DLL generates an access violation. To ensure that you do not unload a DLL with queued work items, you must reference-count your queued work items: you increment a counter before you call *QueueUserWorkItem* and decrement the counter as your work item function completes. Only if the reference count is 0 is it safe to unload the DLL.

Scenario 2: Call Functions at Timed Intervals

Sometimes applications need to perform certain tasks at certain times. Windows offers a waitable timer kernel object that makes it easy to get a time-based notification. Many programmers create a waitable timer object for each time-based task that the application will perform, but this is unnecessary and wastes system resources. Instead, you can create a single waitable timer, set it to the next due time, and then reset the timer for the next time, and so on. However, the code to accomplish this is tricky to write. Fortunately, you can let the new thread pool functions manage this for you.

To schedule a work item to be executed at a certain time, you first create a timer queue by calling this function:

```
HANDLE CreateTimerQueue();
```

A timer queue organizes a set of timers. For example, imagine a single executable file that hosts several services. Each service might require timers to fire to help it maintain its state, such as when a client is no longer responding, when to gather and update some statistical information, and so on. It is inefficient to have a waitable timer and dedicated thread for each service. Instead, each service can have its own timer queue (a lightweight resource) and share the timer component's thread and waitable timer object. When a service terminates, it can simply delete its timer queue, which deletes all the timers created within it.

Once you have a timer queue, you can create timers in it as follows:

```
BOOL CreateTimerQueueTimer(
   PHANDLE phNewTimer,
   HANDLE hTimerQueue,
   WAITORTIMERCALLBACK pfnCallback,
   PVOID pvContext,
   DWORD dwDueTime,
   DWORD dwPeriod,
   ULONG dwFlags);
```

For the second parameter, you pass the handle of the timer queue that you want to create this timer in. If you are creating just a few timers, you can simply pass NULL for the *hTimerQueue* parameter and avoid the call to *CreateTimerQueue* altogether. Passing NULL tells the function to use a default timer queue and simplifies your coding. The *pfnCallback* and *pvContext* parameters indicate what function should be called and what should be passed to that function when the time comes due. The *dwDueTime* parameter indicates how many milliseconds should pass before the function is called the first time. (The value 0 causes the function to be called as soon as possible, making *CreateTimerQueueTimer* similar to *QueueUserWorkItem*.) The *dwPeriod* parameter indicates how many milliseconds should pass before the function is called in the future. Passing 0 for *dwPeriod* makes this a one-shot timer, causing the work item to be queued only once. The handle of the new timer is returned via the function's *phNewTimer* parameter.

The worker callback function must have the following prototype:

```
VOID WINAPI WaitOrTimerCallback(
   PVOID pvContext,
   BOOL fTimerOrWaitFired);
```

When this function is called, the *fTimerOrWaitFired* parameter is always TRUE, indicating that the timer has fired.

Now let's talk about *CreateTimerQueueTimer*'s *dwFlags* parameter. This parameter tells the function how to queue the work item when the time comes due. You can use WT_EXECUTEDEFAULT if you want a non-I/O component thread to process the work item, WT_EXECUTEINIOTHREAD if you want to issue an asynchronous I/O request at a certain time, or WT_EXECUTEINPERSISTENTTHREAD if you want a thread that never dies to process the work item. You can use WT_EXECUTELONGFUNCTION if you think that your work item will require a long time to execute.

You can also use another flag, WT_EXECUTEINTIMERTHREAD, which requires a bit more explaining. In Table 11-1 on page 400, you can see that the thread pool has a timer component. This component creates the single waitable timer kernel object and manages its due time. The component always consists of a single thread. When you call *CreateTimerQueueTimer*, you cause the timer component's thread to wake up, add your timer to a queue of timers, and reset the waitable timer kernel object. The timer component's thread then goes into an alertable sleep, waiting for the waitable timer to queue an APC to it. After the waitable timer queues the APC, the thread wakes up, updates the timer queue, resets the waitable timer, and then decides what to do with the work item that should now be executed.

Next, the thread checks for the following flags: WT_EXECUTEDEFAULT, WT_EXECUTEINIOTHREAD, WT_EXECUTEINPERSISTENTTHREAD, WT_EXECUTELONGFUNCTION, and WT_EXECUTEINTIMERTHREAD. By now, it should be obvious what the WT_EXECUTEINTIMERTHREAD flag does: it causes the timer component's thread to execute the work item. While this makes execution of the work item more efficient, it is very dangerous! If the work item function blocks for a long time, the timer component's thread can't do anything else. The waitable timer might still be queuing APC entries to the thread, but these work items won't be handled until the currently executing function returns. If you plan to execute code using the timer thread, the code should execute quickly and should not block.

The WT_EXECUTEINIOTHREAD, WT_EXECUTEINPERSISTENT-THREAD, and WT_EXECUTEINTIMERTHREAD flags are mutually exclusive. If you don't pass any of these flags (or use the WT_EXECUTEDEFAULT flag), the work item is queued to the non-I/O component's threads. Also, the WT_EXECUTELONGFUNCTION flag is ignored if the WT_EXECUTEINTIMERTHREAD flag is specified.

When you no longer want a timer to fire, you must delete it by calling the function at the top of page 406.

```
BOOL DeleteTimerQueueTimer(
   HANDLE hTimerQueue,
   HANDLE hTimer,
   HANDLE hCompletionEvent);
```

You must call this function even for one-shot timers that have fired. The *hTimerQueue* parameter indicates which queue the timer is in. The *hTimer* parameter identifies the timer to delete; the handle was returned by an earlier call to *CreateTimerQueueTimer*.

The last parameter, *hCompletionEvent*, tells you when there are no outstanding work items queued because of this timer. If you pass INVALID_HANDLE_VALUE for this parameter, *DeleteTimerQueueTimer* does not return until all queued work items for this timer have completely executed. Think about what this means: if you do a blocking delete of a timer during its own work item processing, you create a deadlock situation, right? You are waiting for the work item to finish processing, but you are halting its processing while waiting for it to finish! A thread can do a blocking delete of a timer only if it isn't the thread processing the timer's work item.

Also, if you are using the timer component's thread, you should not attempt a blocking delete of any timer or a deadlock will occur. Attempting to delete a timer queues an APC notification to the timer component's thread. If this thread is waiting for a timer to be deleted, it can't also be deleting the timer, so a deadlock occurs.

Instead of passing INVALID_HANDLE_VALUE for the *hCompletionEvent* parameter, you can pass NULL. This tells the function that you want the timer deleted as soon as possible. In this case, *DeleteTimerQueueTimer* returns immediately, but you will not know when all of this timer's queued work items have completed processing. Finally, you can pass the handle of an event kernel object as the *hCompletionEvent* parameter. When you do this, *DeleteTimerQueueTimer* returns immediately and the timer component's thread sets the event after all of the timer's queued work items have completed processing. Make sure that before you call *DeleteTimerQueueTimer*, the event is not signaled, or your code will think that the queued work items have executed before they really have.

Once you create a timer, you can alter its due time or period by calling this function:

```
BOOL ChangeTimerQueueTimer(
   HANDLE hTimerQueue,
   HANDLE hTimer,
   ULONG dwDueTime,
   ULONG dwPeriod);
```

Here, you pass the handle of a timer queue and the handle of an existing timer that you want to modify. You can change the timer's *dwDueTime* and *dwPeriod*. Note that attempting to change a one-shot timer that has already fired has no effect. Also note that you can freely call this function without having to worry about deadlocks.

When you no longer need a set of timers, you can delete the timer queue by calling this function:

```
BOOL DeleteTimerQueueEx(
    HANDLE hTimerQueue,
    HANDLE hCompletionEvent);
```

This function takes the handle of an existing timer queue and deletes all of the timers in it so that you don't have to call *DeleteTimerQueueTimer* explicitly for every one. The *hCompletionEvent* parameter has the same semantics here as it does for the *DeleteTimerQueueTimer* function. This means that the same deadlock possibilities exist, so be careful.

Before we move on to another scenario, let me point out a couple of additional items. First, the timer component of the thread pool creates the waitable timer so that it queues APC entries rather than signaling the object. This means that the operating system queues APC entries continuously, and timer events are never lost. So setting a periodic timer guarantees that your work item is queued at every interval. If you create a periodic timer that fires every 10 seconds, your callback function is called every 10 seconds. Be aware that this will happen using multiple threads; you might have to synchronize portions of your work item function.

If you don't like this behavior and would prefer that your work items be queued 10 seconds after each one executes, you should create one-shot timers at the end of your work item function. Or you can create a single timer with a high timeout value and call *ChangeTimerQueueTimer* at the end of the work item function.

The TimedMsgBox Sample Application

The TimedMsgBox application ("11 TimedMsgBox.exe"), listed in Figure 11-1 on page 409, shows how to use the thread pool's timer functions to implement a message box that automatically closes if the user doesn't respond within a certain amount of time. The source code and resource files for the application are in the 11-TimedMsgBox directory on the book's companion CD-ROM.

When you start the program, it sets a global variable, *g_nSecLeft*, to 10. This indicates the number of seconds that the user has to respond to the message box. Then *CreateTimerQueueTimer* is called, instructing the thread pool to call the *MsgBoxTimeout* function every second. Once everything has been initialized, *MessageBox* is called and presents the following message box to the user.

```
Timed Message Box          [X]

You have 10 seconds to respond

        [     OK     ]
```

While waiting for the user to respond, the *MsgBoxTimeout* function is called by a thread pool thread. This function finds the window handle for the message box, decrements the global *g_nSecLeft* variable, and updates the string in the message box. After *MsgBoxTimeout* has been called the first time, the message box looks like this.

```
Timed Message Box          [X]

You have 9 seconds to respond

        [     OK     ]
```

When *MsgBoxTimeout* is called for the tenth time, the *g_nSecLeft* variable becomes 0 and *MsgBoxTimeout* calls *EndDialog* to destroy the message box. The primary thread's call to *MessageBox* returns, *DeleteTimerQueueTimer* is called to tell the thread pool to stop calling the *MsgBoxTimeout* function, and another message box appears, telling the user that he or she didn't respond to the first message box in the allotted period.

```
Result        [X]

Timeout

  [    OK    ]
```

If the user does respond before the time runs out, the following message box appears.

```
Result        [X]

User responded

  [    OK    ]
```

TimedMsgBox.cpp

```
/******************************************************************************
Module:  TimedMsgBox.cpp
Notices: Copyright (c) 2000 Jeffrey Richter
******************************************************************************/


#include "..\CmnHdr.h"      /* See Appendix A. */
#include <tchar.h>


///////////////////////////////////////////////////////////////////////////


// The caption of our message box
TCHAR g_szCaption[] = TEXT("Timed Message Box");


// How many seconds we'll display the message box
int g_nSecLeft = 0;


// This is STATIC window control ID for a message box
#define ID_MSGBOX_STATIC_TEXT    0x0000ffff


///////////////////////////////////////////////////////////////////////////


VOID WINAPI MsgBoxTimeout(PVOID pvContext, BOOLEAN fTimeout) {

   // NOTE: Due to a thread race condition, it is possible (but very unlikely)
   // that the message box will not be created when we get here.
   HWND hwnd = FindWindow(NULL, g_szCaption);

   if (hwnd != NULL) {
      // The window does exist; update the time remaining.
      TCHAR sz[100];
      wsprintf(sz, TEXT("You have %d seconds to respond"), g_nSecLeft--);
      SetDlgItemText(hwnd, ID_MSGBOX_STATIC_TEXT, sz);
```

Figure 11-1. *(continued)*
The TimedMsgBox sample application

Figure 11-1. *continued*

```
        if (g_nSecLeft == 0) {
            // The time is up; force the message box to exit.
            EndDialog(hwnd, IDOK);
        }
    } else {

        // The window does not exist yet; do nothing this time.
        // We'll try again in another second.
    }
}


///////////////////////////////////////////////////////////////////////////


int WINAPI _tWinMain(HINSTANCE hinstExe, HINSTANCE, PTSTR pszCmdLine, int) {

    chWindows9xNotAllowed();

    // How many seconds we'll give the user to respond
    g_nSecLeft = 10;

    // Create a multishot 1-second timer that begins firing after 1 second.
    HANDLE hTimerQTimer;
    CreateTimerQueueTimer(&hTimerQTimer, NULL, MsgBoxTimeout, NULL,
        1000, 1000, 0);

    // Display the message box.
    MessageBox(NULL, TEXT("You have 10 seconds to respond"),
        g_szCaption, MB_OK);

    // Cancel the timer & delete the timer queue
    DeleteTimerQueueTimer(NULL, hTimerQTimer, NULL);

    // Let us know if the user responded or if we timed out.
    MessageBox(NULL,
        (g_nSecLeft == 0) ? TEXT("Timeout") : TEXT("User responded"),
            TEXT("Result"), MB_OK);

    return(0);
}


///////////////////////////////// End of File /////////////////////////////////
```

(continued)

Figure 11-1. *continued*

TimedMsgBox.rc

```
//Microsoft Developer Studio generated resource script.
//
#include "resource.h"

#define APSTUDIO_READONLY_SYMBOLS
/////////////////////////////////////////////////////////////////////////////
//
// Generated from the TEXTINCLUDE 2 resource.
//
#include "afxres.h"


/////////////////////////////////////////////////////////////////////////////
#undef APSTUDIO_READONLY_SYMBOLS


/////////////////////////////////////////////////////////////////////////////
// English (U.S.) resources

#if !defined(AFX_RESOURCE_DLL) || defined(AFX_TARG_ENU)
#ifdef _WIN32
LANGUAGE LANG_ENGLISH, SUBLANG_ENGLISH_US
#pragma code_page(1252)
#endif //_WIN32


/////////////////////////////////////////////////////////////////////////////
//
// Icon
//

// Icon with lowest ID value placed first to ensure application icon
// remains consistent on all systems.
IDI_TIMEDMSGBOX         ICON    DISCARDABLE     "TimedMsgBox.ico"


#ifdef APSTUDIO_INVOKED
/////////////////////////////////////////////////////////////////////////////
//
// TEXTINCLUDE
//

1 TEXTINCLUDE DISCARDABLE
BEGIN
    "resource.h\0"
END
```

(continued)

Figure 11-1. *continued*

```
2 TEXTINCLUDE DISCARDABLE
BEGIN
    "#include ""afxres.h""\r\n"
    "\0"
END

3 TEXTINCLUDE DISCARDABLE
BEGIN
    "\r\n"
    "\0"
END

#endif    // APSTUDIO_INVOKED

#endif    // English (U.S.) resources
/////////////////////////////////////////////////////////////////////////////


#ifndef APSTUDIO_INVOKED
/////////////////////////////////////////////////////////////////////////////
//
// Generated from the TEXTINCLUDE 3 resource.
//


/////////////////////////////////////////////////////////////////////////////
#endif    // not APSTUDIO_INVOKED
```

Scenario 3: Call Functions When Single Kernel Objects Become Signaled

Microsoft discovered that many applications spawn threads simply to wait for a kernel object to become signaled. Once the object is signaled, the thread posts some sort of notification to another thread and then loops back, waiting for the object to signal again. Some developers even write code in which several threads each wait on a single object. This is incredibly wasteful of system resources. Sure, there is a lot less overhead involved in creating threads compared with creating processes, but threads are not free. Each thread has a stack, and a lot of CPU instructions are required to create and destroy threads. You should always try to minimize this.

If you want to register a work item to be executed when a kernel object is signaled, you can use another new thread pooling function:

```
BOOL RegisterWaitForSingleObject(
    PHANDLE phNewWaitObject,
    HANDLE hObject,
    WAITORTIMERCALLBACK pfnCallback,
    PVOID pvContext,
    ULONG dwMilliseconds,
    ULONG dwFlags);
```

This function communicates your parameters to the wait component of the thread pool. You tell this component that you want a work item queued when the kernel object (identified by *hObject*) is signaled. You can also pass a timeout value so that the work item is queued in a certain amount of time even if the kernel object does not become signaled. Timeout values of 0 and INFINITE are legal. Basically, this function works like the familiar *WaitForSingleObject* function (discussed in Chapter 9). After registering a wait, this function returns a handle (via the *phNewWaitObject* parameter) that identifies the wait.

Internally, the wait component uses *WaitForMultipleObjects* to wait for the registered objects and is bound by any limitations that already exist for this function. One such limitation is the inability to wait for a single handle multiple times. So if you want to register a single object multiple times, you must call *DuplicateHandle* and register the original handle and the duplicated handle individually. Of course, *WaitForMultipleObjects* waits for any one of the objects to be signaled, not for all of the objects. If you're familiar with *WaitForMultipleObjects*, you know that it can wait on at most 64 (MAXIMUM_WAIT_OBJECTS) objects at a time. So what happens if you register more than 64 objects with *RegisterWaitForSingleObject*? The wait component adds another thread that also calls *WaitForMultipleObjects*. In reality, after every 63 objects, another thread must be added to this component because the threads need to also wait on a waitable timer object that controls the timeouts.

When the work item is ready to be executed, it is queued to the non-I/O component's threads by default. One of those threads will eventually wake up and call your function, which must have the following prototype:

```
VOID WINAPI WaitOrTimerCallbackFunc(
    PVOID pvContext,
    BOOLEAN fTimerOrWaitFired);
```

The *fTimerOrWaitFired* parameter is TRUE if the wait timed out and FALSE if the object became signaled while waiting.

For *RegisterWaitForSingleObject*'s *dwFlags* parameter, you can pass WT_EXECUTEINWAITTHREAD, which causes one of the wait component's threads to execute the work item function itself. This is more efficient because the work item doesn't have to be queued to the non-I/O component. But it is dangerous because the wait component's thread that is executing your work item function can't wait for other objects to be signaled. You should use this flag only if your work item function executes quickly.

You can also pass WT_EXECUTEINIOTHREAD or WT_EXECUTEIN-PERSISTENTTHREAD if your work item will issue an asynchronous I/O request or perform some operation using a thread that never terminates, respectively. You can also use the WT_EXECUTELONGFUNCTION flag to tell the thread pool that your function might take a long time to execute and that it should consider adding a new thread to the pool. You can use this flag only if the work item is being posted to the non-I/O or I/O components; you should not execute a long function using a wait component's thread.

The last flag that you should be aware of is WT_EXECUTEONLYONCE. Let's say that you register a wait on a process kernel object. Once that process object becomes signaled, it stays signaled. This causes the wait component to continuously queue work items. For a process object, you probably do not want this behavior; you can prevent it by using the WT_EXECUTEONLYONCE flag, which tells the wait component to stop waiting on the object after its work item has executed once.

Now let's say that you're waiting on an auto-reset event kernel object. Once this object becomes signaled, the object is reset to its nonsignaled state and its work item is queued. At this point, the object is still registered, and the wait component waits again for the object to be signaled or for the timeout (which got reset) to expire. When you no longer want the wait component to wait on your registered object, you must unregister it. This is the case even for waits registered with the WT_EXECUTEONLYONCE flag that have queued work items. You unregister a wait by calling this function:

```
BOOL UnregisterWaitEx(
    HANDLE hWaitHandle,
    HANDLE hCompletionEvent);
```

The first parameter indicates a registered wait (as returned from *RegisterWaitForSingleObject*), and the second parameter indicates how you want to be notified when all queued work items for the registered wait have executed. As with the *DeleteTimerQueueTimer* function, you can pass NULL (if you don't want a notification), INVALID_HANDLE_VALUE (to block the call until all queued work items have executed), or the handle of an event object (which gets signaled when the queued work items have executed). For a nonblocking call, if there are no queued work items, *UnregisterWaitEx* returns TRUE; otherwise, it returns FALSE and *GetLastError* returns STATUS_PENDING.

Again, you must be careful to avoid deadlocks when you pass INVALID_HANDLE_VALUE to *UnregisterWaitEx*. A work item function shouldn't block itself while attempting to unregister the wait that caused the work item to execute. This is like saying: suspend my execution until I'm done executing—

deadlock. However, *UnregisterWaitEx* is designed to avoid deadlocking if a wait component's thread executes a work item and the work item unregisters the wait that caused the work item to execute. One more thing: do not close the kernel object's handle until the wait is unregistered. This makes the handle invalid, and the wait component's thread then internally calls *WaitForMultipleObjects*, passing an invalid handle. *WaitForMultipleObjects* always fails immediately, and the entire wait component will not function properly.

Finally, you should not call *PulseEvent* to signal a registered event object. If you do, the wait component's thread will probably be busy doing something and the pulse will be missed. This problem should not be new to you; *PulseEvent* exhibits this problem with almost all threading architectures.

Scenario 4: Call Functions When Asynchronous I/O Requests Complete

The last scenario is a common one: your server application issues some asynchronous I/O requests. When these requests complete, you want to have a pool of threads ready to process the completed I/O requests. This is the architecture that I/O completion ports were originally designed for. If you were managing your own thread pool, you would create an I/O completion port and create a pool of threads that wait on this port. You would also open a bunch of I/O devices and associate their handles with the completion port. As asynchronous I/O requests complete, the device drivers would queue the "work items" to the completion port.

This is a great architecture that allows for a few threads to efficiently handle several work items, and it's fantastic that the thread pooling functions have this built in, saving you a lot of time and effort. To take advantage of this architecture, all you have to do is open your device and associate it with the non-I/O component of the thread pool. Remember that the non-I/O component's threads all wait on an I/O completion port. To associate a device with this component, you call this function:

```
BOOL BindIoCompletionCallback(
   HANDLE hDevice,
   POVERLAPPED_COMPLETION_ROUTINE pfnCallback,
   ULONG dwFlags);
```

Internally, this function calls *CreateIoCompletionPort*, passing it *hDevice* and the handle of the internal completion port. Calling *BindIoCompletion-Callback* also guarantees that at least one thread is always in the non-I/O component. The completion key associated with this device is the address of the overlapped completion routine. This way, when I/O to this device completes, the non-I/O component knows which function to call so that it can process the

415

completed I/O request. The completion routine must have the following prototype:

```
VOID WINAPI OverlappedCompletionRoutine(
    DWORD dwErrorCode,
    DWORD dwNumberOfBytesTransferred,
    POVERLAPPED pOverlapped);
```

You'll notice that you do not pass an OVERLAPPED structure to *BindIo-CompletionCallback*. The OVERLAPPED structure is passed to functions such as *ReadFile* and *WriteFile*. The system keeps track of this overlapped structure internally with the pending I/O request. When the request completes, the system places the address of the structure in the completion port so that it can be passed to your *OverlappedCompletionRoutine*. Also, because the address of the completion routine is the completion key, to get additional context information into the *OverlappedCompletionRoutine* function, you should use the traditional trick of placing the context information at the end of the OVER-LAPPED structure.

You should also be aware that closing a device causes all of its pending I/O requests to complete immediately with an error code. Be prepared to handle this in your callback function. If, after closing the device, you want to make sure that no callbacks are executed, you must do reference counting in your application. In other words, you must increment a counter every time you issue an I/O request and decrement the counter each time an I/O request completes.

Currently, there are no special flags that you can pass to *BindIoCompletion-Callback*'s *dwFlags* parameter, so you must pass 0. I believe that one flag you should be able to pass is WT_EXECUTEINIOTHREAD. If an I/O request completes, this gets queued to a non-I/O component thread. In your *Overlapped-CompletionRoutine* function, you'll probably issue another asynchronous I/O request. But remember that if a thread that issues I/O requests terminates, the I/O requests are also destroyed. Also, the threads in the non-I/O component are created or destroyed depending on the workload. If the workload is low, a thread in this component might terminate with outstanding I/O requests pending. If *BindIoCompletionCallback* supported the WT_EXECUTEINIO-THREAD flag, a thread waiting on the completion port would wake up and post the result to an I/O component thread. Since these threads never die if any I/O requests are pending, you could issue I/O requests without the fear of them being destroyed.

While the WT_EXECUTEINIOTHREAD flag would be nice, you can easily emulate the behavior I just described. In your *OverlappedCompletion-Routine* function, you simply call *QueueUserWorkItem*, passing the WT_EXECUTEINIOTHREAD flag and whatever data you need (at least the overlapped structure, probably). This is all that the thread pooling functions would do for you anyway.

C H A P T E R   T W E L V E

FIBERS

Microsoft added fibers to Windows to make it easy to port existing UNIX server applications to Windows. UNIX server applications are single-threaded (by the Windows definition) but can serve multiple clients. In other words, the developers of UNIX applications have created their own threading architecture library, which they use to simulate pure threads. This threading package creates multiple stacks, saves certain CPU registers, and switches among them to service the client requests.

Obviously, to get the best performance, these UNIX applications must be redesigned; the simulated threading library should be replaced with the pure threads offered by Windows. However, this redesign can take several months or longer to complete, so companies are first porting their existing UNIX code to Windows so they can ship something to the Windows market.

Problems can arise when you port UNIX code to Windows. In particular, the way in which Windows manages a thread stack is much more complex than simply allocating memory. Windows stacks start out with relatively little physical storage and grow as necessary. This process is described in the section titled "A Thread's Stack" in Chapter 16. Porting is also complicated by the structured exception handling mechanism (described in Chapters 23, 24, and 25).

To help companies port their code more quickly and correctly to Windows, Microsoft added fibers to the operating system. In this chapter, we'll examine the concept of a fiber, the functions that manipulate fibers, and how to take advantage of fibers. Keep in mind, of course, that you should avoid fibers in favor of more properly designed applications that use Windows native threads.

Working with Fibers

The first thing to note is that the Windows kernel implements threads. The operating system has intimate knowledge of threads and schedules them according to the algorithm defined by Microsoft. A fiber is implemented in user-mode code; the kernel does not have knowledge of fibers, and they are scheduled according to the algorithm you define. Because you define the fiber-scheduling algorithm, fibers are nonpreemptively scheduled as far as the kernel is concerned.

The next thing to be aware of is that a single thread can contain one or more fibers. As far as the kernel is concerned, a thread is preemptively scheduled and is executing code. However, the thread executes one fiber's code at a time—you decide which fiber. (These concepts will become clearer as we go on.)

The first step you must perform when you use fibers is to turn your existing thread into a fiber. You do this by calling *ConvertThreadToFiber*:

```
PVOID ConvertThreadToFiber(PVOID pvParam);
```

This function allocates memory (about 200 bytes) for the fiber's execution context. This execution context consists of the following elements:

- A user-defined value that is initialized to the value passed to *ConvertThreadToFiber*'s *pvParam* argument

- The head of a structured exception handling chain

- The top and bottom memory addresses of the fiber's stack (When you convert a thread to a fiber, this is also the thread's stack.)

- Various CPU registers, including a stack pointer, an instruction pointer, and others

After you allocate and initialize the fiber execution context, you associate the address of the execution context with the thread. The thread has been converted to a fiber, and the fiber is running on this thread. *ConvertThreadToFiber* actually returns the memory address of the fiber's execution context. You need to use this address later, but you should never read from or write to the execution context data yourself—the fiber functions manipulate the contents of the structure for you when necessary. Now if your fiber (thread) returns or calls *ExitThread*, the fiber and thread both die.

There is no reason to convert a thread to a fiber unless you plan to create additional fibers to run on the same thread. To create another fiber, the thread (currently running fiber) calls *CreateFiber*:

```
PVOID CreateFiber(
   DWORD dwStackSize,
   PFIBER_START_ROUTINE pfnStartAddress,
   PVOID pvParam);
```

CreateFiber first attempts to create a new stack whose size is indicated by the *dwStackSize* parameter. Usually 0 is passed, which, by default, creates a stack that can grow to 1 MB in size but initially has two pages of storage committed to it. If you specify a nonzero size, a stack is reserved and committed using the specified size.

Next, *CreateFiber* allocates a new fiber execution context structure and initializes it. The user-defined value is set to the value passed to *CreateFiber*'s *pvParam*, the top and bottom memory addresses of the new stack are saved, and the memory address of the fiber function (passed as the *pfnStartAddress* argument) is saved.

The *pfnStartAddress* argument specifies the address of a fiber routine that you must implement and that must have the following prototype:

```
VOID WINAPI FiberFunc(PVOID pvParam);
```

When the fiber is scheduled for the first time, this function executes and is passed the *pvParam* value that was originally passed to *CreateFiber*. You can do whatever you like in this fiber function. However, the function is prototyped as returning VOID—not because the return value has no meaning, but because this function should never return at all! If a fiber function does return, the thread and all the fibers created on it are destroyed immediately.

Like *ConvertThreadToFiber*, *CreateFiber* returns the memory address of the fiber's execution context. However, unlike *ConvertThreadToFiber*, this new fiber does not execute because the currently running fiber is still executing. Only one fiber at a time can execute on a single thread. To make the new fiber execute, you call *SwitchToFiber*:

```
VOID SwitchToFiber(PVOID pvFiberExecutionContext);
```

SwitchToFiber takes a single parameter, *pvFiberExecutionContext*, which is the memory address of a fiber's execution context as returned by a previous call to *ConvertThreadToFiber* or *CreateFiber*. This memory address tells the function which fiber to schedule. Internally, *SwitchToFiber* performs the following steps:

1. It saves some of the current CPU registers, including the instruction pointer register and the stack pointer register, in the currently running fiber's execution context.

2. It loads the registers previously saved in the soon-to-be-running fiber's execution context into the CPU registers. These registers include the stack pointer register so that this fiber's stack is used when the thread continues execution.

3. It associates the fiber's execution context with the thread; the thread runs the specified fiber.

4. It sets the thread's instruction pointer to the saved instruction pointer. The thread (fiber) continues execution where this fiber last executed.

SwitchToFiber is the only way for a fiber to get any CPU time. Because your code must explicitly call *SwitchToFiber* at the appropriate times, you are in complete control of the fiber scheduling. Keep in mind that fiber scheduling has nothing to do with thread scheduling. The thread that the fibers run on can always be preempted by the operating system. When the thread is scheduled, the currently selected fiber runs—no other fiber runs unless *SwitchToFiber* is explicitly called.

To destroy a fiber, you call *DeleteFiber*:

```
VOID DeleteFiber(PVOID pvFiberExecutionContext);
```

This function deletes the fiber indicated by the *pvFiberExecutionContext* parameter, which is, of course, the address of a fiber's execution context. This function frees the memory used by the fiber's stack and then destroys the fiber's execution context. But if you pass the address of the fiber that is currently associated with the thread, the function calls *ExitThread* internally, which causes the thread and all the fibers created on the thread to die.

DeleteFiber is usually called by one fiber to delete another. The deleted fiber's stack is destroyed, and the fiber's execution context is freed. Notice the difference here between fibers and threads: threads usually kill themselves by calling *ExitThread*. In fact, it is considered bad form for one thread to terminate another thread using *TerminateThread*. If you do call *TerminateThread*, the system does not destroy the terminated thread's stack. We can take advantage of this ability of a fiber to cleanly delete another fiber—I'll discuss how when I explain the sample application later in this chapter.

Two additional fiber functions are provided for your convenience. A thread can execute a single fiber at a time, and the operating system always knows which fiber is currently associated with the thread. If you want to get the address of the currently running fiber's execution context, you can call *GetCurrentFiber*:

```
PVOID GetCurrentFiber();
```

The other convenience function is *GetFiberData*:

```
PVOID GetFiberData();
```

As I've mentioned, each fiber's execution context contains a user-defined value. This value is initialized with the value that is passed as the *pvParam* argument to *ConvertThreadToFiber* or *CreateFiber*. This value is also passed as an argument to a fiber function. *GetFiberData* simply looks in the currently executing fiber's execution context and returns the saved value.

Both *GetCurrentFiber* and *GetFiberData* are fast and are usually implemented as intrinsic functions, which means that the compiler generates the code for these functions inline.

The Counter Sample Application

The Counter application ("12 Counter.exe") in Figure 12-1 uses fibers to implement background processing. When you run the application, the dialog box below appears. (I recommend that you run the application to really understand what's happening and to see the behavior as you read along.)

You can think of this application as a superminiature spreadsheet consisting of two cells. The first cell is a writable cell implemented as an edit control (labeled Count To), and the second cell is a read-only cell implemented as a static control (labeled Answer). When you change the number in the edit control, the Answer cell automatically recalculates. For this simple application, the recalculation is a counter that starts at 0 and increments slowly until the value in the Answer cell becomes the same value as the entered number. For demonstration purposes, the static control at the bottom of the dialog box updates to indicate which fiber is currently executing. This fiber can be either the user interface fiber or the recalculation fiber.

To test the application, type 5 in the edit control. The Currently Running Fiber field changes to Recalculation, and the number in the Answer field slowly increments from 0 to 5. When the counting is finished, the Currently Running Fiber field changes back to User Interface and the thread goes to sleep. Now, in the edit control, type 0 after the 5 (making 50) and watch the counting start over from 0 and go to 50. But this time, while the Answer field increments, move the window on the screen. You'll notice that the recalculation fiber is preempted and that the user interface fiber is rescheduled so that the application's user interface stays responsive to the user. When you stop moving the window, the recalculation fiber is rescheduled and the Answer field continues counting from where it left off.

One last thing to test: while the recalculation fiber is counting, change the number in the edit control. Again, notice that the user interface is responsive to your input—but also that when you stop typing, the recalculation fiber starts counting from the beginning. This is exactly the kind of behavior that you want in a full-blown spreadsheet application.

Keep in mind that no critical sections or other thread synchronization objects are used in this application—everything is done using a single thread consisting of two fibers.

Let's discuss how this application is implemented. When the process's primary thread starts by executing _*tWinMain* (at the end of the listing), *ConvertThreadToFiber* is called to turn the thread into a fiber and to allow us to create another fiber later. Then a modeless dialog box is created, which is the application's main window. Next, a state variable is initialized to indicate the background processing state (BPS). This state variable is the *bps* member contained in the global *g_FiberInfo* variable. Three states are possible, as described in the following table.

State	Description
BPS_DONE	The recalculation ran to completion, and the user has not changed anything that would require a recalculation.
BPS_STARTOVER	The user has changed something that requires a recalculation to start from the beginning.
BPS_CONTINUE	The recalculation was started but has not finished. Also, the user has not changed anything that would require the recalculation to start over from the beginning.

The background processing state variable is examined in the thread's message loop, which is more complicated than a normal message loop. Here is what the message loop does:

- If a window message exists (the user interface is active), it processes the message. Keeping the user interface responsive is always a higher priority than recalculating values.

- If the user interface has nothing to do, it checks to see whether any recalculations need to be performed. (The background processing state is BPS_STARTOVER or BPS_CONTINUE.)

- If there are no recalculations to do (BPS_DONE), it suspends the thread by calling *WaitMessage*; only a user interface event can cause a recalculation to be required.

If the user interface fiber has nothing to do and the user has just changed the value in the edit control, we need to start the recalculation over from the beginning (BPS_STARTOVER). The first thing to realize is that we might already have a recalculation fiber running. If this is the case, we must delete the fiber and create a new fiber that will start counting from the beginning. The user interface fiber calls *DeleteFiber* to destroy the existing recalculation fiber. This is where fibers (as opposed to threads) come in handy. Deleting the recalculation fiber is perfectly OK: the fiber's stack and execution context are completely and cleanly destroyed. If we were to use threads instead of fibers, the user interface thread would not destroy the recalculation thread cleanly—we'd have to use some form of interthread communication and wait for the recalculation thread to die on its own. Once we know that no recalculation fiber exists, we can create a new recalculation fiber and set the background processing state to BPS_CONTINUE.

When the user interface is idle and the recalculation fiber has something to do, we schedule it time by calling *SwitchToFiber*. *SwitchToFiber* does not return until the recalculation fiber calls *SwitchToFiber* again, passing the address of the user interface fiber's execution context.

The *FiberFunc* function contains the code executed by the recalculation fiber. This fiber function is passed the address of the global *g_FiberInfo* structure so that it knows the handle of the dialog box window, the address of the user interface fiber's execution context, and the current background processing state. The address of this structure need not be passed since it is in a global variable, but I wanted to demonstrate how to pass arguments to fiber functions. Besides, passing the address places fewer dependencies on the code, which is always good practice.

The fiber function first updates the status control in the dialog box to indicate that the recalculation fiber is executing. Then it gets the number in the edit control and enters a loop that starts counting from 0 to the number. Each time the number is about to be incremented, *GetQueueStatus* is called to see whether any messages have shown up in the thread's message queue. (All fibers running on a single thread share the thread's message queue.) When a message shows up, the user interface fiber has something to do; because we want it to take priority over the recalculations, *SwitchToFiber* is called immediately so the user interface fiber can process the message. After the message has been processed, the user interface fiber reschedules the recalculation fiber (as described earlier) and the background processing continues.

When there are no messages to be processed, the recalculation fiber updates the Answer field in the dialog box and then sleeps for 200 milliseconds. In production code, you should remove the call to *Sleep*; I include it here to exaggerate the time required to perform the recalculation.

When the Recalculation fiber finishes calculating the answer, the background processing state variable is set to BPS_DONE and a call to *SwitchToFiber* reschedules the user interface fiber. At this point, if the user interface fiber has nothing to do, it calls *WaitMessage*, suspending the thread so that no CPU time is wasted.

Counter.cpp

```
/****************************************************************************
Module:  Counter.cpp
Notices: Copyright (c) 2000 Jeffrey Richter
****************************************************************************/


#include "..\CmnHdr.h"      /* See Appendix A. */
#include <WindowsX.h>
#include <tchar.h>
#include "Resource.h"



///////////////////////////////////////////////////////////////////////////


// The possible state of the background processing
typedef enum {
   BPS_STARTOVER,  // Start the background processing from the beginning.
   BPS_CONTINUE,   // Continue the background processing.
   BPS_DONE        // There is no background processing to do.
} BKGNDPROCSTATE;


typedef struct {
   PVOID pFiberUI;       // User interface fiber execution context
   HWND  hwnd;           // Handle of main UI window
   BKGNDPROCSTATE bps;   // State of background processing
} FIBERINFO, *PFIBERINFO;


// A global that contains application state information. This
// global is accessed directly by the UI fiber and indirectly
// by the background processing fiber.
FIBERINFO g_FiberInfo;



///////////////////////////////////////////////////////////////////////////


void WINAPI FiberFunc(PVOID pvParam) {
```

Figure 12-1.
The Counter sample application

(continued)

Figure 12-1. *continued*

```
    PFIBERINFO pFiberInfo = (PFIBERINFO) pvParam;

    // Update the window showing which fiber is executing.
    SetDlgItemText(pFiberInfo->hwnd, IDC_FIBER, TEXT("Recalculation"));

    // Get the current count in the EDIT control.
    int nCount = GetDlgItemInt(pFiberInfo->hwnd, IDC_COUNT, NULL, FALSE);

    // Count from 0 to nCount, updating the STATIC control.
    for (int x = 0; x <= nCount; x++) {

        // UI events have higher priority than counting.
        // If there are any UI events, handle them ASAP.
        if (HIWORD(GetQueueStatus(QS_ALLEVENTS)) != 0) {

            // The UI fiber has something to do; temporarily
            // pause counting and handle the UI events.
            SwitchToFiber(pFiberInfo->pFiberUI);

            // The UI has no more events; continue counting.
            SetDlgItemText(pFiberInfo->hwnd, IDC_FIBER, TEXT("Recalculation"));
        }

        // Update the STATIC control with the most recent count.
        SetDlgItemInt(pFiberInfo->hwnd, IDC_ANSWER, x, FALSE);

        // Sleep for a while to exaggerate the effect; remove
        // the call to Sleep in production code.
        Sleep(200);
    }

    // Indicate that counting is complete.
    pFiberInfo->bps = BPS_DONE;

    // Reschedule the UI thread. When the UI thread is running
    // and has no events to process, the thread is put to sleep.
    // NOTE: If we just allow the fiber function to return,
    // the thread and the UI fiber die -- we don't want this!
    SwitchToFiber(pFiberInfo->pFiberUI);
}


///////////////////////////////////////////////////////////////////////////
```

(continued)

Figure 12-1. *continued*

```
BOOL Dlg_OnInitDialog(HWND hwnd, HWND hwndFocus, LPARAM lParam) {

   chSETDLGICONS(hwnd, IDI_COUNTER);

   SetDlgItemInt(hwnd, IDC_COUNT, 0, FALSE);
   return(TRUE);
}



///////////////////////////////////////////////////////////////////////////


void Dlg_OnCommand(HWND hwnd, int id, HWND hwndCtl, UINT codeNotify) {

   switch (id) {
      case IDCANCEL:
         PostQuitMessage(0);
         break;

      case IDC_COUNT:
         if (codeNotify == EN_CHANGE) {

            // When the user changes the count, start the
            // background processing over from the beginning.
            g_FiberInfo.bps = BPS_STARTOVER;
         }
         break;
   }
}



///////////////////////////////////////////////////////////////////////////


INT_PTR WINAPI Dlg_Proc(HWND hwnd, UINT uMsg, WPARAM wParam, LPARAM lParam) {

   switch (uMsg) {
      chHANDLE_DLGMSG(hwnd, WM_INITDIALOG, Dlg_OnInitDialog);
      chHANDLE_DLGMSG(hwnd, WM_COMMAND,    Dlg_OnCommand);
   }
   return(FALSE);
}


///////////////////////////////////////////////////////////////////////////
```

(continued)

Figure 12-1. *continued*

```
int WINAPI _tWinMain(HINSTANCE hinstExe, HINSTANCE, PTSTR pszCmdLine, int) {

   // Counter fiber execution context
   PVOID pFiberCounter = NULL;

   // Convert this thread to a fiber.
   g_FiberInfo.pFiberUI = ConvertThreadToFiber(NULL);

   // Create the application's UI window.
   g_FiberInfo.hwnd = CreateDialog(hinstExe, MAKEINTRESOURCE(IDD_COUNTER),
      NULL, Dlg_Proc);

   // Update the window showing which fiber is executing.
   SetDlgItemText(g_FiberInfo.hwnd, IDC_FIBER, TEXT("User interface"));

   // Initially, there is no background processing to be done.
   g_FiberInfo.bps = BPS_DONE;

   // While the UI window still exists...
   BOOL fQuit = FALSE;
   while (!fQuit) {

      // UI messages are higher priority than background processing.
      MSG msg;
      if (PeekMessage(&msg, NULL, 0, 0, PM_REMOVE)) {

         // If a message exists in the queue, process it.
         fQuit = (msg.message == WM_QUIT);
         if (!IsDialogMessage(g_FiberInfo.hwnd, &msg)) {
            TranslateMessage(&msg);
            DispatchMessage(&msg);
         }

      } else {

         // No UI msgs exist; check the state of the background processing.
         switch (g_FiberInfo.bps) {
            case BPS_DONE:
               // No background processing to do; wait for a UI event.
               WaitMessage();
               break;

            case BPS_STARTOVER:
               // User changed the count; restart the background processing.
```

(continued)

Figure 12-1. *continued*

```
            if (pFiberCounter != NULL) {
                // A recalculation fiber exists; delete it so that
                // background processing starts over from the beginning.
                DeleteFiber(pFiberCounter);
                pFiberCounter = NULL;
            }

            // Create a new recalc fiber that starts from the beginning.
            pFiberCounter = CreateFiber(0, FiberFunc, &g_FiberInfo);

            // The background processing started; it should continue.
            g_FiberInfo.bps = BPS_CONTINUE;

            // Fall through to BPS_CONTINUE case...

        case BPS_CONTINUE:
            // Allow the background processing to execute...
            SwitchToFiber(pFiberCounter);

            // The background processing has been paused
            // (because a UI message showed up) or has been
            // stopped (because the counting has completed).

            // Update the window showing which fiber is executing.
            SetDlgItemText(g_FiberInfo.hwnd, IDC_FIBER,
                TEXT("User interface"));

            if (g_FiberInfo.bps == BPS_DONE) {
                // The background processing ran to completion. Delete the
                // fiber so that processing will restart next time.
                DeleteFiber(pFiberCounter);
                pFiberCounter = NULL;
            }
            break;
        } // switch on background processing state

    } // No UI messages exist
  } // while the window still exists
  DestroyWindow(g_FiberInfo.hwnd);

  return(0); // End the application.
}


/////////////////////////////// End of File ///////////////////////////////////
```

(continued)

Figure 12-1. *continued*

Counter.rc

```
//Microsoft Developer Studio generated resource script.
//
#include "resource.h"

#define APSTUDIO_READONLY_SYMBOLS
/////////////////////////////////////////////////////////////////////////////
//
// Generated from the TEXTINCLUDE 2 resource.
//
#include "afxres.h"


/////////////////////////////////////////////////////////////////////////////
#undef APSTUDIO_READONLY_SYMBOLS


/////////////////////////////////////////////////////////////////////////////
// English (U.S.) resources

#if !defined(AFX_RESOURCE_DLL) || defined(AFX_TARG_ENU)
#ifdef _WIN32
LANGUAGE LANG_ENGLISH, SUBLANG_ENGLISH_US
#pragma code_page(1252)
#endif //_WIN32


/////////////////////////////////////////////////////////////////////////////
//
// Dialog
//

IDD_COUNTER DIALOG DISCARDABLE  0, 0, 156, 37
STYLE DS_3DLOOK | DS_CENTER | WS_MINIMIZEBOX | WS_VISIBLE | WS_CAPTION |
    WS_SYSMENU
CAPTION "Counter"
FONT 8, "MS Sans Serif"
BEGIN
    LTEXT           "Count to:",IDC_STATIC,4,6,34,8
    EDITTEXT        IDC_COUNT,38,4,40,14,ES_AUTOHSCROLL | ES_NUMBER
    LTEXT           "Answer:",IDC_STATIC,90,6,25,8
    RTEXT           "0",IDC_ANSWER,122,6,23,8
    LTEXT           "Currently running fiber:",IDC_STATIC,4,24,75,8
    LTEXT           "Fiber",IDC_FIBER,80,24,72,8
END
```

(continued)

Figure 12-1. *continued*

```
///////////////////////////////////////////////////////////////////////////////////
//
// DESIGNINFO
//

#ifdef APSTUDIO_INVOKED
GUIDELINES DESIGNINFO DISCARDABLE
BEGIN
    IDD_COUNTER, DIALOG
    BEGIN
        LEFTMARGIN, 7
        RIGHTMARGIN, 149
        TOPMARGIN, 7
        BOTTOMMARGIN, 30
    END
END
#endif    // APSTUDIO_INVOKED


#ifdef APSTUDIO_INVOKED
///////////////////////////////////////////////////////////////////////////////////
//
// TEXTINCLUDE
//

1 TEXTINCLUDE DISCARDABLE
BEGIN
    "resource.h\0"
END

2 TEXTINCLUDE DISCARDABLE
BEGIN
    "#include ""afxres.h""\r\n"
    "\0"
END

3 TEXTINCLUDE DISCARDABLE
BEGIN
    "\r\n"
    "\0"
END

#endif    // APSTUDIO_INVOKED
```

(continued)

Figure 12-1. *continued*

```
//////////////////////////////////////////////////////////////////////////
//
// Icon
//

// Icon with lowest ID value placed first to ensure application icon
// remains consistent on all systems.
IDI_COUNTER             ICON    DISCARDABLE     "Counter.ico"
#endif    // English (U.S.) resources
//////////////////////////////////////////////////////////////////////////


#ifndef APSTUDIO_INVOKED
//////////////////////////////////////////////////////////////////////////
//
// Generated from the TEXTINCLUDE 3 resource.
//


//////////////////////////////////////////////////////////////////////////
#endif    // not APSTUDIO_INVOKED
```

MEMORY
MANAGEMENT

CHAPTER THIRTEEN

WINDOWS MEMORY ARCHITECTURE

The memory architecture used by an operating system is the most important key to understanding how the operating system does what it does. When you start working with a new operating system, many questions come to mind. "How do I share data between two applications?" "Where does the system store the information I'm looking for?" and "How can I make my program run more efficiently?" are just a few.

I have found that more often than not, a good understanding of how the system manages memory can help determine the answers to these questions quickly and accurately. This chapter explores the memory architecture used by Microsoft Windows.

A Process's Virtual Address Space

Every process is given its very own virtual address space. For 32-bit processes, this address space is 4 GB, since a 32-bit pointer can have any value from 0x00000000 through 0xFFFFFFFF. This allows a pointer to have one of 4,294,967,296 values, which covers a process's 4-GB range. For 64-bit processes, this address space is 16 EB (exabytes), since a 64-bit pointer can have any value from 0x00000000'00000000 through 0xFFFFFFFF'FFFFFFFF. This allows a pointer to have one of 18,446,744,073,709,551,616 values, which covers a process's 16-EB range. This is quite a range!

Since every process receives its very own private address space, when a thread in a process is running, that thread can access memory that belongs only to its process. The memory that belongs to all other processes is hidden and inaccessible to the running thread.

> **NOTE** In Windows 2000, the memory belonging to the operating system it-self is also hidden from the running thread, which means that the thread cannot accidentally access the operating system's data. In Windows 98, the memory belonging to the operating system is not hidden from the running thread. Therefore, the running thread could accidentally access the operating system's data and corrupt the operating system (potentially causing it to crash). It is *not* possible in Windows 98 for one process's thread to access memory belonging to another process.

As I said, every process has its own private address space. Process A can have a data structure stored in its address space at address 0x12345678, while Process B can have a totally different data structure stored in *its* address space—at address 0x12345678. When threads running in Process A access memory at address 0x12345678, these threads are accessing Process A's data structure. When threads running in Process B access memory at address 0x12345678, these threads are accessing Process B's data structure. Threads running in Process A cannot access the data structure in Process B's address space, and vice versa.

Before you get all excited about having so much address space for your application, keep in mind that this is *virtual* address space—not physical storage. This address space is simply a range of memory addresses. Physical storage needs to be assigned or mapped to portions of the address space before you can successfully access data without raising access violations. We will discuss how this is done later in this chapter.

How a Virtual Address Space Is Partitioned

Each process's virtual address space is split into partitions. The address space is partitioned based on the underlying implementation of the operating system. Partitions vary slightly among the different Windows kernels. Table 13-1 shows how each platform partitions a process's address space.

As you can see, the 32-bit Windows 2000 kernel and 64-bit Windows 2000 kernel have nearly identical partitions; what differs are the partition sizes and locations. On the other hand, you can see that the partitions under the Windows 98 kernel are rather different. Let's examine how the system uses each of these partitions.

Partition	32-Bit Windows 2000 (x86 and Alpha)	32-Bit Windows 2000 (x86 w/3 GB User-Mode)	64-Bit Windows 2000 (Alpha and IA-64)	Windows 98
NULL-Pointer Assignment	0x00000000 0x0000FFFF	0x00000000 0x0000FFFF	0x00000000'00000000 0x00000000'0000FFFF	0x00000000 0x00000FFF
DOS/16-bit Windows Application Compatibility	NA	NA	NA	0x00001000 0x003FFFFF
User-Mode	0x00010000 0x7FFEFFFF	0x00010000 0xBFFEFFFF	0x00000000'00010000 0x000003FF'FFFEFFFF	0x00400000 0x7FFFFFFF
64-KB Off-Limits	0x7FFF0000 0x7FFFFFFF	0xBFFF0000 0xBFFFFFFF	0x000003FF'FFFF0000 0x000003FF'FFFFFFFF	NA
Shared Memory-Mapped File (MMF)	NA	NA	NA	0x80000000 0xBFFFFFFF
Kernel-Mode	0x80000000 0xFFFFFFFF	0xC0000000 0xFFFFFFFF	0x00000400'00000000 0xFFFFFFFF'FFFFFFFF	0xC0000000 0xFFFFFFFF

Table 13-1.
How a process's address space is partitioned

NOTE

Microsoft is actively working on 64-bit Windows 2000. As I write this, however, the system is still under development. You should use the information in this book regarding 64-bit Windows 2000 to influence the design and implementation of your current projects. However, be aware that the details of what I describe in this chapter are quite likely to change by the time 64-bit Windows 2000 ships. With respect to IA-64 (64-bit Intel Architecture) memory management, the specific virtual address ranges for partitions and the system's page size are also likely to change.

Null-Pointer Assignment Partition (Windows 2000 and Windows 98)

This partition of the process's address space, is set aside to help programmers catch NULL-pointer assignments. If a thread in your process attempts to read from or write to a memory address in this partition, the CPU raises an access violation. Protecting this partition is incredibly useful in helping to detect NULL-pointer assignments.

Error checking is often not performed religiously in C/C++ programs. For example, the following code performs no error checking:

```
int* pnSomeInteger = (int*) malloc(sizeof(int));
*pnSomeInteger = 5;
```

If *malloc* cannot find enough memory to satisfy the request, it returns NULL. However, this code doesn't check for that possibility—it assumes that the allocation was successful and proceeds to access memory at address 0x00000000. Because this partition of the address space is off-limits, a memory access violation occurs and the process is terminated. This feature helps developers find bugs in their applications.

MS-DOS/16-Bit Windows Application Compatibility Partition (Windows 98 Only)

This 4-MB region of the process's address space is required by Windows 98 in order to maintain compatibility with MS-DOS and 16-bit Windows applications. We should not attempt to read from or write to this partition from our 32-bit Windows applications. Ideally, the CPU should raise an access violation if a thread in our process touches this memory, but for technical reasons, Microsoft was unable to guard this 4 MB of address space.

In Windows 2000, 16-bit MS-DOS and 16-bit Windows applications run in their own address space and cannot be affected by 32-bit applications.

User-Mode Partition (Windows 2000 and Windows 98)

This partition is where the process's private (unshared) address space resides. One process cannot read from, write to, or in any way access another process's data residing in this partition. For all applications, this partition is where the bulk of the process's data is maintained. Because each process gets its own private, unshared partition for data, applications are far less likely to be corrupted by other applications, making the whole system more robust.

WINDOWS 2000

> In Windows 2000, all .exe and DLL modules load in this area. Each process might load these DLLs at a different address within this partition (although this is very unlikely). The system also maps all memory-mapped files accessible to this process within this partition.

WINDOWS 98

> In Windows 98, the main Win32 system DLLs (Kernel32.dll, AdvAPI32.dll, User32.dll, and GDI32.dll) load in the Shared Memory-Mapped File Partition. The .exe and all other DLL modules load in this user-mode partition. The shared DLLs will be at the same virtual address for all processes, but the other DLLs can load these DLLs at different addresses within the user-mode partition (although this is unlikely). Also, in Windows 98, memory-mapped files never appear in the user-mode partition.

When I first looked at my 32-bit process's address space, I was surprised to see that the amount of usable address space was less than half of my process's overall address space. After all, does the kernel-mode partition really need the top half of the address space? Actually, the answer is yes. The system needs this space for the kernel code, device driver code, device I/O cache buffers, non-paged pool allocations, process page tables, and so on. In fact, Microsoft is squeezing the kernel into this 2-GB space. In 64-bit Windows 2000, the kernel finally gets the room it truly needs.

Getting a 3-GB User-Mode Partition in *x*86 Windows 2000

Over the years, there has been a large outcry from developers for a larger user-mode address space. Microsoft, being attentive to this need, has allowed the *x*86 version of Windows 2000 Advanced Server and Windows 2000 Data Center to increase the user-mode partition to 3 GB. To have all processes use a 3-GB user-mode partition and a 1-GB kernel-mode partition, you need to append the /3GB switch to the desired entry in your system's BOOT.INI file. The "32-Bit Windows 2000 (x86 w/3GB User-mode)" column in Table 13-1 shows how the address space looks when the /3GB switch is used.

Before Microsoft added the /3GB switch, an application could never see a memory pointer where the high bit was set. Some creative developers took it upon themselves to use this high bit as a flag that had meaning only to their applications. Then when the application accessed the memory address, code executed that cleared the high bit of the pointer before the memory address was used. Well, as you can imagine, when an application runs in a 3-GB user-mode environment, the application fails in a blaze of fire.

Microsoft had to create a solution that allowed this application to work in a 3-GB environment. When the system is about to run an application, it checks to see if the application was linked with the /LARGEADDRESSAWARE linker switch. If so, the application is claiming that it does not do anything funny with memory addresses and is fully prepared to take advantage of a 3-GB user-mode address space. On the other hand, if the application was not linked with the /LARGEADDRESSAWARE switch, the operating system reserves the 1-GB area between 0x80000000 and 0xBFFFFFFF. This prevents any memory allocations from being created at a memory address whose high bit is set.

Note that the kernel was squeezed tightly into a 2-GB partition. When using the /3GB switch, the kernel is barely making it into a 1-GB partition. Using the /3GB switch reduces the number of threads, stacks, and other resources that the system can create. In addition, the system can only use a maximum of 16 GB of RAM vs. the normal maximum of 64 GB because there isn't enough virtual address space in kernel mode to manage the additional RAM.

> **NOTE**
>
> An executable's LARGEADDRESSAWARE flag is checked when the operating system creates the process's address space. The system ignores this flag for DLLs. DLLs *must* be written to behave correctly in a 3-GB user-mode partition or their behavior is undefined.

Getting a 2-GB User-Mode Partition in 64-bit Windows 2000

Microsoft realizes that many developers will want to port their existing 32-bit applications to a 64-bit environment as quickly and easily as possible. However, there is a lot of source code in which pointers are assumed to be 32-bit values. Simply rebuilding the application will cause pointer truncation errors and improper memory accesses.

However, if the system could somehow guarantee that no memory allocations would ever be made above 0x00000000'7FFFFFFF, the application would work fine. Truncating a 64-bit address to a 32-bit address when the high 33 bits are 0 causes no problem whatsoever. The system can provide this guarantee by running the application in an *address space sandbox* that limits a process's usable address space to the bottom 2 GB.

By default, when you invoke a 64-bit application, the system reserves all the user-mode address space starting at 0x0000000'80000000. This ensures that all memory allocations are created in the bottom 2 GB of the 64-bit address space. This is the address space sandbox. For most applications, this is more than enough address space anyway. To allow a 64-bit application to access its full 4-TB (terabyte) user-mode partition, the application must be built using the /LARGEADDRESSAWARE linker switch.

> **NOTE** An executable's LARGEADDRESSAWARE flag is checked when the operating system creates the process's 64-bit address space. The system ignores this flag for DLLs. DLLs *must* be written to behave correctly in a full 4-TB user-mode partition or their behavior is undefined.

64-KB Off-Limits Partition (Windows 2000 Only)

This 64-KB partition just above the user-mode partition is off-limits, and any attempt to access memory in this partition causes an access violation. Microsoft reserves this partition because doing so makes implementing the operating system easier for Microsoft. When you pass the address of a block of memory and its length to a Windows function, the function validates the memory block before performing its operation. You could easily imagine code like this (running on a 32-bit Windows 2000 system):

```
BYTE   bBuf[70000];
DWORD dwNumBytesWritten;
WriteProcessMemory(GetCurrentProcess(), (PVOID) 0x7FFEEE90, bBuf,
    sizeof(bBuf), &dwNumBytesWritten);
```

For a function like *WriteProcessMemory*, the memory region being written to is validated by kernel-mode code, which can successfully access memory in the kernel-mode partition (addresses above 0x80000000 on a 32-bit system). If there is memory at the 0x80000000 address, the above call will succeed in writing data to memory that should be accessible only by kernel-mode code. To prevent this while making the validation of such memory regions fast,

Microsoft chose to keep this partition always off-limits; any attempt to read from or write to memory in this region will always cause an access violation.

Shared MMF Partition (Windows 98 Only)

This 1-GB partition is where the system stores data that is shared among all 32-bit processes. For example, the system dynamic-link libraries—Kernel32.dll, AdvAPI32.dll, User32.dll, and GDI32.dll—are all loaded in this address space partition, making them easily available to all 32-bit processes simultaneously. These DLLs are also loaded at the same memory address for every process. In addition, the system maps all memory-mapped files in this partition. Memory-mapped files are discussed in more detail in Chapter 17.

Kernel-Mode Partition (Windows 2000 and Windows 98)

This partition is where the operating system's code resides. The code for thread scheduling, memory management, file systems support, networking support, and all device drivers is loaded in this partition. Everything residing in this partition is shared among all processes. In Windows 2000, these components are completely protected. If you attempt to access memory addresses in this partition, your thread will raise an access violation, causing the system to display a message box to the user and killing your application. See Chapters 23, 24, and 25 for more information about access violations and how to handle them.

WINDOWS 2000

> In 64-bit Windows 2000, the 4-TB user-mode partition looks greatly out of proportion to the 16,777,212-TB kernel-mode partition. It's not that the kernel-mode partition requires all of this virtual address space. It's just that a 64-bit address space is enormous and most of that address space is unused. The system allows our applications to use 4 TB and allows the kernel to use what it needs; the majority of the kernel-mode partition is just not used. Fortunately, the system does not require any internal data structures to maintain the unused portions of the kernel-mode partition.

WINDOWS 98

> Unfortunately, in Windows 98, the data in this partition is not protected—any application can read from or write to this section, potentially corrupting the operating system.

Regions in an Address Space

When a process is created and given its address space, the bulk of this usable address space is *free,* or unallocated. To use portions of this address space, you must allocate regions within it by calling *VirtualAlloc* (discussed in Chapter 15). The act of allocating a region is called *reserving.*

Whenever you reserve a region of address space, the system ensures that the region begins on an *allocation granularity* boundary. The allocation granularity can vary from one CPU platform to another. However, as of this writing, all the CPU platforms (*x*86, 32-bit Alpha, 64-bit Alpha, and IA-64) use the same allocation granularity of 64 KB.

When you reserve a region of address space, the system ensures that the size of the region is a multiple of the system's *page* size. A page is a unit of memory that the system uses in managing memory. Like the allocation granularity, the page size can vary from one CPU to another. The *x*86 uses a 4-KB page size, whereas the Alpha (when running both 32-bit Windows 2000 and 64-bit Windows 2000) uses an 8-KB page size. At the time of this writing, Microsoft expects the IA-64 to also use an 8-KB page size. However, Microsoft might switch to a larger page size (16 KB or higher) if testing indicates better overall system performance.

> **NOTE**
> Sometimes the system reserves regions of address space on behalf of your process. For example, the system allocates a region of address space to store a *process environment block* (PEB). A PEB is a small data structure created, manipulated, and destroyed entirely by the system. When a process is created, the system allocates a region of address space for the PEB.
>
> The system also needs to create *thread environment blocks* (TEBs) to help manage all the threads that currently exist in the process. The regions for these TEBs will be reserved and released as threads in the process are created and destroyed.
>
> Although the system demands that any of your requests to reserve address space regions begin on an allocation granularity boundary (64 KB on all platforms to date), the system itself is not subjected to the same limitation. It is extremely likely that the region reserved for your process's PEB and TEBs will not start on a 64-KB boundary. However, these reserved regions will still have to be a multiple of the CPU's page size.

If you attempt to reserve a 10-KB region of address space, the system will automatically round up your request and reserve a region whose size is a multiple of the page size. This means that on an *x*86, the system will reserve a region that is 12 KB; on an Alpha, the system will reserve a 16-KB region.

When your program's algorithms no longer need to access a reserved region of address space, the region should be freed. This process is called *releasing* the region of address space and is accomplished by calling the *VirtualFree* function.

Committing Physical Storage Within a Region

To use a reserved region of address space, you must allocate physical storage and then map this storage to the reserved region. This process is called *committing* physical storage. Physical storage is always committed in pages. To commit physical storage to a reserved region, you again call the *VirtualAlloc* function.

When you commit physical storage to regions, you do not have to commit physical storage to the entire region. For example, you can reserve a region that is 64 KB and then commit physical storage to the second and fourth pages within the region. Figure 13-1 shows what a process's address space might look like. Notice that the address space is different depending on which CPU platform you're running on. The address space on the left shows what happens on an *x*86 machine (which has a 4-KB page), and the address space on the right shows what happens on an Alpha machine (which has 8-KB pages).

When your program's algorithms no longer need to access committed physical storage in the reserved region, the physical storage should be freed. This process is called *decommitting* the physical storage and is accomplished by calling the *VirtualFree* function.

Physical Storage and the Paging File

In older operating systems, physical storage was considered to be the amount of RAM that you had in your machine. In other words, if you had 16 MB of RAM in your machine, you could load and run applications that used up to 16 MB of RAM. Today's operating systems have the ability to make disk space look like memory. The file on the disk is typically called a *paging file* and it contains the virtual memory that is available to all processes.

Of course, for virtual memory to work, a great deal of assistance is required from the CPU itself. When a thread attempts to access a byte of storage, the CPU must know whether that byte is in RAM or on the disk.

From an application's perspective, a paging file transparently increases the amount of RAM (or storage) that the application can use. If you have 64 MB of RAM in your machine and also have a 100-MB paging file on your hard disk, the applications you're running believe that your machine has a grand total of 164 MB of RAM.

Of course, you don't actually have 164 MB of RAM. Instead, the operating system, in coordination with the CPU, saves portions of RAM to the paging file and loads portions of the paging file back into RAM as the running applications need them. Because a paging file increases the apparent amount of RAM available for applications, the use of a paging file is optional. If you don't have

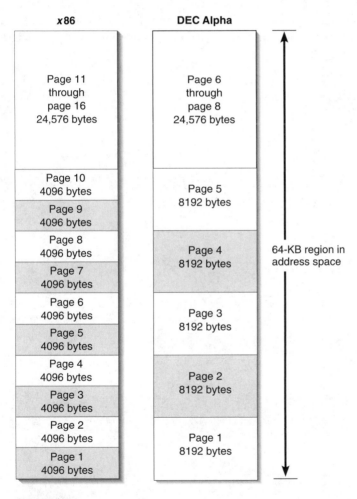

Figure 13-1.
Example process address spaces for different CPUs

a paging file, the system just thinks that there is less RAM available for applications to use. However, users are strongly encouraged to use paging files so that they can run more applications and those applications can work on larger data sets. It is best to think of physical storage as data stored in a paging file on a disk drive (usually a hard disk drive). So when an application commits physical storage to a region of address space by calling the *VirtualAlloc* function, space is actually allocated from a file on the hard disk. The size of the system's paging file is the most important factor in determining how much physical storage is available to applications; the amount of RAM you have has very little effect.

Now, when a thread in your process attempts to access a block of data in the process's address space, one of two things can happen, as shown in the flowchart in Figure 13-2.

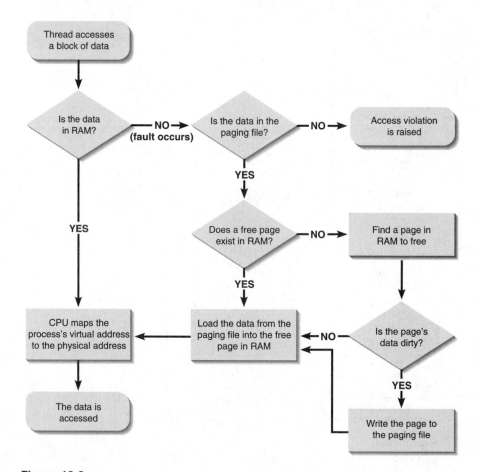

Figure 13-2.
Translating a virtual address to a physical storage address

In the first possibility, the data that the thread is attempting to access is in RAM. In this case, the CPU maps the data's virtual memory address to the physical address in memory, and then the desired access is performed.

In the second possibility, the data that the thread is attempting to access is not in RAM but is contained somewhere in the paging file. In this case, the attempted access is called a page fault, and the CPU notifies the operating system of the attempted access. The operating system then locates a free page of memory in RAM; if a free page cannot be found, the system must free one. If a page has not been modified, the system can simply free the page. But if the system needs to free a page that was modified, it must first copy the page from RAM to the paging file. Next the system goes to the paging file, locates the block of data that needs to be accessed, and loads the data into the free page of memory. The operating system then updates its table indicating that the data's virtual memory address now maps to the appropriate physical memory address in RAM. The CPU now retries the instruction that generated the initial page fault, but this time the CPU is able to map the virtual memory address to a physical RAM address and access the block of data.

The more often the system needs to copy pages of memory to the paging file and vice versa, the more your hard disk thrashes and the slower the system runs. (*Thrashing* means that the operating system spends all its time swapping pages in and out of memory instead of running programs.) Thus by adding more RAM to your computer, you reduce the amount of thrashing necessary to run your applications, which will, of course, greatly improve the system's performance. So, here is a general rule of thumb: to make your machine run faster, add more RAM. In fact, for most situations, you'll get a better performance boost from adding RAM than you will by getting a faster CPU.

Physical Storage Not Maintained in the Paging File

After reading the previous section, you must be thinking that the paging file can get pretty large if many programs are all running at once—especially if you're thinking that every time you run a program the system must reserve regions of address space for the process's code and data, commit physical storage to these regions, and then copy the code and data from the program's file on the hard disk to the committed physical storage in the paging file.

The system does not do what I just described; if it did, it would take a very long time to load a program and start it running. Instead, when you invoke an application, the system opens the application's .exe file and determines the size of the application's code and data. Then the system reserves a region of address space and notes that the physical storage associated with this region is the .exe file itself. That's right—instead of allocating space from the paging file, the system uses the actual contents, or *image*, of the .exe file as the program's reserved region of address space. This, of course, makes loading an application very fast and allows the size of the paging file to remain small.

When a program's file image (that is, an .exe or a DLL file) on the hard disk is used as the physical storage for a region of address space, it is called a *memory-mapped file*. When an .exe or a DLL is loaded, the system automatically reserves a region of address space and maps the file's image to this region. However, the system also offers a set of functions that allow you to map data files to a region of address space. We will talk about memory-mapped files much more in Chapter 17.

Windows 2000 is capable of using multiple paging files. If multiple paging files exist on different physical hard drives, the system can perform much faster because it can write to the multiple drives simultaneously. You can add and remove paging files by opening the System Properties Control Panel applet, choosing the Advanced tab and clicking on the Performance Options button. The following figure shows what this dialog box looks like.

Virtual Memory	? X
Drive [Volume Label]	**Paging File Size (MB)**
C: [System]	144 - 288
D:	

Paging file size for selected drive
Drive: C: [System]
Space available: 649 MB

Initial size (MB): 144

Maximum size (MB): 288   Set

Total paging file size for all drives
Minimum allowed: 2 MB
Recommended: 142 MB
Currently allocated: 144 MB

Registry size
Current registry size: 15 MB

Maximum registry size (MB): 26

OK   Cancel

NOTE

When an .exe or a DLL file is loaded from a floppy disk, both Windows 98 and Windows 2000 copy the entire file from the floppy into the system's RAM. In addition, the system allocates enough storage from the paging file to hold the file's image. This storage is only written to if the system chooses to trim a page of RAM that currently contains a part of the file's image. If the load on the system's RAM is light, the file always runs directly from RAM.

Microsoft was forced to make image files executed from floppies work this way so that setup applications would work correctly. Often a setup program begins with one floppy, which the user removes from the drive in order to insert another floppy. If the system needs to go back to the first floppy to load some of the .exe's or the DLL's code, it is, of course, no longer in the floppy drive. However, because the system copied the file to RAM (and is backed by the paging file), it will have no trouble accessing the setup program.

The system does not copy to RAM image files on other removable media such as CD-ROMs or network drives unless the image is linked using the /SWAPRUN:CD or /SWAPRUN:NET switches. Note that Windows 98 does not support the /SWAPRUN image flags.

Protection Attributes

Individual pages of physical storage allocated can be assigned different protection attributes. The protection attributes are shown in the following table.

Protection Attribute	Description
PAGE_NOACCESS	Attempts to read from, write to, or execute code in this page raise an access violation.
PAGE_READONLY	Attempts to write to or execute code in this page raise an access violation.
PAGE_READWRITE	Attempts to execute code in this page raise an access violation.
PAGE_EXECUTE	Attempts to read or write memory in this page raise an access violation.
PAGE_EXECUTE_READ	Attempts to write to memory in this page raise an access violation.

(continued)

continued

Protection Attribute	Description
PAGE_EXECUTE_READWRITE	There is nothing you can do to this page to raise an access violation.
PAGE_WRITECOPY	Attempts to execute code in this page raise an access violation. Attempts to write to memory in this page cause the system to give the process its own private copy of the page (backed by the paging file).
PAGE_EXECUTE_WRITECOPY	There is nothing you can do to this region to raise an access violation. Attempts to write to memory in this page cause the system to give the process its own private copy of the page (backed by the paging file).

The *x*86 and Alpha CPUs do not support the execute protection attribute, although the operating system software does support this attribute. These CPUs treat read access as execute access. This means that if you assign PAGE_EXECUTE protection to memory, that memory will also have read privileges. Of course, you should not rely on this behavior because Windows implementations on other CPUs might very well treat execute protection as execute-only protection.

Windows 98 supports only the PAGE_NOACCESS, PAGE_READONLY, and PAGE_READWRITE protection attributes.

Copy-On-Write Access

The protection attributes listed in the preceding table should all be fairly self-explanatory except the last two: PAGE_WRITECOPY and PAGE_EXECUTE_WRITECOPY. These attributes exist to conserve RAM usage and paging file space. Windows supports a mechanism that allows two or more processes to share a single block of storage. So, if 10 instances of Notepad are running, all instances share the application's code and data pages. Having all instances share the same storage pages greatly improves the performance of the system—but this does require that all instances consider the storage to be read-only or execute-only. If a thread in one instance wrote to the storage modifying it, the storage as seen by the other instances would also be modified, causing total chaos.

To prevent this chaos, *copy-on-write* protection is assigned to the shared block of storage by the operating system. When an .exe or .dll module is mapped into an address space, the system calculates how many pages are writable. (Usually, the pages containing code are marked as PAGE_EXECUTE_READ while the pages containing data are marked PAGE_READWRITE.) Then, the system allocates storage from the paging file to accommodate these writable pages. This paging file storage is not used unless the module's writable pages are actually written to.

When a thread in one process attempts to write to a shared block, the system intervenes and performs the following steps:

1. The system finds a free page of memory in RAM. Note that this free page will be backed by one of the pages allocated in the paging file when the module was first mapped into the process's address space. Since the system allocated all the potentially required paging file space when the module was first mapped, this step cannot possibly fail.

2. The system copies the contents of the page attempting to be modified to the free page found in step 1. This free page will be assigned either PAGE_READWRITE or PAGE_EXECUTE_READWRITE protection. The original page's protection and data does not change at all.

3. The system then updates the process's page tables so that the accessed virtual address now translates to the new page of RAM.

After the system has performed these steps, the process can access its very own private instance of this page of storage. In Chapter 17, sharing storage and copy-on-write protection are covered in much more detail.

In addition, you should not pass either PAGE_WRITECOPY or PAGE_EXECUTE_WRITECOPY when you are reserving address space or committing physical storage using the *VirtualAlloc* function. Doing so will cause the call to *VirtualAlloc* to fail; calling *GetLastError* returns ERROR_INVALID_PARAMETER. These two attributes are used by the operating system when it maps .exe and DLL file images.

WINDOWS 98

Windows 98 does not support copy-on-write protection. When Windows 98 sees that copy-on-write protection has been requested, it immediately makes copies of the data instead of waiting for an attempted memory write.

Special Access Protection Attribute Flags

In addition to the protection attributes already discussed, there are three protection attribute flags: PAGE_NOCACHE, PAGE_WRITECOMBINE, and PAGE_GUARD. You use these three flags by bitwise ORing them with any of the protection attributes except PAGE_NOACCESS.

The first of these protection attribute flags, PAGE_NOCACHE, disables caching of the committed pages. This flag is not recommended for general use—it exists mostly for hardware device driver developers who need to manipulate memory buffers.

The second protection attribute flag, PAGE_WRITECOMBINE, is also for device driver developers. It allows multiple writes to a single device to be combined together in order to improve performance.

The last protection attribute flag, PAGE_GUARD, allows an application to receive a notification (via an exception) when a byte on a page has been written to. There are some clever uses for this flag. Windows 2000 uses this flag when it creates a thread's stack. See the section "A Thread's Stack" in Chapter 16 for more information about this flag.

Windows 98 ignores the PAGE_NOCACHE, PAGE_WRITE-COMBINE, and PAGE_GUARD protection attribute flags.

Bringing It All Home

In this section, we'll bring address spaces, partitions, regions, blocks, and pages all together. The best way to start is by examining a virtual memory map that shows all the regions of address space within a single process. The process happens to be the VMMap sample application presented in Chapter 14. To fully understand the process's address space, we'll begin by discussing the address space as it appears when VMMap is running under Windows 2000 on a 32-bit *x86* machine. A sample address space map is shown in Table 13-2. Later I'll discuss the differences between the Windows 2000 and Windows 98 address spaces.

Base Address	Type	Size	Blocks	Protection Attribute(s)	Description
00000000	Free	65536			
00010000	Private	4096	1	-RW-	
00011000	Free	61440			
00020000	Private	4096	1	-RW-	
00021000	Free	61440			
00030000	Private	1048576	3	-RW-	Thread Stack
00130000	Private	1048576	2	-RW-	
00230000	Mapped	65536	2	-RW-	
00240000	Mapped	90112	1	-R--	\Device\HarddiskVolume1\WINNT\system32\ unicode.nls
00256000	Free	40960			
00260000	Mapped	208896	1	-R--	\Device\HarddiskVolume1\WINNT\system32\ locale.nls
00293000	Free	53248			
002A0000	Mapped	266240	1	-R--	\Device\HarddiskVolume1\WINNT\system32\ sortkey.nls
002E1000	Free	61440			
002F0000	Mapped	16384	1	-R--	\Device\HarddiskVolume1\WINNT\system32\ sorttbls.nls
002F4000	Free	49152			
00300000	Mapped	819200	4	ER--	
003C8000	Free	229376			
00400000	Image	106496	5	ERWC	C:\CD\x86\Debug\14 VMMap.exe
0041A000	Free	24576			
00420000	Mapped	274432	1	-R--	
00463000	Free	53248			
00470000	Mapped	3145728	2	ER--	
00770000	Private	4096	1	-RW-	
00771000	Free	61440			
00780000	Private	4096	1	-RW-	
00781000	Free	61440			
00790000	Private	65536	2	-RW-	
007A0000	Mapped	8192	1	-R--	\Device\HarddiskVolume1\WINNT\system32\ ctype.nls
007A2000	Free	1763893248			
699D0000	Image	45056	4	ERWC	C:\WINNT\System32\PSAPI.dll

Table 13-2.   *(continued)*

A sample address space map showing regions under Windows 2000 on a 32-bit x86 machine

Table 13-2. *continued*

Base Address	Type	Size	Blocks	Protection Attribute(s)	Description
699DB000	Free	238505984			
77D50000	Image	450560	4	ERWC	C:\WINNT\system32\RPCRT4.DLL
77DBE000	Free	8192			
77DC0000	Image	344064	5	ERWC	C:\WINNT\system32\ADVAPI32.dll
77E14000	Free	49152			
77E20000	Image	401408	4	ERWC	C:\WINNT\system32\USER32.dll
77E82000	Free	57344			
77E90000	Image	720896	5	ERWC	C:\WINNT\system32\KERNEL32.dll
77F40000	Image	241664	4	ERWC	C:\WINNT\system32\GDI32.DLL
77F7B000	Free	20480			
77F80000	Image	483328	5	ERWC	C:\WINNT\System32\ntdll.dll
77FF6000	Free	40960			
78000000	Image	290816	6	ERWC	C:\WINNT\system32\MSVCRT.dll
78047000	Free	124424192			
7F6F0000	Mapped	1048576	2	ER--	
7F7F0000	Free	8126464			
7FFB0000	Mapped	147456	1	-R--	
7FFD4000	Free	40960			
7FFDE000	Private	4096	1	ERW-	
7FFDF000	Private	4096	1	ERW-	
7FFE0000	Private	65536	2	-R--	

The address space map in Table 13-2 shows the various regions in the process's address space. There is one region shown per line, and each line contains six columns.

The first, or leftmost, column shows the region's base address. You'll notice that we start walking the process's address space with the region at address 0x00000000 and end with the last region of usable address space, which begins at address 0x7FFE0000. All regions are contiguous. You'll also notice that almost all the base addresses for non-free regions start on a multiple of 64 KB. This is because of the allocation granularity of address space reservation imposed by the system. A region that does not start on an allocation granularity boundary represents a region that was allocated by operating system code on your process's behalf.

The second column shows the region's type, which is one of the four values—Free, Private, Image, or Mapped—described in the following table.

Type	Description
Free	The region's virtual addresses are not backed by any storage. This address space is not reserved; the application can reserve a region either at the shown base address or anywhere within the free region.
Private	The region's virtual addresses are backed by the system's paging file.
Image	The region's virtual addresses were originally backed by a memory-mapped image file (such as an .exe or DLL file). The virtual addresses might not be backed by the image file anymore. For example, when a global variable in a module's image is written to, the copy-on-write mechanism backs the specific page from the paging file instead of the original image file.
Mapped	The region's virtual addresses were originally backed by a memory-mapped data file. The virtual addresses might not be backed by the data file anymore. For example, a data file might be mapped using copy-on-write protection. Any writes to the file cause the specific pages to be backed by the paging file instead of the original data.

The way that my VMMap application calculates this column might lead to misleading results. When the region is not free, the VMMap sample application guesses which of the three remaining values applies—there is no function we can call to request this region's exact usage. I calculate this column's value by scanning all of the blocks within the region and taking an educated guess. You should examine my code in Chapter 14 to better understand the way I calculate a column's value.

The third column shows the number of bytes that were reserved for the region. For example, the system mapped the image of User32.DLL at memory address 0x77E20000. When the system reserved address space for this image, it needed to reserve 401,408 bytes. The number in the third column will always be a multiple of the CPU's page size (4096 bytes for an *x86*).

The fourth column shows the number of blocks within the reserved region. A block is a set of contiguous pages that all have the same protection attributes and that are all backed by the same type of physical storage—I'll talk more about this in the next section of this chapter. For free regions, this value will always be 0 because no storage can be committed within a free region. (Nothing is displayed in the fourth column for a free region.) For the non-free region, this value can be anywhere from 1 to a maximum number of (region size/page size). For example, the region that begins at memory address 0x77E20000 has a region size of 401,408 bytes. Because this process is running on an *x86* CPU, for which the page size is 4096 bytes, the maximum number of different committed blocks is 98 (401,408/4096); the map shows that there are 4 blocks in the region.

The fifth column on the line shows the region's protection attributes. The individual letters represent the following: *E* = execute, *R* = read, *W* = write, *C* = copy-on-write. If the region does not show any of these protection attributes, the region has no access protection. The free regions show no protection attributes because unreserved regions do not have protection attributes associated with them. Neither the guard protection attribute flag nor the no-cache protection attribute flag will ever appear here; these flags have meaning only when associated with physical storage, not reserved address space. Protection attributes are given to a region for the sake of efficiency only and are always overridden by protection attributes assigned to physical storage.

The sixth and last column shows a text description of what's in the region. For free regions, this column will always be blank; for private regions, it will usually be blank because VMMap has no way of knowing why the application reserved this private region of address space. However, VMMap can identify private regions that contain a thread's stack. VMMap can usually detect thread stacks because they will commonly have a block of physical storage within them with the guard protection attribute. However, when a thread's stack is full it will not have a block with the guard protection attribute, and VMMap will be unable to detect it.

For image regions, VMMap displays the full pathname of the file that is mapped into the region. VMMap obtains this information using the ToolHelp functions (mentioned at the end of Chapter 4). In Windows 2000, VMMap can show regions backed by data files by calling the *GetMappedFileName* function (which does not exist in Windows 98).

Inside the Regions

It is possible to break down the regions even further than shown in Table 13-2. Table 13-3 shows the same address space map as Table 13-2, but the blocks contained inside each region are also displayed.

Base Address	Type	Size	Blocks	Protection Attribute(s)	Description
00000000	Free	65536			
00010000	Private	4096	1	-RW-	
00010000	Private	4096		-RW- ---	
00011000	Free	61440			

Table 13-3. *(continued)*
A sample address space map showing regions and blocks under Windows 2000 on a 32-bit x86 machine

Table 13-3. *continued*

Base Address	Type	Size	Blocks	Protection Attribute(s)	Description
00020000	Private	4096	1	-RW-	
00020000	Private	4096		-RW- ---	
00021000	Free	61440			
00030000	Private	1048576	3	-RW-	Thread Stack
00030000	Reserve	905216		-RW- ---	
0010D000	Private	4096		-RW- G--	
0010E000	Private	139264		-RW- ---	
00130000	Private	1048576	2	-RW-	
00130000	Private	36864		-RW- ---	
00139000	Reserve	1011712		-RW- ---	
00230000	Mapped	65536	2	-RW-	
00230000	Mapped	4096		-RW- ---	
00231000	Reserve	61440		-RW- ---	
00240000	Mapped	90112	1	-R--	\Device\HarddiskVolume1\WINNT\system32\unicode.nls
00240000	Mapped	90112		-R-- ---	
00256000	Free	40960			
00260000	Mapped	208896	1	-R--	\Device\HarddiskVolume1\WINNT\system32\locale.nls
00260000	Mapped	208896		-R-- ---	
00293000	Free	53248			
002A0000	Mapped	266240	1	-R--	\Device\HarddiskVolume1\WINNT\system32\sortkey.nls
002A0000	Mapped	266240		-R-- ---	
002E1000	Free	61440			
002F0000	Mapped	16384	1	-R--	\Device\HarddiskVolume1\WINNT\system32\sorttbls.nls
002F0000	Mapped	16384		-R-- ---	
002F4000	Free	49152			
00300000	Mapped	819200	4	ER--	
00300000	Mapped	16384		ER-- ---	
00304000	Reserve	770048		ER-- ---	
003C0000	Mapped	8192		ER-- ---	
003C2000	Reserve	24576		ER-- ---	
003C8000	Free	229376			
00400000	Image	106496	5	ERWC	C:\CD\x86\Debug\14 VMMap.exe
00400000	Image	4096		-R-- ---	
00401000	Image	81920		ER-- ---	
00415000	Image	4096		-R-- ---	
00416000	Image	8192		-RW- ---	
00418000	Image	8192		-R-- ---	

(continued)

Table 13-3. *continued*

Base Address	Type	Size	Blocks	Protection Attribute(s)	Description
0041A000	Free	24576			
00420000	Mapped	274432	1	-R--	
00420000	Mapped	274432		-R-- ---	
00463000	Free	53248			
00470000	Mapped	3145728	2	ER--	
00470000	Mapped	274432		ER-- ---	
004B3000	Reserve	2871296		ER-- ---	
00770000	Private	4096	1	-RW-	
00770000	Private	4096		-RW- ---	
00771000	Free	61440			
00780000	Private	4096	1	-RW-	
00780000	Private	4096		-RW- ---	
00781000	Free	61440			
00790000	Private	65536	2	-RW-	
00790000	Private	20480		-RW- ---	
00795000	Reserve	45056		-RW- ---	
007A0000	Mapped	8192	1	-R--	\Device\HarddiskVolume1\ WINNT\system32\ctype.nls
007A0000	Mapped	8192		-R-- ---	
007A2000	Free	57344			
007B0000	Private	524288	2	-RW-	
007B0000	Private	4096		-RW- ---	
007B1000	Reserve	520192		-RW- ---	
00830000	Free	1763311616			
699D0000	Image	45056	4	ERWC	C:\WINNT\System32\PSAPI.dll
699D0000	Image	4096		-R-- ---	
699D1000	Image	16384		ER-- ---	
699D5000	Image	16384		-RWC ---	
699D9000	Image	8192		-R-- ---	
699DB000	Free	238505984			
77D50000	Image	450560	4	ERWC	C:\WINNT\system32\ RPCRT4.DLL
77D50000	Image	4096		-R-- ---	
77D51000	Image	421888		ER-- ---	
77DB8000	Image	4096		-RW- ---	
77DB9000	Image	20480		-R-- ---	
77DBE000	Free	8192			
77DC0000	Image	344064	5	ERWC	C:\WINNT\system32\ ADVAPI32.dll

(continued)

Table 13-3. *continued*

Base Address	Type	Size	Blocks	Protection Attribute(s)	Description
77DC0000	Image	4096		-R-- ---	
77DC1000	Image	307200		ER-- ---	
77E0C000	Image	4096		-RW- ---	
77E0D000	Image	4096		-RWC ---	
77E0E000	Image	24576		-R-- ---	
77E14000	Free	49152			
77E20000	Image	401408	4	ERWC	C:\WINNT\system32\USER32.dll
77E20000	Image	4096		-R-- ---	
77E21000	Image	348160		ER-- ---	
77E76000	Image	4096		-RW- ---	
77E77000	Image	45056		-R-- ---	
77E82000	Free	57344			
77E90000	Image	720896	5	ERWC	C:\WINNT\system32\KERNEL32.dll
77E90000	Image	4096		-R-- ---	
77E91000	Image	368640		ER-- ---	
77EEB000	Image	8192		-RW- ---	
77EED000	Image	4096		-RWC ---	
77EEE000	Image	335872		-R-- ---	
77F40000	Image	241664	4	ERWC	C:\WINNT\system32\GDI32.DLL
77F40000	Image	4096		-R-- ---	
77F41000	Image	221184		ER-- ---	
77F77000	Image	4096		-RW- ---	
77F78000	Image	12288		-R-- ---	
77F7B000	Free	20480			
77F80000	Image	483328	5	ERWC	C:\WINT\System32\ntdll.dll
77F80000	Image	4096		-R-- ---	
77F81000	Image	299008		ER-- ---	
77FCA000	Image	8192		-RW- ---	
77FCC000	Image	4096		-RWC ---	
77FCD000	Image	167936		-R-- ---	
77FF6000	Free	40960			
78000000	Image	290816	6	ERWC	C:\WINNT\system32\MSVCRT.dll
78000000	Image	4096		-R-- ---	
78001000	Image	208896		ER-- ---	
78034000	Image	32768		-R-- ---	
7803C000	Image	12288		-RW- ---	
7803F000	Image	16384		RWC- ---	
78043000	Image	16384		-R-- ---	
78047000	Free	124424192			
7F6F0000	Mapped	1048576	2	ER--	

(continued)

Table 13-3. *continued*

Base Address	Type	Size	Blocks	Protection Attribute(s)	Description
7F6F0000	Mapped	28672		ER-- ---	
7F6F7000	Reserve	1019904		ER-- ---	
7F7F0000	Free	8126464			
7FFB0000	Mapped	147456	1	-R--	
7FFB0000	Mapped	147456		-R-- ---	
7FFD4000	Free	40960			
7FFDE000	Private	4096	1	ERW-	
7FFDE000	Private	4096		ERW- ---	
7FFDF000	Private	4096	1	ERW-	
7FFDF000	Private	4096		ERW- ---	
7FFE0000	Private	65536	2	-R--	
7FFE0000	Private	4096		-R-- ---	
7FFE1000	Reserve	61440		-R-- ---	

Of course, free regions do not expand at all because they have no committed pages of storage within them. Each block line shows four columns, which I'll explain here.

The first column shows the address of a set of pages all having the same state and protection attributes. For example, a single page (4096 bytes) of memory with read-only protection is committed at address 0x77E20000. At address 0x77E21000, there is a block of 85 pages (348,160 bytes) of committed storage that has execute and read protection. If both of these blocks had the same protection attributes, the two would be combined and would appear as a single 86-page (352,256-byte) entry in the memory map.

The second column shows what type of physical storage is backing the block within the reserved region. One of five possible values can appear in this column: Free, Private, Mapped, Image, or Reserve. A value of Private, Mapped, or Image indicates that the block is backed by physical storage in the paging file, a data file, or a loaded .exe or DLL file, respectively. If the value is Free or Reserve, the block is not backed by any physical storage at all.

For the most part, the same type of physical storage backs all the committed blocks within a single region. However, it is possible for different committed blocks within a single region to be backed by different types of physical storage. For example, a memory-mapped file image will be backed by an .exe or a DLL file. If you were to write to a single page in this region that had PAGE_WRITECOPY or PAGE_EXECUTE_WRITECOPY, the system would make your process a private copy of the page backed by the paging file instead of the file image. This new page would have the same attributes as the original page without the copy-on-write protection attribute.

The third column shows the size of the block. All blocks are contiguous within a region—there will not be any gaps.

The fourth column shows the number of blocks within the reserved region.

The fifth column shows the protection attributes and protection attribute flags of the block. A block's protection attributes override the protection attributes of the region that contains the block. The possible protection attributes are identical to those that can be specified for a region; however, the protection attribute flags PAGE_GUARD, PAGE_NOCACHE, and PAGE_WRITE-COMBINE—which are never associated with a region—can be associated with a block.

Address Space Differences for Windows 98

Table 13-4 shows the address space map when the same VMMap program is executed under Windows 98. To conserve space, the range of virtual addresses between 0x80018000 and 0x85620000 is not shown.

Base Address	Type	Size	Blocks	Protection Attribute(s)	Description
00000000	Free	4194304			
00400000	Private	131072	6	----	C:\CD\X86\DEBUG\14 VMMAP.EXE
00400000	Private	8192		-R-- ---	
00402000	Private	8192		-RW- ---	
00404000	Private	73728		-R-- ---	
00416000	Private	8192		-RW- ---	
00418000	Private	8192		-R-- ---	
0041A000	Reserve	24576		---- ---	
00420000	Private	1114112	4	----	
00420000	Private	20480		-RW- ---	
00425000	Reserve	1028096		---- ---	
00520000	Private	4096		-RW- ---	
00521000	Reserve	61440		---- ---	
00530000	Private	65536	2	-RW-	
00530000	Private	4096		-RW- ---	
00531000	Reserve	61440		-RW- ---	
00540000	Private	1179648	6	----	Thread Stack
00540000	Reserve	942080		---- ---	
00626000	Private	4096		-RW- ---	

Table 13-4.
A sample address space map showing blocks within regions under Windows 98

(continued)

Table 13-4. *continued*

Base Address	Type	Size	Blocks	Protection Attribute(s)	Description
00627000	Reserve	24576		---- ---	
0062D000	Private	4096		---- ---	
0062E000	Private	139264		-RW- ---	
00650000	Reserve	65536		---- ---	
00660000	Private	1114112	4	----	
00660000	Private	20480		-RW- ---	
00665000	Reserve	1028096		---- ---	
00760000	Private	4096		-RW- ---	
00761000	Reserve	61440		---- ---	
00770000	Private	1048576	2	-RW-	
00770000	Private	32768		-RW- ---	
00778000	Reserve	1015808		-RW- ---	
00870000	Free	2004418560			
78000000	Private	262144	3	----	C:\WINDOWS\SYSTEM\ MSVCRT.DLL
78000000	Private	188416		-R-- ---	
7802E000	Private	57344		-RW- ---	
7803C000	Private	16384		-R-- ---	
78040000	Free	133955584			
80000000	Private	4096	1	----	
80000000	Reserve	4096		---- ---	
80001000	Private	4096	1	----	
80001000	Private	4096		-RW- ---	
80002000	Private	4096	1	----	
80002000	Private	4096		-RW- ---	
80003000	Private	4096	1	----	
80003000	Private	4096		-RW- ---	
80004000	Private	65536	2	----	
80004000	Private	32768		-RW- ---	
8000C000	Reserve	32768		---- ---	
80014000	Private	4096	1	----	
80014000	Private	4096		-RW- ---	
80015000	Private	4096	1	----	
80015000	Private	4096		-RW- ---	
80016000	Private	4096	1	----	
80016000	Private	4096		-RW- ---	
80017000	Private	4096	1	----	
80017000	Private	4096		-RW- ---	

(continued)

Table 13-4. *continued*

Base Address	Type	Size	Blocks	Protection Attribute(s)	Description
85620000	Free	9773056			
85F72000	Private	151552	1	- - - -	
85F72000	Private	151552		-R-- ---	
85F97000	Private	327680	1	- - - -	
85F97000	Private	327680		-R-- ---	
85FE7000	Free	22052864			
874EF000	Private	4194304	1	- - - -	
874EF000	Reserve	4194304		- - - - ---	
878EF000	Free	679219200			
B00B0000	Private	880640	3	- - - -	
B00B0000	Private	233472		-R-- ---	
B00E9000	Private	20480		-RW- ---	
B00EE000	Private	626688		-R-- ---	
B0187000	Free	177311744			
BAAA0000	Private	315392	7	- - - -	
BAAA0000	Private	4096		-R-- ---	
BAAA1000	Private	4096		-RW- ---	
BAAA2000	Private	241664		-R-- ---	
BAADD000	Private	4096		-RW- ---	
BAADE000	Private	4096		-R-- ---	
BAADF000	Private	32768		-RW- ---	
BAAE7000	Private	24576		-R-- ---	
BAAED000	Free	86978560			
BFDE0000	Private	20480	1	- - - -	
BFDE0000	Private	20480		-R-- ---	
BFDE5000	Free	45056			
BFDF0000	Private	65536	3	- - - -	
BFDF0000	Private	40960		-R-- ---	
BFDFA000	Private	4096		-RW- ---	
BFDFB000	Private	20480		-R-- ---	
BFE00000	Free	131072			
BFE20000	Private	16384	3	- - - -	
BFE20000	Private	8192		-R-- ---	
BFE22000	Private	4096		-RW- ---	
BFE23000	Private	4096		-R-- ---	
BFE24000	Free	245760			
BFE60000	Private	24576	3	- - - -	
BFE60000	Private	8192		-R-- ---	
BFE62000	Private	4096		-RW- ---	
BFE63000	Private	12288		-R-- ---	

(continued)

Table 13-4. *continued*

Base Address	Type	Size	Blocks	Protection Attribute(s)	Description
BFE66000	Free	40960			
BFE70000	Private	24576	3	- - - -	
BFE70000	Private	8192		-R-- ---	
BFE72000	Private	4096		-RW- ---	
BFE73000	Private	12288		-R-- ---	
BFE76000	Free	40960			
BFE80000	Private	65536	3	- - - -	C:\WINDOWS\SYSTEM\ ADVAPI32.DLL
BFE80000	Private	49152		-R-- ---	
BFE8C000	Private	4096		-RW- ---	
BFE8D000	Private	12288		-R-- ---	
BFE90000	Private	573440	3	- - - -	
BFE90000	Private	425984		-R-- ---	
BFEF8000	Private	4096		-RW- ---	
BFEF9000	Private	143360		-R-- ---	
BFF1C000	Free	16384			
BFF20000	Private	155648	5	- - - -	C:\WINDOWS\SYSTEM\GDI32.DLL
BFF20000	Private	126976		-R-- ---	
BFF3F000	Private	8192		-RW- ---	
BFF41000	Private	4096		-R-- ---	
BFF42000	Private	4096		-RW- ---	
BFF43000	Private	12288		-R-- ---	
BFF46000	Free	40960			
BFF50000	Private	69632	3	- - - -	C:\WINDOWS\SYSTEM\ USER32.DLL
BFF50000	Private	53248		-R-- ---	
BFF5D000	Private	4096		-RW- ---	
BFF5E000	Private	12288		-R-- ---	
BFF61000	Free	61440			
BFF70000	Private	585728	5	- - - -	C:\WINDOWS\SYSTEM\ KERNEL32.DLL
BFF70000	Private	352256		-R-- ---	
BFFC6000	Reserve	12288		- - - - ---	
BFFC9000	Private	16384		-RW- ---	
BFFCD000	Private	90112		-R-- ---	
BFFE3000	Reserve	114688		- - - - ---	
BFFFF000	Free	4096			

The biggest difference between the two address space maps is the lack of information offered under Windows 98. For example, each region and block will reflect whether the area of address space is Free, Reserve, or Private. You will never see the words Mapped or Image because Windows 98 does not offer the additional information indicating whether the physical storage backing the region is a memory-mapped file or is contained in an .exe or a DLL's file image.

You'll notice that most of the region sizes are exact multiples of the allocation granularity (64 KB). If the sizes of the blocks contained within a region do not add up to a multiple of the allocation granularity, there is frequently a block of reserved address space at the end of the region. This block is whatever size is needed to bring the region to an allocation granularity boundary (64 KB). For example, the region starting at address 0x00530000 consists of 2 blocks: a 4-KB committed block of storage and a reserved block that occupies a 60-KB range of memory addresses.

Finally, the protection flags never reflect execute or copy-on-write access because Windows 98 does not support these flags. The three protection attribute flags—PAGE_NOCACHE, PAGE_WRITECOMBINE, and PAGE_GUARD—are also not supported. Because the PAGE_GUARD flag is not supported, VMMap uses a more complicated technique to determine whether a region of address space is reserved for a thread's stack.

You will notice that, unlike Windows 2000, in Windows 98 the region of address space between 0x80000000 and 0xBFFFFFFF can be examined. This is the partition that contains the address space shared by all 32-bit applications. As you can see, the four system DLLs are loaded into this region of address space and are therefore available to all processes.

The Importance of Data Alignment

In this section, we leave the discussion of a process's virtual address space and discuss the important topic of data alignment. Data alignment is not so much a part of the operating system's memory architecture, but it is a part of the CPU's architecture.

CPUs operate most efficiently when they access properly aligned data. Data is aligned when the memory address of the data modulo of the data's size is 0. For example, a WORD value should always start on an address that is evenly divided by 2, a DWORD value should always start on an address that is evenly divided by 4, and so on. When the CPU attempts to read a data value that is not properly aligned, the CPU will do one of two things. It will either raise an exception or the CPU will perform multiple, aligned memory accesses in order to read the full misaligned data value.

Here is some code that accesses misaligned data:

```
VOID SomeFunc(PVOID pvDataBuffer) {

   // The first byte in the buffer is some byte of information
   char c = * (PBYTE) pvDataBuffer;

   // Increment past the first byte in the buffer
   pvDataBuffer = (PVOID)((PBYTE) pvDataBuffer + 1);

   // Bytes 2-5 contain a double-word value
   DWORD dw = * (DWORD *) pvDataBuffer;

   // The line above raises a data misalignment exception on the Alpha
   :
   :

}
```

Obviously, if the CPU performs multiple memory accesses, the performance of your application is hampered. At best, it will take the system twice as long to access a misaligned value as it will to access an aligned value—but the access time could be even worse! To get the best performance for your application, you'll want to write your code so that the data is properly aligned.

Let's take a closer look at how the *x*86 CPU handles data alignment. The *x*86 CPU contains a special bit flag in its EFLAGS register called the AC (alignment check) flag. By default, this flag is set to zero when the CPU first receives power. When this flag is zero, the CPU automatically does whatever it has to in order to successfully access misaligned data values. However, if this flag is set to 1, the CPU issues an INT 17H interrupt whenever there is an attempt to access misaligned data. The *x*86 version of Windows 2000 and Windows 98 never alters this CPU flag bit. Therefore, you will never see a data misalignment exception occur in an application when it is running on an *x*86 processor.

Now, let's turn our attention to the Alpha CPU. The Alpha CPU cannot automatically fix up misaligned data accesses. Instead, when a misaligned data access occurs, the CPU notifies the operating system. Windows 2000 now decides if it should raise a data misalignment exception—or it can execute additional instructions that silently correct the problem and allow your code to continue executing. By default, when you install Windows 2000 on an Alpha machine, the operating system silently corrects any data misalignment accesses. However, you can alter this behavior. When you boot Windows 2000, the system looks in the registry for the following key:

```
HKEY_LOCAL_MACHINE\CurrentControlSet\Control\Session Manager
```

In this key, there might be a value called EnableAlignmentFaultExceptions. If this value doesn't exist (which is the usual case), Windows 2000 silently fixes up misaligned data accesses. However, if this value does exist, the system gets its associated data value. If the data value is 0, the system performs silent fixups. If, however, the data value is 1, the system will not perform the silent fixups but will instead raise a data misalignment exception. You should almost never change the data value of this registry value because some applications can now raise data misalignment exceptions and terminate.

To make it easier to change this registry entry, the Alpha edition of Microsoft Visual C++ includes a small utility called AXPAlign.exe. AXPAlign is used as shown here:

```
Alpha AXP alignment fault exception control

Usage: axpalign [option]

Options:
    /enable    to enable alignment fault exceptions.
    /disable   to disable alignment fault exceptions.
    /show      to display the current alignment exception setting.

Enable alignment fault exceptions:
    In this mode any aligned access to unaligned data will result in a
    data misalignment exception and no automatic operating system fixups
    will occur. The application may be terminated or a debugger can be
    used to locate the source of alignment faults in your code.

    This setting applies to all running processes and thus care should
    be taken since older applications may get exceptions and terminate.

    Note that SetErrorMode(SEM_NOALIGNMENTFAULTEXCEPT) can be used to
    suppress alignment exceptions even in this mode.

Disable alignment fault exceptions:
    This is the default mode with Windows NT for Alpha AXP, versions 3.1
    and 3.5. In this mode the operating system will fixup any misaligned
    data accesses should they occur and applications or debuggers will
    not see them. This may lead to performance degradation if it occurs
    at a high rate. Perfmon or wperf may be used to monitor the rate.
```

This utility simply changes the state of the registry value or shows the current state of the value. After using this utility to change the data value, you'll have to reboot for the change to take effect.

Without using AXPAlign, you can still tell the system to silently correct misaligned data accesses for all threads in your process by having one of your process's threads call the *SetErrorMode* function:

```
UINT SetErrorMode(UINT fuErrorMode);
```

For our discussion, the flag in question is the SEM_NOALIGNMENT-FAULTEXCEPT flag. When this flag is set, the system automatically corrects for misaligned data accesses. When this flag is reset, the system does not correct for misaligned data accesses but instead raises data misalignment exceptions. Note that changing this flag affects all threads contained within the process that owns the thread that makes the call. In other words, changing this flag will not affect any threads contained in any other processes. You should also note that a process's error mode flags are inherited by any child processes. Therefore, you might want to temporarily reset this flag before calling the *CreateProcess* function (although you usually don't do this).

Of course, you can call *SetErrorMode* passing the SEM_NOALIGNMENT-FAULTEXCEPT flag regardless of which CPU platform you are running on. However, the results are not always the same. For *x86* systems, this flag is always on and cannot be turned off. For Alpha systems, you can turn this flag off only if the EnableAlignmentFaultExceptions registry value is set to 1.

You can use the Windows 2000 MMC Performance Monitor snap-in to see how many alignment fixups per second the system is performing. The following figure shows what the Add Counter dialog box looks like just before you add this counter to the chart.

What this counter really shows is the number of times per second the CPU notifies the operating system of misaligned data accesses. If you monitor this counter on an *x*86 machine, you'll see that it always reports zero fixups per second. This is because the *x*86 CPU itself is performing the fixups and doesn't notify the operating system. Because the *x*86 CPU performs the fixup instead of the operating system, accessing misaligned data on an *x*86 machine is not nearly as bad a performance hit as that of CPUs that require software (the Windows 2000 operating system code) to do the fixup.

As you can see, simply calling *SetErrorMode* is enough to make your application work correctly. But this solution is definitely not the most efficient. In fact, the *Alpha Architecture Reference Manual,* published by Digital Press, states that the system's emulation code to silently correct for misaligned data accesses could take as much as 100 times longer to execute! That's quite an overhead to pay. Fortunately, there is a more efficient solution to your problem.

Microsoft's C/C++ compiler for the Alpha supports a special keyword called *__unaligned*. You use the *__unaligned* modifier just as you would use the *const* or *volatile* modifiers except that the *__unaligned* modifier is only meaningful when applied to pointer variables. When you access data via an unaligned pointer, the compiler generates code that assumes that the data is not aligned properly and adds the additional CPU instructions necessary to access the data. The code shown here is a modified version of the code shown earlier. This new version takes advantage of the *__unaligned* keyword.

```
VOID SomeFunc(PVOID pvDataBuffer) {

   // The first byte in the buffer is some byte of information
   char c = * (PBYTE) pvDataBuffer;

   // Increment past the first byte in the buffer
   pvDataBuffer = (PVOID)((PBYTE) pvDataBuffer + 1);

   // Bytes 2-5 contain a double-word value
   DWORD dw = * (__unaligned DWORD *) pvDataBuffer;

   // The line above causes the compiler to generate additional
   // instructions so that several aligned data accesses are performed
   // to read the DWORD.
   // Note that a data misalignment exception is not raised.

   :
   :

}
```

469

When I compile the following line on the Alpha, 7 CPU instructions are generated:

```
DWORD dw = * (__unaligned DWORD *) pvDataBuffer;
```

However, if I remove the *__unaligned* keyword from the line and recompile, only 3 CPU instructions are generated. As you can see, the use of the *__unaligned* keyword on the Alpha causes more than twice the number of CPU instructions to be generated. The instructions added by the compiler are still much more efficient than letting the CPU trap the misaligned data access and having the operating system correct the problem. In fact, if you monitor the Alignment Fixups/sec counter, you'll see that accesses via unaligned pointers have no effect on the chart.

Finally, the *__unaligned* keyword is not supported by the *x*86 version of the Visual C/C++ compiler. I assume that Microsoft felt that this wasn't necessary because of the speed at which the CPU itself can perform the fixups. However, this also means that the *x*86 compiler will generate errors when it encounters the *__unaligned* keyword. So, if you are trying to create a single source code base for your application, you'll want to use the UNALIGNED macro instead of the *__unaligned* keyword. The UNALIGNED macro is defined in WinNT.h as follows:

```
#if defined(_M_MRX000) || defined(_M_ALPHA) || defined(_M_IA64)
#define UNALIGNED __unaligned
#if defined(_WIN64)
#define UNALIGNED64 __unaligned
#else
#define UNALIGNED64
#endif
#else
#define UNALIGNED
#define UNALIGNED64
#endif
```

CHAPTER FOURTEEN

EXPLORING VIRTUAL MEMORY

In the last chapter, we discussed how the system manages virtual memory, how each process receives its own private address space, and what a process's address space looks like. In this chapter, we move away from the abstract and examine some of the Windows functions that give us information about the system's memory management and about the virtual address space in a process.

System Information

Many operating system values are dependent on the host machine: page size, allocation granularity size, and so on. These values should never be hard-coded into your source code. Instead, you should always retrieve these values when your process initializes and use the retrieved values within your source code. The *GetSystemInfo* function retrieves the values relevant to the host machine:

```
VOID GetSystemInfo(LPSYSTEM_INFO psinf);
```

You must pass the address of a SYSTEM_INFO structure to this function. The function will initialize all of the structure's members and return. Here is what the SYSTEM_INFO data structure looks like:

```
typedef struct _SYSTEM_INFO {
   union {
      DWORD dwOemId;   // Obsolete, do not use
      struct {
         WORD wProcessorArchitecture;
         WORD wReserved;
      };
   };
```

(continued)

471

```
  DWORD      dwPageSize;
  LPVOID     lpMinimumApplicationAddress;
  LPVOID     lpMaximumApplicationAddress;
  DWORD_PTR  dwActiveProcessorMask;
  DWORD      dwNumberOfProcessors;
  DWORD      dwProcessorType;
  DWORD      dwAllocationGranularity;
  WORD       wProcessorLevel;
  WORD       wProcessorRevision;
} SYSTEM_INFO, *LPSYSTEM_INFO;
```

When the system boots, it determines what the values of these members should be. For any given system, the values will always be the same, so you will never need to call this function more than once for any given process. *GetSystem-Info* exists so that an application can query these values at run time. Of all the members in the structure, only four of them have anything to do with memory. These four members are explained in the following table.

Member Name	Description
dwPageSize	Shows the CPU's page size. On x86, this value is 4096 bytes; on Alpha CPUs, this value is 8192 bytes; and on IA-64, this value is 8192 bytes.
lpMinimumApplicationAddress	Gives the minimum memory address of every process's usable address space. On Windows 98, this value is 4,194,304, or 0x00400000, because the bottom 4 MB of every process's address space is unusable. On Windows 2000, this value is 65,536, or 0x00010000, because the first 64 KB of every process's address space is always free.
lpMaximumApplicationAddress	Gives the maximum memory address of every process's usable private address space. On Windows 98, this address is 2,147,483,647, or 0x7FFFFFFF, because the shared memory-mapped file region and the shared operating system code are contained in the top 2-GB partition. On Windows 2000, this address is where kernel-mode memory starts, less 64 KB.
dwAllocationGranularity	Shows the granularity of a reserved region of address space. As of this writing, this value is 65,536 on all Windows platforms.

The other members of this structure are not at all related to memory management; I explain them here for completeness.

Member Name	Description
dwOemId	Obsolete, do not reference
wReserved	Reserved for future use, do not reference
dwNumberOfProcessors	Indicates the number of CPUs in the machine
dwActiveProcessorMask	A bitmask indicating which CPUs are active (allowed to run threads)
dwProcessorType	Used for Windows 98 only—not for Windows 2000; indicates the processor type, such as Intel 386, 486, or Pentium
wProcessorArchitecture	Used only for Windows 2000—not for Windows 98; indicates the processor architecture, such as Intel, Alpha, Intel 64-bit, or Alpha 64-bit
wProcessorLevel	Used only for Windows 2000—not for Windows 98; breaks down the process architecture further, such as specifying Intel Pentium Pro or Pentium II
wProcessorRevision	Used only for Windows 2000—not for Windows 98; breaks down the processor level further

The System Information Sample Application

The SysInfo application ("14 SysInfo.exe")—listed in Figure 14-1 and beginning on page 474—is a simple program that calls *GetSystemInfo* and displays the information returned in the SYSTEM_INFO structure. The source code and resource files for the application are in the 14-SysInfo directory on the companion CD-ROM. The following dialog boxes show the results of running the SysInfo application on several different platforms.

System Info			**System Info**	
Processor Architecture:	Intel		Processor Architecture:	Intel
Processor level:	Pentium		Processor level:	Pentium Pro or Pentium II
Processor revision:	(unknown)		Processor revision:	Model 6, Stepping 10
Number of processors:	1		Number of processors:	1
Active processor mask:	0x0000000000000001		Active processor mask:	0x0000000000000001
Allocation granularity:	65,536		Allocation granularity:	65,536
Page size:	4,096		Page size:	4,096
Minimum app. address:	00400000		Minimum app. address:	00010000
Maximum app. address:	7FFFFFFF		Maximum app. address:	7FFEFFFF

Windows 98 on x86   *32-bit Windows 2000 on x86*

473

🖳 System Info	□▭⊠
Processor Architecture:	Alpha
Processor level:	21164
Processor revision:	Model A, Pass 2
Number of processors:	2
Active processor mask:	0x0000000000000003
Allocation granularity:	65,536
Page size:	8,192
Minimum app. address:	65,536
Maximum app. address:	2,147,418,111

🖳 System Info	□▭⊠
Processor Architecture:	Alpha64
Processor level:	21164
Processor revision:	Model A, Pass 2
Number of processors:	1
Active processor mask:	0x0000000000000001
Allocation granularity:	65,536
Page size:	8,192
Minimum app. address:	0000000000010000
Maximum app. address:	000003FFFFFEFFFF

32-bit Windows 2000 on Alpha   *64-bit Windows on Alpha*

SysInfo.cpp

```
/*********************************************************************************
Module:  SysInfo.cpp
Notices: Copyright (c) 2000 Jeffrey Richter
*********************************************************************************/


#include "..\CmnHdr.h"      /* See Appendix A. */
#include <windowsx.h>
#include <tchar.h>
#include <stdio.h>
#include "Resource.h"


///////////////////////////////////////////////////////////////////////////////


// Set to TRUE if the app is running on Windows 9x.
BOOL g_fWin9xIsHost = FALSE;


///////////////////////////////////////////////////////////////////////////////


// This function accepts a number and converts it to a
// string, inserting commas where appropriate.
PTSTR BigNumToString(LONG lNum, PTSTR szBuf) {

   TCHAR szNum[100];
   wsprintf(szNum, TEXT("%d"), lNum);
```

Figure 14-1.
The SysInfo application

(continued)

Figure 14-1. *continued*

```
    NUMBERFMT nf;
    nf.NumDigits = 0;
    nf.LeadingZero = FALSE;
    nf.Grouping = 3;
    nf.lpDecimalSep = TEXT(".");
    nf.lpThousandSep = TEXT(",");
    nf.NegativeOrder = 0;
    GetNumberFormat(LOCALE_USER_DEFAULT, 0, szNum, &nf, szBuf, 100);
    return(szBuf);
}


//////////////////////////////////////////////////////////////////////////


void ShowCPUInfo(HWND hwnd, WORD wProcessorArchitecture, WORD wProcessorLevel,
    WORD wProcessorRevision) {

    TCHAR szCPUArch[64]  = TEXT("(unknown)");
    TCHAR szCPULevel[64] = TEXT("(unknown)");
    TCHAR szCPURev[64]   = TEXT("(unknown)");

    switch (wProcessorArchitecture) {
        case PROCESSOR_ARCHITECTURE_INTEL:
            lstrcpy(szCPUArch, TEXT("Intel"));
            switch (wProcessorLevel) {
            case 3: case 4:
                wsprintf(szCPULevel, TEXT("80%c86"), wProcessorLevel + '0');
                if (!g_fWin9xIsHost)
                    wsprintf(szCPURev, TEXT("%c%d"),
                    HIBYTE(wProcessorRevision) + TEXT('A'),
                    LOBYTE(wProcessorRevision));
                break;

            case 5:
                wsprintf(szCPULevel, TEXT("Pentium"));
                if (!g_fWin9xIsHost)
                    wsprintf(szCPURev, TEXT("Model %d, Stepping %d"),
                        HIBYTE(wProcessorRevision), LOBYTE(wProcessorRevision));
                break;
```

(continued)

475

Figure 14-1. *continued*

```
      case 6:
         wsprintf(szCPULevel, TEXT("Pentium Pro or Pentium II"));
         if (!g_fWin9xIsHost)
            wsprintf(szCPURev, TEXT("Model %d, Stepping %d"),
               HIBYTE(wProcessorRevision), LOBYTE(wProcessorRevision));
         break;
      }
      break;

   case PROCESSOR_ARCHITECTURE_ALPHA:
      lstrcpy(szCPUArch, TEXT("Alpha"));
      wsprintf(szCPULevel, TEXT("%d"), wProcessorLevel);
      wsprintf(szCPURev, TEXT("Model %c, Pass %d"),
         HIBYTE(wProcessorRevision) + TEXT('A'),
         LOBYTE(wProcessorRevision));
      break;

   case PROCESSOR_ARCHITECTURE_IA64:
      lstrcpy(szCPUArch, TEXT("IA-64"));
      wsprintf(szCPULevel, TEXT("%d"), wProcessorLevel);
      wsprintf(szCPURev, TEXT("Model %c, Pass %d"),
         HIBYTE(wProcessorRevision) + TEXT('A'),
         LOBYTE(wProcessorRevision));
      break;

   case PROCESSOR_ARCHITECTURE_ALPHA64:
      lstrcpy(szCPUArch, TEXT("Alpha64"));
      wsprintf(szCPULevel, TEXT("%d"), wProcessorLevel);
      wsprintf(szCPURev, TEXT("Model %c, Pass %d"),
         HIBYTE(wProcessorRevision) + TEXT('A'),
         LOBYTE(wProcessorRevision));
      break;

   case PROCESSOR_ARCHITECTURE_UNKNOWN:
   default:
      wsprintf(szCPUArch, TEXT("Unknown"));
      break;
   }
   SetDlgItemText(hwnd, IDC_PROCARCH,  szCPUArch);
   SetDlgItemText(hwnd, IDC_PROCLEVEL, szCPULevel);
   SetDlgItemText(hwnd, IDC_PROCREV,   szCPURev);
}
```

(continued)

Figure 14-1. *continued*

```
///////////////////////////////////////////////////////////////////////////

BOOL Dlg_OnInitDialog(HWND hwnd, HWND hwndFocus, LPARAM lParam) {

   chSETDLGICONS(hwnd, IDI_SYSINFO);

   SYSTEM_INFO sinf;
   GetSystemInfo(&sinf);

   if (g_fWin9xIsHost) {
      sinf.wProcessorLevel = (WORD) (sinf.dwProcessorType / 100);
   }

   ShowCPUInfo(hwnd, sinf.wProcessorArchitecture,
      sinf.wProcessorLevel, sinf.wProcessorRevision);

   TCHAR szBuf[50];
   SetDlgItemText(hwnd, IDC_PAGESIZE,
      BigNumToString(sinf.dwPageSize, szBuf));

   _stprintf(szBuf, TEXT("%p"), sinf.lpMinimumApplicationAddress);
   SetDlgItemText(hwnd, IDC_MINAPPADDR, szBuf);

   _stprintf(szBuf, TEXT("%p"), sinf.lpMaximumApplicationAddress);
   SetDlgItemText(hwnd, IDC_MAXAPPADDR, szBuf);

   _stprintf(szBuf, TEXT("0x%016I64X"), (__int64) sinf.dwActiveProcessorMask);
   SetDlgItemText(hwnd, IDC_ACTIVEPROCMASK, szBuf);

   SetDlgItemText(hwnd, IDC_NUMOFPROCS,
      BigNumToString(sinf.dwNumberOfProcessors, szBuf));

   SetDlgItemText(hwnd, IDC_ALLOCGRAN,
      BigNumToString(sinf.dwAllocationGranularity, szBuf));

   return(TRUE);
}

///////////////////////////////////////////////////////////////////////////

void Dlg_OnCommand(HWND hwnd, int id, HWND hwndCtl, UINT codeNotify) {

   switch (id) {
      case IDCANCEL:
```

(continued)

Figure 14-1. *continued*

```
        EndDialog(hwnd, id);
        break;
    }
}


///////////////////////////////////////////////////////////////////////////


INT_PTR WINAPI Dlg_Proc(HWND hDlg, UINT uMsg, WPARAM wParam, LPARAM lParam) {

    switch (uMsg) {
        chHANDLE_DLGMSG(hDlg, WM_INITDIALOG, Dlg_OnInitDialog);
        chHANDLE_DLGMSG(hDlg, WM_COMMAND,    Dlg_OnCommand);
    }
    return(FALSE);
}


///////////////////////////////////////////////////////////////////////////


int WINAPI _tWinMain(HINSTANCE hinstExe, HINSTANCE, PTSTR pszCmdLine, int) {

    OSVERSIONINFO vi = { sizeof(vi) };
    GetVersionEx(&vi);
    g_fWin9xIsHost = (vi.dwPlatformId == VER_PLATFORM_WIN32_WINDOWS);

    DialogBox(hinstExe, MAKEINTRESOURCE(IDD_SYSINFO), NULL, Dlg_Proc);
    return(0);
}

/////////////////////////////// End of File ///////////////////////////////
```

SysInfo.rc

```
//Microsoft Developer Studio generated resource script.
//
#include "Resource.h"

#define APSTUDIO_READONLY_SYMBOLS
///////////////////////////////////////////////////////////////////////////
//
```

(continued)

Figure 14-1. *continued*

```
// Generated from the TEXTINCLUDE 2 resource.
//
#include "afxres.h"


/////////////////////////////////////////////////////////////////////////////
#undef APSTUDIO_READONLY_SYMBOLS


/////////////////////////////////////////////////////////////////////////////
// English (U.S.) resources

#if !defined(AFX_RESOURCE_DLL) || defined(AFX_TARG_ENU)
#ifdef _WIN32
LANGUAGE LANG_ENGLISH, SUBLANG_ENGLISH_US
#pragma code_page(1252)
#endif //_WIN32

#ifdef APSTUDIO_INVOKED
/////////////////////////////////////////////////////////////////////////////
//
// TEXTINCLUDE
//

1 TEXTINCLUDE DISCARDABLE
BEGIN
    "Resource.h\0"
END

2 TEXTINCLUDE DISCARDABLE
BEGIN
    "#include ""afxres.h""\r\n"
    "\0"
END

3 TEXTINCLUDE DISCARDABLE
BEGIN
    "\r\n"
    "\0"
END

#endif    // APSTUDIO_INVOKED


/////////////////////////////////////////////////////////////////////////////
//
```

(continued)

Figure 14-1. *continued*

```
// Dialog
//


IDD_SYSINFO DIALOG DISCARDABLE  18, 18, 186, 97
STYLE WS_MINIMIZEBOX | WS_POPUP | WS_VISIBLE | WS_CAPTION | WS_SYSMENU
CAPTION "System Info"
FONT 8, "MS Sans Serif"
BEGIN
    RTEXT           "Processor Architecture:",IDC_STATIC,4,4,88,8,
                    SS_NOPREFIX
    RTEXT           "ID_PROCARCH",IDC_PROCARCH,96,4,84,8,SS_NOPREFIX
    RTEXT           "Processor level:",IDC_STATIC,4,14,88,8,SS_NOPREFIX
    RTEXT           "ID_PROCLEVEL",IDC_PROCLEVEL,96,14,84,8,SS_NOPREFIX
    RTEXT           "Processor revision:",IDC_STATIC,4,24,88,8,SS_NOPREFIX
    RTEXT           "ID_PROCREV",IDC_PROCREV,96,24,84,8,SS_NOPREFIX
    RTEXT           "Number of processors:",IDC_STATIC,4,34,88,8,SS_NOPREFIX
    RTEXT           "ID_NUMOFPROCS",IDC_NUMOFPROCS,96,34,84,8,SS_NOPREFIX
    RTEXT           "Active processor mask:",IDC_STATIC,4,44,88,8,
                    SS_NOPREFIX
    RTEXT           "ID_ACTIVEPROCMASK",IDC_ACTIVEPROCMASK,96,44,84,8,
                    SS_NOPREFIX
    RTEXT           "Allocation granularity:",IDC_STATIC,4,54,88,8,
                    SS_NOPREFIX
    RTEXT           "ID_ALLOCGRAN",IDC_ALLOCGRAN,96,54,84,8,SS_NOPREFIX
    RTEXT           "Page size:",IDC_STATIC,4,64,88,8,SS_NOPREFIX
    RTEXT           "ID_PAGESIZE",IDC_PAGESIZE,96,64,84,8,SS_NOPREFIX
    RTEXT           "Minimum app. address:",IDC_STATIC,4,74,88,8,SS_NOPREFIX
    RTEXT           "ID_MINAPPADDR",IDC_MINAPPADDR,96,74,84,8,SS_NOPREFIX
    RTEXT           "Maximum app. address:",IDC_STATIC,4,84,88,8,SS_NOPREFIX
    RTEXT           "ID_MAXAPPADDR",IDC_MAXAPPADDR,96,84,84,8,SS_NOPREFIX
END


/////////////////////////////////////////////////////////////////////////
//
// Icon
//


// Icon with lowest ID value placed first to ensure application icon
// remains consistent on all systems.
IDI_SYSINFO             ICON    DISCARDABLE     "SysInfo.Ico"


/////////////////////////////////////////////////////////////////////////
//
```

(continued)

Figure 14-1. *continued*

```
// DESIGNINFO
//

#ifdef APSTUDIO_INVOKED
GUIDELINES DESIGNINFO DISCARDABLE
BEGIN
    IDD_SYSINFO, DIALOG
    BEGIN
        RIGHTMARGIN, 170
        BOTTOMMARGIN, 77
    END
END
#endif    // APSTUDIO_INVOKED

#endif    // English (U.S.) resources
/////////////////////////////////////////////////////////////////////////////


#ifndef APSTUDIO_INVOKED
/////////////////////////////////////////////////////////////////////////////
//
// Generated from the TEXTINCLUDE 3 resource.
//


/////////////////////////////////////////////////////////////////////////////
#endif    // not APSTUDIO_INVOKED
```

Virtual Memory Status

A Windows function called *GlobalMemoryStatus* retrieves dynamic information about the current state of memory:

```
VOID GlobalMemoryStatus(LPMEMORYSTATUS pmst);
```

I think that this function is poorly named—*GlobalMemoryStatus* implies that the function is somehow related to the global heaps in 16-bit Windows. I think that *GlobalMemoryStatus* should have been called something like *Virtual-MemoryStatus* instead.

When you call *GlobalMemoryStatus*, you must pass the address of a MEMORYSTATUS structure. The MEMORYSTATUS data structure is shown on the following page.

```
typedef struct _MEMORYSTATUS {
    DWORD dwLength;
    DWORD dwMemoryLoad;
    SIZE_T dwTotalPhys;
    SIZE_T dwAvailPhys;
    SIZE_T dwTotalPageFile;
    SIZE_T dwAvailPageFile;
    SIZE_T dwTotalVirtual;
    SIZE_T dwAvailVirtual;
} MEMORYSTATUS, *LPMEMORYSTATUS;
```

Before calling *GlobalMemoryStatus*, you must initialize the *dwLength* member to the size of the structure in bytes—that is, the size of a MEMORY-STATUS structure. This initialization allows Microsoft to add members to this structure in future versions of Windows without breaking existing applications. When you call *GlobalMemoryStatus*, it will initialize the remainder of the structure's members and return. The VMStat sample application in the next section describes the various members and their meanings.

If you anticipate that your application will run on machines with more than 4 GB of RAM or if the total swap file size might be larger than 4 GB, you may want to use the new *GlobalMemoryStatusEx* function:

```
BOOL GlobalMemoryStatusEx(LPMEMORYSTATUSEX pmst);
```

You must pass to this function the address of the new MEMORY-STATUSEX structure:

```
typedef struct _MEMORYSTATUSEX {
    DWORD dwLength;
    DWORD dwMemoryLoad;
    DWORDLONG ullTotalPhys;
    DWORDLONG ullAvailPhys;
    DWORDLONG ullTotalPageFile;
    DWORDLONG ullAvailPageFile;
    DWORDLONG ullTotalVirtual;
    DWORDLONG ullAvailVirtual;
    DWORDLONG ullAvailExtendedVirtual;
} MEMORYSTATUSEX, *LPMEMORYSTATUSEX;
```

This structure is identical to the original MEMORYSTATUS structure except that all the size members are 64 bits wide, allowing for values greater than 4 GB. The member at the end, *ullAvailExtendedVirtual*, indicates the size of unreserved memory in the very large memory (VLM) portion of the virtual address space of the calling process. This VLM portion applies only to certain CPU architectures in certain configurations.

The Virtual Memory Status Sample Application

The VMStat application ("14 VMStat.exe"), listed in Figure 14-2, displays a simple dialog box that lists the results of a call to *GlobalMemoryStatus*. The information inside the dialog box is updated once every second, so you might want to keep the application running while you work with other processes on your system. The source code and resource files for the application can be found in the 14-VMStat directory on the companion CD-ROM. The figure below shows the result of running this program on Windows 2000 using a 128-MB Intel Pentium II machine.

The *dwMemoryLoad* member (shown as Memory Load) gives a rough estimate of how busy the memory management system is. This number can be anywhere from 0 to 100. The exact algorithm used to calculate this value varies between Windows 98 and Windows 2000. The algorithm is also subject to change in future versions of the operating system. In practice, the value reported by this member variable is useless.

The *dwTotalPhys* member (shown as TotalPhys) indicates the total number of bytes of physical memory (RAM) that exist. On this 128-MB Pentium II machine, this value is 133,677,056, which is just 540,672 bytes under 128 MB. The reason that *GlobalMemoryStatus* does not report the full 128 MB is that the system reserves some storage as a nonpaged pool during the boot process. This memory is not even considered available to the kernel. The *dwAvailPhys* member (shown as AvailPhys) indicates the total number of bytes of physical memory available for allocation.

The *dwTotalPageFile* member (shown as TotalPageFile) indicates the maximum number of bytes that can be contained in the paging file(s) on your hard disk(s). Although VMStat reported that the paging file is currently 318,574,592 bytes, the system can expand and shrink the paging file as it sees fit. The *dwAvailPageFile* member (shown as AvailPageFile) indicates that 233,046,016 bytes in the paging file(s) are not committed to any process and are currently available should a process decide to commit any private storage.

The *dwTotalVirtual* member (shown as TotalVirtual) indicates the total number of bytes that are private in each process's address space. The value 2,147,352,576 is 128 KB short of being exactly 2 GB. The two partitions from 0x00000000 through 0x0000FFFF and from 0x7FFF0000 through 0x7FFFFFFF of inaccessible address space account for the 128-KB difference. If you run VMStat under Windows 98, you'll see that *dwTotalVirtual* comes back with a value of 2,143,289,344, which is just 4 MB short of being exactly 2 GB. The 4-MB difference exists because the system never lets an application gain access to the 4-MB partition from 0x00000000 through 0x003FFFFF.

The last member, *dwAvailVirtual* (shown as AvailVirtual), is the only member of the structure specific to the process calling *GlobalMemoryStatus*—all the other members apply to the system and would be the same regardless of which process was calling *GlobalMemoryStatus*. To calculate this value, *Global-MemoryStatus* adds up all of the free regions in the calling process's address space. The *dwAvailVirtual* value 2,136,846,336 indicates the amount of free address space that is available for VMStat to do with what it wants. If you subtract the *dwAvailVirtual* member from the *dwTotalVirtual* member, you'll see that VMStat has 10,506,240 bytes reserved in its virtual address space.

There is no member that indicates the amount of physical storage currently in use by the process.

 VMStat.cpp

```
/******************************************************************************
Module:  VMStat.cpp
Notices: Copyright (c) 2000 Jeffrey Richter
******************************************************************************/


#include "..\CmnHdr.h"      /* See Appendix A. */
#include <windowsx.h>
#include <tchar.h>
#include <stdio.h>
#include "Resource.h"


///////////////////////////////////////////////////////////////////////////////

// The update timer's ID
#define IDT_UPDATE   1


///////////////////////////////////////////////////////////////////////////////
```

Figure 14-2.
The VMStat application

(continued)

Figure 14-2. *continued*

```
BOOL Dlg_OnInitDialog(HWND hwnd, HWND hwndFocus, LPARAM lParam) {

    chSETDLGICONS(hwnd, IDI_VMSTAT);

    // Set a timer so that the information updates periodically.
    SetTimer(hwnd, IDT_UPDATE, 1 * 1000, NULL);

    // Force a timer message for the initial update.
    FORWARD_WM_TIMER(hwnd, IDT_UPDATE, SendMessage);
    return(TRUE);
}


///////////////////////////////////////////////////////////////////////////


void Dlg_OnTimer(HWND hwnd, UINT id) {

    // Initialize the structure length before calling GlobalMemoryStatus.
    MEMORYSTATUS ms = { sizeof(ms) };
    GlobalMemoryStatus(&ms);

    TCHAR szData[512] = { 0 };
    _stprintf(szData, TEXT("%d\n%d\n%I64d\n%I64d\n%I64d\n%I64d\n%I64d"),
        ms.dwMemoryLoad, ms.dwTotalPhys,
        (__int64) ms.dwAvailPhys,     (__int64) ms.dwTotalPageFile,
        (__int64) ms.dwAvailPageFile, (__int64) ms.dwTotalVirtual,
        (__int64) ms.dwAvailVirtual);
    SetDlgItemText(hwnd, IDC_DATA, szData);
}


///////////////////////////////////////////////////////////////////////////


void Dlg_OnCommand(HWND hwnd, int id, HWND hwndCtl, UINT codeNotify) {

    switch (id) {
        case IDCANCEL:
            KillTimer(hwnd, IDT_UPDATE);
            EndDialog(hwnd, id);
            break;
    }
}


///////////////////////////////////////////////////////////////////////////
```

(continued)

Figure 14-2. *continued*

```
INT_PTR WINAPI Dlg_Proc(HWND hwnd, UINT uMsg, WPARAM wParam, LPARAM lParam) {

    switch (uMsg) {
        chHANDLE_DLGMSG(hwnd, WM_INITDIALOG, Dlg_OnInitDialog);
        chHANDLE_DLGMSG(hwnd, WM_COMMAND,    Dlg_OnCommand);
        chHANDLE_DLGMSG(hwnd, WM_TIMER,      Dlg_OnTimer);
    }
    return(FALSE);
}


//////////////////////////////////////////////////////////////////////////////

int WINAPI _tWinMain(HINSTANCE hinstExe, HINSTANCE, PTSTR pszCmdLine, int) {

    DialogBox(hinstExe, MAKEINTRESOURCE(IDD_VMSTAT), NULL, Dlg_Proc);
    return(0);
}

/////////////////////////////////// End of File //////////////////////////////////
```

VMStat.rc

```
//Microsoft Developer Studio generated resource script.
//
#include "Resource.h"

#define APSTUDIO_READONLY_SYMBOLS
/////////////////////////////////////////////////////////////////////////////
//
// Generated from the TEXTINCLUDE 2 resource.
//
#include "afxres.h"


/////////////////////////////////////////////////////////////////////////////
#undef APSTUDIO_READONLY_SYMBOLS


/////////////////////////////////////////////////////////////////////////////
// English (U.S.) resources

#if !defined(AFX_RESOURCE_DLL) || defined(AFX_TARG_ENU)
#ifdef _WIN32
LANGUAGE LANG_ENGLISH, SUBLANG_ENGLISH_US
```

Figure 14-2. *continued*

```
#pragma code_page(1252)
#endif //_WIN32


#ifdef APSTUDIO_INVOKED
/////////////////////////////////////////////////////////////////////////////
//
// TEXTINCLUDE
//

1 TEXTINCLUDE DISCARDABLE
BEGIN
    "Resource.h\0"
END

2 TEXTINCLUDE DISCARDABLE
BEGIN
    "#include ""afxres.h""\r\n"
    "\0"
END

3 TEXTINCLUDE DISCARDABLE
BEGIN
    "\r\n"
    "\0"
END


#endif    // APSTUDIO_INVOKED


/////////////////////////////////////////////////////////////////////////////
//
// Dialog
//

IDD_VMSTAT DIALOG DISCARDABLE  60, 60, 132, 66
STYLE WS_MINIMIZEBOX | WS_POPUP | WS_VISIBLE | WS_CAPTION | WS_SYSMENU
CAPTION "VMStat"
FONT 8, "MS Sans Serif"
BEGIN
    LTEXT           "Memory load:\nTotalPhys:\nAvailPhys:\nTotalPageFile:\n\
                    AvailPageFile:\nTotalVirtual:\nAvailVirtual:",
                    IDC_STATIC,4,4,51,56
    RTEXT           "Memory load:\nTotalPhys:\nAvailPhys:\nTotalPageFile:\n\
                    AvailPageFile:\nTotalVirtual:\nAvailVirtual:",
                    IDC_DATA,60,4,68,56
END
```

(continued)

Figure 14-2. *continued*

```
/////////////////////////////////////////////////////////////////////////////
//
// Icon
//

// Icon with lowest ID value placed first to ensure application icon
// remains consistent on all systems.
IDI_VMSTAT                  ICON    DISCARDABLE     "VMStat.Ico"


/////////////////////////////////////////////////////////////////////////////
//
// DESIGNINFO
//

#ifdef APSTUDIO_INVOKED
GUIDELINES DESIGNINFO DISCARDABLE
BEGIN
    IDD_VMSTAT, DIALOG
    BEGIN
        RIGHTMARGIN, 108
        BOTTOMMARGIN, 65
    END
END
#endif    // APSTUDIO_INVOKED

#endif    // English (U.S.) resources
/////////////////////////////////////////////////////////////////////////////


#ifndef APSTUDIO_INVOKED
/////////////////////////////////////////////////////////////////////////////
//
// Generated from the TEXTINCLUDE 3 resource.
//


/////////////////////////////////////////////////////////////////////////////
#endif    // not APSTUDIO_INVOKED
```

Determining the State of an Address Space

Windows offers a function that lets you query certain information (for example, size, storage type, and protection attributes) about a memory address in your address space. In fact, the VMMap sample application shown later in this chapter uses this function to produce the virtual memory map dumps that appeared in Chapter 13. This function is called *VirtualQuery*:

```
DWORD VirtualQuery(
   LPCVOID pvAddress,
   PMEMORY_BASIC_INFORMATION pmbi,
   DWORD dwLength);
```

Windows also offers a function that allows one process to query memory information about another process:

```
DWORD VirtualQueryEx(
   HANDLE hProcess,
   LPCVOID pvAddress,
   PMEMORY_BASIC_INFORMATION pmbi,
   DWORD dwLength);
```

The two functions are identical except that *VirtualQueryEx* allows you to pass the handle of a process whose address space you want to query. Debuggers and other utilities most often use this function—nearly all applications will need only to call *VirtualQuery*. When you call *VirtualQuery(Ex)*, the *pvAddress* parameter must contain the virtual memory address that you want information about. The *pmbi* parameter is the address to a MEMORY_BASIC_ INFORMATION structure that you must allocate. This structure is defined in WinNT.h as follows:

```
typedef struct _MEMORY_BASIC_INFORMATION {
   PVOID BaseAddress;
   PVOID AllocationBase;
   DWORD AllocationProtect;
   SIZE_T RegionSize;
   DWORD State;
   DWORD Protect;
   DWORD Type;
} MEMORY_BASIC_INFORMATION, *PMEMORY_BASIC_INFORMATION;
```

The last parameter, *dwLength*, specifies the size of the MEMORY_BASIC_ INFORMATION structure. *VirtualQuery(Ex)* returns the number of bytes copied into the buffer.

Based on the address that you pass in the *pvAddress* parameter, *Virtual-Query(Ex)* fills the MEMORY_BASIC_INFORMATION structure with information about the range of adjoining pages that share the same state, protection attributes, and type. The following table offers a description of the structure's members.

Member Name	Description
BaseAddress	The same value as the *pvAddress* parameter rounded down to a page boundary.
AllocationBase	Identifies the base address of the region containing the address specified in the *pvAddress* parameter.
AllocationProtect	Identifies the protection attribute assigned to the region when it was initially reserved.
RegionSize	Identifies the size, in bytes, for all pages starting at *BaseAddress* that have the same protection attributes, state, and type as the page containing the address specified in the *pvAddress* parameter.
State	Identifies the state (MEM_FREE, MEM_RESERVE, or MEM_COMMIT) for all adjoining pages that have the same protection attributes, state, and type as the page containing the address specified in the *pvAddress* parameter.
	If the state is free, the *AllocationBase*, *AllocationProtect*, *Protect*, and *Type* members are undefined.
	If the state is MEM_RESERVE, the *Protect* member is undefined.
Protect	Identifies the protection attribute (PAGE_*) for all adjoining pages that have the same protection attributes, state, and type as the page containing the address specified in the *pvAddress* parameter.
Type	Identifies the type of physical storage (MEM_IMAGE, MEM_MAPPED, or MEM_PRIVATE) that is backing all adjoining pages that have the same protection attributes, state, and type as the page containing the address specified in the *pvAddress* parameter. For Windows 98, this member will always indicate MEM_PRIVATE.

The *VMQuery* Function

When I was first learning about Windows memory architecture, I used *Virtual-Query* as my guide. In fact, if you examine the first edition of this book, you'll see that the VMMap sample application was much simpler than the new version I present in the next section. In the old version, I had a simple loop that repeatedly called *VirtualQuery*, and for each call I simply constructed a single line containing the members of the MEMORY_BASIC_INFORMATION structure. I studied this dump and tried to piece the memory management architecture together while referring to the SDK documentation (which was rather poor at the time). Well, I've learned a lot since then. While *VirtualQuery* and the MEMORY_BASIC_INFORMATION structure give you a lot of insight into what's going on, I now know that they don't give you enough information to really understand it all.

The problem is that the MEMORY_BASIC_INFORMATION structure does not return all of the information that the system has stored internally. If you have a memory address and want to obtain some simple information about it, *VirtualQuery* is great. If you just want to know whether there is committed physical storage to an address or whether a memory address can be read from or written to, *VirtualQuery* works fine. But if you want to know the total size of a reserved region or the number of blocks in a region or whether a region contains a thread's stack, a single call to *VirtualQuery* is just not going to give you the information you're looking for.

To obtain much more complete memory information, I have created my own function, *VMQuery*:

```
BOOL VMQuery(
    HANDLE hProcess,
    PVOID pvAddress,
    PVMQUERY pVMQ);
```

This function is similar to *VirtualQueryEx* in that it takes a process handle (in *hProcess*), a memory address (in *pvAddress*), and a pointer to a structure that is to be filled (specified by *pVMQ*). This structure is a *VMQUERY* structure that I have also defined:

```
typedef struct {
    // Region information
    PVOID pvRgnBaseAddress;
    DWORD dwRgnProtection;    // PAGE_*
    SIZE_T RgnSize;
    DWORD dwRgnStorage;       // MEM_*: Free, Image, Mapped, Private
    DWORD dwRgnBlocks;
    DWORD dwRgnGuardBlks;     // If > 0, region contains thread stack
    BOOL fRgnIsAStack;        // TRUE if region contains thread stack

    // Block information
    PVOID pvBlkBaseAddress;
    DWORD dwBlkProtection;    // PAGE_*
    SIZE_T BlkSize;
    DWORD dwBlkStorage;       //
 MEM_*: Free, Reserve, Image, Mapped, Private
} VMQUERY, *PVMQUERY;
```

As you can see from just a quick glance, my VMQUERY structure contains much more information than the Windows MEMORY_BASIC_INFORMATION structure. My structure is divided into two distinct parts: region information and block information. The region portion describes information about the region, and the block portion includes information about the block containing the address specified by the *pvAddress* parameter. The following table describes all the members.

Member Name	Description
pvRgnBaseAddress	Identifies the base address of the virtual address space region containing the address specified in the *pvAddress* parameter.
dwRgnProtection	Identifies the protection attribute (PAGE_*) that was assigned to the region of address space when it was initially reserved.
RgnSize	Identifies the size, in bytes, of the region that was reserved.
dwRgnStorage	Identifies the type of physical storage that is used for the bulk of the blocks in the region. The value is one of the following: MEM_FREE, MEM_IMAGE, MEM_MAPPED, or MEM_PRIVATE. Windows 98 doesn't distinguish between different storage types, so this member will always be MEM_FREE or MEM_PRIVATE under Windows 98.
dwRgnBlocks	Identifies the number of blocks contained within the region.
dwRgnGuardBlks	Identifies the number of blocks that have the PAGE_GUARD protection attribute flag turned on. This value will usually be either 0 or 1. If it's 1, that's a good indicator that the region was reserved to contain a thread's stack. Under Windows 98, this member will always be 0.
fRgnIsAStack	Identifies whether the region contains a thread's stack. This value is determined by taking a "best guess" because it is impossible to be 100 percent sure whether a region contains a stack.
pvBlkBaseAddress	Identifies the base address of the block that contains the address specified in the *pvAddress* parameter.
dwBlkProtection	Identifies the protection attribute for the block that contains the address specified in the *pvAddress* parameter.
BlkSize	Identifies the size, in bytes, of the block that contains the address specified in the *pvAddress* parameter.
dwBlkStorage	Identifies the content of the block that contains the address specified in the *pvAddress* parameter. The value is one of the following: MEM_FREE, MEM_RESERVE, MEM_IMAGE, MEM_MAPPED, or MEM_PRIVATE. Under Windows 98, this member will never be MEM_IMAGE or MEM_MAPPED.

No doubt *VMQuery* must do a significant amount of processing, including many calls to *VirtualQueryEx*, in order to obtain all this information—which means it executes much more slowly than *VirtualQueryEx*. For this reason, you should think carefully when deciding which of these two functions to call. If you do not need the extra information obtained by *VMQuery*, call *VirtualQuery* or *VirtualQueryEx*.

The VMQuery.cpp file, listed in Figure 14-3, shows how I obtain and massage all the information needed to set the members of the VMQUERY structure. The VMQuery.cpp and VMQuery.h files are in the 14-VMMap directory on the companion CD-ROM. Rather than go into detail in the text about how I process this data, I'll let my comments (sprinkled liberally throughout the code) speak for themselves.

VMQuery.cpp

```
/******************************************************************************
Module:  VMQuery.cpp
Notices: Copyright (c) 2000 Jeffrey Richter
******************************************************************************/


#include "..\CmnHdr.h"      /* See Appendix A. */
#include <windowsx.h>
#include "VMQuery.h"


///////////////////////////////////////////////////////////////////////////////


// Helper structure
typedef struct {
   SIZE_T RgnSize;
   DWORD  dwRgnStorage;      // MEM_*: Free, Image, Mapped, Private
   DWORD  dwRgnBlocks;
   DWORD  dwRgnGuardBlks;    // If > 0, region contains thread stack
   BOOL   fRgnIsAStack;      // TRUE if region contains thread stack
} VMQUERY_HELP;


// This global, static variable holds the allocation granularity value for
// this CPU platform. Initialized the first time VMQuery is called.
static DWORD gs_dwAllocGran = 0;


///////////////////////////////////////////////////////////////////////////////
```

Figure 14-3. *(continued)*
The VMQuery listings

Figure 14-3. *continued*

```
// Iterates through a region's blocks and returns findings in VMQUERY_HELP
static BOOL VMQueryHelp(HANDLE hProcess, LPCVOID pvAddress,
   VMQUERY_HELP *pVMQHelp) {

   // Each element contains a page protection
   // (i.e.: 0=reserved, PAGE_NOACCESS, PAGE_READWRITE, etc.)
   DWORD dwProtectBlock[4] = { 0 };

   ZeroMemory(pVMQHelp, sizeof(*pVMQHelp));

   // Get address of region containing passed memory address.
   MEMORY_BASIC_INFORMATION mbi;
   BOOL fOk = (VirtualQueryEx(hProcess, pvAddress, &mbi, sizeof(mbi))
      == sizeof(mbi));

   if (!fOk)
      return(fOk);   // Bad memory address, return failure

   // Walk starting at the region's base address (which never changes)
   PVOID pvRgnBaseAddress = mbi.AllocationBase;

   // Walk starting at the first block in the region (changes in the loop)
   PVOID pvAddressBlk = pvRgnBaseAddress;

   // Save the memory type of the physical storage block.
   pVMQHelp->dwRgnStorage = mbi.Type;

   for (;;) {
      // Get info about the current block.
      fOk = (VirtualQueryEx(hProcess, pvAddressBlk, &mbi, sizeof(mbi))
         == sizeof(mbi));
      if (!fOk)
         break;   // Couldn't get the information, end loop.

      // Is this block in the same region?
      if (mbi.AllocationBase != pvRgnBaseAddress)
         break;   // Found a block in the next region; end loop.

      // We have a block contained in the region.

      // The following if statement is for detecting stacks in Windows 98.
      // A Windows 98 stack region's last 4 blocks look like this:
      // reserved block, no access block, read-write block, reserved block
```

(continued)

Figure 14-3. *continued*

```
    if (pVMQHelp->dwRgnBlocks < 4) {
        // 0th through 3rd block, remember the block's protection
        dwProtectBlock[pVMQHelp->dwRgnBlocks] =
            (mbi.State == MEM_RESERVE) ? 0 : mbi.Protect;
    } else {
        // We've seen 4 blocks in this region.
        // Shift the protection values down in the array.
        MoveMemory(&dwProtectBlock[0], &dwProtectBlock[1],
            sizeof(dwProtectBlock) - sizeof(DWORD));

        // Add the new protection value to the end of the array.
        dwProtectBlock[3] = (mbi.State == MEM_RESERVE) ? 0 : mbi.Protect;
    }

    pVMQHelp->dwRgnBlocks++;             // Add another block to the region
    pVMQHelp->RgnSize += mbi.RegionSize; // Add block's size to region size

    // If block has PAGE_GUARD attribute, add 1 to this counter
    if ((mbi.Protect & PAGE_GUARD) == PAGE_GUARD)
        pVMQHelp->dwRgnGuardBlks++;

    // Take a best guess as to the type of physical storage committed to the
    // block. This is a guess because some blocks can convert from MEM_IMAGE
    // to MEM_PRIVATE or from MEM_MAPPED to MEM_PRIVATE; MEM_PRIVATE can
    // always be overridden by MEM_IMAGE or MEM_MAPPED.
    if (pVMQHelp->dwRgnStorage == MEM_PRIVATE)
        pVMQHelp->dwRgnStorage = mbi.Type;

    // Get the address of the next block.
    pvAddressBlk = (PVOID) ((PBYTE) pvAddressBlk + mbi.RegionSize);
}

// After examining the region, check to see whether it is a thread stack
// Windows 2000: Assume stack if region has at least 1 PAGE_GUARD block
// Windows 9x:   Assume stack if region has at least 4 blocks with
//                   3rd block from end: reserved
//                   2nd block from end: PAGE_NOACCESS
//                   1st block from end: PAGE_READWRITE
//                   block at end: another reserved block.
pVMQHelp->fRgnIsAStack =
    (pVMQHelp->dwRgnGuardBlks > 0)          ||
    ((pVMQHelp->dwRgnBlocks >= 4)           &&
    (dwProtectBlock[0] == 0)                &&
```

(continued)

Figure 14-3. *continued*

```
                (dwProtectBlock[1] == PAGE_NOACCESS)  &&
                (dwProtectBlock[2] == PAGE_READWRITE) &&
                (dwProtectBlock[3] == 0));

        return(TRUE);
    }


    ///////////////////////////////////////////////////////////////////////////////


    BOOL VMQuery(HANDLE hProcess, LPCVOID pvAddress, PVMQUERY pVMQ) {

        if (gs_dwAllocGran == 0) {
            // Set allocation granularity if this is the first call
            SYSTEM_INFO sinf;
            GetSystemInfo(&sinf);
            gs_dwAllocGran = sinf.dwAllocationGranularity;
        }


        ZeroMemory(pVMQ, sizeof(*pVMQ));

        // Get the MEMORY_BASIC_INFORMATION for the passed address.
        MEMORY_BASIC_INFORMATION mbi;
        BOOL fOk = (VirtualQueryEx(hProcess, pvAddress, &mbi, sizeof(mbi))
            == sizeof(mbi));

        if (!fOk)
            return(fOk);   // Bad memory address, return failure

        // The MEMORY_BASIC_INFORMATION structure contains valid information.
        // Time to start setting the members of our own VMQUERY structure.

        // First, fill in the block members. We'll fill the region members later.
        switch (mbi.State) {
            case MEM_FREE:          // Free block (not reserved)
                pVMQ->pvBlkBaseAddress = NULL;
                pVMQ->BlkSize = 0;
                pVMQ->dwBlkProtection = 0;
                pVMQ->dwBlkStorage = MEM_FREE;
                break;

            case MEM_RESERVE:       // Reserved block without committed storage in it.
                pVMQ->pvBlkBaseAddress = mbi.BaseAddress;
                pVMQ->BlkSize = mbi.RegionSize;
```

(continued)

Figure 14-3. *continued*

```
        // For an uncommitted block, mbi.Protect is invalid. So we will
        // show that the reserved block inherits the protection attribute
        // of the region in which it is contained.
        pVMQ->dwBlkProtection = mbi.AllocationProtect;
        pVMQ->dwBlkStorage = MEM_RESERVE;
        break;

     case MEM_COMMIT:     // Reserved block with committed storage in it.
        pVMQ->pvBlkBaseAddress = mbi.BaseAddress;
        pVMQ->BlkSize = mbi.RegionSize;
        pVMQ->dwBlkProtection = mbi.Protect;
        pVMQ->dwBlkStorage = mbi.Type;
        break;


     default:
        DebugBreak();
        break;
}

// Now fill in the region data members.
VMQUERY_HELP VMQHelp;
switch (mbi.State) {
   case MEM_FREE:        // Free block (not reserved)
      pVMQ->pvRgnBaseAddress = mbi.BaseAddress;
      pVMQ->dwRgnProtection  = mbi.AllocationProtect;
      pVMQ->RgnSize          = mbi.RegionSize;
      pVMQ->dwRgnStorage     = MEM_FREE;
      pVMQ->dwRgnBlocks      = 0;
      pVMQ->dwRgnGuardBlks   = 0;
      pVMQ->fRgnIsAStack     = FALSE;
      break;

   case MEM_RESERVE:     // Reserved block without committed storage in it.
      pVMQ->pvRgnBaseAddress = mbi.AllocationBase;
      pVMQ->dwRgnProtection  = mbi.AllocationProtect;

      // Iterate through all blocks to get complete region information.
      VMQueryHelp(hProcess, pvAddress, &VMQHelp);

      pVMQ->RgnSize          = VMQHelp.RgnSize;
      pVMQ->dwRgnStorage     = VMQHelp.dwRgnStorage;
      pVMQ->dwRgnBlocks      = VMQHelp.dwRgnBlocks;
      pVMQ->dwRgnGuardBlks   = VMQHelp.dwRgnGuardBlks;
      pVMQ->fRgnIsAStack     = VMQHelp.fRgnIsAStack;
      break;
```

(continued)

Figure 14-3. *continued*

```
      case MEM_COMMIT:      // Reserved block with committed storage in it.
         pVMQ->pvRgnBaseAddress = mbi.AllocationBase;
         pVMQ->dwRgnProtection  = mbi.AllocationProtect;

         // Iterate through all blocks to get complete region information.
         VMQueryHelp(hProcess, pvAddress, &VMQHelp);

         pVMQ->RgnSize          = VMQHelp.RgnSize;
         pVMQ->dwRgnStorage     = VMQHelp.dwRgnStorage;
         pVMQ->dwRgnBlocks      = VMQHelp.dwRgnBlocks;
         pVMQ->dwRgnGuardBlks   = VMQHelp.dwRgnGuardBlks;
         pVMQ->fRgnIsAStack     = VMQHelp.fRgnIsAStack;
         break;

      default:
         DebugBreak();
         break;
   }

   return(fOk);
}


/////////////////////////////// End of File ///////////////////////////////////
```

VMQuery.h

```
/******************************************************************************
Module:  VMQuery.h
Notices: Copyright (c) 2000 Jeffrey Richter
******************************************************************************/


typedef struct {
   // Region information
   PVOID  pvRgnBaseAddress;
   DWORD  dwRgnProtection;    // PAGE_*
   SIZE_T RgnSize;
   DWORD  dwRgnStorage;       // MEM_*: Free, Image, Mapped, Private
   DWORD  dwRgnBlocks;
   DWORD  dwRgnGuardBlks;     // If > 0, region contains thread stack
   BOOL   fRgnIsAStack;       // TRUE if region contains thread stack
   // Block information
   PVOID  pvBlkBaseAddress;
   DWORD  dwBlkProtection;    // PAGE_*
```

(continued)

Figure 14-3. *continued*

```
   SIZE_T BlkSize;
   DWORD  dwBlkStorage;       // MEM_*: Free, Reserve, Image, Mapped, Private
} VMQUERY, *PVMQUERY;

///////////////////////////////////////////////////////////////////////////

BOOL VMQuery(HANDLE hProcess, LPCVOID pvAddress, PVMQUERY pVMQ);

////////////////////////////////// End of File ///////////////////////////////
```

The Virtual Memory Map Sample Application

The VMMap application (14 VMMap.exe), listed in Figure 14-4, walks a process's address space and shows the regions and the blocks within regions. The source code and resource files for the application are in the 14-VMMap directory on the companion CD-ROM. When you start the program, the following window appears.

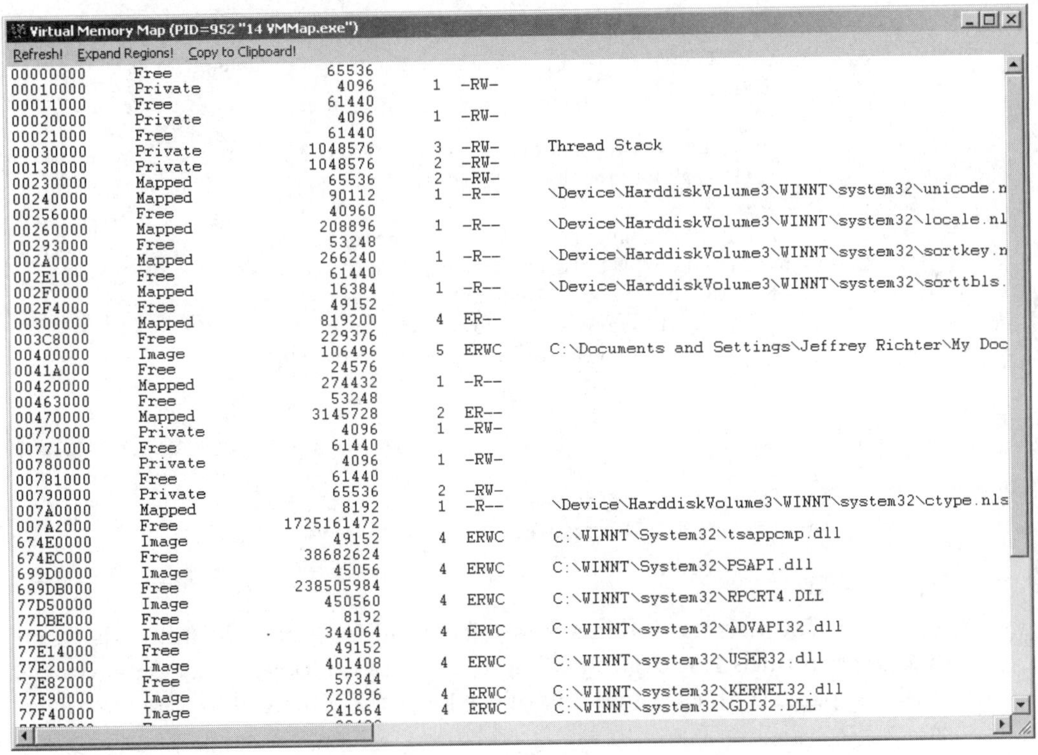

499

I used the contents of this application's list box to produce the virtual memory map dumps presented in Table 13-2 on page 453, Table 13-3 on page 456, and Table 13-4 on page 461 in Chapter 13.

Each entry in the list box shows the result of information obtained by calling my *VMQuery* function. The main loop, in the *Refresh* function, looks like this:

```
BOOL fOk = TRUE;
PVOID pvAddress = NULL;

  :
  :

while (fOk) {

    VMQUERY vmq;
    fOk = VMQuery(hProcess, pvAddress, &vmq);

    if (fOk) {
      // Construct the line to be displayed, and add it to the list box.
      TCHAR szLine[1024];
      ConstructRgnInfoLine(hProcess, &vmq, szLine, sizeof(szLine));
      ListBox_AddString(hwndLB, szLine);

      if (fExpandRegions) {
        for (DWORD dwBlock = 0; fOk && (dwBlock < vmq.dwRgnBlocks);
          dwBlock++) {

          ConstructBlkInfoLine(&vmq, szLine, sizeof(szLine));
          ListBox_AddString(hwndLB, szLine);

          // Get the address of the next region to test.
          pvAddress = ((PBYTE) pvAddress + vmq.BlkSize);
          if (dwBlock < vmq.dwRgnBlocks - 1) {
            // Don't query the memory info after the last block.
            fOk = VMQuery(hProcess, pvAddress, &vmq);
          }
        }
      }

      // Get the address of the next region to test.
      pvAddress = ((PBYTE) vmq.pvRgnBaseAddress + vmq.RgnSize);
    }
}
```

This loop starts walking from virtual address NULL and ends when *VMQuery* returns FALSE, indicating that it can no longer walk the process's address space. With each iteration of the loop, there is a call to *ConstructRgn-*

InfoLine; this function fills a character buffer with information about the region. Then this information is appended to the list box.

Within this main loop is a nested loop that iterates through each block in the region. Each iteration of this loop calls *ConstructBlkInfoLine* to fill a character buffer with information about the region's blocks. Then the information is appended to the list box. It's easy to walk the process's address space using the *VMQuery* function.

 VMMap.cpp

```
/*****************************************************************************
Module:  VMMap.cpp
Notices: Copyright (c) 2000 Jeffrey Richter
*****************************************************************************/


#include "..\CmnHdr.h"        /* See Appendix A. */
#include <psapi.h>
#include <windowsx.h>
#include <tchar.h>
#include <stdio.h>            // For sprintf
#include "..\04-ProcessInfo\Toolhelp.h"
#include "Resource.h"
#include "VMQuery.h"



///////////////////////////////////////////////////////////////////////////


DWORD g_dwProcessId = 0;   // Which process to walk?
BOOL  g_fExpandRegions = FALSE;
CToolhelp g_toolhelp;


// GetMappedFileName is only on Windows 2000 in PSAPI.DLL
// If this function exists on the host system, we'll use it
typedef DWORD (WINAPI* PFNGETMAPPEDFILENAME)(HANDLE, PVOID, PTSTR, DWORD);
static PFNGETMAPPEDFILENAME g_pfnGetMappedFileName = NULL;


///////////////////////////////////////////////////////////////////////////
```

Figure 14-4.   *(continued)*
The VMMap application

Figure 14-4. *continued*

```
// I use this function to obtain the dump figures in the book.
void CopyControlToClipboard(HWND hwnd) {
   TCHAR szClipData[128 * 1024] = { 0 };

   int nCount = ListBox_GetCount(hwnd);
   for (int nNum = 0; nNum < nCount; nNum++) {
      TCHAR szLine[1000];
      ListBox_GetText(hwnd, nNum, szLine);
      _tcscat(szClipData, szLine);
      _tcscat(szClipData, TEXT("\r\n"));
   }

   OpenClipboard(NULL);
   EmptyClipboard();

   // Clipboard accepts only data that is in a block allocated
   // with GlobalAlloc using the GMEM_MOVEABLE and GMEM_DDESHARE flags.
   HGLOBAL hClipData = GlobalAlloc(GMEM_MOVEABLE | GMEM_DDESHARE,
      sizeof(TCHAR) * (_tcslen(szClipData) + 1));
   PTSTR pClipData = (PTSTR) GlobalLock(hClipData);

   _tcscpy(pClipData, szClipData);

#ifdef UNICODE
   BOOL fOk = (SetClipboardData(CF_UNICODETEXT, hClipData) == hClipData);
#else
   BOOL fOk = (SetClipboardData(CF_TEXT, hClipData) == hClipData);
#endif
   CloseClipboard();

   if (!fOk) {
      GlobalFree(hClipData);
      chMB("Error putting text on the clipboard");
   }
}


///////////////////////////////////////////////////////////////////////////////


PCTSTR GetMemStorageText(DWORD dwStorage) {

   PCTSTR p = TEXT("Unknown");
   switch (dwStorage) {
```

(continued)

Figure 14-4. *continued*

```
   case MEM_FREE:    p = TEXT("Free   "); break;
   case MEM_RESERVE: p = TEXT("Reserve"); break;
   case MEM_IMAGE:   p = TEXT("Image  "); break;
   case MEM_MAPPED:  p = TEXT("Mapped "); break;
   case MEM_PRIVATE: p = TEXT("Private"); break;
   }
   return(p);
}


///////////////////////////////////////////////////////////////////////////


PTSTR GetProtectText(DWORD dwProtect, PTSTR szBuf, BOOL fShowFlags) {

   PCTSTR p = TEXT("Unknown");
   switch (dwProtect & ~(PAGE_GUARD | PAGE_NOCACHE | PAGE_WRITECOMBINE)) {
   case PAGE_READONLY:          p = TEXT("-R--"); break;
   case PAGE_READWRITE:         p = TEXT("-RW-"); break;
   case PAGE_WRITECOPY:         p = TEXT("-RWC"); break;
   case PAGE_EXECUTE:           p = TEXT("E---"); break;
   case PAGE_EXECUTE_READ:      p = TEXT("ER--"); break;
   case PAGE_EXECUTE_READWRITE: p = TEXT("ERW-"); break;
   case PAGE_EXECUTE_WRITECOPY: p = TEXT("ERWC"); break;
   case PAGE_NOACCESS:          p = TEXT("----"); break;
   }
   _tcscpy(szBuf, p);
   if (fShowFlags) {
      _tcscat(szBuf, TEXT(" "));
      _tcscat(szBuf, (dwProtect & PAGE_GUARD)        ? TEXT("G") : TEXT("-"));
      _tcscat(szBuf, (dwProtect & PAGE_NOCACHE)      ? TEXT("N") : TEXT("-"));
      _tcscat(szBuf, (dwProtect & PAGE_WRITECOMBINE) ? TEXT("W") : TEXT("-"));
   }
   return(szBuf);
}


///////////////////////////////////////////////////////////////////////////


void ConstructRgnInfoLine(HANDLE hProcess, PVMQUERY pVMQ,
   PTSTR szLine, int nMaxLen) {
```

(continued)

Figure 14-4. *continued*

```
    _stprintf(szLine, TEXT("%p      %s  %16u  "),
      pVMQ->pvRgnBaseAddress,
      GetMemStorageText(pVMQ->dwRgnStorage),
      pVMQ->RgnSize);

    if (pVMQ->dwRgnStorage != MEM_FREE) {
      wsprintf(_tcschr(szLine, 0), TEXT("%5u  "), pVMQ->dwRgnBlocks);
      GetProtectText(pVMQ->dwRgnProtection, _tcschr(szLine, 0), FALSE);
    }

    _tcscat(szLine, TEXT("    "));

    // Try to obtain the module pathname for this region.
    int nLen = _tcslen(szLine);
    if (pVMQ->pvRgnBaseAddress != NULL) {
      MODULEENTRY32 me = { sizeof(me) };

      if (g_toolhelp.ModuleFind(pVMQ->pvRgnBaseAddress, &me)) {
        lstrcat(&szLine[nLen], me.szExePath);
      } else {
        // This is not a module; see if it's a memory-mapped file
        if (g_pfnGetMappedFileName != NULL) {
          DWORD d = g_pfnGetMappedFileName(hProcess,
            pVMQ->pvRgnBaseAddress, szLine + nLen, nMaxLen - nLen);
          if (d == 0) {
            // NOTE: GetMappedFileName modifies the string when it fails
            szLine[nLen] = 0;
          }
        }
      }
    }

    if (pVMQ->fRgnIsAStack) {
      _tcscat(szLine, TEXT("Thread Stack"));
    }
}


/////////////////////////////////////////////////////////////////////////////


void ConstructBlkInfoLine(PVMQUERY pVMQ, PTSTR szLine, int nMaxLen) {

  _stprintf(szLine, TEXT("  %p  %s  %16u          "),
```

(continued)

Figure 14-4. *continued*

```
        pVMQ->pvBlkBaseAddress,
        GetMemStorageText(pVMQ->dwBlkStorage),
        pVMQ->BlkSize);

    if (pVMQ->dwBlkStorage != MEM_FREE) {
        GetProtectText(pVMQ->dwBlkProtection, _tcschr(szLine, 0), TRUE);
    }
}


///////////////////////////////////////////////////////////////////////////


void Refresh(HWND hwndLB, DWORD dwProcessId, BOOL fExpandRegions) {

    // Delete contents of list box & add a horizontal scroll bar
    ListBox_ResetContent(hwndLB);
    ListBox_SetHorizontalExtent(hwndLB, 300 * LOWORD(GetDialogBaseUnits()));

    // Is the process still running?
    HANDLE hProcess = OpenProcess(PROCESS_QUERY_INFORMATION,
        FALSE, dwProcessId);

    if (hProcess == NULL) {
        ListBox_AddString(hwndLB, TEXT(""));   // Blank line, looks better
        ListBox_AddString(hwndLB,
            TEXT("   The process ID identifies a process that is not running"));
        return;
    }

    // Grab a new snapshot of the process
    g_toolhelp.CreateSnapshot(TH32CS_SNAPALL, dwProcessId);

    // Walk the virtual address space, adding entries to the list box.
    BOOL fOk = TRUE;
    PVOID pvAddress = NULL;

    SetWindowRedraw(hwndLB, FALSE);
    while (fOk) {

        VMQUERY vmq;
        fOk = VMQuery(hProcess, pvAddress, &vmq);
```

(continued)

Figure 14-4. *continued*

```
    if (fOk) {
        // Construct the line to be displayed, and add it to the list box.
        TCHAR szLine[1024];
        ConstructRgnInfoLine(hProcess, &vmq, szLine, sizeof(szLine));
        ListBox_AddString(hwndLB, szLine);

        if (fExpandRegions) {
            for (DWORD dwBlock = 0; fOk && (dwBlock < vmq.dwRgnBlocks);
                dwBlock++) {

                ConstructBlkInfoLine(&vmq, szLine, sizeof(szLine));
                ListBox_AddString(hwndLB, szLine);

                // Get the address of the next region to test.
                pvAddress = ((PBYTE) pvAddress + vmq.BlkSize);
                if (dwBlock < vmq.dwRgnBlocks - 1) {
                    // Don't query the memory info after the last block.
                    fOk = VMQuery(hProcess, pvAddress, &vmq);
                }
            }
        }

        // Get the address of the next region to test.
        pvAddress = ((PBYTE) vmq.pvRgnBaseAddress + vmq.RgnSize);
    }
}
SetWindowRedraw(hwndLB, TRUE);
CloseHandle(hProcess);


///////////////////////////////////////////////////////////////////////////////


BOOL Dlg_OnInitDialog(HWND hwnd, HWND hwndFocus, LPARAM lParam) {

    chSETDLGICONS(hwnd, IDI_VMMAP);

    // Show which process we're walking in the window's caption
    TCHAR szCaption[MAX_PATH * 2];
    GetWindowText(hwnd, szCaption, chDIMOF(szCaption));
    g_toolhelp.CreateSnapshot(TH32CS_SNAPALL, g_dwProcessId);
    PROCESSENTRY32 pe = { sizeof(pe) };
    wsprintf(&szCaption[lstrlen(szCaption)], TEXT(" (PID=%u \"%s\")"),
```

(continued)

Figure 14-4. *continued*

```
       g_dwProcessId, g_toolhelp.ProcessFind(g_dwProcessId, &pe)
          ? pe.szExeFile : TEXT("unknown")));
   SetWindowText(hwnd, szCaption);

   // VMMap has so much info to show, let's maximize it by default
   ShowWindow(hwnd, SW_MAXIMIZE);

   // Force the list box to refresh itself
   Refresh(GetDlgItem(hwnd, IDC_LISTBOX), g_dwProcessId, g_fExpandRegions);
   return(TRUE);
}


///////////////////////////////////////////////////////////////////////////


void Dlg_OnSize(HWND hwnd, UINT state, int cx, int cy) {

   // The list box always fills the whole client area
   SetWindowPos(GetDlgItem(hwnd, IDC_LISTBOX), NULL, 0, 0, cx, cy,
      SWP_NOZORDER);
}


///////////////////////////////////////////////////////////////////////////


void Dlg_OnCommand(HWND hwnd, int id, HWND hwndCtl, UINT codeNotify) {

   switch (id) {
      case IDCANCEL:
         EndDialog(hwnd, id);
         break;

      case ID_REFRESH:
         Refresh(GetDlgItem(hwnd, IDC_LISTBOX),
            g_dwProcessId, g_fExpandRegions);
         break;

      case ID_EXPANDREGIONS:
         g_fExpandRegions = g_fExpandRegions ? FALSE: TRUE;
         Refresh(GetDlgItem(hwnd, IDC_LISTBOX),
            g_dwProcessId, g_fExpandRegions);
         break;
```

(continued)

507

Figure 14-4. *continued*

```
        case ID_COPYTOCLIPBOARD:
            CopyControlToClipboard(GetDlgItem(hwnd, IDC_LISTBOX));
            break;
    }
}


///////////////////////////////////////////////////////////////////////////////


INT_PTR WINAPI Dlg_Proc(HWND hwnd, UINT uMsg, WPARAM wParam, LPARAM lParam) {

    switch (uMsg) {
        chHANDLE_DLGMSG(hwnd, WM_INITDIALOG, Dlg_OnInitDialog);
        chHANDLE_DLGMSG(hwnd, WM_COMMAND,    Dlg_OnCommand);
        chHANDLE_DLGMSG(hwnd, WM_SIZE,       Dlg_OnSize);
    }
    return(FALSE);
}


///////////////////////////////////////////////////////////////////////////////


int WINAPI _tWinMain(HINSTANCE hinstExe, HINSTANCE, PTSTR pszCmdLine, int) {

    CToolhelp::EnableDebugPrivilege();

    // Try to load PSAPI.DLL and get the address of GetMappedFileName
    HMODULE hmodPSAPI = LoadLibrary(TEXT("PSAPI"));
    if (hmodPSAPI != NULL) {
#ifdef UNICODE
        g_pfnGetMappedFileName = (PFNGETMAPPEDFILENAME)
            GetProcAddress(hmodPSAPI, "GetMappedFileNameW");
#else
        g_pfnGetMappedFileName = (PFNGETMAPPEDFILENAME)
            GetProcAddress(hmodPSAPI, "GetMappedFileNameA");
#endif
    }

    g_dwProcessId = _ttoi(pszCmdLine);
    if (g_dwProcessId == 0) {
        g_dwProcessId = GetCurrentProcessId();
    }

    DialogBox(hinstExe, MAKEINTRESOURCE(IDD_VMMAP), NULL, Dlg_Proc);
```

(continued)

Figure 14-4. *continued*

```
    if (hmodPSAPI != NULL)
        FreeLibrary(hmodPSAPI); // Free PSAPI.DLL if we loaded it

    return(0);
}



/////////////////////////////// End of File ///////////////////////////////
```

VMMap.rc

```
//Microsoft Developer Studio generated resource script.
//
#include "Resource.h"

#define APSTUDIO_READONLY_SYMBOLS
/////////////////////////////////////////////////////////////////////////////
//
// Generated from the TEXTINCLUDE 2 resource.
//
#include "afxres.h"


/////////////////////////////////////////////////////////////////////////////
#undef APSTUDIO_READONLY_SYMBOLS


/////////////////////////////////////////////////////////////////////////////
// English (U.S.) resources

#if !defined(AFX_RESOURCE_DLL) || defined(AFX_TARG_ENU)
#ifdef _WIN32
LANGUAGE LANG_ENGLISH, SUBLANG_ENGLISH_US
#pragma code_page(1252)
#endif //_WIN32


#ifdef APSTUDIO_INVOKED
/////////////////////////////////////////////////////////////////////////////
//
// TEXTINCLUDE
//

1 TEXTINCLUDE DISCARDABLE
```

(continued)

Figure 14-4. *continued*

```
BEGIN
    "Resource.h\0"
END

2 TEXTINCLUDE DISCARDABLE
BEGIN
    "#include ""afxres.h""\r\n"
    "\0"
END

3 TEXTINCLUDE DISCARDABLE
BEGIN
    "\r\n"
    "\0"
END


#endif    // APSTUDIO_INVOKED


/////////////////////////////////////////////////////////////////////////////
//
// Dialog
//


IDD_VMMAP DIALOG DISCARDABLE  10, 18, 250, 250
STYLE WS_MINIMIZEBOX | WS_MAXIMIZEBOX | WS_POPUP | WS_VISIBLE | WS_CAPTION |
    WS_SYSMENU | WS_THICKFRAME
CAPTION "Virtual Memory Map"
MENU IDR_VMMAP
FONT 8, "Courier"
BEGIN
    LISTBOX         IDC_LISTBOX,0,0,248,248,LBS_NOINTEGRALHEIGHT | NOT
                    WS_BORDER | WS_VSCROLL | WS_HSCROLL | WS_GROUP |
                    WS_TABSTOP
END


/////////////////////////////////////////////////////////////////////////////
//
// Icon
//


// Icon with lowest ID value placed first to ensure application icon
// remains consistent on all systems.
```

(continued)

Figure 14-4. *continued*

```
IDI_VMMAP              ICON    DISCARDABLE    "VMMap.Ico"

/////////////////////////////////////////////////////////////////////////
//
// Menu
//

IDR_VMMAP MENU DISCARDABLE
BEGIN
    MENUITEM "&Refresh!",                ID_REFRESH
    MENUITEM "&Expand Regions!",         ID_EXPANDREGIONS
    MENUITEM "&Copy to Clipboard!",      ID_COPYTOCLIPBOARD
END

#endif    // English (U.S.) resources
/////////////////////////////////////////////////////////////////////////


#ifndef APSTUDIO_INVOKED
/////////////////////////////////////////////////////////////////////////
//
// Generated from the TEXTINCLUDE 3 resource.
//


/////////////////////////////////////////////////////////////////////////
#endif    // not APSTUDIO_INVOKED
```

USING VIRTUAL MEMORY IN YOUR OWN APPLICATIONS

Windows offers three mechanisms for manipulating memory:

- Virtual memory, which is best for managing large arrays of objects or structures
- Memory-mapped files, which are best for managing large streams of data (usually from files) and for sharing data between multiple processes running on a single machine
- Heaps, which are best for managing large numbers of small objects

In this chapter we discuss the first method, virtual memory. Memory-mapped files and heaps are discussed in Chapter 17 and Chapter 18, respectively.

The functions for manipulating virtual memory allow you to directly reserve a region of address space, commit physical storage (from the paging file) to the region, and set your own protection attributes.

Reserving a Region in an Address Space

You reserve a region in your process's address space by calling *VirtualAlloc*:

```
PVOID VirtualAlloc(
   PVOID pvAddress,
   SIZE_T dwSize,
   DWORD fdwAllocationType,
   DWORD fdwProtect);
```

The first parameter, *pvAddress*, contains a memory address specifying where you would like the system to reserve the address space. Most of the time, you'll pass NULL for this parameter. This tells *VirtualAlloc* that the system, which keeps a record of free address ranges, should reserve the region wherever it sees fit. The system can reserve a region from anywhere in your process's address space—there are no guarantees that the system will allocate regions from the bottom of your address space up or vice versa. However, you can have some say over this allocation by using the MEM_TOP_DOWN flag, discussed later in this chapter.

For most programmers, the ability to choose a specific memory address where a region will be reserved is an unusual concept. When you allocated memory in the past, the operating system simply found a block of memory large enough to satisfy the request, allocated the block, and returned its address. But because each process has its own address space, you can specify the base memory address where you would like the operating system to reserve the region.

For example, say that you want to allocate a region starting 50 MBs into your process's address space. In this case, you will pass 52,428,800 (50 × 1024 × 1024) as the *pvAddress* parameter. If this memory address has a free region large enough to satisfy your request, the system will reserve the desired region and return. If a free region does not exist at the specified address, or if the free region is not large enough, the system cannot satisfy your request and *Virtual-Alloc* returns NULL. Note that any address you pass for the *pvAddress* parameter must always reside in your process's user-mode partition or the call to *VirtualAlloc* will fail, causing it to return NULL.

As I mentioned in Chapter 13, regions are always reserved on an allocation granularity boundary (64 KB for all implementations of Windows to date). So if you attempt to reserve a region starting at address 19,668,992 (300 × 65,536 + 8192) in your process's address space, the system rounds that address down to a multiple of 64 KB and will reserve the region starting at address 19,660,800 (300 × 65,536).

If *VirtualAlloc* can satisfy your request, it returns a value indicating the base address of the reserved region. If you passed a specific address as *Virtual-Alloc*'s *pvAddress* parameter, this return value is the same value that you passed to *VirtualAlloc* rounded down (if necessary) to a 64-KB boundary.

VirtualAlloc's second parameter, *dwSize*, specifies the size of the region you want to reserve in bytes. Because the system must always reserve regions in multiples of the CPU's page size, an attempt to reserve a region that spans 62 KB will result in reserving a region that spans 64 KB on machines that use 4-KB, 8-KB, or 16-KB pages.

VirtualAlloc's third parameter, *fdwAllocationType*, tells the system whether you want to reserve a region or commit physical storage. (This distinction is necessary because *VirtualAlloc* is also used to commit physical storage.) To reserve a region of address space, you must pass the MEM_RESERVE identifier as the value for the *fdwAllocationType* parameter.

If you're going to reserve a region that you don't expect to release for a long time, you might want to reserve the region at the highest memory address possible. That way, the region does not get reserved from the middle of your process's address space, where it can potentially cause fragmentation. If you want the system to reserve a region at the highest possible memory address, you must pass NULL for the *pvAddress* parameter and for the *fdwAllocationType* parameter, you must also bitwise OR the MEM_TOP_DOWN flag with the MEM_RESERVE flag.

> **NOTE**
>
> Under Windows 98, the MEM_TOP_DOWN flag is ignored.

The last parameter, *fdwProtect*, indicates the protection attribute that should be assigned to the region. The protection attribute associated with the region has no effect on the committed storage mapped to the region. Regardless of the protection attribute assigned to a region, if no physical storage is committed, any attempt to access a memory address in the range will cause the thread to raise an access violation.

When reserving a region, assign the protection attribute that will be used most often with the storage committed to the region. For example, if you intend to commit physical storage with a protection attribute of PAGE_READWRITE (by far the most common protection attribute), you should reserve the region with PAGE_READWRITE. The system's internal record keeping behaves more efficiently when the region's protection attribute matches the committed storage's protection attribute.

You can use any of the following protection attributes: PAGE_NOACCESS, PAGE_READWRITE, PAGE_READONLY, PAGE_EXECUTE, PAGE_EXECUTE_READ, or PAGE_EXECUTE_READWRITE. However, you cannot specify either the PAGE_WRITECOPY attribute or the PAGE_EXECUTE_WRITECOPY attribute. If you do so, *VirtualAlloc* will not reserve the region and will return NULL. Also, you cannot use the protection attribute flags PAGE_GUARD, PAGE_NOCACHE, or PAGE_WRITECOMBINE when reserving regions—they can be used only with committed storage.

> Windows 98 supports only the PAGE_NOACCESS, PAGE_READ-
> ONLY, and PAGE_READWRITE protection attributes. Attempting to
> reserve a region using PAGE_EXECUTE or PAGE_EXECUTE_READ
> results in a region with PAGE_READONLY protection. Likewise,
> reserving a region using PAGE_EXECUTE_READWRITE results in
> a region with PAGE_READWRITE protection.

Committing Storage in a Reserved Region

After you have reserved a region, you will need to commit physical storage to
the region before you can access the memory addresses contained within it.
The system allocates physical storage committed to a region from the system's
paging file. Physical storage is always committed on page boundaries and in
page-size chunks.

To commit physical storage, you must call *VirtualAlloc* again. This time,
however, you'll pass the MEM_COMMIT identifier instead of the MEM_
RESERVE identifier for the *fdwAllocationType* parameter. You usually pass the
same page protection attribute (most often PAGE_READWRITE) that was used
when *VirtualAlloc* was called to reserve the region, although you can specify a
different protection attribute.

From within the reserved region, you *must* tell *VirtualAlloc* where you
want to commit physical storage and how much physical storage to commit. You
do this by specifying the desired memory address in the *pvAddress* parameter
and the amount of physical storage, in bytes, in the *dwSize* parameter. Note that
you don't have to commit physical storage to the entire region at once.

Let's look at an example of how to commit storage. Say your application
is running on an *x86* CPU and the application reserves a 512-KB region starting at address 5,242,880. You would like your application to commit storage
to the 6-KB portion of the reserved region starting 2 KB into the reserved
region's address space. To do this, call *VirtualAlloc* using the MEM_COMMIT
flag as follows:

```
VirtualAlloc((PVOID) (5242880 + (2 * 1024)), 6 * 1024,
   MEM_COMMIT, PAGE_READWRITE);
```

In this case, the system must commit 8 KB of physical storage, spanning
the address range 5,242,880 through 5,251,071 (5,242,880 + 8 KB – 1 byte).
Both of these committed pages have a protection attribute of PAGE_
READWRITE. Protection attributes are assigned on a whole-page basis only.

It is not possible to use different protection attributes for portions of the same page of storage. However, it is possible for one page in a region to have one protection attribute (such as PAGE_READWRITE) and for another page in the same region to have a different protection attribute (such as PAGE_READONLY).

Reserving a Region and Committing Storage Simultaneously

At times, you'll want to reserve a region and commit storage to it simultaneously. You can do this by placing a single call to *VirtualAlloc* as follows:

```
PVOID pvMem = VirtualAlloc(NULL, 99 * 1024,
   MEM_RESERVE | MEM_COMMIT, PAGE_READWRITE);
```

This call is a request to reserve a 99-KB region and commit 99 KB of physical storage to the region. When the system processes this call, it first searches your process's address space to find a contiguous area of unreserved address space large enough to hold 100 KB (on a 4-KB page machine) or 104 KB (on an 8-KB page machine).

The system searches the address space because I specified NULL as the *pvAddress* parameter. If I had specified a memory address for *pvAddress*, the system would see whether there was enough unreserved address space at that memory address. If the system could not find enough unreserved address space, *VirtualAlloc* would return NULL.

If a suitable region can be reserved, the system commits physical storage to the entire region. Both the region and the committed storage will be assigned PAGE_READWRITE protection.

Finally, *VirtualAlloc* returns the virtual address of the reserved and committed region, which is then saved in the *pvMem* variable. If the system couldn't find a large enough address space or commit the physical storage, *VirtualAlloc* returns NULL.

It is certainly possible when reserving a region and committing physical storage this way to pass a specific address as the *pvAddress* parameter to *Virtual-Alloc*. Or you might need to have the system select a suitable region toward the top of your process's address space by ORing the MEM_TOP_DOWN flag to the *fdwAllocationType* parameter and passing NULL for the *pvAddress* parameter.

When to Commit Physical Storage

Let's pretend you're implementing a spreadsheet application that supports 200 rows by 256 columns. For each cell, you need a CELLDATA structure that describes the contents of the cell. The easiest way for you to manipulate the two-dimensional matrix of cells would be to declare the following variable in your application:

```
CELLDATA CellData[200][256];
```

If the size of a CELLDATA structure were 128 bytes, the two-dimensional matrix would require 6,553,600 (200 × 256 × 128) bytes of physical storage. That's a lot of physical storage to allocate from the paging file right up front for a spreadsheet, especially when you consider that most users put information into only a few spreadsheet cells, leaving the majority unused. The memory usage would be very inefficient.

So, historically, spreadsheets have been implemented using other data structure techniques, such as linked lists. With the linked-list approach, CELLDATA structures have to be created only for the cells in the spreadsheet that actually contain data. Since most cells in a spreadsheet go unused, this method saves a tremendous amount of storage. However, this technique makes it much more difficult to obtain the contents of a cell. If you want to know the contents of the cell in row 5, column 10, you must walk through linked lists in order to find the desired cell, which makes the linked-list method slower than the declared-matrix method.

Virtual memory offers us a compromise between declaring the two-dimensional matrix up front and implementing linked lists. With virtual memory, you get the fast, easy access offered by the declared-matrix technique combined with the superior storage savings offered by the linked-list technique.

For you to obtain the advantages of the virtual memory technique, your program needs to follow these steps:

1. Reserve a region large enough to contain the entire matrix of CELL-DATA structures. Reserving a region uses no physical storage at all.

2. When the user enters data into a cell, locate the memory address in the reserved region where the CELLDATA structure should go. Of course, no physical storage is mapped to this address yet, so any attempts to access memory at this address will raise an access violation.

3. Commit only enough physical storage to the memory address located in step 2 for a CELLDATA structure. (You can tell the system to commit physical storage to specific parts of the reserved region—a region can contain both parts that are mapped to physical storage and parts that are not.)

4. Set the members of the new CELLDATA structure.

Now that physical storage is mapped to the proper location, your program can access the storage without raising an access violation. This virtual memory technique is excellent because physical storage is committed only as the user enters data into the spreadsheet's cells. Because most of the cells in a spreadsheet are empty, most of the reserved region will not have physical storage committed to it.

The one problem with the virtual memory technique is that you must determine when physical storage needs to be committed. If the user enters data into a cell and then simply edits or changes that data, there is no need to commit physical storage—the storage for the cell's CELLDATA structure was committed the first time data was entered.

Also, the system always commits physical storage with page granularity. So when you attempt to commit physical storage for a single CELLDATA structure (as in step 2 above), the system is actually committing a full page of storage. This is not as wasteful as it sounds: committing storage for a single CELLDATA structure has the effect of committing storage for other nearby CELLDATA structures. If the user then enters data into a neighboring cell—which is frequently the case—you might not need to commit additional physical storage.

There are four methods for determining whether to commit physical storage to a portion of a region:

■ Always attempt to commit physical storage. Instead of checking to see whether physical storage is mapped to a portion of the region, have your program try to commit storage every time it calls *Virtual-Alloc*. The system first checks to see whether storage has already been committed and, if so, does not commit additional physical storage. This approach is the easiest but has the disadvantage of making an additional function call every time a CELLDATA structure is altered, which makes your program perform more slowly.

■ Determine (using the *VirtualQuery* function) whether physical storage has already been committed to the address space containing the CELLDATA structure. If it has, do nothing else; if it hasn't, call *VirtualAlloc* to commit the memory. This method is actually worse than the first one: it both increases the size of your code and slows down your program because of the additional call to *VirtualQuery*.

■ Keep a record of which pages have been committed and which haven't. Doing so makes your application run faster: you avoid the call to *VirtualAlloc*, and your code can determine more quickly than the system can whether storage has already been committed. The disadvantage is that you must keep track of the page commit information somehow, which could be either very simple or very difficult depending on your specific situation.

■ Use structured exception handling (SEH)—the best method. SEH is an operating system feature that causes the system to notify your application when certain situations occur. Essentially, you set up your application with an exception handler, and then, whenever an attempt is made to access uncommitted memory, the system notifies your application of the problem. Your application then commits the memory and tells the system to retry the instruction that caused the exception. This time the memory access succeeds, and the program continues running as though there had never been a problem. This method is the most advantageous because it requires the least amount of work from you (meaning less code) and because your program will run at full speed. A complete discussion of the SEH mechanism is saved for Chapters 23, 24, and 25. The Spreadsheet sample application in Chapter 25 illustrates exactly how to use virtual memory as I've just described.

Decommitting Physical Storage and Releasing a Region

To decommit physical storage mapped to a region or release an entire region of address space, call the *VirtualFree* function:

```
BOOL VirtualFree(
    LPVOID pvAddress,
    SIZE_T dwSize,
    DWORD fdwFreeType);
```

Let's first examine the simple case of calling *VirtualFree* to release a reserved region. When your process will no longer be accessing the physical storage within a region, you can release the entire reserved region, and all the physical storage committed to the region, by making a single call to *VirtualFree*.

For this call, the *pvAddress* parameter must be the base address of the region. This address would be the same address that *VirtualAlloc* returned when the region was reserved. The system knows the size of the region at the specified memory address, so you can pass 0 for the *dwSize* parameter. In fact, you must pass 0 for the *dwSize* parameter or the call to *VirtualFree* will fail. For the third parameter, *fdwFreeType*, you must pass MEM_RELEASE to tell the system to decommit all physical storage mapped to the region and to release the region. When releasing a region, you must release all the address space that was reserved by the region. For example, you cannot reserve a 128-KB region and then decide to release only 64 KB of it. You must release all 128 KB.

When you want to decommit some physical storage from the region without releasing the region, you also call *VirtualFree*. To decommit some physical storage, you must pass the memory address that identifies the first page to be decommitted in *VirtualFree*'s *pvAddress* parameter. You must also specify the number of bytes to free in the *dwSize* parameter and the MEM_DECOMMIT identifier in the *fdwFreeType* parameter.

Like committing, decommitting is done with page granularity. That is, specifying a memory address in the middle of a page decommits the entire page. And, of course, if *pvAddress* + *dwSize* falls in the middle of a page, the whole page that contains this address is decommitted as well. So all pages that fall within the range of *pvAddress* to *pvAddress* + *dwSize* are decommitted.

If *dwSize* is 0 and *pvAddress* is the base address for the allocated region, *VirtualFree* will decommit the complete range of allocated pages. After the pages of physical storage have been decommitted, the freed physical storage is available to any other process in the system; any attempt to access the decommitted memory results in an access violation.

When to Decommit Physical Storage

In practice, knowing when it's OK to decommit memory is very tricky. Consider the spreadsheet example again. If your application is running on an *x*86 machine, each page of storage is 4 KB and can hold 32 (4096/128) CELLDATA structures. If the user deletes the contents of *CellData[0][1]*, you might be able to decommit the page of storage as long as cells *CellData[0][0]* through *CellData[0][31]* are also not in use. But how do you know? You can tackle this problem in different ways.

■ Without a doubt, the easiest solution is to design a CELLDATA structure that is exactly 1 page in size. Then, because there is always one structure per page, you can simply decommit the page of physical storage when you no longer need the data in the structure. Even if your data structures were, say, multiples of a page 8 KB or 12 KB for *x*86 CPUs (these would be unusually large structures), decommitting memory would still be pretty easy. Of course, to use this method you must define your data structures to meet the page size of the CPU you're targeting—not how we usually write our programs.

■ A more practical solution is to keep a record of which structures are in use. To save memory, you might use a bitmap. So if you have an array of 100 structures, you also maintain an array of 100 bits. Initially, all the bits are set to 0, indicating that no structures are in use. As you use the structures, you set the corresponding bits to 1. Then, whenever you don't need a structure and you change its bit back to 0, you check the bits of the adjacent structures that fall into the same page of memory. If none of the adjacent structures is in use, you can decommit the page.

■ The last solution implements a garbage collection function. This scheme relies on the fact that the system sets all the bytes in a page to 0 when physical storage is first committed. To use this scheme, you must first set aside a BOOL (perhaps called *fInUse*) in your structure. Then, every time you put a structure in committed memory, you need to ensure that *fInUse* is set to TRUE.

As your application runs, you'll want to call the garbage collection function periodically. This function should traverse all the potential data structures. For each structure, the function first determines whether storage is committed for the structure; if so, the function checks the *fInUse* member to see whether it is 0. A value of 0 means that the structure is not in use, whereas a value of TRUE means that it is in use. After the garbage collection function has checked all the structures that fall within a given page, it calls *VirtualFree* to decommit the storage if all the structures are not in use.

You can call the garbage collection function immediately after a structure is no longer considered to be in use, but doing so might take more time than you want to spend because the function cycles through all the possible structures. An excellent way to implement this function is to have it run as part of a lower-priority thread. In this way, you don't take time away from the thread executing the main application. Whenever the main application is idle or the main application's thread is performing file I/O, the system can schedule time to the garbage collection function.

Of all the methods listed above, the first two are my personal favorites. However, if your structures are small (less than a page), I recommend using the last method.

The Virtual Memory Allocation Sample Application

The VMAlloc application ("15 VMAlloc.exe"), listed in Figure 15-1 beginning on page 525, demonstrates how to use virtual memory techniques for manipulating an array of structures. The source code and resource files for the application are in the 15-VMAlloc directory on the companion CD-ROM. When you start the program, the following window appears.

Initially, no region of address space has been reserved for the array, and all the address space that would be reserved for it is free, as shown by the memory map. When you click the Reserve Region (50, 2 KB Structures) button, VMAlloc calls *VirtualAlloc* to reserve the region, and the memory map is updated to reflect this. After *VirtualAlloc* reserves the region, the remaining buttons become active.

You can now type an index into the edit control to select an index, and then click on the Use button. This has the effect of committing physical storage to the memory address where the array element is to be placed. When a page of storage is committed, the memory map is redrawn to reflect the state of the reserved region for the entire array. So if after reserving the region, you use the Use button to mark array elements 7 and 46 as *in use*, the window will look like the following window (when you are running the program on a 4-KB page machine).

Clicking on the Clear button clears any element that is marked as in use. But doing so does not decommit the physical storage mapped to the array element because each page contains room for multiple structures—just because one is clear doesn't mean the others are too. If the memory were decommitted, the data in the other structures would be lost. Because clicking on Clear doesn't affect the region's physical storage, the memory map is not updated when an array element is cleared.

However, when a structure is cleared, its *fInUse* member is set to FALSE. This setting is necessary so the garbage collection routine can make its pass over all the structures and decommit storage that's no longer in use. If you haven't guessed it by now, the Garbage Collect button tells VMAlloc to execute its garbage collection routine. To keep things simple, I have not implemented the garbage collection routine on a separate thread.

To demonstrate the garbage collection function, clear the array element at index 46. Notice that the memory map does not change. Now click on the Garbage Collect button. The program decommits the page of storage containing element 46, and the memory map is updated to reflect this, as shown in the following window. Note that the *GarbageCollect* function can easily be used in your own applications. I implemented it to work with arrays of any size data structures; the structures do not have to fit exactly in a page. The only requirement is that the first member of your structure must be a BOOL value, which indicates whether the structure is in use.

524

Finally, even though there is no visual display to inform you, all the committed memory is decommitted and the reserved region is freed when the window is destroyed.

This program contains another element that I haven't described yet. The program needs to determine the state of memory in the region's address space in three places:

- After changing the index, the program needs to enable the Use button and disable the Clear button or vice versa.

- In the garbage collection function, the program needs to see whether storage is committed before actually testing to see whether the *fInUse* flag is set.

- When updating the memory map, the program needs to know which pages are free, which are reserved, and which are committed.

VMAlloc performs all these tests by calling the *VirtualQuery* function, discussed in the previous chapter.

VMAlloc.cpp

```
/******************************************************************************
Module:  VMAlloc.cpp
Notices: Copyright (c) 2000 Jeffrey Richter
******************************************************************************/


#include " ..\CmnHdr.h"      /* See Appendix A. */
#include <WindowsX.h>
#include <tchar.h>
#include "Resource.h"


///////////////////////////////////////////////////////////////////////////////


// The number of bytes in a page on this host machine.
UINT g_uPageSize = 0;

// A dummy data structure used for the array.
typedef struct {
  BOOL fInUse;
  BYTE bOtherData[2048 - sizeof(BOOL)];
} SOMEDATA, *PSOMEDATA;
```

Figure 15-1.
The VMAlloc sample application

(continued)

Figure 15-1. *continued*

```
// The number of structures in the array
#define MAX_SOMEDATA    (50)

// Pointer to an array of data structures
PSOMEDATA g_pSomeData = NULL;



// The rectangular area in the window occupied by the memory map
RECT g_rcMemMap;



///////////////////////////////////////////////////////////////////////////////


BOOL Dlg_OnInitDialog(HWND hwnd, HWND hwndFocus, LPARAM lParam) {

   chSETDLGICONS(hwnd, IDI_VMALLOC);

   // Initialize the dialog box by disabling all the nonsetup controls.
   EnableWindow(GetDlgItem(hwnd, IDC_INDEXTEXT),      FALSE);
   EnableWindow(GetDlgItem(hwnd, IDC_INDEX),          FALSE);
   EnableWindow(GetDlgItem(hwnd, IDC_USE),            FALSE);
   EnableWindow(GetDlgItem(hwnd, IDC_CLEAR),          FALSE);
   EnableWindow(GetDlgItem(hwnd, IDC_GARBAGECOLLECT), FALSE);

   // Get the coordinates of the memory map display.
   GetWindowRect(GetDlgItem(hwnd, IDC_MEMMAP), &g_rcMemMap);
   MapWindowPoints(NULL, hwnd, (LPPOINT) &g_rcMemMap, 2);

   // Destroy the window that identifies the location of the memory map
   DestroyWindow(GetDlgItem(hwnd, IDC_MEMMAP));

   // Put the page size in the dialog box just for the user's information.
   TCHAR szBuf[10];
   wsprintf(szBuf, TEXT("("%d KB")"), g_uPageSize / 1024);
   SetDlgItemText(hwnd, IDC_PAGESIZE, szBuf);

   // Initialize the edit control.
   SetDlgItemInt(hwnd, IDC_INDEX, 0, FALSE);


   return(TRUE);
}
```

(continued)

Figure 15-1. *continued*

```
////////////////////////////////////////////////////////////////////////////

void Dlg_OnDestroy(HWND hwnd) {

   if (g_pSomeData != NULL)
      VirtualFree(g_pSomeData, 0, MEM_RELEASE);
}


////////////////////////////////////////////////////////////////////////////

VOID GarbageCollect(PVOID pvBase, DWORD dwNum, DWORD dwStructSize) {

   static DWORD s_uPageSize = 0;

   if (s_uPageSize == 0) {
      // Get the page size used on this CPU.
      SYSTEM_INFO si;
      GetSystemInfo(&si);
      s_uPageSize = si.dwPageSize;

   }


   UINT uMaxPages = dwNum * dwStructSize / g_uPageSize;

   for (UINT uPage = 0; uPage < uMaxPages; uPage++) {
      BOOL fAnyAllocsInThisPage = FALSE;
      UINT uIndex     = uPage  * g_uPageSize / dwStructSize;
      UINT uIndexLast = uIndex + g_uPageSize / dwStructSize;

      for (; uIndex < uIndexLast; uIndex++) {
         MEMORY_BASIC_INFORMATION mbi;
         VirtualQuery(&g_pSomeData[uIndex], &mbi, sizeof(mbi));
         fAnyAllocsInThisPage = ((mbi.State == MEM_COMMIT) &&
            * (PBOOL) ((PBYTE) pvBase + dwStructSize * uIndex));

         // Stop checking this page, we know we can't decommit it.
         if (fAnyAllocsInThisPage) break;
      }
```

(continued)

Figure 15-1. *continued*

```
      if (!fAnyAllocsInThisPage) {
         // No allocated structures in this page; decommit it.
         VirtualFree(&g_pSomeData[uIndexLast - 1], dwStructSize, MEM_DECOMMIT);
      }
   }
}


/////////////////////////////////////////////////////////////////////////////


void Dlg_OnCommand(HWND hwnd, int id, HWND hwndCtl, UINT codeNotify) {

   UINT uIndex = 0;

   switch (id) {
      case IDCANCEL:
         EndDialog(hwnd, id);
         break;

      case IDC_RESERVE:
         // Reserve enough address space to hold the array of structures.
         g_pSomeData = (PSOMEDATA) VirtualAlloc(NULL,
            MAX_SOMEDATA * sizeof(SOMEDATA), MEM_RESERVE, PAGE_READWRITE);

         // Disable the Reserve button and enable all the other controls.
         EnableWindow(GetDlgItem(hwnd, IDC_RESERVE),        FALSE);
         EnableWindow(GetDlgItem(hwnd, IDC_INDEXTEXT),      TRUE);
         EnableWindow(GetDlgItem(hwnd, IDC_INDEX),          TRUE);
         EnableWindow(GetDlgItem(hwnd, IDC_USE),            TRUE);
         EnableWindow(GetDlgItem(hwnd, IDC_GARBAGECOLLECT), TRUE);

         // Force the index edit control to have the focus.
         SetFocus(GetDlgItem(hwnd, IDC_INDEX));

         // Force the memory map to update
         InvalidateRect(hwnd, &g_rcMemMap, FALSE);
         break;

      case IDC_INDEX:
         if (codeNotify != EN_CHANGE)
            break;
```

(continued)

Figure 15-1. *continued*

```
        uIndex = GetDlgItemInt(hwnd, id, NULL, FALSE);
        if ((g_pSomeData != NULL) && chINRANGE(0, uIndex, MAX_SOMEDATA - 1)) {
            MEMORY_BASIC_INFORMATION mbi;
            VirtualQuery(&g_pSomeData[uIndex], &mbi, sizeof(mbi));
            BOOL fOk = (mbi.State == MEM_COMMIT);
            if (fOk)
                fOk = g_pSomeData[uIndex].fInUse;

            EnableWindow(GetDlgItem(hwnd, IDC_USE), !fOk);
            EnableWindow(GetDlgItem(hwnd, IDC_CLEAR), fOk);

        } else {
            EnableWindow(GetDlgItem(hwnd, IDC_USE),   FALSE);
            EnableWindow(GetDlgItem(hwnd, IDC_CLEAR), FALSE);
        }
        break;

    case IDC_USE:
        uIndex = GetDlgItemInt(hwnd, IDC_INDEX, NULL, FALSE);
        if (chINRANGE(0, uIndex, MAX_SOMEDATA - 1)) {

            // NOTE: New pages are always zeroed by the system
            VirtualAlloc(&g_pSomeData[uIndex], sizeof(SOMEDATA),
                MEM_COMMIT, PAGE_READWRITE);

            g_pSomeData[uIndex].fInUse = TRUE;

            EnableWindow(GetDlgItem(hwnd, IDC_USE),   FALSE);
            EnableWindow(GetDlgItem(hwnd, IDC_CLEAR), TRUE);

            // Force the Clear button control to have the focus.
            SetFocus(GetDlgItem(hwnd, IDC_CLEAR));

            // Force the memory map to update
            InvalidateRect(hwnd, &g_rcMemMap, FALSE);
        }
        break;

    case IDC_CLEAR:
        uIndex = GetDlgItemInt(hwnd, IDC_INDEX, NULL, FALSE);
        if ((chINRANGE(0, uIndex, MAX_SOMEDATA - 1)) {
            g_pSomeData[uIndex].fInUse = FALSE;
            EnableWindow(GetDlgItem(hwnd, IDC_USE),   TRUE);
```

(continued)

Figure 15-1. *continued*

```
            EnableWindow(GetDlgItem(hwnd, IDC_CLEAR), FALSE);

            // Force the Use button control to have the focus.
            SetFocus(GetDlgItem(hwnd, IDC_USE));
        }
        break;

    case IDC_GARBAGECOLLECT:
        GarbageCollect(g_pSomeData, MAX_SOMEDATA, sizeof(SOMEDATA));

        // Force the memory map to update
        InvalidateRect(hwnd, &g_rcMemMap, FALSE);
        break;
    }
}


///////////////////////////////////////////////////////////////////////////


void Dlg_OnPaint(HWND hwnd) {      // Update the memory map

    PAINTSTRUCT ps;
    BeginPaint(hwnd, &ps);

    UINT uMaxPages = MAX_SOMEDATA * sizeof(SOMEDATA) / g_uPageSize;
    UINT uMemMapWidth = g_rcMemMap.right - g_rcMemMap.left;

    if (g_pSomeData == NULL) {

        // The memory has yet to be reserved.
        Rectangle(ps.hdc, g_rcMemMap.left, g_rcMemMap.top,
            g_rcMemMap.right - uMemMapWidth % uMaxPages, g_rcMemMap.bottom);

    } else {

        // Walk the virtual address space, painting the memory map
        for (UINT uPage = 0; uPage < uMaxPages; uPage++) {

            UINT uIndex = uPage * g_uPageSize / sizeof(SOMEDATA);
            UINT uIndexLast = uIndex + g_uPageSize / sizeof(SOMEDATA);
            for (; uIndex < uIndexLast; uIndex++) {

                MEMORY_BASIC_INFORMATION mbi;
                VirtualQuery(&g_pSomeData[uIndex], &mbi, sizeof(mbi));
```

(continued)

Figure 15-1. *continued*

```
            int nBrush = 0;
            switch (mbi.State) {
                case MEM_FREE:    nBrush = WHITE_BRUSH; break;
                case MEM_RESERVE: nBrush = GRAY_BRUSH;  break;
                case MEM_COMMIT:  nBrush = BLACK_BRUSH; break;
            }

            SelectObject(ps.hdc, GetStockObject(nBrush));
            Rectangle(ps.hdc,
                g_rcMemMap.left + uMemMapWidth / uMaxPages * uPage,
                g_rcMemMap.top,
                g_rcMemMap.left + uMemMapWidth / uMaxPages * (uPage + 1),
                g_rcMemMap.bottom);

        }
    }
  }

  EndPaint(hwnd, &ps);
}


///////////////////////////////////////////////////////////////////////////


INT_PTR WINAPI Dlg_Proc(HWND hwnd, UINT uMsg, WPARAM wParam, LPARAM lParam) {

  switch (uMsg) {
      chHANDLE_DLGMSG(hwnd, WM_INITDIALOG, Dlg_OnInitDialog);
      chHANDLE_DLGMSG(hwnd, WM_COMMAND,    Dlg_OnCommand);
      chHANDLE_DLGMSG(hwnd, WM_PAINT,      Dlg_OnPaint);
      chHANDLE_DLGMSG(hwnd, WM_DESTROY,    Dlg_OnDestroy);
  }
  return(FALSE);
}


///////////////////////////////////////////////////////////////////////////


int WINAPI _tWinMain(HINSTANCE hinstExe, HINSTANCE, LPTSTR pszCmdLine, int) {

  // Get the page size used on this CPU.
  SYSTEM_INFO si;
  GetSystemInfo(&si);
```

(continued)

Figure 15-1. *continued*

```
    g_uPageSize = si.dwPageSize;

    DialogBox(hinstExe, MAKEINTRESOURCE(IDD_VMALLOC), NULL, Dlg_Proc);
    return(0);
}



////////////////////////////////// End of File /////////////////////////////////////
```

VMAlloc.rc

```
//Microsoft Developer Studio generated resource script.
//
#include "Resource.h"

#define APSTUDIO_READONLY_SYMBOLS
///////////////////////////////////////////////////////////////////////////////
//
// Generated from the TEXTINCLUDE 2 resource.
//
#include "afxres.h"


///////////////////////////////////////////////////////////////////////////////
#undef APSTUDIO_READONLY_SYMBOLS



///////////////////////////////////////////////////////////////////////////////
// English (U.S.) resources


#if !defined(AFX_RESOURCE_DLL) || defined(AFX_TARG_ENU)
#ifdef _WIN32
LANGUAGE LANG_ENGLISH, SUBLANG_ENGLISH_US
#pragma code_page(1252)
#endif //_WIN32


#ifdef APSTUDIO_INVOKED
///////////////////////////////////////////////////////////////////////////////
//
// TEXTINCLUDE
//
```

(continued)

Figure 15-1. *continued*

```
1 TEXTINCLUDE DISCARDABLE
BEGIN
    "Resource.h\0"
END


2 TEXTINCLUDE DISCARDABLE
BEGIN
    "#include ""afxres.h""\r\n"
    "\0"
END


3 TEXTINCLUDE DISCARDABLE
BEGIN
    "\r\n"
    "\0"
END

#endif     // APSTUDIO_INVOKED



/////////////////////////////////////////////////////////////////////////////
//
// Dialog
//

IDD_VMALLOC DIALOG DISCARDABLE  15, 24, 224, 97
STYLE WS_MINIMIZEBOX | WS_POPUP | WS_VISIBLE | WS_CAPTION | WS_SYSMENU
CAPTION "Virtual Memory Allocator"
FONT 8, "MS Sans Serif"
BEGIN
    LTEXT           "Page size:",IDC_STATIC,4,6,34,8
    CONTROL         "16 KB",IDC_PAGESIZE,"Static",SS_LEFTNOWORDWRAP |
                    SS_NOPREFIX | WS_GROUP,50,6,20,8
    DEFPUSHBUTTON   "&Reserve region (50, 2KB structures)",IDC_RESERVE,80,4,
                    140,14,WS_GROUP
    LTEXT           "&Index (0 - 49):",IDC_INDEXTEXT,4,26,45,8
    EDITTEXT        IDC_INDEX,56,24,16,12
    PUSHBUTTON      "&Use",IDC_USE,80,24,32,14
    PUSHBUTTON      "&Clear",IDC_CLEAR,116,24,32,14
    PUSHBUTTON      "&Garbage collect",IDC_GARBAGECOLLECT,160,24,60,14
    GROUPBOX        "Memory map",IDC_STATIC,4,42,216,52
    CONTROL         "",IDC_MEMMAP,"Static",SS_BLACKRECT,8,58,208,16
```

(continued)

Figure 15-1. *continued*

```
        LTEXT           "White: Free",IDC_STATIC,8,80,39,8
        CTEXT           "Grey: Reserved",IDC_STATIC,82,80,52,8
        RTEXT           "Black: Committed",IDC_STATIC,155,80,58,8
END


/////////////////////////////////////////////////////////////////////////////
//
// Icon
//

// Icon with lowest ID value placed first to ensure application icon
// remains consistent on all systems.
IDI_VMALLOC             ICON    DISCARDABLE     "VMAlloc.Ico"
#endif    // English (U.S.) resources
/////////////////////////////////////////////////////////////////////////////


#ifndef APSTUDIO_INVOKED
/////////////////////////////////////////////////////////////////////////////
//
// Generated from the TEXTINCLUDE 3 resource.
//


/////////////////////////////////////////////////////////////////////////////
#endif    // not APSTUDIO_INVOKED
```

Changing Protection Attributes

Although the practice is rare, it is possible to change the protection attributes associated with a page or pages of committed physical storage. For example, say you've developed code to manage a linked list, the nodes of which you are keeping in a reserved region. You could design the functions that process the linked list so that they change the protection attributes of the committed storage to PAGE_READWRITE at the start of each function and then back to PAGE_NOACCESS just before each function terminates.

By doing this, you protect your linked-list data from other bugs hiding in your program. If any other code in your process has a stray pointer that attempts to access your linked-list data, an access violation is raised. Taking advantage of protection attributes can be incredibly useful when you're trying to locate hard-to-find bugs in your application.

You can alter the protection rights of a page of memory by calling *Virtual-Protect*:

```
BOOL VirtualProtect(
    PVOID pvAddress,
    SIZE_T dwSize,
    DWORD flNewProtect,
    PDWORD pflOldProtect);
```

Here, *pvAddress* points to the base address of the memory (which must be in your process's user-mode partition), *dwSize* indicates the number of bytes for which you want to change the protection attribute, and *flNewProtect* can represent any one of the PAGE_* protection attribute identifiers except for PAGE_WRITECOPY and PAGE_EXECUTE_WRITECOPY.

The last parameter, *pflOldProtect*, is the address of a DWORD that *Virtual-Protect* will fill in with the protection attribute originally associated with the byte at *pvAddress*. Even though many applications don't need this information, you must pass a valid address for this parameter, or the function fails.

Of course, protection attributes are associated with entire pages of storage and cannot be assigned to individual bytes. So if you were to call *Virtual-Protect* on a 4-KB page machine using the following code, you would end up assigning PAGE_NOACCESS protection to two pages of storage.

```
VirtualProtect(pvRgnBase + (3 * 1024), 2 * 1024,
    PAGE_NOACCESS, &flOldProtect);
```

WINDOWS 98

Windows 98 supports only the PAGE_NOACCESS, PAGE_READ-ONLY, and PAGE_READWRITE protection attributes. If you attempt to change a page's protection to PAGE_EXECUTE or PAGE_EXECUTE_READ, the page receives PAGE_READONLY protection. Likewise, if you change a page's protection to PAGE_EXECUTE_READWRITE, the page receives PAGE_READWRITE protection.

VirtualProtect cannot be used to change the protection of pages that span different reserved regions. If you have adjoining reserved regions and you want to alter the page protection on the pages within these regions, you must make multiple calls to *VirtualProtect*.

Resetting the Contents of Physical Storage

> Windows 98 does not support the resetting of physical storage.

When you modify the contents of various pages of physical storage, the system tries to keep the changes in RAM as long as possible. However, while applications are running, a demand might be placed on your system's RAM as pages are being loaded from .exe files, DLL files, and/or the paging file. As the system looks for pages of RAM to satisfy recent load requests, the system will have to swap modified pages of RAM to the system's paging file.

Windows 2000 offers a feature that allows an application to improve its performance—the resetting of physical storage. Resetting storage means that you are telling the system that the data on one or more pages of storage is not modified. If the system is searching for a page of RAM and chooses a modified page, the system must write the page of RAM to the paging file. This operation is slow and hurts performance. For most applications, you want the system to preserve your modified pages in the system's paging file.

However, certain applications use storage for short periods of time and then no longer require that the contents of that storage be preserved. To help performance, an application can tell the system not to preserve desired pages of storage in the system's paging file. This is basically a way for an application to tell the system that a data page has not been modified. So if the system chooses to use a page of RAM for another purpose, the page's contents don't have to be preserved in the paging file, thus increasing performance. An application resets storage by calling *VirtualAlloc*, passing the MEM_RESET flag in the third parameter.

If the pages referenced in the call to *VirtualAlloc* are in the paging file, the system discards them. The next time the application accesses the storage, new RAM pages that are first initialized to zeroes are used. If you reset pages that are currently in RAM, they are marked as not modified so that they will never be written to the paging file. Note that although the content of the RAM page is *not* zeroed, you should not continue to read from this page of storage. If the system doesn't need the page of RAM, it will contain the original contents. However, if the system needs the page of RAM, the system can take it. Then when you attempt to access the page's contents, the system will give you a new page that has been zeroed. Since you have no control over this behavior, you must assume that the contents of the page are garbage after you reset the page.

Keep in mind a couple of additional things when you reset storage. First, when you call *VirtualAlloc*, the base address is usually rounded down to a page boundary and the number of bytes is rounded up to an integral number of pages. Rounding the base address and number of bytes this way would be very dangerous to do when resetting storage; therefore, *VirtualAlloc* rounds these values in the opposite direction when you pass MEM_RESET. For example, let's say that you had the following code:

```
PINT pnData = (PINT) VirtualAlloc(NULL, 1024,
   MEM_RESERVE | MEM_COMMIT, PAGE_READWRITE);
pn[0] = 100;
pn[1] = 200;
VirtualAlloc((PVOID) pnData, sizeof(int), MEM_RESET, PAGE_READWRITE);
```

This code commits one page of storage and then says that the first 4 bytes (*sizeof(int)*) are no longer necessary and can be reset. However, as with all storage operations, everything must be done on page boundaries and in page increments. As it turns out, the call to reset the storage above fails (*VirtualAlloc* returns NULL). Why? Because when you pass MEM_RESET to *VirtualAlloc*, the base address that you pass to the function is rounded up to a page boundary and the number of bytes is rounded down to an integral number of pages. This is done to ensure that important data is not thrown away. In the preceding example, rounding the number of bytes down makes it 0, and it is illegal to reset 0 bytes.

The second thing to remember about resetting storage is that the MEM_RESET flag must always be used by itself and cannot be ORed with any other flags. The following call always fails and returns NULL:

```
PVOID pvMem = VirtualAlloc(NULL, 1024,
   MEM_RESERVE | MEM_COMMIT | MEM_RESET, PAGE_READWRITE);
```

It really doesn't make any sense to combine the MEM_RESET flag with any other flag, anyway.

Finally, note that calling *VirtualAlloc* with MEM_RESET requires that you pass a valid page protection value even though this value will not be used by the function.

The MemReset Sample Application

The MemReset application ("15 MemReset.exe"), listed in Figure 15-2 beginning on page 539, demonstrates how the MEM_RESET flag works. The source code and resource files for the application are in the 15-MemReset directory on the companion CD-ROM.

The first thing that the MemReset.cpp code does is reserve and commit a region of physical storage. Since the size passed to *VirtualAlloc* is 1024, the system automatically rounds this value up to the system's page size. Now a string is copied into this buffer using *lstrcpy*, causing the contents of the page to be modified. If the system later decides it needs the page of RAM occupied by our data page, the system will first write the data that is in our page to the system's paging file. When our application later attempts to access this data, the system automatically reloads the page from the paging file into another page of RAM so that we can successfully access the data.

After writing the string to the page of storage, the code presents the user with a message box asking whether the data needs to be accessed at a later time. If the user responds by selecting the No button, the code forces the operating system to believe that the data in the page is not modified by calling *VirtualAlloc* and passing the MEM_RESET flag.

To demonstrate that the storage has been reset, we need to force a heavy demand on the system's RAM. We can do this with the following three-step process:

1. Call *GlobalMemoryStatus* to get the total amount of RAM in the machine.

2. Call *VirtualAlloc* to commit this amount of storage. This operation is very fast because the system doesn't actually allocate RAM for the storage until the process attempts to touch the pages.

3. Call *ZeroMemory* so that the newly committed pages are touched. This will place a heavy burden on the system's RAM, causing some pages that are currently in RAM to be written to the paging file.

If the user indicated that that data will be accessed later, the data is not reset and will be swapped back into RAM later when it is accessed. However, if the user indicated that the data will not be accessed later, the data is reset and the system will not write it out to the paging file, thereby improving our application's performance.

After *ZeroMemory* returns, the code compares the contents of the data page with the string originally written to it. If the data wasn't reset, the contents are guaranteed to be the same. If the data page was reset, the contents might or might not be the same. In the MemReset program, the contents will never be the same because all pages in RAM are forced to be written to the paging file. However, if the dummy region were smaller than the total amount of RAM in the machine, the original contents could possibly still be in RAM. As I pointed out earlier, be careful about this!

MemReset.cpp

```
/****************************************************************************
Module:  MemReset.cpp
Notices: Copyright (c) 2000 Jeffrey Richter
****************************************************************************/


#include..\CmnHdr.h"        /* See Appendix A. */
#include <tchar.h>


/////////////////////////////////////////////////////////////////////////////


int WINAPI _tWinMain(HINSTANCE hinstExe, HINSTANCE, LPTSTR pszCmdLine, int) {

   chWindows9xNotAllowed();

   TCHAR szAppName[]  = TEXT("MEM_RESET tester");
   TCHAR szTestData[] = TEXT("Some text data");

   // Commit a page of storage and modify its contents.
   LPTSTR pszData = (LPTSTR) VirtualAlloc(NULL, 1024,
      MEM_RESERVE | MEM_COMMIT, PAGE_READWRITE);
   lstrcpy(pszData, szTestData);

   if (MessageBox(NULL, TEXT("Do you want to access this data later?"),
      szAppName, MB_YESNO) == IDNO) {

      // We want this page of storage to remain in our process but the
      // contents aren't important to us anymore.
      // Tell the system that the data is not modified.

      // Note: Because MEM_RESET destroys data, VirtualAlloc rounds
      // the base address and size parameters to their safest range.
      // Here is an example:
      //    VirtualAlloc(pvData, 5000, MEM_RESET, PAGE_READWRITE)
      // resets 0 pages on CPUs where the page size is greater than 4 KB
      // and resets 1 page on CPUs with a 4-KB page. So that our call to
      // VirtualAlloc to reset memory below always succeeds, VirtualQuery
      // is called first to get the exact region size.
      MEMORY_BASIC_INFORMATION mbi;
```

Figure 15-2.
The MemReset sample application

(continued)

539

Figure 15-2. *continued*

```
    VirtualQuery(pszData, &mbi, sizeof(mbi));
    VirtualAlloc(pszData, mbi.RegionSize, MEM_RESET, PAGE_READWRITE);
}

// Commit as much storage as there is physical RAM.
MEMORYSTATUS mst;
GlobalMemoryStatus(&mst);
PVOID pvDummy = VirtualAlloc(NULL, mst.dwTotalPhys,
    MEM_RESERVE | MEM_COMMIT, PAGE_READWRITE);

// Touch all the pages in the dummy region so that any
// modified pages in RAM are written to the paging file.
ZeroMemory(pvDummy, mst.dwTotalPhys);

// Compare our data page with what we originally wrote there.
if (lstrcmp(pszData, szTestData) == 0) {

    // The data in the page matches what we originally put there.
    // ZeroMemory forced our page to be written to the paging file.
    MessageBox(NULL, TEXT("Modified data page was saved."),
        szAppName, MB_OK);
} else {

    // The data in the page does NOT match what we originally put there
    // ZeroMemory didn't cause our page to be written to the paging file
    MessageBox(NULL, TEXT("Modified data page was NOT saved."),
        szAppName, MB_OK);
}
return(0);
}


//////////////////////////////// End of File /////////////////////////////////
```

Address Windowing Extensions (Windows 2000 only)

As days go by, applications require more and more memory. This is especially true of server applications: As an increasing number of clients make requests of the server, the server's performance diminishes. To improve performance, the server application needs to keep more of its data in RAM and reduce disk paging.

Other classes of applications—such as database, engineering, and scientific—also require the ability to manipulate large blocks of storage. For all these applications, a 32-bit address space is just not enough room.

To help these applications, Windows 2000 offers a new feature called Address Windowing Extensions (AWE). Microsoft had two goals when creating AWE:

- Allow applications to allocate RAM that is never swapped by the operating system to or from disk.

- Allow an application to access more RAM than fits within the process's address space.

Basically, AWE provides a way for an application to allocate one or more blocks of RAM. When allocated, these blocks are not visible in the process's address space. Then, the application reserves a region of address space (using *VirtualAlloc*), which becomes the address window. The application then calls a function that assigns one RAM block at a time to the address window. Assigning a RAM block to the address window is extremely fast (usually on the order of a few milliseconds).

Obviously only one RAM block at a time can be accessed via a single address window. This makes your code more difficult to implement since you must explicitly call functions within your code to assign different RAM blocks to the address window as you need them.

The code below shows how to use AWE:

```
// First, reserve a 1MB region for the address window
ULONG_PTR ulRAMBytes = 1024 * 1024
PVOID pvWindow = VirtualAlloc(NULL, ulRAMBytes,
   MEM_RESERVE | MEM_PHYSICAL, PAGE_READWRITE);

// Get the number of bytes in a page for this CPU platform
SYSTEM_INFO sinf;
GetSystemInfo(&sinf);

// Calculate the required number of RAM pages for the
// desired number of bytes
ULONG_PTR ulRAMPages = ulRAMBytes / sinf.dwPageSize

// Allocate array for RAM page's page frame numbers
ULONG_PTR aRAMPages[ulRAMPages];
```

(continued)

```
// Allocate the pages of RAM (requires Lock Pages in Memory user right)
AllocateUserPhysicalPages(
    GetCurrentProcess(), // Allocate the storage for our process
    &ulRAMPages,         // Input: # of RAM pages, Output: # pages allocated
    aRAMPages);          // Output: Opaque array indicating pages allocated

// Assign the RAM pages to our window
MapUserPhysicalPages(pvWindow,   // The address of the address window
    ulRAMPages,                  // Number of entries in array
    aRAMPages);                  // Array of RAM pages

// Access the RAM pages via the pvWindow virtual address
    :
    :

// Free the block of RAM pages
FreeUserPhysicalPages(
    GetCurrentProcess(), // Free the RAM allocated for our process
    &ulRAMPages,         // Input: # of RAM pages, Output: # pages freed
    aRAMPages);          // Input: Array indicating the RAM pages to free

// Destroy the address window
VirtualFree(pvWindow, 0, MEM_RELEASE);
```

As you can see, using AWE is simple. Now, let me point out a few interesting things about this code.

The call to *VirtualAlloc* reserves a 1-MB address window. Usually, the address window is much bigger. You must select a size that is appropriate for the size of the RAM blocks your application requires. Of course, the largest contiguous free block available in your address space determines the largest window you can create. The MEM_RESERVE flag indicates that I am just reserving a region of addresses. The MEM_PHYSICAL flag indicates that this region will eventually be backed by physical RAM storage. One limitation of AWE is that all storage mapped to the address window must be readable and writable; hence PAGE_READWRITE is the only valid protection that can be passed to *VirtualAlloc*. In addition, you cannot use the *VirtualProtect* function to alter this protection.

Allocating physical RAM is simply a matter of calling *AllocateUserPhysical-Pages*:

```
BOOL AllocateUserPhysicalPages(
    HANDLE hProcess,
    PULONG_PTR pulRAMPages,
    PULONG_PTR aRAMPages);
```

This function allocates the number of RAM pages specified in the value pointed to by the *pulRAMPages* parameter and assigns these pages to the process identified by the *hProcess* parameter.

Each page of RAM is assigned a *page frame number* by the operating system. As the system selects pages of RAM for the allocation, it populates the array—pointed to by the *aRAMPages* parameter—with each RAM page's page frame number. The page frame numbers themselves are not useful in any way to your application; you should not examine the contents of this array and you most definitely should not alter any of the values in this array. Note that you neither know which pages of RAM were allocated to this block nor should you care. When the address window shows the pages in the RAM block, they appear as a contiguous block of memory. This makes the RAM easy to use and frees you from having to understand exactly what the system is doing internally.

When the function returns, the value in *pulRAMPages* indicates the number of pages that the function successfully allocated. This will usually be the same value that you passed to the function, but it can also be a smaller value.

Only the owning process can use the allocated RAM pages; AWE does not allow the RAM pages to be mapped into another process's address space. Therefore, you cannot share RAM blocks between processes.

> **NOTE**
>
> Of course, physical RAM is a very precious resource and an application can only allocate whatever RAM has not already been dedicated. You should use AWE sparingly or your process and other processes will excessively page storage to and from disk, severely hurting overall performance. In addition, less available RAM adversely affects the system's ability to create new processes, threads, and other resources. An application can use the *GlobalMemoryStatusEx* function to monitor physical memory use.
>
> To help protect the allocation of RAM, the *AllocateUserPhysicalPages* function requires the caller to have the "Lock Pages in Memory" user right granted and enabled or the function fails. By default, this right isn't assigned to any user or group. The right is given to the Local System account, which is typically used for services. If you want to run an interactive application that calls *AllocateUserPhysicalPages*, an administrator must grant you this right before you log on and run the application.

WINDOWS
2000

In Windows 2000 you can turn on the Lock Pages in Memory user right, by performing the following steps:

1. Open the Computer Management MMC console by clicking on the Start button and then selecting the Run menu item. In the Run box, type "compmgmt.msc /a" and click on the OK button.

2. If the Local Computer Policy item is not visible in the left-hand pane, select Add/Remove Snap-in from the Console menu. On the Standalone tab, select Computer Management (Local) from the Snap-ins Added To combo box. Now click on the Add button to display the Add Standalone Snap-in dialog box. Select Group Policy from the Available Standalone Snap-ins list, and click on the Add button. On the Select Group Policy Object dialog box leave the defaults and click on the Finish button. Click on the Close button in the Add Standalone Snap-in dialog box and click on the OK button in the Add/Remove Snap-in dialog box. The Local Computer Policy item should now be visible in the left-hand pane of the Computer Management console.

3. In the left-hand pane of the console, double-click to expand each of the following items: Local Computer Policy, Computer Configuration, Windows Settings, Security Settings, and finally Local Policies. Select the User Rights Assignment item.

4. In the right-hand pane, select the Lock Pages in Memory attribute.

5. Select Security from the Action menu to display the Lock Pages in Memory dialog box. Click on the Add button. Use the Select Users or Groups dialog box to add the users and/or groups that you want to assign the Lock Pages in Memory user right. Exit each of the dialog boxes by clicking on the OK button.

User rights are granted when a user logs on. If you just granted the Lock Pages in Memory right to yourself, you must log off and log back on before it takes effect.

Now that I've created the address window and allocated a RAM block, I assign the block to the window by calling *MapUserPhysicalPages*:

```
BOOL MapUserPhysicalPages(
   PVOID pvAddressWindow,
   ULONG_PTR ulRAMPages,
   PULONG_PTR aRAMPages);
```

The first parameter, *pvAddressWindow*, indicates the virtual address of the address window and the second two parameters, *ulRAMPages* and *aRAMPages*, indicate how many and which pages of RAM to make visible in this address window. If the window is smaller than the number of pages you're attempting to map, the function fails. Microsoft's main goal for this function was to make it execute extremely fast. Typically, *MapUserPhysicalPages* is able to map the RAM block in just a few microseconds.

> **NOTE** You can also call *MapUserPhysicalPages* to un-assign the current RAM block by passing NULL for the *aRAMPages* parameter. Here is an example:
>
> ```
> // Un-assign the RAM block from the address window
> MapUserPhysicalPages(pvWindow, ulRAMPages, NULL);
> ```

Once the RAM block has been assigned to the address window, you can easily access the RAM storage simply by referencing virtual addresses relative to the address window's base address (*pvWindow* in my sample code).

When you no longer need the RAM block, you should free it by calling *FreeUserPhysicalPages*:

```
BOOL FreeUserPhysicalPages(
   HANDLE hProcess,
   PULONG_PTR pulRAMPages,
   PULONG_PTR aRAMPages);
```

The first parameter, *hProcess*, indicates which process owns the RAM pages you're attempting to free. The second two parameters indicate how many pages and the page frame numbers of those pages that are to be freed. If this RAM block is currently mapped to the address window, it is unmapped and then freed.

Finally, to completely clean up, I free the address window merely by calling *VirtualFree* and passing the base virtual address of the window, 0 for the region's size, and MEM_RELEASE.

My simple code example creates a single address window and a single RAM block. This allows my application access to RAM that will not be swapped to or from disk. However, an application can create several address windows and can allocate several RAM blocks. These RAM blocks can be assigned to any of the address windows but the system does not allow a single RAM block to appear in two address windows simultaneously.

64-bit Windows 2000 fully supports AWE; porting a 32-bit application that uses AWE is easy and straightforward. However, AWE is less useful for a 64-bit application since a process's address space is so large. AWE is still useful because it allows the application to allocate physical RAM that is not swapped to or from disk.

The AWE Sample Application

The AWE application ("15 AWE.exe"), listed in Figure 15-3, demonstrates how to create multiple address windows and how to assign different storage blocks to these windows. The source code and resource files for the application are in the 15-AWE directory on the companion CD-ROM. When you start the program, it internally creates two address window regions and allocates two RAM blocks.

Initially, the first RAM block is populated with the string "Text in Storage 0" and the second RAM block is populated with the string "Text in Storage 1." Then the first RAM block is assigned to the first address window and the second RAM block is assigned to the second address window. The application's window reflects this.

Using this window, you can perform some experiments. First, you assign RAM blocks to address windows using each address window's combo box. The combo box also offers a No Storage option that unmaps any storage from the address window. Second, editing the text updates the RAM block currently selected in the address window.

If you attempt to assign the same RAM block to the two address windows simultaneously, the following message box appears since AWE doesn't support this.

```
C:\Documents and Settings\Jeffrey Richter\My Documents\AdvWin\CD\x86\De...   [X]

This storage can be mapped only once.

                        [      OK      ]
```

The source code for this sample application is clear-cut. To make working with AWE easier, I created three C++ classes contained in the Addr-Windows.h file. The first class, CSystemInfo, is a very simple wrapper around the *GetSystemInfo* function. The other two classes each create an instance of the CSystemInfo class.

The second C++ class, CAddrWindow, encapsulates an address window. Basically, the *Create* method reserves an address window, the *Destroy* method destroys the address window, the *UnmapStorage* method unmaps any RAM block currently assigned to the address window, and the PVOID cast operator method simply returns the virtual address of the address window.

The third C++ class, CAddrWindowStorage, encapsulates a RAM block that may be assigned to a CAddrWindow object. The *Allocate* method enables the Lock Pages in Memory user right, attempts to allocate the RAM block, and then disables the user right. The *Free* method frees the RAM block. The *How-ManyPagesAllocated* method returns the number of pages successfully allocated. The *MapStorage* and *UnmapStorage* methods map and unmap the RAM block to or from a CAddrWindow object.

Using these C++ classes made implementing the sample application much easier. The sample application creates two CAddrWindow objects and two CAddrWindowStorage objects. The rest of the code is just a matter of calling the correct method for the proper object at the right time.

AWE.cpp

```
/******************************************************************************
Module:  AWE.cpp
Notices: Copyright (c) 2000 Jeffrey Richter
******************************************************************************/


#include "..\CmnHdr.h"      /* See Appendix A. */
#include <Windowsx.h>
#include <tchar.h>
#include "AddrWindow.h"
#include "Resource.h"
```

Figure 15-3.   *(continued)*
The AWE application

547

Figure 15-3. *continued*

```
//////////////////////////////////////////////////////////////////////////

CAddrWindow g_aw[2];              // 2 memory address windows
CAddrWindowStorage g_aws[2];      // 2 storage blocks
const ULONG_PTR g_nChars = 1024;  // 1024 character buffers


//////////////////////////////////////////////////////////////////////////


BOOL Dlg_OnInitDialog(HWND hwnd, HWND hwndFocus, LPARAM lParam) {

   chSETDLGICONS(hwnd, IDI_AWE);

   // Create the 2 memory address windows
   chVERIFY(g_aw[0].Create(g_nChars * sizeof(TCHAR)));
   chVERIFY(g_aw[1].Create(g_nChars * sizeof(TCHAR)));

   // Create the 2 storage blocks
   if (!g_aws[0].Allocate(g_nChars * sizeof(TCHAR))) {
      chFAIL("Failed to allocate RAM.\nMost likely reason: "
         "you are not granted the Lock Pages in Memory user right.");
   }
   chVERIFY(g_aws[1].Allocate(g_nChars * sizeof(TCHAR)));

   // Put some default text in the 1st storage block
   g_aws[0].MapStorage(g_aw[0]);
   lstrcpy((PSTR) (PVOID) g_aw[0], TEXT("Text in Storage 0"));

   // Put some default text in the 2nd storage block
   g_aws[1].MapStorage(g_aw[0]);
   lstrcpy((PSTR) (PVOID) g_aw[0], TEXT("Text in Storage 1"));

   // Populate the dialog box controls
   for (int n = 0; n <= 1; n++) {
      // Set the combo box for each address window
      int id = ((n == 0) ? IDC_WINDOW0STORAGE : IDC_WINDOW1STORAGE);
      HWND hwndCB = GetDlgItem(hwnd, id);
      ComboBox_AddString(hwndCB, TEXT("No storage"));
      ComboBox_AddString(hwndCB, TEXT("Storage 0"));
      ComboBox_AddString(hwndCB, TEXT("Storage 1"));
```

(continued)

Figure 15-3. *continued*

```
       // Window 0 shows Storage 0, Window 1 shows Storage 1
       ComboBox_SetCurSel(hwndCB, n + 1);
       FORWARD_WM_COMMAND(hwnd, id, hwndCB, CBN_SELCHANGE, SendMessage);
       Edit_LimitText(GetDlgItem(hwnd,
          (n == 0) ? IDC_WINDOW0TEXT : IDC_WINDOW1TEXT), g_nChars);
   }

   return(TRUE);
}


///////////////////////////////////////////////////////////////////////////////


void Dlg_OnCommand(HWND hwnd, int id, HWND hwndCtl, UINT codeNotify) {

   switch (id) {

   case IDCANCEL:
      EndDialog(hwnd, id);
      break;

   case IDC_WINDOW0STORAGE:
   case IDC_WINDOW1STORAGE:
      if (codeNotify == CBN_SELCHANGE) {

         // Show different storage in address window
         int nWindow  = ((id == IDC_WINDOW0STORAGE) ? 0 : 1);
         int nStorage = ComboBox_GetCurSel(hwndCtl) - 1;

         if (nStorage == -1) {    // Show no storage in this window
            chVERIFY(g_aw[nWindow].UnmapStorage());
         } else {
            if (!g_aws[nStorage].MapStorage(g_aw[nWindow])) {
               // Couldn't map storage in window
               chVERIFY(g_aw[nWindow].UnmapStorage());
               ComboBox_SetCurSel(hwndCtl, 0);  // Force "No storage"
               chMB("This storage can be mapped only once.");
            }
         }

         // Update the address window's text display
         HWND hwndText = GetDlgItem(hwnd,
            ((nWindow == 0) ? IDC_WINDOW0TEXT : IDC_WINDOW1TEXT));
         MEMORY_BASIC_INFORMATION mbi;
```

(continued)

Figure 15-3. *continued*

```
        VirtualQuery(g_aw[nWindow], &mbi, sizeof(mbi));
        // Note: mbi.State == MEM_RESERVE if no storage is in address window
        EnableWindow(hwndText, (mbi.State == MEM_COMMIT));
        Edit_SetText(hwndText, IsWindowEnabled(hwndText)
           ? (PCSTR) (PVOID) g_aw[nWindow] : TEXT("(No storage)"));
      }
      break;

   case IDC_WINDOW0TEXT:
   case IDC_WINDOW1TEXT:
      if (codeNotify == EN_CHANGE) {
         // Update the storage in the address window
         int nWindow = ((id == IDC_WINDOW0TEXT) ? 0 : 1);
         Edit_GetText(hwndCtl, (PSTR) (PVOID) g_aw[nWindow], g_nChars);
      }
      break;
   }
}


///////////////////////////////////////////////////////////////////////////////


INT_PTR WINAPI Dlg_Proc(HWND hwnd, UINT uMsg, WPARAM wParam, LPARAM lParam) {

   switch (uMsg) {
      chHANDLE_DLGMSG(hwnd, WM_INITDIALOG, Dlg_OnInitDialog);
      chHANDLE_DLGMSG(hwnd, WM_COMMAND,    Dlg_OnCommand);
   }

   return(FALSE);
}


///////////////////////////////////////////////////////////////////////////////


int WINAPI _tWinMain(HINSTANCE hinstExe, HINSTANCE, PTSTR pszCmdLine, int) {

   chWindows2000Required();

   DialogBox(hinstExe, MAKEINTRESOURCE(IDD_AWE), NULL, Dlg_Proc);
   return(0);
}

///////////////////////////////// End of File /////////////////////////////////
```

(continued)

Figure 15-3. *continued*

AWE.rc

```
//Microsoft Developer Studio generated resource script.
//
#include "resource.h"

#define APSTUDIO_READONLY_SYMBOLS
/////////////////////////////////////////////////////////////////////////////
//
// Generated from the TEXTINCLUDE 2 resource.
//
#include "afxres.h"


/////////////////////////////////////////////////////////////////////////////
#undef APSTUDIO_READONLY_SYMBOLS


/////////////////////////////////////////////////////////////////////////////
// English (U.S.) resources

#if !defined(AFX_RESOURCE_DLL) || defined(AFX_TARG_ENU)
#ifdef _WIN32
LANGUAGE LANG_ENGLISH, SUBLANG_ENGLISH_US
#pragma code_page(1252)
#endif //_WIN32


/////////////////////////////////////////////////////////////////////////////
//
// Dialog
//

IDD_AWE DIALOG DISCARDABLE  0, 0, 288, 45
STYLE DS_SETFOREGROUND | DS_3DLOOK | DS_CENTER | WS_MINIMIZEBOX | WS_VISIBLE |
    WS_CAPTION | WS_SYSMENU
CAPTION "Address Windowing Extensions"
FONT 8, "MS Sans Serif"
BEGIN
    LTEXT           "Window 0:",IDC_STATIC,4,6,35,8
    COMBOBOX        IDC_WINDOW0STORAGE,44,4,80,58,CBS_DROPDOWNLIST |
                    WS_TABSTOP
    EDITTEXT        IDC_WINDOW0TEXT,132,4,152,14,ES_AUTOHSCROLL
    LTEXT           "Window 1:",IDC_STATIC,4,28,35,8
    COMBOBOX        IDC_WINDOW1STORAGE,44,25,80,58,CBS_DROPDOWNLIST |
                    WS_TABSTOP
    EDITTEXT        IDC_WINDOW1TEXT,132,25,152,14,ES_AUTOHSCROLL
END
```

(continued)

Figure 15-3. *continued*

```
///////////////////////////////////////////////////////////////////////////////
//
// DESIGNINFO
//

#ifdef APSTUDIO_INVOKED
GUIDELINES DESIGNINFO DISCARDABLE
BEGIN
    IDD_AWE, DIALOG
    BEGIN
        LEFTMARGIN, 7
        RIGHTMARGIN, 281
        TOPMARGIN, 7
        BOTTOMMARGIN, 38
    END
END
#endif    // APSTUDIO_INVOKED


#ifdef APSTUDIO_INVOKED
///////////////////////////////////////////////////////////////////////////////
//
// TEXTINCLUDE
//

1 TEXTINCLUDE DISCARDABLE
BEGIN
    "resource.h\0"
END

2 TEXTINCLUDE DISCARDABLE
BEGIN
    "#include ""afxres.h""\r\n"
    "\0"
END

3 TEXTINCLUDE DISCARDABLE
BEGIN
    "\r\n"
    "\0"
END

#endif    // APSTUDIO_INVOKED
```

(continued)

Figure 15-3. *continued*

```
///////////////////////////////////////////////////////////////////////////
//
// Icon
//

// Icon with lowest ID value placed first to ensure application icon
// remains consistent on all systems.
IDI_AWE                    ICON    DISCARDABLE      "AWE.ico"
#endif    // English (U.S.) resources
///////////////////////////////////////////////////////////////////////////


#ifndef APSTUDIO_INVOKED
///////////////////////////////////////////////////////////////////////////
//
// Generated from the TEXTINCLUDE 3 resource.
//


///////////////////////////////////////////////////////////////////////////
#endif    // not APSTUDIO_INVOKED
```

AddrWindow.h

```
/***************************************************************************
Module:  AddrWindow.h
Notices: Copyright (c) 2000 Jeffrey Richter
***************************************************************************/


#pragma once


///////////////////////////////////////////////////////////////////////////


#include "..\CmnHdr.h"      /* See Appendix A. */
#include <tchar.h>


///////////////////////////////////////////////////////////////////////////
```

(continued)

Figure 15-3. *continued*

```
class CSystemInfo : public SYSTEM_INFO {
public:
   CSystemInfo() { GetSystemInfo(this); }
};


/////////////////////////////////////////////////////////////////////////////


class CAddrWindow {
public:
   CAddrWindow()  { m_pvWindow = NULL; }
   ~CAddrWindow() { Destroy(); }

   BOOL Create(SIZE_T dwBytes, PVOID pvPreferredWindowBase = NULL) {
      // Reserve address window region to view physical storage
      m_pvWindow = VirtualAlloc(pvPreferredWindowBase, dwBytes,
         MEM_RESERVE | MEM_PHYSICAL, PAGE_READWRITE);
      return(m_pvWindow != NULL);
   }

   BOOL Destroy() {
      BOOL fOk = TRUE;
      if (m_pvWindow != NULL) {
         // Destroy address window region
         fOk = VirtualFree(m_pvWindow, 0, MEM_RELEASE);
         m_pvWindow = NULL;
      }
      return(fOk);
   }

   BOOL UnmapStorage() {
      // Unmap all storage from address window region
      MEMORY_BASIC_INFORMATION mbi;
      VirtualQuery(m_pvWindow, &mbi, sizeof(mbi));
      return(MapUserPhysicalPages(m_pvWindow,
         mbi.RegionSize / sm_sinf.dwPageSize, NULL));
   }

   // Returns virtual address of address window
   operator PVOID() { return(m_pvWindow); }
```

(continued)

Figure 15-3. *continued*

```
private:
   PVOID m_pvWindow;      // Virtual address of address window region
   static CSystemInfo sm_sinf;
};


///////////////////////////////////////////////////////////////////////////


CSystemInfo CAddrWindow::sm_sinf;


///////////////////////////////////////////////////////////////////////////


class CAddrWindowStorage {
public:
   CAddrWindowStorage()  { m_ulPages = 0; m_pulUserPfnArray = NULL; }
   ~CAddrWindowStorage() { Free(); }

   BOOL Allocate(ULONG_PTR ulBytes) {
      // Allocate storage intended for an address window

      Free();  // Cleanup this object's existing address window

      // Calculate number of pages from number of bytes
      m_ulPages = (ulBytes + sm_sinf.dwPageSize) / sm_sinf.dwPageSize;

      // Allocate array of page frame numbers
      m_pulUserPfnArray = (PULONG_PTR)
         HeapAlloc(GetProcessHeap(), 0, m_ulPages * sizeof(ULONG_PTR));

      BOOL fOk = (m_pulUserPfnArray != NULL);
      if (fOk) {
         // The "Lock Pages in Memory" privilege must be enabled
         EnablePrivilege(SE_LOCK_MEMORY_NAME, TRUE);
         fOk = AllocateUserPhysicalPages(GetCurrentProcess(),
            &m_ulPages, m_pulUserPfnArray);
         EnablePrivilege(SE_LOCK_MEMORY_NAME, FALSE);
      }
      return(fOk);
   }
```

(continued)

Figure 15-3. *continued*

```
    BOOL Free() {
        BOOL fOk = TRUE;
        if (m_pulUserPfnArray != NULL) {
            fOk = FreeUserPhysicalPages(GetCurrentProcess(),
                &m_ulPages, m_pulUserPfnArray);
            if (fOk) {
                // Free the array of page frame numbers
                HeapFree(GetProcessHeap(), 0, m_pulUserPfnArray);
                m_ulPages = 0;
                m_pulUserPfnArray = NULL;
            }
        }
        return(fOk);
    }

    ULONG_PTR HowManyPagesAllocated() { return(m_ulPages); }

    BOOL MapStorage(CAddrWindow& aw) {
        return(MapUserPhysicalPages(aw,
            HowManyPagesAllocated(), m_pulUserPfnArray));
    }

    BOOL UnmapStorage(CAddrWindow& aw) {
        return(MapUserPhysicalPages(aw,
            HowManyPagesAllocated(), NULL));
    }

private:
    static BOOL EnablePrivilege(PCTSTR pszPrivName, BOOL fEnable = TRUE) {

        BOOL fOk = FALSE;      // Assume function fails
        HANDLE hToken;

        // Try to open this process's access token
        if (OpenProcessToken(GetCurrentProcess(),
            TOKEN_ADJUST_PRIVILEGES, &hToken)) {

            // Attempt to modify the "Lock pages in Memory" user right
            TOKEN_PRIVILEGES tp = { 1 };
            LookupPrivilegeValue(NULL, pszPrivName, &tp.Privileges[0].Luid);
            tp.Privileges[0].Attributes = fEnable ? SE_PRIVILEGE_ENABLED : 0;
            AdjustTokenPrivileges(hToken, FALSE, &tp, sizeof(tp), NULL, NULL);
```

(continued)

Figure 15-3. *continued*

```
            fOk = (GetLastError() == ERROR_SUCCESS);
            CloseHandle(hToken);
        }
        return(fOk);
    }

private:
    ULONG_PTR  m_ulPages;          // Number of storage pages
    PULONG_PTR m_pulUserPfnArray;  // Page frame number array

private:
    static CSystemInfo sm_sinf;
};


///////////////////////////////////////////////////////////////////////////


CSystemInfo CAddrWindowStorage::sm_sinf;


/////////////////////////////// End of File ///////////////////////////////
```

A THREAD'S STACK

Sometimes the system reserves regions in your own process's address space. I mentioned in Chapter 13 that this happens for process and thread environment blocks. Another time that the system reserves regions in your own process's address space is for a thread's stack.

Whenever a thread is created, the system reserves a region of address space for the thread's stack (each thread gets its very own stack) and also commits some physical storage to this reserved region. By default, the system reserves 1 MB of address space and commits 2 pages of storage. However, these defaults can be changed by specifying the /STACK option to Microsoft's linker when you link your application:

```
/STACK:reserve[,commit]
```

When a thread's stack is created, the system reserves a region of address space indicated by the linker's /STACK switch. However, you can override the amount of storage that is initially committed when you call the *CreateThread* or the *_beginthreadex* function. Both functions have a parameter that allows you to override the storage that is initially committed to the stack's address space region. If you specify 0 for this parameter, the system uses the commit size indicated by the /STACK switch. For the remainder of this discussion, I'll assume we're using the default stack sizes: 1 MB of reserved region with storage committed one page at a time.

Figure 16-1 shows what a stack region (reserved starting at address 0x08000000) might look like on a machine whose page size is 4 KB. The stack's region and all of the physical storage committed to it have a page protection of PAGE_READWRITE.

After reserving this region, the system commits physical storage to the top 2 pages of the region. Just before allowing the thread to begin execution, the system sets the thread's stack pointer register to point to the end of the top page of the stack region (an address very close to 0x08100000). This page is where the thread will begin using its stack. The second page from the top is called the *guard page*. As the thread increases its call tree by calling more functions, the thread needs more stack space.

Memory Address	State of Page
0x080FF000	Top of stack: committed page
0x080FE000	Committed page with guard protection attribute flag
0x080FD000	Reserved page
0x08003000	Reserved page
0x08002000	Reserved page
0x08001000	Reserved page
0x08000000	Bottom of stack: reserved page

Figure 16-1.
What a thread's stack region looks like when it is first created

Whenever the thread attempts to access storage in the guard page, the system is notified. In response, the system commits another page of storage just below the guard page. Then the system removes the guard page protection flag from the current guard page and assigns it to the newly committed page of storage. This technique allows the stack storage to increase only as the thread requires it. Eventually, if the thread's call tree continues to expand, the stack region will look like Figure 16-2.

Referring to Figure 16-2, assume that the thread's call tree is very deep and that the stack pointer CPU register points to the stack memory address 0x08003004. Now, when the thread calls another function, the system has to commit more physical storage. However, when the system commits physical storage to the page at address 0x08001000, the system does not do exactly what it did when committing physical storage to the rest of the stack's memory region. Figure 16-3 shows what the stack's reserved memory region looks like.

Memory Address	State of Page
0x080FF000	Top of stack: committed page
0x080FE000	Committed page
0x080FD000	Committed page
0x08003000	Committed page
0x08002000	Committed page with guard protection attribute flag
0x08001000	Reserved page
0x08000000	Bottom of stack: reserved page

Figure 16-2.
A nearly full thread's stack region

As you'd expect, the page starting at address 0x08002000 has the guard attribute removed, and physical storage is committed to the page starting at 0x08001000. The difference is that the system does not apply the guard attribute to the new page of physical storage (0x08001000). This means that the stack's reserved address space region contains all the physical storage that it can ever contain. The bottommost page is always reserved and never gets committed. I will explain the reason for this shortly.

The system performs one more action when it commits physical storage to the page at address 0x08001000—it raises an EXCEPTION_STACK_OVERFLOW exception (defined as 0xC00000FD in WinNT.h). By using structured exception handling (SEH), your program will be notified of this condition and can recover gracefully. For more information on SEH, see Chapters 23, 24, and 25. The Summation sample at the end of this chapter demonstrates how to recover gracefully from stack overflows.

Memory Address	State of Page
0x080FF000	Top of stack: committed page
0x080FE000	Committed page
0x080FD000	Committed page
0x08003000	Committed page
0x08002000	Committed page
0x08001000	Committed page
0x08000000	Bottom of stack: reserved page

Figure 16-3.
A full thread stack region

If the thread continues to use the stack after the stack overflow exception is raised, all the memory in the page at 0x08001000 will be used and the thread will attempt to access memory in the page starting at 0x08000000. When the thread attempts to access this reserved (uncommitted) memory, the system raises an access violation exception. If this access violation exception is raised while the thread is attempting to access the stack, the thread is in deep trouble. The system takes control at this point and terminates the process—not just the thread, but also the whole process. The system doesn't even show a message box to the user—the whole process just disappears!

Now I will explain why the bottommost page of a stack's region is always reserved. Doing so protects against accidental overwriting of other data being used by the process. You see, it's possible that at address 0x07FFF000 (one page below 0x08000000) another region of address space has committed physical storage. If the page at 0x08000000 contained physical storage, the system would not catch attempts by the thread to access the reserved stack region. If the stack were to dip below the reserved stack region, the code in your thread would overwrite other data in your process's address space—a very, very difficult bug to catch.

A Thread's Stack Under Windows 98

Under Windows 98, stacks behave similarly to their Windows 2000 counterparts. However, there are some significant differences.

Figure 16-4 shows what a stack region (reserved starting at address 0x00530000) might look like for a 1-MB stack under Windows 98.

Memory Address	Size	State of Page
0x00640000	16 pages (65,536 bytes)	Top of stack: reserved for stack underflow
0x0063F000	1 page (4096 bytes)	Committed page with PAGE_READWRITE protection; stack in use
0x0063E000	1 page (4096 bytes)	PAGE_NOACCESS page to simulate PAGE_GUARD flag
0x00638000	6 pages (24,576 bytes)	Reserved pages for stack overflow
0x00637000	1 page (4096 bytes)	Committed page with PAGE_READWRITE protection for 16-bit component compatibility
0x00540000	247 pages (1,011,712 bytes)	Reserved pages to allow stack to grow
0x00530000	16 pages (65,536 bytes)	Bottom of stack: reserved for stack overflow

Figure 16-4.
What a thread's stack region looks like when it is first created under Windows 98

First notice that the region is actually 1 MB plus 128 KB in size, even though we wanted to create a stack that was only up to 1 MB in size. In Windows 98, whenever a region is reserved for a stack, the system actually reserves a region that is 128 KB larger than the requested size. The stack is in the middle of this region, with a 64-KB block before the stack and another 64-KB block after the stack.

The 64 KB at the beginning of the stack are there to catch stack overflow conditions, while the 64 KB at the end of the stack are there to catch stack underflow conditions. To see why stack underflow detection is useful, examine the following code fragment:

```
int WINAPI WinMain (HINSTANCE hinstExe, HINSTANCE,
   PSTR pszCmdLine, int nCmdShow) {

   char szBuf[100];
   szBuf[10000] = 0; // Stack underflow

   return(0);
}
```

When this function's assignment statement is executed, an attempt is made to access beyond the end of the thread's stack. Of course, the compiler and the linker will not catch the bug in the code above, but if your application is running under Windows 98, an access violation will be raised when the statement executes. This is a nice feature of Windows 98 that is not offered by Windows 2000. On Windows 2000, it is possible to have another region immediately after your thread's stack. If this happens and you attempt to access memory beyond your stack, you might corrupt memory related to another part of your process—and the system will *not* detect this corruption.

The second significant difference to note is that no pages have the PAGE_GUARD protection attribute flag. Because Windows 98 does not support this flag, it uses a slightly different technique to expand a thread's stack. Windows 98 marks the committed page immediately below the stack with the PAGE_NOACCESS protection attribute (address 0x0063E000 in Figure 16-4). Then when the thread touches the page below the read/write pages, an access violation occurs. The system catches this, changes the no access page to a read/write page, and commits a new "guard" page just below the previous guard page.

The third difference to notice is the single page of PAGE_READWRITE storage at address 0x00637000 in Figure 16-4. This page exists for 16-bit Windows compatibility. Although Microsoft never documented it, developers found out that the 16 bytes at the beginning of a 16-bit application's stack segment (SS) contain information about the 16-bit application's stack, local heap, and local atom table. Because Win32 applications running on Windows 98 frequently call 16-bit DLL components, and some of these 16-bit components assume that this information is available at the beginning of the stack segment, Microsoft was forced to simulate these bytes in Windows 98. When 32-bit code thunks to 16-bit code, Windows 98 maps a 16-bit CPU selector to the 32-bit stack and sets the stack segment register to point to the page at address 0x00637000. The 16-bit code can then access the 16 bytes at the beginning of the stack segment and continue executing without any problems.

Now, as Windows 98 grows the thread's stack, it continues to grow the block at address 0x0063F000; it also keeps moving the guard page down until 1 MB of stack storage is committed, and then the guard page disappears—just as it does under Windows 2000. The system also continues to move the page for 16-bit Windows component compatibility down, and eventually this page goes into the 64-KB block at the beginning of the stack region. So a fully committed stack in Windows 98 looks like Figure 16-5.

Memory Address	Size	State of Page
0x00640000	16 pages (65,536 bytes)	Top of stack: reserved for stack underflow
0x00540000	256 pages (1 MB)	Committed pages with PAGE_READWRITE protection; stack in use
0x00539000	7 pages (28,672 bytes)	Reserved pages for stack overflow
0x00538000	1 page (4096 bytes)	Committed page with PAGE_READWRITE protection for 16-bit component compatibility
0x00530000	8 pages (32,768 bytes)	Bottom of stack: reserved for stack overflow

Figure 16-5.
A full thread stack region under Windows 98

The C/C++ Run-Time Library's Stack-Checking Function

The C/C++ run-time library contains a stack-checking function. As your source code is compiled, the compiler generates calls to this function automatically when necessary. The purpose of the stack-checking function is to make sure that pages are appropriately committed to your thread's stack. Let's look at an example.

Here's a small function that requires a lot of memory for its local variables:

```
void SomeFunction () {
   int nValues[4000];

   // Do some processing with the array.
   nValues[0] = 0;  // Some assignment
}
```

This function will require at least 16,000 bytes (4000 × sizeof(int); each integer is 4 bytes) of stack space to accommodate the array of integers. Usually the code a compiler generates to allocate this stack space simply decrements the CPU's stack pointer by 16,000 bytes. However, the system does not commit physical storage to this lower area of the stack's region until an attempt is made to access the memory address.

On a system with a 4-KB or 8-KB page size, this limitation could cause a problem. If the first access to the stack is at an address that is below the guard page (as shown on the assignment line in the code above), the thread will be accessing reserved memory and the system will raise an access violation. To ensure that you can successfully write functions like the one shown above, the compiler inserts calls to the C run-time library's stack-checking function.

When compiling your program, the compiler knows the page size for the CPU system you are targeting. The *x*86 compiler knows that pages are 4 KB, and the Alpha compiler knows that pages are 8 KB. As the compiler encounters each function in your program, it determines the amount of stack space required for the function; if the function requires more stack space than the target system's page size, the compiler automatically inserts a call to the stack-checking function.

The following pseudocode shows what the stack-checking function does. I say *pseudocode* because this function is usually implemented in assembly language by the compiler vendors.

```
// The C run-time library knows the page size for the target system.
#ifdef _M_ALPHA
#define PAGESIZE    (8 * 1024)    // 8-KB page
#else
#define PAGESIZE    (4 * 1024)    // 4-KB page
#endif

void StackCheck(int nBytesNeededFromStack) {
   // Get the stack pointer position.
   // At this point, the stack pointer has NOT been decremented
   // to account for the function's local variables.
   PBYTE pbStackPtr = (CPU's stack pointer);
```

(continued)

```
while (nBytesNeededFromStack >= PAGESIZE) {
    // Move down a page on the stack--should be a guard page.
    pbStackPtr -= PAGESIZE;

    // Access a byte on the guard page--forces new page to be
    // committed and guard page to move down a page.
    pbStackPtr[0] = 0;

    // Reduce the number of bytes needed from the stack.
    nBytesNeededFromStack -= PAGESIZE;
}

// Before returning, the StackCheck function sets the CPU's
// stack pointer to the address below the function's
// local variables.
}
```

Microsoft Visual C++ does offer a compiler switch that allows you to control the page-size threshold that the compiler uses to determine when to add the automatic call to *StackCheck*. You should use this compiler switch only if you know exactly what you are doing and have a special need for it. For 99.99999 percent of all applications and DLLs written, this switch should not be used.

The Summation Sample Application

The Summation ("16 Summation.exe") sample application in Figure 16-6 beginning on page 570 demonstrates how to use exception filters and exception handlers to recover gracefully from a stack overflow. The source code and resource files for the application are in the 16-Summation directory on the companion CD-ROM. You might want to review the chapters on SEH in order to fully understand how this application works.

The Summation application sums all of the numbers from 0 through *x*, where *x* is a number entered by the user. Of course, the simplest way to do this would be to create a function called *Sum* that simply performs the following calculation:

```
Sum = (x * (x + 1)) / 2;
```

However, for this sample, I have written the *Sum* function to be recursive so that it uses a lot of stack space if you enter large numbers.

When the program starts, it displays the dialog box shown here.

567

In this dialog box, you can enter a number in the edit control and then click on the Calculate button. This causes the program to create a new thread whose sole responsibility is to total all of the numbers between 0 and *x*. While the new thread is running, the program's primary thread waits for the result by calling *WaitForSingleObject* passing the new thread's handle. When the new thread terminates, the system wakes the primary thread. The primary thread retrieves the sum by getting the new thread's exit code through a call to *GetExitCodeThread*. Finally—and this is extremely important—the primary thread closes its handle to the new thread so that the system can completely destroy the thread object and so that our application does not have a resource leak.

Now the primary thread examines the summation thread's exit code. The exit code UINT_MAX indicates that an error occurred—the summation thread overflowed the stack while totaling the numbers—and the primary thread will display a message box to this effect. If the exit code is not UINT_MAX, the summation thread completed successfully and the exit code is the summation. In this case, the primary thread will simply put the summation answer in the dialog box.

Now let's turn to the summation thread. The thread function for this thread is called *SumThreadFunc*. When the primary thread creates this thread, it is passed the number of integers that it should total as its only parameter, *pvParam*. The function then initializes the *uSum* variable to UINT_MAX, which means that the function is assuming that it will not complete successfully. Next *SumThreadFunc* sets up SEH so that it can catch any exception that might be raised while the thread executes. The recursive *Sum* function is then called to calculate the sum.

If the sum is calculated successfully, *SumThreadFunc* simply returns the value of the *uSum* variable; this is the thread's exit code. However, if an exception is raised while the *Sum* function is executing, the system will immediately evaluate the SEH filter expression. In other words, the system will call the *FilterFunc* function and pass it the code that identifies the raised exception. For a stack overflow exception, this code is EXCEPTION_STACK_OVERFLOW. If you want to see the program gracefully handle a stack overflow exception, tell the program to sum the first 44,000 numbers.

My *FilterFunc* function is simple. It checks to see if a stack overflow exception was raised, and if not, it returns EXCEPTION_CONTINUE_SEARCH. Otherwise, the filter returns EXCEPTION_EXECUTE_HANDLER. This indicates to the system that the filter was expecting this exception and that the code contained in the *except* block should execute. For this sample application, the exception handler has nothing special to do but allows the thread to exit gracefully with a return code of UINT_MAX (the value in *uSumNum*). The parent thread will see this special return value and display a warning message to the user.

The final thing that I want to discuss is why I execute the *Sum* function in its own thread instead of just setting up an SEH block in the primary thread and calling the *Sum* function from within the *try* block. I created this additional thread for three reasons.

First, each time a thread is created, it gets its very own 1-MB stack region. If I called the *Sum* function from within the primary thread, some of the stack space would already be in use and the *Sum* function would not be able to use its full 1 MB of stack space. Granted, my sample is a simple program and is probably not using all that much stack, but other programs will probably be more complicated. I can easily imagine a situation in which *Sum* might successfully total the integers from 0 through 1000. Then when *Sum* is called again later, the stack might be deeper, causing a stack overflow to occur when *Sum* is trying only to total the integers from 0 through 750. So to make the *Sum* function behave more consistently, I ensure that it has a full stack that has not been used by any other code.

The second reason for using a separate thread is that a thread is notified only once of a stack overflow exception. If I called the *Sum* function in the primary thread and a stack overflow occurred, the exception could be trapped and handled gracefully. However, at this point all of the stack's reserved address space is committed with physical storage, and there are no more pages with the guard protection flag turned on. If the user performs another sum, the *Sum* function could overflow the stack and a stack overflow exception would not be raised. Instead, an access violation exception would be raised, and it would be too late to handle this situation gracefully.

The final reason for using a separate stack is so that the physical storage for the stack can be freed. Take this scenario as an example: The user asks the *Sum* function to calculate the sum of the integers from 0 through 30,000. This will require quite a bit of physical storage to be committed to the stack region. Then the user might do several summations in which the highest number is only 5000. In this case, a large amount of storage is committed to the stack region but is no longer being used. This physical storage is allocated from the paging file. Rather than leave this storage committed, it's better to free the storage, giving it back to the system and other processes. By having the *SumThreadFunc* thread terminate, the system automatically reclaims the physical storage that was committed to the stack's region.

Summation.cpp

```
/******************************************************************************
Module:  Summation.cpp
Notices: Copyright (c) 2000 Jeffrey Richter
******************************************************************************/


#include "..\CmnHdr.h"        /* See Appendix A. */
#include <windowsx.h>
#include <limits.h>
#include <process.h>          // For _beginthreadex
#include <tchar.h>
#include "Resource.h"


///////////////////////////////////////////////////////////////////////////////


// An example of calling Sum for uNum = 0 through 9
// uNum: 0 1 2 3  4  5  6  7  8  9 ...
// Sum:  0 1 3 6 10 15 21 28 36 45 ...
UINT Sum(UINT uNum) {

   // Call Sum recursively.
   return((uNum == 0) ? 0 : (uNum + Sum(uNum - 1)));
}


///////////////////////////////////////////////////////////////////////////////


LONG WINAPI FilterFunc(DWORD dwExceptionCode) {

   return((dwExceptionCode == STATUS_STACK_OVERFLOW)
      ? EXCEPTION_EXECUTE_HANDLER : EXCEPTION_CONTINUE_SEARCH);
}


///////////////////////////////////////////////////////////////////////////////
// The separate thread that is responsible for calculating the sum.
// I use a separate thread for the following reasons:
//    1. A separate thread gets its own 1 MB of stack space.
//    2. A thread can be notified of a stack overflow only once.
//    3. The stack's storage is freed when the thread exits.
DWORD WINAPI SumThreadFunc(PVOID pvParam) {

   // The parameter pvParam, contains the number of integers to sum.
   UINT uSumNum = PtrToUlong(pvParam);
```

Figure 16-6.
The Summation sample application

(continued)

Figure 16-6. *continued*

```
   // uSum contains the summation of the numbers from 0 through uSumNum.
   // If the sum cannot be calculated, a sum of UINT_MAX is returned.
   UINT uSum = UINT_MAX;

   __try {
      // To catch the stack overflow exception, we must
      // execute the Sum function while inside an SEH block.
      uSum = Sum(uSumNum);
   }
   __except (FilterFunc(GetExceptionCode())) {
      // If we get in here, it's because we have trapped a stack overflow.
      // We can now do whatever is necessary to gracefully continue execution.
      // This sample application has nothing to do, so no code is placed
      // in this exception handler block.
   }

   // The thread's exit code is the sum of the first uSumNum
   // numbers, or UINT_MAX if a stack overflow occurred.
   return(uSum);
}

///////////////////////////////////////////////////////////////////////////////

BOOL Dlg_OnInitDialog(HWND hwnd, HWND hwndFocus, LPARAM lParam) {

   chSETDLGICONS(hwnd, IDI_SUMMATION);

   // Don't accept integers more than 9 digits long.
   Edit_LimitText(GetDlgItem(hwnd, IDC_SUMNUM), 9);

   return(TRUE);
}

///////////////////////////////////////////////////////////////////////////////

void Dlg_OnCommand(HWND hwnd, int id, HWND hwndCtl, UINT codeNotify) {

   switch (id) {
      case IDCANCEL:
         EndDialog(hwnd, id);
         break;

      case IDC_CALC:
         // Get the number of integers the user wants to sum.
         UINT uSum = GetDlgItemInt(hwnd, IDC_SUMNUM, NULL, FALSE);
```

(continued)

Figure 16-6. *continued*

```
         // Create a thread (with its own stack) that is
         // responsible for performing the summation.
         DWORD dwThreadId;
         HANDLE hThread = chBEGINTHREADEX(NULL, 0,
            SumThreadFunc, (PVOID) (UINT_PTR) uSum, 0, &dwThreadId);

         // Wait for the thread to terminate.
         WaitForSingleObject(hThread, INFINITE);

         // The thread's exit code is the resulting summation.
         GetExitCodeThread(hThread, (PDWORD) &uSum);

         // Allow the system to destroy the thread kernel object
         CloseHandle(hThread);

         // Update the dialog box to show the result.
         if (uSum == UINT_MAX) {
            // If result is UINT_MAX, a stack overflow occurred.
            SetDlgItemText(hwnd, IDC_ANSWER, TEXT("Error"));
            chMB("The number is too big, please enter a smaller number");
         } else {
            // The sum was calculated successfully;
            SetDlgItemInt(hwnd, IDC_ANSWER, uSum, FALSE);
         }
         break;
   }
}


///////////////////////////////////////////////////////////////////////////////


INT_PTR WINAPI Dlg_Proc(HWND hwnd, UINT uMsg, WPARAM wParam, LPARAM lParam) {

   switch (uMsg) {
      chHANDLE_DLGMSG(hwnd, WM_INITDIALOG, Dlg_OnInitDialog);
      chHANDLE_DLGMSG(hwnd, WM_COMMAND,    Dlg_OnCommand);
   }
   return(FALSE);
}


///////////////////////////////////////////////////////////////////////////////
```

(continued)

Figure 16-6. *continued*

```
int WINAPI _tWinMain(HINSTANCE hinstExe, HINSTANCE, PTSTR pszCmdLine, int) {

   DialogBox(hinstExe, MAKEINTRESOURCE(IDD_SUMMATION), NULL, Dlg_Proc);
   return(0);
}


/////////////////////////////// End of File ///////////////////////////////////
```

Summation.rc

```
//Microsoft Developer Studio generated resource script.
//
#include "Resource.h"

#define APSTUDIO_READONLY_SYMBOLS
/////////////////////////////////////////////////////////////////////////////
//
// Generated from the TEXTINCLUDE 2 resource.
//
#define APSTUDIO_HIDDEN_SYMBOLS
#include "windows.h"
#undef APSTUDIO_HIDDEN_SYMBOLS


/////////////////////////////////////////////////////////////////////////////
#undef APSTUDIO_READONLY_SYMBOLS


/////////////////////////////////////////////////////////////////////////////
// English (U.S.) resources

#if !defined(AFX_RESOURCE_DLL) || defined(AFX_TARG_ENU)
#ifdef _WIN32
LANGUAGE LANG_ENGLISH, SUBLANG_ENGLISH_US
#pragma code_page(1252)
#endif //_WIN32


/////////////////////////////////////////////////////////////////////////////
//
// Icon
//
```

(continued)

Figure 16-6. *continued*

```
// Icon with lowest ID value placed first to ensure application icon
// remains consistent on all systems.
IDI_SUMMATION              ICON    DISCARDABLE      "Summation.ico"


/////////////////////////////////////////////////////////////////////////////
//
// Dialog
//

IDD_SUMMATION DIALOG DISCARDABLE  18, 18, 162, 41
STYLE WS_POPUP | WS_CAPTION | WS_SYSMENU
CAPTION "Summation"
FONT 8, "MS Sans Serif"
BEGIN
    LTEXT              "Calculate the sum of the numbers from 0 through &x, where x is: ",
                       IDC_STATIC,4,4,112,20
    EDITTEXT           IDC_SUMNUM,120,8,40,13,ES_AUTOHSCROLL
    DEFPUSHBUTTON      "&Calculate",IDC_CALC,4,28,56,12
    LTEXT              "Answer:",IDC_STATIC,68,30,30,8
    LTEXT              "?",IDC_ANSWER,104,30,56,8
END


#ifdef APSTUDIO_INVOKED
/////////////////////////////////////////////////////////////////////////////
//
// TEXTINCLUDE
//

1 TEXTINCLUDE DISCARDABLE
BEGIN
    "Resource.h\0"
END

2 TEXTINCLUDE DISCARDABLE
BEGIN
    "#define APSTUDIO_HIDDEN_SYMBOLS\r\n"
    "#include ""windows.h""\r\n"
    "#undef APSTUDIO_HIDDEN_SYMBOLS\r\n"
    "\0"
END

3 TEXTINCLUDE DISCARDABLE
BEGIN
    "\r\n"
    "\0"
END
```

(continued)

Figure 16-6. *continued*

```
#endif     // APSTUDIO_INVOKED

#endif     // English (U.S.) resources
/////////////////////////////////////////////////////////////////////////////


#ifndef APSTUDIO_INVOKED
/////////////////////////////////////////////////////////////////////////////
//
// Generated from the TEXTINCLUDE 3 resource.
//


/////////////////////////////////////////////////////////////////////////////
#endif     // not APSTUDIO_INVOKED
```

MEMORY-MAPPED FILES

Working with files is something almost every application must do, and it's always a hassle. Should your application open the file, read it, and close the file, or should it open the file and use a buffering algorithm to read from and write to different portions of the file? Microsoft Windows offers the best of both worlds: memory-mapped files.

Like virtual memory, memory-mapped files allow you to reserve a region of address space and commit physical storage to the region. The difference is that the physical storage comes from a file that is already on the disk instead of the system's paging file. Once the file has been mapped, you can access it as if the whole file were loaded in memory.

Memory-mapped files are used for three different purposes:

■ The system uses memory-mapped files to load and execute .exe and DLL files. This greatly conserves both paging file space and the time required for an application to begin executing.

■ You can use memory-mapped files to access a data file on disk. This shelters you from performing file I/O operations on the file and from buffering the file's contents.

■ You can use memory-mapped files to allow multiple processes running on the same machine to share data with each other. Windows does offer other methods for communicating data among processes—but these other methods are implemented using memory-mapped files, making memory-mapped files the most efficient way for multiple processes on a single machine to communicate with one another.

In this chapter, we will examine each of these uses for memory-mapped files.

Memory-Mapped Executables and DLLs

When a thread calls *CreateProcess*, the system performs the following steps:

1. The system locates the .exe file specified in the call to *CreateProcess*. If the .exe file cannot be found, the process is not created and *CreateProcess* returns FALSE.

2. The system creates a new process kernel object.

3. The system creates a private address space for this new process.

4. The system reserves a region of address space large enough to contain the .exe file. The desired location of this region is specified inside the .exe file itself. By default, an .exe file's base address is 0x00400000 (this address might be different for a 64-bit application running on 64-bit Windows 2000). However, you can override this when you create your application's .exe file by using the linker's /BASE option when you link your application.

5. The system notes that the physical storage backing the reserved region is in the .exe file on disk instead of the system's paging file.

After the .exe file has been mapped into the process's address space, the system accesses a section of the .exe file that lists the DLLs containing functions that the code in the .exe calls. The system then calls *LoadLibrary* for each of these DLLs, and if any of the DLLs require additional DLLs, the system calls *LoadLibrary* to load those DLLs as well. Every time *LoadLibrary* is called to load a DLL, the system performs steps similar to steps 4 and 5 above:

1. The system reserves a region of address space large enough to contain the DLL file. The desired location of this region is specified inside the DLL file itself. By default, Microsoft Visual C++ makes the DLL's base address 0x10000000 (this address might be different for a 64-bit DLL running on 64-bit Windows 2000). However, you can override this when you build your DLL by using the linker's /BASE option. All the standard system DLLs that ship with Windows have different base addresses so that they don't overlap if loaded into a single address space.

2. If the system is unable to reserve a region at the DLL's preferred base address, either because the region is occupied by another DLL or .exe or because the region just isn't big enough, the system will then try to find another region of address space to reserve for the

DLL. It is unfortunate when a DLL cannot load at its preferred base address for two reasons. First, the system might not be able to load the DLL if it does not have relocation information. (You can remove relocation information from a DLL when it is created by using the linker's /FIXED switch. This makes the DLL file smaller, but it also means that the DLL *must* load at its preferred address or it can't load at all.) Second, the system must perform some relocations within the DLL. In Windows 98, the system can apply the relocations as pages are swapped into RAM. In Windows 2000, these relocations require additional storage from the system's paging file; they also increase the amount of time needed to load the DLL.

3. The system notes that the physical storage backing the reserved region is in the DLL file on disk instead of in the system's paging file. If Windows 2000 has to perform relocations because the DLL could not load at its preferred base address, the system also notes that some of the physical storage for the DLL is mapped to the paging file.

If for some reason the system is unable to map the .exe and all the required DLLs, the system displays a message box to the user and frees the process's address space and the process object. *CreateProcess* will return FALSE to its caller; the caller can call *GetLastError* to get a better idea of why the process could not be created.

After all the .exe and DLL files have been mapped into the process's address space, the system can begin executing the .exe file's startup code. After the .exe file has been mapped, the system takes care of all the paging, buffering, and caching. For example, if code in the .exe causes it to jump to the address of an instruction that isn't loaded into memory, a fault will occur. The system detects the fault and automatically loads the page of code from the file's image into a page of RAM. Then the system maps the page of RAM to the proper location in the process's address space and allows the thread to continue executing as though the page of code were loaded all along. Of course, all this is invisible to the application. This process is repeated each time any thread in the process attempts to access code or data that is not loaded into RAM.

Static Data Is Not Shared
by Multiple Instances of an Executable or a DLL

When you create a new process for an application that is already running, the system simply opens another memory-mapped view of the file-mapping object that identifies the executable file's image and creates a new process object and a new thread object (for the primary thread). The system also assigns new process and thread IDs to these objects. By using memory-mapped files, multiple running instances of the same application can share the same code and data in RAM.

Note one small problem here. Processes use a flat address space. When you compile and link your program, all the code and data are thrown together as one large entity. The data is separated from the code but only to the extent that it follows the code in the .exe file.[1] The following illustration shows a simplified view of how the code and data for an application are loaded into virtual memory and then mapped into an application's address space.

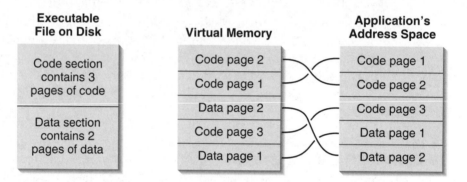

As an example, let's say that a second instance of an application is run. The system simply maps the pages of virtual memory containing the file's code and data into the second application's address space, as shown here.

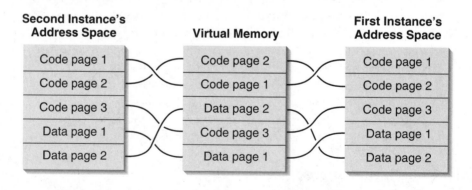

---

1. Actually, the contents of a file are broken down into sections. The code is in one section, and the global variables are in another. Sections are aligned on page boundaries. An application can determine the page size being used by calling *GetSystemInfo*. In the .exe or DLL file, the code section usually precedes the data section.

If one instance of the application alters some global variables residing in a data page, the memory contents for all instances of the application change. This type of change could cause disastrous effects and must not be allowed.

The system prohibits this by using the copy-on-write feature of the memory management system. Any time an application attempts to write to its memory-mapped file, the system catches the attempt, allocates a new block of memory for the page containing the memory the application is trying to write to, copies the contents of the page, and allows the application to write to this newly allocated memory block. As a result, no other instances of the same application are affected. The following illustration shows what happens when the first instance of an application attempts to change a global variable in data page 2.

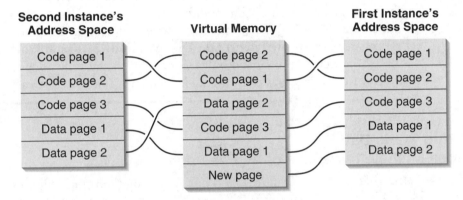

The system allocated a new page of virtual memory and copied the contents of data page 2 into it. The first instance's address space is changed so that the new data page is mapped into the address space at the same location as the original address page. Now the system can let the process alter the global variable without fear of altering the data for another instance of the same application.

A similar sequence of events occurs when an application is being debugged. Let's say that you're running multiple instances of an application and want to debug only one instance. You access your debugger and set a breakpoint in a line of source code. The debugger modifies your code by changing one of your assembly language instructions to an instruction that causes the debugger to activate itself. So you have the same problem again. When the debugger modifies the code, it causes all instances of the application to activate the debugger when the changed assembly instruction is executed. To fix this situation, the system again uses copy-on-write memory. When the system senses that the debugger is attempting to change the code, it allocates a new block of memory, copies the page containing the instruction into the new page, and allows the debugger to modify the code in the page copy.

When a process is loaded, the system examines all the file image's pages. The system commits storage in the paging file immediately for those pages that would normally be protected with the copy-on-write attribute. These pages are simply committed; they are not touched in any way. When a page in the file image is accessed, the system loads the appropriate page. If that page is never modified, it can be discarded from memory and reloaded when necessary. If the file's page is modified, however, the system swaps the modified page to one of the previously committed pages in the paging file.

The only difference in behavior between Windows 2000 and Windows 98 occurs when you have two copies of a module loaded and the writable data hasn't been modified. In this case, processes running under Windows 2000 share the data, while under Windows 98 each process receives its own copy of the data. Windows 2000 and Windows 98 behave exactly the same if only one copy of the module is loaded or if the writable data has been modified (which is normally the case).

Sharing Static Data
Across Multiple Instances of an Executable or a DLL

The fact that global and static data is not shared by multiple mappings of the same .exe or DLL is a safe default. However, on some occasions it is useful and convenient for multiple mappings of an .exe to share a single instance of a variable. For example, Windows offers no easy way to determine whether the user is running multiple instances of an application. But if you could get all the instances to share a single global variable, this global variable could reflect the number of instances running. When the user invoked an instance of the application, the new instance's thread could simply check the value of the global variable (which had been updated by another instance), and if the count were greater than 1, the second instance could notify the user that only one instance of the application is allowed to run and the second instance would terminate.

This section discusses a technique that allows you to share variables among all instances of an .exe or a DLL. But before we dive too deeply into the details, you'll need a little background information....

Every .exe or DLL file image is composed of a collection of sections. By convention, each standard section name begins with a period. For example, when you compile your program, the compiler places all the code in a section called *.text*. The compiler also places all the uninitialized data in a *.bss* section and all the initialized data in a *.data* section.

Each section has a combination of the following attributes associated with it, as shown in the following table.

Attribute	Meaning
READ	The bytes in the section can be read from.
WRITE	The bytes in the section can be written to.
EXECUTE	The bytes in the section can be executed.
SHARED	The bytes in the section are shared across multiple instances. (This attribute effectively turns off the copy-on-write mechanism.)

Using Microsoft Visual Studio's DumpBin utility (with the /Headers switch), you can see the list of sections in an .exe or DLL image file. The following excerpt was generated by running DumpBin on an executable file:

```
SECTION HEADER #1
   .text name
   11A70 virtual size
    1000 virtual address
   12000 size of raw data
    1000 file pointer to raw data
       0 file pointer to relocation table
       0 file pointer to line numbers
       0 number of relocations
       0 number of line numbers
60000020 flags
         Code
         Execute Read

SECTION HEADER #2
  .rdata name
     1F6 virtual size
   13000 virtual address
    1000 size of raw data
   13000 file pointer to raw data
       0 file pointer to relocation table
       0 file pointer to line numbers
       0 number of relocations
       0 number of line numbers
40000040 flags
         Initialized Data
         Read Only
```

(continued)

```
SECTION HEADER #3
   .data name
      560 virtual size
    14000 virtual address
     1000 size of raw data
    14000 file pointer to raw data
        0 file pointer to relocation table
        0 file pointer to line numbers
        0 number of relocations
        0 number of line numbers
 C0000040 flags
          Initialized Data
          Read Write

SECTION HEADER #4
  .idata name
      58D virtual size
    15000 virtual address
     1000 size of raw data
    15000 file pointer to raw data
        0 file pointer to relocation table
        0 file pointer to line numbers
        0 number of relocations
        0 number of line numbers
 C0000040 flags
          Initialized Data
          Read Write

SECTION HEADER #5
  .didat name
      7A2 virtual size
    16000 virtual address
     1000 size of raw data
    16000 file pointer to raw data
        0 file pointer to relocation table
        0 file pointer to line numbers
        0 number of relocations
        0 number of line numbers
 C0000040 flags
          Initialized Data
          Read Write
```

(continued)

```
SECTION HEADER #6
   .reloc name
      26D virtual size
    17000 virtual address
     1000 size of raw data
    17000 file pointer to raw data
        0 file pointer to relocation table
        0 file pointer to line numbers
        0 number of relocations
        0 number of line numbers
 42000040 flags
          Initialized Data
          Discardable
          Read Only

   Summary
       1000 .data
       1000 .didat
       1000 .idata
       1000 .rdata
       1000 .reloc
      12000 .text
```

The following table shows some of the more common section names and explains each section's purpose.

Section Name	Purpose
.bss	Uninitialized data
.CRT	Read-only C run-time data
.data	Initialized data
.debug	Debugging information
.didata	Delay imported names table
.edata	Exported names table
.idata	Imported names table
.rdata	Read-only run-time data
.reloc	Relocation table information
.rsrc	Resources
.text	.exe's or DLL's code
.tls	Thread-local storage
.xdata	Exception handling table

In addition to the standard sections created by the compiler and the linker, you can create your own sections when you compile using the following directive:

```
#pragma data_seg("sectionname")
```

So, for example, I can create a section called "Shared" that contains a single LONG value, as follows:

```
#pragma data_seg("Shared")
LONG g_lInstanceCount = 0;
#pragma data_seg()
```

When the compiler compiles this code, it creates a new section called Shared and places all the *initialized* data variables that it sees after the pragma in this new section. In the example above, the variable is placed in the Shared section. Following the variable, the *#pragma dataseg()* line tells the compiler to stop putting initialized variables in the Shared section and to start putting them back in the default data section. It is extremely important to remember that the compiler will store only initialized variables in the new section. For example, if I had removed the initialization from the previous code fragment (as shown in the following code), the compiler would have put this variable in a section other than the Shared section:

```
#pragma data_seg("Shared")
LONG g_lInstanceCount;
#pragma data_seg()
```

The Microsoft Visual C++ 6.0 compiler offers an *allocate* declaration specifier, however, that does allow you to place uninitialized data in any section you desire. Take a look at the following code:

```
// Create Shared section & have compiler place initialized data in it.
#pragma data_seg("Shared")

// Initialized, in Shared section
int a = 0;

// Uninitialized, not in Shared section
int b;

// Have compiler stop placing initialized data in Shared section.
#pragma data_seg()

// Initialized, in Shared section
__declspec(allocate("Shared")) int c = 0;
```

(continued)

```
// Uninitialized, in Shared section
__declspec(allocate("Shared")) int d;

// Initialized, not in Shared section
int e = 0;

// Uninitialized, not in Shared section
int f;
```

The comments above make it clear as to which section the specified variable will be placed in. For the *allocate* declaration specification to work properly, the section must first be created. Therefore, the code above would not compile if the first *#pragma data_seg* line in the preceding code were removed.

Probably the most common reason to put variables in their own section is to share them among multiple mappings of an .exe or a DLL. By default, each mapping of an .exe or a DLL gets its very own set of variables. However, you can group into their own section any variables that you want to share among all mappings of that module. When you group variables, the system doesn't create new instances of the variables for every mapping of the .exe or the DLL.

Simply telling the compiler to place certain variables in their own section is not enough to share those variables. You must also tell the linker that the variables in a particular section are to be shared. You can do this by using the /SECTION switch on the linker's command line:

```
/SECTION:name,attributes
```

Following the colon, place the name of the section for which you want to alter attributes. In our example, we want to change the attributes of the Shared section. So we'd construct our linker switch as follows:

```
/SECTION:Shared,RWS
```

After the comma, we specify the desired attributes: use *R* for READ, *W* for WRITE, *E* for EXECUTE, and *S* for SHARED. The switch above indicates that the data in the Shared section is readable, writable, and shared. If you want to change the attributes of more than one section, you must specify the /SECTION switch multiple times—once for each section for which you want to change attributes.

You can also embed linker switches right inside your source code using this syntax:

```
#pragma comment(linker, "/SECTION:Shared,RWS")
```

This line tells the compiler to embed the above string inside a special section named ".drectve". When the linker combines all the .obj modules together, the linker examines each .obj module's ".drectve" section and pretends that all the strings were passed to the linker as command-line arguments. I use this technique all the time because it is so convenient—if you move a source code file into a new project, you don't have to remember to set linker switches in Visual C++'s Project Settings dialog box.

Although you can create shared sections, Microsoft discourages the use of shared sections for two reasons. First, sharing memory in this way can potentially violate security. Second, sharing variables means that an error in one application can affect the operation of another application because there is no way to protect a block of data from being randomly written to by an application.

Imagine that you have written two applications, each requiring the user to enter a password. However, you decide to add a feature to your applications that makes things a little easier on the user: If the user is already running one of the applications when the second is started, the second application examines the contents of shared memory to get the password. This way, the user doesn't need to re-enter the password if one of the programs is already being used.

This sounds innocent enough. After all, no other applications but your own load the DLL and know where to find the password contained within the shared section. However, hackers lurk about, and if they want to get your password, all they need to do is write a small program of their own to load your company's DLL and monitor the shared memory blocks. When the user enters a password, the hacker's program can learn the user's password.

An industrious program such as the hacker's might also try to guess repeatedly at passwords and write them to the shared memory. Once the program guesses the correct password, it can send all kinds of commands to one of the two applications. Perhaps this problem could be solved if there were a way to grant access to only certain applications for loading a particular DLL. But currently this is not the case—any program can call *LoadLibrary* to explicitly load a DLL.

The AppInst Sample Application

The AppInst sample application ("17 AppInst.exe"), listed in Figure 17-1, shows how an application can know how many instances of itself are running at any one time. The source code and resource files for the application are in the 17-AppInst directory on this book's companion CD-ROM. When you run the AppInst program, its dialog box appears, indicating that one instance of the application is running.

If you run a second instance of the application, both instance's dialog boxes change to reflect that two instances are now running.

You can run and kill as many instances as you like—the number will always be accurately reflected in whichever instances remain.

Near the top of AppInst.cpp, you'll see the following lines:

```
// Tell the compiler to put this initialized variable in its own Shared
// section so it is shared by all instances of this application.
#pragma data_seg("Shared")
volatile LONG g_lApplicationInstances = 0;
#pragma data_seg()

// Tell the linker to make the Shared section
// readable, writable, and shared.
#pragma comment(linker, "/Section:Shared,RWS")
```

These lines create a section called Shared that will have read, write, and shared protection. Within this section is one variable: *g_lApplicationInstances*. All instances of this application share this variable. Note that the variable is *volatile* so that the optimizer doesn't get too smart for our own good.

When each instance's *_tWinMain* function executes, the *g_lApplication- Instances* variable is incremented by 1; and before *_tWinMain* exits, this variable is decremented by 1. I use *InterlockedExchangeAdd* to alter this variable since multiple threads will access this shared resource.

When each instance's dialog box appears, the *Dlg_OnInitDialog* function is called. This function broadcasts to all top-level windows a registered window message (whose message ID is contained in the *g_aMsgAppInstCountUpdate* variable):

```
PostMessage(HWND_BROADCAST, g_aMsgAppInstCountUpdate, 0, 0);
```

All the windows in the system will ignore this registered window message except for AppInst windows. When one of our windows receives this message, the code in *Dlg_Proc* simply updates the number in the dialog box to reflect the current number of instances (maintained in the shared *g_lApplicationInstances* variable).

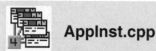

AppInst.cpp

```
/*****************************************************************************
Module:  AppInst.cpp
Notices: Copyright (c) 2000 Jeffrey Richter
*****************************************************************************/


#include "..\CmnHdr.h"        /* See Appendix A. */
#include <windowsx.h>
#include <tchar.h>
#include "Resource.h"


///////////////////////////////////////////////////////////////////////////


// The system-wide unique window message
UINT g_uMsgAppInstCountUpdate = INVALID_ATOM;


///////////////////////////////////////////////////////////////////////////


// Tell the compiler to put this initialized variable in its own Shared
// section so it is shared by all instances of this application.
#pragma data_seg("Shared")
volatile LONG g_lApplicationInstances = 0;
#pragma data_seg()

// Tell the linker to make the Shared section readable, writable, and shared.
#pragma comment(linker, "/Section:Shared,RWS")


///////////////////////////////////////////////////////////////////////////


BOOL Dlg_OnInitDialog(HWND hwnd, HWND hwndFocus, LPARAM lParam) {

   chSETDLGICONS(hwnd, IDI_APPINST);

   // Force the static control to be initialized correctly.
   PostMessage(HWND_BROADCAST, g_uMsgAppInstCountUpdate, 0, 0);
   return(TRUE);
}
```

Figure 17-1.   *(continued)*
The AppInst sample application

Figure 17-1. *continued*

```
//////////////////////////////////////////////////////////////////////////


void Dlg_OnCommand(HWND hwnd, int id, HWND hwndCtl, UINT codeNotify) {

   switch (id) {
      case IDCANCEL:
         EndDialog(hwnd, id);
         break;
   }
}



//////////////////////////////////////////////////////////////////////////


INT_PTR WINAPI Dlg_Proc(HWND hwnd, UINT uMsg, WPARAM wParam, LPARAM lParam) {

   if (uMsg == g_uMsgAppInstCountUpdate) {
      SetDlgItemInt(hwnd, IDC_COUNT, g_lApplicationInstances, FALSE);
   }

   switch (uMsg) {
      chHANDLE_DLGMSG(hwnd, WM_INITDIALOG, Dlg_OnInitDialog);
      chHANDLE_DLGMSG(hwnd, WM_COMMAND,    Dlg_OnCommand);
   }
   return(FALSE);
}



//////////////////////////////////////////////////////////////////////////


int WINAPI _tWinMain(HINSTANCE hinstExe, HINSTANCE, LPTSTR pszCmdLine, int) {

   // Get the numeric value of the systemwide window message used to notify
   // all top-level windows when the module's usage count has changed.
   g_uMsgAppInstCountUpdate =
      RegisterWindowMessage(TEXT("MsgAppInstCountUpdate"));

   // There is another instance of this application running.
   InterlockedExchangeAdd((PLONG) &g_lApplicationInstances, 1);

   DialogBox(hinstExe, MAKEINTRESOURCE(IDD_APPINST), NULL, Dlg_Proc);
```

(continued)

Figure 17-1. *continued*

```
    // This instance of the application is terminating.
    InterlockedExchangeAdd((PLONG) &g_lApplicationInstances, -1);

    // Have all other instances update their display.
    PostMessage(HWND_BROADCAST, g_uMsgAppInstCountUpdate, 0, 0);

    return(0);
}


//////////////////////////////// End of File /////////////////////////////////
```

AppInst.rc

```
//Microsoft Developer Studio generated resource script.
//
#include "Resource.h"

#define APSTUDIO_READONLY_SYMBOLS
/////////////////////////////////////////////////////////////////////////////
//
// Generated from the TEXTINCLUDE 2 resource.
//
#include "afxres.h"


/////////////////////////////////////////////////////////////////////////////
#undef APSTUDIO_READONLY_SYMBOLS


/////////////////////////////////////////////////////////////////////////////
// English (U.S.) resources

#if !defined(AFX_RESOURCE_DLL) || defined(AFX_TARG_ENU)
#ifdef _WIN32
LANGUAGE LANG_ENGLISH, SUBLANG_ENGLISH_US
#pragma code_page(1252)
#endif //_WIN32

#ifdef APSTUDIO_INVOKED
/////////////////////////////////////////////////////////////////////////////
//
// TEXTINCLUDE
//
```

Figure 17-1. *continued*

```
1 TEXTINCLUDE DISCARDABLE
BEGIN
    "Resource.h\0"
END

2 TEXTINCLUDE DISCARDABLE
BEGIN
    "#include ""afxres.h""\r\n"
    "\0"
END

3 TEXTINCLUDE DISCARDABLE
BEGIN
    "\r\n"
    "\0"
END

#endif    // APSTUDIO_INVOKED


/////////////////////////////////////////////////////////////////////////////
//
// Dialog
//

IDD_APPINST DIALOG DISCARDABLE  0, 0, 140, 21
STYLE WS_MINIMIZEBOX | WS_VISIBLE | WS_CAPTION | WS_SYSMENU
CAPTION "Application Instances"
FONT 8, "MS Sans Serif"
BEGIN
    LTEXT           "Number of instances running:",IDC_STATIC,12,4,93,8,
                    SS_NOPREFIX
    RTEXT           "#",IDC_COUNT,112,4,16,12,SS_NOPREFIX
END


/////////////////////////////////////////////////////////////////////////////
//
// Icon
//

// Icon with lowest ID value placed first to ensure application icon
// remains consistent on all systems.
IDI_APPINST             ICON    DISCARDABLE     "AppInst.Ico"
```

(continued)

Figure 17-1. *continued*

```
////////////////////////////////////////////////////////////////////////
//
// DESIGNINFO
//

#ifdef APSTUDIO_INVOKED
GUIDELINES DESIGNINFO DISCARDABLE
BEGIN
    IDD_APPINST, DIALOG
    BEGIN
        RIGHTMARGIN, 76
        BOTTOMMARGIN, 20
    END
END
#endif    // APSTUDIO_INVOKED

#endif    // English (U.S.) resources
////////////////////////////////////////////////////////////////////////


#ifndef APSTUDIO_INVOKED
////////////////////////////////////////////////////////////////////////
//
// Generated from the TEXTINCLUDE 3 resource.
//


////////////////////////////////////////////////////////////////////////
#endif    // not APSTUDIO_INVOKED
```

Memory-Mapped Data Files

The operating system makes it possible to memory map a data file into your process's address space. Thus it is very convenient to manipulate large streams of data.

To understand the power of using memory-mapped files this way, let's look at four possible methods of implementing a program to reverse the order of all the bytes in a file.

Method 1: One File, One Buffer

The first and theoretically simplest method involves allocating a block of memory large enough to hold the entire file. The file is opened, its contents are read into the memory block, and the file is closed. With the contents in memory, we can now reverse all the bytes by swapping the first byte with the last, the second byte with the second-to-last, and so on. This swapping continues until you reach the middle of the file. After all the bytes have been swapped, you reopen the file and overwrite its contents with the contents of the memory block.

This method is pretty easy to implement but has two major drawbacks. First, a memory block the size of the file must be allocated. This might not be so bad if the file is small, but what if the file is huge—say, 2 GB? A 32-bit system will not allow the application to commit a block of physical storage that large. Large files require a different method.

Second, if the process is interrupted in the middle—while the reversed bytes are being written back out to the file—the contents of the file will be corrupted. The simplest way to guard against this is to make a copy of the original file before reversing its contents. If the whole process succeeds, you can delete the copy of the file. Unfortunately, this safeguard requires additional disk space.

Method 2: Two Files, One Buffer

In the second method, you open the existing file and create a new file of 0 length on the disk. Then you allocate a small internal buffer—say, 8 KB. You seek to the end of the original file minus 8 KB, read the last 8 KB into the buffer, reverse the bytes, and write the buffer's contents to the newly created file. The process of seeking, reading, reversing, and writing repeats until you reach the beginning of the original file. Some special—but not extensive—handling is required if the file's length is not an exact multiple of 8 KB. After the original file is fully processed, both files are closed and the original file is deleted.

This method is a bit more complicated to implement than the first one. It uses memory much more efficiently because only an 8-KB chunk is ever allocated, but it has two big problems. First, the processing is slower than in the first method because on each iteration you must perform a seek on the original file before performing a read. Second, this method can potentially use an enormous amount of hard disk space. If the original file is 400 MB, the new file will grow to be 400 MB as the process continues. Just before the original file is deleted, the two files will occupy 800 MB of disk space. This is 400 MB more than should be required—a disadvantage that leads us to the next method.

Method 3: One File, Two Buffers

For this method, let's say the program initializes by allocating two separate 8-KB buffers. The program reads the first 8 KB of the file into one buffer and the last 8 KB of the file into the other buffer. The process then reverses the contents of both buffers and writes the contents of the first buffer back to the end of the file and the contents of the second buffer back to the beginning of the same file. Each iteration continues by moving blocks from the front and back of the file in 8-KB chunks. Some special handling is required if the file's length is not an exact multiple of 16 KB and the two 8-KB chunks overlap. This special handling is more complex than the special handling in the previous method, but it's nothing that should scare off a seasoned programmer.

Compared with the previous two methods, this method is better at conserving hard disk space. Because everything is read from and written to the same file, no additional disk space is required. As for memory use, this method is also not too bad, using only 16 KB. Of course, this method is probably the most difficult to implement. Like the first method, this method can result in corruption of the data file if the process is somehow interrupted.

Now let's take a look at how this process might be accomplished using memory-mapped files.

Method 4: One File, Zero Buffers

When using memory-mapped files to reverse the contents of a file, you open the file and then tell the system to reserve a region of virtual address space. You tell the system to map the first byte of the file to the first byte of this reserved region. You can then access the region of virtual memory as though it actually contained the file. In fact, if there were a single 0 byte at the end of the file, you could simply call the C run-time function _strrev_ to reverse the data in the file.

This method's great advantage is that the system manages all the file caching for you. You don't have to allocate any memory, load file data into memory, write data back to the file, or free any memory blocks. Unfortunately, the possibility that an interruption such as a power failure could corrupt data still exists with memory-mapped files.

Using Memory-Mapped Files

To use a memory-mapped file, you must perform three steps:

1. Create or open a file kernel object that identifies the file on disk that you want to use as a memory-mapped file.

2. Create a file-mapping kernel object that tells the system the size of the file and how you intend to access the file.

3. Tell the system to map all or part of the file-mapping object into your process's address space.

When you are finished using the memory-mapped file, you must perform three steps to clean up:

1. Tell the system to unmap the file-mapping kernel object from your process's address space.

2. Close the file-mapping kernel object.

3. Close the file kernel object.

The next five sections discuss all these steps in more detail.

Step 1: Creating or Opening a File Kernel Object

To create or open a file kernel object, always call the *CreateFile* function:

```
HANDLE CreateFile(
    PCSTR pszFileName,
    DWORD dwDesiredAccess,
    DWORD dwShareMode,
    PSECURITY_ATTRIBUTES psa,
    DWORD dwCreationDisposition,
    DWORD dwFlagsAndAttributes,
    HANDLE hTemplateFile);
```

The *CreateFile* function takes quite a few parameters. For this discussion, I'll concentrate only on the first three: *pszFileName*, *dwDesiredAccess*, and *dwShareMode*.

As you might guess, the first parameter, *pszFileName*, identifies the name (including an optional path) of the file that you want to create or open. The second parameter, *dwDesiredAccess*, specifies how you intend to access the contents of the file. You can specify one of the four following values.

Value	Meaning
0	You cannot read from or write to the file's contents. Specify 0 when you just want to get a file's attributes.
GENERIC_READ	You can read from the file.
GENERIC_WRITE	You can write to the file.
GENERIC_READ | GENERIC_WRITE	You can read from the file and write to the file.

When creating or opening a file for use as a memory-mapped file, select the access flag or flags that make the most sense for how you intend to access the file's data. For memory-mapped files, you must open the file for read-only access or read-write access, so you'll want to specify either GENERIC_READ or GENERIC_READ | GENERIC_WRITE, respectively.

The third parameter, *dwShareMode*, tells the system how you want to share this file. You can specify one of the four following values for *dwShareMode*.

Value	Meaning
0	Any other attempts to open the file fail.
FILE_SHARE_READ	Other attempts to open the file using GENERIC_WRITE fail.
FILE_SHARE_WRITE	Other attempts to open the file using GENERIC_READ fail.
FILE_SHARE_READ | FILE_SHARE_WRITE	Other attempts to open the file succeed.

If *CreateFile* successfully creates or opens the specified file, a handle to a file kernel object is returned; otherwise, INVALID_HANDLE_VALUE is returned.

> **NOTE**
>
> Most Windows functions that return a handle return NULL when they are unsuccessful. *CreateFile*, however, returns INVALID_HANDLE_VALUE, which is defined as ((HANDLE) –1).

Step 2: Creating a File-Mapping Kernel Object

Calling *CreateFile* tells the operating system the location of the file mapping's physical storage. The pathname that you pass indicates the exact location on the disk (or on the network or the CD-ROM, for example) of the physical storage that is backing the file mapping. Now you must tell the system how much physical storage the file-mapping object requires. You do this by calling *CreateFileMapping*:

```
HANDLE CreateFileMapping(
    HANDLE hFile,
    PSECURITY_ATTRIBUTES psa,
    DWORD fdwProtect,
    DWORD dwMaximumSizeHigh,
    DWORD dwMaximumSizeLow,
    PCTSTR pszName);
```

The first parameter, *hFile*, identifies the handle of the file you want mapped into the process's address space. This handle is returned by the previous call to *CreateFile*. The *psa* parameter is a pointer to a SECURITY_ATTRIBUTES structure for the file-mapping kernel object; usually NULL is passed (which provides default security and the returned handle is noninheritable).

As I pointed out at the beginning of this chapter, creating a memory-mapped file is just like reserving a region of address space and then committing physical storage to the region. It's just that the physical storage for a memory-mapped file comes from a file on a disk rather than from space allocated from the system's paging file. When you create a file-mapping object, the system does not reserve a region of address space and map the file's storage to the region. (I'll describe how to do this in the next section.) However, when the system does map the storage to the process's address space, the system must know what protection attribute to assign to the pages of physical storage. *CreateFileMapping*'s *fdwProtect* parameter allows you to specify the protection attributes. Most of the time, you will specify one of the three protection attributes listed in the table on the following page.

Protection Attribute	Meaning
PAGE_READONLY	When the file-mapping object is mapped, you can read the file's data. You must have passed GENERIC_READ to *CreateFile*.
PAGE_READWRITE	When the file-mapping object is mapped, you can read and write the file's data. You must have passed GENERIC_READ | GENERIC_WRITE to *CreateFile*.
PAGE_WRITECOPY	When the file-mapping object is mapped, you can read and write the file's data. Writing causes a private copy of the page to be created. You must have passed either GENERIC_READ or GENERIC_READ | GENERIC_WRITE to *CreateFile*.

Under Windows 98, you can pass the PAGE_WRITECOPY flag to *CreateFileMapping*; this tells the system to commit storage from the paging file. This paging file storage is reserved for a copy of the data file's data; only modified pages are actually written to the paging file. Any changes you make to the file's data are not propagated back to the original data file. The end result is that the PAGE_WRITECOPY flag has the same effect on both Windows 2000 and Windows 98.

In addition to the above page protections, there are four section attributes that you can bitwise OR in the *CreateFileMapping* function's *fdwProtect* parameter. A section is just another word for a memory mapping.

The first of these attributes, SEC_NOCACHE, tells the system that none of the file's memory-mapped pages are to be cached. So as you write data to the file, the system will update the file's data on the disk more often than it normally would. This flag, like the PAGE_NOCACHE protection attribute, exists for the device driver developer and is not usually used by applications.

Windows 98 ignores the SEC_NOCACHE flag.

The second section attribute, SEC_IMAGE, tells the system that the file you are mapping is a portable executable (PE) file image. When the system maps this file into your process's address space, the system examines the file's contents to determine which protection attributes to assign to the various pages of the mapped image. For example, a PE file's code section (.text) is usually mapped with PAGE_EXECUTE_READ attributes, whereas the PE file's data section (.data) is usually mapped with PAGE_READWRITE attributes. Specifying the SEC_IMAGE attribute tells the system to map the file's image and to set the appropriate page protections.

**WINDOWS
98**

> Windows 98 ignores the SEC_IMAGE flag.

The last two attributes, SEC_RESERVE and SEC_COMMIT, are mutually exclusive and do not apply when you are using a memory-mapped data file. These two flags will be discussed in the section "Sparsely Committed Memory-Mapped Files" later in this chapter. When creating a memory-mapped data file, you should not specify either of these flags. *CreateFileMapping* will ignore them.

CreateFileMapping's next two parameters, *dwMaximumSizeHigh* and *dwMaximumSizeLow*, are the most important parameters. The main purpose of the *CreateFileMapping* function is to ensure that enough physical storage is available for the file-mapping object. These two parameters tell the system the maximum size of the file in bytes. Two 32-bit values are required because Windows supports file sizes that can be expressed using a 64-bit value; the *dwMaximumSizeHigh* parameter specifies the high 32 bits, and the *dwMaximum-SizeLow* parameter specifies the low 32 bits. For files that are 4 GB or less, *dwMaximumSizeHigh* will always be 0.

Using a 64-bit value means that Windows can process files as large as 16 EB (exabytes). If you want to create the file-mapping object so that it reflects the current size of the file, you can pass 0 for both parameters. If you intend only to read from the file or to access the file without changing its size, pass 0 for both parameters. If you intend to append data to the file, you will want to choose a maximum file size that leaves you some breathing room. If the file on disk currently contains 0 bytes, you can't pass two zeros to *CreateFileMapping*'s *dwMaximumSizeHigh* and *dwMaximumSizeLow* parameters. Doing so tells the system that you want a file-mapping object with 0 bytes of storage in it. This is an error and *CreateFileMapping* will return NULL.

If you've paid attention so far, you must be thinking that something is terribly wrong here. It's nice that Windows supports files and file-mapping objects that can be anywhere up to 16 EB, but how are you ever going to map a file that big into a 32-bit process's address space, which has a maximum limit of 4 GB (little of which is even usable)? I'll explain how you can accomplish this in the next section. Of course, a 64-bit process has a 16-EB address space so you can work with much larger file mappings, but a similar limitation still exists if the file is super-big.

To really understand how *CreateFile* and *CreateFileMapping* work, I suggest you try the following experiment. Take the code below, build it, and then run it in a debugger. As you single-step through each statement, jump to a command shell and execute a "dir" command on the C:\ directory. Notice the changes that are appearing in the directory as you execute each statement in the debugger.

```
int WINAPI _tWinMain(HINSTANCE hinstExe, HINSTANCE,
   PTSTR pszCmdLine, int nCmdShow) {

   // Before executing the line below, C:\ does not have
   // a file called "MMFTest.Dat."
   HANDLE hfile = CreateFile("C:\\MMFTest.dat",
      GENERIC_READ | GENERIC_WRITE,
      FILE_SHARE_READ | FILE_SHARE_WRITE, NULL, CREATE_ALWAYS,
      FILE_ATTRIBUTE_NORMAL, NULL);

   // Before executing the line below, the MMFTest.Dat
   // file does exist but has a file size of 0 bytes.
   HANDLE hfilemap = CreateFileMapping(hfile, NULL, PAGE_READWRITE,
      0, 100, NULL);

   // After executing the line above, the MMFTest.Dat
   // file has a size of 100 bytes.

   // Cleanup
   CloseHandle(hfilemap);
   CloseHandle(hfile);

   // When the process terminates, MMFTest.Dat remains
   // on the disk with a size of 100 bytes.
   return(0);
}
```

If you call *CreateFileMapping*, passing the PAGE_READWRITE flag, the system will check to make sure that the associated data file on the disk is at least the same size as the size specified in the *dwMaximumSizeHigh* and *dwMaximumSizeLow* parameters. If the file is smaller than the specified size,

CreateFileMapping will make the file on the disk larger by extending its size. This enlargement is required so that the physical storage will already exist when the file is used later as a memory-mapped file. If the file-mapping object is being created with the PAGE_READONLY or the PAGE_WRITECOPY flag, the size specified to *CreateFileMapping* must be no larger than the physical size of the disk file. This is because you won't be able to append any data to the file.

The last parameter of *CreateFileMapping*, *pszName*, is a zero-terminated string that assigns a name to this file-mapping object. The name is used to share the object with another process. (An example of this is shown later in this chapter. Chapter 3 also discusses kernel object sharing in greater detail.) A memory-mapped data file usually doesn't need to be shared; therefore, this parameter is usually NULL.

The system creates the file-mapping object and returns a handle identifying the object back to the calling thread. If the system cannot create the file-mapping object, a NULL handle value is returned. Again, please remember that *CreateFile* returns INVALID_HANDLE_VALUE (defined as –1) when it fails and *CreateFileMapping* returns NULL when it fails. Don't get these error values confused.

Step 3: Mapping the File's Data into the Process's Address Space

After you have created a file-mapping object, you still need to have the system reserve a region of address space for the file's data and commit the file's data as the physical storage that is mapped to the region. You do this by calling *MapViewOfFile*:

```
PVOID MapViewOfFile(
    HANDLE hFileMappingObject,
    DWORD dwDesiredAccess,
    DWORD dwFileOffsetHigh,
    DWORD dwFileOffsetLow,
    SIZE_T dwNumberOfBytesToMap);
```

The *hFileMappingObject* parameter identifies the handle of the file-mapping object, which was returned by the previous call to either *Create-FileMapping* or *OpenFileMapping* (discussed later in this chapter). The *dwDesiredAccess* parameter identifies how the data can be accessed. That's right, we must again specify how we intend to access the file's data. You can specify one of four possible values shown in the table on the following page.

Value	Meaning
FILE_MAP_WRITE	You can read and write file data. *CreateFileMapping* had to be called by passing PAGE_READWRITE.
FILE_MAP_READ	You can read file data. *CreateFileMapping* could be called with any of the protection attributes: PAGE_READONLY, PAGE_READWRITE, or PAGE_WRITECOPY.
FILE_MAP_ALL_ACCESS	Same as FILE_MAP_WRITE.
FILE_MAP_COPY	You can read and write file data. Writing causes a private copy of the page to be created. In Windows 2000, *CreateFileMapping* could be called with any of the protection attributes: PAGE_READONLY, PAGE_READWRITE, or PAGE_WRITECOPY. Windows 98 requires that *CreateFileMapping* be called with PAGE_WRITECOPY.

It certainly seems strange and annoying that Windows requires all these protection attributes to be set over and over again. I assume this was done to give an application as much control as possible over data protection.

The remaining three parameters have to do with reserving the region of address space and mapping the physical storage to the region. When you map a file into your process's address space, you don't have to map the entire file at once. Instead, you can map only a small portion of the file into the address space. A portion of a file that is mapped into your process's address space is called a *view*, which explains how *MapViewOfFile* got its name.

When you map a view of a file into your process's address space, you must specify two things. First, you must tell the system which byte in the data file should be mapped as the first byte in the view. You do this using the *dwFileOffsetHigh* and *dwFileOffsetLow* parameters. Because Windows supports files that can be up to 16 EB, you must specify this byte-offset using a 64-bit value of which the high 32 bits are passed in the *dwFileOffsetHigh* parameter and the low 32 bits are passed in the *dwFileOffsetLow* parameter. Note that the offset in the file must be a multiple of the system's allocation granularity. (To date, all implementations of Windows have an allocation granularity of 64 KB.) The section "System Information" in Chapter 14 shows how to obtain the allocation granularity value for a given system.

Second, you must tell the system how much of the data file to map into the address space. This is the same thing as specifying how large a region of address space to reserve. You specify this size using the *dwNumberOfBytesToMap* parameter. If you specify a size of 0, the system will attempt to map a view starting with the specified offset within the file to the end of the entire file.

In Windows 98, if *MapViewOfFile* cannot find a region large enough to contain the entire file-mapping object, *MapViewOfFile* returns NULL regardless of the size of the view requested.

In Windows 2000, *MapViewOfFile* needs only to find a region large enough for the view requested, regardless of the size of the entire file-mapping object.

If you specify the FILE_MAP_COPY flag when calling *MapViewOfFile*, the system commits physical storage from the system's paging file. The amount of space committed is determined by the *dwNumberOfBytesToMap* parameter. As long as you do nothing more than read from the file's mapped view, the system never uses these committed pages in the paging file. However, the first time any thread in your process writes to any memory address within the file's mapped view, the system will grab one of the committed pages from the paging file, copy the page of original data to this paging-file page, and then map this copied page into your process's address space. From this point on, the threads in your process are accessing a local copy of the data and cannot read or modify the original data.

When the system makes the copy of the original page, the system changes the protection of the page from PAGE_WRITECOPY to PAGE_READWRITE. The following code fragment explains it all:

```
// Open the file that we want to map.
HANDLE hFile = CreateFile(pszFileName, GENERIC_READ | GENERIC_WRITE, 0, NULL,
    OPEN_ALWAYS, FILE_ATTRIBUTE_NORMAL, NULL);

// Create a file-mapping object for the file.
HANDLE hFileMapping = CreateFileMapping(hFile, NULL, PAGE_WRITECOPY,
    0, 0, NULL);

// Map a copy-on-write view of the file; the system will commit
// enough physical storage from the paging file to accommodate
// the entire file. All pages in the view will initially have
// PAGE_WRITECOPY access.
PBYTE pbFile = (PBYTE) MapViewOfFile(hFileMapping, FILE_MAP_COPY,
    0, 0, 0);
```

(continued)

```
// Read a byte from the mapped view.
BYTE bSomeByte = pbFile[0];
// When reading, the system does not touch the committed pages in
// the paging file. The page keeps its PAGE_WRITECOPY attribute.

// Write a byte to the mapped view.
pbFile[0] = 0;
// When writing for the first time, the system grabs a committed
// page from the paging file, copies the original contents of the
// page at the accessed memory address, and maps the new page
// (the copy) into the process's address space. The new page has
// an attribute of PAGE_READWRITE.

// Write another byte to the mapped view.
pbFile[1] = 0;
// Because this byte is now in a PAGE_READWRITE page, the system
// simply writes the byte to the page (backed by the paging file).

// When finished using the file's mapped view, unmap it.
// UnmapViewOfFile is discussed in the next section.
UnmapViewOfFile(pbFile);
// The system decommits the physical storage from the paging file.
// Any writes to the pages are lost.

// Clean up after ourselves.
CloseHandle(hFileMapping);
CloseHandle(hFile);
```

WINDOWS 98

As mentioned earlier, Windows 98 must commit storage in the paging file for the memory-mapped file up front. However, it will write modified pages to the paging file only as necessary.

Step 4: Unmapping the File's Data from the Process's Address Space

When you no longer need to keep a file's data mapped to a region of your process's address space, you can release the region by calling

```
BOOL UnmapViewOfFile(PVOID pvBaseAddress);
```

The only parameter, *pvBaseAddress*, specifies the base address of the returned region. This value must be the same value returned from a call to *MapViewOfFile*. You must remember to call *UnmapViewOfFile*. If you do not call this function, the reserved region won't be released until your process terminates. Whenever you call *MapViewOfFile*, the system always reserves a new region within your process's address space—any previously reserved regions are *not* released.

In the interest of speed, the system buffers the pages of the file's data and doesn't update the disk image of the file immediately while working with the file's mapped view. If you need to ensure that your updates have been written to disk, you can force the system to write a portion or all of the modified data back to the disk image by calling *FlushViewOfFile*:

```
BOOL FlushViewOfFile(
   PVOID pvAddress,
   SIZE_T dwNumberOfBytesToFlush);
```

The first parameter is the address of a byte contained within a view of a memory-mapped file. The function rounds down the address you pass here to a page boundary. The second parameter indicates the number of bytes that you want flushed. The system will round this number up so that the total number of bytes is an integral number of pages. If you call *FlushViewOfFile* and none of the data has been changed, the function simply returns without writing anything to the disk.

For a memory-mapped file whose storage is over a network, *FlushViewOfFile* guarantees that the file's data has been written from the workstation. However, *FlushViewOfFile* cannot guarantee that the server machine that is sharing the file has written the data to the remote disk drive because the server might be caching the file's data. To ensure that the server writes the file's data, you should pass the FILE_FLAG_WRITE_THROUGH flag to the *CreateFile* function whenever you create a file-mapping object for the file and then map the view of the file-mapping object. If you use this flag to open the file, *FlushViewOfFile* will return only when all of the file's data has been stored on the server's disk drive.

Keep in mind one special characteristic of the *UnmapViewOfFile* function. If the view was originally mapped using the FILE_MAP_COPY flag, any changes you made to the file's data were actually made to a copy of the file's data stored in the system's paging file. In this case, if you call *UnmapViewOfFile*, the function has nothing to update on the disk file and simply causes the pages in the paging file to be freed—the data is lost.

If you want to preserve the changed data, you must take additional measures yourself. For example, you might want to create another file-mapping object (using PAGE_READWRITE) from the same file and map this new file-mapping object into your process's address space using the FILE_MAP_WRITE flag. Then you could scan the first view looking for pages with the

PAGE_READWRITE protection attribute. Whenever you found a page with this attribute, you could examine its contents and decide whether to write the changed data to the file. If you do not want to update the file with the new data, keep scanning the remaining pages in the view until you reach the end. If you do want to save the changed page of data, however, just call *MoveMemory* to copy the page of data from the first view to the second view. Because the second view is mapped with PAGE_READWRITE protection, the *MoveMemory* function will be updating the actual contents of the file on the disk. You can use this method to determine changes and preserve your file's data.

WINDOWS 98

> Windows 98 does not support the copy-on-write protection attribute, so you cannot test for pages marked with the PAGE_READWRITE flag when scanning the first view of the memory-mapped file. You will have to devise a method of your own for determining which pages in the first view you have actually modified.

Steps 5 and 6: Closing the File-Mapping Object and the File Object

It goes without saying that you should always close any kernel objects you open. Forgetting to do so will cause resource leaks while your process continues to run. Of course, when your process terminates, the system automatically closes any objects your process opened but forgot to close. But if your process does not terminate for a while, you will accumulate resource handles. You should always write clean, "proper" code that closes any objects you have opened. To close the file-mapping object and the file object, you simply need to call the *CloseHandle* function twice—once for each handle.

Let's look at this process a little more closely. The following pseudocode shows an example of memory-mapping a file:

```
HANDLE hFile = CreateFile(...);
HANDLE hFileMapping = CreateFileMapping(hFile, ...);
PVOID pvFile = MapViewOfFile(hFileMapping, ...);

// Use the memory-mapped file.

UnmapViewOfFile(pvFile);
CloseHandle(hFileMapping);
CloseHandle(hFile);
```

The above code shows the "expected" method for manipulating memory-mapped files. However, what it does not show is that the system increments the usage counts of the file object and the file-mapping object when you call *MapViewOfFile*. This side effect is significant because it means that we could rewrite the code fragment on the preceding page as follows:

```
HANDLE hFile = CreateFile(...);
HANDLE hFileMapping = CreateFileMapping(hFile, ...);
CloseHandle(hFile);
PVOID pvFile = MapViewOfFile(hFileMapping, ...);
CloseHandle(hFileMapping);

// Use the memory-mapped file.

UnmapViewOfFile(pvFile);
```

When you work with memory-mapped files, you will commonly open the file, create the file-mapping object, and then use the file-mapping object to map a view of the file's data into the process's address space. Because the system increments the internal usage counts of the file object and the file-mapping object, you can close these objects at the beginning of your code and eliminate potential resource leaks.

If you will be creating additional file-mapping objects from the same file or mapping multiple views of the same file-mapping object, you cannot call *CloseHandle* early—you'll need the handles later to make the additional calls to *CreateFileMapping* and *MapViewOfFile*, respectively.

The File Reverse Sample Application

The FileRev application ("17 FileRev.exe") listed in Figure 17-2 beginning on page 612 demonstrates how to use memory-mapped files to reverse the contents of an ANSI or a Unicode text file. The source code and resource files for the application are in the 17-FileRev directory on the companion CD-ROM. When you start the program, the following window appears.

FileRev first allows you to select a file and then, when you click on the Reverse File Contents button, the function reverses all of the characters contained within the file. The program will work correctly only on text files; it will not work correctly on binary files. FileRev determines whether the text file is ANSI or Unicode by calling the *IsTextUnicode* function (discussed in Chapter 2).

> In Windows 98, the *IsTextUnicode* function has no useful implemen-
> tation and simply returns FALSE; calling *GetLastError* returns
> ERROR_CALL_NOT_IMPLEMENTED. This means that the FileRev
> sample application always thinks that it is manipulating an ANSI text
> file when it is run under Windows 98.

When you click on the Reverse File Contents button, FileRev makes a copy
of the specified file called FileRev.dat. It does this so that the original file won't
become unusable because its contents have been reversed. Next FileRev calls
the *FileReverse* function, which is responsible for reversing the file; *FileReverse*
calls the *CreateFile* function, opening FileRev.dat for reading and writing.

As I said earlier, the easiest way to reverse the contents of the file is to call
the C run-time function *_strrev*. As with all C strings, the last character of the
string must be a zero terminator. Because text files do not end with a zero
character, FileRev must append one to the file. It does so by first calling
GetFileSize:

```
dwFileSize = GetFileSize(hFile, NULL);
```

Now that you're armed with the length of the file, you can create the file-
mapping object by calling *CreateFileMapping*. The file-mapping object is created with a length of *dwFileSize* plus the size of a wide character (for the zero
character). After the file-mapping object is created, a view of the object is mapped
into FileRev's address space. The *pvFile* variable contains the return value from
MapViewOfFile and points to the first byte of the text file.

The next step is to write a zero character at the end of the file and to reverse the string:

```
PSTR pchANSI = (PSTR) pvFile;
pchANSI[dwFileSize / sizeof(CHAR)] = 0;
```

In a text file, every line is terminated by a return character ('\r') followed
by a newline character ('\n'). Unfortunately, when we call *_strrev* to reverse the
file, these characters also get reversed. For the reversed text file to be loaded into
a text editor, every occurrence of the "\n\r" pair needs to be converted back to
its original "\r\n" order. This conversion is the job of the following loop:

```
while (pchANSI != NULL) {
   // We have found an occurrence....
   *pchANSI++ = '\r';    // Change '\n' to '\r'.
   *pchANSI++ = '\n';    // Change '\r' to '\n'.
   pchANSI = strchr(pchANSI, '\n'); // Find the next occurrence.
}
```

When you examine simple code like this, you can easily forget that you are actually manipulating the contents of a file on a disk drive (which shows you how powerful memory-mapped files are).

After the file has been reversed, FileRev must clean up by unmapping the view of the file-mapping object and closing all the kernel object handles. In addition, FileRev must remove the zero character added to the end of the file (remember that _strrev_ doesn't reverse the position of the terminating zero character). If you don't remove the zero character, the reversed file would be 1 character larger, and calling FileRev again would not reverse the file back to its original form. To remove the trailing zero character, you need to drop back a level and use the file-management functions instead of manipulating the file through memory mapping.

Forcing the reversed file to end at a specific location requires positioning the file pointer at the desired location (the end of the original file) and calling the *SetEndOfFile* function:

```
SetFilePointer(hFile, dwFileSize, NULL, FILE_BEGIN);
SetEndOfFile(hFile);
```

NOTE

> *SetEndOfFile* must be called after the view is unmapped and the file-mapping object is closed; otherwise, the function returns FALSE and *GetLastError* returns ERROR_USER_MAPPED_FILE. This error indicates that the end-of-file operation cannot be performed on a file that is associated with a file-mapping object.

The last thing FileRev does is spawn an instance of Notepad so that you can look at the reversed file. The window on the following page shows the result of running FileRev on its own FileRev.cpp file.

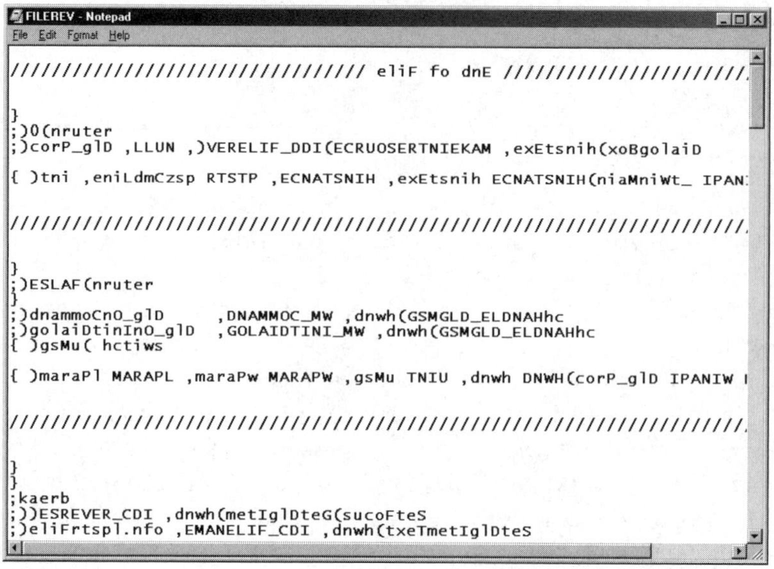

FileRev.cpp

```
/******************************************************************************
Module:  FileRev.cpp
Notices: Copyright (c) 2000 Jeffrey Richter
******************************************************************************/


#include "..\CmnHdr.h"     /* See Appendix A. */
#include <windowsx.h>
#include <tchar.h>
#include <commdlg.h>
#include <string.h>        // For _strrev
#include "Resource.h"


///////////////////////////////////////////////////////////////////////////////


#define FILENAME  TEXT("FILEREV.DAT")


///////////////////////////////////////////////////////////////////////////////
```

Figure 17-2. *(continued)*
The FileRev sample application

Figure 17-2. *continued*

```
BOOL FileReverse(PCTSTR pszPathname, PBOOL pfIsTextUnicode) {

   *pfIsTextUnicode = FALSE;  // Assume text is Unicode.

   // Open the file for reading and writing.
   HANDLE hFile = CreateFile(pszPathname, GENERIC_WRITE | GENERIC_READ, 0,
      NULL, OPEN_EXISTING, FILE_ATTRIBUTE_NORMAL, NULL);

   if (hFile == INVALID_HANDLE_VALUE) {
      chMB("File could not be opened.");
      return(FALSE);
   }

   // Get the size of the file (I assume the whole file can be mapped).
   DWORD dwFileSize = GetFileSize(hFile, NULL);

   // Create the file-mapping object. The file-mapping object is 1 character
   // bigger than the file size so that a zero character can be placed at the
   // end of the file to terminate the string (file). Because I don't yet know
   // if the file contains ANSI or Unicode characters, I assume worst case
   // and add the size of a WCHAR instead of CHAR.
   HANDLE hFileMap = CreateFileMapping(hFile, NULL, PAGE_READWRITE,
      0, dwFileSize + sizeof(WCHAR), NULL);

   if (hFileMap == NULL) {
      chMB("File map could not be opened.");
      CloseHandle(hFile);
      return(FALSE);
   }

   // Get the address where the first byte of the file is mapped into memory.
   PVOID pvFile = MapViewOfFile(hFileMap, FILE_MAP_WRITE, 0, 0, 0);

   if (pvFile == NULL) {
      chMB("Could not map view of file.");
      CloseHandle(hFileMap);
      CloseHandle(hFile);
      return(FALSE);
   }

   // Does the buffer contain ANSI or Unicode?
   int iUnicodeTestFlags = -1;   // Try all tests.
   *pfIsTextUnicode = IsTextUnicode(pvFile, dwFileSize, &iUnicodeTestFlags);
```

(continued)

Figure 17-2. *continued*

```
if (!*pfIsTextUnicode) {
    // For all the file manipulations below, we explicitly use ANSI
    // functions because we are processing an ANSI file.

    // Put a zero character at the very end of the file.
    PSTR pchANSI = (PSTR) pvFile;
    pchANSI[dwFileSize / sizeof(CHAR)] = 0;

    // Reverse the contents of the file.
    _strrev(pchANSI);

    // Convert all "\n\r" combinations back to "\r\n" to
    // preserve the normal end-of-line sequence.
    pchANSI = strchr(pchANSI, '\n'); // Find first '\n'.

    while (pchANSI != NULL) {
        // We have found an occurrence....
        *pchANSI++ = '\r';   // Change '\n' to '\r'.
        *pchANSI++ = '\n';   // Change '\r' to '\n'.
        pchANSI = strchr(pchANSI, '\n'); // Find the next occurrence.
    }

} else {
    // For all the file manipulations below, we explicitly use Unicode
    // functions because we are processing a Unicode file.

    // Put a zero character at the very end of the file.
    PWSTR pchUnicode = (PWSTR) pvFile;
    pchUnicode[dwFileSize / sizeof(WCHAR)] = 0;

    if ((iUnicodeTestFlags & IS_TEXT_UNICODE_SIGNATURE) != 0) {
        // If the first character is the Unicode BOM (byte-order-mark),
        // 0xFEFF, keep this character at the beginning of the file.
        pchUnicode++;
    }

    // Reverse the contents of the file.
    _wcsrev(pchUnicode);

    // Convert all "\n\r" combinations back to "\r\n" to
    // preserve the normal end-of-line sequence.
    pchUnicode = wcschr(pchUnicode, L'\n'); // Find first '\n'.

    while (pchUnicode != NULL) {
        // We have found an occurrence....
        *pchUnicode++ = L'\r';   // Change '\n' to '\r'.
```

(continued)

614

Figure 17-2. *continued*

```
          *pchUnicode++ = L'\n';    // Change '\r' to '\n'.
          pchUnicode = wcschr(pchUnicode, L'\n'); // Find the next occurrence.
      }
   }

   // Clean up everything before exiting.
   UnmapViewOfFile(pvFile);
   CloseHandle(hFileMap);

   // Remove trailing zero character added earlier.
   SetFilePointer(hFile, dwFileSize, NULL, FILE_BEGIN);
   SetEndOfFile(hFile);
   CloseHandle(hFile);

   return(TRUE);
}


///////////////////////////////////////////////////////////////////////////////


BOOL Dlg_OnInitDialog(HWND hwnd, HWND hwndFocus, LPARAM lParam) {

   chSETDLGICONS(hwnd, IDI_FILEREV);

   // Initialize the dialog box by disabling the Reverse button.
   EnableWindow(GetDlgItem(hwnd, IDC_REVERSE), FALSE);
   return(TRUE);
}


///////////////////////////////////////////////////////////////////////////////


void Dlg_OnCommand(HWND hwnd, int id, HWND hwndCtl, UINT codeNotify) {

   TCHAR szPathname[MAX_PATH];

   switch (id) {
      case IDCANCEL:
         EndDialog(hwnd, id);
         break;

      case IDC_FILENAME:
         EnableWindow(GetDlgItem(hwnd, IDC_REVERSE),
            Edit_GetTextLength(hwndCtl) > 0);
         break;
```

(continued)

Figure 17-2. *continued*

```
        case IDC_REVERSE:
            GetDlgItemText(hwnd, IDC_FILENAME, szPathname, chDIMOF(szPathname));

            // Make a copy of input file so that we don't destroy it.
            if (!CopyFile(szPathname, FILENAME, FALSE)) {
                chMB("New file could not be created.");
                break;
            }

            BOOL fIsTextUnicode;
            if (FileReverse(FILENAME, &fIsTextUnicode)) {
                SetDlgItemText(hwnd, IDC_TEXTTYPE,
                    fIsTextUnicode ? TEXT("Unicode") : TEXT("ANSI"));

                // Spawn Notepad to see the fruits of our labors.
                STARTUPINFO si = { sizeof(si) };
                PROCESS_INFORMATION pi;
                TCHAR sz[] = TEXT("Notepad ") FILENAME;
                if (CreateProcess(NULL, sz,
                    NULL, NULL, FALSE, 0, NULL, NULL, &si, &pi)) {

                    CloseHandle(pi.hThread);
                    CloseHandle(pi.hProcess);
                }
            }
            break;

        case IDC_FILESELECT:
            OPENFILENAME ofn = { OPENFILENAME_SIZE_VERSION_400 };
            ofn.hwndOwner = hwnd;
            ofn.lpstrFile = szPathname;
            ofn.lpstrFile[0] = 0;
            ofn.nMaxFile = chDIMOF(szPathname);
            ofn.lpstrTitle = TEXT("Select file for reversing");
            ofn.Flags = OFN_EXPLORER | OFN_FILEMUSTEXIST;
            GetOpenFileName(&ofn);
            SetDlgItemText(hwnd, IDC_FILENAME, ofn.lpstrFile);
            SetFocus(GetDlgItem(hwnd, IDC_REVERSE));
            break;
    }
}
```

//

(continued)

Figure 17-2. *continued*

```
INT_PTR WINAPI Dlg_Proc(HWND hwnd, UINT uMsg, WPARAM wParam, LPARAM lParam) {

   switch (uMsg) {
      chHANDLE_DLGMSG(hwnd, WM_INITDIALOG,  Dlg_OnInitDialog);
      chHANDLE_DLGMSG(hwnd, WM_COMMAND,     Dlg_OnCommand);
   }
   return(FALSE);
}


///////////////////////////////////////////////////////////////////////////////


int WINAPI _tWinMain(HINSTANCE hinstExe, HINSTANCE, PTSTR pszCmdLine, int) {

   DialogBox(hinstExe, MAKEINTRESOURCE(IDD_FILEREV), NULL, Dlg_Proc);
   return(0);
}


///////////////////////////////// End of File ///////////////////////////////////
```


FileRev.rc

```
//Microsoft Developer Studio generated resource script.
//
#include "Resource.h"

#define APSTUDIO_READONLY_SYMBOLS
///////////////////////////////////////////////////////////////////////////////
//
// Generated from the TEXTINCLUDE 2 resource.
//
#include "afxres.h"


///////////////////////////////////////////////////////////////////////////////
#undef APSTUDIO_READONLY_SYMBOLS


///////////////////////////////////////////////////////////////////////////////
// English (U.S.) resources

#if !defined(AFX_RESOURCE_DLL) || defined(AFX_TARG_ENU)
```

(continued)

Figure 17-2. *continued*

```
#ifdef _WIN32
LANGUAGE LANG_ENGLISH, SUBLANG_ENGLISH_US
#pragma code_page(1252)
#endif //_WIN32


/////////////////////////////////////////////////////////////////////////////
//
// Icon
//

// Icon with lowest ID value placed first to ensure application icon
// remains consistent on all systems.
IDI_FILEREV             ICON    DISCARDABLE     "FileRev.Ico"

#ifdef APSTUDIO_INVOKED
/////////////////////////////////////////////////////////////////////////////
//
// TEXTINCLUDE
//

1 TEXTINCLUDE DISCARDABLE
BEGIN
    "Resource.h\0"
END

2 TEXTINCLUDE DISCARDABLE
BEGIN
    "#include ""afxres.h""\r\n"
    "\0"
END

3 TEXTINCLUDE DISCARDABLE
BEGIN
    "\r\n"
    "\0"
END

#endif    // APSTUDIO_INVOKED


/////////////////////////////////////////////////////////////////////////////
//
// Dialog
//
```

(continued)

Figure 17-2. *continued*

```
IDD_FILEREV DIALOG DISCARDABLE  15, 24, 216, 46
STYLE WS_MINIMIZEBOX | WS_POPUP | WS_VISIBLE | WS_CAPTION | WS_SYSMENU
CAPTION "File Reverse"
FONT 8, "MS Sans Serif"
BEGIN
    LTEXT           "&Pathname:",IDC_STATIC,4,4,35,8
    EDITTEXT        IDC_FILENAME,44,4,168,12,ES_AUTOHSCROLL
    PUSHBUTTON      "&Browse...",IDC_FILESELECT,4,16,36,12,WS_GROUP
    DEFPUSHBUTTON   "&Reverse file contents",IDC_REVERSE,4,32,80,12
    LTEXT           "Type of characters in file:",IDC_STATIC,88,34,80,8
    LTEXT           "(unknown)",IDC_TEXTTYPE,172,34,34,8
END


/////////////////////////////////////////////////////////////////////////
//
// DESIGNINFO
//

#ifdef APSTUDIO_INVOKED
GUIDELINES DESIGNINFO DISCARDABLE
BEGIN
    IDD_FILEREV, DIALOG
    BEGIN
        RIGHTMARGIN, 192
        BOTTOMMARGIN, 42
    END
END
#endif    // APSTUDIO_INVOKED

#endif    // English (U.S.) resources
/////////////////////////////////////////////////////////////////////////


#ifndef APSTUDIO_INVOKED
/////////////////////////////////////////////////////////////////////////
//
// Generated from the TEXTINCLUDE 3 resource.
//


/////////////////////////////////////////////////////////////////////////
#endif    // not APSTUDIO_INVOKED
```

Processing a Big File Using Memory-Mapped Files

In an earlier section, I said I would tell you how to map a 16-EB file into a small address space. Well, you can't. Instead, you must map a view of the file that contains only a small portion of the file's data. You should start by mapping a view of the very beginning of the file. When you've finished accessing the first view of the file, you can unmap it and then map a new view starting at an offset deeper within the file. You'll need to repeat this process until you access the complete file. This certainly makes dealing with large memory-mapped files less convenient, but fortunately most files are small enough that this problem doesn't usually come up.

Let's look at an example using an 8-GB file and a 32-bit address space. Here is a routine that counts all the 0 bytes in a binary data file in several steps:

```
__int64 Count0s(void) {

   // Views must always start on a multiple
   // of the allocation granularity
   SYSTEM_INFO sinf;
   GetSystemInfo(&sinf);

   // Open the data file.
   HANDLE hFile = CreateFile("C:\\HugeFile.Big", GENERIC_READ,
      FILE_SHARE_READ, NULL, OPEN_EXISTING, FILE_FLAG_SEQUENTIAL_SCAN, NULL);

   // Create the file-mapping object.
   HANDLE hFileMapping = CreateFileMapping(hFile, NULL,
      PAGE_READONLY, 0, 0, NULL);

   DWORD dwFileSizeHigh;
   __int64 qwFileSize = GetFileSize(hFile, &dwFileSizeHigh);
   qwFileSize += (((__int64) dwFileSizeHigh) << 32);

   // We no longer need access to the file object's handle.
   CloseHandle(hFile);

   __int64 qwFileOffset = 0, qwNumOf0s = 0;

   while (qwFileSize > 0) {

      // Determine the number of bytes to be mapped in this view
      DWORD dwBytesInBlock = sinf.dwAllocationGranularity;
      if (qwFileSize < sinf.dwAllocationGranularity)
         dwBytesInBlock = (DWORD) qwFileSize;
```

(continued)

620

```
        PBYTE pbFile = (PBYTE) MapViewOfFile(hFileMapping, FILE_MAP_READ,
            (DWORD) (qwFileOffset >> 32),              // Starting byte
            (DWORD) (qwFileOffset & 0xFFFFFFFF),       // in file
            dwBytesInBlock);                           // # of bytes to map

        // Count the number of Js in this block.
        for (DWORD dwByte = 0; dwByte < dwBytesInBlock; dwByte++) {
            if (pbFile[dwByte] == 0)
            qwNumOf0s++;
        }

        // Unmap the view; we don't want multiple views
        // in our address space.
        UnmapViewOfFile(pbFile);

        // Skip to the next set of bytes in the file.
        qwFileOffset += dwBytesInBlock;
        qwFileSize -= dwBytesInBlock;
    }

    CloseHandle(hFileMapping);
    return(qwNumOf0s);
}
```

This algorithm maps views of 64 KB (the allocation granularity size) or less. Also, remember that *MapViewOfFile* requires that the file offset parameters be a multiple of the allocation granularity size. As each view is mapped into the address space, the scanning for zeros continues. After each 64-KB chunk of the file has been mapped and scanned, it's time to tidy up by closing the file-mapping object.

Memory-Mapped Files and Coherence

The system allows you to map multiple views of the same data of a file. For example, you can map the first 10 KB of a file into a view and then map the first 4 KB of that same file into a separate view. As long as you are mapping the same file-mapping object, the system ensures that the viewed data is *coherent*. For example, if your application alters the contents of the file in one view, all other views are updated to reflect the changes. This is because even though the page is mapped into the process's virtual address space more than once, the system really has the data in only a single page of RAM. If multiple processes are mapping views of a single data file, the data is still coherent because there is still only one instance of each page of RAM within the data file—it's just that the pages of RAM are mapped into multiple process address spaces.

> **NOTE** Windows allows you to create several file-mapping objects that are backed by a single data file. Windows does *not* guarantee that views of these different file-mapping objects will be coherent. It guarantees only that multiple views of a single file-mapping object will be coherent.

When we're working with files, however, there is no reason why another application can't call *CreateFile* to open the same file that another process has mapped. This new process can then read from and write to the file using the *ReadFile* and *WriteFile* functions. Of course, whenever a process makes these calls, it must be either reading file data from or writing file data to a memory buffer. This memory buffer must be one the process itself created, *not* the memory that is being used by the mapped files. Problems can arise when two applications have opened the same file: one process can call *ReadFile* to read a portion of the file, modify the data, and write it back out using *WriteFile* without the file-mapping object of the second process being aware of the first process's actions. For this reason, it is recommended that when you call *CreateFile* for files that will be memory mapped, you specify 0 as the value of the *dwShareMode* parameter. Doing so tells the system that you want exclusive access to the file and that no other process can open it.

Read-only files do not have coherence problems, making them good candidates for memory-mapped files. Memory-mapped files should never be used to share writable files over a network because the system cannot guarantee coherent views of the data. If someone's computer updates the contents of the file, someone else's computer with the original data in memory will not know that the information has changed.

Specifying the Base Address of a Memory-Mapped File

Just as you can use the *VirtualAlloc* function to suggest an initial address to reserve address space, you can also use the *MapViewOfFileEx* function instead of the *MapViewOfFile* function to suggest that a file be mapped into a particular address.

```
PVOID MapViewOfFileEx(
    HANDLE hFileMappingObject,
    DWORD dwDesiredAccess,
    DWORD dwFileOffsetHigh,
    DWORD dwFileOffsetLow,
    SIZE_T dwNumberOfBytesToMap,
    PVOID pvBaseAddress);
```

All the parameters and the return value for this function are identical to those of the *MapViewOfFile* function with the single exception of the last parameter, *pvBaseAddress*. In this parameter, you specify a target address for the file you're mapping. As with *VirtualAlloc*, the target address you specify should be on an allocation granularity boundary (64 KB); otherwise, *MapViewOfFileEx* returns NULL, indicating an error.

Under Windows 2000, specifying an address that is not a multiple of the allocation granularity causes the function to fail, and *GetLastError* will return 1132 (ERROR_MAPPED_ALIGNMENT). In Windows 98, the address will be rounded down to an allocation granularity boundary.

If the system can't map the file at this location (usually because the file is too large and would overlap another reserved address space), the function fails and returns NULL. *MapViewOfFileEx* does not attempt to locate another address space that can accommodate the file. Of course, you can specify NULL as the *pvBaseAddress* parameter, in which case *MapViewOfFileEx* behaves exactly the same as *MapViewOfFile*.

MapViewOfFileEx is useful when you're using memory-mapped files to share data with other processes. As an example, you might need a memory-mapped file at a particular address when two or more applications are sharing a group of data structures containing pointers to other data structures. A linked list is a perfect example. In a linked list, each node, or element, of the list contains the memory address of another element in the list. To walk the list, you must know the address of the first element and then reference the member of the element that contains the address of the next element. This can be a problem when you're using memory-mapped files.

If one process prepares the linked list in a memory-mapped file and then shares this file with another process, it is possible that the other process will map the file into a completely different location in its address space. When the second process attempts to walk the linked list, it looks at the first element of the list, retrieves the memory address of the next element, and then tries to reference this next element. However, the address of the next element in the first node will be incorrect for this second process.

You can solve this problem in two ways. First, the second process can simply call *MapViewOfFileEx* instead of *MapViewOfFile* when it maps the memory-mapped file containing the linked list into its own address space. Of course, this method requires that the second process know where the first process originally mapped the file when constructing the linked list. When the two applications have been designed to interact with each other—which is most likely the case—this isn't a problem: the address can be hard-coded into both, or one process can notify the other process using another form of interprocess communication, such as sending a message to a window.

The second method for solving the problem is for the process that creates the linked list to store in each node the offset from within the address space where the next node is located. This requires that the application add the offset to the base address of the memory-mapped file in order to access each node. This method is not great: it can be slow, it makes the program bigger (because of the additional code the compiler generates to perform all the calculations), and it can be quite error prone. However, it is certainly a viable method, and the Microsoft compiler offers assistance for based-pointers using the __*based* keyword.

When calling *MapViewOfFileEx*, you must specify an address that is between 0x80000000 and 0xBFFFFFFF, or *MapViewOfFileEx* will return NULL.

WINDOWS 2000

When calling *MapViewOfFileEx*, you must specify an address that is in your process's user-mode partition, or *MapViewOfFileEx* will return NULL.

Implementation Details of Memory-Mapped Files

Windows 98 and Windows 2000 implement memory-mapped files differently. You need to be aware of these differences because they can affect the way you write your code and how other applications can adversely manipulate your data.

Under Windows 98, a view is always mapped in the address space partition that ranges from 0x80000000 to 0xBFFFFFFF. Because of this, all successful calls to *MapViewOfFile* return an address within this range. You might recall that all processes share the data in this partition. This means that if a process maps a view of a file-mapping object, the data of the file-mapping object is physically accessible to all processes whether or not they have mapped a view of the file-mapping object. If another process calls *MapViewOfFile* using the same file-mapping object, Windows 98 will return the same memory address to the second process that it did to the first process. The two processes are accessing the same data, and the views are coherent.

In Windows 98, it is possible for one process to call *MapViewOfFile* and pass the returned memory address to another process's thread using some form of interprocess communication. Once this thread has received the memory address, there is nothing to stop the thread from successfully accessing the same view of the file-mapping object. However, you should not do this for two reasons:

- Your application will not run under Windows 2000, for reasons I'll describe shortly.

- If the first process calls *UnmapViewOfFile*, the address space region will revert to the free state; this means that the second process's thread will raise an access violation when it attempts to access the memory where the view once was.

For the second process to access the view of the memory-mapped file, a thread in the second process should call *MapViewOfFile* on its own behalf. When the second process does this, the system increments a usage count for the memory-mapped view. So if the first process calls *UnmapViewOfFile*, the system will not release the region of address space occupied by the view until the second process also calls *UnmapViewOfFile*.

When the second process calls *MapViewOfFile*, the address returned will be the same address that was returned to the first process. This averts the need for the first process to send the memory address to the second process using interprocess communication.

The Windows 2000 implementation of memory-mapped files is better than the Windows 98 implementation because Windows 2000 *requires* a process to call *MapViewOfFile* before the file's data is accessible in the process's address space. If one process calls *MapViewOfFile*, the system reserves a region of address space for the view in the calling process's address space—no other process can see the view. If another process wants to access the data in the same file-mapping object, a thread in the second process must call *MapViewOfFile*, and the system will reserve a region for the view in the second process's address space.

It is important to note that the memory address returned by the first process's call to *MapViewOfFile* will most likely *not* be the same memory address returned by the second process's call to *MapViewOfFile*. This is true even though both processes are mapping a view of the same file-mapping object. In Windows 98, the memory addresses returned from *MapViewOfFile* are the same—but you should absolutely not *count* on them being the same if you want your application to run under Windows 2000!

Let's look at another implementation difference. Here is a small program that maps two views of a single file-mapping object:

```
#include <Windows.h>

int WINAPI WinMain (HINSTANCE hinstExe, HINSTANCE,
   PTSTR pszCmdLine, int nCmdShow) {

   // Open an existing file-it must be bigger than 64 KB.
   HANDLE hFile = CreateFile(pszCmdLine, GENERIC_READ | GENERIC_WRITE,
      0, NULL, OPEN_ALWAYS, FILE_ATTRIBUTE_NORMAL, NULL);

   // Create a file-mapping object backed by the data file.
   HANDLE hFileMapping = CreateFileMapping(hFile, NULL,
      PAGE_READWRITE, 0, 0, NULL);

   // Map a view of the whole file into our address space.
   PBYTE pbFile = (PBYTE) MapViewOfFile(hFileMapping,
      FILE_MAP_WRITE, 0, 0, 0);

   // Map a view of the file (starting 64 KB in) into our address space
   PBYTE pbFile2 = (PBYTE) MapViewOfFile(hFileMapping,
      FILE_MAP_WRITE, 0, 65536, 0);

   if ((pbFile + 65536) == pbFile2) {
      // If the addresses overlap, there is one address
      // space region for both views: this must be Windows 98.
      MessageBox(NULL, "We are running under Windows 98", NULL, MB_OK);
   } else {
      // If the addresses do not overlap, each view has its own
      // address space region: this must be Windows 2000.
      MessageBox(NULL, "We are running under Windows 2000", NULL, MB_OK);
   }

   UnmapViewOfFile(pbFile2);
   UnmapViewOfFile(pbFile);
   CloseHandle(hFileMapping);
   CloseHandle(hFile);

   return(0);
}
```

In Windows 98, when a view of a file-mapping object is mapped, the system reserves enough address space for the entire file-mapping object. This happens even if *MapViewOfFile* is called with parameters that indicate that you want the system to map only a small portion of the file-mapping object. This means that you can't map a 1-GB file-mapping object to a view even if you specify that only a 64-KB portion of the object be mapped.

Whenever any process calls *MapViewOfFile*, the function returns an address within the address space region that was reserved for the *entire* file-mapping object. So in the preceding code segment, the first call to *MapViewOfFile* returns the base address of the region that contains the entire mapped file. The second call to *MapViewOfFile* returns an address that is 64 KB into the same address space region.

The Windows 2000 implementation is again quite different. The two calls to *MapViewOfFile* in the preceding code segment cause Windows 2000 to reserve two different address space regions. The size of the first region is the size of the file-mapping object, and the size of the second region is the size of the file-mapping object minus 64 KB. Even though there are two different regions, the data is guaranteed to be coherent because both views are made from the same file-mapping object. Under Windows 98, the views are coherent because it *is* the same memory.

Using Memory-Mapped Files to Share Data Among Processes

Windows has always excelled at offering mechanisms that allow applications to share data and information quickly and easily. These mechanisms include RPC, COM, OLE, DDE, window messages (especially WM_COPYDATA), the clipboard, mailslots, pipes, sockets, and so on. In Windows, the lowest-level mechanism for sharing data on a single machine is the memory-mapped file. That's right, all of the mechanisms I mention ultimately use memory-mapped files to do their dirty work if all the processes communicating are on the same machine. If you require high-performance with low overhead, the memory-mapped file is the hands-down best mechanism to use.

This data sharing is accomplished by having two or more processes map views of the same file-mapping object, which means they are sharing the same pages of physical storage. As a result, when one process writes to data in a view of a shared file-mapping object, the other processes see the change instantly in their views. Note that for multiple processes to share a single file-mapping object, all processes must use exactly the same name for the file-mapping object.

627

Let's look at an example: starting an application. When an application starts, the system calls *CreateFile* to open the .exe file on the disk. The system then calls *CreateFileMapping* to create a file-mapping object. Finally the system calls *MapViewOfFileEx* (with the SEC_IMAGE flag) on behalf of the newly created process so that the .exe file is mapped into the process's address space. *MapViewOfFileEx* is called instead of *MapViewOfFile* so that the file's image is mapped to the base address stored in the .exe file's image. The system creates the process's primary thread, puts the address of the first byte of executable code of this mapped view in the thread's instruction pointer, and then lets the CPU start executing the code.

If the user runs a second instance of the same application, the system sees that a file-mapping object already exists for the desired .exe file and doesn't create a new file object or file-mapping object. Instead, the system maps a view of the file a second time, this time in the context of the newly created process's address space. What the system has done is map the identical file into two address spaces simultaneously. Obviously, this is a more efficient use of memory because both processes are sharing the same pages of physical storage containing portions of the code that are executing.

As with all kernel objects, you can use three techniques to share the objects with multiple processes: handle inheritance, naming, and handle duplication. See Chapter 3 for a detailed explanation of all three techniques.

Memory-Mapped Files Backed by the Paging File

So far I've discussed techniques that allow you to map a view of a file that resides on a disk drive. Many applications create some data while they run and need to transfer the data or share it with another process. It would be terribly inconvenient if the applications had to create a data file on a disk drive and store the data there in order to share it.

Microsoft realized this and added the ability to create memory-mapped files that are backed by the system's paging file rather than a dedicated hard disk file. This method is almost identical to the method for creating a memory-mapped disk file except that it's even easier. For one thing, there is no need to call *CreateFile* since you will not be creating or opening a dedicated file. Instead, you simply call *CreateFileMapping* as you would normally and pass INVALID_HANDLE_VALUE as the *hFile* parameter. This tells the system that you are not creating a file-mapping object whose physical storage resides in a file on the disk;

instead, you want the system to commit physical storage from the system's paging file. The amount of storage allocated is determined by *CreateFileMapping*'s *dwMaximumSizeHigh* and *dwMaximumSizeLow* parameters.

After you have created this file-mapping object and mapped a view of it into your process's address space, you can use it as you would any region of memory. If you want to share this data with other processes, call *CreateFileMapping* and pass a zero-terminated string as the *pszName* parameter. Then other processes that want to access the storage can call *CreateFileMapping* or *OpenFileMapping* and pass the same name.

When a process no longer needs access to the file-mapping object, that process should call *CloseHandle*. When all the handles are closed, the system will reclaim the committed storage from the system's paging file.

NOTE

Here is an interesting problem that has caught unsuspecting programmers by surprise. Can you guess what is wrong with the following code fragment?

```
HANDLE hFile = CreateFile(...);
HANDLE hMap = CreateFileMapping(hFile, ...);
if (hMap == NULL)
    return(GetLastError());
    ⋮
```

If the call to *CreateFile* above fails, it returns INVALID_HANDLE_VALUE. However, the unsuspecting programmer who wrote this code didn't test to check whether the file was created successfully. When *CreateFileMapping* is called, INVALID_HANDLE_VALUE is passed in the *hFile* parameter, which causes the system to create a file mapping using storage from the paging file instead of the intended disk file. Any additional code that uses the memory-mapped file will work correctly. However, when the file-mapping object is destroyed, all the data that was written to the file-mapping storage (the paging file) will be destroyed by the system. At this point, the developer sits and scratches his or her head, wondering what went wrong! You must always check *CreateFile*'s return value to see if an error occurred because *CreateFile* can fail for so many reasons!

The Memory-Mapped File Sharing Sample Application

The MMFShare application ("17 MMFShare.exe") listed in Figure 17-3 demonstrates how to use memory-mapped files to transfer data among two or more separate processes. The source code and resource files for the application are in the 17-MMFShare directory on the companion CD-ROM.

You're going to need to execute at least two instances of MMFShare. Each instance creates its own dialog box, shown here.

To transfer data from one instance of MMFShare to another, type the data to be transferred into the Data edit box. Then click on the Create Mapping Of Data button. When you do, MMFShare calls *CreateFileMapping* to create a 4-KB memory-mapped file object backed by the system's paging file and names the object *MMFSharedData*. If MMFShare sees that a file-mapping object with this name already exists, it displays a message box notifying you that it could not create the object. If, on the other hand, MMFShare succeeds in creating the object, it proceeds to map a view of the file into the process's address space and copies the data from the edit control into the memory-mapped file.

After the data has been copied, MMFShare unmaps the view of the file, disables the Create Mapping Of Data button, and enables the Close Mapping Of Data button. At this point, a memory-mapped file named *MMFSharedData* is just sitting somewhere in the system. No processes have mapped a view to the data contained in the file.

If you now go to another instance of MMFShare and click on this instance's Open Mapping And Get Data button, MMFShare attempts to locate a file-mapping object called *MMFSharedData* by calling *OpenFileMapping*. If an object of this name cannot be found, MMFShare notifies you by displaying another message box. If MMFShare finds the object, it maps a view of the object into its process's address space, copies the data from the memory-mapped file into the edit control of the dialog box, and unmaps and closes the file-mapping object. Voilà! You have transferred data from one process to another.

The Close Mapping Of Data button in the dialog box is used to close the file-mapping object, which frees up the storage in the paging file. If no file-mapping object exists, no other instance of MMFShare will be able to open one and get data from it. Also, if one instance has created a memory-mapped file, no other instance is allowed to create one and overwrite the data contained within the file.

MMFShare.cpp

```
/****************************************************************************
Module:  MMFShare.cpp
Notices: Copyright (c) 2000 Jeffrey Richter
****************************************************************************/


#include "..\CmnHdr.h"      /* See Appendix A. */
#include <windowsx.h>
#include <tchar.h>
#include "Resource.h"


///////////////////////////////////////////////////////////////////////////


BOOL Dlg_OnInitDialog(HWND hwnd, HWND hwndFocus, LPARAM lParam) {

   chSETDLGICONS(hwnd, IDI_MMFSHARE);

   // Initialize the edit control with some test data.
   Edit_SetText(GetDlgItem(hwnd, IDC_DATA), TEXT("Some test data"));

   // Disable the Close button because the file can't
   // be closed if it was never created or opened.
   Button_Enable(GetDlgItem(hwnd, IDC_CLOSEFILE), FALSE);
   return(TRUE);
}


///////////////////////////////////////////////////////////////////////////


void Dlg_OnCommand(HWND hwnd, int id, HWND hwndCtl, UINT codeNotify) {

   // Handle of the open memory-mapped file
   static HANDLE s_hFileMap = NULL;
```

Figure 17-3.   *(continued)*
The MMFShare application

Figure 17-3. *continued*

```
switch (id) {
   case IDCANCEL:
      EndDialog(hwnd, id);
      break;

   case IDC_CREATEFILE:
      if (codeNotify != BN_CLICKED)
         break;

      // Create a paging file-backed MMF to contain the edit control text.
      // The MMF is 4 KB at most and is named MMFSharedData.
      s_hFileMap = CreateFileMapping(INVALID_HANDLE_VALUE, NULL,
         PAGE_READWRITE, 0, 4 * 1024, TEXT("MMFSharedData"));

      if (s_hFileMap != NULL) {

         if (GetLastError() == ERROR_ALREADY_EXISTS) {
            chMB("Mapping already exists - not created.");
            CloseHandle(s_hFileMap);

         } else {

            // File mapping created successfully.

            // Map a view of the file into the address space.
            PVOID pView = MapViewOfFile(s_hFileMap,
               FILE_MAP_READ | FILE_MAP_WRITE, 0, 0, 0);

            if (pView != NULL) {
               // Put edit text into the MMF.
               Edit_GetText(GetDlgItem(hwnd, IDC_DATA),
                  (LPTSTR) pView, 4 * 1024);

               // Protect the MMF storage by unmapping it.
               UnmapViewOfFile(pView);

               // The user can't create another file right now.
               Button_Enable(hwndCtl, FALSE);

               // The user closed the file.
               Button_Enable(GetDlgItem(hwnd, IDC_CLOSEFILE), TRUE);

            } else {
               chMB("Can't map view of file.");
            }
         }
```

(continued)

Figure 17-3. *continued*

```
      } else {
         chMB("Can't create file mapping.");
      }
      break;

   case IDC_CLOSEFILE:
      if (codeNotify != BN_CLICKED)
         break;

      if (CloseHandle(s_hFileMap)) {
         // User closed the file; fix up the buttons.
         Button_Enable(GetDlgItem(hwnd, IDC_CREATEFILE), TRUE);
         Button_Enable(hwndCtl, FALSE);
      }
      break;

   case IDC_OPENFILE:
      if (codeNotify != BN_CLICKED)
         break;

      // See if a memory-mapped file named MMFSharedData already exists.
      HANDLE hFileMapT = OpenFileMapping(FILE_MAP_READ | FILE_MAP_WRITE,
         FALSE, TEXT("MMFSharedData"));

      if (hFileMapT != NULL) {
         // The MMF does exist; map it into the process's address space.
         PVOID pView = MapViewOfFile(hFileMapT,
            FILE_MAP_READ | FILE_MAP_WRITE, 0, 0, 0);

         if (pView != NULL) {

            // Put the contents of the MMF into the edit control.
            Edit_SetText(GetDlgItem(hwnd, IDC_DATA), (LPTSTR) pView);
            UnmapViewOfFile(pView);
         } else {
            chMB("Can't map view.");
         }

         CloseHandle(hFileMapT);

      } else {
         chMB("Can't open mapping.");
      }
      break;
   }
}
```

(continued)

Figure 17-3. *continued*

```
//////////////////////////////////////////////////////////////////////////


INT_PTR WINAPI Dlg_Proc(HWND hwnd, UINT uMsg, WPARAM wParam, LPARAM lParam) {

   switch (uMsg) {
      chHANDLE_DLGMSG(hwnd, WM_INITDIALOG, Dlg_OnInitDialog);
      chHANDLE_DLGMSG(hwnd, WM_COMMAND,    Dlg_OnCommand);
   }
   return(FALSE);
}



//////////////////////////////////////////////////////////////////////////


int WINAPI _tWinMain(HINSTANCE hinstExe, HINSTANCE, PTSTR pszCmdLine, int) {

   DialogBox(hinstExe, MAKEINTRESOURCE(IDD_MMFSHARE), NULL, Dlg_Proc);
   return(0);
}



/////////////////////////////// End of File //////////////////////////////
```

MMFShare.rc

```
//Microsoft Developer Studio generated resource script.
//
#include "Resource.h"

#define APSTUDIO_READONLY_SYMBOLS
//////////////////////////////////////////////////////////////////////////
//
// Generated from the TEXTINCLUDE 2 resource.
//
#include "afxres.h"


//////////////////////////////////////////////////////////////////////////
#undef APSTUDIO_READONLY_SYMBOLS


//////////////////////////////////////////////////////////////////////////
// English (U.S.) resources
```

(continued)

Figure 17-3. *continued*

```
#if !defined(AFX_RESOURCE_DLL) || defined(AFX_TARG_ENU)
#ifdef _WIN32
LANGUAGE LANG_ENGLISH, SUBLANG_ENGLISH_US
#pragma code_page(1252)
#endif //_WIN32


/////////////////////////////////////////////////////////////////////////////
//
// Dialog
//

IDD_MMFSHARE DIALOG DISCARDABLE  38, 36, 186, 61
STYLE WS_MINIMIZEBOX | WS_POPUP | WS_VISIBLE | WS_CAPTION | WS_SYSMENU
CAPTION "Memory-Mapped File Sharing"
FONT 8, "MS Sans Serif"
BEGIN
    PUSHBUTTON      "&Create mapping of Data",IDC_CREATEFILE,4,4,84,14,
                    WS_GROUP
    PUSHBUTTON      "&Close mapping of Data",IDC_CLOSEFILE,96,4,84,14
    LTEXT           "&Data:",IDC_STATIC,4,26,18,8
    EDITTEXT        IDC_DATA,28,24,153,12
    PUSHBUTTON      "&Open mapping and get Data",IDC_OPENFILE,40,44,104,14,
                    WS_GROUP
END


/////////////////////////////////////////////////////////////////////////////
//
// Icon
//

// Icon with lowest ID value placed first to ensure application icon
// remains consistent on all systems.
IDI_MMFSHARE            ICON    DISCARDABLE     "MMFShare.Ico"


#ifdef APSTUDIO_INVOKED
/////////////////////////////////////////////////////////////////////////////
//
// TEXTINCLUDE
//

1 TEXTINCLUDE DISCARDABLE
BEGIN
    "Resource.h\0"
END
```

(continued)

Figure 17-3. *continued*

```
2 TEXTINCLUDE DISCARDABLE
BEGIN
    "#include ""afxres.h""\r\n"
    "\0"
END

3 TEXTINCLUDE DISCARDABLE
BEGIN
    "\r\n"
    "\0"
END

#endif    // APSTUDIO_INVOKED

#endif    // English (U.S.) resources
/////////////////////////////////////////////////////////////////////////////


#ifndef APSTUDIO_INVOKED
/////////////////////////////////////////////////////////////////////////////
//
// Generated from the TEXTINCLUDE 3 resource.
//


/////////////////////////////////////////////////////////////////////////////
#endif    // not APSTUDIO_INVOKED
```

Sparsely Committed Memory-Mapped Files

In all the discussion of memory-mapped files so far, we see that the system requires that all storage for the memory-mapped file be committed either in the data file on disk or in the paging file. This means that we can't use storage as efficiently as we might like. Let's return to the discussion of the spreadsheet from the section "When to Commit Physical Storage" in Chapter 15. Let's say that you want to share the entire spreadsheet with another process. If we were to use memory-mapped files, we would need to commit the physical storage for the entire spreadsheet:

```
CELLDATA CellData[200][256];
```

If a CELLDATA structure is 128 bytes, this array requires 6,553,600 (200 × 256 × 128) bytes of physical storage. As I said in Chapter 15, "That's a lot of physical storage to allocate from the paging file right up front for a spread-sheet, especially when you consider that most users put information into only a few spreadsheet cells, leaving the majority unused."

It should be obvious that we would prefer to share the spreadsheet as a file-mapping object without having to commit all of the physical storage up front. *CreateFileMapping* offers a way to do this by specifying either the SEC_RESERVE or the SEC_COMMIT flag in the *fdwProtect* parameter.

These flags are meaningful only if you're creating a file-mapping object that is backed by the system's paging file. The SEC_COMMIT flag causes *CreateFileMapping* to commit storage from the system's paging file. This is also the result if you specify neither flag.

When you call *CreateFileMapping* and pass the SEC_RESERVE flag, the system does not commit physical storage from the system's paging file; it just returns a handle to the file-mapping object. You can now call *MapViewOfFile* or *MapViewOfFileEx* to create a view of this file-mapping object. *MapViewOfFile* and *MapViewOfFileEx* will reserve a region of address space and will not com-mit any physical storage to back the region. Any attempts to access a memory address in the reserved region will cause the thread to raise an access violation.

What we have here is a region of reserved address space and a handle to a file-mapping object that identifies the region. Other processes can use the same file-mapping object to map a view of the same region of address space. Physi-cal storage is still not committed to the region, and if threads in other processes attempt to access a memory address of the view in their regions, these threads will raise access violations.

Now here is where things get exciting. To commit physical storage to the shared region, all a thread has to do is call *VirtualAlloc*:

```
PVOID VirtualAlloc(
   PVOID pvAddress,
   SIZE_T dwSize,
   DWORD fdwAllocationType,
   DWORD fdwProtect);
```

We already discussed this function in great detail in Chapter 15. Calling *VirtualAlloc* to commit physical storage to the memory-mapped view region is just like calling *VirtualAlloc* to commit storage to a region initially reserved by a simple call to *VirtualAlloc* using the MEM_RESERVE flag. And just as you can commit storage sparsely in a region reserved with *VirtualAlloc*, you can also commit storage sparsely within a region reserved by *MapViewOfFile* or *MapViewOfFileEx*. However, when you commit storage to a region reserved by *MapViewOfFile* or *MapViewOfFileEx*, all the processes that have mapped a view of the same file-mapping object can now successfully access the committed pages.

Using the SEC_RESERVE flag and *VirtualAlloc*, we can successfully share the spreadsheet application's *CellData* matrix with other processes—and use physical storage quite efficiently.

WINDOWS 98

> Normally, *VirtualAlloc* will fail when you pass it a memory address outside 0x00400000 through 0x7FFFFFFF. However, when committing physical storage to a memory-mapped file created using the SEC_RESERVE flag, you have to call *VirtualAlloc*, passing a memory address that is between 0x80000000 and 0xBFFFFFFF. Windows 98 knows that you are committing storage to a reserved memory-mapped file and allows the call to succeed.

NOTE

> Under Windows 2000, you cannot use the *VirtualFree* function to decommit storage from a memory-mapped file that was reserved with the SEC_RESERVE flag. However, Windows 98 does allow you to call *VirtualFree* to decommit storage in this case.

The NT File System (NTFS 5) offers support for sparse files. This is a terrific new feature. Using this new sparse file feature, you can easily create and work with sparse memory-mapped files in which the storage is contained in a normal disk file rather than in the system's paging file.

Here is an example of how you could use this: Let's say that you want to create an MMF to store recorded audio data. As the user speaks, you want to write the digital audio data into a memory buffer and have that buffer be backed by a file on the disk. A sparse MMF would certainly be the easiest and most efficient way to implement this in your code. The problem is that you don't know how long the user will speak before clicking on the Stop button. You might need a file large enough for five minutes of data or five hours—a pretty big difference! When using a sparse MMF, however, size really doesn't matter.

The Sparse Memory-Mapped File Sample Application

The MMFSparse application ("17 MMFSparse.exe"), listed in Figure 17-4, demonstrates how to create a memory-mapped file backed by an NTFS 5 sparse file. The source code and resource files for the application are in the 17-MMFSparse directory on the companion CD-ROM. When you start the program, the following window appears.

When you click on the Create a 1MB (1024 KB) Sparse MMF button, the program attempts to create a sparse file called "C:\MMFSparse". If your C drive is not an NTFS 5 volume, this will fail and the process will terminate. If your NTFS 5 volume is on another drive letter, you'll have to modify the source code and rebuild it to see how the application works.

Once the sparse file is created, it is mapped into the process's address space. The Allocated Ranges edit control at the bottom shows which parts of the file are actually backed by disk storage. Initially, the file will have no storage in it and the edit control will contain the text "No allocated ranges in the file."

To read a byte, simply enter a number into the Offset edit box and click on the Read Byte button. The number you enter is multiplied by 1024 (1 KB), and the byte at that location is read and placed in the Byte edit box. If you read from any portion that has no backing storage, you will always read a zero byte. If you read from a portion of the file that does have backing storage, you will read whatever byte is there.

To write a byte, simply enter a number into the Offset edit box and also enter a byte value (0-255) into the Byte edit box. Then, when you click on the Write Byte button, the offset number is multiplied by 1024 and the byte at that location is changed to reflect the specified byte value. This write can cause the file system to commit backing storage for a portion of the file. After any read or write operation, the Allocated Ranges edit control is always updated to show you which portions of the file are actually backed by storage. The window on the following page shows what the dialog box looks like after writing just a single byte at offset 1,024,000 (1000 * 1024).

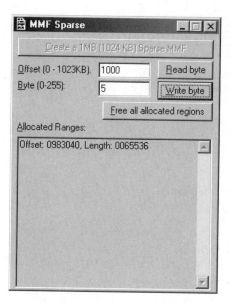

In this figure, notice that there is just one allocated range starting at logical offset 983,040 bytes into the file and that 65,536 bytes of backing storage have been allocated. You can also use Explorer to locate the file C:\MMFSparse and display its property page, as shown here.

Notice that the property page indicates that the file's size is 1 MB (this is the virtual size of the file), but the file actually occupies only 64 KB of disk space.

The last button, Free All Allocated Regions, causes the program to free all of the storage for the file; this feature frees up disk space and makes all the bytes in the file appear as zeros.

Let's talk about how the program works. To make things easier, I created a *CSparseStream* C++ class (implemented in the SparseStream.h file). This class encapsulates the tasks that you can perform with a sparse file or stream. Then, in the MMFSparse.cpp file, I created another C++ class, *CMMFSparse*, that is derived from the *CSparseStream* class. So a *CMMFSparse* object will have all of the features of a *CSparseStream* plus a few more that are specific to using a sparse stream as a memory-mapped file. The process has a single, global instance of a *CMMFSparse* object called *g_mmf*. The application references this global variable throughout its code in order to manipulate the sparse memory-mapped file.

When the user clicks on the Create a 1MB (1024 KB) Sparse MMF button, *CreateFile* is called to create a new file on the NTFS 5 disk partition. This is a normal, ordinary file. But then I use my global *g_mmf* object and call its *Initialize* method, passing the handle of this file and the maximum size of the file (1 MB). Internally, the *Initialize* method calls *CreateFileMapping* to create the file-mapping kernel object using the specified size and then calls *MapViewOfFile* to make the sparse file visible in the process's address space.

When the *Initialize* method returns, the *Dlg_ShowAllocatedRanges* function is called. This function internally calls Windows functions that enumerate the logical ranges of the sparse files that have storage actually allocated to them. The starting offset and length of each allocated range is shown in the edit control at the bottom of the dialog box. When the *g_mmf* object is first initialized, the file on the disk actually has 0 bytes of physical storage allocated for it; the edit control will reflect this.

At this point, the user can attempt to read from or write to bytes within the sparse memory-mapped file. For an attempted write, the user's offset and byte values are obtained from their respective edit controls, and the memory address within the *g_mmf* object is written to. Writing to *g_mmf* can cause the file system to allocate storage to this logical portion of the file, but the allocation is transparent to the application.

If the user attempts to read a byte from the *g_mmf* object, the read might attempt to read a logical byte within the file where storage has been allocated or the byte might identify a byte where storage has not been allocated. If the byte does not have storage allocated, reading the byte returns 0. Again, this is transparent to the application. If storage does exist for the byte being read, the actual value is of course returned.

The last thing that the application demonstrates is how to reset the file so that all of its allocated ranges are freed and the file doesn't actually require any disk storage. The user frees all the allocated ranges by clicking on the Free All Allocated Regions button. Windows cannot free all the allocated ranges for a file that is memory-mapped, so the first thing that the application does is call the *g_mmf* object's *ForceClose* method. Internally, the *ForceClose* method calls *UnmapViewOfFile* and then calls *CloseHandle,* passing the handle of the file-mapping kernel object.

Next the *DecommitPortionOfStream* method is called, freeing all storage allocated for logical bytes 0 through 1 MB in the file. Finally the *Initialize* method is called again on the *g_mmf* object, which reinitializes the memory-mapped file into the process's address space. To prove that the file has had all its allocated storage freed, the *Dlg_ShowAllocatedRanges* function is called, which will display the "No allocated ranges in the file" string in the edit control.

One last thing: If you are using a sparse memory-mapped file in a real-life application, you might want to truncate the logical size of the file when you close it. Trimming the end of a sparse file that contains zero bytes doesn't actually affect the disk space, but it's still a nice thing to do—Explorer and the command shell's DIR command can report a more accurate file size to the user. To set the end of a file marker for a file, you can call the *SetFilePointer* and *SetEndOfFile* functions after calling the *ForceClose* method.

MMFSparse.cpp

```
/**********************************************************************************
Module:  MMFSparse.cpp
Notices: Copyright (c) 2000 Jeffrey Richter
**********************************************************************************/


#include "..\CmnHdr.h"        /* See Appendix A. */
#include <tchar.h>
#include <WindowsX.h>
#include <WinIoCtl.h>
#include "SparseStream.h"
#include "Resource.h"


//////////////////////////////////////////////////////////////////////////////
```

Figure 17-4.
The MMFSparse application

(continued)

Figure 17-4. *continued*

```
// This class makes it easy to work with memory-mapped sparse files.
class CMMFSparse : public CSparseStream {
private:
   HANDLE m_hfilemap;        // File-mapping object
   PVOID  m_pvFile;          // Address to start of mapped file

public:
   // Creates a Sparse MMF and maps it in the process's address space.
   CMMFSparse(HANDLE hstream = NULL, SIZE_T dwStreamSizeMax = 0);

   // Closes a Sparse MMF.
   virtual ~CMMFSparse() { ForceClose(); }

   // Creates a sparse MMF and maps it in the process's address space.
   BOOL Initialize(HANDLE hstream, SIZE_T dwStreamSizeMax);

   // MMF to BYTE cast operator returns address of first byte
   // in the memory-mapped sparse file.
   operator PBYTE() const { return((PBYTE) m_pvFile); }

   // Allows you to explicitly close the MMF without having
   // to wait for the destructor to be called.
   VOID ForceClose();
};


///////////////////////////////////////////////////////////////////////////


CMMFSparse::CMMFSparse(HANDLE hstream, SIZE_T dwStreamSizeMax) {

   Initialize(hstream, dwStreamSizeMax);
}


///////////////////////////////////////////////////////////////////////////


BOOL CMMFSparse::Initialize(HANDLE hstream, SIZE_T dwStreamSizeMax) {

   if (m_hfilemap != NULL)
      ForceClose();

   // Initialize to NULL in case something goes wrong.
   m_hfilemap = m_pvFile = NULL;
```

(continued)

Figure 17-4. *continued*

```
    BOOL fOk = TRUE;   // Assume success.

    if (hstream != NULL) {
       if (dwStreamSizeMax == 0) {
          DebugBreak();  // Illegal stream size
       }

       CSparseStream::Initialize(hstream);
       fOk = MakeSparse();  // Make the stream sparse.
       if (fOk) {
          // Create a file-mapping object
          m_hfilemap = ::CreateFileMapping(hstream, NULL, PAGE_READWRITE,
             (DWORD) (dwStreamSizeMax >> 32i64), (DWORD) dwStreamSizeMax, NULL);

          if (m_hfilemap != NULL) {
             // Map the stream into the process's address space.
             m_pvFile = ::MapViewOfFile(m_hfilemap,
                FILE_MAP_WRITE | FILE_MAP_READ, 0, 0, 0);
          } else {
             // Failed to map the file; clean up
             CSparseStream::Initialize(NULL);
             ForceClose();
             fOk = FALSE;
          }
       }
    }
    return(fOk);
}


//////////////////////////////////////////////////////////////////////////////


VOID CMMFSparse::ForceClose() {

    // Clean up everything that was done successfully
    if (m_pvFile != NULL) {
       ::UnmapViewOfFile(m_pvFile);
       m_pvFile = NULL;
    }
    if (m_hfilemap != NULL) {
       ::CloseHandle(m_hfilemap);
       m_hfilemap = NULL;
    }
}
```

(continued)

Figure 17-4. *continued*

```
//////////////////////////////////////////////////////////////////////


#define STREAMSIZE      (1 * 1024 * 1024)    // 1 MB (1024 KB)
TCHAR szPathname[] = TEXT("C:\\MMFSparse.");
HANDLE g_hstream = INVALID_HANDLE_VALUE;
CMMFSparse g_mmf;


//////////////////////////////////////////////////////////////////////


BOOL Dlg_OnInitDialog(HWND hwnd, HWND hwndFocus, LPARAM lParam) {

   chSETDLGICONS(hwnd, IDI_MMFSPARSE);

   // Initialize the dialog box controls.
   EnableWindow(GetDlgItem(hwnd, IDC_OFFSET), FALSE);
   Edit_LimitText(GetDlgItem(hwnd, IDC_OFFSET), 4);
   SetDlgItemInt(hwnd, IDC_OFFSET, 1000, FALSE);

   EnableWindow(GetDlgItem(hwnd, IDC_BYTE), FALSE);
   Edit_LimitText(GetDlgItem(hwnd, IDC_BYTE), 3);
   SetDlgItemInt(hwnd, IDC_BYTE, 5, FALSE);

   EnableWindow(GetDlgItem(hwnd, IDC_WRITEBYTE), FALSE);
   EnableWindow(GetDlgItem(hwnd, IDC_READBYTE), FALSE);
   EnableWindow(GetDlgItem(hwnd, IDC_FREEALLOCATEDREGIONS), FALSE);

   return(TRUE);
}


//////////////////////////////////////////////////////////////////////


void Dlg_ShowAllocatedRanges(HWND hwnd) {

   // Fill in the Allocated Ranges edit control
   DWORD dwNumEntries;
   FILE_ALLOCATED_RANGE_BUFFER* pfarb =
      g_mmf.QueryAllocatedRanges(&dwNumEntries);

   if (dwNumEntries == 0) {
      SetDlgItemText(hwnd, IDC_FILESTATUS,
         TEXT("No allocated ranges in the file"));
```

(continued)

Figure 17-4. *continued*

```
    } else {
      TCHAR sz[4096] = { 0 };
      for (DWORD dwEntry = 0; dwEntry < dwNumEntries; dwEntry++) {
        wsprintf(_tcschr(sz, 0), TEXT("Offset: %7.7u, Length: %7.7u\r\n"),
           pfarb[dwEntry].FileOffset.LowPart, pfarb[dwEntry].Length.LowPart);
      }
      SetDlgItemText(hwnd, IDC_FILESTATUS, sz);
    }
    g_mmf.FreeAllocatedRanges(pfarb);
}


///////////////////////////////////////////////////////////////////////////////


void Dlg_OnCommand(HWND hwnd, int id, HWND hwndCtl, UINT codeNotify) {

  switch (id) {
    case IDCANCEL:
      if (g_hstream != INVALID_HANDLE_VALUE)
        CloseHandle(g_hstream);
      EndDialog(hwnd, id);
      break;

    case IDC_CREATEMMF:
      // Create the file
      g_hstream = CreateFile(szPathname, GENERIC_READ | GENERIC_WRITE,
        0, NULL, CREATE_ALWAYS, FILE_ATTRIBUTE_NORMAL, NULL);
      if (g_hstream == INVALID_HANDLE_VALUE) {
        chFAIL("Failed to create file.");
      }

      // Create a 1 MB (1024 KB) MMF using the file
      if (!g_mmf.Initialize(g_hstream, STREAMSIZE)) {
        chFAIL("Failed to initialize Sparse MMF.");
      }
      Dlg_ShowAllocatedRanges(hwnd);

      // Enable/disable the other controls.
      EnableWindow(GetDlgItem(hwnd, IDC_CREATEMMF), FALSE);
      EnableWindow(GetDlgItem(hwnd, IDC_OFFSET),    TRUE);
      EnableWindow(GetDlgItem(hwnd, IDC_BYTE),      TRUE);
      EnableWindow(GetDlgItem(hwnd, IDC_WRITEBYTE), TRUE);
      EnableWindow(GetDlgItem(hwnd, IDC_READBYTE),  TRUE);
      EnableWindow(GetDlgItem(hwnd, IDC_FREEALLOCATEDREGIONS), TRUE);
```

(continued)

Figure 17-4. *continued*

```
        // Force the Offset edit control to have the focus.
        SetFocus(GetDlgItem(hwnd, IDC_OFFSET));
        break;

    case IDC_WRITEBYTE:
        {
        BOOL fTranslated;
        DWORD dwOffset = GetDlgItemInt(hwnd, IDC_OFFSET, &fTranslated, FALSE);
        if (fTranslated) {
            g_mmf[dwOffset * 1024] = (BYTE)
                GetDlgItemInt(hwnd, IDC_BYTE, NULL, FALSE);
            Dlg_ShowAllocatedRanges(hwnd);
        }
        }
        break;

    case IDC_READBYTE:
        {
        BOOL fTranslated;
        DWORD dwOffset = GetDlgItemInt(hwnd, IDC_OFFSET, &fTranslated, FALSE);
        if (fTranslated) {
            SetDlgItemInt(hwnd, IDC_BYTE, g_mmf[dwOffset * 1024], FALSE);
            Dlg_ShowAllocatedRanges(hwnd);
        }
        }
        break;

    case IDC_FREEALLOCATEDREGIONS:
        // Normally the destructor causes the file-mapping to close.
        // But, in this case, we wish to force it so that we can reset
        // a portion of the file back to all zeroes.
        g_mmf.ForceClose();

        // We call ForceClose above because attempting to zero a portion of
        // the file while it is mapped causes DeviceIoControl to fail with
        // error ERROR_USER_MAPPED_FILE ("The requested operation cannot
        // be performed on a file with a user-mapped section open.")
        g_mmf.DecommitPortionOfStream(0, STREAMSIZE);
        g_mmf.Initialize(g_hstream, STREAMSIZE);
        Dlg_ShowAllocatedRanges(hwnd);
        break;
    }
}
```

(continued)

Figure 17-4. *continued*

```
///////////////////////////////////////////////////////////////////////////////


INT_PTR WINAPI Dlg_Proc(HWND hwnd, UINT uMsg, WPARAM wParam, LPARAM lParam) {

   switch (uMsg) {
      chHANDLE_DLGMSG(hwnd, WM_INITDIALOG, Dlg_OnInitDialog);
      chHANDLE_DLGMSG(hwnd, WM_COMMAND,    Dlg_OnCommand);
   }
   return(FALSE);
}



///////////////////////////////////////////////////////////////////////////////


int WINAPI _tWinMain(HINSTANCE hinstExe, HINSTANCE, PTSTR pszCmdLine, int) {

   chWindows2000Required();

   DialogBox(hinstExe, MAKEINTRESOURCE(IDD_MMFSPARSE), NULL, Dlg_Proc);
   return(0);
}


/////////////////////////////// End of File ///////////////////////////////////
```

MMFSparse.rc

```
//Microsoft Developer Studio generated resource script.
//
#include "Resource.h"

#define APSTUDIO_READONLY_SYMBOLS
///////////////////////////////////////////////////////////////////////////////
//
// Generated from the TEXTINCLUDE 2 resource.
//
#include "afxres.h"


///////////////////////////////////////////////////////////////////////////////
#undef APSTUDIO_READONLY_SYMBOLS
```

(continued)

Figure 17-4. *continued*

```
/////////////////////////////////////////////////////////////////////////
// English (U.S.) resources

#if !defined(AFX_RESOURCE_DLL) || defined(AFX_TARG_ENU)
#ifdef _WIN32
LANGUAGE LANG_ENGLISH, SUBLANG_ENGLISH_US
#pragma code_page(1252)
#endif //_WIN32


/////////////////////////////////////////////////////////////////////////
//
// Dialog
//

IDD_MMFSHARE DIALOG DISCARDABLE  38, 36, 186, 61
STYLE WS_MINIMIZEBOX | WS_POPUP | WS_VISIBLE | WS_CAPTION | WS_SYSMENU
CAPTION "Memory-Mapped File Sharing"
FONT 8, "MS Sans Serif"
BEGIN
    PUSHBUTTON      "&Create mapping of Data",IDC_CREATEFILE,4,4,84,14,
                    WS_GROUP
    PUSHBUTTON      "&Close mapping of Data",IDC_CLOSEFILE,96,4,84,14
    LTEXT           "&Data:",IDC_STATIC,4,24,18,8
    EDITTEXT        IDC_DATA,28,24,153,12
    PUSHBUTTON      "&Open mapping and get Data",IDC_OPENFILE,40,44,104,14,
                    WS_GROUP
END


/////////////////////////////////////////////////////////////////////////
//
// Icon
//

// Icon with lowest ID value placed first to ensure application icon
// remains consistent on all systems.
IDI_MMFSHARE            ICON    DISCARDABLE     "MMFShare.Ico"

#ifdef APSTUDIO_INVOKED
/////////////////////////////////////////////////////////////////////////
//
// TEXTINCLUDE
//
```

(continued)

Figure 17-4. *continued*

```
1 TEXTINCLUDE DISCARDABLE
BEGIN
    "Resource.h\0"
END

2 TEXTINCLUDE DISCARDABLE
BEGIN
    "#include ""afxres.h""\r\n"
    "\0"
END

3 TEXTINCLUDE DISCARDABLE
BEGIN
    "\r\n"
    "\0"
END

#endif    // APSTUDIO_INVOKED

#endif    // English (U.S.) resources
/////////////////////////////////////////////////////////////////////////////


#ifndef APSTUDIO_INVOKED
/////////////////////////////////////////////////////////////////////////////
//
// Generated from the TEXTINCLUDE 3 resource.
//


/////////////////////////////////////////////////////////////////////////////
#endif    // not APSTUDIO_INVOKED
```

SparseStream.h

```
/******************************************************************************
Module:  SparseStream.h
Notices: Copyright (c) 2000 Jeffrey Richter
******************************************************************************/
```

(continued)

Figure 17-4. *continued*

```
#include "..\CmnHdr.h"      /* See Appendix A. */
#include <WinIoCtl.h>


///////////////////////////////////////////////////////////////////////////////


#pragma once


///////////////////////////////////////////////////////////////////////////////


class CSparseStream {
public:
   static BOOL DoesFileSystemSupportSparseStreams(PCTSTR pszVolume);
   static BOOL DoesFileContainAnySparseStreams(PCTSTR pszPathname);

public:
   CSparseStream(HANDLE hstream = INVALID_HANDLE_VALUE) {
      Initialize(hstream);
   }

   virtual ~CSparseStream() { }

   void Initialize(HANDLE hstream = INVALID_HANDLE_VALUE) {
      m_hstream = hstream;
   }

public:
   operator HANDLE() const { return(m_hstream); }

public:
   BOOL IsStreamSparse() const;
   BOOL MakeSparse();
   BOOL DecommitPortionOfStream(
      __int64 qwFileOffsetStart, __int64 qwFileOffsetEnd);

   FILE_ALLOCATED_RANGE_BUFFER* QueryAllocatedRanges(PDWORD pdwNumEntries);
   BOOL FreeAllocatedRanges(FILE_ALLOCATED_RANGE_BUFFER* pfarb);

private:
   HANDLE m_hstream;
```

(continued)

Figure 17-4. *continued*

```
private:
   static BOOL AreFlagsSet(DWORD fdwFlagBits, DWORD fFlagsToCheck) {
      return((fdwFlagBits & fFlagsToCheck) == fFlagsToCheck);
   }
};


/////////////////////////////////////////////////////////////////////////////


inline BOOL CSparseStream::DoesFileSystemSupportSparseStreams(
   PCTSTR pszVolume) {

   DWORD dwFileSystemFlags = 0;
   BOOL fOk = GetVolumeInformation(pszVolume, NULL, 0, NULL, NULL,
      &dwFileSystemFlags, NULL, 0);
   fOk = fOk && AreFlagsSet(dwFileSystemFlags, FILE_SUPPORTS_SPARSE_FILES);
   return(fOk);
}


/////////////////////////////////////////////////////////////////////////////


inline BOOL CSparseStream::IsStreamSparse() const {

   BY_HANDLE_FILE_INFORMATION bhfi;
   GetFileInformationByHandle(m_hstream, &bhfi);
   return(AreFlagsSet(bhfi.dwFileAttributes, FILE_ATTRIBUTE_SPARSE_FILE));
}


/////////////////////////////////////////////////////////////////////////////


inline BOOL CSparseStream::MakeSparse() {

   DWORD dw;
   return(DeviceIoControl(m_hstream, FSCTL_SET_SPARSE,
      NULL, 0, NULL, 0, &dw, NULL));
}


/////////////////////////////////////////////////////////////////////////////


inline BOOL CSparseStream::DecommitPortionOfStream(
   __int64 qwOffsetStart, __int64 qwOffsetEnd) {

   // NOTE: This function does not work if this file is memory-mapped.
   DWORD dw;
   FILE_ZERO_DATA_INFORMATION fzdi;
   fzdi.FileOffset.QuadPart = qwOffsetStart;
   fzdi.BeyondFinalZero.QuadPart = qwOffsetEnd + 1;
```

(continued)

Figure 17-4. *continued*

```
   return(DeviceIoControl(m_hstream, FSCTL_SET_ZERO_DATA, (LPVOID) &fzdi,
      sizeof(fzdi), NULL, 0, &dw, NULL));
}

///////////////////////////////////////////////////////////////////////////////

inline BOOL CSparseStream::DoesFileContainAnySparseStreams(
   PCTSTR pszPathname) {

   DWORD dw = GetFileAttributes(pszPathname);
   return((dw == 0xffffffff)
      ? FALSE : AreFlagsSet(dw, FILE_ATTRIBUTE_SPARSE_FILE));
}

///////////////////////////////////////////////////////////////////////////////

inline FILE_ALLOCATED_RANGE_BUFFER* CSparseStream::QueryAllocatedRanges(
   PDWORD pdwNumEntries) {

   FILE_ALLOCATED_RANGE_BUFFER farb;
   farb.FileOffset.QuadPart = 0;
   farb.Length.LowPart =
      GetFileSize(m_hstream, (PDWORD) &farb.Length.HighPart);

   // There is no way to determine the correct memory block size prior to
   // attempting to collect this data, so I just picked 100 * sizeof(*pfarb)
   DWORD cb = 100 * sizeof(farb);
   FILE_ALLOCATED_RANGE_BUFFER* pfarb = (FILE_ALLOCATED_RANGE_BUFFER*)
      HeapAlloc(GetProcessHeap(), HEAP_ZERO_MEMORY, cb);

   DeviceIoControl(m_hstream, FSCTL_QUERY_ALLOCATED_RANGES,
      &farb, sizeof(farb), pfarb, cb, &cb, NULL);
   *pdwNumEntries = cb / sizeof(*pfarb);
   return(pfarb);
}

///////////////////////////////////////////////////////////////////////////////

inline BOOL CSparseStream::FreeAllocatedRanges(
   FILE_ALLOCATED_RANGE_BUFFER* pfarb) {

   // Free the queue entry's allocated memory
   return(HeapFree(GetProcessHeap(), 0, pfarb));
}

/////////////////////////////// End Of File /////////////////////////////////
```

HEAPS

The third and last mechanism for manipulating memory is the use of heaps. Heaps are great for allocating lots of small blocks of data. For example, linked lists and trees are best managed using heaps rather than the virtual memory techniques discussed in Chapter 15 or the memory-mapped file techniques discussed in Chapter 17. The advantage of heaps is that they allow you to ignore all the allocation granularity and page boundary stuff and concentrate on the task at hand. The disadvantage of heaps is that allocating and freeing memory blocks is slower than the other mechanisms and you lose the direct control over the committing and decommitting of physical storage.

Internally, a heap is a region of reserved address space. Initially, most of the pages within the reserved region are not committed with physical storage. As you make more allocations from the heap, the heap manager commits more physical storage to the heap. This physical storage is always allocated from the system's paging file. As you free blocks within a heap, the heap manager decommits the physical storage.

Microsoft does not document the exact rules that the heap follows for committing and decommitting storage—and the rules are different for Microsoft Windows 98 and Windows 2000. I can tell you this: Windows 98 is more concerned with memory usage, so it decommits heap storage as soon as possible. Windows 2000 is more concerned with speed, so it tends to hold on to physical storage longer and returns it to the paging file only after the pages have gone unused for some period of time. Microsoft is constantly performing stress tests and running different scenarios to determine the rules that work best most of the time. As applications and the hardware that runs them change, these rules will change. If this knowledge is critical to your application, don't use heaps. Instead, use the virtual memory functions (that is, *VirtualAlloc* and *VirtualFree*) so you can control these rules yourself.

A Process's Default Heap

When a process initializes, the system creates a heap in the process's address space. This heap is called the process's *default heap*. By default, this heap's region of address space is 1 MB in size. However, the system can grow a process's default heap so that it becomes larger than this. You can change the default region size of 1 MB using the /HEAP linker switch when you create an application. Because a DLL does not have a heap associated with it, you should not use the /HEAP switch when you are linking a DLL. The /HEAP switch has the following syntax:

```
/HEAP:reserve[,commit]
```

Many Windows functions require the process's default heap. For example, the core functions in Windows 2000 perform all of their operations using Unicode characters and strings. If you call an ANSI version of a Windows function, this ANSI version must convert the ANSI strings to Unicode strings and then call the Unicode version of the same function. To convert the strings, the ANSI function needs to allocate a block of memory to hold the Unicode version of the string. This block of memory is allocated from your process's default heap. Many other Windows functions require the use of temporary memory blocks; these blocks are allocated from the process's default heap. Also, the old 16-bit Windows functions *LocalAlloc* and *GlobalAlloc* make their memory allocations from the process's default heap.

Because the process's default heap is used by many of the Windows functions, and because your application has many threads simultaneously calling the various Windows functions, access to the default heap is serialized. In other words, the system guarantees that only one thread at a time can allocate or free blocks of memory in the default heap at any given time. If two threads attempt to simultaneously allocate a block of memory in the default heap, only one thread will be able to allocate a block; the other thread will be forced to wait until the first thread's block is allocated. Once the first thread's block is allocated, the heap functions will allow the second thread to allocate a block. This serialized access causes a small performance hit. If your application has only one thread and you want to have the fastest possible access to a heap, you should create your own separate heap and not use the process's default heap. Unfortunately, you cannot tell the Windows functions not to use the default heap, so their accesses to the heap are always serialized.

A single process can have several heaps at once. These heaps can be created and destroyed during the lifetime of the process. The default heap, however, is created before the process begins execution and is destroyed automatically when the process terminates. You cannot destroy the process's default heap. Each heap is identified with its own heap handle, and all of the heap functions that allocate and free blocks within a heap require this heap handle as a parameter.

You can obtain the handle to your process's default heap by calling *GetProcessHeap*:

```
HANDLE GetProcessHeap();
```

Reasons to Create Additional Heaps

In addition to the process's default heap, you can create additional heaps in your process's address space. You would want to create additional heaps in your own applications for the following reasons:

- Component protection
- More efficient memory management
- Local access
- Avoiding thread synchronization overhead
- Quick Free

Let's examine each reason in detail.

Component Protection

Imagine that your application needs to process two components: a linked list of NODE structures and a binary tree of BRANCH structures. You have two source code files: LnkLst.cpp, which contains the functions that process the linked list of NODEs, and BinTree.cpp, which contains the functions that process the binary tree of BRANCHes.

If the NODEs and the BRANCHes are stored together in a single heap, the combined heap might look like Figure 18-1.

Now let's say that a bug in the linked-list code causes the 8 bytes after NODE 1 to be accidentally overwritten, which in turn causes the data in BRANCH 3 to be corrupted. When the code in BinTree.cpp later attempts to traverse the binary tree, it will probably fail because of this memory corruption. Of course, this will lead you to believe that there is a bug in your binary-tree code when in fact the bug exists in the linked-list code. Because the different types of objects are mixed together in a single heap, tracking down and isolating bugs becomes significantly more difficult.

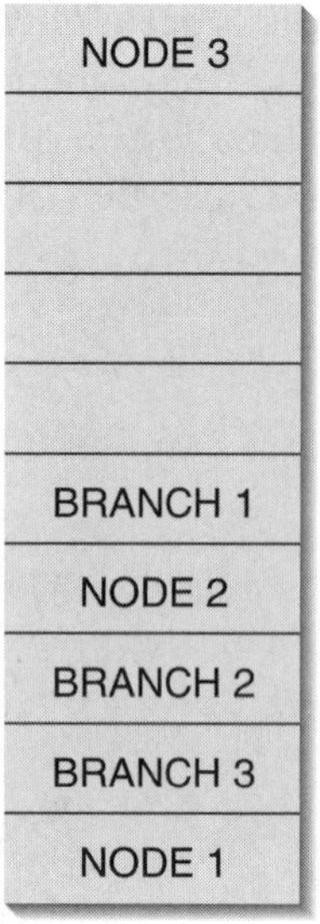

Figure 18-1.
A single heap that stores NODEs and BRANCHes together

By creating two separate heaps—one for NODEs and the other for BRANCHes—you localize your problems. A small bug in your linked-list code does not compromise the integrity of your binary tree, and vice versa. It is still possible to have a bug in your code that causes a wild memory write to another heap, but this is a far less likely scenario.

More Efficient Memory Management

Heaps can be managed more efficiently by allocating objects of the same size within them. For example, let's say that every NODE structure requires 24 bytes and every BRANCH structure requires 32 bytes. All of these objects are allocated from a single heap. Figure 18-2 shows a fully occupied single heap with several NODE and BRANCH objects allocated within it. If NODE 2 and NODE 4 are freed, memory in the heap becomes fragmented. If you then attempt to allocate a BRANCH structure, the allocation will fail even though 48 bytes are available and a BRANCH needs only 32 bytes.

If each heap consisted only of objects that were the same size, freeing an object would guarantee that another object would fit perfectly into the freed object's space.

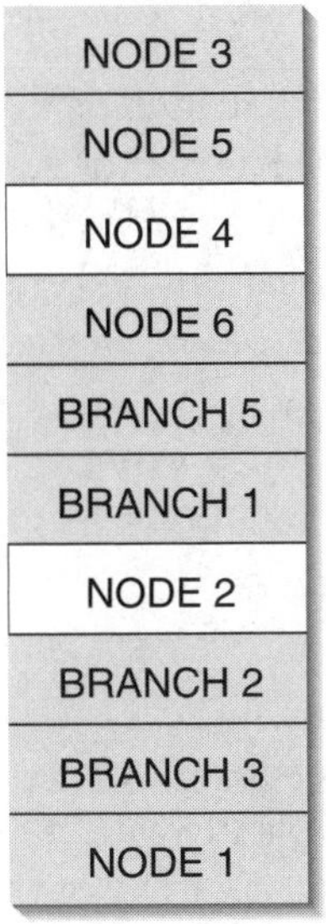

| NODE 3 |
| NODE 5 |
| NODE 4 |
| NODE 6 |
| BRANCH 5 |
| BRANCH 1 |
| NODE 2 |
| BRANCH 2 |
| BRANCH 3 |
| NODE 1 |

Figure 18-2.
A single fragmented heap that contains several NODE and BRANCH objects

Local Access

There is a huge performance penalty whenever the system must swap a page of RAM to and from the system's paging file. If you keep accesses to memory localized to a small range of addresses, it is less likely that the system will need to swap pages between RAM and disk.

So, in designing an application, it's a good idea to allocate things close to each other if they will be accessed together. Returning to our linked list and binary tree example, traversing the linked list is not related in any way to traversing the binary tree. By keeping all the NODEs close together (in one heap), you can keep the NODEs in adjoining pages; in fact, it's likely that several NODEs will fit within a single page of physical memory. Traversing the linked list will not require that the CPU refer to several different pages of memory for each NODE access.

If you were to allocate both NODEs and BRANCHes in a single heap, the NODEs would not necessarily be close together. In a worst-case situation, you might be able to have only one NODE per page of memory, with the remainder of each page occupied by BRANCHes. In this case, traversing the linked list could cause page faults for each NODE, which would make the process extremely slow.

Avoiding Thread Synchronization Overhead

As I'll explain shortly, heaps are serialized by default so that there is no chance of data corruption if multiple threads attempt to access the heap at the same time. However, the heap functions must execute additional code in order to keep the heap thread-safe. If you are performing lots of heap allocations, executing this additional code can really add up, taking a toll on your application's performance. When you create a new heap, you can tell the system that only one thread will access the heap and therefore the additional code will not execute. However, be careful—you are now taking on the responsibility of keeping the heap thread-safe. The system will not be looking out for you.

Quick Free

Finally, using a dedicated heap for some data structures allows you to free the entire heap without having to free each memory block explicitly within the heap. For example, when Windows Explorer walks the directory hierarchy of your hard drive, it must build a tree in memory. If you tell Windows Explorer to refresh its display, it could simply destroy the heap containing the tree and start over (assuming, of course, that it has used a dedicated heap only for the directory tree information). For many applications, this can be extremely convenient— and they'll run faster too.

How to Create an Additional Heap

You can create additional heaps in your process by having a thread call *HeapCreate*:

```
HANDLE HeapCreate(
    DWORD fdwOptions,
    SIZE_T dwInitialSize,
    SIZE_T dwMaximumSize);
```

The first parameter, *fdwOptions*, modifies how operations are performed on the heap. You can specify 0, HEAP_NO_SERIALIZE, HEAP_GENERATE_ EXCEPTIONS, or a combination of the two flags.

By default, a heap will serialize access to itself so that multiple threads can allocate and free blocks from the heap without the danger of corrupting the heap. When an attempt is made to allocate a block of memory from the heap, the *HeapAlloc* function (discussed later) must do the following:

1. Traverse the linked list of allocated and freed memory blocks

2. Find the address of a free block

3. Allocate the new block by marking the free block as allocated

4. Add a new entry to the linked list of memory blocks

Here's an example that illustrates why you should avoid using the HEAP_NO_SERIALIZE flag. Let's say that two threads attempt to allocate blocks of memory from the same heap at the same time. Thread 1 executes steps 1 and 2 above and gets the address of a free memory block. However, before Thread 1 can execute step 3, it is preempted and Thread 2 gets a chance to execute steps 1 and 2. Because Thread 1 has not yet executed step 3, Thread 2 finds the address to the same free memory block.

With both threads having found what they believe to be a free memory block in the heap, Thread 1 updates the linked list, marking the new block as allocated. Thread 2 then also updates the linked list, marking the *same* block as allocated. Neither thread has detected a problem so far, but both threads receive an address to the exact same block of memory.

This type of bug can be very difficult to track down because it usually doesn't manifest itself immediately. Instead, the bug waits in the background until the most inopportune moment. Potential problems are

- The linked list of memory blocks has been corrupted. This problem will not be discovered until an attempt to allocate or free a block is made.

- Both threads are sharing the same memory block. Thread 1 and Thread 2 might both write information to the same block. When Thread 1 examines the contents of the block, it will not recognize the data introduced by Thread 2.

- One thread might proceed to use the block and free it, causing the other thread to overwrite unallocated memory. This will corrupt the heap.

The solution to these problems is to allow a single thread exclusive access to the heap and its linked list until the thread has performed all necessary operations on the heap. The absence of the HEAP_NO_SERIALIZE flag does exactly this. It is safe to use the HEAP_NO_SERIALIZE flag only if one or more of the following conditions are true for your process:

- Your process uses only a single thread.

- Your process uses multiple threads, but only a single thread accesses the heap.

■ Your process uses multiple threads, but manages access to the heap itself by using other forms of mutual exclusion, such as critical sections, mutexes, and semaphores (as discussed in Chapters 8 and 9).

If you're not sure whether to use the HEAP_NO_SERIALIZE flag, don't use it. Not using it will cause your threads to take a slight performance hit whenever a heap function is called, but you won't risk corrupting your heap and its data.

The other flag, HEAP_GENERATE_EXCEPTIONS, causes the system to raise an exception whenever an attempt to allocate or reallocate a block of memory in the heap fails. An exception is just another way for the system to notify your application that an error has occurred. Sometimes it's easier to design your application to look for exceptions rather than to check for return values. Exceptions are discussed in Chapters 23, 24, and 25.

The second parameter of *HeapCreate*, *dwInitialSize*, indicates the number of bytes initially committed to the heap. If necessary, *HeapCreate* rounds this value up to a multiple of the CPU's page size. The final parameter, *dwMaximumSize*, indicates the maximum size to which the heap can expand (the maximum amount of address space the system can reserve for the heap). If *dwMaximumSize* is greater than 0, you are creating a heap that has a maximum size. If you attempt to allocate a block that would cause the heap to go over its maximum, the attempt to allocate the block fails.

If *dwMaximumSize* is 0, you are creating a growable heap, which has no inherent limit. Allocating blocks from the heap simply makes the heap grow until physical storage is exhausted. If the heap is created successfully, *HeapCreate* returns a handle identifying the new heap. This handle is used by the other heap functions.

Allocating a Block of Memory from a Heap

Allocating a block of memory from a heap is simply a matter of calling *HeapAlloc*:

```
PVOID HeapAlloc(
   HANDLE hHeap,
   DWORD fdwFlags,
   SIZE_T dwBytes);
```

The first parameter, *hHeap*, identifies the handle of the heap from which an allocation should be made. The *dwBytes* parameter specifies the number of bytes that are to be allocated from the heap. The middle parameter, *fdwFlags*, allows you to specify flags that affect the allocation. Currently only three flags are supported: HEAP_ZERO_MEMORY, HEAP_GENERATE_EXCEPTIONS, and HEAP_NO_SERIALIZE.

The purpose of the HEAP_ZERO_MEMORY flag should be fairly obvious. This flag causes the contents of the block to be filled with zeros before *HeapAlloc* returns. The second flag, HEAP_GENERATE_EXCEPTIONS, causes the *HeapAlloc* function to raise a software exception if insufficient memory is available in the heap to satisfy the request. When creating a heap with *Heap-Create*, you can specify the HEAP_GENERATE_EXCEPTIONS flag, which tells the heap that an exception should be raised when a block cannot be allocated. If you specify this flag when calling *HeapCreate*, you don't need to specify it when calling *HeapAlloc*. On the other hand, you might want to create the heap without using this flag. In this case, specifying this flag to *HeapAlloc* affects only the single call to *HeapAlloc*, not every call to this function.

If *HeapAlloc* fails and then raises an exception, the exception raised will be one of the two shown in the following table.

Identifier	Meaning
STATUS_NO_MEMORY	The allocation attempt failed because of insufficient memory.
STATUS_ACCESS_VIOLATION	The allocation attempt failed because of heap corruption or improper function parameters.

If the block has been successfully allocated, *HeapAlloc* returns the address of the block. If the memory could not be allocated and HEAP_GENERATE_EXCEPTIONS was not specified, *HeapAlloc* returns NULL.

The last flag, HEAP_NO_SERIALIZE, allows you to force this individual call to *HeapAlloc* to not be serialized with other threads that are accessing the same heap. You should use this flag with extreme caution because the heap could become corrupted if other threads are manipulating the heap at the same time. Never use this flag when making an allocation from your process's default heap, as data could become corrupted: Other threads in your process could access the default heap at the same time.

WINDOWS 98

Calling *HeapAlloc* and requesting a block larger than 256 MB is considered by Windows 98 an error—the call fails. Note that in this case, the function always returns NULL and will not raise an exception, even if you used the HEAP_GENERATE_EXCEPTIONS flag when creating the heap or when attempting to allocate the block.

> **NOTE** It is recommended that you use *VirtualAlloc* when allocating large blocks (around 1 MB or more). Avoid using the heap functions for such large allocations.

Changing the Size of a Block

Often it's necessary to alter the size of a memory block. Some applications initially allocate a larger than necessary block and then, after all the data has been placed into the block, reduce the size of the block. Some applications begin by allocating a small block of memory and then attempting to enlarge the block when more data needs to be copied into it. Resizing a memory block is accomplished by calling the *HeapReAlloc* function:

```
PVOID HeapReAlloc(
    HANDLE hHeap,
    DWORD fdwFlags,
    PVOID pvMem,
    SIZE_T dwBytes);
```

As always, the *hHeap* parameter indicates the heap containing the block you want to resize. The *fdwFlags* parameter specifies the flags that *HeapReAlloc* should use when attempting to resize the block. Only the following four flags are available: HEAP_GENERATE_EXCEPTIONS, HEAP_NO_SERIALIZE, HEAP_ZERO_MEMORY, and HEAP_REALLOC_IN_PLACE_ONLY.

The first two flags have the same meaning as when they are used with *HeapAlloc*. The HEAP_ZERO_MEMORY flag is useful only when you are resizing a block to make it larger. In this case, the additional bytes in the block will be zeroed. This flag has no effect if the block is being reduced.

The HEAP_REALLOC_IN_PLACE_ONLY flag tells *HeapReAlloc* that it is not allowed to move the memory block within the heap, which *HeapReAlloc* might attempt to do if the memory block were growing. If *HeapReAlloc* is able to enlarge the memory block without moving it, it will do so and return the original address of the memory block. On the other hand, if *HeapReAlloc* must move the contents of the block, the address of the new, larger block is returned. If the block is made smaller, *HeapReAlloc* returns the original address of the memory block. You would want to specify the HEAP_REALLOC_IN_PLACE_ONLY flag if the block were part of a linked list or tree. In this case, other nodes in the list or tree might have pointers to this node, and relocating the node in the heap would corrupt the integrity of the linked list.

The remaining two parameters, *pvMem* and *dwBytes*, specify the current address of the block that you want to resize and the new size—in bytes—

of the block. *HeapReAlloc* returns either the address of the new, resized block or NULL if the block cannot be resized.

Obtaining the Size of a Block

After a memory block has been allocated, the *HeapSize* function can be called to retrieve the actual size of the block:

```
SIZE_T HeapSize(
    HANDLE hHeap,
    DWORD fdwFlags,
    LPCVOID pvMem);
```

The *hHeap* parameter identifies the heap, and the *pvMem* parameter indicates the address of the block. The *fdwFlags* parameter can be either 0 or HEAP_NO_SERIALIZE.

Freeing a Block

When you no longer need the memory block, you can free it by calling *HeapFree*:

```
BOOL HeapFree(
    HANDLE hHeap,
    DWORD fdwFlags,
    PVOID pvMem);
```

HeapFree frees the memory block and returns TRUE if successful. The *fdwFlags* parameter can be either 0 or HEAP_NO_SERIALIZE. Calling this function might cause the heap manager to decommit some physical storage, but there are no guarantees.

Destroying a Heap

If your application no longer needs a heap that it created, you can destroy the heap by calling *HeapDestroy*:

```
BOOL HeapDestroy(HANDLE hHeap);
```

Calling *HeapDestroy* causes all the memory blocks contained within the heap to be freed and also causes the physical storage and reserved address space region occupied by the heap to be released back to the system. If the function is successful, *HeapDestroy* returns TRUE. If you don't explicitly destroy the heap before your process terminates, the system will destroy it for you. However, a heap is destroyed only when a process terminates. If a thread creates a heap, the heap won't be destroyed when the thread terminates.

The system will not allow the process's default heap to be destroyed until the process completely terminates. If you pass the handle to the process's default heap to *HeapDestroy*, the system simply ignores the call.

Using Heaps with C++

One of the best ways to take advantage of heaps is to incorporate them into existing C++ programs. In C++, calling the *new* operator—instead of the normal C run-time routine *malloc*—performs class-object allocation. Then, when we no longer need the class object, the *delete* operator is called instead of the normal C run-time routine *free*. For example, let's say we have a class called CSomeClass and we want to allocate an instance of this class. To do this, we would use syntax similar to the following:

```
CSomeClass* pSomeClass = new CSomeClass;
```

When the C++ compiler examines this line, it first checks whether the CSomeClass class contains a member function for the *new* operator; if it does, the compiler generates code to call this function. If the compiler doesn't find a function overloading the *new* operator, the compiler generates code to call the standard C++ *new* operator function.

After you're done using the allocated object, you can destroy it by calling the *delete* operator:

```
delete pSomeClass;
```

By overloading the *new* and *delete* operators for our C++ class, we can easily take advantage of the heap functions. To do this, let's define our CSomeClass class in a header file like this:

```
class CSomeClass {
private:

    static HANDLE s_hHeap;
    static UINT s_uNumAllocsInHeap;

    // Other private data and member functions
    :
    :

public:
    void* operator new (size_t size);
    void operator delete (void* p);
    // Other public data and member functions
    :
    :

};
```

In this code fragment, I've declared two member variables, *s_hHeap* and *s_uNumAllocsInHeap*, as static variables. Because they are static, C++ will make all instances of CSomeClass share the same variables; that is, C++ will *not* allocate separate *s_hHeap* and *s_uNumAllocsInHeap* variables for each instance of the class that is created. This fact is important to us because we want all of our instances of CSomeClass to be allocated within the same heap.

The *s_hHeap* variable will contain the handle to the heap within which CSomeClass objects should be allocated. The *s_uNumAllocsInHeap* variable is simply a counter of how many CSomeClass objects have been allocated within the heap. Every time a new CSomeClass object is allocated in the heap, *s_uNum-AllocsInHeap* is incremented, and every time a CSomeClass object is destroyed, *s_uNumAllocsInHeap* is decremented. When *s_uNumAllocsInHeap* reaches 0, the heap is no longer necessary and is freed. The code to manipulate the heap should be included in a .cpp file that looks like this:

```
HANDLE CSomeClass::s_hHeap = NULL;
UINT CSomeClass::s_uNumAllocsInHeap = 0;

void* CSomeClass::operator new (size_t size) {
   if (s_hHeap == NULL) {
      // Heap does not exist; create it.
      s_hHeap = HeapCreate(HEAP_NO_SERIALIZE, 0, 0);

      if (s_hHeap == NULL)
         return(NULL);
   }
   // The heap exists for CSomeClass objects.
   void* p = HeapAlloc(s_hHeap, 0, size);

   if (p != NULL) {
      // Memory was allocated successfully; increment
      // the count of CSomeClass objects in the heap.
      s_uNumAllocsInHeap++;
   }

   // Return the address of the allocated CSomeClass object.
   return(p);
}
```

Notice that I first defined the two static member variables, *s_hHeap* and *s_uNum-AllocsInHeap*, at the top and initialized them as NULL and 0, respectively.

The C++ *new* operator receives one parameter—*size*. This parameter indicates the number of bytes required to hold a CSomeClass object. The first task for our *new* operator function is to create a heap if one hasn't been created already. This is simply a matter of checking the *s_hHeap* variable to see whether it is NULL. If it is, a new heap is created by calling *HeapCreate*, and the handle that *HeapCreate* returns is saved in *s_hHeap* so that the next call to the *new* operator will not create another heap but rather will use the heap we have just created.

When I called the *HeapCreate* function above, I used the HEAP_NO_ SERIALIZE flag because the remainder of the sample code is not multithread-safe. The other two parameters in the call to *HeapCreate* indicate the initial size and the maximum size of the heap, respectively. I chose 0 and 0 here. The first 0 means that the heap has no initial size; the second 0 means that the heap expands as needed. Depending on your needs, you might want to change either or both of these values.

You might think it would be worthwhile to pass the *size* parameter to the *new* operator function as the second parameter to *HeapCreate*. In this way, you could initialize the heap so that it is large enough to contain one instance of the class. Then, the first time that *HeapAlloc* is called, it would execute faster because the heap wouldn't have to resize itself to hold the class instance. Unfortunately, things don't always work the way you want them to. Because each allocated memory block within the heap has an associated overhead, the call to *HeapAlloc* will still have to resize the heap so that it is large enough to contain the one class instance and its associated overhead.

Once the heap has been created, new CSomeClass objects can be allocated from it using *HeapAlloc*. The first parameter is the handle to the heap, and the second parameter is the size of the CSomeClass object. *HeapAlloc* returns the address to the allocated block.

When the allocation is performed successfully, I increment the *s_uNumAllocsInHeap* variable so that I know there is one more allocation in the heap. The last thing the *new* operator does is return the address of the newly allocated CSomeClass object.

Well, that's it for creating a new CSomeClass object. Let's turn our attention to destroying a CSomeClass object when our application no longer needs it. This is the responsibility of the *delete* operator function, coded as follows:

```
void CSomeClass::operator delete (void* p) {
   if (HeapFree(s_hHeap, 0, p)) {
      // Object was deleted successfully.
      s_uNumAllocsInHeap--;
   }

   if (s_uNumAllocsInHeap == 0) {
      // If there are no more objects in the heap,
      // destroy the heap.
```

```
    if (HeapDestroy(s_hHeap)) {
        // Set the heap handle to NULL so that the new operator
        // will know to create a new heap if a new CSomeClass
        // object is created.
        s_hHeap = NULL;
    }
  }
}
```

The *delete* operator function receives only one parameter: the address of the object being deleted. The first thing the function does is call *HeapFree*, passing it the handle of the heap and the address of the object to be freed. If the object is freed successfully, *s_uNumAllocsInHeap* is decremented, indicating that one fewer CSomeClass object is in the heap. Next the function checks whether *s_uNumAllocsInHeap* is 0. If it is, the function calls *HeapDestroy*, passing it the heap handle. If the heap is destroyed successfully, *s_hHeap* is set to NULL. This is extremely important because our program might attempt to allocate another CSomeClass object sometime in the future. When it does, the *new* operator will be called and will examine the *s_hHeap* variable to determine whether it should use an existing heap or create a new one.

This example demonstrates a convenient scheme for using multiple heaps. The example is easy to set up and can be incorporated into several of your classes. You will probably want to give some thought to inheritance, however. If you derive a new class using CSomeClass as a base class, the new class will inherit CSomeClass's *new* and *delete* operators. The new class will also inherit CSomeClass's heap, which means that when the *new* operator is applied to the derived class, the memory for the derived class object will be allocated from the same heap that CSomeClass is using. Depending on your situation, this might or might not be what you want. If the objects are very different in size, you might be setting yourself up for a situation in which the heap could fragment badly. You might also be making it harder to track down bugs in your code, as mentioned in the sections "Component Protection" and "More Efficient Memory Management" earlier in this chapter.

If you want to use a separate heap for derived classes, simply duplicate what I did in the CSomeClass class. More specifically, include another set of *s_hHeap* and *s_uNumAllocsInHeap* variables, and copy the code over for the *new* and *delete* operators. When you compile, the compiler will see that you have overloaded the *new* and *delete* operators for the derived class and will make calls to those functions instead of to the ones in the base class.

The only advantage to not creating a heap for each class is that you won't need to devote overhead and memory to each heap. However, the amount of overhead and memory the heaps tie up is not great and is probably worth the potential gains. The compromise might be to have each class use its own heap and to let derived classes share the base class's heap when your application has been well tested and is close to shipping. But be aware that fragmentation might still be a problem.

Miscellaneous Heap Functions

In addition to the heap functions I've already mentioned, Windows offers several more. In this section, I'll just briefly mention them.

The ToolHelp functions (mentioned at the end of Chapter 4) allow you to enumerate a process's heaps as well as the allocations within those heaps. For more information, look up the following functions in the Platform SDK documentation: *Heap32First*, *Heap32Next*, *Heap32ListFirst*, and *Heap32ListNext*. What's great about the ToolHelp functions is that they are available in both Windows 98 and Windows 2000.

The remaining heap functions discussed in this section exist only in Windows 2000.

Since a process can have multiple heaps within its address space, the *Get-ProcessHeaps* function allows you to get the handles of the existing heaps:

```
DWORD GetProcessHeaps(
   DWORD dwNumHeaps,
   PHANDLE pHeaps);
```

To call *GetProcessHeaps*, you must first allocate an array of HANDLEs and then call the function as follows:

```
HANDLE hHeaps[25];
DWORD dwHeaps = GetProcessHeaps(25, hHeaps);
if (dwHeaps > 25) {
   // More heaps are in this process than we expected.
} else {
   // hHeaps[0] through hHeap[dwHeaps - 1]
   // identify the existing heaps.
}
```

Note that the handle of your process's default heap is also included in the array of heap handles when this function returns. The *HeapValidate* function validates the integrity of a heap:

```
BOOL HeapValidate(
   HANDLE hHeap,
   DWORD fdwFlags,
   LPCVOID pvMem);
```

You will usually call this function by passing a heap handle, a flag of 0 (the only other legal flag is HEAP_NO_SERIALIZE), and NULL for *pvMem*. This function will then walk the blocks within the heap, making sure that no blocks are corrupt. To make the function execute faster, you might want to pass the address of a specific block for the *pvMem* parameter. Doing so causes the function to check the validity of only the single block.

To coalesce free blocks within a heap and also decommit any pages of storage that do not contain allocated heap blocks, you can call

```
UINT HeapCompact(
    HANDLE hHeap,
    DWORD fdwFlags);
```

Normally, you'll pass 0 for the *fdwFlags* parameter, but you can also pass HEAP_NO_SERIALIZE.

The next two functions, *HeapLock* and *HeapUnlock*, are used together:

```
BOOL HeapLock(HANDLE hHeap);
BOOL HeapUnlock(HANDLE hHeap);
```

These functions are for thread synchronization purposes. When you call *HeapLock*, the calling thread becomes the owner of the specified heap. If any other thread calls a heap function (specifying the same heap handle), the system will suspend the calling thread and not allow it to wake until the heap is unlocked by calling *HeapUnlock*.

Functions such as *HeapAlloc*, *HeapSize*, *HeapFree*, and so on call *HeapLock* and *HeapUnlock* internally to make sure that access to the heap is serialized. It would be unusual for you ever to have to call *HeapLock* or *HeapUnlock* yourself.

The final heap function is *HeapWalk*:

```
BOOL HeapWalk(
    HANDLE hHeap,
    PPROCESS_HEAP_ENTRY pHeapEntry);
```

This function is useful for debugging purposes only. It allows you to walk the contents of a heap. You will call this function multiple times. Each time, you'll pass in the address of a PROCESS_HEAP_ENTRY structure that you must allocate and initialize:

```
typedef struct _PROCESS_HEAP_ENTRY {
    PVOID lpData;
    DWORD cbData;
    BYTE cbOverhead;
```

(continued)

```
      BYTE iRegionIndex;
      WORD wFlags;
      union {
         struct {
            HANDLE hMem;
            DWORD dwReserved[ 3 ];
         } Block;
         struct {
            DWORD dwCommittedSize;
            DWORD dwUnCommittedSize;
            LPVOID lpFirstBlock;
            LPVOID lpLastBlock;
         } Region;
      };
   } PROCESS_HEAP_ENTRY, *LPPROCESS_HEAP_ENTRY, *PPROCESS_HEAP_ENTRY;
```

When you start enumerating the blocks in the heap, you'll have to set the *lpData* member to NULL. This tells *HeapWalk* to initialize the members inside the structure. You can examine the members of the structure after each successful call to *HeapWalk*. To get to the next block in the heap, you just call *HeapWalk* again, passing the same heap handle and the address of the PROCESS_HEAP_ENTRY structure you passed on the previous call. When *HeapWalk* returns FALSE, there are no more blocks in the heap. See the Platform SDK documentation for a description of the members in the structure.

You will probably want to use the *HeapLock* and *HeapUnlock* functions around your *HeapWalk* loop so that other threads cannot allocate and free blocks of memory inside the heap while you're walking it.

PART IV

DYNAMIC-LINK LIBRARIES

CHAPTER NINETEEN

DLL Basics

Dynamic-link libraries (DLLs) have been the cornerstone of Microsoft Windows since the first version of the operating system. All the functions in the Windows API are contained in DLLs. The three most important DLLs are Kernel32.dll, which contains functions for managing memory, processes, and threads; User32.dll, which contains functions for performing user-interface tasks such as window creation and message sending; and GDI32.dll, which contains functions for drawing graphical images and displaying text.

Windows also comes with several other DLLs that offer functions for performing more specialized tasks. For example, AdvAPI32.dll contains functions for object security, registry manipulation, and event logging; ComDlg32.dll contains the common dialog boxes (such as File Open and File Save); and ComCtl32.DLL supports all of the common window controls.

In this chapter, you'll learn how to create DLLs for your own applications. Here are some reasons for using DLLs:

- **They extend the features of an application.**   Since DLLs can be dynamically loaded into a process's address space, an application can determine at run time what actions to perform and then load the code to execute those actions on demand. For example, a DLL is useful when one company creates a product and wants to allow other companies to extend or enhance the product.

- **They can be written in many programming languages.**   You can choose the best language for the job at hand. Perhaps your application's user interface is best programmed with Microsoft Visual Basic, but the business logic is better handled by C++. The system allows a Visual Basic program to load a C++ DLL, a Cobol DLL, a Fortran DLL, and so on.

- **They simplify project management.** If different groups work on different modules during the development process, the project is easier to manage. However, an application should ship with as few files as possible. I know of one company that shipped a product with one hundred DLLs—up to five DLLs per programmer. The application's initialization time was horribly slow because the system had to open one hundred disk files before the program could do anything.

- **They help conserve memory.** If two or more applications use the same DLL, the DLL has its pages in RAM once and the pages are shared by all of the applications. The C/C++ run-time library is a perfect example. Many applications use this library. If all these applications link to the static library, the code for functions such as *sprintf*, *strcpy*, *malloc*, and so on exist in memory multiple times. However, if all these applications link to the DLL C/C++ run-time library, the code for these functions is in memory only once, which means that memory is used more efficiently.

- **They facilitate resource sharing.** DLLs can contain resources such as dialog box templates, strings, icons, and bitmaps. Multiple applications can use DLLs to share these resources.

- **They facilitate localization.** Applications frequently use DLLs to localize themselves. For example, an application that contains only code and no user interface components can load the DLL containing localized user interface components.

- **They help resolve platform differences.** The various versions of Windows offer different functions. Frequently, developers want to call new functions if they exist on the host version. However, if your source code contains a call to a new function and your application is about to run on a version of Windows that doesn't offer that function, the operating system loader will refuse to run your process. This is true even if you never actually call the function. If you keep these new functions in a DLL, however, applications can load on an older version of Windows. Of course, you still cannot successfully call the function.

- **They can serve special purposes.** Windows makes certain features available only to DLLs. For example, you can install certain hooks (set using *SetWindowsHookEx* and *SetWinEventHook*) only if the hook notification function is contained in a DLL. You can extend Windows Explorer's shell by creating COM objects that must live inside a DLL. The same is true for ActiveX controls that can be loaded by a Web browser to create rich Web pages.

DLLs and a Process's Address Space

It is often easier to create a DLL than to create an application because a DLL usually consists of a set of autonomous functions that any application can use. There is usually no support code for processing message loops or creating windows within DLLs. A DLL is simply a set of source code modules, with each module containing a set of functions that an application (executable file) or another DLL will call. After all the source code files have been compiled, they are linked by the linker just as an application's executable file would be. However, for a DLL you must specify the /DLL switch to the linker. This switch causes the linker to emit slightly different information into the resulting DLL file image so that the operating system loader recognizes the file image as a DLL rather than an application.

Before an application (or another DLL) can call functions in a DLL, the DLL's file image must be mapped into the calling process's address space. You can do this using one of two methods: implicit load-time linking or explicit run-time linking. Implicit linking is discussed later in this chapter; explicit linking is discussed in Chapter 20.

Once a DLL's file image is mapped into the calling process's address space, the DLL's functions are available to all the threads running within the process. In fact, the DLL loses almost all of its identity as a DLL: To the threads in the process, the DLL's code and data simply look like additional code and data that happen to be in the process's address space. When a thread calls a DLL function, the DLL function looks at the thread's stack to retrieve its passed parameters and uses the thread's stack for any local variables that it needs. In addition, any objects created by code in the DLL's functions are owned by the calling thread or process—a DLL never owns anything.

For example, if *VirtualAlloc* is called by a function in a DLL, the region of address space is reserved from the address space of the calling thread's process. If the DLL is later unmapped from the process's address space, the address space region remains reserved because the system does not keep track of the fact that a function in the DLL reserved the region. The reserved region is owned by the process and is freed only if a thread somehow calls the *VirtualFree* function or if the process terminates.

As you know, the global and static variables of an executable file are not shared between multiple running instances of the same executable. Windows 98 ensures this by allocating storage for the executable file's global and static variables when the executable file is mapped into the process's address space; Windows 2000 ensures this by using the copy-on-write mechanism discussed in Chapter 13. Global and static variables in a DLL are handled in exactly the same way. When one process maps a DLL image file into its address space, the system creates instances of the global and static data variables as well.

> **NOTE**
>
> It is important to realize that a single address space consists of one executable module and several DLL modules. Some of these modules can link to a static version of the C/C++ run-time library, some of these modules might link to a DLL version of the C/C++ run-time library, and some of these modules (if not written in C/C++) might not require the C/C++ run-time library at all. Many developers make a common mistake because they forget that several C/C++ run-time libraries can be present in a single address space. Examine the following code:
>
> ```
> VOID EXEFunc() {
>    PVOID pv = DLLFunc();
>    // Access the storage pointed to by pv...
>    // Assumes that pv is in EXE's C/C++ run-time heap
>    free(pv);
> }
>
> PVOID DLLFunc() {
>    // Allocate block from DLL's C/C++ run-time heap
>    return(malloc(100));
> }
> ```
>
> So, what do you think? Does the code above work correctly? Is the block allocated by the DLL's function freed by the EXE's function? The answer is: maybe. The code shown does not give you enough information. If both the EXE and the DLL link to the DLL C/C++ run-time library, the code above works just fine. However, if one or both of the modules link to the static C/C++ run-time library, the call to *free* fails. I have seen developers write code similar to this too many times, and it has burned them all.
>
> There is an easy fix for this problem. When a module offers a function that allocates memory, the module must also offer a function that frees memory. Let me rewrite the code above:

(continued)

```
VOID EXEFunc() {
    PVOID pv = DLLFunc();
    // Access the storage pointed to by pv...
    // Makes no assumptions about C/C++ run-time heap
    DLLFreeFunc(pv);
}

PVOID DLLFunc() {
    // Allocate block from DLL's C/C++ run-time heap
    PVOID pv = malloc(100);
    return(pv);
}

BOOL DLLFreeFunc(PVOID pv) {
    // Free block from DLL's C/C++ run-time heap
    return(free(pv));
}
```

This code is correct and will always work. When you write a module, don't forget that functions in other modules might not even be written in C/C++ and therefore might not use *malloc* and *free* for memory allocations. Be careful not to make these assumptions in your code. By the way, this same argument holds true for the C++ *new* and *delete* operators while calling *malloc* and *free* internally.

The Overall Picture

To fully understand how DLLs work and how you and the system use DLLs, let's start out by examining the whole picture. Figure 19-1 summarizes how the components fit together.

For now, we'll concentrate on how executable and DLL modules implicitly link to one another. Implicit linking is by far the most common type of linking. Windows also supports explicit linking (which we'll discuss in Chapter 20).

As you can see in Figure 19-1, several files and components come into play when a module (such as an executable file) makes use of functions and variables in a DLL. To simplify the discussion, I'll refer to "executable modules" as importing functions and variables from a DLL and "DLL modules" as exporting functions and variables for an executable module. However, be aware that DLL modules can (and often do) import functions and variables that are contained in other DLL modules.

679

BUILDING THE DLL

1) Header with *exported* prototypes/structures/symbols
2) C/C++ source files implementing exported functions/variables
3) Compiler produces .obj file for each C/C++ source file
4) Linker combines .obj module producing DLL
5) Linker also produces .lib file if at least one function/variable is exported

BUILDING THE EXE

6) Header with *imported* prototypes/structures/symbols
7) C/C++ source files referencing imported functions/variables
8) Compiler produces .obj file for each C/C++ source file
9) Linker combines .obj modules resolving references to imported functions/variables using .lib file producing .exe (containing import table-list of required DLLs and imported symbols)

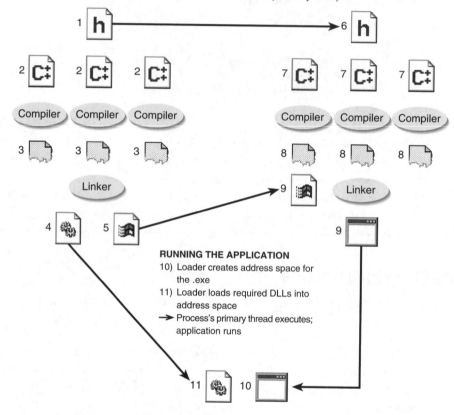

RUNNING THE APPLICATION

10) Loader creates address space for the .exe
11) Loader loads required DLLs into address space
→ Process's primary thread executes; application runs

Figure 19-1.
How a DLL is created and implicitly linked by an application

To build an executable module that imports functions and variables from a DLL module, you must first build the DLL module. Then you can build the executable module.

Building a DLL requires the following steps:

1. You must first create a header file, which contains the function prototypes, structures, and symbols that you want to export from the DLL. This header file is included by all of your DLL's source code modules to help build the DLL. As you'll see later, this same header file is required when you build an executable module (or modules) that uses the functions and variables contained in your DLL.

2. You create the C/C++ source code module (or modules) that implements the functions and variables that you want in the DLL module. Since these source code modules are not required to build an executable module, the DLL company's source code can remain a company secret.

3. Building the DLL module causes the compiler to process each source code module, producing an .obj module (one .obj module per source code module).

4. After all of the .obj modules are created, the linker combines the contents of all the .obj modules and produces a single DLL image file. This image file (or module) contains all the binary code and global/static data variables for the DLL. This file is required in order to execute the executable module.

5. If the linker detects that the DLL's source code module exports at least one function or variable, the linker also produces a single .lib file. This .lib file is small because it contains no functions or variables. It simply lists all the exported function and variable symbol names. This file is required in order to build the executable module.

Once you build the DLL module, you can build the executable module. These steps are

6. In all of the source modules that reference functions, variables, data structures, or symbols, you must include the header file created by the DLL developer.

7. You create the C/C++ source code module (or modules) that implements the functions and variables that you want in the executable module. The code can, of course, reference functions and variables defined in the DLL's header file.

8. Building the executable module causes the compiler to process each source code module, producing an .obj module (one .obj module per source code module).

9. After all of the .obj modules are created, the linker combines the contents of all the .obj modules and produces a single executable image file. This image file (or module) contains all the binary code and global/static data variables for the executable. The executable module also contains an import section that lists all the DLL module names required by this executable. (See Chapter 17 for more on sections.) In addition, for each DLL name listed, the section indicates which function and variable symbols are referenced by the executable's binary code. The operating system loader parses the import section, as you'll see in a moment.

Once the DLL and the executable modules are built, a process can execute. When you attempt to run the executable module, the operating system's loader performs the following steps:

10. The loader creates a virtual address space for the new process. The executable module is mapped into the new process's address space. The loader parses the executable module's import section. For every DLL name listed in the section, the loader locates the DLL module on the user's system and maps that DLL into the process's address space. Note that since a DLL module can import functions and variables from another DLL module, a DLL module might have its own import section. To fully initialize a process, the loader parses every module's import section and maps all required DLL modules into the process's address space. As you can see, initializing a process can be time consuming.

Once the executable module and all of the DLL modules have been mapped into the process's address space, the process's primary thread can start executing and the application can run. The next few sections go into the process in further detail.

Building the DLL Module

When you create a DLL, you create a set of functions that an executable module (or other DLLs) can call. A DLL can export variables, functions, or C++ classes to other modules. In real life, you should avoid exporting variables because this removes a level of abstraction in your code and makes it more difficult to maintain your DLL's code. In addition, C++ classes can be exported only if the modules importing the C++ class are compiled using a compiler from the same vendor. For this reason, you should also avoid exporting C++ classes unless you know that the executable module developers use the same tools as the DLL module developers.

When you create a DLL, you should first establish a header file that contains the variables (type and name) and functions (prototype and name) that you want to export. This header file must also define any symbols and data structures that are used with the exported functions and variables. All of your DLL's source code modules should include this header file. Also, you must distribute this header file so that it can be included in any source code that might import these functions or variables. Having a single header file used by the DLL builder and the executable builder makes maintenance much easier.

Here is how you should code the single header file to include in both the executable and the DLL's source code files:

```
/****************************************************************************
Module:  MyLib.h
****************************************************************************/


#ifdef MYLIBAPI

// MYLIBAPI should be defined in all of the DLL's source
// code modules before this header file is included.

// All functions/variables are being exported.

#else

// This header file is included by an EXE source code module.
// Indicate that all functions/variables are being imported.
#define MYLIBAPI extern "C" __declspec(dllimport)

#endif


///////////////////////////////////////////////////////////////////////////
```

(continued)

```
// Define any data structures and symbols here.

///////////////////////////////////////////////////////////////////////////////

// Define exported variables here. (NOTE: Avoid exporting variables.)
MYLIBAPI int g_nResult;

///////////////////////////////////////////////////////////////////////////////

// Define exported function prototypes here.
MYLIBAPI int Add(int nLeft, int nRight);

//////////////////////////// End of File /////////////////////////////////////
```

In each of your DLL's source code files, you should include the header file as follows:

```
/******************************************************************************
Module: MyLibFile1.cpp
******************************************************************************/


// Include the standard Windows and C-Runtime header files here.
#include <windows.h>


// This DLL source code file exports functions and variables.
#define MYLIBAPI extern "C" __declspec(dllexport)

// Include the exported data structures, symbols, functions, and variables.
#include "MyLib.h"

///////////////////////////////////////////////////////////////////////////////

// Place the code for this DLL source code file here.
int g_nResult;


int Add(int nLeft, int nRight) {
   g_nResult = nLeft + nRight;
   return(g_nResult);
}


//////////////////////////// End of File /////////////////////////////////////
```

When the DLL source code file above is compiled, MYLIBAPI is defined using __*declspec(dllexport)* before the MyLib.h header file. When the compiler sees __*declspec(dllexport)* modifying a variable, function, or C++ class, it knows that this variable, function, or C++ class is to be exported from the resulting DLL module. Notice that the MYLIBAPI identifier is placed in the header file before the definition of the variable to export and before the function to export.

Also notice that inside the source code file (MyLibFile1.cpp), the MYLIBAPI identifier does not appear before the exported variable and function. The MYLIBAPI identifier is not necessary here because the compiler remembers which variables or functions to export when it parses the header file.

You'll notice that the MYLIBAPI symbol includes the *extern "C"* modifier. You should use this modifier only if you are writing C++ code, not straight C code. Normally, C++ compilers mangle function and variable names, which can lead to severe linker problems. For example, imagine writing a DLL in C++ and an executable in straight C. When you build the DLL, the function name is mangled, but when you build the executable, the function name is not mangled. When the linker attempts to link the executable, it will complain that the executable refers to a symbol that does not exist. Using *extern "C"* tells the compiler not to mangle the variable or function names and thereby make the variable or function accessible to executable modules written in C, C++, or any other programming language.

So now you see how the DLL's source code files use this header file. But what about the executable's source code files? Well, executable source code files should not define MYLIBAPI before this header file. Since MYLIBAPI is not defined, the header file defines MYLIBAPI as __*declspec(dllimport)*. The compiler sees that the executable's source code imports variables and functions from the DLL module.

If you examine Microsoft's standard Windows header files, such as WinBase.h, you'll see that Microsoft uses basically the same technique that I've just described.

What Exporting Really Means

The only truly interesting thing I introduced in the previous section was the __*declspec(dllexport)* modifier. When Microsoft's C/C++ compiler sees this modifier before a variable, function prototype, or C++ class, it embeds some additional information in the resulting .obj file. The linker parses this information when all of the .obj files for the DLL are linked.

When the DLL is linked, the linker detects this embedded information about the exported variable, function, or class and automatically produces a .lib file. This .lib file contains the list of symbols exported by the DLL. This .lib file is, of course, required to link any executable module that references this DLL's exported symbols. In addition to creating the .lib file, the linker embeds a table of exported symbols in the resulting DLL file. This *export section* contains the list (in alphabetical order) of exported variables, functions, and class symbols. The linker also places the relative virtual address (RVA) indicating where each symbol can be found in the DLL module.

Using Microsoft Visual Studio's DumpBin.exe utility (with the -exports switch), you can see what a DLL's export section looks like. The following is a fragment of Kernel32.dll's export section. (I've removed some of DUMPBIN's output so that it won't occupy too many pages in this book.)

```
C:\WINNT\SYSTEM32>DUMPBIN -exports Kernel32.DLL

Microsoft (R) COFF Binary File Dumper Version 6.00.8168
Copyright (C) Microsoft Corp 1992-1998. All rights reserved.


Dump of file kernel32.dll

File Type: DLL

  Section contains the following exports for KERNEL32.dll

           0 characteristics
    36DB3213 time date stamp Mon Mar 01 16:34:27 1999
        0.00 version
           1 ordinal base
         829 number of functions
         829 number of names

    ordinal hint RVA      name

          1    0 0001A3C6 AddAtomA
          2    1 0001A367 AddAtomW
          3    2 0003F7C4 AddConsoleAliasA
          4    3 0003F78D AddConsoleAliasW
          5    4 0004085C AllocConsole
          6    5 0002C91D AllocateUserPhysicalPages
          7    6 00005953 AreFileApisANSI
          8    7 0003F1A0 AssignProcessToJobObject
          9    8 00021372 BackupRead
         10    9 000215CE BackupSeek
         11    A 00021F21 BackupWrite
         :
         :
```

```
828   33B  00003200  lstrlenA
829   33C  000040D5  lstrlenW
```

Summary

```
 3000  .data
 4000  .reloc
4D000  .rsrc
59000  .text
```

As you can see, the symbols are in alphabetical order and the numbers under the RVA column identify the offset in the DLL file image where the exported symbol can be found. The ordinal column is for backward compatibility with 16-bit Windows source code and should not be used in modern-day applications. The hint column is used by the system to improve performance and is not important for our discussion.

> Many developers are used to exporting DLL functions by assigning functions an ordinal value. This is especially true of those who come from a 16-bit Windows background. However, Microsoft does not publish ordinal values for the system DLLs. When your executable or DLL links to any Windows function, Microsoft wants you to link using the symbol's name. If you link by ordinal, you run the risk that your application will not run on other or future Windows platforms.
>
> In fact, this has happened to me. I published a sample application that used ordinal numbers in the *Microsoft Systems Journal*. My application ran fine on Windows NT 3.1, but when Windows NT 3.5 came out, my application did not run correctly. To fix the problem, I had to replace the ordinal numbers with function names. Now the application runs on both Windows NT 3.1 and all later versions.
>
> I asked Microsoft why it is getting away from ordinals and got this response: "We feel that the Portable Executable file format provides the benefit of ordinals (fast lookup) with the flexibility of import by name. We can add functions at any time. Ordinals are very hard to manage in a large project with multiple implementations."
>
> You can use ordinals for any DLLs that you create and have your executable files link to these DLLs by ordinal. Microsoft guarantees that this method will work even in future versions of the operating system. However, I am avoiding the use of ordinals in my own work and will link by name only from now on.

Creating DLLs for Use with Non–Visual C++ Tools

If you are using Microsoft Visual C++ to build both a DLL and an executable that will link to the DLL, you can safely skip this entire section. However, if you are building a DLL with Visual C++ that is to be linked with an executable file built using any vendor's tools, you must perform some additional work.

I already mentioned the issue of using the *extern "C"* modifier when you mix C and C++ programming. I also mentioned the issue of C++ classes and how because of name mangling you must use the same compiler vendor's tools. Another issue comes up even when you use straight C programming with multiple tool vendors. The problem is that Microsoft's C compiler mangles C functions even if you're not using C++ at all. This happens only if your function uses the *__stdcall* (WINAPI) calling convention. Unfortunately, this calling convention is the most popular type. When C functions are exported using *__stdcall*, Microsoft's compiler mangles the function names by prepending a leading underscore and adding a suffix of an @ sign followed by a number that indicates the count of bytes that are passed to the function as parameters. For example, this function is exported as *_MyFunc@8* in the DLL's export section.

```
__declspec(dllexport) LONG __stdcall MyFunc(int a, int b);
```

If you build an executable using another vendor's tools, it will attempt to link to a function named *MyFunc*—a function that does not exist in the Microsoft compiler–built DLL—and the link will fail.

To build a DLL with Microsoft's tools that is to be linked with other compiler vendor's tools, you must tell Microsoft's compiler to export the function names without mangling. You can do this in two ways. The first way is to create a .def file for your project and include in the .def file an EXPORTS section like this:

```
EXPORTS
    MyFunc
```

When Microsoft's linker parses this .def file, it sees that both *_MyFunc@8* and *MyFunc* are being exported. Because these two function names match (except for the mangling), the linker exports the function using the .def file name of *MyFunc* and does not export a function with the name of *_MyFunc@8* at all.

Now, you might think that if you build an executable with Microsoft's tools and attempt to link to the DLL containing the unmangled name, the linker will fail because it will try to link to a function called *_MyFunc@8*. Well, you'll be pleased to know that Microsoft's linker does the right thing and links the executable to the function named *MyFunc*.

If you want to avoid using a .def file, you can use the second way of exporting an unmangled version of the function. Inside one of the DLL's source code modules, you add a line like this:

```
#pragma comment(linker, "/export:MyFunc=_MyFunc@8")
```

This line causes the compiler to emit a linker directive telling the linker that a function called *MyFunc* is to be exported with the same entry point as a function called *_MyFunc@8*. This second technique is a bit less convenient than the first because you must mangle the function name yourself to construct the line. Also, when you use this second technique, the DLL actually exports two symbols identifying a single function—*MyFunc* and *_MyFunc@8*—whereas the first technique exports only the *MyFunc* symbol. The second technique doesn't buy you much—it just lets you avoid using a .def file.

Building the Executable Module

The following code fragment shows an executable source code file that imports the DLL's exported symbols and references those symbols in the code.

```
/**************************************************************************
Module:  MyExeFile1.cpp
**************************************************************************/


// Include the standard Windows and C-Runtime header files here.
#include <windows.h>


// Include the exported data structures, symbols, functions, and variables.
#include "MyLib\MyLib.h"

///////////////////////////////////////////////////////////////////////////

int WINAPI WinMain(HINSTANCE hinstExe, HINSTANCE, LPTSTR pszCmdLine, int) {

   int nLeft = 10, nRight = 25;

   TCHAR sz[100];
   wsprintf(sz, TEXT("%d + %d = %d"), nLeft, nRight, Add(nLeft, nRight));
   MessageBox(NULL, sz, TEXT("Calculation"), MB_OK);

   wsprintf(sz, TEXT("The result from the last Add is: %d"), g_nResult);
   MessageBox(NULL, sz, TEXT("Last Result"), MB_OK);
   return(0);
}

/////////////////////////////// End of File ///////////////////////////////
```

When you develop executable source code files, you must include the DLL's header file. Without it, the imported symbols will not be defined and the compiler will issue a lot of warnings and errors.

The executable source code file should not define MYLIBAPI before the DLL's header file. When the executable source code file shown on the previous page is compiled, MYLIBAPI is defined using *__declspec(dllimport)* by the MyLib.h header file. When the compiler sees *__declspec(dllimport)* modifying a variable, function, or C++ class, it knows that this symbol is to be imported from some DLL module. It doesn't know which DLL module, and it doesn't care. The compiler just wants to be sure that you access these imported symbols in the right way. Now, in the source code, you can simply refer to the imported symbols and everything will work.

Next, the linker must combine all the .obj modules to create the resulting executable module. The linker must determine which DLLs contain all of the imported symbols that the code references. So you have to pass the DLL's .lib file to the linker. As mentioned before, the .lib file simply contains the list of symbols that a DLL module exports. The linker simply wants to know that a referenced symbol exists and which DLL module contains that symbol. If the linker resolves all the external symbol references, an executable module is born.

What Importing Really Means

The previous section introduced the *__declspec(dllimport)* modifier. When you import a symbol, you do not have to use the *__declspec(dllimport)* keyword—you can simply use the standard C *extern* keyword. However, the compiler can produce slightly more efficient code if it knows ahead of time that the symbol you are referencing will be imported from a DLL's .lib file. So I highly recommend that you use the *__declspec(dllimport)* keyword for imported function and data symbols. Microsoft does this for you when you call any of the standard Windows functions.

When the linker resolves the imported symbols, it embeds a special section called the *imports section* in the resulting executable module. The imports section lists the DLL modules required by this module and the symbols referenced from each DLL module.

Using Visual Studio's DumpBin.exe utility (with the *-imports* switch), you can see what a module's import section looks like. The following is a fragment of Calc.exe's import section. (Again, I've removed some of DUMPBIN's output so that it would not occupy too many pages in this book.)

```
C:\WINNT\SYSTEM32>DUMPBIN -imports Calc.EXE

Microsoft (R) COFF Binary File Dumper Version 6.00.8168
Copyright (C) Microsoft Corp 1992-1998. All rights reserved.


Dump of file calc.exe

File Type: EXECUTABLE IMAGE

  Section contains the following imports:

    SHELL32.dll
              10010F4 Import Address Table
              1012820 Import Name Table
             FFFFFFFF time date stamp
             FFFFFFFF Index of first forwarder reference

      77C42983     7A  ShellAboutW

    MSVCRT.dll
              1001094 Import Address Table
              10127C0 Import Name Table
             FFFFFFFF time date stamp
             FFFFFFFF Index of first forwarder reference

       78010040    295  memmove
       78018124     42  _EH_prolog
       78014C34    2D1  toupper
       78010F6E    2DD  wcschr
       78010668    2E3  wcslen
    .
    .
    .

    ADVAPI32.dll
              1001000 Import Address Table
              101272C Import Name Table
             FFFFFFFF time date stamp
             FFFFFFFF Index of first forwarder reference

       779858F4    19A  RegQueryValueExA
       77985196    190  RegOpenKeyExA
       77984BA1    178  RegCloseKey

    KERNEL32.dll
              100101C Import Address Table
              1012748 Import Name Table
```

(continued)

```
             FFFFFFFF time date stamp
             FFFFFFFF Index of first forwarder reference

    77ED4134    336  lstrcpyW
    77ED33E8    1E5  LocalAlloc
    77EDEF36     DB  GetCommandLineW
    77ED1610    15E  GetProfileIntW
    77ED4BA4    1EC  LocalReAlloc
  :
  :

Header contains the following bound import information:
    Bound to SHELL32.dll [36E449E0] Mon Mar 08 14:06:24 1999
    Bound to MSVCRT.dll [36BB8379] Fri Feb 05 15:49:13 1999
    Bound to ADVAPI32.dll [36E449E1] Mon Mar 08 14:06:25 1999
    Bound to KERNEL32.dll [36DDAD55] Wed Mar 03 13:44:53 1999
    Bound to GDI32.dll [36E449E0] Mon Mar 08 14:06:24 1999
    Bound to USER32.dll [36E449E0] Mon Mar 08 14:06:24 1999

Summary

     2000 .data
     3000 .rsrc
    13000 .text
```

As you can see, the section has an entry for each DLL that Calc.exe requires: Shell32.dll, MSVCRt.dll, AdvAPI32.dll, Kernel32.dll, GDI32.dll, and User32.dll. Under each DLL's module name is the list of symbols that Calc.exe is importing from that particular module. For example, Calc calls the following functions contained in Kernel32.dll: *lstrcpyW*, *LocalAlloc*, *GetCommandLineW*, *GetProfileIntW*, and so on.

The number immediately to the left of the symbol name indicates the *hint* value of the symbol and is not pertinent to our discussion. The number on the far left of each symbol's line indicates the memory address where the symbol is located in the process's address space. This memory address appears only if the executable module is bound. You can see some additional binding information toward the end of DumpBin's output. (Binding is discussed in Chapter 20.)

Running the Executable Module

When an executable file is invoked, the operating system loader creates the virtual address space for the process. Then the loader maps the executable module into the process's address space. The loader examines the executable's import section and attempts to locate and map any required DLLs into the process's address space.

Since the import section contains just a DLL name without its pathname, the loader must search the user's disk drives for the DLL. Here is the loader's search order:

1. The directory containing the executable image file

2. The process's current directory

3. The Windows system directory

4. The Windows directory

5. The directories listed in the PATH environment variable

Be aware that other things can affect how the loader searches for a DLL. (See Chapter 20 for more information.) As the DLL modules are mapped into the process's address space, the loader checks each DLL's import section as well. If an import section exists (and usually it does), the loader continues to map the additional required DLL modules into the process's address space. The loader keeps track of the DLL modules that it is loading and maps a module only once even if multiple modules require that module.

If the loader cannot locate a required DLL module, the user sees one of the two following message boxes: either the one on top for Windows 2000 or the one on the bottom for Windows 98.

After all of the DLL modules have been located and mapped into the process's address space, the loader fixes up all references to imported symbols. To do this, it again looks in each module's import section. For each symbol listed, the loader examines the designated DLL's export section to see if the symbol exists. If the symbol does not exist (which is very rare), the loader displays a message box similar to the following two boxes: either the one on top for Windows 2000 or the one on the bottom for Windows 98.

22 DIPS.exe - Application Error

The application failed to initialize properly (0xc000007b). Click on OK to terminate the application.

OK

Error Starting Program

The 22 DIPS.EXE file is
linked to missing export 22 DIPSLIB.DLL:?SetDIPSHook@@YGHK@Z.

OK

It would be nice if the Windows 2000 version of this message box indicated which function was missing instead of the non-user-friendly error code of 0xC000007B. Oh well—maybe the next version of Windows will do this.

If the symbol does exist, the loader retrieves the RVA of the symbol and adds the virtual address of where the DLL module is loaded (the location of the symbol in the process's address space). It then saves this virtual address in the executable module's import section. Now, when the code references an imported symbol, it looks in the calling module's import section and grabs the address of the imported symbol, and it can thus successfully access the imported variable, function, or C++ class member function. Voila—the dynamic link is complete, the process's primary thread begins executing, and the application is finally running!

Naturally, it takes the loader quite a bit of time to load all these DLL modules and fix up every module's import section with the proper addresses of all the imported symbols. Since all this work is done when the process initializes, there is no run-time performance hit for the application. For many applications, however, a slow initialization is unacceptable. To help improve your application's load time, you should rebase and bind your executable and DLL modules. Few developers know how to do this, which is unfortunate because these techniques are extremely important. The system would run much better if every company performed these techniques. In fact, I believe that operating systems should ship with a utility that automatically performs these operations. I'll discuss rebasing and binding in the next chapter.

CHAPTER TWENTY

DLL ADVANCED TECHNIQUES

In the previous chapter, we discussed the basics of DLL linking and concentrated specifically on implicit linking, which is by far the most common form of DLL linking. The information in that chapter is all you'll ever need for most applications. However, you can do a lot more with DLLs. In this chapter, we'll discuss a hodgepodge of techniques that relate to DLLs. Most applications will not require these techniques, but they can be extremely useful, so you should know about them. I encourage you to at least read the "Rebasing Modules" and "Binding Modules" sections in this chapter because the techniques they describe can significantly improve the performance of your entire system.

Explicit DLL Module Loading and Symbol Linking

In order for a thread to call a function in a DLL module, the DLL's file image must be mapped into the address space of the calling thread's process. You can accomplish this in two ways. The first way is to have your application's source code simply reference symbols contained in the DLL. This causes the loader to implicitly load (and link) the required DLL when the application is invoked.

The second way is for the application to explicitly load the required DLL and explicitly link to the desired exported symbol while the application is running. In other words, while the application is running, a thread within it can decide that it wants to call a function within a DLL. That thread can explicitly load the DLL into the process's address space, get the virtual memory address of a function contained within the DLL, and then call the function using this memory address. The beauty of this technique is that everything is done while the application is running.

Figure 20-1 shows how an application explicitly loads a DLL and links to a symbol within it.

BUILDING THE DLL

1) Header with *exported* prototypes/structures/ symbols
2) C/C++ source files implementing exported functions/variables
3) Compiler produces .obj file for each C/C++ source file
4) Linker combines .obj modules producing DLL
5) Linker also produces .lib file if at least 1 function/variable is exported
   NOTE: This .lib file is not used for explicit llinking

BUILDING THE EXE

6) Header with *imported* prototypes/structures/ symbols (optional)
7) C/C++ source files that DO NOT reference inported functions/variables
8) Compiler produces .obj file for each C/C++ source file
9) Linker combines .obj modules producing .exe module
   NOTE: DLL's .lib file is not needed since there are no direct references to exported symbols. The .exe file does not contain an import table

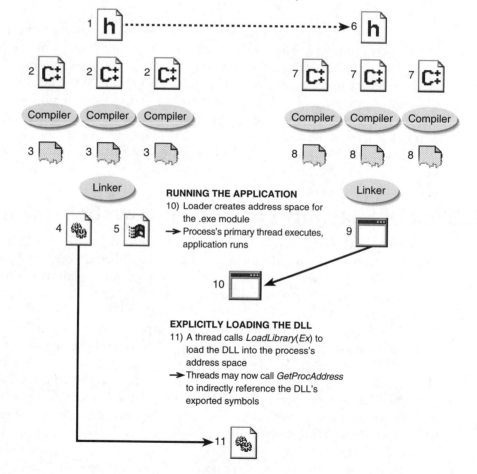

RUNNING THE APPLICATION

10) Loader creates address space for the .exe module
→ Process's primary thread executes, application runs

EXPLICITLY LOADING THE DLL

11) A thread calls *LoadLibrary(Ex)* to load the DLL into the process's address space
→ Threads may now call *GetProcAddress* to indirectly reference the DLL's exported symbols

Figure 20-1.
How a DLL is created and explicitly linked by an application

696

Explicitly Loading the DLL Module

At any time, a thread in the process can decide to map a DLL into the process's address space by calling one of these two functions:

```
HINSTANCE LoadLibrary(PCTSTR pszDLLPathName);

HINSTANCE LoadLibraryEx(
    PCTSTR pszDLLPathName,
    HANDLE hFile,
    DWORD dwFlags);
```

Both of these functions locate a file image on the user's system (using the search algorithm discussed in the previous chapter) and attempt to map the DLL's file image into the calling process's address space. The HINSTANCE value returned from both functions identifies the virtual memory address where the file image is mapped. If the DLL cannot be mapped into the process's address space, NULL is returned. To get more information about the error, you can call *GetLastError*.

You'll notice that the *LoadLibraryEx* function has two additional parameters: *hFile* and *dwFlags*. The *hFile* parameter is reserved for future use and must be NULL for now. For the *dwFlags* parameter, you must specify 0 or a combination of the DONT_RESOLVE_DLL_REFERENCES, LOAD_LIBRARY_AS_DATAFILE, and LOAD_WITH_ALTERED_SEARCH_PATH flags, which are discussed briefly below.

DONT_RESOLVE_DLL_REFERENCES

The DONT_RESOLVE_DLL_REFERENCES flag tells the system to map the DLL into the calling process's address space. Normally, when a DLL is mapped into a process's address space, the system calls a special function in the DLL, usually *DllMain* (discussed later in this chapter), which is used to initialize the DLL. The DONT_RESOLVE_DLL_REFERENCES flag causes the system to simply map the file image without calling *DllMain*.

In addition, a DLL might import functions contained in another DLL. When the system maps a DLL into a process's address space, it also checks to see whether the DLL requires any additional DLLs and automatically loads these as well. When the DONT_RESOLVE_DLL_REFERENCES flag is specified, the system does not automatically load any of these additional DLLs into the process's address space.

LOAD_LIBRARY_AS_DATAFILE

The LOAD_LIBRARY_AS_DATAFILE flag is similar to the DONT_RESOLVE_DLL_REFERENCES flag in that the system simply maps the DLL into the process's address space as if it were a data file. The system spends no

697

additional time preparing to execute any code in the file. For example, when a DLL is mapped into a process's address space, the system examines some information in the DLL to determine which page protection attributes should be assigned to different sections of the file. If you don't specify the LOAD_LIBRARY_AS_DATAFILE flag, the system sets the page protection attributes in the same way that it would if it were expecting to execute code in the file.

This flag is useful for several reasons. First, if you have a DLL that contains only resources and no functions, you can specify this flag so that the DLL's file image is mapped into the process's address space. You can then use the HINSTANCE value returned from *LoadLibraryEx* in calls to functions that load resources. Also, you can use the LOAD_LIBRARY_AS_DATAFILE flag if you want to use resources that are contained in an .exe file. Normally, loading an .exe file starts a new process, but you can also use the *LoadLibraryEx* function to map an .exe file's image into a process's address space. With the mapped .exe file's HINSTANCE value, you can access resources within it. Because an .exe file doesn't have the *DllMain* function, you must specify the LOAD_LIBRARY_AS_DATAFILE flag when you call *LoadLibraryEx* to load an .exe file.

LOAD_WITH_ALTERED_SEARCH_PATH

The LOAD_WITH_ALTERED_SEARCH_PATH flag changes the search algorithm that *LoadLibraryEx* uses to locate the specified DLL file. Normally, *LoadLibraryEx* searches for files in the order shown on page 693 in Chapter 19. However, if the LOAD_WITH_ALTERED_SEARCH_PATH flag is specified, *LoadLibraryEx* searches for the file using the following algorithm:

1. The directory specified in the *pszDLLPathName* parameter
2. The process's current directory
3. The Windows system directory
4. The Windows directory
5. The directories listed in the PATH environment variable

Explicitly Unloading the DLL Module

When the threads in the process no longer want to reference symbols in a DLL, you can explicitly unload the DLL from the process's address space by calling this function:

```
BOOL FreeLibrary(HINSTANCE hinstDll);
```

You must pass the HINSTANCE value that identifies the DLL you want to unload. This value was returned by an earlier call to *LoadLibrary(Ex)*.

You can also unload a DLL module from a process's address space by calling this function:

```
VOID FreeLibraryAndExitThread(
   HINSTANCE hinstDll,
   DWORD dwExitCode);
```

This function is implemented in Kernel32.dll as follows:

```
VOID FreeLibraryAndExitThread(HINSTANCE hinstDll, DWORD dwExitCode) {
   FreeLibrary(hinstDll);
   ExitThread(dwExitCode);
}
```

At first glance, this doesn't look like a big deal, and you might wonder why Microsoft went to the trouble of creating the *FreeLibraryAndExitThread* function. The reason has to do with the following scenario: Suppose you are writing a DLL that, when it is first mapped into a process's address space, creates a thread. When the thread finishes its work, it can unmap the DLL from the process's address space and terminate by calling *FreeLibrary* and then immediately calling *ExitThread*.

But if the thread calls *FreeLibrary* and *ExitThread* individually, a serious problem occurs. The problem, of course, is that the call to *FreeLibrary* unmaps the DLL from the process's address space immediately. By the time the call to *FreeLibrary* returns, the code that contains the call to *ExitThread* is no longer available and the thread will attempt to execute nothing. This causes an access violation, and the entire process is terminated!

However, if the thread calls *FreeLibraryAndExitThread*, this function calls *FreeLibrary*, causing the DLL to be immediately unmapped. The next instruction executed is in Kernel32.dll, not in the DLL that has just been unmapped. This means that the thread can continue executing and can call *ExitThread*. *ExitThread* causes the thread to terminate and does not return.

Granted, you probably won't have much need for the *FreeLibraryAndExitThread* function. I've needed it only once, and I was performing a very specialized task. Also, I was writing code for Microsoft Windows NT 3.1, which did not offer this function. So I was glad to see that Microsoft had added it to more recent versions of Windows.

In reality, the *LoadLibrary* and *LoadLibraryEx* functions increment a per-process usage count associated with the specified library, and the *FreeLibrary* and *FreeLibraryAndExitThread* functions decrement the library's per-process usage count. For example, the first time you call *LoadLibrary* to load a DLL, the system maps the DLL's file image into the calling process's address space and sets the DLL's usage count to 1. If a thread in the same process later calls *LoadLibrary* to load the same DLL file image, the system does not map the DLL file image into the process's address space a second time. Instead, it simply increments the usage count associated with the DLL for that process.

In order for the DLL file image to be unmapped from the process's address space, threads in the process must call *FreeLibrary* twice—the first call simply decrements the DLL's usage count to 1, and the second call decrements the DLL's usage count to 0. When the system sees that a DLL's usage count has reached 0, it unmaps the DLL's file image from this process's address space. Any thread that attempts to call a function in the DLL raises an access violation because the code at the specified address is no longer mapped into the process's address space.

The system maintains a DLL's usage count on a per-process basis; that is, if a thread in Process A makes the following call and then a thread in Process B makes the same call, MyLib.dll is mapped into both processes' address spaces—the DLL's usage count for Process A and for Process B are both 1.

```
HINSTANCE hinstDll = LoadLibrary("MyLib.dll");
```

If a thread in Process B later calls the following function, the DLL's usage count for Process B becomes 0, and the DLL is unmapped from Process B's address space. However, the mapping of the DLL in Process A's address space is unaffected, and the DLL's usage count for Process A remains 1.

```
FreeLibrary(hinstDll);
```

A thread can determine whether a DLL is already mapped into its process's address space by calling the *GetModuleHandle* function:

```
HINSTANCE GetModuleHandle(PCTSTR pszModuleName);
```

For example, the following code loads MyLib.dll only if it is not already mapped into the process's address space:

```
HINSTANCE hinstDll = GetModuleHandle("MyLib"); // DLL extension assumed
if (hinstDll == NULL) {
   hinstDll = LoadLibrary("MyLib"); // DLL extension assumed
}
```

You can also determine the full pathname of a DLL (or an .exe) if you have only the DLL's HINSTANCE value by using the *GetModuleFileName* function:

```
DWORD GetModuleFileName(
   HINSTANCE hinstModule,
   PTSTR pszPathName,
   DWORD cchPath);
```

The first parameter is the DLL's (or .exe's) HINSTANCE. The second parameter, *pszPathName*, is the address of the buffer where the function puts the file image's full pathname. The third parameter, *cchPath*, specifies the size of the buffer in characters.

Explicitly Linking to an Exported Symbol

Once a DLL module has been explicitly loaded, the thread must get the address of the symbol that it wants to reference by calling this function:

```
FARPROC GetProcAddress(
   HINSTANCE hinstDll,
   PCSTR pszSymbolName);
```

The *hinstDll* parameter, returned from a call to *LoadLibrary(Ex)* or *GetModuleHandle*, specifies the handle of the DLL containing the symbol. The *pszSymbolName* parameter can take one of two forms. The first form is the address of a zero-terminated string containing the name of the symbol whose address you want:

```
FARPROC pfn = GetProcAddress(hinstDll, "SomeFuncInDll");
```

Notice that the *pszSymbolName* parameter is prototyped as a PCSTR, as opposed to a PCTSTR. This means that the *GetProcAddress* function accepts only ANSI strings—you never pass Unicode strings to this function because the compiler/linker always stores symbol names as ANSI strings in the DLL's export section.

The second form of the *pszSymbolName* parameter indicates the ordinal number of the symbol whose address you want:

```
FARPROC pfn = GetProcAddress(hinstDll, MAKEINTRESOURCE(2));
```

This usage assumes that you know that the desired symbol name was assigned the ordinal value of 2 by the creator of the DLL. Again, let me reiterate that Microsoft strongly discourages the use of ordinals, so you won't often see this second usage of *GetProcAddress*.

Either method provides the address to the desired symbol contained in the DLL. If the requested symbol does not exist in the DLL module's export section, *GetProcAddress* returns NULL to indicate failure.

You should be aware that the first method of calling *GetProcAddress* is slower than the second because the system must perform string comparisons and searches on the symbol name string that was passed. With the second method, if you pass an ordinal number that hasn't been assigned to any of the exported functions, *GetProcAddress* might return a non-NULL value. This return value will trick your application into thinking that you have a valid address when you don't. Attempting to call this address will almost certainly cause the thread to raise an access violation. Early in my Windows programming career, I didn't fully understand this behavior and was burned by it several times—so watch out. (This behavior is yet another reason to avoid ordinals in favor of symbol names.)

The DLL's Entry-Point Function

A DLL can have a single entry-point function. The system calls this entry-point
function at various times, which I'll discuss shortly. These calls are informational
and are usually used by a DLL to perform any per-process or per-thread initialization and cleanup. If your DLL doesn't require these notifications, you do not
have to implement this function in your DLL source code. For example, if you
create a DLL that contains only resources, you do not need to implement this
function. If you do want to receive notifications in your DLL, you can implement an entry-point function that looks like this:

```
BOOL WINAPI DllMain(HINSTANCE hinstDll, DWORD fdwReason, PVOID fImpLoad) {

   switch (fdwReason) {
      case DLL_PROCESS_ATTACH:
         // The DLL is being mapped into the process's address space.
         break;

      case DLL_THREAD_ATTACH:
         // A thread is being created.
         break;

      case DLL_THREAD_DETACH:
         // A thread is exiting cleanly.
         break;

      case DLL_PROCESS_DETACH:
         // The DLL is being unmapped from the process's address space.
         break;
   }
   return(TRUE);  // Used only for DLL_PROCESS_ATTACH
}
```

> **NOTE** The function name *DllMain* is case-sensitive. Many developers acciden-
> tally call the function *DLLMain* instead. This is an easy mistake to make
> since the term *DLL* is frequently represented in all capital letters. If you
> call the entry-point function anything but *DllMain*, your code will
> compile and link; however, your entry-point function will never be called
> and your DLL will never initialize.

The *hinstDll* parameter contains the instance handle of the DLL. Like the
hinstExe parameter to *(w)WinMain*, this value identifies the virtual memory
address of where the DLL's file image was mapped in the process's address space.
You usually save this parameter in a global variable so you can use it in calls that

load resources, such as *DialogBox* and *LoadString*. The last parameter, *fImpLoad*, is nonzero if the DLL is implicitly loaded and zero if the DLL is explicitly loaded.

The *fdwReason* parameter indicates why the system is calling the function. This parameter can have one of four values: DLL_PROCESS_ATTACH, DLL_PROCESS_DETACH, DLL_THREAD_ATTACH, or DLL_THREAD_DETACH. These are discussed in the following sections.

> **NOTE**
>
> You must remember that DLLs use *DllMain* functions to initialize themselves. When your *DllMain* executes, other DLLs in the same address space probably haven't executed their *DllMain* functions yet. This means that they have not initialized, so you should avoid calling functions imported from other DLLs. In addition, you should avoid calls to *LoadLibrary(Ex)* and *FreeLibrary* from inside *DllMain* because these functions can create dependency loops.
>
> The Platform SDK documentation states that your *DllMain* should perform only simple initialization such as setting up thread local storage (discussed in Chapter 21), creating kernel objects, and opening files. You must also avoid calls to User, Shell, ODBC, COM, RPC, and socket functions (or functions that call these functions) because their DLLs might not have initialized yet or the functions might call *LoadLibrary(Ex)* internally, again creating a dependency loop.
>
> Also be aware that the same problems exist if you create global or static C++ objects because the constructor or destructor for these objects is called at the same time as your *DllMain* function.

The DLL_PROCESS_ATTACH Notification

When a DLL is first mapped into a process's address space, the system calls the DLL's *DllMain* function, passing it a value of DLL_PROCESS_ATTACH for the *fdwReason* parameter. This happens only when the DLL's file image is first mapped. If a thread later calls *LoadLibrary(Ex)* for a DLL that is already mapped into the process's address space, the operating system simply increments the DLL's usage count; it does not call the DLL's *DllMain* function again with a value of DLL_PROCESS_ATTACH.

When processing DLL_PROCESS_ATTACH, a DLL should perform any process-relative initialization required by functions contained within the DLL. For example, the DLL might contain functions that need to use their own heap (created in the process's address space). The DLL's *DllMain* function can create this heap by calling *HeapCreate* during its processing of the DLL_PROCESS_ATTACH notification. The handle to the created heap can be saved in a global variable that the DLL functions have access to.

When *DllMain* processes a DLL_PROCESS_ATTACH notification, *DllMain*'s return value indicates whether the DLL's initialization was successful. If, for example, the call to *HeapCreate* was successful, *DllMain* should return TRUE. If the heap could not be created, it should return FALSE. For any of the other *fdwReason* values—DLL_PROCESS_DETACH, DLL_THREAD_ATTACH, and DLL_THREAD_DETACH—the system ignores the return value from *DllMain*.

Of course, some thread in the system must be responsible for executing the code in the *DllMain* function. When a new process is created, the system allocates the process's address space and then maps the .exe file image and all of the required DLL file images into the process's address space. Then it creates the process's primary thread and uses this thread to call each of the DLL's *DllMain* functions with a value of DLL_PROCESS_ATTACH. After all of the mapped DLLs have responded to this notification, the system causes the process's primary thread to begin executing the executable module's C/C++ run-time startup code, followed by the executable module's entry-point function (*main*, *wmain*, *WinMain*, or *wWinMain*). If any of the DLL's *DllMain* functions return FALSE, indicating unsuccessful initialization, the system terminates the entire process, removing all the file images from its address space and displaying a message box to the user stating that the process could not be started. The message box for Windows 2000 is shown below, followed by the message box for Windows 98.

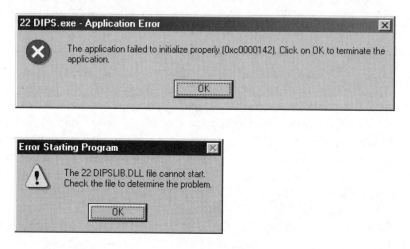

Now let's look at what happens when a DLL is loaded explicitly. When a thread in a process calls *LoadLibrary*(*Ex*), the system locates the specified DLL and maps the DLL into the process's address space. Then the system calls the DLL's *DllMain* function with a value of DLL_PROCESS_ATTACH, using the thread that placed the call to *LoadLibrary*(*Ex*). After the DLL's *DllMain*

function has processed the notification, the system allows the call to *LoadLibrary(Ex)* to return, and the thread continues processing as normal. If the *DllMain* function returns FALSE, indicating that the initialization was unsuccessful, the system automatically unmaps the DLL's file image from the process's address space and the call to *LoadLibrary(Ex)* returns NULL.

The DLL_PROCESS_DETACH Notification

When a DLL is unmapped from a process's address space, the system calls the DLL's *DllMain* function, passing it an *fdwReason* value of DLL_PROCESS_DETACH. A DLL should perform any process-relative cleanup when it processes this value. For example, a DLL might call *HeapDestroy* to destroy a heap that it created during the DLL_PROCESS_ATTACH notification. Note that if a *DllMain* function returns FALSE when it receives a DLL_PROCESS_ATTACH notification, the *DllMain* function is not called with a DLL_PROCESS_DETACH notification. If the DLL is being unmapped because the process is terminating, the thread that calls the *ExitProcess* function is responsible for executing the *DllMain* function's code. Under normal circumstances, this is the application's primary thread. When your entry-point function returns to the C/C++ run-time library's startup code, the startup code explicitly calls the *ExitProcess* function to terminate the process.

If the DLL is being unmapped because a thread in the process called *FreeLibrary* or *FreeLibraryAndExitThread*, the thread that made the call executes the *DllMain* function code. If *FreeLibrary* is used, the thread does not return from this call until after the *DllMain* function has finished executing the DLL_PROCESS_DETACH notification.

Note that a DLL can prevent the process from dying. For example, *DllMain* might enter an infinite loop when it receives the DLL_PROCESS_DETACH notification. The operating system actually kills the process only after every DLL has completed processing the DLL_PROCESS_DETACH notification.

> **NOTE**
>
> If a process terminates because some thread in the system calls *Terminate-Process*, the system does not call the DLL's *DllMain* function with a value of DLL_PROCESS_DETACH. This means that any DLLs mapped into the process's address space do not have a chance to perform any cleanup before the process terminates. This can result in the loss of data. You should use the *TerminateProcess* function only as a last resort!

Figure 20-2 shows the steps that are performed when a thread calls *LoadLibrary*. Figure 20-3 shows the steps that are performed when a thread calls *FreeLibrary*.

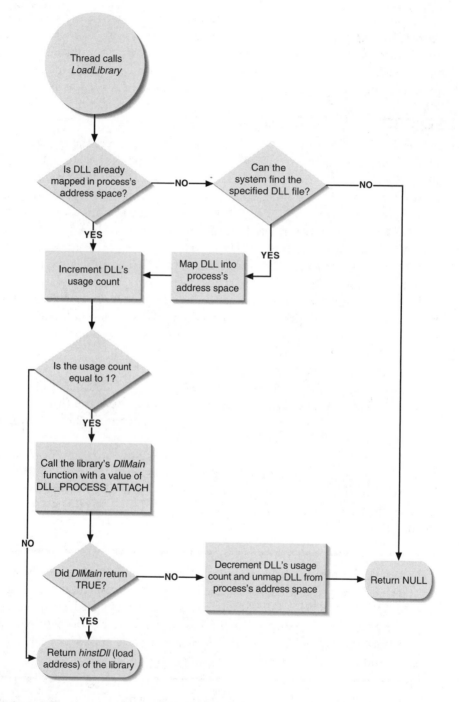

Figure 20-2.
The steps performed by the system when a thread calls LoadLibrary

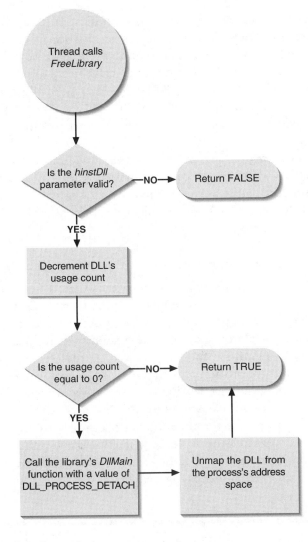

Figure 20-3.
The steps performed by the system when a thread calls FreeLibrary

The DLL_THREAD_ATTACH Notification

When a thread is created in a process, the system examines all of the DLL file images currently mapped into the process's address space and calls each one's *DllMain* function with a value of DLL_THREAD_ATTACH. This tells all the DLLs to perform any per-thread initialization. The newly created thread is re-sponsible for executing the code in all of the DLLs' *DllMain* functions. Only after all the DLLs have had a chance to process this notification does the system allow the new thread to begin executing its thread function.

If a process already has several threads running in it when a new DLL is mapped into its address space, the system does not call the DLL's *DllMain* function with a value of DLL_THREAD_ATTACH for any of the existing threads. It calls the DLL's *DllMain* with a value of DLL_THREAD_ATTACH only if the DLL is mapped into the process's address space when a new thread is created.

Also note that the system does not call any *DllMain* functions with a value of DLL_THREAD_ATTACH for the process's primary thread. Any DLLs that are mapped into the process's address space when the process is first invoked receive the DLL_PROCESS_ATTACH notification but not the DLL_THREAD_ATTACH notification.

The DLL_THREAD_DETACH Notification

The preferred way for a thread to terminate is to have its thread function return. This causes the system to call *ExitThread* to kill the thread. *ExitThread* tells the system that the thread wants to die, but the system does not kill the thread right away. Instead, it takes the soon-to-be-dead thread and has it call all the mapped DLL's *DllMain* functions with a reason of DLL_THREAD_DETACH. This notification tells all the DLLs to perform any per-thread cleanup. For example, the DLL version of the C/C++ run-time library frees the data block that it uses to manage multithreaded applications.

Note that a DLL can prevent the thread from dying. For example, the *DllMain* function can enter an infinite loop when it receives the DLL_THREAD_DETACH notification. The operating system actually kills the thread only after every DLL has completed processing the DLL_THREAD_DETACH notification.

> **NOTE** If a thread terminates because a thread in the system calls *TerminateThread*, the system does not call all of the DLLs' *DllMain* functions with a value of DLL_THREAD_DETACH. This means that any DLLs mapped into the process's address space do not have a chance to perform any cleanup before the thread terminates. This can result in the loss of data. As with *TerminateProcess*, use the *TerminateThread* function only as a last resort!

If any threads are still running when the DLL is detached, *DllMain* is not called with DLL_THREAD_DETACH for any of the threads. You might want to check for this in your DLL_PROCESS_DETACH processing so that you can perform any necessary cleanup.

Because of the rules stated above, the following situation might occur: A thread in a process calls *LoadLibrary* to load a DLL, causing the system to call the DLL's *DllMain* function with a value of DLL_PROCESS_ATTACH. (Note that the DLL_THREAD_ATTACH notification is not sent for this thread.) Next, the thread that loaded the DLL exits, causing the DLL's *DllMain* function to be called again, this time with a value of DLL_THREAD_DETACH. Notice that the DLL is notified that the thread is detaching even though it never received a DLL_THREAD_ATTACH notifying the library that the thread had attached. For this reason, you must be extremely careful when you perform any thread-specific cleanup. Fortunately, most programs are written so that the thread that calls *LoadLibrary* is the same thread that calls *FreeLibrary*.

Serialized Calls to *DllMain*

The system serializes calls to a DLL's *DllMain* function. To understand what this means, consider the following scenario. A process has two threads, Thread A and Thread B. The process also has a DLL, SomeDLL.dll, mapped into its address space. Both threads are about to call the *CreateThread* function to create two more threads, Thread C and Thread D.

When Thread A calls *CreateThread* to create Thread C, the system calls SomeDLL.dll's *DllMain* function with a value of DLL_THREAD_ATTACH. While Thread C executes the code in the *DllMain* function, Thread B calls *CreateThread* to create Thread D. The system must call *DllMain* again with a value of DLL_THREAD_ATTACH, this time having Thread D execute the code. However, calls to *DllMain* are serialized by the system, and the system suspends Thread D until Thread C has completely processed the code in *DllMain* and returned.

After Thread C finishes processing *DllMain*, it can begin executing its thread function. Now the system wakes up Thread D and allows it to process the code in *DllMain*. When it returns, Thread D begins processing its thread function.

Normally, you don't even think about this *DllMain* serialization. The reason I'm making a big deal out of it is that I worked with someone who had a bug in his code caused by *DllMain* serialization. His code looked something like the code on the following page.

```
BOOL WINAPI DllMain(HINSTANCE hinstDll, DWORD fdwReason, PVOID fImpLoad) {

   HANDLE hThread;
   DWORD dwThreadId;

   switch (fdwReason) {
   case DLL_PROCESS_ATTACH:
      // The DLL is being mapped into the process's address space.

      // Create a thread to do some stuff.
      hThread = CreateThread(NULL, 0, SomeFunction, NULL,
         0, &dwThreadId);

      // Suspend our thread until the new thread terminates.
      WaitForSingleObject(hThread, INFINITE);

      // We no longer need access to the new thread.
      CloseHandle(hThread);
      break;

   case DLL_THREAD_ATTACH:
      // A thread is being created.
      break;

   case DLL_THREAD_DETACH:
      // A thread is exiting cleanly.
      break;

   case DLL_PROCESS_DETACH:
      // The DLL is being unmapped from the process's address space.
      break;
   }
   return(TRUE);
}
```

It took us several hours to discover the problem with this code. Can you see it? When *DllMain* receives a DLL_PROCESS_ATTACH notification, a new thread is created. The system must call *DllMain* again with a value of DLL_THREAD_ATTACH. However, the new thread is suspended because the thread that caused the DLL_PROCESS_ATTACH notification to be sent to *DllMain* has not finished processing. The problem is the call to *WaitForSingleObject*. This function suspends the currently executing thread until the new thread terminates. However, the new thread never gets a chance to run, let alone terminate, because it is suspended—waiting for the current thread to exit the *DllMain* function. What we have here is a deadlock situation. Both threads are suspended forever!

When I first started thinking about how to solve this problem, I discovered the *DisableThreadLibraryCalls* function:

```
BOOL DisableThreadLibraryCalls(HINSTANCE hinstDll);
```

DisableThreadLibraryCalls tells the system that you do not want DLL_THREAD_ATTACH and DLL_THREAD_DETACH notifications sent to the specified DLL's *DllMain* function. It seemed reasonable to me that, if we told the system not to send DLL notifications to the DLL, the deadlock situation would not occur. However, when I tested my solution, which follows, I soon discovered that it didn't solve the problem.

```
BOOL WINAPI DllMain(HINSTANCE hinstDll, DWORD fdwReason, PVOID fImpLoad) {

   HANDLE hThread;
   DWORD dwThreadId;

   switch (fdwReason) {
   case DLL_PROCESS_ATTACH:
      // The DLL is being mapped into the process's address space.

      // Prevent the system from calling DllMain
      // when threads are created or destroyed.
      DisableThreadLibraryCalls(hinstDll);

      // Create a thread to do some stuff.
      hThread = CreateThread(NULL, 0, SomeFunction, NULL,
         0, &dwThreadId);

      // Suspend our thread until the new thread terminates.
      WaitForSingleObject(hThread, INFINITE);

      // We no longer need access to the new thread.
      CloseHandle(hThread);
      break;

   case DLL_THREAD_ATTACH:
      // A thread is being created.
      break;

   case DLL_THREAD_DETACH:
      // A thread is exiting cleanly.
      break;

   case DLL_PROCESS_DETACH:
      // The DLL is being unmapped from the process's address space.
      break;
   }
   return(TRUE);
}
```

Upon further research, I discovered the problem. When a process is created, the system also creates a mutex object. Each process has its own mutex object—multiple processes do not share the mutex object. This mutex object synchronizes all of a process's threads when the threads call the *DllMain* functions of the DLLs mapped into the process's address space.

When the *CreateThread* function is called, the system first creates the thread kernel object and the thread's stack. Then it internally calls the *WaitForSingleObject* function, passing the handle of the process's mutex object. Once the new thread has ownership of the mutex, the system makes the new thread call each DLL's *DllMain* function with a value of DLL_THREAD_ATTACH. Only then does the system call *ReleaseMutex* to relinquish ownership of the process's mutex object. Because the system works this way, adding the call to *DisableThreadLibraryCalls* does not prevent the threads from deadlocking. The only way I could think of to prevent the threads from being suspended was to redesign this part of the source code so that *WaitForSingleObject* is not called inside any DLL's *DllMain* function.

DllMain and the C/C++ Run-Time Library

In the discussion of the *DllMain* function above, I have assumed that you are using the Microsoft Visual C++ compiler to build your DLL. When you write a DLL, you'll probably need some startup assistance from the C/C++ run-time library. For example, say that you are building a DLL that contains a global variable and that this global variable is an instance of a C++ class. Before you can safely use the global variable inside your *DllMain* function, the variable must have its constructor called. This is a job for the C/C++ run-time library's DLL startup code.

When you link your DLL, the linker embeds the address of the DLL's entry-point function in the resulting DLL file image. You specify the address of this function using the linker's /ENTRY switch. By default, when you use Microsoft's linker and specify the /DLL switch, the linker assumes that the entry function is called *_DllMainCRTStartup*. This function is contained inside the C/C++ run-time's library file and is statically linked in your DLL file's image when you link your DLL. (The function is statically linked even if you use the DLL version of the C/C++ run-time library.)

When your DLL file image is mapped into a process's address space, the system actually calls this *_DllMainCRTStartup* function instead of your *DllMain* function. The *_DllMainCRTStartup* function initializes the C/C++ run-time library and ensures that any global or static C++ objects are constructed when *_DllMainCRTStartup* receives the DLL_PROCESS_ATTACH notification. After any C/C++ run-time initialization has been performed, the *_DllMainCRTStartup* function calls your *DllMain* function.

When the DLL receives a DLL_PROCESS_DETACH notification, the system again calls the _DllMainCRTStartup function. This time, the function calls your *DllMain* function, and when *DllMain* returns, _*DllMainCRTStartup* calls any destructors for any global or static C++ objects in the DLL. The _*DllMainCRTStartup* function doesn't do any special processing when it receives a DLL_THREAD_ATTACH notification. But for a DLL_THREAD_DETACH notification, the C/C++ run-time frees a thread's *tiddata* memory block, if one exists. Normally, however, this *tiddata* memory block should not exist because a properly written thread function returns to the C/C++ run-time's _*threadstartex* function (discussed in Chapter 6) which internally calls _*endthreadex*, which frees the memory block before the thread attempts to call *ExitThread*.

However, consider the case in which an application written in Pascal calls functions in a DLL written in C/C++. In this scenario, the Pascal application creates a thread and does not use _*beginthreadex*. So the thread knows nothing about the C/C++ run-time library. Now the thread calls a function in the DLL, which in turn calls a C run-time function. As you'll recall, the C run-time function creates a *tiddata* memory block for this thread and associates it with the thread on the fly. This means that a Pascal application can create threads that successfully call C run-time functions! When the Pascal-written thread function returns, *ExitThread* is called. The C/C++ run-time library DLL receives the DLL_THREAD_DETACH notification and frees the *tiddata* memory block so that no memory leaks occur. This stuff was pretty well thought out, huh?

I mentioned earlier that you do not have to implement a *DllMain* function in your DLL's source code. If you don't have your own *DllMain* function, you can use the C/C++ run-time library's implementation of a *DllMain* function, which looks like this (if you're statically linking to the C/C++ run-time library):

```
BOOL WINAPI DllMain(HINSTANCE hinstDll, DWORD fdwReason, PVOID fImpLoad) {

   if (fdwReason == DLL_PROCESS_ATTACH)
      DisableThreadLibraryCalls(hinstDll);
   return(TRUE);
}
```

When the linker links your DLL, it links the C/C++ run-time library's implementation of the *DllMain* function if the linker cannot find a *DllMain* function in your DLL's .obj files. If you don't supply your own *DllMain* function, the C/C++ run-time library rightfully assumes that you don't care about DLL_THREAD_ATTACH and DLL_THREAD_DETACH notifications. To improve the performance of creating and destroying threads, *DisableThreadLibraryCalls* is called.

Delay-Loading a DLL

Microsoft Visual C++ 6.0 offers a fantastic new feature to make working with DLLs easier: delay-load DLLs. A delay-load DLL is a DLL that is implicitly linked but not actually loaded until your code attempts to reference a symbol contained within the DLL. Delay-load DLLs are helpful in these situations:

■ If your application uses several DLLs, its initialization time might be slow because the loader maps all of the required DLLs into the process's address space. One way to alleviate this problem is to spread out the loading of the DLLs as the process executes. Delay-load DLLs let you accomplish this easily.

■ If you call a new function in your code and then try to run your application on an older version of the system in which the function does not exist, the loader reports an error and does not allow the application to run. You need a way to allow your application to run and then, if you detect (at run time) that the application is running on an older system, you don't call the missing function. For example, let's say that an application wants to use the PSAPI functions when running on Windows 2000 and the ToolHelp functions (like *Process32Next*) when running on Windows 98. When the application initializes, it calls *GetVersionEx* to determine the host operating system and properly calls the appropriate functions. Attempting to run this application on Windows 98 causes the loader to display an error message because the PSAPI.dll module doesn't exist on Windows 98. Again, delay-load DLLs let you solve this problem easily.

I've spent quite a bit of time playing with the delay-load DLL feature of Visual C++ 6.0, and I must say that Microsoft has done an excellent job in implementing it. It offers many features and works equally well on both Windows 98 and Windows 2000.

Let's start with the easy stuff: getting delay-load DLLs to work. First, you create a DLL just as you normally would. You also create an executable as you normally would but you do have to change a couple of linker switches and relink the executable. Here are the two linker switches you need to add:

/Lib:DelayImp.lib
/DelayLoad:MyDll.dll

The /Lib switch tells the linker to embed a special function, __*delayLoadHelper*, into your executable. The second switch tells the linker the following things:

- Remove MyDll.dll from the executable module's import section so that the operating system loader does not implicitly load the DLL when the process initializes.

- Embed a new Delay Import section (called .didata) in the executable indicating which functions are being imported from MyDll.dll.

- Resolve calls to the delay-loaded functions by having calls jump to the _ _*delayLoadHelper* function.

When the application runs, a call to a delay-loaded function actually calls the _ _*delayLoadHelper* function instead. This function references the special Delay Import section and knows to call *LoadLibrary* followed by *GetProcAddress*. Once the address of the delay-loaded function is obtained, _ _*delayLoadHelper* fixes up calls to that function so future calls go directly to the delay-loaded function. Note that other functions in the same DLL still have to be fixed up the first time you call them. Also note that you can specify the /DelayLoad linker switch multiple times—once for every DLL that you want to delay-load.

OK, that's it. It's that simple! It is, really. But you should also consider a couple of other issues. Normally, when the operating system loader loads your executable, it tries to load the required DLLs. If a DLL can't be loaded, the loader displays an error message. But for delay-loaded DLLs, the existence of the DLL is not checked at initialization time. If the DLL can't be found when a delay-loaded function is called, the _ _*delayLoadHelper* function raises a software exception. You can trap this exception using structured exception handling (SEH) and keep your application running. If you don't trap the exception, your process is terminated. (SEH is discussed in Chapters 23, 24, and 25.)

Another problem can occur when _ _*delayLoadHelper* does find your DLL but the function you're trying to call isn't in the DLL. This can happen if the loader finds an old version of the DLL, for example. In this case, _ _*delayLoadHelper* also raises a software exception and the same rules apply. The sample application presented in the next section shows how to properly write the SEH code to handle these errors.

You'll notice a lot of other stuff in the code that has nothing to do with SEH and error handling. It has to do with additional features that are available when you use delay-load DLLs. I'll describe these features shortly. If you don't use the more advanced features, you can delete this additional code.

As you can see, the Visual C++ team has defined two software exception codes: *VcppException(ERROR_SEVERITY_ERROR, ERROR_MOD_NOT_FOUND)* and *VcppException(ERROR_SEVERITY_ERROR, ERROR_PROC_NOT_FOUND)*. These indicate that the DLL module was not found and that the function was not found, respectively. My exception filter function, *DelayLoadDllExceptionFilter*, checks for these two exception codes. If neither code is thrown, the filter returns EXCEPTION_CONTINUE_SEARCH, as any good filter should. (Never swallow exceptions that you don't know how to handle.) However, if one of these codes is thrown, the *__delayLoadHelper* function provides a pointer to a *DelayLoadInfo* structure containing some additional information. The *DelayLoadInfo* structure is defined in Visual C++'s DelayImp.h file as follows:

```
typedef struct DelayLoadInfo {
    DWORD           cb;         // Size of structure
    PCImgDelayDescr pidd;       // Raw data (everything is there)
    FARPROC *       ppfn;       // Points to address of function to load
    LPCSTR          szDll;      // Name of dll
    DelayLoadProc   dlp;        // Name or ordinal of procedure
    HMODULE         hmodCur;    // hInstance of loaded library
    FARPROC         pfnCur;     // Actual function that will be called
    DWORD           dwLastError;// Error received
} DelayLoadInfo, * PDelayLoadInfo;
```

This data structure is allocated and initialized by the *__delayLoadHelper* function. As the function progresses through its work of dynamically loading the DLL and getting the address of the called function, it populates the members of this structure. Inside your SEH filter, the *szDll* member points to the name of the DLL you're attempting to load and the function you're attempting to look up is in the *dlp* member. Since you can look up functions by ordinal or by name, the *dlp* member looks like this:

```
typedef struct DelayLoadProc {
    BOOL fImportByName;
    union {
        LPCSTR szProcName;
        DWORD  dwOrdinal;
    };
} DelayLoadProc;
```

If the DLL successfully loads but does not contain the desired function, you might also look at the *hmodCur* member to see the memory address where the DLL is loaded. You can also check the *dwLastError* member to see what error caused the exception to be raised, but this probably isn't necessary for an exception filter because the exception code tells you what happened. The *pfnCur* member contains the address of the desired function. This is always set to NULL in the exception filter because *__delayLoadHelper* couldn't find the address of the function.

Of the remaining members, *cb* is for versioning, *pidd* points to the section embedded in the module that contains the list of delay-load DLLs and functions, and *ppfn* is the address where the function's address will go if the function is found. These last two members are used by the *__delayLoadHelper* function internally. They are for super-advanced use; it is extremely unlikely that you will ever have to examine or understand them.

So far, I've explained the basics of using delay-load DLLs and properly recovering from error conditions. However, Microsoft's implementation of delay-load DLLs goes beyond what I have discussed so far. Your application can unload a delay-loaded DLL, for example. Let's say that your application requires a special DLL to print the user's document. This DLL is a perfect candidate to be a delay-load DLL because most of the time it probably won't be used. However, if the user chooses the Print command, you can call a function in the DLL and it will automatically load. This is great, but after the document is printed, the user probably won't print another document immediately, so you can unload the DLL and free system resources. If the user decides to print another document, the DLL will again be loaded on demand.

To unload a delay-loaded DLL, you must do two things. First, you must specify an additional linker switch (*/Delay:unload*) when you build your executable file. Second, you must modify your source code and place a call to the *__FUnloadDelayLoadedDLL* function at the point where you want the DLL to be unloaded:

```
BOOL __FUnloadDelayLoadedDLL(PCSTR szDll);
```

The */Delay:unload* linker switch tells the linker to place another section inside the file. This section contains the information necessary to reset the functions you have already called so that they again call the *__delayLoadHelper* function. When you call *__FUnloadDelayLoadedDLL*, you pass it the name of the delay-load DLL that you want to unload. The function then goes to the unload section in the file and resets all of the DLL's function addresses. Then *__FUnloadDelayLoadedDLL* calls *FreeLibrary* to unload the DLL.

Let me point out a few important items. First, make sure that you don't call *FreeLibrary* yourself to unload the DLL or the function's address will not be reset; this will cause an access violation the next time you attempt to call a function in the DLL. Second, when you call *__FUnloadDelayLoadedDLL*, the DLL name you pass should not include a path and the letters in the name must be the same case that was used when you passed the DLL name to the */DelayLoad* linker switch; otherwise, *__FUnloadDelayLoadedDLL* will fail. Third, if you never intend to unload a delay-loaded DLL, do not specify the */Delay:unload* linker switch and your executable file will be smaller in size. Lastly, if you call *__FUnloadDelayLoadedDLL* from a module that was not built with the */Delay:unload* switch, nothing bad happens: *__FUnloadDelayLoadedDLL* simply does nothing and returns FALSE.

Another feature of the delay-load DLLs is that by default, the functions that you call are bindable to memory addresses where the system thinks the function will be in a process's address. (I'll discuss binding later in this chapter.) Since creating bindable delay-load DLL sections makes your executable file bigger, the linker also supports a */Delay:nobind* switch. Since binding is generally preferred, most applications should not use this linker switch.

The last feature of delay-load DLLs is for advanced users and really shows Microsoft's attention to detail. As the *__delayLoadHelper* function executes, it can call hook functions that you provide. These functions receive notifications of *__delayLoadHelper*'s progress and notifications of errors. In addition, these functions can override how the DLL is loaded and how the function's virtual memory address is obtained.

To get the notification or override behavior, you must do two things to your source code. First, you must write a hook function that looks like the *DliHook* function in Figure 20-6. The *DliHook* skeleton function does not affect *__delayLoadHelper*'s operation. To alter the behavior, start with the *DliHook* function and then modify it as necessary. Then tell *__delayLoadHelper* the address of the function.

Inside the DelayImp.lib static-link library, two global variables are defined: *__pfnDliNotifyHook* and *__pfnDliFailureHook*. Both of these variables are of type *PfnDliHook*:

```
typedef FARPROC (WINAPI *PfnDliHook)(
   unsigned dliNotify,
   PDelayLoadInfo pdli);
```

As you can see, this is a function data type and matches the prototype of my *DliHook* function. Inside DelayImp.lib, the two variables are initialized to NULL, which tells *__delayLoadHelper* not to call any hook functions. To have your hook function called, you must set one of these variables to your hook function's address. In my code, I simply add these two lines of code at global scope:

```
PfnDliHook __pfnDliNotifyHook  = DliHook;
PfnDliHook __pfnDliFailureHook = DliHook;
```

As you can see, *__delayLoadHelper* actually works with two callback functions. It calls one to report notifications and the other to report failures. Since the prototypes are identical for both functions, and the first parameter, *dliNotify*, tells why the function is being called, I always make life simpler by creating a single function and setting both variables to point to my one function.

This new delay-load DLL feature of Visual C++ 6.0 is pretty cool, and I know a lot of developers who wish that they had this feature years ago. I can think of a lot of applications (especially Microsoft applications) that will take advantage of this mechanism.

The DelayLoadApp Sample Application

The DelayLoadApp application ("20 DelayLoadApp.exe"), listed in Figure 20-6, shows everything you need to do to take full advantage of delay-load DLLs. For demonstration purposes, a simple DLL is required; the code for that is in the 20-DelayLoadLib directory.

Since the application loads the "20 DelayLoadLib" module, the loader does not map this module into the process's address space when you run the application. Inside the application, I periodically call the *IsModuleLoaded* function. This function simply displays a message box notifying you whether a module is loaded into the process's address space. When the application first starts, the "20 DelayLoadLib" module is not loaded, causing the message box in Figure 20-4 to appear.

Figure 20-4.
DelayLoadApp indicating that the "20 DelayLoadLib" module is not loaded

The application then calls a function imported from the DLL, which causes the *__delayLoadHelper* function to automatically load the DLL. When the function returns, the message box in Figure 20-5 is displayed.

Figure 20-5.
DelayLoadApp indicating that the "20 DelayLoadLib" module is loaded

When this message box is dismissed, another function in the DLL is called. Since this function is in the same DLL, the DLL does not get loaded in the address space again, but the address of this new function is resolved and called.

At this point, *__FUnloadDelayLoadedDLL* is called; it unloads the "20 DelayLoadLib" module. Again, the call to *IsModuleLoaded* shows the message box in Figure 20-4. Finally, an imported function is again called, which reloads the "20 DelayLoadLib" module, causing the last call to *IsModuleLoaded* to show the message box in Figure 20-5.

If all is OK, the application will work as I've described. However, if you delete the "20 DelayLoadLib" module before running the application or if the module doesn't contain one of the imported functions, exceptions will be raised. The sample code shows how to recover "gracefully" (so to speak) from this situation.

Finally, the application shows how to properly set a delay load hook function. My skeleton *DliHook* function doesn't do anything of interest. However, it does trap various notifications and shows what you can do when you receive these notifications.

 DelayLoadApp.cpp

```
/*****************************************************************************
Module:  DelayLoadApp.cpp
Notices: Copyright (c) 2000 Jeffrey Richter
*****************************************************************************/


#include "..\CmnHdr.h"      /* See Appendix A. */
#include <Windowsx.h>
#include <tchar.h>


///////////////////////////////////////////////////////////////////////////


#include <Delayimp.h>    // For error handling & advanced features
#include "..\20-DelayLoadLib\DelayLoadLib.h"    // My DLL function prototypes


///////////////////////////////////////////////////////////////////////////
```

Figure 20-6.
The DelayLoadApp sample application
(continued)

720

Figure 20-6. *continued*

```
// Statically link __delayLoadHelper/__FUnloadDelayLoadedDLL
#pragma comment(lib, "Delayimp.lib")

// Tell the linker that my DLL should be delay loaded
// Note the 2 (\") because the filename has a space in it
#pragma comment(linker, "/DelayLoad:\"20 DelayLoadLib.dll\"")

// Tell the linker that I want to be able to unload my DLL
#pragma comment(linker, "/Delay:unload")

// Tell the linker to make the delay load DLL unbindable
// You usually want this, so I commented out this line
//#pragma comment(linker, "/Delay:nobind")


// The name of the Delay-Load module (only used by this sample app)
TCHAR g_szDelayLoadModuleName[] = TEXT("20 DelayLoadLib");


////////////////////////////////////////////////////////////////////


// Forward function prototype
LONG WINAPI DelayLoadDllExceptionFilter(PEXCEPTION_POINTERS pep);


////////////////////////////////////////////////////////////////////


void IsModuleLoaded(PCTSTR pszModuleName) {

   HMODULE hmod = GetModuleHandle(pszModuleName);
   char sz[100];
#ifdef UNICODE
   wsprintfA(sz, "Module \"%S\" is %Sloaded.",
      pszModuleName, (hmod == NULL) ? L"not " : L"");
#else
   wsprintfA(sz, "Module \"%s\" is %sloaded.",
      pszModuleName, (hmod == NULL) ? "not " : "");
#endif
   chMB(sz);
}

////////////////////////////////////////////////////////////////////
```

(continued)

721

Figure 20-6. *continued*

```
int WINAPI _tWinMain(HINSTANCE hinstExe, HINSTANCE, PTSTR pszCmdLine, int) {

   // Wrap all calls to delay-load DLL functions inside SEH
   __try {
      int x = 0;

      // If you're in the debugger, try the new Debug.Modules menu item to
      // see that the DLL is not loaded prior to executing the line below
      IsModuleLoaded(g_szDelayLoadModuleName);

      x = fnLib();  // Attempt to call delay-load function

      // Use Debug.Modules to see that the DLL is now loaded
      IsModuleLoaded(g_szDelayLoadModuleName);

      x = fnLib2(); // Attempt to call delay-load function

      // Unload the delay-loaded DLL
      // NOTE: Name must exactly match /DelayLoad:(DllName)
      __FUnloadDelayLoadedDLL("20 DelayLoadLib.dll");

      // Use Debug.Modules to see that the DLL is now unloaded
      IsModuleLoaded(g_szDelayLoadModuleName);

      x = fnLib();  // Attempt to call delay-load function

      // Use Debug.Modules to see that the DLL is loaded again
      IsModuleLoaded(g_szDelayLoadModuleName);
   }
   __except (DelayLoadDllExceptionFilter(GetExceptionInformation())) {
      // Nothing to do in here, thread continues to run normally
   }

   // More code can go here...

   return(0);
}


///////////////////////////////////////////////////////////////////////////////


LONG WINAPI DelayLoadDllExceptionFilter(PEXCEPTION_POINTERS pep) {
```

(continued)

Figure 20-6. *continued*

```
   // Assume we recognize this exception
   LONG lDisposition = EXCEPTION_EXECUTE_HANDLER;

   // If this is a Delay-load problem, ExceptionInformation[0] points
   // to a DelayLoadInfo structure that has detailed error info
   PDelayLoadInfo pdli =
      PDelayLoadInfo(pep->ExceptionRecord->ExceptionInformation[0]);

   // Create a buffer where we construct error messages
   char sz[500] = { 0 };

   switch (pep->ExceptionRecord->ExceptionCode) {
   case VcppException(ERROR_SEVERITY_ERROR, ERROR_MOD_NOT_FOUND):
      // The DLL module was not found at run time
      wsprintfA(sz, "Dll not found: %s", pdli->szDll);
      break;

   case VcppException(ERROR_SEVERITY_ERROR, ERROR_PROC_NOT_FOUND):
      // The DLL module was found, but it doesn't contain the function
      if (pdli->dlp.fImportByName) {
         wsprintfA(sz, "Function %s was not found in %s",
            pdli->dlp.szProcName, pdli->szDll);
      } else {
         wsprintfA(sz, "Function ordinal %d was not found in %s",
            pdli->dlp.dwOrdinal, pdli->szDll);
      }
      break;

   default:
      // We don't recognize this exception
      lDisposition = EXCEPTION_CONTINUE_SEARCH;
      break;
   }

   if (lDisposition == EXCEPTION_EXECUTE_HANDLER) {
      // We recognized this error and constructed a message, show it
      chMB(sz);
   }

   return(lDisposition);
}


/////////////////////////////////////////////////////////////////////////////
```

(continued)

Figure 20-6. *continued*

```
// Skeleton DliHook function that does nothing interesting
FARPROC WINAPI DliHook(unsigned dliNotify, PDelayLoadInfo pdli) {

   FARPROC fp = NULL;   // Default return value

   // NOTE: The members of the DelayLoadInfo structure pointed
   // to by pdli shows the results of progress made so far.

   switch (dliNotify) {
   case dliStartProcessing:
      // Called when __delayLoadHelper attempts to find a DLL/function
      // Return 0 to have normal behavior or nonzero to override
      // everything (you will still get dliNoteEndProcessing)
      break;

   case dliNotePreLoadLibrary:
      // Called just before LoadLibrary
      // Return NULL to have __delayLoadHelper call LoadLibary
      // or you can call LoadLibrary yourself and return the HMODULE
      fp = (FARPROC) (HMODULE) NULL;
      break;

   case dliFailLoadLib:
      // Called if LoadLibrary fails
      // Again, you can call LoadLibary yourself here and return an HMODULE
      // If you return NULL, __delayLoadHelper raises the
      // ERROR_MOD_NOT_FOUND exception
      fp = (FARPROC) (HMODULE) NULL;
      break;

   case dliNotePreGetProcAddress:
      // Called just before GetProcAddress
      // Return NULL to have __delayLoadHelper call GetProcAddress
      // or you can call GetProcAddress yourself and return the address
      fp = (FARPROC) NULL;
      break;

   case dliFailGetProc:
      // Called if GetProcAddress fails
      // You can call GetProcAddress yourself here and return an address
      // If you return NULL, __delayLoadHelper raises the
      // ERROR_PROC_NOT_FOUND exception
      fp = (FARPROC) NULL;
      break;
```

(continued)

Figure 20-6. *continued*

```
   case dliNoteEndProcessing:
      // A simple notification that __delayLoadHelper is done
      // You can examine the members of the DelayLoadInfo structure
      // pointed to by pdli and raise an exception if you desire
      break;
   }

   return(fp);
}


///////////////////////////////////////////////////////////////////////////////


// Tell __delayLoadHelper to call my hook function
PfnDliHook __pfnDliNotifyHook  = DliHook;
PfnDliHook __pfnDliFailureHook = DliHook;


//////////////////////////////// End of File //////////////////////////////////
```

DelayLoadLib.cpp

```
/******************************************************************************
Module:  DelayLoadLib.cpp
Notices: Copyright (c) 2000 Jeffrey Richter
******************************************************************************/


#include "..\CmnHdr.h"      /* See Appendix A. */
#include <Windowsx.h>
#include <tchar.h>


///////////////////////////////////////////////////////////////////////////////


#define DELAYLOADLIBAPI extern "C" __declspec(dllexport)
#include "DelayLoadLib.h"


///////////////////////////////////////////////////////////////////////////////
```

(continued)

Figure 20-6. *continued*

```
int fnLib() {

    return(321);
}



///////////////////////////////////////////////////////////////////////////////



int fnLib2() {

    return(123);
}



///////////////////////////// End of File //////////////////////////////////
```

DelayLoadLib.h

```
/******************************************************************************
Module:  DelayLoadLib.h
Notices: Copyright (c) 2000 Jeffrey Richter
******************************************************************************/


#ifndef DELAYLOADLIBAPI
#define DELAYLOADLIBAPI extern "C" __declspec(dllimport)
#endif



///////////////////////////////////////////////////////////////////////////////



DELAYLOADLIBAPI int fnLib();
DELAYLOADLIBAPI int fnLib2();



///////////////////////////// End of File //////////////////////////////////
```

Function Forwarders

A function forwarder is an entry in a DLL's export section that redirects a function call to another function in another DLL. For example, if you run the Visual C++ DumpBin utility on the Windows 2000 Kernel32.dll, you'll see a part of the output that looks like this:

```
C:\winnt\system32>DumpBin -Exports Kernel32.dll
    (some output omitted)
360  167   HeapAlloc (forwarded to NTDLL.RtlAllocateHeap)
361  168   HeapCompact  (000128D9)
362  169   HeapCreate  (000126EF)
363  16A   HeapCreateTagsW  (0001279E)
364  16B   HeapDestroy  (00012750)
365  16C   HeapExtend  (00012773)
366  16D   HeapFree (forwarded to NTDLL.RtlFreeHeap)
367  16E   HeapLock  (000128ED)
368  16F   HeapQueryTagW  (000127B8)
369  170   HeapReAlloc (forwarded to NTDLL.RtlReAllocateHeap)
370  171   HeapSize (forwarded to NTDLL.RtlSizeHeap)
    (remainder of output omitted)
```

This output shows four forwarded functions. Whenever your application calls *HeapAlloc*, *HeapFree*, *HeapReAlloc*, or *HeapSize*, your executable is dynamically linked with Kernel32.dll. When you invoke your executable, the loader loads Kerenl32.dll and sees that forwarded functions are actually contained inside NTDLL.dll. It then loads the NTDLL.dll module as well. When your executable calls *HeapAlloc*, it is actually calling the *RtlAllocateHeap* function inside NTDLL.dll. A *HeapAlloc* function doesn't exist anywhere in the system!

If you call the following function, *GetProcAddress* looks in Kernel32's export section, sees that *HeapAlloc* is a forwarded function, and then calls *GetProcAddress* recursively, looking for *RtlAllocateHeap* inside NTDLL.dll's export section.

```
GetProcAddress(GetModuleHandle("Kernel32"), "HeapAlloc");
```

You can take advantage of function forwarders in your DLL module as well. The easiest way to do this is by using a *pragma* directive, as shown here:

```
// Function forwarders to functions in DllWork
#pragma comment(linker, "/export:SomeFunc=DllWork.SomeOtherFunc")
```

This *pragma* tells the linker that the DLL being compiled should export a function called *SomeFunc*. But the actual implementation of *SomeFunc* is in another function called *SomeOtherFunc*, which is contained in a module called DllWork.dll. You must create separate *pragma* lines for each function you want to forward.

Known DLLs

Certain operating system–supplied DLLs get special treatment. These are called *known DLLs*. They are just like any other DLL except that the operating system always looks for them in the same directory in order to load them. Inside the registry is the following key:

```
HKEY_LOCAL_MACHINE\SYSTEM\CurrentControlSet\Control\
    Session Manager\KnownDLLs
```

Here's what this subkey looks like on my machine using the RegEdit.exe utility.

As you can see, this key contains a set of value names that are the names of certain DLLs. Each of these value names has value data that happens to be identical to the value name with a .dll file extension. (This does not have to be the case, however, as I'll show you in an upcoming example.) When *LoadLibrary* or *LoadLibraryEx* is called, the functions first check to see whether you are passing a DLL name that includes the .dll extension. If you are not, they search for the DLL using the normal search rules.

If you do specify a .dll extension, these functions remove the extension and then search the *KnownDLLs* registry key to see whether it contains a value name that matches. If no matching name is found, the normal search rules are used. But if a matching value name is found, the system looks up the associated value data and attempts to load a DLL using the value data instead. The system also begins searching for the DLL in the directory indicated by the *DllDirectory* value's data in the registry. By default, the *DllDirectory* value's data is %SystemRoot%\System32 on Windows 2000.

To illustrate, suppose we add the following value to the *KnownDLLs* registry key:

```
Value name: SomeLib
Value data: SomeOtherLib.dll
```

When we call the following function, the system uses the normal search rules to locate the file:

```
LoadLibrary("SomeLib");
```

However, if we call the function below, the system sees that there is a matching value name. (Remember that the system removes the .dll extension when it checks the registry value names.)

```
LoadLibrary("SomeLib.dll");
```

The system therefore attempts to load a library called SomeOtherLib.dll instead of SomeLib.dll. And it first looks for SomeOtherLib.dll in the %SystemRoot%\System32 directory. If it finds the file in this directory, it loads it. If the file is not in this directory, *LoadLibrary(Ex)* fails and returns NULL, and a call to *GetLastError* returns 2 (ERROR_FILE_NOT_FOUND).

DLL Redirection

WINDOWS 98

> Windows 98 does not support DLL redirection.

When Windows was first developed, RAM and disk space were at a premium. So Windows was designed to share as many resources as possible to conserve these precious resources. To this end, Microsoft recommended that any modules shared by multiple applications, such as the C/C++ run-time library and the Microsoft Foundation Classes (MFC) DLLs, be placed in the Windows system directory. This allowed the system to locate the shared files easily.

As time went on, this became a serious problem because setup programs would overwrite files in this directory with older files or newer files that were not completely backward compatible. This prevented the user's other applications from running properly. Today, hard disks are big and cheap and RAM is also quite plentiful and relatively cheap. So Microsoft is now reversing itself and strongly recommending that you place all of your application's files in their own directory and never touch anything in the Windows system directory. This will prevent your application from harming other applications and will keep your application from being harmed by other applications.

To help you, Microsoft has added a DLL redirection feature to Windows 2000. This feature forces the operating system loader to load modules from your application's directory first. Only if the loader cannot find the file there will it search other directories.

To force the loader to always check the application's directory first, all you do is place a file in the application's directory. The contents of the file are ignored but the file must be called AppName.local.

For example, if you have an executable file called SuperApp.exe, the redirection file must be called SuperApp.exe.local.

Internally, *LoadLibrary(Ex)* has been modified to check for the existence of this file. If the file exists in the application's directory, the module in this directory is loaded. If the module doesn't exist in the application's directory, *LoadLibrary(Ex)* works as usual.

This feature is extremely useful for registered COM objects. It allows an application to place its COM object DLLs in its own directory so that other applications registering the same COM objects cannot interfere with your operation.

Rebasing Modules

Every executable and DLL module has a *preferred base address*, which identifies the ideal memory address where the module should get mapped into a process's address space. When you build an executable module, the linker sets the module's preferred base address to 0x00400000. For a DLL module, the linker sets a preferred base address of 0x10000000. Using Visual Studio's DumpBin utility (with the /headers switch), you can see an image's preferred base address. Here is an example of using DumpBin to dump its own header information:

```
C:\>DUMPBIN /headers dumpbin.exe

Microsoft (R) COFF Binary File Dumper Version 6.00.8168
Copyright (C) Microsoft Corp 1992-1998. All rights reserved.


Dump of file dumpbin.exe

PE signature found

File Type: EXECUTABLE IMAGE

FILE HEADER VALUES
            14C machine (i386)
              3 number of sections
       3588004A time date stamp Wed Jun 17 10:43:38 1998
              0 file pointer to symbol table
              0 number of symbols
             E0 size of optional header
            10F characteristics
                   Relocations stripped
                   Executable
                   Line numbers stripped
                   Symbols stripped
                   32 bit word machine


OPTIONAL HEADER VALUES
            10B magic #
           6.00 linker version
           1000 size of code
           2000 size of initialized data
              0 size of uninitialized data
           1320 RVA of entry point
           1000 base of code
           2000 base of data
         400000 image base        <-- Module's preferred base address
           1000 section alignment
           1000 file alignment
           4.00 operating system version
           0.00 image version
           4.00 subsystem version
              0 Win32 version
           4000 size of image
           1000 size of headers
          127E2 checksum
              3 subsystem (Windows CUI)
              0 DLL characteristics
         100000 size of stack reserve
           1000 size of stack commit
        :
        :
```

When this executable module is invoked, the operating system loader creates a virtual address for the new process. Then the loader maps the executable module at memory address 0x00400000 and the DLL module at 0x10000000. Why is this preferred base address so important? Let's look at this code:

```
int g_x;

void Func() {
    g_x = 5;    // This is the important line.
}
```

When the compiler processes the *Func* function, the compiler and linker produce machine code that looks something like this:

```
MOV   [0x00414540], 5
```

In other words, the compiler and linker have created machine code that is actually hard-coded in the address of the *g_x* variable: 0x00414540. This address is in the machine code and absolutely identifies the location of the *g_x* variable in the process's address space. But of course this memory address is correct if and only if the executable module loads at its preferred base address: 0x00400000.

What if we had the exact same code in a DLL module? In that case, the compiler and linker would have generated machine code that looks something like this:

```
MOV   [0x10014540], 5
```

Again, notice that the virtual memory address for the DLL's *g_x* variable is hard-coded in the DLL file's image on the disk drive. And again, this memory address is absolutely correct as long as the DLL does in fact load at its preferred base address.

OK, now let's say that you're designing an application that requires two DLLs. By default, the linker sets the .exe module's preferred base address to 0x00400000 and the linker sets the preferred base address for both DLLs to 0x10000000. If you attempt to run the .exe, the loader creates the virtual address space and maps the .exe module at the 0x00400000 memory address. Then the loader maps the first DLL to the 0x10000000 memory address. But now, when the loader attempts to map the second DLL into the process's address space, it can't possibly map it at the module's preferred base address. It must relocate the DLL module, placing it somewhere else.

Relocating an executable (or DLL) module is an absolutely horrible process, and you should take measures to avoid it. Let's see why. Suppose that the loader relocates the second DLL to address 0x20000000. In that case, the code that changes the *g_x* variable to 5 should be:

```
MOV   [0x20014540], 5
```

But the code in the file's image looks like this:

```
MOV   [0x10014540], 5
```

If the code from the file's image is allowed to execute, some 4-byte value in the first DLL module will be overwritten with the value 5. This can't possibly be allowed. The loader must somehow fix this code. When the linker builds your module, it embeds a relocation section in the resulting file. This section contains a list of byte offsets. Each byte offset identifies a memory address used by a machine code instruction. If the loader can map a module at its preferred base address, the module's relocation section is never accessed by the system. This is certainly what we want—you never want the relocation section to be used.

If, on the other hand, the module cannot be mapped at its preferred base address, the loader opens the module's relocation section and iterates though all the entries. For each entry found, the loader goes to the page of storage that contains the machine code instruction to be modified. It then grabs the memory address that the machine instruction is currently using and adds to the address the difference between the module's preferred base address and the address where the module actually got mapped.

So, in the example above, the second DLL was mapped at 0x20000000 but its preferred base address is 0x10000000. This yields a difference of 0x10000000, which is then added to the address in the machine code instruction, giving us this:

```
MOV   [0x20014540], 5
```

Now this code in the second DLL will reference its *g_x* variable correctly. There are two major drawbacks when a module cannot load at its preferred base address:

- The loader has to iterate through the relocation section and modify a lot of the module's code. This produces a major performance hit and can really hurt an application's initialization time.

- As the loader writes to the module's code pages, the system's copy-on-write mechanism forces these pages to be backed by the system's paging file.

The second point above is truly bad. It means that the module's code pages can no longer be discarded and reloaded from the module's file image on disk. Instead, the pages are swapped to and from the system's paging file as necessary. This hurts performance too. But wait, it gets worse. Since the paging file backs all of the module's code pages, the system has less storage available for all processes running in the system. This restricts the size of users' spreadsheets, word processing documents, CAD drawings, bitmaps, and so on.

By the way, you can create an executable or DLL module that doesn't have a relocation section in it. You do this by passing the /FIXED switch to the linker when you build the module. Using this switch makes the module smaller in bytes but it means that the module cannot be relocated. If the module cannot load at its preferred base address, it cannot load at all. If the loader must relocate a module but no relocation section exists for the module, the loader kills the entire process and displays an "Abnormal Process Termination" message to the user.

For resource-only DLLs, this is a problem. A resource-only DLL contains no code, so linking the DLL using the /FIXED switch makes a lot of sense. However, if the resource-only DLL can't load at its preferred base address, the module can't load at all. This is ridiculous. To solve this problem, the linker allows you to create a module with information embedded in the header indicating that the module contains no relocation information because none is needed. The Windows 2000 loader works with this header information and allows a resource-only DLL to load without incurring any performance or paging file space penalties.

To create an image without any relocations, link the image using the /SUBSYSTEM:WINDOWS, 5.0 switch or /SUBSYSTEM:CONSOLE, 5.0 switch and do not specify the /FIXED switch. If the linker determines that nothing in the module is subject to relocation fixups, it omits the relocation section from the module and turns off a special IMAGE_FILE_RELOCS_STRIPPED flag in the header. When Windows 2000 loads the module, it sees that the module can be relocated (because the IMAGE_FILE_RELOCS_STRIPPED flag is off) but that the module has no relocations (since the relocation section doesn't exist). Note that this is a new feature of the Windows 2000 loader, which explains why the /SUBSYSTEM switch requires the 5.0 at the end.

You now understand the importance of the preferred base address. So if you have multiple modules that you're loading into a single address space, you must set different preferred base addresses for each module. Microsoft Visual Studio's Project Settings dialog box makes this easy. All you do is select the Link tab and then select the Output category. In the Base Address field, which is blank by default, you enter a number. In the following figure, I've set my DLL module's base address to 0x20000000.

By the way, you should always load DLLs from high-memory addresses, working your way down to low-memory addresses to reduce fragmentation of the address space.

NOTE

Preferred base addresses must always start on an allocation-granularity boundary. On all platforms to date, the system's allocation granularity is 64 KB. This could change in the future. Chapter 13 discusses allocation granularity in more detail.

OK, so that's all fine and good. But what if you're loading a lot of modules into a single address space? It would be nice if there were some easy way to set good preferred base addresses for all of them. Fortunately, there is.

Visual Studio ships with a utility called Rebase.exe. If you run Rebase without any command-line arguments, you get the following usage information:

```
usage:
REBASE [switches]
       [-R image-root [-G filename] [-O filename] [-N filename]]
       image-names...

       One of -b and -i switches are mandatory.

       [-a] Used with -x.  extract All debug info into .dbg file
       [-b InitialBase] specify initial base address
       [-c coffbase_filename] generate coffbase.txt
           -C includes filename extensions, -c does not
       [-d] top down rebase
       [-f] Strip relocs after rebasing the image
```

(continued)

```
[-i coffbase_filename] get base addresses from coffbase_filename
[-l logFilePath] write image bases to log file.
[-p] Used with -x.  Remove private debug info when extracting
[-q] minimal output
[-s] just sum image range
[-u symbol_dir] Update debug info in .DBG along this path
[-v] verbose output
[-x symbol_dir] extract debug info into separate .DBG file first
[-z] allow system file rebasing
[-?] display this message

[-R image_root] set image root for use by -G, -O, -N
[-G filename] group images together in address space
[-O filename] overlay images in address space
[-N filename] leave images at their origional address
    -G, -O, -N, may occur multiple times.  File "filename"
    contains a list of files (relative to "image-root")
```

The Rebase utility is described in the Platform SDK documentation, so I won't go into detail here. However, I'll just add that there is nothing magical about this utility. Internally, it simply calls the *ReBaseImage* function repeatedly for each file specified:

```
BOOL ReBaseImage(
    PSTR CurrentImageName,      // Pathname of file to be rebased
    PSTR SymbolPath,            // Symbol file path so debug info
                                // is accurate
    BOOL fRebase,               // TRUE to actually do the work; FALSE
                                // to pretend
    BOOL fRebaseSysFileOk,      // FALSE to not rebase system images
    BOOL fGoingDown,            // TRUE to rebase the image below
                                // an address
    ULONG CheckImageSize,       // Maximum size that image can grow to
    ULONG* pOldImageSize,       // Receives original image size
    ULONG* pOldImageBase,       // Receives original image base address
    ULONG* pNewImageSize,       // Receives new image size
    ULONG* pNewImageBase,       // Receives new image base address
    ULONG TimeStamp);           // New timestamp for image
```

When you execute Rebase, passing it a set of image file names, it does the following:

1. It simulates creating a process's address space.

2. It opens all of the modules that would normally be loaded into this address space. It thus gets the preferred base address and size of each module.

3. It simulates relocating the modules in the simulated address space so that none of the modules overlap.

4. For the relocated modules, it parses that module's relocation section and modifies the code in the module file on disk.

5. It updates the header of each relocated module to reflect the new preferred base address.

Rebase is an excellent tool, and I strongly encourage you to use it. You should run it toward the end of your build cycle, after all of your application's modules are built. Also, if you use Rebase, you can ignore setting the base address in the Project Settings dialog box. The linker will give the DLL a base of 0x10000000, but Rebase will override that.

By the way, you should never, ever rebase any of the modules that ship with the operating system. Microsoft runs Rebase on all the operating system–supplied files before shipping Windows so that none of the operating system modules overlap if you map them all into a single address space.

I added a special feature to the ProcessInfo.exe application presented in Chapter 4. The tool shows you the list of all modules that are in the process's address space. Under the BaseAddr column, you see the virtual memory address where the module is loaded. Right next to the BaseAddr column is the ImagAddr column. Usually this column is blank, which indicates that the module loaded at its preferred base address. You hope to see this for all modules. However, if another address appears in parentheses, the module did not load at its preferred base address and the number indicates the module's preferred base address as read from header information in the module's disk file.

Here is the ProcessInfo.exe tool looking at the Acrord32.exe process. Notice that some of the modules did load at their preferred base address. Some of them did not. You'll also notice that all of these modules had a preferred base address of 0x10000000, indicating that they are DLLs and that the creator of these modules did not worry about rebasing issues—shame on them.

```
Process Information                                          _ □ ×
Processes!  Modules!  VMMap!

ACRORD32.EXE   (0xFFF71E15)                                      ▼

Filename: C:\ACROBAT3\READER\ACRORD32.EXE               ▲
    PID=FFF71E15, ParentPID=FFFE01A5, PriorityClass=8, Thr

Modules Information:
  Usage  BaseAddr(ImagAddr)      Size   Module
      1  70100000              335872   C:\WINDOWS\SYSTEM\
      1  01BF0000(10000000)     90112   C:\ACROBAT3\READER
      1  018A0000(10000000)    286720   C:\ACROBAT3\READER
      1  018F0000(10000000)    892928   C:\ACROBAT3\READER
      1  7FC60000              282624   C:\WINDOWS\SYSTEM\
      1  01760000(10000000)    135168   C:\ACROBAT3\READER
      1  01120000(10000000)    102400   C:\ACROBAT3\READER
      1  65340000              598016   C:\WINDOWS\SYSTEM\
      1  00FD0000(10000000)    233472   C:\ACROBAT3\READER
      1  BFE10000               65536   C:\WINDOWS\SYSTEM\
      1  BFE90000               24576   C:\WINDOWS\SYSTEM\
      1  00EB0000(10000000)     49152   C:\ACROBAT3\READER
      1  7DB30000               90112   C:\WINDOWS\SYSTEM\
      1  79400000              507904   C:\WINDOWS\SYSTEM\
      1  00D80000(10000000)    106496   C:\ACROBAT3\READER ▼
◄                                                           ►
```

Binding Modules

Rebasing is very important and greatly improves the performance of the entire system. However, you can do even more to improve performance. Let's say that you have properly rebased all of your application's modules. Recall from Chapter 19 our discussion about how the loader looks up the address of all the imported symbols. The loader writes the symbol's virtual address into the executable module's import section. This allows references to the imported symbols to actually get to the correct memory location.

Let's think about this for a second. If the loader is writing the virtual addresses of the imported symbol into the .exe module's import section, the pages that back the import section are written to. Since these pages are copy-on-write, the pages are backed by the paging file. So we have a problem that is similar to the rebasing problem: portions of the image file are swapped to and from the system's paging file instead of being discarded and reread from the file's disk image when necessary. Also, the loader has to resolve the addresses of all the imported symbols (for all modules), which can be time-consuming.

You can use the technique of binding a module so your application can initialize faster and use less storage. Binding a module prepares that module's import section with the virtual address of all the imported symbols. To improve initialization time and to use less storage, you must do this before loading the module, of course.

Visual Studio ships with another utility called Bind.exe, which outputs the following information when you run it with no command-line arguments:

```
usage: BIND [switches] image-names...
           [-?] display this message
           [-c] no caching of import dlls
           [-o] disable new import descriptors
           [-p dll search path]
           [-s Symbol directory] update any associated .DBG file
           [-u] update the image
           [-v] verbose output
           [-x image name] exclude this image from binding
           [-y] allow binding on images located above 2G
```

The Bind utility is described in the Platform SDK documentation, so I won't go into detail here. However, like Rebase, this utility isn't magical. Internally, it calls the *BindImageEx* function repeatedly for each file specified:

```
BOOL BindImageEx(
    DWORD dwFlags,         // Flags giving fine control over the function
    PSTR pszImageName,     // Pathname of file to be bound
    PSTR pszDllPath,       // Search path used for locating image files
    PSTR pszSymbolPath,    // Search path used to keep debug info accurate
    PIMAGEHLP_STATUS_ROUTINE StatusRoutine);  // Callback function
```

The last parameter, *StatusRoutine*, is the address of a callback function that is called periodically by *BindImageEx* so that you can monitor the bind process. Here is the prototype of the function:

```
BOOL WINAPI StatusRoutine(
    IMAGEHLP_STATUS_REASON Reason, // Module/procedure not found, etc.
    PSTR pszImageName,       // Pathname of file being bound
    PSTR pszDllName,         // Pathname of DLL
    ULONG_PTR VA,            // Computed virtual address
    ULONG_PTR Parameter);    // Additional info depending on Reason
```

When you execute Bind, passing it an image name, it does the following:

1. It opens the specified image file's import section.

2. For every DLL listed in the import section, it opens the DLL file and looks in its header to determine its preferred base address.

3. It looks up each imported symbol in the DLL's export section.

4. It takes the RVA of the symbol and adds to it the module's preferred base address. It writes the resulting expected virtual address of the imported symbol to the image file's import section.

5. It adds some additional information to the image file's import section. This information includes the name of all DLL modules that the image is bound to and the timestamp of those modules.

In Chapter 19, we used the DumpBin utility to examine Calc.exe's import section. The bottom of this output showed the bound import information added in step 5. Here is the relevant portion of the output again:

```
Header contains the following bound import information:
    Bound to SHELL32.dll [36E449E0] Mon Mar 08 14:06:24 1999
    Bound to MSVCRT.dll [36BB8379] Fri Feb 05 15:49:13 1999
    Bound to ADVAPI32.dll [36E449E1] Mon Mar 08 14:06:25 1999
    Bound to KERNEL32.dll [36DDAD55] Wed Mar 03 13:44:53 1999
    Bound to GDI32.dll [36E449E0] Mon Mar 08 14:06:24 1999
    Bound to USER32.dll [36E449E0] Mon Mar 08 14:06:24 1999
```

You can see which modules Calc.exe was bound to, and the number in square brackets indicates when Microsoft built each DLL module. This 32-bit timestamp value is expanded and shown as a human-readable string after the square brackets.

During this whole process, Bind makes two important assumptions:

■ When the process initializes, the required DLLs actually load at their preferred base address. You can ensure this by using the Rebase utility described earlier.

■ The location of the symbol referenced in the DLL's export section has not changed since binding was performed. The loader verifies this by checking each DLL's timestamp with the timestamp saved in step 5 above.

Of course, if the loader determines that either of these assumptions is false, Bind has not done anything useful and the loader must manually fix up the executable module's import section, just as it normally would. But if the loader sees that the module is bound, the required DLLs did load at their preferred base address, and the timestamps match, it actually has nothing to do. It doesn't have to relocate any modules, and it doesn't have to look up the virtual address of any imported functions. The application can simply start executing!

In addition, no storage is required from the system's paging file. This is fantastic—we have the best of all worlds here. It's amazing how many commercial applications ship today without proper rebasing and binding.

OK, so now you know that you should bind all the modules that you ship with your application. But when should you perform the bind? If you bind your modules at your company, you would bind them to the system DLLs that you've installed, which are unlikely to be what the user has installed. Since you don't know if your user is running Windows 98, Windows NT, or Windows 2000, or whether these have service packs installed, you should perform binding as part of your application's setup.

Of course, if the user dual-boots Windows 98 and Windows 2000, the bound modules will be incorrect for one of the operating systems. Also, if the user installs your application under Windows 2000 and then upgrades to a service pack, the bind is also incorrect. There isn't much you or the user can do in these situations. Microsoft should ship a utility with the operating system that automatically rebinds every module after an operating system upgrade. But alas, no such utility exists.

CHAPTER TWENTY-ONE

THREAD-LOCAL STORAGE

Sometimes it's helpful to associate data with an instance of an object. For example, window extra bytes associate data with a specific window by using the *SetWindowWord* and *SetWindowLong* functions. You can use thread-local storage (TLS) to associate data with a specific thread of execution. For example, you can associate the creation time of a thread with a thread. Then, when the thread terminates, you can determine the thread's lifetime.

The C/C++ run-time library uses TLS. Because the library was designed years before multithreaded applications, most functions in the library are intended for use with single-threaded applications. The *strtok* function is an excellent example. The first time an application calls *strtok*, the function passes the address to a string and saves the address of the string in its own static variable. When you make future calls to *strtok*, passing NULL, the function refers to the saved string address.

In a multithreaded environment, one thread might call *strtok*, and then, before it can make another call, another thread might also call *strtok*. In this case, the second thread causes *strtok* to overwrite its static variable with a new address without the first thread's knowledge. The first thread's future calls to *strtok* use the second thread's string, which can lead to all kinds of bugs that are difficult to find and to fix.

To address this problem, the C/C++ run-time library uses TLS. Each thread is assigned its own string pointer that is reserved for use by the *strtok* function. Other C/C++ run-time functions that require the same treatment include *asctime* and *gmtime*.

TLS can be a lifesaver if your application relies heavily on global or static variables. Fortunately, developers tend to minimize the use of such variables and rely much more on automatic (stack-based) variables and data passing via function parameters. This is good because stack-based variables are always associated with a particular thread.

The standard C run-time library has been implemented and reimplemented by various compiler vendors; a C compiler wouldn't be worth buying if it didn't include the standard C library. Programmers have used it for years and will continue to do so, which means that the prototype and behavior of functions such as *strtok* must remain exactly as the standard C library describes them. If the C run-time library were to be redesigned today, it would be designed for environments that support multithreaded applications, and extreme measures would be taken to avoid the use of global and static variables.

In my own software projects, I avoid global variables as much as possible. If your application uses global and static variables, I strongly suggest that you examine each variable and investigate the possibilities for changing it to a stack-based variable. This effort can save you an enormous amount of time if you decide to add threads to your application, and even single-threaded applications can benefit.

You can use the two TLS techniques discussed in this chapter—dynamic TLS and static TLS—in both applications and DLLs. However, they're generally more useful when you create DLLs because DLLs often don't know the structure of the application to which they are linked. When you write an application, however, you typically know how many threads will be created and how those threads will be used. You can then create makeshift methods or, better yet, use stack-based methods (local variables) for associating data with each created thread. Nevertheless, application developers can also benefit from the information in this chapter.

Dynamic TLS

An application takes advantage of dynamic TLS by calling a set of four functions. These functions are actually most often used by DLLs. Figure 21-1 shows the internal data structures that Windows uses for managing TLS.

The figure shows a single set of in-use flags for each process running in the system. Each flag is set to either FREE or INUSE, indicating whether the TLS slot is in use. Microsoft guarantees that at least TLS_MINIMUM_ AVAILABLE bit flags are available. By the way, TLS_MINIMUM_AVAILABLE is defined as 64 in WinNT.h. Windows 2000 has expanded this flag array to allow more than 1000 TLS slots! This should be more than enough slots for any application.

To use dynamic TLS, you must first call *TlsAlloc*:

```
DWORD TlsAlloc();
```

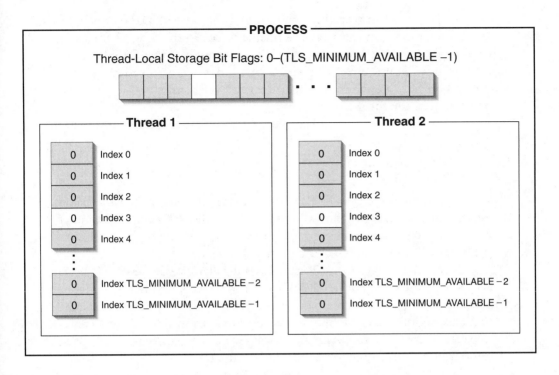

Figure 21-1.
Internal data structures that manage TLS

This function instructs the system to scan the bit flags in the process and locate a FREE flag. The system then changes the flag from FREE to INUSE, and *TlsAlloc* returns the index of the flag in the bit array. A DLL (or an application) usually saves the index in a global variable. This is one of those times when a global variable is actually the better choice because the value is used on a per-process basis rather than a per-thread basis.

If *TlsAlloc* cannot find a FREE flag in the list, it returns TLS_OUT_OF_INDEXES (defined as 0xFFFFFFFF in WinBase.h). The first time *TlsAlloc* is called, the system recognizes that the first flag is FREE and changes the flag to INUSE and *TlsAlloc* returns 0. That's 99 percent of what *TlsAlloc* does. I'll get to the other 1 percent later.

When a thread is created, an array of TLS_MINIMUM_AVAILABLE PVOID values is allocated, initialized to 0, and associated with the thread by the system. As Figure 21-1 shows, each thread gets its own array and each PVOID in the array can store any value.

Before you can store information in a thread's PVOID array, you must know which index in the array is available for use—this is what the earlier call to *TlsAlloc* is for. Conceptually, *TlsAlloc* reserves an index for you. If *TlsAlloc* returns index 3, it is effectively saying that index 3 is reserved for you in every thread currently executing in the process as well as in any threads that might be created in the future.

To place a value in a thread's array, you call the *TlsSetValue* function:

```
BOOL TlsSetValue(
   DWORD dwTlsIndex,
   PVOID pvTlsValue);
```

This function puts a PVOID value, identified by the *pvTlsValue* parameter, into the thread's array at the index identified by the *dwTlsIndex* parameter. The value of *pvTlsValue* is associated with the thread making the call to *TlsSetValue*. If the call is successful, TRUE is returned.

A thread changes its own array when it calls *TlsSetValue*. But it cannot set a TLS value for another thread. I wish that there were another *Tls* function that allowed one thread to store data in another thread's array, but no such function exists. Currently, the only way to pass data from one thread to another is to pass a single value to *CreateThread* or *_beginthreadex*, which then passes the value to the thread function as its only parameter.

When you call *TlsSetValue*, you should always pass an index returned from an earlier call to *TlsAlloc*. Microsoft designed these functions to be as fast as possible and, in so doing, gave up error checking. If you pass an index that was never allocated by a call to *TlsAlloc*, the system stores the value in the thread's array anyway—no error check is performed.

To retrieve a value from a thread's array, you call *TlsGetValue*:

```
PVOID TlsGetValue(DWORD dwTlsIndex);
```

This function returns the value that was associated with the TLS slot at index *dwTlsIndex*. Like *TlsSetValue*, *TlsGetValue* looks only at the array that belongs to the calling thread. And again like *TlsSetValue*, *TlsGetValue* does not perform any test to check the validity of the passed index.

When you come to a point in your process where you no longer need to reserve a TLS slot among all threads, you should call *TlsFree*:

```
BOOL TlsFree(DWORD dwTlsIndex);
```

This function simply tells the system that this slot no longer needs to be reserved. The INUSE flag managed by the process's bit flags array is set to FREE again and might be allocated in the future if a thread later calls *TlsAlloc*. *TlsFree* returns TRUE if the function is successful. Attempting to free a slot that was not allocated results in an error.

Using Dynamic TLS

Usually, if a DLL uses TLS, it calls *TlsAlloc* when its *DllMain* function is called with DLL_PROCESS_ATTACH, and it calls *TlsFree* when *DllMain* is called with DLL_PROCESS_DETACH. The calls to *TlsSetValue* and *TlsGetValue* are most likely made during calls to functions contained within the DLL.

One method for adding TLS to an application is to add it when you need it. For example, you might have a function in a DLL that works similarly to *strtok*. The first time your function is called, the thread passes a pointer to a 40-byte structure. You must save this structure so that future calls can reference it. You might code your function like this:

```
DWORD g_dwTlsIndex; // Assume that this is initialized
                    // with the result of a call to TlsAlloc.
    .
    .
    .
void MyFunction(PSOMESTRUCT pSomeStruct) {
    if (pSomeStruct != NULL) {
        // The caller is priming this function.

        // See if we already allocated space to save the data.
        if (TlsGetValue(g_dwTlsIndex) == NULL) {
            // Space was never allocated. This is the first
            // time this function has ever been called by this thread.
            TlsSetValue(g_dwTlsIndex,
                HeapAlloc(GetProcessHeap(), 0, sizeof(*pSomeStruct)));
        }

        // Memory already exists for the data;
        // save the newly passed values.
        memcpy(TlsGetValue(g_dwTlsIndex), pSomeStruct,
            sizeof(*pSomeStruct));

    } else {

        // The caller already primed the function. Now it
        // wants to do something with the saved data.

        // Get the address of the saved data.
        pSomeStruct = (PSOMESTRUCT) TlsGetValue(g_dwTlsIndex);

        // The saved data is pointed to by pSomeStruct; use it.
        .
        .
        .
    }
```

If the application's thread never calls *MyFunction*, a memory block is never allocated for the thread.

It might seem that 64 TLS locations are more than you'll ever need. However, keep in mind that an application can dynamically link to several DLLs. One DLL can allocate 10 TLS indexes, a second DLL can allocate 5 indexes, and so on. So it is always best to reduce the number of TLS indexes you need. The best way to do this is to use the same method that *MyFunction* uses on the previous page. Sure, I can save all 40 bytes in multiple TLS indexes, but doing so is not only wasteful, it makes working with the data difficult. Instead, you should allocate a memory block for the data and simply save the pointer in a single TLS index just as *MyFunction* does. As I mentioned earlier, Windows 2000 allows for more than 1000 TLS slots. Microsoft increased this limit because many developers took a cavalier attitude toward using the slots, which denied slots to other DLLs and caused them to fail.

When I discussed the *TlsAlloc* function earlier, I described only 99 percent of what it did. To help you understand the remaining 1 percent, look at this code fragment:

```
DWORD dwTlsIndex;
PVOID pvSomeValue;

    :
    :

dwTlsIndex = TlsAlloc();
TlsSetValue(dwTlsIndex, (PVOID) 12345);
TlsFree(dwTlsIndex);

// Assume that the dwTlsIndex value returned from
// this call to TlsAlloc is identical to the index
// returned by the earlier call to TlsAlloc.
dwTlsIndex = TlsAlloc();

pvSomeValue = TlsGetValue(dwTlsIndex);
```

What do you think *pvSomeValue* contains after this code executes? 12345? The answer is 0. *TlsAlloc*, before returning, cycles through every thread in the process and places 0 in each thread's array at the newly allocated index.

This is fortunate because an application might call *LoadLibrary* to load a DLL, and the DLL might call *TlsAlloc* to allocate an index. Then the thread might call *FreeLibrary* to remove the DLL. The DLL should free its index with a call to *TlsFree*, but who knows which values the DLL code placed in any of the thread's arrays? Next, a thread calls *LoadLibrary* to load a different DLL into memory. This DLL also calls *TlsAlloc* when it starts and gets the same index used by the previous DLL. If *TlsAlloc* didn't set the returned index for all threads in the process, a thread might see an old value and the code might not execute correctly.

For example, this new DLL might want to check whether memory for a thread has ever been allocated by calling *TlsGetValue*, as in the code fragment on page 748. If *TlsAlloc* doesn't clear out the array entry for every thread, the old data from the first DLL is still available. If a thread calls *MyFunction*, *MyFunction* thinks that a memory block has already been allocated and calls *memcpy* to copy the new data into what it thinks is a memory block. This could have disastrous results, but fortunately *TlsAlloc* initializes the array elements so that such a disaster can never happen.

Static TLS

Like dynamic TLS, static TLS associates data with a thread. However, static TLS is much easier to use in your code because you don't have to call any functions to take advantage of it.

Let's say that you want to associate a start time with every thread created by your application. All you do is declare the start-time variable as follows:

```
__declspec(thread) DWORD gt_dwStartTime = 0;
```

The *__declspec(thread)* prefix is a modifier that Microsoft added to the Visual C++ compiler. It tells the compiler that the corresponding variable should be placed in its own section in the executable or DLL file. The variable following *__declspec(thread)* must be declared as either a global variable or a static variable inside (or outside) a function. You can't declare a local variable to be of type *__declspec(thread)*. This shouldn't be a problem because local variables are always associated with a specific thread anyway. I use the *gt_* prefix for global TLS variables and *st_* for static TLS variables.

When the compiler compiles your program, it puts all the TLS variables into their own section, which is named, unsurprisingly enough, .tls. The linker combines all the .tls sections from all the object modules to produce one big .tls section in the resulting executable or DLL file.

For static TLS to work, the operating system must get involved. When your application is loaded into memory, the system looks for the .tls section in your executable file and dynamically allocates a block of memory large enough to hold all the static TLS variables. Every time the code in your application refers to one of these variables, the reference resolves to a memory location contained in the allocated block of memory. As a result, the compiler must generate additional

749

code to reference the static TLS variables, which makes your application both larger in size and slower to execute. On an *x*86 CPU, three additional machine instructions are generated for every reference to a static TLS variable.

If another thread is created in your process, the system traps it and automatically allocates another block of memory to contain the new thread's static TLS variables. The new thread has access only to its own static TLS variables and cannot access the TLS variables belonging to any other thread.

That's basically how static TLS works. Now let's add DLLs to the story. It's likely that your application will use static TLS variables and that you'll link to a DLL that also wants to use static TLS variables. When the system loads your application, it first determines the size of your application's .tls section and adds the value to the size of any .tls sections in any DLLs to which your application links. When threads are created in your process, the system automatically allocates a block of memory large enough to hold all the TLS variables required by your application and all the implicitly linked DLLs. This is pretty cool.

But let's look at what happens when your application calls *LoadLibrary* to link to a DLL that also contains static TLS variables. The system must look at all the threads that already exist in the process and enlarge their TLS memory blocks to accommodate the additional memory requirements of the new DLL. Also, if *FreeLibrary* is called to free a DLL containing static TLS variables, the memory block associated with each thread in the process should be compacted.

Alas, this is too much for the operating system to manage. The system allows libraries containing static TLS variables to be explicitly loaded at run time; however, the TLS data isn't properly initialized, and any attempt to access it might result in an access violation. This is the only disadvantage of using static TLS; this problem doesn't occur when you use dynamic TLS. Libraries that use dynamic TLS can be loaded at run time and freed at run time with no problems at all.

CHAPTER TWENTY-TWO

DLL INJECTION
AND API HOOKING

In Microsoft Windows, each process gets its own private address space. When you use pointers to reference memory, the value of the pointer refers to a memory address in your own process's address space. Your process cannot create a pointer that references memory belonging to another process. So if your process has a bug that overwrites memory at a random address, the bug can't affect the memory used by another process.

WINDOWS 98

> Processes running under Windows 98 share the 2-GB address space from 0x80000000 through 0xFFFFFFFF. Only memory-mapped files and system components are mapped into this region. For more information, see Chapters 13, 14, and 17.

Separate address spaces are a great advantage for both developers and users. For developers, the system is more likely to catch wild memory reads and writes. For users, the operating system is more robust because one application cannot bring down another process or the operating system. Of course, this robustness comes at a price: it is much harder to write applications that can communicate with or manipulate other processes.

Situations that require breaking through process boundary walls to access another process's address space include the following:

- When you want to subclass a window created by another process

- When you need debugging aids (for example, when you need to determine which DLLs another process is using)

- When you want to hook other processes

In this chapter, I'll show you several mechanisms you can use to inject a DLL into another process's address space. Once your DLL code is in another address space, you can wreak unlimited havoc on the other process. This should scare you—always think twice about whether this is something you really need to do.

DLL Injection: An Example

Let's say that you want to subclass an instance of a window created by another process. You might recall that subclassing allows you to alter the behavior of a window. To do this, you simply call *SetWindowLongPtr* to change the window procedure address in the window's memory block to point to a new (your own) *WndProc*. The Platform SDK documentation states that an application cannot subclass a window created by another process. This is not exactly true. The problem with subclassing another process's window really has to do with process address space boundaries.

When you call *SetWindowLongPtr* to subclass a window, as shown below, you tell the system that all messages sent or posted to the window specified by *hwnd* should be directed to *MySubclassProc* instead of the window's normal window procedure.

```
SetWindowLongPtr(hwnd, GWLP_WNDPROC, MySubclassProc);
```

In other words, when the system needs to dispatch a message to the specified window's *WndProc*, it looks up the address and then makes a direct call to *WndProc*. In this example, the system sees that the address of the *MySubclassProc* function is associated with the window and makes a direct call to *MySubclassProc* instead.

The problem with subclassing a window created by another process is that the subclass procedure is in another address space. Figure 22-1 shows a simplified view of how a window procedure receives messages. Process A is running and has created a window. The User32.dll file is mapped into the address space of Process A. This mapping of User32.dll is responsible for receiving and dispatching all sent and posted messages destined for any window created by any thread running in Process A. When this mapping of User32.dll detects a message, it first determines the address of the window's *WndProc* and then calls it, passing the window handle, the message, and the *wParam* and *lParam* values. After *WndProc* processes the message, User32.dll loops back around and waits for another window message to be processed.

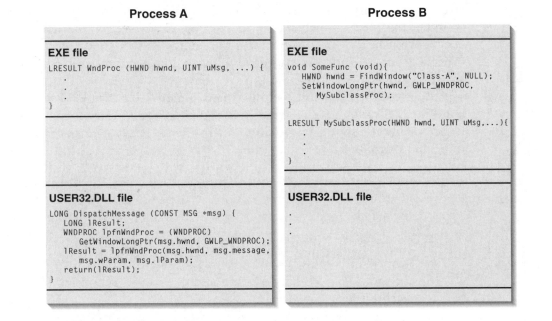

Figure 22-1.
A thread in Process B attempting to subclass a window created by a thread in Process A

Now suppose that your process is Process B and you want to subclass a window created by a thread in Process A. Your code in Process B must first determine the handle to the window you want to subclass. This can happen in a variety of ways. The example shown in Figure 22-1 simply calls *FindWindow* to obtain the desired window. Next, the thread in Process B calls *SetWindowLongPtr* in an attempt to change the address of the window's *WndProc*. Notice that I said "attempt." This call does nothing and simply returns NULL. The code in *SetWindowLongPtr* checks to see whether one process is attempting to change the *WndProc* address for a window created by another process and simply ignores the call.

What if the *SetWindowLongPtr* function could change the window's *WndProc*? The system would associate the address of *MySubclassProc* with the specified window. Then, when this window was sent a message, the User32 code in Process A would retrieve the message, get the address of *MySubclassProc*, and attempt to call this address. But then you'd have a big problem. *MySubclassProc* would be in Process B's address space, but Process A would be the active process. Obviously, if User32 were to call this address, it would be calling an address in Process A's address space, and this would probably result in a memory access violation.

To avoid this problem, you want the system to know that *MySubclassProc* is in Process B's address space and then have the system perform a context switch before calling the subclass procedure. Microsoft did not implement this additional functionality for several reasons:

- Applications rarely need to subclass windows created by threads in other processes. Most applications subclass windows that they create, and the memory architecture of Windows does not hinder this.

- Switching active processes is very expensive in terms of CPU time.

- A thread in Process B would have to execute the code in *MySubclassProc*. Which thread should the system try to use? An existing thread or a new thread?

- How would User32.dll be able to tell whether the address associated with the window was for a procedure in another process or in the same process?

Because there are no great solutions to these problems, Microsoft decided not to allow *SetWindowLongPtr* to change the window procedure of a window created by another process.

However, you can subclass a window created by another process—you simply go about it in a different way. The question isn't really about subclassing—it's about process address space boundaries. If you could somehow get the code for your subclass procedure into Process A's address space, you could easily call *SetWindowLongPtr* and pass Process A's address to *MySubclassProc*. I call this technique "injecting" a DLL into a process's address space. I know several ways to do this. We'll discuss each of these in turn.

Injecting a DLL Using the Registry

If you've been using Windows for any length of time, you should be familiar with the registry. The configuration for the entire system is maintained in the registry, and you can alter the behavior of the system by tweaking its settings. The entry I'll discuss is in the following key:

```
HKEY_LOCAL_MACHINE\Software\Microsoft
    \Windows NT\CurrentVersion\Windows\AppInit_DLLs
```

WINDOWS 98

Windows 98 ignores this registry key, so you cannot use this technique to inject a DLL under Windows 98.

The window below shows what the entries in this key look like when viewed with Registry Editor. The value for this key might contain a single DLL filename or a set of DLL filenames (separated by spaces or commas). Since spaces delimit filenames, you must avoid filenames that contain spaces. The first DLL filename listed might include a path, but any other DLLs that contain a path are ignored. For this reason, it is usually best to place your DLL in the Windows system directory so that paths need not be specified. In the window, I have set the value to a single DLL pathname, C:\MyLib.dll.

When you restart your machine and Windows initializes, the system saves the value of this key. Then, when the User32.dll library is mapped into a process, it receives a DLL_PROCESS_ATTACH notification. When this notification is processed, User32.dll retrieves the saved value of this key and calls *LoadLibrary* for each DLL specified in the string. As each library is loaded, the library's associated *DllMain* is called with an *fdwReason* value of DLL_PROCESS_ATTACH so that each library can initialize itself. Because the injected DLL is loaded so early in the process's lifetime, you must exercise caution when calling functions. There should be no problem calling functions in Kernel32.dll, but calling functions in some other DLL might cause problems.

User32.dll does not check whether each library has been successfully loaded or initialized.

Of all the methods for injecting a DLL, this is by far the easiest. All you do is add a value to an already existing registry key. But this technique also has some disadvantages:

- Because the system reads the value of this key during initialization, you must restart your computer after changing this value. Even logging off and logging back on won't work—you must restart. Of course, the opposite is also true: if you remove a DLL from this key's value, the system won't stop mapping the library until the computer is restarted.

- Your DLL is mapped only into processes that use User32.dll. All GUI-based applications use User32.dll, but most CUI-based applications do not. So if you need to inject your DLL into a compiler or linker, this method won't work.

- Your DLL is mapped into every GUI-based application, but you probably need to inject your library into only one or a few processes. The more processes your DLL is mapped into, the greater the chance of crashing the "container" processes. After all, threads running in these processes are executing your code. If your code enters an infinite loop or accesses memory incorrectly, you affect the behavior and robustness of the processes in which your code runs. Therefore, it is best to inject your library into as few processes as possible.

- Your DLL is mapped into every GUI-based application for its entire lifetime. This is similar to the previous problem. Ideally, your DLL should be mapped into just the processes you need, and it should be mapped into those processes for the minimum amount of time. Suppose that when the user invokes your application, you want to subclass WordPad's main window. Your DLL doesn't have to be mapped into WordPad's address space until the user invokes your application. If the user later decides to terminate your application, you'll want to unsubclass WordPad's main window. In this case, your DLL no longer needs to be injected into WordPad's address space. It's best to keep your DLL injected only when necessary.

Injecting a DLL Using Windows Hooks

You can inject a DLL into a process's address space using hooks. To get hooks to work as they do in 16-bit Windows, Microsoft was forced to devise a mechanism that allows a DLL to be injected into the address space of another process.

Let's look at an example. Process A (a utility similar to Microsoft Spy++) installs a WH_GETMESSAGE hook to see messages processed by windows in the system. The hook is installed by calling *SetWindowsHookEx* as follows:

```
HHOOK hHook = SetWindowsHookEx(WH_GETMESSAGE, GetMsgProc,
   hinstDll, 0);
```

The first parameter, *WH_GETMESSAGE*, indicates the type of hook to install. The second parameter, *GetMsgProc*, identifies the address (in your address space) of the function that the system should call when a window is about to process a message. The third parameter, *hinstDll*, identifies the DLL that contains the *GetMsgProc* function. In Windows, a DLL's *hinstDll* value identifies the virtual memory address where the DLL is mapped into the process's address space. The last parameter, *0*, identifies the thread to hook. It is possible for one thread to call *SetWindowsHookEx* and to pass the ID of another thread in the system. By passing *0* for this parameter, we tell the system that we want to hook all GUI threads in the system.

Now let's take a look at what happens:

1. A thread in Process B prepares to dispatch a message to a window.

2. The system checks to see whether a WH_GETMESSAGE hook is installed on this thread.

3. The system checks to see whether the DLL containing the *GetMsgProc* function is mapped into Process B's address space.

4. If the DLL has not been mapped, the system forces the DLL to be mapped into Process B's address space and increments a lock count on the DLL's mapping in Process B.

5. The system looks at the DLL's *hinstDll* as it applies to Process B and checks to see whether the DLL's *hinstDll* is at the same location as it is when it applies to Process A.

If the *hinstDll*s are the same, the memory address of the *GetMsgProc* function is also the same in the two process address spaces. In this case, the system can simply call the *GetMsgProc* function in Process A's address space.

If the *hinstDll*s are different, the system must determine the virtual memory address of the *GetMsgProc* function in Process B's address space. This address is determined using the following formula:

```
GetMsgProc B = hinstDll B + (GetMsgProc A - hinstDll A)
```

By subtracting *hinstDll* A from *GetMsgProc* A, you get the offset in bytes for the *GetMsgProc* function. Adding this offset to *hinstDll* B gives the location of the *GetMsgProc* function as it applies to the DLL's mapping in Process B's address space.

6. The system increments a lock count on the DLL's mapping in Process B.

7. The system calls the *GetMsgProc* function in Process B's address space.

8. When *GetMsgProc* returns, the system decrements a lock count on the DLL's mapping in Process B.

Note that when the system injects or maps the DLL containing the hook filter function, the whole DLL is mapped, not just the hook filter function. This means that any and all functions contained in the DLL now exist and can be called from threads running in Process B's context.

So, to subclass a window created by a thread in another process, you can first set a WH_GETMESSAGE hook on the thread that created the window, and then, when the *GetMsgProc* function is called, call *SetWindowLongPtr* to subclass the window. Of course, the subclass procedure must be in the same DLL as the *GetMsgProc* function.

Unlike the Registry method of injecting a DLL, this method allows you to unmap the DLL when it is no longer needed in the other process's address space by simply calling the following:

```
BOOL UnhookWindowsHookEx(HHOOK hhook);
```

When a thread calls the *UnhookWindowsHookEx* function, the system cycles through its internal list of processes into which it had to inject the DLL and decrements the DLL's lock count. When the lock count reaches 0, the DLL is automatically unmapped from the process's address space. You'll recall that just before the system calls the *GetMsgProc* function, it increments the DLL's lock count. (See step 6 above.) This prevents a memory access violation. If this lock count is not incremented, another thread running in the system can call *UnhookWindowsHookEx* while Process B's thread attempts to execute the code in the *GetMsgProc* function.

All of this means that you can't subclass the window and immediately unhook the hook. The hook must stay in effect for the lifetime of the subclass.

The Desktop Item Position Saver (DIPS) Utility

The DIPS.exe application, listed in Figure 22-2 (starting on page 763), uses windows hooks to inject a DLL into Explorer.exe's address space. The source code and resource files for the application and DLL are in the 22-DIPS and 22-DIPSLib directories on the companion CD-ROM.

I generally use my computer for business-related tasks, and I find that a screen resolution of 1152 x 864 works best for me. However, I occasionally play games on my computer, and most games are designed for 640 x 480 resolution. So when I feel like playing a game, I go to the Control Panel's Display applet and change the resolution to 640 x 480. When I'm done playing the game, I go back to the Display applet and change the resolution back to 1152 x 864.

This ability to change the display resolution on the fly is awesome and a welcome feature of Windows. However, I do despise one thing about changing the display resolution: the desktop icons don't remember where they were. I have several icons on my desktop to access applications immediately and to get to files that I use frequently. I have these icons positioned on my desktop just so. When I change the display resolution, the desktop window changes size and my icons are rearranged in a way that makes it impossible for me to find anything. Then, when I change the display resolution back, all my icons are rearranged again, in some new order. To fix this, I have to manually reposition all the desktop icons back to the way I like them—how annoying!

I hated manually rearranging these icons so much that I created the Desktop Item Position Saver utility, DIPS. DIPS consists of a small executable and a small DLL. When you run the executable, the following message box appears.

This message box shows how to use the utility. When you pass S as the command-line argument to DIPS, it creates the following registry subkey and adds a value for each item on your desktop window:

```
HKEY_CURRENT_USER\Software\Richter\Desktop Item Position Saver
```

Each item has a position value saved with it. You run DIPS S just before you change the screen resolution to play a game. When you're done playing the game, you change the screen resolution back to normal and run DIPS R. This causes DIPS to open the registry subkey, and for each item on your desktop that matches an item saved in the registry, the item's position is set back to where it was when you ran DIPS S.

At first, you might think that DIPS would be fairly easy to implement. After all, you simply get the window handle of the desktop's ListView control, send it messages to enumerate the items, get their positions, and then save this information in the registry. However, if you try this, you'll see that it is not quite this simple. The problem is that most common control window messages, such as LVM_GETITEM and LVM_GETITEMPOSITION, do not work across process boundaries.

Here's why: the LVM_GETITEM message requires that you pass the address of an LV_ITEM data structure for the message's *LPARAM* parameter. Because this memory address is meaningful only to the process that is sending the message, the process receiving the message cannot safely use it. So to make DIPS work as advertised, you must inject code into Explorer.exe that sends LVM_GETITEM and LVM_GETITEMPOSITION messages successfully to the desktop's ListView control.

> **NOTE**
>
> You can send window messages across process boundaries to interact with built-in controls (such as button, edit, static, combo box, list box, and so on), but you can't do so with the new common controls. For example, you can send a list box control created by a thread in another process an LB_GETTEXT message where the *LPARAM* parameter points to a string buffer in the sending process. This works because Microsoft checks specifically to see whether an LB_GETTEXT message is being sent, and if so, the operating system internally creates memory-mapped files and copies the string data across process boundaries.
>
> Why did Microsoft decide to do this for the built-in controls and not for the new common controls? The answer is portability. In 16-bit Windows, in which all applications run in a single address space, one

(continued)

application could send an LB_GETTEXT message to a window created by another application. To port these 16-bit applications to Win32 easily, Microsoft went to the extra effort of making sure that this still works. However, the new common controls do not exist in 16-bit Windows and therefore there was no porting issue involved, so Microsoft chose not to do the additional work for the common controls.

When you run DIPS.exe, it first gets the window handle of the desktop's ListView control:

```
// The Desktop ListView window is the
// grandchild of the ProgMan window.
hwndLV = GetFirstChild(
    GetFirstChild(FindWindow(__TEXT("ProgMan"), NULL)));
```

This code first looks for a window whose class is ProgMan. Even though no Program Manager application is running, the new shell creates a window of this class for backward compatibility with applications that were designed for older versions of Windows. This ProgMan window has a single child window whose class is SHELLDLL_DefView. This child window also has a single child window whose class is SysListView32. This SysListView32 window is the desktop's ListView control window. (By the way, I obtained all this information using Spy++.)

Once I have the ListView's window handle, I can determine the ID of the thread that created the window by calling *GetWindowThreadProcessId*. I pass this ID to the *SetDIPSHook* function (implemented inside DIPSLib.cpp). *SetDIPSHook* installs a WH_GETMESSAGE hook on this thread and calls the following function to force Windows Explorer's thread to wake up:

```
PostThreadMessage(dwThreadId, WM_NULL, 0, 0);
```

Because I have installed a WH_GETMESSAGE hook on this thread, the operating system automatically injects my DIPSLib.dll file into Explorer's address space and calls my *GetMsgProc* function. This function first checks to see whether it is being called for the first time; if so, it creates a hidden window with a caption of "Richter DIPS." Keep in mind that Explorer's thread is creating this hidden window. While it does this, the DIPS.exe thread returns from *SetDIPSHook* and then calls this function:

```
GetMessage(&msg, NULL, 0, 0);
```

This call puts the thread to sleep until a message shows up in the queue. Even though DIPS.exe does not create any windows of its own, it still has a message queue, and messages can be placed in this queue only by calling

PostThreadMessage. If you look at the code in DIPSLib.cpp's *GetMsgProc* function, you'll see that immediately after the call to *CreateDialog* is a call to *PostThreadMessage* that causes the DIPS.exe thread to wake up again. The thread ID was saved in a shared variable inside the *SetDIPSHook* function.

Notice that I use the thread's message queue for thread synchronization. There is absolutely nothing wrong with doing this, and sometimes it's much easier to synchronize threads in this way rather than using the various kernel objects (mutexes, semaphores, events, and so on). Windows has a rich API; take advantage of it.

When the thread in the DIPS executable wakes up, it knows that the server dialog box has been created and calls *FindWindow* to get the window handle. We now can use window messages to communicate between the client (the DIPS applications) and the server (the hidden dialog box). Because a thread running inside the context of Windows Explorer's process created the dialog box, we do face a few limitations on what we can do to Windows Explorer.

To tell our dialog box to save or restore the desktop icon positions, we simply send a message:

```
// Tell the DIPS window which ListView window to manipulate
// and whether the items should be saved or restored.
SendMessage(hwndDIPS, WM_APP, (WPARAM) hwndLV, fSave);
```

I have coded the dialog box's dialog box procedure to look for the WM_APP message. When it receives this message, the *WPARAM* parameter indicates the handle of the ListView control that is to be manipulated, and the *LPARAM* parameter is a Boolean value indicating whether the current item positions should be saved to the registry or whether the items should be repositioned based on the saved information read from the registry.

Because I use *SendMessage* instead of *PostMessage*, the function does not return until the operation is complete. If you want, you can add messages to the dialog's dialog box procedure to give the program more control over the Explorer process. When I finish communicating with the dialog box and want to terminate the server (so to speak), I send a WM_CLOSE message that tells the dialog box to destroy itself.

Finally, just before the DIPS application terminates, it calls *SetDIPSHook* again but passes 0 as the thread ID. The 0 is a sentinel value that tells the function to unhook the WH_GETMESSAGE hook. When the hook is uninstalled, the operating system automatically unloads the DIPSLib.dll file from Explorer's address space, which means that the dialog box's dialog box procedure is no longer inside Explorer's address space. It is important that the dialog box be destroyed first, before the hook is uninstalled; otherwise, the next message received by the dialog box causes Explorer's thread to raise an access violation.

If this happens, Explorer is terminated by the operating system. You must be very careful when using DLL injection!

Dips.cpp

```
/*********************************************************************
Module:  DIPS.cpp
Notices: Copyright (c) 2000 Jeffrey Richter
*********************************************************************/


#include "..\CmnHdr.h"     /* See Appendix A. */
#include <WindowsX.h>
#include <tchar.h>
#include "Resource.h"
#include "..\22-DIPSLib\DIPSLib.h"


///////////////////////////////////////////////////////////////////


BOOL Dlg_OnInitDialog(HWND hwnd, HWND hwndFocus, LPARAM lParam) {

   chSETDLGICONS(hwnd, IDI_DIPS);
   return(TRUE);
}


///////////////////////////////////////////////////////////////////


void Dlg_OnCommand(HWND hwnd, int id, HWND hwndCtl, UINT codeNotify) {

   switch (id) {
      case IDC_SAVE:
      case IDC_RESTORE:
      case IDCANCEL:
         EndDialog(hwnd, id);
         break;
   }
}

///////////////////////////////////////////////////////////////////
```

Figure 22-2. *(continued)*
The DIPS utility

Figure 22-2. *continued*

```
BOOL WINAPI Dlg_Proc(HWND hwnd, UINT uMsg, WPARAM wParam, LPARAM lParam) {

   switch (uMsg) {
      chHANDLE_DLGMSG(hwnd, WM_INITDIALOG, Dlg_OnInitDialog);
      chHANDLE_DLGMSG(hwnd, WM_COMMAND,    Dlg_OnCommand);
   }

   return(FALSE);
}


///////////////////////////////////////////////////////////////////////////////


int WINAPI _tWinMain(HINSTANCE hinstExe, HINSTANCE, PTSTR pszCmdLine, int) {

   // Convert command-line character to uppercase.
   CharUpperBuff(pszCmdLine, 1);
   TCHAR cWhatToDo = pszCmdLine[0];

   if ((cWhatToDo != TEXT('S')) && (cWhatToDo != TEXT('R'))) {

      // An invalid command-line argument; prompt the user.
      cWhatToDo = 0;
   }

   if (cWhatToDo == 0) {
      // No command-line argument was used to tell us what to
      // do; show usage dialog box and prompt the user.
      switch (DialogBox(hinstExe, MAKEINTRESOURCE(IDD_DIPS), NULL, Dlg_Proc)) {
         case IDC_SAVE:
            cWhatToDo = TEXT('S');
            break;

         case IDC_RESTORE:
            cWhatToDo = TEXT('R');
            break;
      }
   }

   if (cWhatToDo == 0) {
      // The user doesn't want to do anything.
      return(0);
   }
```

(continued)

Figure 22-2. *continued*

```
   // The Desktop ListView window is the grandchild of the ProgMan window.
   HWND hwndLV = GetFirstChild(GetFirstChild(
      FindWindow(TEXT("ProgMan"), NULL)));
   chASSERT(IsWindow(hwndLV));

   // Set hook that injects our DLL into the Explorer's address space. After
   // setting the hook, the DIPS hidden modeless dialog box is created. We
   // send messages to this window to tell it what we want it to do.
   chVERIFY(SetDIPSHook(GetWindowThreadProcessId(hwndLV, NULL)));

   // Wait for the DIPS server window to be created.
   MSG msg;
   GetMessage(&msg, NULL, 0, 0);

   // Find the handle of the hidden dialog box window.
   HWND hwndDIPS = FindWindow(NULL, TEXT("Richter DIPS"));

   // Make sure that the window was created.
   chASSERT(IsWindow(hwndDIPS));

   // Tell the DIPS window which ListView window to manipulate
   // and whether the items should be saved or restored.
   SendMessage(hwndDIPS, WM_APP, (WPARAM) hwndLV, (cWhatToDo == TEXT('S')));

   // Tell the DIPS window to destroy itself. Use SendMessage
   // instead of PostMessage so that we know the window is
   // destroyed before the hook is removed.
   SendMessage(hwndDIPS, WM_CLOSE, 0, 0);

   // Make sure that the window was destroyed.
   chASSERT(!IsWindow(hwndDIPS));

   // Unhook the DLL, removing the DIPS dialog box procedure
   // from the Explorer's address space.
   SetDIPSHook(0);

   return(0);
}


/////////////////////////////////// End of File ///////////////////////////////////
```

(continued)

Figure 22-2. *continued*

DIPSLib.cpp

```
/*****************************************************************************
Module:  DIPSLib.cpp
Notices: Copyright (c) 2000 Jeffrey Richter
*****************************************************************************/


#include "..\CmnHdr.h"      /* See Appendix A. */
#include <WindowsX.h>
#include <CommCtrl.h>

#define DIPSLIBAPI __declspec(dllexport)
#include "DIPSLib.h"
#include "Resource.h"


///////////////////////////////////////////////////////////////////////////


#ifdef _DEBUG
// This function forces the debugger to be invoked
void ForceDebugBreak() {
   __try { DebugBreak(); }
   __except(UnhandledExceptionFilter(GetExceptionInformation())) { }
}
#else
#define ForceDebugBreak()
#endif


///////////////////////////////////////////////////////////////////////////


// Forward references
LRESULT WINAPI GetMsgProc(int nCode, WPARAM wParam, LPARAM lParam);

INT_PTR WINAPI Dlg_Proc(HWND hwnd, UINT uMsg, WPARAM wParam, LPARAM lParam);


///////////////////////////////////////////////////////////////////////////


// Instruct the compiler to put the g_hhook data variable in
```

(continued)

Figure 22-2. *continued*

```
// its own data section called Shared. We then instruct the
// linker that we want to share the data in this section
// with all instances of this application.
#pragma data_seg("Shared")
HHOOK g_hhook = NULL;
DWORD g_dwThreadIdDIPS = 0;
#pragma data_seg()

// Instruct the linker to make the Shared section
// readable, writable, and shared.
#pragma comment(linker, "/section:Shared,rws")


///////////////////////////////////////////////////////////////////////////


// Nonshared variables
HINSTANCE g_hinstDll = NULL;


///////////////////////////////////////////////////////////////////////////


BOOL WINAPI DllMain(HINSTANCE hinstDll, DWORD fdwReason, PVOID fImpLoad) {

   switch (fdwReason) {

      case DLL_PROCESS_ATTACH:
         // DLL is attaching to the address space of the current process.
         g_hinstDll = hinstDll;
         break;

      case DLL_THREAD_ATTACH:
         // A new thread is being created in the current process.
         break;

      case DLL_THREAD_DETACH:
         // A thread is exiting cleanly.
         break;

      case DLL_PROCESS_DETACH:
         // The calling process is detaching the DLL from its address space.
         break;
   }
```

(continued)

Figure 22-2. *continued*

```
    return(TRUE);
}

////////////////////////////////////////////////////////////////////////////

BOOL WINAPI SetDIPSHook(DWORD dwThreadId) {

   BOOL fOk = FALSE;

   if (dwThreadId != 0) {
      // Make sure that the hook is not already installed.
      chASSERT(g_hhook == NULL);

      // Save our thread ID in a shared variable so that our GetMsgProc
      // function can post a message back to the thread when the server
      // window has been created.
      g_dwThreadIdDIPS = GetCurrentThreadId();

      // Install the hook on the specified thread
      g_hhook = SetWindowsHookEx(WH_GETMESSAGE, GetMsgProc, g_hinstDll,
         dwThreadId);

      fOk = (g_hhook != NULL);
      if (fOk) {
         // The hook was installed successfully; force a benign message to
         // the thread's queue so that the hook function gets called.
         fOk = PostThreadMessage(dwThreadId, WM_NULL, 0, 0);
      }
   } else {

      // Make sure that a hook has been installed.
      chASSERT(g_hhook != NULL);
      fOk = UnhookWindowsHookEx(g_hhook);
      g_hhook = NULL;
   }

   return(fOk);
}

////////////////////////////////////////////////////////////////////////////

LRESULT WINAPI GetMsgProc(int nCode, WPARAM wParam, LPARAM lParam) {

   static BOOL fFirstTime = TRUE;
```

(continued)

Figure 22-2. *continued*

```
    if (fFirstTime) {
        // The DLL just got injected.
        fFirstTime = FALSE;

        // Uncomment the line below to invoke the debugger
        // on the process that just got the injected DLL.
        // ForceDebugBreak();

        // Create the DTIS Server window to handle the client request.
        CreateDialog(g_hinstDll, MAKEINTRESOURCE(IDD_DIPS), NULL, Dlg_Proc);

        // Tell the DIPS application that the server is up
        // and ready to handle requests.
        PostThreadMessage(g_dwThreadIdDIPS, WM_NULL, 0, 0);
    }

    return(CallNextHookEx(g_hhook, nCode, wParam, lParam));
}


///////////////////////////////////////////////////////////////////////////


void Dlg_OnClose(HWND hwnd) {

    DestroyWindow(hwnd);
}


///////////////////////////////////////////////////////////////////////////


static const TCHAR g_szRegSubKey[] =
    TEXT("Software\\Richter\\Desktop Item Position Saver");


///////////////////////////////////////////////////////////////////////////


void SaveListViewItemPositions(HWND hwndLV) {

    int nMaxItems = ListView_GetItemCount(hwndLV);

    // When saving new positions, delete the old position
    // information that is currently in the registry.
    LONG l = RegDeleteKey(HKEY_CURRENT_USER, g_szRegSubKey);

    // Create the registry key to hold the info
    HKEY hkey;
```

(continued)

769

Figure 22-2. *continued*

```
    1 = RegCreateKeyEx(HKEY_CURRENT_USER, g_szRegSubKey, 0, NULL,
        REG_OPTION_NON_VOLATILE, KEY_SET_VALUE, NULL, &hkey, NULL);
    chASSERT(1 == ERROR_SUCCESS);

    for (int nItem = 0; nItem < nMaxItems; nItem++) {

        // Get the name and position of a ListView item.
        TCHAR szName[MAX_PATH];
        ListView_GetItemText(hwndLV, nItem, 0, szName, chDIMOF(szName));

        POINT pt;
        ListView_GetItemPosition(hwndLV, nItem, &pt);

        // Save the name and position in the registry.
        1 = RegSetValueEx(hkey, szName, 0, REG_BINARY, (PBYTE) &pt, sizeof(pt));
        chASSERT(1 == ERROR_SUCCESS);
    }
    RegCloseKey(hkey);
}

/////////////////////////////////////////////////////////////////////////////////

void RestoreListViewItemPositions(HWND hwndLV) {

    HKEY hkey;
    LONG 1 = RegOpenKeyEx(HKEY_CURRENT_USER, g_szRegSubKey,
        0, KEY_QUERY_VALUE, &hkey);
    if (1 == ERROR_SUCCESS) {

        // If the ListView has AutoArrange on, temporarily turn it off.
        DWORD dwStyle = GetWindowStyle(hwndLV);
        if (dwStyle & LVS_AUTOARRANGE)
            SetWindowLong(hwndLV, GWL_STYLE, dwStyle & ~LVS_AUTOARRANGE);

        1 = NO_ERROR;
        for (int nIndex = 0; 1 != ERROR_NO_MORE_ITEMS; nIndex++) {
            TCHAR szName[MAX_PATH];
            DWORD cbValueName = chDIMOF(szName);

            POINT pt;
            DWORD cbData = sizeof(pt), nItem;

            // Read a value name and position from the registry.
            DWORD dwType;
```

(continued)

Figure 22-2. *continued*

```
        l = RegEnumValue(hkey, nIndex, szName, &cbValueName,
           NULL, &dwType, (PBYTE) &pt, &cbData);

        if (l == ERROR_NO_MORE_ITEMS)
           continue;

        if ((dwType == REG_BINARY) && (cbData == sizeof(pt))) {
           // The value is something that we recognize; try to find
           // an item in the ListView control that matches the name.
           LV_FINDINFO lvfi;
           lvfi.flags = LVFI_STRING;
           lvfi.psz = szName;
           nItem = ListView_FindItem(hwndLV, -1, &lvfi);
           if (nItem != -1) {
              // We found a match; change the item's position.
              ListView_SetItemPosition(hwndLV, nItem, pt.x, pt.y);
           }
        }
     }
     // Turn AutoArrange back on if it was originally on.
     SetWindowLong(hwndLV, GWL_STYLE, dwStyle);
     RegCloseKey(hkey);
  }
}


///////////////////////////////////////////////////////////////////////////

INT_PTR WINAPI Dlg_Proc(HWND hwnd, UINT uMsg, WPARAM wParam, LPARAM lParam) {

   switch (uMsg) {
      chHANDLE_DLGMSG(hwnd, WM_CLOSE, Dlg_OnClose);

      case WM_APP:
         // Uncomment the line below to invoke the debugger
         // on the process that just got the injected DLL.
         // ForceDebugBreak();

         if (lParam)
            SaveListViewItemPositions((HWND) wParam);
         else
            RestoreListViewItemPositions((HWND) wParam);
         break;
   }
```

(continued)

Figure 22-2. *continued*

```
    return(FALSE);
}



//////////////////////////// End of File ///////////////////////////////////////
```

DIPSLib.h

```
/******************************************************************************
Module:  DIPSLib.h
Notices: Copyright (c) 2000 Jeffrey Richter
******************************************************************************/


#if !defined(DIPSLIBAPI)
#define DIPSLIBAPI __declspec(dllimport)
#endif


///////////////////////////////////////////////////////////////////////////////


// External function prototypes
DIPSLIBAPI BOOL WINAPI SetDIPSHook(DWORD dwThreadId);


//////////////////////////// End of File ///////////////////////////////////////
```

DIPSLib.rc

```
//Microsoft Developer Studio generated resource script.
//
#include "resource.h"

#define APSTUDIO_READONLY_SYMBOLS
///////////////////////////////////////////////////////////////////////////////
//
// Generated from the TEXTINCLUDE 2 resource.
//
#include "afxres.h"
```

(continued)

Figure 22-2. *continued*

```
////////////////////////////////////////////////////////////////////////////
#undef APSTUDIO_READONLY_SYMBOLS


////////////////////////////////////////////////////////////////////////////
// English (U.S.) resources

#if !defined(AFX_RESOURCE_DLL) || defined(AFX_TARG_ENU)
#ifdef _WIN32
LANGUAGE LANG_ENGLISH, SUBLANG_ENGLISH_US
#pragma code_page(1252)
#endif //_WIN32


////////////////////////////////////////////////////////////////////////////
//
// Dialog
//

IDD_DIPS DIALOG DISCARDABLE  0, 0, 132, 13
STYLE WS_CAPTION
CAPTION "Richter DIPS"
FONT 8, "MS Sans Serif"
BEGIN
END


#ifdef APSTUDIO_INVOKED
////////////////////////////////////////////////////////////////////////////
//
// TEXTINCLUDE
//

1 TEXTINCLUDE DISCARDABLE
BEGIN
    "resource.h\0"
END

2 TEXTINCLUDE DISCARDABLE
BEGIN
    "#include ""afxres.h""\r\n"
    "\0"
END

3 TEXTINCLUDE DISCARDABLE
BEGIN
    "\r\n"
    "\0"
END
```

(continued)

Figure 22-2. *continued*

```
#endif    // APSTUDIO_INVOKED

#endif    // English (U.S.) resources
/////////////////////////////////////////////////////////////////////////


#ifndef APSTUDIO_INVOKED
/////////////////////////////////////////////////////////////////////////
//
// Generated from the TEXTINCLUDE 3 resource.
//

/////////////////////////////////////////////////////////////////////////
#endif    // not APSTUDIO_INVOKED
```

Injecting a DLL Using Remote Threads

The third method of injecting a DLL, using remote threads, offers the greatest flexibility. It requires that you understand several Windows features: processes, threads, thread synchronization, virtual memory management, DLLs, and Unicode. (If you're unclear about any of these features, please refer to their respective chapters in this book.) Most Windows functions allow a process to manipulate only itself. This is good because it prevents one process from corrupting another process. However, a handful of functions do allow one process to manipulate another. Most of these functions were originally designed for debuggers and other tools. However, any application can call these functions.

Basically, this DLL injection technique requires that a thread in the target process call *LoadLibrary* to load the desired DLL. Since we can't easily control the threads in a process other than our own, this solution requires that we create a new thread in the target process. Since we create this thread ourselves, we can control what code it executes. Fortunately, Windows offers a function called *CreateRemoteThread* that makes it easy to create a thread in another process:

```
HANDLE CreateRemoteThread(
    HANDLE hProcess,
    PSECURITY_ATTRIBUTES psa,
    DWORD dwStackSize,
    PTHREAD_START_ROUTINE pfnStartAddr,
    PVOID pvParam,
    DWORD fdwCreate,
    PDWORD pdwThreadId);
```

CreateRemoteThread is identical to *CreateThread* except that it has one additional parameter, *hProcess*. This parameter identifies the process that will own the newly created thread. The *pfnStartAddr* parameter identifies the memory address of the thread function. This memory address is, of course, relative to the remote process—the thread function's code cannot be in your own process's address space.

> **NOTE**
>
> In Windows 2000, the more commonly used *CreateThread* function is implemented internally as follows:
>
> ```
> HANDLE CreateThread(PSECURITY_ATTRIBUTES psa, DWORD dwStackSize,
>     PTHREAD_START_ROUTINE pfnStartAddr, PVOID pvParam,
>     DWORD fdwCreate, PDWORD pdwThreadID) {
>
>     return(CreateRemoteThread(GetCurrentProcess(), psa, dwStackSize,
>         pfnStartAddr, pvParam, fdwCreate, pdwThreadID));
> }
> ```

> **WINDOWS 98**
>
> In Windows 98, the *CreateRemoteThread* function has no useful implementation and simply returns NULL; calling *GetLastError* returns ERROR_CALL_NOT_IMPLEMENTED. (The *CreateThread* function contains the complete implementation of the code that creates a thread in the calling process.) Because *CreateRemoteThread* is not implemented, you cannot use this technique to inject a DLL under Windows 98.

OK, so now you know how to create a thread in another process, but how do we get that thread to load our DLL? The answer is simple: we need the thread to call the *LoadLibrary* function:

```
HINSTANCE LoadLibrary(PCTSTR pszLibFile);
```

If you look up *LoadLibrary* in the WinBase.h header file, you'll find the following:

```
HINSTANCE WINAPI LoadLibraryA(LPCSTR  pszLibFileName);
HINSTANCE WINAPI LoadLibraryW(LPCWSTR pszLibFileName);
#ifdef UNICODE
#define LoadLibrary   LoadLibraryW
#else
#define LoadLibrary   LoadLibraryA
#endif // !UNICODE
```

There are actually two *LoadLibrary* functions: *LoadLibraryA* and *LoadLibraryW*. The only difference between them is the type of parameter that you pass to the function. If you have the library's filename stored as an ANSI string, you must call *LoadLibraryA*. (The *A* stands for ANSI.) If the filename is stored as a Unicode string, you must call *LoadLibraryW*. (The *W* stands for wide characters.) No single *LoadLibrary* function exists—only *LoadLibraryA* and *LoadLibraryW*. For most applications, the *LoadLibrary* macro expands to *LoadLibraryA*.

Fortunately, the prototype for the *LoadLibrary* functions and the prototype for a thread function are identical. Here is a thread function's prototype:

```
DWORD WINAPI ThreadFunc(PVOID pvParam);
```

OK, the function prototypes are not exactly identical, but they are close enough. Both functions accept a single parameter and both return a value. Also, both use the same calling convention, WINAPI. This is extremely fortunate because all we have to do is create a new thread and have the thread function address be the address of the *LoadLibraryA* or *LoadLibraryW* function. Basically, all we need to do is execute a line of code that looks like this:

```
HANDLE hThread = CreateRemoteThread(hProcessRemote, NULL, 0,
    LoadLibraryA, "C:\\MyLib.dll", 0, NULL);
```

Or, if you prefer Unicode, the line looks like this:

```
HANDLE hThread = CreateRemoteThread(hProcessRemote, NULL, 0,
    LoadLibraryW, L"C:\\MyLib.dll", 0, NULL);
```

When the new thread is created in the remote process, the thread immediately calls the *LoadLibraryA* (or *LoadLibraryW*) function, passing to it the address of the DLL's pathname. This is easy. But there are two other problems.

The first problem is that you can't simply pass *LoadLibraryA* or *LoadLibraryW* as the fourth parameter to *CreateRemoteThread*, as I've shown above. The reason is quite subtle. When you compile and link a program, the resulting binary contains an import section (described in Chapter 19). This section consists of a series of thunks to imported functions. So when your code calls a function such as *LoadLibraryA*, the linker generates a call to a thunk in your module's import section. The thunk in turn jumps to the actual function.

If you use a direct reference to *LoadLibraryA* in the call to *CreateRemoteThread*, this resolves to the address of the *LoadLibraryA* thunk in your module's import section. Passing the address of the thunk as the starting address of the remote thread causes the remote thread to begin executing who-knows-what. The result is most likely an access violation. To force a direct call to the *LoadLibraryA* function, bypassing the thunk, you must get the exact memory location of *LoadLibraryA* by calling *GetProcAddress*.

The call to *CreateRemoteThread* assumes that Kernel32.dll is mapped to the same memory location in both the local and the remote processes' address spaces. Every application requires Kernel32.dll, and in my experience the system maps Kernel32.dll to the same address in every process. So we have to call *CreateRemoteThread* like this:

```
// Get the real address of LoadLibraryA in Kernel32.dll.
PTHREAD_START_ROUTINE pfnThreadRtn = (PTHREAD_START_ROUTINE)
   GetProcAddress(GetModuleHandle(TEXT("Kernel32")), "LoadLibraryA");

HANDLE hThread = CreateRemoteThread(hProcessRemote, NULL, 0,
   pfnThreadRtn, "C:\\MyLib.dll", 0, NULL);
```

Or, again, if you prefer Unicode, do this:

```
// Get the real address of LoadLibraryW in Kernel32.dll.
PTHREAD_START_ROUTINE pfnThreadRtn = (PTHREAD_START_ROUTINE)
   GetProcAddress(GetModuleHandle(TEXT("Kernel32")), "LoadLibraryW");

HANDLE hThread = CreateRemoteThread(hProcessRemote, NULL, 0,
   pfnThreadRtn, L"C:\\MyLib.dll", 0, NULL);
```

All right, this fixes one problem. But I said that there were two problems. The second problem has to do with the DLL pathname string. The string, "C:\\MyLib.dll", is in the calling process's address space. The address of this string is given to the newly created remote thread, which passes it to *LoadLibraryA*. But when *LoadLibraryA* dereferences the memory address, the DLL pathname string is not there and the remote process's thread will probably raise an access violation; the unhandled exception message box is presented to the user, and the remote process is terminated. That's right, the remote process is terminated—not your process. You will have successfully crashed another process while your process continues to execute just fine!

To fix this, we need to get the DLL's pathname string into the remote process's address space. Then, when *CreateRemoteThread* is called, we need to pass it the address (relative to the remote process) of where we placed the string. Again, Windows offers a function, *VirtualAllocEx*, that allows one process to allocate memory in another process's address space:

```
PVOID VirtualAllocEx(
   HANDLE hProcess,
   PVOID pvAddress,
   SIZE_T dwSize,
   DWORD flAllocationType,
   DWORD flProtect);
```

Another function allows us to free this memory:

```
BOOL VirtualFreeEx(
   HANDLE hProcess,
   PVOID pvAddress,
   SIZE_T dwSize,
   DWORD dwFreeType);
```

Both of these functions are similar to their non-*Ex* versions (which are discussed in Chapter 15). The only difference is that these two functions require a handle to a process as their first argument. This handle indicates the process where the operation is to be performed.

Once we allocate memory for the string, we also need a way to copy the string from our process's address space over to the remote process's address space. Windows offers functions that allow one process to read and write from/to another process's address space:

```
BOOL ReadProcessMemory(
   HANDLE hProcess,
   PVOID pvAddressRemote,
   PVOID pvBufferLocal,
   DWORD dwSize,
   PDWORD pdwNumBytesRead);

BOOL WriteProcessMemory(
   HANDLE hProcess,
   PVOID pvAddressRemote,
   PVOID pvBufferLocal,
   DWORD dwSize,
   PDWORD pdwNumBytesWritten);
```

The remote process is identified by the *hProcess* parameter. The *pvAddress-Remote* parameters indicate the address in the remote process, *pvBufferLocal* is the address of memory in the local process, *dwSize* is the requested number of bytes to transfer, and *pdwNumBytesRead* and *pdwNumBytesWritten* indicate the number of bytes actually transferred and can be examined when the function returns.

Now that you understand all that I'm trying to do, let me summarize the steps you must take:

1. Use the *VirtualAllocEx* function to allocate memory in the remote process's address space.

2. Use the *WriteProcessMemory* function to copy the DLL's pathname to the memory allocated in step 1.

3. Use the *GetProcAddress* function to get the real address (inside Kernel32.dll) of the *LoadLibraryA* or *LoadLibraryW* function.

4. Use the *CreateRemoteThread* function to create a thread in the remote process that calls the proper *LoadLibrary* function, passing it the address of the memory allocated in step 1.

At this point, the DLL has been injected into the remote process's address space, and the DLL's *DllMain* function receives a DLL_PROCESS_ATTACH notification and can execute the desired code. When *DllMain* returns, the remote thread returns from its call to *LoadLibrary* back to the *BaseThreadStart* function (discussed in Chapter 6). *BaseThreadStart* then calls *ExitThread*, causing the remote thread to die.

Now the remote process has the block of storage allocated in step 1 and the DLL still stuck in its address space. To clean this stuff up, we'll need to execute the following steps after the remote thread exists:

5. Use the *VirtualFreeEx* function to free the memory allocated in step 1.

6. Use the *GetProcAddress* function to get the real address (inside Kernel32.dll) of the *FreeLibrary* function.

7. Use the *CreateRemoteThread* function to create a thread in the remote process that calls *FreeLibrary* function, passing the remote DLL's HINSTANCE.

That's basically it. The only downside to this DLL injection technique—the most versatile one we have discussed so far—is that Windows 98 doesn't support a lot of these functions. You can use this technique only on Windows 2000.

The Inject Library Sample Application

The InjLib.exe application, listed in Figure 22-3, injects a DLL using the *CreateRemoteThread* function. The source code and resource files for the application and DLL are in the 22-InjLib and 22-ImgWalk directories on the companion CD-ROM. The program uses the following dialog box to accept the process ID of a running process.

You can obtain a process's ID by using the Task Manager that ships with Windows 2000. Using the ID, the program attempts to open a handle to this running process by calling *OpenProcess,* requesting the appropriate access rights:

```
hProcess = OpenProcess(
   PROCESS_CREATE_THREAD |   // For CreateRemoteThread
   PROCESS_VM_OPERATION |    // For VirtualAllocEx/VirtualFreeEx
   PROCESS_VM_WRITE,         // For WriteProcessMemory
   FALSE, dwProcessId);
```

If *OpenProcess* returns NULL, the application is not running under a security context that allows it to open a handle to the target process. Some processes—such as WinLogon, SvcHost, and Csrss—run under the local system account, which the logged-on user cannot alter. You might be able to open a handle to these processes if you are granted and enable the debug security privilege. The ProcessInfo sample in Chapter 4 demonstrates how to do this.

If *OpenProcess* is successful, a buffer is initialized with the full pathname of the DLL that is to be injected. Then *InjectLib* is called, passing it the handle of the desired remote process and the pathname of the DLL to inject into it. Finally, when *InjectLib* returns, the program displays a message box indicating whether the DLL successfully loaded in the remote process; it then closes the handle to the process. That's all there is to it.

You might notice in the code that I make a special check to see whether the process ID passed is 0. If so, I set the process ID to InjLib.exe's own process ID by calling *GetCurrentProcessId*. This way, when *InjectLib* is called, the DLL is injected into the process's own address space. This makes debugging easier. As you can imagine, when bugs popped up, it was sometimes difficult to determine whether the bugs were in the local process or in the remote process. Originally, I started debugging my code with two debuggers, one watching InjLib and the other watching the remote process. This turned out to be terribly inconvenient. It then dawned on me that InjLib can also inject a DLL into itself—that is, into the same address space as the caller. This made it much easier to debug my code.

As you can see at the top of the source code module, *InjectLib* is really a symbol that expands to either *InjectLibA* or *InjectLibW* depending on how you're compiling the source code. The *InjectLibW* function is where all the magic happens. The comments speak for themselves, and I can't add much here. However, you'll notice that the *InjectLibA* function is short. It simply converts the ANSI DLL pathname to its Unicode equivalent and then calls the *InjectLibW* function to actually do the work. This approach is exactly what I recommended in Chapter 2. It also means that I only had to get the injection code running once—a nice timesaver.

InjLib.cpp

```
/*****************************************************************************
Module:  InjLib.cpp
Notices: Copyright (c) 2000 Jeffrey Richter
*****************************************************************************/


#include "..\CmnHdr.h"     /* See Appendix A. */
#include <windowsx.h>
#include <stdio.h>
#include <tchar.h>
#include <malloc.h>        // For alloca
#include <TlHelp32.h>
#include "Resource.h"


///////////////////////////////////////////////////////////////////////////


#ifdef UNICODE
#define InjectLib InjectLibW
#define EjectLib  EjectLibW
#else
#define InjectLib InjectLibA
#define EjectLib  EjectLibA
#endif   // !UNICODE


///////////////////////////////////////////////////////////////////////////


BOOL WINAPI InjectLibW(DWORD dwProcessId, PCWSTR pszLibFile) {

   BOOL fOk = FALSE; // Assume that the function fails
   HANDLE hProcess = NULL, hThread = NULL;
   PWSTR pszLibFileRemote = NULL;

   __try {
      // Get a handle for the target process.
      hProcess = OpenProcess(
         PROCESS_CREATE_THREAD     |   // For CreateRemoteThread
         PROCESS_VM_OPERATION      |   // For VirtualAllocEx/VirtualFreeEx
```

Figure 22-3.   *(continued)*
The InjLib sample application

Figure 22-3. *continued*

```
        PROCESS_VM_WRITE,                // For WriteProcessMemory
        FALSE, dwProcessId);
    if (hProcess == NULL) __leave;

    // Calculate the number of bytes needed for the DLL's pathname
    int cch = 1 + lstrlenW(pszLibFile);
    int cb  = cch * sizeof(WCHAR);

    // Allocate space in the remote process for the pathname
    pszLibFileRemote = (PWSTR)
        VirtualAllocEx(hProcess, NULL, cb, MEM_COMMIT, PAGE_READWRITE);
    if (pszLibFileRemote == NULL) __leave;

    // Copy the DLL's pathname to the remote process's address space
    if (!WriteProcessMemory(hProcess, pszLibFileRemote,
        (PVOID) pszLibFile, cb, NULL)) __leave;

    // Get the real address of LoadLibraryW in Kernel32.dll
    PTHREAD_START_ROUTINE pfnThreadRtn = (PTHREAD_START_ROUTINE)
        GetProcAddress(GetModuleHandle(TEXT("Kernel32")), "LoadLibraryW");
    if (pfnThreadRtn == NULL) __leave;

    // Create a remote thread that calls LoadLibraryW(DLLPathname)
    hThread = CreateRemoteThread(hProcess, NULL, 0,
        pfnThreadRtn, pszLibFileRemote, 0, NULL);
    if (hThread == NULL) __leave;

    // Wait for the remote thread to terminate
    WaitForSingleObject(hThread, INFINITE);

    fOk = TRUE; // Everything executed successfully
}
__finally { // Now, we can clean everthing up

    // Free the remote memory that contained the DLL's pathname
    if (pszLibFileRemote != NULL)
        VirtualFreeEx(hProcess, pszLibFileRemote, 0, MEM_RELEASE);

    if (hThread  != NULL)
        CloseHandle(hThread);

    if (hProcess != NULL)
        CloseHandle(hProcess);
}
```

(continued)

Figure 22-3. *continued*

```
   return(fOk);
}


//////////////////////////////////////////////////////////////////////////////


BOOL WINAPI InjectLibA(DWORD dwProcessId, PCSTR pszLibFile) {

   // Allocate a (stack) buffer for the Unicode version of the pathname
   PWSTR pszLibFileW = (PWSTR)
      _alloca((lstrlenA(pszLibFile) + 1) * sizeof(WCHAR));

   // Convert the ANSI pathname to its Unicode equivalent
   wsprintfW(pszLibFileW, L"%S", pszLibFile);

   // Call the Unicode version of the function to actually do the work.
   return(InjectLibW(dwProcessId, pszLibFileW));
}


//////////////////////////////////////////////////////////////////////////////


BOOL WINAPI EjectLibW(DWORD dwProcessId, PCWSTR pszLibFile) {

   BOOL fOk = FALSE; // Assume that the function fails
   HANDLE hthSnapshot = NULL;
   HANDLE hProcess = NULL, hThread = NULL;

   __try {
      // Grab a new snapshot of the process
      hthSnapshot = CreateToolhelp32Snapshot(TH32CS_SNAPMODULE, dwProcessId);
      if (hthSnapshot == NULL) __leave;

      // Get the HMODULE of the desired library
      MODULEENTRY32W me = { sizeof(me) };
      BOOL fFound = FALSE;
      BOOL fMoreMods = Module32FirstW(hthSnapshot, &me);
      for (; fMoreMods; fMoreMods = Module32NextW(hthSnapshot, &me)) {
         fFound = (lstrcmpiW(me.szModule,  pszLibFile) == 0) ||
                  (lstrcmpiW(me.szExePath, pszLibFile) == 0);
         if (fFound) break;
      }
```

(continued)

Figure 22-3. *continued*

```
        if (!fFound) __leave;

        // Get a handle for the target process.
        hProcess = OpenProcess(
            PROCESS_CREATE_THREAD
            | PROCESS_VM_OPERATION,  // For CreateRemoteThread
            FALSE, dwProcessId);
        if (hProcess == NULL) __leave;

        // Get the real address of LoadLibraryW in Kernel32.dll
        PTHREAD_START_ROUTINE pfnThreadRtn = (PTHREAD_START_ROUTINE)
            GetProcAddress(GetModuleHandle(TEXT("Kernel32")), "FreeLibrary");
        if (pfnThreadRtn == NULL) __leave;

        // Create a remote thread that calls LoadLibraryW(DLLPathname)
        hThread = CreateRemoteThread(hProcess, NULL, 0,
            pfnThreadRtn, me.modBaseAddr, 0, NULL);
        if (hThread == NULL) __leave;

        // Wait for the remote thread to terminate
        WaitForSingleObject(hThread, INFINITE);

        fOk = TRUE; // Everything executed successfully
    }
    __finally { // Now we can clean everything up

        if (hthSnapshot != NULL)
            CloseHandle(hthSnapshot);

        if (hThread     != NULL)
            CloseHandle(hThread);

        if (hProcess    != NULL)
            CloseHandle(hProcess);
    }

    return(fOk);
}


///////////////////////////////////////////////////////////////////////////////


BOOL WINAPI EjectLibA(DWORD dwProcessId, PCSTR pszLibFile) {
```

(continued)

Figure 22-3. *continued*

```
   // Allocate a (stack) buffer for the Unicode version of the pathname
   PWSTR pszLibFileW = (PWSTR)
      _alloca((lstrlenA(pszLibFile) + 1) * sizeof(WCHAR));

   // Convert the ANSI pathname to its Unicode equivalent
   wsprintfW(pszLibFileW, L"%S", pszLibFile);

   // Call the Unicode version of the function to actually do the work.
   return(EjectLibW(dwProcessId, pszLibFileW));
}


///////////////////////////////////////////////////////////////////////////


BOOL Dlg_OnInitDialog(HWND hwnd, HWND hwndFocus, LPARAM lParam) {

   chSETDLGICONS(hwnd, IDI_INJLIB);
   return(TRUE);
}


///////////////////////////////////////////////////////////////////////////


void Dlg_OnCommand(HWND hwnd, int id, HWND hwndCtl, UINT codeNotify) {

   switch (id) {
      case IDCANCEL:
         EndDialog(hwnd, id);
         break;

      case IDC_INJECT:
         DWORD dwProcessId = GetDlgItemInt(hwnd, IDC_PROCESSID, NULL, FALSE);
         if (dwProcessId == 0) {
            // A process ID of 0 causes everything to take place in the
            // local process; this makes things easier for debugging.
            dwProcessId = GetCurrentProcessId();
         }

         TCHAR szLibFile[MAX_PATH];
         GetModuleFileName(NULL, szLibFile, sizeof(szLibFile));
         _tcscpy(_tcsrchr(szLibFile, TEXT('\\')) + 1, TEXT("22 ImgWalk.DLL"));
```

(continued)

Figure 22-3. *continued*

```
        if (InjectLib(dwProcessId, szLibFile)) {
            chVERIFY(EjectLib(dwProcessId, szLibFile));
            chMB("DLL Injection/Ejection successful.");
        } else {
            chMB("DLL Injection/Ejection failed.");
        }
        break;
   }
}


///////////////////////////////////////////////////////////////////////////


INT_PTR WINAPI Dlg_Proc(HWND hwnd, UINT uMsg, WPARAM wParam, LPARAM lParam) {

   switch (uMsg) {
      chHANDLE_DLGMSG(hwnd, WM_INITDIALOG, Dlg_OnInitDialog);
      chHANDLE_DLGMSG(hwnd, WM_COMMAND,    Dlg_OnCommand);
   }
   return(FALSE);
}


///////////////////////////////////////////////////////////////////////////


int WINAPI _tWinMain(HINSTANCE hinstExe, HINSTANCE, PTSTR pszCmdLine, int) {

   chWindows9xNotAllowed();
   DialogBox(hinstExe, MAKEINTRESOURCE(IDD_INJLIB), NULL, Dlg_Proc);
   return(0);
}


///////////////////////////// End of File //////////////////////////////////
```

InjLib.rc

```
//Microsoft Developer Studio generated resource script.
//
#include "resource.h"
```

(continued)

Figure 22-3. *continued*

```
#define APSTUDIO_READONLY_SYMBOLS
/////////////////////////////////////////////////////////////////////////////
//
// Generated from the TEXTINCLUDE 2 resource.
//
#include "afxres.h"


/////////////////////////////////////////////////////////////////////////////
#undef APSTUDIO_READONLY_SYMBOLS


/////////////////////////////////////////////////////////////////////////////
// English (U.S.) resources

#if !defined(AFX_RESOURCE_DLL) || defined(AFX_TARG_ENU)
#ifdef _WIN32
LANGUAGE LANG_ENGLISH, SUBLANG_ENGLISH_US
#pragma code_page(1252)
#endif //_WIN32


/////////////////////////////////////////////////////////////////////////////
//
// Icon
//

// Icon with lowest ID value placed first to ensure application icon
// remains consistent on all systems.
IDI_INJLIB              ICON    DISCARDABLE     "InjLib.ico"

#ifdef APSTUDIO_INVOKED
/////////////////////////////////////////////////////////////////////////////
//
// TEXTINCLUDE
//

1 TEXTINCLUDE DISCARDABLE
BEGIN
    "resource.h\0"
END

2 TEXTINCLUDE DISCARDABLE
BEGIN
    "#include ""afxres.h""\r\n"
    "\0"
END
```

(continued)

Figure 22-3. *continued*

```
3 TEXTINCLUDE DISCARDABLE
BEGIN
    "\r\n"
    "\0"
END


#endif    // APSTUDIO_INVOKED



/////////////////////////////////////////////////////////////////////////////
//
// Dialog
//


IDD_INJLIB DIALOG DISCARDABLE  15, 24, 158, 24
STYLE DS_3DLOOK | DS_CENTER | WS_MINIMIZEBOX | WS_VISIBLE | WS_CAPTION |
    WS_SYSMENU
CAPTION "Inject Library Tester"
FONT 8, "MS Sans Serif"
BEGIN
    LTEXT           "&Process Id (decimal):",-1,4,6,69,8
    EDITTEXT        IDC_PROCESSID,78,4,36,12,ES_AUTOHSCROLL
    DEFPUSHBUTTON   "&Inject",IDC_INJECT,120,4,36,12,WS_GROUP
END



/////////////////////////////////////////////////////////////////////////////
//
// DESIGNINFO
//


#ifdef APSTUDIO_INVOKED
GUIDELINES DESIGNINFO DISCARDABLE
BEGIN
    IDD_INJLIB, DIALOG
    BEGIN
        RIGHTMARGIN, 134
        BOTTOMMARGIN, 20
    END
END
#endif    // APSTUDIO_INVOKED


#endif    // English (U.S.) resources
/////////////////////////////////////////////////////////////////////////////
```

(continued)

Figure 22-3. *continued*

```
#ifndef APSTUDIO_INVOKED
/////////////////////////////////////////////////////////////////////////////
//
// Generated from the TEXTINCLUDE 3 resource.
//


/////////////////////////////////////////////////////////////////////////////
#endif    // not APSTUDIO_INVOKED
```

The Image Walk DLL

ImgWalk.dll, listed in Figure 22-4, is a DLL that, once injected into a process's address space, can report on all the DLLs that the process is using. (The source code and resource files for the DLL are in the 22-ImgWalk directory on the companion CD-ROM.) For example, if I first run Notepad and then run InjLib, passing it Notepad's process ID, InjLib injects ImgWalk.dll into Notepad's address space. Once there, ImgWalk determines which file images (executables and DLLs) are being used by Notepad and displays the following message box, which shows the results.

ImgWalk walks through a process's address space looking for mapped file images by repeatedly calling *VirtualQuery* to fill a MEMORY_BASIC_INFORMATION structure. With each iteration of the loop, ImgWalk checks for a file pathname to concatenate with a string. This string appears in the message box.

789

```
char szBuf[MAX_PATH * 100] = { 0 };

PBYTE pb = NULL;
MEMORY_BASIC_INFORMATION mbi;
while (VirtualQuery(pb, &mbi, sizeof(mbi)) == sizeof(mbi)) {

   int nLen;
   char szModName[MAX_PATH];

   if (mbi.State == MEM_FREE)
      mbi.AllocationBase = mbi.BaseAddress;

   if ((mbi.AllocationBase == hinstDll) ||
      (mbi.AllocationBase != mbi.BaseAddress) ||
      (mbi.AllocationBase == NULL)) {

      // Do not add the module name to the list
      // if any of the following is true:
      // 1. This region contains this DLL.
      // 2. This block is NOT the beginning of a region.
      // 3. The address is NULL.
      nLen = 0;
   } else {
      nLen = GetModuleFileNameA((HINSTANCE) mbi.AllocationBase,
         szModName, chDIMOF(szModName));
   }

   if (nLen > 0) {
      wsprintfA(strchr(szBuf, 0), "\n%08X-%s",
         mbi.AllocationBase, szModName);
   }

   pb += mbi.RegionSize;
}
chMB(&szBuf[1]);
```

First, I check to see whether the region's base address matches the base address of the injected DLL. If it matches, I set *nLen* to 0 so that the injected library does not appear in the message box. If it doesn't match, I attempt to get the filename for the module loaded at the region's base address. If the *nLen* variable is greater than 0, the system recognizes that the address identifies a loaded module and the system fills the *szModName* buffer with the full pathname of the module. I then concatenate the module's HINSTANCE (base address) and its pathname with the *szBuf* string that will eventually be displayed in the message box. When the loop is finished, the DLL presents a message box with the final string as its contents.

ImgWalk.cpp

```
/*****************************************************************************
Module:  ImgWalk.cpp
Notices: Copyright (c) 2000 Jeffrey Richter
*****************************************************************************/


#include "..\CmnHdr.h"      /* See Appendix A. */
#include <tchar.h>



///////////////////////////////////////////////////////////////////////////


BOOL WINAPI DllMain(HINSTANCE hinstDll, DWORD fdwReason, PVOID fImpLoad) {

   if (fdwReason == DLL_PROCESS_ATTACH) {
      char szBuf[MAX_PATH * 100] = { 0 };

      PBYTE pb = NULL;
      MEMORY_BASIC_INFORMATION mbi;
      while (VirtualQuery(pb, &mbi, sizeof(mbi)) == sizeof(mbi)) {

         int nLen;
         char szModName[MAX_PATH];

         if (mbi.State == MEM_FREE)
            mbi.AllocationBase = mbi.BaseAddress;

         if ((mbi.AllocationBase == hinstDll) ||
             (mbi.AllocationBase != mbi.BaseAddress) ||
             (mbi.AllocationBase == NULL)) {
            // Do not add the module name to the list
            // if any of the following is true:
            // 1. If this region contains this DLL
            // 2. If this block is NOT the beginning of a region
            // 3. If the address is NULL
            nLen = 0;
         } else {
            nLen = GetModuleFileNameA((HINSTANCE) mbi.AllocationBase,
               szModName, chDIMOF(szModName));
         }
```

Figure 22-4.   *(continued)*
Source code for ImgWalk.dll

Figure 22-4. *continued*

```
        if (nLen > 0) {
            wsprintfA(strchr(szBuf, 0), "\n%p-%s",
                mbi.AllocationBase, szModName);
        }

        pb += mbi.RegionSize;
    }

    chMB(&szBuf[1]);
  }

  return(TRUE);
}



//////////////////////////////// End of File //////////////////////////////////
```

Injecting a DLL with a Trojan DLL

Another way to inject a DLL is to replace a DLL that you know a process will load. For example, if you know that a process will load Xyz.dll, you can create your own DLL and give it the same filename. Of course, you must rename the original Xyz.dll to something else.

Inside your Xyz.dll, you must export all the same symbols that the original Xyz.dll exported. You can do this easily using function forwarders (described in Chapter 20), which make it trivially simple to hook certain functions, but you should avoid using this technique because it is not version-resilient. If you replace a system DLL, for example, and Microsoft adds new functions in the future, your DLL will not have function forwarders for them. Applications that reference these new functions will be unable to load and execute.

If you have just a single application in which you want to use this technique, you can give your DLL a unique name and change the import section of the application's .exe module. More specifically, the import section contains the names of the DLLs required by a module. You can rummage through this import section in the file and alter it so that the loader loads your own DLL. This technique is not too bad, but you have to be pretty familiar with the .exe and DLL file formats.

Injecting a DLL as a Debugger

A debugger can perform special actions on a debuggee process. When a debuggee loads, the system automatically notifies the debugger when the debuggee's address space is ready but before the debuggee's primary thread executes any code. At this point, the debugger can force some code into the debuggee's address space (using *WriteProcessMemory*, for example) and then cause the debuggee's primary thread to execute that code.

This technique requires that you manipulate the debuggee thread's CONTEXT structure, which means that you must write CPU-specific code. You have to modify your source code to work correctly on different CPU platforms. In addition, you probably have to hand-code the machine language instructions that you want the debuggee to execute. Also, the relationship between a debugger and its debuggee is solid. If the debugger terminates, Windows automatically kills the debuggee. You cannot prevent this.

Injecting Code with a Memory-Mapped File on Windows 98

Injecting your own code on Windows 98 is actually trivial. All 32-bit Windows applications running on Windows 98 share the same top 2 GB of address space. If you allocate some storage up there, that storage is available in every process's address space. To allocate storage above 2 GB, you simply use memory-mapped files (discussed in Chapter 17). You create a memory-mapped file and then call *MapViewOfFile* to make it visible. Then you populate that area of your address space (which is the same area in all process's address space). You probably have to resort to hand-coded machine language to make this work, which makes the solution difficult to port to other CPU platforms. But if you're doing this, you probably don't care about different CPU platforms since Windows 98 only runs on *x*86 anyway.

What makes this technique difficult is that you still have to get a thread in the other process to execute the code in the memory-mapped file. To do this, you need some way to control the thread in the remote process. *CreateRemoteThread* would work nicely, but Windows 98 doesn't support it. Unfortunately, I have no solution to offer you here.

Injecting Code with *CreateProcess*

If your process is spawning the process into which you want to inject code, things get a little easier. For one, your process (the parent process) can create the new process suspended. This allows you to alter the child process's state without affecting its execution since it hasn't started executing anything yet. But the parent process also gets a handle to the child process's primary thread. Using this handle, you can alter what code the thread executes. You can solve the problem mentioned in the previous section since you can set the thread's instruction pointer to execute the code in the memory-mapped file.

Here is one way for your process to control what code the child process's primary thread executes:

1. Have your process spawn the child process suspended.

2. Retrieve the primary thread's starting memory address from the .exe module's file header.

3. Save the machine instructions at this memory address.

4. Force some hand-coded machine instructions at this address. The instructions should call *LoadLibrary* to load a DLL.

5. Resume the child process's primary thread so that this code executes.

6. Restore the original instructions back into the starting address.

7. Let the process continue execution from the starting address as if nothing had happened.

Steps 6 and 7 above are tricky to get right because you have to change the code that you are currently executing. It is possible, however—I've seen it done.

This technique offers a lot of benefits. First, it gets the address space before the application executes. Second, it works on both Windows 98 and Windows 2000. Third, since you're not a debugger, you can easily debug the application with the injected DLL. And finally, this technique works on both console and GUI applications.

Of course, this technique also has some disadvantages. You can inject the DLL only if your code is the parent process. And, of course, this technique is not CPU-independent; you must make modifications for different CPU platforms.

API Hooking: An Example

Injecting a DLL into a process's address space is a wonderful way to determine what's going on within a process. However, simply injecting a DLL doesn't give you enough information. You'll often want to know exactly how threads in a particular process are calling various functions, and you might want to modify what a Windows function does.

For example, I know of a company that produced a DLL that was loaded by a database product. The DLL's job was to enhance and extend the capabilities of the database product. When the database product was terminated, the DLL received a DLL_PROCESS_DETACH notification and only then executed all of its cleanup code. The DLL would call functions in other DLLs to close socket connections, files, and other resources, but by the time it received the DLL_PROCESS_DETACH notification, other DLLs in the process's address space had already gotten their DLL_PROCESS_DETACH notifications. So when the company's DLL tried to clean up, many of the functions it called would fail because the other DLLs had already uninitialized.

The company hired me to help them solve this problem, and I suggested that we hook the *ExitProcess* function. As you know, calling *ExitProcess* causes the system to notify the DLLs with DLL_PROCESS_DETACH notifications. By hooking the *ExitProcess* function, we ensured that the company's DLL was notified when *ExitProcess* was called. This notification would come in before any DLLs got a DLL_PROCESS_DETACH notification; therefore, all of the DLLs in the process were still initialized and functioning properly. At this point, the company's DLL would know that the process was about to terminate and could perform all of its cleanup successfully. Then the operating system's *ExitProcess* function would be called, causing all of the DLLs to receive their DLL_PROCESS_DETACH notifications and clean up. The company's DLL would have no special cleanup to perform when it received this notification since it had already done what it needed to do.

In this example, injecting the DLL came for free: the database application was already designed to allow this, and it loaded the company's DLL. When the company's DLL was loaded, it had to scan all the loaded executable and DLL modules for calls to *ExitProcess*. When it found calls to *ExitProcess*, the DLL had to modify the modules so that they would call a function in the company's DLL instead of the operating system's *ExitProcess* function. (This process is a lot simpler than it sounds.) Once the company's *ExitProcess* replacement function (or hook function, as it's more commonly called) executed its cleanup code, the operating system's *ExitProcess* function (in Kernel32.dll) was called.

This example shows a typical use for API hooking. It solved a very real problem with very little code.

API Hooking by Overwriting Code

API hooking isn't new—developers have been using API hooking methods for years. When it comes to solving the problem I just described, the first "solution" that everyone comes to is to hook by overwriting code. Here's how this works:

1. You locate the address of the function you want to hook in memory (say *ExitProcess* in Kernel32.dll).

2. You save the first few bytes of this function in some memory of your own.

3. You overwrite the first few bytes of this function with a JUMP CPU instruction that jumps to the memory address of your replacement function. Of course, your replacement function must have exactly the same signature as the function you're hooking: all the parameters must be the same, the return value must be the same, and the calling convention must be the same.

4. Now, when a thread calls the hooked function, the JUMP instruction will actually jump to your replacement function. At this point, you can execute whatever code you'd like.

5. You unhook the function by taking the saved bytes (from step 2) and placing them back at the beginning of the hooked function.

6. You call the hooked function (which is no longer hooked), and the function performs its normal processing.

7. When the original function returns, you execute steps 2 and 3 again so that your replacement function will be called in the future.

This method was heavily used by 16-bit Windows programmers and worked just fine in that environment. Today, this method has several serious shortcomings, and I strongly discourage its use. First, it is CPU-dependent: JUMP instructions on *x*86, Alpha, and other CPUs are different, and you must use hand-coded machine instructions to get this technique to work. Second, this method doesn't work at all in a preemptive, multithreaded environment. It takes time for a thread to overwrite the code at the beginning of a function. While the code is being overwritten, another thread might attempt to call the same function. The results are disastrous! So this method works only if you know that no more than one thread will attempt to call a particular function at any given time.

**WINDOWS
98**

> On Windows 98, the main Windows DLLs (Kernel32, AdvAPI32, User32, and GDI32) are protected in such a way that an application cannot overwrite their code pages. You can get around this by writing a virtual device driver (VxD).

API Hooking by Manipulating a Module's Import Section

As it turns out, another API hooking technique solves both of the problems I've mentioned. This technique is easy to implement and is quite robust. But to understand it, you must understand how dynamic linking works. In particular, you must understand what's contained in a module's imports section. While I haven't gone into the nitty-gritty details of data structures and the like, I did spend a good bit of Chapter 19 explaining how this section is generated and what's in it. You can refer back to that chapter as you read the information that follows.

As you know, a module's import section contains the set of DLLs that the module requires in order to run. In addition, it contains the list of symbols that the module imports from each of the DLLs. When the module places a call to an imported function, the thread actually grabs the address of the desired imported function from the module's import section and then jumps to that address.

So, to hook a particular function, all you do is change the address in the module's import section. That's it. No CPU-dependent stuff. And since you're not modifying the function's code in any way, you don't need to worry about any thread synchronization issues.

The following function performs the magic. It looks in one module's import section for a reference to a symbol at a specific address. If such a reference exists, it changes the address of the symbol.

```
void ReplaceIATEntryInOneMod(PCSTR pszCalleeModName,
   PROC pfnCurrent, PROC pfnNew, HMODULE hmodCaller) {

   ULONG ulSize;
   PIMAGE_IMPORT_DESCRIPTOR pImportDesc = (PIMAGE_IMPORT_DESCRIPTOR)
      ImageDirectoryEntryToData(hmodCaller, TRUE,
      IMAGE_DIRECTORY_ENTRY_IMPORT, &ulSize);

   if (pImportDesc == NULL)
      return;  // This module has no import section.

   // Find the import descriptor containing references
   // to callee's functions.
   for (; pImportDesc->Name; pImportDesc++) {
      PSTR pszModName = (PSTR)
         ((PBYTE) hmodCaller + pImportDesc->Name);
      if (lstrcmpiA(pszModName, pszCalleeModName) == 0)
         break;
   }

   if (pImportDesc->Name == 0)
      // This module doesn't import any functions from this callee.
      return;

   // Get caller's import address table (IAT)
   // for the callee's functions.
   PIMAGE_THUNK_DATA pThunk = (PIMAGE_THUNK_DATA)
      ((PBYTE) hmodCaller + pImportDesc->FirstThunk);

   // Replace current function address with new function address.
   for (; pThunk->u1.Function; pThunk++) {

      // Get the address of the function address.
      PROC* ppfn = (PROC*) &pThunk->u1.Function;

      // Is this the function we're looking for?
      BOOL fFound = (*ppfn == pfnCurrent);

      // See the sample code for some tricky Windows 98
      // stuff that goes here.

      if (fFound) {
         // The addresses match; change the import section address.
         WriteProcessMemory(GetCurrentProcess(), ppfn, &pfnNew,
            sizeof(pfnNew), NULL);
         return;  // We did it; get out.
      }
   }

   // If we get to here, the function
   // is not in the caller's import section.
}
```

To see how you call this function, let me first start by explaining a potential environment. Let's say that we have a module called DataBase.exe. The code in this module calls the *ExitProcess* function contained in Kernel32.dll, but we want it to call the *MyExitProcess* function contained in my DBExtend.dll module. To accomplish this, we call *ReplaceIATEntryInOneMod* as follows:

```
PROC pfnOrig = GetProcAddress(GetModuleHandle("Kernel32"),
   "ExitProcess");
HMODULE hmodCaller = GetModuleHandle("DataBase.exe");

void ReplaceIATEntryInOneMod(
   "Kernel32.dll", // Module containing the function (ANSI)
   pfnOrig,        // Address of function in callee
   MyExitProcess,  // Address of new function to be called
   hmodCaller);    // Handle of module that should call the new function
```

The first thing that *ReplaceIATEntryInOneMod* does is locate the *hmodCaller* module's import section by calling *ImageDirectoryEntryToData*, passing it IMAGE_DIRECTORY_ENTRY_IMPORT. If this function returns NULL, the DataBase.exe module has no import section and there is nothing to do.

If the DataBase.exe module has an import section, *ImageDirectoryEntry-ToData* returns the address of the import section, which is a pointer of type PIMAGE_IMPORT_DESCRIPTOR. We must now look in the module's import section for the DLL that contains the imported function that we want to change. In this example, we're looking for the symbols that are being imported from "Kernel32.dll" (the first parameter passed to the *ReplaceIATEntry-InOneMod* function). The *for* loop scans for the DLL module's name. Notice that all strings in a module's import sections are written in ANSI (never Unicode). This is why I explicitly call the *lstrcmpiA* function instead of using the *lstrcmpi* macro.

If the loop terminates without locating any references to symbols inside "Kernel32.dll", the function returns and again does nothing. If the module's import section does reference symbols in "Kernel32.dll", we get the address to an array of IMAGE_THUNK_DATA structures that contains information about the imported symbols. Then we iterate through all of the import symbols from "Kernel32.dll" looking for an address that matches the current address of the symbol. In our example, we're looking for an address that matches the address of the *ExitProcess* function.

If no address matches what we're looking for, this module must not import the desired symbol, and *ReplaceIATEntryInOneMod* simply returns. If the address is found, *WriteProcessMemory* is called to change the address of the replacement function. I use *WriteProcessMemory* instead of *InterlockedExchangePointer* because *WriteProcessMemory* changes the bytes no matter what page protections exist on those bytes. For example, if the page has PAGE_READONLY protection, *InterlockedExchangePointer* raises an access violation; *WriteProcessMemory*, on the other hand, handles all of the page protection changes and just works.

From now on, when any thread executes code inside DataBase.exe's module that calls *ExitProcess*, the thread calls our replacement function. From this function, we can easily get the address of the real *ExitProcess* function inside Kernel32.dll and call it when we want the normal *ExitProcess* processing.

Note that the *ReplaceIATEntryInOneMod* function alters calls to functions made from code within a single module. But another DLL might be in the address space, and that DLL might have calls to *ExitProcess* as well. If a module other than DataBase.exe attempts to call *ExitProcess*, its call will succeed at calling the *ExitProcess* function in Kernel32.dll.

If you want to trap all calls to *ExitProcess* from all modules, you must call *ReplaceIATEntryInOneMod* once for each module loaded in the process's address space. To this end, I've written another function called *ReplaceIATEntryInAllMods*. This function simply uses the toolhelp functions to enumerate all the modules loaded in the process's address space and then calls *ReplaceIATEntryInOneMod* for each module, passing it the appropriate module handle for the last parameter.

Problems can occur in a few other places. For example, what if a thread calls *LoadLibrary* to load a new DLL after you call *ReplaceIATEntryInAllMods*? In this case, the newly loaded DLL might have calls to *ExitProcess* that you have not hooked. To solve this problem, you must hook the *LoadLibraryA*, *LoadLibraryW*, *LoadLibraryExA*, and *LoadLibraryExW* functions so that you can trap these calls and call *ReplaceIATEntryInOneMod* for the newly loaded module.

The last problem has to do with *GetProcAddress*. Say a thread executes this:

```
typedef int (WINAPI *PFNEXITPROCESS)(UINT uExitCode);
PFNEXITPROCESS pfnExitProcess = (PFNEXITPROCESS) GetProcAddress(
   GetModuleHandle("Kernel32"), "ExitProcess");
pfnExitProcess(0);
```

This code tells the system to get the real address of *ExitProcess* in Kernel32.dll and then call that address. If a thread executes this code, your replacement function is not called. To get around this problem, you must also hook the *GetProcAddress* function. If it is called and is about to return the address of a hooked function, you must return the address of the replacement function instead.

The sample application presented in the next section shows how to do API hooking and solves all of the *LoadLibrary* and *GetProcAddress* problems as well.

The LastMsgBoxInfo Sample Application

The LastMsgBoxInfo application ("22 LastMsgBoxInfo.exe"), listed in Figure 22-5, demonstrates API hooking. It hooks all calls to the *MessageBox* function contained in User32.dll. To hook this function in all processes, the application performs DLL injection using the Windows hook technique. The source code and resource files for the application and DLL are in the 22-LastMsgBoxInfo and 22-LastMsgBoxInfoLib directories on the companion CD-ROM.

When you run the application, the following dialog box appears.

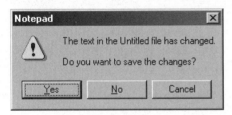

At this point, the application is waiting. Now run any application and cause it to display a message box. For testing purposes, I always run Notepad, enter some text, and then try to close Notepad without saving the text. This causes Notepad to display this message box.

When you dismiss this message box, the LastMsgBoxInfo dialog box looks like this.

As you can see, the LastMsgBoxInfo application can see exactly how other processes have called the *MessageBox* function.

The code for displaying and managing the Last MessageBox Info dialog box is quite simple. The setting up of API hooking is where all of the hard work takes place. To make API hooking easier, I created a CAPIHook C++ class. The class definition is in APIHook.h and the class implementation is in APIHook.cpp. The class is easy to use since there are only a few public member functions: a

801

constructor, a destructor, and a function that returns the address of the original function.

To hook a function, you simply create an instance of this C++ class as follows:

```
CAPIHook g_MessageBoxA("User32.dll", "MessageBoxA",
   (PROC) Hook_MessageBoxA, TRUE);

CAPIHook g_MessageBoxW("User32.dll", "MessageBoxW",
   (PROC) Hook_MessageBoxW, TRUE);
```

Notice that I have to hook two functions: *MessageBoxA* and *MessageBoxW*. User32.dll contains both functions. When *MessageBoxA* is called, I want my *Hook_MessageBoxA* to be called instead; when *MessageBoxW* is called, I want my *Hook_MessageBoxW* function called instead.

The constructor for my CAPIHook class simply remembers what API you've decided to hook and calls *ReplaceIATEntryInAllMods* to actually perform the hooking.

The next public member function is the destructor. When a CAPIHook object goes out of scope, the destructor calls *ReplaceIATEntryInAllMods* to reset the symbol's address back to its original address in every module—the function is no longer hooked.

The third public member returns the address of the original function. This member function is usually called from inside the replacement function in order to call the original function. Here is the code inside the *Hook_MessageBoxA* function:

```
int WINAPI Hook_MessageBoxA(HWND hWnd, PCSTR pszText,
   PCSTR pszCaption, UINT uType) {

   int nResult = ((PFNMESSAGEBOXA)(PROC) g_MessageBoxA)
      (hWnd, pszText, pszCaption, uType);
   SendLastMsgBoxInfo(FALSE, (PVOID) pszCaption, (PVOID) pszText, nResult);
   return(nResult);
}
```

This code refers to the global *g_MessageBoxA* CAPIHook object. Casting this object to a PROC data type causes the member function to return the address of the original *MessageBoxA* function inside User32.dll.

If you use this C++ class, that's all there is to hooking and unhooking imported functions. If you examine the code toward the bottom of the CAPIHook.cpp file, you'll notice that the C++ class automatically instantiates CAPIHook objects to trap *LoadLibraryA*, *LoadLibraryW*, *LoadLibraryExA*, *LoadLibraryExW*, and *GetProcAddress*. In this way, the CAPIHook class automatically takes care of the problems mentioned earlier.

LastMsgBoxInfo.cpp

```
/*********************************************************************************
Module:  LastMsgBoxInfo.cpp
Notices: Copyright (c) 2000 Jeffrey Richter
*********************************************************************************/


#include "..\CmnHdr.h"      /* See Appendix A. */
#include <windowsx.h>
#include <tchar.h>
#include "Resource.h"
#include "..\22-LastMsgBoxInfoLib\LastMsgBoxInfoLib.h"


///////////////////////////////////////////////////////////////////////////////


BOOL Dlg_OnInitDialog(HWND hwnd, HWND hwndFocus, LPARAM lParam) {

   chSETDLGICONS(hwnd, IDI_LASTMSGBOXINFO);
   SetDlgItemText(hwnd, IDC_INFO,
      TEXT("Waiting for a Message Box to be dismissed"));
   return(TRUE);
}


///////////////////////////////////////////////////////////////////////////////


void Dlg_OnSize(HWND hwnd, UINT state, int cx, int cy) {

   SetWindowPos(GetDlgItem(hwnd, IDC_INFO), NULL,
      0, 0, cx, cy, SWP_NOZORDER);
}


///////////////////////////////////////////////////////////////////////////////


void Dlg_OnCommand(HWND hwnd, int id, HWND hwndCtl, UINT codeNotify) {
```

Figure 22-5. *(continued)*
The LastMsgBoxInfo sample application

Figure 22-5. *continued*

```
   switch (id) {
      case IDCANCEL:
         EndDialog(hwnd, id);
         break;
   }
}


//////////////////////////////////////////////////////////////////////////////


BOOL Dlg_OnCopyData(HWND hwnd, HWND hwndFrom, PCOPYDATASTRUCT pcds) {

   // Some hooked process sent us some message box info, display it
   SetDlgItemTextA(hwnd, IDC_INFO, (PCSTR) pcds->lpData);
   return(TRUE);
}


//////////////////////////////////////////////////////////////////////////////


INT_PTR WINAPI Dlg_Proc(HWND hwnd, UINT uMsg, WPARAM wParam, LPARAM lParam) {

   switch (uMsg) {
      chHANDLE_DLGMSG(hwnd, WM_INITDIALOG, Dlg_OnInitDialog);
      chHANDLE_DLGMSG(hwnd, WM_SIZE,       Dlg_OnSize);
      chHANDLE_DLGMSG(hwnd, WM_COMMAND,    Dlg_OnCommand);
      chHANDLE_DLGMSG(hwnd, WM_COPYDATA,   Dlg_OnCopyData);
   }
   return(FALSE);
}


//////////////////////////////////////////////////////////////////////////////


int WINAPI _tWinMain(HINSTANCE hinstExe, HINSTANCE, PTSTR pszCmdLine, int) {

   DWORD dwThreadId = 0;
#ifdef _DEBUG
   HWND hwnd = FindWindow(NULL, TEXT("Untitled - Paint"));
   dwThreadId = GetWindowThreadProcessId(hwnd, NULL);
#endif
```

(continued)

Figure 22-5. *continued*

```
    LastMsgBoxInfo_HookAllApps(TRUE, dwThreadId);
    DialogBox(hinstExe, MAKEINTRESOURCE(IDD_LASTMSGBOXINFO), NULL, Dlg_Proc);
    LastMsgBoxInfo_HookAllApps(FALSE, 0);
    return(0);
}


/////////////////////////////// End of File //////////////////////////////////
```

LastMsgBoxInfo.rc

```
//Microsoft Developer Studio generated resource script.
//
#include "resource.h"

#define APSTUDIO_READONLY_SYMBOLS
/////////////////////////////////////////////////////////////////////////////
//
// Generated from the TEXTINCLUDE 2 resource.
//
#include "afxres.h"


/////////////////////////////////////////////////////////////////////////////
#undef APSTUDIO_READONLY_SYMBOLS


/////////////////////////////////////////////////////////////////////////////
// English (U.S.) resources

#if !defined(AFX_RESOURCE_DLL) || defined(AFX_TARG_ENU)
#ifdef _WIN32
LANGUAGE LANG_ENGLISH, SUBLANG_ENGLISH_US
#pragma code_page(1252)
#endif //_WIN32


/////////////////////////////////////////////////////////////////////////////
//
// Dialog
//


IDD_LASTMSGBOXINFO DIALOG DISCARDABLE  0, 0, 379, 55
STYLE DS_CENTER | WS_MINIMIZEBOX | WS_MAXIMIZEBOX | WS_VISIBLE | WS_CAPTION |
    WS_SYSMENU | WS_THICKFRAME
```

(continued)

Figure 22-5. *continued*

```
CAPTION "Last MessageBox Info"
FONT 8, "MS Sans Serif"
BEGIN
    EDITTEXT        IDC_INFO,0,0,376,52,ES_MULTILINE | ES_AUTOVSCROLL |
                    ES_AUTOHSCROLL | ES_READONLY | WS_VSCROLL | WS_HSCROLL
END


/////////////////////////////////////////////////////////////////////////////
//
// DESIGNINFO
//

#ifdef APSTUDIO_INVOKED
GUIDELINES DESIGNINFO DISCARDABLE
BEGIN
    IDD_LASTMSGBOXINFO, DIALOG
    BEGIN
        LEFTMARGIN, 7
        RIGHTMARGIN, 372
        TOPMARGIN, 7
        BOTTOMMARGIN, 48
    END
END
#endif    // APSTUDIO_INVOKED


#ifdef APSTUDIO_INVOKED
/////////////////////////////////////////////////////////////////////////////
//
// TEXTINCLUDE
//

1 TEXTINCLUDE DISCARDABLE
BEGIN
    "resource.h\0"
END

2 TEXTINCLUDE DISCARDABLE
BEGIN
    "#include ""afxres.h""\r\n"
    "\0"
END
```

(continued)

Figure 22-5. *continued*

```
3 TEXTINCLUDE DISCARDABLE
BEGIN
    "\r\n"
    "\0"
END

#endif    // APSTUDIO_INVOKED


/////////////////////////////////////////////////////////////////////////////
//
// Icon
//

// Icon with lowest ID value placed first to ensure application icon
// remains consistent on all systems.
IDI_LASTMSGBOXINFO    ICON    DISCARDABLE    "LastMsgBoxInfo.ico"
#endif    // English (U.S.) resources
/////////////////////////////////////////////////////////////////////////////



#ifndef APSTUDIO_INVOKED
/////////////////////////////////////////////////////////////////////////////
//
// Generated from the TEXTINCLUDE 3 resource.
//


/////////////////////////////////////////////////////////////////////////////
#endif    // not APSTUDIO_INVOKED
```

LastMsgBoxInfoLib.cpp

```
/******************************************************************************
Module:  LastMsgBoxInfoLib.cpp
Notices: Copyright (c) 2000 Jeffrey Richter
******************************************************************************/


#define WINVER        0x0500
#include "..\CmnHdr.h"
```

(continued)

Figure 22-5. *continued*

```
#include <WindowsX.h>
#include <tchar.h>
#include <stdio.h>
#include "APIHook.h"

#define LASTMSGBOXINFOLIBAPI extern "C" __declspec(dllexport)
#include "LastMsgBoxInfoLib.h"

///////////////////////////////////////////////////////////////////////////////

// Prototypes for the hooked functions
typedef int (WINAPI *PFNMESSAGEBOXA)(HWND hWnd, PCSTR pszText,
   PCSTR pszCaption, UINT uType);

typedef int (WINAPI *PFNMESSAGEBOXW)(HWND hWnd, PCWSTR pszText,
   PCWSTR pszCaption, UINT uType);


// We need to reference these variables before we create them.
extern CAPIHook g_MessageBoxA;
extern CAPIHook g_MessageBoxW;

///////////////////////////////////////////////////////////////////////////////

// This function sends the MessageBox info to our main dialog box
void SendLastMsgBoxInfo(BOOL fUnicode,
   PVOID pvCaption, PVOID pvText, int nResult) {

   // Get the pathname of the process displaying the message box
   char szProcessPathname[MAX_PATH];
   GetModuleFileNameA(NULL, szProcessPathname, MAX_PATH);

   // Convert the return value into a human-readable string
   PCSTR pszResult = "(Unknown)";
   switch (nResult) {
      case IDOK:      pszResult = "Ok";     break;
      case IDCANCEL:  pszResult = "Cancel"; break;
      case IDABORT:   pszResult = "Abort";  break;
      case IDRETRY:   pszResult = "Retry";  break;
      case IDIGNORE:  pszResult = "Ignore"; break;
      case IDYES:     pszResult = "Yes";    break;
      case IDNO:      pszResult = "No";     break;
      case IDCLOSE:   pszResult = "Close";  break;
      case IDHELP:    pszResult = "Help";   break;
```

(continued)

808

Figure 22-5. *continued*

```
    case IDTRYAGAIN: pszResult = "Try Again"; break;
    case IDCONTINUE: pszResult = "Continue";  break;
  }

  // Construct the string to send to the main dialog box
  char sz[2048];
  wsprintfA(sz, fUnicode
    ? "Process: (%d) %s\r\nCaption: %S\r\nMessage: %S\r\nResult: %s"
    : "Process: (%d) %s\r\nCaption: %s\r\nMessage: %s\r\nResult: %s",
    GetCurrentProcessId(), szProcessPathname,
    pvCaption, pvText, pszResult);

  // Send the string to the main dialog box
  COPYDATASTRUCT cds = { 0, lstrlenA(sz) + 1, sz };
  FORWARD_WM_COPYDATA(FindWindow(NULL, TEXT("Last MessageBox Info")),
    NULL, &cds, SendMessage);
}


///////////////////////////////////////////////////////////////////////////////


// This is the MessageBoxW replacement function
int WINAPI Hook_MessageBoxW(HWND hWnd, PCWSTR pszText, LPCWSTR pszCaption,
  UINT uType) {

  // Call the original MessageBoxW function
  int nResult = ((PFNMESSAGEBOXW)(PROC) g_MessageBoxW)
    (hWnd, pszText, pszCaption, uType);

  // Send the information to the main dialog box
  SendLastMsgBoxInfo(TRUE, (PVOID) pszCaption, (PVOID) pszText, nResult);

  // Return the result back to the caller
  return(nResult);
}


///////////////////////////////////////////////////////////////////////////////


// This is the MessageBoxA replacement function
int WINAPI Hook_MessageBoxA(HWND hWnd, PCSTR pszText, PCSTR pszCaption,
  UINT uType) {

  // Call the original MessageBoxA function
  int nResult = ((PFNMESSAGEBOXA)(PROC) g_MessageBoxA)
    (hWnd, pszText, pszCaption, uType);
```

(continued)

809

Figure 22-5. *continued*

```
    // Send the information to the main dialog box
    SendLastMsgBoxInfo(FALSE, (PVOID) pszCaption, (PVOID) pszText, nResult);

    // Return the result back to the caller
    return(nResult);
}


///////////////////////////////////////////////////////////////////////////////


// Hook the MessageBoxA and MessageBoxW functions
CAPIHook g_MessageBoxA("User32.dll", "MessageBoxA",
    (PROC) Hook_MessageBoxA, TRUE);

CAPIHook g_MessageBoxW("User32.dll", "MessageBoxW",
    (PROC) Hook_MessageBoxW, TRUE);


// Since we do DLL injection with Windows' hooks, we need to save the hook
// handle in a shared memory block (Windows 2000 actually doesn't need this)
#pragma data_seg("Shared")
HHOOK g_hhook = NULL;
#pragma data_seg()
#pragma comment(linker, "/Section:Shared, rws")


///////////////////////////////////////////////////////////////////////////////


static LRESULT WINAPI GetMsgProc(int code, WPARAM wParam, LPARAM lParam) {

    // NOTE: On Windows 2000, the 1st parameter to CallNextHookEx can
    // be NULL.  On Windows 98, it must be the hook handle.
    return(CallNextHookEx(g_hhook, code, wParam, lParam));
}


///////////////////////////////////////////////////////////////////////////////


// Returns the HMODULE that contains the specified memory address
static HMODULE ModuleFromAddress(PVOID pv) {

    MEMORY_BASIC_INFORMATION mbi;
    return((VirtualQuery(pv, &mbi, sizeof(mbi)) != 0)
        ? (HMODULE) mbi.AllocationBase : NULL);
}


///////////////////////////////////////////////////////////////////////////////
```

(continued)

Figure 22-5. *continued*

```
BOOL WINAPI LastMsgBoxInfo_HookAllApps(BOOL fInstall, DWORD dwThreadId) {

   BOOL fOk;

   if (fInstall) {

      chASSERT(g_hhook == NULL); // Illegal to install twice in a row

      // Install the Windows' hook
      g_hhook = SetWindowsHookEx(WH_GETMESSAGE, GetMsgProc,
         ModuleFromAddress(LastMsgBoxInfo_HookAllApps), dwThreadId);

      fOk = (g_hhook != NULL);
   } else {

      chASSERT(g_hhook != NULL); // Can't uninstall if not installed
      fOk = UnhookWindowsHookEx(g_hhook);
      g_hhook = NULL;
   }

   return(fOk);
}


//////////////////////////// End of File ///////////////////////////////////
```

LastMsgBoxInfoLib.h

```
/******************************************************************************
Module:  LastMsgBoxInfoLib.h
Notices: Copyright (c) 2000 Jeffrey Richter
******************************************************************************/


#ifndef LASTMSGBOXINFOLIBAPI
#define LASTMSGBOXINFOLIBAPI extern "C" __declspec(dllimport)
#endif


///////////////////////////////////////////////////////////////////////////


LASTMSGBOXINFOLIBAPI BOOL WINAPI LastMsgBoxInfo_HookAllApps(BOOL fInstall,
```

(continued)

Figure 22-5. *continued*

```
    DWORD dwThreadId);


/////////////////////////////// End of File ///////////////////////////////
```

APIHook.cpp

```
/******************************************************************************
Module:  APIHook.cpp
Notices: Copyright (c) 2000 Jeffrey Richter
******************************************************************************/


#include "..\CmnHdr.h"
#include <ImageHlp.h>
#pragma comment(lib, "ImageHlp")

#include "APIHook.h"
#include "..\04-ProcessInfo\Toolhelp.h"


///////////////////////////////////////////////////////////////////////////////

// When an application runs on Windows 98 under a debugger, the debugger
// makes the module's import section point to a stub that calls the desired
// function. To account for this, the code in this module must do some crazy
// stuff. These variables are needed to help with the crazy stuff.


// The highest private memory address (used for Windows 98 only)
PVOID CAPIHook::sm_pvMaxAppAddr = NULL;
const BYTE cPushOpCode = 0x68;    // The PUSH opcode on x86 platforms


///////////////////////////////////////////////////////////////////////////////

// The head of the linked-list of CAPIHook objects
CAPIHook* CAPIHook::sm_pHead = NULL;


///////////////////////////////////////////////////////////////////////////////

CAPIHook::CAPIHook(PSTR pszCalleeModName, PSTR pszFuncName, PROC pfnHook,
    BOOL fExcludeAPIHookMod) {

    if (sm_pvMaxAppAddr == NULL) {
```

(continued)

Figure 22-5. *continued*

```
    // Functions with address above lpMaximumApplicationAddress require
    // special processing (Windows 98 only)
    SYSTEM_INFO si;
    GetSystemInfo(&si);
    sm_pvMaxAppAddr = si.lpMaximumApplicationAddress;
}


m_pNext  = sm_pHead;     // The next node was at the head
sm_pHead = this;         // This node is now at the head


// Save information about this hooked function
m_pszCalleeModName    = pszCalleeModName;
m_pszFuncName         = pszFuncName;
m_pfnHook             = pfnHook;
m_fExcludeAPIHookMod  = fExcludeAPIHookMod;
m_pfnOrig             = GetProcAddressRaw(
    GetModuleHandleA(pszCalleeModName), m_pszFuncName);
chASSERT(m_pfnOrig != NULL);  // Function doesn't exist


if (m_pfnOrig > sm_pvMaxAppAddr) {
    // The address is in a shared DLL; the address needs fixing up
    PBYTE pb = (PBYTE) m_pfnOrig;
    if (pb[0] == cPushOpCode) {
        // Skip over the PUSH op code and grab the real address
        PVOID pv = * (PVOID*) &pb[1];
        m_pfnOrig = (PROC) pv;
    }
}


// Hook this function in all currently loaded modules
ReplaceIATEntryInAllMods(m_pszCalleeModName, m_pfnOrig, m_pfnHook,
    m_fExcludeAPIHookMod);
}


///////////////////////////////////////////////////////////////////////////


CAPIHook::~CAPIHook() {

    // Unhook this function from all modules
    ReplaceIATEntryInAllMods(m_pszCalleeModName, m_pfnHook, m_pfnOrig,
        m_fExcludeAPIHookMod);

    // Remove this object from the linked list
    CAPIHook* p = sm_pHead;
```

(continued)

Figure 22-5. *continued*

```
      if (p == this) {        // Removing the head node
         sm_pHead = p->m_pNext;
      } else {

         BOOL fFound = FALSE;

         // Walk list from head and fix pointers
         for (; !fFound && (p->m_pNext != NULL); p = p->m_pNext) {
            if (p->m_pNext == this) {
               // Make the node that points to us point to the our next node
               p->m_pNext = p->m_pNext->m_pNext;
               break;
            }
         }
         chASSERT(fFound);
      }
}


///////////////////////////////////////////////////////////////////////////


// NOTE: This function must NOT be inlined
FARPROC CAPIHook::GetProcAddressRaw(HMODULE hmod, PCSTR pszProcName) {

   return(::GetProcAddress(hmod, pszProcName));
}


///////////////////////////////////////////////////////////////////////////


// Returns the HMODULE that contains the specified memory address
static HMODULE ModuleFromAddress(PVOID pv) {

   MEMORY_BASIC_INFORMATION mbi;
   return((VirtualQuery(pv, &mbi, sizeof(mbi)) != 0)
      ? (HMODULE) mbi.AllocationBase : NULL);
}


///////////////////////////////////////////////////////////////////////////


void CAPIHook::ReplaceIATEntryInAllMods(PCSTR pszCalleeModName,
   PROC pfnCurrent, PROC pfnNew, BOOL fExcludeAPIHookMod) {

   HMODULE hmodThisMod = fExcludeAPIHookMod
      ? ModuleFromAddress(ReplaceIATEntryInAllMods) : NULL;
```

(continued)

814

Figure 22-5. *continued*

```
   // Get the list of modules in this process
   CToolhelp th(TH32CS_SNAPMODULE, GetCurrentProcessId());

   MODULEENTRY32 me = { sizeof(me) };
   for (BOOL fOk = th.ModuleFirst(&me); fOk; fOk = th.ModuleNext(&me)) {

      // NOTE: We don't hook functions in our own module
      if (me.hModule != hmodThisMod) {

         // Hook this function in this module
         ReplaceIATEntryInOneMod(
            pszCalleeModName, pfnCurrent, pfnNew, me.hModule);
      }
   }
}


///////////////////////////////////////////////////////////////////////////////

void CAPIHook::ReplaceIATEntryInOneMod(PCSTR pszCalleeModName,
   PROC pfnCurrent, PROC pfnNew, HMODULE hmodCaller) {

   // Get the address of the module's import section
   ULONG ulSize;
   PIMAGE_IMPORT_DESCRIPTOR pImportDesc = (PIMAGE_IMPORT_DESCRIPTOR)
      ImageDirectoryEntryToData(hmodCaller, TRUE,
      IMAGE_DIRECTORY_ENTRY_IMPORT, &ulSize);

   if (pImportDesc == NULL)
      return;  // This module has no import section


   // Find the import descriptor containing references to callee's functions
   for (; pImportDesc->Name; pImportDesc++) {
      PSTR pszModName = (PSTR) ((PBYTE) hmodCaller + pImportDesc->Name);
      if (lstrcmpiA(pszModName, pszCalleeModName) == 0)
         break;   // Found
   }

   if (pImportDesc->Name == 0)
      return;  // This module doesn't import any functions from this callee

   // Get caller's import address table (IAT) for the callee's functions
   PIMAGE_THUNK_DATA pThunk = (PIMAGE_THUNK_DATA)
      ((PBYTE) hmodCaller + pImportDesc->FirstThunk);
```

(continued)

Figure 22-5. *continued*

```
   // Replace current function address with new function address
   for (; pThunk->u1.Function; pThunk++) {

      // Get the address of the function address
      PROC* ppfn = (PROC*) &pThunk->u1.Function;

      // Is this the function we're looking for?
      BOOL fFound = (*ppfn == pfnCurrent);

      if (!fFound && (*ppfn > sm_pvMaxAppAddr)) {

         // If this is not the function and the address is in a shared DLL,
         // then maybe we're running under a debugger on Windows 98. In this
         // case, this address points to an instruction that may have the
         // correct address.

         PBYTE pbInFunc = (PBYTE) *ppfn;
         if (pbInFunc[0] == cPushOpCode) {
            // We see the PUSH instruction, the real function address follows
            ppfn = (PROC*) &pbInFunc[1];

            // Is this the function we're looking for?
            fFound = (*ppfn == pfnCurrent);
         }
      }

      if (fFound) {
         // The addresses match, change the import section address
         WriteProcessMemory(GetCurrentProcess(), ppfn, &pfnNew,
            sizeof(pfnNew), NULL);
         return;  // We did it, get out
      }
   }

   // If we get to here, the function is not in the caller's import section
}


///////////////////////////////////////////////////////////////////////////////

// Hook LoadLibrary functions and GetProcAddress so that hooked functions
// are handled correctly if these functions are called.

CAPIHook CAPIHook::sm_LoadLibraryA  ("Kernel32.dll", "LoadLibraryA",
   (PROC) CAPIHook::LoadLibraryA, TRUE);
```

(continued)

Figure 22-5. *continued*

```
CAPIHook CAPIHook::sm_LoadLibraryW  ("Kernel32.dll", "LoadLibraryW",
   (PROC) CAPIHook::LoadLibraryW, TRUE);

CAPIHook CAPIHook::sm_LoadLibraryExA("Kernel32.dll", "LoadLibraryExA",
   (PROC) CAPIHook::LoadLibraryExA, TRUE);

CAPIHook CAPIHook::sm_LoadLibraryExW("Kernel32.dll", "LoadLibraryExW",
   (PROC) CAPIHook::LoadLibraryExW, TRUE);

CAPIHook CAPIHook::sm_GetProcAddress("Kernel32.dll", "GetProcAddress",
   (PROC) CAPIHook::GetProcAddress, TRUE);


///////////////////////////////////////////////////////////////////////////


void CAPIHook::FixupNewlyLoadedModule(HMODULE hmod, DWORD dwFlags) {

   // If a new module is loaded, hook the hooked functions
   if ((hmod != NULL) && ((dwFlags & LOAD_LIBRARY_AS_DATAFILE) == 0)) {

      for (CAPIHook* p = sm_pHead; p != NULL; p = p->m_pNext) {
         ReplaceIATEntryInOneMod(p->m_pszCalleeModName,
            p->m_pfnOrig, p->m_pfnHook, hmod);
      }
   }
}


///////////////////////////////////////////////////////////////////////////


HMODULE WINAPI CAPIHook::LoadLibraryA(PCSTR pszModulePath) {

   HMODULE hmod = ::LoadLibraryA(pszModulePath);
   FixupNewlyLoadedModule(hmod, 0);
   return(hmod);
}


///////////////////////////////////////////////////////////////////////////


HMODULE WINAPI CAPIHook::LoadLibraryW(PCWSTR pszModulePath) {

   HMODULE hmod = ::LoadLibraryW(pszModulePath);
   FixupNewlyLoadedModule(hmod, 0);
   return(hmod);
}
```

(continued)

817

Figure 22-5. *continued*

```
///////////////////////////////////////////////////////////////////////////

HMODULE WINAPI CAPIHook::LoadLibraryExA(PCSTR pszModulePath,
   HANDLE hFile, DWORD dwFlags) {

   HMODULE hmod = ::LoadLibraryExA(pszModulePath, hFile, dwFlags);
   FixupNewlyLoadedModule(hmod, dwFlags);
   return(hmod);
}


///////////////////////////////////////////////////////////////////////////

HMODULE WINAPI CAPIHook::LoadLibraryExW(PCWSTR pszModulePath,
   HANDLE hFile, DWORD dwFlags) {

   HMODULE hmod = ::LoadLibraryExW(pszModulePath, hFile, dwFlags);
   FixupNewlyLoadedModule(hmod, dwFlags);
   return(hmod);
}


///////////////////////////////////////////////////////////////////////////

FARPROC WINAPI CAPIHook::GetProcAddress(HMODULE hmod, PCSTR pszProcName) {

   // Get the true address of the function
   FARPROC pfn = GetProcAddressRaw(hmod, pszProcName);

   // Is it one of the functions that we want hooked?
   CAPIHook* p = sm_pHead;
   for (; (pfn != NULL) && (p != NULL); p = p->m_pNext) {

      if (pfn == p->m_pfnOrig) {

         // The address to return matches an address we want to hook
         // Return the hook function address instead
         pfn = p->m_pfnHook;
         break;
      }
   }

   return(pfn);
}


//////////////////////////////// End of File ////////////////////////////////
```

(continued)

Figure 22-5. *continued*

APIHook.h

```
/******************************************************************************
Module:  APIHook.h
Notices: Copyright (c) 2000 Jeffrey Richter
******************************************************************************/


#pragma once

///////////////////////////////////////////////////////////////////////////////

class CAPIHook {
public:
   // Hook a function in all modules
   CAPIHook(PSTR pszCalleeModName, PSTR pszFuncName, PROC pfnHook,
      BOOL fExcludeAPIHookMod);

   // Unhook a function from all modules
   ~CAPIHook();

   // Returns the original address of the hooked function
   operator PROC() { return(m_pfnOrig); }

public:
   // Calls the real GetProcAddress
   static FARPROC WINAPI GetProcAddressRaw(HMODULE hmod, PCSTR pszProcName);

private:
   static PVOID sm_pvMaxAppAddr; // Maximum private memory address
   static CAPIHook* sm_pHead;    // Address of first object
   CAPIHook* m_pNext;            // Address of next object

   PCSTR m_pszCalleeModName;     // Module containing the function (ANSI)
   PCSTR m_pszFuncName;          // Function name in callee (ANSI)
   PROC  m_pfnOrig;              // Original function address in callee
   PROC  m_pfnHook;              // Hook function address
   BOOL  m_fExcludeAPIHookMod;   // Hook module w/CAPIHook implementation?

private:
   // Replaces a symbol's address in a module's import section
   static void WINAPI ReplaceIATEntryInAllMods(PCSTR pszCalleeModName,
      PROC pfnOrig, PROC pfnHook, BOOL fExcludeAPIHookMod);
```

(continued)

Figure 22-5. *continued*

```
    // Replaces a symbol's address in all module's import sections
    static void WINAPI ReplaceIATEntryInOneMod(PCSTR pszCalleeModName,
        PROC pfnOrig, PROC pfnHook, HMODULE hmodCaller);

private:
    // Used when a DLL is newly loaded after hooking a function
    static void    WINAPI FixupNewlyLoadedModule(HMODULE hmod, DWORD dwFlags);

    // Used to trap when DLLs are newly loaded
    static HMODULE WINAPI LoadLibraryA(PCSTR  pszModulePath);
    static HMODULE WINAPI LoadLibraryW(PCWSTR pszModulePath);
    static HMODULE WINAPI LoadLibraryExA(PCSTR  pszModulePath,
        HANDLE hFile, DWORD dwFlags);
    static HMODULE WINAPI LoadLibraryExW(PCWSTR pszModulePath,
        HANDLE hFile, DWORD dwFlags);

    // Returns address of replacement function if hooked function is requested
    static FARPROC WINAPI GetProcAddress(HMODULE hmod, PCSTR pszProcName);

private:
    // Instantiates hooks on these functions
    static CAPIHook sm_LoadLibraryA;
    static CAPIHook sm_LoadLibraryW;
    static CAPIHook sm_LoadLibraryExA;
    static CAPIHook sm_LoadLibraryExW;
    static CAPIHook sm_GetProcAddress;
};


/////////////////////////////// End of File ////////////////////////////////
```

STRUCTURED EXCEPTION HANDLING

CHAPTER TWENTY·THREE

TERMINATION HANDLERS

Close your eyes for a moment and imagine writing your application as though your code could never fail. That's right—there's always enough memory, no one ever passes you an invalid pointer, and the files you count on always exist. Wouldn't it be a pleasure to write your code if you could make these assumptions? Your code would be so much easier to write, to read, and to understand. No more fussing with *if* statements here and *goto*s there—in each function, you'd just write your code top to bottom.

If this kind of straightforward programming environment seems like a dream to you, you'll love structured exception handling (SEH). The virtue of SEH is that as you write your code, you can focus on getting your task done. If something goes wrong at run time, the system catches it and notifies you of the problem.

With SEH, you can't totally ignore the possibility of an error in your code, but you can separate the main job from the error-handling chores. This division makes it easy to concentrate on the problem at hand and focus on possible errors later.

One of Microsoft's main motivations for adding SEH to Windows was to ease the development of the operating system itself. The developers of the operating system use SEH to make the system more robust. We can use SEH to make our own applications more robust.

The burden of getting SEH to work falls more on the compiler than on the operating system. Your compiler must generate special code when exception blocks are entered into and exited from. The compiler must produce tables of support data structures to handle SEH. The compiler also must supply callback functions that the operating system can call so that exception blocks can be traversed. And the compiler is responsible for preparing stack frames and other internal information that is used and referenced by the operating system. Adding SEH support to a compiler is not an easy task. It shouldn't surprise you that different compiler vendors implement SEH in different ways. Fortunately, we can ignore compiler implementation details and just use the compiler's SEH capabilities.

Differences among compiler implementations could make it difficult to discuss the advantages of SEH in specific ways with specific code examples. However, most compiler vendors follow Microsoft's suggested syntax. The syntax and keywords I use in my examples might differ from those of another company's compiler, but the main SEH concepts are the same. I'll use the Microsoft Visual C++ compiler's syntax throughout this chapter.

> **NOTE**
>
> Don't confuse structured exception handling with C++ exception handling. C++ exception handling is a different form of exception handling, a form that makes use of the C++ keywords *catch* and *throw*. Microsoft's Visual C++ also supports C++ exception handling and is implemented internally by taking advantage of the structured exception handling capabilities already present in the compiler and in Windows operating systems.

SEH really consists of two main capabilities: termination handling and exception handling. We'll discuss termination handlers in this chapter and exception handling in the next chapter.

A termination handler guarantees that a block of code (the termination handler) will be called and executed regardless of how another section of code (the guarded body) is exited. The syntax (using the Microsoft Visual C++ compiler) for a termination handler is as follows:

```
__try {
   // Guarded body
   :
   :
}
__finally {
   // Termination handler
   :
   :
}
```

The *__try* and *__finally* keywords delineate the two sections of the termination handler. In the code fragment above, the operating system and the compiler work together to guarantee that the *__finally* block code in the termination handler will be executed no matter how the guarded body is exited.

Regardless of whether you put a *return*, a *goto*, or even a call to *longjump* in the guarded body, the termination handler will be called. I'll show you several examples demonstrating this.

Understanding Termination Handlers by Example

Because the compiler and the operating system are intimately involved with the execution of your code when you use SEH, I believe that the best way to demonstrate how SEH works is by examining source code samples and discussing the order in which the statements execute in each example.

Therefore, the next few sections show different source code fragments, and the text associated with each fragment explains how the compiler and operating system alter the execution order of your code.

Funcenstein1

To appreciate the ramifications of using termination handlers, let's examine a more concrete coding example.

```
DWORD Funcenstein1() {
   DWORD dwTemp;

   // 1. Do any processing here.
   :
   :
   __try {
      // 2. Request permission to access
      //    protected data, and then use it.
      WaitForSingleObject(g_hSem, INFINITE);

      g_dwProtectedData = 5;
      dwTemp = g_dwProtectedData;
   }
   __finally {
      // 3. Allow others to use protected data.
      ReleaseSemaphore(g_hSem, 1, NULL);
   }

   // 4. Continue processing.
   return(dwTemp);
}
```

The numbered comments above indicate the order in which your code will execute. In *Funcenstein1*, using the *try-finally* blocks isn't doing much for you. The code will wait for a semaphore, alter the contents of the protected data, save the new value in the local variable *dwTemp*, release the semaphore, and return the new value to the caller.

Funcenstein2

Now let's modify the function a little and see what happens:

```
DWORD Funcenstein2() {
    DWORD dwTemp;

    // 1. Do any processing here.
    :
    :

    __try {
        // 2. Request permission to access
        //    protected data, and then use it.
        WaitForSingleObject(g_hSem, INFINITE);

        g_dwProtectedData = 5;
        dwTemp = g_dwProtectedData;

        // Return the new value.
        return(dwTemp);
    }
    __finally {
        // 3. Allow others to use protected data.
        ReleaseSemaphore(g_hSem, 1, NULL);
    }

    // Continue processing--this code
    // will never execute in this version.
    dwTemp = 9;
    return(dwTemp);
}
```

In *Funcenstein2*, a *return* statement has been added to the end of the *try* block. This *return* statement tells the compiler that you want to exit the function and return the contents of the *dwTemp* variable, which now contains the value 5. However, if this *return* statement had been executed, the thread would not have released the semaphore—and no other thread would ever regain control of the semaphore. As you can imagine, this kind of sequence can become a really big problem because threads waiting for the semaphore might never resume execution.

However, by using the termination handler, you have avoided the premature execution of the *return* statement. When the *return* statement attempts to exit the *try* block, the compiler makes sure that the code in the *finally* block executes first. The code inside the *finally* block is guaranteed to execute before the *return* statement in the *try* block is allowed to exit. In *Funcenstein2*, putting the call to *ReleaseSemaphore* into a termination handler block ensures that the semaphore will always be released. There is no chance for a thread to accidentally retain ownership of the semaphore, which would mean that all other threads waiting for the semaphore would never be scheduled CPU time.

After the code in the *finally* block executes, the function does, in fact, return. Any code appearing below the *finally* block doesn't execute because the function returns in the *try* block. Therefore, this function returns the value 5, not the value 9.

You might be asking yourself how the compiler guarantees that the *finally* block executes before the *try* block can be exited. When the compiler examines your source code, it sees that you have coded a *return* statement inside a *try* block. Having seen this, the compiler generates code to save the return value (5 in our example) in a temporary variable created by the compiler. The compiler then generates code to execute the instructions contained inside the *finally* block; this is called a *local unwind*. More specifically, a local unwind occurs when the system executes the contents of a *finally* block because of the premature exit of code in a *try* block. After the instructions inside the *finally* block execute, the value in the compiler's temporary variable is retrieved and returned from the function.

As you can see, the compiler must generate additional code and the system must perform additional work to pull this whole thing off. On different CPUs, the steps needed for termination handling to work vary. The Alpha processor, for example, must execute several hundred or even several thousand CPU instructions to capture the *try* block's premature return and call the *finally* block. You should avoid writing code that causes premature exits from the *try* block of a termination handler because the performance of your application could be adversely impacted. Later in this chapter, I'll discuss the __*leave* keyword, which can help you avoid writing code that forces local unwinds.

Exception handling is designed to capture exceptions—the exceptions to the rule that you expect to happen infrequently (in our example, the premature *return*). If a situation is the norm, checking for the situation explicitly is much more efficient than relying on the SEH capabilities of the operating system and your compiler to trap common occurrences.

Note that when the flow of control naturally leaves the *try* block and enters the *finally* block (as shown in *Funcenstein1*), the overhead of entering the *finally* block is minimal. On the *x*86 CPUs using Microsoft's compiler, a single machine instruction is executed as execution leaves the *try* block to enter the *finally* block—I doubt that you will even notice this overhead in your application. When the compiler has to generate additional code and the system has to perform additional work, as in *Funcenstein2*, the overhead is much more noticeable.

Funcenstein3

Now let's modify the function again and take a look at what happens:

```
DWORD Funcenstein3() {
   DWORD dwTemp;

   // 1. Do any processing here.
   .
   .
   .
   __try {
      // 2. Request permission to access
      //    protected data, and then use it.
      WaitForSingleObject(g_hSem, INFINITE);

      g_dwProtectedData = 5;
      dwTemp = g_dwProtectedData;

      // Try to jump over the finally block.
      goto ReturnValue;
   }

   __finally {
      // 3. Allow others to use protected data.
      ReleaseSemaphore(g_hSem, 1, NULL);
   }

   dwTemp = 9;
   // 4. Continue processing.
   ReturnValue:
   return(dwTemp);
}
```

In *Funcenstein3*, when the compiler sees the *goto* statement in the *try* block, it generates a local unwind to execute the contents of the *finally* block first. However, this time, after the code in the *finally* block executes, the code after the *ReturnValue* label is executed because no return occurs in either the *try* or the *finally* block. This code causes the function to return a 5. Again, because you have interrupted the natural flow of control from the *try* block into the *finally* block, you could incur a high performance penalty depending on the CPU your application is running on.

Funcfurter1

Now let's look at another scenario in which termination handling really proves its value. Look at this function:

```
DWORD Funcfurter1() {
    DWORD dwTemp;

    // 1. Do any processing here.
    :
    :
    __try {
        // 2. Request permission to access
        //    protected data, and then use it.
        WaitForSingleObject(g_hSem, INFINITE);

        dwTemp = Funcinator(g_dwProtectedData);
    }
    __finally {
        // 3. Allow others to use protected data.
        ReleaseSemaphore(g_hSem, 1, NULL);
    }

    // 4. Continue processing.
    return(dwTemp);
}
```

Now imagine that the *Funcinator* function called in the *try* block contains a bug that causes an invalid memory access. Without SEH, this situation would present the user with the ever-popular Application Error dialog box. When the user dismissed the error dialog box, the process would be terminated. When the process is terminated (because of an invalid memory access), the semaphore would still be owned and would never be released—any threads in other processes that were waiting for this semaphore would never be scheduled CPU time. But placing the call to *ReleaseSemaphore* in a *finally* block guarantees that the semaphore gets released even if some other function causes a memory access violation.

If termination handlers are powerful enough to capture a process while terminating because of an invalid memory access, we should have no trouble believing that they will also capture *setjump* and *longjump* combinations and, of course, simple statements such as *break* and *continue*.

Pop Quiz Time: *FuncaDoodleDoo*

Now for a test. Can you determine what the following function returns?

```
DWORD FuncaDoodleDoo() {
   DWORD dwTemp = 0;

   while (dwTemp < 10) {

      __try {
         if (dwTemp == 2)
            continue;

         if (dwTemp == 3)
            break;
      }
      __finally {
         dwTemp++;
      }

      dwTemp++;
   }

   dwTemp += 10;
   return(dwTemp);
}
```

Let's analyze what the function does step by step. First *dwTemp* is set to 0. The code in the *try* block executes, but neither of the *if* statements evaluates to TRUE. Execution moves naturally to the code in the *finally* block, which increments *dwTemp* to 1. Then the instruction after the *finally* block increments *dwTemp* again, making it 2.

When the loop iterates, *dwTemp* is 2 and the *continue* statement in the *try* block will execute. Without a termination handler to force execution of the *finally* block before exit from the *try* block, execution would immediately jump back up to the *while* test, *dwTemp* would not be changed, and we would have started an infinite loop. With a termination handler, the system notes that the *continue* statement causes the flow of control to exit the *try* block prematurely and moves execution to the *finally* block. In the *finally* block, *dwTemp* is incremented to 3. However, the code after the *finally* block doesn't execute because the flow of control moves back to *continue* and thus to the top of the loop.

Now we are processing the loop's third iteration. This time, the first *if* statement evaluates to FALSE, but the second *if* statement evaluates to TRUE. The system again catches our attempt to break out of the *try* block and executes the code in the *finally* block first. Now *dwTemp* is incremented to 4. Because a *break* statement was executed, control resumes after the loop. Thus, the code after the *finally* block and still inside the loop doesn't execute. The code below

830

the loop adds 10 to *dwTemp* for a grand total of 14—the result of calling this function. It should go without saying that you should never actually write code like *FuncaDoodleDoo*. I placed the *continue* and *break* statements in the middle of the code only to demonstrate the operation of the termination handler.

Although a termination handler will catch most situations in which the *try* block would otherwise be exited prematurely, it can't cause the code in a *finally* block to be executed if the thread or process is terminated. A call to *ExitThread* or *ExitProcess* will immediately terminate the thread or process without executing any of the code in a *finally* block. Also, if your thread or process should die because some application called *TerminateThread* or *TerminateProcess*, the code in a *finally* block again won't execute. Some C run-time functions (such as *abort*) that in turn call *ExitProcess* again preclude the execution of *finally* blocks. You can't do anything to prevent another application from terminating one of your threads or processes, but you can prevent your own premature calls to *ExitThread* and *ExitProcess*.

Funcenstein4

Let's take a look at one more termination handling scenario.

```
DWORD Funcenstein4() {
    DWORD dwTemp;
    // 1. Do any processing here.
    :
    :
    __try {
        // 2. Request permission to access
        //    protected data, and then use it.
        WaitForSingleObject(g_hSem, INFINITE);

        g_dwProtectedData = 5;
        dwTemp = g_dwProtectedData;

        // Return the new value.
        return(dwTemp);
    }
    __finally {
        // 3. Allow others to use protected data.
        ReleaseSemaphore(g_hSem, 1, NULL);
        return(103);
    }

    // Continue processing--this code will never execute.
    dwTemp = 9;
    return(dwTemp);
}
```

In *Funcenstein4*, the *try* block will execute and try to return the value of *dwTemp* (5) back to *Funcenstein4*'s caller. As noted in the discussion of *Funcenstein2*, trying to return prematurely from a *try* block causes the generation of code that puts the return value into a temporary variable created by the compiler. Then the code inside the *finally* block is executed. Notice that in this variation on *Funcenstein2* I have added a *return* statement to the *finally* block. Will *Funcenstein4* return 5 or 103 to the caller? The answer is 103 because the *return* statement in the *finally* block causes the value 103 to be stored in the same temporary variable in which the value 5 has been stored, overwriting the 5. When the *finally* block completes execution, the value now in the temporary variable (103) is returned from *Funcenstein4* to its caller.

We've seen termination handlers do an effective job of rescuing execution from a premature exit of the *try* block, and we've also seen termination handlers produce an unwanted result because they prevented a premature exit of the *try* block. A good rule of thumb is to avoid any statements that would cause a premature exit of the *try* block part of a termination handler. In fact, it is always best to remove all *return*s, *continue*s, *break*s, *goto*s, and so on from inside both the *try* and the *finally* blocks of a termination handler and to put these statements outside the handler. Such a practice will cause the compiler to generate both a smaller amount of code—because it won't have to catch premature exits from the *try* block—and faster code, because it will have fewer instructions to execute in order to perform the local unwind. In addition, your code will be much easier to read and maintain.

Funcarama1

We've pretty much covered the basic syntax and semantics of termination handlers. Now let's look at how a termination handler could be used to simplify a more complicated programming problem. Let's look at a function that doesn't take advantage of termination handlers at all:

```
BOOL Funcarama1() {
   HANDLE hFile = INVALID_HANDLE_VALUE;
   PVOID pvBuf = NULL;
   DWORD dwNumBytesRead;
   BOOL fOk;

   hFile = CreateFile("SOMEDATA.DAT", GENERIC_READ,
      FILE_SHARE_READ, NULL, OPEN_EXISTING, 0, NULL);
   if (hFile == INVALID_HANDLE_VALUE) {
      return(FALSE);
   }
```

```
   pvBuf = VirtualAlloc(NULL, 1024, MEM_COMMIT, PAGE_READWRITE);
   if (pvBuf == NULL) {
      CloseHandle(hFile);
      return(FALSE);
   }

   fOk = ReadFile(hFile, pvBuf, 1024, &dwNumBytesRead, NULL);
   if (!fOk || (dwNumBytesRead == 0)) {
      VirtualFree(pvBuf, MEM_RELEASE | MEM_DECOMMIT);
      CloseHandle(hFile);
      return(FALSE);
   }

   // Do some calculation on the data.
   :
   :

   // Clean up all the resources.
   VirtualFree(pvBuf, MEM_RELEASE | MEM_DECOMMIT);
   CloseHandle(hFile);
   return(TRUE);
}
```

All the error checking in *Funcarama1* makes the function difficult to read, which also makes the function difficult to understand, maintain, and modify.

Funcarama2

Of course, it's possible to rewrite *Funcarama1* so that it is a little cleaner and easier to understand:

```
BOOL Funcarama2() {
   HANDLE hFile = INVALID_HANDLE_VALUE;
   PVOID pvBuf = NULL;
   DWORD dwNumBytesRead;
   BOOL fOk, fSuccess = FALSE;

   hFile = CreateFile("SOMEDATA.DAT", GENERIC_READ,
      FILE_SHARE_READ, NULL, OPEN_EXISTING, 0, NULL);

   if (hFile != INVALID_HANDLE_VALUE) {

      pvBuf = VirtualAlloc(NULL, 1024, MEM_COMMIT, PAGE_READWRITE);

      if (pvBuf != NULL) {

         fOk = ReadFile(hFile, pvBuf, 1024, &dwNumBytesRead, NULL);
```

(continued)

```
            if (fOk && (dwNumBytesRead != 0)) {
                // Do some calculation on the data.
                :
                :
                fSuccess = TRUE;
            }

        }

        VirtualFree(pvBuf, MEM_RELEASE | MEM_DECOMMIT);
    }

    CloseHandle(hFile);
    return(fSuccess);
}
```

Although easier to understand than *Funcarama1*, *Funcarama2* is still difficult to modify and maintain. Also, the indentation level gets to be pretty extreme as more conditional statements are added; with such a rewrite, you soon end up writing code on the far right of your screen and wrapping statements after every five characters!

Funcarama3

Let's rewrite the first version, *Funcarama1*, to take advantage of an SEH termination handler:

```
DWORD Funcarama3() {

    // IMPORTANT: Initialize all variables to assume failure.
    HANDLE hFile = INVALID_HANDLE_VALUE;
    PVOID pvBuf = NULL;

    __try {
        DWORD dwNumBytesRead;
        BOOL fOk;

        hFile = CreateFile("SOMEDATA.DAT", GENERIC_READ,
            FILE_SHARE_READ, NULL, OPEN_EXISTING, 0, NULL);
        if (hFile == INVALID_HANDLE_VALUE) {
            return(FALSE);
        }

        pvBuf = VirtualAlloc(NULL, 1024, MEM_COMMIT, PAGE_READWRITE);
        if (pvBuf == NULL) {
            return(FALSE);
        }

        fOk = ReadFile(hFile, pvBuf, 1024, &dwNumBytesRead, NULL);
        if (!fOk || (dwNumBytesRead != 1024)) {
```

```
        return(FALSE);
      }

      // Do some calculation on the data.
      :
      :

    }

    __finally {
      // Clean up all the resources.
      if (pvBuf != NULL)
        VirtualFree(pvBuf, MEM_RELEASE | MEM_DECOMMIT);
      if (hFile != INVALID_HANDLE_VALUE)
        CloseHandle(hFile);
    }
    // Continue processing.
    return(TRUE);
}
```

The real virtue of the *Funcarama3* version is that all of the function's cleanup code is localized in one place and one place only: the *finally* block. If we ever need to add some additional code to this function, we can simply add a single cleanup line in the *finally* block—we won't have to go back to every possible location of failure and add our cleanup line to each failure location.

Funcarama4: The Final Frontier

The real problem with the *Funcarama3* version is the overhead. As I mentioned after the discussion of *Funcenstein4*, you really should avoid putting *return* statements into a *try* block as much as possible.

To help make such avoidance easier, Microsoft added another keyword, *__leave*, to its C/C++ compiler. Here is the *Funcarama4* version, which takes advantage of the *__leave* keyword:

```
DWORD Funcarama4() {

    // IMPORTANT: Initialize all variables to assume failure.
    HANDLE hFile = INVALID_HANDLE_VALUE;
    PVOID pvBuf = NULL;

    // Assume that the function will not execute successfully.
    BOOL fFunctionOk = FALSE;

    __try {
      DWORD dwNumBytesRead;
      BOOL fOk;
```

(continued)

```
    hFile = CreateFile("SOMEDATA.DAT", GENERIC_READ,
      FILE_SHARE_READ, NULL, OPEN_EXISTING, 0, NULL);
    if (hFile == INVALID_HANDLE_VALUE) {
      __leave;
    }

    pvBuf = VirtualAlloc(NULL, 1024, MEM_COMMIT, PAGE_READWRITE);

    if (pvBuf == NULL) {
      __leave;
    }

    fOk = ReadFile(hFile, pvBuf, 1024, &dwNumBytesRead, NULL);
    if (!fOk || (dwNumBytesRead == 0)) {
      __leave;
    }

    // Do some calculation on the data.
      :
      :

    // Indicate that the entire function executed successfully.
    fFunctionOk = TRUE;
  }
  __finally {
    // Clean up all the resources.
    if (pvBuf != NULL)
      VirtualFree(pvBuf, MEM_RELEASE | MEM_DECOMMIT);
    if (hFile != INVALID_HANDLE_VALUE)
      CloseHandle(hFile);
  }
  // Continue processing.
  return(fFunctionOk);
}
```

The use of the *__leave* keyword in the *try* block causes a jump to the end of the *try* block. You can think of it as jumping to the *try* block's closing brace. Because the flow of control will exit naturally from the *try* block and enter the *finally* block, no overhead is incurred. However, it was necessary to introduce a new Boolean variable, *fFunctionOk*, to indicate the success or failure of the function. That's a relatively small price to pay.

When designing your functions to take advantage of termination handlers in this way, remember to initialize all of your resource handles to invalid values before entering your *try* block. Then, in the *finally* block, you can check to see which resources have been allocated successfully so that you'll know which ones to free. Another popular method for tracking which resources will need to be freed is to set a flag when a resource allocation is successful. Then the code in the *finally* block can examine the state of the flag to determine whether the resource needs freeing.

Notes About the *finally* Block

So far we have explicitly identified two scenarios that force the *finally* block to be executed:

- Normal flow of control from the *try* block into the *finally* block

- Local unwind: premature exit from the *try* block (*goto, longjump, continue, break, return,* and so on) forcing control to the *finally* block

A third scenario—a *global unwind*—occurred without explicit identification as such in the *Funcfurter1* function we saw earlier in the chapter. Inside the *try* block of this function was a call to the *Funcinator* function. If the *Funcinator* function caused a memory access violation, a global unwind caused *Funcfurter1*'s *finally* block to execute. We'll look at global unwinding in greater detail in the next chapter.

Code in a *finally* block always starts executing as a result of one of these three situations. To determine which of the three possibilities caused the *finally* block to execute, you can call the intrinsic function[1] *AbnormalTermination*:

```
BOOL AbnormalTermination();
```

This intrinsic function can be called only from inside a *finally* block and returns a Boolean value indicating whether the *try* block associated with the *finally* block was exited prematurely. In other words, if the flow of control leaves the *try* block and naturally enters the *finally* block, *AbnormalTermination* will return FALSE. If the flow of control exits the *try* block abnormally—usually because a local unwind has been caused by a *goto, return, break,* or *continue* statement or because a global unwind has been caused by a memory access violation or another exception—a call to *AbnormalTermination* will return TRUE. It is impossible to determine whether a *finally* block is executing because of a global or a local unwind. This is usually not a problem because you have, of course, avoided writing code that performs local unwinds.

---

1. An intrinsic function is a special function recognized by the compiler. The compiler generates the code for the function inline rather than generating code to call the function. For example, *memcpy* is an intrinsic function (if the /Oi compiler switch is specified). When the compiler sees a call to *memcpy*, it puts the *memcpy* code directly into the function that called *memcpy* instead of generating a call to the *memcpy* function. This usually has the effect of making your code run faster at the expense of code size.

   The intrinsic *AbnormalTermination* function is different from the intrinsic *memcpy* function in that it exists only in an intrinsic form. No C run-time library contains the *AbnormalTermination* function.

Funcfurter2

Here is *Funcfurter2*, which demonstrates use of the *AbnormalTermination* intrinsic function:

```
DWORD Funcfurter2() {
    DWORD dwTemp;

    // 1. Do any processing here.
    :
    :

    __try {
        // 2. Request permission to access
        //    protected data, and then use it.
        WaitForSingleObject(g_hSem, INFINITE);

        dwTemp = Funcinator(g_dwProtectedData);
    }
    __finally {
        // 3. Allow others to use protected data.
        ReleaseSemaphore(g_hSem, 1, NULL);

        if (!AbnormalTermination()) {
            // No errors occurred in the try block, and
            // control flowed naturally from try into finally.
            :
            :

        } else {
            // Something caused an exception, and
            // because there is no code in the try block
            // that would cause a premature exit, we must
            // be executing in the finally block
            // because of a global unwind.

            // If there were a goto in the try block,
            // we wouldn't know how we got here.
            :
            :

        }
    }

    // 4. Continue processing.
    return(dwTemp);
}
```

Now that you know how to write termination handlers, you'll see that they can be even more useful and important when we look at exception filters and exception handlers in the next chapter. Before we move on, let's review the reasons for using termination handlers:

- They simplify error processing because all cleanup is in one location and is guaranteed to execute.

- They improve program readability.

- They make code easier to maintain.

- They have minimal speed and size overhead if used correctly.

The SEH Termination Sample Application

The SEHTerm application, "23 SEHTerm.exe" (listed in Figure 23-1), demonstrates how termination handlers work. The source code and resource files for the application are in the 23-SEHTerm directory on the companion CD-ROM.

When you run the application, the primary thread enters a *try* block. Inside this *try* block, the following message box is displayed.

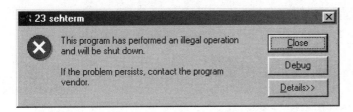

This message box asks whether you want the program to access an invalid byte in memory. (Most applications aren't as considerate as this; they usually just access invalid memory without asking.) Let's examine what happens if you click on the Yes button. In this case, the thread attempts to write a 5 to memory address NULL. Writing to address NULL always causes an access violation exception. When the thread raises an access violation, the system displays the message box shown below on Windows 98.

On Windows 2000, the message box shown on the following page is displayed.

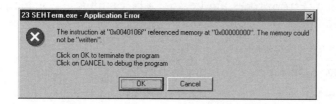

If you now click on the Close button (in Windows 98) or the OK button (in Windows 2000), the process will be terminated. However, there is a *finally* block in the source code, so the *finally* block executes before the process terminates. The finally block displays this message box.

The *finally* block is executing because its associated *try* block exited abnormally. When this message box is dismissed, the process does, in fact, terminate.

OK, now let's run the application again. This time, however, let's click on the No button so that we do not attempt to access invalid memory. When you click No, the thread naturally flows out of the *try* block and enters the *finally* block. Again, the *finally* block displays a message box.

Notice, however, that this time the message box indicates that the *try* block exited normally. When we dismiss this message box, the thread leaves the *finally* block and displays one last message box.

When this message box is dismissed, the process terminates naturally, because *WinMain* returns. Notice that you do not see this last message box when the process is terminated because of an access violation.

SEHTerm.cpp

```
/******************************************************************************
Module:  SEHTerm.cpp
Notices: Copyright (c) 2000 Jeffrey Richter
******************************************************************************/


#include "..\CmnHdr.h"      /* See Appendix A. */
#include <tchar.h>


///////////////////////////////////////////////////////////////////////////////


int WINAPI _tWinMain(HINSTANCE hinstExe, HINSTANCE, PTSTR pszCmdLine, int) {

   __try {
      int n = MessageBox(NULL, TEXT("Perform invalid memory access?"),
         TEXT("SEHTerm: In try block"), MB_YESNO);

      if (n == IDYES) {
         * (PBYTE) NULL = 5;  // This causes an access violation.
      }
   }
   __finally {
      PCTSTR psz = AbnormalTermination()
         ? TEXT("Abnormal termination") : TEXT("Normal termination");
      MessageBox(NULL, psz, TEXT("SEHTerm: In finally block"), MB_OK);
   }

   MessageBox(NULL, TEXT("Normal process termination"),
      TEXT("SEHTerm: After finally block"), MB_OK);

   return(0);
}


//////////////////////////////// End of File ///////////////////////////////////
```

Figure 23-1.
The SEHTerm sample application

EXCEPTION HANDLERS AND SOFTWARE EXCEPTIONS

An exception is an event you don't expect. In a well-written application, you don't expect attempts to access an invalid memory address or divide a value by 0. Nevertheless, such errors do occur. The CPU is responsible for catching invalid memory accesses and divides by 0, and it will raise an exception in response to these errors. When the CPU raises an exception, it's known as a *hardware exception*. Later in this chapter, we'll see that the operating system and your applications can raise their own exceptions, known as *software exceptions*.

When a hardware or software exception is raised, the operating system offers your application the opportunity to see what type of exception was raised and allows the application to handle the exception itself. Here is the syntax for an exception handler:

```
__try {
   // Guarded body
   .
   .
   .
}
__except (exception filter) {
   // Exception handler
   .
   .
   .
}
```

Notice the *__except* keyword. Whenever you create a *try* block, it must be followed by either a *finally* block or an *except* block. A *try* block can't have both a *finally* block and an *except* block, and a *try* block can't have multiple *finally* or *except* blocks. However, it is possible to nest *try-finally* blocks inside *try-except* blocks and vice versa.

Understanding Exception Filters and Exception Handlers by Example

Unlike termination handlers (discussed in the previous chapter), exception filters and exception handlers are executed directly by the operating system—the compiler has little to do with evaluating exception filters or executing exception handlers. The next several sections illustrate the normal execution of *try-except* blocks, explain how and why the operating system evaluates exception filters, and show the circumstances under which the operating system executes the code inside an exception handler.

Funcmeister1

Here's a more concrete coding example of a *try-except* block:

```
DWORD Funcmeister1() {
   DWORD dwTemp;

   // 1. Do any processing here.
   :
   :

   __try {
      // 2. Perform some operation.
      dwTemp = 0;
   }
   __except (EXCEPTION_EXECUTE_HANDLER) {
      // Handle an exception; this never executes.
      :
      :
      :
   }

   // 3. Continue processing.
   return(dwTemp);
}
```

In the *Funcmeister1 try* block, we simply move a 0 into the *dwTemp* variable. This operation will never cause an exception to be raised, so the code inside the *except* block will never execute. Note this difference from *try-finally* behavior. After *dwTemp* is set to 0, the next instruction to execute is the *return* statement.

Although *return*, *goto*, *continue*, and *break* statements are strongly discouraged in the *try* block of a termination handler, no speed or code-size penalty is associated with using these statements inside the *try* block of an exception handler. Such a statement in the *try* block associated with an *except* block won't incur the overhead of a local unwind.

Funcmeister2

Let's modify the function and see what happens:

```
DWORD Funcmeister2() {
   DWORD dwTemp = 0;

   // 1. Do any processing here.
   :
   :

   __try {
      // 2. Perform some operation(s).
      dwTemp = 5 / dwTemp;      // Generates an exception
      dwTemp += 10;            // Never executes
   }
   __except ( /* 3. Evaluate filter. */ EXCEPTION_EXECUTE_HANDLER) {
      // 4. Handle an exception.

      MessageBeep(0);
      :
      :

   }

   // 5. Continue processing.
   return(dwTemp);
}
```

In *Funcmeister2*, an instruction inside the *try* block calls for the attempt to divide 5 by 0. The CPU will catch this event and raise a hardware exception. When this exception is raised, the system will locate the beginning of the *except* block and evaluate the exception filter expression, an expression that must evaluate to one of the following three identifiers as defined in the Windows' Excpt.h file.

Identifier	Defined As
EXCEPTION_EXECUTE_HANDLER	1
EXCEPTION_CONTINUE_SEARCH	0
EXCEPTION_CONTINUE_EXECUTION	−1

In the next few sections, we'll discuss how each of these identifiers alters the thread's execution. While reading these sections, you can refer to Figure 24-1, which summarizes how the system processes an exception.

845

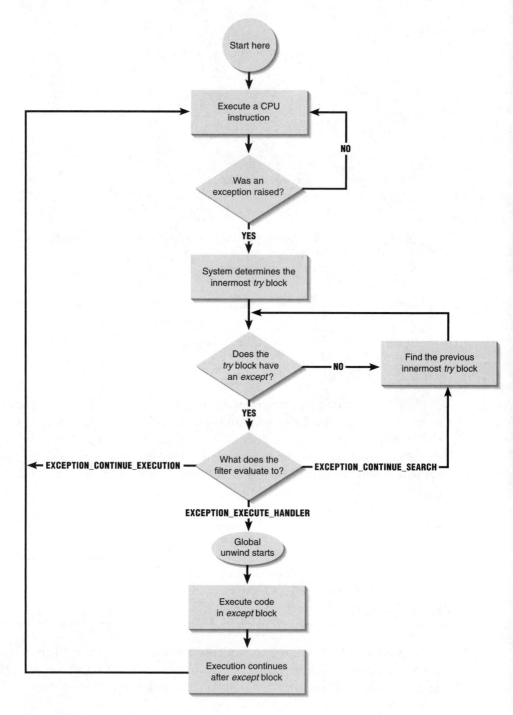

Figure 24-1.
How the system processes an exception

EXCEPTION_EXECUTE_HANDLER

In *Funcmeister2*, the exception filter expression evaluates to EXCEPTION_ EXECUTE_HANDLER. This value basically says to the system, "I recognize the exception. That is, I had a feeling that this exception might occur some time, and I've written some code to deal with it that I'd like to execute now." At this point, the system performs a global unwind (discussed later in this chapter) and then execution jumps to the code inside the *except* block (the exception handler code). After the code in the *except* block has executed, the system considers the exception to be handled and allows your application to continue executing. This mechanism allows Windows applications to trap errors, handle them, and continue running without the user ever knowing that the error happened.

But, once the *except* block has executed, where in the code should execution resume? With a little bit of thought, we can easily imagine several possibilities.

The first possibility would be for execution to resume after the CPU instruction that generates the exception. In *Funcmeister2*, execution would resume with the instruction that adds 10 to *dwTemp*. This might seem like a reasonable thing to do, but in reality, most programs are written so that they cannot continue executing successfully if one of the earlier instructions fails to execute.

In *Funcmeister2*, the code can continue to execute normally; however, *Funcmeister2* is not the normal situation. Most likely, your code will be structured so that the CPU instructions following the instruction that generates the exception will expect a valid return value. For example, you might have a function that allocates memory, in which case a whole series of instructions will be executed to manipulate that memory. If the memory cannot be allocated, all the lines will fail, making the program generate exceptions repeatedly.

Here is another example of why execution cannot continue after the failed CPU instruction. Let's replace the C statement that generated the exception in *Funcmeister2* with the following line:

```
malloc(5 / dwTemp);
```

For the line above, the compiler generates CPU instructions to perform the division, pushes the result on the stack, and calls the *malloc* function. If the division fails, the code can't continue executing properly. The system has to push something on the stack; if it doesn't, the stack gets corrupted.

Fortunately, Microsoft has not made it possible for us to have the system resume execution on the instruction following the instruction that generates the exception. This decision saves us from potential problems like these.

The second possibility would be for execution to resume with the instruction that generated the exception. This is an interesting possibility. What if inside the *except* block you had this statement:

```
dwTemp = 2;
```

With this assignment in the *except* block, you could resume execution with the instruction that generated the exception. This time, you would be dividing 5 by 2, and execution would continue just fine without raising another exception. You can alter something and have the system retry the instruction that generated the exception. However, you should be aware that this technique could result in some subtle behaviors. We'll discuss this technique in the "EXCEPTION_CONTINUE_EXECUTION" section.

The third and last possibility would be for execution to pick up with the first instruction following the *except* block. This is actually what happens when the exception filter expression evaluates to EXCEPTION_EXECUTE_HANDLER. After the code inside the *except* block finishes executing, control resumes at the first instruction after the *except* block.

Some Useful Examples

Let's say that you want to implement a totally robust application that needs to run 24 hours a day, 7 days a week. In today's world, with software so complex and so many variables and factors to affect an application's performance, I think that it's impossible to implement a totally robust application without the use of SEH. Let's look at a simple example: the C run-time function *strcpy*:

```
char* strcpy(
   char* strDestination,
   const char* strSource);
```

This is a pretty simple function, huh? How could little old *strcpy* ever cause a process to terminate? Well, if the caller ever passes NULL (or any bad address) for either of these parameters, *strcpy* raises an access violation and the whole process is terminated.

Using SEH, it's possible to create a totally robust *strcpy* function:

```
char* RobustStrCpy(char* strDestination, const char* strSource) {

   __try {
      strcpy(strDestination, strSource);
   }
```

```
  __except (EXCEPTION_EXECUTE_HANDLER) {
     // Nothing to do here
  }

  return(strDestination);
}
```

All this function does is place the call to *strcpy* inside a structured exception-handling frame. If *strcpy* executes successfully, the function just returns. If *strcpy* raises an access violation, the exception filter returns EXCEP-TION_EXECUTE_HANDLER, causing the thread to execute the handler code. In this function, the handler code does nothing and so again, *RobustStrCpy* just returns to its caller. *RobustStrCpy* will never cause the process to terminate!

Let's look at another example. Here's a function that returns the number of space-delimited tokens in a string:

```
int RobustHowManyToken(const char* str) {

  int nHowManyTokens = -1;  // -1 indicates failure
  char* strTemp = NULL;     // Assume failure

  __try {

     // Allocate a temporary buffer
     strTemp = (char*) malloc(strlen(str) + 1);

     // Copy the original string to the temporary buffer
     strcpy(strTemp, str);

     // Get the first token
     char* pszToken = strtok(strTemp, " ");

     // Iterate through all the tokens
     for (; pszToken != NULL; pszToken = strtok(NULL, " "))
        nHowManyTokens++;

     nHowManyTokens++;      // Add 1 since we started at -1
  }
  __except (EXCEPTION_EXECUTE_HANDLER) {
     // Nothing to do here
  }
```

(continued)

```
      // Free the temporary buffer (guaranteed)
      free(strTemp);

      return(nHowManyTokens);
}
```

This function allocates a temporary buffer and copies a string into it. Then the function uses the C run-time function *strtok* to obtain the tokens within the string. The temporary buffer is necessary because *strtok* modifies the string it's tokenizing.

Thanks to SEH, this deceptively simple function handles all kinds of possibilities. Let's see how this function performs under a few different circumstances.

First, if the caller passes NULL (or any bad memory address) to the function, *nHowManyTokens* is initialized to −1. The call to *strlen,* inside the *try* block, raises an access violation. The exception filter gets control and passes it to the *except* block, which does nothing. After the *except* block, *free* is called to release the temporary block of memory. However, this memory was never allocated, so we end up calling *free*, passing it NULL. ANSI C explicitly states that it is legal to call *free,* passing it NULL, in which case *free* does nothing—so this is not an error. Finally, the function returns −1, indicating failure. Note that the process is not terminated.

Second, the caller might pass a good address to the function but the call to *malloc* (inside the *try* block) can fail and return NULL. This will cause the call to *strcpy* to raise an access violation. Again, the exception filter is called, the *except* block executes (which does nothing), *free* is called passing it NULL (which does nothing), and −1 is returned, indicating to the caller that the function failed. Note that the process is not terminated.

Finally, let's assume that the caller passes a good address to the function and the call to *malloc* also succeeds. In this case, the remaining code will also succeed in calculating the number of tokens in the *nHowManyTokens* variable. At the end of the *try* block, the exception filter will not be evaluated, the code in the *except* block will not be executed, the temporary memory buffer will be freed, and *nHowManyTokens* will be returned to the caller.

Using SEH is pretty cool. The *RobustHowManyToken* function demonstrates how to have guaranteed cleanup of a resource without using *try-finally*. Any code that comes after an exception handler is also guaranteed to be executed (assuming that the function does not return from within a *try* block—a practice that should be avoided).

Let's look at one last and particularly useful example of SEH. Here's a function that duplicates a block of memory:

```
PBYTE RobustMemDup(PBYTE pbSrc, size_t cb) {

   PBYTE pbDup = NULL;        // Assume failure

   __try {

      // Allocate a buffer for the duplicate memory block
      pbDup = (PBYTE) malloc(cb);

      memcpy(pbDup, pbSrc, cb);
   }
   __except (EXCEPTION_EXECUTE_HANDLER) {
      free(pbDup);
      pbDup = NULL;
   }

   return(pbDup);
}
```

This function allocates a memory buffer and copies the bytes from the source block into the destination block. Then the function returns the address of the duplicate memory buffer to the caller (or NULL if the function fails). The caller is expected to free the buffer when it no longer needs it. This is the first example in which we actually have some code inside the *except* block. Let's see how this function performs under different circumstances.

- If the caller passes a bad address in the *pbSrc* parameter or if the call to *malloc* fails (returning NULL), *memcpy* will raise an access violation. The access violation executes the filter, which passes control to the *except* block. Inside the *except* block, the memory buffer is freed and *pbDup* is set to NULL so that the caller will know that the function failed. Again, note that ANSI C allows *free* to be passed NULL.

- If the caller passes a good address to the function and if the call to *malloc* is successful, the address of the newly allocated memory block is returned to the caller.

Global Unwinds

When an exception filter evaluates to EXCEPTION_EXECUTE_HANDLER, the system must perform a *global unwind*. The global unwind causes all of the outstanding *try-finally* blocks that started executing below the *try-except* block that handles the exception to resume execution. Figure 24-2 shows a flowchart that describes how the system performs a global unwind. Please refer to this figure while I explain the following example.

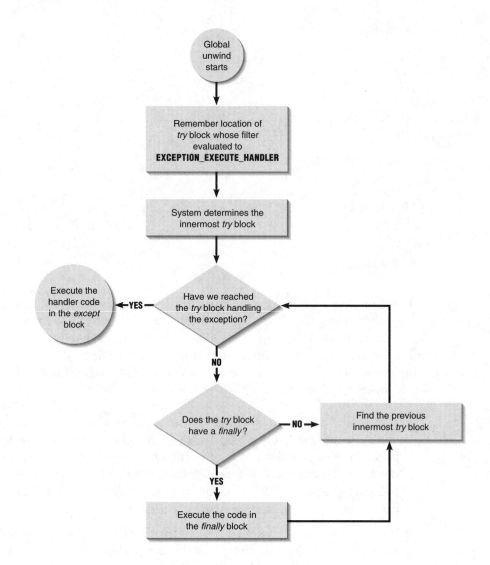

Figure 24-2.
How the system performs a global unwind

```
void FuncOStimpy1() {

    // 1. Do any processing here.
    .
    .

    __try {
        // 2. Call another function.
        FuncORen1();

        // Code here never executes.
    }

    __except ( /* 6. Evaluate filter. */ EXCEPTION_EXECUTE_HANDLER) {
        // 8. After the unwind, the exception handler executes.
        MessageBox(…);
    }

    // 9. Exception handled--continue execution.
    .
    .

}
void FuncORen1() {
    DWORD dwTemp = 0;

    // 3. Do any processing here.
    .
    .

    __try {
        // 4. Request permission to access protected data.
        WaitForSingleObject(g_hSem, INFINITE);

        // 5. Modify the data.
        //    An exception is generated here.
        g_dwProtectedData = 5 / dwTemp;
    }
    __finally {
        // 7. Global unwind occurs because filter evaluated
        //     to EXCEPTION_EXECUTE_HANDLER.

        // Allow others to use protected data.
        ReleaseSemaphore(g_hSem, 1, NULL);
    }

    // Continue processing--never executes.
    .
    .

}
```

Together, *FuncOStimpy1* and *FuncORen1* illustrate the most confusing aspects of SEH. The numbers that begin the comments show the order of execution, but let's hold hands and walk through it together anyway.

FuncOStimpy1 begins execution by entering its *try* block and calling *FuncORen1*. *FuncORen1* starts by entering its own *try* block and waiting to obtain a semaphore. Once it has the semaphore, *FuncORen1* tries to alter the global data variable *g_dwProtectedData*. However, the division by 0 causes an exception to be generated. The system grabs control now and searches for a *try* block matched with an *except* block. Since the *try* block in *FuncORen1* is matched by a *finally* block, the system searches upward for another *try* block. This time, it finds the *try* block in *FuncOStimpy1*, and it sees that *Func-OStimpy1*'s *try* block is matched by an *except* block.

The system now evaluates the exception filter associated with *Func-OStimpy1*'s *except* block and waits for the return value. When the system sees that the return value is EXCEPTION_EXECUTE_HANDLER, the system begins a global unwind in *FuncORen1*'s *finally* block. Note that the unwind takes place *before* the system begins execution of the code in *FuncOStimpy1*'s *except* block. For a global unwind, the system starts back at the bottom of all outstanding *try* blocks and searches this time for *try* blocks associated with *finally* blocks. The *finally* block that the system finds here is the one contained inside *FuncORen1*.

When the system executes the code in *FuncORen1*'s *finally* block, you can clearly see the power of SEH. Because *FuncORen1*'s *finally* block releases the semaphore, another thread is allowed to resume execution. If the call to *Release-Semaphore* were not contained inside the *finally* block, the semaphore would never be released.

After the code contained in the *finally* block has executed, the system continues walking upward, looking for outstanding *finally* blocks that need to be executed. This example has none. The system stops walking upward when it reaches the *try-except* block that decided to handle the exception. At this point, the global unwind is complete, and the system can execute the code contained inside the *except* block.

That's how structured exception handling works. SEH can be difficult to understand because the system gets quite involved with the execution of your code. No longer does the code flow from top to bottom—the system makes sections of code execute according to its notions of order. This order of execution is complex but predictable, and by following the flowcharts in Figure 24-1 and Figure 24-2, you should be able to use SEH with confidence.

To better understand the order of execution, let's look at what happened from a slightly different perspective. When a filter returns EXCEPTION_

EXECUTE_HANDLER, the filter is telling the operating system that the thread's instruction pointer should be set to the code inside the *except* block. However, the instruction pointer was inside *FuncORen1*'s *try* block. From Chapter 23, you'll recall that whenever a thread leaves the *try* portion of a *try-finally* block, the code in the *finally* block is guaranteed to execute. The global unwind is the mechanism that ensures this rule when exceptions are raised.

Halting Global Unwinds

It's possible to stop the system from completing a global unwind by putting a *return* statement inside a *finally* block. Let's look at the code here:

```
void FuncMonkey() {
   __try {
      FuncFish();
   }
   __except (EXCEPTION_EXECUTE_HANDLER) {
      MessageBeep(0);
   }
   MessageBox(…);
}

void FuncFish() {
   FuncPheasant();
   MessageBox(…);
}

void FuncPheasant() {

   __try {
      strcpy(NULL, NULL);
   }

   __finally {
      return;
   }
}
```

When the *strcpy* function is called in *FuncPheasant*'s *try* block, a memory access violation exception is raised. When this happens, the system starts scanning to see whether any exception filters exist that can handle the exception. The system will find that the exception filter in *FuncMonkey* wants to handle the exception, and the system initiates a global unwind.

The global unwind starts by executing the code inside *FuncPheasant*'s *finally* block. However, this block of code contains a *return* statement. The *return* statement causes the system to stop unwinding, and *FuncPheasant* will actually end up returning to *FuncFish*. *FuncFish* will continue executing and will display a message box on the screen. *FuncFish* will then return to *FuncMonkey*. The code in *FuncMonkey* continues executing by calling *MessageBox*.

Notice that the code inside *FuncMonkey*'s exception block never executes the call to *MessageBeep*. The *return* statement in *FuncPheasant*'s *finally* block causes the system to stop unwinding altogether, and execution continues as though nothing ever happened.

Microsoft deliberately designed SEH to work this way. You might occasionally want to stop unwinding and allow execution to continue. This method allows you to do so, although it usually isn't the sort of thing you want to do. As a rule, be careful to avoid putting *return* statements inside *finally* blocks.

EXCEPTION_CONTINUE_EXECUTION

Let's take a closer look at the exception filter to see how it evaluates to one of the three exception identifiers defined in Excpt.h. In the section called "*Funcmeister2*", the EXCEPTION_EXECUTE_HANDLER identifier is hard-coded directly into the filter for simplicity's sake, but you can make the filter call a function that will determine which of the three identifiers should be returned. Here's another code example:

```
char g_szBuffer[100];

void FunclinRoosevelt1() {
   int x = 0;
   char *pchBuffer = NULL;

   __try {
      *pchBuffer = 'J';
      x = 5 / x;
   }
   __except (OilFilter1(&pchBuffer)) {
      MessageBox(NULL, "An exception occurred", NULL, MB_OK);
   }
   MessageBox(NULL, "Function completed", NULL, MB_OK);
}

LONG OilFilter1(char **ppchBuffer) {
   if (*ppchBuffer == NULL) {
      *ppchBuffer = g_szBuffer;
      return(EXCEPTION_CONTINUE_EXECUTION);
   }
   return(EXCEPTION_EXECUTE_HANDLER);
}
```

We first run into a problem when we try to put a 'J' into the buffer pointed to by *pchBuffer*. Unfortunately, we didn't initialize *pchBuffer* to point to our global buffer *g_szBuffer*; *pchBuffer* points to NULL instead. The CPU will generate an exception and evaluate the exception filter in the *except* block associated with the *try* block in which the exception occurred. In the *except* block, the *OilFilter1* function is passed the address of the *pchBuffer* variable.

When *OilFilter1* gets control, it checks to see whether **ppchBuffer* is NULL and, if it is, sets it to point to the global buffer *g_szBuffer*. The filter then returns EXCEPTION_CONTINUE_EXECUTION. When the system sees that the filter evaluated to EXCEPTION_CONTINUE_EXECUTION, it jumps back to the instruction that generated the exception and tries to execute it again. This time, the instruction will succeed, and 'J' will be put into the first byte of *g_szBuffer*.

As the code continues to execute, we run up against the divide by 0 problem in the *try* block. Again the system evaluates the exception filter. This time, *OilFilter1* sees that **ppchBuffer* is not NULL and returns EXCEPTION_EXECUTE_HANDLER, which tells the system to execute the *except* block code. This causes a message box to appear with text indicating that an exception occurred.

As you can see, you can do an awful lot of work inside an exception filter. Of course, the filter must return one of the three exception identifiers, but it can also perform any other tasks you want it to.

Use EXCEPTION_CONTINUE_EXECUTION with Caution

As it turns out, trying to correct the situation shown in the *FunclinRoosevelt1* function and having the system continue execution might or might not work—it depends on the target CPU for your application, on how your compiler generates instructions for C/C++ statements, and on your compiler options.

A compiler might generate two machine instructions for the following C/C++ statement:

```
*pchBuffer = 'J';
```

The machine instructions might look like this:

```
MOV EAX, [pchBuffer]    // Move the address into a register
MOV [EAX], 'J'          // Move 'J' into the address
```

This second instruction generates the exception. The exception filter would catch the exception, correct the value in *pchBuffer*, and tell the system to re-execute the second CPU instruction. The problem is that the contents of the register wouldn't be changed to reflect the new value loaded into *pchBuffer*, and re-executing the CPU instruction would therefore generate another exception. We'd have an infinite loop!

Continuing execution might be fine if the compiler optimizes the code but might fail if the compiler doesn't optimize the code. This can be an incredibly difficult bug to fix, and you will have to examine the assembly language generated for your source code to determine what has gone wrong in your application. The moral of this story is to be *extremely* careful when returning EXCEPTION_CONTINUE_EXECUTION from an exception filter.

In one situation, EXCEPTION_CONTINUE_EXECUTION is guaranteed to work every time, all the time: when you are committing storage sparsely to a reserved region. In Chapter 15, we discussed how to reserve a large address space and then commit storage sparsely to this address space. The VMAlloc sample application demonstrated this. A better way to have written the VMAlloc application would have been to use SEH to commit the storage as necessary instead of calling *VirtualAlloc* all the time.

In Chapter 16, we talked about thread stacks. In particular, I showed you how the system reserved a 1-MB region of address space for the thread's stack and how the system automatically commits new storage to the stack as the thread needs it. To make this work, the system has internally set up an SEH frame. When your thread attempts to touch stack storage that doesn't exist, an exception is raised. The system's exception filter determines that the exception was due to an attempt to touch a stack's reserved address space. The exception filter then calls *VirtualAlloc* internally to commit more storage to your thread's stack and the filter returns EXCEPTION_CONTINUE_EXECUTION. At this point, the CPU instruction that attempted to touch the stack storage will now succeed and the thread continues running.

You can write some incredibly fast-performing and efficient applications when you combine virtual memory techniques with structured exception handling. The Spreadsheet sample application shown in the next chapter demonstrates how to efficiently implement the memory management portions of a spreadsheet application using SEH. This code is also designed to perform extremely fast.

EXCEPTION_CONTINUE_SEARCH

The examples have been pretty tame so far. Let's shake things up a bit by adding a function call:

```
char g_szBuffer[100];

void FunclinRoosevelt2() {
```

```
   char *pchBuffer = NULL;

   __try {
      FuncAtude2(pchBuffer);
   }
   __except (OilFilter2(&pchBuffer)) {
      MessageBox(…);
   }
}

void FuncAtude2(char *sz) {
   *sz = 0;
}

LONG OilFilter2 (char **ppchBuffer) {
   if (*ppchBuffer == NULL) {
      *ppchBuffer = g_szBuffer;
      return(EXCEPTION_CONTINUE_EXECUTION);
   }
   return(EXCEPTION_EXECUTE_HANDLER);
}
```

When *FunclinRoosevelt2* executes, it calls *FuncAtude2*, passing it NULL. When *FuncAtude2* executes, an exception is raised. Just as before, the system evaluates the exception filter associated with the most recently executing *try* block. In this example, the *try* block inside *FunclinRoosevelt2* is the most recently executing *try* block, so the system calls the *OilFilter2* function to evaluate the exception filter—even though the exception was generated inside the *FuncAtude2* function.

Now let's stir things up a little more by adding another *try-except* block.

```
char g_szBuffer[100];

void FunclinRoosevelt3() {

   char *pchBuffer = NULL;

   __try {
      FuncAtude3(pchBuffer);
   }
   __except (OilFilter3(&pchBuffer)) {
      MessageBox(…);
   }
}
```

(continued)

```
void FuncAtude3(char *sz) {
   __try {
      *sz = 0;
   }
   __except (EXCEPTION_CONTINUE_SEARCH) {
      // This never executes.
         .
         .
         .
   }
}


LONG OilFilter3(char **ppchBuffer) {
   if (*ppchBuffer == NULL) {
      *ppchBuffer = g_szBuffer;
      return(EXCEPTION_CONTINUE_EXECUTION);
   }
   return(EXCEPTION_EXECUTE_HANDLER);
}
```

Now when *FuncAtude3* tries to fill address NULL with 0, an exception is still raised but *FuncAtude3*'s exception filter will get executed. *FuncAtude3*'s exception filter is very simple and evaluates to EXCEPTION_ CONTINUE_SEARCH. This identifier tells the system to walk up to the previous *try* block that's matched with an *except* block and call this previous *try* block's exception filter.

Because *FuncAtude3*'s filter evaluates to EXCEPTION_CONTINUE_ SEARCH, the system will walk up to the previous *try* block (in *FunclinRoosevelt3*) and evaluate its exception filter, *OilFilter3*. *OilFilter3* will see that *pchBuffer* is NULL, will set *pchBuffer* to point to the global buffer, and will then tell the system to resume execution on the instruction that generated the exception. This will allow the code inside *FuncAtude3*'s *try* block to execute, but unfortunately, *FuncAtude3*'s local *sz* variable will not have been changed, and resuming execution on the failed instruction will simply cause another exception to be generated. What we have here is another infinite loop!

You'll notice I said that the system walks up to the most recently executing *try* block that's matched with an *except* block and evaluates its filters. This means that any *try* blocks that are matched with *finally* blocks instead of *except* blocks are skipped by the system while it walks up the chain. The reason for this should be pretty obvious: *finally* blocks don't have exception filters and therefore give the system nothing to evaluate. If *FuncAtude3* in the last example contained a *finally* block instead of its *except* block, the system would have started evaluating exception filters beginning with *FunclinRoosevelt3*'s *OilFilter3*.

Chapter 25 offers more information about EXCEPTION_CONTINUE_ SEARCH.

GetExceptionCode

Often an exception filter must analyze the situation before it can determine which value to return. For example, your handler might know what to do if a divide by 0 exception occurs, but it might not know how to handle a memory access exception. The exception filter has the responsibility for examining the situation and returning the appropriate value.

This code demonstrates a method for identifying the kind of exception that has occurred:

```
__try {
   x = 0;
   y = 4 / x;
}

__except ((GetExceptionCode() == EXCEPTION_INT_DIVIDE_BY_ZERO) ?
   EXCEPTION_EXECUTE_HANDLER : EXCEPTION_CONTINUE_SEARCH) {
   // Handle divide by zero exception.
}
```

The *GetExceptionCode* intrinsic function returns a value identifying the kind of exception that has occurred:

```
DWORD GetExceptionCode();
```

The following list of all predefined exceptions and their meanings is adapted from the Platform SDK documentation. The exception identifiers can be found in the WinBase.h file. I have grouped the exceptions together by category.

Memory-Related Exceptions

- **EXCEPTION_ACCESS_VIOLATION** The thread tried to read from or write to a virtual address for which it doesn't have the appropriate access. This is the most common exception.

- **EXCEPTION_DATATYPE_MISALIGNMENT** The thread tried to read or write data that is misaligned on hardware that doesn't provide alignment. For example, 16-bit values must be aligned on 2-byte boundaries, 32-bit values on 4-byte boundaries, and so on.

- **EXCEPTION_ARRAY_BOUNDS_EXCEEDED** The thread tried to access an array element that is out of bounds, and the underlying hardware supports bounds checking.

- **EXCEPTION_IN_PAGE_ERROR** A page fault couldn't be satisfied because the file system or a device driver returned a read error.

■ **EXCEPTION_GUARD_PAGE** A thread attempted to access a page of memory that has the PAGE_GUARD protection attribute. The page is made accessible, and an EXCEPTION_GUARD_PAGE exception is raised.

■ **EXCEPTION_STACK_OVERFLOW** The thread has used all of its allotted stack.

■ **EXCEPTION_ILLEGAL_INSTRUCTION** A thread executed an invalid instruction. This exception is defined by the specific CPU architecture; executing an invalid instruction can cause a trap error on different CPUs.

■ **EXCEPTION_PRIV_INSTRUCTION** The thread tried to execute an instruction whose operation is not allowed in the current machine mode.

Exception-Related Exceptions

■ **EXCEPTION_INVALID_DISPOSITION** An exception filter returned a value other than EXCEPTION_EXECUTE_HANDLER, EXCEPTION_CONTINUE_SEARCH, or EXCEPTION_CONTINUE_EXECUTION.

■ **EXCEPTION_NONCONTINUABLE_EXCEPTION** An exception filter returned EXCEPTION_CONTINUE_EXECUTION in response to a noncontinuable exception.

Debugging-Related Exceptions

■ **EXCEPTION_BREAKPOINT** A breakpoint was encountered.

■ **EXCEPTION_SINGLE_STEP** A trace trap or other single-instruction mechanism signaled that one instruction has been executed.

■ **EXCEPTION_INVALID_HANDLE** A function was passed an invalid handle.

Integer-Related Exceptions

■ **EXCEPTION_INT_DIVIDE_BY_ZERO** The thread tried to divide an integer value by an integer divisor of 0.

■ **EXCEPTION_INT_OVERFLOW** The result of an integer operation caused a carry out of the most significant bit of the result.

Floating Point–Related Exceptions

- **EXCEPTION_FLT_DENORMAL_OPERAND** One of the operands in a floating-point operation is denormal. A denormal value is one that is too small to represent a standard floating-point value.

- **EXCEPTION_FLT_DIVIDE_BY_ZERO** The thread tried to divide a floating-point value by a floating-point divisor of 0.

- **EXCEPTION_FLT_INEXACT_RESULT** The result of a floating-point operation can't be represented exactly as a decimal fraction.

- **EXCEPTION_FLT_INVALID_OPERATION** Represents any floating-point exception not included in this list.

- **EXCEPTION_FLT_OVERFLOW** The exponent of a floating-point operation is greater than the magnitude allowed by the corresponding type.

- **EXCEPTION_FLT_STACK_CHECK** The stack overflowed or underflowed as the result of a floating-point operation.

- **EXCEPTION_FLT_UNDERFLOW** The exponent of a floating-point operation is less than the magnitude allowed by the type.

The *GetExceptionCode* intrinsic function can be called only in an exception filter (between the parentheses following *__except*) or inside an exception handler. The following code is legal:

```
__try {
   y = 0;
   x = 4 / y;
}

__except (
   ((GetExceptionCode() == EXCEPTION_ACCESS_VIOLATION) ||
    (GetExceptionCode() == EXCEPTION_INT_DIVIDE_BY_ZERO)) ?
   EXCEPTION_EXECUTE_HANDLER : EXCEPTION_CONTINUE_SEARCH) {

   switch (GetExceptionCode()) {
      case EXCEPTION_ACCESS_VIOLATION:
         // Handle the access violation.
         :
         :
         break;
```

(continued)

```
        case EXCEPTION_INT_DIVIDE_BY_ZERO:
            // Handle the integer divide by 0.
                :
                :

            break;
        }
    }
```

However, you cannot call *GetExceptionCode* from inside an exception filter function. To help you catch such errors, the compiler will produce a compilation error if you try to compile the following code:

```
__try {
    y = 0;
    x = 4 / y;
}

__except (CoffeeFilter()) {

    // Handle the exception.
        :
        :

}

LONG CoffeeFilter (void) {
    // Compilation error: illegal call to GetExceptionCode.
    return((GetExceptionCode() == EXCEPTION_ACCESS_VIOLATION) ?
        EXCEPTION_EXECUTE_HANDLER : EXCEPTION_CONTINUE_SEARCH);
}
```

You can get the desired effect by rewriting the code this way:

```
__try {
    y = 0;
    x = 4 / y;
}

__except (CoffeeFilter(GetExceptionCode())) {

    // Handle the exception.
        :
        :

}

LONG CoffeeFilter (DWORD dwExceptionCode) {
    return((dwExceptionCode == EXCEPTION_ACCESS_VIOLATION) ?
        EXCEPTION_EXECUTE_HANDLER : EXCEPTION_CONTINUE_SEARCH);
}
```

Exception codes follow the rules for error codes as defined inside the WinError.h file. Each DWORD is divided as shown in Table 24-1.

Bits	31–30	29	28	27–16	15–0
Contents	Severity	Microsoft/ customer	Reserved	Facility code	Exception code
Meaning	0=Success 1=Informational 2=Warning 3=Error	0=Microsoft-defined code 1=customer-defined code	Must be 0	Microsoft-defined (see table below)	Microsoft/ customer-defined

Table 24-1.
The composition of an error code

Currently, Microsoft defines the following facility codes.

Facility Code	Value	Facility Code	Value
FACILITY_NULL	0	FACILITY_CONTROL	10
FACILITY_RPC	1	FACILITY_CERT	11
FACILITY_DISPATCH	2	FACILITY_INTERNET	12
FACILITY_STORAGE	3	FACILITY_MEDIASERVER	13
FACILITY_ITF	4	FACILITY_MSMQ	14
FACILITY_WIN32	7	FACILITY_SETUPAPI	15
FACILITY_WINDOWS	8	FACILITY_SCARD	16
FACILITY_SECURITY	9	FACILITY_COMPLUS	17

So here's what we get if we pick apart the EXCEPTION_ACCESS_VIOLATION exception code. Looking up EXCEPTION_ACCESS_VIOLATION in WinBase.h, we see that it has a value of 0xC0000005:

```
   C    0    0    0    0    0    0    5   (hexadecimal)
1100 0000 0000 0000 0000 0000 0000 0101  (binary)
```

Bits 30 & 31 are both set to 1, indicating that an access violation is an error (the thread cannot continue running). Bit 29 is 0, meaning that Microsoft has defined this code. Bit 28 is 0 because it is reserved for future use. Bits 16 through 27 are 0, indicating FACILITY_NULL (an access violation can happen anywhere in the system; it is not an exception that only occurs when using certain facilities). Bits 0 through 15 contain the value 5, which just means that Microsoft defined an access violation as code 5.

GetExceptionInformation

When an exception occurs, the operating system pushes the following three structures on the stack of the thread that raised the exception: the EXCEPTION_RECORD structure, the CONTEXT structure, and the EXCEPTION_POINTERS structure.

The EXCEPTION_RECORD structure contains CPU-independent information about the raised exception, and the CONTEXT structure contains CPU-dependent information about the raised exception. The EXCEPTION_POINTERS structure has only two data members that are pointers to the pushed EXCEPTION_RECORD and CONTEXT data structures:

```
typedef struct _EXCEPTION_POINTERS {
   PEXCEPTION_RECORD ExceptionRecord;
   PCONTEXT ContextRecord;
} EXCEPTION_POINTERS, *PEXCEPTION_POINTERS;
```

To retrieve this information and use it in your own application, you will need to call the *GetExceptionInformation* function:

```
PEXCEPTION_POINTERS GetExceptionInformation();
```

This intrinsic function returns a pointer to an EXCEPTION_POINTERS structure.

The most important thing to remember about the *GetException-Information* function is that it can be called only in an exception filter—because the CONTEXT, EXCEPTION_RECORD, and EXCEPTION_POINTERS data structures are valid only during the exception filter processing. Once control has been transferred to the exception handler, the data on the stack is destroyed.

Though this situation is rarely necessary, if you need to access the exception information from inside your exception handler block, you must save the EXCEPTION_RECORD data structure and/or CONTEXT data structure pointed to by the EXCEPTION_POINTERS structure in one or more variables that you create. The following code demonstrates how to save both the EXCEPTION_RECORD and CONTEXT data structures:

```
void FuncSkunk() {
    // Declare variables that we can use to save the exception
    // record and the context if an exception should occur.
    EXCEPTION_RECORD SavedExceptRec;
    CONTEXT SavedContext;
        .
        .
        .
    __try {

        .
        .

    }


    __except (
        SavedExceptRec =
            *(GetExceptionInformation())->ExceptionRecord,
        SavedContext =
            *(GetExceptionInformation())->ContextRecord,
        EXCEPTION_EXECUTE_HANDLER) {

        // We can use the SavedExceptRec and SavedContext
        // variables inside the handler code block.
        switch (SavedExceptRec.ExceptionCode) {
            .
            .
            .
        }
    }
        .
        .
        .
}
```

Notice the use of the C language's comma (,) operator in the exception filter. Many programmers aren't used to seeing this operator. It tells the compiler to execute the comma-separated expressions from left to right. When all of the expressions have been evaluated, the result of the last (or rightmost) expression is returned.

In *FuncSkunk*, the left expression will execute, causing the EXCEPTION_RECORD structure on the stack to be stored in the *SavedExceptRec* local variable. The result of this expression is the value of *SavedExceptRec*. However, this result is discarded and the next expression to the right is evaluated. This second expression causes the CONTEXT structure on the stack to be stored in the *SavedContext* local variable. The result of the second expression is *SavedContext*, and again, this expression is discarded as the third expression is evaluated. This is a very simple expression that evaluates to EXCEPTION_EXECUTE_ HANDLER. The result of this rightmost expression is the result of the entire comma-separated expression.

Because the exception filter evaluated to EXCEPTION_EXECUTE_ HANDLER, the code inside the *except* block executes. At this point, the *Saved-ExceptRec* and *SavedContext* variables have been initialized and can be used inside the *except* block. Keep in mind it is important that the *SavedExceptRec* and *SavedContext* variables be declared outside the *try* block.

As you've probably guessed, the *ExceptionRecord* member of the EXCEPTION_POINTERS structure points to an EXCEPTION_RECORD structure:

```
typedef struct _EXCEPTION_RECORD {
   DWORD ExceptionCode;
   DWORD ExceptionFlags;
   struct _EXCEPTION_RECORD *ExceptionRecord;
   PVOID ExceptionAddress;
   DWORD NumberParameters;
   ULONG_PTR ExceptionInformation[EXCEPTION_MAXIMUM_PARAMETERS];
} EXCEPTION_RECORD;
```

The EXCEPTION_RECORD structure contains detailed, CPU-independent information about the exception that has most recently occurred:

- *ExceptionCode* contains the code of the exception. This is the same information that is returned from the *GetExceptionCode* intrinsic function.

- *ExceptionFlags* contains flags about the exception. Currently the only two values are 0 (which indicates a continuable exception) and EXCEPTION_NONCONTINUABLE (which indicates a noncontinuable exception). Any attempt to continue execution after a noncontinuable exception causes an EXCEPTION_NONCON-TINUABLE_EXCEPTION exception to be raised.

- *ExceptionRecord* points to an EXCEPTION_RECORD structure for another unhandled exception. While handling one exception, it is possible to raise another exception. For example, the code in your exception filter could attempt to divide a number by 0. Exception records can be chained to provide additional information when nested exceptions occur. A nested exception occurs if an exception is generated during the processing of an exception filter. If there are no unhandled exceptions, this member will contain NULL.

- *ExceptionAddress* specifies the address of the CPU instruction that generated the exception.

- *NumberParameters* specifies the number of parameters (0 to 15) associated with the exception. This is the number of defined elements in the *ExceptionInformation* array. For almost all exceptions, this value will be 0.

- *ExceptionInformation* specifies an array of additional arguments that describe the exception. For almost all exceptions, the array elements are undefined.

The last two members of the EXCEPTION_RECORD structure, *NumberParameters* and *ExceptionInformation*, offer the exception filter some additional information about the exception. Currently only one type of exception offers additional information: EXCEPTION_ACCESS_VIOLATION. All other possible exceptions will have the *NumberParameters* member set to 0. You examine the *NumberParameters* array member to look at the additional information about a generated exception.

For an EXCEPTION_ACCESS_VIOLATION exception, *ExceptionInformation[0]* contains a flag that indicates the type of operation that caused the access violation. If this value is 0, the thread tried to read the inaccessible data. If this value is 1, the thread tried to write to inaccessible data. *ExceptionInformation[1]* specifies the address of the inaccessible data.

By using these members, you can produce exception filters that offer a significant amount of information about your application. For example, you might write an exception filter like this:

```
__try {
   .
   .
}
__except (ExpFltr(GetExceptionInformation()->ExceptionRecord)) {
   .
   .
}

LONG ExpFltr (PEXCEPTION_RECORD pER) {
   char szBuf[300], *p;
   DWORD dwExceptionCode = pER->ExceptionCode;

   sprintf(szBuf, "Code = %x, Address = %p",
      dwExceptionCode, pER->ExceptionAddress);
```

(continued)

869

```
    // Find the end of the string.
    p = strchr(szBuf, 0);

    // I used a switch statement in case Microsoft adds
    // information for other exception codes in the future.
    switch (dwExceptionCode) {
        case EXCEPTION_ACCESS_VIOLATION:
            sprintf(p, "Attempt to %s data at address %p",
                pER->ExceptionInformation[0] ? "write" : "read",
                pER->ExceptionInformation[1]);
            break;

        default:
            break;
    }

    MessageBox(NULL, szBuf, "Exception", MB_OK | MB_ICONEXCLAMATION);

    return(EXCEPTION_CONTINUE_SEARCH);
}
```

The *ContextRecord* member of the EXCEPTION_POINTERS structure points to a CONTEXT structure (discussed in Chapter 7). This structure is platform-dependent; that is, the contents of this structure will differ from one CPU platform to another.

Basically, this structure contains one member for each of the registers available on the CPU. When an exception is raised, you can find out even more information by examining the members of this structure. Unfortunately, realizing the benefit of such a possibility requires you to write platform-dependent code that recognizes the machine it's running on and uses the appropriate CONTEXT structure. The best way to handle this is to put *#ifdef*s into your code. The CONTEXT structures for the various CPUs supported by Windows are in the WinNT.h file.

Software Exceptions

So far, we have been discussing hardware exceptions in which the CPU catches an event and raises an exception. It is also possible for your code to forcibly raise an exception. This is another way for a function to indicate failure to its caller. Traditionally, functions that can fail return some special value to indicate failure. The caller of the function is supposed to check for this special value and take an alternative course of action. Frequently, the caller has to clean up what it's doing and return its own failure code back to its caller. This propagating of error codes causes your source code to become much more difficult to write and to maintain.

An alternative approach is to have functions raise exceptions when they fail. With this approach, the code is much easier to write and to maintain. Plus, the code typically performs better without all of the error testing code being executed. In fact, the error-testing code only executes if there is a failure, and this is the exceptional case.

Unfortunately, most developers do not get into the habit of using exceptions for error handling. There are two basic reasons for this. The first reason is that most developers are unfamiliar with SEH. Even if one developer is acquainted with it, other developers might not be. If one developer writes a function that raises an exception but other developers don't write SEH frames to trap the exception, the process will be terminated by the operating system.

The second reason why developers avoid SEH is that it is not portable to other operating systems. Many companies target multiple operating systems and would like to have a single source code base for their products, which is certainly understandable. SEH is a Windows-specific technology.

However, if you decide to return errors via exceptions, I applaud your decision and this section is for you. First, let's look at the Windows Heap functions such as *HeapCreate*, *HeapAlloc*, and so on. You'll recall from Chapter 18 that these functions offer developers a choice. Normally when any of the heap functions fail, they return NULL to indicate failure. You can, however, pass the HEAP_GENERATE_EXCEPTIONS flag to any of these heap functions. If you use this flag and the function fails, the function does not return NULL; instead, the function raises a STATUS_NO_MEMORY software exception that other parts of your code can catch with an SEH frame.

If you want to take advantage of this exception, you can code your *try* block as though the memory allocation will always succeed; if the allocation fails, you can either handle the exception by using an *except* block or have your function clean up by matching the *try* block with a *finally* block. How convenient!

Your application traps software exceptions exactly the same way that it traps hardware exceptions. In other words, everything I said in the last chapter applies equally well to software exceptions.

What we want to concentrate on in this section is how to have your own functions forcibly raise software exceptions as a method for indicating failure. In fact, you can implement your functions similarly to Microsoft's implementation of the heap functions: have your callers pass a flag that tells your function how it should indicate failures.

Raising a software exception couldn't be easier. You simply call the *Raise-Exception* function:

```
VOID RaiseException(
   DWORD dwExceptionCode,
   DWORD dwExceptionFlags,
   DWORD nNumberOfArguments,
   CONST ULONG_PTR *pArguments);
```

The first parameter, *dwExceptionCode*, must be a value that identifies the raised exception. The *HeapAlloc* function passes STATUS_NO_MEMORY for this parameter. If you define your own exception identifiers, you should follow the same format as the standard Windows error codes as defined in the WinError.h file. Recall that each DWORD is divided as shown in Table 24-1 on page 865.

If you create your own exception code, fill out all four fields of the DWORD:

- Bits 31 and 30 will contain the severity.

- Bit 29 will be 1 (0 is reserved for Microsoft-created exceptions, such as *HeapAlloc*'s STATUS_NO_MEMORY).

- Bit 28 is 0.

- Bits 27 through 16 will be one of Microsoft's predefined facility codes.

- Bits 15 through 0 will be an arbitrary value that you choose to identify the section of your application that raised the exception.

RaiseException's second parameter, *dwExceptionFlags*, must be either 0 or EXCEPTION_NONCONTINUABLE. Basically, this flag indicates whether it is legal for an exception filter to return EXCEPTION_CONTINUE_EXECUTION in response to this raised exception. If you do not pass the EXCEPTION_NONCONTINUABLE flag to *RaiseException*, the filter can return EXCEPTION_CONTINUE_EXECUTION. Normally, this would cause the thread to re-execute the same CPU instruction that raised the software exception. However, Microsoft has done some trickery so that execution continues after the call to the *RaiseException* function.

If you do pass the EXCEPTION_NONCONTINUABLE flag to *Raise-Exception*, you're telling the system that the type of exception you are raising can't be continued. This flag is used internally in the operating system to signal fatal (nonrecoverable) errors. In addition, when *HeapAlloc* raises the STATUS_

NO_MEMORY software exception, it uses the EXCEPTION_NON-CONTINUABLE flag to tell the system that this exception cannot be continued. This makes sense: there is no way to force the memory to be allocated and continue running.

If a filter ignores the EXCEPTION_NONCONTINUABLE flag and returns EXCEPTION_CONTINUE_EXECUTION anyway, the system raises a new exception: EXCEPTION_NONCONTINUABLE_EXCEPTION.

It is possible for an exception to be raised while the application is trying to process another exception. This makes sense, of course. While we're at it, let's note that it's also possible for an invalid memory access to occur inside a *finally* block, an exception filter, or an exception handler. When this happens, the system stacks exceptions. Remember the *GetExceptionInformation* function? This function returns the address of an EXCEPTION_POINTERS structure. The *ExceptionRecord* member of the EXCEPTION_POINTERS structure points to an EXCEPTION_RECORD structure that contains another *ExceptionRecord* member. This member is a pointer to another EXCEPTION_RECORD, which contains information about the previously raised exception.

Usually the system is processing only one exception at a time, and the *ExceptionRecord* member is NULL. However, if during the processing of one exception another exception is raised, the first EXCEPTION_RECORD structure contains information about the most recently raised exception and the *ExceptionRecord* member of this first EXCEPTION_RECORD structure points to the EXCEPTION_RECORD structure for the previously raised exception. If additional exceptions have not been processed completely, you can continue to walk this linked-list of EXCEPTION_RECORD structures to determine how to handle the exception.

RaiseException's third and fourth parameters, *nNumberOfArguments* and *pArguments*, are used to pass additional information about the raised exception. Usually, there is no need for additional arguments—you can simply pass NULL for the *pArguments* parameter, in which case *RaiseException* ignores the *nNumberOfArguments* parameter. If you do want to pass additional arguments, the *nNumberOfArguments* parameter must indicate the number of elements in the ULONG_PTR array pointed to by the *pArguments* parameter. This parameter cannot exceed EXCEPTION_MAXIMUM_PARAMETERS, which is defined in WinNT.h as 15.

During the processing of this exception, you can have an exception filter refer to the *NumberParameters* and *ExceptionInformation* members of the EXCEPTION_RECORD structure to examine the information in the *nNumberOfArguments* and *pArguments* parameters.

873

You might want to generate your own software exceptions in your application for any of several reasons. For example, you might want to send informational messages to the system's event log. Whenever a function in your application sensed some sort of problem, you could call *RaiseException* and have some exception handler further up the call tree look for certain exceptions and either add them to the event log or pop up a message box. You might also want to create software exceptions to signal internal fatal errors in your application.

UNHANDLED EXCEPTIONS AND C++ EXCEPTIONS

In the previous chapter, we discussed what happens when a filter returns EXCEPTION_CONTINUE_SEARCH. Returning this tells the system to continue walking up the call tree looking for additional exception filters. But what happens if every filter returns EXCEPTION_CONTINUE_SEARCH? In this case, we have what's called an *unhandled exception*.

Remember from Chapter 6 that every thread truly begins executing with a function inside Kernel32.dll called *BaseProcessStart* or *BaseThreadStart*. These two functions are practically identical; the only difference is that one function is used for a process's primary thread:

```
VOID BaseProcessStart(PPROCESS_START_ROUTINE pfnStartAddr) {
   __try {
      ExitThread((pfnStartAddr)());
   }
   __except (UnhandledExceptionFilter(GetExceptionInformation())) {
      ExitProcess(GetExceptionCode());
   }
   // NOTE: We never get here
}
```

The other function is used for all of a process's secondary threads:

```
VOID BaseThreadStart(PTHREAD_START_ROUTINE pfnStartAddr, PVOID pvParam) {
   __try {
      ExitThread((pfnStartAddr)(pvParam));
   }
   __except (UnhandledExceptionFilter(GetExceptionInformation())) {
      ExitProcess(GetExceptionCode());
   }
   // NOTE: We never get here
}
```

Notice that both of these functions contain an SEH frame. Both functions enter a *try* block and from within the *try* block call your primary or secondary thread's entry-point function. So, if your thread raises an exception and if all your filters return EXCEPTION_CONTINUE_SEARCH, the system has provided a special filter function that will be called for you automatically: *UnhandledExceptionFilter*.

```
LONG UnhandledExceptionFilter(PEXCEPTION_POINTERS pExceptionInfo);
```

This function is responsible for displaying the message box that indicates that a thread in your process has an unhandled exception and allows the user to terminate or debug the process. This message box looks similar to the following in Windows 98.

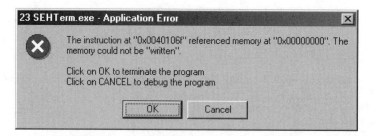

In Windows 2000, it looks like this.

In the Windows 2000 message box, the first paragraph of text indicates which exception occurred and the address of the instruction in the process's address space that generated the exception. It just so happens that a memory access violation caused this message box to appear, so the system can report the invalid memory address that was accessed and specify that an attempt to read the memory caused the exception. The *UnhandledExceptionFilter* function gets this additional information from the *ExceptionInformation* member of the EXCEPTION_RECORD structure generated for this exception.

Following the description of the exception, the message box indicates the user's two choices. The first choice is to click on the OK button, which causes *UnhandledExceptionFilter* to return EXCEPTION_EXECUTE_HANDLER. This, of course, causes a global unwind to occur so that any *finally* blocks that you have are executed, and then the handler in *BaseProcessStart or BaseThread-Start* executes. Both of these handlers call *ExitProcess,* which is why your process terminates. Note that the process's exit code will be the exception code. Also note that it is your process's thread that is killing your process—the operating system is not doing it! This means that you have control over this behavior and can alter it.

The second choice, clicking on the Cancel button, is a developer's dream come true. When you click on the Cancel button, *UnhandledExceptionFilter* attempts to load a debugger and attaches the debugger to the process. With the debugger attached to the process, you can examine the state of global, local, and static variables, set breakpoints, examine the call tree, restart the process, and do anything else you would normally do when you debug a process.

The real boon is that you can handle the failure of your application when it occurs. Under most other operating systems, you must invoke your application through the debugger to debug it. If an exception occurs in a process on one of these other operating systems, you have to terminate the process, start a debugger, and invoke the application—again using the debugger. The problem is that you would have to try to reproduce the bug before you could fix it. And who knows what the values of the different variables were when the problem originally occurred? It's much harder to resolve a bug this way. The ability to dynamically attach a debugger to a process as it runs is one of the best features in Windows.

WINDOWS 2000

This book concentrates solely on user-mode application development. However, you might find it interesting to know what happens when a thread running in kernel-mode raises an unhandled exception. Exceptions in kernel mode are handled exactly the same as exceptions in user mode. If a low-level virtual memory function generates an exception, the system checks whether any kernel-mode exception filters are prepared to handle the exception. If the system cannot find an exception

(continued)

> filter to handle the exception, the exception is unhandled. In the case of a kernel-mode exception, the unhandled exception is in the operating system or (more likely) in a device driver and not in an application. Such an unhandled exception identifies a serious bug!
>
> It isn't safe for the system to continue running if an unhandled exception occurs in kernel mode, so the system doesn't call the *UnhandledExceptionFilter* function in such a case; instead, the system shows what is typically called the Blue Screen of Death. The display switches video mode to a blue screen containing nothing but text and the computer is halted. The text displays which device drivers are loaded and the module containing the code that raised the unhandled violation. You should jot down this information and send it to Microsoft or to the device driver vendor so that the bug can be fixed. Since the computer is halted, you'll need to reboot your machine before you can do anything else; any unsaved work is lost.

Just-In-Time Debugging

The ability to connect a debugger to any process at any time is called *just-in-time debugging*. Here's a little more information about how this works: when you click on the Cancel button, you're telling the *UnhandledExceptionFilter* function that you want to debug the process.

Internally, *UnhandledExceptionFilter* invokes the debugger by looking into the following registry subkey:

```
HKEY_LOCAL_MACHINE\SOFTWARE\Microsoft\Windows NT\CurrentVersion\AeDebug
```

Inside this subkey, there is a data value named Debugger, which is typically set to the following value when you install Visual Studio:

```
"C:\Program Files\Microsoft Visual Studio\Common\MSDev98\Bin\msdev.exe"
  -p %ld -e %ld
```

WINDOWS 98

> In Windows 98, these values are not stored in the registry—they are stored in the Win.ini file.

This line tells the system which program (MSDev.exe) to run as the debugger. Of course, you can change this to the debugger of your choice. *UnhandledExceptionFilter* also passes two parameters on the command line to the debugger. The first parameter is the ID of the process that is to be debugged.

The second parameter identifies an inheritable manual-reset event that was created in the nonsignaled state by the *UnhandledExceptionFilter* function. Vendors must implement their debuggers so that they recognize the *-p* and *-e* switches as identifying the process ID and the event handle.

After the process ID and event handle are merged into the string, *UnhandledExceptionFilter* executes the debugger by calling *CreateProcess*. At this point, the debugger process starts running and checks its command-line arguments. If the *-p* switch exists, the debugger grabs the process ID and attaches itself to the process by calling *DebugActiveProcess*:

```
BOOL DebugActiveProcess(DWORD dwProcessID);
```

Once the debugger attaches itself, the operating system informs the debugger of the debuggee's state. For example, the system will tell the debugger how many threads are in the debuggee and which DLLs are loaded in the debuggee's address space. It takes time for the debugger to accumulate all of this data as it prepares to debug the process. While all of this preparation is going on, the thread inside *UnhandledExceptionFilter* must wait. It does this by calling *WaitForSingleObject*, passing the handle of the manual-reset event that it had created. You'll recall that this event was created in the nonsignaled state, and therefore, the debuggee's thread is immediately suspended waiting for the event.

After the debugger has fully initialized, it again checks its command line looking for the *-e* switch. If this switch exists, the debugger gets the handle of the event and calls *SetEvent*. The debugger can use the event's handle value directly because the event's handle was created inheritable and because the debuggee's call to the *UnhandledExceptionFilter* function spawned the debugger process as a child process.

Setting the event causes the debuggee's thread to wake up. The thread communicates the information about the unhandled exception to the debugger. The debugger receives this notification and loads the proper source code file, positioning itself at the instruction that raised the exception. Wow, this is all very cool!

By the way, you don't have to wait for an exception before you can debug a process. You can always connect a debugger to any process at any time by running "MSDEV –p *PID*" where PID is the ID of the process you want to debug. In fact, the Windows 2000 Task Manager makes this easy for you. When viewing the Process tab, you can select a process, click the right mouse button, and choose the Debug menu option. This causes the Task Manager to look at the same registry subkey we just discussed and call *CreateProcess*, passing the ID of the selected process. In this case, the Task Manager passes 0 for the event handle.

Turning Off the Exception Message Box

There might be times when you don't want the exception message box to be displayed if an exception occurs. For example, you might not want the message box to appear in the shipping version of your product. If it did appear, it could easily lead an end user to accidentally start debugging your application. An end user needs only to click on the Cancel button in the message box to enter unfamiliar, scary territory—the debugger. You can use a variety of methods to prevent this message box from appearing.

Forcing the Process to Die

To prevent *UnhandledExceptionFilter* from displaying the exception message box, you can call the *SetErrorMode* function shown here, passing it the SEM_NOGPFAULTERRORBOX identifier:

```
UINT SetErrorMode(UINT fuErrorMode);
```

Then, when *UnhandledExceptionFilter* is called to handle the exception, it sees that you have turned on this flag and immediately returns EXCEPTION_EXECUTE_HANDLER. This causes the global unwind and then executes the handler in *BaseProcessStart* or *BaseThreadStart*. The handler terminates the process.

I personally don't like this method because the user is given absolutely no warning; the application just vanishes.

Wrapping a Thread Function

Another method you can use to disable the message box is to place a *try-except* block around the entire contents of your primary thread's entry-point function (*main*, *wmain*, *WinMain*, or *wWinMain*). Make sure that the exception filter always evaluates to EXCEPTION_EXECUTE_HANDLER so that the exception is handled, preventing the system from calling the *UnhandledExceptionFilter* function.

In your exception handler, you can display a dialog box with some diagnostic information. The user can copy the information and report it to your customer service lines to help you track the sources of problems in your application. You should create the dialog box so that the user can only terminate the application and not invoke the debugger.

The problem with this method is that it catches only exceptions that occur in your process's primary thread. If any other threads are running, and an unhandled exception occurs in one of these threads, the system calls the built-in

UnhandledExceptionFilter function. To fix this, you would need to include *try-except* blocks in all your secondary thread entry-point functions as well.

Wrapping All Thread Functions

Windows offers another function, *SetUnhandledExceptionFilter*, which allows you to wrap all your thread functions in an SEH frame:

```
PTOP_LEVEL_EXCEPTION_FILTER SetUnhandledExceptionFilter(
    PTOP_LEVEL_EXCEPTION_FILTER pTopLevelExceptionFilter);
```

After your process calls this function, an unhandled exception occurring in any of your process's threads causes your own exception filter to be called. You need to pass the address of your filter as the parameter to *SetUnhandledExceptionFilter*. The prototype of your filter function must look like this:

```
LONG UnhandledExceptionFilter(PEXCEPTION_POINTERS pExceptionInfo);
```

You'll notice that this function is identical in form to the *UnhandledExceptionFilter* function. You can perform any processing you desire in your exception filter as long as you return one of the three EXCEPTION_* identifiers. The following table shows what happens when each identifier is returned.

Identifier	What Happens
EXCEPTION_EXECUTE_HANDLER	The process simply terminates because the system doesn't perform any action in its exception handler block.
EXCEPTION_CONTINUE_EXECUTION	Execution continues at the instruction that raised the exception. You can modify the exception information referenced by the PEXCEPTION_POINTERS parameter.
EXCEPTION_CONTINUE_SEARCH	The normal Windows *UnhandledExceptionFilter* function executes.

To make the *UnhandledExceptionFilter* function the default filter again, you can simply call *SetUnhandledExceptionFilter* and pass it NULL. Also, whenever you set a new unhandled exception filter, *SetUnhandledExceptionFilter* returns the address of the previously installed exception filter. This address will be NULL if *UnhandledExceptionFilter* was the currently installed filter. If your own filter is about to return EXCEPTION_CONTINUE_SEARCH, you should call the previously installed filter whose address was returned by the *SetUnhandledExceptionFilter* function.

Automatically Invoking the Debugger

Here is the last method for turning off *UnhandledExceptionFilter*'s message box. In the same registry subkey mentioned earlier, there is another data value named Auto. This value indicates whether *UnhandledExceptionFilter* should display the message box or simply start the debugger. If Auto is set to 1, *Unhandled-ExceptionFilter* does not display a message box showing the user the exception and immediately invokes the debugger. If the Auto subkey is set to 0, *UnhandledExceptionFilter* displays the exception message box first and operates as described earlier.

Calling *UnhandledExceptionFilter* Yourself

The *UnhandledExceptionFilter* function is a fully documented Windows function that you can call directly from within your own code. Here is an example of how you can use it:

```
void Funcadelic() {
   __try {
      .
      .
      .
   }
   __except (ExpFltr(GetExceptionInformation())) {
      .
      .
      .
   }
}

LONG ExpFltr(PEXCEPTION_POINTERS pEP) {
   DWORD dwExceptionCode = pEP->ExceptionRecord.ExceptionCode;

   if (dwExceptionCode == EXCEPTION_ACCESS_VIOLATION) {
      // Do some work here....
      return(EXCEPTION_CONTINUE_EXECUTION);
   }

   return(UnhandledExceptionFilter(pEP));
}
```

In the *Funcadelic* function, an exception in the *try* block causes the *ExpFltr* function to be called. The *ExpFltr* function is passed the return value from *GetExceptionInformation*. Inside the exception filter, the exception code is determined and compared with EXCEPTION_ACCESS_VIOLATION. If an access violation has occurred, the exception filter corrects the situation and returns EXCEPTION_CONTINUE_EXECUTION from the filter. The return value causes the system to continue execution at the instruction that originally caused the exception in the first place.

If any other exception has occurred, *ExpFltr* calls *UnhandledException-Filter*, passing it the address of the EXCEPTION_POINTERS structure. *UnhandledExceptionFilter* then displays a message box that allows you to terminate the process or to begin debugging the process. The return value from *UnhandledExceptionFilter* is returned from *ExpFltr*.

Inside the *UnhandledExceptionFilter* Function

When I first started working with exceptions, I believed that a lot of information could be gained from understanding exactly what the system's *Unhandled-ExceptionFilter* function did. So, I researched this function in great detail. The following steps describe exactly what *UnhandledExceptionFilter* does internally:

1. If an access violation occurred and it was due to an attempted write (versus a read), the system checks to see if you're attempting to modify a resource in an .exe or DLL module. By default, resources are (and should be) read-only; attempting to modify a resource raises an access violation. However, 16-bit Windows allows resources to be modified, and for backward compatibility this should work in 32-bit and 64-bit Windows as well. Thus, if you are attempting to modify a resource, *UnhandledExceptionFilter* calls *VirtualProtect* to change the protection on the resource's page to PAGE_READWRITE and returns EXCEPTION_CONTINUE_EXECUTION.

2. If you have called *SetUnhandledExceptionFilter* to specify your own filter, *UnhandledExceptionFilter* calls your filter function. If your filter function returns EXCEPTION_EXECUTE_HANDLER or EXCEPTION_CONTINUE_EXECUTION, the *Unhandled-ExceptionFilter* returns this value back to the system. If you have not set your own unhandled exception filter or if your unhandled exception filter returns EXCEPTION_CONTINUE_SEARCH, processing continues with step 3.

> Windows 98 has the following bug: it only calls your own unhandled
> exception filter function if the process is not being debugged. This made
> it impossible for me to debug the Spreadsheet sample application pre-
> sented later in this chapter.

3. If your process is under the care of a debugger, EXCEPTION_
    CONTINUE_SEARCH is returned. This should seem odd to you
    because the system is already executing the highest *try* or *except*
    frame for the thread; there is no other exception filter to continue
    searching for higher up. When the system sees that the highest filter
    returns EXCEPTION_CONTINUE_SEARCH, the system knows
    to contact the debugger and tell the debugger that the debuggee has
    just had an unhandled exception. In response, the debugger displays
    a message box and allows you to debug the process. (By the way, the
    IsDebuggerPresent function is used to determine if a process is being
    debugged.)

4. If a thread in the process had called *SetErrorMode* passing the
    SEM_NOGPFAULTERRORBOX flag, *UnhandledExceptionFilter*
    returns EXCEPTION_EXECUTE_HANDLER.

5. If the process is in a job (see Chapter 5) and the job's limit informa-
    tion has the JOB_OBJECT_LIMIT_DIE_ON_UNHANDLED_
    EXCEPTION flag turned on, *UnhandledExceptionFilter* returns
    EXCEPTION_EXECUTE_HANDLER.

> Windows 98 doesn't support jobs so this step is skipped.

6. *UnhandledExceptionFilter* looks in the registry and grabs the value
    of the Auto value. If this value is 1, jump to step 7. If this value is 0,
    the message box is displayed to the user. The message box indicates
    which exception was raised. If the registry subkey also contains the
    Debugger value, the message box has both OK and Cancel buttons.
    If the registry subkey does not have the Debugger value, the mes-
    sage box contains only an OK button. If the user clicks on the OK
    button, *UnhandledExceptionFilter* returns EXCEPTION_
    EXECUTE_HANDLER. If the Cancel button is available and the
    user clicks on it, processing continues with step 7.

In Windows 98, these values are not stored in the registry—they are stored in the Win.ini file.

7. *UnhandledExceptionFilter* is now going to spawn the debugger. It first calls *CreateEvent* to create a nonsignaled, manual-reset event. The handle of this event is inheritable. Next it grabs the Debugger value out of the registry and calls *sprintf* to paste in the process ID (obtained by calling the *GetCurrentProcessId* function) and the event handle. The STARTUPINFO's *lpDesktop* member is also set to "Winsta0\\Default" so that the debugger appears on the interactive desktop. *CreateProcess* is then called with its *fInheritHandles* parameter set to TRUE, which invokes the debugger process and allows it to inherit the event object's handle. *UnhandledExceptionFilter* now waits for the debugger to initialize by calling *WaitForSingleObjectEx*, passing the event's handle. Note that *WaitForSingleObjectEx* is used instead of *WaitForSingleObject* so that the thread can wait in an alertable state. This allows any queued asynchronous procedure calls (APCs) for the thread to be processed.

8. When the debugger is fully initialized, it sets the event handle, which causes the thread inside *UnhandledExceptionFilter* to wake up. Now that the process is under the care of a debugger, *Unhandled-ExceptionFilter* returns EXCEPTION_CONTINUE_SEARCH. Notice that this is exactly what happened in step 3.

Exceptions and the Debugger

The Microsoft Visual C++ debugger has fantastic support for debugging exceptions. When a process's thread raises an exception, the operating system immediately notifies a debugger (if a debugger is attached). This notification is called a *first-chance notification*. Normally, the debugger responds to a first-chance notification by telling the thread to search for exception filters. If all of the exception filters return EXCEPTION_CONTINUE_SEARCH, the operating system notifies the debugger again with a *last-chance notification*. These two notifications exist in order to give the software developer more control over debugging an exception.

You use the debugger's Exceptions dialog box (shown on the next page) to tell the debugger how to react to first-chance exception notifications.

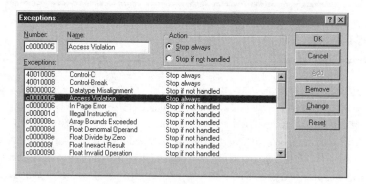

As you can see, the dialog box consists of a list of all the system-defined exceptions. Each exception's 32-bit code is shown, followed by a text description and the debugger's action. In the window above, I have selected the access violation exception and changed its action to Stop Always. Now, whenever a thread in the debuggee raises an access violation, the debugger receives its first-chance notification and displays a message box similar to the following.

At this point, the thread has *not* had a chance to search for exception filters. I can now place breakpoints in the code, check variables, or examine the thread's call stack. No exception filters have executed yet; the exception has just occurred. If I now use the debugger to single-step through the code, I am prompted with the following message box.

Clicking on Cancel returns you to the debugger. Clicking on No tells the debuggee's thread to retry the CPU instruction that failed. For most exceptions, retrying the instruction will just raise the exception again and is not useful.

However, for an exception raised with the *RaiseException* function, this tells the thread to continue executing as though the exception was never raised. Continuing in this manner can be particularly useful for debugging C++ programs: it would be as though a C++ *throw* statement never executed. C++ exception handling is discussed more toward the end of this chapter.

Finally, clicking on Yes allows the debuggee's thread to search for exception filters. If an exception filter is found that returns EXCEPTION_EXECUTE_HANDLER or EXCEPTION_CONTINUE_EXECUTION, all is well and the thread continues executing its code. However, if all filters return EXCEPTION_CONTINUE_SEARCH, the debugger receives a last-chance notification and displays a message box similar to the following.

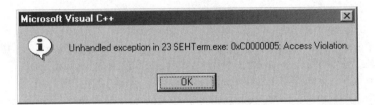

At this point, you must debug the application or terminate it.

I have just shown you what happens if the debugger's action is set to Stop Always. However, for most exceptions, Stop If Not Handled is the default action. So, if a thread in the debuggee raises an exception, the debugger receives a first-chance notification. If the action is set to Stop If Not Handled, the debugger simply displays a string in the debugger's Output window indicating that it received the notification.

![Screenshot of AdvWin - Microsoft Visual C++ [break] showing SEHTERM.Cpp source code with the line `* (PBYTE) 0 = 0;` and an Output window displaying "First-chance exception in 23 SEHTerm.exe: 0xC0000005: Access Violation."]

If the action for an access violation is set to Stop If Not Handled, the debugger allows the thread to search for exception filters. Only if the exception is not handled will the debugger display the message box shown here.

NOTE

The important point to remember is that first-chance notifications do *not* indicate problems or bugs in the application. In fact, this notification can only appear when your process is being debugged. The debugger is simply reporting that an exception was raised, but if the debugger does not display the message box, a filter handled the exception and the application continues to run just fine. A last-chance notification means that your code has a problem or bug that must be fixed.

Before leaving this section, I'd like to point out just one more thing about the debugger's Exceptions dialog box. This dialog box fully supports any software exceptions that you yourself define. All you have to do is enter your unique software exception code number, a string name for your exception, your preferred action, and then click on the Add button to add your exception to the list. The window below illustrates how I made the debugger aware of my own software exception.

The Spreadsheet Sample Application

The Spreadsheet sample application ("25 Spreadsheet.exe") listed in Figure 25-1 beginning on page 892 shows how to sparsely commit storage to a reserved address space region using structured exception handling. The source code and resource files for the application are in the "25-Spreadsheet" directory on the companion CD-ROM. When you execute the Spreadsheet sample, the following dialog box appears.

Internally, the application reserved a region for a two-dimensional spreadsheet. The spreadsheet contains 256 rows by 1024 columns and each cell is 1024 bytes in size. If the application were to commit storage up front for the entire spreadsheet, 268,435,456 bytes, or 256 MB, of storage would be required. In order to conserve precious storage space, the application reserves a 256-MB region of address space without committing any storage backing this region.

Let's say that the user attempts to place the value 12345 in a cell existing at row 100, column 100 (as shown in the previous window). When the user clicks on the Write Cell button, the application code tries to write to that location in the spreadsheet. Of course, this attempted write raises an access violation. However, since I'm using SEH in the application, my exception filter detects the attempted write, displays the "Violation: Attempting to Write" message at the bottom of the dialog box, commits storage for the cell, and has the CPU re-execute the instruction that raised the violation. Since storage has been committed, the value is written to the spreadsheet's cell.

Let's try another experiment. Try to read the value in the cell at row 5, column 20. When you attempt to read from this cell, an access violation is again raised. For an attempted read, the exception filter doesn't commit storage, but it does display the "Violation: Attempting to Read" message in the dialog box. The program gracefully recovers from the failed read by removing the number in the Value field of the dialog box, as shown here.

For our third experiment, try to read the cell value in row 100, column 100. Since storage was committed for this cell, no violation will occur and no exception filter is executed (improving the performance). The dialog box looks like this.

Now for our fourth and last experiment: Try to write the value 54321 into the cell at row 100, column 101. When you attempt this, no violation occurs because this cell is on the same storage page as the cell at (100, 100). We can verify this with the "No Violation raised" message at the bottom of the dialog box shown here.

I tend to use virtual memory and SEH quite a bit in my own projects. After a while, I decided to create a templated C++ class, CVMArray, which encapsulates all of the hard work. You can find the source code for this C++ class in the VMArray.h file (part of the Spreadsheet sample shown in Figure 25-1). You can work with the CVMArray class in two ways. First, you can just create an instance of this class passing the maximum number of elements in the array to the constructor. The class automatically sets up a process-wide unhandled exception filter so whenever any code in any thread accesses a memory address in the virtual memory array, the unhandled exception filter calls *VirtualAlloc* to commit storage for the new element and returns EXCEPTION_CONTINUE_EXECUTION. Using the CVMArray class in this way allows you to use sparse storage with just a few lines of code, and you don't have to sprinkle SEH frames throughout your source code. The only downside to this approach is that your application can't recover gracefully if for some reason storage cannot be committed when needed.

The second way to use the CVMArray class is to derive your own C++ class from it. If you use the derived class, you still get all of the benefits of the base class—but now you also get to add features of your own. For example, you can now handle insufficient storage problems more gracefully by overloading the virtual *OnAccessViolation* function. The Spreadsheet sample application shows how a CVMArray-derived class can add these features.

Spreadsheet.cpp

```
/******************************************************************************
Module:  Spreadsheet.cpp
Notices: Copyright (c) 2000 Jeffrey Richter
******************************************************************************/


#include "..\CmnHdr.h"        /* See Appendix A. */
#include <windowsx.h>
#include <tchar.h>
#include "Resource.h"
#include "VMArray.h"



///////////////////////////////////////////////////////////////////////////////


HWND g_hwnd;    // Global window handle used for SEH reporting

const int g_nNumRows = 256;
const int g_nNumCols = 1024;
```

Figure 25-1. *(continued)*
The Spreadsheet sample application

Figure 25-1. *continued*

```
// Declare the contents of a single cell in the spreadsheet
typedef struct {
   DWORD dwValue;
   BYTE  bDummy[1020];
} CELL, *PCELL;


// Declare the data type for an entire spreadsheet
typedef CELL SPREADSHEET[g_nNumRows][g_nNumCols];
typedef SPREADSHEET *PSPREADSHEET;


///////////////////////////////////////////////////////////////////////////////


// A spreadsheet is a 2-dimensional array of CELLs
class CVMSpreadsheet : public CVMArray<CELL> {
public:
   CVMSpreadsheet() : CVMArray<CELL>(g_nNumRows * g_nNumCols) {}

private:
   LONG OnAccessViolation(PVOID pvAddrTouched, BOOL fAttemptedRead,
      PEXCEPTION_POINTERS pep, BOOL fRetryUntilSuccessful);
};


///////////////////////////////////////////////////////////////////////////////


LONG CVMSpreadsheet::OnAccessViolation(PVOID pvAddrTouched, BOOL fAttemptedRead,
   PEXCEPTION_POINTERS pep, BOOL fRetryUntilSuccessful) {

   TCHAR sz[200];
   wsprintf(sz, TEXT("Violation: Attempting to %s"),
      fAttemptedRead ? TEXT("Read") : TEXT("Write"));
   SetDlgItemText(g_hwnd, IDC_LOG, sz);

   LONG lDisposition = EXCEPTION_EXECUTE_HANDLER;
   if (!fAttemptedRead) {

      // Return whatever the base class says to do
      lDisposition = CVMArray<CELL>::OnAccessViolation(pvAddrTouched,
         fAttemptedRead, pep, fRetryUntilSuccessful);
   }
```

(continued)

Figure 25-1. *continued*

```
    return(lDisposition);
}

//////////////////////////////////////////////////////////////////////////


// This is the global CVMSpreadsheet object
static CVMSpreadsheet g_ssObject;

// Create a global pointer that points to the entire spreadsheet region
SPREADSHEET& g_ss = * (PSPREADSHEET) (PCELL) g_ssObject;


//////////////////////////////////////////////////////////////////////////


BOOL Dlg_OnInitDialog(HWND hwnd, HWND hwndFocus, LPARAM lParam) {

    chSETDLGICONS(hwnd, IDI_SPREADSHEET);

    g_hwnd = hwnd; // Save for SEH reporting

    // Put default values in the dialog box controls
    Edit_LimitText(GetDlgItem(hwnd, IDC_ROW),    3);
    Edit_LimitText(GetDlgItem(hwnd, IDC_COLUMN), 4);
    Edit_LimitText(GetDlgItem(hwnd, IDC_VALUE),  7);
    SetDlgItemInt(hwnd, IDC_ROW,     100,   FALSE);
    SetDlgItemInt(hwnd, IDC_COLUMN,  100,   FALSE);
    SetDlgItemInt(hwnd, IDC_VALUE,   12345, FALSE);
    return(TRUE);
}


//////////////////////////////////////////////////////////////////////////


void Dlg_OnCommand(HWND hwnd, int id, HWND hwndCtl, UINT codeNotify) {

    int nRow, nCol;

    switch (id) {
      case IDCANCEL:
          EndDialog(hwnd, id);
          break;
```

(continued)

Figure 25-1. *continued*

```
case IDC_ROW:
    // User modified the row, update the UI
    nRow = GetDlgItemInt(hwnd, IDC_ROW, NULL, FALSE);
    EnableWindow(GetDlgItem(hwnd, IDC_READCELL),
        chINRANGE(0, nRow, g_nNumRows - 1));
    EnableWindow(GetDlgItem(hwnd, IDC_WRITECELL),
        chINRANGE(0, nRow, g_nNumRows - 1));
    break;

case IDC_COLUMN:
    // User modified the column, update the UI
    nCol = GetDlgItemInt(hwnd, IDC_COLUMN, NULL, FALSE);
    EnableWindow(GetDlgItem(hwnd, IDC_READCELL),
        chINRANGE(0, nCol, g_nNumCols - 1));
    EnableWindow(GetDlgItem(hwnd, IDC_WRITECELL),
        chINRANGE(0, nCol, g_nNumCols - 1));
    break;

case IDC_READCELL:
    // Try to read a value from the user's selected cell
    SetDlgItemText(g_hwnd, IDC_LOG, TEXT("No violation raised"));
    nRow = GetDlgItemInt(hwnd, IDC_ROW, NULL, FALSE);
    nCol = GetDlgItemInt(hwnd, IDC_COLUMN, NULL, FALSE);
    __try {
        SetDlgItemInt(hwnd, IDC_VALUE, g_ss[nRow][nCol].dwValue, FALSE);
    }
    __except (
        g_ssObject.ExceptionFilter(GetExceptionInformation(), FALSE)) {

        // The cell is not backed by storage, the cell contains nothing.
        SetDlgItemText(hwnd, IDC_VALUE, TEXT(""));
    }
    break;

case IDC_WRITECELL:
    // Try to read a value from the user's selected cell
    SetDlgItemText(g_hwnd, IDC_LOG, TEXT("No violation raised"));
    nRow = GetDlgItemInt(hwnd, IDC_ROW, NULL, FALSE);
    nCol = GetDlgItemInt(hwnd, IDC_COLUMN, NULL, FALSE);

    // If the cell is not backed by storage, an access violation is
    // raised causing storage to automatically be committed.
    g_ss[nRow][nCol].dwValue =
        GetDlgItemInt(hwnd, IDC_VALUE, NULL, FALSE);
    break;
```

(continued)

Figure 25-1. *continued*

```
    }
}


///////////////////////////////////////////////////////////////////////////


INT_PTR WINAPI Dlg_Proc(HWND hwnd, UINT uMsg, WPARAM wParam, LPARAM lParam) {

    switch (uMsg) {
        chHANDLE_DLGMSG(hwnd, WM_INITDIALOG, Dlg_OnInitDialog);
        chHANDLE_DLGMSG(hwnd, WM_COMMAND,    Dlg_OnCommand);
    }
    return(FALSE);
}


///////////////////////////////////////////////////////////////////////////


int WINAPI _tWinMain(HINSTANCE hinstExe, HINSTANCE, PTSTR pszCmdLine, int) {

    DialogBox(hinstExe, MAKEINTRESOURCE(IDD_SPREADSHEET), NULL, Dlg_Proc);
    return(0);
}

////////////////////////////// End of File //////////////////////////////////
```

Spreadsheet.rc

```
//Microsoft Developer Studio generated resource script.
//
#include "Resource.h"

#define APSTUDIO_READONLY_SYMBOLS
///////////////////////////////////////////////////////////////////////////
//
// Generated from the TEXTINCLUDE 2 resource.
//
#include "afxres.h"


///////////////////////////////////////////////////////////////////////////
```

(continued)

Figure 25-1. *continued*

```
#undef APSTUDIO_READONLY_SYMBOLS

/////////////////////////////////////////////////////////////////////////////
// English (U.S.) resources

#if !defined(AFX_RESOURCE_DLL) || defined(AFX_TARG_ENU)
#ifdef _WIN32
LANGUAGE LANG_ENGLISH, SUBLANG_ENGLISH_US
#pragma code_page(1252)
#endif //_WIN32

#ifdef APSTUDIO_INVOKED
/////////////////////////////////////////////////////////////////////////////
//
// TEXTINCLUDE
//

1 TEXTINCLUDE DISCARDABLE
BEGIN
    "Resource.h\0"
END

2 TEXTINCLUDE DISCARDABLE
BEGIN
    "#include ""afxres.h""\r\n"
    "\0"
END

3 TEXTINCLUDE DISCARDABLE
BEGIN
    "\r\n"
    "\0"
END

#endif    // APSTUDIO_INVOKED


/////////////////////////////////////////////////////////////////////////////
//
// Dialog
//

IDD_SPREADSHEET DIALOG DISCARDABLE  18, 18, 164, 165
STYLE DS_CENTER | WS_MINIMIZEBOX | WS_VISIBLE | WS_CAPTION | WS_SYSMENU
```

(continued)

Figure 25-1. *continued*

```
CAPTION "Spreadsheet"
FONT 8, "MS Sans Serif"
BEGIN
    LTEXT           "Cell size:\nRows:\nColumns:\nTotal size:",IDC_STATIC,4,
                    4,36,36
    LTEXT           "1024 bytes\n256\n1024\n256 MB (268,435,456 bytes)",
                    IDC_STATIC,44,4,104,36
    LTEXT           "R&ow (0-255):",IDC_STATIC,4,56,42,8
    EDITTEXT        IDC_ROW,60,52,40,14,ES_AUTOHSCROLL | ES_NUMBER
    LTEXT           "&Column (0-1023):",IDC_STATIC,4,76,54,8
    EDITTEXT        IDC_COLUMN,60,72,40,14,ES_AUTOHSCROLL | ES_NUMBER
    PUSHBUTTON      "&Read Cell",IDC_READCELL,108,72,50,14
    LTEXT           "&Value:",IDC_STATIC,4,96,21,8
    EDITTEXT        IDC_VALUE,60,92,40,14,ES_AUTOHSCROLL | ES_NUMBER
    PUSHBUTTON      "&Write Cell",IDC_WRITECELL,108,92,50,14
    LTEXT           "Execution lo&g:",IDC_STATIC,4,118,48,8
    EDITTEXT        IDC_LOG,4,132,156,28,ES_MULTILINE | ES_AUTOHSCROLL |
                    ES_READONLY
END


/////////////////////////////////////////////////////////////////////////
//
// Icon
//

// Icon with lowest ID value placed first to ensure application icon
// remains consistent on all systems.
IDI_SPREADSHEET         ICON    DISCARDABLE     "Spreadsheet.Ico"
#endif    // English (U.S.) resources
/////////////////////////////////////////////////////////////////////////




#ifndef APSTUDIO_INVOKED
/////////////////////////////////////////////////////////////////////////
//
// Generated from the TEXTINCLUDE 3 resource.
//



/////////////////////////////////////////////////////////////////////////
#endif    // not APSTUDIO_INVOKED
```

(continued)

Figure 25-1. *continued*

VMArray.h

```
/*****************************************************************************
Module:  VMArray.h
Notices: Copyright (c) 2000 Jeffrey Richter
*****************************************************************************/


#pragma once


///////////////////////////////////////////////////////////////////////////


// NOTE: This C++ class is not thread safe. You cannot have multiple threads
// creating and destroying objects of this class at the same time.

// However, once created, multiple threads can access different CVMArray
// objects simultaneously and you can have multiple threads accessing a single
// CVMArray object if you manually synchronize access to the object yourself.


///////////////////////////////////////////////////////////////////////////


template <class TYPE>
class CVMArray {
public:
   // Reserves sparse array of elements
   CVMArray(DWORD dwReserveElements);

   // Frees sparse array of elements
   virtual ~CVMArray();

   // Allows accessing an element in the array
   operator TYPE*()             { return(m_pArray); }
   operator const TYPE*() const { return(m_pArray); }

   // Can be called for fine-tuned handling if commit fails
   LONG ExceptionFilter(PEXCEPTION_POINTERS pep,
      BOOL fRetryUntilSuccessful = FALSE);

protected:
   // Override this to fine-tune handling of access violation
```

(continued)

Figure 25-1. *continued*

```
      virtual LONG OnAccessViolation(PVOID pvAddrTouched, BOOL fAttemptedRead,
         PEXCEPTION_POINTERS pep, BOOL fRetryUntilSuccessful);

private:
   static CVMArray* sm_pHead;      // Address of first object
   CVMArray* m_pNext;              // Address of next  object

   TYPE* m_pArray;                 // Pointer to reserved region array
   DWORD m_cbReserve;              // Size of reserved region array (in bytes)

private:
   // Address of previous unhandled exception filter
   static PTOP_LEVEL_EXCEPTION_FILTER sm_pfnUnhandledExceptionFilterPrev;

   // Our global unhandled exception filter for instances of this class
   static LONG WINAPI UnhandledExceptionFilter(PEXCEPTION_POINTERS pep);
};


///////////////////////////////////////////////////////////////////////////////


// The head of the linked-list of objects
template <class TYPE>
CVMArray<TYPE>* CVMArray<TYPE>::sm_pHead = NULL;

// Address of previous unhandled exception filter
template <class TYPE>
PTOP_LEVEL_EXCEPTION_FILTER CVMArray<TYPE>::sm_pfnUnhandledExceptionFilterPrev;


///////////////////////////////////////////////////////////////////////////////


template <class TYPE>
CVMArray<TYPE>::CVMArray(DWORD dwReserveElements) {

   if (sm_pHead == NULL) {
      // Install our global unhandled exception filter when
      // creating the first instance of the class.
      sm_pfnUnhandledExceptionFilterPrev =
         SetUnhandledExceptionFilter(UnhandledExceptionFilter);
   }
```

(continued)

Figure 25-1. *continued*

```
   m_pNext = sm_pHead;   // The next node was at the head
   sm_pHead = this;      // This node is now at the head

   m_cbReserve = sizeof(TYPE) * dwReserveElements;

   // Reserve a region for the entire array
   m_pArray = (TYPE*) VirtualAlloc(NULL, m_cbReserve,
      MEM_RESERVE | MEM_TOP_DOWN, PAGE_READWRITE);
   chASSERT(m_pArray != NULL);
}


///////////////////////////////////////////////////////////////////////////


template <class TYPE>
CVMArray<TYPE>::~CVMArray() {

   // Free the array's region (decommitting all storage within it)
   VirtualFree(m_pArray, 0, MEM_RELEASE);

   // Remove this object from the linked list
   CVMArray* p = sm_pHead;
   if (p == this) {      // Removing the head node
      sm_pHead = p->m_pNext;
   } else {

      BOOL fFound = FALSE;

      // Walk list from head and fix pointers
      for (; !fFound && (p->m_pNext != NULL); p = p->m_pNext) {
         if (p->m_pNext == this) {
            // Make the node that points to us point to the next node
            p->m_pNext = p->m_pNext->m_pNext;
            break;
         }
      }
      chASSERT(fFound);
   }
}


///////////////////////////////////////////////////////////////////////////
```

(continued)

Figure 25-1. *continued*

```
// Default handling of access violations attempts to commit storage
template <class TYPE>
LONG CVMArray<TYPE>::OnAccessViolation(PVOID pvAddrTouched,
   BOOL fAttemptedRead, PEXCEPTION_POINTERS pep, BOOL fRetryUntilSuccessful) {

   BOOL fCommittedStorage = FALSE;  // Assume committing storage fails

   do {
      // Attempt to commit storage
      fCommittedStorage = (NULL != VirtualAlloc(pvAddrTouched,
         sizeof(TYPE), MEM_COMMIT, PAGE_READWRITE));

      // If storage could not be committed and we're supposed to keep trying
      // until we succeed, prompt user to free storage
      if (!fCommittedStorage && fRetryUntilSuccessful) {
         MessageBox(NULL,
            TEXT("Please close some other applications and Press OK."),
            TEXT("Insufficient Memory Available"), MB_ICONWARNING | MB_OK);
      }
   } while (!fCommittedStorage && fRetryUntilSuccessful);

   // If storage committed, try again. If not, execute the handler
   return(fCommittedStorage
      ? EXCEPTION_CONTINUE_EXECUTION : EXCEPTION_EXECUTE_HANDLER);
}


///////////////////////////////////////////////////////////////////////////////


// The filter associated with a single CVMArray object
template <class TYPE>
LONG CVMArray<TYPE>::ExceptionFilter(PEXCEPTION_POINTERS pep,
   BOOL fRetryUntilSuccessful) {

   // Default to trying another filter (safest thing to do)
   LONG lDisposition = EXCEPTION_CONTINUE_SEARCH;

   // We only fix access violations
   if (pep->ExceptionRecord->ExceptionCode != EXCEPTION_ACCESS_VIOLATION)
      return(lDisposition);

   // Get address of attempted access and get attempted read or write
   PVOID pvAddrTouched = (PVOID) pep->ExceptionRecord->ExceptionInformation[1];
   BOOL fAttemptedRead = (pep->ExceptionRecord->ExceptionInformation[0] == 0);
```

(continued)

Figure 25-1. *continued*

```
    // Is attempted access within this VMArray's reserved region?
    if ((m_pArray <= pvAddrTouched) &&
        (pvAddrTouched < ((PBYTE) m_pArray + m_cbReserve)))) {

        // Access is in this array, try to fix the problem
        lDisposition = OnAccessViolation(pvAddrTouched, fAttemptedRead,
            pep, fRetryUntilSuccessful);
    }

    return(lDisposition);
}

///////////////////////////////////////////////////////////////////////////

// The filter associated with all CVMArray objects
template <class TYPE>
LONG WINAPI CVMArray<TYPE>::UnhandledExceptionFilter(PEXCEPTION_POINTERS pep) {

    // Default to trying another filter (safest thing to do)
    LONG lDisposition = EXCEPTION_CONTINUE_SEARCH;

    // We only fix access violations
    if (pep->ExceptionRecord->ExceptionCode == EXCEPTION_ACCESS_VIOLATION) {

        // Walk all the nodes in the linked-list
        for (CVMArray* p = sm_pHead; p != NULL; p = p->m_pNext) {

            // Ask this node if it can fix the problem.
            // NOTE: The problem MUST be fixed or the process will be terminated!
            lDisposition = p->ExceptionFilter(pep, TRUE);

            // If we found the node and it fixed the problem, stop the loop
            if (lDisposition != EXCEPTION_CONTINUE_SEARCH)
                break;
        }
    }

    // If no node fixed the problem, try the previous exception filter
    if (lDisposition == EXCEPTION_CONTINUE_SEARCH)
        lDisposition = sm_pfnUnhandledExceptionFilterPrev(pep);

    return(lDisposition);
}

///////////////////////////// End of File /////////////////////////////
```

(continued)

C++ Exceptions Versus Structured Exceptions

Developers frequently ask me whether they should use structured exceptions or C++ exceptions when developing their applications. I'd like to offer an answer in this section.

Let me start by reminding you that SEH is an operating system facility available in any programming language, while C++ EH can only be used when writing C++ code. If you're writing a C++ application, you should use C++ exceptions instead of structured exceptions. The reason is that C++ exceptions are part of the language and therefore the compiler knows what a C++ class object is. This means that the compiler automatically generates code to call C++ object destructors in order to guarantee object cleanup.

However, you should know that Microsoft's Visual C++ compiler has implemented C++ exception handling using the operating system's structured exception handling. So, when you create a C++ *try* block, the compiler is generating an SEH __*try* block. A C++ *catch* test becomes an SEH exception filter and the code in the *catch* block becomes the code in the SEH __*except* block. In fact, when you write a C++ *throw* statement, the compiler generates a call to the Windows *RaiseException* function. The variable used in the *throw* statement is passed as an additional argument to *RaiseException*.

The following code fragment will help make all of this a little clearer. The function on the left uses C++ exception handling and the function on the right demonstrates how the C++ compiler generates the equivalent structured exception handling.

```
void ChunkyFunky() {              void ChunkyFunky() {
   try {                             __try {
      // Try body                       // Try body
         :                                  :
         :                                  :

      throw 5;                          RaiseException(Code=0xE06D7363,
                                           Flag=EXCEPTION_NONCONTINUABLE,
                                           Args=5);
   }                                 }
   catch (int x) {                   __except ((ArgType == Integer) ?
                                        EXCEPTION_EXECUTE_HANDLER :
                                        EXCEPTION_CONTINUE_SEARCH) {
      // Catch body                      // Catch body
         :                                  :
         :                                  :

   }                                 }
      :                                  :
      :                                  :

}                                 }
```

You'll notice a few interesting details about the code above. First, notice that *RaiseException* is called with an exception code of 0xE06D7363. This is the software exception code selected by the Visual C++ team to be used when throwing C++ exceptions. In fact, you can verify this if you open the debugger's Exceptions dialog box and scroll to the bottom of the exceptions list, shown here.

Exceptions			
Number: `e06d7363`	Name: `Microsoft C++ Exception`	Action: ○ Stop always ● Stop if not handled	OK / Cancel
Exceptions:			Add
c0000026	Invalid Disposition	Stop if not handled	Remove
c0000094	Integer Divide by Zero	Stop if not handled	
c0000095	Integer Overflow	Stop if not handled	Change
c0000096	Privileged Instruction	Stop if not handled	
c00000fd	Stack Overflow	Stop if not handled	Reset
c0000135	DLL Not Found	Stop if not handled	
c0000142	DLL Initialization Failed	Stop if not handled	
c06d007e	Module Not Found	Stop if not handled	
c06d007f	Procedure Not Found	Stop if not handled	
c0000008	Invalid Handle	Stop always	
e06d7363	Microsoft C++ Exception	Stop if not handled	

You'll also notice that the EXCEPTION_NONCONTINUABLE flag is always used when a C++ exception is thrown. C++ exceptions can never be re-executed, and it would be an error for a filter diagnosing a C++ exception to return EXCEPTION_CONTINUE_EXECUTION. In fact, if you look at the *__except* filter in the function on the right, you'll see that it is only capable of evaluating to EXCEPTION_EXECUTE_HANDLER or EXCEPTION_CONTINUE_SEARCH.

The remaining parameters to *RaiseException* are used as the mechanism that actually throws the specified variable. Exactly how the thrown variable information is passed to *RaiseException* is not documented, but it's not too hard to imagine ways that the compiler team could have implemented this.

The last thing I'd like to point out is the *__except* filter. The purpose of this filter is to compare the *throw* variables data type with the variable type used in the C++ *catch* statement. If the data types are the same, the filter returns EXCEPTION_EXECUTE_HANDLER, causing the statements in the *catch* block (*__except* block) to execute. If the data types are different, the filter returns EXCEPTION_CONTINUE_SEARCH, allowing *catch* filters farther up the call tree to be evaluated.

Since C++ exceptions are implemented internally via structured exceptions, you can use both mechanisms in a single application. For example, I love using virtual memory to commit storage when access violations are raised. The C++ language does not support this type of *resumptive exception handling* at all. However, I can use structured exception handling in the parts of my code where I want to take advantage of this and have my own __*except* filter return EXCEPTION_CONTINUE_EXECUTION. For all other parts of my code that do not require resumptive exception handling, I'll stick with C++ exception handling.

Catching Structured Exceptions with C++

Normally, C++ exception handling does not allow an application to recover from a hard exception such as an access violation or a division by 0. However, Microsoft has added this support to their compiler. For example, the following code will prevent the process from terminating abnormally:

```
void main() {
   try {
      * (PBYTE) 0 = 0;        // Access violation
   }
   catch (...) {
      // This code handles the access-violation exception
   }
   // The process is terminating normally
}
```

This is nice, since it allows your application to recover gracefully from hard exceptions. However, it would also be nice if the catch's exception-declaration could somehow distinguish between different exception codes. For example, it would be nice to be able to write code like this:

```
void Functastic() {

   try {
      * (PBYTE) 0 = 0;        // Access violation

      int x = 0;
      x = 5 / x;              // Division by zero
   }
   catch (StructuredException) {
      switch (StructuredExceptionCode) {
         case EXCEPTION_ACCESS_VIOLATION:
```

```
      // This code handles an access-violation exception
      break;

   case EXCEPTION_INT_DIVIDE_BY_ZERO:
      // This code handles a division-by-zero exception
      break;

   default:
      // We don't handle any other exceptions
      throw;    // Maybe another catch is looking for this
      break;    // Never executes
   }
 }
}
```

Well, you'll be happy to know that Visual C++ has a mechanism that makes this possible. Here's what you need to do. Create your own C++ class to use in your code to identify structured exceptions. Here is an example:

```
#include <eh.h>              // For _set_se_translator
 :
 :
class CSE {
public:
   // Call this function for each thread.
   static void MapSEtoCE() { _set_se_translator(TranslateSEtoCE); }

   operator DWORD() { return(m_er.ExceptionCode); }

private:
   CSE(PEXCEPTION_POINTERS pep) {
      m_er      = *pep->ExceptionRecord;
      m_context = *pep->ContextRecord;
   }

   static void _cdecl TranslateSEtoCE(UINT dwEC,
      PEXCEPTION_POINTERS pep) {
      throw CSE(pep);
   }

private:
   EXCEPTION_RECORD m_er;       // CPU independent exception information
   CONTEXT          m_context; // CPU dependent exception information
};
```

907

Inside each of your thread's entry-point functions, call the static member function *MapSEtoCE*. This function calls the C run-time function *_set_se_translator* passing it the address of the CSE class's *TranslateSEtoCE* function. By calling *_set_se_translator*, you're telling the C++ run time to call the *TranslateSEtoCE* function whenever a structured exception is raised. This function constructs a CSE class object and initializes the two data members to contain the CPU-independent and CPU-dependent information about the exception. After the CSE object is constructed, it is thrown just as any normal variable can be thrown. Now, your C++ code can handle structured exceptions by catching a variable of this type.

Here's an example of how to catch this C++ object:

```
void Functastic() {

    CSE::MapSEtoCE(); // Must be called before any exceptions are raised

    try {
        * (PBYTE) 0 = 0;          // Access violation

        int x = 0;
        x = 5 / x;                // Division by zero
    }
    catch (CSE se) {
        switch (se) {      // Calls the operator DWORD() member function
            case EXCEPTION_ACCESS_VIOLATION:
                // This code handles an access-violation exception
                break;

            case EXCEPTION_INT_DIVIDE_BY_ZERO:
                // This code handles a division-by-zero exception
                break;

            default:
                // We don't handle any other exceptions
                throw;   // Maybe another catch is looking for this
                break;   // Never executes
        }
    }
}
```

PART VI

WINDOWING

WINDOW MESSAGING

This chapter describes how the Microsoft Windows messaging system works for applications that present a graphical user interface. When designing the windowing system used by Windows 2000 and Windows 98, Microsoft had two major goals in mind:

- Keep as much backward compatibility with 16-bit Windows as possible, making it easy for developers to port their existing 16-bit Windows applications.

- Make the windowing system robust so that one thread cannot adversely affect other threads in the system.

Unfortunately, these goals are in direct conflict with one another. In 16-bit Windows, sending a message to a window is always performed synchronously: the sender cannot continue running until the window receiving the message has completely processed it. This is usually a desired featured. However, if the window receiving the message takes a long time to process the message or if it hangs, the sender can no longer execute. This means that the system is not robust.

This conflict made for some interesting challenges for Microsoft's design team. Their solution is not perfect, but it is an excellent compromise between the two aforementioned goals. If you keep these goals in mind as you read this chapter, you'll understand why Microsoft made the design choices it did.

Let's start off with some ground rules. Windows allows a single process to create up to 10,000 different types of User objects: icons, cursors, window classes, menus, accelerator tables, and more. When a thread calls a function that creates one of these objects, the object is owned by the thread's process. So, if the process terminates without a thread explicitly destroying the object, the operating system will automatically destroy the object. However, two User objects—windows and hooks—are owned by the thread that creates the window or installs the hook. So, if a thread creates a window or installs a hook and then that thread terminates, the operating system automatically destroys the window or uninstalls the hook.

This concept of thread ownership has an important impact on windows: the thread that creates a window must be the thread that handles all messages for the window. To make this concept more concrete, imagine a thread that creates a window and then terminates. In this case, the window will not receive a WM_DESTROY or WM_NCDESTROY message because the thread has terminated and cannot possibly be used to allow the window to receive and process these messages.

This also means that every thread that creates at least one window is assigned a message queue by the system. This queue is used for window message dispatching. In order for the window to receive these messages, the thread *must* have its very own message loop. In this chapter, we examine each thread's message queue. In particular, we'll see how messages are placed in this queue and how a thread extracts messages from this queue and processes them.

A Thread's Message Queue

As I have already said, one of the main goals of Windows is to offer a robust environment for all the applications running. To meet this goal, each thread must run in an environment in which it believes that it is the only thread running. More specifically, each thread must have message queues that are totally unaffected by other threads. In addition, each thread must have a simulated environment that allows the thread to maintain its own notion of keyboard focus, window activation, mouse capture, and so on.

When a thread is first created, the system assumes that the thread will not be used for any user interface–related tasks. This reduces the system resources required by the thread. However, as soon as the thread calls a graphical UI-related function (such as checking its message queue or creating a window) the system automatically allocates some additional resources for the thread so that it can perform its UI-related tasks. Specifically, the system allocates a THREADINFO structure and associates this data structure with the thread.

This THREADINFO structure contains a set of member variables that are used to make the thread think that it is running in its very own environment. The THREADINFO structure is an internal, undocumented data structure that identifies the thread's posted-message queue, send-message queue, reply-message queue, virtualized-input queue, and wake flags, as well as a number of variables that are used for the thread's local input state. Figure 26-1 illustrates how THREADINFO structures are associated with three threads.

This THREADINFO structure is the cornerstone of the windows messaging system and you should refer to this figure as you read the following sections.

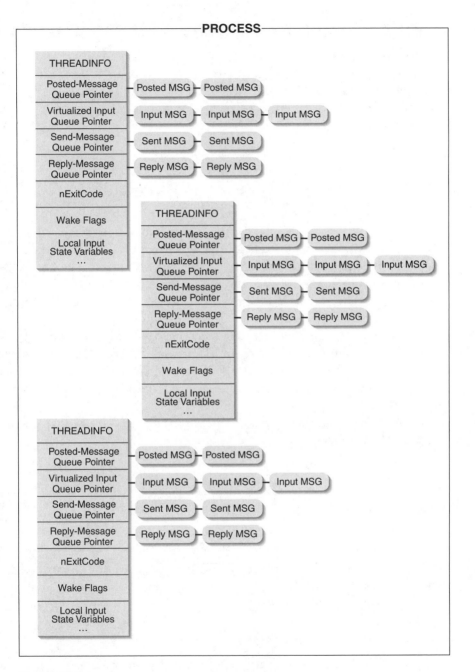

Figure 26-1.
Three threads with their respective THREADINFO structures

Posting Messages to a Thread's Message Queue

Once a thread has a THREADINFO structure associated with it, the thread also has its very own set of message queues. If a single process creates three threads and all these threads call *CreateWindow*, there will be three message queue sets. Messages are placed in a thread's posted-message queue by calling the *PostMessage* function:

```
BOOL PostMessage(
   HWND hwnd,
   UINT uMsg,
   WPARAM wParam,
   LPARAM lParam);
```

When a thread calls this function, the system determines which thread created the window identified by the *hwnd* parameter. The system then allocates a block of memory, stores the message parameters in this block of memory, and appends the block of memory to the appropriate thread's posted-message queue. In addition, the function sets the QS_POSTMESSAGE wake bit (I'll discuss this shortly). *PostMessage* returns immediately after posting the message—the calling thread has no idea whether the posted message was processed by the specified window's window procedure. In fact, it is possible that the specified window will never receive the posted message. This could happen if the thread that created the specified window were somehow to terminate before processing all of the messages in its queue.

A message can also be placed in a thread's posted-message queue by calling *PostThreadMessage*:

```
BOOL PostThreadMessage(
   DWORD dwThreadId,
   UINT uMsg,
   WPARAM wParam,
   LPARAM lParam);
```

> **NOTE**
>
> You can determine which thread created a window by calling *Get-WindowThreadProcessId*:
>
> ```
> DWORD GetWindowThreadProcessId(
>    HWND hwnd,
>    PDWORD pdwProcessId);
> ```
>
> This function returns the system-wide unique ID of the thread that created the window identified by the *hwnd* parameter. You can also get

> the system-wide unique ID of the process that owns this thread by pass-
> ing the address of a DWORD for the *pdwProcessId* parameter. Usually,
> we do not need the process ID and simply pass NULL for this parameter.

The desired thread is identified by the first parameter, *dwThreadId*. When
this message is placed in the queue, the *hwnd* member in the MSG structure
will be set to NULL. This function is usually called when an application performs some special processing in its main message loop.

The main message loop for the thread is written so that, after *GetMessage*
or *PeekMessage* retrieves a message, the code checks for an *hwnd* of NULL and
can examine the *msg* member of the MSG structure to perform the special
processing. If the thread determines that this message is not destined for a window, *DispatchMessage* is not called, and the message loop iterates to retrieve the
next message.

Like the *PostMessage* function, *PostThreadMessage* returns immediately after
posting the message to the thread's queue. The calling thread has no idea when
or if the message gets processed.

The last function that posts a message to a thread's queue is *PostQuitMessage*:

```
VOID PostQuitMessage(int nExitCode);
```

You call this function in order to terminate a thread's message loop. Calling
PostQuitMessage is similar to calling

```
PostThreadMessage(GetCurrentThreadId(), WM_QUIT, nExitCode, 0);
```

However, *PostQuitMessage* doesn't really post a message to any of the
THREADINFO structure's queues. Internally *PostQuitMessage* just turns on the
QS_QUIT wake flag (which I'll discuss later) and sets the *nExitCode* member
of the THREADINFO structure. Since these actions can never fail, *PostQuit-
Message* is prototyped as returning VOID.

Sending Messages to a Window

Window messages can be sent directly to a window procedure by using the
SendMessage function:

```
LRESULT SendMessage(
   HWND hwnd,
   UINT uMsg,
   WPARAM wParam,
   LPARAM lParam);
```

The window procedure will process the message. Only after the message has been processed will *SendMessage* return to the caller. Because of its synchronous nature, *SendMessage* is used more frequently than either *PostMessage* or *PostThreadMessage*. The calling thread knows that the window message has been completely processed before the next line of code executes.

Here is how *SendMessage* works. If the thread calling *SendMessage* is sending a message to a window created by the same thread, *SendMessage* is simple: it just calls the specified window's window procedure as a subroutine. When the window procedure is finished processing the message, it returns a value back to *SendMessage*. *SendMessage* returns this value to the calling thread.

However, if a thread is sending a message to a window created by another thread, the internal workings of *SendMessage* are far more complicated.[1] Windows requires that the thread that created the window process the window's message. So if you call *SendMessage* to send a message to a window created by another process, and therefore to another thread, your thread cannot possibly process the window message because your thread is not running in the other process's address space and therefore does not have access to the window procedure's code and data. In fact, your thread is suspended while the other thread is processing the message. So in order to send a window message to a window created by another thread, the system must perform the actions I'll discuss next.

First, the sent message is appended to the receiving thread's send-message queue, which has the effect of setting the QS_SENDMESSAGE flag (which I'll discuss later) for that thread. Second, if the receiving thread is already executing code and isn't waiting for messages (on a call to *GetMessage*, *PeekMessage*, or *WaitMessage*), the sent message can't be processed—the system won't interrupt the thread to process the message immediately. When the receiving thread is waiting for messages, the system first checks to see whether the QS_SENDMESSAGE wake flag is set, and if it is, the system scans the list of messages in the send-message queue to find the first sent message. It is possible that several sent messages could pile up in this queue. For example, several threads could each send a message to a single window at the same time. When this happens, the system simply appends these messages to the receiving thread's send-message queue.

---

1. This is true even if the two threads are in the same process.

When the receiving thread is waiting for messages, the system extracts the first message in the send-message queue and calls the appropriate window procedure to process the message. If no more messages are in the send-message queue, the QS_SENDMESSAGE wake flag is turned off. While the receiving thread is processing the message, the thread that called *SendMessage* is sitting idle, waiting for a message to appear in its reply-message queue. After the sent message is processed, the window procedure's return value is posted to the sending thread's reply-message queue. The sending thread will now wake up and retrieve the return value contained inside the reply message. This return value is the value that is returned from the call to *SendMessage*. At this point, the sending thread continues execution as normal.

While a thread is waiting for *SendMessage* to return, it basically sits idle. It is, however, allowed to perform one task: if another thread in the system sends a message to a window created by a thread that is waiting for *SendMessage* to return, the system will process the sent message immediately. The system doesn't have to wait for the thread to call *GetMessage*, *PeekMessage*, or *WaitMessage* in this case.

Because Windows uses this method to handle the sending of interthread messages, it's possible that your thread could hang. For example, let's say that the thread processing the sent message has a bug and enters an infinite loop. What happens to the thread that called *SendMessage*? Will it ever be resumed? Does this mean that a bug in one application can cause another application to hang? The answer is yes!

Four functions—*SendMessageTimeout*, *SendMessageCallback*, *SendNotifyMessage*, and *ReplyMessage*—allow you to write code defensively to protect yourself from this situation. The first function is *SendMessageTimeout*:

```
LRESULT SendMessageTimeout(
    HWND hwnd,
    UINT uMsg,
    WPARAM wParam,
    LPARAM lParam,
    UINT fuFlags,
    UINT uTimeout,
    PDWORD_PTR pdwResult);
```

The *SendMessageTimeout* function allows you to specify the maximum amount of time you are willing to wait for another thread to reply to your message. The first four parameters are the same parameters that you pass to *SendMessage*. For the *fuFlags* parameter, you can pass SMTO_NORMAL (defined as 0), SMTO_ABORTIFHUNG, SMTO_BLOCK, SMTO_NOTIMEOUTIFNOTHUNG, or a combination of these flags.

The SMTO_ABORTIFHUNG flag tells *SendMessageTimeout* to check whether the receiving thread is in a hung state[2] and, if so, to return immediately. The SMTO_NOTIMEOUTIFNOTHUNG flag causes the function to ignore the timeout value if the receiving thread is not hung. The SMTO_BLOCK flag causes the calling thread not to process any other sent messages until *SendMessageTimeout* returns. The SMTO_NORMAL flag is defined as 0 in WinUser.h; this is the flag to use if you don't specify any combination of the other flags.

Earlier in this section I said that a thread could be interrupted while waiting for a sent message to return so that it can process another sent message. Using the SMTO_BLOCK flag stops the system from allowing this interruption. You should use this flag only if your thread could not process a sent message while waiting for its sent message to be processed. Using SMTO_BLOCK could create a deadlock situation until the timeout expires—for example, if you send a message to another thread and that thread needs to send a message to your thread. In this case, neither thread can continue processing and both threads are forever suspended.

The *uTimeout* parameter specifies the number of milliseconds you are willing to wait for the reply message. If the function is successful, TRUE is returned and the result of the message is copied into the buffer whose address you specify in the *pdwResult* parameter.

By the way, this function is prototyped incorrectly in the header file of WinUser.h. The function should be prototyped simply as returning a BOOL since the LRESULT is actually returned via a parameter to the function. This raises some problems because *SendMessageTimeout* will return FALSE if you pass an invalid window handle or if it times out. The only way to know for sure why the function failed is by calling *GetLastError*. However, *GetLastError* will be 0 (ERROR_SUCCESS) if the function fails because of a timeout. If you pass an invalid handle, *GetLastError* will be 1400 (ERROR_INVALID_WINDOW_HANDLE).

---

2. The operating system considers a thread to be hung if the thread stops processing messages for more than 5 seconds.

If you call *SendMessageTimeout* to send a message to a window created by the calling thread, the system simply calls the window procedure and places the return value in *pdwResult*. Because all processing must take place with one thread, the code following the call to *SendMessageTimeout* cannot start executing until after the message has been processed.

The second function that can help send interthread messages is *Send-MessageCallback*:

```
BOOL SendMessageCallback(
   HWND hwnd,
   UINT uMsg,
   WPARAM wParam,
   LPARAM lParam,
   SENDASYNCPROC pfnResultCallBack,
   ULONG_PTR dwData);
```

Again, the first four parameters are the same as those used by the *SendMessage* function. When a thread calls *SendMessageCallback*, the function sends the message off to the receiving thread's send-message queue and immediately returns so that your thread can continue processing. When the receiving thread has finished processing the message, a message is posted to the sending thread's reply-message queue. Later, the system notifies your thread of the reply by calling a function that you write using the following prototype:

```
VOID CALLBACK ResultCallBack(
   HWND hwnd,
   UINT uMsg,
   ULONG_PTR dwData,
   LRESULT lResult);
```

You must pass the address to this function as the *pfnResultCallBack* parameter of *SendMessageCallback*. When this function is called, it is passed the handle of the window that finished processing the message and the message value in the first two parameters. The third parameter, *dwData*, will always be the value that you passed in the *dwData* parameter to *SendMessageCallback*. The system simply takes whatever you specify here and passes it directly to your *ResultCallBack* function. The last parameter passed to your *ResultCallBack* function is the result from the window procedure that processed the message.

Because *SendMessageCallback* returns immediately when performing an interthread send, the callback function is not called as soon as the receiving thread finishes processing the message. Instead, the receiving thread posts a message to the sending thread's reply-message queue. The next time the sending thread calls *GetMessage*, *PeekMessage*, *WaitMessage*, or one of the *SendMessage** functions, the message is pulled from the reply-message queue and your *ResultCallBack* function is executed.

The *SendMessageCallback* function has another use. Windows offers a method by which you can broadcast a message to all the existing overlapped windows in the system by calling *SendMessage* and passing HWND_ BROADCAST (defined as −1) as the *hwnd* parameter. Use this method only to broadcast a message whose return value you aren't interested in, because the function can return only a single LRESULT. But by using the *SendMessage-Callback* function, you can broadcast a message to every overlapped window and see the result of each. Your *ResultCallBack* function will be called with the result of every window processing the message.

If you call *SendMessageCallback* to send a message to a window created by the calling thread, the system immediately calls the window procedure, and then, after the message is processed, the system calls the *ResultCallBack* function. After the *ResultCallBack* function returns, execution begins at the line following the call to *SendMessageCallback*.

The third function that can help send interthread messages is *SendNotifyMessage*:

```
BOOL SendNotifyMessage(
    HWND hwnd,
    UINT uMsg,
    WPARAM wParam,
    LPARAM lParam);
```

SendNotifyMessage places a message in the send-message queue of the receiving thread and returns to the calling thread immediately. This should sound familiar because it is exactly what the *PostMessage* function does. However, *SendNotifyMessage* differs from *PostMessage* in two ways.

First, if *SendNotifyMessage* sends a message to a window created by another thread, the sent message has higher priority than posted messages placed in the receiving thread's queue. In other words, messages that the *SendNotifyMessage* function places in a queue are always retrieved before messages that the *Post-Message* function posts to a queue.

Second, when you are sending a message to a window created by the calling thread, *SendNotifyMessage* works exactly like the *SendMessage* function: *SendNotifyMessage* doesn't return until the message has been processed.

As it turns out, most messages sent to a window are used for notification purposes; that is, the message is sent because the window needs to be aware that a state change has occurred so that it can perform some processing before you carry on with your work. For example, WM_ACTIVATE, WM_DESTROY, WM_ENABLE, WM_SIZE, WM_SETFOCUS, and WM_MOVE (to name just a few) are all notifications that are sent to a window by the system instead of being posted. However, these messages are notifications to the window; the system doesn't have to stop running so that the window procedure can process these messages. In contrast, when the system sends a WM_CREATE message to a window, the system must wait until the window has finished processing the message. If the return value is −1, the window is not created.

The fourth function that can help in sending interthread messages is *ReplyMessage*:

```
BOOL ReplyMessage(LRESULT lResult);
```

This function is different from the three functions we just discussed. Whereas *SendMessageTimeout*, *SendMessageCallback*, and *SendNotifyMessage* are used by the thread sending a message to protect itself from hanging, *ReplyMessage* is called by the thread receiving the window message. When a thread calls *ReplyMessage*, it is telling the system that it has completed enough work to know the result of the message and that the result should be packaged up and posted to the sending thread's reply-message queue. This allows the sending thread to wake up, get the result, and continue executing.

The thread calling *ReplyMessage* specifies the result of processing the message in the *lResult* parameter. After *ReplyMessage* is called, the thread that sent the message resumes, and the thread processing the message continues to process the message. Neither thread is suspended; both can continue executing normally. When the thread processing the message returns from its window procedure, any value that it returns is simply ignored.

The problem with *ReplyMessage* is that it has to be called from within the window procedure that is receiving the message and not by the thread that called one of the *Send** functions. So you are better off writing defensive code by replacing your calls to *SendMessage* with one of the three *Send** functions discussed previously instead of relying on the implementer of a window procedure to make calls to *ReplyMessage*.

You should also be aware that *ReplyMessage* does nothing if you call it while processing a message sent from the same thread. In fact, this is what *ReplyMessage*'s return value indicates. *ReplyMessage* returns TRUE if you call it while you are processing an interthread send and FALSE if you are processing an intrathread send.

At times, you might want to know if you are processing an interthread or an intrathread sent message. You can find this out by calling *InSendMessage*:

```
BOOL InSendMessage();
```

The name of this function does not accurately explain what it does. At first glance, you would think that this function returns TRUE if the thread is processing a sent message and FALSE if it's processing a posted message. You would be wrong. The function returns TRUE if the thread is processing an interthread sent message and FALSE if it is processing an intrathread sent or posted message. The return values of *InSendMessage* and *ReplyMessage* are identical.

There is another function that you can call to determine what type of message your window procedure is processing:

```
DWORD InSendMessageEx(PVOID pvReserved);
```

When you call this function, you must pass NULL for the *pvReserved* parameter. The function's return value indicates what type of message you are processing. If the return value is ISMEX_NOSEND (defined as 0), the thread is processing an intrathread sent or posted message. If the return value is not ISMEX_NOSEND, it is a combination of the bit flags described in the following table.

Flag	Description
ISMEX_SEND	The thread is processing an interthread sent message sent using either the *SendMessage* or *SendMessage-Timeout* function. If the ISMEX_REPLIED flag is not set, the sending thread is blocked waiting for the reply.
ISMEX_NOTIFY	The thread is processing an interthread sent message sent using the *SendNotifyMessage* function. The sending thread is not waiting for a reply and is not blocked.
ISMEX_CALLBACK	The thread is processing an interthread sent message sent using the *SendMessageCallback* function. The sending thread is not waiting for a reply and is not blocked.
ISMEX_REPLIED	The thread is processing an interthread sent message and has already called *ReplyMessage*. The sending thread is not blocked.

Waking a Thread

When a thread calls *GetMessage* or *WaitMessage* and there are no messages for the thread or windows created by the thread, the system can suspend the thread so that it is not scheduled any CPU time. However, when a message is posted or sent to the thread, the system sets a wake flag indicating that the thread should now be scheduled CPU time to process the message. Under normal circumstances, the user is not typing or moving the mouse and no messages are being sent to any of the windows. This means that most of the threads in the system are not being scheduled any CPU time.

The Queue Status Flags

When a thread is running, it can query the status of its queues by calling the *GetQueueStatus* function:

```
DWORD GetQueueStatus(UINT fuFlags);
```

The *fuFlags* parameter is a flag or a set of flags ORed together that allows you to test for specific wake bits. The following table shows the possible flag values and their meanings.

Flag	Message in the Queue
QS_KEY	WM_KEYUP, WM_KEYDOWN, WM_SYSKEYUP, or WM_SYSKEYDOWN
QS_MOUSEMOVE	WM_MOUSEMOVE
QS_MOUSEBUTTON	WM_?BUTTON* (Where ? is L, M, or R, and * is DOWN, UP, or DBLCLK)
QS_MOUSE	Same as QS_MOUSEMOVE | QS_MOUSEBUTTON
QS_INPUT	Same as QS_MOUSE | QS_KEY
QS_PAINT	WM_PAINT
QS_TIMER	WM_TIMER
QS_HOTKEY	WM_HOTKEY
QS_POSTMESSAGE	Posted message (other than from a hardware input event). This flag is identical to QS_ALLPOST-MESSAGE except that this flag is cleared when the queue has no posted messages in the desired message filter range.
QS_ALLPOSTMESSAGE	Posted message (other than from a hardware input event). This flag is identical to QS_POSTMESSAGE except that this flag is only cleared when the queue has absolutely no posted messages (regardless of any message filter range).
QS_ALLEVENTS	Same as QS_INPUT | QS_POSTMESSAGE | QS_TIMER | QS_PAINT | QS_HOTKEY
QS_QUIT	*PostQuitMessage* has been called. Note that this flag is not documented and does not exist in the WinUser.h file. It is used internally by the system.
QS_SENDMESSAGE	Message sent by another thread
QS_ALLINPUT	Same as QS_ALLEVENTS | QS_SENDMESSAGE

When you call the *GetQueueStatus* function, the *fuFlags* parameter tells *GetQueueStatus* the types of messages to check for in the queues. The fewer the number of QS_* identifiers you OR together, the faster the call executes. Then when *GetQueueStatus* returns, the types of messages currently in the thread's queues can be found in the high word of the return value. This returned set of flags will always be a subset of what you asked for. For example, let's say you make the following call:

```
BOOL fPaintMsgWaiting = HIWORD(GetQueueStatus(QS_TIMER)) & QS_PAINT;
```

The value of *fPaintMsgWaiting* will always be FALSE whether or not a WM_PAINT message is waiting in the queue, because QS_PAINT was not specified as a flag in the parameter passed to *GetQueueStatus*.

The low word of *GetQueueStatus*'s return value indicates the types of messages that have been added to the queue and that haven't been processed since the last call to *GetQueueStatus*, *GetMessage*, or *PeekMessage*.

Not all the wake flags are treated equally by the system. For the QS_MOUSEMOVE flag, the flag is turned on as long as an unprocessed WM_MOUSEMOVE message exists in the queue. When *GetMessage* or *PeekMessage* (with PM_REMOVE) pulls the last WM_MOUSEMOVE message from the queue, the flag is turned off until a new WM_MOUSEMOVE message is placed in the input queue. The QS_KEY, QS_MOUSEBUTTON, and QS_HOTKEY flags work in the same way for their respective messages.

The QS_PAINT flag is handled differently. If a window created by the thread has an invalid region, the QS_PAINT flag is turned on. When the area occupied by all windows created by this thread becomes validated (usually by a call to *ValidateRect*, *ValidateRegion*, or *BeginPaint*), the QS_PAINT flag is turned off. This flag is turned off only when all windows created by the thread are validated. Calling *GetMessage* or *PeekMessage* has no effect on this wake flag.

The QS_POSTMESSAGE flag is set whenever at least one message is in the thread's posted-message queue. This doesn't include hardware event messages that are in the thread's virtualized input queue. When all the messages in the thread's posted-message queue have been processed and the queue is empty, this flag is reset.

The QS_TIMER flag is set whenever a timer (created by the thread) goes off. After *GetMessage* or *PeekMessage* returns the WM_TIMER event, the QS_TIMER flag is reset until the timer goes off again.

The QS_SENDMESSAGE flag indicates that a message is in the thread's send-message queue. This flag is used by the system internally to identify and process messages being sent from one thread to another. It is not set for messages that a thread sends to itself. Although you can use the QS_SENDMESSAGE flag, you'd rarely need to. I've never seen an application use this flag.

There is another queue status flag that is not documented—QS_QUIT. When a thread calls *PostQuitMessage*, the QS_QUIT flag is turned on. The system does not actually append a WM_QUIT message to the thread's message queue. The *GetQueueStatus* function does not return the state of this flag.

The Algorithm for Extracting Messages from a Thread's Queue

When a thread calls *GetMessage* or *PeekMessage*, the system must examine the state of the thread's queue status flags and determine which message should be processed. Figure 26-2 and the following steps illustrate how the system determines which message the thread should process next.

1. If the QS_SENDMESSAGE flag is turned on, the system sends the message to the proper window procedure. Both the *GetMessage* and *PeekMessage* functions handle this processing internally and do not return to the thread after the window procedure has processed the message; instead, these functions sit and wait for another message to process.

2. If messages are in the thread's posted-message queue, *GetMessage* and *PeekMessage* fill the MSG structure passed to these functions, and then the functions return. The thread's message loop usually calls *DispatchMessage* at this point to have the message processed by the appropriate window procedure.

3. If the QS_QUIT flag is turned on, *GetMessage* and *PeekMessage* return a WM_QUIT message (where the *wParam* parameter is the specified exit code) and reset the QS_QUIT flag.

4. If messages are in the thread's virtualized input queue, *GetMessage* and *PeekMessage* return the hardware input message.

5. If the QS_PAINT flag is turned on, *GetMessage* and *PeekMessage* return a WM_PAINT message for the proper window.

6. If the QS_TIMER flag is turned on, *GetMessage* and *PeekMessage* return a WM_TIMER message.

Although you might find it hard to believe, there's a reason for this madness. The big assumption that Microsoft made when designing this algorithm was that applications should be user-driven and that the user would drive the applications by creating hardware input events (keyboard and mouse operations). While using an application, the user might press a mouse button, causing a sequence of events to occur. An application makes each of the individual events occur by posting messages to the thread's message queue.

So if you press the mouse button, the window that processes the WM_LBUTTONDOWN message might post three messages to different windows. Because it is the hardware event that sparks these three software events, the system processes the software events before retrieving the user's next hardware event. This explains why the posted-message queue is checked before the virtualized input queue.

An excellent example of this sequence of events is a call to the *Translate-Message* function. This function checks whether a WM_KEYDOWN or a WM_SYSKEYDOWN message was retrieved from the input queue. If one of these messages was retrieved, the system checks whether the virtual key information can be converted to a character equivalent. If the virtual key information can be converted, *TranslateMessage* calls *PostMessage* to place a WM_CHAR message or a WM_SYSCHAR message in the posted-message queue. The next time *GetMessage* is called, the system first checks the contents of the posted-message queue and, if a message exists there, pulls the message from the queue and returns it. The returned message will be the WM_CHAR message or the WM_SYSCHAR message. The next time *GetMessage* is called, the system checks the posted-message queue and finds it empty. The system then checks the input queue, where it finds the WM_(SYS)KEYUP message. *GetMessage* returns this message.

Because the system works this way, the following sequence of hardware events WM_KEYDOWN WM_KEYUP generates the following sequence of messages to your window procedure (assuming that the virtual key information can be converted to a character equivalent):

```
WM_KEYDOWN
WM_CHAR
WM_KEYUP
```

Now let's get back to discussing how the system decides what messages to return from *GetMessage* and *PeekMessage*. After the system checks the posted-message queue—but before it checks the virtualized input queue—it checks the QS_QUIT flag. Remember that the QS_QUIT flag is set when the thread calls *PostQuitMessage*. Calling *PostQuitMessage* is similar (but not identical) to calling *PostThreadMessage*, which places the message at the end of the message queue and causes the message to be processed before the input queue is checked. So why does *PostQuitMessage* set a flag instead of placing a WM_QUIT message in the message queue? There are two reasons.

First, it is possible that posting a message could fail in very low memory situations. If an application wants to quit, it should be allowed to quit—even (or especially) in low-memory situations. The second reason is that using a flag allows the thread to finish processing all the other posted messages before the

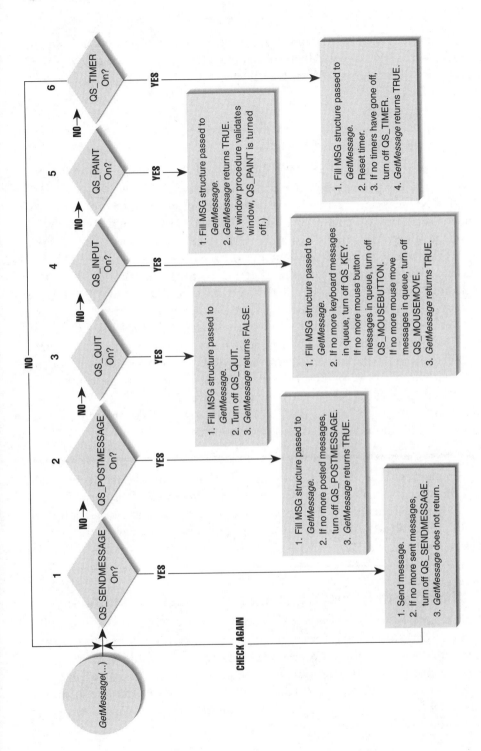

Figure 26-2.
The algorithm for extracting messages from a thread's queue

thread's message loop terminates. So if you have the following code fragment, the WM_USER message will be retrieved from the queue before a WM_QUIT message, even though the WM_USER message is posted to the queue after *PostQuitMessage* is called.

```
case WM_CLOSE:
   PostQuitMessage(0);
   PostMessage(hwnd, WM_USER, 0, 0);
```

The last two messages are WM_PAINT and WM_TIMER. A WM_PAINT message has low priority because painting the screen is a slow process. If a WM_PAINT message were sent every time a window became invalid, the system would be too slow to use. By placing WM_PAINT messages after keyboard input, the system runs much faster. For example, you can select a menu item that invokes a dialog box, choose an item from the box, and press Enter all before the dialog box even appears on the screen. If you type fast enough, your keystroke messages will always be pulled from the queue before any WM_PAINT messages. When you press Enter to accept the dialog box options, the dialog box window is destroyed and the system resets the QS_PAINT flag.

The last message, WM_TIMER, has an even lower priority than a WM_PAINT message. To understand why, think about an application that updates its display with every WM_TIMER message. If the timer messages came in too fast, the display would not get a chance to repaint itself. By processing WM_PAINT messages before WM_TIMER messages, this problem is avoided and the application is always able to update its display.

> **NOTE**
>
> Remember that the *GetMessage* and *PeekMessage* functions check only the wake flags and message queues of the calling thread. This means that threads can never retrieve messages from a queue that is attached to another thread—including messages for threads that are part of the same process.

Waking a Thread with Kernel Objects or with Queue Status Flags

The *GetMessage* and *PeekMessage* functions cause a thread to sleep until the thread needs to process a UI-related task. Sometimes, it's convenient to have a thread that can wake up to process a UI-related task or some other task. For example, a thread could start some long operation and give the user the ability to cancel the operation. This thread needs to know when the operation has completed (a non-UI-related task), or if the user clicks on a Cancel button (a UI-related task) to terminate the operation.

A thread can call the *MsgWaitForMultipleObjects* or *MsgWaitForMultiple-ObjectsEx* functions to cause the thread to wait for its own messages:

```
DWORD MsgWaitForMultipleObjects(
    DWORD nCount,
    PHANDLE phObjects,
    BOOL fWaitAll,
    DWORD dwMilliseconds,
    DWORD dwWakeMask);

DWORD MsgWaitForMultipleObjectsEx(
    DWORD nCount,
    PHANDLE phObjects,
    DWORD dwMilliseconds,
    DWORD dwWakeMask,
    DWORD dwFlags);
```

These functions are similar to the *WaitForMultipleObjects* function (discussed in Chapter 9). The difference is that these functions allow a thread to be scheduled when a kernel object becomes signaled or when a window message needs dispatching to a window created by the calling thread.

Internally, the system is just adding an event kernel object to the array of kernel handles. The *dwWakeMask* parameter tells the system when you want the event to be signaled. The legal domain of possible values that can be specified in *dwWakeMask* parameter is the same as the values that can be passed to the *GetQueueStatus* function.

Normally, when the *WaitForMultipleObjects* function returns, it returns the index of the object that became signaled to satisfy the call (WAIT_OBJECT_0 to WAIT_OBJECT_0 + $nCount - 1$). Adding the *dwWakeMask* parameter is like adding another handle to the call. If *MsgWaitForMultipleObjects(Ex)* is satisfied because of the wake mask, the return value will be WAIT_OBJECT_0 + *nCount*.

Here's an example demonstrating how to call *MsgWaitForMultipleObjects*:

```
MsgWaitForMultipleObjects(0, NULL, TRUE, INFINITE, QS_INPUT);
```

This statement says that we're not passing any handles of synchronization objects, as indicated by passing 0 and NULL for the *nCount* and *phObjects* parameters. We're telling the function to wait for all objects to be signaled. But because we're specifying only one object to wait on, the *fWaitAll* parameter could have easily been FALSE without altering the effect of this call. We are also telling the system that we want to wait—however long it takes—until either a keyboard message or a mouse message is available in the calling thread's input queue.

As soon as you start getting creative using *MsgWaitForMultipleObjects*, you realize that this function lacks many important features. This is why Microsoft was forced to create the *MsgWaitForMultipleObjectsEx* function. This *MsgWait-ForMultipleObjectsEx* function is a superset of *MsgWaitForMultipleObjects*. The new features come by way of the *dwFlags* parameter. For this parameter, you can specify any combination of the following flags.

Flag	Description
MWMO_WAITALL	The function waits for all the kernel objects to become signaled and for the specified messages to appear in the thread's queue. Without this flag, the function waits until any kernel object becomes signaled or for the specified message to appear in the thread's queue.
MWMO_ALERTABLE	The function waits in an alertable state.
MWMO_INPUTAVAILABLE	The function wakes if any of the specified messages are in the thread's queue. (I'll explain this in more detail a little later on in this section.)

If you don't want any of these additional features, you just pass zero (0) for the *dwFlags* parameter.

Here are the important things to note about *MsgWaitForMultiple-Objects(Ex)*:

- Since this function just appends an internal event kernel object to the array of kernel handles, the maximum value of the *nCount* parameter is MAXIMUM_WAIT_OBJECTS minus 1, or 63.

- When you pass FALSE for the *fWaitAll* parameter, the function returns when either a kernel object is signaled or when the specified message type appears in the thread's queue.

- When you pass TRUE for the *fWaitAll* parameter, the function returns when all of the kernel objects are signaled *and* the specified message type appears in the thread's queue. This behavior seems to catch many developers by surprise. Many developers want a way to have their thread wake up when all the kernel objects are signaled *or* when the specified message type appears in the thread's queue. There is no function that is capable of the latter.

- When you call either of these functions, they actually check to see if *new* messages of the specified type have been placed into the calling thread's queue.

Note that the last point also catches many developers by surprise. Here's an example of the problem. Let's say that a thread's queue currently contains two keystroke messages in it. If the thread were to now call *MsgWaitForMultipleObjects(Ex)* with the *dwWakeMask* parameter set to QS_INPUT, the thread would wake up, pull the first keystroke message from the queue, and process the message. Now, if the thread were to call *MsgWaitForMultipleObjects(Ex)* again, the thread would not wake up because there is no *new* message in the thread's queue.

This has become such a major problem for developers that Microsoft added the MWMO_INPUTAVAILABLE flag, which can be used only with *MsgWaitForMultipleObjectsEx*, not *MsgWaitForMultipleObjects*.

Here is an example of how to properly code a message loop using *MsgWaitForMultipleObjectsEx*:

```
BOOL  fQuit = FALSE;          // Should the loop terminate?

while (!fQuit) {

   // Wake when the kernel object is signaled OR
   // if we have to process a UI message.
   DWORD dwResult = MsgWaitForMultipleObjectsEx(1, &hEvent,
      INFINITE, QS_ALLEVENTS, MWMO_INPUTAVAILABLE);

   switch (dwResult) {
      case WAIT_OBJECT_0:      // The event became signaled.
         break;

      case WAIT_OBJECT_0 + 1:  // A message is in our queue.

         // Dispatch all of the messages.
         MSG msg;
         while (PeekMessage(&msg, NULL, 0, 0, PM_REMOVE)) {

            if (msg.message == WM_QUIT) {
               // A WM_QUIT message, exit the loop
               fQuit = TRUE;
            } else {
               // Translate and dispatch the message.
               TranslateMessage(&msg);
               DispatchMessage(&msg);
            }
         } // Our queue is empty.
         break;
   }
}   // End of while loop
```

931

Sending Data with Messages

In this section, we'll examine how the system transfers data between processes using window messages. Some window messages specify the address of a block of memory in their *lParam* parameter. For example, the WM_SETTEXT message uses the *lParam* parameter as a pointer to a zero-terminated string that identifies the new text for the window. Consider the following call:

```
SendMessage(FindWindow(NULL, "Calculator"), WM_SETTEXT,
    0, (LPARAM) "A Test Caption");
```

This call seems harmless enough—it determines the window handle of the Calculator application's window and attempts to change its caption to *A Test Caption*. But let's take a closer look at what happens here.

The string of the new title is contained in your process's address space. So the address of this string in your process space will be passed as the *lParam* parameter. When the window procedure for Calculator's window receives this message, it looks at the *lParam* parameter and attempts to manipulate what it thinks is a zero-terminated string in order to make it the new title.

But the address in *lParam* points to a string in your process's address space—not in Calculator's address space. This is a big problem because a memory access violation is sure to occur. But if you execute the line above, you'll see that it works successfully. How can this be?

The answer is that the system looks specifically for the WM_SETTEXT message and handles it differently from the way it handles most other messages. When you call *SendMessage*, the code in the function checks whether you are trying to send a WM_SETTEXT message. If you are, it packs the zero-terminated string from your address space into a memory-mapped file that it is going to share with the other process. Then it sends the message to the thread in the other process. When the receiving thread is ready to process the WM_SETTEXT message, it determines the location, in its own address space, of the shared memory-mapped file that contains a copy of the new window text. The *lParam* parameter is initialized to point to this address, and the WM_SETTEXT message is dispatched to the appropriate window procedure. After the message is processed, the memory-mapped file is destroyed. Boy, doesn't this seem like a lot of work?

Fortunately, most messages don't require this type of processing—it takes place only when an application sends interprocess messages. Special processing such as this has to be performed for any message whose *wParam* or *lParam* parameters represent a pointer to a data structure.

Let's look at another case that requires special handling by the system—the WM_GETTEXT message. Suppose your application contains the following code:

```
char szBuf[200];
SendMessage(FindWindow(NULL, "Calculator"), WM_GETTEXT,
   sizeof(szBuf), (LPARAM) szBuf);
```

The WM_GETTEXT message requests that Calculator's window procedure fill the buffer pointed to by *szBuf* with the title of its window. When you send this message to a window in another process, the system must actually send two messages. First the system sends a WM_GETTEXTLENGTH message to the window. The window procedure responds by returning the number of characters required to hold the window's title. The system can use this count to create a memory-mapped file that will end up being shared between the two processes.

Once the memory-mapped file has been created, the system can send the WM_GETTEXT message to fill it. Then the system switches back to the process that called *SendMessage* in the first place, copies the data from the shared memory-mapped file into the buffer pointed to by *szBuf*, and returns from the call to *SendMessage*.

Well, all this is fine and good if you are sending messages that the system is aware of. But what if you create your own (WM_USER + x) message that you want to send from one process to a window in another? The system will not know that you want it to use memory-mapped files and to update pointers when sending. However, Microsoft has created a special window message, WM_COPYDATA, for exactly this purpose:

```
COPYDATASTRUCT cds;
SendMessage(hwndReceiver, WM_COPYDATA,
   (WPARAM) hwndSender, (LPARAM) &cds);
```

COPYDATASTRUCT is a structure defined in WinUser.h, and it looks like this:

```
typedef struct tagCOPYDATASTRUCT {
   ULONG_PTR dwData;
   DWORD cbData;
   PVOID lpData;
} COPYDATASTRUCT;
```

When you're ready to send some data to a window in another process, you must first initialize the COPYDATASTRUCT structure. The *dwData* member is reserved for your own use. You can place any value in it. For example, you might have occasion to send different types or categories of data to the other process. You can use this value to indicate the content of the data you are sending.

The *cbData* member specifies the number of bytes that you want to transfer to the other process, and the *lpData* member points to the first byte of the data. The address pointed to by *lpData* is, of course, in the sender's address space.

933

When *SendMessage* sees that you are sending a WM_COPYDATA message, it creates a memory-mapped file *cbData* bytes in size and copies the data from your address space to the memory-mapped file. It then sends the message to the destination window. When the receiving window procedure processes this message, the *lParam* parameter points to a COPYDATASTRUCT that exists in the address space of the receiving process. The *lpData* member of this structure points to the view of the shared memory-mapped file in the receiving process's address space.

You should remember three important things about the WM_COPYDATA message:

- Always send this message; never post it. You can't post a WM_COPYDATA message because the system must free the memory-mapped file after the receiving window procedure has processed the message. If you post the message, the system doesn't know when the WM_COPYDATA message is processed, and therefore it can't free the copied block of memory.

- It takes some time for the system to make a copy of the data in the other process's address space. This means that you shouldn't have another thread that modifies the contents of the memory block running in the sending application until the call to *SendMessage* returns.

- The WM_COPYDATA message allows a 16-bit application to communicate with a 32-bit application and vice versa. It also allows a 32-bit application to talk to a 64-bit application and vice versa. This is an incredibly easy way to have newer applications talk to older applications. Also note that WM_COPYDATA is fully supported on Windows 2000 and Windows 98. Unfortunately, if you are still writing 16-bit Windows applications, Microsoft Visual C++ 1.52 does not have a definition for the WM_COPYDATA message or the COPYDATASTRUCT structure. You will need to add them manually:

```
// Manually include this in your 16-bit Windows source code.
#define WM_COPYDATA    0x004A

typedef VOID FAR* PVOID;
typedef struct tagCOPYDATASTRUCT {
   DWORD dwData;
   DWORD cbData;
   PVOID lpData;
} COPYDATASTRUCT, FAR* PCOPYDATASTRUCT;
```

The WM_COPYDATA message is an incredible device that could save many developers hours of time when trying to solve interprocess communication problems. It's a shame it's not used more frequently. For an example that demonstrates an excellent use of the WM_COPYDATA message, see the LastMsgBoxInfo sample application presented in Chapter 22.

The CopyData Sample Application

The CopyData application ("26 CopyData.exe"), listed in Figure 26-3, demonstrates how to use the WM_COPYDATA message to send a block of data from one application to another. The source code and resource files for the application are in the 26-CopyData directory on the companion CD-ROM. You'll need to have at least two copies of CopyData running to see it work. Each time you start a copy of CopyData, it presents a dialog box that looks like this.

To see data copied from one application to another, first change the text in the Data1 and Data2 edit controls. Then click on one of the two Send Data* To Other Windows buttons, and the program sends the data to all the running instances of CopyData. Each instance updates the contents of its own edit box to reflect the new data.

The list below describes how CopyData works. When a user clicks on one of the two buttons, CopyData performs the following actions.

1. Initializes the *dwData* member of COPYDATASTRUCT with 0 if the user clicked on the Send Data1 To Other Windows button, or with 1 if the user clicked on the Send Data2 To Other Windows button.

2. Retrieves the length of the text string (in characters) from the appropriate edit box and adds 1 for a zero-terminating character. This value is converted from a number of characters to a number of bytes by multiplying by *sizeof(TCHAR)*. The result is then placed in the *cbData* member of COPYDATASTRUCT.

3. Calls _*alloca* to allocate a block of memory large enough to hold the length of the string in the edit box plus its zero-terminating character. The address of this block is stored in the *lpData* member of COPYDATASTRUCT.

4. Copies the text from the edit box into this memory block.

At this point, everything is ready to be sent to the other windows. To determine which windows to send the WM_COPYDATA message to, CopyData calls *FindWindowEx* passing the caption of its dialog box so that only other instances of the CopyData application are enumerated. As each instance's window is found, the WM_COPYDATA message is forwarded so that each instance updates its edit controls.

CopyData.cpp

```
/******************************************************************************
Module:  CopyData.cpp
Notices: Copyright (c) 2000 Jeffrey Richter
******************************************************************************/


#include "..\CmnHdr.h"      /* See Appendix A. */
#include <windowsx.h>
#include <tchar.h>
#include <malloc.h>
#include "Resource.h"



///////////////////////////////////////////////////////////////////////////////


// WindowsX.h doesn't have a prototype for Cls_OnCopyData, so here it is.
/* BOOL Cls_OnCopyData(HWND hwnd, HWND hwndFrom, PCOPYDATASTRUCT pcds) */


///////////////////////////////////////////////////////////////////////////////


BOOL Dlg_OnCopyData(HWND hwnd, HWND hwndFrom, PCOPYDATASTRUCT cds) {

   Edit_SetText(GetDlgItem(hwnd, cds->dwData ? IDC_DATA2 : IDC_DATA1),
      (PTSTR) cds->lpData);

   return(TRUE);
}
```

Figure 26-3.
The CopyData sample application

(continued)

Figure 26-3. *continued*

```
//////////////////////////////////////////////////////////////////////////////


BOOL Dlg_OnInitDialog(HWND hwnd, HWND hwndFocus, LPARAM lParam) {

   chSETDLGICONS(hwnd, IDI_COPYDATA);

   // Initialize the edit controls with some test data.
   Edit_SetText(GetDlgItem(hwnd, IDC_DATA1), TEXT("Some test data"));
   Edit_SetText(GetDlgItem(hwnd, IDC_DATA2), TEXT("Some more test data"));
   return(TRUE);
}



//////////////////////////////////////////////////////////////////////////////


void Dlg_OnCommand(HWND hwnd, int id, HWND hwndCtl, UINT codeNotify) {

   switch (id) {
      case IDCANCEL:
         EndDialog(hwnd, id);
         break;

      case IDC_COPYDATA1:
      case IDC_COPYDATA2:
         if (codeNotify != BN_CLICKED)
            break;

         HWND hwndEdit = GetDlgItem(hwnd,
            (id == IDC_COPYDATA1) ? IDC_DATA1 : IDC_DATA2);

         // Prepare the COPYDATASTRUCT.
         COPYDATASTRUCT cds;

         // Indicate which data field we're sending (0=ID_DATA1, 1=ID_DATA2)
         cds.dwData = (DWORD) ((id == IDC_COPYDATA1) ? 0 : 1);

         // Get the length (in bytes) of the data block we're sending.
         cds.cbData = (Edit_GetTextLength(hwndEdit) + 1) * sizeof(TCHAR);

         // Allocate a block of memory to hold the string.
         cds.lpData = _alloca(cds.cbData);
```

(continued)

Figure 26-3. *continued*

```
            // Put the edit control's string in the data block.
            Edit_GetText(hwndEdit, (PTSTR) cds.lpData, cds.cbData);

            // Get the caption of our window.
            TCHAR szCaption[100];
            GetWindowText(hwnd, szCaption, chDIMOF(szCaption));

            // Enumerate through all the top-level windows with the same caption.
            HWND hwndT = NULL;
            do {
                hwndT = FindWindowEx(NULL, hwndT, NULL, szCaption);
                if (hwndT != NULL) {
                    FORWARD_WM_COPYDATA(hwndT, hwnd, &cds, SendMessage);
                }
            } while (hwndT != NULL);
            break;
    }
}


///////////////////////////////////////////////////////////////////////////////


INT_PTR WINAPI Dlg_Proc(HWND hwnd, UINT uMsg, WPARAM wParam, LPARAM lParam) {

    switch (uMsg) {
        chHANDLE_DLGMSG(hwnd, WM_INITDIALOG, Dlg_OnInitDialog);
        chHANDLE_DLGMSG(hwnd, WM_COMMAND,   Dlg_OnCommand);
        chHANDLE_DLGMSG(hwnd, WM_COPYDATA,  Dlg_OnCopyData);
    }
    return(FALSE);
}


///////////////////////////////////////////////////////////////////////////////


int WINAPI _tWinMain(HINSTANCE hinstExe, HINSTANCE, PTSTR pszCmdLine, int) {

    DialogBox(hinstExe, MAKEINTRESOURCE(IDD_COPYDATA), NULL, Dlg_Proc);
    return(0);
}

//////////////////////////////// End of File ///////////////////////////////////
```

(continued)

938

Figure 26-3. *continued*

CopyData.rc

```
//Microsoft Developer Studio generated resource script.
//
#include "Resource.h"

#define APSTUDIO_READONLY_SYMBOLS
/////////////////////////////////////////////////////////////////////////////
//
// Generated from the TEXTINCLUDE 2 resource.
//
#include "afxres.h"


/////////////////////////////////////////////////////////////////////////////
#undef APSTUDIO_READONLY_SYMBOLS


/////////////////////////////////////////////////////////////////////////////
// English (U.S.) resources

#if !defined(AFX_RESOURCE_DLL) || defined(AFX_TARG_ENU)
#ifdef _WIN32
LANGUAGE LANG_ENGLISH, SUBLANG_ENGLISH_US
#pragma code_page(1252)
#endif //_WIN32


/////////////////////////////////////////////////////////////////////////////
//
// Dialog
//

IDD_COPYDATA DIALOG DISCARDABLE  38, 36, 220, 42
STYLE WS_MINIMIZEBOX | WS_VISIBLE | WS_CAPTION | WS_SYSMENU
CAPTION "CopyData Application"
FONT 8, "MS Sans Serif"
BEGIN
    LTEXT           "Data&1:",IDC_STATIC,4,4,24,12
    EDITTEXT        IDC_DATA1,28,4,76,12
    PUSHBUTTON      "&Send Data1 to other windows",IDC_COPYDATA1,112,4,104,
                    14,WS_GROUP
    LTEXT           "Data&2:",IDC_STATIC,4,24,24,12
    EDITTEXT        IDC_DATA2,28,24,76,12
    PUSHBUTTON      "Send &Data2 to other windows",IDC_COPYDATA2,112,24,104,
                    14,WS_GROUP
END
```

(continued)

Figure 26-3. *continued*

```
///////////////////////////////////////////////////////////////////////////
//
// Icon
//

// Icon with lowest ID value placed first to ensure application icon
// remains consistent on all systems.
IDI_COPYDATA              ICON    DISCARDABLE      "CopyData.Ico"

#ifdef APSTUDIO_INVOKED
///////////////////////////////////////////////////////////////////////////
//
// TEXTINCLUDE
//

1 TEXTINCLUDE DISCARDABLE
BEGIN
    "Resource.h\0"
END

2 TEXTINCLUDE DISCARDABLE
BEGIN
    "#include ""afxres.h""\r\n"
    "\0"
END

3 TEXTINCLUDE DISCARDABLE
BEGIN
    "\r\n"
    "\0"
END

#endif    // APSTUDIO_INVOKED

#endif    // English (U.S.) resources
///////////////////////////////////////////////////////////////////////////

#ifndef APSTUDIO_INVOKED
///////////////////////////////////////////////////////////////////////////
//
// Generated from the TEXTINCLUDE 3 resource.
//

///////////////////////////////////////////////////////////////////////////
#endif    // not APSTUDIO_INVOKED
```

How Windows Handle
ANSI/Unicode Characters and Strings

WINDOWS 98

Windows 98 only supports ANSI window classes and ANSI window procedures.

When you register a new window class, you must tell the system the address of the window procedure responsible for processing messages for this class. For certain messages (such as WM_SETTEXT), the *lParam* parameter for the message is a pointer to a string. The system needs to know whether the window procedure requires that the string be in ANSI or Unicode before dispatching the message so that the message will be processed correctly.

You tell the system whether a window procedure expects ANSI strings or Unicode strings depending on which function you use to register the window class. If you construct the WNDCLASS structure and call *RegisterClassA*, the system thinks that the window procedure expects all strings and characters to be ANSI. Registering the window class with *RegisterClassW* causes the system to dispatch only Unicode strings and characters to the window procedure. Of course, the macro *RegisterClass* expands to either *RegisterClassA* or *RegisterClassW*, depending on whether UNICODE is defined when you compile the source module.

If you have a handle to a window, you can determine what type of characters and strings the window procedure expects by calling

```
BOOL IsWindowUnicode(HWND hwnd);
```

If the window procedure for the specified window expects Unicode, the function returns TRUE; otherwise, FALSE is returned.

If you create an ANSI string and send a WM_SETTEXT message to a window whose window procedure expects Unicode strings, the system will automatically convert the string for you before sending the message. You'll rarely need to call the *IsWindowUnicode* function.

The system will also perform automatic translations if you subclass a window procedure. Let's say that the window procedure for an edit control expects its characters and strings to be in Unicode. Then somewhere in your program you create an edit control and subclass the window's procedure by calling

```
LONG_PTR SetWindowLongPtrA(
   HWND hwnd,
   int nIndex,
   LONG_PTR dwNewLong);
```

or

```
LONG_PTR SetWindowLongPtrW(
    HWND hwnd,
    int nIndex,
    LONG_PTR dwNewLong);
```

and passing GCLP_WNDPROC as the *nIndex* parameter and the address to your subclass procedure as the *dwNewLong* parameter. But what happens if your subclass procedure expects ANSI characters and strings? This could potentially create a big problem. The system determines how to convert the strings and characters depending on which of the two functions above you use to perform the subclassing. If you call *SetWindowLongPtrA*, you're telling the system that the new window procedure (your subclass procedure) is to receive ANSI characters and strings. In fact, if you were to call *IsWindowUnicode* after calling *SetWindowLongPtrA*, you would see that it would return FALSE, indicating that the subclassed edit window procedure no longer expects Unicode characters and strings.

But now we have a new problem: how do we ensure that the original window procedure gets the correct type of characters and strings? The system needs to have two pieces of information to correctly convert the characters and strings. The first is the form that the characters and strings are currently in. We inform the system by calling either *CallWindowProcA* or *CallWindowProcW*:

```
LRESULT CallWindowProcA(
    WNDPROC wndprcPrev,
    HWND hwnd,
    UINT uMsg,
    WPARAM wParam,
    LPARAM lParam);

LRESULT CallWindowProcW(
    WNDPROC wndprcPrev,
    HWND hwnd,
    UINT uMsg,
    WPARAM wParam,
    LPARAM lParam);
```

If the subclass procedure has ANSI strings that it wants to pass to the original window procedure, the subclass procedure must call *CallWindowProcA*. If the subclass procedure has Unicode strings that it wants to pass to the original window procedure, the subclass procedure must call *CallWindowProcW*.

The second piece of information that the system needs is the type of characters and strings that the original window procedure expects. The system gets this information from the address of the original window procedure. When you call the *SetWindowLongPtrA* or the *SetWindowLongPtrW* function, the system checks to see whether you are subclassing a Unicode window procedure with an ANSI subclass procedure or vice versa. If you're not changing the type of strings expected, *SetWindowLongPtr* simply returns the address of the original window procedure. If you're changing the type of characters and strings that the window procedure expects, *SetWindowLongPtr* doesn't return the actual address of the original window procedure; instead, it returns a handle to an internal subsystem data structure.

This structure contains the address of the original window procedure and a value that indicates whether that procedure expects Unicode or ANSI strings. When you call *CallWindowProc*, the system checks whether you are passing a handle of one of the internal data structures or the address of a window procedure. If you're passing the address of a window procedure, the original window procedure is called and no character and string conversions need to be performed.

If, on the other hand, you're passing the handle of an internal data structure, the system converts the characters and strings to the appropriate type (Unicode or ANSI) and then calls the original window procedure.

CHAPTER TWENTY-SEVEN

THE HARDWARE INPUT MODEL AND LOCAL INPUT STATE

In this chapter, I'll discuss the system's hardware input model. Specifically, we'll examine how keystrokes and mouse events enter the system and get dispatched to the appropriate window procedure. One of Microsoft's main goals for the input model was to ensure that one thread's action could not adversely affect another thread's actions. Here's an example from 16-bit Windows: If a task entered an infinite loop, all tasks were hung and could no longer respond to the user. The user had to reboot the computer. This gave too much control to a single task. Robust operating systems, such as Windows 2000 and Windows 98, do not allow a hung thread to prevent other threads in the system from receiving hardware input.

The Raw Input Thread

Figure 27-1 summarizes the system's hardware input model. When the system initializes, it creates a special thread known as the *raw input thread* (RIT). In addition, the system creates a queue called the *system hardware input queue* (SHIQ). The RIT and the SHIQ compose the heart of the system's hardware input model.

The RIT usually sleeps, waiting for an entry to appear in the SHIQ. When the user presses and releases a key, presses and releases a mouse button, or moves the mouse, the device driver for the hardware device appends a hardware event to the SHIQ, which wakes up the RIT. The RIT then extracts the entry from the SHIQ and translates the event into the appropriate WM_KEY*, WM_?BUTTON*, or WM_MOUSEMOVE message. The translated message is then appended to the appropriate thread's virtualized input queue (VIQ) (discussed in Chapter 26). The RIT then loops back to wait for more messages to appear in the SHIQ. Because the RIT executes code written only by Microsoft—and because this code is heavily tested—the RIT can never stop responding to hardware input events.

So how does the RIT know which thread's virtualized input queue to append the hardware input messages to? Well, for mouse messages, the RIT simply determines which window is under the mouse cursor. Using the window, the RIT calls *GetWindowThreadProcessId* to find out which thread created the window. The thread ID returned identifies which thread gets the mouse message.

Things work a bit differently for keystroke hardware events. At any given time, one thread is "connected" to the RIT. This thread is called the *foreground thread* because it created the window that the user is interacting with and this thread's windows are in the foreground with respect to windows created by other threads.

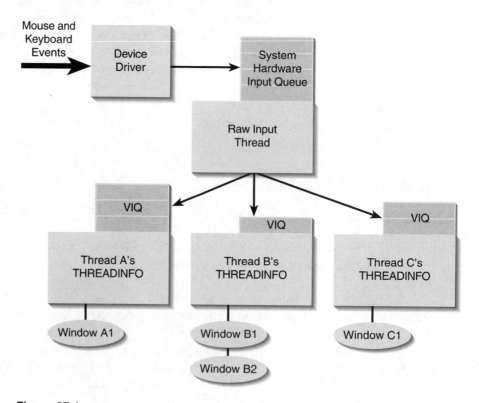

Figure 27-1.
The system's hardware input model

When a user logs on to the system, the Windows Explorer process has a thread that creates the taskbar and the desktop. This thread is connected to the RIT. If you now spawn Calculator, it has a thread that creates a window, and this thread becomes connected to the RIT. Note that Windows Explorer's thread is no longer connected to the RIT since the RIT can only have one thread connected to it at a time. So now, when a keystroke message enters the SHIQ, the RIT simply wakes up, translates the event into the appropriate keystroke message, and places the message in the connected thread's virtualized input queue.

So how do different thread's get connected to the RIT? Well, as I've just explained, when a process is spawned, this process's thread can create a window. This window comes to the foreground and its thread gets connected to the RIT. In addition, the RIT is responsible for handling special key sequences such as Alt+Tab, Alt+Esc, and Ctrl+Alt+Del. Since the RIT handles these key sequences internally, users are guaranteed that they can always activate windows with the keyboard; there is no way for an application to intercept and discard these key sequences. When the user presses one of the special key sequences, the RIT activates the selected window and connects its thread to the RIT. Windows also offers functions that activate a window, causing the window's thread to be connected to the RIT. These functions will be discussed later in this chapter.

From Figure 27-1, you can see how threads are protected from one another. If the RIT dispatches a message for Window B1 or Window B2, the message goes in Thread B's virtualized input queue. When processing the message, Thread B could enter an infinite loop or deadlock while synchronizing on a kernel object. If this happens, Thread B is still connected to the RIT and more messages might be appended to Thread B's virtualized input queue.

However, the user will probably notice that both Windows B1 and B2 are not responding and might want to switch to Window A1. To make the switch, the user presses Alt+Tab. Since the RIT handles the Alt+Tab keystroke combination, the user can always switch to another window without a problem. After selecting Window A1, Thread A is connected to the RIT. At this point, the user can enter input into Window A1 even though Thread B and both its windows are not responding.

Local Input State

Having threads independently handle input—preventing one thread from adversely affecting another thread—is just part of what makes the input model robust. However, this feature alone is not enough to keep threads isolated from one another, so the system has additional infrastructure. This additional infrastructure is called *local input state*.

Each thread has its own local input state, which is managed inside a thread's THREADINFO structure (discussed in Chapter 26). This input state consists of the thread's virtualized input queue as well as a set of variables. These variables keep track of the following input state management information:

Keyboard input and window focus information, such as

- Which window has keyboard focus
- Which window is active
- Which keys are considered pressed down
- The state of the caret

The variables also keep track of mouse cursor management information, such as

- Which window has mouse capture
- The shape of the mouse cursor
- The visibility of the mouse cursor

Because each thread gets its very own set of input state variables, each thread has a different notion of focus window, mouse capture window, and so on. From a thread's perspective, either one of its windows has keyboard focus or no window in the system has keyboard focus, either one of its windows has mouse capture or no window has mouse capture, and so on. As you might expect, this separatism has some ramifications, which we'll discuss in this chapter.

Keyboard Input and Focus

As we know, the RIT directs the user's keyboard input to a thread's virtualized input queue—not to a window. The RIT places the keyboard events into the thread's virtualized input queue without referring to a particular window. When the thread calls *GetMessage*, the keyboard event is removed from the queue and assigned to the window (created by the thread) that currently has input focus. Figure 27-2 illustrates this process.

To instruct a different window to accept keyboard input, you need to specify to which thread's virtualized input queue the RIT should direct keyboard input *and* you need to tell the thread's input state variables which window will have keyboard focus. Calling *SetFocus* alone does not accomplish both tasks. If

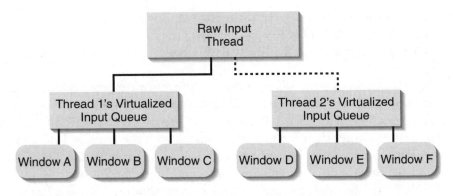

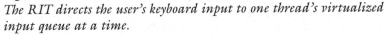

Figure 27-2.
The RIT directs the user's keyboard input to one thread's virtualized input queue at a time.

Thread 1 is currently receiving input from the RIT, a call to *SetFocus*—passing the handle of Window A, Window B, or Window C—causes the focus to change. The window losing focus removes its focus rectangle or hides its caret, and the window gaining focus draws a focus rectangle or shows its caret.

However, let's say that Thread 1 is still receiving input from the RIT, and it calls *SetFocus*, passing the handle of Window E. In this case, the system prevents the call to *SetFocus* from doing anything because the window for which you are trying to set focus is not using the virtualized input queue that is currently "connected" to the RIT. After Thread 1 executes this call, there is no change in focus, and the appearance of the screen doesn't change.

In another situation, Thread 1 might be connected to the RIT and Thread 2 might call *SetFocus*, passing the handle of Window E. In this case, Thread 2's local input state variables are updated to reflect that Window E is the window to receive keyboard input the next time the RIT directs keystrokes to Thread 2. The call doesn't cause the RIT to direct input to Thread 2's virtualized input queue.

Because Window E now has focus for Thread 2, it receives a WM_ SETFOCUS message. If Window E is a pushbutton, it draws a focus rectangle for itself, so two windows with focus rectangles (Window A and Window E) might appear on the screen. This can be quite disconcerting to an end user. You should be careful when you call *SetFocus* so that this situation doesn't occur. Call *SetFocus* only if your thread is connected to the RIT.

By the way, if you give focus to a window that displays a caret when it receives a WM_SETFOCUS message, you can produce several windows on the screen that simultaneously display flashing carets. This can be a bit bewildering to a user.

When focus is transferred from one window to another using conventional methods (such as clicking on a window with the mouse), the window losing focus receives a WM_KILLFOCUS message. If the window receiving focus belongs to a thread other than the thread associated with the window losing focus, the local input state variables of the thread that created the window losing focus are updated to reflect that no window has focus. Calling *GetFocus* at this time returns NULL, which makes the thread think that no window currently has the focus.

The *SetActiveWindow* function activates a top-level window in the system and sets focus to that window:

```
HWND SetActiveWindow(HWND hwnd);
```

Like the *SetFocus* function, this function does nothing if the calling thread did not create the window passed to it.

The complement of *SetActiveWindow* is the *GetActiveWindow* function:

```
HWND GetActiveWindow();
```

This function works just like the *GetFocus* function except that it returns the handle of the active window indicated by the calling thread's local input state variables. So if the active window is owned by another thread, *GetActiveWindow* returns NULL.

Other functions that can alter a window's z-order, activation status, and focus status include *BringWindowToTop* and *SetWindowPos*:

```
BOOL BringWindowToTop(HWND hwnd);

BOOL SetWindowPos(
   HWND hwnd,
   HWND hwndInsertAfter,
   int x,
   int y,
   int cx,
   int cy,
   UINT fuFlags);
```

These two functions work identically (in fact, *BringWindowToTop* calls *SetWindowPos* internally, passing HWND_TOP as the second parameter). If the thread calling these functions is not connected to the RIT, the functions do nothing. However, if the thread calling these functions is connected to the RIT, the system activates the specified window. Note that this works even if the calling thread did not create the specified window. This means that the window becomes active and the thread that created the specified window is connected to the RIT. This also causes the calling thread's and the newly connected thread's local input state variables to be updated.

At times, a thread wants to have its window come to the foreground. For example, you might have a meeting scheduled using Microsoft Outlook. About a half hour before the meeting time, Outlook pops up a dialog box reminding you that the meeting is coming up soon. If Outlook's thread is not connected to the RIT, this dialog box will come up behind another window and you will not see it. There needs to be some way to draw the user's attention to windows even if the user is using another application's window.

The following function brings a window to the foreground and connects its thread to the RIT:

```
BOOL SetForegroundWindow(HWND hwnd);
```

The system also activates the window and gives it the focus. The complementary function is *GetForegroundWindow*:

```
HWND GetForegroundWindow();
```

This function returns the window handle that is currently in the foreground.

In earlier versions of windows, the *SetForegroundWindow* function always worked. That is, the thread calling this function could always bring the specified window to the foreground (even if the window was not created by the calling thread). However, developers started abusing this capability and were popping up windows on top of each other. For example, I would be writing a magazine article and all of a sudden the Print Job Finished dialog box would pop up on the screen. If I wasn't looking at the screen, I wouldn't even see the dialog box and I'd be typing text into it instead of into my document. Even more annoying is when you try to select a menu item and suddenly another window pops up, closing the menu.

To stop these annoyances, Microsoft has added a lot more intelligence to the *SetForegroundWindow* function. In particular, the function only works if the thread calling the function is already connected to the RIT or if the thread currently connected to the RIT has not received any input in a certain amount of time (the time is controlled using the *SystemParametersInfo* function and the

SPI_SETFOREGROUNDLOCKTIMEOUT value). In addition, the function fails if a menu is active.

If *SetForegroundWindow* is not allowed to bring the window to the foreground, it flashes the window's caption and the window's button on the taskbar. The user will see the taskbar button flashing and know that the window is trying to get the user's attention. The user will have to manually activate the window to see what information it has to report. The *SystemParametersInfo* function is also used to control the flashing using the SPI_SETFOREGROUND-FLASHCOUNT value.

Because of this new behavior, the system offers some additional functions. The first function (listed below) allows a thread in the specified process to successfully call *SetForegroundWindow* if the thread calling *AllowSetForeground-Window* can successfully call *SetForegroundWindow*. To allow any process to pop a window up over your thread's windows, pass ASFW_ANY (defined as −1) for the *dwProcessId* parameter:

```
BOOL AllowSetForegroundWindow(DWORD dwProcessId);
```

In addition, a thread can lock the *SetForegroundWindow* function so that it always fails by calling *LockSetForegroundWindow*:

```
BOOL LockSetForegroundWindow(UINT uLockCode);
```

You can pass either LSFW_LOCK or LSFW_UNLOCK for the *uLockCode* parameter. This function is called by the system internally when a menu is activated so that a window attempting to come to the foreground does not close the menu. Windows Explorer needs to call these functions explicitly when it displays the Start menu, since this is not a built-in menu.

The system automatically unlocks the *SetForegroundWindow* function when the user presses the Alt key or if the user explicitly brings a window to the foreground. This prevents an application from keeping *SetForegroundWindow* locked all the time.

Another aspect of keyboard management and the local input state is that of the synchronous key state array. Every thread's local input state variables include a synchronous key state array, but all threads share a single asynchronous key state array. These arrays reflect the state of all keys on a keyboard at any given time. The *GetAsyncKeyState* function determines whether the user is currently pressing a key on the keyboard:

```
SHORT GetAsyncKeyState(int nVirtKey);
```

The *nVirtKey* parameter identifies the virtual key code of the key to check. The high bit of the result indicates whether the key is currently pressed (1) or not (0). I have often used this function during the processing of a single message to check whether the user has released the primary mouse button. I pass the virtual key value VK_LBUTTON and wait for the high bit of the return value to be 0. Note that *GetAsyncKeyState* always returns 0 (not pressed) if the thread calling the function did not create the window that currently has the input focus.

The *GetKeyState* function, which follows, differs from the *GetAsyncKeyState* function because it returns the keyboard state at the time the most recent keyboard message was removed from the thread's queue:

```
SHORT GetKeyState(int nVirtKey);
```

This function is not affected by which window has input focus and can be called at any time.

Mouse Cursor Management

Mouse cursor management is another component of the local input state. Because the mouse, like the keyboard, must be shared among all the different threads, Windows must not allow a single thread to monopolize the mouse cursor by altering its shape or confining it to a small area of the screen. In this section, we'll take a look at how the mouse cursor is managed by the system.

One aspect of mouse cursor management is the cursor's hide/show capability. If a thread calls *ShowCursor(FALSE)*, the mouse cursor is hidden when it is over any window created by this thread. If the mouse cursor is moved over a window created by another thread, the mouse cursor is visible.

Another aspect of mouse cursor management is the ability to clip the cursor to a rectangular region of the screen using the *ClipCursor* function:

```
BOOL ClipCursor(CONST RECT *prc);
```

This function causes the mouse to be constrained within the screen coordinates specified in the rectangle pointed to by the *prc* parameter. When a thread calls *ClipCursor*, what should the system do? Allowing the cursor to be clipped could adversely affect other threads, and preventing the cursor from being clipped would adversely affect the calling thread. Microsoft has implemented a compromise. When a thread calls this function, the system does clip the mouse cursor to the specified rectangle. However, if an asynchronous activation event occurs (when the user clicks on another application's window, when a call to *SetForegroundWindow* is made, or when Ctrl+Esc is pressed), the system stops clipping the cursor's movement, allowing the cursor to move freely across the entire screen.

Now we move to the issue of mouse capture. When a window "captures" the mouse (by calling *SetCapture*), it requests that all mouse messages be directed from the RIT to the thread's virtualized input queue and that all mouse messages from the virtualized input queue be directed to the window that set capture. This capturing of mouse messages continues until the application later calls *ReleaseCapture*.

Again, capturing the mouse compromises the robustness of the system—there must be a compromise. When an application calls *SetCapture*, the RIT is directed to place all mouse messages in the thread's virtualized input queue. *SetCapture* also sets the local input state variables for the thread that called *SetCapture*.

Usually an application calls *SetCapture* when the user presses a mouse button. However, there is no reason why a thread could not call *SetCapture* even if a mouse button is not down. If *SetCapture* is called when a mouse button is down, capture is performed system-wide. However, when the system detects that no mouse buttons are down, the RIT no longer directs mouse messages solely to the thread's virtualized input queue. Instead, the RIT directs mouse messages to the input queue associated with the window that is directly beneath the mouse cursor. This is normal behavior when the mouse is not captured.

However, the thread that originally called *SetCapture* still thinks that mouse capture is in effect. Thus whenever the mouse is positioned over any window created by the thread that has capture set, the mouse messages will be directed to the capture window for that thread. In other words, when the user releases all mouse buttons, mouse capture is no longer performed on a system-wide level—it is now performed on a thread-local level.

In addition, if the user attempts to activate a window created by another thread, the system automatically sends mouse button down and mouse button up messages to the thread that sets capture. Then the system updates the thread's local input state variables to indicate that the thread no longer has mouse capture. It is clear from this implementation that Microsoft expects mouse clicking and dragging to be the most common reason for using mouse capture.

The final local input state variable pertaining to the mouse is its cursor shape. Whenever a thread calls *SetCursor* to change the shape of the mouse cursor, the local input state variables are updated to reflect the mouse cursor shape. In other words, the local input state variables always remember the most recent shape of the mouse cursor set by the thread.

Let's say that the user moves the mouse over your window, your window receives a WM_SETCURSOR message, and you call *SetCursor* to change the mouse cursor to an hourglass. After the call to *SetCursor*, you have code that enters into a lengthy process. (An infinite loop is a good example of a lengthy process.) Now the user moves the mouse cursor out of your window and over a window belonging to another application. When the mouse moves over the other window, that window can control the cursor's shape.

Local input state variables are not required for accomplishing this change. But now let's move the mouse cursor back into your window, which is still executing its lengthy procedure. The system wants to send WM_SETCURSOR messages to the window, but the window is unable to retrieve them because it is still looping. So the system looks at the most recently set mouse cursor shape (contained in the thread's local input state variables) and automatically sets the mouse cursor back to this shape (the hourglass, in this example). This gives the user visual feedback that the process is still working and that the user must wait.

Attaching Virtualized Input Queues and Local Input State Together

You can see from our discussion that the input model is robust because each thread has its own local input state environment and that each thread connects to and disconnects from the RIT when necessary. At times you might want to have two or more threads share a single set of local input state variables and share a single virtualized input queue.

You can force two or more threads to share the same virtualized input queue and local input state variables by using the *AttachThreadInput* function:

```
BOOL AttachThreadInput(
   DWORD idAttach,
   DWORD idAttachTo,
   BOOL fAttach);
```

The first parameter, *idAttach*, is the ID of the thread containing the virtualized input queue (and local input state variables) you no longer want to use. The second parameter, *idAttachTo*, is the ID of the thread containing the virtualized input queue (and local input state variables) you want the threads to share. The last parameter, *fAttach*, is TRUE if you want the sharing to occur or FALSE if you want to separate the two threads' virtualized input queues and local input state variables. You can tell several threads to share the same virtualized input queue and local input state variables by making multiple calls to the *AttachThreadInput* function.

Returning to the earlier example, let's say that Thread A calls *Attach-ThreadInput*, passing Thread A's ID as the first parameter, Thread B's ID as the second parameter, and TRUE as the last parameter:

```
AttachThreadInput(idThreadA, idThreadB, TRUE);
```

Now every hardware input event destined for Window A1, Window B1, or Window B2 will be appended to Thread B's virtualized input queue as shown in Figure 27-3. Thread A's virtualized input queue will no longer receive input events unless the two queues are detached by calling *AttachThreadInput* a second time, passing FALSE as the *fAttach* parameter.

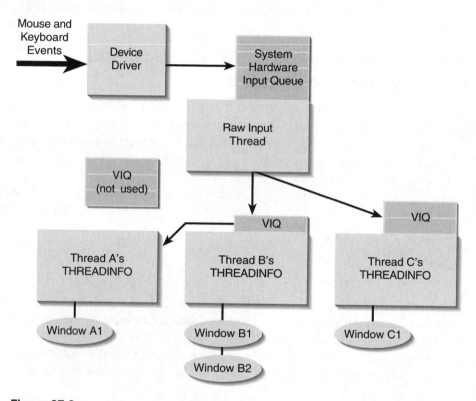

Figure 27-3.
Hardware messages for Window A1, Window B1, and Window B2 go in Thread B's virtualized input queue.

When you attach two threads' input together, you make the threads share a single virtualized input queue and a single set of local input state variables. The threads still use their own posted-message queue, send-message queue, reply-message queue, and wake flags (as discussed in Chapter 26).

If you make all threads share a single queue, you severely curtail the robustness of the system. If one thread receives a keystroke and hangs, another thread can't receive any input. So you should avoid using the *AttachThread-Input* function.

On a few occasions the system implicitly attaches two threads together. The first occasion is when a thread installs a journal record hook or journal playback hook. When the hook is uninstalled, the system automatically restores all the threads so that they use the same input queues they used before the hook was installed.

When a thread installs a journal record hook, it tells the system that it wants to be notified of all hardware events entered by the user. The thread usually saves or records this information in a file. Since the user's input must be recorded in the same order as entered, every thread in the system shares a single virtualized input queue, making all input processing synchronous.

There is one other instance in which the system implicitly calls *Attach-ThreadInput* on your behalf. Let's say you have an application that creates two threads. The first thread creates a dialog box. After the dialog box has been created, the second thread calls *CreateWindow*, using the WS_CHILD style, and passes the handle of the dialog box to be the child's parent. The system calls *AttachThreadInput* with the child window's thread to tell the child's thread that it should use the same input queue that the dialog box thread is using. This action forces input to be synchronized among all the child windows in the dialog box.

The Local Input State Laboratory (LISLab) Sample Application

The LISLab application ("27 LISLab.exe"), listed in Figure 27-4 beginning on page 965, is a laboratory that allows you to experiment with local input states. The source code and resource files for the application are in the 27-LISLab directory on the companion CD-ROM.

To experiment with local input states, you need two threads as guinea pigs. The LISLab process has one thread, and I decided to make Notepad's thread be another. If Notepad is not running when LISLab is started, LISLab will start Notepad. After LISLab has initialized, you'll see the following dialog box.

In the upper left corner is the Windows group box. The five entries in this box are updated twice per second—that is, the dialog box receives a WM_ TIMER message twice every second, and in response, it calls the following functions: *GetFocus, GetActiveWindow, GetForegroundWindow, GetCapture,* and *GetClipCursor.* The first four functions return window handles. From these window handles, I can determine the window's class and caption and display this information. Remember that these window handles are being retrieved from my own thread's local input state variables.

If I activate another application (for example, Notepad), the Focus and Active entries change to (No Window) and the Foreground entry changes to [Notepad] Untitled - Notepad. Notice that by activating Notepad you make LISLab think that no window has focus and that no window is active.

Next you can experiment with changing the window focus. First select SetFocus from the Function combo box at the upper right corner of the Local Input State Lab dialog box. Then enter the delay time (in seconds) that you want LISLab to wait before calling *SetFocus.* For this experiment, you'll probably want to specify a delay of 0 seconds. I'll explain shortly how the Delay field is used.

Next select a window that you want to pass in the call to *SetFocus.* You select a window using the Notepad Windows And Self list box on the left side of the Local Input State Lab dialog box. For this experiment, select [Notepad] Untitled - Notepad in the list box. Now you are ready to call *SetFocus.* Simply click on the Delay button and watch what happens to the Windows group box—nothing. The system does not perform a focus change.

If you really want *SetFocus* to change focus to Notepad, you can click on the Attach To Notepad button. Clicking on this button causes LISLab to call the following function:

```
AttachThreadInput(GetWindowThreadProcessId(g_hwndNotepad, NULL),
   GetCurrentThreadId(), TRUE);
```

This call tells LISLab's thread to use the same virtualized input queue as that of Notepad. In addition, LISLab's thread will also share the same local input state variables used by Notepad.

If after clicking on the Attach To Notepad button you click on Notepad's window, LISLab's dialog box looks like this.

Notice that now, because the input queues are attached, LISLab can follow window focus changes made in Notepad. The above dialog box shows that the Edit control currently has the focus. If we display the File Open dialog box in Notepad, LISLab will continue to update its display and show us which Notepad window has focus, which window is active, and so on.

Now we can move back to LISLab, click on the Delay button, and have *SetFocus* attempt to give Notepad focus. This time the call to *SetFocus* succeeds because the input queues are attached.

You can continue to experiment by placing calls to *SetActiveWindow*, *SetForegroundWindow*, *BringWindowToTop*, and *SetWindowPos* by selecting the desired function from the Function combo box. Try calling these functions both when the input queues are attached and when they are detached and notice the differences.

Now I'll explain why I include the delay option. This option causes LISLab to call the specified function after the number of seconds indicated. An example will help illustrate why you need it. First make sure that LISLab is detached from Notepad by clicking on the Detach From Notepad button. Then select ---> This Dialog Box <--- from the Notepad Windows And Self list box. Next select Set-Focus from the Function combo box, and enter a delay of 10 seconds. Finally, click on the Delay button, and then quickly click on Notepad's window to make it active. You must make Notepad active before the 10 seconds elapse.

While LISLab is waiting for the 10 seconds to elapse, it displays the word Pending to the right of the seconds value. After the 10 seconds, Pending is replaced by Executed and the result of calling the function is displayed. If you watch carefully, you'll see that LISLab will give focus to the Function combo box and show that the combo box now has the focus. But Notepad will still be receiving your keystrokes. LISLab's thread thinks that the combo box has the focus, and Notepad's thread thinks that one of its windows has the focus. However, the RIT remains "connected" to Notepad's thread.

One final point about windows and the focus: Both the *SetFocus* and *Set-ActiveWindow* functions return the handle to the window that originally had the focus or was active. The information for this window is displayed in the PrevWnd field in the LISLab dialog box. Also, just before LISLab calls *SetForegroundWindow*, it calls *GetForegroundWindow* to get the handle of the window that was originally in the foreground. This information is also displayed in the PrevWnd field.

It's time to move on to experiments involving the mouse cursor. Whenever you move the mouse over LISLab's dialog box (but not over any of its child windows), the mouse is displayed as a vertical arrow. As mouse messages are sent to the dialog box, they are also added to the Mouse Messages Received list box. This is how you know when the dialog box is receiving mouse messages. If you move the mouse outside the dialog box or over one of its child windows, you'll see that messages are no longer added to the list box.

Now move the mouse to the right of the dialog box—over the text Click Right Mouse Button To Set Capture—and click and hold the right mouse button. When you do this, LISLab calls *SetCapture* and passes the handle of LISLab's dialog box. Notice that LISLab reflects that it has capture by updating the Windows group box at the top.

Without releasing the right mouse button, move the mouse over LISLab's child windows and watch the mouse messages being added to the list box. Notice that if you move the mouse outside of LISLab's dialog box, LISLab continues to be notified of mouse messages. The mouse cursor retains its vertical arrow shape no matter where you move the mouse on the screen.

Now we're ready to see where the system behaves differently. Release the right mouse button and watch what happens. The capture window reflected at the top of LISLab continues to show that LISLab thinks it still has mouse capture. However, if you move the mouse outside of LISLab's dialog box, the cursor no longer remains a vertical arrow and mouse messages stop going to the Mouse Messages Received list box. If you move the mouse over any of LISLab's child windows, you'll see that capture is still in effect because all the windows are using the same set of local input state variables.

When you're done experimenting with mouse capture, you can turn it off using one of two techniques:

■ Double-click the right mouse button anywhere in the Local Input State Lab dialog box to have LISLab place a call to *ReleaseCapture*.

■ Click on a window created by a thread other than LISLab's thread. When you do this, the system automatically sends mouse button up and mouse button down messages to LISLab's dialog box.

Regardless of which method you choose, watch how the Capture field in the Windows group box changes to reflect that no window has mouse capture.

There are only two more mouse-related experiments: one experiment involves clipping the mouse cursor's movement to a rectangle, and the other involves cursor visibility. When you click on the Top, Left button, LISLab executes the following code:

```
RECT rc;
   :
   :
SetRect(&rc, 0, 0, GetSystemMetrics(SM_CXSCREEN) / 2,
   GetSystemMetrics(SM_CYSCREEN) / 2);
```

This causes the mouse cursor to be confined to the top left quarter of the screen. If you use Alt+Tab to select another application's window, you'll notice that the clipping rectangle stays in effect. The system automatically stops clipping the mouse and allows it to traverse the entire screen when you perform any of the following operations:

Windows 98	Click on another application's title bar and move the window.
Windows 2000	Click on another application's title bar. (You don't have to move the window.)
Windows 2000	Invoke and dismiss the Task Manager using Ctrl+Shift+Esc.

You can also click on the Remove button in the Local Input State Lab dialog box (assuming that the button is in the clipping rectangle) to remove the clipping rectangle.

Clicking on the Hide or Show Cursor button causes LISLab to execute the following code:

```
ShowCursor(FALSE);
```

or

```
ShowCursor(TRUE);
```

When you hide the mouse cursor, it doesn't appear when you move the mouse over LISLab's dialog box. But the moment you move the mouse outside this dialog box, the cursor appears again. Use the Show button to counteract the effect of the Hide button. Note that the effects of hiding the cursor are cumulative; that is, if you click on the Hide button five times, you must click on the Show button five times to make the cursor visible.

The last experiment involves using the Infinite Loop button. When you click on this button, LISLab executes the following code:

```
SetCursor(LoadCursor(NULL, IDC_NO));
for (;;)
   ;
```

The first line changes the mouse cursor to a slashed circle, and the second line executes an infinite loop. After you click on the Infinite Loop button,

LISLab stops responding to any input whatsoever. If you move the mouse over LISLab's dialog box, the cursor remains as the slashed circle. However, if you move the mouse outside the dialog box, the cursor changes to reflect the cursor of the window over which it is located. You can use the mouse to manipulate these other windows.

If you move the mouse back over LISLab's dialog box, the system sees that LISLab is not responding and automatically changes the cursor back to its most recent shape—the slashed circle. You can see that a thread executing an infinite loop is an inconvenience to the user but other windows can be used.

Notice that if you move a window over the hung Local Input State Lab dialog box and then move it away, the system sends LISLab a WM_PAINT message. But the system also realizes that the thread is not responding. The system helps out here by repainting the window for the unresponsive application. Of course, the system cannot repaint the window correctly because it doesn't know what the application is supposed to be doing, so the system simply erases the window's background and redraws the frame.

Now the problem is that we have a window on the screen that isn't responding to anything we do. How do we get rid of it? In Windows 98, we must first press Ctrl+Alt+Del to display the Close Program window shown here.

And in Windows 2000, you can either right-click on the application's button on the Taskbar or you can display the Task Manager window shown here.

Then we simply select the application we want to terminate—Local Input State Lab, in this case—and click on the End Task button. The system will attempt to terminate LISLab in a nice way (by sending a WM_CLOSE message) but will notice that the application isn't responding. This causes the system to display the following dialog box in Windows 98.

In Windows 2000 it looks like this.

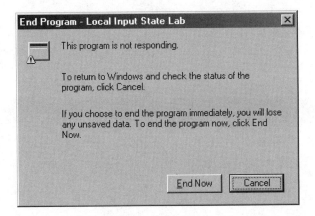

Choosing End Task (for Windows 98) or End Now (Windows 2000) causes the system to forcibly remove LISLab from the system. The Cancel button tells the system that you changed your mind and no longer want to terminate the application. Choose End Task or End Now to remove LISLab from the system.

The whole point of these experiments is to show you the system's robustness. It's impossible for one application to place the operating system in a state that would render the other applications unusable. Also note that both Windows 98 and Windows 2000 automatically free all resources that were allocated by threads in the terminated process—there are no memory leaks!

LISLab.cpp

```
/*****************************************************************************
Module:  LISLab.cpp
Notices: Copyright (c) 2000 Jeffrey Richter
*****************************************************************************/


#include "..\CmnHdr.h"     /* See Appendix A. */
#include <windowsx.h>
#include <tchar.h>
#include <string.h>
#include "Resource.h"


//////////////////////////////////////////////////////////////////////////////
```

Figure 27-4.
The LISLab sample application

(continued)

965

Figure 27-4. *continued*

```
#define TIMER_DELAY (500)  // Half a second

UINT_PTR g_uTimerId = 1;
int      g_nEventId = 0;
DWORD    g_dwEventTime = 0;
HWND     g_hwndSubject = NULL;
HWND     g_hwndNotepad = NULL;


///////////////////////////////////////////////////////////////////////////


void CalcWndText(HWND hwnd, PTSTR szBuf, int nLen) {

   TCHAR szClass[50], szCaption[50], szBufT[150];

   if (hwnd == (HWND) NULL) {
      _tcscpy(szBuf, TEXT("(no window)"));
      return;
   }


   if (!IsWindow(hwnd)) {
      _tcscpy(szBuf, TEXT("(invalid window)"));
      return;
   }

   GetClassName(hwnd, szClass, chDIMOF(szClass));
   GetWindowText(hwnd, szCaption, chDIMOF(szCaption));

   wsprintf(szBufT, TEXT("[%s] %s"), (PTSTR) szClass,
      (*szCaption == 0) ? (PTSTR) TEXT("(no caption)") : (PTSTR) szCaption);
   _tcsncpy(szBuf, szBufT, nLen - 1);
   szBuf[nLen - 1] = 0; // Force zero-terminated string
}


///////////////////////////////////////////////////////////////////////////


// To minimize stack use, one instance of WALKWINDOWTREEDATA
// is created as a local variable in WalkWindowTree() and a
// pointer to it is passed to WalkWindowTreeRecurse.
```

(continued)

Figure 27-4. *continued*

```
// Data used by WalkWindowTreeRecurse
typedef struct {
   HWND  hwndLB;        // Handle to the output list box
   HWND  hwndParent;    // Handle to the parent
   int   nLevel;        // Nesting depth
   int   nIndex;        // List box item index
   TCHAR szBuf[100];    // Output buffer
   int   iBuf;          // Index into szBuf
} WALKWINDOWTREEDATA, *PWALKWINDOWTREEDATA;


void WalkWindowTreeRecurse(PWALKWINDOWTREEDATA pWWT) {

   if (!IsWindow(pWWT->hwndParent))
      return;

   pWWT->nLevel++;
   const int nIndexAmount = 2;

   for (pWWT->iBuf = 0; pWWT->iBuf < pWWT->nLevel * nIndexAmount; pWWT->iBuf++)
      pWWT->szBuf[pWWT->iBuf] = TEXT(' ');

   CalcWndText(pWWT->hwndParent, &pWWT->szBuf[pWWT->iBuf],
      chDIMOF(pWWT->szBuf) - pWWT->iBuf);
   pWWT->nIndex = ListBox_AddString(pWWT->hwndLB, pWWT->szBuf);
   ListBox_SetItemData(pWWT->hwndLB, pWWT->nIndex, pWWT->hwndParent);

   HWND hwndChild = GetFirstChild(pWWT->hwndParent);
   while (hwndChild != NULL) {
      pWWT->hwndParent = hwndChild;
      WalkWindowTreeRecurse(pWWT);
      hwndChild = GetNextSibling(hwndChild);
   }

   pWWT->nLevel--;
}


///////////////////////////////////////////////////////////////////////////


void WalkWindowTree(HWND hwndLB, HWND hwndParent) {

   WALKWINDOWTREEDATA WWT;
```

(continued)

Figure 27-4. *continued*

```
    WWT.hwndLB = hwndLB;
    WWT.hwndParent = hwndParent;
    WWT.nLevel = -1;

    WalkWindowTreeRecurse(&WWT);
}


///////////////////////////////////////////////////////////////////////////////


BOOL Dlg_OnInitDialog(HWND hwnd, HWND hwndFocus, LPARAM lParam) {

    chSETDLGICONS(hwnd, IDI_LISLAB);

    // Associate the Up arrow cursor with the dialog box's client area
    SetClassLongPtr(hwnd, GCLP_HCURSOR,
        (LONG_PTR) LoadCursor(NULL, IDC_UPARROW));

    g_uTimerId = SetTimer(hwnd, g_uTimerId, TIMER_DELAY, NULL);

    HWND hwndT = GetDlgItem(hwnd, IDC_WNDFUNC);
    ComboBox_AddString(hwndT, TEXT("SetFocus"));
    ComboBox_AddString(hwndT, TEXT("SetActiveWindow"));
    ComboBox_AddString(hwndT, TEXT("SetForegroundWnd"));
    ComboBox_AddString(hwndT, TEXT("BringWindowToTop"));
    ComboBox_AddString(hwndT, TEXT("SetWindowPos-TOP"));
    ComboBox_AddString(hwndT, TEXT("SetWindowPos-BTM"));
    ComboBox_SetCurSel(hwndT, 0);

    // Fill the windows list box with our window
    hwndT = GetDlgItem(hwnd, IDC_WNDS);
    ListBox_AddString(hwndT, TEXT("---> This dialog box <---"));

    ListBox_SetItemData(hwndT, 0, hwnd);
    ListBox_SetCurSel(hwndT, 0);

    // Now add Notepad's windows
    g_hwndNotepad = FindWindow(TEXT("Notepad"), NULL);
    if (g_hwndNotepad == NULL) {

        // Notepad isn't running; run it.
        STARTUPINFO si = { sizeof(si) };
```

(continued)

Figure 27-4. *continued*

```
    PROCESS_INFORMATION pi;
    TCHAR szCommandLine[] = TEXT("Notepad");
    if (CreateProcess(NULL, szCommandLine, NULL, NULL, FALSE, 0,
        NULL, NULL, &si, &pi)) {

        // Wait for Notepad to create all its windows.
        WaitForInputIdle(pi.hProcess, INFINITE);
        CloseHandle(pi.hProcess);
        CloseHandle(pi.hThread);
        g_hwndNotepad = FindWindow(TEXT("Notepad"), NULL);
    }
}
WalkWindowTree(hwndT, g_hwndNotepad);

return(TRUE);
}


///////////////////////////////////////////////////////////////////////////


void Dlg_OnCommand(HWND hwnd, int id, HWND hwndCtl, UINT codeNotify) {

    HWND hwndT;

    switch (id) {

        case IDCANCEL:
            if (g_uTimerId != 0)
                KillTimer(hwnd, g_uTimerId);
            EndDialog(hwnd, 0);
            break;

        case IDC_FUNCSTART:
            g_dwEventTime = GetTickCount() + 1000 *
                GetDlgItemInt(hwnd, IDC_DELAY, NULL, FALSE);
            hwndT = GetDlgItem(hwnd, IDC_WNDS);
            g_hwndSubject = (HWND)
                ListBox_GetItemData(hwndT, ListBox_GetCurSel(hwndT));
            g_nEventId = ComboBox_GetCurSel(GetDlgItem(hwnd, IDC_WNDFUNC));
            SetWindowText(GetDlgItem(hwnd, IDC_EVENTPENDING), TEXT("Pending"));
            break;
```

(continued)

Figure 27-4. *continued*

```
      case IDC_THREADATTACH:
         AttachThreadInput(GetWindowThreadProcessId(g_hwndNotepad, NULL),
            GetCurrentThreadId(), TRUE);
         break;

      case IDC_THREADDETACH:
         AttachThreadInput(GetWindowThreadProcessId(g_hwndNotepad, NULL),
            GetCurrentThreadId(), FALSE);
         break;

      case IDC_REMOVECLIPRECT:
         ClipCursor(NULL);
         break;

      case IDC_HIDECURSOR:
         ShowCursor(FALSE);
         break;

      case IDC_SHOWCURSOR:
         ShowCursor(TRUE);
         break;

      case IDC_INFINITELOOP:
         SetCursor(LoadCursor(NULL, IDC_NO));
         for (;;)
            ;
         break;

      case IDC_SETCLIPRECT:
         RECT rc;
         SetRect(&rc, 0, 0, GetSystemMetrics(SM_CXSCREEN) / 2,
            GetSystemMetrics(SM_CYSCREEN) / 2);
         ClipCursor(&rc);
         break;
   }
}


///////////////////////////////////////////////////////////////////////////


void AddStr(HWND hwndLB, PCTSTR szBuf) {

   int nIndex;
```

(continued)

Figure 27-4. *continued*

```
  do {
     nIndex = ListBox_AddString(hwndLB, szBuf);
     if (nIndex == LB_ERR)
         ListBox_DeleteString(hwndLB, 0);
  } while (nIndex == LB_ERR);

  ListBox_SetCurSel(hwndLB, nIndex);
}


///////////////////////////////////////////////////////////////////////////


int Dlg_OnRButtonDown(HWND hwnd, BOOL fDoubleClick,
   int x, int y, UINT keyFlags) {

   TCHAR szBuf[100];
   wsprintf(szBuf,
      TEXT("Capture=%-3s, Msg=RButtonDown, DblClk=%-3s, x=%5d, y=%5d"),
      (GetCapture() == NULL) ? TEXT("No") : TEXT("Yes"),
      fDoubleClick ? TEXT("Yes") : TEXT("No"), x, y);

   AddStr(GetDlgItem(hwnd, IDC_MOUSEMSGS), szBuf);
   if (!fDoubleClick) SetCapture(hwnd);
   else ReleaseCapture();
   return(0);
}


///////////////////////////////////////////////////////////////////////////


int Dlg_OnRButtonUp(HWND hwnd, int x, int y, UINT keyFlags) {

   TCHAR szBuf[100];
   wsprintf(szBuf, TEXT("Capture=%-3s, Msg=RButtonUp,   x=%5d, y=%5d"),
      (GetCapture() == NULL) ? TEXT("No") : TEXT("Yes"), x, y);

   AddStr(GetDlgItem(hwnd, IDC_MOUSEMSGS), szBuf);
   return(0);
}


///////////////////////////////////////////////////////////////////////////
```

(continued)

971

Figure 27-4. *continued*

```
int Dlg_OnLButtonDown(HWND hwnd, BOOL fDoubleClick,
   int x, int y, UINT keyFlags) {

   TCHAR szBuf[100];
   wsprintf(szBuf,
      TEXT("Capture=%-3s, Msg=LButtonDown, DblClk=%-3s, x=%5d, y=%5d"),
      (GetCapture() == NULL) ? TEXT("No") : TEXT("Yes"),
      fDoubleClick ? TEXT("Yes") : TEXT("No"), x, y);

   AddStr(GetDlgItem(hwnd, IDC_MOUSEMSGS), szBuf);
   return(0);
}


/////////////////////////////////////////////////////////////////////////////


void Dlg_OnLButtonUp(HWND hwnd, int x, int y, UINT keyFlags) {

   TCHAR szBuf[100];
   wsprintf(szBuf,
      TEXT("Capture=%-3s, Msg=LButtonUp,   x=%5d, y=%5d"),
      (GetCapture() == NULL) ? TEXT("No") : TEXT("Yes"), x, y);

   AddStr(GetDlgItem(hwnd, IDC_MOUSEMSGS), szBuf);
}


/////////////////////////////////////////////////////////////////////////////


void Dlg_OnMouseMove(HWND hwnd, int x, int y, UINT keyFlags) {

   TCHAR szBuf[100];
   wsprintf(szBuf, TEXT("Capture=%-3s, Msg=MouseMove,   x=%5d, y=%5d"),
      (GetCapture() == NULL) ? TEXT("No") : TEXT("Yes"), x, y);

   AddStr(GetDlgItem(hwnd, IDC_MOUSEMSGS), szBuf);
}


/////////////////////////////////////////////////////////////////////////////
```

(continued)

Figure 27-4. *continued*

```
void Dlg_OnTimer(HWND hwnd, UINT id) {

   TCHAR szBuf[100];

   CalcWndText(GetFocus(), szBuf, chDIMOF(szBuf));
   SetWindowText(GetDlgItem(hwnd, IDC_WNDFOCUS), szBuf);

   CalcWndText(GetCapture(), szBuf, chDIMOF(szBuf));
   SetWindowText(GetDlgItem(hwnd, IDC_WNDCAPTURE), szBuf);

   CalcWndText(GetActiveWindow(), szBuf, chDIMOF(szBuf));
   SetWindowText(GetDlgItem(hwnd, IDC_WNDACTIVE), szBuf);

   CalcWndText(GetForegroundWindow(), szBuf, chDIMOF(szBuf));
   SetWindowText(GetDlgItem(hwnd, IDC_WNDFOREGROUND), szBuf);

   RECT rc;
   GetClipCursor(&rc);
   wsprintf(szBuf, TEXT("left=%d, top=%d, right=%d, bottom=%d"),
      rc.left, rc.top, rc.right, rc.bottom);
   SetWindowText(GetDlgItem(hwnd, IDC_CLIPCURSOR), szBuf);


   if ((g_dwEventTime == 0) || (GetTickCount() < g_dwEventTime))
      return;

   HWND hwndT;
   switch (g_nEventId) {
      case 0:  // SetFocus
         g_hwndSubject = SetFocus(g_hwndSubject);
         break;

      case 1:  // SetActiveWindow
         g_hwndSubject = SetActiveWindow(g_hwndSubject);
         break;

      case 2:  // SetForegroundWindow
         hwndT = GetForegroundWindow();
         SetForegroundWindow(g_hwndSubject);
         g_hwndSubject = hwndT;
         break;
```

(continued)

Figure 27-4. *continued*

```
        case 3:  // BringWindowToTop
          BringWindowToTop(g_hwndSubject);
          break;

        case 4:  // SetWindowPos w/HWND_TOP
          SetWindowPos(g_hwndSubject, HWND_TOP, 0, 0, 0, 0,
            SWP_NOMOVE | SWP_NOSIZE);
          g_hwndSubject = (HWND) 1;
          break;

        case 5:  // SetWindowPos w/HWND_BOTTOM
          SetWindowPos(g_hwndSubject, HWND_BOTTOM, 0, 0, 0, 0,
            SWP_NOMOVE | SWP_NOSIZE);
          g_hwndSubject = (HWND) 1;
          break;
     }

  if (g_hwndSubject == (HWND) 1) {
     SetWindowText(GetDlgItem(hwnd, IDC_PREVWND), TEXT("Can't tell."));
  } else {
     CalcWndText(g_hwndSubject, szBuf, chDIMOF(szBuf));
     SetWindowText(GetDlgItem(hwnd, IDC_PREVWND), szBuf);
  }

  g_hwndSubject = NULL; g_nEventId = 0; g_dwEventTime = 0;
  SetWindowText(GetDlgItem(hwnd, IDC_EVENTPENDING), TEXT("Executed"));
}


///////////////////////////////////////////////////////////////////////////


INT_PTR WINAPI Dlg_Proc(HWND hwnd, UINT uMsg, WPARAM wParam, LPARAM lParam) {

  switch (uMsg) {
     chHANDLE_DLGMSG(hwnd, WM_INITDIALOG,     Dlg_OnInitDialog);
     chHANDLE_DLGMSG(hwnd, WM_COMMAND,        Dlg_OnCommand);

     chHANDLE_DLGMSG(hwnd, WM_MOUSEMOVE,      Dlg_OnMouseMove);

     chHANDLE_DLGMSG(hwnd, WM_LBUTTONDOWN,    Dlg_OnLButtonDown);
     chHANDLE_DLGMSG(hwnd, WM_LBUTTONDBLCLK,  Dlg_OnLButtonDown);
     chHANDLE_DLGMSG(hwnd, WM_LBUTTONUP,      Dlg_OnLButtonUp);
```

(continued)

Figure 27-4. *continued*

```
      chHANDLE_DLGMSG(hwnd, WM_RBUTTONDOWN,    Dlg_OnRButtonDown);
      chHANDLE_DLGMSG(hwnd, WM_RBUTTONDBLCLK, Dlg_OnRButtonDown);
      chHANDLE_DLGMSG(hwnd, WM_RBUTTONUP,      Dlg_OnRButtonUp);

      chHANDLE_DLGMSG(hwnd, WM_TIMER,          Dlg_OnTimer);
   }
   return(FALSE);
}


///////////////////////////////////////////////////////////////////////////////


int WINAPI _tWinMain(HINSTANCE hinstExe, HINSTANCE, PTSTR pszCmdLine, int) {

   DialogBox(hinstExe, MAKEINTRESOURCE(IDD_LISLAB), NULL, Dlg_Proc);
   return(0);
}


//////////////////////////////// End of File //////////////////////////////////
```

LISLab.rc

```
//Microsoft Developer Studio generated-resource script.
//
#include "Resource.h"

#define APSTUDIO_READONLY_SYMBOLS
/////////////////////////////////////////////////////////////////////////////
//
// Generated from the TEXTINCLUDE 2 resource.
//
#include "afxres.h"


/////////////////////////////////////////////////////////////////////////////
#undef APSTUDIO_READONLY_SYMBOLS

/////////////////////////////////////////////////////////////////////////////
// English (U.S.) resources
```

(continued)

975

Figure 27-4. *continued*

```
#if !defined(AFX_RESOURCE_DLL) || defined(AFX_TARG_ENU)
#ifdef _WIN32
LANGUAGE LANG_ENGLISH, SUBLANG_ENGLISH_US
#pragma code_page(1252)
#endif //_WIN32


/////////////////////////////////////////////////////////////////////////////
//
// Icon
//

// Icon with lowest ID value placed first to ensure application icon
// remains consistent on all systems.
IDI_LISLAB              ICON    DISCARDABLE     "LISLab.Ico"


/////////////////////////////////////////////////////////////////////////////
//
// Dialog
//

IDD_LISLAB DIALOG DISCARDABLE  12, 38, 286, 178
STYLE WS_MINIMIZEBOX | WS_VISIBLE | WS_CAPTION | WS_SYSMENU
CAPTION "Local Input State Lab"
FONT 8, "MS Sans Serif"
BEGIN
    GROUPBOX        "Windows",IDC_STATIC,4,0,192,56
    LTEXT           "Focus:",IDC_STATIC,8,12,23,8
    LTEXT           "Focus window info",IDC_WNDFOCUS,52,12,140,8
    LTEXT           "Active:",IDC_STATIC,8,20,24,8
    LTEXT           "Active window info",IDC_WNDACTIVE,52,20,140,8
    LTEXT           "Foreground:",IDC_STATIC,8,28,40,8
    LTEXT           "Foreground window info",IDC_WNDFOREGROUND,52,28,140,8
    LTEXT           "Capture:",IDC_STATIC,8,36,29,8
    LTEXT           "Capture window info",IDC_WNDCAPTURE,52,36,140,8
    LTEXT           "Clip Cursor:",IDC_STATIC,8,44,39,8
    LTEXT           "Cursor clipping info",IDC_CLIPCURSOR,52,44,140,8
    LTEXT           "&Function:",IDC_STATIC,200,4,32,8
    COMBOBOX        IDC_WNDFUNC,200,14,82,54,CBS_DROPDOWNLIST | WS_VSCROLL |
                    WS_TABSTOP
    PUSHBUTTON      "Dela&y:",IDC_FUNCSTART,200,30,26,14
    EDITTEXT        IDC_DELAY,228,30,24,12,ES_AUTOHSCROLL
    LTEXT           "Executed",IDC_EVENTPENDING,252,30,32,10
    LTEXT           "PrevWnd:",IDC_STATIC,200,46,34,8
    LTEXT           "Previous window info",IDC_PREVWND,208,54,76,18
```

(continued)

Figure 27-4. *continued*

```
     LTEXT           "&Notepad windows and Self:",IDC_STATIC,4,62,90,8
     LISTBOX         IDC_WNDS,4,72,192,32,WS_VSCROLL | WS_TABSTOP
     PUSHBUTTON      "&Attach to Notepad",IDC_THREADATTACH,200,72,80,12
     PUSHBUTTON      "&Detach from Notepad",IDC_THREADDETACH,200,88,80,12
     LTEXT           "&Mouse messages received:",IDC_STATIC,4,102,89,8
     LISTBOX         IDC_MOUSEMSGS,4,112,192,32,WS_VSCROLL | WS_TABSTOP
     LTEXT           "Click right mouse button to set capture.\n\nDouble-click
right mouse button to release capture.",
                     IDC_STATIC,200,110,80,40
     LTEXT           "Clipping rect:",IDC_STATIC,4,148,44,8
     PUSHBUTTON      "&Top, left",IDC_SETCLIPRECT,52,146,56,14
     PUSHBUTTON      "&Remove",IDC_REMOVECLIPRECT,112,146,56,12
     LTEXT           "Cursor visibility:",IDC_STATIC,4,164,47,8
     PUSHBUTTON      "&Hide",IDC_HIDECURSOR,52,162,56,12
     PUSHBUTTON      "&Show",IDC_SHOWCURSOR,112,162,56,12
     PUSHBUTTON      "&Infinite loop",IDC_INFINITELOOP,200,162,80,12,WS_GROUP |
                     NOT WS_TABSTOP
END


#ifdef APSTUDIO_INVOKED
/////////////////////////////////////////////////////////////////////////////
//
// TEXTINCLUDE
//

1 TEXTINCLUDE DISCARDABLE
BEGIN
    "Resource.h\0"
END

2 TEXTINCLUDE DISCARDABLE
BEGIN
    "#include ""afxres.h""\r\n"
    "\0"
END

3 TEXTINCLUDE DISCARDABLE
BEGIN
    "\r\n"
    "\0"
END

#endif    // APSTUDIO_INVOKED
```

(continued)

977

```
//////////////////////////////////////////////////////////////////////////////
//
// DESIGNINFO
//

#ifdef APSTUDIO_INVOKED
GUIDELINES DESIGNINFO DISCARDABLE
BEGIN
    IDD_LISLAB, DIALOG
    BEGIN
        RIGHTMARGIN, 283
        BOTTOMMARGIN, 170
    END
END
#endif    // APSTUDIO_INVOKED

#endif    // English (U.S.) resources
//////////////////////////////////////////////////////////////////////////////
```

```
#ifndef APSTUDIO_INVOKED
//////////////////////////////////////////////////////////////////////////////
//
// Generated from the TEXTINCLUDE 3 resource.
//


//////////////////////////////////////////////////////////////////////////////
#endif    // not APSTUDIO_INVOKED
```

The Local Input State Watch (LISWatch) Sample Application

The LISWatch application ("27 LISWatch.exe"), listed in Figure 27-5 beginning on page 981, is a useful utility that monitors the active window, the focus window, and the mouse capture window. The source code and resource files for the application are in the 27-LISWatch directory on the companion CD-ROM.

When you run LISWatch, it displays the dialog box shown here.

```
LISWatch                                          _ □ ×
Thread:   System-wide              HELP: Click right mouse button
Focus:    [Static] Thread:
Active:   [#32770] LISWatch
Capture:  [no window]
Foregrnd: [#32770] LISWatch
```

When this dialog box receives a WM_INITDIALOG message, it calls *Set-Timer* to set a timer that fires twice every second. When the WM_TIMER message is received, the contents of the dialog box update to reflect which window is active, which window has focus, and which window has captured the mouse. At the bottom of the dialog box, you also see which window is the foreground window. You can experiment with this utility by simply clicking on windows created by different applications. As you move around, you'll notice that LISWatch is able to accurately report the proper window information regardless of which thread has created the various windows.

The interesting part of the utility executes when a WM_TIMER message is received, so you might want to refer to the *Dlg_OnTimer* function as I go through this explanation. Also, assume for now that the global variable, *g_dwThreadIdAttachTo*, is set to zero. I'll explain the purpose of this variable later.

Since each thread has its own local input state, *Dlg_OnTimer* first calls *GetForegroundWindow* to determine which window the user is interacting with. Note that *GetForegroundWindow* always returns a valid window handle regardless of which thread in the system created this window or calls this function.

This returned window handle is then passed to *GetWindowThreadProcessId* to determine which thread is connected to the RIT. Now, LISWatch attaches its own thread's local input state to the local input state of the thread connected to the RIT by calling *AttachThreadInput*. After the local input states are attached, LISWatch's thread can call *GetFocus*, *GetActiveWindow*, and *GetCapture*—all of which return valid window handles. The helper function, *CalcWndText*, constructs a string containing each window's class name and window text. Each window's string is then updated in LISWatch's dialog box. Finally, just before *Dlg_OnTimer* returns, it again calls *AttachThreadInput* but this time passes FALSE for the last parameter so that the two threads' local input states are detached from one another.

This explains the basics of LISWatch. However, I have added another feature to LISWatch that I'd like to explain now. When you start LISWatch, it monitors window activation changes that occur anywhere in the system. This is what the "System-wide" means at the top of the dialog box. However, LISWatch also allows you to restrict it to watching a single thread's local input state changes. With this feature enabled, LISWatch is able to report to you exactly what a single thread sees as its local input state.

To have LISWatch monitor a single thread's local input state, all you have to do is click the left mouse button on LISWatch's window, drag the mouse cursor over a window created by another thread, and then release the mouse button. After you release the mouse button, LISWatch sets the global *g_dwThreadIdAttachTo* variable to the ID of the selected thread. This thread ID will replace "System-wide" at the top of LISWatch's dialog box. When this global variable is not zero, *Dlg_OnTimer* alters its behavior slightly. Instead of always attaching its local input state to that of the foreground thread, LISWatch attaches itself to the selected thread. This way, its calls to *GetActive-Window*, *GetFocus*, and *GetCapture* all reflect what the selected thread's local input state sees.

Let's try an experiment. Run Calculator, and use LISWatch to select its window. When you activate Calculator's window, LISWatch updates its display as shown here.

For me, Calculator's thread ID is 0x000004ec. LISWatch is currently set up to monitor this one thread's local input state changes. If I click on any of Calculator's radio buttons or check boxes, LISWatch can show you these focus changes because all of these windows were created by thread 0x000004ec.

However, if you now activate a window created by another application (Notepad in my example), LISWatch looks like this.

Here LISWatch is reporting that Calculator thread's local input state is reporting that no window in the system has focus, no window is active, and no window has captured the mouse.

To really understand exactly how all this local input state stuff works, you should run multiple instances of LISWatch and set up all the instances so that they are monitoring the local input states of different threads. Then start clicking on various windows to see what each thread's local input state reflects.

LISWatch.cpp

```
/*****************************************************************************
Module:  LISWatch.cpp
Notices: Copyright (c) 2000 Jeffrey Richter
*****************************************************************************/


#include "..\CmnHdr.h"      /* See Appendix A. */
#include <tchar.h>
#include <windowsx.h>
#include "Resource.h"


///////////////////////////////////////////////////////////////////////////


#define TIMER_DELAY (500)         // Half a second

UINT_PTR g_uTimerId = 1;
DWORD g_dwThreadIdAttachTo = 0;   // 0=System-wide; Non-zero=specifc thread


///////////////////////////////////////////////////////////////////////////


BOOL Dlg_OnInitDialog(HWND hwnd, HWND hwndFocus, LPARAM lParam) {

   chSETDLGICONS(hwnd, IDI_LISWATCH);

   // Update our contents periodically
   g_uTimerId = SetTimer(hwnd, g_uTimerId, TIMER_DELAY, NULL);

   // Make our window on top of all others
   SetWindowPos(hwnd, HWND_TOPMOST, 0, 0, 0, 0, SWP_NOMOVE | SWP_NOSIZE);
   return(TRUE);
}


///////////////////////////////////////////////////////////////////////////


void Dlg_OnRButtonDown(HWND hwnd, BOOL fDoubleClick, int x, int y,
   UINT keyFlags) {
```

Figure 27-5. (continued)
The LISWatch sample application

Figure 27-5. *continued*

```
    chMB("To monitor a specific thread, click the left mouse button in "
        "the main window and release it in the desired window.\n"
        "To monitor all threads, double-click the left mouse button in "
        "the main window.");
}


///////////////////////////////////////////////////////////////////////////////


void Dlg_OnLButtonDown(HWND hwnd, BOOL fDoubleClick, int x, int y,
    UINT keyFlags) {

    // If we're attached to a thread, detach from it
    if (g_dwThreadIdAttachTo != 0)
        AttachThreadInput(GetCurrentThreadId(), g_dwThreadIdAttachTo, FALSE);

    // Set capture to ourself and change the mouse cursor
    SetCapture(hwnd);
    SetCursor(LoadCursor(GetModuleHandle(NULL), MAKEINTRESOURCE(IDC_EYES)));
}


///////////////////////////////////////////////////////////////////////////////


void Dlg_OnLButtonUp(HWND hwnd, int x, int y, UINT keyFlags) {

    if (GetCapture() == hwnd) {

        // If we had mouse capture set, get the ID of the thread that
        // created the window that is under the mouse cursor.
        POINT pt;
        pt.x = LOWORD(GetMessagePos());
        pt.y = HIWORD(GetMessagePos());
        ReleaseCapture();
        g_dwThreadIdAttachTo = GetWindowThreadProcessId(
            ChildWindowFromPointEx(GetDesktopWindow(), pt, CWP_SKIPINVISIBLE),
            NULL);

        if (g_dwThreadIdAttachTo == GetCurrentThreadId()) {
```

(continued)

Figure 27-5. *continued*

```
            // The mouse button is released on one of our windows;
            // monitor local-input state on a system-wide basis.
            g_dwThreadIdAttachTo = 0;

        } else {

            // The mouse button is released on a window that our thread didn't
            // create; monitor local input state for that thread only.
            AttachThreadInput(GetCurrentThreadId(), g_dwThreadIdAttachTo, TRUE);
        }
    }
}


///////////////////////////////////////////////////////////////////////////////


static void CalcWndText(HWND hwnd, PTSTR szBuf, int nLen) {

    if (hwnd == (HWND) NULL) {
        lstrcpy(szBuf, TEXT("(no window)"));
        return;
    }

    if (!IsWindow(hwnd)) {
        lstrcpy(szBuf, TEXT("(invalid window)"));
        return;
    }

    TCHAR szClass[50], szCaption[50], szBufT[150];
    GetClassName(hwnd, szClass, chDIMOF(szClass));
    GetWindowText(hwnd, szCaption, chDIMOF(szCaption));
    wsprintf(szBufT, TEXT("[%s] %s"), (PTSTR) szClass,
        (szCaption[0] == 0) ? (PTSTR) TEXT("(no caption)") : (PTSTR) szCaption);
    _tcsncpy(szBuf, szBufT, nLen - 1);
    szBuf[nLen - 1] = 0; // Force zero-terminated string
}


/////////////////////////////////////////////////////////////////////


void Dlg_OnTimer(HWND hwnd, UINT id) {
```

(continued)

Figure 27-5. *continued*

```
    TCHAR szBuf[100] = TEXT("System-wide");
    HWND hwndForeground = GetForegroundWindow();
    DWORD dwThreadIdAttachTo = g_dwThreadIdAttachTo;

    if (dwThreadIdAttachTo == 0) {

        // If monitoring local input state system-wide, attach our input
        // state to the thread that created the current foreground window.
        dwThreadIdAttachTo =
            GetWindowThreadProcessId(hwndForeground, NULL);
        AttachThreadInput(GetCurrentThreadId(), dwThreadIdAttachTo, TRUE);

    } else {

        wsprintf(szBuf, TEXT("0x%08x"), dwThreadIdAttachTo);
    }

    SetWindowText(GetDlgItem(hwnd, IDC_THREADID), szBuf);

    CalcWndText(GetFocus(), szBuf, chDIMOF(szBuf));
    SetWindowText(GetDlgItem(hwnd, IDC_WNDFOCUS), szBuf);

    CalcWndText(GetActiveWindow(), szBuf, chDIMOF(szBuf));
    SetWindowText(GetDlgItem(hwnd, IDC_WNDACTIVE), szBuf);

    CalcWndText(GetCapture(), szBuf, chDIMOF(szBuf));
    SetWindowText(GetDlgItem(hwnd, IDC_WNDCAPTURE), szBuf);

    CalcWndText(hwndForeground, szBuf, chDIMOF(szBuf));
    SetWindowText(GetDlgItem(hwnd, IDC_WNDFOREGRND), szBuf);

    if (g_dwThreadIdAttachTo == 0) {
        // If monitoring local input state system-wide, detach our input
        // state from the thread that created the current foreground window.
        AttachThreadInput(GetCurrentThreadId(), dwThreadIdAttachTo, FALSE);
    }
}


////////////////////////////////////////////////////////////////////////////


void Dlg_OnCommand(HWND hwnd, int id, HWND hwndCtl, UINT codeNotify) {

    switch (id) {
        case IDCANCEL:
```

(continued)

Figure 27-5. *continued*

```
        EndDialog(hwnd, id);
        break;
    }
}


//////////////////////////////////////////////////////////////////////////


INT_PTR WINAPI Dlg_Proc(HWND hwnd, UINT uMsg, WPARAM wParam, LPARAM lParam) {

   switch (uMsg) {
       chHANDLE_DLGMSG(hwnd, WM_INITDIALOG,  Dlg_OnInitDialog);
       chHANDLE_DLGMSG(hwnd, WM_COMMAND,     Dlg_OnCommand);
       chHANDLE_DLGMSG(hwnd, WM_TIMER,       Dlg_OnTimer);
       chHANDLE_DLGMSG(hwnd, WM_RBUTTONDOWN, Dlg_OnRButtonDown);
       chHANDLE_DLGMSG(hwnd, WM_LBUTTONDOWN, Dlg_OnLButtonDown);
       chHANDLE_DLGMSG(hwnd, WM_LBUTTONUP,   Dlg_OnLButtonUp);
   }
   return(FALSE);
}


//////////////////////////////////////////////////////////////////////////


int WINAPI _tWinMain(HINSTANCE hinstExe, HINSTANCE, PTSTR pszCmdLine, int) {

   DialogBox(hinstExe, MAKEINTRESOURCE(IDD_LISWATCH), NULL, Dlg_Proc);
   return(0);
}


///////////////////////////////// End of File ///////////////////////////////
```

LISWatch.rc

```
//Microsoft Developer Studio generated resource script.
//
#include "resource.h"

#define APSTUDIO_READONLY_SYMBOLS
```

(continued)

Figure 27-5. *continued*

```
/////////////////////////////////////////////////////////////////////////////
//
// Generated from the TEXTINCLUDE 2 resource.
//
#include "afxres.h"


/////////////////////////////////////////////////////////////////////////////
#undef APSTUDIO_READONLY_SYMBOLS


/////////////////////////////////////////////////////////////////////////////
// English (U.S.) resources

#if !defined(AFX_RESOURCE_DLL) || defined(AFX_TARG_ENU)
#ifdef _WIN32
LANGUAGE LANG_ENGLISH, SUBLANG_ENGLISH_US
#pragma code_page(1252)
#endif //_WIN32

#ifdef APSTUDIO_INVOKED
/////////////////////////////////////////////////////////////////////////////
//
// TEXTINCLUDE
//

1 TEXTINCLUDE DISCARDABLE
BEGIN
    "resource.h\0"
END

2 TEXTINCLUDE DISCARDABLE
BEGIN
    "#include ""afxres.h""\r\n"
    "\0"
END

3 TEXTINCLUDE DISCARDABLE
BEGIN
    "\r\n"
    "\0"
END

#endif    // APSTUDIO_INVOKED
```

(continued)

Figure 27-5. *continued*

```
///////////////////////////////////////////////////////////////////////////
//
// Dialog
//

IDD_LISWATCH DIALOG DISCARDABLE  32768, 5, 240, 41
STYLE WS_MINIMIZEBOX | WS_VISIBLE | WS_CAPTION | WS_SYSMENU
CAPTION "LISWatch"
FONT 8, "MS Sans Serif"
BEGIN
    LTEXT           "Thread:",IDC_STATIC,4,0,31,8
    LTEXT           "ThreadId",IDC_THREADID,36,0,100,8
    LTEXT           "Focus:",IDC_STATIC,4,8,31,8
    LTEXT           "Focus window",IDC_WNDFOCUS,36,8,204,8
    LTEXT           "Active:",IDC_STATIC,4,16,31,8
    LTEXT           "Active window",IDC_WNDACTIVE,36,16,204,8
    LTEXT           "Capture:",IDC_STATIC,4,24,31,8
    LTEXT           "Capture window",IDC_WNDCAPTURE,36,24,204,8
    LTEXT           "Foregrnd:",IDC_STATIC,4,32,31,8
    LTEXT           "Foreground window",IDC_WNDFOREGRND,36,32,204,8
    LTEXT           "HELP: Click right mouse button",IDC_STATIC,140,0,99,8
END


///////////////////////////////////////////////////////////////////////////
//
// Icon
//

// Icon with lowest ID value placed first to ensure application icon
// remains consistent on all systems.
IDI_LISWATCH            ICON    DISCARDABLE     "LISWatch.ico"


///////////////////////////////////////////////////////////////////////////
//
// Cursor
//

IDC_EYES                CURSOR  DISCARDABLE     "Eyes.cur"


///////////////////////////////////////////////////////////////////////////
//
// DESIGNINFO
//
```

(continued)

987

Figure 27-5. *continued*

```
#ifdef APSTUDIO_INVOKED
GUIDELINES DESIGNINFO DISCARDABLE
BEGIN
    IDD_LISWATCH, DIALOG
    BEGIN
        RIGHTMARGIN, 190
        BOTTOMMARGIN, 10
    END
END
#endif     // APSTUDIO_INVOKED


#endif     // English (U.S.) resources
/////////////////////////////////////////////////////////////////////////////


#ifndef APSTUDIO_INVOKED
/////////////////////////////////////////////////////////////////////////////
//
// Generated from the TEXTINCLUDE 3 resource.
//


/////////////////////////////////////////////////////////////////////////////
#endif     // not APSTUDIO_INVOKED
```

A P P E N D I X   A

THE BUILD ENVIRONMENT

To build the sample applications in this book, you must deal with compiler and linker switch settings. I have tried to isolate these details from the sample applications by putting almost all of these settings in a single header file, called CmnHdr.h, which is included in all of the sample application source code files.

Since I wasn't able to put all of the settings in this header file, I made some changes to each sample application's project settings. For each project, I displayed the Project Settings dialog box and then made the following changes:

- On the General tab, I set the Output Files directory so that all final .exe and .dll files go to a single directory.

- On the C/C++ tab, I selected the Code Generation category and selected Multithreaded DLL for the Use Run-Time Library field.

That's it. These are the only two settings that I explicitly changed; I accepted the default settings for everything else. Note that I made the two changes above for both the Debug and Release builds of each project. I was able to set all other compiler and linker settings in the source code, so these settings will be in effect if you use any of my source code modules in your projects.

The CmnHdr.h Header File

All of the sample programs include the CmnHdr.h header file before any other header file. I wrote CmnHdr.h, which is listed in Figure A-1 beginning on page 997, to make my life a little easier. The file contains macros, linker directives, and other code that is common across all the applications. When I want to try something, all I do is modify CmnHdr.h and rebuild all the sample applications. CmnHdr.h is in the root directory on the companion CD-ROM.

The remainder of this appendix discusses each section of the CmnHdr.h header file. I'll explain the rationale for each section and describe how and why you might want to make changes before rebuilding all the sample applications.

Windows Version Build Option

Because some of the sample applications call functions that are new in Microsoft Windows 2000, this section of CmnHdr.h defines the _WIN32_WINNT symbol as follows:

```
#define _WIN32_WINNT 0x0500
```

I have to do this because the new Windows 2000 functions are prototyped in the Windows header files like this:

```
#if (_WIN32_WINNT >= 0x0500)
⋮

WINBASEAPI
BOOL
WINAPI
AssignProcessToJobObject(
    IN HANDLE hJob,
    IN HANDLE hProcess
    );
⋮

#endif /* _WIN32_WINNT >= 0x0500 */
```

Unless you specifically define _WIN32_WINNT as I have (before including Windows.h), the prototypes for the new functions will not be declared and the compiler will generate errors if you attempt to call these functions. Microsoft has protected these functions with the _WIN32_WINNT symbol to help ensure that applications you develop can run on multiple versions of Microsoft Windows NT and Windows 98.

Unicode Build Option

I wrote all the sample applications so that they can be compiled as either ANSI or Unicode. When you compile the applications for the *x*86 CPU architecture, ANSI is the default so that the applications will execute on Windows 98. However, Unicode is used when you build the applications for any other CPU architecture so the applications will use less memory and execute faster.

To create Unicode versions for the *x*86 architecture, you simply uncomment the single line that defines UNICODE and rebuild. By defining the UNICODE macro in CmnHdr.h, you can easily control how you build the sample applications. For more information on Unicode, see Chapter 2.

Windows Definitions and Warning Level 4

When I develop software, I always try to ensure that the code compiles free of errors and warnings. I also like to compile at the highest possible warning level so that the compiler does the most work for me and examines even the most minute details of my code. For the Microsoft C/C++ compilers, this means that I built all the sample applications using warning level 4.

Unfortunately, Microsoft's operating systems group doesn't share my sentiments about compiling using warning level 4. As a result, when I set the sample applications to compile at warning level 4, many lines in the Windows header files cause the compiler to generate warnings. Fortunately, these warnings do not represent problems in the code. Most are generated by unconventional uses of the C language that rely on compiler extensions that almost all vendors of Windows-compatible compilers implement.

In this section of CmnHdr.h, I make sure that the warning level is set to 3 and that CmnHdr.h includes the standard Windows.h header file. Once Windows.h is included, I set the warning level to 4 when I compile the rest of the code. At warning level 4, the compiler emits "warnings" for things that I don't consider problems, so I explicitly tell the compiler to ignore certain benign warnings by using the *#pragma warning* directive.

The Pragma Message Helper Macro

When I work on code, I often like to get something working immediately and then make it bulletproof later. To remind myself that some code needs additional attention, I used to include a line like this:

```
#pragma message("Fix this later")
```

When the compiler compiled this line, it would output a string reminding me that I had some more work to do. This message was not that helpful, however. I decided to find a way for the compiler to output the name of the source code file and the line number that the *pragma* appears on. Not only would I know that I had additional work to do, but I could also locate the surrounding code immediately.

To get this behavior, you have to trick the *pragma message* directive using a series of macros. The result is that you can use the chMSG macro like this:

```
#pragma chMSG(Fix this later)
```

When the line above is compiled, the compiler produces a line that looks like this:

```
C:\CD\CmnHdr.h(82):Fix this later
```

Now, using Microsoft Visual Developer Studio, you can double-click on this line in the output window and be automatically positioned at the correct place in the correct file.

As a convenience, the chMSG macro does not require quotes to be used around the text string.

The chINRANGE and chDIMOF Macros

I frequently use these two handy macros in my applications. The first one, chINRANGE, checks to see whether a value is between two other values. The second macro, chDIMOF, simply returns the number of elements in an array. It does this by using the *sizeof* operator to first calculate the size of the entire array in bytes. It then divides this number by the number of bytes required for a single entry in the array.

The chBEGINTHREADEX Macro

All the multithreaded samples in this book use the *_beginthreadex* function, which is in Microsoft's C/C++ run-time library, instead of the operating system's *CreateThread* function. I use this function because the *_beginthreadex* function prepares the new thread so that it can use the C/C++ run-time library functions and because it ensures that the per-thread C/C++ run-time library information is destroyed when the thread returns. (See Chapter 6 for more details.) Unfortunately, the *_beginthreadex* function is prototyped as follows:

```
unsigned long __cdecl _beginthreadex(
    void *,
    unsigned,
    unsigned (__stdcall *)(void *),
    void *,
    unsigned,
    unsigned *);
```

Although the parameter values for *_beginthreadex* are identical to the parameter values for the *CreateThread* function, the parameters' data types do not match. Here is the prototype for the *CreateThread* function:

```
typedef DWORD (WINAPI *PTHREAD_START_ROUTINE)(PVOID pvParam);

HANDLE CreateThread(
    PSECURITY_ATTRIBUTES psa,
    DWORD cbStack,
    PTHREAD_START_ROUTINE pfnStartAddr,
    PVOID pvParam,
    DWORD fdwCreate,
    PDWORD pdwThreadId);
```

Microsoft did not use the Windows data types when creating the _beginthreadex_ function's prototype because Microsoft's C/C++ run-time group does not want to have any dependencies on the operating system group. I commend this decision; however, this makes using the _beginthreadex_ function more difficult.

There are really two problems with the way Microsoft prototyped the _beginthreadex_ function. First, some of the data types used for the function do not match the primitive types used by the _CreateThread_ function. For example, the Windows data type DWORD is defined as follows:

```
typedef unsigned long DWORD;
```

This data type is used for _CreateThread_'s _cbStack_ parameter as well as for its _fdwCreate_ parameter. The problem is that _beginthreadex_ prototypes these two parameters as _unsigned_, which really means _unsigned int_. The compiler considers an _unsigned int_ to be different from an _unsigned long_ and generates a warning. Because the _beginthreadex_ function is not a part of the standard C/C++ run-time library and exists only as an alternative to calling the _CreateThread_ function, I believe that Microsoft should have prototyped _beginthreadex_ this way so that warnings are not generated:

```
unsigned long __cdecl _beginthreadex(
    void *psa,
    unsigned long cbStack,
    unsigned (__stdcall *) (void *pvParam),
    void *pvParam,
    unsigned long fdwCreate,
    unsigned long *pdwThreadId);
```

The second problem is just a small variation of the first. The _beginthreadex_ function returns an _unsigned long_ representing the handle of the newly created thread. An application typically wants to store this return value in a data variable of type HANDLE as follows:

```
HANDLE hThread = _beginthreadex(...);
```

993

The code above causes the compiler to generate another warning. To avoid the compiler warning, you must rewrite the line above, introducing a cast as follows:

```
HANDLE hThread = (HANDLE) _beginthreadex(...);
```

Again, this is inconvenient. To make life a little easier, I defined a chBEGIN-THREADEX macro in CmnHdr.h to perform all of this casting for me:

```
typedef unsigned (__stdcall *PTHREAD_START) (void *);

#define chBEGINTHREADEX(psa, cbStack, pfnStartAddr, \
    pvParam, fdwCreate, pdwThreadId)                \
        ((HANDLE)_beginthreadex(                    \
            (void *)        (psa),                  \
            (unsigned)      (cbStack),              \
            (PTHREAD_START) (pfnStartAddr),         \
            (void *)        (pvParam),              \
            (unsigned)      (fdwCreate),            \
            (unsigned *)    (pdwThreadId)))
```

DebugBreak Improvement for *x86* Platforms

I sometimes want to force a breakpoint in my code even if the process is not running under a debugger. You can do this in Windows by having a thread call the *DebugBreak* function. This function, which resides in Kernel32.dll, lets you attach a debugger to the process. Once the debugger is attached, the instruction pointer is positioned on the CPU instruction that caused the breakpoint. This instruction is contained in the *DebugBreak* function in Kernel32.dll, so to see my source code I must single-step out of the *DebugBreak* function.

On the *x86* architecture, you perform a breakpoint by executing an "int 3" CPU instruction. So, on *x86* platforms, I redefine *DebugBreak* as this inline assembly language instruction. When my *DebugBreak* is executed, I do not call into Kernel32.dll; the breakpoint occurs right in my code and the instruction pointer is positioned to the next C/C++ language statement. This just makes things a little more convenient.

Creating Software Exception Codes

When you work with software exceptions, you must create your own 32-bit exception codes. These codes follow a specific format (discussed in Chapter 24). To make creating these codes easier, I use the MAKESOFTWAREEXCEPTION macro.

The chMB Macro

The chMB macro simply displays a message box. The caption is the full pathname of the executable file for the calling process.

The chASSERT and chVERIFY Macros

To find potential problems as I developed the sample applications, I sprinkled chASSERT macros throughout the code. This macro tests whether the expression identified by x is TRUE and, if it isn't, displays a message box indicating the file, line, and the expression that failed. In release builds of the applications, this macro expands to nothing. The chVERIFY macro is almost identical to the chASSERT macro except that the expression is evaluated in release builds as well as in debug builds.

The chHANDLE_DLGMSG Macro

When you use message crackers with dialog boxes, you should not use the HANDLE_MSG macro from Microsoft's WindowsX.h header file because it doesn't return TRUE or FALSE to indicate whether a message was handled by the dialog box procedure. My chHANDLE_DLGMSG macro massages the window message's return value and handles it properly for use in a dialog box procedure.

The chSETDLGICONS Macro

Because most of the sample applications use a dialog box as their main window, you must change the dialog box icon manually so that it is displayed correctly on the Taskbar, in the task switch window, and in the application's caption itself. The chSETDLGICONS macro is always called when dialog boxes receive a WM_INITDIALOG message so that the icons are set correctly.

The OS Version Check Inline Functions

Most of the sample applications run on all platforms, but some of them require features that are not supported in Windows 95 and Windows 98; some of them require features that are present only in Windows 2000. Each application checks the version of the host system when initializing and displays a notice if a more capable operating system is required.

For sample applications that do not run on Windows 95 and Windows 98, you'll see a call to my *chWindows9xNotAllowed* function in the application's *_tWinMain* function. For sample applications that require Windows 2000, you'll see a call to my *chWindows2000Required* function in the application's *_tWinMain* function.

Making Sure the Host System Supports Unicode

Windows 98 does not support Unicode as completely as does Windows 2000. In fact, applications that call Unicode functions do not run on Windows 98! Unfortunately, Windows 98 does not give any notification if an application compiled for Unicode is invoked. For the applications in this book, this means that the applications start and terminate with no indication that they ever attempted to execute.

This drove me absolutely nuts! I needed a way to know that my application was built for Unicode but was running on a Windows 98 system, so I created a CUnicodeSupported C++ class. This class's constructor simply checks to see whether the host system has good Unicode support; if not, a message box is displayed and the process terminates.

You'll notice that in CmnHdr.h, I create a global, static instance of this class. When my application starts, the C/C++ run-time library startup code calls this object's constructor. If the constructor detects that the operating system has full Unicode support, it returns and the application continues running. By creating a global instance of this class, I did not have to put any special code in each sample application's source code modules. For non-Unicode builds, I do not declare or instantiate the C++ class. This allows the application to just run.

Forcing the Linker to Look for a (*w*)*WinMain* Entry-Point Function

Some readers of previous editions of this book who added my source code modules to a new Visual C++ project received linker errors when building the project. The problem was that they created a Win32 Console Application project, causing the linker to look for a (*w*)*main* entry-point function. Since all of the book's sample applications are GUI applications, my source code has a *_tWinMain* entry-point function instead; this is why the linker complained.

My standard reply to readers was that they should delete the project and create a new Win32 Application project (note that the word "Console" doesn't appear in this project type) with Visual C++ and add my source code files to it. The linker looks for a (*w*)*WinMain* entry-point function, which I do supply in my code, and the project will build properly.

To reduce the amount of e-mail I get on this issue, I added a *pragma* to CmnHdr.h that forces the linker to look for the (*w*)*WinMain* entry-point function even if you create a Win32 Console Application project with Visual C++.

996

In Chapter 4, I go into great detail about what the Visual C++ project types are all about, how the linker chooses which entry-point function to look for, and how to override the linker's default behavior.

CmnHdr.h

```
/*****************************************************************************
Module:  CmnHdr.h
Notices: Copyright (c) 2000 Jeffrey Richter
Purpose: Common header file containing handy macros and definitions
         used throughout all the applications in the book.
         See Appendix A.
*****************************************************************************/


#pragma once    // Include this header file once per compilation unit


///////////////////////// Windows Version Build Option /////////////////////////


#define _WIN32_WINNT 0x0500
//#define WINVER       0x0500


///////////////////////////// Unicode Build Option /////////////////////////////


// If we are not compiling for an x86 CPU, we always compile using Unicode.
#ifndef _M_IX86
#define UNICODE
#endif

// To compile using Unicode on the x86 CPU, uncomment the line below.
//#define UNICODE

// When using Unicode Windows functions, use Unicode C-Runtime functions too.
#ifdef UNICODE
#define _UNICODE
#endif


///////////////////////// Include Windows Definitions /////////////////////////
```

Figure A-1.
The CmnHdr.h header file

(continued)

Figure A-1. *continued*

```
#pragma warning(push, 3)
#include <Windows.h>
#pragma warning(pop)
#pragma warning(push, 4)


/////////////// Verify that the proper header files are being used ///////////////


#ifndef WT_EXECUTEINPERSISTENTTHREAD
#pragma message("You are not using the latest Platform SDK header/library ")
#pragma message("files. This may prevent the project from building correctly.")
#endif


/////////////// Allow code to compile cleanly at warning level 4 ///////////////

/* nonstandard extension 'single line comment' was used */
#pragma warning(disable:4001)

// unreferenced formal parameter
#pragma warning(disable:4100)

// Note: Creating precompiled header
#pragma warning(disable:4699)

// function not inlined
#pragma warning(disable:4710)

// unreferenced inline function has been removed
#pragma warning(disable:4514)

// assignment operator could not be generated
#pragma warning(disable:4512)


/////////////////////////// Pragma message helper macro ///////////////////////////


/*
When the compiler sees a line like this:
   #pragma chMSG(Fix this later)
```

(continued)

Figure A-1. *continued*

```
it outputs a line like this:

  c:\CD\CmnHdr.h(82):Fix this later

You can easily jump directly to this line and examine the surrounding code.
*/

#define chSTR2(x)        #x
#define chSTR(x)    chSTR2(x)
#define chMSG(desc) message(__FILE__ "(" chSTR(__LINE__) "):" #desc)


///////////////////////////// chINRANGE Macro //////////////////////////////////


// This macro returns TRUE if a number is between two others.
#define chINRANGE(low, Num, High) (((low) <= (Num)) && ((Num) <= (High)))


////////////////////////////// chDIMOF Macro //////////////////////////////////


// This macro evaluates to the number of elements in an array.
#define chDIMOF(Array) (sizeof(Array) / sizeof(Array[0]))


////////////////////////// chBEGINTHREADEX Macro ///////////////////////////


// This macro function calls the C runtime's _beginthreadex function.
// The C runtime library doesn't want to have any reliance on Windows' data
// types such as HANDLE. This means that a Windows programmer needs to cast
// values when using _beginthreadex. Since this is terribly inconvenient,
// I created this macro to perform the casting.
typedef unsigned (__stdcall *PTHREAD_START) (void *);

#define chBEGINTHREADEX(psa, cbStack, pfnStartAddr, \
   pvParam, fdwCreate, pdwThreadId)                  \
      ((HANDLE)_beginthreadex(                        \
         (void *)          (psa),                     \
         (unsigned)        (cbStack),                 \
         (PTHREAD_START) (pfnStartAddr),              \
         (void *)          (pvParam),                 \
```

(continued)

Figure A-1. *continued*

```
        (unsigned)      (fdwCreate),                \
        (unsigned *)    (pdwThreadId)))


/////////////////// DebugBreak Improvement for x86 platforms ////////////////////


#ifdef _X86_
#define DebugBreak()    _asm { int 3 }
#endif


/////////////////////////// Software Exception Macro ///////////////////////////


// Useful macro for creating your own software exception codes
#define MAKESOFTWAREEXCEPTION(Severity, Facility, Exception) \
   ((DWORD) ( \
   /* Severity code    */  (Severity       ) |    \
   /* MS(0) or Cust(1) */  (1          << 29) |    \
   /* Reserved(0)      */  (0          << 28) |    \
   /* Facility code    */  (Facility << 16) |    \
   /* Exception code   */  (Exception << 0)))


/////////////////////////// Quick MessageBox Macro ///////////////////////////


inline void chMB(PCSTR s) {
   char szTMP[128];
   GetModuleFileNameA(NULL, szTMP, chDIMOF(szTMP));
   MessageBoxA(GetActiveWindow(), s, szTMP, MB_OK);
}


/////////////////////////// Assert/Verify Macros ///////////////////////////


inline void chFAIL(PSTR szMsg) {
   chMB(szMsg);
   DebugBreak();
}
```

(continued)

Figure A-1. *continued*

```
// Put up an assertion failure message box.
inline void chASSERTFAIL(LPCSTR file, int line, PCSTR expr) {
   char sz[128];
   wsprintfA(sz, "File %s, line %d : %s", file, line, expr);
   chFAIL(sz);
}


// Put up a message box if an assertion fails in a debug build.
#ifdef _DEBUG
#define chASSERT(x) if (!(x)) chASSERTFAIL(__FILE__, __LINE__, #x)
#else
#define chASSERT(x)
#endif


// Assert in debug builds, but don't remove the code in retail builds.
#ifdef _DEBUG
#define chVERIFY(x) chASSERT(x)
#else
#define chVERIFY(x) (x)
#endif


////////////////////////// chHANDLE_DLGMSG Macro //////////////////////////////


// The normal HANDLE_MSG macro in WindowsX.h does not work properly for dialog
// boxes because DlgProc return a BOOL instead of an LRESULT (like
// WndProcs). This chHANDLE_DLGMSG macro corrects the problem:
#define chHANDLE_DLGMSG(hwnd, message, fn)                         \
   case (message): return (SetDlgMsgResult(hwnd, uMsg,      \
      HANDLE_##message((hwnd), (wParam), (lParam), (fn))))


////////////////////////// Dialog Box Icon Setting Macro //////////////////////////


// Sets the dialog box icons
inline void chSETDLGICONS(HWND hwnd, int idi) {
   SendMessage(hwnd, WM_SETICON, TRUE,  (LPARAM)
      LoadIcon((HINSTANCE) GetWindowLongPtr(hwnd, GWLP_HINSTANCE),
         MAKEINTRESOURCE(idi)));
```

(continued)

Figure A-1. *continued*

```
    SendMessage(hwnd, WM_SETICON, FALSE, (LPARAM)
       LoadIcon((HINSTANCE) GetWindowLongPtr(hwnd, GWLP_HINSTANCE),
       MAKEINTRESOURCE(idi)));
}


/////////////////////////// OS Version Check Macros ////////////////////////////


inline void chWindows9xNotAllowed() {
    OSVERSIONINFO vi = { sizeof(vi) };
    GetVersionEx(&vi);
    if (vi.dwPlatformId == VER_PLATFORM_WIN32_WINDOWS) {
       chMB("This application requires features not present in Windows 9x.");
       ExitProcess(0);
    }
}


inline void chWindows2000Required() {
    OSVERSIONINFO vi = { sizeof(vi) };
    GetVersionEx(&vi);
    if ((vi.dwPlatformId != VER_PLATFORM_WIN32_NT) && (vi.dwMajorVersion < 5)) {
       chMB("This application requires features present in Windows 2000.");
       ExitProcess(0);
    }
}


/////////////////////////// UNICODE Check Macro ////////////////////////////


// Since Windows 98 does not support Unicode, issue an error and terminate
// the process if this is a native Unicode build running on Windows 98.

// This is accomplished by creating a global C++ object. Its constructor is
// executed before WinMain.

#ifdef UNICODE

class CUnicodeSupported {
public:
    CUnicodeSupported() {
```

(continued)

Figure A-1. *continued*

```
      if (GetWindowsDirectoryW(NULL, 0) <= 0) {
         chMB("This application requires an OS that supports Unicode.");
         ExitProcess(0);
      }
   }
};

// "static" stops the linker from complaining that multiple instances of the
// object exist when a single project contains multiple source files.
static CUnicodeSupported g_UnicodeSupported;

#endif


////////////////////////// Force Windows subsystem ////////////////////////////


#pragma comment(linker, "/subsystem:Windows")


///////////////////////////////// End of File /////////////////////////////////
```

MESSAGE CRACKERS, CHILD CONTROL MACROS, AND API MACROS

When I go to conferences, I frequently ask people if they're using message crackers, and the response is usually "no." When I probe further, I discover that they don't know what message crackers do or even what they are. By using C/C++ with message crackers to present the sample code in this book, I get to introduce these little-known but useful macros to many people who might not know about them.

Message crackers are in the WindowsX.h file supplied with Microsoft Visual C++. You usually include this file immediately after the Windows.h file. The WindowsX.h file is nothing more than a bunch of *#define* directives that create a set of macros for you to use. The macros in WindowsX.h are actually divided into three groups: message crackers, child control macros, and API macros. These macros help you in the following ways:

- They reduce the amount of casting you need to do in an application and make the casting that is required error-free. One of the big problems with programming for Windows in C/C++ has been the amount of casting required. You hardly ever see a call to a Windows function that doesn't require some sort of cast. You should avoid casts because they prevent the compiler from catching potential errors in your code. A cast tells the compiler, "I know I'm passing the wrong type here, but that's OK; I know what I'm doing." When you do a lot of casting, it's easy to make a mistake. The compiler should do as much work as possible to help out.

- They make your code more readable.

- They simplify porting between 16-bit Windows, 32-bit Windows, and 64-bit Windows.

- They're easy to understand. (They're just macros, after all.)

- They're easy to incorporate into existing code. You can leave old code alone and immediately use the macros in new code. You don't have to retrofit an entire application.

- You can use them in C and C++ code, although they're not necessary if you're using a C++ class library.

- If you need a feature that the macros don't support, you can easily write your own macros based on the ones in the header file.

- You don't need to reference or remember obscure Windows constructs. For example, many functions in Windows expect a long parameter where the value in the long's high-word means one thing and the value in its low-word means something else. Before calling these functions, you must construct a long value out of the two individual values. You usually do this by using the MAKELONG macro from WinDef.h. But I can't tell you how many times I've accidentally reversed the two values, causing an incorrect value to be passed to a function. The macros in WindowsX.h come to the rescue.

Message Crackers

Message crackers make it easier to write window procedures. Typically, window procedures are implemented as one huge *switch* statement. In my travels, I've seen window procedure *switch* statements that contained well over 500 lines of code. We all know that implementing window procedures in this way is bad practice, but we do it anyway. I've been known to do it myself on occasion. Message crackers force you to break up your *switch* statements into smaller functions—one function per window message. This makes your code much more manageable.

Another problem with window procedures is that every message has *wParam* and *lParam* parameters, and depending on the message, these parameters have different meanings. In some cases, such as a WM_COMMAND message, *wParam* contains two different values. The high-word of the *wParam* parameter is the notification code, and the low-word is the ID of the control. Or is it the other way around? I always forget. If you use message crackers, you don't have to remember or look up any of this. Message crackers are so named because they crack apart the parameters for any given message. To process the WM_COMMAND message, you simply write a function that looks like this:

```
void Cls_OnCommand(HWND hwnd, int id, HWND hwndCtl,
   UINT codeNotify) {

   switch (id) {

      case ID_SOMELISTBOX:
         if (codeNotify != LBN_SELCHANGE)
         break;

         // Do LBN_SELCHANGE processing.
         break;

      case ID_SOMEBUTTON:
         break;
      :
      :

   }
}
```

Look how easy it is! The crackers look at the message's *wParam* and *lParam* parameters, break the parameters apart, and call your function.

To use message crackers, you must make some changes to your window procedure's *switch* statement. Take a look at the window procedure here:

```
LRESULT WndProc (HWND hwnd, UINT uMsg,
   WPARAM wParam, LPARAM lParam) {

   switch (uMsg) {
      HANDLE_MSG(hwnd, WM_COMMAND, Cls_OnCommand);
      HANDLE_MSG(hwnd, WM_PAINT,   Cls_OnPaint);
      HANDLE_MSG(hwnd, WM_DESTROY, Cls_OnDestroy);
      default:
         return(DefWindowProc(hwnd, uMsg, wParam, lParam));
   }
}
```

The HANDLE_MSG macro is defined as follows in WindowsX.h:

```
#define HANDLE_MSG(hwnd, message, fn) \
   case (message): \
      return HANDLE_##message((hwnd), (wParam), (lParam), (fn));
```

For a WM_COMMAND message, the preprocessor expands this line to read as follows:

```
case (WM_COMMAND):
   return HANDLE_WM_COMMAND((hwnd), (wParam), (lParam),
      (Cls_OnCommand));
```

The HANDLE_WM_* macros, which are also defined in WindowsX.h, are actually message crackers. They crack the contents of the *wParam* and *lParam* parameters, perform all the necessary casting, and call the appropriate message function, such as the *Cls_OnCommand* function shown earlier. The macro for HANDLE_WM_COMMAND is as follows:

```
#define HANDLE_WM_COMMAND(hwnd, wParam, lParam, fn) \
    ( (fn) ((hwnd), (int) (LOWORD(wParam)), (HWND)(lParam), \
    (UINT) HIWORD(wParam)), 0L)
```

When the preprocessor expands this macro, the result is a call to the *Cls_On-Command* function with the contents of the *wParam* and *lParam* parameters broken down into their respective parts and cast appropriately.

Before you use message cracker macros to process a message, you should open the WindowsX.h file and search for the message you want to process. For example, if you search for WM_COMMAND, you'll see the part of the file that contains these lines:

```
/* void Cls_OnCommand(HWND hwnd, int id, HWND hwndCtl,
    UINT codeNotify); */
#define HANDLE_WM_COMMAND(hwnd, wParam, lParam, fn) \
    ((fn)((hwnd), (int)(LOWORD(wParam)), (HWND)(lParam), \
    (UINT)HIWORD(wParam)), 0L)
#define FORWARD_WM_COMMAND(hwnd, id, hwndCtl, codeNotify, fn) \
    (void)(fn)((hwnd), WM_COMMAND, \
    MAKEWPARAM((UINT)(id),(UINT)(codeNotify)), \
    (LPARAM)(HWND)(hwndCtl))
```

The first line is a comment that shows you the prototype of the function you have to write. The next line is the HANDLE_WM_* macro, which we've already discussed. The last line is a message forwarder. Let's say that during your processing of the WM_COMMAND message you want to call the default window procedure to have it do some work for you. This function would look like this:

```
void Cls_OnCommand (HWND hwnd, int id, HWND hwndCtl,
    UINT codeNotify) {

    // Do some normal processing.

    // Do default processing.
    FORWARD_WM_COMMAND(hwnd, id, hwndCtl, codeNotify,
        DefWindowProc);
}
```

The FORWARD_WM_* macro takes the cracked message parameters and reconstructs them to their *wParam* and *lParam* equivalents. The macro then calls a function that you supply. In the example above, the macro calls the *DefWindowProc* function, but you can just as easily use *SendMessage* or *Post-Message*. In fact, if you want to send (or post) a message to any window in the system, you can use a FORWARD_WM_* macro to help combine the individual parameters.

Child Control Macros

The child control macros make it easier to send messages to child controls. They are very similar to the FORWARD_WM_* macros. Each macro starts with the type of control you are sending the message to, followed by an underscore and the name of the message. For example, to send an LB_GETCOUNT message to a list box, you use the following macro from WindowsX.h:

```
#define ListBox_GetCount(hwndCtl) \
    ((int)(DWORD)SendMessage((hwndCtl), LB_GETCOUNT, 0, 0L))
```

Let me point out a couple of things about this macro. First, it takes only one parameter, *hwndCtl*, which is the window handle of the list box. Because the LB_GETCOUNT message ignores the *wParam* and *lParam* parameters, you don't need to bother with them. The macro passes zeros, as you can see above. Second, when *SendMessage* returns, the result is cast to an *int* so you don't have to supply your own cast.

The one thing I don't like about the child control macros is that they take the handle of the control window. Most of the time, the controls you need to send messages to are children of a dialog box. So you end up having to call *GetDlgItem* all the time, producing code like this:

```
int n = ListBox_GetCount(GetDlgItem(hDlg, ID_LISTBOX));
```

This code doesn't run any slower than it would if you used *SendDlgItemMessage*, but your application will contain some extra code because of the additional call to *GetDlgItem*. If you need to send several messages to the same control, you might want to call *GetDlgItem* once, save the child window's handle, and then call all the macros you need, as shown in the following code:

```
HWND hwndCtl = GetDlgItem(hDlg, ID_LISTBOX);
int n = ListBox_GetCount(hwndCtl);
ListBox_AddString(hwndCtl, "Another string");
  .
  .
  .
```

If you design your code in this way, your application will run faster because it won't have to repeatedly call *GetDlgItem*. *GetDlgItem* can be a slow function if your dialog box has many controls and the control you are looking for is toward the end of the z-order.

API Macros

The API macros simplify certain common operations, such as creating a new font, selecting the font into a device context, and saving the handle of the original font. The code looks something like this:

```
HFONT hfontOrig = (HFONT) SelectObject(hdc, (HGDIOBJ) hfontNew);
```

This statement requires two casts to get a warning-free compilation. One of the macros in WindowsX.h was designed for exactly this purpose:

```
#define SelectFont(hdc, hfont) \
    ((HFONT) SelectObject( (hdc), (HGDIOBJ) (HFONT) (hfont)))
```

If you use this macro, the line of code in your program becomes the following:

```
HFONT hfontOrig = SelectFont(hdc, hfontNew);
```

This code is easier to read and is much less error-prone.

Several other API macros in WindowsX.h help with common Windows tasks. I urge you to examine them and use them.

INDEX

Italic page-number references indicate figures, listings, or tables.

Symbols and Numbers

, (comma) operator in an exception filter, 867

% (percent sign), indicating replaceable strings, 76

0xC000007 error code, 694

/3GB switch, appending in the BOOT.INI file, 440

3-GB user-mode partition on *x*86 Windows 2000, *437, 439–40*

16-bit code

accessing 16 bytes at the beginning of stack segments, 565

supporting error handling in Windows 98, 6

16-bit Windows applications

communicating with 32-bit, 934

CreateWindowEx and, 28

running in separate VDMs, 98

sending a message to a window, 911

32-bit applications, communicating with 16-bit, 934

32-bit processes, virtual address space for, 435

32-bit Windows 2000

partitioning of the kernel, 436, *437*

system information on an Alpha, *474*

system information on an *x*86, *473*

64-bit processes, virtual address space for, 435

64-bit Windows 2000, 438. *See also* Windows 2000

getting a 2-GB user-mode partition, 440–41

partitioning of the kernel, 436, *437*

support of AWE, 546

system information on an Alpha, *474*

user-mode partition compared to kernel-mode, 442

64-KB off-limits partition, *437*, 441–42

1132 (ERROR_MAPPED_ALIGNMENT), 623

A

abandoned mutexes, 318

AbnormalTermination intrinsic function, 837, *838*

above normal priority class, *231*, 232

ABOVE_NORMAL_PRIORITY_CLASS identifier, *99*, 235

above normal thread priority, 232, *233*

abstract layer over the system scheduler, 230

access violation exception, 562

access violations, *449–50*

accounting information

maintaining for jobs, 143–44

querying, 151–55

AC (alignment check) flag, 466

ActiveProcessLimit member of JOBOBJECT_BASIC_LIMIT_INFORMATION, *141, 142*

ActiveProcess member of JOBOBJECT_BASIC_ACCOUNTING_INFORMATION, *152*

ActiveProcessorMask member of the SYSTEM_INFO data structure, *473*

active window, monitoring in LISWatch, 978–80, *981–88*

Add Counters dialog box, 468–69, *468*

address space. *See also* private address space; virtual address space

advantages of separate, 751

creating for a process, 182

determining the state of an, 489–501

mapping file's data into a process's, 603–6

mapping regions and blocks within regions, 499

in a process, 69, 677

regions in, 443–44

reserving a region in, 513–16

address space, *continued*

reserving for DLLs, 578–79

several DLL modules in, 678

specifying for a thread's stack, 187

unmapping a file's data from, 606–8

address space map

blocks within regions under Windows 98, 461, *461–64*, 465

regions and blocks under Windows 2000 on a 32-bit *x86* machine, 453–56, *453–54*, *456–60*, 460–61

address space sandbox. *See* sandbox

Address Windowing Extensions. *See* AWE (Address Windowing Extensions)

address windows

assigning RAM blocks to, 541, 542, *542*

creating multiple, 546

encapsulating, 547

freeing, 545

AdvAPI32.dll, 675

affinities, 250–55

affinity mask, 251–52

Affinity member of JOBOBJECT_BASIC_LIMIT_INFORMATION, *141, 143*

affinity restrictions, 144

algorithms

scheduling threads, 213

waking up multiple threads, 292

alignment errors, porting code from *x86* processors, 308

Alignment Fixups/sec counter, *468,* 470

allocate declaration specifier, 586–87, *586–87*

Allocated Ranges edit control in the MMF Sparse dialog box, 639

AllocateUserPhysicalPages function, 542–43

allocation granularity boundary, 443, 514

AllowSetForegroundWindow function, 952

Alpha CPU

address space for, 444, *445*

definition of CONTEXT_FULL, *227*

handling data alignment, 466–68

interlocked functions on, 261

page size of, 443

support of the execute protection attribute, 450

Alt+Esc, handling by the RIT, 947

Alt key, pressing to unlock the *SetForegroundWindow* function, 952

Alt+Tab, handling by the RIT, 947

ANSI

compiling sample applications as, 990

registering strings and characters as, 941

saving text files as, 34

ANSI C

allowing *free* to be passed NULL, 850, 851

string functions, *23–24*

ANSI characters, identifying in text files, 34–35

ANSI strings

accepted by *GetProcAddress*, 701

Windows 98 and, 21

in Windows 2000, 20

ANSI/Unicode

generic data types, 26

generic source code files, 24

versions of entry-point functions, 186

ANSI versions of functions, 38, *39*

APC entries

queuing continuously, 407

queuing waitable timers, 309–11

API hooking

creating a C++ class for, 801–2

an example of, 795–96

manipulating a module's import section, 797–800

overwriting code, 796–97

API macros, 1010

Append method in the Queue sample application, 321

AppInst sample application, 588–89, *590–94*

applications

  16-bit communicating with 32-bit, 934

  adding TLS to, 747

  in the background, 183

  binding during setup, 741

  causing another to hang, 917

  changing the base address for, 76

  creating multithreaded, 399

  debugging as failures occur, 877

  debugging multiple instances of, 581

  designing multithreaded, 183–84

  determining the system version of Windows, 86–90

  disadvantages of multithreaded, 184–85

  driving by creating hardware input events, 925–26

  extending the features of, 675

  forcing keystrokes into, 333

  grouping data for cache lines, 265

  implementing totally robust, 848

  initialization of, 694

  initializing with delay-load DLLs, 714

  for international markets, 17

  knowing how many instances are running, 588–89

  localizing with DLLs, 676

  making ANSI- and Unicode-ready, 29–40

  optimizing performance for, 240

  placing all files in their own directory, 730

  querying the number of CPUs, 251

  running, *680,* 682

  running a second instance of the same, 628

  running in an address space sandbox, 441

  running on an older system, 714

  sending interprocess messages, 932

applications, *continued*

  specifying the starting priority of, 236

  starting, 628

  types of, 71

  writing your first, 71–90

__argc global variable, *75,* 78

__argv global variable, *75,* 78

array, macro for returning the number of elements in, 992

array of structures, using virtual memory techniques for manipulating, 523–25

AssignProcessToJobObject function, 149–50

asynchronous activation event, stopping clipping of the mouse cursor, 953

asynchronous device I/O, 332

asynchronous function, 110, 192

asynchronous I/O requests, 402

asynchronous key state array, 952

asynchronous procedure call. *See* APC entries

atomic access, 258

AttachThreadInput function, 955–57, 979

attributes, 583, 587

AutoExec.bat file, modifying with SET lines, 80

auto-reset events, 293

  compared with manual-reset events, 296–97, *296*

  creating objects, 298

  demonstrating the use of, 297

  successful wait side effect rule for, 294

  thread synchronization behavior, *331*

auto-reset timer, 306, *331*

AvailPageFile, 483, *483*

AvailPhys, 483, *483*

AvailVirtual, *483,* 484

AWE (Address Windowing Extensions), 541–42, *541–42,* 546

AWE sample application, 546–47, *547–57*

AXPAlign.exe utility, 467, *467*

B

background processes, 240

background processing, implementing with fibers, 421

background processing state (BPS), 422

background services, optimizing performance for, 240

base address

for an executable file, 76–77

for regions, 454

specifying for a memory-mapped file, 622–24

specifying for reserving a region, 514

/BASE: *address* linker switch, 76

based pointers, assistance for, 624

/BASE option, overriding base addresses, 578

base priority level of a thread, 238

BaseProcessStart function, 197, *197*, 875–76, *875*

BaseThreadStart function, 195–96, *196*, 197, 875–76, *875*

_beginthreadex function, 187

calling *CreateThread* instead, 208

calling instead of *CreateThread*, 200

compared with *CreateThread*, 992–94

linking to a single-thread run-time library, 200–201

pseudocode version of the source code, 201, *201*

_beginthread function, 208–9, *208*

below normal priority class, *231*, 232

BELOW_NORMAL_PRIORITY_CLASS identifier, *99*, 235

below normal thread priority, *232*, *233*

binary data file, 620–21, *620–21*

Bind.exe utility, 739–41

BindImageEx function, 739

binding, 738–41

BindIoCompletionCallback function, 415–16

binheritHandles parameter of *CreateProcess*, 94

bit flags. *See* flags

blocking deletes of timers, 406

blocks. *See* memory blocks

Blue Screen of Death, 878

BOOL data type, *3*

Boot.ini file for a dual processor machine, 256, *256*

BPS_CONTINUE state, *422*, 423

BPS_DONE state, *422*, 423

BPS_STARTOVER, *422*

BPS (background processing state) variable, 422

BRANCHes

allocating in a single heap with NODEs, 659

storing with NODEs, 657–58, *658*

breakpoints, forcing in code, 994

BringWindowToTop function, 950–51, 960

broadcasting, messages to overlapped windows, 920

.bss section, 582, *585*

built-in controls, 760–61

byte offsets, listed in a relocation section, 733

C

C run-time functions, 24

C run-time library

global variables in, 74, *75*

Unicode support in, 23–26

C run-time memory allocation functions, 74

C run-time string functions, 23, *23–24*

C++, catching structured exceptions with, 906–8, *906–7, 908*

C++, using heaps with, 666–70

C++ classes

creating to identify structured exceptions, 907–8, *907*

exporting from DLL modules, 683

C++ compiler. *See* Visual C++ compiler

C++ exception handling, compared with SEH, 824

C++ exceptions versus structured, 904–8

C++ programs, debugging, 887

C/C++ applications, *ExitProcess* function or *ExitThread* and, 108, *108–9*

C/C++ programs, error checking in, 438

C/C++ run-time libraries
  DllMain and, 712–13
  dynamically linked version of, 207
  implementation of a *DllMain* function, 713
  multithreaded applications and, 199
  multithreaded version of, 207
  several in a single address space, 678
  shipping with Visual C++, 198–209
  single-threaded version of the statically linked, 207
  stack checking function in, 565–67, *566–67*
  use of TLS, 743
C/C++ run-time startup functions, 72, 74–75
C/C++ source code modules, 681
CACHE_ALIGN macro, 266
cache lines, 262–63, 265–67
caching, no memory-mapped pages, 600
CAddrWindow class, 547
CAddrWindowStorage class, 547
CalcWndText function in LISWatch, 979
callback timers, 312
calloc function, 74
call tree, increasing for a thread, 560
CallWindowProcA function, 942
CallWindowProc function, 943
CallWindowProcW function, 942
CancelWaitableTimer function, 309
CAPIHook C++ class, 801–2
carets, simultaneously displaying flashing, 950
casting, 1005
cast operator member function in the CWhenZero class, 358
catalyst process, 61
cbStack parameter for *CreateThread*, 187–88
CD-ROM with this book
  AppInst application, 588
  AWE application, 546
  CmnHdr.h header file, 989
  CopyData application, 935

CD-ROM with this book, *continued*
  DelayLoad application, 719
  Desktop Item Position Saver (DIPS) utility, 759
  ErrorShow application, 9
  FileRev application, 609
  Handshake application, 297
  ImgWalk.dll, 789
  Inject Library application, 779
  InterlockedType application, 358
  LastMsgBoxInfo application, 801
  LISLab application, 957
  LISWatch application, 978
  MemReset application, 537
  MMFShare application, 630
  MMFSparse application, 638
  Optex sample application, 340
  ProcessInfo application, 115
  Queue application, 319
  Scheduling Lab application, 241
  SEHTerm application, 839
  Spreadsheet application, 889
  Summation application, 567
  SWMRG application, 371
  SysInfo application, 473
  TimedMsgBox application, 407
  VMAlloc application, 523
  VMMap application, 499
  VMQuery function, 493
  VMStat application, 483
  WaitForMultipleExpressions application, 382
CellData matrix, sharing with other processes, 638
CELLDATA structure, 518, 636–37
  committing physical storage for, 519
  designing to be exactly 1 page in size, 522
CGuard class in CResGuard, 354
ChangeDisplaySettings function, *146*
ChangeTimerQueueTimer function, 406–7
character sets, 17–20
CharLowerBuff function, 32

CharLower function, 32

CharNext function, 18

CharPrev function, 18

CharUpperBuff function, 32

CharUpper function, 32

chASSERT macros, 995

chBEGINTHREADEX macro, 200, 992–94

chDIMOF macro, 992

_chdir function, 85

chHANDLE_DLGMSG macro, 995

child control macros, 1009–10

child controls, 1009

child processes. *See also* processes

    debugging, 96

    handle tables for, 52–53, *52*

    inheriting environment variables, 81

    inheriting process affinity, 251

    passing environment blocks to, 86

    passing handle values to, 53

    preventing error mode inheritance, 84

    running detached, 114

    setting the current drive and directory, 100

    spawning, 50, 112–14

chINRANGE macro, 992

chMB macro, 995

chMSG macro, 992

chSETDLGICONS macro, 995

chVERIFY macro, 995

CInterlockedScalar class, 356

CInterlockedString class, 359

CInterlockedType class, 354–56

class-object allocation, 666

cleanup code, localizing, 835

Click Right Mouse Button To Set Capture in the LISLab dialog box, 960–61

client, communicating with the server, 298

client sessions, name spaces for, 59

Client Threads list box in the Queue sample application, *319,* 320

clipboard, preventing processes from reading or erasing, *146*

ClipCursor function, 953

clipping rectangle, 961–62

CloseHandle function, 48–49, 105

    calling when the event kernel is no longer required, 294

    closing file-mapping objects and file objects, 608–9, *608, 609*

    raising an exception to closing a protected handle, 54

Close Program window, displaying in Windows 98, 963, *963*

CMMFSparse class, 641

CmnHdr.h header file, 989–97, *997–1003*

code

    forcibly raising exceptions, 870–74

    injecting with *CreateProcess*, 794

    injecting with memory-mapped files, 793

code points in Unicode, 19–20

code section of a file, *580*

coherence, memory-mapped files and, 621–22

COM, Unicode strings in, 22–23

ComCtl32.dll, 675

ComDlg32.dll, 675

command lines, 78–79

command-line string, passing and interpreting by an application, 78

CommandLineToArgvW function, 78–79

command shell, spawning child processes, 159

comma (,) operator in an exception filter, 867

committing physical storage, 444, 514–15

committing storage in a reserved region, 516–17

common controls, interacting with, 760–61

COM object DLLs, placing registered, 730

CompareString function, 30–32

compilers

    EXCEPTION_CONTINUE_EXECUTION identifier and, 858

    guaranteeing execution of the *finally* block, 827

compilers, *continued*
  implementation of SEH capabilities, 823–24
  processing functions, 732
compiler settings for the sample applications in
    this book, 989
completion port
  associating jobs or objects with, 156
  sending job event notifications to, *157*
component protection, 657–58
console input, thread synchronization behavior,
    331
console user interface (CUI). *See* CUI-based
    applications
console window
  creating, 97
  specifying the window title for, *101*
ConstructBlkInfoLine function, 501
ConstructRgnInfoline function, 500–501, *500*
content indexing service, 182
CONTEXT_FULL, 227, *227*
contexts of threads, 195, 226
CONTEXT structure, 866, 870
  changing members in, 227
  initializing the *ContextFlags* member of, 226,
    226, 227, *227–28*, 228
  manipulating, 793
  role in thread scheduling, 223
  saving, 866–68, *867*
  for threads, 195, 213
  for an *x*86 CPU, 223, *223–25*
context switch, 213
control registers, 225
ConvertThreadToFiber function, 418
Coordinated Universal Time (UTC), 307
COptex class, 338, 340
COptex object, 338
CopyData sample application, 935–36, *936–40*
COPYDATASTRUCT structure, 933–34

copy-on-write feature, 450–51
  forcing pages to be backed by the paging file,
    733–34
  of the memory management system, 581
Counter sample application, 421–23, *424–31*
CPU cache lines, 265–67
CPU-dependent code, 227
CPU registers
  grabbing the current, 225
  for threads, 195
CPUs
  accessing properly aligned data, 465
  bitmask indicating active, *473*
  keeping busy, 182–83
  limiting the number used by Windows 2000 on
    an *x*86 machine, 256
  number in the machine, *473*
  page sizes of, 443, *472*
  process address spaces for different, *445*
  setting for an ideal, 254
CPU-specific data structure, 223
CPU time, wasting with spinlocks, 262–63
CQueue class in the Queue sample application,
    320, *320*
CREATE_BREAKAWAY_FROM_JOB flag,
    98, 150
CREATE_DEFAULT_ERROR_MODE flag,
    84, 97
CreateDesktop function, *146*
CreateEvent function, 293
CreateFiber function, 418–19
CreateFile function, 28
  calling for memory-mapped files, 622
  checking the return value for, 629
  creating or opening a file kernel object, 597–99
  debugger code for understanding, 602–3, *602*
  returning INVALID_HANDLE_VALUE, 603
CreateFileMapping function, 41
  calling, 599–603

CreateFileMapping function, *continued*
creating file-mapping objects, 610
debugger code for understanding, 602–3, *602*
sharing a spreadsheet as a file-mapping object, 637
CREATE_FORCEDOS flag, 98
*Create** functions, 55–57, *55–56,* 58
CreateIcon function, 45
CreateJobObject function, *140*
CreateMutex function, 57, 316
CREATE_NEW_CONSOLE flag, 97
CREATE_NEW_PROCESS_GROUP flag, 97
CREATE_NO_WINDOW flag, 97
CreateProcess function, 28, 51, 90–107, 578
injecting code with, 794
searching for an executable, 92–93
CreateRemoteThread function
calling, 776–77
compared with *CreateThread,* 775
creating a thread in another process, 774–75
CreateSemaphore function, 314
CREATE_SEPARATE_WOW_VDM flag, 97–98
CREATE_SHARED_WOW_VDM flag, 98
CREATE_SUSPENDED flag, 96–97, 190, 214
checking for, 215
passing to *CreateThread,* 196, 237
CreateThread function, 186–90
calling instead of *_beginthreadex,* 208
compared with *_beginthreadex,* 992–94
compared with *CreateRemoteThread,* 775
thread pool and, 401
CreateTimerQueue function, 404
CreateTimerQueueTimer function, 312, 404–5
CREATE_UNICODE_ENVIRONMENT flag, 98
CreateWaitableTimer function, 305
CreateWindowEx functions, 26–28
CreateWindowEx macro, 27–28
creation time, returned by *GetThreadTimes, 220*

CResGuard class, 354
CResGuard object, 355
CRITICAL_SECTION data structure, *271,* 272, *273–74*
allocating, 274
creating for each resource, 272
in the CResGuard class, 354, *354*
initializing members within, 274
manipulating, 274
resetting variables inside, 274
critical sections, 269–77, 337
changing the spin count for, 277–78
characteristics of, *319*
code using, *271*
compared with mutex kernel objects, 315, 338
contention for, 338
error handling and, 278–79
implementing, 338
mutex kernel objects and, 318–19, *319*
spinlocks and, 277–78
thread synchronization behavior, *331*
tips and techniques, 279–81
CriticalSectionTimeout data value, 276
CRITICAL_SECTION variable, 279–81
cross-process optex, 338, 339, 340
CRt0.c file, 74
.CRT section, *585*
CSE class objects, constructing, 908, *908*
CSparseStream C++ class, 641
CStopwatch class, *222*
CSWMRG class, 370, *370–71,* 371
CSystemInfo class, 547
CToolhelp C++ class, 118
Ctrl+Alt+Del, handling by the RIT, 947
Ctrl+Break, modifying the list of processes notified, 97
Ctrl+C, modifying the list of processes notified, 97
CUI-based applications, 71

CUI-based processes, blocking access to parent console windows, 97

CUnicodeSupported C++ class, 996

current directories, handling for multiple drives, 85

Currently Running Fiber field in the Counter sample application, 421

current resource count, 313, 314, 315

cursor. *See* mouse cursor

CVMArray C++ class, 891–92

CWhenZero class, 357–58

CWhenZero object, 359

D

data
  associating with instances of an object, 743
  sending with messages, 932–40

data alignment, importance of, 465–70

data files
  accessing on disk, 577
  counting all the 0 bytes in, 620–21, *620–21*
  memory mapping into address space for processes, 594–96

data members, new syntax for aligning, 266

data objects. *See also* kernel objects; User objects
  endowing with thread safety, 353

.data section, *580*, 582, *585*

data structures
  "atomic" access of more sophisticated, 267
  keeping a record of which are in use, 522

DBCSs (double-byte character sets), 18

deadlock situations, 403, 710, *710*

DebugActiveProcess function, 879

DebugBreak function, 340, 994

debugger
  automatically invoking, 882
  connecting to any process at any time, 879
  dynamically attaching to a process, 877
  Exceptions dialog box, 885–86, *886*, 888, *888*
  executing, 879

debugger, *continued*
  forcing code into the debuggee's address space, 793
  Output window, 887, *887*
  spawning by *UnhandledExceptionFilter*, 885
  support for debugging exceptions, 885–88
  waiting for debug events, 334

Debugger data value, 878

debugging
  C++ programs, 887
  just-in-time, 878–79
  monitoring the last error code, 6–7, *7*
  multiple instances of an application, 581

debugging-related exceptions, 862

Debug menu option in the Task Manager, 879

DEBUG_ONLY_THIS_PROCESS flag, 96

DEBUG_PROCESS flag, 96

debug registers, identifying for a CPU, 225

.debug section, *585*

declared-matrix method, 518

__*declspec (dllimport)* keyword, 690

__*declspec (dllexport)* modifier, 685

__*declspec (thread)* prefix, 749

DecommitPortionOfStream method in MMFSparse, 642

decommitting physical storage, 444

dedicated heaps for data structures, 660

default heaps for processes, 656–57

default security for kernel objects, 43

.def file, EXPORTS section in, 688

#*define* directives in the WindowsX.h file, 1005

DefWindowProc function, 1009

DelayImp.lib static-link library, global variables defined in, 718

DelayLoadApp sample application, 719–20, *720–26*

__*delayLoadHelper* function
  callback functions with, 718–19
  embedding, 714
  jumping calls to, 715

DelayLoadInfo structure, 716

delay-loading DLLs, 714–26

/DelayLoad linker switch, 714–15

/Delay:nobind linker switch, 718

delay option in LISLab, 960

/Delay:unload linker switch, 717–18

DeleteCriticalSection function, 274

DeleteFiber function, 420

delete operator in C++, 666, 668–69, *668–69*

DeleteTimerQueueEx function, 407

DeleteTimerQueueTimer function, 405–6

denormal operand value, 863

derived classes, using a separate heap for, 669

desktop, identifying for an application, *101*

Desktop Item Position Saver (DIPS) utility, 759–63, *763–74*

detached processes, 114

DETACHED_PROCESS flag, 97

Developer Studio, stopping a build in progress, 150

device I/O, asynchronous, 332

device objects, 332

devices, closing with no callbacks, 416

dialog box icons, changing manually, 995

.didata section, *585*, 715

DIPS (Desktop Item Position Saver) utility, 759–63, *763–74*

DisableThreadLibraryCalls function, 711, 713

disk defragmenting software, running in the background, 183

DispatchMessage function, 915, 925

display resolution, changing on the fly, 759

Dlg_OnInitDialog function, 589

Dlg_OnTimer function in LISWatch, 979, 980

DliHook skeleton function, 718, 720

DllDirectory value, 729

.dll extension, 729

DLL file image, 582, 681

DLL files
  loading and executing, 577
  loading from floppy disk, 449

DLL functions, exporting by assigning ordinal values, 687

_DllMainCRTStartup function, 712–13

DllMain function, *702*, 703
  C/C++ run-time libraries and, 712–13
  mapping a file image without calling, 697
  serialized calls to, 709–12

DLL modules, 679
  building, *680, 681*, 683–89
  creating with no relocation section, 734
  explicitly loading, 695, *696*, 697–98
  explicitly unloading, 698–700
  mapping by the loader, 693
  relocating, 732–33

DLL_PROCESS_ATTACH notification, 703–5, 709, 755

DLL_PROCESS_DETACH notification, 705–7, 795

DLLs (dynamic-link libraries), 675, 677
  3-GB user-mode partition and, 440
  building, *696*
  creating for use with non–Visual C++ tools, 688–89
  creating with two exported functions, 28
  delay-loading, 714–26
  determining the full pathname of, 700
  entry-point functions for, 702–13, *702*
  features available only to, 676–77
  in a full 4-TB user-mode partition, 441
  getting the pathname string into the remote process's address space, 777
  global and static variables in, 678
  injecting as a debugger, 793
  injecting into another process's address space, 752
  injecting using remote threads, 774–89

DLLs (dynamic-link libraries), *continued*
  injecting using the registry, 754–56
  injecting with a Trojan DLL, 792
  known, 728–29
  loading by calling *LoadLibrary*, 578–79
  loading from high-memory addresses, 735
  maintaining a usage count on a per-process
    basis, 700
  mapping, 682
  not loading additional, 697
  performing per-thread cleanup, 708
  performing per-thread initialization, 707
  performing process-relative cleanup, 705
  preferred base address for, 730
  preventing processes from dying, 705
  preventing threads from dying, 708
  a process's address space and, 677–79
  reasons for using, 675–77
  receiving notification of thread termination, 193
  redirection of, 729–30
  reporting on all in use by a process, 789
  resource-only, 734
  search order by the loader, 693
  startup code, 712
  unloading, 403
/DLL switch, specifying to the linker, 677
DLL_THREAD_ATTACH notification, 707–8
DLL_THREAD_DETACH notification, 208,
    708–9
dlp member of the *DelayLoadInfo* structure, 716
DONT_RESOLVE_DLL_REFERENCES flag
    with *LoadLibraryEx*, 697
DOS/16-bit Windows application compatibility
    partition, *437*, 438
double-byte character sets (DBCSs), 18
DumpBin utility, 583, *583–85*
  displaying preferred base addresses, 730–32, *731*
  with the -exports switch, 686–87, *686–87*
  with the -imports switch, 690–92, *691–92*

DUPLICATE_CLOSE_SOURCE flag, 61
DuplicateHandle function, 60–65, 211
  processes involved with, 64, *64*
  registering a single object multiple times, 413
DUPLICATE_SAME_ACCESS flag, 61, 63
dwAllocationGranularity member of the
    SYSTEM_INFO data structure, *472*
dwFlags member of STARTUPINFO structure,
    102–3
dwFlags parameter
  in *CreateTimerQueueTimer* function, 405
  for *RegisterWaitForSingleObject*, 413
dwNumberOfProcessors member of the SYSTEM_
    INFO data structure, *473*
DWORD data type, *4*
dwPageSize member of the SYSTEM_INFO data
    structure, *472*
dwProcessorType member of the SYSTEM_INFO
    data structure, *473*
dynamic-link libraries (DLLs). *See* DLLs
    (dynamic-link libraries)
dynamic priority range for threads, 238
dynamic TLS, 744
  compared with static TLS, 750
  using, 747–49

E

.edata section, *585*
edit control, writable cell implemented as, 421
ELEMENT structure in the Queue sample
    application, 321
EnableAlignmentFaultExceptions registry value,
    467, 468
endless recursion bugs, 188
end of a file marker, 642
_endthreadex function, 192, 205–6, *205*
_endthread function, 208–9, *208*
EnterCriticalSection function, 272–73,
    274–76, 277

entry-point functions, 72
  calling, 74–75, 182
  for DLLs, 702–13, *702*
  returning for a primary thread, 107–8
  for secondary threads, 185–86
EnumProcesses function, 115
_environ global variable, *75*
environment block, 79
environment variables
  creating an initial set for Windows 98, 80
  determining the existence and value of, 82
  inheritance of, 81
  for processes, 79–83
  users and, 82
Environment Variables dialog box in Windows
    2000, 80–81, *81*
"@err,hr" in Visual Studio's Watch Window, 6, *7*
errno global variable, 199, 206
error codes
  composition of, 865, *865*
  converting into text descriptions, 7–8
  creating a master list for Windows functions, 8
  monitoring the last, 6
  setting the last, for threads, 8–9
  for Windows functions, 4
error handling
  critical sections and, 278–79
  performed by Windows functions, 3–16
  using exceptions for, 871
ERROR_INVALID_HANDLE, 48
ERROR_INVALID_PARAMETER, 451
Error Lookup utility, 7
error modes for processes, 83–84
ERROR_SECRET_TOO_LONG, *382*
ErrorShow sample application, 9–10, *11–16*
Error Starting Program message boxes, *693, 694,*
    704
ERROR_TOO_MANY_SECRETS, *382*

event kernel objects, 293–97
except block
  in an exception handler, 843
  executing code in, 847
__*except* filter with *RaiseException*, 905
EXCEPTION_ACCESS_VIOLATION exception,
    861, 865–66, 869
EXCEPTION_ARRAY_BOUNDS_EXCEEDED
    exception, 861
EXCEPTION_BREAKPOINT exception, 862
exception codes, creating, 872
EXCEPTION_CONTINUE_EXECUTION
    identifier, 845, 856–58, 872, 881
EXCEPTION_CONTINUE_SEARCH identifier,
    845, 858–60, 881
  every filter returning, 875
  returning, 716
EXCEPTION_DATATYPE_MISALIGNMENT
    exception, 308, 861
EXCEPTION_EXECUTE_HANDLER identifier,
    845, 847–56
  returning from *SetUnhandledExceptionFilter*,
    881
exception filters
  execution of, 844
  writing, 869–70, *869–70*
EXCEPTION_FLT_DENORMAL_OPERAND
    exception, 863
EXCEPTION_FLT_DIVIDE_BY_ZERO
    exception, 863
EXCEPTION_FLT_INEXACT_RESULT
    exception, 863
EXCEPTION_FLT_INVALID_OPERATION
    exception, 863
EXCEPTION_FLT_OVERFLOW exception, 863
EXCEPTION_FLT_STACK_CHECK exception,
    863
EXCEPTION_FLT_UNDERFLOW exception,
    863
EXCEPTION_GUARD_PAGE exception, 862

exception handlers, 843
 creating, 880–82
 execution of, 844
 setting up applications with, 520
exception handling
 forms of, 824
 resumptive, 906
exception identifiers, 872
EXCEPTION_* identifiers, returning from
 SetUnhandledExceptionFilter, 881
EXCEPTION_ILLEGAL_INSTRUCTIONS
 exception, 862
exception information, accessing from inside an
 exception handler block, 866–67
EXCEPTION_IN_PAGE_ERROR exception, 861
EXCEPTION_INT_DIVIDE_BY_ZERO
 exception, 862
EXCEPTION_INT_OVERFLOW exception, 862
EXCEPTION_INVALID_DISPOSITION
 exception, 862
EXCEPTION_INVALID_HANDLE exception,
 862
EXCEPTION_MAXIMUM_PARAMETERS, 873
exception message box, turning off, 880–82
EXCEPTION_NONCONTINUABLE_EXCEPTION
 exception, 862, 873
EXCEPTION_NONCONTINUABLE flag, 868
 passing, 872–73
 using when a C++ exception is thrown, 905
EXCEPTION_POINTERS structure, 866, 873
EXCEPTION_PRIV_INSTRUCTION exception,
 862
EXCEPTION_RECORD structure, 866
 contents of, 868–69
 pointing to, 868
 saving, 866–68, *867*
exception-related exceptions, 862
exceptions, 662, 843
 C++ versus structured, 904–8
 capturing, 827

exceptions, *continued*
 for error handling, 871
 identifying, 861
 in kernel mode, 877–78
 listing of all predefined, 861–63
 listing of system-defined, 886
 processing of, 845, *846*
 raising while handling exceptions, 868
 raising while processing another exception, 873
 resuming execution after, 847–48
 stacking, 873
Exceptions dialog box in the debugger, 885–86,
 886, 888, *888*
EXCEPTION_SINGLE_STEP exception, 862
EXCEPTION_STACK_OVERFLOW exception,
 561, 568, 862
__*except* keyword, 843
executable files
 searching for, with *CreateProcess*, 93
 setting processor affinity in, 254, *254*
 .tls sections in, 749
executable image file, 682
executable modules, 679
 building, *680*, 681–82, 689–92, *689*
 creating with no relocation section, 734
 preferred base address for, 730
 relocating, 732–33
 running, 692–94
EXECUTE attribute for a section, *583*
execution context
 for a fiber, 418
 getting the address of the current fiber's, 420
 returning the save value from, 420
execution times for threads, 219–22
.exe file
 accessing resources contained in, 698
 executing startup code, 579
 image of, 448
 loading and executing, 577

.exe file, *continued*
   locating with *CreateProcess*, 578
   mapping into address space for processes, 578
   sections composing, 582
exit code
   setting for a thread, 192
   for threads, 186
exit function, 75
ExitProcess function, 108–9
   calling, 75
   hooking, 795–96
   making explicit calls to, 109
   terminating threads, 193
   trapping all calls to, from all modules, 800
ExitThread function, 191–92, 193
   calling, 108, 197, 206, 699, 708
   making explicit calls to, 109
exit time, returned by *GetThreadTimes*, 220
ExpandEnvironmentStrings function, 82–83
explicitly linking to exported symbols, 701
explicitly loading DLL modules, 695, *696*,
      697–98
explicitly unloading DLL modules, 698–700
Explorer. *See* Windows Explorer
exported symbols, explicitly linking to, 701
export section in a DLL file, 686
EXPORTS section in the .def file, 688
extended registers, identifying for a CPU, 225
extern "C" modifier, 685

F
facility codes, listing of, 865
FACILITY_NULL facility code, 865, 866
fatal errors, 872
fdwCreate parameter
   of *CreateProcess*, 96–99
   of *CreateThread*, 190
fFunctionOk Boolean variable, 836, *836*
FiberFunc function, 423

fibers, 417–20
field types in *printf* functions, 33
file change notifications, *331*
file data, preserving changed, 607–8
FILE_FLAG_WRITE_THROUGH flag, 607
file image for a DLL, 677
file kernel objects, 597–99
FILE_MAP_ALL_ACCESS value in
      MapViewOfFile, 604
FILE_MAP_COPY value
   file data changes and, 607
   in *MapViewOfFile*, 604
   specifying with *MapViewOfFile*, 605
file-mapping objects, 599–603
   assigning names to, 603
   closing, 608–9
   coherence of, 622
   creating, 610
   mapping two views of a single, *626*
   returning a handle to, 637
   sharing, 627
   sharing spreadsheets as, 637
FILE_MAP_READ value in *MapViewOfFile*, 604
FILE_MAP_WRITE flag, 607
FILE_MAP_WRITE value, in *MapViewOfFile*, 604
file objects, closing, 608–9
FileRev application, 609–11, *612–19*
FileReverse function in FileRev, 610
files
   mapping multiple views of the same data, 621
   mapping views of large, 620–21
   methods for reversing the contents of, 595–96
   setting the end of file marker, 642
   setting the maximum size of, 601
   thread synchronization behavior, *331*
   unmapping data from the process's address
      space, 606–8
FILE_SHARE_READ value in *CreateFile*, 598
FILE_SHARE_WRITE value in *CreateFile*, 598

FILETIME structure, compared with LARGE_
    INTEGER, 307
FilterFunc function, 568
finally block
    calling *ReleaseSemaphore*, 829
    forcing execution of, 830, 837
    guaranteeing the execution of, 827
    overhead of entering, 827
    placing a *return* statement inside to halt global
        unwinds, *855*, 855–56
__*finally* keyword in a termination handler, 824
FindWindowEx function, calling in CopyData, 936
first-chance exception notifications, 885–86, 888
FirstFunc function in the Optex sample
    application, 340
"first in, first out" algorithm, 292
/FIXED switch, 579, 734
flags
    affecting process creation, 96–99
    changing for kernel object handles, 53–55
flashing carets, simultaneously displaying, 950
flat address space, 580
floating-point registers, 225
floating-point–related exceptions, 863
FlushViewOfFile function, 607
focus, transferring from one window to another,
    950
focus window, monitoring in LISWatch, 978–80,
    981–88
ForceClose method in MMFSparse, 642
foreground, bringing windows to, 951
foreground process, tweaking the scheduler for,
    240–41
foreground thread, 946
foreground window, monitoring in LISWatch, 979
FORMAT_MESSAGE_ALLOCATE_BUFFER
    flag, 10
FORMAT_MESSAGE_FROM_SYSTEM flag, 10
FormatMessage function, 7–8, 10
FORWARD_WM_* macro, 1009

fragmented heaps, 658, *659*
free, calling and passing it NULL, 850, 851
free address space, 443
Free All Allocated Regions button in the
    MMFSparse dialog box, 641, 642
FreeEnvironmentStrings function, 99
FREE flag, 744, 745
FreeLibraryAndExitThread function, 699–700
FreeLibrary function, 698–700, 705, *707*
free regions, 455
Free type
    of physical storage, 460
    of region, 455
FreeUserPhysicalPages function, 545
FuncaDoodleDoo function, 830–31
Funcarama1 function, 832–33, *832–33*
Funcarama2 function, 833–34, *833–34*
Funcarama3 function, 834–35, *834–35*
Funcarama4 function, 835–36, *835–36*
Funcenstein1 function, 825
Funcenstein2 function, 826–27
Funcenstein3 function, 828
Funcenstein4 function, 831–32
Funcfurter1 function, 829
Funcfurter2 function, 838, *838*
Funcmeister1 function, 844
Funcmeister2 function, 845
FuncORen1 function, *853*, 854
FuncOStimpy1 function, *853*, 854
function calls, redirecting, 727
function forwarders, 727–28
function parameters in thread functions, 186
functions
    calling, 3
    calling asynchronously, 401–3
    calling at timed intervals, 403–12
    calling in a DLL, 677
    calling when asynchronous I/O requests
        complete, 415–16

functions, *continued*

calling when single kernel objects become signaled, 412–15

creating a master list of, 8

creating kernel objects, 46–48, *47*

designing to take advantage of termination handlers, 836

entry-point, 72

error codes for, 4

error handling performed by, 3–16

hooking and unhooking imported, 802

intrinsic, 420

performing non-I/O-related tasks asynchronously, 402

raising exceptions upon failure, 871

returning the reason for success, 6

return types for, *3–4*

used for memory allocations, 679

writing Unicode and ANSI versions of, 38–40, *38, 39*

__*FUnloadDelayLoadedDLL* function, 717–18

G

Garbage Collect button in the Virtual Memory Allocator window, 524

GarbageCollect function, 524

garbage collection function, 522–23

GCLP_WNDPROC, passing as the *nIndex* parameter, 942

GDI32.dll, 675

GDI objects, 45

general-protection-fault message box, 84

GENERIC_READ value in *CreateFile*, *598, 600*

GENERIC_WRITE value in *CreateFile*, *598*

GetActiveWindow function, 950

GetAsyncKeyState function, 952–53

GetCommandLine function, 78

GetCurrentDirectory function, 85

GetCurrentFiber function, 420

GetCurrentProcess function, 64, *65*

GetCurrentProcessId function, 210, 780

GetCurrentThreadId function, 210

GetDlgItem function, 1009–10

GetEnvironmentStrings function, 99

GetEnvironmentVariable function, 53, 82

GetExceptionCode intrinsic function, 861, 863–64, *863–64*

GetExceptionInformation intrinsic function, 866, *867*

GetExitCodeProcess function, 111–12, *113*

GetExitCodeThread function, 194

GetFiberData function, 420

GetFileSize function in FileRev, 610

GetForegroundWindow function, 951, 960, 979

GetFullPathName function, 86

GetHandleInformation function, 55

GetKeyState function, 953

GetLastError function, 4, 6

GetMessage function, 915

calling, 761–62

checking the calling thread, 927

returning messages from, 926

GetModuleFileName function, 700

GetModuleHandle function, 77, 700

GetModulePreferredBaseAddr function, 118

GetNotZeroHandle member function, 358

GetPriorityClass function, *143*, 235

GetProcAddress function, *696*, 701, 800

GetProcessAffinityMask function, 251–52

GetProcessHeap function, 657

GetProcessHeaps function, 670

GetProcessIoCounters function, 152–53

GetProcessPriorityBoost function, 239

GetProcessTimes function, 210, *210*, 221, 222

_*getptd* function, *205, 205*

GetQueuedCompletionStatus function, 156–57, *157*, 402

GetQueueStatus function, 423, 923–25

GetStartupInfo function, 104

GetSystemInfo function, 471, 472

GetThreadContext function, 225–26, *225,* 227, 228

GetThreadLocale function, 31

GetThreadPriorityBoost function, 239

GetThreadPriority function, 237

GetThreadTimes function, 210, *210,* 220–21, *220–21,* 222

GetVal functions in the CInterlockedType class, 355–56

GetVersionEx function, 87

GetVersion function, 86–87

GetWindowThreadProcessId function, 761, 914–15
  determining which thread created a window, 946
  in LISWatch, 979

/Gf and /GF compiler switches in Visual C++, 92

GlobalAlloc function, 656

global atom table, *146*

GlobalMemoryStatusEx function, 482, 543

GlobalMemoryStatus function, 481–82

global name space, 59, 60

"Global\" prefix, 60

global unwinds, 837
  halting, *853,* 855–56
  performing, 851–55, *852, 853*

global variables
  for C/C++ run time, 74, *75*
  changing for multiple instances of an application, 581
  changing to stack-based, 744
  in DLLs, 678
  running inside *DllMain* functions, 712
  sharing among all instances of an .exe or a DLL, 582
  in thread functions, 186

grandchild processes, spawning child processes, 52

granularity of reserved regions of address space, *472*

graphical user interface (GUI), 71

Graphics Device Interface (GDI) objects, 45

growable heap, 662

guard page, 560

guard page protection flag, 560

guard protection attribute flag, *560, 561*

GUI-based applications, 71

H

handle/base address, 77

HANDLE data type, *3*

HANDLE_FLAG_PROTECT_FROM_CLOSE flag, 54–55

HANDLE_MSG macro, 995, 1007

handles
  closing for processes, 105
  controlling the inheritance of, 54–55
  converting pseudo-handles to, 210–12, *212*
  creating inheritable, 50–51
  passing an array of, 381
  returning process-relative, 47

handle tables
  for child processes, 52–53, *52*
  for kernel objects, 46–49, *46*

handle values, 47–48
  assigning to mutex objects, 57
  passing to child processes, 53

HANDLE_WM_COMMAND macro, 1008

HANDLE_WM_* macros, 1008

Handshake sample application, 297–99, *299–305*

hard affinities, 251, 253

hard disks, thrashing of, 447

hard drives, multiple paging files on different, 448

hard exceptions, recovering from, 906

hardware
  events generating messages, 926
  exceptions, 843

hardware, *continued*
    input events driving applications, 925–26
    input model, 945, *946*
header files
    creating for a DLL module, 681, 683, *683–84*
    data types defined by, 26
/Headers switch in the DumpBin utility, 583
Heap32First function, 670
Heap32ListFirst function, 670
Heap32ListNext function, 670
Heap32Next function, 670
HeapAlloc function, 660–61, 662–63, *667,* 668
HeapCompact function, 671
HeapCreate function, 660–62
    calling, *667,* 668
    HEAP_GENERATE_EXCEPTIONS flag, 663
HeapDestroy function, 665, 669
HeapFree function, 79, 665, 669
heap functions, passing HEAP_GENERATE_
    EXCEPTIONS flag to, 871
HEAP_GENERATE_EXCEPTIONS flag, 660,
    662
    with *HeapAlloc,* 663
    with *HeapCreate,* 663
    with *HeapReAlloc,* 664
    passing to heap functions, 871
/HEAP linker switch, 656
HeapLock function, 671
heap manager, 655
HEAP_NO_SERIALIZE flag, 660–62
    avoiding, 661
    with *HeapAlloc,* 663
    with *HeapCreate,* 667, 668
    with *HeapReAlloc,* 664
HeapReAlloc function, 664–65
HEAP_REALLOC_IN_PLACE_ONLY flag, 664
heaps, 513, 655
    allocating a block of memory from, 662–64
    allowing exclusive thread access to, 661
    bytes initially committed to, 662

heaps, *continued*
    coalescing free blocks within, 671
    creating additional, 660–70
    creating growable, 662
    dedicated, 660
    destroying, 665
    enumerating a process's, 670
    fragmented, 658, *659*
    getting the handles of existing, 670
    keeping thread-safe, 660
    managing more efficiently, 658–59
    maximum size of, 662
    modifying how operations are performed on,
      660
    reasons for creating additional, 657–60
    rules for committing and decommitting storage,
      655
    scheme for using multiple, 669
    using with C++, 666–70
    validating the integrity of, 670–71
    walking the contents of, 671–72
HeapSize function, 665
HeapUnlock function, 671
HeapValidate function, 670–71
HeapWalk function, 671
HEAP_ZERO_MEMORY flag
    with *HeapAlloc,* 663
    with *HeapReAlloc,* 664
hide/show capability of the mouse cursor, 953
highest thread priority, 232, *233*
high-memory addresses, loading DLLs from, 735
high priority class, *231,* 231–32
HIGH_PRIORITY_CLASS identifier, *99, 235*
high-resolution performance functions, 222
HINSTANCE parameter type, 76
hinstDll value, 757–58
hinstExe parameter in *(w) WinMain,* 76
HMODULE parameter type, 76
hook functions, 718, 796
hooks, 757–74

I

.idata section, *585*

idle priority class, 231, *231*

IDLE_PRIORITY_CLASS identifier, *99, 235*

idle relative thread priority, 237–38, *237*

idle thread priority, 232, *233*

ID numbers for process kernel and thread kernel objects, 106

IDs, obtaining for processes, 780

#ifdefs, placing in code, 870

ImageCfg.exe utility, 254–55

IMAGE_FILE_RELOCS_STRIPPED flag, 734

image files, executing from floppies, 449

image of the .exe file, 448

images, creating without relocations, 734

Image type
   of physical storage, 460
   of region, 455

ImgWalk.dll, 789–90, *791–92*

implicit linking, 679

implicit load-time linking, 677

import section
   locating in a module, 799
   of a module, 797

imports section in an executable module, 690

Increase Scheduling Priority privilege, 232

indexing service, 182

inert processes, 69, 181

INFINITE
   passing as the second parameter to *WaitForSingleObject*, 288
   passing in the *Sleep* function, 218

Infinite Loop button in LISLab, 962–63

inheritable handles, 50–51

inheritance of kernel object handles, 94, *95–96*

Inherit.c program, *95–96*

initialization of applications, 694

initialization values, passing to thread functions, 188–89

InitializeCriticalSectionAndSpinCount function, 277

InitializeCriticalSection function, 274, 278

Inject Library sample application, 779–80, *781–89*

InSendMessageEx function, 922

InSendMessage function, 921–22

instance handles, 76–78

instruction pointer register for a thread, 195

"int 3" CPU function, 994

INT 17H interrupt, 466

integer registers, identifying for a CPU, 225

integer-related exceptions, 862

InterlockedCompareExchange function, 263–64, *264*

InterlockedCompareExchangePointer function, 264

InterlockedDecrement function, 264

InterlockedExchangeAdd function, 260, *260*, 261

InterlockedExchange function, 262, 262–63

InterlockedExchangePointer function, 262, 800

interlocked functions, 259–64
   running on different CPUs, 260–61
   speed of execution of, 261
   thread synchronization and, 331

Interlocked.h file, *361–66*

InterlockedIncrement function, 264

InterlockedType.rc file, *366–68*

InterlockedType sample application, 358–59, *359–68*

international markets, producing applications for, 17

interprocess messages, 932

interthread messages, 917–22

interthread sent message, 921, 922

IntLockTest.cpp file, *359–61*

intrathread sent message, 921, 922

intrinsic functions, 420, 837

INUSE flag, 744, 745, 746

INVALID_HANDLE_VALUE, *3*

  avoiding deadlocks passing to
    UnregisterWaitEx, 414

  comparing function return values with, 48

  passing in *CreateFileMapping*, 628–29

  returned by *CreateFile*, 598, 599

inverse semaphores, 353

I/O accounting information, querying, 152–53

I/O-bound tasks, allowing separate threads for,
  183

I/O completion port kernel object, 156

I/O completion ports, 415

I/O components of thread pools, queuing work
  items to, 402

IO_COUNTERS structure, 152

IoInfo member of the JOBOBJECT_
  EXTENDED_LIMIT_INFORMATION
  structure, 145

I/O requests

  calling functions when asynchronous, complete,
    415

  queued by threads to device drivers, 402

isalaph function, 32–33

IsDBCSLeadByte function, 18

IsDebuggerPresent function, 884

islower function, 32–33

ISMEX_CALLBACK flag, *922*

ISMEX_NOSEND value, 922

ISMEX_NOTIFY flag, *922*

ISMEX_REPLIED flag, *922*

ISMEX_SEND flag, *922*

IsModuleLoaded function, 719

IsSingleProcessOptex function, 339

IsTextUnicode function, 34–35, 609–10

isupper function, 32–33

IsWindowUnicode function, 941

J

JobLab sample application, 158–60, *160–79*

JobMemoryLimit member of the JOBOBJECT_
  EXTENDED_LIMIT_INFORMATION
  structure, 145

JOBOBJECT_BASIC_ACCOUNTING_
  INFORMATION structure, 151–52, *151–52*

JOBOBJECT_BASIC_AND_IO_
  ACCOUNTING_INFORMATION
  structure, 152

JOBOBJECT_BASIC_LIMIT_INFORMATION
  structure, 141, *141–43*, 143–44, 145

JOBOBJECT_BASIC_PROCESS_ID_LIST
  structure, 153

JOBOBJECT_BASIC_UI_RESTRICTIONS
  structure, *141*, 145, *145–46*, 146–47

JOB_OBJECT_BREAKAWAY_OK flag, 150

job object counters, 154, *154*

job object details counters, 154, *155*

JOBOBJECT_END_OF_JOB_TIME_
  INFORMATION structure, *158*

JOBOBJECT_EXTENDED_LIMIT_
  INFORMATION structure, *141*, 145, *145*

JOB_OBJECT_LIMIT_ACTIVE_PROCESS flag
  in the *LimitFlags* member, 142

JOB_OBJECT_LIMIT_AFFINITY flag in the
  LimitFlags member, *143*, 144

JOB_OBJECT_LIMIT_DIE_ON_
  UNHANDLED_EXCEPTION limit flag, 145

JOB_OBJECT_LIMIT_JOB_MEMORY flag, 145

JOB_OBJECT_LIMIT_JOB_TIME flag in the
  LimitFlags member, 142, 144

JOB_OBJECT_LIMIT_PRESERVE_JOB_TIME
  flag in the *LimitFlags* member, 144

JOB_OBJECT_LIMIT_PRIORITY_CLASS flag
  in the *LimitFlags* member, *143*

JOB_OBJECT_LIMIT_PROCESS_MEMORY
  flag, 145

JOB_OBJECT_LIMIT_SCHEDULING_CLASS
  flag in the *LimitFlags* member, *143*

JOB_OBJECT_LIMIT_WORKINGSET flag in
  the *LimitFlags* member, 142
JOB_OBJECT_MSG events, *157,* 158
job objects. *See* jobs
JOBOBJECT_SECURITY_LIMIT_
  INFORMATION structure, *141,* 148, *148*
JOB_OBJECT_SILENT_BREAKAWAY_OK flag,
  150
JOB_OBJECT_TERMINATE_AT_END_OF_
  JOB value, 158
JOB_OBJECT_UILIMIT_DESKTOP flag, *146*
JOB_OBJECT_UILIMIT_DISPLAYSETTINGS
  flag, *146*
JOB_OBJECT_UILIMIT_EXITWINDOWS flag,
  146
JOB_OBJECT_UILIMIT_GLOBALATOMS
  flag, *146*
JOB_OBJECT_UILIMIT_HANDLES flag,
  146–47, *146*
JOB_OBJECT_UILIMIT_READCLIPBOARD
  flag, *146*
JOB_OBJECT_UILIMIT_
  SYSTEMPARAMETERS flag, *146*
JOB_OBJECT_UILIMIT_WRITECLIPBOARD
  flag, *146*
jobs, 137
  application for experimenting with, 158–60,
    160–79
  bit flags for basic user-interface restrictions, *146*
  changing the relative scheduling of, 144
  event notifications, *157*
  getting statistical information about, 151–55
  maintaining accounting information, 143–44
  notifications for, 155–58
  placing processes in, 137, 149–50
  placing restrictions on processes, 140–49
  placing security restrictions on, 148
  signaling when the allotted time has expired,
    155–56
  terminating processes in, 150–51
  thread synchronization behavior, *331*

JobToken member of JOB_OBJECT_SECURITY_
  LIMIT_INFORMATION, *148*
journal record hook, 957
JUMP CPU instruction, 796–97
just-in-time debugging, 878–79

K

kanji, working with double-byte character sets, 18
Kernel32.dll, 675
  implementation of *FreeLibararyAndExitThread,*
    699
  mapping of, 777
kernel mode
  transitioning threads to, 285
  unhandled exceptions in, 877–78
kernel-mode CPU time, total used by processes,
  151
kernel-mode partition, *437,* 439, 442
kernel object handles
  controlling the inheritance of, 54–55
  inheritance of, 94, *95–96*
kernel objects, 41. *See also* data objects; User
    objects
  assigning names to, 56
  calling, when single becomes signaled, 412–15
  closing, 48–49, 608
  creating, 46–48
  creating unnamed (anonymous), 56
  destroying during process termination, 111
  differentiating from User objects and GDI
    objects, 45
  gaining access to existing, 44
  handle tables for, *46*
  manipulating, 42
  mechanisms for sharing among processes, 50–65
  multiple name spaces for, in Terminal Server, 59
  naming, 55–60
  in processes, 69
  protecting with security descriptors, 43–45

kernel objects, *continued*
   restricting access to, 44
   sharing across process boundaries, 49–65
   signaled or nonsignaled state of, 285–87
   signaling and waiting on, 334–36
   for threads, 181
   thread synchronization with, 285–87
   usage counts for, 42–43
   waking threads with, 928–31
kernel time, returned by *GetThreadTimes*, 220
keyboard buffer, identifying, *102*
keyboard events, assigning to windows, 948–49, *949*
keyboard input and focus information, 948–53
keys, determining currently pressed, 952–53
keystroke hardware events, appending to virtualized input queues, 946–47
keystrokes, forcing into applications, 333
known DLLs, 728–29

L

L, before a literal string, 25
LARGEADDRESSAWARE flag, 440, 441
/LARGEADDRESSAWARE linker switch, 440, 441
LARGE_INTEGER structure, 307
last-chance exception notification, 885, 888
LastMessageBox Info dialog box, 801–2, *801*
LastMsgBoxInfo sample application, 801–2, *803–20*
LB_GETCOUNT message, sending to a list box, 1009
LCID, comparing two strings, 31
LeaveCriticalSection function, 272–73, 275, 276–77
__*leave* keyword, 827, 835–36
LibCD.lib, *198*
LibC.lib, *198*
LibCMtD.lib, *198*

LibCMt.lib, *198*
.lib file, 681, 685–86, *696*
/Lib linker switch, 714
LimitFlags member
   of JOBOBJECT_BASIC_LIMIT_INFORMATION, *141, 142*
   setting bits in, 143
linked-list approach for spreadsheets, 518
linked lists
   synchronizing access to, 271
   walking with memory-mapped files, 623–24
linker directive for exporting functions, 689
linkers
   default base addresses for, 76
   forcing to look for the *(w)WinMain* entry-point function, 996–97
linker switches
   adding for delay-load DLLs, 714
   embedding in source code, 587–88
   settings for the sample applications in this book, 989
   setting up for application projects, 71–72
Link tab of the Project Settings dialog box, 74
LISLab application, 957–65, *965–78*
ListView control
   getting the window handle of, 761, *761*
   LVM_GETITEM and LVM_GETITEMPOSITION messages to, 760
LISWatch application, 978–80, *981–88*
literal characters, using the _TEXT macro for, 26
loader
   forcing to always check the application's directory first, 730
   for the operating system, 682
   search order for DLLs, 693
LoadIcon function, 76
LoadLibraryA function, 776
LOAD_LIBRARY_AS_DATAFILE flag, 697–98
LoadLibraryEx function, 697–98

LoadLibrary(Ex) function, *696*

LoadLibrary function, 697

    calling with a thread, 775–77

    incrementing a per-process usage count, 699–700

    loading DLLs, 578–79

    steps performed when a thread calls, 705, *706*

LoadLibraryW function, 776

LOAD_WITH_ALTERED_SEARCH_PATH flag, 698

LocalAlloc function, 656

locale, assigning to a thread, 31

locale ID (LCID), 31

LocalFileTimeToFileTime function, 307

local input state, 947–55

Local Input State Lab dialog box, *958, 959*

Local Input State Laboratory sample application. *See* LISLab application

local input states, laboratory for experimenting with, 957–65, *965–78*

Local Input State Watch sample application, 957–65, *965–78*

localization

    facilitating with DLLs, 676

    problem with, 17–18

localized access to memory, 659

"Local\" prefix, 60

local unwind, 827, 837

local variables, 186. *See also* stack-based variables

Lock Pages in Memory user right, 544

LockSetForegroundWindow function, 952

LONG data type, *4*

lowest thread priority, 232, *233*

lpMaximumApplicationAddress member of the SYSTEM_INFO data structure, *472*

lpMinimumApplicationAddress member of the SYSTEM_INFO data structure, *472*

lstrcat function, *30*

lstrcmp function, *30*

lstrcmpi function, *30*

lstrcpy function, *30*

lstrlen function, *30*

LVM_GETITEM messages, 760

M

mainCRTStartup function, 73

main entry point function, *72, 73*

MAKESOFTWAREEXCEPTION macro, 994

malloc function, 74

manual-reset events, 293

    compared with auto-reset events, 296–97, *296*

    thread synchronization behavior, *331*

manual-reset timer, 306

manual-reset waitable timer, *331*

Mapped type

    of physical storage, 460

    of region, 455

MapSEtoCE static member function, 908

MapUserPhysicalPages function, 545

MapViewOfFileEx function

    calling to create views of file-mapping objects, 637

    committing physical storage sparsely to a shared region, 637

    mapping a file into a particular address, 622–23

MapViewOfFile function, 603–6

    calling, 606–7, 625–26

    calling to create views of file-mapping objects, 637

    committing physical storage sparsely to a shared region, 637

    file offset parameter requirements, 621

    making memory-mapped files of visible, 793

maximum file size, 601

maximum memory address of usable private address spaces, *472*

maximum resource count, 313

MAXIMUM_SUSPEND_COUNT, 216

MAXIMUM_WAIT_OBJECTS, 289

MaximumWorkingSetSize member of
JOBOBJECT_BASIC_LIMIT_
INFORMATION, *141, 142*

members of a memory block, 41–42

MEM_COMMIT identifier, 516

memcpy function, 837

memory

    allocating in another process's address space, 777

    architecture used by Microsoft Windows, 435

    conserving with DLLs, 676

    fixing alignment faults, 84

    freeing in another process's address space, 778

    function duplicating a block of, 850–51, *851*

    functions used for allocations, 679

    leaks, 49

    localized access to, 659

    mechanisms for manipulating, 513

    retrieving dynamic information about the status
of, 481–82

memory address, querying information about, 489

MEMORY_BASIC_INFORMATION structure,
489–90, *490, 491*

memory blocks, 455

    accessing with threads, 316

    allocating from heaps, 662–64

    allocating large, 664

    changing the size of, 664–65

    corrupting a linked list of, 661

    displaying in an address space map, 456,
456–60, 460–61

    freeing, 665

    members of, 41–42

    retrieving the actual size of, 665

Memory Load, displaying in the VMStat
application, 483, *483*

memory management, more efficient, 658–59

memory management system, copy-on-write
feature of, 581

memory-mapped executables and DLLs, 578–94

memory-mapped files, 448, 513, 577, 594–96,
597–619

    backed by the paging file, 628–36

    coherence and, 621–22

    implementation details of, 624–27

    processing a big file using, 620–21

    purposes for, 577

    reversing the contents of a file, 596, 609

    running multiple instances of the same
application, 580–81

    sharing data with other processes, 623, 627–28

    sparsely committed, 636–53

    specifying the base address of, 622–24

    transferring data among two or more separate
processes, 630

Memory-Mapped File Sharing sample application,
630–31, *631–36*

memory-related exceptions, 861–62

MEMORYSTATUS data structure, 481–82

MEMORYSTATUSEX structure, 482

memory updates, effect of cache lines on, 265

MEM_PHYSICAL flag, 542

MEM_RESERVE flag, 542

MEM_RESERVE identifier, 515

MEM_RESET flag with *VirtualAlloc*, 536, 537,
537, 538, *539–40*

MemReset sample application, 537–38, *539–40*

MEM_TOP_DOWN flag, 515

message boxes

    displaying for unhandled exceptions, 876

    macro for displaying, 995

MessageBox function, hooking all calls to, 801

message crackers, 1005, 1006–9

message loops, properly coding with
MsgWaitForMultipleObjectsEx, 931

message queues

    assigning to threads, 912

    posting messages to, 914–15

messages
  broadcasting to all existing overlapped
    windows, 920
  creating, 933
  extracting from a thread's queue, 925–28, *927*
  low memory situation and, 926
  posting to a thread's message queue, 914–15
  sending data with, 932–40
  sending for notification purposes, 920–21
  sending to a window created by another thread,
    916–17
  sending to a window procedure, 915–22
  sending to child controls, 1009
Microsoft Management Console Performance
  Monitor, *154, 155*
Microsoft's C compiler, effect on functions
  exported with __*stdcall*, 688
Microsoft Spy++
  running jobs restricting access to UI handles,
    146–47, *147*
  Thread Properties dialog box, 213, *213*
Microsoft Visual C++, setting up linker switches,
  71–72
Microsoft Visual C++ compiler
  allocate declaration specifier, 586–87, *586–87*
  syntax of, 824
Microsoft Visual C++ debugger. *See* debugger
Microsoft Visual Studio 6.0. *See* Visual Studio 6.0
Microsoft Windows
  compared with a real-time operating system, 214
  determining the version for applications, 86–90
  ground rules for programming, 911
  memory architecture used by, 435
Microsoft Windows 2000. *See* Windows 2000
minimum memory address of usable address
  space, *472*
MinimumWorkingSetSize member of
  JOBOBJECT_BASIC_LIMIT_
  INFORMATION, *141, 142*
misaligned data value, 465–66, *466*

MMC Performance Monitor
  job object counters, *154*
  job object details counters, *155*
MMFShare application, 630–31, *631–36*
MMFSparse application, 638–42, *642–53*
modules
  binding, 738–41
  rebasing executable and DLL, 730–38
mouse capture, turning off, 961
mouse capture window, monitoring in LISWatch,
  978–80, *981–88*
mouse cursor
  capturing in a window, 954
  changing the shape of, 954–55
  clipping to a rectangular region of the screen,
    953, 961–62
  controlling while invoking new processes, 103
  hiding or showing, 962
  management of, 953–55
  moving over LISLab's dialog box, 960
mouse messages, appending to virtualized input
  queues, 946
MoveMemory function, 608
MS-DOS/16-bit Windows application
  compatibility partition, *437,* 438
MsgBoxTimeout function, 408
MsgWaitForMultipleObjectsEx function, 333–34,
  929–31
MsgWaitForMultipleObjects function, 312,
  333–34, 929–31
MSVCRtD.lib, *198*
MSVCRt.lib, *198*
_MT identifier, 206
multibyte-character strings, 36–38
MultiByteToWideChar function, 35–36
multiple heaps, 669. *See also* heaps
multiple paging files, 448. *See also* paging file
multiprocessor machines
  spinlocks on, 263
  with Windows 2000, 70

multithreaded applications, 184–85, 399

multithreaded environments, standard C/C++ run-time library and, 199

multithreading, allowing simplified user interfaces, 183

mutexes
  abandoned, 318
  not supported with *WaitForMultipleExpressions*, 386
  special exception to signaled/nonsignaled rules, 317, 318

mutex kernel objects, 315–18
  characteristics of, *319*
  compared with critical sessions, 338
  creating, 316
  creating and naming, 56
  critical sections and, 318–19, *319*
  releasing, 317
  thread ownership concept of, 317–18
  thread synchronization behavior, *331*

mutex object for a process, 712

MWMO_* flags with *MsgWaitForMultipleObjectsEx*, 930

N

named objects, 55–60

names, assigning to kernel objects, 56

nanoseconds, 308

nested exceptions, 868

NetMsg.dll module, 10

new operator in C++, 666, 667–68, *667*

NODEs
  allocating in a single heap with BRANCHes, 659
  storing with BRANCHes, 657–58, *658*

noncontinuable exception, 862

non-I/O components, associating a device with, 415–16

nonsignaled state of kernel objects, 285–87

Non-Uniform Memory Access (NUMA), 250–51, *251*

normal priority class, 230–31, *231*

NORMAL_PRIORITY_CLASS identifier, *99, 235*

normal processes, bringing to the foreground, 240

normal thread priority, 232, *233*

NORM_IGNORE* flags in *CompareString*, 31

Notepad
  File Save As dialog box, *34*
  property page for a shortcut running, *104*
  spawning an instance of, 611, *612*

notification purposes for messages sent to windows, 920–21

notifications for jobs, 155–58

NT File System (NTFS 5), support for sparse files, 638

NULL-pointer assignment partition, *437*, 438

NUMA computer architecture, 250–51, *251*

/NumProcs=1 switch, 256

O

object chart for thread synchronization, 331

object handle inheritance, 50–55

object handles, duplicating, 60–65

object names, creating unique, 59

objects. *See* data objects; kernel objects

.obj modules, producing, 681, 682

off-limits partition, 441–42

OnValChanged function, 356, 357

OpenEvent function, 293

OpenFile function, avoiding, 28

OpenFileMapping function, 44

Open functions, 58, *58*

OpenJobObject function, 139–40

OpenMutex function, 316

OpenProcess function, 780

OpenSemaphore function, 314

OpenThread function, 217–18, *217*

OpenWaitableTimer function, 305–6

operating system code, location of, 442

operating system loader. *See* loader

optex, 338, 339, *339*

Optex sample application, 340–41, *341–52*

optimized mutex. *See* optex

order of execution, using SEH, 854–55

ordinals with *GetProcAddress*, 701

ordinal values, linking DLLs with, 687

OS string functions, 28–29

_*osver* global variable, *75*

OS version check inline functions, 995–96

OSVERSIONINFOEX structure, 87, *88, 89*

OSVERSIONINFO structure, 87

Output window of the debugger, 887, *887*

OverlappedCompletionRoutine function, 416

OVERLAPPED structure, 416

P

PAGE_EXECUTE protection attribute, *449*, 516

PAGE_EXECUTE_READ protection attribute, *449*, 516

PAGE_EXECUTE_READWRITE protection attribute, *450*, 516

PAGE_EXECUTE_WRITECOPY protection attribute, 450, *450*, 451

page faults, *152*, 447

page frame numbers, 543

page granularity, decommitting with, 521

PAGE_GUARD flag, 452, 465

PAGE_GUARD protection attribute flag, 492

  accessing a page having, 862

  not supported in Windows 98, 564

PAGE_NOACCESS protection attribute, *449*

PAGE_NOCACHE flag, 452

PAGE_NOCACHE protection attribute, 600

PAGE_READONLY flag, 603

PAGE_READONLY protection attribute, *449*, *600, 604*

PAGE_READWRITE flag, 602–3, *602*

PAGE_READWRITE protection attribute, *449*, 515, *604*

  in *CreateFileMapping*, 600, 604

  looking for pages with, 608

PAGE_READWRITE storage, single page in Windows 98, 564–65

pages, 443

  altering protection rights of, 534–35

  calculating writable, 451

page sizes, 443, *472*

PAGE_WRITECOMBINE flag, 452

PAGE_WRITECOPY flag, 603

PAGE_WRITECOPY protection attribute, 450, *450*, 451, *604*

  changing to PAGE_READWRITE, 605, *605–6*

  in *CreateFileMapping*, *600*

paging file, 444

  backing memory-mapped files, 628–36

  committing storage from, 637

  committing storage in Windows 98, 582

  not maintaining physical storage in, 447–49

  physical storage and, 444–49

parent processes, 50

  calling *WaitForInputIdle*, 332

  controlling code executed by child processes, 794

  controlling the inheritance of environment variables, 81

  passing environment blocks to child processes, 86

  preventing error mode inheritance in child processes, 84

  querying, 106

  setting the child's current drive and directory, 100

  spawning child processes, 51–52

partitions of virtual address space, 436

Pascal application, calling functions in a DLL, 713

PCSTR data type, prototyping as, with *GetProcAddress*, 701

PCTSTR data type, 26

PCWSTR data type, 26

PDH.dll, 115

pdwThreadID for *CreateThread*, 190

PeakJobMemoryUsed member of the JOBOBJECT_EXTENDED_LIMIT_INFORMATION structure, 145

PeakProcessMemoryUsed member of the JOBOBJECT_EXTENDED_LIMIT_INFORMATION structure, 145

PEB (process environment block), 443

PeekMessage function, 915
    checking the calling thread, 927
    returning messages from, 926

PE file, 601

Pentium floating-point bug, 253

percent sign (%), indicating replaceable strings, 82

performance, optimizing in Windows 2000, 240

performance counters, 154

Performance Data database, 114–15

Performance Data Helper, 115

performance functions, 222

Performance Options dialog box in Windows 2000, 240, *240*

PerJobUserTimeLimit member of JOBOBJECT_BASIC_LIMIT_INFORMATION, *141, 142*

per-process usage count, 699–700

PerProcessUserTimeLimit member of JOBOBJECT_BASIC_LIMIT_INFORMATION, *141, 142*

per-thread initialization, performing by DLLs, 707

__*pfnDliFailureHook*, 718

__*pfnDliNotifyHook*, 718

pfnStartAddr parameter for *CreateThread*, 188–90

_pgmptr global variable, *75*

physical memory, displaying in the VMStat application, 483

physical RAM, 542. *See also* RAM

physical storage
    backing blocks in reserved regions, 460
    committing, 516–17, 518–20
    committing from the paging file, 605
    committing within a region, 444
    compared with virtual address space, 436
    decommitting, 520–34
    freeing for stacks, 569
    identifying the type of, 490
    methods for determining whether to commit, 519–20
    not maintaining in the paging file, 447–49
    paging file and, 444–49
    resetting the contents of, 536–40
    when to decommit, 521–23

physical storage address, translating a virtual address to, *446*

platform differences, resolving with DLLs, 676

pointers
    obtaining to complete command lines, 78
    referencing memory, 751

polling method, 268, 269

portable executable (PE) file image, 601

PostMessage function, 914

PostQueuedCompletionStatus function
    equivalent performed by *QueueUserWorkItem*, 402
    forcing an event to a thread, 312

PostQuitMessage function, 915, 925, 926, 927

PostThreadMessage function, 761, 762, 914–15, 926

power failure, memory-mapped files and, 596

ppiProcInfo parameter of *CreateProcess*, 105–7

#pragma dataseg() directive, storing initialized variables, 586–87, *586*

pragma directive, taking advantage of function forwarders in DLL modules, 727–28

pragma message directive, tricking with a series of macros, 992

#*pragma warning* directive, ignoring benign warnings, 991

predefined exceptions, listing of all, 861–63

preemptive multithreaded operating system, 214

preemptive multithreading system, 189

preferred base addresses, 730

    for DLLs, 579

    drawbacks of not loading at, 733

    setting different, 734

    starting on allocation-granularity boundaries, 735

primary thread, 70, 182

    allocating and initializing a data block for, 207

    returning the entry-point function for, 107–8

    in the Summation sample application, 568

    suspending, 96–97, 242

printf functions, 33

priorities

    programming, 235–50

    for threads, 228–34

priority 31 thread, 229

priority classes, 230–32, *231*

    assigning to processes, 235

    specifying, 98–99, *99*

priority class identifiers, 235

PriorityClass member of JOBOBJECT_ BASIC_LIMIT_INFORMATION, *141, 143*

priority levels

    boosting dynamically for threads, 238–39

    for threads in Windows 2000, 233–34, *234*

private address space, 435–36, 751

Private type

    of physical storage, 460

    of region, 455

PrivilegesToDelete member of JOB_OBJECT_ SECURITY_LIMIT_INFORMATION, *148*

procedures, subclassing for windows, 941–42

Process32First function, 115

Process32Next function, 115

process address spaces for different CPUs, *445*

PROCESSENTRY32 structure, 106

process environment block (PEB), 443

processes, 69. *See also* child processes

    allowing multiple to share data, 577

    all threads dying in, 110–11

    altering their own priority classes, 235

    command lines passed to new, 78–79

    communicating with or manipulating other, 751

    creating for applications already running, 579–82

    creating with *CreateProcess*, 90–107

    current drive and directory for, 84–86

    default heaps for, 656–57

    dynamically attaching a debugger to, 877

    enumerating running, 114–18

    environment blocks associated with, 79

    environment variables for, 79–83

    error modes for, 83–84

    flat address space needed by, 580

    forcing to die, 880

    handle tables for, 46

    handling current directories for multiple drives, 85

    identifying by unique system-wide IDs, 210

    inert, 181

    initializing, 682

    instance handles, 76–77

    mapping into address space, 603–6

    memory leaks and, 49

    methods for transferring data between, 113

    mutex objects for, 712

    obtaining the ID for, 780

    placing in jobs, 149–50

processes, *continued*

    preventing job objects from killing, 158

    previous instance handles for, *77–78*

    private address space for, 439, 751

    querying parent, 106

    reserving regions of address space for, 443

    returning times applying to, 221

    sharing a block of storage, 450

    sharing data among, using memory-mapped files, 627–28

    sharing kernel objects across, 49–65

    sharing RAM blocks not allowed between, 543

    sharing the same optex, 341

    suspending and resuming, 216–18

    terminating, 107–12, 150–51

    threads and, 181–82

    thread synchronization behavior, *331*

    total number in a job, *152*

    total number killed, *152*

    transferring data between, using window messages, 932–40

    treating as a single group, 137

    virtual address space for, 435

Processes tab of the Windows 2000 Task Manager, 236

process groups, 97

PROCESS_HEAP_ENTRY structure, 671–72

process IDs, 106–7, 153, *153*

PROCESS_INFORMATION structure, 105–6

ProcessInfo sample application, 115–18, *118–36, 737–38, 738*

process kernel objects, 60

    ID numbers for, 106

    nonsignaled or signaled state of, 286

    specifying security for, 94

ProcessMemoryLimit member of the JOBOBJECT_EXTENDED_LIMIT_ INFORMATION structure, 145

process objects, signaling, 113

processor affinity, 83, 254

Processor Affinity dialog box in Windows 2000 Task Manager, 255

processor architecture, indicating for Windows 2000, *473*

processor type, indicating for Windows 98, *473*

process priority class, 234

process-relative cleanup, performing by DLLs, 705

process-relative handles, 47

process-relative handle values, assigning to mutex objects, 57

process-relative initialization, performing for functions contained within the DLL, 703

process-relative kernel object handles, 49–50

Process Status functions, 115

programming languages, writing DLLs in many, 675

programs, creating for both Unicode and ANSI, 30

project management, simplifying with DLLs, 676

Project Settings dialog box, 198

    Link tab, 74

    in Visual Studio, 734, *735*

properties for a thread, 213, *213*

property pages for shortcuts, 103–4, *104*

protection attribute flags, 452, 461

protection attributes, 449–50, *449–50*

    assigning to regions, 515–16

    changing for pages of memory, 534–35

    identifying for all adjoining pages, 490

    for regions, 456

    specifying in *CreateFileMapping*, 599–600, *600*

psa parameter for *CreateThread*, 187

PSAPI.dll, 115

psaProcess parameter of *CreateProcess*, 94

psaThread parameter of *CreateProcess*, 94

pseudo-handles

    converting ambiguous, 212

    converting to real handles, 210–12, *212*

pseudo-handles, *continued*
  passing, 210
  returning, 209
psiStartInfo parameter of *CreateProcess*, 100
pszApplicationName parameter of *CreateProcess*, 91
pszCommandLine parameter of *CreateProcess*, 91–94
pszCurDir parameter of *CreateProcess*, 100
PTSTR data type, 26, 91–92
PulseEvent function, 297
  signaling a registered event object, 415
  SignalObjectAndWait function and, 335–36
pvEnvironment parameter of *CreateProcess*, 99
PVOID arrays, 745, 746
PVOID cast operator method, 547
PVOID data type, *3*
pvParam parameter for *CreateThread*, 188–90
PWSTR data type, 26

Q

QS_ALLEVENTS flag, *923*
QS_ALLINPUT flag, *923*
QS_ALLPOSTMESSAGE flag, *923*
QS_HOTKEY flag, *923*, 924
QS_INPUT flag, *923*
QS_KEY flag, *923*, 924
QS_MOUSEBUTTON flag, *923*, 924
QS_MOUSE flag, *923*
QS_MOUSEMOVE flag, *923*, 924
QS_PAINT flag, *923*, 924, 925
QS_POSTMESSAGE flag, *923*, 924
QS_POSTMESSAGE wake bit, 914
QS_QUIT flag, 915, *923*, 925, 926
QS_SENDMESSAGE flag, *923*, 924, 925
  setting, 916
  turning off, 917
QS_TIMER flag, *923*, 924, 925
quantums, 70, *70*

QueryInformationJobObject function, 149, 156
  getting IDs for currently running processes, 153
  getting statistical information about jobs, 151
QueryPerformanceCounter function, 222
QueryPerformanceFrequency function, 222
queues, querying the status of, 923
Queue sample application, 319–22, *322–30*
queue status flags, 923–25
  examining the state of, 925
  waking threads with, 928–31
QueueUserAPC function, 385
QueueUserWorkItem function, 401–3
Quick Free, 660

R

RaiseException function, 872–73, 904–5, *904*
RAM
  adding for better performance, 447
  allocating one or more blocks of, 541
  allocating physical, 542
  forcing a heavy demand on, 538
RAM blocks
  encapsulating, 547
  freeing, 545
  un-assigning the current, 545
raw input thread (RIT), 945–47
.rdata section, *585*
READ attribute for a section, *583*
read-only files, coherence and, 622
ReadProcessMemory function, 778
real-time operating systems, 214
real-time priority class, *231*, 232
REALTIME_PRIORITY_CLASS identifier, *99*, 235
real-time range for threads, 238–39
Rebase.exe utility, 735–37, *735–36*
ReBaseImage function, 736, *736*
rebasing, executable and DLL modules, 730–38

recalculation fiber
   in the Counter sample application, 421
   deleting, 422–23
recalculation thread, destroying, 423
recursion bugs, catching endless, 188
recursion counter in a mutex, 315
redirection of DLLs, 729–30
Refresh function, 500–501, *500*
regions
   in an address space, 443–44
   assigning protection attributes to, 515–16
   committing physical storage within, 444
   number of blocks within reserved, 455
   number of bytes reserved for, 455
   protection attributes for, 456
   releasing, 520–34
   reserving and committing storage
      simultaneously, 517
   reserving at the highest memory address
      possible, 515
   reserving in address spaces, 513–16
   text description of, 456
   types of, 454–55, *455*
   in Unicode, 19, *19*
registers, getting a thread's important, 226, *226–27*
RegisterWaitForSingleObject function, 413–14
registry, injecting DLLs using, 754–56
Registry Editor, viewing the \AppInit_DLLs key,
   755
Registry entries for environment variables in
   Windows 2000, 80–81
RegNotifyChangeKeyValue function, 402
relative thread priority, 237
relative virtual address (RVA), 686, *686*, 687
ReleaseCapture function, 954, 961
ReleaseMutex function, 317, 318
ReleaseSemaphore function, 315
   calling in a *finally* block, 829
   in the Queue sample application, 321, 322

relocation information, removing from a DLL, 579
relocation sections, building in modules, 733
.reloc section, *585*
remote processes, copying strings to the address
   space of, 778
remote threads, injecting DLLs, 774–89
Remove method in the Queue sample application,
   321–22
replaceable strings, 82
ReplaceIATEntryInAllMods function, 800
ReplaceIATEntryInOneMod function, 797, *798*,
   799–800
ReplyMessage function, 921
reserved regions, 455
   committing storage in, 516–17
   releasing by calling *VirtualFree*, 521
Reserve type of physical storage, 460
reserving address space regions, 443
reserving regions, compared with committing
   physical storage, 514–15
ResetEvent function, 294
resetting storage, 536
resource guard class, 354
resource-only DLLs, 734
resources
   accessing multiple simultaneously, 281
   "atomically" manipulating, 269–70
   counting, 313
   creating a CRITICAL_SECTION structure for
      each, 272
   making thread-safe, 353
   string values in, 33–34
   synchronizing access to, 399
   writing code for shared, 273
resource sharing, facilitating with DLLs, 676
RestrictedSids member of JOB_OBJECT_
   SECURITY_LIMIT_INFORMATION, *148*
restrictions, placing on job processes, 140–49
ResultCallBack function, 919, 920

Result message box in the TimedMsgBox
  application, 408
ResumeThread function, 215, 237–38
resumptive exception handling, 906
return statement
  avoiding the premature execution of, 826
  putting inside a *finally* block to halt global
    unwinds, 855–56, *855*
return value data types for Windows functions, *3–4*
Reverse file contents button in the FileRev
  application, 609, *609*
RIT (raw input thread), 945–47
RobustHowManyToken function, 849–50, *849*
RobustMemDup function, 850–51, *851*
.rsrc section, *585*
RTL_CRITICAL_SECTION structure, 274
runaway processes, killing, *231*
running threads, operating system memory
  and, 436
run-time libraries, linking projects with, 198–99,
  198
RVA (relative virtual address), 686, *686*, 687

S

sandbox, 137, 441
  creating a really secure, 147
  setting up, 140
scalar data type, creating a thread-safe, 356
schedulable threads, 214–15
scheduling algorithm, 230
SchedulingClass member of JOBOBJECT_BASIC_
  LIMIT_INFORMATION, *141*, *143*, 144
Scheduling Lab sample application, 241–42,
  243–50
screen resolution, 759
search order, altering for DLLs, 698
Search Results window in the content indexing
  service, 182

SEC_COMMIT attribute, 601
SEC_COMMIT flag with *CreateFileMapping*, 637
SEC_IMAGE attribute, 600–601
SEC_NOCACHE attribute, 600
secondary threads, 185–87
SEC_RESERVE attribute, 601
SEC_RESERVE flag
  with *CreateFileMapping*, 637
  with *VirtualAlloc*, 638
section attributes in *CreateFileMapping*, 600–601
sections
  breaking the contents of a file into, *580*
  composing .exe or DLL file images, 582–83
  creating, 586
  listing in an .exe or DLL image file, 583, *583–85*
  names for common, *585*
  shared, 588
/SECTION switch on the linker's command line,
  587
security access flags, selecting proper, 45
SECURITY_ATTRIBUTES structure, 43–44, 94
  initializing, 50
  pointers to, 43, 187
security descriptors, protecting kernel objects,
  43–45
SecurityLimitFlags member of JOB_OBJECT_
  SECURITY_LIMIT_INFORMATION, *148*
security restrictions, placing on jobs, 148
segment registers, identifying for a CPU, 225
SEH (structured exception handling), 520, 823–24
  creating a totally robust *strcpy* function, 848–49
  order of execution using, 854–55
  portability of, 871
SEH code with __*delayLoadHelper*, 715
SEH frame
  placing around thread functions, 205
  setting up around thread functions, 196
SEHTerm application, 839–41, *841*

semaphore kernel objects, 313–15
  creating, 314
  thread synchronization behavior, *331*
semaphores, inverse, 353
SEM_FAILCRITICALERRORS flag, 84
SEM_NOALIGNMENTFAULTEXCEPT flag, 84, 468
SEM_NOGPFAULTERRORBOX flag, 84
SEM_NOGPFAULTERRORBOX identifier, 880
SEM_NOOPENFILEERRORBOX flag, 84
SendMessageCallback function, 919–20
SendMessage function, 762, 915–17
send-message queues, 920
SendMessageTimeout function, 917–19
SendNotifyMessage function, 920–21
serialized calls to *DllMain*, 709–12
server, communicating with the client, 298
Server Threads list box in the Queue sample application, *319*, 320
Session keyword, 60
SetActiveWindow function, 950, 960
SetCapture function, 954, 961
SetCriticalSectionSpinCount function, 277–78, 339
SetCurrentDirectory function, 85
SetCursor function, 954
SetDIPSHook function, 761
SetEndOfFile function in FileRev, 611
SetEnvironmentVariable function, 83
SetErrorMode function, 83–84
  correcting misaligned data accesses, 468
  efficiency of, 469
  forcing processes to die, 880
  passing the SEM_NOALIGNMENTFAULTEXCEPT flag, 468
SetEvent function, 294, 295, 296–97
SetFocus function, 948–49, 959, 960
SetForegroundWindow function, 951–52, 960
SetHandleInformation function, 54–55

SetInformationJobObject function, 141, 149, *156*, 157
SET lines, placing in an AutoExec.bat file, 80
SetPriorityClass function, *143*, 235
SetProcessAffinityMask function, 251
SetProcessPriorityBoost function, 239
__set_se_translator function, 908
SetThreadAffinityMask function, 252–53
SetThreadContext function, 227, *227*, 228
SetThreadIdealProcessor function, 254
SetThreadPriorityBoost function, 239
SetThreadPriority function, *143*, 237
SetTimer function, 979
SetUnhandledExceptionFilter function, 881
SetVal functions in the CInterlockedType class, 355–56
SetWaitableTimer function, 306–9, *306–7, 308–9*
SetWindowHookEx function, 757–58
SetWindowLongPtrA function, 941, 942, 943
SetWindowLongPtr function, 752–54
SetWindowLongPtrW function, 942, 943
SetWindowPos function, 950–51, 960
SHARED attribute for a section, *583*
shared blocks, assigning copy-on-write protection to, 451
Shared MemoryMapped File Partition, 439
shared MMF partition, *437*, 442
shared regions, committing physical storage to, 637
shared resources
  using one CRITICAL_SECTION variable per, 279–81
  writing code for, 273
Shared section, creating in AppInst, 589
shared sections, 588
SHIQ (system hardware input queue), 945
ShlWApi.h header file, 29
shortcuts, property pages for, 103–4, *104*

SidsToDisable member of JOB_OBJECT_
SECURITY_LIMIT_INFORMATION, *148*

signaled state of kernel objects, 285–87

signal function, 205, 207

SignalObjectAndWait function, 334–36

single-process optex, 339, 340

single writer/multiple reader guard. *See*
CSWMRG class; SWMRG sample application

single-writer/multiple-readers scenario, 368

Sleep field in the Scheduling Lab application, *241,*
242

Sleep function, 218–19, *262, 263*

SMTO_* flags with *SendMessageTimeout*, 918

soft affinity, assigning threads to processors, 250

software exception codes, 994

software exceptions, 843, 870–74
generating, 874
trapping, 871

SORT_STRINGSORT flag in *CompareString, 31*

source code
embedding linker switches in, 587–88
writing for Unicode, 23–29

source code files
compiling automatically, 183
including the header file, *684,* 684–85

source code modules, processing, 681

source process, 61

space-delimited tokens in a string, returning the
number of, *849,* 849–50

spaces, significance in environment variables,
79–80

sparse files, NT File System (NTFS 5) support for,
638

sparsely committed memory-mapped files, 636–53

Sparse Memory-Mapped File sample application.
See MMFSparse application

sparse MMF, 638

SPI_GETFOREGROUNDFLASHCOUNT
value, 952

SPI_GETFOREGROUNDLOCKTIMEOUT
value, 952

spinlocks, 269
avoiding on single-CPU machines, 263
critical sections and, 277–78
implementing, 262
on multiprocessor machines, 263
wasting CPU time, 262–63

spreadsheets
declared-matrix method, 518
linked-list approach for, 518
sharing as file-mapping objects, 637
sharing with another process, 636
superminiature, 421
virtual memory technique for, 518–19

Spreadsheet sample application, 889–92, *892–903*

stack-based variables, 743, 744. *See also* local
variables

stack checking function in the C++ run-time
library, 565–67, *566–67*

stack limit, 188

/STACK linker switch, 187–88

/STACK option, specifying to Microsoft's linker,
559

stack overflows
catching in Windows 98, 564
recovering from, 562, 567–69, *570–75*

stack pointer for a thread, 195

stack regions
differences for threads under Windows 98,
563–65
for threads, 559, *560, 561*

standard C run-time library, 744

Start command, switches for priority classes, 236

STARTF_FORCEOFFFEEDBACK flag, 103

STARTF_FORCEONFEEDBACK flag, 103

STARTF_RUN_FULLSCREEN flag, *102*

STARTF_USECOUNTCHARS flag, *102*

STARTF_USEFILLATTRIBUTE flag, *102*

STARTF_USEPOSITION flag, *102*

STARTF_USESHOWWINDOW flag, *102*

STARTF_USESIZE flag, *102*

STARTF_USESTDHANDLES flag, *102*

start glass cursor, 103

StartRestrictedProcess function, 149–50

StartRestrictProcess function, 137, *138–39*, 139–40

start time, associating with every thread, 749

startup code, executing for an .exe file, 579

STARTUPINFO structure, 100–104

starvation, 229

starved thread, 275–76

starving threads, 219, 239

state variables in the Count sample application, 422

static control, read-only cell implemented as, 421

static data

    not sharing by multiple instances of an executable or DLL, 579–82

    sharing across multiple instances of an executable or DLL, 582–88

static TLS, 749–50

static variables

    in DLLs, 678

    in thread functions, 186

statistical information about jobs, 151–55

STATUS_ACCESS_VIOLATION exception with *HeapAlloc*, 663

STATUS_NO_MEMORY exception

EXCEPTION_NONCONTINUABLE flag and, 872

    with *HeapAlloc*, 663

    raising, 871

__*stdcall* (WINAPI) calling convention, exporting functions, 688

STILL_ACTIVE identifier, 112

Stop Always, setting the debugger's action to, 886–87

Stop If Not Handled, setting the debugger's action to, 887–88

stopwatch timer, *222*

storage, committing sparsely, 637–38, 858, 889

strcmp function, compared with a Windows function, 30

strcmpi function, compared with a Windows function, 30

strcpy function, creating a totally robust, 848–49

string manipulation functions. *See* Windows string functions

strings

    converting in Windows 2000, 20

    modifying arithmetic problems, 29

    representing in Unicode, 19

    translating between Unicode and ANSI, 35–40

string values in resources, 33–34

str prefix, replacing with *wcs*, 24

_*strrev* run-time function, 610

strtok function, 743, 849–50, *849–50*

structured exception handling. *See* SEH (structured exception handling)

structured exceptions

    vs. C++, 904–8

    catching with C++, 906–8, *906–7, 908*

    creating a C++ class identifying, 907–8, *907*

subclassing an instance of a window created by another process, 752–54

/SUBSYSTEM:CONSOLE linker switch, 71, 73, 74, 734

/SUBSYSTEM linker switch, 73, 74

/SUBSYSTEM:WINDOWS linker switch, 71, 73, 74, 734

successful wait side effects, 291, 294

Sum function, executing in its own thread, 569

Summation sample application, 567–69, *570–75*

summation thread, 568

suspend and resume, supporting with *SetWaitableTimer*, 309

Suspend button in the Scheduling Lab sample application, 242 suspend count for a thread, 215

suspended threads, 214

SuspendProcess function, 216–18, *217*

SuspendThread function, 216, 226

/SWAPRUN image flags, 449

SwitchDesktop function, *146*

switch statements

    implementing window procedures, 1006

    making changes to use message crackers, 1007

SwitchToFiber function, 419–20, 423

SwitchToThread function, 219

SWMRG sample application, 371–72, *372–80*

symbols, fixing references to imported, 693–94

synchronization

    of threads accessing a shared resource, 368–69

    user-mode, 399

synchronization primitives, placing around certain functions, 207

synchronous key state array, 952

SysInfo application, 473, *473–81*

system-defined exceptions, listing of all, 886

system hardware input queue (SHIQ), 945

SYSTEM_INFO data structure, 471–73, *472, 473*

system information, retrieving, 471–81

System Information sample application. *See* SysInfo application

SystemParametersInfo function

    controlling flashing, 952

    controlling input time, 951

    preventing processes from changing system parameters via, *146*

System Properties Control Panel applet, 448

SYSTEMTIME structure, *306, 307*

System Variables list in the Environment Variables dialog box, 81, *81*

system version of Windows, determining for applications, 86–90

"System-wide" monitoring in LISWatch, 979

T

target process, 61

Task Manager

    allowing users to alter CPU affinity, 255

    changing the priority classes of processes, 236

    Debug menu option, 879

    obtaining a process's ID, 780

Task Manager window, displaying in Windows 2000, 964

TCHAR data type, 25

TChar.h file, 24

    _tcspy macro, 24–25

    _TEXT macro, 25–26

TEBs (thread environment blocks), 443

Terminal Server, name spaces in, 59–60

TerminateJobObject function, 151

TerminateProcess function, 110

    DllMain and, 705

    terminating threads, 193

TerminateThread function, 192–93, 708

termination handlers, 824–25

    reasons for using, 838–39

    understanding by example code samples, 825–41

termination handling on different CPUs, 827

text files

    determining if ANSI or Unicode, 34–35

    identifying characters in, 34–35

    line termination of, 610–11

    reversing the contents of, 609

_TEXT macro in TChar.h, 25–26

.text section, 582, *585*

text strings, coding, 17

ThisPeriodTotalKernelTime member of JOBOBJECT_BASIC_ACCOUNTING_INFORMATION, *152*

ThisPeriodTotalUserTime member of JOBOBJECT_BASIC_ACCOUNTING_INFORMATION, *151* thrashing, 447

thread environment blocks (TEBs), 443

thread functions, 185–86

  calling, 196

  passing initialization values to, 188–89

  returning from, for thread termination, 191

  wrapping all in an SEH frame, 881–82

  wrapping the primary, 880

thread IDs, 106–7

THREADINFO structure, 912, *913*

thread kernel objects, 94, 186

  creating, 194

  ID numbers for, 106

  life of, 185

  nonsignaled or signaled state of, 286

thread-local level, performing mouse capture, 954

thread-local storage. *See* TLS (thread-local storage)

thread ownership concept for mutexes, 317–18

thread pool

  components of, 399–400, *400*

  forcing to create new threads, 403

  overhead of using, 400–401

thread priorities, 232–33

THREAD_PRIORITY* identifiers, *237*

Thread Properties dialog box in Microsoft Spy++, 213, *213*

threads

  accessing memory blocks, 316

  algorithm for scheduling, 213

  algorithm for waking up multiple, 292

  all dying in a process, 110–11

  allowing exclusive access to heaps, 661

  allowing lower-priority to execute, 219

  assigning a locale to, 31

  assigning message queues to, 912

  associating a start time with, 749

  communicating with each other, 257

  components of, 181

threads, *continued*

  connecting to the RIT, 947

  contexts of, 226

  control over the running of, 214

  CPU registers for, 195

  creating, 182–85, *400*

  creating and initializing, 194–96, *195*

  creating in another process, 774–75

  creating stack regions for, 559–60, *560, 561*

  creating suspended, 214, 215–16

  destroying, *400*

  determining which created a window, 914

  disabling the dynamic boosting of priority levels, 239

  dynamically boosting the priority levels of, 238–39

  entry-point functions for, 185–86

  errno variables and, 199

  execution times for, 219–22

  exit code for, 186

  extracting messages from a queue, 925–28, *927*

  factors affecting the creation of, *400*

  forcing unserialized calls to heaps, 663

  gaining access to resources, 314, 316–17

  identifying by unique system-wide IDs, 210

  implicitly attaching together, 957

  internals of, 194–97

  keeping available to handle requests, 403

  killing, 708

  managing the creation and destruction of, 399

  misuse of, 184–85

  monitoring local input state for a single, 979–80

  ownership of, 912

  passing data from one to another, 746

  performing blocking deletes of timers, 406

  placing a value in the PVOID array, 746

  preempting lower priority, 229

  priorities for, 228–34

  in processes, 69

threads, *continued*

processes and, 181–82

properties for, 213, *213*

protecting from one another, *946, 947*

querying thread times, 210

queuing work items to, 401

rescheduling with the *Sleep* function, 218–19

reserving regions of address space for, 559

reserving the bottommost page of the stack, 563

retrieving a value from the PVOID array, 746

returning the priority level of, 238

running simultaneously, 189–90, *189*

scenarios for scheduling, 144

scheduling CPU time for, 70, *70*

scheduling for time slices, 238

scheduling multiple, 213–14

setting affinity masks for individual, 252

setting the last error code, 8–9

setting the relative priority of, 237

sharing memory blocks in linked lists, 661

sharing virtualized input queues and local input state variables, 955–57

signaled/nonsignaled state of, 286

starved, 275–76

starving, 219

storing IDs for, 190

suspending, 922

suspending and resuming, 215–16

suspending several times, 215–16

suspending themselves, 332

switching to another, 219

synchronization accessing a shared resource, 368–69

synchronizing, 762

terminating, 191–94

termination actions, 193–94

thread synchronization behavior, *331*

transitioning from user mode to kernel mode, 277, 285

threads, *continued*

turning into fibers, 418

waiting, *400*

waiting for their own messages, 333–34, 929

waking, *400*, 922–31, 928–31

thread-safe data object, 354–55

thread-safe heaps, 660

thread safety, endowing data objects with, 353

thread-safe variables, 356–57

thread scheduler, algorithm for, 230

thread scheduling, role of context structure in, 223

thread stacks, 181

allocating memory for, 194–95, *195*

SEH frames and, 858

_threadstartex function, 202, 204–5, *204*

thread synchronization, 257–58

advanced, 267–69

avoiding overhead, 660

object chart for, *331*

user-mode, 285

using the thread's message queue for, 762

thunking, source code for *CreateWindowExA* under Windows 2000, 28

tiddata memory block, 713

tiddata structure, 202, *202–3*

time-critical thread priority, 232

timed intervals, calling functions at, 403–12

Timed Message Box, 408

TimedMsgBox sample application, 407–8, *409–12*

time-outs, handling in *WaitForMultipleExpressions*, 385, *385–86*

time quantum, adjusting for threads, 144

timer APC routine, 310–11

TimerAPCRoutine function, 310–11, *310–11*

timer queue, 404, 407

timers, 312–13

altering due time or period, 406–7

APCs and, 311

creating in a timer queue, 404

setting in LISWatch, 979

time slices
  scheduling threads for, 238
  for threads, 70, *70*
time values, returned by *GetThreadTimes*, 220, *220*
TLS (thread-local storage), 4, 204, 743
  adding to an application, 747
  assigning string pointers to run-time functions, 743
  dynamic, 744–49
  internal data structures used for managing, 744, *745*
  static, 749–50
TlsAlloc function, 744–46, 748–49, *748*
TlsFree function, 746
TlsGetValue function, 205, *205*, 746
TLS_MINIMUM_AVAILABLE bit flags, 744, *745*
TLS_OUT_OF_INDEXES, returning by *TlsAlloc*, 745
.tls section, *585*, 749
TlsSetValue function, 746
TLS slots, allowed by Windows 2000, 748
tokens in a string, returning the number of space-delimited, 849–50, *849–50*
tolower function, Unicode strings and, 32
ToolHelp API, 115
ToolHelp functions, 115, 670
  enumerating lists of threads, 217
  querying parent processes, 106
  working with, 118
Toolhelp.h file with ProcessInfo, *130–36*
TotalKernelTime member of JOBOBJECT_BASIC_ACCOUNTING_INFORMATION, *151*
TotalPageFaultCount member of JOBOBJECT_BASIC_ACCOUNTING_INFORMATION, *152*
TotalPageFile, displaying in the VMStat application, 483, *483*
TotalPhys, displaying in the VMStat application, 483, *483*

TotalProcesses member of JOBOBJECT_BASIC_ACCOUNTING_INFORMATION, *152*
TotalTerminatedProcesses member of JOBOBJECT_BASIC_ACCOUNTING_INFORMATION, *152*
TotalUserTime member of JOBOBJECT_BASIC_ACCOUNTING_INFORMATION, *151*
TotalVirtual, displaying in the VMStat application, *483*, 484
toupper function, Unicode strings and, 32
TranslateMessage function, 926
TranslateSEtoCE function, 908
Trojan DLLs, 792
try block
  in an exception handler, 843
  returning prematurely from, 832
TryEnterCriticalSection function, 276, 339
try-except blocks, 844–61
__*try* keyword in a termination handler, 824

U

UI handles, running jobs restricting access to, 146–47, *147*
UI-related tasks, waking threads to process, 928
UIRestrictionsClass member of JOBOBJECT_BASIC_UI_RESTRICTIONS, *145*, 146
unaligned data references, 308
__*unaligned* keyword with the Alpha CPU, 469–70, *469*
UNALIGNED macro, 470
unallocated address space, 443
"unhandled exception" dialog box, turning off, 145
UnhandledExceptionFilter function, 876–78
  calling, 882–83, *882*
  compared with *SetUnhandledExceptionFilter*, 881
  invoking the debugger, 878–79

UnhandledExceptionFilter function, *continued*
  making the default filter again, 881–82
  steps performed by, 883–85
unhandled exceptions, 875
  displaying message boxes indicating, 876
  in kernel mode, 877–78
UnhookWindowsHookEx function, 758–59
Unicode, 18–20
  code points, 19–20
  considering, 17
  making sure the host system supports, 996
  reasons for using, 20
  regions in, 19, *19*
  registering strings and characters as, 941
  representing strings, 19
  saving text files as, 34
  Windows 98 and, 21
  Windows 2000 and, 20
  Windows CE and, 22
  writing source code, 23–29
Unicode/ANSI generic data type, 26
Unicode/ANSI generic source code files, 24
Unicode build option in the Hdr.h header file,
  990–91
Unicode characters, identifying in text files, 34–35
Unicode consortium, 18–19
Unicode data types, defined by Windows, 26
_UNICODE macro, 23, 24–26
Unicode-ready applications, guidelines for, 29
Unicode standard, 18–19
Unicode strings, 30–33
Unicode versions of functions, 38, *38*
unique object names, 59
UNIX server applications, porting to Windows,
  417
UnmapStorage method, unmapping RAM blocks,
  547
UnmapViewOfFile function, 606–7
unnamed (anonymous) kernel objects, 56

UnregisterWaitEx function, 414
"unresolved external symbol" error, 73
updates, writing to disk, 607
usage counts for kernel objects, 42–43
User32.dll file, 675
  mapping DLLs into processes using, 754–56
  mapping of, 752–53, *753*
UserHandleGrantAccess function, 148
user-interface fiber in the Counter sample
    application, 421
user interface threads, 184–85
user-mode context, 226
user-mode CPU time, total used by processes, *151*
user-mode functions, thread synchronization and,
    331
user-mode partition, *437*, 439–41
user-mode synchronization, 399
user-mode thread synchronization, 285
user-mode time, specifying to processes, *142*
User objects. *See also* data objects; kernel objects
  differentiating from kernel objects, 45
  granting or denying access to, 148
user time, returned by *GetThreadTimes*, *220*
User timers, compared with waitable timers,
    312–13
UTC (Coordinated Universal Time), converting
    to, 307

V

variables
  avoiding exporting, 683
  modifying shared, 260
  sharing, 582, 588
  volatile, 589
VcppException exception codes, 715–16
VDM (Virtual DOS Machine), 97–98
VerifyVersionInfo function, 88–89, 90
VER_SET_CONDITION macro, 89
very large memory portion, 482

view of a file, 603–6

virtual address, translating to a physical storage address, *446*

virtual address space, 436

   calculating bytes reserved in, 484

   partitioning, 436–42

   for processes, 435

VirtualAllocEx function, 777

VirtualAlloc function, 513–16, 517

   for allocating large blocks, 664

   committing physical storage, 444, 516–17, 637

   resetting storage, 536–37

Virtual DOS Machine (VDM), 97–98

VirtualFreeEx function, 778

VirtualFree function, 520–21

   decommitting storage, 444, 638

   freeing the address window, 545

   releasing address space, 444

virtualized input queue, appending hardware messages to, 945–46

virtual memory, 444, 513

virtual memory addresses, 732

Virtual Memory Allocation sample application. *See* VMAlloc application

Virtual Memory Allocator window, *523, 524*

Virtual Memory dialog box, *448*

Virtual Memory Map sample application. *See* VMMap application

VirtualMemoryStatus. See GlobalMemoryStatus function

Virtual Memory Status sample application, 483–84, *484–88*

virtual memory techniques

   combining with SEH, 858

   for spreadsheets, 518–19

VirtualProtect function, 535

VirtualQueryEx function, 489

VirtualQuery function, 489, 525

Visual C++, run-time libraries shipping with, 198–209

Visual C++ compiler, 904

Visual C++ linker, default base address of, 76

Visual C++ run-time library

   _beginthreadex function, 187

   _endthreadex function, 192

Visual Studio 6.0

   configuring to show the last error code number, 6–7, *7*

   Error Lookup utility, 7

   Rebase.exe utility, 735–37, *735–36*

VLM portion, 482

VMAlloc application, 523–25, *525–34,* 858

VMArray.h file, 891, *899–903*

VMMap application, 116, 452, 499–501, *501–11*

VMQuery.cpp file, *493–98*

VMQuery function, 491–93

VMQuery.h file, *498–99*

VMQUERY structure, 491–92, *492*

VMStat application, 483–84, *484–88*

VOID data type, *3*

volatile type qualifier, *268, 269*

volatile variables, 589

W

WAIT_ABANDONED value, 318

waitable timers, 305, 403–4

   compared with User timers, 312–13

   queuing APC entries, 309–11

WaitForDebugEvent function, 334

WaitForInputIdle function, 53, 332–33

WaitForMultExp.cpp file, *387–91*

WaitForMultExp.h file, *391*

WaitForMultipleExpressions function, 337, 380–82

   implementing, 383–86

   mutexes not supported, 386

   testing, 382

WaitForMultipleExpressions sample application, 382–86, *387–98*

WaitForMultipleObjectsEx function, 384

WaitForMultipleObjects function, 289–90, *290*, 383
  compared with *MsgWaitForMultipleObjects*, 929
  compared with *RegisterWaitForSingleObject*, 413
  improving, 380
  performing operations atomically, 291–92
  performing thread synchronization, 332

WaitForSingleObject function, 113, 287–89, *288*
  calling, 295
  not calling inside any DLL's *DllMain* function, 712
  performing thread synchronizations, 332

wait functions, 287–90

WaitOrTimerCallback function, 404–5

wake bits, testing for specific, 923

wake flags, 922

__*wargv* global variable, 75

warning level 4, sample applications built using, 991

Watch window, configuring to show the last error code number, 6–7, *7*

WCHAR data type, 26

wchar_t data type in the C run-time library, 23

wcscmpi function, compared with a Windows function, 30

wcsmp function, compared with a Windows function, 30

wcs prefix for Unicode functions, 24

Web browsers, communicating in the background, 183

_*wenviron* global variable, *75*

WfMETest.cpp file, *391–96*

WfMETest.rc file, *396–98*

WH_GETMESSAGE hook, 757

wide-character strings, 35–36

WideCharToMultiByte function, 36–38

_WIN32_WINNT, defining in Hdr.h header file, 990

window activation changes, monitoring anywhere in the system, 979

window-based timers, 312

window class, registering a new, 941

Window helper functions for manipulating DBCS strings, 18

window procedures, problems with, 1006

windows
  activating a top-level and setting focus, 950
  assigning keyboard events to, 948–49, *949*
  bringing to the foreground, 951
  capturing the mouse, 954
  changing the focus of, 958
  flashing the caption and button on the taskbar, 952
  getting rid of nonresponsive, 963–64
  handling ANSI/Unicode characters and strings, 941–43
  sending messages across process boundaries, 760–61
  sending messages to, 915–22
  specifying the width and length of, *101–2*
  subclassing instances of, 752–54
  subclassing procedures, 941–42

Windows. *See* Microsoft Windows

Windows 95, *pdwThreadID* parameter and, 190

Windows 98
  address space differences for, 461, *461–64*, 465
  address space shared by processes, 751
  ANSI window classes and procedures, 941
  calling *HeapAlloc*, 663
  calling *MapViewOfFileEx*, 624
  calling your own unhandled exception filter, 884
  committing storage in the paging file, 606
  copy-on-write attribute and, 582
  copy-on-write protection and, 451, 608
  CreateRemoteThread function and, 775
  CreateWindowEx and, 28

Windows 98, *continued*

creating an initial set of environment variables, 80

C run-time functions in, 24

DLL redirection not supported, 729

FileRev and, 610

implementation of functions in 16-bit code, 6

implementing memory-mapped files, 624–27

inheritance supported by, 50

injecting code with a memory-mapped file, 793

IsTextUnicode function under, 35

jobs not supported by, 137

kernel-mode partition not protected, 442

maintaining compatibility with MS-DOS and 16-bit Windows applications, 438

MapViewOfFile and, 605

message box for unhandled exceptions, 876

no support for jobs, 884

operating system memory and running threads, 436

partitioning of the kernel, 436, *437*

passing security functions, 44–45

passing the PAGE_WRITECOPY flag to *CreateFileMapping*, 600

pdwThreadID parameter and, 190

pressing Ctrl+Alt+Del to display the Close Program window, 963, *963*

protection attribute flags and, 452

protection attributes supported, 450, 535

protection of the main Windows DLLs, 797

resetting of physical storage and, 536–40

rules for heaps, 655

running 16-bit Windows applications, 98

scheduling threads, 71

security features not implemented in, 43

shared MMF partition, *437*, 442

stopping mouse cursor clipping, 962

system information on an *x*86, *473*

Windows 98, *continued*

a thread's stack under, 563–65

Unicode and, 21, 996

user-mode partition, 439

VirtualAlloc memory addresses and, 638

Windows 2000. *See also* 64-bit Windows 2000

calling *MapViewOfFileEx*, 624

content indexing service shipping with, 182

CreateThread function in, 775

CreateWindowEx and, 28

displaying the Task Manager window, 964

environment variables in, 80–81

hiding operating system memory from running threads, 436

implementing memory-mapped files, 625

limiting the number of CPUs on an *x*86 machine, 256

MapViewOfFile and, 605

message box for unhandled exceptions, 876–77

with multiple CPUs, 70

multiple paging files in, 448

pdwThreadID parameter and, 190

priority levels for threads, 233–34, *234*

resetting of physical storage, 536

rules for heaps, 655

specifying an address that is not a multiple of the allocation granularity, 623

stopping mouse cursor clipping, 962

testing whether the host system is exactly, 90

TLS slots allowed by, 748

turning on the Lock Pages in Memory user right, 544

Unicode and, 20

user-mode partition, 439

VirtualFree function and, 638

Windows 2000 Advanced Server, 3-GB user-mode partition, 439

Windows 2000 Data Center, 3-GB user-mode partition, 439

Windows 2000 MMC Performance Monitor snap-in, viewing alignment fixups per second, 468

Windows 2000 Notepad. *See* Notepad

Windows 2000 Task Manager. *See* Task Manager

Windows API for Unicode, design of, 23

Windows applications. *See* applications

Windows CE, Unicode and, 22

Windows definitions, warning level 4 and, 991

Windows Explorer
creating the taskbar and desktop, 947
high priority class and, 231–32

Windows functions. *See* functions

Windows header files. *See* header files

Windows hooks. *See* hooks

Windows messaging system, 911

Windows string functions, 28–29, 30–33

Windows version build option in the CmnHdr.h header file, 990

WindowsX.h file, 1005

WinError.h file, error codes defined in, 865

WinError.h header file, 4, *4–5*, 6

WinExec function, avoiding, 28

WinMainCRTStartup function, 73

WinMain entry point function, *72*, 996–97

WinMain functions, 77–78, *77*

WinMain's hinstExe parameter in *(w)WinMain*, 76

_winmajor global variable, *75*

_winminor global variable, *75*

WinUser.h, prototyping of *SendMessageTimeout*, 918

_winver global variable, *75*

wmainCRTStartup function, 73

wmain entry point function, *72, 73*

WM_CHAR message, placing in the posted-message queue, 926

WM_COMMAND message, 1006–7, *1007*

WM_COPYDATA message, 933–35

WM_CREATE message, 921

WM_GETTEXTLENGTH message, 933

WM_GETTEXT message, 932–33

WM_KEYDOWN message, 926

WM_KEY* messages, 333

WM_(SYS)KEYUP message, 926

WM_KILLFOCUS message, 950

WM_LBUTTONDOWN message, 926

WM_PAINT message, 927

WM_QUIT message, 927

WM_SETCURSOR message, 955

WM_SETTEXT message, 932

WM_SYSCHAR message, 926

WM_SYSKEYDOWN message, 926

WM_TIMER messages
generated by User timers, 312, 313
in LISWatch, 979
priority of, 927

WM_USER message, 927

work items, 401
executing with the timer's component thread, 405
queuing to thread pools, 402
registering for execution, 412–13

_wpgmptr global variable, *75*

wProcessorArchitecture member of the SYSTEM_INFO data structure, *473*

wProcessorLevel member of the SYSTEM_INFO data structure, *473*

wProcessorRevision member of the SYSTEM_INFO data structure, *473*

writable files, coherence and, 622

writable pages, calculating, 451

WRITE attribute for a section, *583*

WriteProcessMemory function, 441, 778, 799–800

wShowWindow member of STARTUPINFO, 103

WT_EXECUTEDEFAULT flag, 402, 405

WT_EXECUTEINIOTHREAD flag, 402, 405, 414, 416

WT_EXECUTEINPERSISTENTTHREAD flag, 402, 405, 414

WT_EXECUTEINTIMERTHREAD flag, 405

WT_EXECUTEINWAITTHREAD flag, 413–14

WT_EXECUTELONGFUNCTION flag, *400*, 403, 405, 414

WT_EXECUTEONLYONCE flag, 414

wWinMainCRTStartup function, 73

wWinMain entry point function, *72*

X

*x*86 architecture, creating Unicode versions for, 991

*x*86 CPU
   address space for, 444, *445*

*x*86 CPU, *continued*
   CONTEXT structure for, 223, *223–25*
   dealing with unaligned data references, 308
   DebugBreak function and, 994
   definition of CONTEXT_FULL, *227*
   handling data alignment, 466
   page size of, 443
   performing alignment fixups, 469
   support of the execute protection attribute, 450

*x*86 family of CPUs, interlocked functions in, 260–61

.xdata section, *585*

Z

ZeroMemory function, 538

zero page thread, 229

About the author...

Jeffrey Richter gives programming seminars (*http://www.SolSem.com*) to software developers and is available for consulting (*http://www.JeffreyRichter.com*). His clients include such companies as Allen-Bradley, AT&T, Caterpillar, Digital, DreamWorks, GE Medical Systems, Hewlett-Packard, IBM, Intel, Intuit, Microsoft, Pitney Bowes, Sybase, Tandem, and Unisys.

Jeff also speaks regularly at industry conferences, including Software Development and COMDEX, Boston University's WinDev, Microsoft's Professional Developer's Conference, and Tech-Ed. Jeff is also a contributing editor to *Microsoft Systems Journal,* for which he authors the Win32 Q & A column and has written several feature articles.

Jeff lives in Bellevue, Washington. His hobbies include helicopter flying, magic, and drumming. He loves *The Simpsons* and has a few animation cells. He also has a passion for classic rock and jazz-fusion bands.

The manuscript for this book was prepared and submitted to Microsoft Press in electronic form. Text files were prepared using Microsoft Word 97. Pages were composed by Microsoft Press using Adobe PageMaker 6.52 for Windows, with text in Galliard and display type in Helvetica bold. Composed pages were delivered to the printer as electronic prepress files.

Cover Graphic Designer
Girvin | Strategic Branding & Design

Cover Illustrator
Glen Mitsui

Interior Graphic Artist
Rob Nance

Principal Compositors
Barb Runyan
Carl Diltz

Indexer
Richard Strout

ou'll love his EXPERT Seminars!

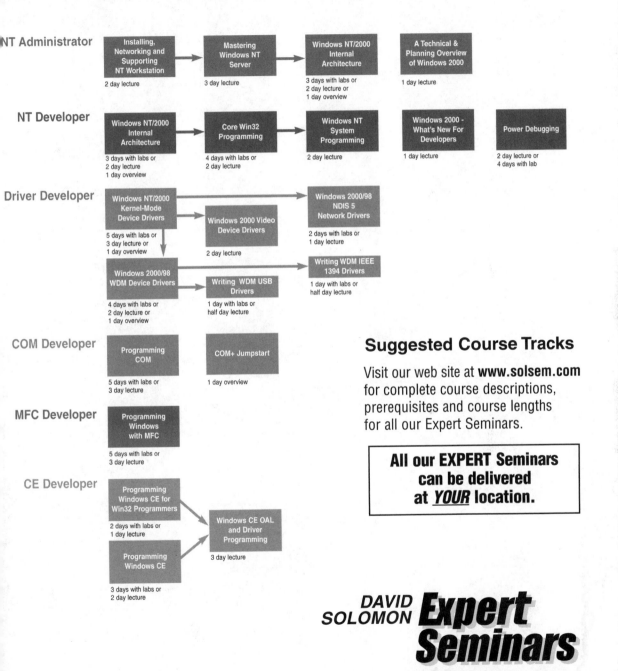

NT Administrator

| Installing, Networking and Supporting NT Workstation | Mastering Windows NT Server | Windows NT/2000 Internal Architecture | A Technical & Planning Overview of Windows 2000 |

2 day lecture

3 day lecture

3 days with labs or
2 day lecture or
1 day overview

1 day lecture

NT Developer

Windows NT/2000 Internal Architecture
3 days with labs or
2 day lecture
1 day overview

Core Win32 Programming
4 days with labs or
2 day lecture

Windows NT System Programming
2 day lecture

Windows 2000 - What's New For Developers
1 day lecture

Power Debugging
2 day lecture or
4 days with lab

Driver Developer

Windows NT/2000 Kernel-Mode Device Drivers
5 days with labs or
3 day lecture or
1 day overview

Windows 2000 Video Device Drivers
2 day lecture

Windows 2000/98 NDIS 5 Network Drivers
2 days with labs or
1 day lecture

Windows 2000/98 WDM Device Drivers
4 days with labs or
2 day lecture or
1 day overview

Writing WDM USB Drivers
1 day with labs or
half day lecture

Writing WDM IEEE 1394 Drivers
1 day with labs or
half day lecture

COM Developer

Programming COM
5 days with labs or
3 day lecture

COM+ Jumpstart
1 day overview

Suggested Course Tracks

Visit our web site at **www.solsem.com** for complete course descriptions, prerequisites and course lengths for all our Expert Seminars.

MFC Developer

Programming Windows with MFC
5 days with labs or
3 day lecture

All our EXPERT Seminars can be delivered at _YOUR_ location.

CE Developer

Programming Windows CE for Win32 Programmers
2 days with labs or
1 day lecture

Programming Windows CE
3 days with labs or
2 day lecture

Windows CE OAL and Driver Programming
3 day lecture

DAVID SOLOMON Expert Seminars

www.solsem.com

The
definitive
guide
to the **Win32 API**

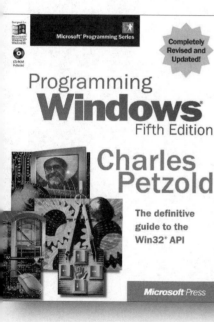

"Look it up in Petzold" remains the decisive last word in answering questions about Microsoft® Windows® development. And in PROGRAMMING WINDOWS, Fifth Edition, the esteemed Windows Pioneer Award winner revises his classic text with authoritative coverage of the latest versions of the Windows operating system—once again drilling down to the essential API heart of Win32® programming. Packed as always with definitive examples, this newest Petzold delivers the ultimate sourcebook and tutorial for Windows programmers at all levels working with Windows 95, Windows 98, or Windows NT® No aspiring or experienced developer can afford to be without it.

Microsoft®

mspress.microsoft.com

Learn how
COM+

can simplify your
development tasks

Wouldn't it be great to have an enterprise application's infrastructure so that you could inherit what you need and spend your time writing your own business logic? COM+ is what you've been waiting for—an advanced development environment that provides prefabricated solutions to common enterprise application problems. UNDERSTANDING COM+ is a succinct, entertaining book that offers an overview of COM+ and key COM+ features, explains the role of COM+ in enterprise development, and describes the services it can provide for your components and clients. You'll learn how COM+ can streamline application development to help you get enterprise applications up and running and out the door.

mspress.microsoft.com

Get a **Free**
e-mail newsletter, updates,
special offers, links to related books,
and more when you

register on line!

Register your Microsoft Press® title on our Web site and you'll get a FREE subscription to our e-mail newsletter, *Microsoft Press Book Connections.* You'll find out about newly released and upcoming books and learning tools, online events, software downloads, special offers and coupons for Microsoft Press customers, and information about major Microsoft® product releases. You can also read useful additional information about all the titles we publish, such as detailed book descriptions, tables of contents and indexes, sample chapters, links to related books and book series, author biographies, and reviews by other customers.

Registration is easy. Just visit this Web page and fill in your information:

http://www.microsoft.com/mspress/register

Microsoft

- -

Proof of Purchase

Use this page as proof of purchase if participating in a promotion or rebate offer on this title. Proof of purchase must be used in conjunction with other proof(s) of payment such as your dated sales receipt—see offer details.

Programming Applications for Microsoft® Windows®

1-57231-996-8

CUSTOMER NAME

Microsoft Press, PO Box 97017, Redmond, WA 98073-9830

MICROSOFT LICENSE AGREEMENT

Book Companion CD

)FTWARE PRODUCT LICENSE

user manual, in "online" documentation, and/or in other Microsoft-provided materials. Any supplemental software code provided to you as part of the Support Services shall be considered part of the SOFTWARE PRODUCT and subject to the terms and conditions of this EULA. With respect to technical information you provide to Microsoft as part of the Support Services, Microsoft may use such information for its business purposes, including for product support and development. Microsoft will not utilize such technical information in a form that personally identifies you.

- **Software Transfer.** You may permanently transfer all of your rights under this EULA, provided you retain no copies, you transfer all of the SOFTWARE PRODUCT (including all component parts, the media and printed materials, any upgrades this EULA, and, if applicable, the Certificate of Authenticity), **and** the recipient agrees to the terms of this EULA.

- **Termination.** Without prejudice to any other rights, Microsoft may terminate this EULA if you fail to comply with the terms and conditions of this EULA. In such event, you must destroy all copies of the SOFTWARE PRODUCT and all of i component parts.

3. **COPYRIGHT.** All title and copyrights in and to the SOFTWARE PRODUCT (including but not limited to any images, photographs, animations, video, audio, music, text, SAMPLE CODE, REDISTRIBUTABLES, and "applets" incorporated ir the SOFTWARE PRODUCT) and any copies of the SOFTWARE PRODUCT are owned by Microsoft or its suppliers. The SOFTWARE PRODUCT is protected by copyright laws and international treaty provisions. Therefore, you must treat the SOFTWARE PRODUCT like any other copyrighted material **except** that you may install the SOFTWARE PRODUCT on a single computer provided you keep the original solely for backup or archival purposes. You may not copy the printed materi; accompanying the SOFTWARE PRODUCT.

4. **U.S. GOVERNMENT RESTRICTED RIGHTS.** The SOFTWARE PRODUCT and documentation are provided with RESTRICTED RIGHTS. Use, duplication, or disclosure by the Government is subject to restrictions as set forth in subpara- graph (c)(1)(ii) of the Rights in Technical Data and Computer Software clause at DFARS 252.227-7013 or subparagraphs (c)(1) and (2) of the Commercial Computer Software—Restricted Rights at 48 CFR 52.227-19, as applicable. Manufacturer i Microsoft Corporation/One Microsoft Way/Redmond, WA 98052-6399.

5. **EXPORT RESTRICTIONS.** You agree that you will not export or re-export the SOFTWARE PRODUCT, any part thereof or any process or service that is the direct product of the SOFTWARE PRODUCT (the foregoing collectively referred to as tl "Restricted Components"), to any country, person, entity, or end user subject to U.S. export restrictions. You specifically agr not to export or re-export any of the Restricted Components (i) to any country to which the U.S. has embargoed or restricted the export of goods or services, which currently include, but are not necessarily limited to, Cuba, Iran, Iraq, Libya, North Korea, Sudan, and Syria, or to any national of any such country, wherever located, who intends to transmit or transport the Restricted Components back to such country; (ii) to any end user who you know or have reason to know will utilize the Restricted Components in the design, development, or production of nuclear, chemical, or biological weapons; or (iii) to any end user who has been prohibited from participating in U.S. export transactions by any federal agency of the U.S. governmen You warrant and represent that neither the BXA nor any other U.S. federal agency has suspended, revoked, or denied your export privileges.

DISCLAIMER OF WARRANTY

NO WARRANTIES OR CONDITIONS. MICROSOFT EXPRESSLY DISCLAIMS ANY WARRANTY OR CONDITION FOR THE SOFTWARE PRODUCT. THE SOFTWARE PRODUCT AND ANY RELATED DOCUMENTATION ARE PROVIDED "A IS" WITHOUT WARRANTY OR CONDITION OF ANY KIND, EITHER EXPRESS OR IMPLIED, INCLUDING, WITHOUT LIMITATION, THE IMPLIED WARRANTIES OF MERCHANTABILITY, FITNESS FOR A PARTICULAR PURPOSE, OR NONINFRINGEMENT. THE ENTIRE RISK ARISING OUT OF USE OR PERFORMANCE OF THE SOFTWARE PRODUCT REMAINS WITH YOU.

LIMITATION OF LIABILITY. TO THE MAXIMUM EXTENT PERMITTED BY APPLICABLE LAW, IN NO EVENT SHAL MICROSOFT OR ITS SUPPLIERS BE LIABLE FOR ANY SPECIAL, INCIDENTAL, INDIRECT, OR CONSEQUENTIAL DAMAGES WHATSOEVER (INCLUDING, WITHOUT LIMITATION, DAMAGES FOR LOSS OF BUSINESS PROFITS, BUSINESS INTERRUPTION, LOSS OF BUSINESS INFORMATION, OR ANY OTHER PECUNIARY LOSS) ARISING OUT (THE USE OF OR INABILITY TO USE THE SOFTWARE PRODUCT OR THE PROVISION OF OR FAILURE TO PROVIDE SUPPORT SERVICES, EVEN IF MICROSOFT HAS BEEN ADVISED OF THE POSSIBILITY OF SUCH DAMAGES. IN ANY CASE, MICROSOFT'S ENTIRE LIABILITY UNDER ANY PROVISION OF THIS EULA SHALL BE LIMITED TO THE GREATER OF THE AMOUNT ACTUALLY PAID BY YOU FOR THE SOFTWARE PRODUCT OR US$5.00; PROVIDED, HOWEVER, IF YOU HAVE ENTERED INTO A MICROSOFT SUPPORT SERVICES AGREEMENT, MICROSOFT'S ENTIRE LIABILITY REGARDING SUPPORT SERVICES SHALL BE GOVERNED BY THE TERMS OF THAT AGREEMENT. BECAUSE SOME STATES AND JURISDICTIONS DO NOT ALLOW THE EXCLUSION OR LIMITATION OF LIABILITY, THE ABOVE LIMITATION MAY NOT APPLY TO YOU.

MISCELLANEOUS

This EULA is governed by the laws of the State of Washington USA, except and only to the extent that applicable law mandat governing law of a different jurisdiction.

Should you have any questions concerning this EULA, or if you desire to contact Microsoft for any reason, please contact tl Microsoft subsidiary serving your country, or write: Microsoft Sales Information Center/One Microsoft Way/Redmond, W 98052-6399.